Lecture Notes in Computer Science 15484

Founding Editors

Gerhard Goos
Juris Hartmanis

AF147333

The series Lecture Notes in Computer Science (LNCS), including its subseries Lecture Notes in Artificial Intelligence (LNAI) and Lecture Notes in Bioinformatics (LNBI), has established itself as a medium for the publication of new developments in computer science and information technology research, teaching, and education.

LNCS enjoys close cooperation with the computer science R & D community, the series counts many renowned academics among its volume editors and paper authors, and collaborates with prestigious societies. Its mission is to serve this international community by providing an invaluable service, mainly focused on the publication of conference and workshop proceedings and postproceedings. LNCS commenced publication in 1973.

Kai-Min Chung · Yu Sasaki
Editors

Advances in Cryptology – ASIACRYPT 2024

30th International Conference on the Theory
and Application of Cryptology and Information Security
Kolkata, India, December 9–13, 2024
Proceedings, Part I

 Springer

Editors
Kai-Min Chung 🆔
Academia Sinica
Taipei, Taiwan

Yu Sasaki 🆔
NTT Social Informatics Laboratories
Tokyo, Japan

ISSN 0302-9743   ISSN 1611-3349 (electronic)
Lecture Notes in Computer Science
ISBN 978-981-96-0874-4   ISBN 978-981-96-0875-1 (eBook)
https://doi.org/10.1007/978-981-96-0875-1

This Springer imprint is published by the registered company Springer Nature Singapore Pte Ltd.
The registered company address is: 152 Beach Road, #21-01/04 Gateway East, Singapore 189721, Singapore

If disposing of this product, please recycle the paper.

Preface

The 30th Annual International Conference on the Theory and Application of Cryptology and Information Security (Asiacrypt 2024) was held in Kolkata, India, on December 9–13, 2024. The conference covered all technical aspects of cryptology and was sponsored by the International Association for Cryptologic Research (IACR).

We received a record 433 paper submissions for Asiacrypt from around the world. The Program Committee (PC) selected 127 papers for publication in the proceedings of the conference. As in the previous year, the Asiacrypt 2024 program had three tracks.

The two program chairs are greatly indebted to the six area chairs for their great contributions throughout the paper selection process. The area chairs were Siyao Guo for Information-Theoretic and Complexity-Theoretic Cryptography, Bo-Yin Yang for Efficient and Secure Implementations, Goichiro Hanaoka for Public-Key Cryptography Algorithms and Protocols, Arpita Patra for Multi-Party Computation and Zero-Knowledge, Prabhanjan Ananth for Public-Key Primitives with Advanced Functionalities, and Tetsu Iwata for Symmetric-Key Cryptography. The area chairs helped suggest candidates to form a strong program committee, foster and moderate discussions together with the PC members assigned as paper discussion leads to form consensus, suggest decisions on submissions in their areas, and nominate outstanding PC members. We are sincerely grateful for the invaluable contributions of the area chairs.

To review and evaluate the submissions, while keeping the load per PC member manageable, we selected the PC members consisting of 105 leading experts from all over the world, in all six topic areas of cryptology, and we also had approximately 468 external reviewers, whose input was critical to the selection of papers. The review process was conducted using double-blind peer review. The conference operated a two-round review system with a rebuttal phase. This year, we continued the interactive rebuttal from Asiacrypt 2023. After the reviews and first-round discussions, PC members and area chairs selected 264 submissions to proceed to the second round. The remaining 169 papers were rejected, including two desk-rejects. Then, the authors were invited to participate in a two-step interactive rebuttal phase, where the authors needed to submit a rebuttal in five days and then interact with the reviewers to address questions and concerns the following week. We believe the interactive form of the rebuttal encouraged discussions between the authors and the reviewers to clarify the concerns and contributions of the submissions and improved the review process. Then, after several weeks of second-round discussions, the committee selected the final 127 papers to appear in these proceedings. This year, we received seven resubmissions from the revise-and-resubmit experiment from Crypto 2024, of which five were accepted. The nine volumes of the conference proceedings contain the revised versions of the 127 papers that were selected. The final revised versions of papers were not reviewed again and the authors are responsible for their contents.

The PC nominated and voted for three papers to receive the Best Paper Awards. The Best Paper Awards went to Mariya Georgieva Belorgey, Sergiu Carpov, Nicolas Gama,

Sandra Guasch and Dimitar Jetchev for their paper "Revisiting Key Decomposition Techniques for FHE: Simpler, Faster and More Generic", Xiaoyang Dong, Yingxin Li, Fukang Liu, Siwei Sun and Gaoli Wang for their paper "The First Practical Collision for 31-Step SHA-256", and Valerio Cini and Hoeteck Wee for their paper "Unbounded ABE for Circuits from LWE, Revisited". The authors of those three papers were invited to submit extended versions of their papers to the Journal of Cryptology.

The program of Asiacrypt 2024 also featured the 2024 IACR Distinguished Lecture, delivered by Paul Kocher, as well as an invited talk by Dakshita Khurana. Following Eurocrypt 2024, we selected seven PC members for the Distinguished PC Members Awards, nominated by the area chairs and program chairs. The Distinguished PC Members Awards went to Sherman S. M. Chow, Elizabeth Crites, Matthias J. Kannwischer, Mustafa Khairallah, Ruben Niederhagen, Maciej Obremski and Keita Xagawa.

Following Crypto 2024, Asiacrypt 2024 included an artifact evaluation process for the first time. Authors of accepted papers were invited to submit associated artifacts, such as software or datasets, for archiving alongside their papers; 14 artifacts were submitted. Rei Ueno was the Artifact Chair and led an artifact evaluation committee of 10 members listed below. In the interactive review process between authors and reviewers, the goal was not just to evaluate artifacts but also to improve them. Artifacts that passed successfully through the artifact review process were publicly archived by the IACR at https://artifacts.iacr.org/.

Numerous people contributed to the success of Asiacrypt 2024. We would like to thank all the authors, including those whose submissions were not accepted, for submitting their research results to the conference. We are very grateful to the area chairs, PC members, and external reviewers for contributing their knowledge and expertise, and for the tremendous amount of work that was done with reading papers and contributing to the discussions. We are greatly indebted to Bimal Kumar Roy, the General Chairs, for their efforts in organizing the event, to Kevin McCurley and Kay McKelly for their help with the website and review system, and to Jhih-Wei Shih for the assistance with the use of the review system. We thank the Asiacrypt 2024 advisory committee members Bart Preneel, Huaxiong Wang, Bo-Yin Yang, Goichiro Hanaoka, Jian Guo, Ron Steinfeld, and Michel Abdalla for their valuable suggestions. We are also grateful for the helpful advice and organizational material provided to us by Crypto 2024 PC co-chairs Leonid Reyzin and Douglas Stebila, Eurocrypt 2024 PC co-chairs Marc Joye and Gregor Leander, and TCC 2023 chair Hoeteck Wee. We also thank the team at Springer for handling the publication of these conference proceedings.

December 2024

Kai-Min Chung
Yu Sasaki

Organization

General Chair

Bimal Kumar Roy   TCG CREST Kolkata, India

Program Committee Chairs

Kai-Min Chung   Academia Sinica, Taiwan
Yu Sasaki   NTT Social Informatics Laboratories Tokyo
         (Japan) and National Institute of Standards and
         Technology, USA

Area Chairs

Prabhanjan Ananth   University of California, Santa Barbara, USA
Siyao Guo   NYU Shanghai, China
Goichiro Hanaoka   National Institute of Advanced Industrial Science
         and Technology, Japan
Tetsu Iwata   Nagoya University, Japan
Arpita Patra   Indian Institute of Science Bangalore, India
Bo-Yin Yang   Academia Sinica, Taiwan

Program Committee

Akshima   NYU Shanghai, China
Bar Alon   Ben-Gurion University, Israel
Elena Andreeva   TU Wien, Austria
Nuttapong Attrapadung   AIST, Japan
Subhadeep Banik   University of Lugano, Switzerland
Zhenzhen Bao   Tsinghua University, China
James Bartusek   University of California, Berkeley, USA
Hanno Becker   Amazon Web Services, UK
Sonia Belaïd   CryptoExperts, France
Ward Beullens   IBM Research, Switzerland
Andrej Bogdanov   University of Ottawa, Canada

Pedro Branco   Max Planck Institute for Security and Privacy,
                                  Germany
Gaëtan Cassiers   UCLouvain, Belgium
Céline Chevalier   CRED, Université Paris-Panthéon-Assas, and
                                  DIENS, France
Avik Chakraborti   Institute for Advancing Intelligence TCG CREST,
                                  India
Nishanth Chandran   Microsoft Research India, India
Jie Chen   East China Normal University, China
Yu Long Chen   KU Leuven and National Institute of Standards
                                  and Technology, Belgium
Mahdi Cheraghchi   University of Michigan, USA
Nai-Hui Chia   Rice University, USA
Wonseok Choi   Purdue University, USA
Tung Chou   Academia Sinica, Taiwan
Arka Rai Choudhuri   NTT Research, USA
Sherman S. M. Chow   Chinese University of Hong Kong, China
Chitchanok Chuengsatiansup   University of Melbourne, Australia
Michele Ciampi   University of Edinburgh, UK
Valerio Cini   NTT Research, USA
Elizabeth Crites   Web3 Foundation, Switzerland
Nico Döttling   CISPA Helmholtz Center, Germany
Avijit Dutta   Institute for Advancing Intelligence TCG CREST,
                                  India
Daniel Escudero   JP Morgan AlgoCRYPT CoE and JP Morgan AI
                                  Research, USA
Thomas Espitau   PQShield, France
Jun Furukawa   NEC Corporation, Japan
Rosario Gennaro   CUNY, USA
Junqing Gong   East China Normal University, China
Rishab Goyal   University of Wisconsin-Madison, USA
Julia Hesse   IBM Research Europe, Switzerland
Akinori Hosoyamada   NTT Social Informatics Laboratories, Japan
Michael Hutter   PQShield, Austria
Takanori Isobe   University of Hyogo, Japan
Joseph Jaeger   Georgia Institute of Technology, USA
Matthias J. Kannwischer   Chelpis Quantum Corp, Taiwan
Bhavana Kanukurthi   Indian Institute of Science, India
Shuichi Katsumata   PQShield and AIST, Japan
Jonathan Katz   Google and University of Maryland, USA
Mustafa Khairallah   Lund University, Sweden
Fuyuki Kitagawa   NTT Social Informatics Laboratories, Japan

Katerina Sotiraki	Yale University, USA
Akshayaram Srinivasan	University of Toronto, Canada
Marc Stöttinger	Hochschule RheinMain, Germany
Akira Takahashi	J.P. Morgan AI Research and AlgoCRYPT CoE, USA
Qiang Tang	University of Sydney, Australia
Aishwarya Thiruvengadam	IIT Madras, India
Emmanuel Thomé	Inria Nancy, France
Junichi Tomida	NTT Social Informatics Laboratories, Japan
Monika Trimoska	Eindhoven University of Technology, Netherlands
Huaxiong Wang	Nanyang Technological University, Singapore
Meiqin Wang	Shandong University, China
Qingju Wang	Telecom Paris, Institut Polytechnique de Paris, France
David Wu	UT Austin, USA
Keita Xagawa	Technology Innovation Institute, United Arab Emirates
Chaoping Xing	Shanghai Jiaotong University, China
Shiyuan Xu	University of Hong Kong, China
Anshu Yadav	IST, Austria
Shota Yamada	AIST, Japan
Yu Yu	Shanghai Jiao Tong University, China
Mark Zhandry	NTT Research, USA
Hong-Sheng Zhou	Virginia Commonwealth University, USA

Additional Reviewers

Hugo Aaronson	Jiawei Bao
Damiano Abram	Jyotirmoy Basak
Hamza Abusalah	Nirupam Basak
Abtin Afshar	Gabrielle Beck
Siddharth Agarwal	Hugo Beguinet
Navid Alamati	Amit Behera
Miguel Ambrona	Mihir Bellare
Parisa Amiri Eliasi	Tamar Ben David
Ravi Anand	Aner Moshe Ben Efraim
Saikrishna Badrinarayanan	Fabrice Benhamouda
Chen Bai	Tyler Besselman
David Balbás	Tim Beyne
Brieuc Balon	Rishabh Bhadauria
Gustavo Banegas	Divyanshu Bhardwaj
Laasya Bangalore	Shivam Bhasin

Amit Singh Bhati
Loïc Bidoux
Alexander Bienstock
Jan Bobolz
Alexandra Boldyreva
Maxime Bombar
Nicolas Bon
Carl Bootland
Jonathan Bootle
Giacomo Borin
Cecilia Boschini
Jean-Philippe Bossuat
Mariana Botelho da Gama
Christina Boura
Pierre Briaud
Jeffrey Burdges
Fabio Campos
Yibo Cao
Pedro Capitão
Ignacio Cascudo
David Cash
Wouter Castryck
Anirban Chakrabarthi
Debasmita Chakraborty
Suvradip Chakraborty
Kanad Chakravarti
Ayantika Chatterjee
Rohit Chatterjee
Jorge Chavez-Saab
Binyi Chen
Bohang Chen
Long Chen
Mingjie Chen
Shiyao Chen
Xue Chen
Yu-Chi Chen
Chen-Mou Cheng
Jiaqi Cheng
Ashish Choudhury
Miranda Christ
Qiaohan Chu
Eldon Chung
Hao Chung
Léo Colisson
Daniel Collins

Jolijn Cottaar
Murilo Coutinho
Eric Crockett
Bibhas Chandra Das
Nayana Das
Pratish Datta
Alex Davidson
Hannah Davis
Leo de Castro
Luca De Feo
Thomas Decru
Giovanni Deligios
Ning Ding
Fangqi Dong
Minxin Du
Qiuyan Du
Jesko Dujmovic
Moumita Dutta
Pranjal Dutta
Duyen
Marius Eggert
Solane El Hirch
Andre Esser
Hülya Evkan
Sebastian Faller
Yanchen Fan
Niklas Fassbender
Hanwen Feng
Xiutao Feng
Dario Fiore
Scott Fluhrer
Danilo Francati
Shiuan Fu
Georg Fuchsbauer
Shang Gao
Rachit Garg
Gayathri Garimella
Pierrick Gaudry
François Gérard
Paul Gerhart
Riddhi Ghosal
Shibam Ghosh
Ashrujit Ghoshal
Shane Gibbons
Valerie Gilchrist

Xinxin Gong
Lorenzo Grassi
Scott Griffy
Chaowen Guan
Aurore Guillevic
Sam Gunn
Felix Günther
Kanav Gupta
Shreyas Gupta
Kamil Doruk Gur
Jincheol Ha
Hossein Hadipour
Tovohery Hajatiana Randrianarisoa
Shai Halevi
Shuai Han
Tobias Handirk
Yonglin Hao
Zihan Hao
Keisuke Hara
Keitaro Hashimoto
Aditya Hegde
Andreas Hellenbrand
Paul Hermouet
Minki Hhan
Hilder Lima
Taiga Hiroka
Ryo Hiromasa
Viet Tung Hoang
Charlotte Hoffmann
Clément Hoffmann
Man Hou Hong
Wei-Chih Hong
Alexander Hoover
Fumitaka Hoshino
Patrick Hough
Yao-Ching Hsieh
Chengcong Hu
David Hu
Kai Hu
Zihan Hu
Hai Huang
Mi-Ying Huang
Yu-Hsuan Huang
Zhicong Huang
Shih-Han Hung

Yuval Ishai
Ryoma Ito
Amit Jana
Ashwin Jha
Xiaoyu Ji
Yanxue Jia
Mingming Jiang
Lin Jiao
Haoxiang Jin
Zhengzhong Jin
Chris Jones
Eliran Kachlon
Giannis Kaklamanis
Chethan Kamath
Soumya Kanti Saha
Sabyasachi Karati
Harish Karthikeyan
Andes Y. L. Kei
Jean Kieffer
Jiseung Kim
Seongkwang Kim
Sebastian Kolby
Sreehari Kollath
Dimitris Kolonelos
Venkata Koppula
Abhiram Kothapalli
Stanislav Kruglik
Anup Kumar Kundu
Péter Kutas
Norman Lahr
Qiqi Lai
Yi-Fu Lai
Abel Laval
Guirec Lebrun
Byeonghak Lee
Changmin Lee
Hyung Tae Lee
Joohee Lee
Keewoo Lee
Yeongmin Lee
Yongwoo Lee
Andrea Lesavourey
Baiyu Li
Jiangtao Li
Jianqiang Li

Junru Li
Liran Li
Minzhang Li
Shun Li
Songsong Li
Weihan Li
Wenzhong Li
Yamin Li
Yanan Li
Yu Li
Yun Li
Zeyong Li
Zhe Li
Chuanwei Lin
Fuchun Lin
Yao-Ting Lin
Yunhao Ling
Eik List
Fengrun Liu
Fukang Liu
Hanlin Liu
Hongqing Liu
Rui Liu
Tianren Liu
Xiang Liu
Xiangyu Liu
Zeyu Liu
Paul Lou
George Lu
Zhenghao Lu
Ting-Gian Lua
You Lyu
Jack P. K. Ma
Yiping Ma
Varun Madathil
Lorenzo Magliocco
Avishek Majumder
Nikolaos Makriyannis
Varun Maram
Chloe Martindale
Elisaweta Masserova
Jake Massimo
Loïc Masure
Takahiro Matsuda
Christian Matt

Subhra Mazumdar
Nikolas Melissaris
Michael Meyer
Ankit Kumar Misra
Anuja Modi
Deep Inder Mohan
Charles Momin
Johannes Mono
Hart Montgomery
Ethan Mook
Thorben Moos
Tomoyuki Morimae
Hiraku Morita
Tomoki Moriya
Aditya Morolia
Christian Mouchet
Nicky Mouha
Tamer Mour
Changrui Mu
Arindam Mukherjee
Pratyay Mukherjee
Anne Müller
Alice Murphy
Shyam Murthy
Kohei Nakagawa
Barak Nehoran
Patrick Neumann
Lucien K. L. Ng
Duy Nguyen
Ky Nguyen
Olga Nissenbaum
Anca Nitulescu
Julian Nowakowski
Frederique Oggier
Jean-Baptiste Orfila
Emmanuela Orsini
Tapas Pal
Ying-yu Pan
Roberto Parisella
Aditi Partap
Alain Passelègue
Alice Pellet-Mary
Zachary Pepin
Octavio Perez Kempner
Edoardo Perichetti

Léo Perrin
Naty Peter
Richard Petri
Rafael del Pino
Federico Pintore
Erik Pohle
Simon Pohmann
Guru Vamsi Policharla
Daniel Pollman
Yuriy Polyakov
Alexander Poremba
Eamonn Postlethwaite
Sihang Pu
Luowen Qian
Tian Qiu
Rajeev Raghunath
Srinivasan Raghuraman
Mostafizar Rahman
Mahesh Rajasree
Somindu Chaya Ramanna
Simon Rastikian
Anik Raychaudhuri
Martin Rehberg
Michael Reichle
Krijn Reijnders
Doreen Riepel
Guilherme Rito
Matthieu Rivain
Bhaskar Roberts
Marc Roeschlin
Michael Rosenberg
Paul Rösler
Arnab Roy
Lawrence Roy
Luigi Russo
Keegan Ryan
Markku-Juhani Saarinen
Éric Sageloli
Dhiman Saha
Sayandeep Saha
Yusuke Sakai
Kosei Sakamoto
Subhabrata Samajder
Simona Samardjiska
Maria Corte-Real Santos

Sina Schaeffler
André Schrottenloher
Jacob Schuldt
Mark Schultz
Mahdi Sedaghat
Jae Hong Seo
Yannick Seurin
Aein Shahmirzadi
Girisha Shankar
Yixin Shen
Rentaro Shiba
Ardeshir Shojaeinasab
Jun Jie Sim
Mark Simkin
Jaspal Singh
Benjamin Smith
Yongha Son
Fang Song
Yongsoo Song
Pratik Soni
Pierre-Jean Spaenlehauer
Matthias Johann Steiner
Lukas Stennes
Roy Stracovsky
Takeshi Sugawara
Adam Suhl
Siwei Sun
Elias Suvanto
Koutarou Suzuki
Erkan Tairi
Atsushi Takayasu
Kaoru Takemure
Abdullah Talayhan
Quan Quan Tan
Gang Tang
Khai Hanh Tang
Tianxin Tang
Yi Tang
Stefano Tessaro
Sri AravindaKrishnan Thyagarajan
Yan Bo Ti
Jean-Pierre Tillich
Toi Tomita
Aleksei Udovenko
Arunachalaeswaran V.

Artifact Chair

Artifact Evaluation Committee

Contents – Part I

Digital Signatures

Advanced Primitives

Signature-Based Witness Encryption
with Compact Ciphertext

Gennaro Avitabile[1] , Nico Döttling[2] , Bernardo Magri[3,4] ,
Christos Sakkas[3] , and Stella Wohnig[2,5(✉)]

[1] IMDEA Software Institute, Madrid, Spain
gennaro.avitabile@imdea.org
[2] CISPA Helmholtz Center for Information Security, Saarbrücken, Germany
doettling@cispa.de, stella.wohnig.crypto@gmail.com
[3] University of Manchester, Manchester, UK
{bernardo.magri,christos.sakkas}@manchester.ac.uk
[4] Primev, Manchester, UK
[5] Saarland University, Saarbrücken, Germany

Abstract. Signature-based witness encryption (SWE) is a recently proposed notion that allows to encrypt a message with respect to a tag T and a set of signature verification keys. The resulting ciphertext can only be decrypted by a party who holds at least k different valid signatures w.r.t. T and k different verification keys out of the n keys specified at encryption time. Natural applications of this primitive involve distributed settings (e.g., blockchains), where multiple parties sign predictable messages, such as polling or randomness beacons. However, known SWE schemes without trusted setup have ciphertexts that scale linearly in the number of verification keys. This quickly becomes a major bottleneck as the system gets more distributed and the number of parties increases.

Towards showing the feasibility of SWE with ciphertext size sub-linear in the number of keys, we give a construction based on indistinguishability obfuscation (iO) for Turing machines and strongly puncturable signatures (SPS).

1 Introduction

Threshold cryptography focuses on distributing the security of a cryptosystem among multiple parties, ensuring that a minimum number of these parties, known as the threshold, is required to operate the system. In recent years, threshold schemes have garnered significant attention from the community [5,7,9,16,24,27], primarily due to their applications in decentralized systems like blockchains. A recent example is the notion of threshold signature-based witness encryption (SWE) that was first introduced by Döttling et al. [9]. It allows to encrypt a plaintext with respect to a tag and a set of verification keys for a signature scheme. Once a sufficient number of signatures of this tag under these verification keys are provided, these signatures can be used to efficiently decrypt the SWE ciphertext. The main application of SWE described in [9] is to build a

K.-M. Chung and Y. Sasaki (Eds.): ASIACRYPT 2024, LNCS 15484, pp. 3–31, 2025.
https://doi.org/10.1007/978-981-96-0875-1_1

time-release encryption scheme by combining SWE with a proof-of-stake (PoS) blockchain: The idea is to use the verification keys of the blockchain committee members that sign every new block created in the chain as the SWE verification keys, and the block number of a block in the chain as the tag; then, once a block with that number is built the signatures of the committee members on that number can be used to decrypt the SWE ciphertext. Madathil *et al.* [27] construct an almost equivalent primitive called *verifiable witness encryption based on threshold signatures* (VweTS), and provide another compelling use-case for such a scheme: They facilitate blockchain transactions conditioned on "real life" events that happen outside of the blockchain system, by requiring a threshold number of oracles' signatures (third-party services that certify real-world events like weather data, outcomes of bets etc.) to unlock data to complete the transaction.

Conceptually, the notion of SWE can be seen as an interesting special case of witness encryption [15] which allows one to encrypt a message under any NP statement such that a witness for that statement allows to decrypt the ciphertext.

Another seemingly related notion is the one of threshold encryption schemes [8,12]. They are encryption schemes where decryption takes place with the help of a threshold of decryption servers. A significant difference w.r.t. SWE is that in threshold encryption a setup phase is assumed. During this setup, a public key for the scheme and correlated secret keys for the decryption servers are computed via a protocol. Furthermore, it is necessary to communicate with these servers in order to decrypt the message. A simple approach to threshold encryption [8] is to create the correlated secret keys as t-of-n linear secret shares a_i of an ElGamal secret key a, the corresponding public key is g^a. When a client gets an encryption (g^r, mg^{ar}) of m under g^a, they send g^r to each of the decryption servers and receive back decryption shares $g^{r(a_i^{-1})}$. The client then recombines the shares to get $g^{r(a^{-1})}$ given that at least t servers participate.

A big advantage of SWE over the above approach is that SWE does not require to setup correlated keys or communication between decryptors and signers. In fact, the servers may even be unaware that encryptions are being made w.r.t. signatures they may release in the future. This requirement is in line with the original application of SWE in the blockchain setting, as no additional load should be put on the blockchain committee other than simply producing a signature.

A common feature of the applications of SWE is the potentially large set of signers, as it is desirable that the members of blockchain committees or the number of trusted oracles can increase as much as possible to tackle centralization. Therefore, a critical drawback of the SWE/VweTS constructions in [9,27] is that the size of their ciphertexts grows linearly with the number of verification keys used in the signing procedure. A natural question to ask is whether it is possible to construct an SWE scheme that does not suffer from this limitation, and neither relies on a (long) trusted setup nor on strong ideal models (such as the programmable generic group model [33]). In this work, we answer this question in the affirmative by introducing the notion of *compact signature-*

based witness encryption (cSWE). In a cSWE scheme, the size of the ciphertext only grows poly-logarithmically in the number of verification keys. We provide a formal definition of cSWE and present a construction based on Turing-machine indistinguishability obfuscation and strongly puncturable signatures. In the next section, we describe our contributions in more detail.

1.1   Our Contributions

Compact SWE. In this work, we construct the first cSWE scheme that allows one to encrypt a message m with respect to a reference tag T and a set of verification keys $V = (\mathsf{vk}_1, \ldots, \mathsf{vk}_n)$ such that the ciphertext size only scales poly-logarithmically in n. Importantly, our construction does not rely on a trusted setup. The construction is based on indistinguishability obfuscation for Turing Machines [17, 25] and it achieves ciphertext size in the order of $\mathcal{O}(\mathsf{poly}(\lambda \cdot \log n))$. We prove security of our construction w.r.t. non-adaptive adversaries where the reference tag T and the indices of the corrupt verification keys are known ahead of time. Our result establishes principal feasibility of this notion in the non-adaptive setting and may pave the way towards a more efficient implementation of cSWE in the future.

1.2   Technical Overview

We will now provide an outline of our constructions and techniques.

Compact SWE. We start by reviewing the high-level idea of the SWE construction given in [9]. To encrypt a message m w.r.t. a reference tag T and a set of verification keys $V = (\mathsf{vk}_1, \ldots, \mathsf{vk}_n)$, the message m is first encrypted under a symmetric encryption scheme using a freshly sampled key K. The key K is then secret-shared using a t-of-n linear secret sharing scheme, in the case of [9] this is the Shamir scheme [32][1] where the shares $s_1, \ldots, s_n$ of K satisfy $\sum_{j=1}^{t} s_{i_j} \cdot L_{i_j} = K$ for Lagrange coefficients L_{i_j}. The ciphertext is structured in a way such that for each individual share, two elements are added to the ciphertext to ensure that the share s_i can be retrieved given a valid signature of T under the verification key vk_i.

In a bit more detail, the SWE construction of [9] uses BLS [2] as the underlying signature scheme. In BLS, a valid signature σ on T under vk must satisfy the equation $e(\sigma, g_2) = e(H(T), \mathsf{vk})$, where e is a bilinear map from groups G_1, G_2 into G_T, and g_2 is a generator of G_2. Then, for each share s_i, they create an encryption of that share by choosing some randomness $r_i \in \mathbb{Z}_p$, and outputting $(g_2^{r_i}, e(H(T), \mathsf{vk})^{r_i} \cdot s_i)$. Note that, having a signature σ_i of message T under key vk_i, a decryptor can compute $e(H(T), \mathsf{vk})^{r_i} = e(\sigma_i, g_2^{r_i})$, and thus easily get s_i. However, without such a signature the value $e(H(T), \mathsf{vk})^{r_i}$ is indistinguishable from random under the bilinear Diffie-Hellman assumption.

---

[1] This means $s_i = K + \sum_{j=1}^{t} r_j(\xi_i)^j \mod p$ for a prime p, random r_j and distinct evaluation points $\xi_i \in \mathbb{Z}_p$.

We will base our techniques on the above idea of encrypting each share s_i, such that it can be individually retrieved if a signature of T under vk_i is given. However, we will need to depart from the BLS-based approach [9] to achieve a ciphertext size independent of n.

The (non-compact) SWE construction of [9] achieves *adaptive fully malicious security*; the adversary can corrupt any unqualified set of signers and even choose their verification keys in a fully malicious manner.

Compact SWE and Adaptive Security. There seems, however, to be a substantial barrier for achieving adaptive security for *compact* SWE, and in fact it seems that a heuristic such as e.g. programmable random oracle model or the programmable generic group model may be necessary in this setting (see the discussion on [16] in the related works section below). From an information theoretic perspective, e.g. for a threshold of $k = n/2$, a ciphertext of size $o(n)$ is too small to even encode the set of corrupted parties, which requires $\Omega(n)$ bits. Hence, it seems hard to make a ciphertext behave differently for honest and corrupted keys as the ciphertext cannot "know" which keys are corrupted and which are not.

Hence, somewhat expectedly guessing-based transformations from non-adaptive to adaptive security fail in this setting. If we guess the set of corrupted parties ahead of time, we need to compensate for a security loss of order $2^{\Omega(n)}$. But this means that the underlying primitives need to at least provide $\Omega(n)$ bits of security, which in turn results in a ciphertext of size $\Omega(n)$, which is not compact by our definition.

A similar situation occurs in the setting of *adaptively secure succinct non-interactive arguments of knowledge (SNARGs)*: The object in question, in this case a certificate π, is so small that it cannot encode a sufficient amount of information about an adaptively chosen false statement x, hence the guessing-based non-adaptive to adaptive security transformation incurs a security loss incompatible with the succinctness requirement.

Gentry and Wichs [18] provided a formal barrier result which shows that there is no construction of adaptive SNARGs with a black-box security reduction from any falsifiable assumption [28]. While we do not provide a formal argument as this is beyond the scope of our work, the basic idea of this argument (likely) carries over to the setting of compact SWE. In fact, the Gentry-Wichs result [18] holds even for designated verifier SNARGs, and any succinct witness encryption scheme immediately gives rise to a designated verifier SNARG for the same language.

Somewhat surprisingly, a recent work by Wu and Waters [34] showed that this security loss can be "pushed into a CRS". That is by making the CRS scale with the logarithm of the security loss, the size of the certificate π can be kept small. Since we are interested in compact SWE constructions without setup, this is not an option in our setting.

Non-adaptive Security. Hence, we will focus on a notion of non-adaptive security in this work. Specifically, in this notion we require that the adversary chooses the reference message T and the indices of the corrupted keys ahead of time. Only after that does the adversary get $t - 1$ honestly generated pairs of verification and signing keys (at the corrupted positions) and $n - t - 1$ honestly chosen verification keys for the honest parties. We then give the adversary access to a signing oracle which will sign for all honest keys and all messages except the challenge tag T. Under these constraints we ask for indistinguishability security for the signature witness encryption, i.e. the adversary should not be able to distinguish SWE encryptions with respect to $\mathsf{vk}_1, \ldots, \mathsf{vk}_n$ and T of two distinct messages $m_0 \neq m_1$.

Constructions with Structured Common Reference String. Before we discuss our construction in the plain model, we will briefly discuss how we can construct compact SWE if we are allowed to shift the burden into a *long and structured CRS*. The basic idea is similar to the construction of zero-knowledge SNARGs of Sahai and Waters [31]: We can *delegate* the task of generating and decrypting compact SWE ciphertexts to a pair of (large) obfuscated circuits given in the CRS. The first circuit takes verification keys $\mathsf{vk}_1, \ldots, \mathsf{vk}_n$, the tag T, the message m as well as additional random coins and produces a ciphertext c and a succinct commitment h binding to the vk_i and c. The second obfuscated circuit takes as input $\mathsf{vk}_1, \ldots, \mathsf{vk}_n$ and c, an opening of h to these values, as well as signatures σ_i for some $I \subset [n]$ of size at least k. The circuit checks if each σ_i is a valid signature of T under vk_i and if so returns the message m. We can establish security of this construction using a standard puncturing argument and relying on standard tools such as puncturable PRFs and SSB hashing. This construction uses a long and structured CRS (consisting of obfuscated programs) in a critical way.

A First Attempt. In order to achieve a compact SWE construction without trusted setup, we have to depart from the above blueprint. Our basic idea is to adapt the construction of witness encryption from iO [14] to the setting of compact SWE, but this raises several challenges. Hence, consider the following attempt to construct a cSWE. The ciphertext consists of a symmetric key encryption of the message m under key K and an obfuscated circuit C. The circuit C pseudorandomly generates the secret shares under say the Shamir scheme of key K on demand; on input an index i and a valid signature σ for T under vk_i, the circuit produces the i-th share of the key K. The randomness for generating shares is taken from a puncturable PRF.

There are two evident issues with this approach. (1) A minor issue is that we cannot hardwire all the verification keys vk_i into the circuit C, as this would require the circuit size growing linearly with n, contradicting our compactness requirement. (2) Computing individual Shamir shares inside the circuit C implies evaluating a degree $t - 1$ polynomial (that takes time $\Theta(n)$), requiring a circuit of size $\Omega(n)$, again contradicting our compactness requirement.

There will be, however a more subtle third issue which surfaces when trying to prove security of this construction: If we were to rely on standard puncturing techniques to *erase* the shares of honest parties in the challenge ciphertext, we would need to puncture the above circuit $n - k$ times. But this would again require an obfuscated circuit of size $\Omega(n)$!

Our Basic Approach. Starting from the above sketch, we will address issues (1) and (2) above as follows. To address the issue (1), we will rely on somewhere statistically binding (SSB) hashing [22]. An SSB hash function is a keyed commitment scheme, which allows to succinctly produce a committing hash h of a database of size n. The key generation algorithm takes an index $i \in [n]$, and outputs a hashing key guaranteeing that the hash is computationally binding on all indices and statistically binding on i. The binding index is hidden by the commitment scheme. We use the SSB scheme to commit to all verification keys $(i, \mathsf{vk}_i)_{i \in [n]}$ and force the decryptor to input $(i, \mathsf{vk}_i, \sigma)$ and a valid opening τ for the SSB hash. This ensures, that except with negligible probability, on input $(i, \mathsf{vk}, \sigma, \tau)$, vk actually is the i-th key and σ is a signature for vk_i, so outputting s_i is justified. To address issue (2), we will rely on iO for Turing machines [17,25] (TM). The size of an obfuscated Turing machine depends polynomially on its description size, but only poly-logarithmically on its runtime.

Towards Proving Security. The intuition for the security proof is that we want to replace the obfuscated TM M with an equivalent TM M' which has no information about the shares or the shared key. The basic idea of the hybrid argument is as follows.

Since we are in a setting of non-adaptive security, the security reduction knows which signers will be corrupted even before their corresponding verification keys are generated. We will use a standard SSB argument to go through a sequence of hybrids, where in hybrid i we make the SSB hash statistically binding to the i-th *uncorrupted* verification key, call this key vk_i. We would like to argue that since the adversary never obtains a signature σ_i of T under vk_i, he cannot make the obfuscated TM output a share s_i of the message m_i. However, standard EUF-CMA security seems far too weak to guarantee this: In order to use indistinguishability security of iO, we need to move into a situation where it is *impossible* (rather than computationally hard) to make the TM accept some signature σ_i for T under vk_i and output the corresponding share s_i. To address this issue, we use strongly puncturable signatures (Sect. 3). These allow a special key generation $\mathsf{PKeyGen}(T)$, which outputs a punctured key pair $(\mathsf{vk}, \mathsf{sk})$ at message T. With overwhelming probability, no valid signature exists for message T, while the verification key remains indistinguishable from a standard non-punctured key. This type of signatures was introduced under the name of all-but-one signatures in [20] where various instantiations based on different number-theoretic assumptions (e.g., RSA, pairing-based assumptions, LWE) were proposed. Equipped with this tool, the reduction can now replace all honest keys with punctured keys, punctured at T. Hence, by additionally relying on SSB hashing as explained above we can rely on iO security to gradually replace the TM M by a TM M' which never outputs shares s_i for indices i of honest parties.

The Final Scheme. However, this transformation does not quite suffice to establish security. Recall that the shares s_i of the message m are generated *pseudorandomly*, that is an adversary with access to a plain description of the TM M' described above could still easily recover the PRF key $\tilde{K}$ used to generate the shares and just generate them by himself. Note also that iO security by itself does not guarantee that $\tilde{K}$ is hidden. The standard tool commonly used to argue security in this setting is puncturing: If we were to puncture the key $\tilde{K}$ in a suitable manner, then we might be able to ensure that this punctured key does not leak information about the shares of honest parties. While there are some minor issues with this idea, such as the fact that the shares s_i are correlated and a contrived puncturing argument would be necessary, the big issue here is we would need to puncture at $n - k = \Omega(n)$ points, which once again contradicts our compactness requirement! The reason why we need to remove all honest shares simultaneously is that otherwise Shamir secret sharing offers no security! Removing one share at a time is useless, as this share could easily be recomputed from the other shares. Hence, puncturing will not help us, and we need to depart from the puncturing approach. But where could we store shares of the message m instead? Observe that our ciphertext already includes an SSB commitment to all the verification keys vk_i, and we will precisely leverage this feature in our solution: We will augment the verification keys vk_i by some additional auxiliary information which contains a sufficiently large slot to encode a Shamir share. In the real world this auxiliary information is just a random string. But in the security reduction we can embed an encryption of the corresponding share s_i into vk_i. We then use iO security to switch to a machine M' that reads its shares from the input, limiting its internal computation to checking the validity of the input SSB opening and the signature. Upon success, it decrypts and outputs the share in vk_i; otherwise, it aborts. This switch between computational models is feasible because we bind the SSB hash to each index $i^* \in [n]$. This ensures that on input $(i^*, \mathsf{vk}, \sigma, \tau)$, if the obfuscated machine produces an output, then $\mathsf{vk} = \mathsf{vk}_{i^*}$ must hold. Consequently, the correct share is obtained by decrypting vk, and the output remains consistent whether the shares are computed internally or decrypted from the public keys.

While this outlines our main technical ideas, there are other subtle technical challenges which our construction in Sect. 4 needs to address.

On the Use of iO. Our construction uses iO for Turing Machines in a crucial way. Specifically, we use iO to delegate the generation of shares to the decrypter, the ciphertexts in our scheme constitute compressed versions of a pseudorandom share vector. This type of compression is currently beyond the scope of other compact delegation techniques (e.g. Laconic Function Evaluation [30]), and in fact general purpose delegation schemes with even a weak amount of output compression imply iO [26].

1.3   Related Work

Signature-Based Witness Encryption. The only known construction of signature-based witness encryption [9] grows linearly in the number of verification keys input to the encryption procedure. The same is true for verifiable witness encryption based on threshold signatures [27]. While the ciphertext's size of these constructions is asymptotically worse than ours, their main focus is on concrete efficiency. However, both [9,27] rely on specific assumptions in idealized models, i.e. the bilinear Diffie-Hellman assumption and the random oracle model, whereas we focus on a compact-ciphertext construction in the plain model. Furthermore, we point out that these previous works achieve fully adaptive security notions, as opposed to our non-adaptive security as discussed in Sect. 1.2. There exist also concretely efficient schemes (in the ROM) with constant-size ciphertexts [13], but they can handle only the special case of $t = n$.

Threshold Encryption. Threshold encryption schemes [8,12] are encryption schemes where decryption can take part only with the cooperation of a threshold number of decryption servers. These constructions achieve constant ciphertext size. However, they require a correlated set up of decryptors' secret keys. Furthermore, decryption requires communicating with t servers to get partial decryptions that are then aggregated to get the plaintext. Recently, [7] a scheme with efficient batch-decryption for threshold encryption was proposed. This solution still requires a correlated set up of secret keys, but a server can output partial decryptions for many ciphertexts at once, reducing the communication overhead. In their scheme, the keys are generated by a trusted dealer.

In [16] the notion of silent setup for threshold encryption is introduced. This means, that the involved decryption servers are now able to choose their key pairs independently and encryptors can deterministically aggregate the public keys of their chosen decryption servers into a single succinct encryption key, which can be used to encrypt a message. Dropping correlated key creation is achieved by pushing the complexity into a highly structured CRS and "hints", which can be seen as extensions of the public keys of each party. Both the CRS and the hints are linear in the size of maximum decryption servers. For each decryption procedure direct communication with the decryption servers is still required. Their scheme achieves adaptive security in the *programmable* generic group model.

Witness Encryption and Committe-Based Witness Encryption. Witness Encryption [15] is defined for an NP language $\mathcal{L}$ with poly-time relation $\mathcal{R}$. Encryption of a message m is w.r.t a statement x and decryption is possible with a witness w s.t. $(x, w) \in \mathcal{R}$. Security intuitively says that a ciphertext does not reveal any information about m if $x \notin \mathcal{L}$. Security is extended in [19] in the form of *extractable* witness encryption, which also offers security guarantees even when $x \in \mathcal{L}$. In [21] extractable witness encryption on the blockchain (eWEB) is introduced. In this scheme, a message encrypted with respect to a statement x is secret-shared among several committee members and labeled with x. The decryptor must interact with a threshold number of committee members, proving they have a valid witness to collect the shares and decrypt the message. However, the storage complexity for each committee member increases with the number of shares they hold. This limitation is addressed by [10], which proposes creating a joint public key for encryption while giving each committee member a share of a correlated secret key. Another work [11] further improves this by hiding the statement w.r.t. encryption is done. Their ciphertext size is independent of the number of keys. However, they require a correlated key setup where the committee has a single public key and the secret key is shared among the members. In another work, [4], blockchain witness encryption is independently introduced, serving a similar function to [21], but it requires deploying a smart contract on the blockchain for each encryption. The critical difference between SWE and these works is that in SWE committee keys are independently sampled, and decryption relies solely on the availability of signatures from the committee.

2   Preliminaries

Notation. We denote by $\lambda \in \mathbb{N}$ the security parameter and by $x \leftarrow \mathcal{A}(\mathsf{in}; r)$ the output of the algorithm $\mathcal{A}$ on input in where $\mathcal{A}$ is randomized with $r \leftarrow \{0,1\}^*$ as its randomness. We omit this randomness when it is obvious or not explicitly required. By $\mathcal{A}^O$ we denote, that we run $\mathcal{A}$ with oracle access to O, that is it may query the oracle on inputs of its choice and only receives the corresponding outputs. We denote by $x \leftarrow_\$ S$ an output x being chosen uniformly at random from a set S. We denote the set $\{1, \ldots, n\}$ by $[n]$ and $x[i]$ denotes the i-th bit of x. PPT denotes probabilistic polynomial time. Also, $\mathsf{poly}(x), \mathsf{negl}(x)$ respectively denote any polynomial or negligible function in parameter x.

In the following, we define the cryptographic building blocks necessary for our protocol.

Symmetric Encryption Scheme. A symmetric encryption scheme SKE is a tuple of three efficient algorithms $\mathsf{SKE} = (\mathsf{SKE.KeyGen}, \mathsf{SKE.Enc}, \mathsf{SKE.Dec})$ such that

- $K \leftarrow_\$ \mathsf{SKE.KeyGen}(1^\lambda)$: The probabilistic key generation algorithm on input the security parameter 1^λ outputs a key $K \in \{0,1\}^*$.
- $\mathsf{ct} \leftarrow_\$ \mathsf{SKE.Enc}(K, m)$: The probabilistic encryption algorithm takes as input the key K and a message $m \in \{0,1\}^*$ and outputs a ciphertext $\mathsf{ct} \in \{0,1\}^*$.
- $m \leftarrow \mathsf{SKE.Dec}(K, \mathsf{ct})$: The deterministic decryption algorithm takes as input the key K and a ciphertext ct and outputs a message m.

We require a symmetric encryption scheme to fulfill correctness, IND-CPA security and pseudorandom ciphertexts as defined below:

Definition 1 (Correctness). *We say that a symmetric encryption scheme is correct, if for all $\lambda \in \mathbb{N}$ and all $m \in \{0,1\}^*$, we have*

$$\Pr\left[\mathsf{SKE.Dec}(K, \mathsf{SKE.Enc}(K, m)) = m \mid K \leftarrow_\$ \mathsf{SKE.KeyGen}(1^\lambda)\right] = 1.$$

Definition 2 (Security). *We say that a symmetric encryption scheme is IND-CPA secure, if no adversary $\mathcal{A}$ has more than negligible advantage in the following experiment* $\mathsf{Exp}_{\mathsf{IND\text{-}CPA}}(\mathcal{A}, 1^\lambda)$:

- *The experiment samples $b \leftarrow_\$ \{0,1\}$ and $K \leftarrow_\$ \mathsf{SKE.KeyGen}(1^\lambda)$.*
- *$\mathcal{A}$ gets access to an encryption oracle $O(K, \cdot)$, which on input m outputs $\mathsf{Enc}(K, m)$, which it may use during the whole experiment.*
- *$\mathcal{A}$ chooses two challenge messages m_0, m_1 with $|m_0| = |m_1|$.*
- *The challenger sends $\mathsf{ct} = \mathsf{SKE.Enc}(K, m_b)$ to $\mathcal{A}$.*
- *$\mathcal{A}$ outputs a bit b'.*

The advantage of $\mathcal{A}$ is defined as

$$\mathsf{Adv}^{\mathcal{A}}_{\mathsf{IND\text{-}CPA}} := \left| \Pr\left[\mathsf{Exp}_{\mathsf{IND\text{-}CPA}}(\mathcal{A}, 1^\lambda) \right] - \frac{1}{2} \right|.$$

Pseudo-Random Functions. A keyed family of functions $\mathsf{PRF}_K : \{0,1\}^\mu \to \{0,1\}^\nu$ for keys $K \in \{0,1\}^*$ and some $\mu, \nu = \mathsf{poly}(|K|)$ is a pseudo-random function (PRF) family, if

- given K, m the function $\mathsf{PRF}_K(m)$ is efficiently computable and
- for every PPT distinguisher $\mathcal{D}$, it holds $\mathcal{D}^{\mathsf{PRF}_K(\cdot)} \approx_c \mathcal{D}^{F(\cdot)}$, where $K \leftarrow_\$ \{0,1\}^\lambda$ and F is chosen randomly from all functions from $\{0,1\}^{\mu(\lambda)}$ to $\{0,1\}^{\nu(\lambda)}$.

We also write $\mathsf{PRF}(K, m)$ for $\mathsf{PRF}_K(m)$.

Puncturable Pseudo-Random Functions. A puncturable family of PRFs PPRF mapping strings of length $\mu(\cdot)$ to $\nu(\cdot)$ is given by a triple of algorithms $(\mathsf{KeyGen}, \mathsf{Puncture}, \mathsf{Eval})$, satisfying the following conditions:

Definition 3 (Pseudorandomness). *For every PPT distinguisher $\mathcal{D}$, it holds $\mathcal{D}^{\mathsf{Eval}(K, \cdot)} \approx_c \mathcal{D}^{F(\cdot)}$, where $K \leftarrow_\$ \mathsf{KeyGen}$ and F is chosen randomly from all functions from $\{0,1\}^{\mu(\lambda)}$ to $\{0,1\}^{\nu(\lambda)}$.*

Definition 4 (Functionality Preserved Under Puncturing). *For every PPT adversary A such that $A(1^\lambda)$ outputs a set $S \subseteq \{0,1\}^{\mu(\lambda)}$, then for all $x \in \{0,1\}^{\mu(\lambda)}$ where $x \notin S$, we have that:*

$$\Pr\left[\mathsf{Eval}(K, x) = \mathsf{Eval}(K_S, x) : K \leftarrow \mathsf{KeyGen}(1^\lambda), K_S \leftarrow \mathsf{Puncture}(K, S)\right] = 1$$

Definition 5 (Pseudorandom at Punctured Points). *For every PPT adversary (A_1, A_2) such that $A_1(1^\lambda)$ outputs a set $S \subseteq \{0,1\}^{\mu(\lambda)}$ and state σ, consider an experiment where $K \leftarrow \mathsf{KeyGen}(1^\lambda)$ and $K_S \leftarrow \mathsf{Puncture}(K, S)$. Then, the following is negligible in λ:*

$$\left| \Pr\left[A_2\left(\sigma, K_S, S, \mathsf{Eval}(K, S)\right) = 1\right] - \Pr\left[A_2\left(\sigma, K_S, S, U_{\nu(\lambda) \cdot |S|}\right) = 1\right] \right|$$

Here, $S = \{x_1, \ldots, x_k\}$ is the enumeration of the elements of S in lexicographic order, U_ℓ denotes the uniform distribution over ℓ bits and $\mathsf{Eval}(K, S)$ denotes the concatenation of $(\mathsf{Eval}(K, x_1), \ldots, \mathsf{Eval}(K, x_k))$.

In abuse of notation, we write $\mathsf{PPRF}(K, m)$ to denote $\mathsf{PPRF.Eval}(K, m)$. The construction given in [3] fulfills the following efficiency guarantees:

- A key punctured at a single point is of size $\mu \cdot \mathsf{poly}(\lambda)$.
- Evaluation of PPRF at a key punctured at most a single point runs in $\mathcal{O}(\mu \cdot \mathsf{poly}(\lambda))$.

Somewhere Statistically Binding Hashing. Somewhere statistically binding (SSB) hashing was initially introduced by [22] and several constructions of SSB hashing followed. [29]

Definition 6. *A somewhere statistically binding (SSB) scheme* SSB *is composed of the following algorithms:*

- $\mathsf{hk} \leftarrow \mathsf{KeyGen}(1^\lambda, n, i)$ *takes as input the security parameter* λ, $n \in \mathbb{N}$ *and an index* $i \in [n]$. *It outputs a hashing key* hk.
- $h \leftarrow \mathsf{Hash}(\mathsf{hk}, D)$ *takes as input a hashing key* hk *and a database* $D = (x_i)_{i \in [n]}$. *It outputs a digest* h.
- $\tau \leftarrow \mathsf{Open}(\mathsf{hk}, D, i)$ *takes as input a hashing key* hk, *a database* $D = (x_i)_{i \in [n]}$ *and an index* i. *It outputs a proof* τ.
- $b \leftarrow \mathsf{Vrfy}(\mathsf{hk}, h, i, x, \tau)$ *takes as input a hashing key* hk, *a digest* h, *an index* $i \in [n]$, *a value* x *and a proof* τ. *It outputs a bit* b.

We require that an SSB hashing scheme fulfills the following efficiency guarantees:

1. The length ℓ_{hk} of the hashing key hk and the length ℓ_τ of proof τ are both of size $\mathcal{O}(\mathsf{poly}(\lambda) \cdot \log n)$;
2. The Vrfy algorithm can be represented by a Turing machine of description size and runtime $\mathcal{O}(\mathsf{poly}(\lambda) \cdot \log n)$.
3. The hash h is of size $\ell_h(\lambda) = \mathcal{O}(\mathsf{poly}(\lambda))$.

Additionally, an SSB hashing scheme fulfills the following properties.

Definition 7 (Correctness). *We say that an SSB hashing scheme is correct if for all* $\lambda \in \mathbb{N}$, *all* $n = \mathsf{poly}(\lambda)$, *all databases* D *of size* n, *all indices* $j, i \in [n]$ *we have that*

$$\Pr\left[1 \leftarrow \mathsf{Vrfy}(\mathsf{hk}, h, i, x, \tau) : \begin{array}{c} \mathsf{hk} \leftarrow \mathsf{KeyGen}(1^\lambda, n, j) \\ h \leftarrow \mathsf{Hash}(\mathsf{hk}, D) \\ \tau \leftarrow \mathsf{Open}(\mathsf{hk}, D, i) \end{array}\right] = 1.$$

Definition 8 (Somewhere Statistically Binding). *We say that an SSB hashing scheme is somewhere statistically binding if for all $\lambda \in \mathbb{N}$, all $n = \mathsf{poly}(\lambda)$, all databases D of size n, all indices $i \in [n]$, all database values x and all proofs τ we have that*

$$\Pr \left[D_i = x : \begin{array}{l} \mathsf{hk} \leftarrow \mathsf{KeyGen}(1^\lambda, n, i) \\ h \leftarrow \mathsf{Hash}(\mathsf{hk}, D) \\ 1 \leftarrow \mathsf{Vrfy}(\mathsf{hk}, h, i, x, \tau) \end{array} \right] = 1.$$

Definition 9 (Index Hiding). *We say that an SSB hashing scheme is index hiding if for all $\lambda \in \mathbb{N}$ and all PPT adversaries $\mathcal{A} = (\mathcal{A}_1, \mathcal{A}_2)$ we have that*

$$\left| \Pr \left[b \leftarrow \mathcal{A}_2(\mathsf{hk}, aux) : \begin{array}{l} (n, i_0, i_1, aux) \leftarrow \mathcal{A}_1(1^\lambda) \\ b \leftarrow_\$ \{0, 1\} \\ \mathsf{hk} \leftarrow \mathsf{KeyGen}(1^\lambda, n, i_b) \end{array} \right] - \frac{1}{2} \right| = \mathsf{negl}(\lambda).$$

Secret Sharing. We will introduce linear secret sharings and the well-known Shamir secret sharing [32].

Definition 10 (Linear Secret Sharing). *Let $t \leq n$. A (t, n)-linear secret sharing (LSS) LSS scheme is composed of the following algorithms:*

- $(s_1, \ldots, s_n) \leftarrow \mathsf{Share}(m)$ *takes as input a message m. It outputs n shares $(s_1, \ldots, s_n)$.*
- $m \leftarrow \mathsf{Reconstruct}(s_{i_1}, \ldots, s_{i_t})$ *takes as input t shares $(s_{i_1}, \ldots, s_{i_t})$. It outputs a message m.*

We expect an (t, n)-LSS to be correct and t-private.

Definition 11 (Correctness). *An LSS scheme LSS is said to be correct if for all messages m and all subsets $\{i_1, \ldots, i_t\} \subseteq [n]$*

$$\Pr \left[m = \mathsf{Reconstruct}(s_{i_1}, \ldots, s_{i_t}) : (s_1, \ldots, s_n) \leftarrow \mathsf{Share}(m) \right] = 1.$$

Definition 12 (Privacy). *We say that a (t, n)-LSS scheme LSS is t-private if for all subsets $\{i_1, \ldots, i_z\} \subset [n]$ where $z < t$, all pairs of messages (m_0, m_1) and all PPT adversaries $\mathcal{A}$ we have that*

$$\left| \begin{array}{l} \Pr \left[1 \leftarrow \mathcal{A}(s_{0,i_1}, \ldots, s_{0,i_z}) : (s_{0,1}, \ldots, s_{0,n}) \leftarrow \mathsf{Share}(m_0) \right] - \\ \Pr \left[1 \leftarrow \mathcal{A}(s_{1,i_1}, \ldots, s_{1,i_z}) : (s_{1,1}, \ldots, s_{1,n}) \leftarrow \mathsf{Share}(m_1) \right] \end{array} \right| = \mathsf{negl}(\lambda).$$

One such LSS scheme is the popular Shamir secret sharing [32]. Let $\mathbb{Z}_p$ be the finite field of prime order p and fix distinct elements $\xi = \xi_1, \ldots, \xi_n \in \mathbb{Z}_p$.

Shamir.Share(m) picks a random degree $t - 1$ polynomial f with $f(0) = m$ and sets $s_i = f(\xi_i)$ for $i \in [n]$ as its shares.

To reconstruct, we use **Lagrange Interpolation**: For a set of supporting points $\chi_1, \ldots, \chi_k$ from a finite field $\mathbb{Z}_p$, where $p \in \mathbb{N}$ is prime, the Lagrange basis polynomials are given by $L_1, \ldots, L_k$, where

$$L_i(x) = \prod_{j \in [k]; j \neq i} \frac{x - \chi_j}{\chi_i - \chi_j}.$$

These are chosen such that $L_i(\chi_j) = 1$ iff $i = j$ and 0 otherwise. Consequently, given a set of k data points (ξ_i, y_i), we can output a polynomial $f_L(x) = \Sigma_{i \in [k]} L_i(x) \cdot y_i$ that will run through these points and which has degree at most k-1. This process is called Lagrange Interpolation. Hence, if $k > t-1$, we will get back the original polynomial used in sharing and can evaluate $f(0) = m$.

Indistinguishability Obfuscation for Turing Machines. Indistinguishability Obfuscation $(i\mathcal{O})$ [14] is a primitive to encode functionalities (usually represented as circuits) in a way such that the encodings of functionally equivalent circuits are indistinguishable.

In this work we need indistinguishability obfuscation for Turing Machines as constructed in [17,25]. This is defined in [17] as follows:

Definition 13 (Succinct Indistinguishability Obfuscator). *A succinct indistinguishability obfuscator for a machine class $\{\mathcal{M}_\lambda\}_{\lambda \in \mathbb{N}}$ consists of a uniform PPT machine iOM as follows:*

- obM $\leftarrow$ iOM $\left(1^\lambda, 1^n, t, M\right)$*: iOM takes as input the security parameter 1^λ, a description M of the Turing machine to obfuscate, and an input length n and time bound t for M.*
- *iOM outputs a machine obM, which is an obfuscation of M corresponding to input length n and time bound t. obM takes as input $x \in \{0,1\}^n$ and $t' \leq t$.*

The scheme should satisfy the following three requirements:

- ***Correctness:*** *For all security parameters $\lambda \in \mathbb{N}$, for all $M \in \mathcal{M}_\lambda$, for all inputs $x \in \{0,1\}^n$, time bounds t and $t' \leq t$, let y be the output of M on t' steps, then we have that:*

$$\Pr\left[\text{obM}\,(x,t') = y : \text{obM} \leftarrow i\mathcal{O}\text{M}\left(1^\lambda, 1^n, t, M\right)\right] = 1$$

- ***Security:*** *For any (not necessarily uniform) PPT distinguisher D, there exists a negligible function α such that the following holds: For all security parameters $\lambda \in \mathbb{N}$, time bounds t, and pairs of machines $M_0, M_1 \in \mathcal{M}_\lambda$ of the same size such that for all running times $t' \leq t$ and for all inputs x, $M_0(x) = M_1(x)$ when M_0 and M_1 are executed for time t', we have that for obM$_b \leftarrow i\mathcal{O}\text{M}\left(1^\lambda, 1^n, t, M_b\right)$ for $b \in \{0,1\}$:*

$$|\Pr\left[D(\text{ob}M_0) = 1\right] - \Pr\left[D(\text{ob}M_1) = 1\right]| \leq \alpha(\lambda)$$

- ***Efficiency and Succinctness:*** *We require that the running time of iOM and the length of its output, namely the obfuscated machine obM, is in $\mathcal{O}(\text{poly}(|M|, \log t, n, \lambda))$. We also require that the obfuscated machine on input x and t' runs in time $\mathcal{O}(\text{poly}\left(|M|, t', n, \log t, \lambda\right))$.*

3   Strongly Puncturable Signatures

Strongly puncturable signature (SPS) schemes are signature schemes with additional features and were introduced in [20] under the name of all-but-one signatures. In particular, such a scheme comes with a punctured key generation algorithm that, on input a message m^*, generates a pair of punctured keys $(\mathsf{vk}^*, \mathsf{sk}^*)$ at message m^*. A SPS scheme has to satisfy: (1) *puncturability*, meaning that given a punctured key $(\mathsf{vk}^*, \mathsf{sk}^*)$ w.r.t. a message m^* there *does not exist*, except with negligible probability, a valid signature for m^* w.r.t. the key vk^*; (2) *punctured-key indistinguishability* ensuring that punctured verification keys are indistinguishable from regular verification keys, as long as no signature on m^* is requested. Additionally, an SPS has to satisfy the usual correctness and EUF-CMA unforgeability properties of digital signatures.

We call this type of signature *strongly* puncturable to remark the difference with other notions of puncturable signatures [1,6,23] where a verifying signature for the punctured message m^* might exist, but it is infeasible to compute (given e.g. a punctured signing key).

In [20], various instantiations that can be based on different number-theoretic assumptions (e.g., RSA, pairing-based assumptions, LWE) were proposed. In the full version of this paper, we propose an alternative instantiation based on simulation-sound non-interactive zero-knowledge (NIZK) proofs and pseudorandom generators (PRGs).

Definition 14 (Strongly Puncturable Signature Scheme).
A strongly puncturable signature scheme $\mathsf{Sig} = (\mathsf{KeyGen}, \mathsf{PKeyGen}, \mathsf{Sign}, \mathsf{Vrfy})$ *consists of the following algorithms:*

- $(\mathsf{vk}, \mathsf{sk}) \leftarrow_\$ \mathsf{KeyGen}(1^\lambda)$: *On input the security parameter* 1^λ, *the key generation algorithm* KeyGen *returns a verification key* vk *and a signing key* sk.
- $(\mathsf{vk}, \mathsf{sk}) \leftarrow_\$ \mathsf{PKeyGen}(1^\lambda, m^*)$: *On input the security parameter* 1^λ, *a message* m^* *to puncture at, the punctured key generation algorithm* $\mathsf{PKeyGen}$ *returns a verification key* vk *and a signing key* sk, *that allows to sign any message except* m^*.
- $\sigma \leftarrow_\$ \mathsf{Sign}(\mathsf{sk}, m)$: *On input a signing key* sk *and a message* m, *it outputs a signature* σ.
- $d \leftarrow \mathsf{Vrfy}(\mathsf{vk}, \sigma, m)$, $d \in \{0,1\}$: *On input a verification key* vk, *a signature* σ *and a message* m, *the verification algorithm* Vrfy *returns a bit* $d \in \{0,1\}$.

A strongly puncturable signature scheme has the following properties:

Definition 15 (Correctness). *For all* λ *and all messages* m *in the underlying message space*

$$\Pr\left[\mathsf{Vrfy}(\mathsf{vk}, \mathsf{Sign}(\mathsf{sk}, m), m) = 1 \mid (\mathsf{vk}, \mathsf{sk}) \leftarrow_\$ \mathsf{KeyGen}(1^\lambda)\right] = 1.$$

Definition 16 (Puncturability). *For all* λ *and for all messages* m^*, *we require that the following probability is negligible in* λ:

$$\Pr\left[\exists \sigma \text{ s.t. } \mathsf{Vrfy}(\mathsf{vk}^*, \sigma, m^*) = 1 \mid (\mathsf{vk}^*, \mathsf{sk}^*) \leftarrow_\$ \mathsf{PKeyGen}(1^\lambda, m^*)\right]$$

Definition 17 (Punctured-Key Indistinguishability). *We say that a strongly puncturable signature scheme* Sig = (KeyGen, PKeyGen, Sign, Vrfy) *has key indistinguishability, if no PPT adversary $\mathcal{A}$ has more than negligible advantage in the experiment* $\mathsf{Exp}_{\mathsf{IND\text{-}SPS}}(\mathcal{A}, 1^\lambda)$. *We define $\mathcal{A}$'s advantage by*

$$\mathsf{Adv}^{\mathcal{A}}_{\mathsf{IND\text{-}SPS}} := \left| \Pr[\mathsf{Exp}_{\mathsf{IND\text{-}SPS}}(\mathcal{A}, 1^\lambda) = 1] - \frac{1}{2} \right|.$$

Experiment $\mathsf{Exp}_{\mathsf{IND\text{-}SPS}}(\mathcal{A}, 1^\lambda)$

1. *Adversary $\mathcal{A}$ provides a message m^* to puncture at.*
2. *The challenger picks a challenge bit $b \leftarrow_{\$} \{0, 1\}$. If $b = 0$, then* (vk, sk) $\leftarrow_{\$}$ KeyGen(1^λ). *If $b = 1$, then* (vk, sk) $\leftarrow_{\$}$ PKeyGen($1^\lambda, m^*$). *The verification key* vk *is returned to $\mathcal{A}$.*
3. *$\mathcal{A}$ gets oracle-access to* Sign$_{m^*}$(sk, ·). *The oracle signs any message under the secret key* sk, *except m^*.*
4. *$\mathcal{A}$ returns a guess bit b' and wins iff $b' = b$.*

Note that we can leverage punctured-key indistinguishability combined with a guessing argument to achieve standard EUF-CMA security. We omit this definition as it is not necessary for our work.

4   Compact Threshold SWE

In this section we introduce a compact t-of-n SWE scheme. This is a special purpose (threshold) witness encryption where we encrypt with regard to a set of signature verification keys $V = (\mathsf{vk}_1, \ldots, \mathsf{vk}_n)$ and a reference message T, such that decryption becomes available upon receiving t signatures $(\sigma_{i_j})_{j \in [t]}$ which verify for the reference message under t of the verification keys i.e. Sig.Vrfy($\mathsf{vk}_{i_j}, \sigma_{i_j}, T) = 1$. We say that such a scheme is compact if its ciphertext size grows polylogarithmically in the number of verification keys n, and we say it is secure if IND-CPA security holds in the absence of at least t such signatures.

4.1   Definition

Compared to the original proposal of SWE in [9], we have relaxed the definitions here in the following ways:

- The security is non-adaptive as discussed in Sect. 1.2.
- The underlying signature in this work needs to be puncturable and we take multiple signatures instead of one aggregated signature[2] as arguments.

---

[2] The original paper uses BLS signatures, which allow to compress multiple signatures on different messages and from different signers into a single aggregated signature, that can be efficiently checked against all messages/signers in one step.

Definition 18 (Compact Signature-Based Witness Encryption). *A t-out-of-n cSWE for a strongly puncturable signature scheme* Sig = (KeyGen, PKeyGen, Sign, Vrfy) *is a tuple of two algorithms* (Enc, Dec) *where:*

- ct ← Enc($1^\lambda, V = (vk_1, \ldots, vk_n), T, m$): *Encryption takes as input a security parameter λ, a set V of n verification keys of the underlying scheme* Sig, *a reference signing message T and a message m of arbitrary length $\ell \in$ poly(λ). It outputs a ciphertext* ct.
- $m \leftarrow$ Dec(ct, $(\sigma_i)_{i \in I}, I, V$): *Decryption takes as input a ciphertext* ct, *a list of signatures $(\sigma_i)_{i \in I}$, an index set $I \subseteq [n]$ and a set V of verification keys of the underlying scheme* Sig. *It outputs a message m.*

We require such a scheme to fulfill three properties: correctness, compactness and security.

Definition 19 (Correctness). *A t-out-of-n cSWE scheme* cSWE = (Enc, Dec) *for a strongly puncturable signature scheme* Sig = (KeyGen, PKeyGen, Sign, Vrfy) *is correct if $\forall \lambda \in \mathbb{N}$, sets of keys $V = (vk_1, \ldots, vk_n)$, index sets $I \subseteq [n]$ with $|I| \geq t$, messages m, T and signatures $(\sigma_i)_{i \in I}$ with* Sig.Vrfy$(vk_i, \sigma_i, T) = 1$ *for all $i \in I$, it holds* Dec(Enc($1^\lambda, V, T, m$), $(\sigma_i)_{i \in I}, I, V$) = m.

Definition 20 (Compactness). *Given* ct ← Enc($1^\lambda, V, T, m$), *its size $|$ct$|$ is $\mathcal{O}($poly$(\lambda, \log n))$, where $n = |V|$.*

Definition 21 (Security). *A t-out-of-n cSWE scheme* cSWE = (Enc, Dec) *for a strongly puncturable signature scheme* Sig = (KeyGen, PKeyGen, Sign, Vrfy) *is secure if for all $\lambda \in \mathbb{N}$, all $t, n =$ poly$(\lambda), t < n$, there is no PPT adversary $\mathcal{A}$ that has more than negligible advantage in the experiment* $\mathsf{Exp}_{\mathsf{Sec}}(\mathcal{A}, 1^\lambda)$.

Experiment $\mathsf{Exp}_{\mathsf{Sec}}(\mathcal{A}, 1^\lambda)$

1. *The adversary $\mathcal{A}$ specifies signing reference message T^* and indices $J \subset [n]$ with $|J| \leq t - 1$.*
2. *The experiment generates n key pairs for $i \in [n]$ as $(vk_i, sk_i) \leftarrow$ Sig.KeyGen(1^λ) and provides $V = (vk_1, \ldots, vk_n)$ to $\mathcal{A}$, as well as all sk_i for $i \in J$.*
3. *$\mathcal{A}$ gets to make signing queries for pairs (i, T). If $i \in J$ or $T = T^*$, the experiment aborts, else it returns* Sig.Sign(sk_i, T).
4. *$\mathcal{A}$ announces challenge messages m_0, m_1 with $|m_0| = |m_1|$.*
5. *The experiment flips a bit $b \leftarrow_{\$} \{0, 1\}$, and sends* Enc($1^\lambda, V, T^*, m_b$) *to $\mathcal{A}$.*
6. *$\mathcal{A}$ gets to make further signing queries for pairs (i, T). If $i \in J$ or $T = T^*$, the experiment aborts, else it returns* Sig.Sign(sk_i, T).
7. *Finally, $\mathcal{A}$ outputs a guess b'.*
8. *If $b = b'$, the experiment outputs 1, else 0.*

We define $\mathcal{A}$'s advantage by $\mathsf{Adv}^{\mathcal{A}}_{\mathsf{Sec}} := \left| \Pr\left[\mathsf{Exp}_{\mathsf{Sec}}(\mathcal{A}, 1^\lambda) = 1 \right] - \frac{1}{2} \right|$.

4.2   Construction

Our construction relies on indistinguishability obfuscation for Turing Machines and a Strongly Puncturable Signature scheme. The following scheme works for $n = \mathsf{poly}(\lambda)$ potential signers and requires t-of-n signatures to decrypt. Given a strongly puncturable signature scheme Sig, our protocol will work for a slightly altered signature scheme Sig'. We define Sig' to behave exactly as Sig, but additionally the public keys vk output by $(\mathsf{vk}, \mathsf{sk}) \leftarrow \mathsf{Sig}'.\mathsf{KeyGen}(1^\lambda)$ have a random part $R_i \leftarrow_\$ \mathbb{Z}_p$ appended to vk_i, hence its keys are of the form (vk_i, R_i). Let $\ell_{vk} = |(\mathsf{vk}_i, R_i)|$ be the size of its keys, $\mathcal{M}$ its message space, and ℓ_σ be the length of its signatures. Let

- $p > 2^\lambda$ be a prime number.
- $\mathsf{PRF} : \{0,1\}^\lambda \times \{0,1\}^\mu \to \mathbb{Z}_p$ be a PRF with $\log n \le \mu \le \log p$.
- $\mathsf{PPRF} = (\mathsf{KeyGen}, \mathsf{Puncture}, \mathsf{Eval})$ with $\mathsf{Eval} : \{0,1\}^\lambda \times \{0,1\}^\mu \to \mathbb{Z}_p$ be a PPRF and ℓ_{pkey} be the size of any key punctured at most one point.
- SKE be a symmetric key encryption scheme
- SSB be an SSB-hashing scheme and $\ell_{\mathsf{hk}}, \ell_\tau, \ell_h$ be the length of the hashing keys hk, proofs τ and hashes h of SSB on input a database D with length n and with a maximum size of its entries of ℓ_{vk}.
- $\mathsf{ob}M$ be an indistinguishability obfuscator for the class of machines $\mathcal{TM}_\lambda = \{M_{i^*}[K, K_1, h, T, \mathsf{hk}, K_2, U, \mathsf{ind}_2](\mathsf{ind}, (\mathsf{vk}, R), \tau, \sigma')\}$ where each such machine takes: indices $i^*, \mathsf{ind}_2 \in \{0, \ldots, n+1\}$, values $K, K_1 \in \{0,1\}^\lambda$, $h \in \{0,1\}^{\ell_h}, T \in \mathcal{M}, \mathsf{hk} \in \{0,1\}^{\ell_{hk}}$, a PPRF key $K_2 \in \{0,1\}^\ell_{pkey}$ and a value $U \in \mathbb{Z}_p$ as hardwired inputs and an index $\mathsf{ind} \in [n]$, values vk, R of combined length ℓ_{vk}, as well as $\tau \in \{0,1\}^{\ell_\tau}$ and $\sigma \in \{0,1\}^{\ell_\sigma}$ as run-time inputs. $M_{i^*}[K, K_1, h, T, \mathsf{hk}, K_2, U, \mathsf{ind}_2](\mathsf{ind}, (\mathsf{vk}, R), \tau, \sigma')$ is defined as:
  - If $\mathsf{ind} < 1$ or $\mathsf{ind} > n$, abort and output $\bot$.
  - If $0 - \mathsf{SSB.Vrfy}(\mathsf{hk}, h, \mathsf{ind}, (\mathsf{vk}, R), \tau)$, abort and output $\bot$.
  - If $0 = \mathsf{Sig.Vrfy}(\mathsf{vk}, \sigma', T)$, abort and output $\bot$.
  - If $\mathsf{ind} = \mathsf{ind}_2$: Output $R + U \mod p$ and halt.
  - If $\mathsf{ind} \le i^*$: Output $R + \mathsf{PPRF}(K_2, \mathsf{ind}) \mod p$ and halt.
  - Else if $\mathsf{ind} > i^*$:
    * Write on the tape variables $i = 1, R = 0, X = 1, S = K$.
    * While $i < t$: Set $R = \mathsf{PRF}(K_1, i)$, $X = X \cdot \mathsf{ind} \mod p$, $S = S + X \cdot R \mod p$, $i = i + 1$.
    * Output S.

Note that all these machines have the same description size. Let ℓ_{inp} be shorthand for its input size and $T_{\mathcal{TM}}$ denote the maximum runtime within this machine class. It is syntactically clear that these machines always halt, so $T_{\mathcal{TM}}$ is well-defined.

Protocol Compact cSWE for Sig' - from iO

$\text{cSWE.Enc}(1^\lambda, V = (\text{vk}_i, R_i)_{i \in [n]}, T, m)$:
- Generate PRF key $K_1 \leftarrow \text{PRF.KeyGen}(1^\lambda)$
- Generate symmetric key $K \leftarrow \text{SKE.KeyGen}(1^\lambda)$
- Generate PPRF key $K_2 \leftarrow \text{PPRF.KeyGen}(1^\lambda)$
- Generate a hashing key $\text{hk} \leftarrow \text{SSB.KeyGen}(1^\lambda, n, 1)$
- Set $h = \text{SSB.Hash}(\text{hk}, (\text{vk}_i, R_i)_{i \in [n]})$
- Choose $U \leftarrow_\$ \mathbb{Z}_p$.
- Let $M' = M_0[K, K_1, h, T, \text{hk}, K_2, U, 0](\cdot, (\cdot, \cdot), \cdot, \cdot)$.
- Compute $\text{ob}M \leftarrow i\mathcal{O}M(1^\lambda, M', \ell_{inp}, T_{T\mathcal{M}})$.
- Compute $\text{ct}' = \text{SKE.Enc}(K, m)$
- Output $(\text{ob}M, \text{ct}', \text{hk})$

$\text{cSWE.Dec}(\text{ct}, (\sigma), I, V = (\text{vk}_i, R_i)_{i \in [n]})$:
- Parse $\text{ct} = (\text{ob}M, \text{ct}', \text{hk})$
- If $|I| < t$, abort.
- Parse $\sigma = (\sigma_i)_{i \in I}$.
- For $i \in I$:
  - Compute $\tau_i = \text{Open}(\text{hk}, V, i)$
  - Run $c_i = \text{ob}M(i, (\text{vk}_i, R_i), \tau, \sigma_i)$
  - Notice $c_i = K + \Sigma_{j=1}^{t-1} \text{PRF}(K_1, j) \cdot i^j$ i.e. evaluations $S_i = f(i)$ on polynomial $f = K + \Sigma_{j=1}^{t-1} \text{PRF}(K_1, j) \cdot x^j$.
- Compute $K' = \sum_{i \in I} c_i \cdot L_i$ where $L_i = \prod_{j \in I; j \neq i} \frac{-j}{i-j}$.
- Output $m = \text{SKE.Dec}(K', \text{ct}')$.

We point out that by encrypting a symmetric encryption key, we can get an encryption scheme that allows messages m of arbitrary length without impacting the size of $\text{ob}M$.

4.3 Proofs

Theorem 1. *Our construction* cSWE *is correct, given that the underlying primitives* Sig', SKE, SSB *and* $\text{ob}M$ *are correct.*

Proof. Let $\lambda \in \mathbb{N}$, a set of keys $V = (\text{vk}_1, \ldots, \text{vk}_n)$, an index set $I \subseteq [n]$ with $|I| \geq t$, messages m, T and signatures $(\sigma_i)_{i \in I}$ be given such that for all $i \in I$, we have $\text{Sig.Vrfy}(\text{vk}_i, \sigma_i, T) = 1$. Let us show $\text{Dec}(\text{Enc}(1^\lambda, V, T, m), (\sigma_i)_{i \in I}, I, V) = m$. $\text{Enc}(1^\lambda, V, T, m)$ yields an output $(\text{ob}M, \text{ct}', \text{hk})$. In $\text{Dec}((\text{ob}M, \text{ct}', \text{hk}), (\sigma_i)_{i \in I}, I, V)$, we do not abort before calling $\text{ob}M$, as $|I| \geq t$ by requirement. We compute for $i \in I$: $\tau_i = \text{Open}(\text{hk}, V, i)$, $c_i = \text{ob}M(i, (\text{vk}_i, R_i), \tau, \sigma_i)$. By correctness of $\text{ob}M$, this outputs the value generated by $M_0[K, K_1, h, T, \text{hk}, K_2, U, 0](i, (\text{vk}_i, R_i), \tau, \sigma_i)$, which runs the following code:

- If $i < 1$ or $i > n$, abort and output $\perp$.

- If $0 = \mathsf{SSB.Vrfy}(\mathsf{hk}, h, i, (\mathsf{vk}_i, R_i), \tau)$, abort and output $\bot$.
- If $0 = \mathsf{Sig.Vrfy}(\mathsf{vk}_i, \sigma_i, T)$, abort and output $\bot$.
- If $i = 0$: Output $R + U \mod p$ and halt.
- If $i \leq 0$: Output $R + \mathsf{PPRF}(K_2, i) \mod p$ and halt.
- Else if $i > 0$:
  - Write on the tape variables $j = 1, R = 0, X = 1, S = K$
  - While $j < t$:
    * Set $R = \mathsf{PRF}(K_1, j)$, $X = X \cdot i \mod p$, $S = S + X \cdot R \mod p$, $j = j + 1$.
  - Output S

And has hardcoded values $K_1 \leftarrow \mathsf{PRF.KeyGen}(1^\lambda)$, $K \leftarrow \mathsf{SKE.KeyGen}(1^\lambda)$, $K_2 \leftarrow \mathsf{PPRF.KeyGen}(1^\lambda)$, $\mathsf{hk} \leftarrow \mathsf{SSB.KeyGen}(1^\lambda, n, 1)$, $h = \mathsf{SSB.Hash}(\mathsf{hk}, (\mathsf{vk}_i, R_i)_{i \in [n]})$.

Clearly $1 \leq i \leq n$. $\mathsf{SSB.Vrfy}(\mathsf{hk}, h, i, (\mathsf{vk}_i, R_i), \tau) = 1$ holds by correctness of SSB since hk, V in Dec are the same as in the call to Enc. $\mathsf{Sig.Vrfy}(\mathsf{vk}_i, \sigma_i, T)$ holds by definition.

This means we get for $i \in I$ $c_i = K + \Sigma_{j=1}^{t-1}\mathsf{PRF}(K_1, j) \cdot i^j$ i.e. evaluations $c_i = f(i)$ of a polynomial $f = K + \Sigma_{j=1}^{t-1}\mathsf{PRF}(K_1, j) \cdot x^j$ with $f(0) = K$. By computing $K' = \sum_{i \in I} c_i \cdot L_i$ with $L_i = \prod_{j \in I; j \neq i} \frac{-j}{i-j}$ being the Langrange polynomials for supporting points $i \in I$ evaluated at 0, we are guaranteed $K' = f(0) = K$.

So Dec finally outputs $\mathsf{SKE.Dec}(K, \mathsf{ct}')$, but since $\mathsf{ct}' = \mathsf{SKE.Enc}(K, m)$, by the correctness of SKE, we output the original message m. $\square$

Theorem 2. *Our construction cSWE is compact.*

Proof. The bottleneck of our ciphertext size is the size of the obfuscated Turing machine, which depends polynomially on its description size and polylogarithmically on its runtime. We notice, that we can describe all inputs (runtime as well as hardwired ones) in $\mathcal{O}(\mathsf{poly}(\lambda) \cdot \log n)$ All operations (comparisons, modular arithmetic in $\mathbb{Z}_p$, SSB verification, signature verification and (P)PRF evaluations) can be described and evaluated in size/time $\mathcal{O}(\mathsf{poly}(\lambda) \cdot \log n)$ and we can describe the whole code including the while-loop in $\mathcal{O}(\mathsf{poly}(\log n \cdot \lambda))$, while the maximum runtime is in $\mathcal{O}(n \cdot \mathsf{poly}(\log n \cdot \lambda))$, leading to the desired size.

In more detail, the output of $\mathsf{cSWE'.Enc}(1^\lambda, V = (\mathsf{vk}_i, R_i)_{i \in [n]}, T, m)$ is $(\mathsf{ob}M, \mathsf{ct}', \mathsf{hk})$, where $\mathsf{hk} = \mathsf{SSB.Hash}(\mathsf{hk}, (\mathsf{vk}_i, R_i)_{i \in [n]})$, $|\mathsf{hk}| = \ell_{hk} = \mathcal{O}(\mathsf{poly}(\lambda) \cdot \log n)$ by the efficiency guarantees on SSB.

And $\mathsf{ct}' = \mathsf{SKE.Enc}(K, m)$, so $|\mathsf{ct}'| = \mathcal{O}(\mathsf{poly}(\lambda) \cdot |m|) = \mathcal{O}(\mathsf{poly}(\lambda))$. It remains to show that $\mathsf{ob}M$ is in $\mathcal{O}(\mathsf{poly}(\lambda, \log n))$.

$\mathsf{ob}M \leftarrow i\mathcal{O}M(1^\lambda, M', \ell_{inp}, T_{T\mathcal{M}})$ with $M' = M_{i^*=0}[K, K_1, h, T, \mathsf{hk}, K_2, U, \mathsf{ind}_2 = 0]$ By the efficiency requirements on $i\mathcal{O}M$, $|\mathsf{ob}M|$ is in $\mathcal{O}(\mathsf{poly}(|M'|, \log T_{T\mathcal{M}}, \ell_{inp}, \lambda))$, where $|M'|$ is the description size, $T_{T\mathcal{M}}$ the maximum runtime and ℓ_{inp} the maximum input size of machines in $T\mathcal{M}_\lambda$. The machines in this class are defined as
$M_{i^*}[K, K_1, h, T, \mathsf{hk}, K_2, U, \mathsf{ind}_2](\mathsf{ind}, (\mathsf{vk}, R), \tau, \sigma')$:

- If $\mathsf{ind} < 1$ or $\mathsf{ind} > n$, abort and output $\bot$.
- If $0 = \mathsf{SSB.Vrfy}(\mathsf{hk}, h, \mathsf{ind}, (\mathsf{vk}, R), \tau)$, abort and output $\bot$.

- If $0 = \mathsf{Sig.Vrfy}(\mathsf{vk}, \sigma', T)$, abort and output $\perp$.
- If $\mathsf{ind} = \mathsf{ind}_2$: Output $R + U \mod p$ and halt.
- If $\mathsf{ind} \leq i^*$: Output $R + \mathsf{PPRF}(K_2, \mathsf{ind}) \mod p$ and halt.
- Else if $\mathsf{ind} > i^*$:
  - Write on the tape variables $i = 1, R = 0, X = 1, S = K$
  - While $i < t$: Set $R = \mathsf{PRF}(K_1, i)$, $X = X \cdot \mathsf{ind} \mod p$, $S = S + X \cdot R \mod p$, $i = i + 1$.
  - Output S

By construction, the sizes of hardwired inputs are as follows: $|i^*|, |\mathsf{ind}_2| = \log n$, $|K|, |K_1| = \lambda$, $|h| = \ell_h = \mathcal{O}(\mathsf{poly}(\lambda))$ by efficiency of SSB, $|T| = \mathcal{O}(\mathsf{poly}(\lambda))$ as $T \in \mathcal{M}$ is from the message space of Sig with security parameter λ, $|\mathsf{hk}| = \ell_{hk} = \mathcal{O}(\mathsf{poly}(\lambda) \cdot \log n)$ by the efficiency guarantees on SSB, $|K_2| = \ell_{pkey} = \mu \cdot \mathsf{poly}(\lambda)$ by the efficiency guarantees of PPRF and $|U| = \log p$.

The **runtime inputs** are bounded in size as follows: $\mathsf{ind} = \log n$, $|(\mathsf{vk}, R)| = \ell_{\mathsf{vk}} = \lambda + \log p$, $|\tau| = \ell_\tau = \mathcal{O}(\mathsf{poly}(\lambda)) \cdot \log n$ by efficiency of SSB and $|\sigma| = \ell_\sigma = \mathsf{poly}(\lambda)$.

We can bound $\mu, \log p = \mathcal{O}(\mathsf{poly}(\log n, \lambda))$, as we only required $\log p > \lambda, \log p \geq \mu \geq \log n$. So, we see directly that the input size is bounded as

$$\ell_{inp} = \mathcal{O}(\mathsf{poly}(\lambda \cdot \log n)).$$

Towards analysing the **maximum runtime** $T_{\mathcal{TM}}$: Comparisons with ind, i^* can be executed in time $\mathcal{O}(\mathsf{poly}(\log n))$. The Turing machine code for $\mathsf{SSB.Vrfy}(\mathsf{hk}, h, \mathsf{ind}, (\mathsf{vk}, R), \tau)$ has runtime $\mathcal{O}(\mathsf{poly}(\lambda) \cdot \log n)$ by efficiency of SSB. The code for $\mathsf{Sig.Vrfy}(\mathsf{vk}, \sigma', T)$ has runtime $\mathcal{O}(\mathsf{poly}(\lambda))$. Modular arithmetic in $\mathbb{Z}_p$ can be executed in time $\mathsf{poly}(\log p) = \mathcal{O}(\mathsf{poly}(\lambda, \log n))$. $\mathsf{PPRF}(K_2, \mathsf{ind})$ can be executed in $\mathcal{O}(\mu \cdot \mathsf{poly}(\lambda)) = \mathcal{O}(\mathsf{poly}(\log n \cdot \lambda))$ by our efficiency requirements on PPRF and so can $\mathsf{PRF}(K_1, i)$. Since $t \leq n$, the while-loop has runtime in $\mathcal{O}(n \cdot \mathsf{poly}(\log n \cdot \lambda))$. So the maximum runtime is bounded by

$$T_{\mathcal{TM}} = \mathcal{O}(n \cdot \mathsf{poly}(\log n \cdot \lambda)).$$

Towards analysing the **description size** $|M'|$: Comparisons with ind, i^* can be described in size $\mathcal{O}(\mathsf{poly}(\log n))$. The Turing machine code for $\mathsf{SSB.Vrfy}(\mathsf{hk}, h, \mathsf{ind}, (\mathsf{vk}, R), \tau)$ has size $\mathcal{O}(\mathsf{poly}(\lambda) \cdot \log n)$ by efficiency of SSB. The code for $\mathsf{Sig.Vrfy}(\mathsf{vk}, \sigma', T)$ has size $\mathcal{O}(\mathsf{poly}(\lambda))$. Modular arithmetic in $\mathbb{Z}_p$ can be described in size $\mathsf{poly}(\log p) = \mathcal{O}(\mathsf{poly}(\lambda, \log n))$. $\mathsf{PPRF}(K_2, \mathsf{ind})$ can be described in $\mathcal{O}(\mu \cdot \mathsf{poly}(\lambda)) = \mathcal{O}(\mathsf{poly}(\log n \cdot \lambda))$ by our efficiency requirements on PPRF and so can $\mathsf{PRF}(K_1, i)$. Since $\log t \leq \log n$, the while-loop can be described in size $\log n + \mathcal{O}(\mathsf{poly}(\log n \cdot \lambda))$. We conclude that the description size is bounded by

$$|M'| = \mathcal{O}(\mathsf{poly}(\log n \cdot \lambda)).$$

Thus, $|\mathsf{ob}M| = \mathcal{O}(\mathsf{poly}(|M'|, \log T_{\mathcal{TM}}, \ell_{inp}, \lambda)) = \mathcal{O}(\mathsf{poly}(\mathsf{poly}(\log n \cdot \lambda), \log(n \cdot \mathsf{poly}(\log n \cdot \lambda)), \mathsf{poly}(\lambda \cdot \log n), \lambda)) = \mathcal{O}(\mathsf{poly}(\log n, \lambda))$.

So the whole ciphertext is in size $\mathcal{O}(\mathsf{poly}(\log n, \lambda))$.   □

Theorem 3. *Our construction of* cSWE *is secure, given that* Sig *is punctured key indistinguishable and puncturable,* SSB *is index hiding and somewhere perfectly binding,* obM *is secure,* SKE *is correct, IND-CPA secure and has pseudorandom ciphertexts,* PRF *is a pseudorandom function and* PPRF *is a puncturable pseudorandom function.*

Proof. We define a series of indistinguishable hybrids and show, that an adversary $\mathcal{A}$ with non-negligible advantage in the last hybrid could break IND-CPA security of SKE. Our strategy is to puncture all honest keys at message T^*, then gradually move each party's shares from being computed inside the Turing machine into being embedded in the key part R_i in encrypted form. The Turing machine should in the end only have to decrypt the shares from its input and can forget the key K that it was supposed to share. Then, we can observe, that it never decrypts the honest parties' shares, as there is no accepting signature due to puncturability of our signing scheme. We bind the SSB hash to each honest position i^*, puncture the PPRF at i^* to forget the decryption key, hardwire the output share s_{i^*} into the machine instead and replace the share s_{i^*} with an encryption of garbage inside R_{i^*}. Then, we observe, that by SSB binding and puncturability, no input exists anymore for which s_{i^*} is output and we can forget the hardwired value again. Lastly, we notice that we now need less than t shares of K to run this experiment and can therefore replace them with shares of an unrelated key K' by t-privacy. What remains is a single encryption of m under K, where K is not known or used in any other part of the output.

Full Proof: Let $\lambda \in \mathbb{N}$, such that $t = \mathsf{poly}(\lambda)$. Let $\mathcal{A}$ be an adversary for $\mathsf{Exp}_{\mathsf{Sec}}(\mathcal{A}, 1^\lambda)$ with more than negligible advantage.

$\mathcal{H}_0 = \mathcal{H}_1^0$: This game is identical to $\mathsf{Exp}_{\mathsf{Sec}}(\mathcal{A}, 1^\lambda)$.

To recap, we get indices $J \subset [n]$, $|J| \leq t - 1$ and reference message T^* from $\mathcal{A}$, then the experiment generates key pairs for $i \in [n]$ as $(\mathsf{vk}_i, \mathsf{sk}_i) \leftarrow \mathsf{Sig.KeyGen}(1^\lambda)$, $R_i \leftarrow \mathbb{Z}_p$ and provides $V = ((\mathsf{vk}_1, R_1), \ldots, (\mathsf{vk}_n, R_n))$ to $\mathcal{A}$, as well as all sk_i for $i \in J$. We allow any signing queries for honest keys $\mathsf{vk}_i, i \in [n] \setminus J$ on any message except T^*, before and after the adversary announces challenge messages m_0, m_1 and the experiment replies to this challenge by choosing $b \leftarrow_\$ \{0,1\}$, and sending $\mathsf{Enc}(1^\lambda, V, T^*, m_b)$ to $\mathcal{A}$.
    In the end, $\mathcal{A}$ outputs a guess b' to our choice bit b.

$\mathcal{H}_1^{i^*}$ for $i^* \in \{1, \ldots, n\}$:
  - If $i^* \in J$, this is identical to $\mathcal{H}_1^{i^*-1}$.
  - Else, it is identical to $\mathcal{H}_1^{i^*-1}$, except that the key vk_{i^*} is created as a punctured key as $(\mathsf{vk}_{i^*}, \mathsf{sk}_{i^*}) \leftarrow_\$ \mathsf{Sig.PKeyGen}(1^\lambda, T^*)$ for the signing reference messsage T^* specified by $\mathcal{A}$ instead of $(\mathsf{vk}_{i^*}, \mathsf{sk}_{i^*}) \leftarrow_\$ \mathsf{Sig.KeyGen}(1^\lambda)$.

We observe that our experiment never needs to compute signatures of T^* for honest keys vk_i with $i \notin J$. So clearly, $\mathcal{H}_1^{i^*}$ and $\mathcal{H}_1^{i^*-1}$ are indistinguishable by the punctured-key indistinguishability of Sig'. In the last hybrid $\mathcal{H}_1^n$, all honest keys will be chosen punctured at message T^*.

We define an event

$$\mathbf{bad} = \{\exists \sigma, i \in [n] \setminus J \text{ such that } \mathsf{Sig.Vrfy}(\mathsf{vk}_i, \sigma, T^*) = 1\}.$$

Note that by puncturability of Sig, it holds

$$\Pr[\mathbf{bad}] \leq \Sigma_{i \in [n] \setminus J} \Pr \left[\begin{array}{l} \exists \sigma \text{ s.t. } \mathsf{Vrfy}(\mathsf{vk}^*, \sigma, T^*) = 1 : \\ (\mathsf{vk}^*, \mathsf{sk}^*) \leftarrow_\$ \mathsf{PKeyGen}(1^\lambda, T^*) \end{array} \right] \leq n \cdot \mathsf{negl}(\lambda),$$

which is negligble. In the following we condition on $\mathbf{bad}$ not happening.

$\mathcal{H}_2$: This is identical to $\mathcal{H}_1^n$ except for conceptual changes:
- The reduction computes already at the start of the experiment the keys K, K_1, K_2 it will use in the call to $\mathsf{Enc}(1^\lambda, V, T^*, m_b)$.
- We define the polynomial $f' = K + \Sigma_{j=1}^{t-1} \mathsf{PRF}(K_1, j) \cdot x^j$ and $s_i = f'(i)$ for $i \in [n]$. Note that s_{ind} corresponds to the output of M' on an accepting input $(\mathsf{ind}, (\mathsf{vk}_{\mathsf{ind}}, R_{\mathsf{ind}}), \tau, \sigma')$, where $1 = \mathsf{SSB.Vrfy}(\mathsf{hk}, h, \mathsf{ind}, (\mathsf{vk}_{\mathsf{ind}}, R_{\mathsf{ind}}), \tau)$ and $1 = \mathsf{Sig.Vrfy}(\mathsf{vk}_{\mathsf{ind}}, \sigma', T)$ for $\mathsf{ind} \in [n]$. The shares s_i for $i \in J$ correspond to the outputs the adversary is guaranteed to get by just signing T^* himself and following the decryption procedure.

We will now loop through $\mathcal{H}_3^i, \mathcal{H}_4^i, \ldots, \mathcal{H}_7^i$ to gradually replace all honest verification keys by punctured ones and switch to a setting where the obfuscated machine pulls all of its outputs out of the R_i key parts instead of computing them itself. We start with $\mathcal{H}_7^0 = \mathcal{H}_2$ for notational convenience.

$\mathcal{H}_3^{i^*}$ for $i^* \in \{1, \ldots, n\}$: This is identical to $\mathcal{H}_7^{i^*-1}$ (with $\mathcal{H}_7^0 = \mathcal{H}_2$) except that we generate $\mathsf{hk} \leftarrow \mathsf{SSB.KeyGen}(1^\lambda, n, i^*)$ binding to i^*.

This is clearly indistinguishable from $\mathcal{H}_7^{i^*-1}$ by SSB being index hiding.

$\mathcal{H}_4^{i^*}$ for $i^* \in \{1, \ldots, n\}$: This is identical to $\mathcal{H}_3^{i^*}$ except in the way we choose R_{i^*} in vk_{i^*}. We sample $u_{i^*} \leftarrow_\$ \mathbb{Z}_p$ and set $R_{i^*} = s_{i^*} - u_{i^*} \mod p$ with s_{i^*} defined as above instead of $R_{i^*} \leftarrow \mathbb{Z}_p$.

This is indistinguishable from $\mathcal{H}_3^{i^*}$ as $s_{i^*} - u_{i^*}$ is still uniform in $\mathbb{Z}_p$.

$\mathcal{H}_5^{i^*}$ for $i^* \in \{1, \ldots, n\}$: This is identical to $\mathcal{H}_4^{i^*}$ except we generate $K_{\{i^*\}} \leftarrow \mathsf{PPRF.Puncture}(K_2, \{i^*\})$ the machine M' we use is replaced by $M' = M_{i^*}[K, K_1, h, T^*, \mathsf{hk}, K_{\{i^*\}}, u_{i^*}, i^*]$ instead of $M' = M_{i^*-1}[K, K_1, h, T^*, \mathsf{hk}, K_2, U, 0]$.

This is indistinguishable from $\mathcal{H}_4^{i^*}$ by security of $\mathsf{ob}M$. To show this, let us argue, that $M_0 := M_{i^*}[K, K_1, h, T^*, \mathsf{hk}, K_{\{i^*\}}, u_{i^*}, i^*]$ and $M_1 := M_{i^*-1}[K, K_1, h, T^*, \mathsf{hk}, K_2, U, 0]$ are functionally equivalent. We recall that $M_{i^*}[K, K_1, h, T, \mathsf{hk}, K_2, U, \mathsf{ind}_2](\mathsf{ind}, (\mathsf{vk}, R), \tau, \sigma')$ is defined as follows:

- If $0 = $ SSB.Vrfy$(\mathsf{hk}, h, \mathsf{ind}, (\mathsf{vk}, R), \tau)$, abort and output $\bot$.
- If $0 = $ Sig.Vrfy$(\mathsf{vk}, \sigma', T)$, abort and output $\bot$.
- If $\mathsf{ind} = \mathsf{ind}_2$: Output $R + U \mod p$ and halt.
- If $\mathsf{ind} \leq i^*$: Output $R + $ PPRF$(K_2, \mathsf{ind}) \mod p$ and halt.
- Else if $\mathsf{ind} > i^*$:
  - Write on the tape variables $i = 1, R = 0, X = 1, S = K$
  - While $i < t$:
    * Set $R = $ PRF(K_1, i), $X = X \cdot \mathsf{ind} \mod p$, $S = S + X \cdot R \mod p$, $i = i + 1$.
  - Output S (Note that $S = f'(\mathsf{ind}) = s_{\mathsf{ind}}$.)

Assuming that there is an input $(\mathsf{ind}^*, (\mathsf{vk}^*, R^*), \tau^*, \sigma^*)$ for which M_0, M_1 produce different outputs, then $1 = $ SSB.Vrfy$(\mathsf{hk}, h, \mathsf{ind}^*, (\mathsf{vk}^*, R^*), \tau^*)$, $1 = $ Sig.Vrfy$(\mathsf{vk}^*, \sigma^*, T^*)$, $0 < \mathsf{ind} \leq n$ must hold. Otherwise they both output $\bot$. We distinguish 3 cases:

$\mathsf{ind}^* > i^*$ In this case both machines output s_{ind}^*.

$\mathsf{ind}^* = i^*$ In this case M_1 outputs s_{ind}^*, but M_0 outputs $R^* + u_{i^*} \mod p$. We note that $\mathsf{hk} \leftarrow $ SSB.KeyGen$(1^\lambda, n, i^*)$ and $h = $ SSB.Hash$(\mathsf{hk}, (\mathsf{vk}_i, R_i)_{i \in [n]})$ are honestly created by the reduction and so since SSB is somewhere statistically binding, we know that $\mathsf{vk}^* = \mathsf{vk}_{i^*}, R^* = R_{i^*}$. That means that M_0 outputs $R_{i^*} + u_{i^*} = s_{i^*}$, which is the same output as in M_1.

$\mathsf{ind}^* < i^*$ In this case M_0 outputs $R^* + $ PPRF$(K_{\{i^*\}}, \mathsf{ind}^*) \mod p$, while M_1 outputs $R^* + $ PPRF$(K_2, \mathsf{ind}^*) \mod p$. As $\mathsf{ind} \neq i^*$ and $K_{\{i^*\}} \leftarrow $ PPRF.Puncture$(K_2, \{i^*\})$, we can conclude that these outputs are identical by the PPRF preserving functionality under puncturing.

It follows that there does not exist an input that makes M_0 and M_1 have a different output, thus $\mathcal{H}_5^{i^*}$ and $\mathcal{H}_4^{i^*}$ are indistinguishable.

$\mathcal{H}_6^{i^*}$ for $i^* \in \{1, \ldots, n\}$: This is identical to $\mathcal{H}_5^{i^*}$ except that we now choose $R_{i^*} = s_{i^*} - $ PPRF$(K_2, i^*) \mod p$ instead of $R_{i^*} = s_{i^*} - u_{i^*} \mod p$ and $M' = M_{i^*}[K, K_1, h, T^*, \mathsf{hk}, K_{\{i^*\}}, $ PPRF$(K_2, i^*), i^*]$ instead of $M' = M_{i^*} [K, K_1, h, T^*, \mathsf{hk}, K_{\{i^*\}}, u_{i^*}, i^*]$

$\mathcal{H}_6^{i^*}$ and $\mathcal{H}_5^{i^*}$ are indistinguishable as PPRF is pseudorandom at the punctured point i^*. Given $K_{\{i^*\}}, i^*$ and either a uniform value $\bar{u} \leftarrow \mathbb{Z}_p$ or PPRF(K_2, i^*), we can obliviously emulate either $\mathcal{H}_5^{i^*}$ or $\mathcal{H}_6^{i^*}$ to build a distinguisher for pseudorandomness at punctured points of PPRF.

$\mathcal{H}_7^{i^*}$ for $i^* \in \{1, \ldots, n\}$: This is identical to $\mathcal{H}_6^{i^*}$ except that we now choose $M' = M_{i^*}[K, K_1, h, T^*, \mathsf{hk}, K_2, U, 0]$ instead of $M' = M_{i^*}[K, K_1, h, T^*, \mathsf{hk}, K_{\{i^*\}}, $ PPRF$(K_2, i^*), i^*]$

This is indistinguishable from $\mathcal{H}_6^{i*}$ by security of obM.

To show this, let us argue, that $M_0 := M_{i*}[K, K_1, h, T^*, \mathsf{hk}, K_2, U, 0]$ and $M_1 := M_{i*}[K, K_1, h, T^*, \mathsf{hk}, K_{\{i*\}}, \mathsf{PPRF}(K_2, i^*), i^*]$ are functionally equivalent.

Assuming that there is an input $(\mathsf{ind}^*, (\mathsf{vk}^*, R^*), \tau^*, \sigma^*)$ for which M_0, M_1 produce different outputs, then $1 = \mathsf{SSB.Vrfy}(\mathsf{hk}, h, \mathsf{ind}^*, (\mathsf{vk}^*, R^*), \tau^*)$, $1 = \mathsf{Sig.Vrfy}(\mathsf{vk}^*, \sigma^*, T^*)$, $0 < \mathsf{ind} \leq n$ must hold.

We distinguish 3 cases:

$\mathsf{ind}^* > i^*$ In this case both machines output s_{ind}^*.
$\mathsf{ind}^* = i^*$ In this case both machines output $R^* + \mathsf{PPRF}(K_2, i^*) \mod p$.
$\mathsf{ind}^* < i^*$ In this case M_0 outputs $R^* + \mathsf{PPRF}(K_2, \mathsf{ind}^*) \mod p$, while M_1 outputs $R^* + \mathsf{PPRF}(K_{\{i*\}}, \mathsf{ind}^*) \mod p$.
   As $\mathsf{ind} \neq i^*$ and $K_{\{i*\}} \leftarrow \mathsf{PPRF.Puncture}(K_2, \{i^*\})$, we can conclude that these outputs are identical by the PPRF preserving functionality under puncturing.

This means such a resulting in different outputs can not exist - $\mathcal{H}_6^{i*}$ and $\mathcal{H}_7^{i*}$ are indeed indistinguishable.

$\mathcal{H}_8$: This is identical to $\mathcal{H}_7^n$, except that we use $M' = M_n[\emptyset, \emptyset, h, T^*, \mathsf{hk}, K_2, U, 0]$ which is the same as the previous machine, except of it having dummy inputs instead of K, K_1.

As the output of M' does no longer depend on K, K_1 in $\mathcal{H}_7^n$, this is indistinguishable from the previous hybrid by security of obM.

$\mathcal{H}_9 =:$ This is identical to $\mathcal{H}_8$ except that we set the $s_i^* = (K + \Sigma_{j=1}^{t-1} r_j \cdot (i)^j))$ in $R_i = s_i^* - \mathsf{PPRF}(K_2, i) \mod p$ for $i \in [n]$, where we pick $r_j \leftarrow \{0,1\}^\mu$ randomly instead of $s_i^* = (K + \Sigma_{j=1}^{t-1} \mathsf{PRF}(K_1, j) \cdot (i)^j))$.

This is indistinguishable from $\mathcal{H}_8$ by pseudorandomness of PRF.

Now we will almost "revert" the moves in $\mathcal{H}_3$ to $\mathcal{H}_7$ again to put random values into R_i for $i \notin J$, but this time we do not let M' keep the information to decrypt them - we rely on the puncturability of Sig to make sure that the case of decryptions would never have been reached anyways and invoke security of obM. This deletes all traces of honest shares in R_i.

$\mathcal{H}_{10}^{i*}$ for $i^* \in \{1, \ldots, n\}$: This is identical to $\mathcal{H}_{13}^{i*-1}$ (with $\mathcal{H}_{13}^0 = \mathcal{H}_9$) except that we generate $\mathsf{hk} \leftarrow \mathsf{SSB.KeyGen}(1^\lambda, n, i^*)$ binding to i^*.

This is clearly indistinguishable from $\mathcal{H}_{13}^{i*-1}$ by SSB being index hiding.

$\mathcal{H}_{11}^{i*}$ for $i^* \in \{1, \ldots, n\}$: If $i^* \in J$, this is identical to $\mathcal{H}_{10}^{i*}$.
   Else, this is identical to $\mathcal{H}_{10}^{i*}$ except that the machine M' we use is replaced by $M' = M_n[\emptyset, \emptyset, h, T^*, \mathsf{hk}, K_{\{i*\}}, \mathsf{PPRF}(K_2, i^*), i^*]$ instead of $M' = M_n[\emptyset, \emptyset, h, T^*, \mathsf{hk}, K_2, U, 0]$.

This is indistinguishable from $\mathcal{H}_{10}^{i*}$ by security of obM and the argument is analogous to $\mathcal{H}_7^{i*}$ and $\mathcal{H}_6^{i*}$ being indistinguishable.

$\mathcal{H}_{12}^{i^*}$ for $i^* \in \{1,\ldots,n\}$: If $i^* \in J$, this is identical to $\mathcal{H}_{11}^{i^*}$.

Else this is identical to $\mathcal{H}_{11}^{i^*}$ except that we now choose $R_{i^*} = s_{i^*} - u_{i^*} \bmod p$ instead of $R_{i^*} = s_{i^*} - \mathsf{PPRF}(K_2, i^*) \bmod p$ and $M' = M_n[\emptyset, \emptyset, h, T^*, \mathsf{hk}, K_{\{i^*\}}, u_{i^*}, i^*]$ instead of $M' = M_n[\emptyset, \emptyset, h, T^*, \mathsf{hk}, K_{\{i^*\}}, \mathsf{PPRF}(K_2, i^*), i^*]$.

$\mathcal{H}_{12}^{i^*}$ and $\mathcal{H}_{11}^{i^*}$ are indistinguishable by PPRF being pseudorandom at punctured points and the argument is analogous to $\mathcal{H}_6^{i^*}$ and $\mathcal{H}_5^{i^*}$ being indistinguishable.

$\mathcal{H}_{13}^{i^*}$ for $i^* \in \{1,\ldots,n\}$: If $i^* \in J$, this is identical to $\mathcal{H}_{12}^{i^*}$.

This is identical to $\mathcal{H}_{12}^{i^*}$ except that we now choose $M' = M_n[\emptyset, \emptyset, h, T^*, \mathsf{hk}, K_2, U, 0]$ instead of $M' = M_n[\emptyset, \emptyset, h, T^*, \mathsf{hk}, K_{\{i^*\}}, u_{i^*}, i^*]$.

This is indistinguishable from $\mathcal{H}_{12}^{i^*}$ by security of obM.

To show this, let us argue, that $M_0 := M_n[\emptyset, \emptyset, h, T^*, \mathsf{hk}, K_2, U, 0]$ and $M_1 := M_n[\emptyset, \emptyset, h, T^*, \mathsf{hk}, K_{\{i^*\}}, u_{i^*}, i^*]$ are functionally equivalent.

Assuming that there is an input $(\mathsf{ind}^*, (\mathsf{vk}^*, R^*), \tau^*, \sigma^*)$ for which M_0, M_1 produce different outputs, then $1 = \mathsf{SSB.Vrfy}(\mathsf{hk}, h, \mathsf{ind}^*, (\mathsf{vk}^*, R^*), \tau^*)$, $1 = \mathsf{Sig.Vrfy}(\mathsf{vk}^*, \sigma^*, T^*)$, $0 < \mathsf{ind} \le n$ must hold.

We distinguish 2 cases:

$\mathsf{ind}^* \ne i^*$ In this case M_0 outputs $R^* + \mathsf{PPRF}(K_2, \mathsf{ind}^*) \bmod p$, while M_1 outputs $R^* + \mathsf{PPRF}(K_{\{i^*\}}, \mathsf{ind}^*) \bmod p$. We can conclude that these outputs are identical by the PPRF preserving functionality under puncturing.

$\mathsf{ind}^* = i^*$ We claim, that no input $(i^*, (\mathsf{vk}^*, R^*), \tau^*, \sigma^*)$ exists where $1 = \mathsf{SSB.Vrfy}(\mathsf{hk}, h, i^*, (\mathsf{vk}^*, R^*), \tau^*)$ and $1 = \mathsf{Sig.Vrfy}(\mathsf{vk}^*, \sigma^*, T^*)$ hold, hence the output is always $\perp$ in both machines.

Let us assume towards contradiction, that such an input exists. By SSB being somewhere statistically binding, we know $\mathsf{vk}^* = \mathsf{vk}_{i^*}$, $R^* = R_{i^*}$. So, it must hold $1 = \mathsf{Sig.Vrfy}(\mathsf{vk}_{i^*}, \sigma^*, T^*)$ for $i^* \in J$ - As the event **bad** has not happened, no such σ^* can exist.

This means such an input with differing output can not exist - $\mathcal{H}_{12}^{i^*}$ and $\mathcal{H}_{13}^{i^*}$ are indeed indistinguishable.

$\mathcal{H}_{14}$ This is identical to $\mathcal{H}_{13}^n$ except that we now compute $R_i \leftarrow_\$ \mathbb{Z}_p$ for all $i \in [n] \setminus J$ instead of $R_i = s_i - u_i \bmod p$ for $u_i \leftarrow_\$ \mathbb{Z}_p$ being a fresh uniform value for each $i \in [n] \setminus J$.

As the u_{i^*} are not re-used anywhere in the experiment, this is indistinguishable from $\mathcal{H}_{13}^n$ as both distributions lead to uniform R_i for all honest indices $i \in [n] \setminus J$.

It is clear now, that we only ever compute $|J| \le t - 1$ shares of the key K, which are of the from $R_i = K + \Sigma_{j=1}^{t-1} r_j \cdot (i)^j + \mathsf{PPRF}(K_2, i) \bmod p$. This clearly corresponds to $|J|$ Shamir shares corresponding to interpolation points $i \in J$ out of a t-of-n sharing for points $i \in [n]$. So in the next hybrid, we can make the key K disappear.

$\mathcal{H}_{15}$: This is identical to $\mathcal{H}_{14}$, except that we choose a random $K' \leftarrow \{0,1\}^\lambda$ and make $R_i = K' + \Sigma_{j=1}^{t-1} r_j \cdot (i)^j + \mathsf{PPRF}(K_2, i) \mod p$ for $i \in J$. Where $r_j \leftarrow \mathbb{Z}_p$ randomly.

This is indistinguishable from $\mathcal{H}_{14}$ by the t-privacy of the Shamir secret sharing scheme. Let us assume that there is an adversary $\mathcal{A}$ which breaks security of cSWE with probability ε. Conditioned on **bad** not happening, $\mathcal{A}$ has negligible advantage $n'(\lambda)$ of distinguishing the real experiment from $\mathcal{H}_{15}$. In hybrid $\mathcal{H}_{15}$, there is no information about K except in the ciphertext $\mathsf{ct}' = \mathsf{SKE.Enc}(K, m_b)$. So we can make an IND-CPA distinguisher $\mathcal{D}$, that simulates $\mathcal{H}_{15}$ by asking the IND-CPA security game of SKE for an encryption with challenge messages m_0, m_1, receiving a ciphertext ct^* and then making all the outputs in $\mathcal{H}_{15}$ honestly, except setting ciphertext part $\mathsf{ct}' = \mathsf{ct}^*$ and outputting whatever $\mathcal{A}$ does.

The advantage we get from this distinguisher in the IND-CPA game is guaranteed to be $\mathsf{Adv}(\mathcal{D}) \geq \varepsilon - n'(\lambda) - \Pr[\mathbf{bad}] = \varepsilon - \mathsf{negl}(\lambda)$. This means that ε must be negligible due to SKE being IND-CPA secure. $\qquad\square$

Acknowledgements. We thank the reviewer B of Asiacrypt 2024 for pointing out the existence of the notion and constructions of all-but-one signatures. Gennaro Avitabile received funding from the European Research Council (ERC) under the European Union's Horizon 2020 research and innovation program under project PICOCRYPT (grant agreement No. 101001283), and from the Spanish Government under projects PRODIGY (TED2021-132464B-I00) and ESPADA (PID2022-142290OB-I00). The last two projects are co-funded by European Union EIE, and NextGenerationEU/PRTR funds. Nico Döttling: Funded by the European Union (ERC, LACONIC, 101041207). Views and opinions expressed are however those of the author(s) only and do not necessarily reflect those of the European Union or the European Research Council. Neither the European Union nor the granting authority can be held responsible for them.

References

1. Bellare, M., Stepanovs, I., Waters, B.: New negative results on differing-inputs obfuscation. In: Fischlin, M., Coron, JS. (eds.) Advances in Cryptology, EUROCRYPT 2016. LNCS, vol. 9666, pp. 792–821. Springer, Berlin, Heidelberg (2016). https://doi.org/10.1007/978-3-662-49896-5_28
2. Boneh, D., Lynn, B., Shacham, H.: Short signatures from the Weil pairing. In: Boyd, C. (ed.) ASIACRYPT 2001. LNCS, vol. 2248, pp. 514–532. Springer, Heidelberg (Dec 2001). https://doi.org/10.1007/3-540-45682-1_30
3. Boyle, E., Goldwasser, S., Ivan, I.: Functional signatures and pseudorandom functions. In: Krawczyk, H. (ed.) PKC 2014. LNCS, vol. 8383, pp. 501–519. Springer, Heidelberg (2014). https://doi.org/10.1007/978-3-642-54631-0_29
4. Campanelli, M., David, B., Khoshakhlagh, H., Konring, A., Nielsen, J.B.: Encryption to the future : a paradigm for sending secret messages to future (anonymous) committees. In: Agrawal, S., Lin, D. (eds.) ASIACRYPT 2022, Part III. LNCS, vol. 13793, pp. 151–180. Springer, Heidelberg (2022). https://doi.org/10.1007/978-3-031-22969-5_6

5. Cerulli, A., Connolly, A., Neven, G., Preiss, F.S., Shoup, V.: VETKeys: how a blockchain can keep many secrets. Cryptology ePrint Archive, Paper 2023/616 (2023). https://eprint.iacr.org/2023/616

6. Chakraborty, S., Prabhakaran, M., Wichs, D.: Witness maps and applications. In: Kiayias, A., Kohlweiss, M., Wallden, P., Zikas, V. (eds.) PKC 2020, Part I. LNCS, vol. 12110, pp. 220–246. Springer, Heidelberg (May 2020). https://doi.org/10.1007/978-3-030-45374-9_8

7. Choudhuri, A.R., Garg, S., Piet, J., Policharla, G.V.: Mempool privacy via batched threshold encryption: attacks and defenses. In: 33rd USENIX Security Symposium (USENIX Security 24), pp. 3513–3529. USENIX Association, Philadelphia, PA (2024). https://www.usenix.org/conference/usenixsecurity24/presentation/choudhuri

8. Desmedt, Y., Frankel, Y.: Threshold cryptosystems. In: Brassard, G. (ed.) CRYPTO'89. LNCS, vol. 435, pp. 307–315. Springer, Heidelberg (1990). https://doi.org/10.1007/0-387-34805-0_28

9. Döttling, N., Hanzlik, L., Magri, B., Wohnig, S.: McFly: verifiable encryption to the future made practical. In: Baldimtsi, F., Cachin, C. (eds.) Financial Cryptography and Data Security, FC 2023. LNCS, vol. 13950, pp. 252–269. Springer, Cham (2024). https://doi.org/10.1007/978-3-031-47754-6_15

10. Erwig, A., Faust, S., Riahi, S.: Large-scale non-interactive threshold cryptosystems through anonymity. Cryptology ePrint Archive, Report 2021/1290 (2021). https://eprint.iacr.org/2021/1290

11. Faust, S., Hazay, C., Kretzler, D., Schlosser, B.: Statement-oblivious threshold witness encryption. In: CSF 2023 Computer Security Foundations Symposium, pp. 17–32. IEEE Computer Society Press (2023). https://doi.org/10.1109/CSF57540.2023.00026

12. Frankel, Y.: A practical protocol for large group oriented networks. In: Quisquater, J.J., Vandewalle, J. (eds.) EUROCRYPT'89. LNCS, vol. 434, pp. 56–61. Springer, Heidelberg (1990). https://doi.org/10.1007/3-540-46885-4_8

13. Gailly, N., Melissaris, K., Romailler, Y.: tlock: practical timelock encryption from threshold BLS. Cryptology ePrint Archive, Paper 2023/189 (2023). https://eprint.iacr.org/2023/189

14. Garg, S., Gentry, C., Halevi, S., Raykova, M., Sahai, A., Waters, B.: Candidate indistinguishability obfuscation and functional encryption for all circuits. In: 54th FOCS, pp. 40–49. IEEE Computer Society Press (2013). https://doi.org/10.1109/FOCS.2013.13

15. Garg, S., Gentry, C., Sahai, A., Waters, B.: Witness encryption and its applications. In: Boneh, D., Roughgarden, T., Feigenbaum, J. (eds.) 45th ACM STOC, pp. 467–476. ACM Press (2013). https://doi.org/10.1145/2488608.2488667

16. Garg, S., Kolonelos, D., Policharla, G.V., Wang, M.: Threshold encryption with silent setup. Cryptology ePrint Archive, Paper 2024/263 (2024). https://eprint.iacr.org/2024/263

17. Garg, S., Srinivasan, A.: A simple construction of iO for Turing machines. In: Beimel, A., Dziembowski, S. (eds.) TCC 2018, Part II. LNCS, vol. 11240, pp. 425–454. Springer, Heidelberg (Nov 2018). https://doi.org/10.1007/978-3-030-03810-6_16

18. Gentry, C., Wichs, D.: Separating succinct non-interactive arguments from all falsifiable assumptions. In: Fortnow, L., Vadhan, S.P. (eds.) 43rd ACM STOC, pp. 99–108. ACM Press (2011). https://doi.org/10.1145/1993636.1993651

19. Goldwasser, S., Kalai, Y.T., Popa, R.A., Vaikuntanathan, V., Zeldovich, N.: How to run Turing machines on encrypted data. In: Canetti, R., Garay, J.A. (eds.) CRYPTO 2013, Part II. LNCS, vol. 8043, pp. 536–553. Springer, Heidelberg (2013). https://doi.org/10.1007/978-3-642-40084-1_30

20. Goyal, R., Vusirikala, S., Waters, B.: Collusion resistant broadcast and trace from positional witness encryption. In: Lin, D., Sako, K. (eds.) PKC 2019, Part II. LNCS, vol. 11443, pp. 3–33. Springer, Heidelberg (2019). https://doi.org/10.1007/978-3-030-17259-6_1

21. Goyal, V., Kothapalli, A., Masserova, E., Parno, B., Song, Y.: Storing and retrieving secrets on a blockchain. In: Hanaoka, G., Shikata, J., Watanabe, Y. (eds.) PKC 2022, Part I. LNCS, vol. 13177, pp. 252–282. Springer, Heidelberg (2022). https://doi.org/10.1007/978-3-030-97121-2_10

22. Hubacek, P., Wichs, D.: On the communication complexity of secure function evaluation with long output. In: Roughgarden, T. (ed.) ITCS 2015, pp. 163–172. ACM (2015). https://doi.org/10.1145/2688073.2688105

23. Jiang, M., Duong, D.H., Susilo, W.: Puncturable signature: a generic construction and instantiations. In: Computer Security - ESORICS 2022: 27th European Symposium on Research in Computer Security, Copenhagen, Denmark, September 26–30, 2022, Proceedings, Part II, pp. 507–527. Springer-Verlag, Berlin, Heidelberg (2022). https://doi.org/10.1007/978-3-031-17146-8_25

24. Kondi, Y., Magri, B., Orlandi, C., Shlomovits, O.: Refresh when you wake up: proactive threshold wallets with offline devices. In: 2021 IEEE Symposium on Security and Privacy, pp. 608–625. IEEE Computer Society Press (2021). https://doi.org/10.1109/SP40001.2021.00067

25. Koppula, V., Lewko, A.B., Waters, B.: Indistinguishability obfuscation for Turing machines with unbounded memory. In: Servedio, R.A., Rubinfeld, R. (eds.) 47th ACM STOC, pp. 419–428. ACM Press (2015). https://doi.org/10.1145/2746539.2746614

26. Lin, H., Pass, R., Seth, K., Telang, S.: Indistinguishability obfuscation with nontrivial efficiency. In: Cheng, C.M., Chung, K.M., Persiano, G., Yang, B.Y. (eds.) PKC 2016, Part II. LNCS, vol. 9615, pp. 447–462. Springer, Heidelberg (2016). https://doi.org/10.1007/978-3-662-49387-8_17

27. Madathil, V., Thyagarajan, S.A.K., Vasilopoulos, D., Fournier, L., Malavolta, G., Moreno-Sanchez, P.: Cryptographic Oracle-based conditional payments. In: 30th Annual Network and Distributed System Security Symposium, NDSS 2023, San Diego, California, USA, February 27–March 3, 2023. The Internet Society (2023). https://www.ndss-symposium.org/ndss-paper/cryptographic-oracle-based-conditional-payments/

28. Naor, M.: On cryptographic assumptions and challenges (invited talk). In: Boneh, D. (ed.) CRYPTO 2003. LNCS, vol. 2729, pp. 96–109. Springer, Heidelberg (2003). https://doi.org/10.1007/978-3-540-45146-4_6

29. Okamoto, T., Pietrzak, K., Waters, B., Wichs, D.: New realizations of somewhere statistically binding hashing and positional accumulators. In: Iwata, T., Cheon, J.H. (eds.) ASIACRYPT 2015, Part I. LNCS, vol. 9452, pp. 121–145. Springer, Heidelberg (2015). https://doi.org/10.1007/978-3-662-48797-6_6

30. Quach, W., Wee, H., Wichs, D.: Laconic function evaluation and applications. In: Thorup, M. (ed.) 59th FOCS, pp. 859–870. IEEE Computer Society Press (2018). https://doi.org/10.1109/FOCS.2018.00086

31. Sahai, A., Waters, B.: How to use indistinguishability obfuscation: deniable encryption, and more. In: Shmoys, D.B. (ed.) 46th ACM STOC, pp. 475–484. ACM Press (2014). https://doi.org/10.1145/2591796.2591825

32. Shamir, A.: How to share a secret. Commun. ACM **22**(11), 612–613 (1979)
33. Shoup, V.: Lower bounds for discrete logarithms and related problems. In: Fumy, W. (ed.) EUROCRYPT'97. LNCS, vol. 1233, pp. 256–266. Springer, Heidelberg (1997). https://doi.org/10.1007/3-540-69053-0_18
34. Waters, B., Wu, D.J.: Adaptively-sound succinct arguments for np from indistinguishability obfuscation. Cryptology ePrint Archive, Paper 2024/165 (2024). https://eprint.iacr.org/2024/165

Bounded Collusion-Resistant Registered Functional Encryption for Circuits

Yijian Zhang[1,3], Jie Chen[1,2(✉)], Debiao He[4], and Yuqing Zhang[5,6]

[1] Shanghai Key Laboratory of Trustworthy Computing, School of Software Engineering, East China Normal University, Shanghai, China
[2] Institute for Math & AI, Wuhan University, Wuhan, China
s080001@e.ntu.edu.sg
[3] Institute of Cybersecurity and Cryptology, School of Computing and Information Technology, University of Wollongong, Wollongong NSW, Australia
[4] School of Cyber Science and Engineering, Wuhan University, Wuhan, China
[5] National Computer Network Intrusion Protection Center, University of Chinese Academy of Sciences, Beijing, China
[6] School of Cyberspace Security, Hainan University, Haikou, China

Abstract. As an emerging primitive, *Registered Functional Encryption* (RFE) eliminates the key-escrow issue that threatens numerous works for functional encryption, by replacing the trusted authority with a transparent key curator and allowing each user to sample their decryption keys locally. In this work, we present a new black-box approach to construct RFE for all polynomial-sized circuits. It considers adaptive simulation-based security in the bounded collusion model (Gorbunov et al. - CRYPTO'12), where the security can be ensured only if there are no more than $Q \geq 1$ corrupted users and Q is fixed at the setup phase. Unlike earlier works, we do not employ unpractical *Indistinguishability Obfuscation* ($i\mathcal{O}$). Conversely, it can be extended to support unbounded users, which is previously only known from $i\mathcal{O}$.

Technically, our general compiler exploits garbled circuits and a novel variant of slotted *Registered Broadcast Encryption* (RBE), namely global slotted RBE. This primitive is similar to slotted RBE, but needs *optimally compact* public parameters and ciphertext, so as to satisfy the efficiency requirement of the resulting RFE. Then we present two concrete global slotted RBE from pairings and lattices, respectively. With proposed compiler, we hence obtain two bounded collusion-resistant RFE schemes. Here, the first scheme relies on k-Lin assumption, while the second one supports unbounded users under LWE and evasive LWE assumptions.

Keywords: Functional Encryption · Registered Encryption · Bounded Collusion Model · Simulation-Based Security

1 Introduction

Registered Functional Encryption (RFE) [22,25] has emerged as a rising public-key cryptographic primitive recently. Unlike standard *Functional Encryption*

© International Association for Cryptologic Research 2025
K.-M. Chung and Y. Sasaki (Eds.): ASIACRYPT 2024, LNCS 15484, pp. 32–64, 2025.
https://doi.org/10.1007/978-981-96-0875-1_2

(FE) [17], RFE is particularly initiated to eliminate key-escrow problem that a lot of FE schemes have suffered for many years. In RFE, a common random string crs is initialized by the key curator who broadcasts crs to all users later. Then this curator is just responsible for providing registration service for each user, without holding any secret. With crs, a newly joined user can produce a pair of public key pk and secret key sk locally, then he submits a specified function f along with pk to the curator for registration. After receiving (f, pk), the curator updates current master public key mpk and helper secret key hsk for the new user. For encryption, the data provider uses mpk to generate a ciphertext ct associated with private data x, and the user can perform decryption algorithm over ct with (sk, hsk) to learn $f(x)$ and nothing else. During this process, it is required that (i) all registration procedures are deterministic and auditable, and (ii) mpk and hsk must be compact (i.e., polylogarithmic in the total number of user) and updates for mpk and hsk should be efficient.

Previously, lots of significant progress have been made on constructing RFE for various kinds of limited functionality. Focusing on identity-based policy, Garg et al. [29] put forth the first registration-based encryption construction, which inspired a line of subsequent works enhancing the security [23,33] and efficiency [31] of this primitive. In addition, a more generic subclass of RFE, i.e., registered attribute-based encryption (RABE), was built relying on general assumptions over bilinear groups [34,45], and then it was also achieved from lattice-based assumptions [26].

In light of these notable achievements, it is natural to ask how to construct RFE for more powerful and generic functionality, i.e., polynomial-sized circuits. Unfortunately, all existing constructions [22,25] are built upon the existence of *Indistinguishability Obfuscation* ($i\mathcal{O}$). An exception is Branco et al.'s work [18], which proposed a generic framework based on RFE for linear function (also called linear RFE in short), but we observe the security of their result is pretty weak, only achieving selective indistinguishablility-based (IND) security against adversary with single corrupt key. In their definition, the adversary is forced to submit the challenge message and specify the corrupted user set in advance, and IND security is actually inadequate for some cases as noted in [17]. For FE, stronger simulation-based (SIM) security is more desirable and up to now has facilitated a series of beneficial applications [3,13,35,36]. Thus, Zhu et al. [44] formalized the definition of SIM secure RFE and presented concrete realizations, whereas they also considered the selective setting and only focused on linear/quadratic function. Given all these, an open question that arises is

Can we construct a registered functional encryption for all polynomial-sized circuits that achieves SIM security without assistance of $i\mathcal{O}$?

Bounded Collusion Model. In this work, we will focus on bounded collusion-resistant RFE for circuits from weak assumptions, and consider stronger adaptive SIM security. Compared to plain RFE, bounded collusion-resistant RFE additionally requires that a prior-bound Q^1 of the number of corrupted users should be declared at the setup phase. The adversary cannot extract any useful information about encrypted data x (except for $C_1(x), \ldots, C_Q(x)$) even when he is able to adaptively query secret keys with respect to circuits $C_1, \ldots, C_Q$.

Bounded collusion-resistant FE has been studied extensively, and a number of works gained satisfactory results from general cryptographic tools, including public-key encryption (PKE) [39], multi-party computation (MPC) [11,32] and FE for linear/quadratic function [6,8]. This model is firstly proposed to construct FE for circuits without $i\mathcal{O}$, since several works [10,16] have shown that fully collusion-resistant FE for circuits exactly implies $i\mathcal{O}$, making itself difficult to be deduced from weak assumptions. This rule may also work on RFE, imagine that RFE can trivially simulate FE if the key curator acts as central authority by preparing sufficient secret keys for all possible functions and then distributing each to matched users.

1.1   Results

As a matter of fact, the notion of RFE should be naturally "bounded" since the user number L is fixed during initialization. A crucial point is the size of master public key and helper secret key, which should be $\mathsf{poly}(C, \log L)$ (here, C denotes the size of circuit), namely *compactness*. However, if we think of that in bounded collusion model, the overhead of all parameters could be $\mathsf{poly}(L)$. Such fact contradicts to compactness, so we decide to slightly relax it by considering a lower collusion bound $Q \ll L$ and allowing master public key and helper key of size $\mathsf{poly}(C, Q, \log L)$.

In this work, we manage to answer above question and conclude our contributions as follows:

– We propose a new black-box approach to construct bounded collusion-resilient RFE for all polynomial-sized circuits. It mainly contains two ingredients, i.e., garbled circuits and global slotted registered broadcast encryption, where the latter can be regarded as a compact variant of slotted registered broadcast encryption. Furthermore, our approach would also be useful when constructing RFE with unbounded users property, i.e., all parameters of size not scaling with L. Prior to this work, only $i\mathcal{O}$-based works [22,25] are known to realize unbounded users.
– With above general compiler, we obtain two bounded collusion-resistant RFE constructions, both of which are adaptively SIM secure (without malicious case). The first one is provably secure under k-Lin assumption in the standard model. Another one is secure in the random oracle model, relying on LWE and evasive LWE assumptions [40]. The second RFE could be extended to

---

[1] Generally speaking, the collusion bound Q is implied by the security parameter 1^λ. Since [32] defined bounded collusion-resistant FE, it has been widely accepted that Q is an integer much less than the total number of system users, which means not many users collude with adversary. In this work, our bounded collusion-resistant RFE also inherits this assumption as default.

support unbounded users. Compared to selective security, adaptive security does not require the adversary commit any challenge information, as well as the queried input to oracles.

Table 1. Comparison among existing RFE for circuits. In the column of "Security", "AD" and "SEL" denote adaptive and selective security, respectively. In the column of "Assumption", "SSB" represents somewhere statistically binding hash functions, and "RO" represents random oracle. The column "Unbounded" and "Full" denote unbounded users and full collusion-resistance.

Reference	Security	Assumption	Unbounded	Full
[22, 25]	AD-IND	SSB + $i\mathcal{O}$	✓	✓
[18]	SEL-IND	q-type DDH	✗	✗
Ours	AD-SIM	k-Lin	✗	✗
	AD-SIM	LWE + evasive LWE + RO	✓	✗

As shown in Table 1, it is clear that our technique greatly differs from current works. Instead of unpractical $i\mathcal{O}$, our results are based on more general assumptions, and achieve adaptive SIM security.

Prior to this work, adaptively secure RFE for circuits can also be gained from a generic framework introduced by Branco et al. [18]. Nevertheless, following this line, it would at least require a linear RFE with same security level. As we mentioned before, Zhu et al. [44] provided several schemes with SIM security, whereas they considered weaker selective settings. On the other hand, if post-quantum security or unbounded users are additionally required, linear RFE with comparable features ought to be ready. However, all existing linear RFE rely on pairing-based assumptions and only support a finite number of users.

1.2 Technique Overview

As introduced in [25, 34], RFE can be generically derived from slotted RFE via "power-of-two" transformation. In slotted RFE, the key curator is replaced by a stateless aggregator who aggregates all public keys and functions to generates mpk and hsk's at once. In a similar sense, bounded collusion RFE can be gained from bounded collusion slotted RFE using the same method.

We adopt the notion of Q-bound L-slot RFE, i.e., slotted RFE supporting L users and against collusion attack from Q users. In Q-bound L-slot RFE for circuits, after collecting all $\{(\mathsf{pk}_i, C_i)\}_{i\in[L]}$, the aggregator would publish master public key mpk and helper secret keys $\{\mathsf{hsk}_j\}_{j\in[L]}$. Assume the adversary holds the set of secret keys $\mathsf{sk}_{c_1}, \ldots, \mathsf{sk}_{c_Q}$ (where $c_1, \ldots, c_Q \in [L]$), SIM security requires that it cannot distinguish the challenge ciphertext ct^* that is either normally generated from message x^*, or simulated using $(\mathsf{mpk}, \{\mathsf{hsk}_j\}_{j\in[L]},$ $\{\mathsf{sk}_{c_j}\}_{j\in[Q]}, \{C_{c_j}(x^*)\}_{j\in[Q]})$. If we additionally consider malicious case, ct^* should be simulated without $\{\mathsf{sk}_{c_j}\}_{j\in[Q]}$. Here, we ignore this stringent case. For efficiency, we require mpk and hsk of size $\mathsf{poly}(C, Q, \log L)$, where C denotes the circuit size.

Roadmap. Our technical line somewhat deviates from current RFE for limited functionality where they always start from 1-slot case and then generalize to L-slot. We will follow the roadmap:

$$1\text{-bound 1-slot RFE} \xrightarrow[\text{[26,45]}]{\text{Step 1}} 1\text{-bound } L\text{-slot RFE} \xrightarrow[\text{[32]}]{\text{Step 2}} Q\text{-bound } L\text{-slot RFE}$$

Start Point: 1-Bound 1-Slot RFE. First, we propose a new and straightforward construction for 1-bound 1-slot RFE supporting all polynomial circuits. Initially, Sahai et al. [39] built the first 1-bound FE for circuits from standard assumptions, which was later evolved into Q-bound FE by Gorbunov et al. [32]. Here, we also start from [39], but stand by a new perspective. Our first observation is: the worry-free encryption in [39] will yield a 1-bound 1-slot RFE after slight adaptions. An overview is depicted as below.

In 1-bound 1-slot RFE, only single user is going to register his circuit C. Suppose C can be translated into a bit string of length n, given public key encryption scheme $\mathsf{PKE} = (\mathsf{Setup}, \mathsf{Enc}, \mathsf{Dec})$ and garbled circuit algorithms $(\mathsf{Garble}, \mathsf{Eval}, \widehat{\mathsf{Garble}})$ [15,42], the aggregator initially samples a sequence of public keys $\{\widehat{\mathsf{pk}}_w\}_{w \in [n]}$ by running algorithm $\mathsf{PKE.Setup}$ n times. Then it sets $\mathsf{crs} = (\{\widehat{\mathsf{pk}}_w\}_{w \in [n]})$. To register circuit C, the user samples public key pairs $\{(\mathsf{pk}_w, \mathsf{sk}_w)\}_{w \in [n]}$. He keeps $\mathsf{sk} = (\{\mathsf{sk}_w\}_{w \in [n]})$ as decryption key and sends $(\mathsf{C}, \{\mathsf{pk}_w\}_{w \in [n]})$ to aggregator. Thereafter, the aggregator would produce $(\mathsf{mpk}, \mathsf{hsk})$ in the following form:

$$\mathsf{mpk} = \begin{pmatrix} \overline{\mathsf{pk}}_{1,0} & \cdots & \overline{\mathsf{pk}}_{n,0} \\ \overline{\mathsf{pk}}_{1,1} & \cdots & \overline{\mathsf{pk}}_{n,1} \end{pmatrix} \quad \text{and} \quad \mathsf{hsk} = \perp,$$

where for each $w \in [n]$ and $b \in \{0,1\}$, set $\overline{\mathsf{pk}}_{w,b} = \mathsf{pk}_w$ when $\mathsf{C}[w] = b$; otherwise, set $\overline{\mathsf{pk}}_{w,b} = \widehat{\mathsf{pk}}_w$.

Next, to encrypt data x, let $\mathsf{U}(\cdot, \cdot)$ be the universal circuit such that $\mathsf{U}(\mathsf{C}, x) = \mathsf{C}(x)$ for any circuit C and data x. Then run $(\tilde{\mathsf{U}}, \{\mathsf{lab}_{w,b}\}_{w \in [n], b \in \{0,1\}}) \leftarrow \mathsf{Garble}(1^\lambda, \mathsf{U}[x])$ where $\mathsf{U}[x]$ is a universal circuit with x hard-wired. With mpk, the ciphertext is defined as:

$$\mathsf{ct} = \left(\tilde{\mathsf{U}}, \begin{pmatrix} \mathsf{PKE.Enc}(\overline{\mathsf{pk}}_{1,0}, \mathsf{lab}_{1,0}) & \cdots & \mathsf{PKE.Enc}(\overline{\mathsf{pk}}_{n,0}, \mathsf{lab}_{n,0}) \\ \mathsf{PKE.Enc}(\overline{\mathsf{pk}}_{1,1}, \mathsf{lab}_{1,1}) & \cdots & \mathsf{PKE.Enc}(\overline{\mathsf{pk}}_{n,1}, \mathsf{lab}_{n,1}) \end{pmatrix} \right).$$

For decryption, since $\overline{\mathsf{pk}}_{w,b} = \mathsf{pk}_w$ when $\mathsf{C}[w] = b$, the user can recover labels $\{\mathsf{lab}_{w,\mathsf{C}[w]}\}_{w \in [n]}$ by performing algorithm $\mathsf{PKE.Dec}$ n times. Finally, he obtains $\mathsf{C}(x) \leftarrow \mathsf{Eval}(\tilde{\mathsf{U}}, \{\mathsf{lab}_{w,\mathsf{C}[w]}\}_{w \in [n]})$. As for security, our analysis is listed as follows:

– In corrupt case, the registered user has colluded with adversary. Then adversary obtains labels $\{\mathsf{lab}_{w,\mathsf{C}[w]}\}_{w \in [n]}$, whereas he is unable to acquire other labels which are encrypted by public keys issued from aggregator. Thus, following the security of garbled circuits, the adversary cannot learn any information about x except for $\mathsf{C}(x)$;

- In honest case, the adversary has no idea about sk, so he cannot obtain any label according to the semantic security of PKE. Thus, the privacy of x is preserved.

Actually, above construction would immediately lead to 1-bound FE enduring multiple users, by rendering a trusted authority to generate all public keys $\{\overline{\mathsf{pk}}_{w,b}\}$ and then distributing secret key corresponding to each user's circuit. However, in the context of registration, such idea is unrealistic since the aggregator must store no long-term secret. Most importantly, L users will generate L different public keys by themselves, so our problem is how to adapt above construction to accommodate more than one user.

Step 1: 1-Bound L-Slot RFE. Next, we proceed to convert 1-bound 1-slot RFE into 1-bound L-slot RFE that allows L users to register their circuits $\mathsf{C}_1, \ldots, \mathsf{C}_L$. Apparently, public key encryption is insufficient to accommodate all these circuits in mpk, so our idea is to replace it with a more powerful tool, i.e., slotted registered broadcast encryption (RBE). In slotted RBE, each user will register his slot index into mpk, and ciphertext is associated with a broadcast set (that is denoted by a bit string $S \in \{0,1\}^L$) and a message m. For a user indexed by i, the decryption algorithm will recover m properly only when $S[i] = 1$. As for security, we just need "minimal" IND security, which states that the adversary cannot distinguish the ciphertext encrypted by either m_0 or m_1 given public parameters. The reason why we call minimal security is that the adversary is assumed to be unable to collude with any registered user. Let $\mathsf{sRBE} = (\mathsf{Setup}, \mathsf{Gen}, \mathsf{Ver}, \mathsf{Agg}, \mathsf{Enc}, \mathsf{Dec})$ be a slotted RBE with minimal security, we depict 1-bound L-slot RFE as follows.

First, the aggregator initializes $2n$ instances of sRBE and obtains a sequence of common random strings $\{\mathsf{crs}_{w,b}\}_{w\in[n],b\in\{0,1\}}$. For each instance, it runs $\mathsf{sRBE}.\mathsf{Gen}$ to generate L public keys $\{\widehat{\mathsf{pk}}_{i,w,b}\}_{i\in[L],w\in[n],b\in\{0,1\}}$. Then set

$$\mathsf{crs} = (\{\mathsf{crs}_{w,b}\}_{w\in[n],b\in\{0,1\}}, \{\widehat{\mathsf{pk}}_{i,w,b}\}_{i\in[L],w\in[n],b\in\{0,1\}}).$$

For a user with slot index i, he samples $(\mathsf{pk}_{i,w,b}, \mathsf{sk}_{i,w,b}) \leftarrow \mathsf{sRBE}.\mathsf{Gen}(\mathsf{crs}_{w,b}, i)$ for each instance. Then set public key and secret key as

$$\mathsf{pk}_i = (\{\mathsf{pk}_{i,w,b}\}_{w\in[n],b\in\{0,1\}}), \quad \mathsf{sk}_i = (\{\mathsf{sk}_{i,w,b}\}_{w\in[n],b\in\{0,1\}}).$$

Upon receiving $\{\mathsf{pk}_i, \mathsf{C}_i\}_{i\in[L]}$, the aggregator will initialize broadcast sets $S_{w,b} \in \{0,1\}^L$ for each $w \in [n]$ and $b \in \{0,1\}$, then define master public key mpk and helper secret key hsk_j (for slot $j \in [L]$) as follows:

$$\mathsf{mpk} = \begin{pmatrix} \mathsf{mpk}_{1,0} & \cdots & \mathsf{mpk}_{n,0} \\ \mathsf{mpk}_{1,1} & \cdots & \mathsf{mpk}_{n,1} \end{pmatrix} \text{ and } \mathsf{hsk}_j = \begin{pmatrix} \mathsf{hsk}_{j,1,0} & \cdots & \mathsf{hsk}_{j,n,0} \\ \mathsf{hsk}_{j,1,1} & \cdots & \mathsf{hsk}_{j,n,1} \end{pmatrix},$$

where for each $w \in [n]$ and $b \in \{0,1\}$, it involves two steps:

(i) for all $i \in [L]$, set

$$(\overline{\mathsf{pk}}_{i,w,b}, S_{w,b}[i]) := \begin{cases} (\mathsf{pk}_{i,w,b}, 1), & \text{when } \mathsf{C}_i[w] = b, \\ (\widehat{\mathsf{pk}}_{i,w,b}, 0), & \text{otherwise.} \end{cases}$$

(ii) run $(\mathsf{mpk}'_{w,b}, \{\mathsf{hsk}_{j,w,b}\}_{j\in[L]}) \leftarrow \mathsf{sRBE.Agg}(\mathsf{crs}_{w,b}, \{i, \overline{\mathsf{pk}}_{i,w,b}\}_{i\in[L]})$ and set $\mathsf{mpk}_{w,b} = (\mathsf{mpk}'_{w,b}, S_{w,b})$.

The encryption algorithm works in a similar way. Briefly, we run algorithm sRBE.Enc to generate the ciphertext:

$$\mathsf{ct} = \left(\tilde{\mathsf{U}}, \begin{pmatrix} \mathsf{sRBE.Enc}(\mathsf{mpk}_{1,0}, \mathsf{lab}_{1,0}) & \cdots & \mathsf{sRBE.Enc}(\mathsf{mpk}_{n,0}, \mathsf{lab}_{n,0}) \\ \mathsf{sRBE.Enc}(\mathsf{mpk}_{1,1}, \mathsf{lab}_{1,1}) & \cdots & \mathsf{sRBE.Enc}(\mathsf{mpk}_{n,1}, \mathsf{lab}_{n,1}) \end{pmatrix} \right),$$

where $\left(\tilde{\mathsf{U}}, \{\mathsf{lab}_{w,b}\}_{w\in[n],b\in\{0,1\}} \right) \leftarrow \mathsf{Garble}(1^\lambda, \mathsf{U}[x])$ and note that broadcast set $S_{w,b}$ has been contained in $\mathsf{mpk}_{w,b}$. The decryption follows algorithms sRBE.Dec and Eval. At last, the security analysis is as follows:

- In corrupt case, suppose C^* is the unique corrupted circuit, let $b_w = \mathsf{C}^*[w]$ and $\bar{b}_w = 1 - \mathsf{C}^*[w]$, then we have

$$\tilde{\mathsf{U}}, \left\{\mathsf{sRBE.Enc}(\mathsf{mpk}_{w,b_w}, \mathsf{lab}_{w,b_w})\right\}_{w\in[n]}, \left\{\mathsf{sRBE.Enc}(\mathsf{mpk}_{w,\bar{b}_w}, \mathsf{lab}_{w,\bar{b}_w})\right\}_{w\in[n]}$$

$$\approx \tilde{\mathsf{U}}, \left\{\mathsf{sRBE.Enc}(\mathsf{mpk}_{w,b_w}, \mathsf{lab}_{w,b_w})\right\}_{w\in[n]}, \left\{\mathsf{sRBE.Enc}(\mathsf{mpk}_{w,\bar{b}_w}, \mathrm{Random})\right\}_{w\in[n]}$$

$$\approx \widetilde{\mathsf{U}}, \left\{\mathsf{sRBE.Enc}(\mathsf{mpk}_{w,b_w}, \widetilde{\mathsf{lab}}_{w,b_w})\right\}_{w\in[n]}, \left\{\mathsf{sRBE.Enc}(\mathsf{mpk}_{w,\bar{b}_w}, \mathrm{Random})\right\}_{w\in[n]}$$

where $\left(\widetilde{\mathsf{U}}, \{\widetilde{\mathsf{lab}}_{w,b_w}\}_{w\in[n]} \right) \leftarrow \widetilde{\mathsf{Garble}}(1^\lambda, \mathsf{C}^*(x))$. The first $\approx$ follows the IND security of slotted RBE, and the second $\approx$ follows the simulation security of garbled circuits.
- In honest case, since the adversary has no idea about the secret key for some honest circuit $\mathsf{C}_i \neq \mathsf{C}^*$, he cannot acquire all labels $\{\mathsf{lab}_{w,\mathsf{C}_i[w]}\}_{w\in[n]}$. Thus, it is impossible to learn other information about x, including $\mathsf{C}_i(x)$.

Efficiency. It seems that 1-bound L-slot RFE is almost accomplished, because slotted RBE with minimal security can be directly obtained from recent works [26,34,45]. However, we observe above transformation has a vital drawback. Recall that the compactness of slotted RBE requires mpk and hsk of size $\mathsf{poly}(P, \log L)$ where P denotes the size of broadcast space. Considering broadcast space is exactly $[L]$ and broadcast set for encryption contains L bits, it is completely reasonable that slotted RBE has the following properties:

$$\underbrace{|\mathsf{mpk}| = \mathsf{poly}(L), \ |\mathsf{hsk}| = \mathsf{poly}(L),}_{\text{Real compactness}} \ \underbrace{|\mathsf{ct}| = \mathsf{poly}(L)}_{\text{Real encryption}}.$$

Unfortunately, applying such slotted RBE will immediately lead to mpk and hsk of size $\mathsf{poly}(L)$ in our resulting construction since it does not reach the compactness goal of slotted RFE, i.e.,

$$\underbrace{|\mathsf{mpk}| = \mathsf{poly}(C, \log L), \ |\mathsf{hsk}| = \mathsf{poly}(C, \log L)}_{\text{Ideal compactness}}.$$

Besides, the encryption algorithm would be extremely inefficient when L is a large number.

To address this issue, we have to severely restrict the efficiency of underlying slotted RBE. Specifically, we expect that the underlying slotted RBE provides

- *Optimal compactness.* It means $|\mathsf{mpk}| = \mathsf{poly}(\log L), |\mathsf{hsk}| = \mathsf{poly}(\log L)$ and $\mathsf{ct} = \mathsf{poly}(\log L)$. Thus, our 1-bound L-slot RFE naturally enjoys mpk and hsk of size $\mathsf{poly}(C, \log L)$, as well as compact ciphertext.

However, it seems rather tough to carry above thought into practice, because such efficiency requirement (especially compact ciphertext) is too restrictive. As an alternative solution, we pay attention to a weaker variant of RBE, called *global slotted RBE*. Concretely, this primitive is identical to slotted RBE except that its encryption always sets $S = 1^L$ as default. This is inspired by the fact that the aggregator is generally assumed to be honest and transparent (implied by common reference string model [34]). Therefore, it is unnecessary to assign broadcast sets $\{S_{w,b}\}_{w\in[n], b\in\{0,1\}}$ for each component in ct, so we can directly fixed them at 1^L, which relieves us of the difficult task of designing broadcast strategy in highly compact ciphertext.

In summary, a global slotted RBE with optimal compactness will yield a 1-bound L-slot RFE for circuits through our transformation (in Sect. 5). Then the next question is how to obtain a concrete global slotted RBE. We claim that this thing is not technically harder than constructing an RABE scheme. In particular, global slotted RBE can be derived from RABE by applying the generic transformation in [26] which was used to build flexible BE. This reflects the universality of the primitive we proposed because several RABE schemes [26, 45] from suitable assumptions have been provided. Nevertheless, we remark that this transformation seems a bit cumbersome, requiring a pair of dummy attribute and policy for functionality and thus causing extra overhead on performance. In this work, we present two global slotted RBE schemes (in Sects. 3 and 4) that do not need any dummy attribute/policy while still achieving optimal compactness and adaptive security.

As a result, we obtain two concrete 1-bound L-slot RFE for circuits that are adaptively SIM secure under k-Lin assumption and (evasive) LWE assumption, respectively[2]. Comparatively, although [18] has given a concrete 1-bound L-slot RFE for circuits, it just achieves weaker selective IND security, relying on q-type DDH assumption.

Step 2: Q-Bound L-Slot RFE. Here, we adopt Gorbunov et al.'s generic transformation [32]. In essence, it exploits a reusable dynamic MPC protocol [11] to upgrade 1-bound FE to Q-bound FE. This methodology is as well suitable for the conversion from 1-bound L-slot RFE to Q-bound L-slot RFE (without malicious case).

---

[2] Our pairing-based construction has the same structure as the k-Lin distributed BE in [37], because both of them are based on the BE scheme in [30]. Our lattice-based construction can also be seen as a new application of witness encryption.

Roughly speaking, we improves 1-bound security to Q-bound security by implementing N instances of 1-bound slotted RFE in parallel, where N is a system parameter dependent on Q. To resist the adversary colluding with Q users, the encryption algorithm will divide data x into N secret shares, then use these instances to encrypt each share. In the meantime, we restrict each user only register into a part of N instances. For decryption, the user first computes multiple local parts of $\mathsf{C}(x)$ using secret keys, then recovers the whole $\mathsf{C}(x)$ by aggregating these local parts. In security reduction, Q-bound security are based on the security of underlying 1-bound L-slot RFE and MPC protocol. Finally, we manage to build a Q-bound L-slot RFE for circuits (in Sect. 6) which can be later transformed into a full-fledged Q-bound RFE via "power-of-two" [25,34].

Towards Unbounded Users. As we can see, above generic construction only supports a finite number of users, due to crs of size $\mathsf{poly}(L)$. Even so, we point out that it can also be utilized to construct RFE supporting an arbitrary number of users, as long as the underlying global slotted RBE supports unbounded users as well. This can be done in **Step 1** by removing all public keys $\{\widehat{\mathsf{pk}}_{i,w,b}\}$ in crs and directly aggregating all public keys from users to generate mpk and hsk. In this way, crs only consists of a limited number of global slotted RBE instances, so the size of crs will naturally not scale with L if the crs of global slotted RBE does not grow with L. Thereby, we obtain a concrete RFE for circuits enjoying unbounded users property. Considering all parameters of size unavoidably growing with Q, our unbounded notion is a bit weaker than earlier works [26,34], but this will not be an issue due to the fact that $Q \ll L$.

1.3   Disscussion

Malicious Case. The technical barrier to tackle malicious case in Q-bound slotted RFE lies on the fact that the challenger cannot ensure adversary generates secret key with right randomness. Although non-interactive zero-knowledge arguments (NIZK) [18,45] would be helpful in simulating challenge ciphertext with only public keys, the adversary can still control the generation of randomness which is essential to the upgradation from 1-bound security to Q-bound security. Previously, only $i\mathcal{O}$-based solution is known to resist malicious users, and it aims at weak IND security. Therefore, we leave seeking new technology to tackle malicious case in RFE for circuits without $i\mathcal{O}$ as a future work.

Dynamic Bounded Collusion Model. Recently, Agrawal et al. [7] and Garg et al. [28] initiated the notion of *dynamic bounded collusion model*, where Q is given in the encryption algorithm (instead of setup algorithm) and hence enable to more flexibly select collusion bound while balancing performance. Comparatively, our RFE is static bounded collusion-resistant. At a high level, it is feasible to spread the concept of dynamic bounded collusion-resistance to the registering setting, then there is no need to require all parameters of size relevant to Q. However, to our best knowledge, it seems necessary to build a dynamic bounded RFE based on the existence of static bounded RFE [27]. Therefore, we believe this work will motivate the study of dynamic bounded collusion-resistant RFE.

Succinctness. One may want to ask whether it is possible to achieve succinct RFE, i.e., the encryption overhead sublinear in the size of the circuit. Intuitively, we can build a succinct 1-bound slotted RFE from our 1-bound slotted RFE and a *Laconic Function Evaluation* (LFE). It is analogous to Quach et al.'s transformation [38] applying on non-succinct 1-bound FE. Concretely, LFE can be used to deterministically compress the large-sized registered circuit into a short digest, then succinctness is guaranteed by performing RFE encryption with respect to LFE encryption, as the overhead of LFE encryption is small.

1.4 Related Work

We mention other works to remove the trusted authority in FE. Chandran et al. [19] introduced the notion of multi-authority functional encryption (MAFE), then proposed a MAFE for arbitrary polynomial-time function based on subexponentially secure $i\mathcal{O}$ and injective one-way functions. On the other hand, Chotard et al. [20] formalized the notion of decentralized muliti-client functional encryption (DMCFE) and gave the first instance supporting inner-product computation, afterwards an elegant line of work [1,2,4] are devoted to this filed, while all of them only focus on linear function. Furthermore, Chotard et al. [21] formalized a new extension called dynamic decentralized functional encryption (DDFE) that allows multiple users to join the system dynamically and generate secret keys in a decentralized fashion. Beyond linear function, a recent work [9] provided the first DDFE for attributed-weighted sums that includes arithmetic branch programs. In addition, Agrawal et al. [5] initiated the study of multi-party functional encryption (MPFE) that unifies a wide range of FE variants, including but not limited to MAFE, DMCFE and DDFE.

2   Preliminaries

For a finite set S, we write $s \leftarrow S$ to denote that s is picked uniformly from finite set S. Then, we use $|S|$ to denote the size of S. Let $\approx_s$ stand for two distributions being statistically indistinguishable, and $\approx_c$ denote two distributions being computationally indistinguishable. For any $x \in \{0,1\}^n$, we use $x[w]$ to denote the w-th bit of x.

2.1   Prime-Order Bilinear Groups

A generator $\mathcal{G}$ takes as input a security parameter 1^λ and outputs a description $\mathbb{G} := (p, \mathbb{G}_1, \mathbb{G}_2, \mathbb{G}_T, e)$, where p is a prime, $\mathbb{G}_1$, $\mathbb{G}_2$ and $\mathbb{G}_T$ are cyclic groups of order p, and $e : \mathbb{G}_1 \times \mathbb{G}_2 \rightarrow \mathbb{G}_T$ is a non-degenerate bilinear map. Group operations in $\mathbb{G}_1, \mathbb{G}_2, \mathbb{G}_T$ and bilinear map e are computable in deterministic polynomial time in λ. Let $g_1 \in \mathbb{G}_1$, $g_2 \in \mathbb{G}_2$ and $g_T = e(g_1, g_2) \in \mathbb{G}_T$ be the respective generators, we employ *implicit representation* of group elements: for a matrix $\mathbf{M}$ over $\mathbb{Z}_p$, we define $[\mathbf{M}]_s = g_s^{\mathbf{M}}, \forall s \in \{1, 2, T\}$, where exponentiation is carried out component-wise. Given $[\mathbf{A}]_1, [\mathbf{B}]_2$ where $\mathbf{A}$ and $\mathbf{B}$ have proper sizes, we let $e([\mathbf{A}]_1, [\mathbf{B}]_2) = [\mathbf{AB}]_T$. We review *matrix decisional Diffie-Hellman (MDDH) assumption*, which is implied by k-Lin [24].

Assumption 1 $((k, \ell, d)$-**MDDH over** $\mathbb{G}_s$, $s \in \{1, 2\})$. *Let $k, \ell, d \in \mathbb{N}$ with $k < \ell$. We say that the (k, ℓ, d)-MDDH assumption holds in $\mathbb{G}_s$ if for all efficient adversaries $\mathcal{A}$, the following advantage function is negligible in λ.*

$$\mathsf{Adv}^{\mathrm{MDDH}}_{\mathcal{A}, s, k, \ell, d}(\lambda) = \big| \Pr[\mathcal{A}(\mathbb{G}, [\mathbf{M}]_s, [\mathbf{SM}]_s) = 1] - \Pr[\mathcal{A}(\mathbb{G}, [\mathbf{M}]_s, [\mathbf{U}]_s) = 1] \big|$$

where $\mathbb{G} := (p, \mathbb{G}_1, \mathbb{G}_2, \mathbb{G}_T, e) \leftarrow \mathcal{G}(1^\lambda)$, $\mathbf{M} \leftarrow \mathbb{Z}_p^{k \times \ell}$, $\mathbf{S} \leftarrow \mathbb{Z}_p^{d \times k}$ *and* $\mathbf{U} \leftarrow \mathbb{Z}_p^{d \times \ell}$.

2.2 Garbled Circuits

Algorithms. A garbled circuit scheme [15, 42] (with input $x \in \{0, 1\}^n$ and circuit family C) consists of two efficient algorithms as follows:

- $\mathsf{Garble}(1^\lambda, \mathsf{C}) \to (\tilde{\mathsf{C}}, \{\mathsf{lab}_{w,b}\}_{w \in [n], b \in \{0,1\}})$. It takes as input security parameter 1^λ and a circuit $\mathsf{C} \in C$, and then outputs a garbled circuit $\tilde{\mathsf{C}}$ and labels $\{\mathsf{lab}_{w,b}\}_{w \in [n], b \in \{0,1\}}$.
- $\mathsf{Eval}(\tilde{\mathsf{C}}, \{\mathsf{lab}_{w,x[w]}\}_{w \in [n]}) \to z$. It takes as input a garbled circuit $\tilde{\mathsf{C}}$ and a sequence of input labels $\{\mathsf{lab}_{w,x[w]}\}_{w \in [n]}$, and then deterministically outputs a value z.

Without loss of generality, we assume that the size of each label $\mathsf{lab}_{w,b}$ is $O(\lambda)$. Note that above definition from Yao's garbled circuits suffices for our construction, while the performance of garbled circuits may be further improved through the techniques of [14, 43].

Correctness. For all λ, for any circuit C and input $x \in \{0, 1\}^n$, we have

$$\Pr[\mathsf{Eval}(\tilde{\mathsf{C}}, \{\mathsf{lab}_{w,x[w]}\}_{w \in [n]}) = \mathsf{C}(x) \mid (\tilde{\mathsf{C}}, \{\mathsf{lab}_{w,b}\}_{w \in [n], b \in \{0,1\}}) \leftarrow \mathsf{Garble}(1^\lambda, \mathsf{C})] = 1.$$

Security. There exists a simulator $\widetilde{\mathsf{Garble}}$ such that for any circuit C and input $x \in \{0, 1\}^n$, we have

$$\left(\tilde{\mathsf{C}}, \{\mathsf{lab}_{w,x[w]}\}_{w \in [n]} \right) \approx_c \widetilde{\mathsf{Garble}}(1^\lambda, \mathsf{C}(x))$$

where $(\tilde{\mathsf{C}}, \{\mathsf{lab}_{w,b}\}_{w \in [n], b \in \{0,1\}}) \leftarrow \mathsf{Garble}(1^\lambda, \mathsf{C})$.

2.3 Global Slotted Registered Broadcast Encryption

Algorithms. A global slotted registered broadcast encryption (global slotted RBE for short) consists of six efficient algorithms as follows:

- $\mathsf{Setup}(1^\lambda, 1^L) \to \mathsf{crs}$. It takes as input the security parameter 1^λ, the upper bound 1^L of the number of slots, outputs a common reference string crs.
- $\mathsf{Gen}(\mathsf{crs}, i) \to (\mathsf{pk}_i, \mathsf{sk}_i)$. It takes as input crs and $i \in [L]$, outputs a key pair $(\mathsf{pk}_i, \mathsf{sk}_i)$.

- $\mathsf{Ver}(\mathsf{crs}, i, \mathsf{pk}_i) \to 0/1$. It takes as input $\mathsf{crs}, i, \mathsf{pk}_i$, outputs a bit indicating whether pk_i is valid.
- $\mathsf{Agg}(\mathsf{crs}, \{i, \mathsf{pk}_i\}_{i \in [L]}) \to (\mathsf{mpk}, \{\mathsf{hsk}_j\}_{j \in [L]})$. It takes as input crs and a series of pk_i with slot index i for all $i \in [L]$, outputs master public key mpk and a series of helper keys hsk_j for all $j \in [L]$.
- $\mathsf{Enc}(\mathsf{mpk}, \mathsf{m}) \to \mathsf{ct}$. It takes as input mpk and a message m, outputs a ciphertext ct.
- $\mathsf{Dec}(\mathsf{hsk}_{i^*}, \mathsf{sk}_{i^*}, \mathsf{ct}) \to \mathsf{m}/\bot$. It takes as input $\mathsf{hsk}_{i^*}, \mathsf{sk}_{i^*}, \mathsf{ct}$, outputs m or an empty symbol $\bot$.

Completeness. For all $\lambda, L \in \mathbb{N}$, and all $i \in [L]$, we have

$$\Pr\left[\mathsf{Ver}(\mathsf{crs}, i, \mathsf{pk}_i) = 1 | \mathsf{crs} \leftarrow \mathsf{Setup}(1^\lambda, 1^L); (\mathsf{pk}_i, \mathsf{sk}_i) \leftarrow \mathsf{Gen}(\mathsf{crs}, i)\right] = 1.$$

Correctness. For all $\lambda, L \in \mathbb{N}$, and all $i^* \in [L]$, all $\mathsf{crs} \leftarrow \mathsf{Setup}(1^\lambda, 1^L)$, all $(\mathsf{pk}_{i^*}, \mathsf{sk}_{i^*}) \leftarrow \mathsf{Gen}(\mathsf{crs}, i^*)$, all $\{\mathsf{pk}_i\}_{i \in [L] \setminus \{i^*\}}$ such that $\mathsf{Ver}(\mathsf{crs}, i, \mathsf{pk}_i) = 1$, and all m, we have

$$\Pr\left[\mathsf{Dec}(\mathsf{hsk}_{i^*}, \mathsf{sk}_{i^*}, \mathsf{ct}) = \mathsf{m} \,\middle|\, \begin{array}{l} (\mathsf{mpk}, \{\mathsf{hsk}_j\}_{j \in [L]}) \leftarrow \mathsf{Agg}(\mathsf{crs}, \{i, \mathsf{pk}_i\}_{i \in [L]}) \\ \mathsf{ct} \leftarrow \mathsf{Enc}(\mathsf{mpk}, m) \end{array}\right] = 1.$$

Optimal Compactness. For all $\lambda, L \in \mathbb{N}$, and all $i \in [L]$, it holds that

$$|\mathsf{mpk}| = \mathsf{poly}(\lambda, \log L) \text{ and } |\mathsf{hsk}_i| = \mathsf{poly}(\lambda, \log L).$$

In addition, it requires $|\mathsf{ct}| = \mathsf{poly}(\lambda, \log L)$.

Indistinguishability-Based (IND) Security. For all $\lambda \in \mathbb{N}$ and all efficient adversaries $\mathcal{A}$, the indistinguishability-based security requires the advantage

$$\left| \Pr\left[b' = b \,\middle|\, \begin{array}{l} L \leftarrow \mathcal{A}(1^\lambda); \mathsf{crs} \leftarrow \mathsf{Setup}(1^\lambda, 1^L) \\ (\{i, \mathsf{pk}_i^*\}_{i \in [L]}, \mathsf{m}_0^*, \mathsf{m}_1^*) \leftarrow \mathcal{A}^{\mathsf{OGen}(\cdot), \mathsf{OCor}(\cdot)}(\mathsf{crs}) \\ (\mathsf{mpk}, \{\mathsf{hsk}_j\}_{j \in [L]}) \leftarrow \mathsf{Agg}(\mathsf{crs}, \{i, \mathsf{pk}_i^*\}_{i \in L}) \\ b \leftarrow \{0, 1\}; \mathsf{ct}^* \leftarrow \mathsf{Enc}(\mathsf{mpk}, \mathsf{m}_b^*); b' \leftarrow \mathcal{A}(\mathsf{ct}^*) \end{array} \right] - \frac{1}{2} \right|$$

is negligible in λ, where oracles $\mathsf{OGen}, \mathsf{OCor}$ work with initial setting $\{\mathcal{D}_i = \emptyset\}_{i \in [L]}, \mathcal{C} = \emptyset$ as follows:

- $\mathsf{OGen}(i)$: run $(\mathsf{pk}, \mathsf{sk}) \leftarrow \mathsf{Gen}(\mathsf{crs}, i)$, set $\mathcal{D}_i[\mathsf{pk}] = \mathsf{sk}$ and return pk.
- $\mathsf{OCor}(i, \mathsf{pk})$: return $\mathcal{D}_i[\mathsf{pk}]$ and update $\mathcal{C} = \mathcal{C} \cup \{(i, \mathsf{pk})\}$.

and for all $i \in [L]$, we require $\mathcal{D}_i[\mathsf{pk}_i^*] \neq \bot$ and $(i, \mathsf{pk}_i^*) \notin \mathcal{C}$.

Indeed, global slotted RBE can be seen as a plain slotted RBE which always set broadcast set as 1^L and achieves the minimal security, i.e., IND security only under honest case.

2.4   Q-Bound Slotted Registered Functional Encryption

Algorithms. A Q-bound slotted registered functional encryption (Q-bound slotted RFE for short) for circuit family $C : X \to Z$ consists of six efficient algorithms as follows:

- Setup$(1^\lambda, 1^L, 1^Q, C) \to$ crs. It takes as input the security parameter 1^λ, upper bound 1^L of the number of slots, collusion bound 1^Q and circuit family C, outputs a common reference string crs.
- Gen$($crs$, i) \to ($pk$_i,$ sk$_i)$. It takes as input crs and slot index $i \in [L]$, outputs a key pair $($pk$_i,$ sk$_i)$.
- Ver$($crs$, i,$ pk$_i) \to 0/1$. It takes as input crs$, i,$ pk$_i$, outputs a bit indicating whether pk$_i$ is valid.
- Agg$($crs$, \{$pk$_i,$ C$_i\}_{i \in [L]}) \to ($mpk$, \{$hsk$_j\}_{j \in [L]})$. It takes as input crs and a series of pk$_i$ with C$_i \in C$ for all $i \in [L]$, outputs master public key mpk and a series of helper keys hsk$_j$ for all $j \in [L]$. This algorithm is deterministic.
- Enc$($mpk$, x) \to$ ct. It takes as input mpk$, x \in X$, outputs a ciphertext ct.
- Dec$($hsk$_{i^*},$ sk$_{i^*},$ ct$) \to z/ \perp$. It takes as input hsk$_{i^*},$ sk$_{i^*},$ ct, outputs $z \in Z$ or an empty symbol $\perp$.

Completeness. For all $\lambda, L \in \mathbb{N}$, all $Q \ll L$ and all C, and all $i \in [L]$, we have

$$\Pr\left[\mathsf{Ver}(\mathsf{crs}, i, \mathsf{pk}_i) = 1 | \mathsf{crs} \leftarrow \mathsf{Setup}(1^\lambda, 1^L, 1^Q, C); (\mathsf{pk}_i, \mathsf{sk}_i) \leftarrow \mathsf{Gen}(\mathsf{crs}, i)\right] = 1.$$

Correctness. For all $\lambda, L \in \mathbb{N}$, all $Q \ll L$ and all C, and all $i^* \in [L]$, all crs $\leftarrow$ Setup$(1^\lambda, 1^L, 1^Q, C)$, all $($pk$_{i^*},$ sk$_{i^*}) \leftarrow$ Gen$($crs$, i^*)$, all $\{$pk$_i\}_{i \in [L] \setminus \{i^*\}}$ such that Ver$($crs$, i,$ pk$_i) = 1$, all $x \in X$ and C$_1, \ldots,$ C$_L \in C$, we have

$$\Pr\left[\mathsf{Dec}(\mathsf{hsk}_{i^*}, \mathsf{sk}_{i^*}, \mathsf{ct}) = \mathsf{C}_{i^*}(x) \,\middle|\, \begin{array}{l} (\mathsf{mpk}, \{\mathsf{hsk}_j\}_{j \in [L]}) \leftarrow \mathsf{Agg}(\mathsf{crs}, \{\mathsf{pk}_i, \mathsf{C}_i\}_{i \in [L]}) \\ \mathsf{ct} \leftarrow \mathsf{Enc}(\mathsf{mpk}, x) \end{array}\right] = 1.$$

Compactness. For all $\lambda, L \in \mathbb{N}$, all $Q \ll L$ and all C, and all $i \in [L]$, it holds that

$$|\mathsf{mpk}| = \mathsf{poly}(\lambda, C, Q, \log L) \text{ and } |\mathsf{hsk}_i| = \mathsf{poly}(\lambda, C, Q, \log L).$$

Simulation-Based (SIM) Security. For all $\lambda \in \mathbb{N}$ and all efficient adversaries $\mathcal{A}$, the adaptive simulation-based security requires that there exists simulator $\widetilde{\mathsf{Enc}}$ such that:

$$\left| \begin{array}{l} (L, Q) \leftarrow \mathcal{A}(1^\lambda); \mathsf{crs} \leftarrow \mathsf{Setup}(1^\lambda, 1^L, 1^Q, C) \\ (\{\mathsf{pk}_i^*, \mathsf{C}_i^*\}_{i \in [L]}, x^*) \leftarrow \mathcal{A}^{\mathsf{OGen}(\cdot), \mathsf{OCor}(\cdot)}(\mathsf{crs}) \\ (\mathsf{mpk}, \{\mathsf{hsk}_j\}_{j \in [L]}) \leftarrow \mathsf{Agg}(\mathsf{crs}, \{\mathsf{pk}_i^*, \mathsf{C}_i^*\}_{i \in L}) \\ \mathsf{ct}^* \leftarrow \mathsf{Enc}(\mathsf{mpk}, x^*); \alpha \leftarrow \mathcal{A}(\mathsf{ct}^*) \end{array} \right| \approx_c \left| \begin{array}{l} (L, Q) \leftarrow \mathcal{A}(1^\lambda); \mathsf{crs} \leftarrow \mathsf{Setup}(1^\lambda, 1^L, 1^Q, C) \\ (\{\mathsf{pk}_i^*, \mathsf{C}_i^*\}_{i \in [L]}, x^*) \leftarrow \mathcal{A}^{\mathsf{OGen}(\cdot), \mathsf{OCor}(\cdot)}(\mathsf{crs}) \\ (\mathsf{mpk}, \{\mathsf{hsk}_j\}_{j \in [L]}) \leftarrow \mathsf{Agg}(\mathsf{crs}, \{\mathsf{pk}_i^*, \mathsf{C}_i^*\}_{i \in L}) \\ \widetilde{\mathsf{ct}}^* \leftarrow \widetilde{\mathsf{Enc}}(\mathsf{mpk}, \mathcal{K}); \alpha \leftarrow \mathcal{A}(\widetilde{\mathsf{ct}}^*) \end{array} \right|$$

where oracles OGen, OCor work with initial setting $\{\mathcal{D}_i = \emptyset\}_{i \in [L]}, \mathcal{C} = \emptyset$ and $\mathcal{K} = \emptyset$ as follows:

- OGen(i): run $($pk$,$ sk$) \leftarrow$ Gen$($crs$, i)$, set $\mathcal{D}_i[$pk$] =$ sk and return pk.

– OCor(i, pk): return $\mathcal{D}_i[\text{pk}]$ and update $\mathcal{C} = \mathcal{C} \cup \{(i, \text{pk})\}$.

Here, We consider the notion of Q-bound SIM security without malicious case. More concretely, it requires (i) $\mathcal{D}_i[\text{pk}_i^*] \neq \perp$ for all $i \in [L]$; (ii) for each $(i, \text{pk}_i^*) \in \mathcal{C}$ where $|\mathcal{C}| \leq Q^3$, set $\mathcal{K} = \mathcal{K} \cup \{(i, \mathsf{C}_i^*, \mathsf{C}_i^*(x^*), \mathcal{D}_i[\text{pk}_i^*])\}$.

2.5   Q-Bound Registered Functional Encryption

Algorithms. A Q-bound registered functional encryption (Q-bound RFE for short) for circuit family $C : X \to Z$ consists of six efficient algorithms as follows:

– Setup($1^\lambda, 1^L, 1^Q, C$) $\to$ crs. It takes as input the security parameter 1^λ, the maximum number of users 1^L, collusion bound 1^Q and circuit family C, outputs a common reference string crs.
– Gen(crs, aux) $\to$ (pk, sk). It takes as input crs and state aux, outputs key pair (pk, sk).
– Reg(crs, aux, pk, C) $\to$ (mpk, aux'). It takes as input crs, aux, pk along with $C \in C$, outputs master public key mpk and updated state aux'.
– Upd(crs, aux, pk) $\to$ hsk. It takes as input crs, aux, pk, outputs a helper key hsk.
– Enc(mpk, x) $\to$ ct. It takes as input mpk, $x \in X$, outputs a ciphertext ct.
– Dec(hsk, sk, ct) $\to$ $z/ \perp /$getupd. It takes as input hsk, sk, ct, outputs $z \in Z$ or an empty symbol $\perp$ to indicate a decryption failure, or a symbol getupd to indicate the need of an updated helper key.

Correctness. For all stateful adversary $\mathcal{A}$, the following advantage function is negligible in λ:

$$\Pr[b = 1 | \text{crs} \leftarrow \text{Setup}(1^\lambda, 1^L, 1^Q, C); b = 0; \mathcal{A}^{\text{ORegNT}(\cdot,\cdot),\text{ORegT}(\cdot),\text{OEnc}(\cdot,\cdot),\text{ODec}(\cdot)}(\text{crs})]$$

where the oracles work as follows with initial setting aux $= \perp$, $\mathcal{E} = \emptyset$, $\mathcal{R} = \emptyset$ and $t = \perp$:

– ORegNT(pk, C): run (mpk, aux') $\leftarrow$ Reg(crs, aux, pk, C), update aux $=$ aux', append (mpk, aux) to $\mathcal{R}$ and return $(|\mathcal{R}|, \text{mpk}, \text{aux})$;
– ORegT(C^*):
run (pk*, sk*) $\leftarrow$ Gen(crs, aux), (mpk, aux') $\leftarrow$ Reg(crs, aux, pk*, C^*), update aux $=$ aux', compute hsk* $\leftarrow$ Upd(crs, aux, pk*), append (mpk, aux) to $\mathcal{R}$, return $(t = |\mathcal{R}|, \text{mpk}, \text{aux}, \text{pk}^*, \text{sk}^*, \text{hsk}^*)$;
– OEnc(i, x): let $\mathcal{R}[i] = (\text{mpk}, \cdot)$ and run ct $\leftarrow$ Enc(mpk, x), append (x, ct) to $\mathcal{E}$ and return $(|\mathcal{E}|, \text{ct})$;
– ODec(j): let $\mathcal{E}[j] = (x_j, \text{ct}_j)$, compute $z_j \leftarrow$ Dec(hsk*, sk*, ct$_j$). If $z_j =$ getupd, run hsk* $\leftarrow$ Upd(crs, aux, pk*) and recompute $z_j \leftarrow$ Dec(hsk*, sk*, ct$_j$). Set $b = 1$ when $z_j \neq C^*(x_j)$.

---

[3] Here, we consider the bounded collusion model in a weak sense, i.e., the number of corruption queries is restricted. Nevertheless, our 1-bound RFE construction is still secure, even allowing arbitrary polynomial number of corruption queries and the existence of malicious user.

with the following restrictions:

- there exists one query to ORegT;
- for query (i, x) to OEnc, it holds that $t \geq i, \mathcal{R}[i] \neq \bot$;
- for query (j) to ODec, it holds that $\mathcal{E}[j] \neq \bot$.

Compactness and Update Efficiency. For all $\lambda, L \in \mathbb{N}$, all $Q \ll L$ and all C, it holds that

$$|\mathsf{mpk}| = \mathsf{poly}(\lambda, C, Q, \log L) \text{ and } |\mathsf{hsk}| = \mathsf{poly}(\lambda, C, Q, \log L).$$

Furthermore, the number of invocations of Upd in ODec is at most $O(\log |\mathcal{R}|)$ and each invocation costs $\mathsf{poly}(\log |\mathcal{R}|)$ time.

Simulation-Based (SIM) Security. For all $\lambda \in \mathbb{N}$ and all efficient adversaries $\mathcal{A}$, the adaptive simulation-based security requires that there exists simulator $\widetilde{\mathsf{Enc}}$ such that:

$$\begin{vmatrix} \mathsf{crs} \leftarrow \mathsf{Setup}(1^\lambda, 1^L, 1^Q, C) \\ x^* \leftarrow \mathcal{A}^{\mathsf{ORegHK}(\cdot), \mathsf{OCorHK}(\cdot)}(\mathsf{crs}) \\ \mathsf{ct}^* \leftarrow \mathsf{Enc}(\mathsf{mpk}, x^*) \\ \mathcal{A}^{\mathsf{OCorHK}(\cdot)}(\mathsf{ct}^*); \alpha \leftarrow \mathcal{A}(\mathsf{ct}^*) \end{vmatrix} \approx_c \begin{vmatrix} \mathsf{crs} \leftarrow \mathsf{Setup}(1^\lambda, 1^L, 1^Q, C) \\ x^* \leftarrow \mathcal{A}^{\mathsf{ORegHK}(\cdot), \mathsf{OCorHK}(\cdot)}(\mathsf{crs}) \\ \widetilde{\mathsf{ct}}^* \leftarrow \widetilde{\mathsf{Enc}}(\mathsf{mpk}, \mathcal{K}); \\ \mathcal{A}^{\mathsf{OCorHK}(\cdot)}(\widetilde{\mathsf{ct}}^*); \alpha \leftarrow \mathcal{A}(\widetilde{\mathsf{ct}}^*) \end{vmatrix}$$

where oracles ORegHK, OCorHK work with initial setting $\mathsf{mpk} = \bot, \mathsf{aux} = \bot, \mathcal{R} = \emptyset, \mathcal{C} = \emptyset, \mathcal{K} = \emptyset$ and $\mathcal{D}$ being a dictionary with $\mathcal{D}[\mathsf{pk}] = \emptyset$ for all possible pk:

- ORegHK(C):
  run $(\mathsf{pk}, \mathsf{sk}) \leftarrow \mathsf{Gen}(\mathsf{crs}, \mathsf{aux})$ and $(\mathsf{mpk}', \mathsf{aux}') \leftarrow \mathsf{Reg}(\mathsf{crs}, \mathsf{aux}, \mathsf{pk}, C)$, update $\mathsf{mpk} = \mathsf{mpk}', \mathsf{aux} = \mathsf{aux}', \mathcal{D}[\mathsf{pk}] = \mathcal{D}[\mathsf{pk}] \cup \{C\}$, append $(\mathsf{pk}, \mathsf{sk})$ to $\mathcal{R}$ and return $(|\mathcal{R}|, \mathsf{mpk}, \mathsf{aux}, \mathsf{pk})$;
- OCorHK(i): let $\mathcal{R}[i] = (\mathsf{pk}, \mathsf{sk})$ and $C = \mathcal{D}[\mathsf{pk}]$, append pk to $\mathcal{C}$ and return sk.

Similarly, we require the Q-bound SIM security without malicious case. More concretely, it requires (i) $\mathcal{R}[i] \neq \bot$ for each query i to OCorHK; (ii) for each $(i, \mathsf{pk}_i^*) \in \mathcal{C}$ where $|\mathcal{C}| \leq Q$, let $\mathcal{R}[i] = (\mathsf{pk}_i^*, \mathsf{sk}_i^*)$ and $C_i = \mathcal{D}[\mathsf{pk}_i^*]$, set $\mathcal{K} = \mathcal{K} \cup \{(i, C_i^*, C_i^*(x^*), \mathsf{sk}_i^*)\}$.

3 Pairing-Based Global Slotted RBE

In this section, we present a global slotted RBE relying on MDDH assumption.

3.1 Construction

Our construction works as follows:

- $\mathsf{Setup}(1^\lambda, 1^L)$: Generate $\mathbb{G} := (p, \mathbb{G}_1, \mathbb{G}_2, \mathbb{G}_T, e) \leftarrow \mathcal{G}(1^\lambda)$ and sample

$$\mathbf{A} \leftarrow \mathbb{Z}_p^{k \times (k+1)}, \mathbf{B} \leftarrow \mathbb{Z}_p^{(k+1) \times k}, \mathbf{k} \leftarrow \mathbb{Z}_p^{1 \times (k+1)}.$$

For all $i \in [L]$, sample $\mathbf{V}_i \leftarrow \mathbb{Z}_p^{(k+1) \times (k+1)}$, $\mathbf{r}_i \leftarrow \mathbb{Z}_p^{1 \times k}$. Output

$$\mathsf{crs} = \begin{pmatrix} [\mathbf{A}]_1, \{[\mathbf{AV}_i]_1, [\mathbf{Br}_i^\top, \mathbf{V}_i\mathbf{Br}_i^\top + \mathbf{k}^\top]_2\}_{i \in [L]}, \\ \{[\mathbf{V}_i\mathbf{Br}_j^\top]_2\}_{j \in [L], i \in [L] \setminus \{j\}}, [\mathbf{Ak}^\top]_T \end{pmatrix}.$$

- $\mathsf{Gen}(\mathsf{crs}, i)$: Sample $\mathbf{U}_i \leftarrow \mathbb{Z}_p^{(k+1) \times (k+1)}$, output $\mathsf{pk}_i = ([\mathbf{AU}_i]_1, \{[\mathbf{U}_i\mathbf{Br}_j^\top]_2\}_{j \in [L] \setminus \{i\}})$ and $\mathsf{sk}_i = \mathbf{U}_i$.
- $\mathsf{Ver}(\mathsf{crs}, i, \mathsf{pk}_i)$: Parse the public key $\mathsf{pk}_i = ([\mathbf{AU}_i]_1, \{[\mathbf{U}_i\mathbf{Br}_j^\top]_2\}_{j \in [L] \setminus \{i\}})$. For each $j \in [L] \setminus \{i\}$, check

$$e([\mathbf{A}]_1, [\mathbf{U}_i\mathbf{Br}_j^\top]_2) \stackrel{?}{=} e([\mathbf{AU}_i]_1, [\mathbf{Br}_j^\top]_2).$$

If above checks pass, output 1; otherwise, output 0.
- $\mathsf{Agg}(\mathsf{crs}, \{i, \mathsf{pk}_i\}_{i \in [L]})$: For all $i \in [L]$, parse $\mathsf{pk}_i = ([\mathbf{AU}_i]_1, \{[\mathbf{U}_i\mathbf{Br}_j^\top]_2\}_{j \in [L] \setminus \{i\}})$. Output

$$\mathsf{mpk} = \left([\mathbf{A}]_1, [\mathbf{Ak}^\top]_T, \left[\sum_{j \in [L]} (\mathbf{AV}_j + \mathbf{AU}_j) \right]_1 \right),$$

and for all $i \in [L]$, output

$$\mathsf{hsk}_i = \left(\underbrace{[\mathbf{Br}_i^\top]_2}_{\mathbf{k}_0^\top}, \underbrace{[\mathbf{V}_i\mathbf{Br}_i^\top + \mathbf{k}^\top]_2}_{\mathbf{k}_1^\top}, \underbrace{\left[\sum_{j \in [L] \setminus \{i\}} (\mathbf{V}_j\mathbf{Br}_i^\top + \mathbf{U}_j\mathbf{Br}_i^\top) \right]_2}_{\mathbf{k}_2^\top} \right).$$

- $\mathsf{Enc}(\mathsf{mpk}, \mathsf{m})$: Parse $\mathsf{mpk} = \left([\mathbf{A}]_1, [\mathbf{Ak}^\top]_T, \left[\sum_{j \in [L]} (\mathbf{AV}_j + \mathbf{AU}_j) \right]_1 \right)$. Sample $\mathbf{s} \leftarrow \mathbb{Z}_p^{1 \times k}$, output

$$\mathsf{ct} = \left(\underbrace{[\mathbf{sA}]_1}_{\mathbf{c}_0}, \underbrace{\left[\sum_{j \in [L]} (\mathbf{sAV}_j + \mathbf{sAU}_j) \right]_1}_{\mathbf{c}_1}, \underbrace{[\mathbf{sAk}^\top]_T \cdot \mathsf{m}}_{C} \right).$$

- $\mathsf{Dec}(\mathsf{hsk}_{i^*}, \mathsf{sk}_{i^*}, \mathsf{ct})$: Parse $\mathsf{sk}_{i^*} = \mathbf{U}_{i^*}$, $\mathsf{hsk}_{i^*} = ([\mathbf{k}_0^\top]_2, [\mathbf{k}_1^\top]_2, [\mathbf{k}_2^\top]_2)$ and $\mathsf{ct} = ([\mathbf{c}_0]_1, [\mathbf{c}_1]_1, C)$. Compute

$$\begin{aligned} [z_1]_T &= e([\mathbf{c}_1]_1, [\mathbf{k}_0^\top]_2), \quad [z_2]_T = e([\mathbf{c}_0]_1, [\mathbf{k}_2^\top]_2), \\ [z_3]_T &= e([\mathbf{c}_0\mathbf{U}_{i^*}]_1, [\mathbf{k}_0^\top]_2), \quad [z_4]_T = e([\mathbf{c}_0]_1, [\mathbf{k}_1^\top]_2), \\ [z_5]_T &= [z_1 - z_2 - z_3 - z_4]_T, \end{aligned}$$

and output $z = C \cdot [z_5]_T$.

Completeness and Optimal Compactness. For completeness, it just follows the definition of bilinear map e and the fact $\mathbf{A} \cdot \mathbf{U}_i \mathbf{Br}_j^\top = \mathbf{AU}_i \cdot \mathbf{Br}_j^\top$. As for optimal compactness, it is easy to see that the above construction satisfies our requirements, i.e., $|\mathsf{mpk}| = \mathsf{poly}(\lambda, \log L), |\mathsf{hsk}_i| = \mathsf{poly}(\lambda, \log L)$ and $|\mathsf{ct}| = \mathsf{poly}(\lambda, \log L)$.

Correctness. For all $\lambda, L \in \mathbb{N}$, all P, all $i^* \in [L]$, all $\mathsf{crs} \leftarrow \mathsf{Setup}(1^\lambda, 1^L)$, all $(\mathsf{pk}_{i^*}, \mathsf{sk}_{i^*}) \leftarrow \mathsf{Gen}(\mathsf{crs}, i^*)$, all $\{\mathsf{pk}_i\}_{i \in [L] \setminus \{i^*\}}$ such that $\mathsf{Ver}(\mathsf{crs}, i, \mathsf{pk}_i) = 1$, for all m, we have

$$\mathsf{hsk}_{i^*} = ([\mathbf{k}_0^\top]_2, [\mathbf{k}_1^\top]_2, [\mathbf{k}_2^\top]_2), \quad \mathsf{ct} = ([\mathbf{c}_0]_1, [\mathbf{c}_1]_1, C).$$

We obtain

$$z_1 = \sum_{i \in [L]} (\mathbf{sAV}_i \mathbf{Br}_{i^*}^\top + \mathbf{sAU}_i \mathbf{Br}_{i^*}^\top),$$
$$z_2 = \sum_{i \in [L] \setminus \{i^*\}} (\mathbf{sAV}_i \mathbf{Br}_{i^*}^\top + \mathbf{sAU}_i \mathbf{Br}_{i^*}^\top),$$
$$z_3 = \mathbf{sAU}_{i^*} \mathbf{Br}_{i^*}^\top,$$
$$z_4 = \mathbf{sAV}_{i^*} \mathbf{Br}_{i^*}^\top + \mathbf{sAk}^\top,$$

and then

$$z_5 = z_1 - z_2 - z_3 - z_4 = -\mathbf{sAk}^\top.$$

Finally, we have $z = C \cdot [z_5]_T = \mathsf{m}$. This proves the correctness.

3.2   Security

Theorem 1. *Assume MDDH assumption holds, our pairing-based global slotted RBE achieves the IND security in the standard model as defined in Sect. 2.3.*

Proof. The proof is presented in the full version.   □

4   Lattice-Based Global Slotted RBE

In this section, we give a global slotted RBE construction based on function-binding hash function (relying on LWE assumption) [26] and witness encryption (relying on evasive LWE assumption) [40]. This construction is adapted from slotted RABE (with a public randomized aggregation procedure) in [26]. Concretely, we initially construct a global slotted RBE construction that achieves adaptive security subject to the restriction that adversary does not make any corruption queries. Then we use the "two-key" technology [30] to remove this restriction and obtain a global slotted RBE that achieves the adaptive security (as defined in Sect. 2) in the random oracle.

4.1 Construction Without Corruption

Assume a public key encryption $\mathsf{PKE} = (\mathsf{Setup}, \mathsf{Enc}, \mathsf{Dec})$ with all parameters of size $\mathsf{poly}(\lambda)$, a function-binding hash function $\mathsf{FBH} = (\mathsf{Setup}, \mathsf{Hash}, \mathsf{Open}, \mathsf{Ver})$ with block size $m_{\mathrm{in}} = \lambda + \log L$, and a witness encryption $\mathsf{WE} = (\mathsf{Enc}, \mathsf{Dec})$ for a NP language $\mathcal{L}$ with witness relation $\mathcal{R}$ defined as follows:

$$\mathcal{R}((\mathsf{hk}, \mathsf{pk}, \mathsf{dig}), (i, \mathsf{ct}, r, \pi)) = 1$$
$$\Leftrightarrow \mathsf{ct} = \mathsf{PKE.Enc}(\mathsf{pk}, 1; r) \;\wedge\; \mathsf{FBH.Ver}(\mathsf{hk}, \mathsf{dig}, \{i\}, \{(i, (i, \mathsf{ct}))\}, \pi) = 1$$

our construction is as follows:

- $\mathsf{Setup}(1^\lambda, 1^L)$: Run $(\mathsf{pk}, \mathsf{sk}) \leftarrow \mathsf{PKE.Setup}(1^\lambda)$ and $\mathsf{hk} \leftarrow \mathsf{FBH.Setup}(1^\lambda, L)$, and output the common reference string $\mathsf{crs} = (\mathsf{pk}, \mathsf{hk})$.
- $\mathsf{Gen}(\mathsf{crs}, i)$: Parse $\mathsf{crs} = (\mathsf{pk}, \mathsf{hk})$. Sample $r \leftarrow \{0,1\}^\lambda$ and run $\mathsf{ct} \leftarrow \mathsf{PKE.Enc}(\mathsf{pk}, 1; r)$, then output $\mathsf{pk}_i = \mathsf{ct}$ and $\mathsf{sk}_i = r$.
- $\mathsf{Ver}(\mathsf{crs}, i, \mathsf{pk}_i)$: Check whether pk_i is a valid ciphertext of PKE. If so, output 1; otherwise, output 0.
- $\mathsf{Agg}(\mathsf{crs}, \{i, \mathsf{pk}_i\}_{i \in [L]})$: Parse $\mathsf{crs} = (\mathsf{pk}, \mathsf{hk})$. Then run

$$\mathsf{dig} \leftarrow \mathsf{FBH.Hash}(\mathsf{hk}, ((1, \mathsf{pk}_1), \ldots, (L, \mathsf{pk}_L))),$$
$$\pi_i \leftarrow \mathsf{FBH.Open}(\mathsf{hk}, ((1, \mathsf{pk}_1), \ldots, (L, \mathsf{pk}_L)), \{i\}), \forall\, i = 1, \ldots, L.$$

  Output the master public key $\mathsf{mpk} = (\mathsf{crs}, \mathsf{dig})$ and the helper secret key $\mathsf{hsk}_j = (j, \pi_j, \mathsf{pk}_j)$ for all $j \in [L]$.
- $\mathsf{Enc}(\mathsf{mpk}, m)$: Parse $\mathsf{mpk} = ((\mathsf{pk}, \mathsf{hk}), \mathsf{dig})$. Output the ciphertext

$$\mathsf{ct} \leftarrow \mathsf{WE.Enc}(1^\lambda, (\mathsf{hk}, \mathsf{pk}, \mathsf{dig}), m).$$

- $\mathsf{Dec}(\mathsf{hsk}_{i^*}, \mathsf{sk}_{i^*}, \mathsf{ct})$: Parse $\mathsf{hsk}_{i^*} = (i^*, \pi_{i^*}, \mathsf{pk}_{i^*})$. Output

$$m = \mathsf{WE.Dec}(\mathsf{ct}, (i^*, \mathsf{pk}_{i^*}, \mathsf{sk}_{i^*}, \pi_{i^*})).$$

Optimal Compactness and Unbounded Users. Note that $|\mathsf{crs}| = |\mathsf{pk}| + |\mathsf{hk}| = \mathsf{poly}(\lambda, \log L)$, $|\mathsf{mpk}| = |\mathsf{crs}| + |\mathsf{dig}| = \mathsf{poly}(\lambda, \log L)$, $|\mathsf{hsk}_j| = |j| + |\pi_j| + |\mathsf{pk}_j| = \mathsf{poly}(\lambda, \log L)$, and the runtime for algorithms $\mathsf{PKE.Enc}$ and $\mathsf{FBH.Ver}$ are at most $\mathsf{poly}(\lambda, \log L)$, so above construction supports optimal compactness and unbounded users.

Correctness. For all $\lambda, L \in \mathbb{N}$, all C, and all $i^* \in [L]$, all $\mathsf{crs} \leftarrow \mathsf{Setup}(1^\lambda, 1^L, C)$ where $\mathsf{crs} = (\mathsf{pk}, \mathsf{hk})$, all $(\mathsf{pk}_{i^*}, \mathsf{sk}_{i^*}) \leftarrow \mathsf{Gen}(\mathsf{crs}, i^*)$, all $\{\mathsf{pk}_i\}_{i \in [L] \setminus \{i^*\}}$ such that $\mathsf{Ver}(\mathsf{crs}, i, \mathsf{pk}_i) = 1$, and all message m, we have $\mathsf{mpk} = (\mathsf{crs}, \mathsf{dig})$ and $\mathsf{hsk}_{i^*} = (i^*, \pi_{i^*}, \mathsf{pk}_{i^*})$, where

$$\mathsf{dig} \leftarrow \mathsf{FBH.Hash}(\mathsf{hk}, ((1, \mathsf{pk}_1), \ldots, (L, \mathsf{pk}_L))),$$
$$\pi_{i^*} \leftarrow \mathsf{FBH.Open}(\mathsf{hk}, ((1, \mathsf{pk}_1), \ldots, (L, \mathsf{pk}_L)), \{i^*\}).$$

Then the ciphertext is computed as

$$\mathsf{ct} \leftarrow \mathsf{WE.Enc}(1^\lambda, (\mathsf{hk}, \mathsf{pk}, \mathsf{dig}), \mathsf{m}).$$

For decryption, we state that $\mathsf{hsk}_{i^*} = (i^*, \pi_{i^*}, \mathsf{pk}_{i^*})$ along with sk_{i^*} is a valid witness for the statement $(\mathsf{hk}, \mathsf{pk}, \mathsf{dig})$, because $\mathsf{pk}_{i^*} = \mathsf{PKE.Enc}(\mathsf{pk}, 1; \mathsf{sk}_{i^*})$, and $\mathsf{FBH.Ver}(\mathsf{hk}, \mathsf{dig}, \{i^*\}, \{(i^*, (i^*, \mathsf{pk}_{i^*}))\}, \pi_{i^*}) = 1$ by the completeness of FBH. Thus, by the correctness of witness encryption, we have

$$\mathsf{WE.Dec}(\mathsf{ct}, (i^*, \mathsf{pk}_{i^*}, \mathsf{sk}_{i^*}, \pi_{i^*})) = \mathsf{m}.$$

4.2   Security

Theorem 2. *Assume* $\mathsf{PKE} = (\mathsf{Setup}, \mathsf{Enc}, \mathsf{Dec})$ *is a public key encryption with semantic security,* $\mathsf{FBH} = (\mathsf{Setup}, \mathsf{Hash}, \mathsf{Open}, \mathsf{Ver})$ *is a function-binding hash function with function hiding and function bind properties, and* $\mathsf{WE} = (\mathsf{Enc}, \mathsf{Dec})$ *is a secure witness encryption, our global slotted RBE achieves the adaptive IND security without corruption.*

Proof. The proof is presented in the full version.   □

4.3   Final Construction

Assume a hash function $\mathsf{H} : \{0,1\}^* \rightarrow \{0,1\}^L$ that can be modeled as random oracle, a global slotted RBE without corruption $\mathsf{gsRBE}_{\mathrm{wc}} = (\mathsf{Setup}, \mathsf{Gen}, \mathsf{Ver}, \mathsf{Agg}, \mathsf{Enc}, \mathsf{Dec})$ that all parameters are of size $\mathrm{poly}(\lambda)$, our final construction is as follows:

- $\mathsf{Setup}(1^\lambda, 1^L)$: Run $\mathsf{crs} \leftarrow \mathsf{gsRBE}_{\mathrm{wc}}.\mathsf{Setup}(1^\lambda)$ and output the common reference string crs.
- $\mathsf{Gen}(\mathsf{crs}, i)$: Sample two pairs of public key and secret

$$(\mathsf{pk}_0, \mathsf{sk}_0) \leftarrow \mathsf{gsRBE}_{\mathrm{wc}}.\mathsf{Gen}(\mathsf{crs}, i), \quad (\mathsf{pk}_1, \mathsf{sk}_1) \leftarrow \mathsf{gsRBE}_{\mathrm{wc}}.\mathsf{Gen}(\mathsf{crs}, i).$$

  Then sample a random bit $\beta \leftarrow \{0,1\}$ and $s \leftarrow \{0,1\}^\lambda$, output $\mathsf{pk}_i = (\mathsf{pk}_0, \mathsf{pk}_1, s), \mathsf{sk}_i = (\beta, \mathsf{sk}_\beta)$.
- $\mathsf{Ver}(\mathsf{crs}, i, \mathsf{pk}_i)$: Parse $\mathsf{pk}_i = (\mathsf{pk}_{i,0}, \mathsf{pk}_{i,1}, s_i)$. If both $\mathsf{pk}_{i,0}$ and $\mathsf{pk}_{i,1}$ pass the check of algorithm $\mathsf{gsRBE}_{\mathrm{wc}}.\mathsf{Ver}$, and $s_i \in \{0,1\}^\lambda$, output 1; otherwise, output 0.
- $\mathsf{Agg}(\mathsf{crs}, \{i, \mathsf{pk}_i\}_{i \in [L]})$: Parse $\mathsf{pk}_i = (\mathsf{pk}_{i,0}, \mathsf{pk}_{i,1}, s_i)$. Compute $(h_1, \dots, h_L) \leftarrow \mathsf{H}(\mathsf{crs}, (1, \mathsf{pk}_1), \dots, (L, \mathsf{pk}_L))$ and let $\overline{h}_i = 1 - h_i$ for all $i \in [L]$. Then run

$$(\mathsf{mpk}_0, \{\mathsf{hsk}_{j,0}\}_{j \in [L]}) \leftarrow \mathsf{gsRBE}_{\mathrm{wc}}.\mathsf{Agg}(\mathsf{crs}, ((1, \mathsf{pk}_{1,h_1}), \dots, (L, \mathsf{pk}_{L,h_L}))),$$
$$(\mathsf{mpk}_1, \{\mathsf{hsk}_{j,1}\}_{j \in [L]}) \leftarrow \mathsf{gsRBE}_{\mathrm{wc}}.\mathsf{Agg}(\mathsf{crs}, ((1, \mathsf{pk}_{1,\overline{h}_1}), \dots, (L, \mathsf{pk}_{L,\overline{h}_L}))).$$

  Output the master public key $\mathsf{mpk} = (\mathsf{mpk}_0, \mathsf{mpk}_1)$ and the helper secret key $\mathsf{hsk}_j = (h_j, \mathsf{hsk}_{j,0}, \mathsf{hsk}_{j,1})$ for all $j \in [L]$.

- Enc(mpk, m) : Parse $\mathsf{mpk} = (\mathsf{mpk}_0, \mathsf{mpk}_1)$, output $\mathsf{ct} = (\mathsf{ct}_0, \mathsf{ct}_1)$, where $\mathsf{ct}_0 \leftarrow \mathsf{gsRBE}_{\mathrm{WC}}.\mathsf{Enc}(\mathsf{mpk}_0, m)$ and $\mathsf{ct}_1 \leftarrow \mathsf{gsRBE}_{\mathrm{WC}}.\mathsf{Enc}(\mathsf{mpk}_1, m)$.
- Dec($\mathsf{hsk}_{i^*}, \mathsf{sk}_{i^*}, \mathsf{ct}$) : Parse $\mathsf{hsk}_{i^*} = (h_{i^*}, \mathsf{hsk}_{i^*,0}, \mathsf{hsk}_{i^*,1})$, $\mathsf{sk}_{i^*} = (\beta_{i^*}, \mathsf{sk}_{\beta_{i^*}})$ and $\mathsf{ct} = (\mathsf{ct}_0, \mathsf{ct}_1)$. If $\beta_{i^*} = h_{i^*}$, output $m = \mathsf{gsRBE}_{\mathrm{WC}}.\mathsf{Dec}(\mathsf{hsk}_{i^*,0}, \mathsf{sk}_{i^*,\beta_{i^*}}, \mathsf{ct}_0)$; otherwise, output $m = \mathsf{gsRBE}_{\mathrm{WC}}.\mathsf{Dec}(\mathsf{hsk}_{i^*,1}, \mathsf{sk}_{i^*,\beta_{i^*}}, \mathsf{ct}_1)$.

Optimal Compactness and Unbounded Users. Note that the final construction consists of two instances for $\mathsf{gsRBE}_{\mathrm{WC}}$, so it will meet optimal compactness (resp., unbounded users) as long as $\mathsf{gsRBE}_{\mathrm{WC}}$ meets optimal compactness (resp., unbounded users).

Correctness. Informally, the public key $\mathsf{pk}_{i^*,\beta_{i^*}}$ corresponding to secret key $\mathsf{sk}_{i^*,\beta_{i^*}}$ is either registered into mpk_0 (when $\beta_{i^*} = h_{i^*}$) or mpk_1 (when $\beta_{i^*} = \overline{h}_{i^*}$), then it can recover message m properly following the correctness of $\mathsf{gsRBE}_{\mathrm{WC}}$.

As for security, this construction achieves the adaptive IND security in random oracle model and it allows the query to corruption oracle OCor. The proof strategy is analogous to [26]. The difference lies on the fact that we do not require any challenge policy, so our construction is naturally adaptively IND secure.

Finally, we obtain an Q-bound slotted RFE for circuits via the compiler in Sects. 5 and 6, and we can modify the compiler to achieve unbounded users by eliminating all $\{\widehat{\mathsf{pk}}_{i,w,b}\}$ of crs and just setting $\overline{\mathsf{pk}}_{i,w,b} = \mathsf{pk}_{i,w,b}$ only when $C_i[w] = b$. Here, due to the good traits of FBH, algorithm sRBE.Agg still works as usual when the number of registered public keys is less than L.

5 1-Bound Slotted RFE for Circuits

With global slotted RBE, we present a slotted RFE scheme for circuits with adaptive 1-bound SIM security.

5.1 Construction

For some circuit family $C : X \rightarrow Z$, let $\mathsf{U}(\cdot, \cdot)$ be the universal circuit such that $\mathsf{U}(\mathsf{C}, x) = \mathsf{C}(x)$ for any circuit $\mathsf{C} \in C$ and input $x \in X$. Assume a garbled circuit scheme $\mathsf{GC} = (\mathsf{Garble}, \mathsf{Eval})$ where n is the input length of the circuit, and a global slotted registered broadcast encryption $\mathsf{gsRBE} = (\mathsf{Setup}, \mathsf{Gen}, \mathsf{Ver}, \mathsf{Agg}, \mathsf{Enc}, \mathsf{Dec})$, then our 1-bound slotted RFE for circuits (set $Q = 1$ as default) works as follows:

- Setup($1^\lambda, 1^L, C$) : Run $\mathsf{gsRBE}.\mathsf{Setup}(1^\lambda, 1^L)$ $2n$ times and obtain $\{\mathsf{crs}_{w,b}\}_{w \in [n], b \in \{0,1\}}$. For all $w \in [n]$ and $b \in \{0,1\}$, run $\mathsf{gsRBE}.\mathsf{Gen}(\mathsf{crs}_{w,b}, i)$ for all $i \in [L]$, omit secret keys and obtain valid public keys $\{\widehat{\mathsf{pk}}_{i,w,b}\}_{i \in [L], w \in [n], b \in \{0,1\}}$. Output

$$\mathsf{crs} = (\{\mathsf{crs}_{w,b}\}_{w \in [n], b \in \{0,1\}}, \{\widehat{\mathsf{pk}}_{i,w,b}\}_{i \in [L], w \in [n], b \in \{0,1\}}).$$

- $\mathsf{Gen}(\mathsf{crs}, i)$: For all $w \in [n]$ and $b \in \{0,1\}$, run $(\mathsf{pk}_{i,w,b}, \mathsf{sk}_{i,w,b}) \leftarrow \mathsf{gsRBE.Gen}(\mathsf{crs}_{w,b}, i)$. Output

$$\mathsf{pk}_i = (\{\mathsf{pk}_{i,w,b}\}_{w\in[n], b\in\{0,1\}}), \ \mathsf{sk}_i = (\{\mathsf{sk}_{i,w,b}\}_{w\in[n], b\in\{0,1\}}).$$

- $\mathsf{Ver}(\mathsf{crs}, i, \mathsf{pk}_i)$: For all $w \in [n]$ and $b \in \{0,1\}$, run $\beta_{w,b} \leftarrow \mathsf{gsRBE.Ver}(\mathsf{crs}_{w,b}, i, \mathsf{pk}_{i,w,b})$, and if $\beta_{w,b} = 0$, output 0 and abort. Otherwise, output 1.

- $\mathsf{Agg}(\mathsf{crs}, \{\mathsf{pk}_i, \mathsf{C}_i\}_{i\in[L]})$: Parse $\mathsf{C}_i = (\mathsf{C}_i[1], \ldots, \mathsf{C}_i[n]) \in \{0,1\}^n$ and $\mathsf{pk}_i = (\{\mathsf{pk}_{i,w,b}\}_{w\in[n], b\in\{0,1\}})$. For all $i \in [L]$ and all $w \in [n], b \in \{0,1\}$, set

$$\overline{\mathsf{pk}}_{i,w,b} := \begin{cases} \mathsf{pk}_{i,w,b}, & \text{when } \mathsf{C}_i[w] = b, \\ \widehat{\mathsf{pk}}_{i,w,b}, & \text{otherwise.} \end{cases}$$

Then run $(\mathsf{mpk}_{w,b}, \{\mathsf{hsk}_{j,w,b}\}_{j\in[L]}) \leftarrow \mathsf{gsRBE.Agg}(\mathsf{crs}_{w,b}, \{i, \overline{\mathsf{pk}}_{i,w,b}\}_{i\in[L]})$. Output

$$\mathsf{mpk} = (\{\mathsf{mpk}_{w,b}\}_{w\in[n], b\in\{0,1\}}), \ \mathsf{hsk}_j = (\mathsf{C}_j, \{\mathsf{hsk}_{j,w,b}\}_{w\in[n], b\in\{0,1\}}).$$

- $\mathsf{Enc}(\mathsf{mpk}, x)$: Let $\mathsf{U}[x]$ be the universal circuit with x hard-wired. Run

$$(\tilde{\mathsf{U}}, \{\mathsf{lab}_{w,b}\}_{w\in[n], b\in\{0,1\}}) \leftarrow \mathsf{GC.Garble}(1^\lambda, \mathsf{U}[x]).$$

For all $w \in [n], b \in \{0,1\}$, run

$$\mathsf{ct}_{w,b} \leftarrow \mathsf{gsRBE.Enc}(\mathsf{mpk}_{w,b}, \mathsf{lab}_{w,b}).$$

Output $\mathsf{ct} = (\tilde{\mathsf{U}}, \{\mathsf{ct}_{w,b}\}_{w\in[n], b\in\{0,1\}})$.

- $\mathsf{Dec}(\mathsf{hsk}_{i^*}, \mathsf{sk}_{i^*}, \mathsf{ct})$: Parse $\mathsf{hsk}_{i^*} = (\mathsf{C}_{i^*}, \{\mathsf{hsk}_{i^*,w,b}\}_{w\in[n], b\in\{0,1\}})$ and $\mathsf{sk}_{i^*} = (\{\mathsf{sk}_{i^*,w,b}\}_{w\in[n], b\in\{0,1\}})$. For all $w \in [n]$, let $b_w = \mathsf{C}_{i^*}[w]$ and run

$$m_{w,b_w} \leftarrow \mathsf{gsRBE.Dec}(\mathsf{hsk}_{i^*,w,b_w}, \mathsf{sk}_{i^*,w,b_w}, \mathsf{ct}_{w,b_w}).$$

Thus, we output

$$z \leftarrow \mathsf{GC.Eval}(\tilde{\mathsf{U}}, \{m_{w,b_w}\}_{w\in[n]}).$$

Remark. The above generic construction can be instantiated by any global slotted RBE scheme, but it does not support unbounded users, i.e., crs not scaling with L. Indeed, if we adopt the construction in Sect. 4, we can improve it into the one supporting unbounded users by removing all public keys $\{\widehat{\mathsf{pk}}_{i,w,b}\}$ in algorithm Setup and directly letting $\overline{\mathsf{pk}}_{i,w,b} = \mathsf{pk}_{i,w,b}$ when $\mathsf{C}_i[w] = b$.

Completeness and Compactness. For completeness, it follows the underlying slotted RBE. In other words, if slotted RBE in above construction meets completeness, then it holds that

$$\Pr[\mathsf{gsRBE.Ver}(\mathsf{crs}_{w,b}, i, \mathsf{pk}_i) = 1] = 1$$

for all $w \in [n]$ and all $b \in \{0, 1\}$. Thus, the completeness of our construction follows readily.

For compactness, thanks to the optimal compactness of gsRBE, our 1-bound slotted RFE scheme has the following properties:

$$|\mathsf{mpk}| = 2n \cdot \mathsf{poly}(\lambda, \log L), \quad |\mathsf{hsk}_j| = 2n \cdot \mathsf{poly}(\lambda, \log L)$$

where n is related to circuit family C. Thus, our construction meets the compactness requirement.

Correctness. For all $\lambda, L \in \mathbb{N}$, all C, and all $i^* \in [L]$, all $\mathsf{crs} \leftarrow \mathsf{Setup}(1^\lambda, 1^L, C)$, all $(\mathsf{pk}_{i^*}, \mathsf{sk}_{i^*}) \leftarrow \mathsf{Gen}(\mathsf{crs}, i^*)$, all $\{\mathsf{pk}_i\}_{i \in [L] \setminus \{i^*\}}$ such that $\mathsf{Ver}(\mathsf{crs}, i, \mathsf{pk}_i) = 1$, all $x \in X$ and $C_1, \ldots, C_L \in C$, we have $\mathsf{sk}_{i^*} = (\{\mathsf{sk}_{i,w,b}\}_{w \in [n], b \in \{0,1\}})$ and

$$\mathsf{ct} = \left(\tilde{\mathsf{U}}, \begin{pmatrix} \mathsf{gsRBE.Enc}(\mathsf{mpk}_{1,0}, \mathsf{lab}_{1,0}) & \cdots & \mathsf{gsRBE.Enc}(\mathsf{mpk}_{n,0}, \mathsf{lab}_{n,0}) \\ \mathsf{gsRBE.Enc}(\mathsf{mpk}_{1,1}, \mathsf{lab}_{1,1}) & \cdots & \mathsf{gsRBE.Enc}(\mathsf{mpk}_{n,1}, \mathsf{lab}_{n,1}) \end{pmatrix} \right).$$

Here, each $\mathsf{mpk}_{w,b}$ is generated from $\{i, \overline{\mathsf{pk}}_{i,w,b}\}_{i \in [L]}$. Note that in algorithm Enc, we have

$$\overline{\mathsf{pk}}_{i,w,b} := \begin{cases} \mathsf{pk}_{i,w,b}, & \text{when } C_i[w] = b, \\ \widehat{\mathsf{pk}}_{i,w,b}, & \text{otherwise.} \end{cases}$$

Here, $\mathsf{sk}_{i^*,w,b}$ is the secret key of $\overline{\mathsf{pk}}_{i^*,w,b}$ only when $C_{i^*}[w] = b$. Thus, after computing all $m_{w,b}$, nothing else can be obtained except for $\{\mathsf{lab}_{i^*,w,b_w}\}_{w \in [n]}$. Then it follows the correctness of garbled circuits to compute $z = \mathsf{U}(C_{i^*}, x) = C_{i^*}(x)$. Therefore, the correctness follows readily.

5.2 Security

Theorem 3. *Assume* $\mathsf{GC} = (\mathsf{Garble}, \mathsf{Eval})$ *is a secure garbled circuits scheme and* $\mathsf{gsRBE} = (\mathsf{Setup}, \mathsf{Gen}, \mathsf{Ver}, \mathsf{Agg}, \mathsf{Enc}, \mathsf{Dec})$ *is a global slotted RBE scheme with optimal compactness which achieves the IND security defined in Sect. 2.3, our construction achieves the 1-bound SIM security defined in Sect. 2.4.*

Proof. let C^* be the circuit corresponding to the unique corrupted user. Just as the security analysis presented in Sect. 1.2, our proof strategy follows the security of underlying global slotted RBE and garbled circuits. Concretely, we randomize all labels $\{\mathsf{lab}_{w,1-C^*[w]}\}_{w \in [n]}$ one by one (from $\mathsf{Game}_{1,\kappa-1}$ to $\mathsf{Game}_{1,\kappa}$), via the IND security of global slotted RBE. Then we can simulate rest labels (from $\mathsf{Game}_{1,n}$ to Game_2) via the security of garbled circuits. In final game, the challenge ciphertext will only disclose $C^*(x^*)$ and nothing else. Here, we define the simulator $\widetilde{\mathsf{Enc}}$ that works as follows:

– $\widetilde{\mathsf{Enc}}(\mathsf{mpk}, (i^*, C^*, C^*(x^*), \mathsf{sk}_{i^*}))$: Parse $\mathsf{mpk} = (\{\mathsf{mpk}_{w,b}\}_{w \in [n], b \in \{0,1\}})$. Run

$$\left(\tilde{C}^*, \{\widetilde{\mathsf{lab}}_{w, C^*[w]}\}_{w \in [n]} \right) \leftarrow \widetilde{\mathsf{Garble}}(1^\lambda, C^*(x)).$$

Then sample $\widetilde{\mathsf{lab}}_{w,1-C^*[w]} \leftarrow \{0,1\}^\lambda$ for all $w \in [n]$. Set

$$
\mathsf{ct}^* = \left(\tilde{\mathsf{C}}^*, \begin{pmatrix} \mathsf{ct}^*_{1,0} & \cdots & \mathsf{ct}^*_{n,0} \\ \mathsf{ct}^*_{1,1} & \cdots & \mathsf{ct}^*_{n,1} \end{pmatrix} \right)
$$

$$
= \left(\tilde{\mathsf{C}}^*, \begin{pmatrix} \mathsf{gsRBE.Enc}(\mathsf{mpk}_{1,0}, \widetilde{\mathsf{lab}}_{1,0}) & \cdots & \mathsf{gsRBE.Enc}(\mathsf{mpk}_{n,0}, \widetilde{\mathsf{lab}}_{n,0}) \\ \mathsf{gsRBE.Enc}(\mathsf{mpk}_{1,1}, \widetilde{\mathsf{lab}}_{1,1}) & \cdots & \mathsf{gsRBE.Enc}(\mathsf{mpk}_{n,1}, \widetilde{\mathsf{lab}}_{n,1}) \end{pmatrix} \right).
$$

The algorithm $\widetilde{\mathsf{Enc}}$ actually does not need sk_{i^*}, so our resulting construction can resist single malicious user.

Game Sequence. We prove Theorem 3 via a sequence of games as follows:

- Game_0: this game is identical to the real experiment of adaptive 1-SIM security. Recall that
  - crs has the form:

  $$
  \mathsf{crs} = (\{\mathsf{crs}_{w,b}\}_{w\in[n],b\in\{0,1\}}, \{\widehat{\mathsf{pk}}_{i,w,b}\}_{i\in[L],w\in[n],b\in\{0,1\}}).
  $$

  where $\mathsf{crs}_{w,b}$ and $\widehat{\mathsf{pk}}_{i,w,b}$ are generated from the underlying slotted RBE algorithms $\mathsf{gsRBE.Setup}$ and $\mathsf{gsRBE.Gen}$, respectively.
  - For each $i \in [L]$, $(\mathsf{pk}_i, \mathsf{sk}_i)$ are in the form:

  $$
  \mathsf{pk}_i = (\{\mathsf{pk}_{i,w,b}\}_{w\in[n],b\in\{0,1\}}), \quad \mathsf{sk}_i = (\{\mathsf{sk}_{i,w,b}\}_{w\in[n],b\in\{0,1\}}).
  $$

  where $(\mathsf{pk}_{i,w,b}, \mathsf{sk}_{i,w,b})$ are sampled from algorithm $\mathsf{gsRBE.Gen}$.
  - The master public key mpk and helper secret key hsk_j has the form

  $$
  \mathsf{mpk} = \begin{pmatrix} \mathsf{mpk}_{1,0} & \cdots & \mathsf{mpk}_{n,0} \\ \mathsf{mpk}_{1,1} & \cdots & \mathsf{mpk}_{n,1} \end{pmatrix}, \quad \mathsf{hsk}_j = \left(\mathsf{C}_j, \begin{pmatrix} \mathsf{hsk}_{j,1,0} & \cdots & \mathsf{hsk}_{j,n,0} \\ \mathsf{hsk}_{j,1,1} & \cdots & \mathsf{hsk}_{j,n,1} \end{pmatrix} \right),
  $$

  where for each $w \in [n], b \in \{0,1\}$, $\mathsf{mpk}_{w,b}$ is computed as

  $$
  \overline{\mathsf{pk}}_{i,w,b} := \begin{cases} \mathsf{pk}_{i,w,b}, & \text{when } \mathsf{C}_i[w] = b \\ \widehat{\mathsf{pk}}_{i,w,b}, & \text{otherwise.} \end{cases}
  $$

  Then obtain $(\mathsf{mpk}_{w,b}, \{\mathsf{hsk}_{j,w,b}\}_{j\in[L]}) \leftarrow \mathsf{gsRBE.Agg}(\mathsf{crs}_{w,b}, \{i, \overline{\mathsf{pk}}_{i,w,b}\}_{i\in[L]})$.
  - The challenge ciphertext ct^* has the form

  $$
  \mathsf{ct}^* = \left(\tilde{\mathsf{U}}, \begin{pmatrix} \mathsf{ct}^*_{1,0} & \cdots & \mathsf{ct}^*_{n,0} \\ \mathsf{ct}^*_{1,1} & \cdots & \mathsf{ct}^*_{n,1} \end{pmatrix} \right)
  $$

  $$
  = \left(\tilde{\mathsf{U}}, \begin{pmatrix} \mathsf{gsRBE.Enc}(\mathsf{mpk}_{1,0}, \mathsf{lab}_{1,0}) & \cdots & \mathsf{gsRBE.Enc}(\mathsf{mpk}_{n,0}, \mathsf{lab}_{n,0}) \\ \mathsf{gsRBE.Enc}(\mathsf{mpk}_{1,1}, \mathsf{lab}_{1,1}) & \cdots & \mathsf{gsRBE.Enc}(\mathsf{mpk}_{n,1}, \mathsf{lab}_{n,1}) \end{pmatrix} \right),
  $$

  where $(\tilde{\mathsf{U}}, \{\mathsf{lab}_{w,b}\}_{w\in[n],b\in\{0,1\}}) \leftarrow \mathsf{GC.Garble}(1^\lambda, \mathsf{U}[x^*])$.

– $\mathsf{Game}_{1.\kappa}(\kappa \in [n])$: $\mathsf{Game}_{1.\kappa}$ is identical to Game_0 except that for each $w \leq \kappa$, set $b_w = \mathsf{C}^*[w]$ and $\overline{b}_w = 1 - \mathsf{C}^*[w]$, we have

$$\mathsf{ct}^*_{w,b_w} \leftarrow \mathsf{gsRBE.Enc}(\mathsf{mpk}_{w,b_w}, s_{w,b_w}, \mathsf{lab}_{w,b_w}),$$

$$\mathsf{ct}^*_{w,\overline{b}_w} \leftarrow \mathsf{gsRBE.Enc}(\mathsf{mpk}_{w,\overline{b}_w}, s_{w,\overline{b}_w}, \widetilde{\mathsf{lab}}_{w,\overline{b}_w}),$$

where $\widetilde{\mathsf{lab}}_{w,\overline{b}_w}$ is randomly sampled from $\{0,1\}^\lambda$.

– Game_2: this game is identical to $\mathsf{Game}_{1,n}$ except that it replaces Enc with $\widetilde{\mathsf{Enc}}$ to generate the challenge ciphertext ct^*.

Lemma 1 ($\mathsf{Game}_{1,\kappa-1} \approx_c \mathsf{Game}_{1,\kappa}$). *For any efficient adversary $\mathcal{A}$, there exists an algorithm $\mathcal{B}_1$ with close running time to $\mathcal{A}$ such that*

$$|\mathsf{Adv}^{1,\kappa-1}_{\mathcal{A}}(\lambda) - \mathsf{Adv}^{1,\kappa}_{\mathcal{A}}(\lambda)| \leq 2 \cdot \mathsf{Adv}^{\mathsf{gsRBE}}_{\mathcal{B}_1}(\lambda) + \mathsf{negl}(\lambda).$$

Proof. Initially, $\mathcal{B}_1$ receives upper bound L from $\mathcal{A}$. Then $\mathcal{B}_1$ flips a coin $\beta \leftarrow \{0,1\}$ and sends L to the challenger of gsRBE. Then $\mathcal{B}_1$ proceeds following phases:

Setup. After receiving the $\mathsf{crs}_{\kappa,\beta}$ from the challenger of gsRBE, initialize $2n-1$ slotted RBE instances by itself, and obtain $\{\mathsf{crs}_{w,b}\}_{w\in[n],b\in\{0,1\}}$. For all $w \in [n]$ and all $b \in \{0,1\}$, if $w = \kappa$ and $b = \beta$, query the oracle $\mathsf{OGen}(i)$ of gsRBE to obtain $\widehat{\mathsf{pk}}_{i,\kappa,\beta}$ for all $i \in [L]$; otherwise, run $\mathsf{gsRBE.Gen}(\mathsf{crs}_{w,b}, i)$ by itself for all $i \in [L]$. Then omit all secret keys and obtain public keys $\{\widehat{\mathsf{pk}}_{i,w,b}\}_{i\in[L],w\in[n],b\in\{0,1\}}$. Output

$$\mathsf{crs} = (\{\mathsf{crs}_{w,b}\}_{w\in[n],b\in\{0,1\}}, \{\widehat{\mathsf{pk}}_{i,w,b}\}_{i\in[L],w\in[n],b\in\{0,1\}}).$$

Query. Here, $\mathcal{A}$ can query oracles as below:

– $\mathsf{OGen}(i)$: For all $w \in [n]$ and all $b \in \{0,1\}$, if $w = \kappa$ and $b = \beta$, query the oracle $\mathsf{OGen}(i)$ of gsRBE to obtain $\mathsf{pk}_{i,\kappa,\beta}$; otherwise, run $(\mathsf{pk}_{i,w,b}, \mathsf{sk}_{i,w,b}) \leftarrow \mathsf{gsRBE.Gen}(\mathsf{crs}_{w,b}, i)$ by itself. Output $\mathsf{pk} = (\{\mathsf{pk}_{i,w,b}\}_{w\in[n],b\in\{0,1\}})$ and set $\mathcal{D}_i[\mathsf{pk}] = \{\mathsf{sk}_{i,w,b}\}_{w\in[n]\setminus\{\kappa\},b\in\{0,1\}} \cup \{\mathsf{sk}_{i,\kappa,1-\beta}\}$.

– $\mathsf{OCor}(i,\mathsf{pk})$: Parse $\mathsf{pk} = (\{\mathsf{pk}_{i,w,b}\}_{w\in[n],b\in\{0,1\}})$. Query the oracle $\mathsf{OCor}(i, \mathsf{pk}_{\kappa,\beta})$ of gsRBE to obtain $\mathsf{sk}_{i,\kappa,\beta}$. Then return $\mathcal{D}_i[\mathsf{pk}] \cup \{\mathsf{sk}_{i,\kappa,\beta}\}$. Update $\mathcal{C} = \mathcal{C} \cup \{(i,\mathsf{pk})\}$.

Challenge. $\mathcal{B}_1$ receives challenge public keys $\{\mathsf{pk}^*_i\}_{i\in[L]}$ where $\mathsf{pk}^*_i = \{\mathsf{pk}^*_{i,w,b}\}_{w\in[n],b\in\{0,1\}}$. Combining with challenge circuits $\{\mathsf{C}^*_i\}_{i\in[L]}$, we assume that the unique corrupted user registering the circuit $\mathsf{C}^* \in \{\mathsf{C}^*_i\}_{i\in[L]}$, and C^* is linked to the public key $\mathsf{pk}^* \in \{\mathsf{pk}^*_i\}_{i\in[L]}$. If $\mathsf{C}^*[\kappa] = \beta$, then abort the experiment immediately; otherwise, it means that all public keys that has registered in gsRBE are not corrupted. Thus, for all $i \in [L]$ and all $w \in [n], b \in \{0,1\}$, set

$$\overline{\mathsf{pk}}_{i,w,b} := \begin{cases} \mathsf{pk}^*_{i,w,b}, & \text{when } \mathsf{C}_i[w] = b, \\ \widehat{\mathsf{pk}}_{i,w,b}, & \text{otherwise.} \end{cases}$$

After that, run $(\tilde{U}, \{\mathsf{lab}_{w,b}\}_{w\in[n],b\in\{0,1\}}) \leftarrow \mathsf{GC.Garble}(1^\lambda, U[x^*])$ and for each $w \le \kappa$, pick $\widetilde{\mathsf{lab}}_{w,1-\mathsf{C}^*[w]} \leftarrow \{0,1\}^\lambda$. For all $w \in [n], b \in \{0,1\}$, if $w = \kappa$ and $b = \beta$, send $(\{i, \overline{\mathsf{pk}}_{i,\kappa,\beta}\}_{i\in[L]}, \mathsf{lab}_{\kappa,\beta}, \widetilde{\mathsf{lab}}_{\kappa,\beta})$ to the challenger, and obtain $(\mathsf{mpk}_{\kappa,\beta}, \{\mathsf{hsk}_{j,\kappa,\beta}\}_{j\in[L]})$; otherwise, run $(\mathsf{mpk}_{w,b}, \{\mathsf{hsk}_{j,w,b}\}_{j\in[L]}) \leftarrow \mathsf{gsRBE.Agg}(\mathsf{crs}_{w,b}, \{i, \overline{\mathsf{pk}}_{i,w,b}\}_{i\in[L]})$. Set

$$\mathsf{mpk} = (\{\mathsf{mpk}_{w,b}\}_{w\in[n],b\in\{0,1\}}), \quad \mathsf{hsk}_j = (\mathsf{C}_j^*, \{\mathsf{hsk}_{j,w,b}\}_{w\in[n],b\in\{0,1\}}).$$

Then $\mathcal{B}_1$ receives the challenge ciphertext $\mathsf{ct}_{\kappa,\beta}^*$ and computes other $\mathsf{ct}_{w,b}^*$ as follows:

$$\mathsf{ct}_{w,b}^* = \begin{cases} \mathsf{gsRBE.Enc}(\mathsf{mpk}_{w,b}, \widetilde{\mathsf{lab}}_{w,b}), & \text{when } w < \kappa \wedge \mathsf{C}^*[w] = 1-b, \\ \mathsf{gsRBE.Enc}(\mathsf{mpk}_{w,b}, \mathsf{lab}_{w,b}), & \text{otherwise.} \end{cases}$$

Finally, return the challenge ciphertext

$$\mathsf{ct}^* = \left(\tilde{U}, \begin{pmatrix} \mathsf{ct}_{1,0}^* \cdots \mathsf{ct}_{n,0}^* \\ \mathsf{ct}_{1,1}^* \cdots \mathsf{ct}_{n,1}^* \end{pmatrix} \right).$$

Observe that if $\mathsf{ct}_{\kappa,\beta}^*$ is generated under message $\widetilde{\mathsf{lab}}_{\kappa,\beta}$, $\mathcal{B}_1$ simulates $\mathsf{Game}_{1,\kappa}$; otherwise, it simulates $\mathsf{Game}_{1,\kappa-1}$. Thus, this readily proves the lemma. $\qquad\square$

Lemma 2 ($\mathsf{Game}_{1,n} \approx_c \mathsf{Game}_2$). *For any efficient adversary $\mathcal{A}$, there exists an algorithm $\mathcal{B}_2$ with close running time to $\mathcal{A}$ such that*

$$|\mathsf{Adv}_{\mathcal{A}}^{1,n}(\lambda) - \mathsf{Adv}_{\mathcal{A}}^2(\lambda)| \le \mathsf{Adv}_{\mathcal{B}_2}^{\mathsf{GC}}(\lambda) + \mathsf{negl}(\lambda).$$

Proof. The only difference between $\mathsf{Game}_{1,n}$ and Game_2 is the generation of ct^*. Obviously, if the underlying garbled circuits scheme is secure, the output of algorithm Enc in $\mathsf{Game}_{1,n}$ is indistinguishable from the output of algorithm $\widetilde{\mathsf{Enc}}$ in Game_2 from the view of $\mathcal{A}$. $\qquad\square$

Analysis for Honest and Corrupt Cases. Without loss of generality, we assume that all challenge circuits are different from each other. Let C^* be the corrupted circuit for slot i^*. For some honest slot i, there must exist at least a different bit (assume index w') between C_i^* and C^*. In this way, even if $\mathcal{A}$ owns the secret key of slot i^*, it will only obtain $\{\widetilde{\mathsf{lab}}_{w,\mathsf{C}_i^*[w]}\}_{w\in[n]\backslash\{w'\}} \cup \{\widetilde{\mathsf{lab}}_{w',\mathsf{C}_i^*[w']}\}$. Here, $\{\widetilde{\mathsf{lab}}_{w,\mathsf{C}_i^*[w]}\}_{w\in[n]\backslash\{w'\}}$ are simulated using 1^λ and $\mathsf{C}^*(x^*)$, while $\widetilde{\mathsf{lab}}_{w',\mathsf{C}_i^*[w']}$ is a random string independent from other labels. According to the privacy of garbled circuits, $\mathcal{A}$ cannot extract any useful information about $\mathsf{C}_i^*(x^*)$.

For corrupt case, $\mathcal{A}$ can only obtain $\left(\tilde{\mathsf{C}}^*, \{\widetilde{\mathsf{lab}}_{w,\mathsf{C}^*[w]}\}_{w\in[n]} \right)$ that are simulated using just 1^λ and $\mathsf{C}^*(x^*)$. Thus, only $\mathsf{C}^*(x^*)$ is revealed. At last, the proof of Theorem 3 is completed. $\qquad\square$

6   Q-Bound Slotted RFE for Circuits

In this section, we roughly follow the approach of [32] in order to upgrade the construction in Sect. 5 from 1-bound security to Q-bound security. Here, we only present an Q-bound secure RFE for NC1 circuits because it can be trivially bootstrapped into RFE for all polynomial-sized circuits using computational randomized encodings [12]. With slotted RFE for circuits, we can convert it into a full-fledged RFE construction via "power-of-two" approach (presented in the full version).

6.1   Construction

Let $C := \text{NC1}$ be a circuit family with circuits of degree D and size n. Our construction is additionally parameterized with S, N, t and v. For any circuit $\mathsf{C} \in C$ and set $\Delta \subseteq [S]$, we define a new circuit $\mathsf{G} \in G$ takes as input $\mathbf{x} = (x, r_1, \ldots, r_S)$ as follows:

$$\mathsf{G}(\mathbf{x}) = \mathsf{C}(x) + \sum_{j \in \Delta} r_j. \tag{1}$$

Assume a 1-bound slotted registered function encryption $\mathsf{osRFE} = (\mathsf{Setup}, \mathsf{Gen}, \mathsf{Ver}, \mathsf{Agg}, \mathsf{Enc}, \mathsf{Dec})$, our Q-bound slotted RFE for circuit family C works as follows:

- $\mathsf{Setup}(1^\lambda, 1^L, 1^Q, C)$: Initialize N 1-bound slotted RFE instances by running $\mathsf{osRFE}.\mathsf{Setup}(1^\lambda, 1^L, G)$ for N times, and obtain $\{\mathsf{crs}_k\}_{k \in [N]}$. Output

$$\mathsf{crs} = (\{\mathsf{crs}_k\}_{k \in [N]}).$$

- $\mathsf{Gen}(\mathsf{crs}, i)$: Parse $\mathsf{crs} = (\{\mathsf{crs}_k\}_{k \in [N]})$, then it proceeds as follows:
  - Sample uniformly random set $\Gamma_i \subseteq [N]$ of size $tD + 1$ and random set $\Delta_i \subseteq [S]$ of size v, where Δ_i can be translated into a bit string δ_i of length $v \log S$. Set $n' = n + v \log S$;
  - For all $k \in [N]$, run $(\mathsf{pk}_{k,i}, \mathsf{sk}_{k,i}) \leftarrow \mathsf{osRFE}.\mathsf{Gen}(\mathsf{crs}_k, i)$. Here, based on the construction presented in Sect. 5, for each $k \in [N]$, we have $\mathsf{pk}_{k,i} = (\{\mathsf{pk}_{k,i,w,b}\}_{w \in [n'], b \in \{0,1\}})$ and $\mathsf{sk}_{k,i} = (\{\mathsf{sk}_{k,i,w,b}\}_{w \in [n'], b \in \{0,1\}})$, where $(\mathsf{pk}_{k,i,w,b}, \mathsf{sk}_{k,i,w,b})$ are sampled from the key-generation algorithm of global slotted RBE. Then omit secret keys $\mathsf{sk}_{k,i}$ for all $k \notin \Gamma_i$, and for all $k \in \Gamma_i$, update

$$\mathsf{sk}_{k,i} = (\{\mathsf{sk}_{k,i,w,b}\}_{w \le n} \cup \{\mathsf{sk}_{k,i,w,\delta_i[w]}\}_{w > n}).$$

  Output

$$\mathsf{pk}_i = (\{\mathsf{pk}_{k,i}\}_{k \in [N]}), \quad \mathsf{sk}_i = (\{\mathsf{sk}_{k,i}\}_{k \in \Gamma_i}, \Gamma_i, \Delta_i).$$

- $\mathsf{Ver}(\mathsf{crs}, i, \mathsf{pk}_i)$: For all $k \in [N]$, run $\beta_k \leftarrow \mathsf{osRFE}.\mathsf{Ver}(\mathsf{crs}_k, i, \mathsf{pk}_{k,i})$, and if $\beta_k = 0$, output 0 and abort; otherwise, output 1.

– $\mathsf{Agg}(\mathsf{crs}, \{\mathsf{pk}_i, \mathsf{C}_i\}_{i \in [L]})$: Parse $\mathsf{pk}_i = (\{\mathsf{pk}_{k,i}\}_{k \in [N]})$ for each $i \in [L]$. For all $k \in [N]$, run $(\mathsf{mpk}_k, \{\mathsf{hsk}_{k,j}\}_{j \in [L]}) \leftarrow \mathsf{osRFE.Agg}(\mathsf{crs}_k, \{\mathsf{pk}_{k,i}, \mathsf{G}_i\}_{i \in [L]})$, where G_i is defined as in (1) given constant C_i and Δ_i. Here, algorithm $\mathsf{osRFE.Agg}$ works as in construction 5.1 except that all submitted public keys associated with Δ_i are directly registered into $\{\mathsf{mpk}_k\}_{k \in [N]}$ to ensure the cover freeness. Then output

$$\mathsf{mpk} = (\{\mathsf{mpk}_k\}_{k \in [N]}), \quad \mathsf{hsk}_j = (\{\mathsf{hsk}_{k,j}\}_{k \in [N]})$$

– $\mathsf{Enc}(\mathsf{mpk}, x)$: It proceeds as follows:
  - Sample a random degree t polynomial $\mu(\cdot)$ whose constant term is x;
  - For all $j \in [S]$, sample a random degree Dt polynomial $\zeta_j(\cdot)$ whose constant term is 0;
  - For all $k \in [N]$, compute $\mathbf{x}_k = (\mu(k), \zeta_1(k), \ldots, \zeta_S(k))$ and run $\mathsf{ct}_k \leftarrow \mathsf{osRFE.Enc}(\mathsf{mpk}_k, \mathbf{x}_k)$.

  Then output

$$\mathsf{ct} = (\mathsf{ct}_1, \ldots, \mathsf{ct}_N).$$

– $\mathsf{Dec}(\mathsf{hsk}_{i^*}, \mathsf{sk}_{i^*}, \mathsf{ct})$:   Parse $\mathsf{hsk}_{i^*} = (\{\mathsf{hsk}_{k,i^*}\}_{k \in [N]}), \mathsf{sk}_{i^*} = (\{\mathsf{sk}_{k,i^*}\}_{k \in \Gamma_{i^*}}, \Gamma_{i^*}, \Delta_{i^*})$. For all $k \in \Gamma_{i^*}$, run

$$z_k \leftarrow \mathsf{osRFE.Dec}(\mathsf{hsk}_{k,i^*}, \mathsf{sk}_{k,i^*}, \mathsf{ct}_k).$$

Then use $\{z_k\}_{k \in \Gamma_{i^*}}$ to recover a degree Dt polynomial $\psi(\cdot)$ such that $\psi(k) = z_k$. Output $\psi(0)$.

Remark. For the range of parameters S, N, t and v, we let $v = O(\lambda)$. Suppose there are Q corrupted users whose slot numbers are collected in set $\{c_1, \ldots, c_Q\} \subseteq [L]$, then we set $t = O(Q^2\lambda)$ and $N = O(D^2Q^2t)$ to ensure small pairwise intersections [32]. In other words, for all $\Gamma_{c_1}, \ldots, \Gamma_{c_Q}$, it holds that

$$\Pr\left[\left|\bigcup_{i \neq j}(\Gamma_{c_i} \cap \Gamma_{c_j})\right| > t\right] \leq \mathsf{negl}(\lambda).$$

Besides, we set $S = O(Q^2v)$ to ensure cover freeness [32]. In other words, for all $\Delta_{c_1}, \ldots, \Delta_{c_Q}$ and all $i \in [Q]$, it holds that

$$\Pr\left[\Delta_{c_i} \setminus \left(\bigcup_{j \neq i}\Delta_{c_j}\right) = \emptyset\right] \leq \mathsf{negl}(\lambda).$$

On the other hand, we can trivially bootstrap above construction into RFE for all polynomial-sized circuits instead of NC1 circuits. For any polynomial-sized circuit C_i, this can be done by modifying the definition of circuit G_i into generating a randomized encoding of C_i that is computable by a constant-degree circuit with fresh randomness generated from weak pseudo-random function. Here, we omit more details and only discuss the NC1 case.

Completeness and Compactness. For completeness, it follows the underlying 1-bound slotted RFE. For compactness, combining the compactness analysis of osRFE, it holds that

$$|\mathsf{mpk}| = N \cdot 2n \cdot \mathsf{poly}(\lambda, \log L), \ |\mathsf{hsk}_j| = N \cdot 2n \cdot \mathsf{poly}(\lambda, \log L)$$

where N depends on the corruption bound Q, and n is related to circuit family C. Thus, our construction meets the compactness requirement.

Correctness. By the correctness of underlying 1-bound slotted RFE, for all $k \in \Gamma_{i^*}$ we have

$$\psi(k) = \mathsf{G}_{i^*}(\mathbf{x}_k) = \mathsf{C}_{i^*}(\mu(k)) + \sum_{j \in \Delta_{i^*}} \zeta_j(k).$$

Since $|\Gamma_{i^*}| = Dt + 1$, we can recover the polynomial $\psi(\cdot)$ of degree Dt, and then evaluate $\psi(0) = \mathsf{C}_{i^*}(\mu(0)) = \mathsf{C}_{i^*}(x)$. Indeed, above computation exactly corresponds to BGW MPC protocol [41]. Therefore, the correctness follows readily.

6.2 Security

Theorem 4. *Assume* $\mathsf{osRFE} = (\mathsf{Setup}, \mathsf{Gen}, \mathsf{Ver}, \mathsf{Agg}, \mathsf{Enc}, \mathsf{Dec})$ *is a slotted RFE scheme which achieves the 1-bound SIM security, the above construction achieves the Q-bound SIM security.*

Proof. Our proof strategy is analogous to [32]. Suppose the adversary $\mathcal{A}$ colludes with Q corrupted users whose slot indices are collected in set $\{c_1, \ldots, c_Q\} \subseteq [L]$. Let $\mathcal{T}$ denote the set $\bigcup_{i \neq j}(\Gamma_{c_i} \cap \Gamma_{c_j})$, and note that $\mathcal{A}$ has no idea about other $\Gamma_i \notin \{\Gamma_{o_1}, \ldots, \Gamma_{c_Q}\}$ under honest slots. With challenge ciphertext $\mathsf{ct}^* = (\mathsf{ct}_1^*, \ldots, \mathsf{ct}_N^*)$ and secret key $\mathsf{sk}_i = (\{\mathsf{sk}_{k,i}\}_{k \in \Gamma_i}, \Gamma_i, \Delta_i)$ for $k \in [N]$, then the proof strategy is organized as follows:

- If $k \notin \mathcal{T}$, it means there exists at most a set Γ_{c_i} such that $k \in \Gamma_{c_i}$ and $k \notin \Gamma_{c_j}$ for other j. In particular, ct_k^* can be just decrypted correctly by a corrupted user with slot i. Thus, it can rely on the 1-bound SIM security of underlying construction;
- Otherwise, it means that $\mathcal{A}$ holds more than one secret keys that are used to decrypt ct_k^* correctly. In this way, 1-bound SIM security would be broken, and the security would in turn rely on the underlying MPC protocol. In this case, $\mathcal{A}$ will obtain no valid information about the challenge message x^* as long as small pairwise intersections and cover freeness hold.

Then we define the simulator $\widetilde{\mathsf{Enc}}$ that works as follows:

- $\widetilde{\mathsf{Enc}}(\mathsf{mpk}, \mathcal{K})$: Parse $\mathcal{K} = \{(c_i, \mathsf{C}_{c_i}^*, \mathsf{C}_{c_i}^*(x^*), \mathsf{sk}_{c_i})\}_{i \in [Q]}$. Here, we obtain $\Gamma_{c_1}, \ldots, \Gamma_{c_Q}, \Delta_{c_1}, \ldots, \Delta_{c_Q}$ from sk_i. Then it proceeds as follows:
  - Sample a uniformly random degree t polynomial $\mu(\cdot)$ whose constant term is 0;

- For all $j \in [Q]$, fix some $a_j^* \in \Delta_{c_j} \setminus \left(\bigcup_{j \neq k} \Delta_{c_k} \right)$ based on the cover freeness. For other $a \in (\Delta_{c_1} \cup \cdots \cup \Delta_{c_Q}) \setminus \{a_j^*\}_{j \in [Q]}$, sample a uniformly random degree Dt polynomial $\zeta_a(\cdot)$ whose constant term is 0. For all $j \in [Q]$, pick a random degree Dt polynomial $\psi_{c_j}(\cdot)$ whose constant term is $\mathsf{C}_{c_j}(x^*)$ and adjust the evaluation of $\zeta_{a_j^*}$ such that for all $k \in \mathcal{T}$, we have

$$\psi_{c_j}(k) = \mathsf{C}_{c_j}(\mu(k)) + \sum_{a \in \Delta_{c_j}} \zeta_a(k).$$

- For all $k \notin \mathcal{T}$, suppose there is at most a set Γ_{c_i} such that $k \in \Gamma_{c_i}$ and $k \notin \Gamma_{c_j}$ for all $j \neq i$, then we simulate ct_k^* as follows:

$$\mathsf{ct}_k^* \leftarrow \mathsf{osRFE.\widetilde{Enc}}(\mathsf{mpk}_k, (c_i, \mathsf{G}_{c_i}, \psi_{c_i}(k), \mathsf{sk}_{c_i})).$$

- For all $k \in \mathcal{T}$, we generate ct_k^* as in real experiment:

$$\mathsf{ct}_k^* \leftarrow \mathsf{osRFE.Enc}(\mathsf{mpk}_k, (\mu(k), \zeta_1(k), \ldots, \zeta_S(k))).$$

Finally, output

$$\mathsf{ct}^* = (\mathsf{ct}_1^*, \ldots, \mathsf{ct}_N^*).$$

Game Sequence. We prove Theorem 4 via a sequence of games as follows:

- Game_0: Real Game.
- Game_1: this game is identical to Game_0 except that it samples $\zeta_1, \ldots, \zeta_S, \psi_1, \ldots, \psi_Q$ as in $\widetilde{\mathsf{Enc}}$ and simulates all $\{\mathsf{ct}_k^*\}_{k \notin \mathcal{T}}$ as in algorithm $\widetilde{\mathsf{Enc}}$.
- Game_2: this game is identical to Game_1 except that it replaces Enc with $\widetilde{\mathsf{Enc}}$ to generate the challenge ciphertext ct^*.

Lemma 3 ($\mathsf{Game}_0 \approx_c \mathsf{Game}_1$). *For any adversary $\mathcal{A}$, there exists an algorithm $\mathcal{B}$ with close running time to $\mathcal{A}$ such that*

$$|\mathsf{Adv}_{\mathcal{A}}^0(\lambda) - \mathsf{Adv}_{\mathcal{A}}^1(\lambda)| \leq \mathsf{Adv}_{\mathcal{B}}^{\mathsf{osRFE}}(\lambda) + \mathsf{negl}(\lambda).$$

Proof. Informally, thanks to cover freeness, we observe that the distribution of $\zeta_1, \ldots, \zeta_S, \psi_1, \ldots, \psi_Q$ in $\widetilde{\mathsf{Enc}}$ are essentially identical to those in Enc, and then we can follow the 1-bound SIM security of underlying slotted RFE scheme to simulate all $\{\mathsf{ct}_k^*\}_{k \notin \mathcal{T}}$ as in $\widetilde{\mathsf{Enc}}$. Thus, it holds that Game_0 is computationally indistinguishable from Game_1. □

Lemma 4 ($\mathsf{Game}_1 \approx_s \mathsf{Game}_2$). *For any adversary $\mathcal{A}$, we have*

$$|\mathsf{Adv}_{\mathcal{A}}^1(\lambda) - \mathsf{Adv}_{\mathcal{A}}^2(\lambda)| \leq \mathsf{negl}(\lambda).$$

Proof. The only difference between Game_1 and Game_2 is the distributions of μ. We claim that the distributions of $\{\mu(k)\}_{k \in \mathcal{T}}$ in Game_1 are essentially identical to those in Game_2 as long as small pairwise intersections holds, i.e., $|\mathcal{T}| \leq t$. Thus, this readily proves the lemma. $\qquad\square$

Acknowledgements. Thank Yin Zhu for his useful advice. We also thank all anonymous reviewers for their helpful comments. This work was supported in part by National Natural Science Foundation of China (62372180, 62325209, U2336203), Innovation Program of Shanghai Municipal Education Commission (2021-01-07-00-08-E00101), the "Digital Silk Road" Shanghai International Joint Lab of Trustworthy Intelligent Software (22510750100), the Australian Research Council Discovery Early Career Researcher Award DE240100282, the Major Program (JD) of Hubei Province (No. 2023BAA027), and the Key Research and Development Science and Technology of Hainan Province (GHYF2022010).

References

1. Michel Abdalla, Fabrice Benhamouda, and Romain Gay. From single-input to multi-client inner-product functional encryption. In Steven D. Galbraith and Shiho Moriai, editors, *ASIACRYPT 2019, Part III*, volume 11923 of *LNCS*, pages 552–582. Springer, Heidelberg, 2019.

2. Michel Abdalla, Fabrice Benhamouda, Markulf Kohlweiss, and Hendrik Waldner. Decentralizing inner-product functional encryption. In Dongdai Lin and Kazue Sako, editors, *PKC 2019, Part II*, volume 11443 of *LNCS*, pages 128–157. Springer, Heidelberg, 2019.

3. Shashank Agrawal and David J. Wu. Functional encryption: Deterministic to randomized functions from simple assumptions. In Jean-Sébastien Coron and Jesper Buus Nielsen, editors, *EUROCRYPT 2017, Part II*, volume 10211 of *LNCS*, pages 30–61. Springer, Heidelberg, April / May 2017.

4. Shweta Agrawal, Michael Clear, Ophir Frieder, Sanjam Garg, Adam O'Neill, and Justin Thaler. Ad hoc multi-input functional encryption. In Thomas Vidick, editor, *ITCS 2020*, volume 151, pages 40:1–40:41. LIPIcs, January 2020.

5. Shweta Agrawal, Rishab Goyal, and Junichi Tomida. Multi-party functional encryption. In Kobbi Nissim and Brent Waters, editors, *TCC 2021, Part II*, volume 13043 of *LNCS*, pages 224–255. Springer, Heidelberg, 2021.

6. Shweta Agrawal, Benoît Libert, and Damien Stehlé. Fully secure functional encryption for inner products, from standard assumptions. In Matthew Robshaw and Jonathan Katz, editors, *CRYPTO 2016, Part III*, volume 9816 of *LNCS*, pages 333–362. Springer, Heidelberg, 2016.

7. Shweta Agrawal, Monosij Maitra, Narasimha Sai Vempati, and Shota Yamada. Functional encryption for turing machines with dynamic bounded collusion from LWE. In Tal Malkin and Chris Peikert, editors, *CRYPTO 2021, Part IV*, volume 12828 of *LNCS*, pages 239–269, Virtual Event, August 2021. Springer, Heidelberg.

8. Shweta Agrawal and Alon Rosen. Functional encryption for bounded collusions, revisited. In Yael Kalai and Leonid Reyzin, editors, *TCC 2017, Part I*, volume 10677 of *LNCS*, pages 173–205. Springer, Heidelberg, 2017.

9. Shweta Agrawal, Junichi Tomida, and Anshu Yadav. Attribute-based multi-input fe (and more) for attribute-weighted sums. In *Annual International Cryptology Conference*, pages 464–497. Springer, 2023.

10. Prabhanjan Ananth and Abhishek Jain. Indistinguishability obfuscation from compact functional encryption. In Rosario Gennaro and Matthew J. B. Robshaw, editors, *CRYPTO 2015, Part I*, volume 9215 of *LNCS*, pages 308–326. Springer, Heidelberg, August 2015.

11. Prabhanjan Ananth and Vinod Vaikuntanathan. Optimal bounded-collusion secure functional encryption. In Dennis Hofheinz and Alon Rosen, editors, *TCC 2019, Part I*, volume 11891 of *LNCS*, pages 174–198. Springer, Heidelberg, 2019.

12. Benny Applebaum, Yuval Ishai, and Eyal Kushilevitz. Computationally private randomizing polynomials and their applications. *computational complexity*, 15(2):115–162, 2006.

13. Giuseppe Ateniese, Danilo Francati, David Nuñez, and Daniele Venturi. Match me if you can: Matchmaking encryption and its applications. In Alexandra Boldyreva and Daniele Micciancio, editors, *CRYPTO 2019, Part II*, volume 11693 of *LNCS*, pages 701–731. Springer, Heidelberg, 2019.

14. Donald Beaver, Silvio Micali, and Phillip Rogaway. The round complexity of secure protocols. In *Proceedings of the twenty-second annual ACM symposium on Theory of computing*, pages 503–513, 1990.

15. Mihir Bellare, Viet Tung Hoang, and Phillip Rogaway. Foundations of garbled circuits. In Ting Yu, George Danezis, and Virgil D. Gligor, editors, *ACM CCS 2012*, pages 784–796. ACM Press, October 2012.

16. Nir Bitansky and Vinod Vaikuntanathan. Indistinguishability obfuscation from functional encryption. In Venkatesan Guruswami, editor, *56th FOCS*, pages 171–190. IEEE Computer Society Press, October 2015.

17. Dan Boneh, Amit Sahai, and Brent Waters. Functional encryption: Definitions and challenges. In Yuval Ishai, editor, *TCC 2011*, volume 6597 of *LNCS*, pages 253–273. Springer, Heidelberg, 2011.

18. Pedro Branco, Russell WF Lai, Monosij Maitra, Giulio Malavolta, Ahmadreza Rahimi, and Ivy KY Woo. Traitor tracing without trusted authority from registered functional encryption. *Cryptology ePrint Archive*, 2024.

19. Nishanth Chandran, Vipul Goyal, Aayush Jain, and Amit Sahai. Functional encryption: Decentralised and delegatable. Cryptology ePrint Archive, Report 2015/1017, 2015. https://eprint.iacr.org/2015/1017.

20. Jérémy Chotard, Edouard Dufour Sans, Romain Gay, Duong Hieu Phan, and David Pointcheval. Decentralized multi-client functional encryption for inner product. In Thomas Peyrin and Steven Galbraith, editors, *ASIACRYPT 2018, Part II*, volume 11273 of *LNCS*, pages 703–732. Springer, Heidelberg, 2018.

21. Jérémy Chotard, Edouard Dufour-Sans, Romain Gay, Duong Hieu Phan, and David Pointcheval. Dynamic decentralized functional encryption. In Daniele Micciancio and Thomas Ristenpart, editors, *CRYPTO 2020, Part I*, volume 12170 of *LNCS*, pages 747–775. Springer, Heidelberg, 2020.

22. Pratish Datta and Tapas Pal. Registration-based functional encryption. *IACR Cryptol. ePrint Arch.*, 2023:457, 2023.

23. Nico Döttling, Dimitris Kolonelos, Russell WF Lai, Chuanwei Lin, Giulio Malavolta, and Ahmadreza Rahimi. Efficient laconic cryptography from learning with errors. In *Annual International Conference on the Theory and Applications of Cryptographic Techniques*, pages 417–446. Springer, 2023.

24. Alex Escala, Gottfried Herold, Eike Kiltz, Carla Ràfols, and Jorge Villar. An algebraic framework for Diffie-Hellman assumptions. In Ran Canetti and Juan A. Garay, editors, *CRYPTO 2013, Part II*, volume 8043 of *LNCS*, pages 129–147. Springer, Heidelberg, 2013.

25. Danilo Francati, Daniele Friolo, Monosij Maitra, Giulio Malavolta, Ahmadreza Rahimi, and Daniele Venturi. Registered (inner-product) functional encryption. In *International Conference on the Theory and Application of Cryptology and Information Security*, pages 98–133. Springer, 2023.
26. Cody Freitag, Brent Waters, and David J Wu. How to use (plain) witness encryption: Registered abe, flexible broadcast, and more. In *Annual International Cryptology Conference*, pages 498–531. Springer, 2023.
27. Rachit Garg, Rishab Goyal, and George Lu. Dynamic collusion functional encryption and multi-authority attribute-based encryption. In *IACR International Conference on Public-Key Cryptography*, pages 69–104. Springer, 2024.
28. Rachit Garg, Rishab Goyal, George Lu, and Brent Waters. Dynamic collusion bounded functional encryption from identity-based encryption. In Orr Dunkelman and Stefan Dziembowski, editors, *EUROCRYPT 2022, Part II*, volume 13276 of *LNCS*, pages 736–763. Springer, Heidelberg, May / June 2022.
29. Sanjam Garg, Mohammad Hajiabadi, Mohammad Mahmoody, and Ahmadreza Rahimi. Registration-based encryption: Removing private-key generator from IBE. In Amos Beimel and Stefan Dziembowski, editors, *TCC 2018, Part I*, volume 11239 of *LNCS*, pages 689–718. Springer, Heidelberg, 2018.
30. Craig Gentry and Brent Waters. Adaptive security in broadcast encryption systems (with short ciphertexts). In Antoine Joux, editor, *EUROCRYPT 2009*, volume 5479 of *LNCS*, pages 171–188. Springer, Heidelberg, 2009.
31. Noemi Glaeser, Dimitris Kolonelos, Giulio Malavolta, and Ahmadreza Rahimi. Efficient registration-based encryption. In *Proceedings of the 2023 ACM SIGSAC Conference on Computer and Communications Security*, pages 1065–1079, 2023.
32. Sergey Gorbunov, Vinod Vaikuntanathan, and Hoeteck Wee. Functional encryption with bounded collusions via multi-party computation. In Reihaneh Safavi-Naini and Ran Canetti, editors, *CRYPTO 2012*, volume 7417 of *LNCS*, pages 162–179. Springer, Heidelberg, 2012.
33. Rishab Goyal and Satyanarayana Vusirikala. Verifiable registration-based encryption. In Daniele Micciancio and Thomas Ristenpart, editors, *CRYPTO 2020, Part I*, volume 12170 of *LNCS*, pages 621–651. Springer, Heidelberg, 2020.
34. Susan Hohenberger, George Lu, Brent Waters, and David J. Wu. Registered attribute-based encryption. In Carmit Hazay and Martijn Stam, editors, *EUROCRYPT 2023, Part III*, volume 14006 of *LNCS*, pages 511–542. Springer, Heidelberg, 2023.
35. Aayush Jain, Huijia Lin, Ji Luo, and Daniel Wichs. The pseudorandom oracle model and ideal obfuscation. In *Annual International Cryptology Conference*, pages 233–262. Springer, 2023.
36. Sam Kim and David J. Wu. Access control encryption for general policies from standard assumptions. In Tsuyoshi Takagi and Thomas Peyrin, editors, *ASIACRYPT 2017, Part I*, volume 10624 of *LNCS*, pages 471–501. Springer, Heidelberg, 2017.
37. Dimitris Kolonelos, Giulio Malavolta, and Hoeteck Wee. Distributed broadcast encryption from bilinear groups. In *International Conference on the Theory and Application of Cryptology and Information Security*, pages 407–441. Springer, 2023.
38. Willy Quach, Hoeteck Wee, and Daniel Wichs. Laconic function evaluation and applications. In Mikkel Thorup, editor, *59th FOCS*, pages 859–870. IEEE Computer Society Press, October 2018.
39. Amit Sahai and Hakan Seyalioglu. Worry-free encryption: functional encryption with public keys. In Ehab Al-Shaer, Angelos D. Keromytis, and Vitaly Shmatikov, editors, *ACM CCS 2010*, pages 463–472. ACM Press, October 2010.

40. Hoeteck Wee. Optimal broadcast encryption and CP-ABE from evasive lattice assumptions. In Orr Dunkelman and Stefan Dziembowski, editors, *EUROCRYPT 2022, Part II*, volume 13276 of *LNCS*, pages 217–241. Springer, Heidelberg, May / June 2022.
41. Avi Wigderson, MB Or, and S Goldwasser. Completeness theorems for noncryptographic fault-tolerant distributed computations. In *Proceedings of the 20th Annual Symposium on the Theory of Computing (STOC'88)*, pages 1–10, 1988.
42. Andrew Chi-Chih Yao. How to generate and exchange secrets. In *27th annual symposium on foundations of computer science (Sfcs 1986)*, pages 162–167. IEEE, 1986.
43. Samee Zahur, Mike Rosulek, and David Evans. Two halves make a whole - reducing data transfer in garbled circuits using half gates. In Elisabeth Oswald and Marc Fischlin, editors, *EUROCRYPT 2015, Part II*, volume 9057 of *LNCS*, pages 220–250. Springer, Heidelberg, 2015.
44. Ziqi Zhu, Jiangtao Li, Kai Zhang, Junqing Gong, and Haifeng Qian. Registered functional encryptions from pairings. In *EUROCRYPT*, 2024.
45. Ziqi Zhu, Kai Zhang, Junqing Gong, and Haifeng Qian. Registered abe via predicate encodings. In *International Conference on the Theory and Application of Cryptology and Information Security*, pages 66–97. Springer, 2023.

Registered FE Beyond Predicates: (Attribute-Based) Linear Functions and More

Pratish Datta[1]([✉]), Tapas Pal[2]([✉]), and Shota Yamada[3]

[1] NTT Research, Sunnyvale, CA 94085, USA
pratish.datta@ntt-research.com
[2] Karlsruhe Institute of Technology, KASTEL SRL, 76131 Karlsruhe, Germany
tapas.pal@kit.edu
[3] National Institute of Advanced Industrial Science and Technology (AIST),
Tokyo 135-0064, Japan
yamada-shota@aist.go.jp

Abstract. This paper introduces the *first* registered functional encryption RFE scheme tailored for *linear functions*. Distinctly different from classical functional encryption (FE), RFE addresses the key-escrow issue and negates the master key exfiltration attack. Instead of relying on a centralized trusted authority, it introduces a "key curator" - a fully transparent entity that does not retain secrets. In an RFE framework, users independently generate secret keys and subsequently register their respective public keys, along with their authorized functions, with the key curator. This curator consolidates public keys from various users into a unified, concise master public key. For decryption, users occasionally secure helper decryption keys from the key curator, which they use in conjunction way with their private keys. It is imperative that the aggregate public key, helper decryption keys, ciphertexts, and the times for encryption/decryption are polylogarithmic in the number of registered users.

All existing RFE designs were confined to predicates where given the correct credentials a user can retrieve the entire payload from a ciphertext or gain no information about it otherwise. Contrarily, our RFE scheme facilitates the computation of linear functions on encrypted content and extraction of only the computation results. Recognizing potential leaks from linear functions, we further enhance our RFE by incorporating an attribute-based access control mechanism. The outcome is the *first* registered attribute-based linear FE (RABIPFE), which supports access policies depicted as linear secret sharing schemes LSSS. Our proposed schemes are realized in the common reference string (CRS) model as introduced by Hohenberger et al.[EUROCRYPT 2023], employ simple tools and black-box methods. Specifically, our constructions operate in asymmetric prime-order bilinear group setting and are proven secure in the generic bilinear group model. Aligning with all pre-existing black-box RFE designs within the CRS model, our schemes cater to a predetermined maximum user count. A notable variant of our RABIPFE scheme

T. Pal—This work was done while the author was affiliated with NTT Social Informatics Laboratories, Tokyo, Japan.

K.-M. Chung and Y. Sasaki (Eds.): ASIACRYPT 2024, LNCS 15484, pp. 65–104, 2025.
https://doi.org/10.1007/978-981-96-0875-1_3

also yields the *first* efficient registered ABE (RABE) system for LSSS access policies in asymmetric prime-order bilinear groups. Conclusively, demonstrating feasibility, we formulated an RFE blueprint that supports general functionalities and an infinite user base, leveraging indistinguishability obfuscation and one-way functions.

1   Introduction

Functional Encryption: Functional Encryption (FE) [32,101] expands upon the traditional public-key encryption paradigm by introducing fine-grained access control over encrypted data. In an FE scheme, a central authority possesses a master secret key and issues a corresponding master public key. Leveraging its master secret key, this authority furnishes users with secret keys corresponding to diverse legitimate functions. Conversely, any party can encrypt data using the master public key. Given a secret key for a function f and a ciphertext of a message x, decryption unveils $f(x)$ without revealing further details about x.

The FE paradigm holds vast potential, presenting myriad applications, both as a standalone solution and as a foundational element for other cryptographic primitives [15,16,20,26,27,58,60,67,72,97]. Given its broad utility, FE and its various subclasses have garnered significant attention in the research community. Below is a non-exhaustive list of notable results in the field [2,3,5–11,13,14,17–19,21,24,25,28–31,34–37,40–42,44,54,59,62–66,68,70, 75,76,79,81,84,87,88,90–93,99,100,104,107,109,111,113–118]

The Key-Escrow Challenge: While FE offers a powerful means for achieving precise control over encrypted data, it distinctly alters the trust dynamic when juxtaposed with standard public-key encryption. Specifically, in FE, a central, trusted entity is tasked with distributing the secret decryption keys tailored to each user. This central entity must safely maintain a long-term master secret key. A compromise of this authority could grant adversaries the power to decrypt every ciphertext in the system, revealing all encrypted messages. This inherent vulnerability to key exfiltration attacks necessitates meticulous protection of the master secret key for the system's duration. By contrast, with traditional public-key encryption, users autonomously generate their own key pairs without entrusting their secret keys to a central figure. This decentralization eliminates a single point of failure. The amalgamation of inherent key escrow and susceptibility to key exfiltration remains a significant barrier to FE adoption.

Registered FE: Addressing the key-escrow and master key exfiltration vulnerabilities inherent in FE, recent efforts have delved into an innovative encryption framework known as Registered FE (RFE). RFE replaces the central authority with a fully transparent entity known as a "key curator", which does not retain any secrets. Contrary to issuing secret decryption keys, the key curator's primary role revolves around consolidating public keys from registered users into a concise master public key. Elaborating, within an RFE framework, users autonomously generate their public and secret key pairs (mirroring traditional public-key encryption practices). They subsequently register their public keys, along with the functions they are sanctioned for, with the key curator. This entity, in turn, refreshes the scheme's master public key. Analogous to conventional FE, this master public key can encrypt any message x in the system. A registered user, authorized for a specific function f, can decrypt the ciphertext, gleaning solely $f(x)$, utilizing their secret key. This is aided by a publicly computable helper decryption key, which connects the user's public key with the prevailing master public key. Given the dynamic nature of the RFE system, where the master public key evolves as new users are onboarded, it is imperative for users to intermittently update their helper decryption keys throughout the system's lifespan. It is worth noting that these updates for each user can be determined publicly. From an efficiency perspective, if L users are registered, each user should only be tasked with updating their decryption key a maximum of $O(\log L)$ times throughout the system's existence. Further, the magnitude of each update must remain succinct, preferably within the realm of $\mathsf{poly}(\lambda, \log L)$, where λ symbolizes a security parameter. Aligning with standard FE, it is also crucial that the master public key maintains a compact footprint, sized approximately $\mathsf{poly}(\lambda, \log L)$.

Initial Results: Non-black-Box Constructions: Early research work spearheaded by Garg et al. [38,56,57,69], established RFE schemes within the context of Identity-Based Encryption (IBE), a subclass of FE. These were developed using well-studied computational assumptions, including CDH, factoring, and LWE. This new primitive was named Registration-Based Encryption (RBE) in those works. However, these constructions extensively relied on non-black-box cryptographic techniques, making them largely infeasible, even when considering subsequent optimization efforts [38].

Non-black-Box Constructions and the CRS Model: A seminal advancement in the domain of RFE was marked by the recent contributions of Hohenberger et al. [73]. Their work elucidated the concept of Registered ABE (RABE), examining RFE within the broader framework of Attribute-Based Encryption (ABE).

Moreover, the research devised innovative techniques for realizing RABE (with RBE as a specific case) using purely black-box cryptographic methods. Impressively, they designed an efficient RABE scheme for access structures represented as Linear Secret Sharing Schemes (LSSS) in composite order bilinear groups, based on the same established static assumptions for IBE [88] and ABE [87].

Yet, this black-box approach did require one significant trade-off: the one-time trusted generation of a structured Common Reference String (CRS). At a cursory look, this might seem like a mere transposition of trust. However, it is crucial to underscore that this CRS setup is a one-off process, potentially executed via a multi-party computation protocol, and remains reusable across diverse systems. Importantly, post this setup, the CRS remains the sole trusted element. All subsequent activities of the key curator are both deterministic and auditable. The system's security remains intact unless the initial CRS setup is jeopardized. This is markedly different from conventional FE wherein the central authority's long-term master secret key demands perpetual trust. Any breach, resulting in the unauthorized acquisition of this secret key, grants the perpetrator unfettered access to decrypt every system ciphertext. Hence, this CRS-based RFE framework considerably reduces the inherent trust requisites compared to its traditional FE counterpart.

This innovative approach, focusing on creating efficient black-box RFE architectures within the CRS paradigm using simple cryptographic tools, has catalyzed a renaissance of interest in the cryptographic sphere. This has culminated in a flurry of very recent findings [46,51–53,82,120], majority of which are actually concurrent to our work [51,52,82,120]. These investigations have spearheaded the development of registration-adapted variants of assorted FE subclasses, such as broadcast encryption [53,82], IBE (tailored for large identities) [46]([51]), ABE designed for access policies represented as LSSS and arithmetic branching programs [120], and Inner-Product Predicate Encryption (IPE) [52,120]. Notably, these constructions [51,52,82,120] are characterized by their black-box nature, efficiency, and reliance on simple tools like bilinear pairings.

Limitation of the State of the Art: While the advancements in the field have been commendable, the subclasses of FE for which registration-based variations have been constructed predominantly fall within the realm of predicate encryption (PE). PE, a subclass of FE, associates a secret key with an ID/attribute string, while a ciphertext encrypts a predicate-payload pair (or vice-versa). The decryption process unveils the payload only if the predicate is satisfied by the attribute string; otherwise, a unique null symbol, $\perp$, is revealed. Although PE facilitates fine-grained access controls to encrypted content, its capabilities are restricted. Specifically, it can only expose encrypted data entirely or partially to eligible users and keep concealed from unauthorized ones. In contrast, more potent FE subclasses permit privacy-focused computations on encrypted data, emphasizing the extraction of computational outcomes over the raw data. Despite the massive developments in the field, currently, constructing RFE for functionalities beyond predicates remains an unresolved challenge.

Inner-Product FE: This study pivots to what is arguably one of the simplest function classes richly covered in literature: linear functions or inner-products [1–3,10,11,24,25,34,40,48,80,94,106,108–110,115]. An Inner-Product FE (IPFE) scheme involves encrypting vectors over a specific finite field, with secret keys also devised for vectors within that field. The decryption process discloses the inner product of the message and secret key vectors. The practicality of inner product functions spans diverse applications, from computing weighted means in descriptive statistics, evaluating polynomials, determining exact thresholds [2], facilitating hidden-weight coin flips [39], to biometric authentication and encrypted data's nearest-neighbour search [80]. Moreover, IPFE can serve as foundational for creating FE schemes that support advanced function categories, such as quadratic functions [21, 59]. Regrettably, as with other FE subclasses, the key-escrow issue poses a significant challenge to the deployment of IPFE.

Attribute-Based IPFE: FE has further evolved to support even more advanced function classes, merging the attribute-based access control of PE with the evaluation of linear functions on encrypted data. Although IPFE offers broad practical applications, its underlying nature is fragile, with each new secret key release leaking sensitive information. To counteract this vulnerability, Abdalla et al. [3] proposed attribute-based IPFE (ABIPFE), a concept that embeds access policies into ciphertext while facilitating linear function evaluations. In an ABIPFE framework, each vector is encrypted under certain access policies, while its secret key corresponds to a combination of an attribute stream and a vector. Successful decryption unveils the inner product of the message and key vector, contingent upon the access policy being met by the attribute. Numerous subsequent studies [5, 42–44, 47, 85, 102] have explored ABIPFE across diverse access policy categories using established tools such as bilinear groups and lattices. Despite such advancements, the threat of master key exfiltration attacks continues to overshadow ABIPFE. Hence, in this work, we pose a pivotal question that has largely remained elusive.

Open Problem. *Is it possible to design efficient black-box RFE schemes for function classes beyond predicates, such as for Attribute-Based Linear Function Evaluation?*

Our Results

In this paper, we offer a positive response to the aforementioned open question. Indeed, for the first time in the literature, we formulate the notion of RFE[1], and the design of the primitive for function classes that transcend simple predicates. Specifically, we presented the *first* registered IPFE (RIPFE) and ABIPFE (RABIPFE) schemes. Developed within the CRS model and leveraging simple tools and black-box methodologies, our designs operate within asymmetric prime-order bilinear group setting, which is known to be faster and more secure compared to its other variants [23, 61, 77, 78]. Security is assured within the generic bilinear group model (GGM) [105]. The proposed RABIPFE system incorporates LSSS access policies, the zenith of policy expressiveness achieved by current ABE/ABIPFE constructions rooted in bilinear groups, even within conventional centralized frameworks. As a special case of our RABIPFE construc-

---

[1] All existing studies in this field have specifically defined the concept of RFE in accordance with the particular function classes they explored, often under varied terminologies. For instance, Garg et al. [56] utilized the term "registration-based encryption (RBE)". Hohenberger et al. [73] introduced the term "registered ABE (RABE)". Kolonelos et al. [82] put forth the concept of "distributed broadcast encryption (DBE)". Similarly, Freitag et al. [53] coined the term "flexible broadcast encryption (FBE)", and the list goes on. What distinguishes our work is the formal definition of RFE in its broadest sense, encompassing all existing registration-based primitives as particular instances of this overarching notion.

tion, we also present the first registered ABE (RABE) system in a prime-order bilinear group setting.

Our schemes are tailored to accommodate a pre-determined number of users. Specifically, the structured CRS dimensions are quadratically proportional to user numbers, while registration performance is linearly dependent on user count, aligning with existing black-box RFE structures within the CRS model. Further, analogous to the current CRS-based RFE schemes, we necessitate a thorough verification of user public keys before their registration in the system to address concerns regarding malicious public keys. Similar to the existing RABE scheme, our RABIPFE system can accommodate an attribute within access policies either singularly or within set limitations, with parameter dimensions expanding linearly based on repetition limits via a simple encoding technique similar to this [89,112]. Existing techniques for handling arbitrary repetitions of the same attributes within an access policy from centralized ABE literature [83,91,92] seemingly lack direct applicability in the registration-based context, leaving ample room for future investigation.

As our objective veers towards designing RFEs with functionalities surpassing predicates, we have to devise a different randomization strategy than existing works. While prior works like [73] naturally separated the masking component from the CRS into random shares to oversee predicate validation and membership verification, this does not work in our setting. Broadly speaking, the challenge arises from the distinction that, in the context of predicates, each user's decryption result is either zero or one. However, in our setting, the decryption results for different users can diverge significantly. To resolve this issue, our approach directly randomizes the component concealing the inner-product value during decryption. This novel process however, inherently risks the intermingling of decryption threads, potentially leading to vulnerabilities. To navigate these challenges, our refined randomization process, in essence, links the key vector to pertinent users while concurrently managing functional evaluation and membership validation in an integrated fashion. Such technique was previously used implicitly by Waters [112] in the context of centralized ABE for handling separation of computation threads arising from multi-use of attributes within policies. We not only extend this method beyond predicates but also adapt it to the registration-based framework, while presenting it in a more explicit manner (see Sect. 2 for further details).

Further, beyond the prime-order bilinear group-centric schemes, we also detail the blueprint for an RFE system catering to an indefinite number of users and supporting general functionalities via indistinguishability obfuscation (IO) and one-way functions (OWFs). An obfuscator, as defined in [22], is a tool that converts a circuit into an equivalent one, *i.e.* preserving its input-output behaviour, while concealing the original circuit's confidential data. Indistinguishability obfuscator [22] is a specific type of obfuscator ensuring that any two equivalent circuits' obfuscations are indistinguishable. Coupled with the seminal work of Jain et al. [75,76], realizing IO from falsifiable assumptions, this leads to an RFE system for arbitrary functionalities and user counts grounded in falsifiable assumptions. This latter achievement stands as a testament to the potential of RFE systems to accommodate versatile functionalities and an expansive user base.

Concurrent Works: Concurrently to our work, Francati et al. [52] also formulated the notion of RFE[2]. They additionally provided robust attribute hiding registered *zero* inner-product PE scheme, in prime-order bilinear group under the generic bilinear group model (GGM). However, this RFE remains within the context of RFE for predicates as previously described, and fully discloses payload data to authorized individuals. Contrasting this, our RFE scheme for linear or inner-product functionality does not just reveal encrypted data. Instead, it computes and outputs the inner-product of encrypted content.

Further, just like our work, Francati et al. [52] also presented an RFE scheme for general functionalities and supporting an arbitrary number of users from IO and OWFs. The differences between the two constructions are as follows. Francati et al. [52] essentially observed that the construction of RABE due to Hohenberger et al. [73] for general access policies and an arbitrary number of users from IO and OWFs actually works as a full pleaded RFE that can support arbitrary functionalities beyond predicates. On the other hand, we tweak the RABE scheme of [73] by introducing a Naor-Yung style [95] "double-encryption" mechanism inspired by the techniques of Garg et al. [56]. However, rather than using a simulation *sound* non-interactive zero-knowledge (NIZK) proof system as [56,95], our construction only employs Lamport's one-time signatures [86] which can be realized from OWFs.

In another synchronized study, Zhu et al. [120] constructed RABE schemes suitable for access policies expressed by LSSS and arithmetic branching programs (ABP) as well as attribute-hiding inner-product predicates. They utilized asymmetric prime-order bilinear groups and proved security in the standard model under the k-linear assumption [49]. Again, while both of their schemes primarily address predicates, our registration-based renditions of IPFE and ABIPFE surpass this scope, facilitating the evaluation of linear functions on encrypted data.

Subsequent Works: Subsequently to our work, Zhu et al. [119] proposed RFE schemes for linear and quadratic function in prime-order bilinear groups. The security of those constructions was proven in the standard model under the k-linear and bilateral k-linear assumptions, respectively. In another subsequent work, Branco et al. [33] constructed RFE schemes for quadratic and linear functions, proving their security in weak/selective models within GGM and the standard model under a static q-type assumption respectively.

---

[2] To provide further context on concurrency, please note that the current version of our paper is a major upgrade of an initial version of [45] with new additional results, namely, the RIPFE and RABIPFE constructions. The initial version of [45], which appeared at the same time as [52], nevertheless already contained the same notions of RFE as [52]. The initial version also contained our RFE scheme for general functionalities from IO.

Other Related Works: As different line of works [37,96] studied another decentralized variants of FE called dynamic decentralized functional encryption (DDFE). DDFE combines *multi-client* and *multi-authority* FE in a decentralized setting. In DDFE, there are several clients/encrypters who generate their master secret keys independently and they have to use those *secret keys* to encrypt messages at the slots under their control. When a user wants to evaluate some (multi-input) function on the data encrypted by a set of encrypters, those encrypters *acting as authorities* provide partial secret keys to that user. The user then combines those partial secret keys to obtain its full secret key for the function. Thus, if there exists only one encrypter in a DDFE system it essentially boils down to a *standard single-input secret-key centralized FE*. In contrast, in RFE, there is no designated authority or encrypter. Rather in RFE, when a user wants to evaluate some function on encrypted data it independently generates its public/secret key pair and then registers its public key along with its desired functionality to a key curator. Most importantly, the key curator holds *no secret*. Moreover, encryption does not require any secret information and can be performed by anyone even by parties having no contribution to the aggregated master public key. Thus RFE remains decentralized irrespective of whether the supported functionality is single or multi-input.

2   Technical Overview

In this work, we construct registration-based FE schemes for general as well as specific function classes. Regarding the specific classes, in the registration-based setting, we consider FE for linear functions which is known as IPFE [2] and FE for linear functions with access control which is noted as ABIPFE [4]. Before going to the technical descriptions of the designing of these primitives in the registration-based setting, we first provide an overview of the definition of registered FE for general functions.

2.1   Definition of Registered FE

Let $\mathcal{U}_F$ be the universe of functions and $\mathcal{M}$ be the set of messages supported by the scheme. We also assume that $\mathcal{U}_F$ contains only polynomial-size functions having maximum size ℓ_f in bit-length. There is a one-time trusted setup which samples a common reference string (CRS) crs depending on the security parameter and the bound ℓ_f. We allow the size of crs to be $\mathsf{poly}(\lambda, \ell_f, L)$. The key curator first initializes an empty master public key MPK when there is no user in the system at the beginning. If a user wants to join the system then it first samples a public-secret key pair (pk, sk) using crs, and then sends the public key pk along with a function $f_{\mathsf{pk}} \in \mathcal{U}_F$ to the key curator for registration. The key curator then aggregates the pair (pk, f_{pk}) into the current master public key MPK and outputs an updated one MPK'. Additionally, the user also receives a helper decryption key hsk from the key curator.

The key curator does not hold any secret and the role can be played by anyone in the system as well since the process of aggregation is *deterministic*.

The key generation and registration are both allowed to run in time $\mathsf{poly}(\lambda, \ell_f, L)$. However, in our actual constructions, the key generation process does not depend on ℓ_f. On the other hand, we require that the size of the secret key sk, the master public key MPK (at any stage) and the helper decryption key hsk for each user must be *polylogarithmic* in the total number of users, *i.e.*, $\mathsf{poly}(\lambda, \ell_f, \log L)$. Whenever a new user joins the system, the master public key is updated and as a result, the existing users might need an updated helper decryption key from the key curator. As in existing registration-based systems, we require that the actual number of updates needed for a helper decryption key of each user is essentially $O(\log L)$ throughout the existence of the system.

In our setting, the knowledge of MPK is sufficient for encrypting a message $m \in \mathcal{M}$. Any registered users whose public key-function pair $(\mathsf{pk}, f_{\mathsf{pk}})$ is integrated into the master public key MPK can decrypt the ciphertext ct using their secret keys sk and the helper decryption keys hsk. It is important to note that the large crs is not required at all during encryption or decryption, the information of crs is requested for generating keys of users and at the time of registering a user. This makes the encryption and decryption algorithm much more efficient, both of which run in time $\mathsf{poly}(\lambda, \ell_f, \log L)$ and are comparable to exiting (non-registered) FEs for specific class of functions such as IPFE. We formally define registered FE in Sect. 4.

Slotted Registered FE: We followed the blueprint of Hohenberger et al. [73] for constructing a registered encryption scheme. In particular, we first define and construct a slotted registered FE (SlotRFE) scheme and then use a transformation to achieve the full-fledged RFE scheme described above. A SlotRFE scheme is basically an RFE scheme where the total number of users L is *fixed* at the time of setup, and each user of the system is identified via a slot index $i \in [L]$. Therefore, each slot i is associated with a user-sampled key pair $(\mathsf{pk}_i, \mathsf{sk}_i)$ and a function $f_i \in \mathcal{U}_F$. The aggregation algorithm can be run only when a list of public key-function pair (pk_i, f_i) for all $i \in [L]$ is available. It uses the list to output the aggregated master public key MPK and a helper decryption key hsk_i for each user $i \in [L]$, that is all the users are registered in one shot. Note that, no update of the master public key or helper decryption keys is needed since no new user is allowed to join the system once the registration is over. For a SlotRFE, we require that the sizes of the master public key and helper decryption keys must grow at most poly-logarithmically with the total number of users in the system. The formal definition of SLotRFE is given in Sect. 5.

We present a transformation to go from SlotRFE to RFE. The idea of the conversion essentially follows from the similar transformation used for RABE by Hohenberger et al. [73]. The full detail of how we adapt their transformation into the setting of FE to construct RFE from our SlotRFE is provided in the full version [45]. It depends on a *power-of-two* approach that uses $\ell+1$ many SlotRFE schemes for building an RFE scheme with $L = 2^\ell$ users. Just like the RABE, the public parameters $(\mathsf{crs}, \mathsf{MPK}, \mathsf{hsk})$, ciphertext size and encryption time of the resulting RFE carry an overhead of $O(\log L)$ compared to the underlying SlotRFE scheme. This means that if the CRS of the SlotRFE scales with at most $O(\log L)$ then the RFE can support an exponential number of users. It is exactly the case for our IO-based RFE scheme for general functions. However, our pairing-based RFE schemes can only support a (polynomially) bounded number of users[3] since corresponding slotted versions produce a CRS of size $O(L^2)$.

2.2   Registered FE for (Attribute-Based) Linear Functions

In this subsection, we first provide technical ideas of our registered IPFE where functions and messages are vectors and decryption recovers the inner product between the vectors. Then, we discuss the technical ideas of constructing a registered ABIPFE.

Recap of plain IPFE [2]: Let us first describe the IPFE construction by Abdalla et al. [2], which is not registration-based, but serves as our starting point. Their construction works over groups of prime order without pairings. In their construction, the master public key consists of group elements $\mathsf{MPK} = (g, g^{\boldsymbol{\alpha}})$, where $\boldsymbol{\alpha} \in \mathbb{Z}_p^n$ and n is the dimension of the vectors supported by the scheme. The ciphertext encrypting a vector $\boldsymbol{x} \in \mathbb{Z}_p^n$ is of the form $\mathsf{ct} = (g^{s\boldsymbol{\alpha}+\boldsymbol{x}}, g^s)$, where $s \leftarrow \mathbb{Z}_p$, and a secret key associated with a vector $\boldsymbol{y} \in \mathbb{Z}_p^n$ is $\mathsf{sk} = \langle \boldsymbol{\alpha}, \boldsymbol{y} \rangle$. To decrypt a ciphertext, we first compute $g^{s\langle \boldsymbol{\alpha}+\boldsymbol{x}, \boldsymbol{y} \rangle} = g^{s\langle \boldsymbol{\alpha}, \boldsymbol{y} \rangle + \langle \boldsymbol{x}, \boldsymbol{y} \rangle}$ from $g^{s\boldsymbol{\alpha}+\boldsymbol{x}}$ and remove the masking term $g^{s\langle \boldsymbol{\alpha}, \boldsymbol{y} \rangle}$ using g^s and the secret key $\langle \boldsymbol{\alpha}, \boldsymbol{y} \rangle$. Then, we recover $\langle \boldsymbol{x}, \boldsymbol{y} \rangle$ from $g^{\langle \boldsymbol{x}, \boldsymbol{y} \rangle}$ by the brute-force computation.

Let us briefly discuss the intuition behind the security of the construction. Suppose that the adversary is given secret keys $\{\langle \boldsymbol{\alpha}, \boldsymbol{y}_i \rangle\}_i$ corresponding to vectors $\{\boldsymbol{y}_i\}_i$. Intuitively, only meaningful way to get information of $\boldsymbol{x}$ from the ciphertext is to take linear combination between the ciphertext components to compute $g^{s\langle \boldsymbol{\alpha}+\boldsymbol{x}, \boldsymbol{z} \rangle} = g^{s\langle \boldsymbol{\alpha}, \boldsymbol{z} \rangle + \langle \boldsymbol{x}, \boldsymbol{z} \rangle}$ for some vector $\boldsymbol{z}$ and remove the masking term $g^{s\langle \boldsymbol{\alpha}, \boldsymbol{z} \rangle}$ to recover the information of $\langle \boldsymbol{x}, \boldsymbol{z} \rangle$. Since the adversary is given only $\{\langle \boldsymbol{\alpha}, \boldsymbol{y}_i \rangle\}_i$, it is impossible for her to obtain any information of $\langle \boldsymbol{\alpha}, \boldsymbol{z} \rangle$ when $\boldsymbol{z}$ is outside of the span of the vectors $\{\boldsymbol{y}_i\}_i$. This in turn means that the information of $\langle \boldsymbol{x}, \boldsymbol{z} \rangle$ cannot be obtained if $\boldsymbol{z}$ is outside of the span, as desired.

Attempt 1: In our first attempt, we consider a construction that supports only a single user. Even in this setting, we face the challenge that there is no obvious way to generate a secret key, because the secret key generation of the plain IPFE construction we explained above crucially requires the knowledge of the master secret key. Translated into the setting of registration-based IPFE, this means that the key generation requires the knowledge of a trapdoor corresponding to the CRS, which is not known to the user. To resolve the problem, we observe that what is necessary for the decryption is actually the masking term $g^{s\langle \boldsymbol{\alpha}, \boldsymbol{y} \rangle}$. We construct the scheme so that the masking term can be recovered by the decryptor by exploiting the fact that the master public key can depend on the vector $\boldsymbol{y}$ in the registration-based setting.

---

[3] In fact, all existing pairing-based RABEs have the limitation of supporting only a bounded number of users.

Concretely, the CRS of the construction is the same as the master public key of the IPFE we explained. Namely, we set $\mathsf{crs} = (g, g^\alpha)$. A user who joins the system chooses random $r \leftarrow \mathbb{Z}_p$ and sets the public key as $\mathsf{pk} = g^r$ and the secret key as $\mathsf{sk} = r$. We set the master public key as $\mathsf{MPK} = (g, g^\alpha, W = g^{r + \langle \alpha, y \rangle})$, where y is the vector associated with the user. The ciphertext encrypting x is $\mathsf{ct} = (g^{s\alpha + x}, g^s, W^s = g^{sr + s\langle \alpha, y \rangle})$. A user can therefore recover $g^{s\langle \alpha, y \rangle}$ by computing g^{sr} from g^s and r and then compute W^s / g^{sr}. The rest of the decryption algorithm is the same as the plain IPFE construction explained above.

While the construction works for the single-user setting, the apparent problem is that there is no obvious way to extend the construction to the multi-user case. One could consider a natural attempt where we set $\mathsf{pk}_i = g^{r_i}$ for each user indexed with i and aggregate the public keys to set the master public key as $\mathsf{MPK} = (g, g^\alpha, W = \prod_i g^{r_i + \langle \alpha, y_i \rangle} = g^{\sum_i r_i + \sum_i \langle \alpha, y_i \rangle})$. Suppose that we were able to set the ciphertext and helper decryption key so that the decryption is possible. Then, a collusion of two users should be able to recover $\langle x, y_1 + z \rangle$ and $\langle x, y_1 - z \rangle$ for arbitrary z, which breaks the security of the scheme. This is because $\mathsf{sk}_1 = r_1$ and $\mathsf{sk}_2 = r_2$ are valid secret keys for vectors $y_1 + z$ and $y_2 - z$ respectively, since we have $W = g^{r_1 + \langle \alpha, y_1 + z \rangle} \cdot g^{r_2 + \langle \alpha, y_2 - z \rangle} \cdot g^{\sum_{i \neq 1,2} r_i + \sum_i \langle \alpha, y_i \rangle}$. At a high level, the construction is insecure, since each vector y_i is not bound to the corresponding index i.

Attempt 2: Based on the above observation, in our second attempt, we computationally bind each vector with the corresponding index. Namely, we set $\mathsf{crs} = (g, g^\alpha, g^{\beta_1}, \ldots, g^{\beta_L}, g^{\beta_1 \alpha}, \ldots g^{\beta_L \alpha})$, where L is the number of users in the system and $\beta_i \leftarrow \mathbb{Z}_p$ for each i. We set the secret key for user i as $\mathsf{sk}_i = r_i$ and the corresponding public key as $\mathsf{pk}_i = g^{\beta_i r_i}$. Given the set of public keys $\{\mathsf{pk}_i\}_{i \in [L]}$ and corresponding vectors $\{y_i\}_{i \in [L]}$, the master public key is set as $\mathsf{MPK} = (g, g^\alpha, W = \prod_{i \in [L]} \mathsf{pk}_i \cdot g^{\beta_i \langle \alpha, y_i \rangle} = \prod_{i \in [L]} g^{\beta_i (r_i + \langle \alpha, y_i \rangle)})$. The difference from the previous attempt is that we separate the thread of the computation for each user by the individual randomness β_i. To encrypt the vector x, we compute $\mathsf{ct} = (g^s, g^{s\alpha + x}, \mathsf{MPK}^s = \prod_i g^{s\beta_i (r_i + \langle \alpha, y_i \rangle)})$. Although it seems that now the construction is secure, we do not know how to decrypt the ciphertext. During the decryption, a user indexed with i may want to unmask $g^{s\beta_i r_i}$, but she only knows g^s, g^{β_i}, and r_i and thus this task is impossible. This motivates us to use the (symmetric) pairings in our next attempt.

Attempt 3: In our third attempt, we construct the scheme so that a user who knows r_i can remove the masking term. Towards this goal, we change the CRS as $\mathsf{crs} = (g, g_T^\alpha, g^{\beta_1}, \ldots, g^{\beta_L}, g^{\beta_1 \alpha}, \ldots, g^{\beta_L \alpha}, g^{1/\beta_1}, \ldots, g^{1/\beta_L})$. The forms of the public keys, secret keys, and master public key are the same as the previous attempt except that now the group components are in the source group. We change the form of the ciphertext as $\mathsf{ct} = (g_T^s, g_T^{s\alpha + x}, W^s = \prod_j g^{s\beta_j (r_j + \langle \alpha, y_j \rangle)})$, where $g_T = e(g, g)$. To decrypt the ciphertext, user i computes

$$e(W^s, g^{1/\beta_i}) = e(\prod_j g^{s\beta_j(r_j + \langle \alpha, y_j \rangle)}, g^{1/\beta_i})$$

$$= g_T^{sr_i} \cdot g_T^{s\langle \alpha, y_i \rangle} \cdot \underbrace{\prod_{j \neq i} g_T^{s\beta_j r_j / \beta_i} \cdot \prod_{j \neq i} g_T^{s\beta_j \langle \alpha, y_j \rangle / \beta_i}}_{=\text{Cross term}}.$$

Here, the user can unmask the term $g_T^{sr_i}$ using g_T^s and her secret key r_i. However, to retrieve the desired term $g_T^{s\langle \alpha, y_i \rangle}$, she also has to remove the cross term. In our next attempt, we enforce the users to compute extra components and include them into the public key when they register into the system. These extra components will enable the decryptor to compute the cross term.

Attempt 4: In our fourth attempt, we set $\mathsf{crs} = (g, g^{1/\gamma}, g_T^\alpha, \{g^{\beta_j}, g^{\beta_j \alpha}, g^{1/\beta_j}\}_j,$ $\{g^{\gamma\beta_j/\beta_k}, g^{\gamma\beta_j\alpha/\beta_k}\}_{j \neq k})$, where $\gamma \leftarrow \mathbb{Z}_q$ and the extra components will be used for computing the cross terms. We then enforce user i to compute and publicize $\{g^{\gamma\beta_i r_i/\beta_j}\}_{j \neq i}$ when it registers. Namely, we set $\mathsf{pk}_i = (g^{\beta_i r_i}, \{g^{\gamma\beta_i r_i/\beta_j}\}_{j \neq i})$ and $\mathsf{sk}_i = r_i$. The aggregation algorithm is going to be a bit more complex since it computes helper decryption keys $\{\mathsf{hsk}_i\}_i$ in addition to MPK. Concretely, given the public keys $\{\mathsf{pk}_i\}_i$ and corresponding vectors $\{y_i\}_i$, the aggregation algorithm computes

$$\mathsf{MPK} = \left(g_T, g_T^\alpha, g^{1/\gamma}, W = \prod_{i \in [L]} g^{\beta_i(r_i + \langle \alpha, y_i \rangle)}\right), \quad \mathsf{hsk}_i = \prod_{j \neq i} \left(g^{\beta_j \gamma r_j/\beta_i} \cdot g^{\beta_j \gamma \langle \alpha, y_j \rangle/\beta_i}\right).$$

The ciphertext is now $\mathsf{ct} = (g_T^s, g^{s/\gamma}, g_T^{s\alpha + x}, W^s)$. The cross term then can be recovered by computing

$$e(g^{s/\gamma}, \mathsf{hsk}_i) = \prod_{j \neq i} e\left(g^{s/\gamma}, g^{\beta_j \gamma r_j/\beta_i} \cdot g^{\beta_j \gamma \langle \alpha, y_j \rangle/\beta_i}\right) = \prod_{j \neq i} g_T^{s\beta_j r_j/\beta_i} \cdot \prod_{j \neq i} g_T^{s\beta_j \langle \alpha, y_j \rangle/\beta_i}$$

as desired.

One thing missing from the above discussion is how to check the validity of the public key registered by the user. Given the public key $\mathsf{pk}_i = (U_i, \{V_{i,j}\}_{j \neq i})$, we can check that it is in the valid form in the sense that there exists r_i such that $U_i = g^{\beta_i r_i}$ and $V_{i,j} = g^{\gamma\beta_i r_i/\beta_j}$ by checking $e(U_i, g^{1/\beta_j}) = e(V_{i,j}, g^{1/\gamma})$ for all $j \neq i$. However, this check does not ensure that the user actually followed the protocol to compute U_i: a malicious user might have deviated from the protocol and still have passed the verification. For example, the user might have used g^{β_i} and $g^{\beta_i \alpha}$ to compute U_i as $U_i = g^{\beta_i r_i + \beta_i \langle \alpha, z \rangle}$ for some z and computed corresponding $V_{i,j} = g^{\gamma\beta_i r_i/\beta_j + \gamma\beta_i \langle \alpha, z \rangle/\beta_j}$ from $g^{\gamma\beta_i/\beta_j}$ and $g^{\gamma\beta_i\alpha/\beta_j}$. Such a user can certainly pass the verification. However, the user is able to decrypt the ciphertext with respect to the vector $y_i + z$, namely, it can recover $\langle x, y_i + z \rangle$, even though it registered into the system with the vector y_i, since we have $W = g^{\beta_i(r_i + \langle \alpha, y_i + z \rangle)} \cdot \prod_{j \neq i} g^{\beta_j(r_j + \langle \alpha, y_j \rangle)}$, which is problematic. Therefore, it is not enough to check that the public key is in a valid form. Rather, we have to check that the public key is computed following the exact procedure specified by the protocol. A straightforward solution to ensure this is to use non-interactive zero-knowledge proof of knowledge (NIZK-PoK), where we add the CRS of NIZK-PoK to the CRS (of registration-based IPFE) and let the user i prove the knowledge of r_i when it registers. While this idea may work, it is somewhat indirect and/or introduces additional idealized assumptions. In more detail, if we use Fiat-Shamir [50] transformation for instantiating the NIZK-PoK, it requires random oracle models in addition to GGM, which is not desirable. Another possible way of instantiating the NIZK-PoK is to use the Groth-Sahai proofs [71]. However, this is inefficient and indirect, since the Groth-Sahai proofs cannot handle knowledge of exponent efficiently and requires bit-decomposition. In the next step, we provide a much more direct solution to the problem using asymmetric pairings.

Our Final Construction: We then explain our final construction. In the construction, we use the asymmetric pairing $e : \mathbb{G}_1 \times \mathbb{G}_2 \to \mathbb{G}_T$ with generators $g_1 \in \mathbb{G}_1$ and $g_2 \in \mathbb{G}_2$. In the construction, U_i resides in $\mathbb{G}_1$ and is computed as $U_i = g_1^{\beta_i r_i}$. We let the user compute the copy $\tilde{U}_i = g_2^{\beta_i r_i}$ of U_i in $\mathbb{G}_2$ when it registers, which is meant to serve as a proof that U_i is generated following the honest procedure of the protocol. By carefully placing the group components into $\mathbb{G}_1$ and $\mathbb{G}_2$, we can prevent the above attack. In more detail, we place $\{g_1^{\beta_i}\}_i$ and $\{g_2^{\gamma\beta_i/\beta_j}\}_{i,j}$ in the CRS so that the user can compute U_i and $V_{i,j}$. The CRS also includes $\{g_1^{\beta_i\alpha}\}_i$, which is used for computing the master public key. We further include $\{g_2^{\beta_i}\}_i$ in the CRS so that the copy $\tilde{U}_i$ of U_i can be computed. However, we do *not* include $\{g_2^{\beta_i\alpha}\}_i$ in the CRS and thus the adversary is not able to mount the above attack.

Here, we provide a concrete description of our construction. First, we set

$$\mathsf{crs} = \left(g_1, g_2, g_T^\alpha, g_1^{1/\gamma}, \{g_1^{\beta_i\alpha}, g_1^{\beta_i}, g_2^{\beta_i}, g_2^{1/\beta_i}\}_i, \{g_2^{\gamma\beta_i/\beta_j}, g_2^{\gamma\beta_i\alpha/\beta_j}\}_{i\neq j} \right). \quad (1)$$

When a user with index i registers, it sets the public key as $\mathsf{pk}_i = (U_i = g_1^{\beta_i r_i}, \tilde{U}_i = g_2^{\beta_i r_i}, \{V_{i,j} = g_2^{\gamma r_i\beta_i/\beta_j}\}_{j\neq i})$ and $\mathsf{sk}_i = r_i$. The verification of the public key is done by checking $e(U_i, g_2) = e(g_1, \tilde{U}_i)$ and $e(U_i, g_2^{1/\beta_j}) = e(g_1^{1/\gamma}, V_{i,j})$ for all $j \neq i$. The aggregation algorithm computes

$$\mathsf{MPK} = \left(g_T, g_T^\alpha, g_1^{1/\gamma}, W = \prod_{i\in[L]} g_1^{\beta_i(r_i+\langle\alpha,y_i\rangle)} \right), \quad \mathsf{hsk}_i = \prod_{j\neq i} \left(g_2^{\beta_j\gamma r_j/\beta_i} \cdot g_2^{\beta_j\gamma\langle\alpha,y_j\rangle/\beta_i} \right). \quad (2)$$

A ciphertext encrypting a vector $\boldsymbol{x}$ is

$$\mathsf{ct} = (g_T^s, g_T^{s\alpha+\boldsymbol{x}}, g_1^{-s/\gamma}, W^s).$$

We omit the description of the decryption algorithm here. We observe that the sizes of MPK and hsk_i are compact, both of which are $\mathsf{poly}(\lambda, n, \log L)$[4].

---

[4] We assume that the master public key MPK is implicitly included in each user's helper decryption key hsk_i.

Overview of the Security Proof: We prove the security of our construction in the generic group model. Roughly speaking, in the generic group model, the only way for the adversary to obtain non-trivial information encoded on the exponents of the group elements is to find a non-trivial linear combination of pairing products that equals zero. In the first step of the proof, we show that (1) the only way for the adversary to pass the verification when it registers the public key is to follow the honest key generation procedure. We then show that (2) the only way for the adversary to obtain non-trivial information on the encrypted vectors (*i.e.*, messages) is to follow the honest decryption procedure or take a linear combination between them. These two facts immediately imply the security of the construction.

We first show (1). In particular, we show that when the adversary passes the verification, it should have computed U_i as $U_i = g_1^{\beta_i r_i}$ using r_i. In the proof, we show that if the adversary deviates from the correct procedure of computing U_i, then it cannot compute the associating copy $\tilde{U}_i$ or $\{V_{i,j}\}_{j \neq i}$. For example, suppose that the adversary inserts the term $g_1^{1/\gamma}$ into U_i as $U_i = g_1^{\beta_i r_i} \cdot g_1^{t/\gamma}$ for some $t \in \mathbb{Z}_q$. Then, in order to pass the verification, the adversary has to compute $\tilde{U}_i = g_2^{\beta_i r_i} \cdot g_2^{t/\gamma}$. However, the term $g_2^{1/\gamma}$ is missing from the CRS, there is no way for the adversary to compute $\tilde{U}_i$. Other cases can be dealt with in a similar manner.[5]

We then explain the overview of the proof of (2), which is shown in several steps. In the first step, we show that the ciphertext component W^s should be paired with (linear combination of) $\{g_2^{1/\beta_i}\}_i$ terms, since otherwise the result of the pairing computation includes terms that can never be cancelled by any other pairing products. For example, if we pair W^s with $g_2^{\beta_i}$, the pairing product includes the term of the form $g_T^{s\beta_i\beta_j r_i}$. However, this term cannot be cancelled inside the linear combination of the pairing products, since any other combination of the terms does not yield $g_T^{s\beta_i\beta_j r_i}$ as a result of the pairing computation. This means at a high level that there is no non-trivial information that is obtained by inserting $e(W^s, g_2^{\beta_i})$ into the linear combination.

We then focus on the term $e(W^s, g_2^{1/\beta_i})$. By (1), all the public keys should be correctly generated including the ones that are generated by the adversary. In particular, we have $W = \prod_{i \in [L]} W_i = \prod_{i \in [L]} g_1^{\beta_i(r_i + \langle y_i, \alpha \rangle)}$ for some $\{r_i\}$. We therefore have

$$e(W^s, g_2^{1/\beta_i}) = g_T^{sr_i} \cdot g_T^{s\langle \alpha, y_i \rangle} \cdot \underbrace{\prod_{j \neq i} g_T^{s\beta_j r_j/\beta_i} \cdot \prod_{j \neq i} g_T^{s\beta_j \langle \alpha, y_j \rangle/\beta_i}}_{=\text{Cross term}}. \tag{3}$$

Ignoring the cross terms, the above component is similar to the message-carrying part of the plain IPFE we first introduced. Indeed, our proof from here closely

---

[5] Actually, the adversary can pass the verification by randomizing an honestly generated public key. However, there is no gain for the adversary to perform this type of malicious key generation as we will show in the formal proof. We ignore this subtle point in this overview and defer the full details to the formal proof.

follows the intuition of why the plain IPFE scheme is secure. First, we show that if r_i is not known to the adversary, then it cannot unmask the term $g_T^{sr_i}$. This means that the adversary can insert $e(W^s, g_2^{1/\beta_i})$ into the linear combination only when the index i is corrupted or the public key for this index is generated by the adversary herself. In both cases, the adversary can unmask the term $g_T^{sr_i}$ using the knowledge of r_i. However, she still has to compute and unmask the term $g_T^{s\langle\alpha,y_i\rangle}$. By inspection, we can show that the only possible way to unmask $g_T^{s\langle\alpha,y_i\rangle}$ is to compute $g_T^{s\langle\alpha,y_i\rangle+\langle x,y_i\rangle}$ using $g_T^{s\alpha+x}$ and then subtract the term from it. As a result, we will obtain $g_T^{\langle x,y_i\rangle}$, which only contains the information of $\langle x, y_i\rangle$. To sum up, if the adversary wants to obtain non-trivial information of the encrypted vector x from the ciphertext, it should take the linear combination among the ciphertext components in a way that the information of x is lost except for $\langle x, y_i\rangle$, where i is an index that is corrupted or the corresponding public key is generated by the adversary herself. This means that the information of x does not leak to the adversary more than necessary, since $\langle x, y_i\rangle$ for such i is revealed to the adversary anyway by the correctness of the protocol. The full construction and analysis are provided in Sect. 6.

Barriers for Proving the Security Under Standard Assumptions: Before moving to the overview of the construction of the registered ABIPFE, we briefly discuss the barriers for proving the security of our registered IPFE scheme under standard assumptions. First, even though the IPFE scheme by [2] can be proven secure from the standard assumption, we cannot hope the same for our scheme at least trivially. One obstacle is the usage of the randomness $\{\beta_i\}_{i\in[L]}$ introduced for separating the threads of computation (Please see Attempts 2 and 3 in this subsection). For this randomness to work effectively, we need that they are not known to the reduction algorithm in the clear and should come from the problem instance. However, if this is the case, the security problem on which our scheme depends should be a q-type assumption, where the size of the problem instance is parameterized by L (i.e., the number of randomness β_i). Furthermore, even using non-standard q-type assumptions, we do not know how to prove the security of our scheme because of the following reasons. First, we observe that our proof relies on the argument that the decryption result should be masked by the term $g_T^{sr_i}$ for user index i corresponding to an honest user when we compute $e(W^s, g_2^{1/\beta_i})$ (Please refer to Eq. (3)). Translating this discussion into the standard model case, we may want the term $g_T^{sr_i}$ to be pseudorandom to mask the decryption result, which makes the entire term $e(W^s, g_2^{1/\beta_i})$ pseudorandom as well. On the other hand, for an index i that is corrupted, $e(W^s, g_2^{1/\beta_i})$ should give the decryption result and thus should be structured. Combining these two observations, in the reduction, we need to simulate W^s so that $e(W^s, g_2^{1/\beta_i})$ should be pseudorandom for honest user index i and should be structured for corrupted user index i. It seems that these two contradicting requirements cannot be satisfied simultaneously in the standard model. To resolve this, a possible approach is to replace W^s and g_2^{1/β_i} with an IPFE ciphertext and secret key respectively and to program the decryption results into it in the security proof.

However, this requires the size of the ciphertext to be at least linear in the number of users in the system, which ruins the compactness of the ciphertexts. In the GGM, we only have to argue that the adversary cannot cancel the term $g_T^{sr_i}$, which is enough for arguing that the decryption result is masked.

Registered ABIPFE: Our pairing-based registered ABIPFE scheme provides attribute-based access control over IPFE. In the slotted version, each user is registered with a vector $\boldsymbol{y}_i$ and an attribute set Att_i whereas the encryption of $\boldsymbol{x}$ is performed under an access policy P which is represented by a linear secret sharing scheme (LSSS). We recall that an access structure of LSSS is specified by a matrix $\mathbf{M} \in \mathbb{Z}_p^{K \times N}$ and a mapping ρ which associates distinct attributes to the row indices of $\mathbf{M}$. To share a secret s, we first sample a random vector $\boldsymbol{v} = (s, v_2, \ldots, v_N)$ and compute the shares $\boldsymbol{u} = \mathbf{M}\boldsymbol{v}$. The i-th component of $\boldsymbol{u}$ is the share associated with the attribute $\rho(i)$. The reconstruction of the secret is possible with a set of attributes Att that satisfies the access structure. More specifically, there exists a vector $\boldsymbol{\omega}$ such that $\boldsymbol{\omega}^\top \boldsymbol{u}_{\mathsf{Att}} = \mathbf{M}_{\mathsf{Att}}\boldsymbol{v} = s$ where $\mathbf{M}_{\mathsf{Att}}$ is the matrix formed by the rows of $\mathbf{M}$ associated with the attributes in Att via the mapping ρ and $\boldsymbol{u}_{\mathsf{Att}}$ is the components of $\boldsymbol{u}$ associated with Att.

At a very high level, our slotted registered ABIPFE is a combination of the registered ABE of [73] and our registered IPFE discussed above. Combining the primitives ABE and IPFE, even in the non-registration-based setting, in a completely generic way might be insecure [3,103] since the ABE adversary is not allowed to query any secret key that decrypts the challenge ciphertext. However, this is crucial for the security of ABIPFE. Our approach aims to blend the *attribute-aggregation* procedure devised for the registered ABE of [73] with the *function-aggregation* technique developed in this work for our registered IPFE. The aggregated master public key consists of two aggregated components—one for attributes and another for function vectors—which are randomized using a newly sampled group element during encryption. This additional randomization adds an extra layer of security to the encryption process, making it (computationally) difficult for *unauthorized* users to gain access to the inner product values, even if they possess secret keys.

Let $\mathcal{U}_{\mathsf{att}}$ be the universe of attributes. Then, for each attribute $w \in \mathcal{U}_{\mathsf{att}}$ and slot $i \in [L]$, the setup randomly samples $t_{i,w} \leftarrow \mathbb{Z}_p$ and adds the additional elements $\{g_1^{1/\pi}, \{g_1^{\beta_i t_{i,w}}\}_{i,w}, \{g_2^{\pi \beta_i t_{i,w}/\beta_j}\}_{i \neq j}\}$ to the crs (given in Eq. 1) of the registered IPFE. The users can sample their individual key pairs similar to our registered IPFE. At the aggregation step, each user submits a pair $(\boldsymbol{y}_i, \mathsf{Att}_i)$ comprising of a vector and an attribute set along with its public key pk_i. The aggregation algorithm follows exactly the same way as in IPFE except it adds new components: $\{T_w = \prod_{i \in [L], w \notin \mathsf{Att}_i} g_1^{\beta_i t_{i,w}}\}_w$ to MPK and $\prod_{j \neq i: w \notin \mathsf{Att}_j} g_2^{\pi \beta_j t_{j,w}/\beta_i}$ to hsk_i of Eq. 2. Therefore, the sizes of MPK and hsk_i both are bounded by $\mathsf{poly}(\lambda, |\mathcal{U}_{\mathsf{att}}|, n, \log L)$, meeting the efficiency requirement of a slotted registered FE scheme. A ciphertext encrypting a vector $\boldsymbol{x}$ under a policy $(\mathbf{M}, \rho)$ is computed as follows. Our idea is to randomize the ciphertext component W^s of IPFE with a random element $h \leftarrow \mathbb{G}_1$ as $h^s \cdot W^s$. At the time of decryption, it eventually produces an additional masking factor $e(h, g_2)^{s/\beta_i}$ which can only be cancelled using a secret key sk_i that corresponds to Att_i satisfying the policy $(\mathbf{M}, \rho)$. More specifically, we first sample a random vector $\boldsymbol{v} = (s, v_2, \ldots, v_N)$ and then set the ciphertext

$$\mathsf{ct} = (\ g_T^s, g_T^{s\alpha+x}, g_1^{-s/\gamma}, g_1^{-s/\pi}, h^s W^s, h^{\langle v, m_k \rangle} T_{\rho(k)}^s\ )$$

where $\boldsymbol{m}_k$ denotes the k-th row of $\mathbf{M}$. To decrypt the ciphertext the i-th user first computes a slot-specific component $e(h, g_2)^{s/\beta_i} \cdot e(g_1, g_2)^{s\langle \alpha, y_i \rangle}$ using the ciphertext components $h^s W^s, g_1^{-s/\gamma}$, secret key sk_i and a component (same as the i-th helper decryption key of IPFE shown in Eq. 2) of hsk_i. Next, assuming that Att_i satisfies the policy, the user reconstruct the secret s in the form of $e(h, g_2)^{s/\beta_i}$ via pairing the ciphertext components $h^{\langle v, m_k \rangle} T_{\rho(k)}^s, g_1^{-s/\pi}$ with g_2^{1/β_i} and the newly added helper decryption key component $\prod_{j \neq i: w \notin \mathsf{Att}_j} g_2^{\pi \beta_j t_{j,w}/\beta_i}$ respectively. In this step, we avail a *cross-terms cancellation* approach similar to [73]. Finally, the user recovers the inner product value $\langle \boldsymbol{x}, \boldsymbol{y}_i \rangle$ from $g_T^{s\langle \alpha, y_i \rangle + \langle x, y_i \rangle}$ by unmasking it using the term $g_T^{s\langle \alpha, y_i \rangle}$. To prove the generic security of the scheme, we show that the *only* way for an adversary to recover the masking term $g_T^{s\langle \alpha, y_i \rangle}$ is to make use of a secret key sk_i which corresponds to an attribute set satisfying the challenge policy. We refer to Sect. 7 for a formal description of the construction and analysis of the slotted registered ABIPFE.

2.3   Registered FE for Polynomial-Size Circuits

In this work, we build a registered FE for all polynomial-size circuits from indistinguishability obfuscation and one-way functions. While our pairing-based registered FEs for specific functionalities could only support a bounded number of users, the registered FE for general functions allows an *arbitrary* number of users to join the system. Our registered FE for all circuits generalizes the IO-based registered ABE of Hohenberger et al. [73] that provides access control using any arbitrary circuit predicates. In particular, it is based on IO [22,55] and somewhere statistically binding hash functions (SSB) [74,98]. An overview of the slotted registered FE is as follows. The crs is an SSB hash key hk. In the key generation phase, each user samples a seed s_i and sets the public key as $\mathsf{pk}_i = \mathsf{PRG}(s_i)$ where PRG is a pseudorandom generator. To register a set of L users, the key curator hashes the list of public key-function pairs $\{(\mathsf{pk}_i, f_i)\}_i$ using hk and sets the hash value h to be the master public key MPK. Additionally, it computes an SSB opening π_i for each slot index i, which serves as the helper decryption key hsk_i of the user. The ciphertext of the slotted scheme consists of a ciphertext CT encrypting the message m under a freshly sampled (symmetric) encryption key SK and an obfuscated circuit which is consistent with MPK and SK. The circuit first verifies (a) the opening π using MPK and (b) the public key pk_i by re-computing $\mathsf{PRG}(\mathsf{sk}_i)$, and if the checks pass then it outputs the message m by decrypting the ciphertext CT using SK. The correctness is immediate by the definition of the obfuscated circuit. The compactness of MPK and hsk_i follows from the *succinctness* of SSB. Since the size of crs (or the hash key) scales with $O(\log L)$, our slotted registered FE can be transformed into a registered FE supporting any arbitrary number of users. We give a detailed description of the scheme in Sect. 8.

3   Preliminaries

Notations: Throughout this paper, we use λ as the security parameter. Let $n, m \in \mathbb{Z}$ be two non-negative integers. Then $[n]$ denotes the set $\{1, 2, \ldots, n\}$ if $n > 0$ and $[n, m]$ denotes the set $\{n, n+1, \ldots, m\}$. We use the bold uppercase letters (e.g. $\mathbf{M}$) to denote matrices and the bold lowercase letters (e.g. $\boldsymbol{x}$) to denote vectors. The components of the vectors are denoted by non-boldface letters (e.g. $\boldsymbol{x} = (x_1, \ldots, x_n)$). We write $\mathsf{poly}(\lambda)$ as a polynomial function of λ if it is of the form $O(\lambda^c)$ for some constant $c \in \mathbb{N}$. We say a function $\mathsf{negl}(\lambda)$ is negligible function of λ if it is of the form $O(\lambda^{-c})$ for all $c > 0$.

Bilinear Groups: Assume a bilinear group generator algorithm GG that takes as input 1^λ and outputs a tuple $\mathcal{G} = (\mathbb{G}_1, \mathbb{G}_2, \mathbb{G}_T, p, g_1, g_2, e)$, where $\mathbb{G}_1, \mathbb{G}_2$ are the source groups and $\mathbb{G}_T$ is the target group of the same prime order $p = p(\lambda)$ with generators g_1, g_2 respectively. The map $e : \mathbb{G}_1 \times \mathbb{G}_2 \to \mathbb{G}_T$ satisfies *non-degeneracy*, meaning that $e(g_1, g_2) = g_T$ generates $\mathbb{G}_T$. It also satisfies bilinearity, *i.e.*, for all $a, b \in \mathbb{Z}_p$ it holds that $e(g_1^a, g_2^b) = e(g_1, g_2)^{ab}$. We require that the group operations and the bilinear map are efficiently computable. The backgrounds of the generic bilinear group model can be found in the full version [45].

4   Registered Functional Encryption

In this section, we introduce the notion of registered FE for general class of functions. We generalize the registration-based ABE notion of [73] into the setting of FE which goes beyond the all-or-nothing type paradigm.

Definition 1 (Registered Functional Encryption). Let $\mathcal{U}_F = \{\mathcal{F}_\lambda\}_{\lambda \in \mathbb{N}}$ be the universe of functions and $\mathcal{M}$ be the set of messages. A registered functional encryption scheme with function universe $\mathcal{U}_F$ and message space $\mathcal{M}$ is a tuple of efficient algorithms $\mathsf{RFE} = (\mathsf{Setup}, \mathsf{KeyGen}, \mathsf{RegPK}, \mathsf{Enc}, \mathsf{Update}, \mathsf{Dec})$ that work as follows:

$\mathsf{Setup}(1^\lambda, 1^{\ell_f}) \to \mathsf{crs}$: The setup algorithm takes the security parameter λ, the (maximum) size ℓ_f of the functions in $\mathcal{U}_F$ as inputs and outputs a common reference string crs.

$\mathsf{KeyGen}(\mathsf{crs}, \mathsf{aux}) \to (\mathsf{pk}, \mathsf{sk})$: The key generation algorithm takes the common reference string crs, and a (possibly empty) state aux as inputs and outputs a public key pk and a secret key sk.

RegPK(crs, aux, pk, f_{pk}) → (MPK, aux′): The registration algorithm takes a common reference string crs, a (possibly empty) state aux, a public key pk and a function $f_{pk} \in \mathcal{F}_\lambda$ as inputs and outputs a master public key MPK and an updated state aux′. This is a *deterministic* algorithm. Here the subscript pk in f_{pk} simply underlies the fact that the function f_{pk} is associated with the user whose public key is pk.

Enc(MPK, m) → ct: The encryption algorithm takes a master public key MPK and a message $m \in \mathcal{M}$ as inputs and outputs a ciphertext ct.

Update(crs, aux, pk) → hsk: The update algorithm takes a common reference string crs, a state aux and a public key pk as inputs, and outputs a helper decryption key hsk. This is a *deterministic* algorithm.

Dec(sk, hsk, ct) $\in \mathcal{M} \cup \{\mathsf{GetUpdate}, \bot\}$: The decryption algorithm takes a secret key sk, a helper decryption key hsk and ciphertext ct as inputs. The algorithm either outputs a message $m′ \in \mathcal{M}$, a special symbol $\bot$ indicating decryption failure, or a special message GetUpdate indicating an updated helper decryption key is needed to decrypt the ciphertext. This is a *deterministic* algorithm.

The algorithms must satisfy the following properties:

Correctness, Compactness and Update Efficiency: For all security parameters $\lambda \in \mathbb{N}$, all messages $m \in \mathcal{M}$, all functions $f \in \mathcal{F}_\lambda$, we define the following experiment between an adversary $\mathcal{A}$ and a challenger:

- **Setup phase:** The challenger starts by sampling the common reference string crs ← Setup($1^\lambda, 1^{\ell_f}$). It then initializes the auxiliary input aux ← $\bot$ and initial master public key MPK_0 ← $\bot$. It also initializes a counter ctr[reg] ← 0 to keep track of the number of registration queries and another counter ctr[enc] ← 0 to keep track of the number of encryption queries. Finally, it initializes ctr[reg]* ← ∞ as the index for the target key. It gives crs to $\mathcal{A}$.
- **Query phase:** During the query phase, the adversary $\mathcal{A}$ is able to make the following queries:
  - **Register non-target key query:** In a non-target-key registration query, the adversary $\mathcal{A}$ specifies a public key pk and a function $f \in \mathcal{U}_F$. The challenger first increments the counter ctr[reg] ← ctr[reg] + 1 and then registers the key by computing ($\mathsf{MPK}_{ctr[reg],aux′}$) ← RegPK(crs, aux, pk, f). The challenger updates its auxiliary data by setting aux ← aux′ and replies $\mathcal{A}$ with (ctr[reg], $\mathsf{MPK}_{ctr[reg]}$, aux).
  - **Register target key query:** In a target-key registration query, the adversary specifies a function $f^* \in \mathcal{U}_F$. If the adversary has previously made a target-key registration query, then the challenger replies with $\bot$. Otherwise, the challenger increments the counter ctr[reg] ← ctr[reg] + 1, samples (pk*, sk*) ← KeyGen(1^λ, aux), and registers ($\mathsf{MPK}_{ctr[reg],aux′}$) ← RegPK(crs, aux, pk*, f^*). It computes the helper decryption key hsk* ← Update(crs, aux, pk*). The challenger updates its auxiliary data by setting aux ← aux′, stores the index of the target identity ctr[reg]* ← ctr[reg], and replies to $\mathcal{A}$ with (ctr[reg], $\mathsf{MPK}_{ctr[reg]}$, aux, pk*, hsk*, sk*).

- **Encryption query:** In an encryption query, the adversary submits the index $\mathsf{ctr[reg]}^* \leq i \leq \mathsf{ctr[reg]}$ of a public key[6] and a message $m_{\mathsf{ctr[enc]}} \in \mathcal{M}$. If the adversary has not yet registered a target key the challenger replies with $\perp$. Otherwise, the challenger increments the counter $\mathsf{ctr[enc]} \leftarrow \mathsf{ctr[enc]} + 1$ and computes $\mathsf{ct}_{\mathsf{ctr[enc]}} \leftarrow \mathsf{Enc}(\mathsf{MPK}_i, m)$. The challenger replies to $\mathcal{A}$ with $(\mathsf{ctr[enc]}, \mathsf{ct}_{\mathsf{ctr[enc]}})$.
- **Decryption query:** In a decryption query, the adversary submits a ciphertext index $1 \leq j \leq \mathsf{ctr[enc]}$. The challenger computes $m'_j \leftarrow \mathsf{Dec}(\mathsf{sk}^*, \mathsf{hsk}^*, \mathsf{ct}_j)$. If $m'_j = \mathsf{GetUpdate}$, then the challenger computes an updated helper decryption key $\mathsf{hsk}^* \leftarrow \mathsf{Update}(\mathsf{crs}, \mathsf{aux}, \mathsf{pk}^*)$ and recomputes $m'_j \leftarrow \mathsf{Dec}(\mathsf{sk}^*, \mathsf{hsk}^*, \mathsf{ct}_j)$. If $m'_j \neq f^*(m_j)$, the experiment halts with outputs $b = 1$.

If $\mathcal{A}$ has finished making queries and the experiment has not halted (as a result of a decryption query), then the experiment outputs $b = 0$.

We say that RFE is correct, compact and update efficient if for all adversaries $\mathcal{A}$ making at most polynomial number of queries, the following properties hold:

- **Correctness:** There exists a negligible function $\mathsf{negl}(\cdot)$ such that for all $\lambda \in \mathbb{N}$, $\Pr[b = 1] = \mathsf{negl}(\lambda)$ in the above experiment. We say that the scheme satisfies *perfect correctness* if $\Pr[b = 1] = 0$.
- **Compactness:** Let N be the number of registration queries the adversary makes in the above experiment. There exists a universal polynomial $\mathsf{poly}(\cdot, \cdot, \cdot)$ such that for $i \in [N]$, $|\mathsf{MPK}_i| = \mathsf{poly}(\lambda, \ell_f, \log i)$. We also require that the size of the helper decryption key hsk^* satisfy $\mathsf{hsk}^* = \mathsf{poly}(\lambda, \ell_f, \log N)$ (at *all* point of the experiment).
- **Update efficiency:** Let N be the number of registration queries made by $\mathcal{A}$. Then, in the course of the above experiment, the challenger invokes the update algorithm Update at most $O(\log N)$ times where each invocation runs in $\mathsf{poly}(\log N)$ time in the RAM model of computation. Specially, we model Update as a RAM program that has *random* access to its input; thus, the running time of Update in the RAM model can be *smaller* than the input length.

Security: Let $\mathsf{coin} \in \{0, 1\}$ be a bit. We define the following security experiment $\mathsf{Expt}_{\mathcal{A}}^{\mathsf{RFE}}(1^\lambda, \mathsf{coin})$ played between an adversary $\mathcal{A}$ and a challenger.

- **Setup phase:** The challenger samples a common reference string $\mathsf{crs} \leftarrow \mathsf{Setup}(1^\lambda, 1^{\ell_f})$. It then initializes the auxiliary input $\mathsf{aux} \leftarrow \perp$, the initial master public key $\mathsf{MPK} \leftarrow \perp$, a counter $\mathsf{ctr} \leftarrow 0$ for the number of honest-key-registration queries the adversary has made, an empty set of keys $\mathsf{Cor} \leftarrow \emptyset$ for tracking the honestly generated keys that are corrupted in course of the experiment, an empty set of keys $\mathsf{Mal} \leftarrow \emptyset$ which will be filled with the keys

---

[6] The message is encrypted under a master public key which is registered only after the adversary registers a target key since we require the correctness to hold only for the target key.

generated by the adversary and an empty dictionary $D \leftarrow \emptyset$ mapping public keys to registered function. For notational convenience, if $pk \notin D$, then we define $D[pk] := \emptyset$. The challenger gives the crs to $\mathcal{A}$.

- **Query phase:** The adversary $\mathcal{A}$ is allowed to query the following queries:
  - **Registered malicious key query:** In a corrupted key query, $\mathcal{A}$ specifies a public key pk and a function $f \in \mathcal{U}_F$. The challenger registers the key by computing $(MPK', aux') \leftarrow RegPK(crs, aux, pk, f)$. The challenger updates its copy of the public key $MPK \leftarrow MPK'$, its auxiliary data $aux \leftarrow aux'$, adds pk to Mal, and updates $D[pk] \leftarrow D[pk] \cup \{f\}$. It replies to $\mathcal{A}$ with (MPK', aux').
  - **Registered honest key query:** In an honest key query, $\mathcal{A}$ specifies a function $f \in \mathcal{U}_F$. The challenger increments $ctr \leftarrow ctr + 1$ and samples $(pk_{ctr}, sk_{ctr}) \leftarrow KeyGen(crs, aux)$, and registers the key by computing $(MPK', aux') \leftarrow RegPK(crs, aux, pk_{ctr}, f)$. The challenger updates its public key $MPK \leftarrow MPK'$, its auxiliary data $aux \leftarrow aux'$, adds $D[pk_{ctr}] \leftarrow D[pk_{ctr}] \cup \{f\}$. It replies to $\mathcal{A}$ with $(ctr, MPK', aux', pk_{ctr})$.
  - **Corrupt honest key query:** In a corrupt-honest key query, $\mathcal{A}$ specifies an index $1 \leq i \leq ctr$. Let (pk_i, sk_i) be the i-th public/secret key the challenger samples when responding to the i-th honest-key-registration query. The challenger adds pk_i to Cor and replies to $\mathcal{A}$ with sk_i.
- **Challenge phase:** The adversary $\mathcal{A}$ chooses two messages $m_0^*, m_1^* \in \mathcal{M}$. The challenger replies with the challenge ciphertext $ct^* \leftarrow Enc(MPK, m_{coin}^*)$.
- **Output phase:** At the end of the experiment, $\mathcal{A}$ outputs a bit $coin' \in \{0, 1\}$, which is the output of the experiment.

Let $\mathcal{S} = \{f_{pk} \in D[pk] : pk \in Cor \cup Mal\}$. We say an adversary $\mathcal{A}$ is admissible if for all functions $f_{pk} \in \mathcal{S}$, it holds that $f_{pk}(m_0^*) = f_{pk}(m_1^*)$. The registration-based functional encryption scheme RFE is said to be secure if for all admissible adversaries $\mathcal{A}$, there exists a negligible function $negl(\cdot)$ such that for all $\lambda \in \mathbb{N}$,

$$| \Pr[Expt_{\mathcal{A}}^{RFE}(1^\lambda, 0) = 1] - \Pr[Expt_{\mathcal{A}}^{RFE}(1^\lambda, 1) = 1]| = negl(\lambda).$$

Definition 2 (Bounded Registered FE). We say that a registered FE scheme RFE is bounded if there is an *a-priori* bound on the number of registered users in the system. In a bounded RFE, the setup additionally takes a bound parameter 1^L which specifies the maximum number of registered users that can be joined to the system. Similarly, in the correctness and security definition, the adversary is asked to submit the bound 1^L at the beginning and it is restricted to query up to L queries.

Specific function classes of RFE: In this work, we construct RFE schemes for general (polynomial-size) functions from obfuscation as well as bounded RFE schemes for specific function classes from pairings. We consider the following class of registered FEs:

- *Registered Inner Product FE.* The inner product FE or IPFE [2,12] is a specific class of FE which only allows linear computation over the encrypted data.

The function space $\mathcal{U}_F$ and the message space $\mathcal{M}$ are vectors from the set $\mathbb{Z}^n$ for an integer $n \in \mathbb{N}$. In particular, a user registers the public key pk along with a function $f_{\mathsf{pk}} = \boldsymbol{y} \in \mathbb{Z}^n$ and a message $m = \boldsymbol{x} \in \mathbb{Z}^n$ is encrypted using the master public key. During decryption a user recovers the inner product $\langle \boldsymbol{x}, \boldsymbol{y} \rangle$ between the vectors. As in all existing pairing-based IPFE schemes of the literature, our registered IPFE scheme also requires that the inner product value to lie in a polynomial range for efficient extraction of it from the exponent of the target group.

- *Registered Attribute-Based Inner Product FE.* We consider the attribute-based IPFE or ABIPFE [3] which provides attribute-based access control over IPFE. The secret key and message vectors are additionally associated with an attribute set $\mathsf{Att} \subseteq \mathcal{U}_{\mathsf{att}}$ and a policy $P \in \mathcal{P}$ where $\mathcal{U}_{\mathsf{att}}$ and $\mathcal{P}$ are attribute universe and a set of supported policies respectively, and the recovery of the inner product during decryption depends on whether the attribute set is satisfying the policy. In our registration-based setting, a user registers a public key pk with a function $f_{\mathsf{pk}} = (\mathsf{Att}, \boldsymbol{y}) \in \mathsf{PSet}(\mathcal{U}_{\mathsf{att}}) \times \mathbb{Z}^n (= \mathcal{U}_F)$ [7] and the encryption of the message $m = (P, \boldsymbol{x}) \in \mathcal{P} \times \mathbb{Z}^n$ yields a ciphertext where P is made available with it in the clear. The decryption procedure computes $\langle \boldsymbol{x}, \boldsymbol{y} \rangle$ (also belonging to a polynomial range) using the secret key sk of the user if the associated attribute set Att satisfies the policy, *i.e.*, if $P(\mathsf{Att}) = 1$ holds.

5   Slotted Registered Functional Encryption

In this section, we introduce the notion of slotted registered FE which is the core building block for building the full-fledged registered FE scheme.

Definition 3 (Slotted Registered Functional Encryption). Let $\mathcal{U}_F = \{\mathcal{F}_\lambda\}_{\lambda \in \mathbb{N}}$ be the universe of functions and $\mathcal{M}$ be the set of messages. A slotted registered functional encryption scheme with function universe $\mathcal{U}_F$ and message space $\mathcal{M}$ is a tuple of efficient algorithms $\mathsf{SlotRFE} = (\mathsf{Setup}, \mathsf{KeyGen}, \mathsf{IsValid}, \mathsf{Aggregate}, \mathsf{Enc}, \mathsf{Dec})$ that work as follows:

Setup$(1^\lambda, 1^{\|\mathcal{U}_F\|}, 1^L) \to \mathsf{crs}$: The setup algorithm takes the security parameter λ, the (maximum) size $\|\mathcal{U}_F\|$ of the functions in $\mathcal{U}_F$ and the number of slots L (in unary) as inputs and outputs a common reference string crs.

KeyGen$(\mathsf{crs}, i) \to (\mathsf{pk}_i, \mathsf{sk}_i)$: The key generation algorithm takes the common reference string crs, and a slot index $i \in [L]$ as inputs and outputs a public key pk_i and a secret key sk_i for the slot i.

IsValid$(\mathsf{crs}, i, \mathsf{pk}_i) \in \{0, 1\}$: The key-validation algorithm takes a common reference string crs, a slot index $i \in [L]$ and a public key pk_i as inputs and outputs a bit $b \in \{0, 1\}$. This is a *deterministic* algorithm.

Aggregate$(\mathsf{crs}, (\mathsf{pk}_1, f_1), \ldots, (\mathsf{pk}_L, f_L)) \to (\mathsf{MPK}, \mathsf{hsk}_1, \ldots, \mathsf{hsk}_L)$: The aggregate algorithm takes a common reference string crs, a list of L public key-function

---

[7] Here, $\mathsf{PSet}(X)$ denotes the power set of the set X.

pairs $(\mathsf{pk}_1, f_1), \ldots, (\mathsf{pk}_L, f_L)$ as inputs such that $f_i \in \mathcal{F}_\lambda$ for all $i \in [L]$ and outputs a master public key MPK and a collection of helper decryption keys $\mathsf{hsk}_1, \ldots, \mathsf{hsk}_L$. We assume that the master public key is implicitly provided to the users along with their helper decryption keys. This is a *deterministic* algorithm.

Enc$(\mathsf{MPK}, m) \to \mathsf{ct}$: The encryption algorithm takes a master public key MPK and a message $m \in \mathcal{M}$ as inputs and outputs a ciphertext ct.

Dec$(\mathsf{sk}, \mathsf{hsk}, \mathsf{ct}) \in \mathcal{M} \cup \{\bot\}$: The decryption algorithm takes a secret key sk, a helper decryption key hsk and ciphertext ct as inputs and outputs a message m'. This is a *deterministic* algorithm.

The algorithms must satisfy the following properties:

Completeness: For all $\lambda \in \mathbb{N}$, all function classes $\mathcal{U}_F$, and all indices $i \in [L]$,

$$\Pr\left[\mathsf{IsValid}(\mathsf{crs}, i, \mathsf{pk}_i) = 1 :\ \mathsf{crs} \leftarrow \mathsf{Setup}(1^\lambda, 1^{|\mathcal{U}_F|}, 1^L); (\mathsf{pk}_i, \mathsf{sk}_i) \leftarrow \mathsf{KeyGen}(\mathsf{crs}, i)\right] = 1.$$

Correctness: The SlotRFE is said to be correct if for all security parameters $\lambda \in \mathbb{N}$, all possible lengths $L \in \mathbb{N}$, all indices $i \in [L]$, if we sample $\mathsf{crs} \leftarrow \mathsf{Setup}(1^\lambda, 1^{\|\mathcal{U}_F\|}, 1^L)$, $(\mathsf{pk}_i, \mathsf{sk}_i) \leftarrow \mathsf{KeyGen}(\mathsf{crs}, i)$ and for all collections of public keys $\{\mathsf{pk}_j\}_{j \neq i}$ (which may be correlated to pk_i) where $\mathsf{IsValid}(\mathsf{crs}, j, \mathsf{pk}_j) = 1$, all messages $m \in \mathcal{M}$, all functions $f \in \mathcal{F}_\lambda$, the following holds

$$\Pr\left[\mathsf{Dec}(\mathsf{sk}_i, \mathsf{hsk}_i, \mathsf{ct}) = f(m) : \begin{array}{l} (\mathsf{MPK}, \mathsf{hsk}_1, \ldots, \mathsf{hsk}_L) \leftarrow \mathsf{Aggregate}(\mathsf{MPK}, (\mathsf{pk}_1, f_1), \ldots, (\mathsf{pk}_L, f_L)); \\ \mathsf{ct} \leftarrow \mathsf{Enc}(\mathsf{MPK}, m) \end{array}\right] = 1.$$

Compactness: The SlotRFE is said to be compact if there exists a universal polynomial $\mathsf{poly}(\cdot, \cdot, \cdot)$ such that the length of the master public key and individual helper secret keys output by **Aggregate** are bounded by $\mathsf{poly}(\lambda, \|\mathcal{U}_F\|, \log L)$.

The security model essentially stays the same as in our registered FE scheme (Definition 1) except that the adversary is asked to submit a list of L public key-function pair during the challenge phase and the malicious public keys qualify for aggregation *only* if they pass the validity check. We present the security model of SlotRFE formally in the full version [45].

Theorem 1. *Assuming* SlotRFE *is a secure slotted registered functional encryption scheme then there exists a* RFE *which is secure as per Definition 1.*

6 Slotted Registered IPFE from Pairings

The slotted registered inner product functional encryption SlotRIPFE = (Setup, KeyGen, IsValid, Aggregate, Enc, Dec) for a function universe $\mathcal{U}_F = \mathbb{Z}^n$, and message space $\mathcal{M} = \mathbb{Z}^n$ works as follows:

Setup$(1^\lambda, 1^n, L)$: The setup algorithm takes the security parameter λ, the length n of vectors (in unary) and the number of users L (in binary) as inputs and samples $\mathcal{G} = (\mathbb{G}_1, \mathbb{G}_2, \mathbb{G}_T, p, g_1, g_2, e) \leftarrow \mathsf{GG}(1^\lambda)$. The algorithm computes the following terms:

1. Sample $\boldsymbol{\alpha} \leftarrow \mathbb{Z}_p^n, \gamma, \beta_i \leftarrow \mathbb{Z}_p$ for all $i \in [L]$.
2. Compute $\mathbf{Z} := g_T^{\boldsymbol{\alpha}}$ and $\Gamma := g_1^{1/\gamma}$ where $g_T = e(g_1, g_2)$.
3. For each $i \in [L]$, compute $\mathbf{A}_i := g_1^{\beta_i \boldsymbol{\alpha}}, B_i := g_1^{\beta_i}, \tilde{B}_i := g_2^{\beta_i}, D_i := g_2^{1/\beta_i}$.
4. For each slot $i, j \in [L]$ and $i \neq j$, compute $R_{i,j} := g_2^{\gamma \beta_i/\beta_j}, \mathbf{S}_{i,j} := g_2^{\gamma \beta_i \boldsymbol{\alpha}/\beta_j}$.
5. Output the common reference string as

$$\mathsf{crs} := \left(\begin{array}{c} \mathcal{G}, \; \mathbf{Z} = g_T^{\boldsymbol{\alpha}}, \; \Gamma = g_1^{1/\gamma}, \\ \{\mathbf{A}_i = g_1^{\beta_i \boldsymbol{\alpha}}, \; B_i = g_1^{\beta_i}, \; \tilde{B}_i = g_2^{\beta_i}, \; D_i = g_2^{1/\beta_i}\}_{i \in [L], \ell \in [n]}, \\ \{R_{i,j} = g_2^{\gamma \beta_i/\beta_j}, \; \mathbf{S}_{i,j} = g_2^{\gamma \beta_i \boldsymbol{\alpha}/\beta_j}\}_{i,j \in [L], i \neq j} \end{array} \right).$$

KeyGen(crs, i): The key generation algorithm takes the common reference string crs, and a slot index $i \in [L]$ as inputs and works as follows:

1. Sample $r_i \leftarrow \mathbb{Z}_p$ and compute $U_i := B_i^{r_i}, \tilde{U}_i := \tilde{B}_i^{r_i}, P_{i,j} := R_{i,j}^{r_i}$ for all $j \in [L]$ and $j \neq i$.
2. Output the public and secret keys as

$$\mathsf{pk}_i := \left(U_i = g_1^{\beta_i r_i}, \tilde{U}_i = g_2^{\beta_i r_i}, \; \{P_{i,j} = g_2^{\gamma \beta_i r_i/\beta_j}\}_{j \in [L], j \neq i} \right) \text{ and } \mathsf{sk}_i := r_i.$$

IsValid$(\mathsf{crs}, i, \mathsf{pk}_i)$: The public key verification algorithm takes the common reference string crs, a slot index $i \in [L]$ and a public key $\mathsf{pk}_i = (U_i, \tilde{U}_i, \{P_{i,j}\}_{j \in [L], j \neq i})$, and checks the following:

$$e(U_i, g_2) \overset{?}{=} e(g_1, \tilde{U}_i) \text{ and } e(U_i, D_j) \overset{?}{=} e(\Gamma, P_{i,j}) \; \forall j \in [L] \setminus \{i\}.$$

If the check passes then it outputs 1; otherwise 0.

Aggregate$(\mathsf{crs}, (\mathsf{pk}_1, \boldsymbol{y}_1), \ldots, (\mathsf{pk}_L, \boldsymbol{y}_L))$: The aggregate algorithm takes a common reference string crs, a list of L public key-function pairs $(\mathsf{pk}_1, \boldsymbol{y}_1), \ldots, (\mathsf{pk}_L, \boldsymbol{y}_L)$ as inputs such that $\boldsymbol{y}_i \in \mathbb{Z}^n$ and $\mathsf{pk}_i = (U_i, \tilde{U}_i, \{P_{i,j}\}_{j \in [L], j \neq i})$ for all $i \in [L]$. It proceeds as follows:

1. Using $\mathbf{A}_i, U_i$ and $\boldsymbol{y}_i$, compute $W_i := U_i \cdot \prod_{\ell \in [n]} A_{i,\ell}^{y_{i,\ell}} = U_i \cdot g_1^{\beta_i \langle \boldsymbol{y}_i, \boldsymbol{\alpha} \rangle}$, where $A_{i,\ell}$ denotes the ℓ-th entry of $\mathbf{A}_i$.
2. Using $\mathbf{S}_{i,j}$ and $\boldsymbol{y}_i$, compute $S_{j,i} = \prod_{\ell \in [n]} S_{j,i,\ell}^{y_{j,\ell}} = g_2^{\gamma \beta_j \langle \boldsymbol{y}_j, \boldsymbol{\alpha} \rangle/\beta_i}$ for all $i, j \in [L]$ and $j \neq i$, where $S_{j,i,\ell}$ denotes the ℓ-th entry of $\mathbf{S}_{j,i}$.
3. Compute the component of MPK as $W := \prod_{i \in [L]} W_i$.
4. Compute the components of hsk_i as $S_i := \prod_{j \in [L] \setminus \{i\}} S_{j,i}$ and $P_i := \prod_{j \in [L] \setminus \{i\}} P_{j,i}$.
5. Output the master public key and slot-specific helper decryption keys as

$$\mathsf{MPK} := (\mathcal{G}, \mathbf{Z}, \Gamma, W) \text{ and } \mathsf{hsk}_i := S_i \cdot P_i.$$

Enc(MPK, x): The encryption algorithm takes a master public key MPK and a message $x \in \mathbb{Z}^n$ as inputs and proceeds as follows:

1. Sample $s \leftarrow \mathbb{Z}_p$.
2. Compute $C_0 := g_T^s$ and $\mathbf{C}_1 = (g_T^{x_1} \cdot Z_1^s, \ldots, g_T^{x_n} \cdot Z_n^s) = g_T^{x+s\alpha}$ where Z_ℓ denotes the ℓ-th entry of $\mathbf{Z}$.
3. Compute $C_2 := W^{-s}$ and $C_3 := \Gamma^s$.
4. Output the ciphertext

$$\text{ct} := (C_0, \mathbf{C}_1, C_2, C_3).$$

Dec(sk, hsk, ct): The decryption algorithm takes a secret key $\text{sk} = r$, a helper decryption key hsk for the i-th slot and a ciphertext $\text{ct} := (C_0, \mathbf{C}_1, C_2, C_3)$ as inputs and works as follows:

1. Compute the following terms

$$E := e(C_2, D_i) \cdot e(C_3, \text{hsk}) \quad \text{and} \quad C = \prod_{\ell \in [n]} C_{1,\ell}^{y_{i,\ell}}$$

where $C_{1,\ell}$ denotes the ℓ-th entry of $\mathbf{C}_1$.
2. Output the message as $\log_{g_T} \left(C \cdot C_0^{\text{sk}} \cdot E \right)$.

Completeness: Consider a key pair $(\text{pk}_i, \text{sk}_i)$ generated using $\text{KeyGen}(\text{crs}, i; r)$. Then by construction, we have $\text{pk} = (U_i, \tilde{U}_i, \{P_{i,j}\}_{j \in [L], j \neq i})$ where

$$U_i = B_i^{r_i} = g_1^{\beta_i r_i}, \quad \tilde{U}_i = \tilde{B}_i^{r_i} = g_2^{\beta_i r_i} \quad \text{and} \quad P_{i,j} = R_{i,j}^{r_i} = g_2^{\gamma \beta_i r_i / \beta_j}.$$

Therefore, the validity of pk_i is verified using

$$e(U_i, g_2) = e(g_1, g_2)^{\beta_i r_i} = e(g_1, \tilde{U}_i) \quad \text{and}$$
$$e(U_i, D_j) = e(g_1, g_2)^{\beta_i r_i / \beta_j} = e(\Gamma, P_{i,j}) \quad \forall j \in [L] \setminus \{i\}$$

since $D_j = g_2^{1/\beta_j}$ and $\Gamma = g_1^{1/\gamma}$. The RIPFE satisfies completeness since the public key passes all the pairing equations defined by the IsValid algorithm, *i.e.* $\text{IsValid}(\text{crs}, \text{pk}_i)$ outputs 1.

Correctness: Consider a secret key $\text{sk} = r_i$, a helper decryption key $\text{hsk} = S_i \cdot P_i$ and a ciphertext $\text{ct} = (C_0, \mathbf{C}_1, C_2, C_3)$. Then, by construction, we have

$$\text{hsk} = \prod_{j \neq i} g_2^{\gamma r_j \beta_j / \beta_i} \cdot \prod_{\ell \in [n]} \prod_{j \neq i} g_2^{\gamma y_{j,\ell} \alpha_\ell \beta_j / \beta_i} = \prod_{j \neq i} g_2^{\gamma r_j \beta_j / \beta_i} \cdot \prod_{j \neq i} g_2^{\gamma \langle y_j, \alpha \rangle \beta_j / \beta_i},$$

$$C_2 = \prod_{i \in [L]} W_i^{-s} = \prod_{i \in [L]} U_i^{-s} \prod_{i \in [L]} \cdot \prod_{\ell \in [n]} A_{i,\ell}^{-s y_{i,\ell}} = \prod_{i \in [L]} g_1^{-s r_i \beta_i} \cdot \prod_{i \in [L]} g_1^{-s \langle y_i, \alpha \rangle \beta_i},$$

$$e(C_2, D_i) = \prod_{j \in [L]} e(g_1, g_2)^{-sr_j \beta_j / \beta_i} \cdot \prod_{j \in [L]} e(g_1, g_2)^{-s\langle \boldsymbol{y}_j, \boldsymbol{\alpha} \rangle \beta_j / \beta_i},$$

$$e(C_3, \mathsf{hsk}) = \prod_{j \neq i} e(g_1, g_2)^{sr_j \beta_j / \beta_i} \cdot \prod_{j \neq i} e(g_1, g_2)^{s\langle \boldsymbol{y}_j, \boldsymbol{\alpha} \rangle \beta_j / \beta_i},$$

$$C = \prod_{\ell \in [n]} C_{1,\ell}^{y_{i,\ell}} = g_T^{\langle \boldsymbol{x}, \boldsymbol{y}_i \rangle + s \langle \boldsymbol{y}_i, \boldsymbol{\alpha} \rangle}, \quad C_0^{\mathsf{sk}} = g_T^{sr_i}.$$

Therefore, $E = e(C_2, D_i) \cdot e(C_3, \mathsf{hsk}) = e(g_1, g_2)^{-s(r_i + \langle \boldsymbol{y}_i, \boldsymbol{\alpha} \rangle)}$. Hence, the inner product value is obtained as $\log_{g_T} \left(C \cdot C_0^{\mathsf{sk}} \cdot E \right) = \langle \boldsymbol{x}, \boldsymbol{y}_i \rangle$.

Compactness: The master public key contains $O(n)$ group elements and each group element can be represented using $\mathsf{poly}(\lambda)$ bits. Therefore, the master public key size is bounded by $\mathsf{poly}(\lambda, |\mathcal{U}_F|, \log L)$ where $|\mathcal{U}_F| = n$. The helper decryption key contains a single group element. Since the information of the aggregated master public key is given with the helper decryption key the size is also bounded by $\mathsf{poly}(\lambda, |\mathcal{U}_F|, \log L)$.

Security Analysis: We refer to the full version [45] for detailed security analysis in GGM.

7 Slotted Registered ABIPFE from Pairings

In this section, we present our slotted registered attribute-based IPFE scheme based on pairing. The attribute-based access control is provided by the policies represented by linear secret sharing access structures (LSSS). We present the formal definitions of access structures and linear secret-sharing schemes in the full version [45].

The slotted registered attribute-based IPFE SlotRABIPFE = (Setup, KeyGen, IsValid, Aggregate, Enc, Dec) for an attribute universe $\mathcal{U}_{\mathsf{att}}$, a set of policies $\mathcal{P}$ which contains (one-use) LSSS policies of a monotone access structure on $\mathcal{U}_{\mathsf{att}}$, and a function space $\mathcal{U}_F = \mathsf{PSet}(\mathcal{U}_{\mathsf{att}}) \times \mathbb{Z}^n$, message space $\mathcal{M} = \mathcal{P} \times \mathbb{Z}^n$ works as follows:

Setup$(1^\lambda, 1^n, \mathcal{U}_{\mathsf{att}}, L)$: The setup algorithm takes the security parameter λ, the length n of vectors (in unary), the attribute universe $\mathcal{U}_{\mathsf{att}}$ and the number of users L (in binary) as inputs and samples $\mathcal{G} = (\mathbb{G}_1, \mathbb{G}_2, \mathbb{G}_T, p, g_1, g_2, e) \leftarrow \mathsf{GG}(1^\lambda)$. The algorithm computes the following terms:
  1. Sample $\boldsymbol{\alpha} \leftarrow \mathbb{Z}_p^n, \gamma, \pi, \beta_i \leftarrow \mathbb{Z}_p$ for all $i \in [L]$.
  2. Compute $\mathbf{Z} := g_T^{\boldsymbol{\alpha}}$ and $\Gamma := g_1^{1/\gamma}, \Pi := g_1^{1/\pi}$ where $g_T = e(g_1, g_2)$.
  3. For each $i \in [L]$, compute $\mathbf{A}_i := g_1^{\beta_i \boldsymbol{\alpha}}, B_i := g_1^{\beta_i}, \widetilde{B}_i := g_2^{\beta_i}, D_i := g_2^{1/\beta_i}$.
  4. For each slot $i, j \in [L]$ and $i \neq j$, compute $R_{i,j} := g_2^{\beta_i / \beta_j}, \mathbf{S}_{i,j} := g_2^{\gamma \beta_i \boldsymbol{\alpha} / \beta_j}$.
  5. Sample $t_{i,w} \leftarrow \mathbb{Z}_p$ for all $i \in [L], w \in \mathcal{U}_{\mathsf{att}}$.
  6. For all $i, j \in [L]$ with $i \neq j$ and $w \in \mathcal{U}_{\mathsf{att}}$, compute $T_{i,w} := B_i^{t_{i,w}}, H_{i,j,w} := g_2^{\pi \beta_i t_{i,w} / \beta_j}$.

7. Output the common reference string as

$$\mathsf{crs} := \left(\begin{array}{c} \mathcal{G}, \quad \mathbf{Z} = g_T^{\alpha}, \quad \Gamma = g_1^{1/\gamma}, \quad \Pi = g_1^{1/\pi}, \\ \left\{ \mathbf{A}_i = g_1^{\beta_i \alpha}, \; B_i = g_1^{\beta_i}, \; \{T_{i,w} = g_1^{\beta_i t_{i,w}}\}_{w \in \mathcal{U}_{\mathsf{att}}}, \; \widetilde{B}_i = g_2^{\beta_i}, \; D_i = g_2^{1/\beta_i} \right\}_{i \in [L]}, \\ \left\{ R_{i,j} = g_2^{\gamma \beta_i/\beta_j}, \; \mathbf{S}_{i,j} = g_2^{\gamma \beta_i \alpha/\beta_j}, \; H_{i,j,w} = g_2^{\pi \beta_i t_{i,w}/\beta_j} \right\}_{\substack{i,j \in [L], i \neq j, \\ w \in \mathcal{U}_{\mathsf{att}}}} \end{array} \right)$$

KeyGen(crs, i): The key generation algorithm takes the common reference string crs, and a slot index $i \in [L]$ as inputs and works as follows:

1. Sample $r_i \leftarrow \mathbb{Z}_p$ and compute $U_i := B_i^{r_i}, \widetilde{U} = \widetilde{B}_i^{r_i}, P_{i,j} := R_{i,j}^{r_i}$ for all $j \in [L]$ and $j \neq i$.
2. Output the public and secret keys as

$$\mathsf{pk}_i := \left(U_i = g_1^{\beta_i r_i}, \widetilde{U}_i = g_2^{\beta_i r_i}, \; \{P_{i,j} = g_2^{\gamma \beta_i r_i/\beta_j}\}_{j \in [L], j \neq i} \right) \quad \text{and} \quad \mathsf{sk}_i := r_i.$$

IsValid$(\mathsf{crs}, i, \mathsf{pk}_i)$: The public key verification algorithm takes the common reference string crs, a slot index $i \in [L]$ and a public key $\mathsf{pk}_i = (U_i, \widetilde{U}_i, \{P_{i,j}\}_{j \in [L], j \neq i})$, and checks the following:

$$e(U_i, g_2) \overset{?}{=} e(g_1, \widetilde{U}_i) \quad \text{and} \quad e(U_i, D_j) \overset{?}{=} e(\Gamma, P_{i,j}) \quad \forall j \in [L] \setminus \{i\}.$$

If the check passes then it outputs 1; otherwise 0.

Aggregate$(\mathsf{crs}, (\mathsf{pk}_1, \mathsf{Att}_1, \boldsymbol{y}_1), \dots, (\mathsf{pk}_L, \mathsf{Att}_L, \boldsymbol{y}_L))$: The aggregate algorithm takes a common reference string crs, a list of L public key, attribute, function tuple $(\mathsf{pk}_1, \mathsf{Att}_1, \boldsymbol{y}_1), \dots, (\mathsf{pk}_L, \mathsf{Att}_L, \boldsymbol{y}_L)$ as inputs such that $\mathsf{Att}_i \subseteq \mathcal{U}_{\mathsf{att}}, \boldsymbol{y}_i \in \mathbb{Z}^n$ and $\mathsf{pk}_i = (U_i, \widetilde{U}_i, \{P_{i,j}\}_{j \in [L], j \neq i})$ for all $i \in [L]$. It proceeds as follows:

1. Using $\mathbf{A}_i, U_i$ and $\boldsymbol{y}_i$, compute $W_i := U_i \prod_{\ell \in [n]} A_{i,\ell}^{y_{i,\ell}} = g_1^{\beta_i(r_i + \langle \boldsymbol{y}_i, \boldsymbol{\alpha} \rangle)}$, where $A_{i,\ell}$ denotes the ℓ-th entry of $\mathbf{A}_i$.
2. Using $\mathbf{S}_{i,j}$ and $\boldsymbol{y}_i$, compute $S_{j,i} = \prod_{\ell \in [n]} S_{j,i,\ell}^{y_{j,\ell}} = g_2^{\gamma \beta_j \langle \boldsymbol{y}_j, \boldsymbol{\alpha} \rangle / \beta_i}$ for all $i, j \in [L]$ and $j \neq i$, where $S_{j,i,\ell}$ denotes the ℓ-th entry of $\mathbf{S}_{j,i}$.
3. Compute the component of MPK as $W = \prod_{i \in [L]} W_i = \prod_{i \in [L]} g_1^{\beta_i(r_i + \langle \boldsymbol{y}_i, \boldsymbol{\alpha} \rangle)}$.
4. Compute the component of hsk_i as $F_i = S_i \cdot P_i$ where

$$S_i := \prod_{j \in [L] \setminus \{i\}} S_{j,i} = \prod_{j \in [L] \setminus \{i\}} g_2^{\gamma \beta_j \langle \boldsymbol{y}_j, \boldsymbol{\alpha} \rangle / \beta_i}, \quad P_i := \prod_{j \in [L] \setminus \{i\}} P_{j,i} = \prod_{j \in [L] \setminus \{i\}} g_2^{\gamma \beta_i r_i / \beta_j}$$

5. For each $w \in \mathcal{U}_{\mathsf{att}}, i \in [L]$, compute

$$T_w = \prod_{j \in [L]: w \notin \mathsf{Att}_j} T_{j,w} = \prod_{j \in [L]: w \notin \mathsf{Att}_j} g_1^{\beta_j t_{j,w}}, H_{i,w} = \prod_{j \neq i: w \notin \mathsf{Att}_j} H_{j,i,w} = \prod_{j \neq i: w \notin \mathsf{Att}_j} g_2^{\pi \beta_j t_{j,w}/\beta_i}.$$

6. Output the master public key and slot-specific helper decryption keys as

$$\mathsf{MPK} := (\mathcal{G}, \; \mathbf{Z}, \Gamma, \; W, \; \{T_w\}_{w \in \mathcal{U}}) \quad \text{and} \quad \mathsf{hsk}_i := (\mathsf{Att}_i, D_i, \; F_i, \; \{H_{i,w}\}_{w \in \mathcal{U}_{\mathsf{att}}}).$$

Enc(MPK, $(\mathbf{M}, \rho), \boldsymbol{x}$): The encryption algorithm takes a master public key MPK, a policy $(\mathbf{M} \in \mathbb{Z}_p^{K \times N}, \rho : [K] \to \mathcal{U}_{\mathsf{att}})$ where ρ is an injective function mapping the row indices of $\mathbf{M}$ into the attributes in $\mathcal{U}_{\mathsf{att}}$ and a message $\boldsymbol{x} \in \mathbb{Z}^n$ as inputs and proceeds as follows:

1. Sample $h \leftarrow \mathbb{G}_1$ and $s \leftarrow \mathbb{Z}_p$.
2. Compute $C_0 := g_T^s$ and $\mathbf{C}_1 := (g_T^{x_1} \cdot Z_1^s, \ldots, g_T^{x_n} \cdot Z_n^s) = g_T^{\boldsymbol{x} + s\boldsymbol{\alpha}}$ where Z_ℓ denotes the ℓ-th entry of $\mathbf{Z}$.
3. Compute $C_2 := h^{-s} W^{-s}$, $C_3 := \Gamma^s$ and $C_4 := \Pi^s$.
4. Sample $v_2, \ldots, v_N$ and set $\boldsymbol{v} := (s, v_2, \ldots, v_N)$.
5. For each $k \in [K]$, compute $C_{5,k} := h^{\langle \boldsymbol{v}, \boldsymbol{m}_k \rangle} T_{\rho(k)}^{-s}$.
6. Output the ciphertext $\mathsf{ct} := \left((\mathbf{M}, \rho), \ C_0, \mathbf{C}_1, C_2, C_3, C_4, \{C_{5,k}\}_{k \in [K]} \right)$.

Dec(sk, hsk, ct): The decryption algorithm takes a secret key $\mathsf{sk} = r$, a helper decryption key $\mathsf{hsk} = (\mathsf{Att}_i, D_i, F_i, \{H_{i,w}\}_{w \in \mathcal{U}_{\mathsf{att}}})$ for the i-th slot and a ciphertext $\mathsf{ct} := \left((\mathbf{M}, \rho), \ C_0, \mathbf{C}_1, C_2, C_3, C_4, \{C_{5,k}\}_{k \in [K]} \right)$ as inputs and works as follows. If Att_i does not satisfy the policy $(\mathbf{M}, \rho)$ then output $\perp$. Otherwise, there exists $\boldsymbol{\omega} \in \mathbb{Z}_p^{|I|}$ such that $\boldsymbol{\omega}^\top \mathbf{M}_{\mathsf{Att}_i} = \boldsymbol{e}_1^\top$ where $I = \{k \in [K] : \rho(k) \in \mathsf{Att}_i\} = \{k_\iota : \iota \in [|I|]\}$ and $\mathbf{M}_{\mathsf{Att}_i}$ is formed by taking the subset of rows of $\mathbf{M}$ indexed by I.

1. Compute the following terms

$$E_{\mathsf{slot}} = e(C_2, D_i) \cdot e(C_3, F_i) \cdot C_0^{\mathsf{sk}},$$

$$E_{\mathsf{att}} = \prod_{\iota \in [|I|]} \left(e(C_{5,k_\iota}, D_i) \cdot e(C_4, H_{i,\rho(k_\iota)}) \right)^{\omega_\iota} \quad \text{and} \quad C = \prod_{\ell \in [n]} C_{1,\ell}^{y_{i,\ell}}$$

where $C_{1,\ell}$ denotes the ℓ-th entry of $\mathbf{C}_1$.
2. Output the message as $\log_{g_T} (C \cdot E_{\mathsf{slot}} \cdot E_{\mathsf{att}})$.

We discuss the completeness, correctness, compactness and security analysis in GGM of the slotted registered ABIPFE in the full version [45].

8   Slotted Registered FE from Indistinguishability Obfuscation

8.1   Construction

Construction: We use the following cryptographic tools as building blocks:

- A length doubling PRG $\mathsf{PRG} : \{0,1\}^\lambda \to \{0,1\}^{2\lambda}$.
- A secret key encryption scheme $\mathsf{SKE} = (\mathsf{Setup}, \mathsf{Enc}, \mathsf{Dec})$.
- A somewhere statistically binding hash function $\mathsf{SSB} = (\mathsf{Setup}, \mathsf{Hash}, \mathsf{Open}, \mathsf{Vrfy})$.
- An indistinguishability obfuscation $i\mathcal{O}$ for P/poly.

We provide necessary details about these cryptographic building blocks in the full version [45]. The slotted registered functional encryption $\mathsf{SlotRFE} = (\mathsf{Setup}, \mathsf{KeyGen}, \mathsf{IsValid}, \mathsf{Aggregate}, \mathsf{Enc}, \mathsf{Dec})$ for a function universe $\mathcal{U}_F = \{0,1\}^{\ell_f}$, and message space $\mathcal{M}$ works as follows:

Constants: $\mathsf{MPK} = (\mathsf{hk}, h), \mathsf{SK}_j, V = (v_{k,\beta})_{k \in [2\ell_c], \beta \in \{0,1\}}$
Inputs: $\mathsf{sk}_i \in \{0,1\}^\lambda, i \in [L], \mathsf{pk}_i \in \{0,1\}^{2\lambda}, f_i \in \{0,1\}^{\ell_f}, \pi_i \in \{0,1\}^{\ell_{\mathsf{open}}}$, SKE
ciphertexts $\{\mathsf{CT}_j\}_{j \in \{0,1\}}$ and $\sigma_{\mathsf{CT}} = (u_k)_{k \in [2\ell_c]}$

1. Parse $(\mathsf{CT}_0, \mathsf{CT}_1) = (\beta_1, \ldots, \beta_{\ell_c}, \beta_{\ell_c+1}, \ldots, \beta_{2\ell_c}) \in \{0,1\}^{2\ell_c}$.
2. If $\mathsf{SSB.Vrfy}(\mathsf{hk}, h, i, (\mathsf{pk}_i, f_i), \pi_i) = 1 \wedge \mathsf{PRG}(\mathsf{sk}_i) = \mathsf{pk}_i \wedge (\mathsf{PRG}(u_k) = v_{k,\beta_k})_{k \in [2\ell_c]}$
   a. Compute $\widehat{m} \leftarrow \mathsf{SKE.Dec}(\mathsf{SK}_j, \mathsf{CT}_j)$
   b. Output $f_i(\widehat{m})$
3. Else, output $\bot$

Fig. 1. The circuit $C_j = C_j[\mathsf{MPK}, \mathsf{SK}_j, V]$ for $j \in \{0,1\}$

Setup$(1^\lambda, 1^{\ell_f}, L)$: The setup algorithm takes the security parameter λ, the bit-length ℓ_f of a function in $\mathcal{U}_F$ (in unary) and the number of users L (in binary) as inputs and sets $\ell_{\mathsf{blk}} = \ell_f + 2\lambda$, computes $\mathsf{hk} \leftarrow \mathsf{SSB.Setup}(1^\lambda, 1^{\ell_{\mathsf{blk}}}, L, 1)$ and sets $\mathsf{crs} := \mathsf{hk}$. It outputs crs.

Keygen(crs, i): The key generation algorithm takes the common reference string crs, and a slot index $i \in [L]$ as inputs and samples $s_i \leftarrow \{0,1\}^\lambda$. It outputs the public key as $\mathsf{pk}_i := \mathsf{PRG}(s_i)$ and the secret key as $\mathsf{sk}_i := s_i$.

IsValid$(\mathsf{crs}, i, \mathsf{pk}_i)$: The key-validation algorithm takes a common reference string crs, a slot index $i \in [L]$ and a public key pk_i as inputs and outputs 1 if $\mathsf{pk}_i \in \{0,1\}^{2\lambda}$; otherwise outputs 0.

Aggregate$(\mathsf{crs}, (\mathsf{pk}_1, f_1), \ldots, (\mathsf{pk}_L, f_L))$: The aggregate algorithm takes a common reference string crs, a list of L public key-function pairs $(\mathsf{pk}_1, f_1), \ldots, (\mathsf{pk}_L, f_L)$ as inputs such that $f_i \in \mathcal{U}_F$ for all $i \in [L]$. It computes

$$h \leftarrow \mathsf{SSB.Hash}(\mathsf{hk}, (\mathsf{pk}_1, f_1), \ldots, (\mathsf{pk}_L, f_L))$$

and sets $\mathsf{MPK} := (\mathsf{hk}, h)$. For each user $i \in [L]$, the aggregate algorithm computes

$$\pi_i \leftarrow \mathsf{SSB.Open}(\mathsf{hk}, ((\mathsf{pk}_1, f_1), \ldots, (\mathsf{pk}_L, f_L)), i)$$

where we treat each pair $(\mathsf{pk}_i, f_i) \in \{0,1\}^{\ell_{\mathsf{blk}}}$ as one SSB hash-block. It sets $\mathsf{hsk}_i := (i, \mathsf{pk}_i, f_i, \pi_i)$ and outputs $\mathsf{MPK}, \mathsf{hsk}_1, \ldots, \mathsf{hsk}_L$.

Enc(MPK, m): The encryption algorithm takes MPK, and a message $m \in \mathcal{M}$ as inputs and samples $\mathsf{SK}_0, \mathsf{SK}_1 \leftarrow \mathsf{SKE.Setup}(1^\lambda)$, computes

$$\mathsf{CT}_0 \leftarrow \mathsf{SKE.Enc}(\mathsf{SK}_0, m) \text{ and } \mathsf{CT}_1 \leftarrow \mathsf{SKE.Enc}(\mathsf{SK}_1, \mathbf{0}_{|m|}).$$

It writes $(\mathsf{CT}_0, \mathsf{CT}_1) = (\beta_1, \ldots, \beta_{\ell_c}, \beta_{\ell_c+1}, \ldots, \beta_{2\ell_c}) \in \{0,1\}^{2\ell_c}$. The algorithm samples $u_{k,\beta} \leftarrow \{0,1\}^\lambda$ for all $k \in [2\ell_c], \beta \in \{0,1\}$. It computes $V = (v_{k,\beta} := \mathsf{PRG}(u_{k,\beta}))_{k \in [2\ell_c], \beta \in \{0,1\}}$. It constructs the circuit $C_0 = C[\mathsf{MPK}, \mathsf{SK}_0, V]$ as defined in Fig. 1 and computes $\widetilde{C}_0 \leftarrow i\mathcal{O}(1^\lambda, C_0)$. It outputs the ciphertext $\mathsf{ct} := (\mathsf{CT}_0, \mathsf{CT}_1, \widetilde{C}_0, \sigma_{\mathsf{CT}} := (u_{k,\beta_k})_{k \in [2\ell_c]})$.

$\mathsf{Dec}(\mathsf{sk}_i, \mathsf{hsk}_i, \mathsf{ct})$: The decryption algorithm takes a secret key sk_i, a helper decryption key $\mathsf{hsk}_i = (i, \mathsf{pk}_i, f_i, \pi_i)$ and ciphertext $\mathsf{ct} = (\mathsf{CT}_0, \mathsf{CT}_1, \widetilde{C}_0, \sigma_{\mathsf{CT}})$ as inputs and outputs $\widetilde{C}_0(\mathsf{sk}_i, i, \mathsf{pk}_i, f_i, \pi_i, \mathsf{CT}_0, \mathsf{CT}_1, \sigma_{\mathsf{CT}})$.

We discuss the completeness, correctness, compactness and security analysis of the slotted registered FE in the full version [45].

Acknowledgement. The third author was partly supported by JST AIP Acceleration Research JPMJCR22U5 and JST CREST Grant Number JPMJCR22M1.

References

1. Abdalla, M., Benhamouda, F., Kohlweiss, M., Waldner, H.: Decentralizing inner-product functional encryption. In: Lin, D., Sako, K. (eds.) PKC 2019: 22nd International Conference on Theory and Practice of Public Key Cryptography, Part II. Lecture Notes in Computer Science, vol. 11443, pp. 128–157. Springer, Heidelberg (Apr 2019). https://doi.org/10.1007/978-3-030-17259-6_5
2. Abdalla, M., Bourse, F., De Caro, A., Pointcheval, D.: Simple functional encryption schemes for inner products. In: Katz, J. (ed.) PKC 2015: 18th International Conference on Theory and Practice of Public Key Cryptography. Lecture Notes in Computer Science, vol. 9020, pp. 733–751. Springer, Heidelberg (Mar / Apr 2015). https://doi.org/10.1007/978-3-662-46447-2_33
3. Abdalla, M., Catalano, D., Gay, R., Ursu, B.: Inner-product functional encryption with fine-grained access control. In: Moriai, S., Wang, H. (eds.) Advances in Cryptology – ASIACRYPT 2020, Part III. Lecture Notes in Computer Science, vol. 12493, pp. 467–497. Springer, Heidelberg (Dec 2020). https://doi.org/10.1007/978-3-030-64840-4_16
4. Abdalla, M., Catalano, D., Gay, R., Ursu, B.: Inner-product functional encryption with fine-grained access control. IACR Cryptology ePrint Archive, Report 2020/577 (2020)
5. Abdalla, M., Gong, J., Wee, H.: Functional encryption for attribute-weighted sums from k-Lin. In: Micciancio, D., Ristenpart, T. (eds.) Advances in Cryptology – CRYPTO 2020, Part I. Lecture Notes in Computer Science, vol. 12170, pp. 685–716. Springer, Heidelberg (Aug 2020). https://doi.org/10.1007/978-3-030-56784-2_23
6. Agrawal, S.: Stronger security for reusable garbled circuits, general definitions and attacks. In: Katz, J., Shacham, H. (eds.) Advances in Cryptology – CRYPTO 2017, Part I. Lecture Notes in Computer Science, vol. 10401, pp. 3–35. Springer, Heidelberg (Aug 2017). https://doi.org/10.1007/978-3-319-63688-7_1
7. Agrawal, S., Boneh, D., Boyen, X.: Efficient lattice (H)IBE in the standard model. In: Gilbert, H. (ed.) Advances in Cryptology – EUROCRYPT 2010. Lecture Notes in Computer Science, vol. 6110, pp. 553–572. Springer, Heidelberg (May / Jun 2010). https://doi.org/10.1007/978-3-642-13190-5_28
8. Agrawal, S., Boneh, D., Boyen, X.: Lattice basis delegation in fixed dimension and shorter-ciphertext hierarchical IBE. In: Rabin, T. (ed.) Advances in Cryptology – CRYPTO 2010. Lecture Notes in Computer Science, vol. 6223, pp. 98–115. Springer, Heidelberg (Aug 2010). https://doi.org/10.1007/978-3-642-14623-7_6

9. Agrawal, S., Kitagawa, F., Modi, A., Nishimaki, R., Yamada, S., Yamakawa, T.: Bounded functional encryption for turing machines: Adaptive security from general assumptions. In: Kiltz, E., Vaikuntanathan, V. (eds.) TCC 2022: 20th Theory of Cryptography Conference, Part I. Lecture Notes in Computer Science, vol. 13747, pp. 618–647. Springer, Heidelberg (Nov 2022). https://doi.org/10.1007/978-3-031-22318-1_22

10. Agrawal, S., Libert, B., Maitra, M., Titiu, R.: Adaptive simulation security for inner product functional encryption. In: Kiayias, A., Kohlweiss, M., Wallden, P., Zikas, V. (eds.) PKC 2020: 23rd International Conference on Theory and Practice of Public Key Cryptography, Part I. Lecture Notes in Computer Science, vol. 12110, pp. 34–64. Springer, Heidelberg (May 2020). https://doi.org/10.1007/978-3-030-45374-9_2

11. Agrawal, S., Libert, B., Stehlé, D.: Fully secure functional encryption for inner products, from standard assumptions. Cryptology ePrint Archive, Report 2015/608 (2015), https://eprint.iacr.org/2015/608

12. Agrawal, S., Libert, B., Stehlé, D.: Fully secure functional encryption for inner products, from standard assumptions. In: Robshaw, M., Katz, J. (eds.) Advances in Cryptology – CRYPTO 2016, Part III. Lecture Notes in Computer Science, vol. 9816, pp. 333–362. Springer, Heidelberg (Aug 2016). https://doi.org/10.1007/978-3-662-53015-3_12

13. Agrawal, S., Maitra, M., Vempati, N.S., Yamada, S.: Functional encryption for turing machines with dynamic bounded collusion from LWE. In: Malkin, T., Peikert, C. (eds.) Advances in Cryptology – CRYPTO 2021, Part IV. Lecture Notes in Computer Science, vol. 12828, pp. 239–269. Springer, Heidelberg, Virtual Event (Aug 2021). https://doi.org/10.1007/978-3-030-84259-8_9

14. Agrawal, S., Yamada, S.: Optimal broadcast encryption from pairings and LWE. In: Canteaut, A., Ishai, Y. (eds.) Advances in Cryptology – EUROCRYPT 2020, Part I. Lecture Notes in Computer Science, vol. 12105, pp. 13–43. Springer, Heidelberg (May 2020). https://doi.org/10.1007/978-3-030-45721-1_2

15. Ananth, P., Jain, A.: Indistinguishability obfuscation from compact functional encryption. In: Gennaro, R., Robshaw, M.J.B. (eds.) Advances in Cryptology – CRYPTO 2015, Part I. Lecture Notes in Computer Science, vol. 9215, pp. 308–326. Springer, Heidelberg (Aug 2015). https://doi.org/10.1007/978-3-662-47989-6_15

16. Ananth, P., Jain, A., Sahai, A.: Indistinguishability obfuscation from functional encryption for simple functions. Cryptology ePrint Archive, Report 2015/730 (2015), https://eprint.iacr.org/2015/730

17. Ananth, P., Vaikuntanathan, V.: Optimal bounded-collusion secure functional encryption. In: Hofheinz, D., Rosen, A. (eds.) TCC 2019: 17th Theory of Cryptography Conference, Part I. Lecture Notes in Computer Science, vol. 11891, pp. 174–198. Springer, Heidelberg (Dec 2019). https://doi.org/10.1007/978-3-030-36030-6_8

18. Ananth, P.V., Sahai, A.: Functional encryption for turing machines. In: Kushilevitz, E., Malkin, T. (eds.) TCC 2016-A: 13th Theory of Cryptography Conference, Part I. Lecture Notes in Computer Science, vol. 9562, pp. 125–153. Springer, Heidelberg (Jan 2016). https://doi.org/10.1007/978-3-662-49096-9_6

19. Attrapadung, N.: Dual system encryption via doubly selective security: Framework, fully secure functional encryption for regular languages, and more. In: Nguyen, P.Q., Oswald, E. (eds.) Advances in Cryptology – EUROCRYPT 2014.

Lecture Notes in Computer Science, vol. 8441, pp. 557–577. Springer, Heidelberg (May 2014). https://doi.org/10.1007/978-3-642-55220-5_31

20. Badrinarayanan, S., Goyal, V., Jain, A., Sahai, A.: A note on VRFs from verifiable functional encryption. Cryptology ePrint Archive, Report 2017/051 (2017), https://eprint.iacr.org/2017/051

21. Baltico, C.E.Z., Catalano, D., Fiore, D., Gay, R.: Practical functional encryption for quadratic functions with applications to predicate encryption. In: Katz, J., Shacham, H. (eds.) Advances in Cryptology – CRYPTO 2017, Part I. Lecture Notes in Computer Science, vol. 10401, pp. 67–98. Springer, Heidelberg (Aug 2017). https://doi.org/10.1007/978-3-319-63688-7_3

22. Barak, B., Goldreich, O., Impagliazzo, R., Rudich, S., Sahai, A., Vadhan, S.P., Yang, K.: On the (im)possibility of obfuscating programs. In: Kilian, J. (ed.) Advances in Cryptology – CRYPTO 2001. Lecture Notes in Computer Science, vol. 2139, pp. 1–18. Springer, Heidelberg (Aug 2001). https://doi.org/10.1007/3-540-44647-8_1

23. Barbulescu, R., Gaudry, P., Joux, A., Thomé, E.: A heuristic quasi-polynomial algorithm for discrete logarithm in finite fields of small characteristic. In: Nguyen, P.Q., Oswald, E. (eds.) Advances in Cryptology – EUROCRYPT 2014. Lecture Notes in Computer Science, vol. 8441, pp. 1–16. Springer, Heidelberg (May 2014). https://doi.org/10.1007/978-3-642-55220-5_1

24. Benhamouda, F., Bourse, F., Lipmaa, H.: CCA-secure inner-product functional encryption from projective hash functions. In: Fehr, S. (ed.) PKC 2017: 20th International Conference on Theory and Practice of Public Key Cryptography, Part II. Lecture Notes in Computer Science, vol. 10175, pp. 36–66. Springer, Heidelberg (Mar 2017). https://doi.org/10.1007/978-3-662-54388-7_2

25. Bishop, A., Jain, A., Kowalczyk, L.: Function-hiding inner product encryption. In: Iwata, T., Cheon, J.H. (eds.) Advances in Cryptology – ASIACRYPT 2015, Part I. Lecture Notes in Computer Science, vol. 9452, pp. 470–491. Springer, Heidelberg (Nov / Dec 2015). https://doi.org/10.1007/978-3-662-48797-6_20

26. Bitansky, N.: Verifiable random functions from non-interactive witness-indistinguishable proofs. In: Kalai, Y., Reyzin, L. (eds.) TCC 2017: 15th Theory of Cryptography Conference, Part II. Lecture Notes in Computer Science, vol. 10678, pp. 567–594. Springer, Heidelberg (Nov 2017). https://doi.org/10.1007/978-3-319-70503-3_19

27. Bitansky, N., Vaikuntanathan, V.: Indistinguishability obfuscation from functional encryption. In: Guruswami, V. (ed.) 56th Annual Symposium on Foundations of Computer Science. pp. 171–190. IEEE Computer Society Press (Oct 2015). https://doi.org/10.1109/FOCS.2015.20

28. Boneh, D., Boyen, X.: Secure identity based encryption without random oracles. In: Franklin, M. (ed.) Advances in Cryptology – CRYPTO 2004. Lecture Notes in Computer Science, vol. 3152, pp. 443–459. Springer, Heidelberg (Aug 2004). https://doi.org/10.1007/978-3-540-28628-8_27

29. Boneh, D., Franklin, M.K.: Identity-based encryption from the Weil pairing. In: Kilian, J. (ed.) Advances in Cryptology – CRYPTO 2001. Lecture Notes in Computer Science, vol. 2139, pp. 213–229. Springer, Heidelberg (Aug 2001). https://doi.org/10.1007/3-540-44647-8_13

30. Boneh, D., Gentry, C., Gorbunov, S., Halevi, S., Nikolaenko, V., Segev, G., Vaikuntanathan, V., Vinayagamurthy, D.: Fully key-homomorphic encryption, arithmetic circuit ABE and compact garbled circuits. In: Nguyen, P.Q., Oswald, E. (eds.) Advances in Cryptology – EUROCRYPT 2014. Lecture Notes in Com-

puter Science, vol. 8441, pp. 533–556. Springer, Heidelberg (May 2014). https://doi.org/10.1007/978-3-642-55220-5_30

31. Boneh, D., Gentry, C., Waters, B.: Collusion resistant broadcast encryption with short ciphertexts and private keys. In: Shoup, V. (ed.) Advances in Cryptology – CRYPTO 2005. Lecture Notes in Computer Science, vol. 3621, pp. 258–275. Springer, Heidelberg (Aug 2005). https://doi.org/10.1007/11535218_16

32. Boneh, D., Sahai, A., Waters, B.: Functional encryption: Definitions and challenges. In: Ishai, Y. (ed.) TCC 2011: 8th Theory of Cryptography Conference. Lecture Notes in Computer Science, vol. 6597, pp. 253–273. Springer, Heidelberg (Mar 2011). https://doi.org/10.1007/978-3-642-19571-6_16

33. Branco, P., Lai, R.W.F., Maitra, M., Malavolta, G., Rahimi, A., Woo, I.K.Y.: Traitor tracing without trusted authority from registered functional encryption. Cryptology ePrint Archive, Paper 2024/179 (2024), https://eprint.iacr.org/2024/179

34. Castagnos, G., Laguillaumie, F., Tucker, I.: Practical fully secure unrestricted inner product functional encryption modulo p. In: Peyrin, T., Galbraith, S. (eds.) Advances in Cryptology – ASIACRYPT 2018, Part II. Lecture Notes in Computer Science, vol. 11273, pp. 733–764. Springer, Heidelberg (Dec 2018). https://doi.org/10.1007/978-3-030-03329-3_25

35. Chen, J., Gay, R., Wee, H.: Improved dual system ABE in prime-order groups via predicate encodings. In: Oswald, E., Fischlin, M. (eds.) Advances in Cryptology – EUROCRYPT 2015, Part II. Lecture Notes in Computer Science, vol. 9057, pp. 595–624. Springer, Heidelberg (Apr 2015). https://doi.org/10.1007/978-3-662-46803-6_20

36. Chen, J., Gong, J., Kowalczyk, L., Wee, H.: Unbounded ABE via bilinear entropy expansion, revisited. In: Nielsen, J.B., Rijmen, V. (eds.) Advances in Cryptology – EUROCRYPT 2018, Part I. Lecture Notes in Computer Science, vol. 10820, pp. 503–534. Springer, Heidelberg (Apr / May 2018). https://doi.org/10.1007/978-3-319-78381-9_19

37. Chotard, J., Dufour-Sans, E., Gay, R., Phan, D.H., Pointcheval, D.: Dynamic decentralized functional encryption. In: Micciancio, D., Ristenpart, T. (eds.) Advances in Cryptology – CRYPTO 2020, Part I. Lecture Notes in Computer Science, vol. 12170, pp. 747–775. Springer, Heidelberg (Aug 2020). https://doi.org/10.1007/978-3-030-56784-2_25

38. Cong, K., Eldefrawy, K., Smart, N.P.: Optimizing registration based encryption. Cryptology ePrint Archive, Report 2021/499 (2021), https://eprint.iacr.org/2021/499

39. Connor, R.J., Schuchard, M.: Blind bernoulli trials: A noninteractive protocol for hidden-weight coin flips. In: Heninger, N., Traynor, P. (eds.) USENIX Security 2019: 28th USENIX Security Symposium. pp. 1483–1500. USENIX Association (Aug 2019)

40. Datta, P., Dutta, R., Mukhopadhyay, S.: Functional encryption for inner product with full function privacy. In: Cheng, C.M., Chung, K.M., Persiano, G., Yang, B.Y. (eds.) PKC 2016: 19th International Conference on Theory and Practice of Public Key Cryptography, Part I. Lecture Notes in Computer Science, vol. 9614, pp. 164–195. Springer, Heidelberg (Mar 2016). https://doi.org/10.1007/978-3-662-49384-7_7

41. Datta, P., Okamoto, T., Takashima, K.: Adaptively simulation-secure attribute-hiding predicate encryption. In: Peyrin, T., Galbraith, S. (eds.) Advances in Cryptology – ASIACRYPT 2018, Part II. Lecture Notes in Computer Science, vol.

11273, pp. 640–672. Springer, Heidelberg (Dec 2018). https://doi.org/10.1007/978-3-030-03329-3_22

42. Datta, P., Pal, T.: (Compact) adaptively secure FE for attribute-weighted sums from k-lin. In: Tibouchi, M., Wang, H. (eds.) Advances in Cryptology – ASIACRYPT 2021, Part IV. Lecture Notes in Computer Science, vol. 13093, pp. 434–467. Springer, Heidelberg (Dec 2021). https://doi.org/10.1007/978-3-030-92068-5_15

43. Datta, P., Pal, T.: Decentralized multi-authority attribute-based inner-product FE: Large universe and unbounded. In: Boldyreva, A., Kolesnikov, V. (eds.) PKC 2023: 26th International Conference on Theory and Practice of Public Key Cryptography, Part I. Lecture Notes in Computer Science, vol. 13940, pp. 587–621. Springer, Heidelberg (May 2023). https://doi.org/10.1007/978-3-031-31368-4_21

44. Datta, P., Pal, T., Takashima, K.: Compact FE for unbounded attribute-weighted sums for logspace from SXDH. In: Agrawal, S., Lin, D. (eds.) Advances in Cryptology – ASIACRYPT 2022, Part I. Lecture Notes in Computer Science, vol. 13791, pp. 126–159. Springer, Heidelberg (Dec 2022). https://doi.org/10.1007/978-3-031-22963-3_5

45. Datta, P., Pal, T., Yamada, S.: Registered FE beyond predicates: (attribute-based) linear functions and more. Cryptology ePrint Archive, Paper 2023/457 (2023), https://eprint.iacr.org/2023/457

46. Döttling, N., Kolonelos, D., Lai, R.W.F., Lin, C., Malavolta, G., Rahimi, A.: Efficient laconic cryptography from learning with errors. In: Hazay, C., Stam, M. (eds.) Advances in Cryptology – EUROCRYPT 2023, Part III. Lecture Notes in Computer Science, vol. 14006, pp. 417–446. Springer, Heidelberg (Apr 2023). https://doi.org/10.1007/978-3-031-30620-4_14

47. Dowerah, U., Dutta, S., Mitrokotsa, A., Mukherjee, S., Pal, T.: Unbounded predicate inner product functional encryption from pairings. Journal of Cryptology 36 (2023). https://doi.org/10.1007/s00145-023-09458-2

48. Dufour Sans, E., Pointcheval, D.: Unbounded inner-product functional encryption with succinct keys. In: Deng, R.H., Gauthier-Umaña, V., Ochoa, M., Yung, M. (eds.) ACNS 19: 17th International Conference on Applied Cryptography and Network Security. Lecture Notes in Computer Science, vol. 11464, pp. 426–441. Springer, Heidelberg (Jun 2019). https://doi.org/10.1007/978-3-030-21568-2_21

49. Escala, A., Herold, G., Kiltz, E., Ràfols, C., Villar, J.: An algebraic framework for Diffie-Hellman assumptions. In: Canetti, R., Garay, J.A. (eds.) Advances in Cryptology – CRYPTO 2013, Part II. Lecture Notes in Computer Science, vol. 8043, pp. 129–147. Springer, Heidelberg (Aug 2013). https://doi.org/10.1007/978-3-642-40084-1_8

50. Fiat, A., Shamir, A.: How to prove yourself: Practical solutions to identification and signature problems. In: Odlyzko, A.M. (ed.) Advances in Cryptology – CRYPTO'86. Lecture Notes in Computer Science, vol. 263, pp. 186–194. Springer, Heidelberg (Aug 1987). https://doi.org/10.1007/3-540-47721-7_12

51. Fiore, D., Kolonelos, D., de Perthuis, P.: Cuckoo commitments: Registration-based encryption and key-value map commitments for large spaces. Springer-Verlag (2023)

52. Francati, D., Friolo, D., Maitra, M., Malavolta, G., Rahimi, A., Venturi, D.: Registered (inner-product) functional encryption. In: Guo, J., Steinfeld, R. (eds.) Advances in Cryptology – ASIACRYPT 2023. pp. 98–133. Springer Nature Singapore, Singapore (2023)

53. Freitag, C., Waters, B., Wu, D.J.: How to use (plain) witness encryption: Registered abe, flexible broadcast, and more. Springer-Verlag (2023). https://doi.org/10.1007/978-3-031-38551-3_16

54. Garg, R., Goyal, R., Lu, G., Waters, B.: Dynamic collusion bounded functional encryption from identity-based encryption. In: Dunkelman, O., Dziembowski, S. (eds.) Advances in Cryptology – EUROCRYPT 2022, Part II. Lecture Notes in Computer Science, vol. 13276, pp. 736–763. Springer, Heidelberg (May / Jun 2022). https://doi.org/10.1007/978-3-031-07085-3_25

55. Garg, S., Gentry, C., Halevi, S., Raykova, M., Sahai, A., Waters, B.: Candidate indistinguishability obfuscation and functional encryption for all circuits. In: 54th Annual Symposium on Foundations of Computer Science. pp. 40–49. IEEE Computer Society Press (Oct 2013). https://doi.org/10.1109/FOCS.2013.13

56. Garg, S., Hajiabadi, M., Mahmoody, M., Rahimi, A.: Registration-based encryption: Removing private-key generator from IBE. In: Beimel, A., Dziembowski, S. (eds.) TCC 2018: 16th Theory of Cryptography Conference, Part I. Lecture Notes in Computer Science, vol. 11239, pp. 689–718. Springer, Heidelberg (Nov 2018). https://doi.org/10.1007/978-3-030-03807-6_25

57. Garg, S., Hajiabadi, M., Mahmoody, M., Rahimi, A., Sekar, S.: Registration-based encryption from standard assumptions. In: Lin, D., Sako, K. (eds.) PKC 2019: 22nd International Conference on Theory and Practice of Public Key Cryptography, Part II. Lecture Notes in Computer Science, vol. 11443, pp. 63–93. Springer, Heidelberg (Apr 2019). https://doi.org/10.1007/978-3-030-17259-6_3

58. Garg, S., Pandey, O., Srinivasan, A., Zhandry, M.: Breaking the sub-exponential barrier in obfustopia. In: Coron, J.S., Nielsen, J.B. (eds.) Advances in Cryptology – EUROCRYPT 2017, Part III. Lecture Notes in Computer Science, vol. 10212, pp. 156–181. Springer, Heidelberg (Apr / May 2017). https://doi.org/10.1007/978-3-319-56617-7_6

59. Gay, R.: A new paradigm for public-key functional encryption for degree-2 polynomials. In: Kiayias, A., Kohlweiss, M., Wallden, P., Zikas, V. (eds.) PKC 2020: 23rd International Conference on Theory and Practice of Public Key Cryptography, Part I. Lecture Notes in Computer Science, vol. 12110, pp. 95–120. Springer, Heidelberg (May 2020). https://doi.org/10.1007/978-3-030-45374-9_4

60. Goldwasser, S., Kalai, Y.T., Popa, R.A., Vaikuntanathan, V., Zeldovich, N.: Reusable garbled circuits and succinct functional encryption. In: Boneh, D., Roughgarden, T., Feigenbaum, J. (eds.) 45th Annual ACM Symposium on Theory of Computing. pp. 555–564. ACM Press (Jun 2013). https://doi.org/10.1145/2488608.2488678

61. Göloglu, F., Granger, R., McGuire, G., Zumbrägel, J.: On the function field sieve and the impact of higher splitting probabilities — application to discrete logarithms in $\mathbb{F}_{2^{1971}}$ and $\mathbb{F}_{2^{3164}}$. In: Canetti, R., Garay, J.A. (eds.) Advances in Cryptology – CRYPTO 2013, Part II. Lecture Notes in Computer Science, vol. 8043, pp. 109–128. Springer, Heidelberg (Aug 2013). https://doi.org/10.1007/978-3-642-40084-1_7

62. Gong, J., Waters, B., Wee, H.: ABE for DFA from k-Lin. In: Boldyreva, A., Micciancio, D. (eds.) Advances in Cryptology – CRYPTO 2019, Part II. Lecture Notes in Computer Science, vol. 11693, pp. 732–764. Springer, Heidelberg (Aug 2019). https://doi.org/10.1007/978-3-030-26951-7_25

63. Gong, J., Wee, H.: Adaptively secure ABE for DFA from k-Lin and more. In: Canteaut, A., Ishai, Y. (eds.) Advances in Cryptology – EUROCRYPT 2020,

Part III. Lecture Notes in Computer Science, vol. 12107, pp. 278–308. Springer, Heidelberg (May 2020). https://doi.org/10.1007/978-3-030-45727-3_10

64. Gorbunov, S., Vaikuntanathan, V., Wee, H.: Functional encryption with bounded collusions via multi-party computation. In: Safavi-Naini, R., Canetti, R. (eds.) Advances in Cryptology – CRYPTO 2012. Lecture Notes in Computer Science, vol. 7417, pp. 162–179. Springer, Heidelberg (Aug 2012). https://doi.org/10.1007/978-3-642-32009-5_11

65. Gorbunov, S., Vaikuntanathan, V., Wee, H.: Attribute-based encryption for circuits. In: Boneh, D., Roughgarden, T., Feigenbaum, J. (eds.) 45th Annual ACM Symposium on Theory of Computing. pp. 545–554. ACM Press (Jun 2013). https://doi.org/10.1145/2488608.2488677

66. Gorbunov, S., Vaikuntanathan, V., Wee, H.: Predicate encryption for circuits from LWE. In: Gennaro, R., Robshaw, M.J.B. (eds.) Advances in Cryptology – CRYPTO 2015, Part II. Lecture Notes in Computer Science, vol. 9216, pp. 503–523. Springer, Heidelberg (Aug 2015). https://doi.org/10.1007/978-3-662-48000-7_25

67. Goyal, R., Hohenberger, S., Koppula, V., Waters, B.: A generic approach to constructing and proving verifiable random functions. In: Kalai, Y., Reyzin, L. (eds.) TCC 2017: 15th Theory of Cryptography Conference, Part II. Lecture Notes in Computer Science, vol. 10678, pp. 537–566. Springer, Heidelberg (Nov 2017). https://doi.org/10.1007/978-3-319-70503-3_18

68. Goyal, R., Koppula, V., Waters, B.: Lockable obfuscation. In: Umans, C. (ed.) 58th Annual Symposium on Foundations of Computer Science. pp. 612–621. IEEE Computer Society Press (Oct 2017). https://doi.org/10.1109/FOCS.2017.62

69. Goyal, R., Vusirikala, S.: Verifiable registration-based encryption. In: Micciancio, D., Ristenpart, T. (eds.) Advances in Cryptology – CRYPTO 2020, Part I. Lecture Notes in Computer Science, vol. 12170, pp. 621–651. Springer, Heidelberg (Aug 2020). https://doi.org/10.1007/978-3-030-56784-2_21

70. Goyal, V., Pandey, O., Sahai, A., Waters, B.: Attribute-based encryption for fine-grained access control of encrypted data. In: Juels, A., Wright, R.N., De Capitani di Vimercati, S. (eds.) ACM CCS 2006: 13th Conference on Computer and Communications Security. pp. 89–98. ACM Press (Oct / Nov 2006). https://doi.org/10.1145/1180405.1180418, available as Cryptology ePrint Archive Report 2006/309

71. Groth, J., Sahai, A.: Efficient non-interactive proof systems for bilinear groups. In: Smart, N.P. (ed.) Advances in Cryptology – EUROCRYPT 2008. Lecture Notes in Computer Science, vol. 4965, pp. 415–432. Springer, Heidelberg (Apr 2008). https://doi.org/10.1007/978-3-540-78967-3_24

72. Hemenway, B., Jafargholi, Z., Ostrovsky, R., Scafuro, A., Wichs, D.: Adaptively secure garbled circuits from one-way functions. In: Robshaw, M., Katz, J. (eds.) Advances in Cryptology – CRYPTO 2016, Part III. Lecture Notes in Computer Science, vol. 9816, pp. 149–178. Springer, Heidelberg (Aug 2016). https://doi.org/10.1007/978-3-662-53015-3_6

73. Hohenberger, S., Lu, G., Waters, B., Wu, D.J.: Registered attribute-based encryption. In: Hazay, C., Stam, M. (eds.) Advances in Cryptology – EUROCRYPT 2023, Part III. Lecture Notes in Computer Science, vol. 14006, pp. 511–542. Springer, Heidelberg (Apr 2023). https://doi.org/10.1007/978-3-031-30620-4_17

74. Hubacek, P., Wichs, D.: On the communication complexity of secure function evaluation with long output. In: Roughgarden, T. (ed.) ITCS 2015: 6th Conference

on Innovations in Theoretical Computer Science. pp. 163–172. Association for Computing Machinery (Jan 2015). https://doi.org/10.1145/2688073.2688105

75. Jain, A., Lin, H., Sahai, A.: Indistinguishability obfuscation from well-founded assumptions. In: Khuller, S., Williams, V.V. (eds.) 53rd Annual ACM Symposium on Theory of Computing. pp. 60–73. ACM Press (Jun 2021). https://doi.org/10.1145/3406325.3451093

76. Jain, A., Lin, H., Sahai, A.: Indistinguishability obfuscation from LPN over $\mathbb{F}_p$, DLIN, and PRGs in NC^0. In: Dunkelman, O., Dziembowski, S. (eds.) Advances in Cryptology – EUROCRYPT 2022, Part I. Lecture Notes in Computer Science, vol. 13275, pp. 670–699. Springer, Heidelberg (May / Jun 2022). https://doi.org/10.1007/978-3-031-06944-4_23

77. Joux, A.: Faster index calculus for the medium prime case application to 1175-bit and 1425-bit finite fields. In: Johansson, T., Nguyen, P.Q. (eds.) Advances in Cryptology – EUROCRYPT 2013. Lecture Notes in Computer Science, vol. 7881, pp. 177–193. Springer, Heidelberg (May 2013). https://doi.org/10.1007/978-3-642-38348-9_11

78. Joux, A.: A new index calculus algorithm with complexity $L(1/4 + o(1))$ in small characteristic. In: Lange, T., Lauter, K., Lisonek, P. (eds.) SAC 2013: 20th Annual International Workshop on Selected Areas in Cryptography. Lecture Notes in Computer Science, vol. 8282, pp. 355–379. Springer, Heidelberg (Aug 2014). https://doi.org/10.1007/978-3-662-43414-7_18

79. Katz, J., Sahai, A., Waters, B.: Predicate encryption supporting disjunctions, polynomial equations, and inner products. In: Smart, N.P. (ed.) Advances in Cryptology – EUROCRYPT 2008. Lecture Notes in Computer Science, vol. 4965, pp. 146–162. Springer, Heidelberg (Apr 2008). https://doi.org/10.1007/978-3-540-78967-3_9

80. Kim, S., Lewi, K., Mandal, A., Montgomery, H., Roy, A., Wu, D.J.: Function-hiding inner product encryption is practical. In: Catalano, D., De Prisco, R. (eds.) SCN 18: 11th International Conference on Security in Communication Networks. Lecture Notes in Computer Science, vol. 11035, pp. 544–562. Springer, Heidelberg (Sep 2018). https://doi.org/10.1007/978-3-319-98113-0_29

81. Kitagawa, F., Nishimaki, R., Tanaka, K.: Simple and generic constructions of succinct functional encryption. Journal of Cryptology **34**(3), 25 (Jul 2021). https://doi.org/10.1007/s00145-021-09396-x

82. Kolonelos, D., Malavolta, G., Wee, H.: Distributed broadcast encryption from bilinear groups. Springer-Verlag (2023)

83. Kowalczyk, L., Wee, H.: Compact adaptively secure ABE for NC^1 from k-Lin. In: Ishai, Y., Rijmen, V. (eds.) Advances in Cryptology – EUROCRYPT 2019, Part I. Lecture Notes in Computer Science, vol. 11476, pp. 3–33. Springer, Heidelberg (May 2019). https://doi.org/10.1007/978-3-030-17653-2_1

84. Kowalczyk, L., Wee, H.: Compact adaptively secure ABE for NC^1 from k-Lin. Journal of Cryptology **33**(3), 954–1002 (Jul 2020). https://doi.org/10.1007/s00145-019-09335-x

85. Lai, Q., Liu, F.H., Wang, Z.: New lattice two-stage sampling technique and its applications to functional encryption - stronger security and smaller ciphertexts. In: Canteaut, A., Standaert, F.X. (eds.) Advances in Cryptology – EUROCRYPT 2021, Part I. Lecture Notes in Computer Science, vol. 12696, pp. 498–527. Springer, Heidelberg (Oct 2021). https://doi.org/10.1007/978-3-030-77870-5_18

86. Lamport, L.: Constructing digital signatures from a one way function. Tech. Rep. CSL-98 (October 1979), https://www.microsoft.com/en-us/research/

publication/constructing-digital-signatures-one-way-function/, this paper was published by IEEE in the Proceedings of HICSS-43 in January, 2010.

87. Lewko, A.B., Okamoto, T., Sahai, A., Takashima, K., Waters, B.: Fully secure functional encryption: Attribute-based encryption and (hierarchical) inner product encryption. In: Gilbert, H. (ed.) Advances in Cryptology – EUROCRYPT 2010. Lecture Notes in Computer Science, vol. 6110, pp. 62–91. Springer, Heidelberg (May / Jun 2010). https://doi.org/10.1007/978-3-642-13190-5_4

88. Lewko, A.B., Waters, B.: New techniques for dual system encryption and fully secure HIBE with short ciphertexts. In: Micciancio, D. (ed.) TCC 2010: 7th Theory of Cryptography Conference. Lecture Notes in Computer Science, vol. 5978, pp. 455–479. Springer, Heidelberg (Feb 2010). https://doi.org/10.1007/978-3-642-11799-2_27

89. Lewko, A.B., Waters, B.: Decentralizing attribute-based encryption. In: Paterson, K.G. (ed.) Advances in Cryptology – EUROCRYPT 2011. Lecture Notes in Computer Science, vol. 6632, pp. 568–588. Springer, Heidelberg (May 2011). https://doi.org/10.1007/978-3-642-20465-4_31

90. Lewko, A.B., Waters, B.: New proof methods for attribute-based encryption: Achieving full security through selective techniques. In: Safavi-Naini, R., Canetti, R. (eds.) Advances in Cryptology – CRYPTO 2012. Lecture Notes in Computer Science, vol. 7417, pp. 180–198. Springer, Heidelberg (Aug 2012). https://doi.org/10.1007/978-3-642-32009-5_12

91. Lin, H., Luo, J.: Compact adaptively secure ABE from k-Lin: Beyond NC^1 and towards NL. In: Canteaut, A., Ishai, Y. (eds.) Advances in Cryptology – EUROCRYPT 2020, Part III. Lecture Notes in Computer Science, vol. 12107, pp. 247–277. Springer, Heidelberg (May 2020). https://doi.org/10.1007/978-3-030-45727-3_9

92. Lin, H., Luo, J.: Succinct and adaptively secure ABE for ABP from k-lin. In: Moriai, S., Wang, H. (eds.) Advances in Cryptology – ASIACRYPT 2020, Part III. Lecture Notes in Computer Science, vol. 12493, pp. 437–466. Springer, Heidelberg (Dec 2020). https://doi.org/10.1007/978-3-030-64840-4_15

93. Lin, H., Vaikuntanathan, V.: Indistinguishability obfuscation from DDH-like assumptions on constant-degree graded encodings. In: Dinur, I. (ed.) 57th Annual Symposium on Foundations of Computer Science. pp. 11–20. IEEE Computer Society Press (Oct 2016). https://doi.org/10.1109/FOCS.2016.11

94. Mera, J.M.B., Karmakar, A., Marc, T., Soleimanian, A.: Efficient lattice-based inner-product functional encryption. Cryptology ePrint Archive, Report 2021/046 (2021), https://eprint.iacr.org/2021/046

95. Naor, M., Yung, M.: Public-key cryptosystems provably secure against chosen ciphertext attacks. In: 22nd Annual ACM Symposium on Theory of Computing. pp. 427–437. ACM Press (May 1990). https://doi.org/10.1145/100216.100273

96. Nguyen, K., Pointcheval, D., Schädlich, R.: Dynamic decentralized functional encryption with strong security. Cryptology ePrint Archive, Paper 2022/1532 (2022), https://eprint.iacr.org/2022/1532, https://eprint.iacr.org/2022/1532

97. Nishimaki, R., Wichs, D., Zhandry, M.: Anonymous traitor tracing: How to embed arbitrary information in a key. In: Fischlin, M., Coron, J.S. (eds.) Advances in Cryptology – EUROCRYPT 2016, Part II. Lecture Notes in Computer Science, vol. 9666, pp. 388–419. Springer, Heidelberg (May 2016). https://doi.org/10.1007/978-3-662-49896-5_14

98. Okamoto, T., Pietrzak, K., Waters, B., Wichs, D.: New realizations of somewhere statistically binding hashing and positional accumulators. In: Iwata, T., Cheon,

J.H. (eds.) Advances in Cryptology – ASIACRYPT 2015, Part I. Lecture Notes in Computer Science, vol. 9452, pp. 121–145. Springer, Heidelberg (Nov / Dec 2015). https://doi.org/10.1007/978-3-662-48797-6_6

99. Okamoto, T., Takashima, K.: Fully secure functional encryption with general relations from the decisional linear assumption. In: Rabin, T. (ed.) Advances in Cryptology – CRYPTO 2010. Lecture Notes in Computer Science, vol. 6223, pp. 191–208. Springer, Heidelberg (Aug 2010). https://doi.org/10.1007/978-3-642-14623-7_11

100. Okamoto, T., Takashima, K.: Adaptively attribute-hiding (hierarchical) inner product encryption. In: Pointcheval, D., Johansson, T. (eds.) Advances in Cryptology – EUROCRYPT 2012. Lecture Notes in Computer Science, vol. 7237, pp. 591–608. Springer, Heidelberg (Apr 2012). https://doi.org/10.1007/978-3-642-29011-4_35

101. O'Neill, A.: Definitional issues in functional encryption. Cryptology ePrint Archive, Report 2010/556 (2010), https://eprint.iacr.org/2010/556

102. Pal, T., Dutta, R.: Attribute-based access control for inner product functional encryption from LWE. In: Longa, P., Ràfols, C. (eds.) Progress in Cryptology - LATINCRYPT 2021: 7th International Conference on Cryptology and Information Security in Latin America. Lecture Notes in Computer Science, vol. 12912, pp. 127–148. Springer, Heidelberg, Bogotá, Colombia (Oct 2021). https://doi.org/10.1007/978-3-030-88238-9_7

103. Pal, T., Dutta, R.: Attribute-based access control for inner product functional encryption from LWE. In: Longa, P., Ràfols, C. (eds.) Progress in Cryptology - LATINCRYPT 2021 - 7th International Conference on Cryptology and Information Security in Latin America, Bogotá, Colombia, October 6-8, 2021, Proceedings. Lecture Notes in Computer Science, vol. 12912, pp. 127–148. Springer (2021). https://doi.org/10.1007/978-3-030-88238-9_7, https://doi.org/10.1007/978-3-030-88238-9_7

104. Sahai, A., Waters, B.R.: Fuzzy identity-based encryption. In: Cramer, R. (ed.) Advances in Cryptology – EUROCRYPT 2005. Lecture Notes in Computer Science, vol. 3494, pp. 457–473. Springer, Heidelberg (May 2005). https://doi.org/10.1007/11426639_27

105. Shoup, V.: Lower bounds for discrete logarithms and related problems. In: Fumy, W. (ed.) Advances in Cryptology – EUROCRYPT'97. Lecture Notes in Computer Science, vol. 1233, pp. 256–266. Springer, Heidelberg (May 1997). https://doi.org/10.1007/3-540-69053-0_18

106. Tomida, J.: Tightly secure inner product functional encryption: Multi-input and function-hiding constructions. In: Galbraith, S.D., Moriai, S. (eds.) Advances in Cryptology – ASIACRYPT 2019, Part III. Lecture Notes in Computer Science, vol. 11923, pp. 459–488. Springer, Heidelberg (Dec 2019). https://doi.org/10.1007/978-3-030-34618-8_16

107. Tomida, J.: Unbounded quadratic functional encryption and more from pairings. In: Hazay, C., Stam, M. (eds.) Advances in Cryptology – EUROCRYPT 2023, Part III. Lecture Notes in Computer Science, vol. 14006, pp. 543–572. Springer, Heidelberg (Apr 2023). https://doi.org/10.1007/978-3-031-30620-4_18

108. Tomida, J., Abe, M., Okamoto, T.: Efficient functional encryption for inner-product values with full-hiding security. In: Bishop, M., Nascimento, A.C.A. (eds.) ISC 2016: 19th International Conference on Information Security. Lecture Notes in Computer Science, vol. 9866, pp. 408–425. Springer, Heidelberg (Sep 2016). https://doi.org/10.1007/978-3-319-45871-7_24

109. Tomida, J., Takashima, K.: Unbounded inner product functional encryption from bilinear maps. In: Peyrin, T., Galbraith, S. (eds.) Advances in Cryptology – ASIACRYPT 2018, Part II. Lecture Notes in Computer Science, vol. 11273, pp. 609–639. Springer, Heidelberg (Dec 2018). https://doi.org/10.1007/978-3-030-03329-3_21

110. Wang, Z., Fan, X., Liu, F.H.: FE for inner products and its application to decentralized ABE. In: Lin, D., Sako, K. (eds.) PKC 2019: 22nd International Conference on Theory and Practice of Public Key Cryptography, Part II. Lecture Notes in Computer Science, vol. 11443, pp. 97–127. Springer, Heidelberg (Apr 2019). https://doi.org/10.1007/978-3-030-17259-6_4

111. Waters, B.: Dual system encryption: Realizing fully secure IBE and HIBE under simple assumptions. In: Halevi, S. (ed.) Advances in Cryptology – CRYPTO 2009. Lecture Notes in Computer Science, vol. 5677, pp. 619–636. Springer, Heidelberg (Aug 2009). https://doi.org/10.1007/978-3-642-03356-8_36

112. Waters, B.: Ciphertext-policy attribute-based encryption: An expressive, efficient, and provably secure realization. In: Catalano, D., Fazio, N., Gennaro, R., Nicolosi, A. (eds.) PKC 2011: 14th International Conference on Theory and Practice of Public Key Cryptography. Lecture Notes in Computer Science, vol. 6571, pp. 53–70. Springer, Heidelberg (Mar 2011). https://doi.org/10.1007/978-3-642-19379-8_4

113. Waters, B.: Functional encryption for regular languages. In: Safavi-Naini, R., Canetti, R. (eds.) Advances in Cryptology – CRYPTO 2012. Lecture Notes in Computer Science, vol. 7417, pp. 218–235. Springer, Heidelberg (Aug 2012). https://doi.org/10.1007/978-3-642-32009-5_14

114. Wee, H.: Dual system encryption via predicate encodings. In: Lindell, Y. (ed.) TCC 2014: 11th Theory of Cryptography Conference. Lecture Notes in Computer Science, vol. 8349, pp. 616–637. Springer, Heidelberg (Feb 2014). https://doi.org/10.1007/978-3-642-54242-8_26

115. Wee, H.: Attribute-hiding predicate encryption in bilinear groups, revisited. In: Kalai, Y., Reyzin, L. (eds.) TCC 2017: 15th Theory of Cryptography Conference, Part I. Lecture Notes in Computer Science, vol. 10677, pp. 206–233. Springer, Heidelberg (Nov 2017). https://doi.org/10.1007/978-3-319-70500-2_8

116. Wee, H.: Functional encryption for quadratic functions from k-lin, revisited. In: Pass, R., Pietrzak, K. (eds.) TCC 2020: 18th Theory of Cryptography Conference, Part I. Lecture Notes in Computer Science, vol. 12550, pp. 210–228. Springer, Heidelberg (Nov 2020). https://doi.org/10.1007/978-3-030-64375-1_8

117. Wee, H.: Broadcast encryption with size $N^{1/3}$ and more from k-lin. In: Malkin, T., Peikert, C. (eds.) Advances in Cryptology – CRYPTO 2021, Part IV. Lecture Notes in Computer Science, vol. 12828, pp. 155–178. Springer, Heidelberg, Virtual Event (Aug 2021). https://doi.org/10.1007/978-3-030-84259-8_6

118. Wee, H.: Optimal broadcast encryption and CP-ABE from evasive lattice assumptions. In: Dunkelman, O., Dziembowski, S. (eds.) Advances in Cryptology – EUROCRYPT 2022, Part II. Lecture Notes in Computer Science, vol. 13276, pp. 217–241. Springer, Heidelberg (May / Jun 2022). https://doi.org/10.1007/978-3-031-07085-3_8

119. Zhu, Z., Li, J., Zhang, K., Gong, J., Qian, H.: Registered functional encryptions from pairings. In: Joye, M., Leander, G. (eds.) Advances in Cryptology – EUROCRYPT 2024. pp. 373–402. Springer Nature Switzerland, Cham (2024)

120. Zhu, Z., Zhang, K., Gong, J., Qian, H.: Registered abe via predicate encodings. Springer-Verlag (2023)

Updatable Privacy-Preserving Blueprints

Bernardo David[1]([✉]), Felix Engelmann[2][iD], Tore Frederiksen[3],
Markulf Kohlweiss[4][iD], Elena Pagnin[5][iD], and Mikhail Volkhov[4,6]

[1] IT University of Copenhagen, Copenhagen, Denmark
beda@itu.dk
[2] Lund University, Lund, Sweden
fe-research@nlogn.org
[3] Zama, Paris, France
tore.frederiksen@zama.ai
[4] University of Edinburgh, IOG, Edinburgh, UK
mkohlwei@ed.ac.uk, misha@o1labs.org
[5] Chalmers University of Technology and University of Gothenburg,
Gothenburg, Sweden
elenap@chalmers.se
[6] O1Labs, Edinburgh, UK

Abstract. Privacy-preserving blueprint schemes (Kohlweiss et al.,
EUROCRYPT'23) offer a mechanism for safeguarding user's privacy
while allowing for specific legitimate controls by a designated auditor
agent. These schemes enable users to create *escrows* encrypting the result
of evaluating a function $y = P(t, x)$, with P being publicly known, t a
secret used during the auditor's key generation, and x the user's private
input. Crucially, escrows only disclose the *blueprinting* result $y = P(t, x)$
to the designated auditor, even in cases where the auditor is fully com-
promised. The original definition and construction only support the evaluation of functions P on an input x provided by a *single* user.

We address this limitation by introducing *updatable* privacy-
preserving blueprint schemes (UPPB), which enhance the original notion
with the ability for multiple users to non-interactively update the private
user input x while blueprinting. Moreover, UPPBs contain a proof that
y is the result of a *sequence of valid updates*, while revealing nothing
else about the private inputs $\{x_i\}$ of updates. As in the case of privacy-
preserving blueprints, we first observe that UPPBs can be realized via a
generic construction for arbitrary predicates P based on FHE and NIZKs.
Our main result is uBlu, an efficient instantiation for a specific predicate
comparing the values x and t, where x is the cumulative sum of users'
private inputs and t is a fixed private value provided by the auditor in the
setup phase. This rather specific setting already finds interesting applications such as privacy-preserving anti-money laundering and location
tracking, and can be extended to support more generic predicates.

B. David—Work supported by DIREC and by Independent Research Fund Denmark
grants number 9040-00399B (TrA^{2}C)and 0165-00079B.
F. Engelmann—Part of this work was done while at the IT University of Copenhagen.
T. Frederiksen—Part of this work was done while at the Alexandra Institute.

K.-M. Chung and Y. Sasaki (Eds.): ASIACRYPT 2024, LNCS 15484, pp. 105–139, 2025.
https://doi.org/10.1007/978-981-96-0875-1_4

From the technical perspective, we devise a novel technique to keep the escrow size concise, independent of the number of updates, and reasonable for practical applications. We achieve this via a novel characterization of malleability for the algebraic NIZK by Couteau and Hartmann (CRYPTO'20) that allows for an additive update function.

Keywords: Updatable NIZKs · Privacy-Preserving Blueprints

1   Introduction

Data protection often demands that the actions and personal information of individual users be kept private. At the same time, regulatory organizations should be able to learn about potential violations evidenced by the combined actions of multiple users and track down the misbehaving parties. In such scenarios, cryptographic techniques such as multiparty computation come to mind as potential solutions. While such techniques may trivially reconcile the paradox of privacy vs. accountability, they often impose performance overheads and trust assumptions that are incompatible with the original scenario.

Multiparty computation (MPC) [21,40] is a natural solution for auditing private data without undermining the privacy of users or jeopardizing the audit process by revealing sensitive audit parameters. An auditor could execute an efficient MPC protocol (*e.g.*, [28]) together with users to audit their data while only revealing the final audit result. However, traditional MPC requires *all* participating parties to interact in *each* computation.It is unrealistic to require all users to interact with each other at once, as opposed to only interacting when generating the audit data, as parties may simply be unavailable or technically incapable of executing long-running complex protocols. Moreover, processing large volumes of audit data via traditional MPC would prove prohibitively expensive due to the network interaction required from *all* participating parties.

Privacy-Preserving Blueprints: Adding Updates. A privacy-preserving blueprint scheme [43,48] allows a user to create an *escrow* that encodes the output of a function $P(t, x)$ from a "recipe" data posted earlier by the auditor (called a blueprint[1]),but reveals nothing else about the blueprint inputs. In this setting, P is public, t is a private input from the auditor, and x is a private input from the user. This notion allows an auditor, who sees an escrow for the value $y = P(t, x)$, to non-interactively learn y, allowing for asynchronous audits. However, $P(t, x)$ can only be computed on an input x that is fully known to a single party who generates the escrow. This is clearly insufficient when inputs come from multiple mutually distrusting users and the original constructions of blueprints cannot be efficiently extended to this case. We focus on overcoming this limitation with the notion of *updatable* privacy-preserving blueprints, which allow a party departing

---

[1] We use the term "blueprint" quite informally. The *concrete* data in our protocol is hints, tags, and escrows, where hints are semantically the closest term to "blueprint".

from an initial blueprint for $P(t,x)$ to obtain an updated blueprint for $P(t,x')$, where x' is an output of a function of the current x and the party's private input x_i, without learning anything about t or x. Moreover, our notion allows for parties to check that a sequence of blueprints has been obtained by successive updates done by different parties using their respective private inputs, without learning anything else. Our main construction supports evaluating predicates of the form "output 1 if $x_1 + \cdots + x_n \in [t, t+d)$, and 0 otherwise", where each x_i is added to the blueprint as an update by a different party. Furthermore, we show how updatable blueprints can work with more generic predicates (expressible via multivariate polynomials) and non-binary outputs, allowing more elaborate applications including privacy-preserving location testing.

Applications of Updatable Privacy-Preserving Blueprints. Our new notion can be seen as a type of MPC and therefore can be used in different areas, such as privacy-preserving auditing, financial accountability, reputation systems, private auctions, or voting. The common trait in these applications is that they involve both sensitive audit parameters provided by authorities (or a collective of users) and the private data of multiple individual parties. Current approaches, especially in financial regulation-compliance, sacrifice either privacy (when legally possible) or accuracy, which is lost as a result of auditing incomplete data.

While the notion of updatable privacy-preserving blueprints is generic, our running motivational example is implementing anti-money laundering (AML) policies. Traditional banks mostly do AML by manually inspecting an account if its suspiciousness score (expressing how risky the account is) is above a certain threshold [6]. The score is first computed from private account metadata and updated based only on local account activity, which precludes using valuable information held by other banks (e.g., the reputation of parties transferring money into the account) and results in high false-positive rates. In decentralized finance, AML schemes for privacy-preserving cryptocurrencies either only support auditing users in isolation [32,54] or rely on revocable anonymity [2,26,47], requiring the auditor to learn all information about users' activities, severely undermining their privacy. Updatable blueprints can address these issues in both scenarios by enabling privacy-preserving AML audits on joint data from multiple users.

Intuitively, an updatable blueprint scheme can be used to securely compute and validate a suspiciousness score for the users' bank accounts based on the features of transactions between multiple banks—and the private information these banks hold about their customers. A blueprint is attached to each account to accumulate a score that is based on the reputation of customers at other banks transferring funds into the account. Before such a transfer, the sending bank must receive the up-to-date blueprint of the suspiciousness score from the receiving bank. It then sends, along with the transfer, an updated blueprint that includes the new value x_i corresponding to the transaction and the reputation of the sending account owner. Upon receiving the transfer, the receiving bank records the updated blueprint as the new up-to-date blueprint. At any moment, an auditor (*e.g.* a tax authority) can validate the correctness of this procedure and check if a user's score exceeds a certain threshold without learning the score. If so, the auditor can further request the opening of related commitments held by other banks. Crucially, none of these operations require users or banks to perform any extra rounds of communication, i.e., updatable blueprints only add minimal overhead to the existing communication and computation involved in transfers. A similar idea can be used to enforce limits on the amount of funds transferred in decentralized finance applications using cryptocurrencies.

1.1   Our Contributions

In this work, we introduce the notion of *updatable* privacy-preserving blueprints, constructions, and applications. Our main results are summarized as follows:

Updatable Privacy-Preserving Blueprint: In Sect. 4, we introduce our new notion, extending privacy-preserving blueprints [48] to allow for an auditor to learn a predicate $P(t, x)$ of their own private input t and users' private inputs x such that users can update x in an existing blueprint.

Efficient Construction for Range Predicates: In Sect. 5, we present uBlu, an efficient realization of UPPB for a comparison predicate between private user inputs and a private threshold set by the auditor. This includes an update mechanism that allows users to update the current input value.

Succinct Updatable Algebraic NIZK: As a core technique in our construction, we show in Sect. 3 that we can extend the NIZK proof system of [23] to allow for updating the witness and the instance of an existing NIZK while maintaining its efficiency and security. More details in the full version [29]

Prototype Implementation and Benchmarks: In Sect. 6, we present benchmarks obtained with a prototype implementation of our uBlu construction, which showcase its performance and scalability.

In the full version of this work [29] we further discuss application venues for UPPB, and possible extensions, we provide an overview in Sect. 5.6.

We remark that the main technical contribution of this work is a mechanism for updatable range predicates. At the core of this construction, we perform homomorphic computation of polynomials with coefficients contained in ElGamal ciphertexts (which encode a private threshold t) on a point contained in a Pedersen commitment, which may be updated as needed. Our techniques allow us to construct *sound* blueprints that *do not grow with the number of updates*, and are reasonably sized for practical applications. By investigating and employing the updatability of CH20 NIZK [23], we construct efficient and concise proofs that a given ElGamal ciphertext contains a correct evaluation of a polynomial whose coefficients are contained in other ElGamal ciphertexts on a point x contained in a Pedersen commitment. Furthermore, when the value x in the commitment is updated, our NIZKs can also be updated without revealing the previous x or the polynomial coefficients, while retaining its conciseness and efficiency.

1.2 Overview of Our Techniques

The Notion of Updatable Privacy-Preserving Blueprints. A UPPB scheme is defined in terms of a base commitment scheme and a public predicate $P(t, x)$ taking two private inputs: a fixed value t generated by a designated auditor party; and an aggregate value $x = \mathsf{fold}(x_1, \ldots, x_n)$ where fold is an online streaming algorithm. In our concrete instantiation we employ $\mathsf{fold}(x_1, \ldots, x_n) = \sum_{i=1}^{n} x_i$. Each x_i is provided by a potential different user in *committed* form. UPPBs implement a mechanism that allows users to contribute in generating a sequence of *hints* and *tags*, where each hint-tag pair encodes—among other things—the blueprint value $P(t, x)$. Given a hint, a user can then generate a corresponding *escrow* that proves—to a designated auditor—the blueprint value $P(t, \mathsf{fold}(x_1, \ldots, x_n))$ encoded in the hint, as well as the validity of the sequence of updates applied to the hint (according to fold). Hence, the updatable functionality for blueprints requires several components: escrows esc, tags tag, hints hint, and commitments $\mathfrak{C}$. Usually, one escrow is connected to an ordered sequence of tags, hints and commitments, that we informally refer to as *history*. Next, we elaborate on how these components interact.

Given an escrow esc for a history of commitments $\{\mathfrak{C}_i\}$ to the values $\{x_i\}$, the auditor learns the value of $P(t, \mathsf{fold}(x_1, \ldots, x_n))$ but nothing else, and third parties learn nothing. The auditor generates a key pair $(\mathsf{sk}, \mathsf{pk})$ and an initial blueprint hint_0 for the predicate $P(t, 0)$, where sk and t remain private, pk is published, and hint_0 is passed to the first user. Blueprint hints store the so-far aggregated x, and can be verified against a history of commitments. Specifically, using pk and hint_{i-1}, a user can extend the history with their value x_i, each time deriving an updated hint_i. In our construction, hint_{i-1} will contain an aggregate value $\sum_{j=1}^{i-1} x_j$ that users can update via homomorphic operations to add their private input x_i. A hint_i can be transformed into an escrow, esc, which reveals nothing to the users but can be used by an auditor who knows sk to learn *only* whether $P(t, \sum_{j=1}^{i} x_j) = 1$, while keeping the x_j values private. When a user updates hint_{i-1} to hint_i, they obtain an updated tag_i for verifying the validity and consistency of the commitment history by running $\mathsf{VfHistory}_{\mathsf{pk}}(\{\mathsf{tag}_j, \mathfrak{C}_j\}_{j=1}^{i})$, of the hint by running $\mathsf{VfHint}_{\mathsf{pk}}(\mathsf{hint}_i, \mathsf{tag}_i)$, and of esc by running $\mathsf{VfEscrow}_{\mathsf{pk}}(\mathsf{esc}_i, \mathsf{tag}_i)$. We have the following three properties: (i) tag_i can only verify for a single history, *i.e..*, valid histories do not collide in their tags; (ii) we can extract the openings x_j of all base commitments from a valid history; (iii) if esc verifies with respect to tag_i, then it indeed is an escrow of predicate value $P(t, \sum_{j=1}^{i} x_j)$ for the openings x_j of these base commitments.

We require hints, escrows, and tags derived from valid hints to be hiding. However, as hints contain the aggregate value, $\sum_{j=1}^{i} x_j$, hints are only hiding against adversaries who do not know sk. Thus, hints should only be used for updates between users who cooperate to gain privacy, but must not be given to the auditor as this would leak the current aggregate value. We assume that users trust each other enough to not collude with the auditor, but are otherwise distrusting, e.g. they do not want to share their secret $\{x_i\}$ with each other and want to be able to verify the validity of hints themselves. Finally, our scheme preserves the hiding and binding properties of the base commitment scheme.

A Generic but Inefficient Construction. Building on fully homomorphic encryption (FHE) and generic NIZKs for NP, we can construct a UPPB scheme for arbitrary predicates P and update functions fold as follows. The auditor generates an key pair $(\mathsf{pk}, \mathsf{sk})$ for a circuit private FHE scheme [55], and publishes pk, along with an encryption of t under pk, and an encryption of 0 as the initial hint_0. For any $i > 0$, users can update the blueprint value contained in the hint by first encrypting their private input x_i under pk, and then using the resulting ciphertext c_i to homomorphically evaluate the update function fold on hint_{i-1} and c_i, obtaining a new hint_i. The corresponding update tag_i can be obtained by generating a NIZK proof showing that hint_i was correctly computed by evaluating the update function fold on hint_{i-1} and the ciphertext containing x_i. To generate an escrow esc, a user homomorphically evaluates the predicate $P(t, \mathsf{fold}(x_1, \ldots, x_i))$ using hint_i and the ciphertext containing t published by the auditor; and computes the corresponding tag as a NIZK showing that the predicate was correctly evaluated. Using sk, the auditor can decrypt esc and learn only the output of $P(t, \mathsf{fold}(x_1, \ldots, x_i))$ but nothing else; while the validity of esc can be checked by verifying the NIZK proof in tag. This construction supports arbitrary predicates and updates (beyond additive ones), however, it relies on heavy primitives which are not efficiently instantiatable to date. This is a serious caveat in a setting such as that of AML and location privacy, where hundreds of thousands of updates must be processed per second.

An Efficient Construction for Range Predicates. Range predicates $P(t, X)$ are evaluated over ordered sets and output 1 iff $X \geq t$. To construct a concretely efficient UPPB scheme called uBlu, we will consider the subclass of range predicates $P_d(t, X)$ that can be expressed as a degree d polynomial over $\mathbb{Z}_q$ (for an opportune module q and degree d) with roots at positions $[t, \ldots, t+d-1]$. Here d is the size of the range for which $P(t, X) = 1$ and t is the auditor's secret threshold. The core of our scheme is a mechanism that relies on Pedersen commitments, ElGamal ciphertexts, and NIZKs with updatable witness/instances for predicate evaluations in the multi-user scenario, guaranteeing the soundness of the updates.

In detail, the auditor ElGamal encrypts the powers $(-t)^i$ for $i \in [d]$, in the exponent. The ciphertexts are included in the initial hint hint_0. Users can combine the ciphertexts to homomorphically evaluate the polynomial $P_d(t, x)$ at their input x, in the exponent. Moreover, given hint_{i-1} (containing an encryption of $P_d(t, x)$) a user with input x' can update the hint to hint_i containing an encryption of $P_d(t, x + x')$. This is achieved by an algebraic transformation on the polynomial representation, as described in Sect. 5.1.

When converting hints to escrows esc, users homomorphically reconstruct the ElGamal ciphertext for the value $P_d(t, x)$, and then exponentiate it by a random β obtaining an encryption of $\beta \cdot P_d(t, x)$. If the polynomial evaluates to

0, the randomization has no effect and the auditor is able to decrypt the message G^0 (this is the case where the predicate $P(T, X) = [P_d(T, X) \overset{?}{=} 0]$ outputs 1). Otherwise, if the polynomial evaluation is not a root, the auditor learns nothing.

The main technical achievement of this work is the design of hints that do not grow with the number of updates, and are reasonably sized for practical applications. We make hints linear in the degree d of the polynomial and endow them with *updatable* proofs that attest to hint consistency. Intuitively, this is achieved by including witness-products in the witness and checking the consistency of those products w.r.t. the minimal witness values by using Pedersen commitments and adding extra checks in the relation to ensure input consistency based on these commitments. Thanks to the homomorphic property of Pedersen commitments, our witness and instance are updatable: randomnesses and x values accumulate additively (see Sect. 5.3 for further details).

For the many use cases which *do require* a linear history of proofs-of-updates, we provide a very concise "update history" consisting of update tags tag, which naturally grows in the number of updates, but allows enforcing update accountability.In addition, as we use Pedersen as base commitment, it is easy to integrate our uBlu construction with applications such as credentials and private payment systems: one simply proves *extra* statements about base commitments, *e.g.*, that their values are equal to a credential attribute or a payment transaction value.

1.3 Related Work

Homomorphic commitments [16,25] and functional commitments [17] could potentially support general updates and predicate evaluations for UPPB schemes. However, these operations require knowledge of individual commitment openings, making such schemes unfit for our multi-user setting, where users' inputs must be kept private. The threshold predicate for which we present an efficient uBlu scheme is closely related to Yao's Millionaire's Problem, *i.e.* performing secure comparison. While there are many protocols for secure comparison (*e.g.*, [27,39]) that could be used in this setting, they require continuous online involvement of parties and many rounds of interaction. In our setting, no interaction is required from the auditor or users (after they update commitments).

Updatable NIZKs, such as CH20 [23] used as our prime technical tool, have been previously investigated in [7,18,20,46]. While recursive approach to NIZK updatability becomes more practical over time [8,9,11,13–15,19,51], direct malleability without recursion is more lightweight and thus more suitable for tailored application, such as various signature schemes [10,30,36,46], anonymous credentials [1], scalable mix-nets [45] etc. The malleability of CH20 was observed in [22] to build anonymous credentials and structure-preserving signatures on equivalence classes. It is also worth noting that RO-based NIZKs are essentially non-malleable, unless via recursion [33,38,49]. This is why the CH20 NIZK combining the simplicity of a Schnorr-like proof with a bilinear setup avoiding the ROM limitation, stands out as a natural candidate for direct updatability.

Table 1. Notation used throughout the paper.

Notation	Definition
$\lambda \in \mathbb{N}$	Security parameter (often implicitly used)
PPT	Probabilistic polynomial time
$\xleftarrow{\$}, \uparrow_\$$	Sampling from distribution, uniform if implicit
$x \xleftarrow{\$} \mathsf{Alg}(y)$	Probabilistic execution with uniform randomness
$x \leftarrow \mathsf{Alg}(y; r)$	Specifies algorithm's random coins
$(x, \cdot) \leftarrow \mathsf{Alg}(y)$	Leaves the second output undefined
$F(X, Y) \in \mathbb{Z}[X, Y]$	Polynomials and variables are in capital letters
$[m, n], (resp.[n])$	Discrete interval $\{m, m+1, \ldots, n\}, (resp.[1, n])$
$\overset{?}{=}, (resp. \neq)$	(resp. negation of) Boolean result of an equality check
$[a = b]$	Predicate evaluation, boolean value
$1, (resp.\ 0)$	Generic for boolean values $1, (resp.\ 0)$
$\wedge, (resp.\ \vee)$	Logic AND (resp. OR) operator
assert b	In pseudocode: "if not b, then return 0"
$(\mathbb{G}_1, \mathbb{G}_2, \mathbb{G}_3, \hat{e})$	Type-III bilinear group
$\vec{x}$ or $\mathbf{x}$, $(resp.\ [\vec{x}]_b)$	Vector of $\mathbb{Z}$ (resp. $\mathbb{G}_b$ for $b \in \{1, 2, 3\}$) elements

A series of recent papers explored accountable law enforcement access system [5,35,41,42,48,59]. A different approach to privacy-preserving AML securely computing similarity scores of transaction graphs [37,57]. However, as computing similarity among many accounts is expensive, the authors of [57] suggest that banks pre-select accounts, which can be done utilizing our techniques for computing aggregate suspiciousness scores. Other approaches [31] take advantage of specific structures of a transaction graph to limit the interaction during an MPC computation of a AML algorithm. However, this limited interaction is only achieved for specific graphs and communication/round complexities are still impractical for very large number of users. Our applications are most closely related to a subcategory of these works on abuse-resistant regulation compliance [5,35,48] where users have full privacy against a malicious auditor. As a consequence the auditor's detection policy must be kept private since users can adapt their behavior to avoid detection. Hence, it is necessary to securely compute a function on private inputs from the user and the regulator.

2   Preliminaries

For conciseness, we present our notation in Table 1. Our protocols are in the type-III bilinear group setup. Whenever clear from the context $\mathbb{G} = \mathbb{G}_1 = \langle G \rangle$.

Secure Commitments. Following [48] we use non-interactive commitments to bind inputs to externally committed values.

Definition 1 (Statistically Hiding Non-interactive Commitment). *A pair of algorithms* $(\mathfrak{Setup}, \mathfrak{Commit})$, *defined over message space* $\mathbb{V}$ *and randomness space* $\mathbb{R}$, *constitutes a statistically hiding non-interactive commitment scheme if it satisfies:*

- Statistical hiding, *i.e., for any* pp *output by* $\mathfrak{Setup}(1^\lambda)$, *for any* $m_0, m_1 \in \mathbb{V}$, *the distributions* $D(\mathsf{pp}, m_0)$ *and* $D(\mathsf{pp}, m_1)$ *are statistically close, where* $D(\mathsf{pp}, m) = \{r \xleftarrow{\$} \mathbb{R} : \mathfrak{Commit}_{\mathsf{pp}}(m; r)\}$; *and*
- Computational binding, *i.e. for any* PPT *adversary* $\mathcal{A}$, *there exists a negligible function* $\mathsf{negl}(\lambda)$ *such that* $\Pr[\mathfrak{Commit}_{\mathsf{pp}}(m_0; r_0) = \mathfrak{Commit}_{\mathsf{pp}}(m_1; r_1) \wedge m_0 \neq m_1 : \mathsf{pp} \xleftarrow{\$} \mathfrak{Setup}(1^\lambda); (m_0, r_0, m_1, r_1) \leftarrow \mathcal{A}(\mathsf{pp})] = \mathsf{negl}(\lambda)$.

3 Updatable NIZK Proof Systems

Zero-knowledge proofs enable a prover to convince a verifier of the validity of a statement, without revealing any additional information beyond the truth of the statement itself. Further, non-interactive zero-knowledge proofs (NIZK) remove the need for interaction between prover and verifier: the prover simply outputs a publicly verifiable proof generated from her (secret) witness and a common reference string (crs) [58].

Notation-wise, we will denote languages and relations interchangeably in the following manner: $\mathcal{L_R} = \{\mathsf{x} \mid \exists\, \mathsf{w}. (\mathsf{x}, \mathsf{w}) \in \mathcal{R_L}\}$, where $\mathsf{x} \in X$ is a (public) instance, $\mathsf{w} \in W$ is a (secret) witness, and the relation $\mathcal{R_L}$ is a subset of $X \times W$. Defining $\mathcal{R}$ also determines $\mathcal{L_R}$ uniquely; furthermore we implicitly assume $\mathcal{L}$ uniquely defines $\mathcal{R_L}$.

Definition 2 (Updatable Language). *A language* $\mathcal{L}$ *is updatable w.r.t. the class of transformations* $\mathcal{T}$ *if for all* $T \in \mathcal{T}$, $T = (T_{\mathsf{x}}, T_{\mathsf{w}})$, *and for all* $(\mathsf{x}, \mathsf{w}) \in \mathcal{R_L}$ *it holds that* $(T_{\mathsf{x}}(\mathsf{x}), T_{\mathsf{w}}(\mathsf{w})) \in \mathcal{R_L}$. *We call such* T *valid transformations for* $\mathcal{L}$.

Note that the functions $T_{\mathsf{x}} : X \to X, T_{\mathsf{w}} : W \to W$ are defined independently of any particular instance and witness, i.e. in T_{x} the symbol "x" is only used as a label. All the relations and functions we consider can be evaluated in PPT in the security parameter.

We recall the definitions of standard and updatable NIZK proofs. Updatable NIZKs are known as malleable proofs [7,18] and allow transforming a proof for x into a proof for $T_{\mathsf{x}}(\mathsf{x})$. We prefer the term updatable and make this feature explicit in our syntax.

Definition 3 (Standard and Updatable NIZKs). *An* updatable *NIZK proof system for a language* $\mathcal{L}$ *and a set of transformations* $\mathcal{T}$ *is defined by:*

- $\mathsf{Setup}(1^\lambda) \xrightarrow{\$} (\mathsf{crs}, \mathsf{td})$: *generates a common reference string* crs *and a trapdoor* td *which is used for security definitions;*
- $\mathsf{Prove}(\mathsf{crs}, \mathsf{x}, \mathsf{w}) \xrightarrow{\$} \pi$: *produces a proof for* $(\mathsf{x}, \mathsf{w}) \in \mathcal{R_L}$;
- $\mathsf{Verify}(\mathsf{crs}, \pi, \mathsf{x}) \to 0/1$: *verifies* π *w.r.t. the public instance* x;
- $\mathsf{Update}(\mathsf{crs}, \pi, \mathsf{x}, T) \xrightarrow{\$} \pi'$: *updates the proof* π *for* x *into* π' *for* $T_{\mathsf{x}}(\mathsf{x})$.

A standard *non-updatable NIZK proof system is defined only by the first three algorithms. For conciseness, in what follows we sometimes drop* crs *from the explicit inputs and separate the proof and instance by a semicolon, e.g.,* Verify$(\pi; x)$.

Our NIZKs need to satisfy the standard security definitions—completeness, soundness, and zero-knowledge, given e.g., in [44]—which we defer to. An updatable NIZK must additionally satisfy the following two properties. First, the updated proof must be valid for the updated instance:

Definition 4 (Update Completeness). *An updatable NIZK proof system for $\mathcal{L}$ satisfies* update completeness *w.r.t. a set of transformations $\mathcal{T}$, if given* $(\mathsf{crs}, \cdot) \xleftarrow{\$} \mathsf{Setup}(1^\lambda)$, *for all* x, π *such that* $\mathsf{Verify}(\pi, x) = 1$, *and all* $T = (T_x, \cdot) \in \mathcal{T}$ *it holds that:* $\Pr\left[\mathsf{Verify}(\mathsf{crs}, \mathsf{Update}(\mathsf{crs}, \pi, x, T), T_x(x)) = 1\right] = 1$.

Second, derivation privacy states that updated proofs are distributed similarly to fresh proofs for the new instance.

Definition 5 (Derivation Privacy). *An updatable NIZK proof system for $\mathcal{L}$ satisfies* derivation privacy *w.r.t. $\mathcal{T}$, if given* $(\mathsf{crs}, \cdot) \xleftarrow{\$} \mathsf{Setup}(1^\lambda)$, *for all* $(x, w) \in \mathcal{R}_{\mathcal{L}}$, *all π such that* $\mathsf{Verify}(\mathsf{crs}, \pi, x) = 1$, *and all* $T = (T_x, T_w) \in \mathcal{T}$ *it holds that:* $\left\{ \mathsf{Update}(\mathsf{crs}, \pi, x, T) \right\} \overset{p}{=} \left\{ \mathsf{Prove}(\mathsf{crs}, T_x(x), T_w(w)) \right\}$, *i.e., the two collections are perfectly indistinguishable.*

Because updated proofs are distributed as fresh ones, they can be simulated using the standard simulator guaranteed by zero-knowledge; therefore transformed proofs are also zero-knowledge. This property is inspired by derivation privacy in [18].

NIZKs Used in this Work. We use two NIZK proof systems that work with the same class of languages.

- Π: The standard non-updatable Σ-protocol proof system for equality of discrete logarithm relations [52,60]. It is assumed to be straight-line knowledge-sound after non-interactive transformation, e.g. by encrypting witnesses or using Fischlin's technique [34].
- Π_u: The CH20 NIZK [23], which is Σ-like, but is updatable, works in the bilinear setting, and has a uniform CRS. We discuss CH20 and investigate its updatability in [29].

The Common Algebraic Language. Let $\mathbb{G}$ be a prime ordered group. Define the set of linear polynomials $\mathcal{P} \subset \mathbb{G}[X_1 \dots X_l]$ in l variables with coefficients in $\mathbb{G}$ as $\mathcal{P} = \{a_0 + \sum_{i=1}^{l} a_i X_i \,|\, a_0 \in \mathbb{G}, a_1 \dots a_l \in \mathbb{Z}_q\}$. Both Π and Π_u work with the so-called *algebraic* language[2] $\mathcal{L}_M$:

$$\mathcal{L}_M = \left\{ \vec{x} \in \mathbb{G}^l \,\middle|\, \exists\, \vec{w} \in \mathbb{Z}_p^t : M(\vec{x}) \cdot \vec{w} = \vec{x} \right\}, \text{ where } M(\vec{X}) \in \mathcal{P}^{l \times t}.$$

---

[2] For simplicity, and contrast with [23], we do not consider arbitrary $\Theta(\vec{x})$ such that $M(\vec{x}) \cdot \vec{w} = \Theta(\vec{x})$.

In other words, it is a set of DLOG-like linear equations with a common instance and bases in $M(\vec{X})$ that can potentially depend on the instance x itself. We define the corresponding relation $\mathcal{R}_M$ to be the set $\{(\vec{x}, \vec{w}) \in \mathbb{G}^l \times \mathbb{Z}_p^t \,|\, M(\vec{x}) \cdot \vec{w} = \vec{x}\}$.

Updatability for algebraic languages $\mathcal{L}_M$, due to their group structure, means that there exist four matrices $(T_{\mathsf{xm}}, T_{\mathsf{xa}}, T_{\mathsf{wm}}, T_{\mathsf{wa}})$ such that for all $(\vec{x}, \vec{w}) \in \mathcal{R}_M$ it holds that:

$$(T_{\mathsf{xm}} \cdot \vec{x} + T_{\mathsf{xa}}, T_{\mathsf{wm}} \cdot \vec{w} + T_{\mathsf{wa}}) \in \mathcal{R}_M.$$

The functions $T_{\mathsf{x}}, T_{\mathsf{w}}$ required in Definition 2 are defined as follows: $T_{\mathsf{x}}(\mathsf{x}) := T_{\mathsf{xm}} \cdot \vec{x} + T_{\mathsf{xa}}$ and $T_{\mathsf{w}}(\mathsf{w}) := T_{\mathsf{wm}} \cdot \vec{w} + T_{\mathsf{wa}}$. We will show that the algebraic languages we define in this work are updatable by explicitly providing the matrices and proving they satisfy the equation. For more details see [29].

4   Updatable Privacy-Preserving Blueprints

Updatable privacy-preserving blueprints are like privacy-preserving blueprints [48, Definition 3], in the sense that they are defined for a given function (in our case an efficiently computable predicate) and a given non-interactive commitment scheme. In addition to the basic algorithms, updatable privacy-preserving blueprints have three new algorithms that are necessary for our functionality: Update, VfHistory, and VfHint. Finally, to enable proving external properties about update values we require the commitment scheme to be statistically hiding and computationally binding (see Definition 1). For integration, the commitment scheme additionally has to be compatible with our updatable NIZK system. We also introduce hints and tags which repackage and augment some of the variables used in the original syntax of [48, Definition 3]. For convenience, we will refer to updatable privacy-preserving blueprint schemes as *updatable blueprints* (UPPB), and to the statistically hiding non-interactive NIZK-friendly commitment scheme as *the base commitment scheme* and denote it as $\mathfrak{BC} = (\mathfrak{Setup}, \mathfrak{Commit})$ (with gothic font). We will also employ binary predicates, i.e. functions of the form $P(T, X) : \mathbb{V} \times \mathbb{V} \to \{0, 1\}$.

For a concrete example, consider Pedersen commitments, the CH20 NIZK, $\mathbb{V} = \mathbb{Z}_q$, and the predicate family $\mathcal{P}_\mathbb{V}$ of range checks, i.e., binary predicates that are parameterized by a public distance value $d \in \mathbb{Z}_q$ that return 1 if $x \in [t, t + d - 1]$, and 0 otherwise.

Definition 6 (Updatable Privacy-Preserving Blueprints). *Let* BC $=$ $(\mathfrak{Setup}, \mathfrak{Commit})$ *be a statistically hiding non-interactive commitment scheme defined over* $(\mathbb{V}, \mathbb{R})$, *and* $P(T, X) \in \mathcal{P}_\mathbb{V}$ *be an efficiently computable binary predicate defined over* $\mathbb{V}$. *An updatable blueprint scheme (UPPB) for* $(\mathsf{BC}, P(T, X))$ *is defined by the following set of PPT algorithms:*

Setup$(1^\lambda, \mathsf{pp}) \xrightarrow{\$} (\mathsf{pp}, \mathsf{td})$: *takes as input the security parameter* λ, *and base commitment parameters* $\mathfrak{pp}$ *output by* $\mathfrak{Setup}(1^\lambda)$. *It returns public parameters that contain at least a description of a special value denoted by* 0. *It also returns a trapdoor* td *that is only used in security definitions.* pp *and* $\mathfrak{pp}$ *are implicit inputs to all other algorithms.*

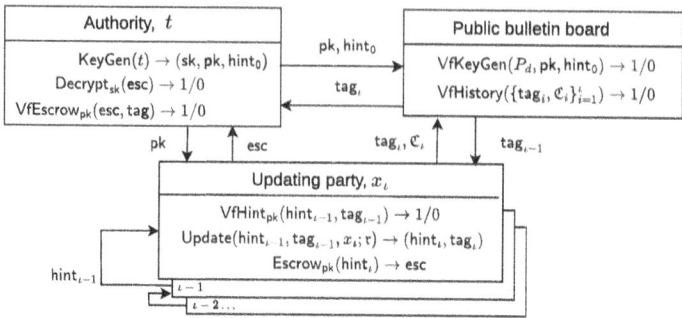

Fig. 1. Illustration of semantics of updatable blueprints in a potential application scenario with a public bulletin board.

$\mathsf{KeyGen}(t) \xrightarrow{\$} (\mathsf{sk}, \mathsf{pk}, \mathsf{hint_0})$: *takes as input a value $t \in \mathbb{V}$. It outputs a key pair $(\mathsf{sk}, \mathsf{pk})$; a hint $\mathsf{hint_0}$ implicitly encoding 0—this first hint is also the only public one.*

$\mathsf{VfKeyGen}(\mathsf{pk}, \mathsf{hint_0}) \to 1/0$: *verifies the validity of the public output of KeyGen.*

$\mathsf{Update_{pk}}(\mathsf{hint}, \mathsf{tag}, x, \mathfrak{r}) \xrightarrow{\$} (\mathsf{hint}', \mathsf{tag}')$: *takes as input a hint and its tag, a value, and external base commitment randomness. When $\mathsf{hint} = \mathsf{hint_0}$, $\mathsf{tag} = \perp$. It returns an updated hint' and the new update tag'. To keep track of the update history (also called trace) of a commitment we introduce an epoch index $\iota \geq 1$, e.g., $\mathsf{Update_{pk}}(\mathsf{hint}_{\iota-1}, \mathsf{tag}_{\iota-1}, x_\iota, \mathfrak{r}_\iota) \xrightarrow{\$} (\mathsf{hint}_\iota, \mathsf{tag}_\iota)$.*

$\mathsf{VfHistory_{pk}}(\{\mathsf{tag}_i, \mathcal{C}_i\}_{i=1}^\iota) \to 1/0$: *takes as input an ordered sequence of update tags and base commitments and verifies the consistency of the update history (also called trace, see Definition 7).*

$\mathsf{VfHint_{pk}}(\mathsf{hint}, \mathsf{tag}) \to 1/0$: *takes as input a hint and the last corresponding update tag. It returns 1 if the inputs are deemed to be consistent (see Definition 7), and 0 otherwise.*

$\mathsf{Escrow_{pk}}(\mathsf{hint}) \xrightarrow{\$} \mathsf{esc}$: *takes as input a hint for the last tag of a history. It returns a predicate escrow esc that prepares the history for audit evaluation.*

$\mathsf{VfEscrow_{pk}}(\mathsf{esc}, \mathsf{tag}) \to 1/0$: *takes as input a predicate escrow esc, and the update tag tag used in the last update. It returns 1 if the inputs are consistent, and 0 otherwise.*

$\mathsf{Decrypt_{sk}}(\mathsf{esc}) \to \top/\perp$: *takes as input the auditor's secret key sk and a predicate escrow. It returns $\top$ if the escrow contains values that satisfy the predicate $P(t, \cdot)$, where t is determined by sk.*

Figure 1 illustrates the semantics of the protocol on the example where history is stored on a public bulletin board. Alternatively, histories can be queried and verified directly by the authority.

The notion of *correctness* covers the honest execution of the protocol. It ensures that: (1) the honestly generated key always verifies, (2) honestly updated histories of base commitments verify, and (3) the result of decrypted escrow is consistent with the evaluation of the predicate on the sum of update values.

Definition 7 (Correctness). *Let* BC *and* $P \in \mathcal{P}_\mathbb{V}$ *be as in Definition 6, and* $\lambda \in \mathbb{N}$*. A UPPB scheme for* (BC, P) *is* correct *if the following statements hold for all* $\mathsf{pp} \xleftarrow{\$} \mathfrak{Setup}(1^\lambda)$*,* $(\mathsf{pp}, \cdot) \xleftarrow{\$} \mathsf{Setup}(1^\lambda, \mathsf{pp})$ *(remember these are implicit in all the algorithms):*

- *Full correctness: for all* $t \in \mathbb{V}$*, all poly-sized sequences of values* $x_1, \dots, x_n \in \mathbb{V}$ *and* $\mathfrak{r}_1, \dots, \mathfrak{r}_n \in \mathbb{R}$*:*

$$
\Pr \left[
\begin{array}{l}
\mathsf{VfKeyGen}(\mathsf{pk}, \mathsf{hint}_0) = 1 \wedge \\
\text{for all } i \in [n]: \\
\quad \mathsf{VfHint}_{\mathsf{pk}}(\mathsf{hint}_i, \mathsf{tag}_i) = 1 \wedge \\
\quad \mathsf{VfHistory}_{\mathsf{pk}}(\{\mathsf{tag}_j, \mathfrak{C}_j\}_{j=1}^i) = 1 \wedge \\
\quad \mathsf{VfEscrow}_{\mathsf{pk}}(\mathsf{esc}_i, \mathsf{tag}_i) = 1 \wedge \\
\quad \mathsf{Decrypt}_{\mathsf{sk}}(\mathsf{esc}_i) = P(t, \sum_{j=1}^i x_j)
\end{array}
\middle| :
\begin{array}{l}
(\mathsf{sk}, \mathsf{pk}, \mathsf{hint}_0) \xleftarrow{\$} \mathsf{KeyGen}(t) \\
\text{for } i \in [n]: \\
\quad (\mathsf{hint}_i, \mathsf{tag}_i) \curvearrowright \$ \\
\quad \mathsf{Update}_{\mathsf{pk}}(\mathsf{hint}_{i-1}, \mathsf{tag}_{i-1}, x_i, \mathfrak{r}_i) \\
\quad \mathsf{esc}_i \xleftarrow{\$} \mathsf{Escrow}_{\mathsf{pk}}(\mathsf{hint}_i) \\
\quad \mathfrak{C}_i \leftarrow \mathfrak{Commit}(x_i; \mathfrak{r}_i)
\end{array}
\right] = 1
$$

- *Update correctness: for all* $\mathsf{pk}, \mathsf{hint}_0$ *s.t.* $\mathsf{VfKeyGen}(\mathsf{pk}, \mathsf{hint}_0) = 1$*, and all* $\mathsf{hint}_n, \{\mathsf{tag}_j, \mathfrak{C}_j\}_{i=1}^n$ *such that* $\mathsf{VfHint}_{\mathsf{pk}}(\mathsf{hint}_n, \mathsf{tag}_n) = 1$ *and* $\mathsf{VfHistory}_{\mathsf{pk}}(\{\mathsf{tag}_j, \mathfrak{C}_j\}_{j=1}^n) = 1$*, and for all* $x \in \mathbb{V}, \mathfrak{r} \in \mathbb{R}$*:*

$$
\Pr \left[
\begin{array}{l}
\mathsf{VfHint}_{\mathsf{pk}}(\mathsf{hint}_{n+1}, \mathsf{tag}_{n+1}) = 1 \wedge \\
\mathsf{VfHistory}_{\mathsf{pk}}(\{\mathsf{tag}_j, \mathfrak{C}_j\}_{j=1}^{n+1}) = 1 \wedge \\
\mathsf{VfEscrow}_{\mathsf{pk}}(\mathsf{esc}_{n+1}, \mathsf{tag}_{n+1}) = 1
\end{array}
\middle| :
\begin{array}{l}
(\mathsf{hint}_{n+1}, \mathsf{tag}_{n+1}) \curvearrowright \$ \\
\quad \mathsf{Update}_{\mathsf{pk}}(\mathsf{hint}_n, \mathsf{tag}_n, x, \mathfrak{r}) \\
\mathsf{esc}_{n+1} \xleftarrow{\$} \mathsf{Escrow}_{\mathsf{pk}}(\mathsf{hint}_{n+1}) \\
\mathfrak{C}_{n+1} \leftarrow \mathfrak{Commit}(x; \mathfrak{r})
\end{array}
\right] = 1
$$

In both statements, the probability is taken over the random coins internally sampled by the randomized algorithms of UPPB.

4.1   Security Properties

We say that a history and predicate escrows are valid if they verify under a verifying public key. Valid histories and escrows must satisfy two properties: history binding and soundness.

History binding enforces that for any valid history, its prefix must also be valid, and no alternative prefix can ever be valid. This means that after verifying a commitment history one can use the last tag as a commitment to the whole history and is guaranteed the validity of each step in the history.

Definition 8 (History Binding). *A UPPB scheme for* (BC, P) *is* history binding *if for all PPT* $\mathcal{A}$*, it holds that* $\Pr[\mathcal{G}_\mathcal{A}(1^\lambda) = 1] \leq \mathsf{negl}(\lambda)$*, where game* $\mathcal{G}_\mathcal{A}(1^\lambda)$ *is as follows:*

$1:$ $\mathsf{pp} \xleftarrow{\$} \mathsf{Setup}(1^\lambda);\ (\mathsf{pp}, \cdot) \xleftarrow{\$} \mathsf{Setup}(1^\lambda, \mathsf{pp})$

$2:$ $(\mathsf{pk}, \mathsf{hint}_0, \{\{\mathsf{tag}_i^{(b)}, \mathcal{C}_i^{(b)}\}_{i=1}^\iota\}_{b \in \{0,1\}}) \xleftarrow{\$} \mathcal{A}(\mathsf{pp})$

$3:$ **return** $\mathsf{VfKeyGen}(\mathsf{pk}, \mathsf{hint}_0) = 1\ \wedge$

$4:$ $\quad \mathsf{VfHistory}_{\mathsf{pk}}(\{\mathsf{tag}_i^{(0)}, \mathcal{C}_i^{(0)}\}_{i=1}^\iota) = 1\ \wedge$

$5:$ $\quad \Big(\mathsf{VfHistory}_{\mathsf{pk}}(\{\mathsf{tag}_i^{(0)}, \mathcal{C}_i^{(0)}\}_{i=1}^{\iota-1}) \neq 1\ \vee$

$6:$ $\quad\quad \mathsf{VfHistory}_{\mathsf{pk}}(\{\mathsf{tag}_i^{(1)}, \mathcal{C}_i^{(1)}\}_{i=1}^\iota) = 1\ \wedge$

$7:$ $\quad\quad \mathsf{tag}_\iota^{(0)} = \mathsf{tag}_\iota^{(1)} \wedge \exists i.\, (\mathsf{tag}_i^{(0)}, \mathcal{C}_i^{(0)}) \neq (\mathsf{tag}_i^{(1)}, \mathcal{C}_i^{(1)})\Big)$

In practice, history binding prevents history manipulation: assuming an updater that produced tag as a "receipt" of their update is later approached by the regulator for presenting their esc, the updater will not be able to deceive the regulator by saying "this tag I produced for a different history". So history binding is crucial for "tracking back" the history of changes done to the esc; it enforces history linearity.

Soundness focuses on what VfEscrow and VfHistory functions mean *together*: (1) any verifying history "contains" a set of update values, and (2) if esc verifies w.r.t. the last tag of this history, it must decrypt to the value of predicate P evaluated on t and the sum of committed values in the history.

Definition 9 (Soundness). *A UPPB scheme for* (BC, P) *is sound if there exists a deterministic poly-time black-box extractor* Ext, *such that for all PPT* $\mathcal{A}$:

1. *Valid history can be explained in terms of base commitments: for all* $\iota > 0$,

$$
\Pr\left[
\begin{array}{l}
\mathsf{VfKeyGen}(\mathsf{pk}, \mathsf{hint}_0) = 1\ \wedge \\
\mathsf{VfHistory}_{\mathsf{pk}}(\{\mathsf{tag}_i, \mathcal{C}_i\}_{i=1}^\iota) = 1\ \wedge \\
\mathcal{C}_\iota \neq \mathsf{Commit}(x_\iota, \mathsf{r}_\iota)
\end{array}
\ :\
\begin{array}{l}
\mathsf{pp} \xleftarrow{\$} \mathsf{Setup}(1^\lambda) \\
(\mathsf{pp}, \mathsf{td}) \xleftarrow{\$} \mathsf{Setup}(1^\lambda, \mathsf{pp}) \\
(\mathsf{pk}, \mathsf{hint}_0, \{\mathsf{tag}_i, \mathcal{C}_i\}_{i=1}^\iota) \uparrow_{\$} \\
\quad\quad\quad\quad\quad\quad\quad\quad\quad \mathcal{A}(\mathsf{pp}) \\
(x_\iota, \mathsf{r}_\iota) \leftarrow \mathsf{Ext}(\mathsf{td}, \mathsf{tag}_\iota)
\end{array}
\right] \leq \mathsf{negl}(\lambda)
$$

2. *Decryption always reveals the predicate computed for the sum of update values: for all* $t \in \mathbb{V}$, $\iota > 0$,

$$
\Pr\left[
\begin{array}{l}
\mathsf{VfHistory}_{\mathsf{pk}}(\{\mathsf{tag}_i, \mathcal{C}_i\}_{i=1}^\iota) = 1\ \wedge \\
\mathsf{VfEscrow}_{\mathsf{pk}}(\mathsf{esc}^\star, \mathsf{tag}_\iota) = 1\ \wedge \\
\mathsf{Decrypt}_{\mathsf{sk}}(\mathsf{esc}^\star) \neq P(t, \sum_{i=1}^\iota x_i)
\end{array}
\ :\
\begin{array}{l}
\mathsf{pp} \xleftarrow{\$} \mathsf{Setup}(1^\lambda) \\
(\mathsf{pp}, \mathsf{td}) \xleftarrow{\$} \mathsf{Setup}(1^\lambda, \mathsf{pp}) \\
(\mathsf{sk}, \mathsf{pk}, \mathsf{hint}_0) \xleftarrow{\$} \mathsf{KeyGen}(t) \\
(\mathsf{esc}^\star, \{\mathsf{tag}_i, \mathcal{C}_i\}_{i=1}^\iota) \uparrow_{\$} \\
\quad\quad\quad\quad\quad\quad \mathcal{A}(\mathsf{pp}, \mathsf{pk}, \mathsf{hint}_0) \\
\text{for } i \in [1, \iota]: \\
\quad (x_i, \mathsf{r}_i) \leftarrow \mathsf{Ext}(\mathsf{td}, \mathsf{tag}_i)
\end{array}
\right] \leq \mathsf{negl}(\lambda)
$$

The extractor is the same in both clauses of the definition and works the same given the same inputs. This means that the two parts are composable: the extracted value in the second part satisfies $\forall i.\ \mathfrak{C}_i = \mathfrak{Commit}(x_i, \mathfrak{r}_i)$ with over-whelming probability. Together with the binding property of BC, this guarantees that any values x_ι that are opened, by revealing $\mathfrak{r}_\iota$ or that are used externally in proofs of knowledge about $\mathfrak{C}_\iota$, must be the same as that used to evaluate P.

The first part of soundness considers dishonest keys (emulating a view of a third party observing the history, e.g. on the bulletin board), while the second part has honest keys because it is viewed from the honest regulator's perspective.

Our *hiding* definitions provide privacy guarantees, capturing the following properties: (1) output of KeyGen does not leak the threshold value t (Definition 10), (2) tags do not leak the update value (Definition 11), (3) hints do not leak the update value, without sk (Definition 12), and (4) escrow values only leak the result of the evaluated predicate (Definition 13).

Threshold hiding states that it is computationally impossible to determine the threshold value t chosen upon key generation from the public key, without the secret key.

Definition 10 (Threshold Hiding). *A UPPB scheme for* (BC, P) *is threshold hiding if for all PPT $\mathcal{A}$ it holds that:*

$$\Pr\left[b \overset{?}{=} b^\star : \begin{array}{l} \mathsf{pp} \overset{\$}{\leftarrow} \mathfrak{Setup}(1^\lambda);\ (\mathsf{pp}, \cdot) \overset{\$}{\leftarrow} \mathsf{Setup}(1^\lambda, \mathsf{pp}) \\ (t_0, t_1) \leftarrow \mathcal{A}(\mathsf{pp}),\ b \overset{\$}{\leftarrow} \{0,1\} \\ (\cdot, \mathsf{pk}, \mathsf{hint}_0) \overset{\$}{\leftarrow} \mathsf{KeyGen}(t_b) \\ b^\star \leftarrow \mathcal{A}(\mathsf{pk}, \mathsf{hint}_0) \end{array} \right] \leq \frac{1}{2} + \mathsf{negl}(\lambda)$$

Tag hiding states that tags do not reveal any additional information than already revealed by $\mathfrak{C}$ itself.

Definition 11 (Tag Hiding). *A UPPB scheme for* BC *defined over* $(\mathbb{V}, \mathbb{R})$ *and* $P(T, X) \in \mathcal{P}_\mathbb{V}$ *is (perfectly) hiding in tags if, for* $(\mathsf{pp}, \mathsf{td}) \overset{\$}{\leftarrow} \mathsf{Setup}(1^\lambda, \mathbb{V}, \mathcal{P})$ *all* $t \in \mathbb{V}$, *all* pk, *all pairs* (hint, tag) *such that* $\mathsf{VfHint}_\mathsf{pk}(\mathsf{hint}, \mathsf{tag}) = 1$, *and for all* $x \in \mathbb{V}$, $\mathfrak{r} \in \mathbb{R}$, *there exists a PPT $\mathcal{S}$ such that:*

$$\left\{ \mathsf{tag}' \mid (\cdot, \mathsf{tag}') \overset{\$}{\leftarrow} \mathsf{Update}_\mathsf{pk}(\mathsf{hint}, \mathsf{tag}, x, \mathfrak{r}) \right\} = \left\{ \mathcal{S}(\mathsf{td}, \mathsf{pk}, \mathsf{tag}, \mathfrak{C} := \mathfrak{Commit}(x, \mathfrak{r})) \right\}$$

where distributions are over the internal randomness of the Update *algorithm and the simulator. For the first update, this holds conditioned on* hint := hint_0, tag := $\bot$.

Note that the simulation-style definition here is dictated by tags being verifiable w.r.t. base commitments in histories. This allows composable reasoning: tags are hiding regardless of the base commitments hiding property; whereas IND-style definition would imply that the base scheme needs to be hiding which we avoid. Tag hiding also implies hiding for any *sequence* of tags, and thus for any history $\{\mathsf{tag}_i, \mathfrak{C}_i\}_{i=1}^\iota$: using $\mathcal{S}$ and $\{\mathfrak{C}_i\}$ we can simulate all the tags one by one, without any hints.

Hint hiding states that without the secret key, hints do not leak information update values.

Definition 12 (Hint Hiding). *A UPPB scheme for* BC *defined over* $(\mathbb{V}, \mathbb{R})$ *and* $P(T, X) \in \mathcal{P}_{\mathbb{V}}$ *is (computationally value) hiding in hints if, for all* $t \in \mathbb{V}$ *and all PPT* $\mathcal{A}$, *it holds that* $\Pr[\mathcal{G}_{\mathcal{A}}(1^{\lambda}) = 1] \leq 1/2 + \mathsf{negl}(\lambda)$, *where game* $\mathcal{G}_{\mathcal{A}}(1^{\lambda})$ *is:*

1: $\mathsf{pp} \xleftarrow{\$} \mathsf{Setup}(1^{\lambda})$; $(\mathsf{pp}, \cdot) \xleftarrow{\$} \mathsf{Setup}(1^{\lambda}, \mathsf{pp})$
2: $(\cdot, \mathsf{pk}, \mathsf{hint}_0) \xleftarrow{\$} \mathsf{KeyGen}(t)$; $b \xleftarrow{\$} \{0, 1\}$
3: $(\mathsf{hint}^{\star}, \mathsf{tag}^{\star}, x^{(0)}, x^{(1)}, \mathfrak{r}) \xleftarrow{\$} \mathcal{A}(\mathsf{pp}, \mathsf{pk}, \mathsf{hint}_0)$
4: $(\mathsf{hint}, \cdot) \xleftarrow{\$} \mathsf{Update}_{\mathsf{pk}}(\mathsf{hint}^{\star}, \mathsf{tag}^{\star}, x^{(b)}, \mathfrak{r})$
5: $b^{\star} \xleftarrow{\$} \mathcal{A}(\mathsf{hint})$
6: **return** $b^{\star} \overset{?}{=} b \wedge \mathsf{VfHint}_{\mathsf{pk}}(\mathsf{hint}^{\star}, \mathsf{tag}^{\star}) \overset{?}{=} 1$

Escrow hiding models that even with the knowledge of the secret key, the escrow esc does not leak anything about the values inside the history besides the predicate result itself.

Definition 13 (Escrow Hiding). *A UPPB scheme for* BC *defined over* $(\mathbb{V}, \mathbb{R})$ *and* $P(T, X) \in \mathcal{P}_{\mathbb{V}}$ *is escrow hiding if there exists a PPT simulator* $\mathcal{S}$ *such that for all PPT* $\mathcal{A}$, *it holds that* $\Pr[\mathcal{G}_{\mathcal{A}}(1^{\lambda}) = 1] \leq 1/2 + \mathsf{negl}(\lambda)$, *where game* $\mathcal{G}_{\mathcal{A}}(1^{\lambda})$ *is as follows:*

1: $(\mathsf{pp}, \mathsf{td}) \xleftarrow{\$} \mathsf{Setup}(1^{\lambda}, \mathbb{V}, \mathcal{P})$.
2: $(t, \mathsf{pk}, \mathsf{hint}_0, \{\mathsf{tag}_i, x_i, \mathfrak{r}_i\}_{i=1}^{\iota}, \mathsf{hint}_{\iota}) \xleftarrow{\$} \mathcal{A}(\mathsf{pp})$
3: $b \xleftarrow{\$} \{0, 1\}$
4: $\mathsf{esc} \leftarrow$ **if** $b = 0$ **then** $\mathsf{Escrow}_{\mathsf{pk}}(\mathsf{hint}_{\iota})$ **else** $\mathcal{S}(\mathsf{td}, \mathsf{pk}, P(t, \sum_{i \in [\iota]} x_i), \mathsf{tag}_{\iota})$
5: $b^{\star} \xleftarrow{\$} \mathcal{A}(\mathsf{esc})$
6: **return** $b^{\star} = b \wedge$
7:     $\mathsf{VfKeyGen}(\mathsf{pk}, \mathsf{hint}_0) = 1 \wedge$
8:     $\mathsf{VfHistory}_{\mathsf{pk}}(\{\mathsf{tag}_i, \mathfrak{Commit}(x_i, \mathfrak{r}_i)\}_{i=1}^{\iota}) = 1 \wedge$
9:     $\mathsf{VfHint}(\mathsf{hint}_{\iota}, \mathsf{tag}_{\iota}) = 1$

5   uBlu: Efficient Realization of Updatable Blueprints

Our efficient uBlu construction is presented in Figs. 3 (main algorithms), 2 (helper functions), and 4 (verification algorithms). The construction is instantiated with Pedersen commitment scheme PedersenC as a base commitment, and the predicate $P_d(T, X)$ that returns 1 if and only if x is in the range $\{t, t+1, \ldots, t+d-1\}$. It also uses the updatable proof system Π_u instantiated by CH20, and a straight-line simulation-extractable Π (instantiated by Fiat-Shamir transformed Σ-protocols for proofs of equality of discrete logarithm representations with encryptions of witnesses). Next, we proceed with an overview that gradually builds intuition on the techniques employed in our construction, and conclude with how to achieve privacy and soundness.

BlindPowers($\{B_i\}_{i \in [d]}, \alpha$)

1: **return** $\{D_i := B_i \cdot W_i^{\alpha}\}_{i \in [d]}$

Evaluate($\{A_i, B_i\}_{i \in [d]}, \beta$)

1: Let $\{U_i\}_{i=1}^d$ be Stirling numbers as defined in Section 5.1.
2: **return**
$$\left(\prod_{i \in [d]} (A_i^{U_i})^{\beta}, \prod_{i \in [d]} (B_i^{U_i})^{\beta} \right)$$

UpdatePowers$_{\mathsf{pk}}$($\{A_{\iota-1,i}, B_{\iota-1,i}\}_{i \in [d]}, x_\iota, \{r_{\iota,i}\}_{i \in [d]}$)

1: Let $V_{i,j}(X) := \binom{i}{j} X^{i-j}$
2: **for** $i \in [d]$ **do**
3: $\quad A_{\iota,i} \leftarrow \left(\prod_{j=1}^i (A_{\iota-1,j})^{V_{i,j}(x_\iota)} \right) G^{r_{\iota,i}}$
4: $\quad B_{\iota,i} \leftarrow \left(G^{x_\iota^i} \prod_{j=1}^i (B_{\iota-1,j})^{V_{i,j}(x_\iota)} \right) H^{r_{\iota,i}}$
5: **return** $\{A_{\iota,i}, B_{\iota,i}\}_{i \in [d]}$

Fig. 2. Helper functions for the main uBlu protocol. The values $\{W_i\}_{i \in [d]}$ are independent bases, being part of the public parameters, and $\{V_{i,j}\}, \{U_i\}_{i \in [d]}$ are public values as defined in Sect. 5.1.

5.1 Achieving Updatable Functionality

The Predicate. We consider the predicate that returns $\top$ if the value x concealed in the escrow is *above* the given threshold t. For efficiency, we limit the check to a reasonable interval, i.e. the escrow is only decryptable if the value x is in $[t, t+d-1]$ for a small value d: for generic X and T the predicate is defined as

$$P_d = P_d(T, X) = \left[\prod_{\delta=0}^{d-1} (X - T - \delta) \stackrel{?}{=} 0 \right] \in \{0, 1\}. \tag{1}$$

Clearly, when evaluated, the predicate $P_d(t, x)$ returns 1 if and only if x is in the "critical range" $[t, t+d-1]$ on which the core polynomial evaluates to 0. The polynomial is built in such a way as to allow for efficient updates as discussed next.

Setup and Key Generation. The setup takes as input a group $\mathbb{G}$, of order q generated by Setup of the base commitment scheme (Pedersen), together with generator $G_1 = G$ and $\mathfrak{H}$. It finishes the bilinear group setup, creating $\mathsf{pp}_{\mathsf{BLG}}$ w.r.t. $\mathbb{G}_1$. It also sets up common reference strings and trapdoors for the NIZK proofs (more on this in Sect. 5.3). Most importantly, it generates d random masking values $W_1, \ldots, W_d \xleftarrow{\$} \mathbb{G}$ which are needed for blinding ElGamal ciphertexts in the hints.

To run the key generation process, the regulator needs to choose a threshold value t. In a nutshell, KeyGen samples $\mathsf{sk} \xleftarrow{\$} \mathbb{Z}_q$ and computes its corresponding DH public key $H \leftarrow G^{\mathsf{sk}}$. The public key consists of H and some additional data to prove consistency. The key generation process additionally returns a hint consisting of: 1) a sequence of d ElGamal ciphertexts encrypting the powers of $t, t^2, \ldots, t^d$ under the public key H; 2) a NIZK consistency proof π_c for these powers; and 3) additional dummy information for correct hint formatting. This allows public verifiability of the correctness of the key generation procedure and of the hints in epoch $\iota = 0$.

Setup(1^λ, pp)

% To ensure $\mathbb{G}_1$ is the same for Pedersen
BCS and the pairing system
1: **parse** pp as $(\mathbb{G}_1, G, \mathfrak{H}, P_d)$
2: $pp_{BLG} \leftarrow BLG.Setup(1^\lambda; \mathbb{G}_1, G)$
   % Blinding factors for $\{D_i\}_{i=1}^d$
   % d comes from the predicate P_d in pp
3: $\{W_i\}_{i \in [d]} \xleftarrow{\$} \mathbb{G}_1$
4: $(crs_\Pi, td_\Pi) \leftarrow \Pi.Setup(1^\lambda, pp_{BLG})$
5: $(crs_{\Pi_u}, td_{\Pi_u}) \leftarrow \Pi_u^{\mathcal{L}c}.Setup(1^\lambda, pp_{BLG})$
6: $pp \leftarrow (pp, pp_{BLG}, \{W_i\}_{i \in [d]}, 0, P_d, crs_\Pi, crs_{\Pi_u})$
7: $td \leftarrow (td_\Pi, td_{\Pi_u})$
8: **return** (pp, td)

KeyGen(t)

1: $sk \xleftarrow{\$} \mathbb{Z}_q$, $H \leftarrow G^{sk}$
2: $\{r_{0,i}\}_{i=1}^d, r_t \xleftarrow{\$} \mathbb{Z}_q$
3: **for** $i \in [d]$ **do**
   % ElGamal encryptions of t^i
4:    $A_{0,i} \leftarrow G^{r_{0,i}}$, $B_{0,i} \leftarrow G^{((-t)^i)} H^{r_{0,i}}$
5: $\mathfrak{T} \leftarrow \mathfrak{Commit}(t; r_t)$ % Pedersen $\mathfrak{T} = G^t \mathfrak{H}^{r_t}$
6: $\mathfrak{X}_0 \leftarrow \mathfrak{Commit}(0; 0)$ % $\mathfrak{X}_0 = 1_{\mathbb{G}_1}$
7: $\mathfrak{A}_0 \leftarrow \mathfrak{Commit}(0; 0)$
8: $x_c \leftarrow (H, \{A_{0,i}, B_{0,i}\}_{i \in [d]}, \mathfrak{T}, \mathfrak{X}_0, \mathfrak{A}_0)$
9: $w_c \leftarrow \begin{pmatrix} t, r_t, \{r_{0,i}\}_{i \in [d]}, \hat{x} := 0, \\ \hat{r}_x := 0, \{r_{0,i} \cdot (0 - t)\}_{i \in [d]}, \\ \alpha := 0, r_\alpha := 0 \\ \alpha \cdot (\hat{x} - t) := 0, r_\alpha(\hat{x} - t) := 0 \end{pmatrix}$
10: $\pi_c \xleftarrow{\$} \Pi_u^{\mathcal{L}c}.Prove(x_c, w_c)$
11: $\pi_{pk} \curlyvee \$$
    $\Pi^{\mathcal{L}_{pk}}.Prove((H, B_{0,1}, \mathfrak{T}), (sk, t, r_{0,1}, r_t))$
12: $pk \leftarrow (H, \mathfrak{T}, \pi_{pk})$
13: $hint_0 \leftarrow (\{A_{0,i}, B_{0,i}\}_{i \in [d]}, \mathfrak{X}_0, \pi_c)$
14: **return** $(sk, pk, hint_0)$

Update$_{pk}$(hint$_{\iota-1}$, tag$_{\iota-1}$, x_ι; r)

1: **parse** $tag_{\iota-1}$ as $(\pi_{t,\iota-1}, \mathfrak{X}_{\iota-1})$
2: $r_{x,\iota} \xleftarrow{\$} \mathbb{Z}_q$
3: $hint_\iota \leftarrow UpdateHint(hint_{\iota-1}, x_\iota, r_{x,\iota})$
4: $\mathfrak{C}_\iota \leftarrow \mathfrak{Commit}(x_\iota, r)$
5: **parse** $hint_{\iota-1}$ as $(\cdot, \mathfrak{X}_{\iota-1}, \cdot)$
6: **parse** $hint_\iota$ as $(\cdot, \mathfrak{X}_\iota, \cdot)$
7: $\pi_{t,\iota} \curlyvee \$$
   $\Pi^{\mathcal{L}_t}.Prove\left(\begin{pmatrix} H, \\ \mathfrak{X}_{\iota-1}, \mathfrak{X}_\iota, \\ \mathfrak{C}_\iota, \pi_{t,\iota-1} \end{pmatrix}, \begin{pmatrix} x_\iota, \\ r_{x,\iota}, \\ r_\iota \end{pmatrix}\right)$
8: $tag_\iota \leftarrow (\pi_{t,\iota}, \mathfrak{X}_\iota)$
9: **return** $(hint_\iota, tag_\iota)$

UpdateHint$_{pk}$(hint$_{\iota-1}$, x_ι, $r_{x,\iota}$) (Helper)

1: **parse** $hint_{\iota-1}$ as $\begin{pmatrix} \{A_{\iota-1,i}, B_{\iota-1,i}\}_{i \in [d]}, \\ \mathfrak{X}_{\iota-1}, \pi_{c,\iota-1} \end{pmatrix}$
2: $\{r_{\iota,i}\}_{i \in [d]} \xleftarrow{\$} \mathbb{Z}_q$
   % $r_{x,\iota}$ is the input to UpdateHint
3: $\mathfrak{X}_\iota \leftarrow \mathfrak{X}_{\iota-1} \cdot \mathfrak{Commit}(x_\iota; r_{x,\iota})$
   % $= \mathfrak{Commit}(\sum_{i \in [\iota]} x_i; \sum r_{x,i})$
4: $\{A_{\iota,i}, B_{\iota,i}\}_{i \in [d]} \curlyvee$
   $UpdatePowers\begin{pmatrix} \{A_{\iota-1,i}, B_{\iota-1,i}\}_{i \in [d]}, \\ x_\iota, \{r_{\iota,i}\}_{i \in [d]} \end{pmatrix}$
5: $x_c \leftarrow \begin{pmatrix} H, \{A_{\iota-1,i}, B_{\iota-1,i}\}_{i \in [d]}, \\ \mathfrak{T}, \mathfrak{X}_{\iota-1}, \mathfrak{A} := 1 \end{pmatrix}$
6: $w_{upd,c} \leftarrow \begin{pmatrix} x_\iota, \{r_{\iota,i}\}_{i \in [d]}, r_{x,\iota}, \\ \alpha := 0, r_\alpha := 0 \end{pmatrix}$
7: $\pi_{c,\iota} \xleftarrow{\$} \Pi_u^{\mathcal{L}c}.Update(\pi_{c,\iota-1}; x_c, \vec{T}_{upd}(w_{upd,c}))$
8: $hint_\iota \leftarrow (\{A_{\iota,i}, B_{\iota,i}\}_{i \in [d]}, \mathfrak{X}_\iota, \pi_{c,\iota})$
9: **return** $hint_\iota$

Escrow$_{pk}$(hint$_\iota$)

   % Partially rerandomize the hint
1: $(\{A_i, B_i\}_{i \in [d]}, \mathfrak{X}, \pi_c) \curlyvee$
   $UpdateHint_{pk}(hint_\iota, 0, 0)$
2: $\alpha, \beta, r_\alpha, r_\beta \xleftarrow{\$} \mathbb{Z}_q^\star$
3: $\mathfrak{A} \leftarrow \mathfrak{Commit}(\alpha; r_\alpha)$
4: $\mathfrak{B} \leftarrow \mathfrak{Commit}(\beta; r_\beta)$
5: $\{D_i\}_{i \in [d]} \leftarrow BlindPowers(\{B_i\}_{i \in [d]}, \alpha)$
6: $(E_1, E_2) \leftarrow Evaluate(\{A_i, B_i\}_{i \in [d]}, \beta)$
7: $x_c \leftarrow (H, \{A_i, B_i\}_{i \in [d]}, \mathfrak{T}, \mathfrak{X}, \mathfrak{A} := 1)$
8: $w_{upd,c} \leftarrow \begin{pmatrix} x_\iota := 0, \{r_{\iota,i} := 0\}_{i \in [d]}, \\ r_{x,\iota} := 0, \alpha, r_\alpha \end{pmatrix}$
9: $\pi_c' \xleftarrow{\$} \Pi_u^{\mathcal{L}c}.Update(\pi_c; x_c, T_{upd}(w_{upd,c}))$
10: $w_e \leftarrow (\alpha, r_\alpha, \beta, r_\beta)$
    % U_i are the Stirling numbers
11: $\pi_e \leftarrow \Pi^{\mathcal{L}_e}.Prove\left(\left(\begin{pmatrix} E_1, E_2, \mathfrak{B}, \mathfrak{A}, \\ \prod A_i^{U_i}, \prod D_i^{U_i} \end{pmatrix}\right), w_e\right)$
12: $esc \leftarrow \begin{pmatrix} E_1, E_2, \pi_e, \pi_c', \mathfrak{X}, \\ \{A_i, D_i\}_{i \in [d]}, \mathfrak{A}, \mathfrak{B} \end{pmatrix}$
13: **return** esc

Decrypt$_{sk}$(esc)

1: **parse** esc as $(E_1, E_2, \cdot)$
2: $M \leftarrow E_1^{-sk} * E_2$
   % ElGamal decryption $M = G^{\beta P(t, \hat{x})}$
3: **return** $[M \stackrel{?}{=} 1_{\mathbb{G}_1}]$

Fig. 3. Our uBlu protocol for $\mathsf{BC} = \mathsf{PedersenC} = (\mathfrak{Setup}, \mathfrak{Commit})$, the predicate $P_d(T, X) = \left[\prod_{\delta=0}^{d-1}(X - T - \delta) \stackrel{?}{=} 0\right]$, and CH20 updatable NIZK. Main Algorithms.

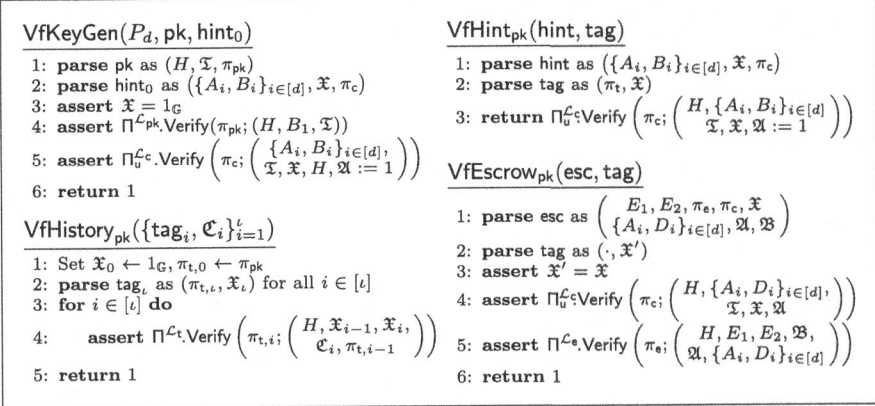

Fig. 4. Verification Algorithms for the uBlu protocol. Continuation of Fig. 3.

Hints and Updatability. Hints are used to update the value concealed in an updatable blueprint.

At each epoch ι hints have two main components: 1) a sequence of d ElGamal ciphertexts in the exponent for a public key H (see Eq. (5) for definition); and 2) a base Pedersen commitment $\mathfrak{X}$ for the accumulated value $\hat{x} = \sum_{i \in [\iota]} x_i$ embedded in the ciphertexts (the meaning of "embedded" will become clear in a moment).

To understand the mechanics behind updatability, we need to look back at the polynomial in our predicates P_d (see Eq. (1)). This is a product of expressions consisting of a sum of a private/unknown value $(X - T)$ and a public value δ. Hence, the polynomial in Eq. (1) can be written as a linear combination of powers of $(X - T)$, namely:

$$\prod_{\delta=0}^{d-1}((X - T) - \delta) = \sum_{i=0}^{d} U_i(X - T)^i \tag{2}$$

where all U_i are well-determined public coefficients that depend solely on i and d.[3] By the binomial theorem, it is possible to rewrite terms on the right side of Eq. (2) as:

$$(X - T + Y)^i = \sum_{j=0}^{i} \left(\binom{i}{j} Y^{i-j} \right) \cdot (X - T)^j. \tag{3}$$

---

[3] To be precise, the U_i are the Stirling coefficients, i.e., Stirling numbers of the first kind are defined as the coefficients in the expansion of the falling factorial polynomial $(x)_n = \prod_{i=0}^{n-1}(x - i) = \sum_{k=0}^{n} s(n,k)x^k$, and have closed form $s(n,k) = \begin{bmatrix} n \\ k \end{bmatrix} = (-1)^{n-k} \cdot \sum_{1 \leq i_1 < \ldots < i_{n-k} \leq n-1} (\prod_{j=1}^{n-k} i_j)$ [50].

Equation (3) shows that we can always build $((x+y)-t)^i$ linearly from (lower powers) $(x-t)^j$ and y. This property is exploited by the UpdatePowers helper function (Fig. 2) to compute hints for $x+y$ as a linear combination of the old hints values (dependent only on x and t), and values dependent only on the new (known) input $y = x_\iota$. For easy reference, we define the y-dependent values as

$$V_{i,j}(y) := \binom{i}{j} y^{i-j} \in \mathbb{Z}_q. \tag{4}$$

Recall that hints contain a sequence of ElGamal ciphertexts, in our construction the initial hint, produced at epoch $\iota = 0$ during key generation, contains encryptions of powers of $-t^i$, i.e. $\{A_{0,i} = G^{r_{0,i}}, B_{0,i} = G^{(-t)^i} H^{r_{0,i}}\}_{i \in [d]}$ where the $\{r_{0,i}\}_{i \in [d]}$ are the random values and t is the regulator's secret threshold for the predicate. Hints get progressively updated (as we show momentarily) into the following form:

$$\{A_{\iota,i} = G^{\hat{r}_{\iota,i}}, B_{\iota,i} = G^{(\hat{x}-t)^i} H^{\hat{r}_{\iota,i}}\}_{i \in [d]}, \tag{5}$$

where $\hat{r}_{0,i}$ denotes accumulated randomness, $\hat{x} = \sum_{i \in [\iota]} x_i$ is the committed value accumulated at epoch ι. (Note that when $\iota = 0$ the ciphertexts conceal the value $(0-t)^i$).

By linear homomorphism, it is possible to add a new known value y to the quantity $(x-t)$ that is concealed in the hints of the previous epoch via the expression:

$$B_{\iota+1,i} = \prod_{j=0}^{i} B_{\iota,j}^{V_{i,j}(y)} = G^{\sum_{j=0}^{i}(x-t)^j \cdot V_{i,j}(y)} \cdot (H^{r_{\iota,i}})^{V_{i,j}(y)} = G^{(x+y-t)^i} H^{r_{\iota,i} V_{i,j}(y)}$$

where the last equality comes for Eq. (3) and the definition in Eq. (4) and $B_{0,0} = G^{t^0} H^0$. Noting that $V_{i,0}(y) = y^i$, each $B_{\iota+1,i}$ can be computed solely from hints of epoch ι with $j > 0$ in the following way:

$$B_{\iota+1,i} = G^{y^i} \prod_{j=1}^{i} B_{\iota,j}^{V_{i,j}(y)}$$

where we isolate the $j = 0$ term $G^{y^i} = B_{\iota,0}^{V_{i,0}(y)}$ to the left.

Preparing Hints for Escrow. This procedure is performed by the Escrow algorithm (Fig. 3). Intuitively, the ElGamal ciphertexts are extracted from the hint, and "evaluated". The Evaluate algorithm raises both ciphertext components to $U_i \cdot \beta$, where β is a random non-zero value (used for masking non-escrow data), and the U_i are the Stirling coefficients described in Sect. 5.1. Specifically:

$$E_1 = \prod_{i \in [d]} (A_i^{U_i})^\beta = G^{\beta \cdot (\sum_{i \in [d]} r_{\iota,i} \cdot U_i)}$$

$$E_2 = \prod_{i \in [d]} (B_i^{U_i})^\beta = \left(G^{\sum_{i \in [d]} U_i (x-t)^i} H^{\sum_{i \in [d]} r_{\iota,i} \cdot U_i} \right)^\beta = G^{\beta \cdot (\prod_{\delta=0}^{d-1}(x-t-\delta))} H^{\beta \cdot (\sum_{i \in [d]} r_{\iota,i} \cdot U_i)}$$

where the last equality comes for Eq. (2). As a result, the holder of the ElGamal secret key cannot efficiently decrypt the evaluated ciphertext. Decryption corresponds to solving the discrete logarithm problem since β is random (and unknown to the authority) unless the ciphertext encrypts the value "0". Note that we built the predicate in such a way that the ciphertext encodes 0 only on the roots of the polynomial, which correspond to values in the "critical range". The Escrow procedure outputs the predicate escrow which, in addition to the evaluated ElGamal ciphertext, contains additional components needed to prove consistency and verify the correctness of the procedure.

Testing the Predicate. This procedure is run by the regulator and simply attempts to decrypt the ciphertext (E_1, E_2) using the secret key sk corresponding to the ElGamal encryption public key H. This entails computing $M = E_2 \cdot (E_1)^{-\mathsf{sk}}$, which by construction is $M = G^{\beta \cdot (\prod_{\delta=0}^{d-1}(X - T - \delta))}$, where the reader should recognize the core polynomial of the predicate (see Eq. (1)). Note that β (unknown to the regulator) acts as a random mask that prevents efficient decryption whenever the polynomial evaluates to a value other than 0. This makes M gibberish unless the predicate P_d evaluates to 1 (the polynomial evaluates to 0), which yields $M = G^0 = 1_{\mathbb{G}}$.

5.2   Achieving Privacy

Up to this point, we discussed the correctness of our construction. Now we focus on how to achieve privacy, i.e., the authority only learns $P_d(t, x)$ and nothing else, and updaters learn nothing about the concealed value.

The IND-CPA property of ElGamal ciphertexts $\{A_i = G^{r_i}, B_i = G^{(x-t)^i} H^{r_i}\}_{i \in [d]}$ prevents updaters from seeing the concealed value. The regulator however can obtain $\{G^{(x-t)^i}\}_{i \in [d]}$ by decrypting the ciphertexts, and even though encoding values in the exponent makes generic decryption inefficient, it does not prevent the regulator from obtaining x by when the encoded values are in small, predictable ranges (which is the setting of our application). To hide x properly, updaters will *blind* hints before sending them to the regulator with the escrow.

The blinding is performed by BlindPowers and consists of multiplying each B_i component by a value W_i^{α}, where the $\{W_i\}_{i=1}^d$ are public group elements generated upon system setup, and α is a freshly sampled random value. Specifically, blinded ciphertexts are of the form: $\{A_i, D_i := B_i \cdot W_i^{\alpha}\}_{i \in [d]}$. To achieve efficient updatable proofs, the α component will be zero while the hints are updated, which means parties will exchange unblinded hints; and α will only be set while the hints are converted to an escrow (more details on this in the upcoming description of updatable proofs).

5.3   Achieving Soundness Using NIZKs

Intuitively speaking, soundness means that whenever the data (primarily hints and escrows) is valid, it must be "good" – bind to the history, contain only updates that are relevant to commitments, etc. As of now, hints and escrows can be malformed and lack these guarantees. We overcome these issues by employing NIZKs to ensure data correctness.

Our construction employs four kinds of proofs. The *key proof* (π_{pk}) will show that the public key was built correctly. The *consistency proof* (π_c) will show the consistency of all the components in a hint, and it will be updatable (details of which are the main technical contribution of the construction). The *trace proof* (π_t) will show that the new hint—obtained updating a hint from the previous epoch—is computed correctly and that the update value is the same as in the external commitment $\mathfrak{C}$. Trace proofs are included in tags tag and form the trace. The *escrow proof* (π_e) will show that the escrow esc was produced correctly from a tag and its hint.

Key Proof (π_{pk}). During the key generation phase, the regulator produces the ElGamal encryptions of the powers of the threshold (as explained in Sect. 5.1), in particular, we will use the first ciphertext $(A_{0,1}, B_{0,1}) := (G^{r_{0,1}}, G^t H^{r_{0,1}})$ that is a standard ElGamal encryption of t for the auditor's public key H. In addition, the regulator computes a Pedersen commitment to the threshold $\mathfrak{T} = G^t \mathfrak{H}^{r_t}$ (which is included in the public key pk). The public key additionally contains π_{pk} that proves knowledge of the sk corresponding to the ElGamal public key $H = G^{\mathsf{sk}}$, and knowledge of a threshold value t and randomnesses that realize the public components $B_{0,1}$ (contained in hint_0) and $\mathfrak{T}$. Specifically, the language $\mathcal{L}_{\mathsf{pk}}$ is defined by:

$$\begin{aligned} \mathsf{x} &= (H, B_{0,1}, \mathfrak{T}) \in \mathbb{G}^3 \\ \mathsf{w} &= (\mathsf{sk}, t, r_{0,1}, r_t) \in \mathbb{Z}_q^4 \end{aligned} \quad \text{and} \quad M(\mathsf{x}) = \begin{bmatrix} G & 0 & 0 & 0 \\ 0 & G & H & 0 \\ 0 & G & 0 & \mathfrak{H} \end{bmatrix}.$$

where witness here and in the following is highlighted in gray.

Consistency Proof (π_c). This proof shows that all the hint values (including the $\{A_{0,i}, B_{0,i}\}$ produced by KeyGen) are indeed encodings of $(\hat{x} - t)^i$, where $\hat{x}$ and t are the current accumulated value and the original threshold selected by the regulator. It works for both unblinded (B_i) and blinded (D_i) hints. This proof is produced (1) originally by the regulator in KeyGen to prove the consistency of powers in $\mathsf{hint}_{\mathsf{pk}}$, and (2) by updating parties to prove that the hints they send further are still consistent, (3) by updating parties to prove to the regulator that the blinded hints in the escrow are consistent. The consistency proof will always refer to $\mathfrak{T}$ (the Pedersen commitment to the threshold included in pk) to make sure that the witness t used in all proof iterations is the same as the initial one.

At epoch ι, the consistency proof π_c proves the following statement: for an instance

$$\mathsf{x} = (H, \{A_{\iota,i}, D_{\iota,i}\}_{i \in [d]}, \mathfrak{T}, \mathfrak{X}_\iota, \mathfrak{A}) \in \mathbb{G}^{2d+4}$$

there exists a witness

$$\mathsf{w} = \begin{pmatrix} t, r_t, \hat{x}_\iota, \hat{r}_{\mathsf{x},\iota}, \alpha, r_\alpha, \{\hat{r}_{\iota,i}\}_{i \in [d]}, \\ (\hat{x}_\iota - t), \{r_{\iota,i}(\hat{x}_\iota - t)\}_{i \in [d-1]}, \alpha(\hat{x}_\iota - t), r_\alpha(\hat{x}_\iota - t) \end{pmatrix} \in \mathbb{Z}_q^{2d+8}$$

such that the following relations are satisfied:

1. $\mathfrak{T} = G^t \mathfrak{H}^{r_t}$ (r_t is the randomness used to create $\mathfrak{T}$, the Pedersen commitment to the threshold)
2. $\mathfrak{X}_\iota = G^{\hat{x}_\iota} \mathfrak{H}^{\hat{r}_{x,\iota}}$ (Pedersen commitment to $\hat{x}_\iota$, the accumulated value)
3. $\mathfrak{A}_\iota = G^\alpha \mathfrak{H}^{r_\alpha}$ (Pedersen commitment to the randomness for blinding factors)
4. $A_{\iota,1} = G^{\hat{r}_{\iota,1}}$ ($r_{\iota,i}$ is the randomness used to create the ElGamal ciphertext)
5. $D_{\iota,1} = G^{\hat{x}_\iota - t} H^{\hat{r}_{\iota,1}} W_1^\alpha$ (the blinded ciphertext encrypts $(\hat{x} - t)$)
6. $\forall\, i \in [2, d]$:

    (a) $A_{\iota,i} = G^{\hat{r}_{\iota,i}}$

    (b) $D_{\iota,i} = (D_{\iota,i-1})^{\hat{x}_\iota - t} (H^{-1})^{\hat{r}_{\iota,i-1}(\hat{x}_\iota - t)} H^{\hat{r}_{\iota,i}} (W_{i-1}^{-1})^{\alpha(\hat{x}_\iota - t)} W_i^\alpha$
7. *Witness products* (needed for step 6):

    (a) $1 = G^{\hat{x}_\iota} (G^{-1})^t (G^{-1})^{\hat{x}_\iota - t}$

    (b) $1 = \mathfrak{A}_\iota^{\hat{x}_\iota - t} (G^{-1})^{\alpha(\hat{x}_\iota - t)} (\mathfrak{H}^{-1})^{r_\alpha(\hat{x}_\iota - t)}$

    (c) $1 = A_{\iota,i}^{\hat{x}_\iota - t} (G^{-1})^{\hat{r}_{\iota,i}(\hat{x}_\iota - t)}$, for $i \in [d-1]$:

The complexity of this formula is due to the fact that we need to prove the relationship between the powers of $(\hat{x} - t)^i$, which we do recursively. Note that we do not store powers as additional witnesses; the only witness is the first power $(\hat{x}_\iota - t)$.

When simplified, the recursive formulas reduce to the following four relations:

$$\mathfrak{T} = G^t \mathfrak{H}^{r_t} \qquad\qquad \mathfrak{X} = G^{\hat{x}} \mathfrak{H}^{\hat{r}_x}$$
$$\mathfrak{A} = G^\alpha \mathfrak{H}^{r_\alpha} \qquad (A_i, D_i) = (G^{\hat{r}_i}, G^{(\hat{x}-t)^i} H^{\hat{r}_i} W_i^\alpha) \text{ for } i \in [d]$$

As briefly mentioned before, we use α in two different ways depending on the scenario: (1) while updating the hints blinding is disabled: users will set $\alpha = r_\alpha = 0$, and thus $\mathfrak{A} = 1$; thus D_i will be actually just B_i; (2) while creating escrow, the blinding values α, r_α will be introduced, $\mathfrak{A} \neq 1$ will be sent to the regulator, but α, r_α will not, which will ensure hiding of the blinding approach.

Therefore, to verify the consistency proof, the party (user or regulator) needs an instance x, which consists of the original $D_{0,1}$ produced during key generation; a collection of ciphertexts $\{(A_{\iota,i}, D_{\iota,i})\}_{i \in [d]}$ (unblinded or blinded); a tag tag_ι containing a commitment $\mathfrak{X}$ to the accumulated $\hat{x}_\iota$; and a special commitment $\mathfrak{A}$ to the blinding randomness α (either trivial $\mathfrak{A} = 1$ for users, or nontrivial for regulator).

Consistency proofs are instantiated by Π_u, which is linear in the size of the hints but is also updatable, meaning that the proof for new hints is a transformation of the previous consistency proof. Practically, this is quite efficient, since otherwise consistency proofs would need to be aggregated, and hints would thus grow in size; this is especially expensive given that the consistency language is linear in d. Because of updatability, no updating party (except for the regulator, who creates the initial proof) ever knows the whole witness "contained" in the proof.

Updating Hints and Consistency Proof. The consistency proof language $\mathcal{L}_{\mathsf{c}}$ is structured in such a way, that it supports a transformation that we will call T_{upd}, which can change all the necessary witnesses, including our target aggregated commitment value $\hat{x}_\iota$. To fit within the algebraic language updatability framework, we must be able to represent the new instance and witness as a linear combination of the old instance and witness values correspondingly.

We first start with the instance, which implicitly defines $T_{\mathsf{xm}}, T_{\mathsf{xa}}$:

- Using the (plaintext) update value x_ι, sample rerandomisation factors $r_{\iota,i}$, and compute the new hints:
  - $A_{\iota,i} = \left(\prod_{j=1}^{i} (A_{\iota-1,j})^{V_{i,j}(x_\iota)} \right) G^{r_{\iota,i}}$.
  - $B_{\iota,i} = G^{x_\iota^i} \left(\prod_{j=1}^{i} (B_{\iota-1,j})^{V_{i,j}(x_\iota)} \right) H^{r_{\iota,i}}$, where $G^{x_\iota^i}$ covers the role of implicit $(B_{\iota-1,0})^{V_{i,0}(x_\iota)}$.
- Sample $r_{\mathsf{x},\iota}$, update the tag commitment $\mathfrak{X}_\iota = \mathfrak{X}_{\iota-1} G^{x_\iota} \mathfrak{H}^{r_{\mathsf{x},\iota}}$.
- Sample α, r_α, create the special commitment $\mathfrak{A} = G^\alpha \mathfrak{H}^{r_\alpha}$ (optionally, or still assume $\mathfrak{A} = 1$).

Next, we show how to update the witness, which implicitly defines $T_{\mathsf{wm}}, T_{\mathsf{wa}}$:

$$\hat{x}_\iota := \hat{x}_{\iota-1} + x_\iota \qquad\qquad \hat{x}_\iota - t := \hat{x}_{\iota-1} - t + x_\iota$$

$$\hat{r}_{\iota,i} := \sum_{j=1}^{i} \hat{r}_{\iota-1,i} \cdot V_{i,j}(x_\iota) + r_{\iota,i} \quad \hat{r}_{\iota,i}(\hat{x}_\iota - t) := \sum_{j=1}^{i} \hat{r}_{\iota-1,i}(\hat{x}_{\iota-1} - t) \cdot V_{i,j}(x_\iota) +$$

$$\sum_{j=1}^{i} \hat{r}_{\iota-1,i} \cdot x_\iota \cdot V_{i,j}(x_\iota) +$$

$$r_{\iota,i} \cdot (\hat{x}_{\iota-1} - t) + r_{\iota,i} x_\iota$$

$$\hat{r}_{\mathsf{x},\iota} := \hat{r}_{\mathsf{x},\iota-1} + r_{\mathsf{x},\iota}$$

$$\hat{\alpha} := \alpha \qquad\qquad \hat{\alpha}(\hat{x}_\iota - t) := \alpha \cdot (\hat{x}_{\iota-1} - t) + \alpha \cdot x_\iota$$

$$\hat{r}_\alpha := r_\alpha \qquad\qquad \hat{r}_\alpha(\hat{x}_\iota - t) := r_\alpha \cdot (\hat{x}_{\iota-1} - t) + r_\alpha \cdot x_\iota$$

The language transformation T_{upd} is formally a set of matrices $(T_{\mathsf{xm}}, T_{\mathsf{xa}}, T_{\mathsf{wm}}, T_{\mathsf{wa}})$ as implicitly defined above, that is parameterized by a vector of update values $\mathsf{w}_{\mathsf{upd,c}} = (x_\iota, \{r_{\iota,i}\}_{i \in [d]}, r_{\mathsf{x},\iota}, \alpha, r_\alpha)$, where all the "product witnesses" can be defined in terms of this tuple.

Note that we do not describe the last four witnesses as "accumulatable"— if we try to update w with (α, r_α) more than once, $\hat{\alpha}$ will not be equal to the sum of previous α unlike e.g. $\hat{r}_{\mathsf{x},\iota}$. This is due to our setup: (1) we apply T_{upd} incrementally parameterized with $(x_\iota, \{r_{\iota,i}\}_{i \in [d]}, r_{\mathsf{x},\iota}, \alpha = 0, r_\alpha = 0)$ with *blinding turned off*; (2) and then, given $\alpha = r_\alpha = 0$ and $\mathfrak{A} = 1$, we can *introduce blinding*, applying T_{upd} parameterized with $\alpha, r_\alpha \neq 0$ only once. This separation is a result of a deeper limitation of Π_{u}, discussion of which we defer to [29]:

Theorem 1 (Validity of T_{upd} (Informal)). *The transformation T_{upd} is valid w.r.t. $\mathcal{L}_{\mathsf{c}}$, and the Π_{u} proof system for $\mathcal{L}_{\mathsf{c}}$ satisfies update completeness* *and derivation privacy w.r.t. T_{upd} when applied according to the two distinct parametrizations described above.*

Trace Proof (π_t). Trace proofs are small aggregatable proofs that allow parties to linearise their updates. At epoch ι, the party performing an update with local value x_ι will prove the following statement. For an instance $x = (H, \mathfrak{X}_{\iota-1}, \mathfrak{X}_\iota, \mathfrak{C}_\iota, \pi_{t,\iota-1})$ (where $\mathfrak{C}_\iota = G^{x_\iota} \mathfrak{H}^r$), there exists a witness $w = (x_\iota, r_{x,\iota}, \mathfrak{r}_\iota)$ such that:

1. $\mathfrak{X}_\iota = \mathfrak{X}_{\iota-1} \cdot G^{x_\iota} \mathfrak{H}^{r_{x,\iota}}$ (the new tag is computed form the previous one, and the updating information is completely known to the updater).
2. $\mathfrak{C}_\iota = \mathrm{Commit}(x_\iota, \mathfrak{r}_\iota)$ (the updated value x_ι is the same as in $\mathfrak{C}_\iota$).

Note that the value $\pi_{t,\iota-1}$ is in the instance, and thus bound by the NIZK being a signature of knowledge, but it does not appear in any equations. In practice, this translates with hashing the additional value when computing a Fiat-Shamir challenge, but not using it otherwise. This proof will be instantiated with a standard non-updatable Π Σ-protocol.

As a potential future-work extension of our scheme, one can consider parties including their signatures on these elements, to sign the update act, which can be used for extending updater accountability w.r.t. the regulator.

Escrow Proof (π_e). This proof is produced upon conversion of a hint into an escrow esc. The esc contains an ElGamal encryption $E = (E_1, E_2)$ of $\beta \cdot P_d(\hat{x}, t)$ for some masking value β (random), an escrow proof, a consistency proof (rerandomized, and with α introduced), and information needed to check the proofs: a commitment $\mathfrak{X}$ to the accumulated value, a commitment $\mathfrak{B}$ to the randomness β, a commitment $\mathfrak{A}$ to the introduced accumulated blinding exponent α, and, most importantly, *blinded* ElGamal ciphertexts $\{A_i, D_i\}_{i \in [d]}$ (with α).

The escrow proof for $\mathcal{L}_e$ proves the following statement. For an instance $x = (E_1, E_2, \mathfrak{B}, \mathfrak{A}, \prod A_i^{U_i}, \prod D_i^{U_i})$, there exists a witness $w = (\alpha, r_\alpha, \beta, r_\beta, \beta\alpha, r_\beta\alpha)$ such that the following conditions are satisfied:

1. $\mathfrak{A} = G^\alpha \mathfrak{H}^{r_\alpha}$
2. $\mathfrak{B} = G^\beta \mathfrak{H}^{r_\beta}$
3. $1 = \mathfrak{B}^\alpha (G^{-1})^{\beta\alpha} (\mathfrak{H}^{-1})^{r_\beta\alpha}$
4. $E_1 = \prod_i (A_i^{U_i})^\beta$
5. $E_2 = \prod_i (D_i^{U_i})^\beta \cdot \prod_i (W_i^{-U_i})^{\beta\alpha}$

The language is compact, so the proof π_e can be created from scratch, and since it doesn't need to be updatable performance-wise we can also use standard Π as a proof system.

5.4   Security of the uBlu Construction

The main security statement of our construction can be summarized as follows.

Theorem 2. *The* uBlu *protocol w.r.t.* (PedersenC, $P_d(T, X)$) *introduced in Sect. 5 is secure according to the security Definitions 8–13 (all in Sect. 4.1) under: hiding and binding of* PedersenC*; DDH in* $\mathbb{G}_1$ *that in particular implies ElGamal IND-CPA; completeness, strong simulation-extractability, and ZK of* Π*; and (update) completeness, soundness, derivation privacy, and ZK of* Π$_u$.

Proof (Summary). The detailed statement of the theorem and its proof are deferred to [29]. Here we present the summary and main intuition.

History Binding is proven by unfolding simulation-extractability of Π, instantiating trace proofs, along the history.

Soundness reduces to KS of Π, soundness of Π$_u$, and binding of PedersenC. The first part of soundness is a trivial application of Π KS, while for the second part, we need to unpack all the NIZKs, using the fact that they are "connected" by binding commitments, to arrive at the statement about correct decryptability of esc.

Threshold Hiding is, first, by ZK of both Π and Π$_u$—and after proofs in pk, hint$_0$ are simulated, we reduce the property directly to IND-CPA of ElGamal, holding under DDH in $\mathbb{G}_1$. *Hint hiding* is very similar to threshold hiding: it holds by IND-CPA of Pedersen (A_i, D_i are hiding), ZK of the NIZKs, but also by derivation privacy of Π$_u$, since Update uses Π$_u$.Update internally. Similarly, *Tag hiding* is a direct consequence of ZK of trace proof and hiding of PedersenC.

Escrow hiding holds under DDH in $\mathbb{G}_1$, security of PedersenC, ZK of Π, Π$_u$, KS of Π, and soundness of Π$_u$. The hardest part in simulating esc is arguing that encryption (E_1, E_2) has a "correct" form, which is similar to the soundness proof.   □

5.5   Adding Range Proofs for Improved Accuracy

For efficiency, construction approximates the predicate $[x > t]$ with a polynomial that has roots in the range $[t, t + d - 1]$, for a reasonably small value d. For the approximation to be accurate, however, we need to ensure that an update does not jump over the range or cause an overflow. In other words, we need an extra range proof ensuring that the value x_i added during the update is not too large.

Range proofs can be conveniently integrated into our protocol which already exposes $\mathfrak{C}_i = G^{x_i} \mathfrak{H}^{\tau_i}$ for exactly this purpose. Among the existing approaches to range proofs on Pedersen commitments, we recall Bulletproofs [12] or "adjusted" Pedersen commitments and square decomposition [24]. These are efficient, with the latter only requiring a constant amount of exponentiations and group elements in the proof.

Here we present a much simpler approach than the aforementioned: committing to bits of x_i, and using Π to prove that (1) $\mathfrak{C}$ contains bit-reconstructed values; and (2) commitments are actually to the bit values $\in \{0, 1\}$. The latter can be done as follows: given $C = G^x H^r$ for H being chosen uniformly at random, note that condition $x \in \{0, 1\}$ is equivalent to $(x - 1)x = 0$, therefore it is enough to prove that $C^{x-1} = H^{r'}$ for some (known to the prover but private) r'. This requires $O(\log(d))$ exponentiations and group elements, which is practically efficient for our choice of d.

With this in mind, every updater can only "adjust" the aggregated rating $\hat{x}$ by $x_\iota \in [0, d]$, which makes our uBlu construction a proper score aggregation system. Other more complicated predicates can be proven similarly about x_ι; commitment $\mathfrak{C}_i$ is used precisely for this kind of external integration of a uBlu scheme with other applications.

5.6   Extensions and Applications

The uBlu protocol we presented in this section is designed for a limited class of predicates (range predicates) to keep the core construction simple. In this section we suggest generalizations of our construction to support arbitrary polynomial predicates and non-binary escrow values.

Arbitrary Polynomial Predicates. Our uBlu protocol targets the "range polynomial" $P_d(T, X)$, that is zero in $[t, t + d - 1]$. We leverage the special structure of P_d to design hints linear in d. Clearly, the uBlu construction can easily be adapted to the case of polynomials $P(T, X)$ that capture $r > 1$ disjoint ranges (e.g. $[t_1, t_1 + d_1]$ *and* $[t_2, t_2 + d_2]$). The cost is r sets of hints that are linear in the corresponding range length.

However, the algebraic trick used in our protocol to construct and update hints can be generalized to *any* polynomial predicate $P(T, X)$ at the cost of a *quadratic* number of hints, each encoding $\{x^i t^j\}_{i,j:i+j \leq d}$, which are updatable in a similar way our linear hints are. An example of using non-interval predicates could be designing P to encode a certain few excluded revealing points, for example representing a certain blocklist of public key hashes.

In detail, assuming $P(T, X) = \sum_{i,j} C_{i,j} X^i T^j$, we can always construct the evaluation of the updated polynomial $P(T, X + Y) = \sum_{i,j} C_{i,j}(X + Y)^i T^j$ from the hints, if we can transform old hints $\{(x^i t^j)\}_{i,j}$ into the new ones $\{(x + y)^i t^j\}_{i,j}$. The latter is always possible since $(x + y)^i t^j = \sum_{k=0}^{i} \binom{i}{k} y^{i-k}(t^j x^k)$ is a linear combination of the previous $(t^j x^k)$, which are known. Quadratic number of hints makes many algorithms much less efficient and generally imposes much stricter upper bounds on d.

Multi-variate Polynomial Predicates. It is possible to extend updatable blueprints to support evaluations of predicates described by multi-variate polynomials, by considering all the necessary cross-term monomials $\{\prod_{i=1}^{n} X_i^{j_i}\}$ as hints.

For example, assume the polynomial is of the form $P(T, X_1, \ldots, X_n) = \sum_i^n P_i(T, X_i)$, and we are running uBlu in parallel for each P_i independently, however with the same starting commitment to t. Updates and the evaluation can still be done in a manner similar to the core protocol. The only significant difference now is the escrow proof will now have to attest to the evaluation of joint $P(T, X_1, \ldots, X_n)$ instead of independent $P_i(T, X_i)$ as in the basic scheme. This, however, can still be encoded as an algebraic relation—now it will take $\{\mathfrak{A}_i\}_{i=1}^{n}$ (one element per each "parallel" run), which will lead to the introduction of $\{\beta\alpha_i\}_{i=1}^{s}$ witnesses and the statement for E_2 will have to change to $E_2 = (\prod_{i=1}^{d} \prod_{j=1}^{n} D_{j,i}^{U_i})^{\beta} \cdot (\prod_{i=1}^{d} W_i)^{\sum_{j=1}^{n} \beta\alpha_j}$.

As a slightly different but instructive example, let us consider evaluating the polynomial corresponding to the computation of the squared Euclidean distance. In this case, we manage the two-variate polynomial $P(T_X, T_Y, X, Y) = (X - T_X)^2 + (Y - T_Y)^2$, where (T_X, T_Y) are the coordinates of a departure point, and X, Y are updates on the respective latitude and longitude deviation from the previous (or initial) position. The regulator needs to commit to T_X, T_Y separately. In order to evaluate $P(t_X, t_Y, x + x', y + y')$ it is sufficient to notice that:

$$
\begin{aligned}
((x' + x) &- t_X)^2 + ((y' - y) - t_y)^2 = \\
= \; & x'^2 + x^2 + t_X^2 + 2(x'(x + t_X) + x t_X) + y'^2 + y^2 + t_Y^2 + 2(y'(y + t_Y) + y t_Y) \\
= \; & x'^2 + 2x'(x + t_X) + (x^2 + t_X^2 + 2x t_X) + y'^2 + 2y'(y + t_Y) + (y^2 + t_Y^2 + 2y t_Y)
\end{aligned}
$$

where in the last line, all terms in parenthesis are computable from the previous hints.

Non-binary Predicate Value. In some applications, *e.g.*, when users are anonymous, it is desirable for $\mathsf{Escrow_{pk}}$ to return not only a binary value but also information about the user (*e.g.* their identity) to enable further investigations. Our uBlu scheme can be modified to achieve this functionality. The core idea is to construct $\mathsf{Escrow_{pk}}$ so that instead of returning an encryption of $\beta P_1(x)$, the algorithm returns $(\beta_1 P_1(x), \beta_2 P_1(x) + P_2(x))$ for random β_1, β_2, which in case $P_1(x) \neq 0$ produces two random points and in the case $P_1(x) = 0$ (*i.e.* if the escrow is decryptable) returns $(0, P_2(x))$. The extra information $y = P_2(x)$ can also be proven to be coming from the pre-computed commitment $\mathfrak{C}_y$ (e.g. coming from an external identity scheme). Since P_1 and P_2 are different predicates, they will have different sets of hints; but assuming that $\deg P_2$ is low, the previous paragraph explained how we can extend the uBlu scheme to support polynomial reconstructions for arbitrary P_2. Naturally, the escrow proof must be modified to attest to the correct evaluation of the escrow.

6 Instantiation and Performance

In this section, we summarise the implementation and performance details of the uBlu construction. We consider an instantiation of our updatable blueprint schemes in the "standard model", with a caveat that we apply the Fiat-Shamir heuristic for the non-updatable proof system Π. The updatable proof system Π_u, which is instantiated by the CH20 [23] NIZK, is non-interactive by design.

Table 2. Complexity of our uBlu construction in terms of the number P of pairing operations and E_1/E_2 the number of multiplicative group scalar exponentiations in $\mathbb{G}_1/\mathbb{G}_2$. Constant d is defining the "explosion" range $[t, t + d - 1]$. Value ι_{cur} stands for the current epoch (history length).

Algorithm	$\#P$	$\#E_1$	$\#E_2$
Setup	0	$O(1)$	$O(1)$
KeyGen	0	$9d + O(1)$	$4d + O(1)$
Update	0	$4d^2 + O(d)$	$1.5d^2 + O(d)$
Escrow	0	$14d + O(1)$	$4d + O(1)$
Decrypt	0	$O(1)$	0
VfKeyGen	$2d + O(1)$	$10d + O(1)$	$6d + O(1)$
VfHint	$2d + O(1)$	$10d + O(1)$	$6d + O(1)$
VfHistory	0	$O(\iota_{cur})$	$O(\iota_{cur})$
VfEscrow	$2d + O(1)$	$10d + O(1)$	$6d + O(1)$

Table 3. Size complexity of the different components of our uBlu construction in terms of the number of group elements (or elements of equivalent size).

Object	pp	sk	pk	hint	tag	esc
$\#\mathbb{G}_1$	$O(d^2)$	1	$O(1)$	$4d + 5$	$O(1)$	$4d + O(1)$
$\#\mathbb{G}_2$	$O(1)$	0	0	$2d + 8$	0	$2d + 8$

Asymptotic Summary. We start our performance evaluation by summarising the minimal computational complexity of the different algorithms of uBlu in Table 2 and the sizes of the different components in Table 3. For this we assume that the public combinatorial values (binomial coefficients for $V_{i,j}$ and Stirling coefficients for U_i) are pre-computed, which requires total auxiliary storage of $2d^2$ elements (added into the cost for Setup). For more details on the asymptotic performance estimates, especially w.r.t. the NIZKs, see [29].

Implementation. We implemented a proof-of-concept prototype[4] of our uBlu scheme using the Rust programming language and benchmark it on a clean bare metal server with a 6 core (12 thread) Xeon® E-2286G CPU @ 4.00GHz, on the fully updated version of Ubuntu 24.04. The choice of Rust is motivated by type safety (which helps prevent bugs), memory safety (preventing most buffer or heap overflow attacks), extensive possibility for static analysis, and relatively high performance; all of which are features valuable for cryptographic implementations, should our code be used in production in the future.

We used the `ark_ec` library from Arkworks for elliptic curve operations since it contains a well-maintained and optimized implementation of common curves

---

[4] Available at https://anonymous.4open.science/r/ublu-impl-20A7/ (anonymized).

such as BLS and Barreto-Naehrig [4]. For our concrete implementation we use BLS12-381 [3] as it is a type III pairing friendly elliptic curve and gives a reasonable compromise between speed and security. We also use this curve to realize the base commitment BC using Pedersen's scheme [56] over $\mathbb{G}_1$.

Code Design. To provide a compromise between readability and ease of efficiency evaluation, our code is implemented generally verbatim from the specification. However, since preliminary benchmarks unsurprisingly showed the main bottleneck in the pairing operations needed for the CH20 proof verifications, we did introduce relevant optimizations. More specifically, since the computation of $\hat{e}([M(\mathsf{x})]_1, [\boldsymbol{d}]_2) \stackrel{?}{=} \hat{e}(\mathsf{x}, [z]_2) \cdot \hat{e}([\boldsymbol{a}]_1, [1]_2)$ requires the multiplication of the result of multiple pairings, we take advantage of the fact that this can be reduced significantly using a Miller loop [53]. Even so, checking the statement above still requires $l = |\mathsf{x}|$ uses of the Miller loop trick. Thus, instead of checking each of the l results of the Miller loop, we instead check a single, randomized linear combination (in the target group). That is, we pick a random scalar coefficient for each of the l rows in M and multiply this with all $\mathbb{G}_1$ pairing inputs and then execute a single Miller loop over everything. Thus the result will be a random linear combination of the coefficients in the target group. This yields an improvement of close to $\times 10$. Along the single-threaded evaluation, we also parallelized the point-scalar exponentiations per row of all matrices using `par_iter` from `rayon`.

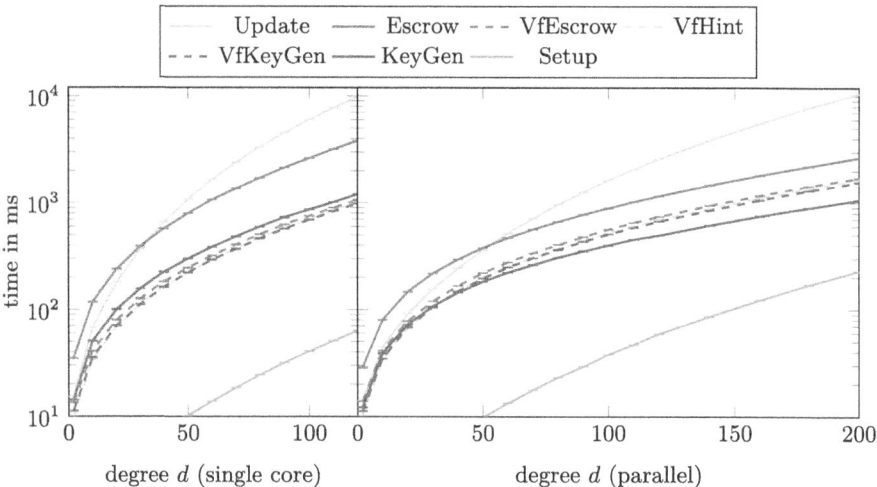

Fig. 5. Benchmark of uBlu, without and with parallelism enabled. VfHistory requires 1.15 ms per update and Decrypt takes below 1 ms, so both are not shown on the figure.

We show the benchmark results in Fig. 5 for all algorithms (except VfHistory and Decrypt which are idependent of d) with d as the variability point on the x-axis. VfHistory scales linearly with 1.15 ms per ι and Decrypt takes less than 1 ms. The benchmarks were run using 'cargo bench' with the `criterion` library and the error-bars represent the standard deviation from at least 10 iterations. From the graphs we see that Update and Escrow are the slowest, mostly updating and generating proofs, with Update clearly exhibiting the quadratic pattern pointed out in the asymptotic analysis. The parallelization approximately allows doubling d while keeping the same runtime compared to single-threaded. The memory usage during any benchmark is low under 50 MB. Finally, we note that there is *still* space for optimisation in our implementation, promising a constant factor decrease on most expensive timings.

References

1. T. Acar and L. Nguyen. "Revocation for Delegatable Anonymous Credentials". In: *PKC 2011*. Ed. by D. Catalano, N. Fazio, R. Gennaro, and A. Nicolosi. Vol. 6571. LNCS. Springer, Heidelberg, Mar. 2011, pp. 423–440. https://doi.org/10.1007/978-3-642-19379-8_26.

2. E. Androulaki, J. Camenisch, A. D. Caro, M. Dubovitskaya, K. Elkhiyaoui, and B. Tackmann. "Privacy-preserving auditable token payments in a permissioned blockchain system". In: *AFT '20: 2nd ACM Conference on Advances in Financial Technologies, New York, NY, USA, October 21-23, 2020*. ACM, 2020, pp. 255–267. https://doi.org/10.1145/3419614.3423259. https://doi.org/10.1145/3419614.3423259.

3. P. S. L. M. Barreto, B. Lynn, and M. Scott. "Constructing Elliptic Curves with Prescribed Embedding Degrees". In: *SCN 02*. Ed. by S. Cimato, C. Galdi, and G. Persiano. Vol. 2576. LNCS. Springer, Heidelberg, Sept. 2003, pp. 257–267. https://doi.org/10.1007/3-540-36413-7_19.

4. P. S. L. M. Barreto and M. Naehrig. "Pairing-Friendly Elliptic Curves of Prime Order". In: *SAC 2005*. Ed. by B. Preneel and S. Tavares. Vol. 3897. LNCS. Springer, Heidelberg, Aug. 2006, pp. 319–331. https://doi.org/10.1007/11693383_22.

5. J. Bartusek, S. Garg, A. Jain, and G.-V. Policharla. "End-to-End Secure Messaging with Traceability Only for Illegal Content". In: *EUROCRYPT 2023*, Part V. Ed. by C. Hazay and M. Stam. Vol. 14008. LNCS. Springer, Heidelberg, Apr. 2023, pp. 35–66. https://doi.org/10.1007/978-3-031-30589-4_2.

6. C. Baum, J. H. Chiang, B. David, and T. K. Frederiksen. "SoK: PrivacyEnhancing Technologies in Finance". In: *5th Conference on Advances in Financial Technologies, AFT 2023, October 23-25, 2023, Princeton, NJ, USA*. Ed. by J. Bonneau and S. M. Weinberg. Vol. 282. LIPIcs. Schloss Dagstuhl - Leibniz-Zentrum für Informatik, 2023, 12:1-12:30. https://doi.org/10.4230/LIPICS.AFT.2023.12. https://doi.org/10.4230/LIPIcs.AFT.2023.12.

7. M. Belenkiy, J. Camenisch, M. Chase, M. Kohlweiss, A. Lysyanskaya, and H. Shacham. "Randomizable Proofs and Delegatable Anonymous Credentials". In: *CRYPTO 2009*. Ed. by S. Halevi. Vol. 5677. LNCS. Springer, Heidelberg, Aug. 2009, pp. 108–125. https://doi.org/10.1007/978-3-642-03356-8_7.

8. E. Ben-Sasson, A. Chiesa, E. Tromer, and M. Virza. "Scalable Zero Knowledge via Cycles of Elliptic Curves". In: *CRYPTO 2014, Part II*. Ed. by J. A. Garay and R. Gennaro. Vol. 8617. LNCS. Springer, Heidelberg, Aug. 2014, pp. 276–294. https://doi.org/10.1007/978-3-662-44381-1_16.

9. N. Bitansky, R. Canetti, A. Chiesa, and E. Tromer. "Recursive composition and bootstrapping for SNARKS and proof-carrying data". In: *45th ACM STOC*. Ed. by D. Boneh, T. Roughgarden, and J. Feigenbaum. ACM Press, June 2013, pp. 111–120. https://doi.org/10.1145/2488608.2488623.

10. O. Blazy, G. Fuchsbauer, D. Pointcheval, and D. Vergnaud. "Signatures on Randomizable Ciphertexts". In: *PKC 2011*. Ed. by D. Catalano, N. Fazio, R. Gennaro, and A. Nicolosi. Vol. 6571. LNCS. Springer, Heidelberg, Mar. 2011, pp. 403–422. https://doi.org/10.1007/978-3-642-19379-8_25.

11. S. Bowe, J. Grigg, and D. Hopwood. *Halo: Recursive Proof Composition without a Trusted Setup*. Cryptology ePrint Archive, Report 2019/1021. https://eprint.iacr.org/2019/1021. 2019.

12. B. Bünz, J. Bootle, D. Boneh, A. Poelstra, P. Wuille, and G. Maxwell. "Bulletproofs: Short Proofs for Confidential Transactions and More". In: *2018 IEEE Symposium on Security and Privacy*. IEEE Computer Society Press, May 2018, pp. 315–334. https://doi.org/10.1109/SP.2018.00020.

13. B. Bünz, A. Chiesa, W. Lin, P. Mishra, and N. Spooner. *Proof-Carrying Data without Succinct Arguments*. Cryptology ePrint Archive, Report 2020/1618. https://eprint.iacr.org/2020/1618. 2020.

14. B. Bünz, A. Chiesa, W. Lin, P. Mishra, and N. Spooner. "Proof-Carrying Data Without Succinct Arguments". In: *CRYPTO 2021, Part I*. Ed. by T. Malkin and C. Peikert. Vol. 12825. LNCS. Virtual Event: Springer, Heidelberg, Aug. 2021, pp. 681–710. https://doi.org/10.1007/978-3-030-84242-0_24.

15. B. Bünz, A. Chiesa, P. Mishra, and N. Spooner. "Recursive Proof Composition from Accumulation Schemes". In: *TCC 2020, Part II*. Ed. by R. Pass and K. Pietrzak. Vol. 12551. LNCS. Springer, Heidelberg, Nov. 2020, pp. 1–18. https://doi.org/10.1007/978-3-030-64378-2_1.

16. I. Cascudo, I. Damgård, B. David, N. Döttling, R. Dowsley, and I. Giacomelli. "Efficient UC Commitment Extension with Homomorphism for Free (and Applications)". In: *ASIACRYPT 2019, Part II*. Ed. by S. D. Galbraith and S. Moriai. Vol. 11922. LNCS. Springer, Heidelberg, Dec. 2019, pp. 606–635. https://doi.org/10.1007/978-3-030-34621-8_22.

17. D. Catalano, D. Fiore, and I. Tucker. "Additive-Homomorphic Functional Commitments and Applications to Homomorphic Signatures". In: *ASIACRYPT 2022, Part IV*. Ed. by S. Agrawal and D. Lin. Vol. 13794. LNCS. Springer, Heidelberg, Dec. 2022, pp. 159–188. https://doi.org/10.1007/978-3-031-22972-5_6.

18. M. Chase, M. Kohlweiss, A. Lysyanskaya, and S. Meiklejohn. "Malleable Proof Systems and Applications". In: *EUROCRYPT 2012*. Ed. by D. Pointcheval and T. Johansson. Vol. 7237. LNCS. Springer, Heidelberg, Apr. 2012, pp. 281–300. https://doi.org/10.1007/978-3-642-29011-4_18.

19. M. Chase, M. Kohlweiss, A. Lysyanskaya, and S. Meiklejohn. "Malleable Signatures: New Definitions and Delegatable Anonymous Credentials". In: *CSF 2014 Computer Security Foundations Symposium*. Ed. by A. Datta and C. Fournet. IEEE Computer Society Press, 2014, pp. 199–213. https://doi.org/10.1109/CSF.2014.22.

20. M. Chase, M. Kohlweiss, A. Lysyanskaya, and S. Meiklejohn. "Succinct Malleable NIZKs and an Application to Compact Shuffles". In: *TCC 2013*. Ed. by A. Sahai. Vol. 7785. LNCS. Springer, Heidelberg, Mar. 2013, pp. 100–119. https://doi.org/10.1007/978-3-642-36594-2_6.

21. D. Chaum, C. Crépeau, and I. Damgård. "Multiparty Unconditionally Secure Protocols (Abstract) (Informal Contribution)". In: *CRYPTO'87*. Ed. by C. Pomerance. Vol. 293. LNCS. Springer, Heidelberg, Aug. 1988, p. 462. https://doi.org/10.1007/3-540-48184-2_43.

22. A. Connolly, P. Lafourcade, and O. Perez-Kempner. "Improved Constructions of Anonymous Credentials from Structure-Preserving Signatures on Equivalence Classes". In: *PKC 2022, Part I*. Ed. by G. Hanaoka, J. Shikata, and Y. Watanabe. Vol. 13177. LNCS. Springer, Heidelberg, Mar. 2022, pp. 409–438. https://doi.org/10.1007/978-3-030-97121-2_15.

23. G. Couteau and D. Hartmann. "Shorter Non-interactive Zero-Knowledge Arguments and ZAPs for Algebraic Languages". In: *CRYPTO 2020, Part III*. Ed. by D. Micciancio and T. Ristenpart. Vol. 12172. LNCS. Springer, Heidelberg, Aug. 2020, pp. 768–798. https://doi.org/10.1007/978-3-030-56877-1_27.

24. G. Couteau, M. Klooß, H. Lin, and M. Reichle. "Efficient Range Proofs with Transparent Setup from Bounded Integer Commitments". In: *EUROCRYPT 2021, Part III*. Ed. by A. Canteaut and F.-X. Standaert. Vol. 12698. LNCS. Springer, Heidelberg, Oct. 2021, pp. 247–277. https://doi.org/10.1007/978-3-030-77883-5_9.

25. I. Damgård, B. M. David, I. Giacomelli, and J. B. Nielsen. "Compact VSS and Efficient Homomorphic UC Commitments". In: *ASIACRYPT 2014, Part II*. Ed. by P. Sarkar and T. Iwata. Vol. 8874. LNCS. Springer, Heidelberg, Dec. 2014, pp. 213–232. https://doi.org/10.1007/978-3-662-45608-8_12.

26. I. Damgård, C. Ganesh, H. Khoshakhlagh, C. Orlandi, and L. Siniscalchi. "Balancing Privacy and Accountability in Blockchain Identity Management". In: *CT-RSA 2021*. Ed. by K. G. Paterson. Vol. 12704. LNCS. Springer, Heidelberg, May 2021, pp. 552–576. https://doi.org/10.1007/978-3-030-75539-3_23

27. I. Damgard, M. Geisler, and M. Kroigard. "Homomorphic encryption and secure comparison". In: *International Journal of Applied Cryptography* 1.1 (2008), pp. 22–31.

28. I. Damgård, V. Pastro, N. P. Smart, and S. Zakarias. "Multiparty Computation from Somewhat Homomorphic Encryption". In: *CRYPTO 2012*. Ed. by R. Safavi-Naini and R. Canetti. Vol. 7417. LNCS. Springer, Heidelberg, Aug. 2012, pp. 643–662. https://doi.org/10.1007/978-3-642-32009-5_38.

29. B. David, F. Engelmann, T. Frederiksen, M. Kohlweiss, E. Pagnin, and M. Volkhov. *Updatable Privacy-Preserving Blueprints*. Cryptology ePrint Archive, Paper 2023/1787. 2023. url: https://print.iacr.org/2023/1787.

30. Y. Dodis, K. Haralambiev, A. López-Alt, and D. Wichs. "Cryptography against Continuous Memory Attacks". In: *51st FOCS*. IEEE Computer Society Press, Oct. 2010, pp. 511–520. https://doi.org/10.1109/FOCS.2010.56.

31. M. B. van Egmond et al. *Privacy-preserving Anti-Money Laundering using Secure Multi-Party Computation*. Cryptology ePrint Archive, Paper 2024/065 (To appear in Financial Cryptography 2024). https://eprint.iacr.org/2024/065. 2024. url: https://eprint.iacr.org/2024/065

32. M. F. Esgin, R. K. Zhao, R. Steinfeld, J. K. Liu, and D. Liu. "MatRiCT: Efficient, Scalable and Post-Quantum Blockchain Confidential Transactions Protocol". In: *ACM CCS 2019*. Ed. by L. Cavallaro, J. Kinder, X. Wang, and J. Katz. ACM Press, Nov. 2019, pp. 567–584. https://doi.org/10.1145/3319535.3354200.

33. S. Faust, M. Kohlweiss, G. A. Marson, and D. Venturi. "On the Nonmalleability of the Fiat-Shamir Transform". In: *INDOCRYPT 2012*. Ed. by S. D. Galbraith and M. Nandi. Vol. 7668. LNCS. Springer, Heidelberg, Dec. 2012, pp. 60–79. https://doi.org/10.1007/978-3-642-34931-7_5.

34. M. Fischlin. "Communication-Efficient Non-interactive Proofs of Knowledge with Online Extractors". In: *CRYPTO 2005*. Ed. by V. Shoup. Vol. 3621. LNCS. Springer, Heidelberg, Aug. 2005, pp. 152–168. https://doi.org/10.1007/11535218_10.

35. J. Frankle, S. Park, D. Shaar, S. Goldwasser, and D. J.Weitzner. "Practical Accountability of Secret Processes". In: *USENIX Security 2018*. Ed. by W. Enck and A. P. Felt. USENIX Association, Aug. 2018, pp. 657–674.

36. G. Fuchsbauer. "Commuting Signatures and Verifiable Encryption". In: *EURO-CRYPT 2011*. Ed. by K. G. Paterson. Vol. 6632. LNCS. Springer, Heidelberg, May 2011, pp. 224–245. https://doi.org/10.1007/978-3-642-20465-4_14.

37. N. Gama et al. "Detecting money laundering activities via secure multiparty computation for structural similarities in flow networks". In: *Real World Cryptography*. 2020. url: https://www.youtube.com/watch?v=4hryY6cMPaM&t=2558s.

38. C. Ganesh, H. Khoshakhlagh, M. Kohlweiss, A. Nitulescu, and M. Zając. "What Makes Fiat–Shamir zkSNARKs (Updatable SRS) Simulation Extractable?" In: *International Conference on Security and Cryptography for Networks*. Springer. 2022, pp. 735–760.

39. J. A. Garay, B. Schoenmakers, and J. Villegas. "Practical and Secure Solutions for Integer Comparison". In: *PKC 2007*. Ed. by T. Okamoto and X. Wang. Vol. 4450. LNCS. Springer, Heidelberg, Apr. 2007, pp. 330–342. https://doi.org/10.1007/978-3-540-71677-8_22.

40. O. Goldreich, S. Micali, and A. Wigderson. "How to Play any Mental Game or A Completeness Theorem for Protocols with Honest Majority". In: *19th ACM STOC*. Ed. by A. Aho. ACM Press, May 1987, pp. 218–229. https://doi.org/10.1145/28395.28420.

41. S. Goldwasser and S. Park. *Public Accountability vs. Secret Laws: Can They Coexist?* Cryptology ePrint Archive, Report 2018/664. https://eprint.iacr.org/2018/664. 2018.

42. M. Green, G. Kaptchuk, and G. V. Laer. "Abuse Resistant Law Enforcement Access Systems". In: *EUROCRYPT 2021, Part III*. Ed. by A. Canteaut and F.-X. Standaert. Vol. 12698. LNCS. Springer, Heidelberg, Oct. 2021, pp. 553–583. https://doi.org/10.1007/978-3-030-77883-5_19.

43. S. Griffy, M. Kohlweiss, A. Lysyanskaya, and M. Sengupta. *Privacy-Preserving Blueprints via Succinctly Verifiable Computation over Additively-Homomorphically Encrypted Data*. Cryptology ePrint Archive, Paper 2024/675. 2024. url: https://eprint.iacr.org/2024/675.

44. J. Groth and A. Sahai. "Efficient Non-interactive Proof Systems for Bilinear Groups". In: *EUROCRYPT 2008*. Ed. by N. P. Smart. Vol. 4965. LNCS. Springer, Heidelberg, Apr. 2008, pp. 415–432. https://doi.org/10.1007/978-3-540-78967-3_24.

45. C. Hébant, D. H. Phan, and D. Pointcheval. "Linearly-Homomorphic Signatures and Scalable Mix-Nets". In: *PKC 2020, Part II*. Ed. by A. Kiayias, M. Kohlweiss, P. Wallden, and V. Zikas. Vol. 12111. LNCS. Springer, Heidelberg, May 2020, pp. 597–627. https://doi.org/10.1007/978-3-030-45388-6_21.

46. M. Khalili, D. Slamanig, and M. Dakhilalian. "Structure-Preserving Signatures on Equivalence Classes from Standard Assumptions". In: *ASIACRYPT 2019, Part III*. Ed. by S. D. Galbraith and S. Moriai. Vol. 11923. LNCS. Springer, Heidelberg, Dec. 2019, pp. 63–93. https://doi.org/10.1007/978-3-030-34618-8_3.

47. A. Kiayias, M. Kohlweiss, and A. Sarencheh. "PEReDi: Privacy-Enhanced, Regulated and Distributed Central Bank Digital Currencies". In: *Proceedings of the 2022 ACM SIGSAC Conference on Computer and Communications Security, CCS 2022, Los Angeles, CA, USA, November 7-11, 2022*. Ed. by H. Yin, A. Stavrou, C. Cremers, and E. Shi. ACM, 2022, pp. 1739–1752. https://doi.org/10.1145/3548606.3560707. url: https://doi.org/10.1145/3548606.3560707.

48. M. Kohlweiss, A. Lysyanskaya, and A. Nguyen. "Privacy-Preserving Blueprints". In: *EUROCRYPT 2023, Part II*. Ed. by C. Hazay and M. Stam. Vol. 14005. LNCS. Springer, Heidelberg, Apr. 2023, pp. 594–625. https://doi.org/10.1007/978-3-031-30617-4_20.

49. M. Kohlweiss and M. Zając. *On Simulation-Extractability of Universal zk-SNARKs*. Cryptology ePrint Archive, Report 2021/511. https://eprint.iacr.org/2021/511. 2021.

50. J. Konvalina. "A unified interpretation of the binomial coefficients, the Stirling numbers, and the Gaussian coefficients". In: *The American Mathematical Monthly* 107.10 (2000), pp. 901–910.

51. A. Kothapalli, S. Setty, and I. Tzialla. *Nova: Recursive Zero-Knowledge Arguments from Folding Schemes*. Cryptology ePrint Archive, Report 2021/370. https://eprint.iacr.org/2021/370. 2021.

52. U. M. Maurer. "Unifying Zero-Knowledge Proofs of Knowledge". In: *AFRICACRYPT 09*. Ed. by B. Preneel. Vol. 5580. LNCS. Springer, Heidelberg, June 2009, pp. 272–286.

53. V. S. Miller. "The Weil Pairing, and Its Efficient Calculation". In: *Journal of Cryptology* 17.4 (Sept. 2004), pp. 235–261. https://doi.org/10.1007/s00145-004-0315-8.

54. N. Narula, W. Vasquez, and M. Virza. "zkLedger: Privacy-Preserving Auditing for Distributed Ledgers". In: *15th USENIX Symposium on Networked Systems Design and Implementation, NSDI 2018, Renton, WA, USA, April 9-11, 2018*. Ed. by S. Banerjee and S. Seshan. USENIX Association, 2018, pp. 65–80. url: https://www.usenix.org/conference/nsdi18/presentation/narula.

55. R. Ostrovsky, A. Paskin-Cherniavsky, and B. Paskin-Cherniavsky. "Maliciously Circuit-Private FHE". In: *CRYPTO 2014, Part I*. Ed. by J. A. Garay and R. Gennaro. Vol. 8616. LNCS. Springer, Heidelberg, Aug. 2014, pp. 536–553. https://doi.org/10.1007/978-3-662-44371-2_30.

56. T. P. Pedersen. "Non-Interactive and Information-Theoretic Secure Verifiable Secret Sharing". In: *CRYPTO'91*. Ed. by J. Feigenbaum. Vol. 576. LNCS. Springer, Heidelberg, Aug. 1992, pp. 129–140. https://doi.org/10.1007/3-540-46766-1_9.

57. P. de Perthuis and D. Pointcheval. "Two-Client Inner-Product Functional Encryption with an Application to Money-Laundering Detection". In: *ACM CCS 2022*. Ed. by H. Yin, A. Stavrou, C. Cremers, and E. Shi. ACM Press, Nov. 2022, pp. 725–737. https://doi.org/10.1145/3548606.3559374.

58. C. Rackoff and D. R. Simon. "Non-Interactive Zero-Knowledge Proof of Knowledge and Chosen Ciphertext Attack". In: *CRYPTO'91*. Ed. by J. Feigenbaum. Vol. 576. LNCS. Springer, Heidelberg, Aug. 1992, pp. 433–444. https://doi.org/10.1007/3-540-46766-1_35.

59. A. Scafuro. "Break-glass Encryption". In: *PKC 2019, Part II*. Ed. by D. Lin and K. Sako. Vol. 11443. LNCS. Springer, Heidelberg, Apr. 2019, pp. 34–62. https://doi.org/10.1007/978-3-030-17259-6_2.

60. C.-P. Schnorr. "Efficient Identification and Signatures for Smart Cards". In: *CRYPTO'89*. Ed. by G. Brassard. Vol. 435. LNCS. Springer, Heidelberg, Aug. 1990, pp. 239–252. https://doi.org/10.1007/0-387-34805-0_22.

Homomorphic Encryption

Faster BGV Bootstrapping
for Power-of-Two Cyclotomics Through
Homomorphic NTT

Shihe Ma[1], Tairong Huang[2], Anyu Wang[2,3,4(✉)] [iD], and Xiaoyun Wang[2,3,4,5,6]

[1] Institute for Network Sciences and Cyberspace, Tsinghua University, Beijing, China
msh24@mails.tsinghua.edu.cn
[2] Institute for Advanced Study, BNRist, Tsinghua University, Beijing, China
huangtr@mail.tsinghua.edu.cn, {anyuwang,xiaoyunwang}@tsinghua.edu.cn
[3] Zhongguancun Laboratory, Beijing, China
[4] National Financial Cryptography Research Center, Beijing, China
[5] Shandong Institute of Blockchain, Jinan, Shandong, China
[6] Key Laboratory of Cryptologic Technology and Information Security (Ministry of Education), School of Cyber Science and Technology, Shandong University, Qingdao, Shandong, China

Abstract. Power-of-two cyclotomics is a popular choice when instantiating the BGV scheme because of its efficiency and compliance with the FHE standard. However, in power-of-two cyclotomics, the linear transformations in BGV bootstrapping cannot be decomposed into subtransformations for acceleration with existing techniques. Thus, they can be highly time-consuming when the number of slots is large, degrading the advantage brought by the SIMD property of the plaintext space. By exploiting the algebraic structure of power-of-two cyclotomics, this paper derives explicit decomposition of the linear transformations in BGV bootstrapping into NTT-like sub-transformations, which are highly efficient to compute homomorphically. Moreover, multiple optimizations are made to evaluate homomorphic linear transformations, including modified BSGS algorithms, trade-offs between level and time, and specific simplifications for thin and general bootstrapping. We implement our method on HElib. With the number of slots ranging from 4096 to 32768, we obtain a 2.4x–55.1x improvement in bootstrapping throughput, compared to previous works or the naive approach.

Keywords: Fully Homomorphic Encryption · BGV · Bootstrapping · NTT

© International Association for Cryptologic Research 2025
K.-M. Chung and Y. Sasaki (Eds.): ASIACRYPT 2024, LNCS 15484, pp. 143–175, 2025.
https://doi.org/10.1007/978-981-96-0875-1_5

1 Introduction

Fully homomorphic encryption (FHE) allows anyone to compute over encrypted data without access to the decryption key or the underlying plaintext. Thus, FHE is useful in privacy-preserving computing like outsourced computation and privacy-preserving machine learning [5,28]. Among the various FHE schemes, when the data to be computed homomorphically are represented as integers, the common choice of the underlying FHE scheme is BGV [7] or BFV [14]. BGV/BFV offers the single instruction multiple data (SIMD) functionality, in which a plaintext encodes an array of elements and homomorphic operations are performed simultaneously on each slot of the array.

The bootstrapping technique first proposed by Gentry [18] plays an important role in FHE. By homomorphically decrypting the ciphertext, it refreshes the noise in the ciphertext before the validity of the ciphertext is corrupted, thus allowing for an unlimited number of homomorphic operations. The bootstrapping of BGV has been studied extensively in the past years [11,16,17,19,22,30], leading to significant improvements in its performance.

From an implementation standpoint, power-of-two cyclotomics are frequently employed to instantiate BGV. A majority of FHE libraries, including SEAL [34], OpenFHE [4], and lattigo [26], exclusively use power-of-two cyclotomics, which is also the only cyclotomics recommended in the FHE standard [1]. However, in the context of power-of-two cyclotomics, the existing techniques [11,17,22] for computing the linear transformations in BGV bootstrapping are highly inefficient when dealing with a large number of slots.

Let M denote the cyclotomic order and p the prime of the plaintext modulus in the BGV scheme. Halevi and Shoup [22] propose a method for enabling fast linear transformations in bootstrapping, which requires M to have multiple distinct prime factors so that the linear transformations can be decomposed into multiple sub-transformations by leveraging the structure of the powerful basis. Each sub-transformation has a dimension much smaller than the entire transformation, making it more computationally efficient. However, this decomposition is impossible when M is a power of two, as M only has a single prime factor 2 and a trivial powerful basis structure. Furthermore, Halevi and Shoup's method requires that $\mathbb{Z}_M^*/\langle p \rangle$ is a cyclic group, which is not the case when M is a power of two and $p \equiv 1 \bmod 4$.

To circumvent the cyclicity constraint on $\mathbb{Z}_M^*/\langle p \rangle$ when M is a power of two, Chen and Han [11] design a linear transformation tailored for thin bootstrapping where each slot stores only an integer. The algorithm is later revised by Geelen and Vercauteren [17]. However, this method still computes the linear transformations as a whole, which means it still suffers from long running time when the number of slots is large.

FHE applications over integers typically seek a large number of slots to fully exploit the SIMD property [12,32]. Given that the dimension of the linear transformations is equal to the number of slots, the poor performance of linear transformations with a large dimension in power-of-two cyclotomics greatly limits the flexibility of BGV bootstrapping, resulting in diminished compatibility with the SIMD feature. This may account for why previous works opt for parameters supporting at most 128 slots for BGV bootstrapping in power-of-two cyclotomics [11,33] and why most FHE libraries (except HElib) do not support BGV/BFV bootstrapping. Therefore, accelerating the linear transformations in BGV bootstrapping is crucial if we want to exploit both the NTT efficiency of power-of-two cyclotomics and the SIMD property of BGV.

1.1   Our Techniques and Results

Our basic observation is that the primary component of the linear transformation in BGV bootstrapping can be interpreted as an NTT, and thus can be decomposed into linear sub-transformations based on fast-NTT algorithms (such as the Cooley-Tukey algorithm [13]). This opens up the potential for an accelerated linear transformation in BGV bootstrapping by considering the homomorphic evaluation of these sub-transformations. Although NTT in plaintext has been extensively studied and various fast-NTT algorithms are known, the scope of homomorphic evaluation presents unique challenges. General BGV linear transformations are typically implemented using a combination of fundamental transformations (i.e., one-dimensional linear transformations [20]). The evaluation complexity of a general linear transformation is determined by its specific form. Therefore, to achieve an efficient linear transformation in BGV bootstrapping, it is essential to first ascertain the feasibility of decomposing the NTT into multiple linear sub-transformations that can be evaluated efficiently. This paper addresses this problem by proposing a concrete construction for such a decomposition. Furthermore, we introduce several novel optimizations to both the decomposition and the evaluation of sub-transformations. Our contributions can be summarized as follows.

(1) We provide an explicit framework for homomorphic NTT in BGV bootstrapping by leveraging the algebraic properties of power-of-two cyclotomics. Specifically, we demonstrate that for any power-of-two M and prime $p > 2$, both the NTT and its inverse can be decomposed into one-dimensional linear sub-transformations. These sub-transformations exhibit different forms for different p, as p affects the hypercube structure and the number of non-zero coefficients in each factor of $X^{M/2} + 1$. For $p \equiv 1 \bmod 4$, these one-dimensional linear transformations all fall within the MatMul1D type as defined in [20]. Furthermore, we show that, based on the specific vector representation of each slot, the matrix for each one-dimensional linear transformation is tridiagonal, which allows for highly efficient homomorphic evaluation. For $p \equiv 3 \bmod 4$, we demonstrate that all but the first one of these one-dimensional linear transformations are of the MatMul1D type, which can be represented as matrices with six or seven diagonals. For further optimization, we illustrate how we can 'fold' multiple non-zero diagonals of the matrices inside a single slot, thereby producing new tridiagonal matrices that correspond to one-dimensional linear transformations of the BlockMatMul1D type. This leads to reduced running time in most cases.

(2) We propose several further optimizations for the homomorphic evaluation of linear transformations. Firstly, we show that the level-collapsing method used in CKKS bootstrapping [10,23] can be adapted to our framework, which allows for a trade-off between the time and depth consumption of homomorphic linear transformations. Secondly, we introduce a modified Baby-Step Giant-Step (BSGS) technique, which accelerates the homomorphic linear transformations under certain conditions. Lastly, we demonstrate that our framework is applicable to both thin and general bootstrapping, each with different optimizations. For thin bootstrapping, where each slot stores an integer, we observe that some sub-transformations can either be omitted or computed on a subfield (or subring) of each slot, thereby reducing the running time. For general bootstrapping, where each slot stores a Galois field/ring element, we reorder the final transformation that moves slot coefficients from the power basis to the normal basis, resulting in improved performance.

(3) We implement our approach for both general and thin bootstrapping based on HElib with the optimization in [30]. The parameters have slot numbers ranging from 4096 to 32768. The performance indicator is the bootstrapping throughput, the ratio between the after-bootstrap capacity and the bootstrapping time. The capacity of a ciphertext is defined as $\log_2$(ciphertext modulus/ bound of ciphertext noise). For thin bootstrapping, we obtain a bootstrapping throughput 2.4x–13.4x that of prior works or the naive approach. For general bootstrapping, the improvement in throughput is 15.2x–55.1x.

1.2   Related Works

FFT Based Linear Transformations in CKKS Bootstrapping. In [10,23], it was shown that the homomorphic linear transformations in CKKS bootstrapping can be decomposed into FFT-like matrices for acceleration. Our idea can be viewed as an analogue of this approach for BGV bootstrapping. However, the decomposition of linear transformations in BGV bootstrapping into NTT-like matrices is significantly more complex than in CKKS. Firstly, as the cyclotomic polynomial $X^{M/2} + 1$ splits in $\mathbb{C}$, the linear transformations evaluated during CKKS bootstrapping closely resemble the standard FFT. Conversely, in BGV, $X^{M/2} + 1$ can be factorized into binomials or trinomials of degrees greater than one, which correspond to incomplete Cooley-Tukey NTT or incomplete Bruun-like NTT [8]. Secondly, each slot in a CKKS ciphertext stores a scalar value in $\mathbb{C}$, while a slot in BGV may store an element in a Galois field or Galois ring, which can be interpreted as a vector of integers modulo the plaintext modulus. Consequently, the linear transformations are purely inter-slot in CKKS bootstrapping, while they are both inter-slot and intra-slot in BGV bootstrapping. This fact complicates the form of the linear transformations and provides multiple design possibilities. Thirdly, the slots in CKKS always form a one-dimensional vector, while slots in BGV can form a hypercube with multiple dimensions. This further complicates the linear transformations in BGV compared to those in CKKS.

Finally, when the plaintext modulus of BGV is a prime power p^r and each slot stores an element in a Galois ring, it remains unexplored whether the factorization of $X^{M/2} + 1$ modulo p^r still enables efficient homomorphic NTT. Although NTT in arbitrary algebras has been investigated by Cantor and Kaltofen, it is realized through root adjoining [9], which is infeasible in the FHE setting.

Optimized Digit Removal for Large Plaintext Prime. In BGV bootstrapping, the digit removal procedure is also a computationally expensive component. This is particularly true when facilitating SIMD for power-of-two cyclotomics, where the plaintext prime p scales with the number of slots. For instance, to achieve 2^A slots, p should be at least $2^{A+1} + 1$ if $p \equiv 1 \bmod 4$, or at least $2^{A+1} - 1$ if $p \equiv 3 \bmod 4$ [31]. As a result, it is necessary to leverage the technique introduced in [30] to expedite the digit removal procedure in BGV bootstrapping with a large p. However, in [30], the powerful basis decomposition method of HElib [22] is employed to compute linear transformations, implying that the linear transformations will dominate the running time of BGV bootstrapping when the slot number is large. Therefore, our approach to accelerate the linear transformations contributes to completing the final piece for efficient BGV bootstrapping for highly-SIMD integer arithmetic in power-of-two cylotomics (e.g., $p = 65537$ with 2^{15} slots for $M = 2^{16}$ cyclotomics).

1.3 Concurrent Works

Since there is an easy and efficient conversion between BGV and BFV ciphertexts [3], advances in BGV bootstrapping directly apply to BFV bootstrapping, and vice versa. Thus, a comparison between concurrent works on BGV/BFV bootstrapping and this work is necessary.

Comparison with Functional BFV Bootstrapping. Both the works by Lee et al. [27] and by Liu and Wang [29] focus on performing functional bootstrapping on BFV ciphertext. The former work achieves functional bootstrapping by decomposing a lookup table as the sum of step functions and computing each step function separately. The latter work achieves functional bootstrapping through Lagrange interpolation. It requires that only a small subset of the plaintext space is used, and exploits such sparsity of plaintext for better efficiency. In contrast, our work focuses on general (non-functional) BGV bootstrapping without imposing any constraints on the plaintext. Since these works have different purposes and constraints from our work, we do not conduct experimental comparisons between them.

Comparison with CKKS-Based BFV Bootstrapping. Kim et al. propose to bootstrap BFV ciphertexts using CKKS bootstrapping [25]. Their method has two main advantages. First, a CKKS plaintext always has $M/4$ slots, which can be larger than that of a BGV/BFV ciphertext if each slot has an extension degree greater than two. This means fewer digit-removal-like operations during bootstrapping and better efficiency. Second, their bootstrapping time and usable levels after bootstrapping are independent of the size or number-theoretic properties of the BGV/BFV plaintext modulus.

The major drawback of their method is that the bootstrapping time is proportional to the 'denoising factor', which is the capacity gained through bootstrapping. In contrast, the running time of our method is only determined by the number-theoretic properties (not the size) of the plaintext modulus. Moreover, in traditional BGV/BFV bootstrapping (including ours), a decrease in the plaintext modulus results in an increase in the denoising factor. Therefore, when comparing the two methods, a decrease in the plaintext modulus implies a larger denoising factor for our method, leading to a longer running time for their method to achieve the same denoising factor.

This is demonstrated by our experiments under plaintext moduli of various sizes. We observe that: their method performs best for very large plaintext modulus, while our method is faster for medium-sized plaintext modulus (e.g., <54bits). We believe these medium-sized moduli are adequate for most BGV/BFV applications. Specifically, our experiments adopt the same ring dimension and security level as Table 4 and 5 in their paper, with a plaintext modulus ranging from 22 bits to 54 bits. The results confirm that our method has a bootstrapping throughput 6.00 times (1.32 times) that of theirs under a plaintext modulus of 22 bits (54 bits). The benchmarking results are available in Supplementary Materials A in the full version of this paper.

1.4   Comparison with Another NTT-Based BGV/BFV Bootstrapping

A recent parallel work by Geelen [15] also accelerates the linear transformations in BGV/BFV bootstrapping in power-of-two cyclotomics by decomposing them into NTT-like matrices. Their and our methods have some slight technical differences, and thus are suitable for different scenarios.

For $p \equiv 1 \mod 4$, as the only difference between the two methods, the last 2D transformation in CoeffToSlot is a MatMul in our method while it is a BlockMatMul in their method, meaning our method is faster.

For $p \equiv 3 \mod 4$, their method is faster than our Radix-2 method since their middle matrices are MatMul1D while ours are BlockMatMul1D. Compared with our Bruun method, matrices in their method also have fewer nonzero diagonals, but their final matrix is a BlockMatMul1D while it is a MatMul1D in our Bruun method. Thus, in the case of $p \equiv 3 \mod 4$, it can be difficult to predict if their method or our Bruun method is faster.

2   Preliminary

2.1   Notations

– Let $\Phi_M(X)$ represent the M-th cyclotomic polynomial, and let R_q be the quotient ring $\mathbb{Z}_q[X]/(\Phi_M(X))$, where $q \geq 2$ is an integer. The Euler function is denoted by $\varphi(\cdot)$, and thus $\deg(\Phi_M) = \varphi(M)$. This paper primarily focuses on the case where M is a power of two, i.e., $\Phi_M(X) = X^{M/2} + 1$.

- Let G be a finite group. The order of any $g \in G$ is denoted by $\mathrm{ord}_G(g)$, and the subgroup generated by $g_1, \ldots, g_l \in G$ is represented as $\langle g_1, \ldots, g_l \rangle$.
- For positive integers a and b, we denote the set $\{0, 1, \ldots, a-1\}$ as $[a]$ and the remainder of a modulo b as $[a]_b \in [b]$. For a set S and an integer a, we denote $a \times S$ for $\{a \cdot s \mid s \in S\}$, $a + S$ for $\{a + s \mid s \in S\}$ and $[S]_a$ for $\{[s]_a \mid s \in S\}$. We use $[a, b]$ to denote the integer interval $[a, b] \cap \mathbb{Z}$ for simplicity.
- Let $a = \sum_{i=0}^{k-1} a_i 2^i$ be the bit decomposition of a k-bit nonnegative integer a, we define $\mathrm{BitRev}_{k,t}(a) = [a]_{2^t} + \sum_{i=t}^{k-1} a_{k-1-i+t} 2^i$ for $0 \le t \le k$, and $\mathrm{BitRev}'_{k,t}(a) = [a]_{2^t} + a_{k-1} 2^{k-1} + \sum_{i=t}^{k-2} a_{k-2-i+t} 2^i$ for $t \in [k]$. In other words, $\mathrm{BitRev}_{k,t}$ reverses all but the lowest t bits in a, while $\mathrm{BitRev}'_{k,t}$ preserves the highest bit and the lowest t bits in a, reversing all other bits.
- Given an array of size 2^k with elements $a_i, i \in [2^k]$, we define $\mathrm{BR}_{k,t}(a_i) = a_{\mathrm{BitRev}_{k,t}(i)}$ and $\mathrm{BR}'_{k,t}(a_i) = a_{\mathrm{BitRev}'_{k,t}(i)}$. Both $\mathrm{BR}_{k,t}$ and $\mathrm{BR}'_{k,t}$ are order-two permutations on the array.
- All vectors are assumed to be column vectors, and all linear transformations correspond to left-multiplying a column vector by a matrix. For a vector $\mathbf{v}$ of length n, its i-th entry is denoted as $\mathbf{v}[i]$ for $i \in [n]$, and the notation $\mathbf{v}[i +: \Delta]$ stands for the Δ-sized subvector $(\mathbf{v}[i], \mathbf{v}[i+1], \ldots, \mathbf{v}[i + \Delta - 1])$. For a polynomial $m(x) = \sum_{i=0}^{n-1} m_i x^i$, the notation $m[i +: \Delta]$ stands for the coefficient vector $(m_i, m_{i+1}, \ldots, m_{i+\Delta-1})$.
- For an $n \times n$ matrix $\mathbf{N}$, the entry at the i-th row and j-th column is denoted by $\mathbf{N}[i, j]$, with $i, j \in [n]$. The i-th diagonal of $\mathbf{N}$ is the vector whose j-th entry is $\mathbf{N}[j, [i+j]_n]$. Note that the i-th and j-th diagonals coincide if $i \equiv j \bmod n$. Let $\mathbf{I}_n$ be the identity matrix of size n.
- The power (standard) basis of R_q consists of X^i for $i \in [\varphi(M)]$. Let $M = M_1 M_2 \ldots M_k$ be the factorization of M into prime powers. The powerful basis of R_q consists of $\prod_{i=1}^{k} X_i^{e_i}$, where $X_i = X^{M/M_i}$ and $e_i \in [\varphi(M_i)]$. We note that the powerful basis is identical to the standard basis when M is a power of 2.

2.2 Galois Fields and Rings

Let p be a prime number. The Galois field with characteristic p and cardinality p^d is denoted by $\mathsf{GF}(p^d)$, and the Galois ring with characteristic p^r and cardinality p^{rd} is denoted by $\mathsf{GR}(p^r; d)$. In the special case where $r = 1$, it has $\mathsf{GR}(p; d) = \mathsf{GF}(p^d)$. We introduce some conclusions about Galois rings that will be used in subsequent proofs. Refer to [35] for the details of the following conclusions.

Hensel's Lemma. Let f be a monic polynomial in $\mathbb{Z}_{p^r}[X]$, and denote $\bar{f} = f \bmod p \in \mathbb{Z}_p[X]$. Assume that $\bar{f} = g_1 g_2 \ldots g_n$, where $g_1, g_2, \ldots, g_n \in \mathbb{Z}_p[X]$ are pairwise coprime monic polynomials. Then Hensel's lemma guarantees that there exist pairwise coprime monic polynomials $f_1, f_2, \ldots, f_n \in \mathbb{Z}_{p^r}[x]$ such that $f = f_1 f_2 \ldots f_n$ and $\bar{f}_i = g_i$ for $1 \le i \le n$.

Hensel's Lemma can be generalized to extension rings. Let f be a monic polynomial in $\mathsf{GR}(p^r;d)[X]$, and denote $\bar{f} = f \bmod p \in \mathsf{GF}(p^d)[X]$. Assume that $\bar{f} = g_1 g_2 \ldots g_n \in \mathsf{GF}(p^d)[X]$, where $g_1, g_2, \ldots, g_n \in \mathsf{GF}(p^d)[X]$ be pairwise coprime monic polynomials. Then there exist pairwise coprime monic polynomials $f_1, f_2, \ldots, f_n \in \mathsf{GR}(p^r;d)[X]$ such that $f = f_1 f_2 \ldots f_n$ and $\bar{f}_i = g_i$ for $1 \le i \le n$.

The Group of Units. Assume p is an odd prime number. Let $R = \mathsf{GR}(p^r;d)$ and let R^* denote the group of multiplicative units in R. Then it has $R^* = G_1 \times G_2$, where G_1 is a cyclic group of order $p^d - 1$ and G_2 is a direct product of d cyclic groups each of order p^{r-1}.

Primitive Element. There exists a nonzero element $\gamma \in \mathsf{GR}(p^r;ml)$ such that

a) γ has multiplicative order $p^{ml} - 1$;
b) γ is a root of a basic primitive polynomial[1] $h(X)$ of degree l over $\mathsf{GR}(p^r;m)$, where $h(X)$ divides $X^{p^{ml}-1} - 1$ over $\mathsf{GR}(p^r;m)$;
c) $\mathsf{GR}(p^r;ml) = \mathsf{GR}(p^r;m)[\gamma] = \{a_0 + a_1\gamma + \ldots + a_{l-1}\gamma^{l-1} : a_i \in \mathsf{GR}(p^r;m)\}$.

Frobenius Automorphism. Let $R = \mathsf{GR}(p^r;m)$ and $R' = \mathsf{GR}(p^r;ml) = R[\gamma]$, where $\gamma \in R'$ is a primitive element. Define a map $\pi : R' \to R'$ by

$$\pi(a_0 + a_1\gamma + \ldots + a_{l-1}\gamma^{l-1}) = a_0 + a_1\gamma^{p^m} + \ldots + a_{l-1}\gamma^{(l-1)p^m}$$

for all $a_0, a_1, \ldots, a_{l-1} \in R$. Then π is an automorphism of R' leaving R fixed elementwise. Moreover, for $\alpha \in R'$, $\pi(\alpha) = \alpha$ if and only if $\alpha \in R$.

Throughout the remainder of this paper, the symbol $\mathcal{E}$ will always denote the Galois ring $\mathsf{GR}(p^r;d)$. If $\mathsf{GF}(p^d)$ is represented as $\mathbb{Z}_p[X]/f(X)$ for some irreducible polynomial $f(X)$, its power basis is defined as X^i for $i \in [d]$. The power basis of a Galois ring is defined similarly. The normal basis of $\mathsf{GF}(p^d)$ is $\{\beta^{p^i} \mid i \in [d]\}$ for some $\beta \in \mathsf{GF}(p^d)$ where $\{\beta^{p^i} \mid i \in [d]\}$ is $\mathbb{F}_p$-linear independent. The notion of normal basis can also be generalized to Galois rings using the Frobenius automorphism.

2.3   BGV Plaintext Space

The BGV plaintext space is $R_{p^r} = \mathbb{Z}_{p^r}[X]/(\Phi_M(X))$, where p is a prime number, M is coprime to p, and r is a positive integer (known as the Hensel lifting parameter). Let $d = \mathrm{ord}_{\mathbb{Z}_M^*}(p)$. It is known that $\Phi_M(X)$ factorizes into $L = \varphi(M)/d$ irreducible and pairewise coprime monic polynomials of degree d over $\mathbb{Z}_{p^r}$, i.e., $\Phi_M(X) = \prod_{i=0}^{L-1} F_i(X)$. The Chinese Reminder Theorem provides an isomorphism between R_{p^r} and $\prod_{0 \le i < L} \mathbb{Z}_{p^r}[X]/(F_i(X))$. Specifically, let

---

[1] A non-constant monic polynomial $h(X)$ over $\mathsf{GR}(p^r;m)$ is a monic basic primitive polynomial if $\bar{h}(X)$ is a primitive polynomial over $\mathsf{GF}(p^m)$.

$\eta = X \bmod F_0(X)$ and let $S \subseteq \mathbb{Z}_M^*$ be a set of representatives of $\mathbb{Z}_M^* / \langle p \rangle$, then for any $m(X) \in R_{p^r}$ the isomorphism can be explicitly expressed as

$$\texttt{Decode}(m(X)) = (m(\eta^{s_0}), \ldots, m(\eta^{s_{L-1}}))_{s_i \in S}.$$

Note that $\mathbb{Z}_{p^r}[X]/(F_i(X)) \cong \mathsf{GR}(p^r; d)$. By denoting $\mathcal{E} = \mathsf{GR}(p^r; d)$, $\texttt{Decode}$ eventually induces an isomorphism between R_{p^r} and $\mathcal{E}^L$, and the L coordinates of $\mathcal{E}^L$ are referred to as *slots* in the plaintext.

In the context of rotation operations in BGV, S is typically expressed as the products of several generators, i.e., $S = \{\prod_{i=1}^n g_i^{e_i} \mid e_i \in [L_i]\}$, where L_i is the order of g_i in $\mathbb{Z}_M^* / \langle p, g_1, \cdots, g_{i-1} \rangle$. By assigning the index $(e_1, \ldots, e_n)$ to the slot $\prod_{i=1}^n g_i^{e_i}$, the L slots can be organized into an n-dimensional *hypercube*. A *hypercolumn along the s-th dimension* is composed of L_s slots, where e_j remains constant for $j \neq s$ and e_s varies from 0 to $L_s - 1$. It is evident that there are L/L_s hypercolumns in the s-th dimension.

A dimension s is referred to as a *good dimension* if $\mathrm{ord}_{\mathbb{Z}_M^*}(g_s) = L_s$, otherwise, it is termed a *bad dimension*. It is known that we can rotate all the L/L_s hypercolumns along the s-th dimension simultaneously with one Galois automorphism in a good dimension, or two in a bad dimension. Specifically, let ρ_s be the rotation-up-by-one-slot operation along the s-th dimension that moves the slot at index $(e_1, \ldots, e_n)$ to $(e_1, \ldots, e_{s-1}, [e_s - 1]_{L_s}, e_{s+1}, \ldots, e_n)$. Let θ_s be the Galois automorphism that sends $m(X)$ to $m(X^{g_s})$. If this dimension is good, it has $\rho_s = \theta_s$. Otherwise, for $i \in [L_s]$, it has $\rho_s^i(m) = \theta_s^i(m) \cdot \mu_s(i) + \theta_s^{i-L_s}(m) \cdot \mu_s(i)'$ for some constants $\mu_s(i)$ and $\mu_s(i)'$ [20,21]. This rotation operation plays a pivotal role in executing homomorphic linear transformations on the slots.

2.4   Homomorphic Linear Transformations

Let T be a linear transformation from $\mathcal{E}^L$ to $\mathcal{E}^L$. We say that T is a one-dimensional linear transformation along the s-th dimension if the value in any slot of $\mathsf{T}(\alpha)$ only depends on the slots of the same hypercolumn along the s-th dimension of α. One-dimensional linear transformations have been studied extensively due to their role as fundamental building blocks of arbitrary linear transformations on slots [20].

The one-dimensional transformations fall into two categories. The first type, called MatMul1D in HElib, is the one-dimensional $\mathcal{E}$-linear transformation. A MatMul1D transformation T along the s-th dimension can be expressed as

$$\mathsf{T}(m) = \sum_{i \in [L_s]} \kappa(i) \rho_s^i(m), \text{ for } m \in R_{p^r}, \tag{1}$$

where $\kappa(i) \in R_{p^r}$ are constants determined by T. When considering the restriction of T on a hypercolumn k along the s-th dimension, it can be represented as a matrix $\mathbf{T}_k \in \mathcal{E}^{L_s \times L_s}$. $\texttt{Decode}(\kappa(i))$ is composed of the i-th diagonals of all $\mathbf{T}_k$'s.

The other type, called BlockMatMul1D, is the one-dimensional $\mathbb{Z}_{p^r}$-linear transformation. Specifically, a BlockMatMul1D transformation T' along the s-th dimension can be expressed as

$$T'(m) = \sum_{j \in [d]} \sum_{i \in [L_s]} \kappa(i,j)\sigma^j(\rho_s^i(m)), \text{ for } m \in R_{p^r}, \tag{2}$$

where $\kappa(i,j) \in R_{p^r}$ are constants determined by T', and σ is the Frobenius automorphism. When considering the restriction of T' on a hypercolumn k along the s-th dimension, it can be represented as an $L_s \times L_s$ matrix $\mathbf{T}'_k$ such that each of its entries is a $\mathbb{Z}_{p^r}$-linear transformation on $\mathcal{E}$. Such an entry can be represented as either a matrix in $\mathbb{Z}_{p^r}^{d \times d}$ or a linearized polynomial $f(v) = \sum_{j \in [d]} a_j \sigma^j(v)$, where $a_j \in \mathcal{E}$. Again, $\mathtt{Decode}(\kappa(i,j))$ is composed of the j-th coefficients of the i-th diagonals in all $\mathbf{T}'_k$'s (in the linearized polynomial form).

For a MatMul1D or BlockMatMul1D type one-dimensional linear transformation T along the s-th dimension, define $\mathrm{DiagSet}_s(T) \subseteq [L_s]$ as the union of the sets of the indices of nonzero diagonals in $\mathbf{T}_k$ for $k \in [L/L_s]$, where $\mathbf{T}_k$ is the restriction of T on a hypercolumn k. Since $\kappa(i)$ in Eq. 1 and $\kappa(i,j)$ in Eq. 2 are composed of the i-th diagonals in all $\mathbf{T}_k$, we can replace '$i \in [L_s]$' with '$i \in \mathrm{DiagSet}_s(T)$' by omitting the zero diagonals. Moreover, for two one-dimensional linear transformations T and T' on the s-th dimension, their composition satisfies

$$\mathrm{DiagSet}_s(T' \circ T) \subseteq \{[a+b]_{L_s} \mid a \in \mathrm{DiagSet}_s(T), b \in \mathrm{DiagSet}_s(T')\}$$

due to Eq. 1 and Eq. 2.

Hoisting. When computing multiple automorphisms on the *same* ciphertext, the hoisting technique could be used to significantly speed up the computation [11,20]. In an ordinary automorphism, the decomposition of the ciphertext before re-linearization is the most expensive part because it requires NTTs. When hoisting is applied, the ciphertext is decomposed and moved into the NTT domain in the first step. Then, we can perform multiple automorphisms on this ciphertext without further decomposition or NTTs.

2.5   BGV Bootstrapping

BGV bootstrapping is categorized into two types, general bootstrapping [19,22] and thin bootstrapping [11]. The general bootstrapping consists of four steps: (1) decryption formula simplification; (2) CoeffToSlot transformation; (3) digit removal; (4) SlotToCoeff. Given $m \in R_{p^r}$, the CoeffToSlot moves the powerful basis coefficients of m into the slots, where each slot is identified as a d-dimension vector space w.r.t. the normal basis of $\mathcal{E}$. In contrast, the SlotToCoeff is almost the inverse of CoeffToSlot, moving the coefficients in slots (w.r.t. the power basis of $\mathcal{E}$) into the powerful basis in R_{p^r}. We omit the descriptions of (1) and (3) because they are not the focus of this work. We can consider a simplified version of CoeffToSlot that homomorphically computes the encoding map $\mathtt{Encode}(\cdot) =$

Decode$^{-1}(\cdot)$, which is the most complicated part of CoeffToSlot and only needs to be composed with lightweight transformations to be converted to the actual CoeffToSlot. SlotToCoeff is also simplified as the decoding map Decode$(\cdot)$.

If each slot stores only an integer instead of a Galois ring/field element, the bootstrapping is called a thin bootstrapping. In thin bootstrapping, the steps come in a different order, namely (4)(1)(2)(3). The input ciphertext to SlotTo-Coeff now encrypts a plaintext whose slots store integers instead of Galois ring elements, which reduces the cost of SlotToCoeff. Since step (1) adds undesired coefficients into the plaintext polynomial, an extra linear map is needed to clear these extra coefficients. This map can be performed after CoeffToSlot in general cyclotomics [22] or before CoeffToSlot in power-of-two cyclotomics [11].

2.6   Number Theoretic Transform (NTT)

In this paper, we focus on the NTT mapping which maps $m \in R_{p^r}$ to $(m \bmod F_0(X), \ldots, m \bmod F_{L-1}(X)) \in \prod_{i \in [L]} \mathbb{Z}_{p^r}[X]/F_i(X)$, where $F_i(X)$'s are the irreducible factors of $\Phi_M(X)$ defined in Sect. 2.3. The inverse NTT (iNTT) is defined as the inverse of this map. There has been plenty of research about the NTT/iNTT on the plaintext [24], and various fast NTT algorithms have been proposed, such as Cooley-Tukey [13] and Bruun [8]. These algorithms typically decompose NTT/iNTT into multiple layers to speed up the computation. We do not delve into their details here, as we will present explicit decompositions of NTT/iNTT within the framework of BGV linear transformations.

3   The Decomposition of Linear Transformations

As discussed previously, this section focuses on the decomposition of Decode and Encode. Let $\Phi_M(X) = \prod_{i=0}^{L-1} F_i(X)$, where $F_i(X)$ is the minimal polynomial of η^{s_i} and $\{s_i\}_{i \in [L]} \subseteq \mathbb{Z}_M^*$ is a set of representatives of $\mathbb{Z}_M^*/\langle p \rangle$. Then Decode can be decomposed into two sub-maps Red and Eval, i.e., Decode = Eval $\circ$ Red, where Red is an NTT map from R_{p^r} to $\prod_{i \in [L]} \mathbb{Z}_{p^r}[X]/F_i(X)$ such that

$$\text{Red}(m) = (m \bmod F_0, m \bmod F_1, \ldots, m \bmod F_{L-1}), \text{ for } m \in R_{p^r},$$

and Eval is a map from $\prod_{i \in [L]} \mathbb{Z}_{p^r}[X]/F_i(X)$ to $\mathcal{E}^L$ such that

$$\text{Eval}(m_0(X), \ldots, m_{L-1}(X)) = (m_0(\eta^{s_0}), \ldots, m_{L-1}(\eta^{s_{L-1}})).$$

Both Red and Eval are $\mathbb{Z}_{p^r}$-linear transformations, and they can be represented as matrices in $(\mathbb{Z}_{p^r}^{d \times d})^{L \times L}$ by identifying the input and output as vectors in $(\mathbb{Z}_{p^r}^d)^L$ via coefficient embedding. Specifically, for $m(X) \in R_{p^r}$, the i-th entry is the vector $m[id +: d]$ for $i \in [L]$. For $(m_i(X))_{i \in [L]} \in \prod_{i \in [L]} \mathbb{Z}_{p^r}[X]/F_i(X)$, the i-th entry is the coefficient vector of $m_i(X)$. For $\mathcal{E}^L$, the i-th entry is the coefficient vector of the i-th slot with respect to the power basis of $\mathcal{E} = \mathbb{Z}_{p^r}[X]/F_0(X)$. When we represent a homomorphic linear transformation as a matrix, each of its entries is an element in $\mathbb{Z}_{p^r}^{d \times d}$.

Clearly `Eval` is a `BlockMatMul1D` type one-dimensional linear transformation such that its main diagonal is the only nonzero diagonal (in terms of an $L \times L$ block matrix). Thus `Eval` and `Eval`$^{-1}$ can be computed by evaluating a linearized polynomial in Eq. 2 with $i = 0$. In the remainder of this section, we focus on the decomposition of `Red` (and `Red`$^{-1}$) into linear sub-transformations for power-of-two cyclotomics.

In the case when M is a power of two, it is known that $\mathbb{Z}_M^* = \langle -1, 5 \rangle \cong \mathbb{Z}_2 \times \mathbb{Z}_{M/4}$. If $p \equiv 1 \bmod 4$, $\mathbb{Z}_M^*/\langle p \rangle = \langle -1, 5 \rangle \cong \mathbb{Z}_2 \times \mathbb{Z}_{M/(4d)}$, implying a 2-by-$\frac{M}{4d}$ sized hypercube generated by $g_1 = -1, g_2 = 5$. The slots are indexed into a 1D array by concatenating the second D-sized hypercolumn to the end of the first one. If $p \equiv 3 \bmod 4$, $\mathbb{Z}_M^*/\langle p \rangle = \langle 5 \rangle \cong \mathbb{Z}_{M/(2d)}$. The hypercube has a single generator $g_1 = 5$ and collapses into a single dimension of size $\frac{M}{2d}$. We call the dimension generated by 5 (in both cases of p) *the major dimension* and denote its size as D, i.e., $D = L/2 = M/(4d)$ for $p = 1 \bmod 4$ and $D = L = M/(2d)$ for $p \equiv 3 \bmod 4$. We call the dimension generated by -1 (in case of $p \equiv 1 \bmod 4$) *the minor dimension*, which has a size of 2. We omit the subscript s in $\rho_s, \theta_s, \mu_s, \mu_s'$, DiagSet$_s$ when they are related to the one-dimensional linear transformations on the major dimension. The main result of this section can be summarized as follows.

Theorem 1. *(1) If $p \equiv 1 \bmod 4$, we have the decomposition*

$$\text{Red}^{-1} = \text{BR}'_{\log_2(2dD),\log_2(d)} \circ \text{Red}_{\text{BR}}^{-1} \text{ and}$$

$$\text{Red}_{\text{BR}}^{-1} = \text{N}_{\log_2(D)+1} \circ \ldots \circ \text{N}_1,$$

where BR$'$ *is interpreted as a permutation on* $(\mathbb{Z}_{p^r}^d)^{2D}$ *in the natural manner. For* $j \in [1, \log_2(D)]$, *both* N_j *and* N_j^{-1} *are MatMul1D transformations on the major dimension with nonzero diagonals indexed by* $2^{-j}D \times \{-1, 0, 1\}$. $\text{N}_{\log_2(D)+1}$ *and its inverse are MatMul1D transformations on the minor dimension.*

(2) If $p \equiv 3 \bmod 4$, we have the Bruun-style decomposition

$$\text{Red}^{-1} = \text{BR}_{\log_2(dD),\log_2(d)} \circ \text{Red}_{\text{BR}}^{-1} \text{ and}$$

$$\text{Red}_{\text{BR}}^{-1} = \text{N}_{\log_2(D)} \circ \ldots \circ \text{N}_1,$$

where N_1 *and* N_1^{-1} *are BlockMatMul1D transformations with nonzero diagonals indexed by* $D/2 \times \{-1, 0, 1\}$. *For* $j \in [2, \log_2(D)]$, N_j *is a MatMul1D transformation with nonzero diagonals indexed by* $2^{-j}D \times [-3, 3]$, *and* N_j^{-1} *is a MatMul1D transformation with nonzero diagonals indexed by* $2^{-j}D \times [-3, 2]$. *Alternatively,* Red^{-1} *can also be decomposed in Radix-2 style into*

$$\text{Red}^{-1} = \text{BR}_{\log_2(dD),\log_2(d)-1} \circ \text{Red}_{\text{BR}}'^{-1} \text{ and}$$

$$\text{Red}_{\text{BR}}'^{-1} = \text{N}'_{\log_2(D)} \circ \ldots \circ \text{N}'_1,$$

where both N'_j *and* N'^{-1}_j *are BlockMatMul1D transformations with nonzero diagonals indexed by* $2^{-j}D \times \{-1, 0, 1\}$ *for* $j \in [1, \log_2(D)]$.

Recall that for a one-dimensional linear transformation $\mathbb{N}$ along the s-th dimension, the number of rotations required to evaluate it equals $|\mathrm{DiagSet}(\mathbb{N})|$. According to Theorem 1, both $|\mathrm{DiagSet}(\mathbb{N}_j)|$ and $|\mathrm{DiagSet}(\mathbb{N}_j^{-1})|$ are small (usually two to three) because they have only a few diagonals. Therefore, the computation time for the linear transformations in bootstrapping can be significantly reduced by utilizing the decomposition presented in Theorem 1. In the subsequent discussion, we provide the derivation of Theorem 1 for two cases of p. Moreover, in Sect. 3.1 and Sect. 3.2 we make the assumption that $r = 1$ in the plaintext modulus, implying that each slot corresponds to the Galois field $\mathsf{GF}(p^d)$. The general case where $r > 1$ (corresponding to the Galois ring case) will be addressed in Sect. 3.3.

3.1   The Case of $p \equiv 1 \bmod 4$

The set of representatives $\{s_i\}_{i\in[L]}$ is chosen to be $s_{e_1 D + e_2} = (-1)^{e_1} 5^{e_2}$ for $e_1 \in [2], e_2 \in [D]$. We note that the minor dimension is always good, while the major dimension is good whenever $p \equiv 1 \bmod M$. By [31], it has $\Phi_M(X) = \prod_{i \in \mathbb{Z}_{4D}^*}(X^d - \zeta^i)$ over $\mathbb{Z}_p$, where $\zeta \in \mathbb{Z}_p$ is a primitive $4D$-th root of unity and each factor is irreducible over $\mathbb{Z}_p$. Without loss of generality, we can assume that $F_0(X) = X^d - \zeta$, which leads to $F_i(X) = X^d - \zeta^{s_i}$ for $i \in [L]$. To begin with, we prove the following lemma.

Lemma 1. Let $F_i^{(0)} = F_i(X)$ for $i \in [L]$, and $F_i^{(j)} = F_i^{(j-1)} F_{i+2^{-j}D}^{(j-1)}$ for $1 \le j \le \log_2(D)$ and $i \in [0, 2^{-j}D) \cup [D, D + 2^{-j}D)$, then it has

$$F_i^{(j)} = X^{d \cdot 2^j} - \zeta^{s_i \cdot 2^j}, \text{ for } j \in [0, \log_2(D)], i \in [0, 2^{-j}D) \cup [D, D + 2^{-j}D).$$

Proof. Clearly, the statement is true for $j = 0$. Now let $1 \le j \le \log_2(D)$ and suppose the statement holds for $j - 1$ and $i \in [0, 2^{-(j-1)}D) \cup [D, D + 2^{-(j-1)}D)$. By the definition of $F_i^{(j)}$ it has

$$F_i^{(j)} = F_i^{(j-1)} F_{i+2^{-j}D}^{(j-1)} = (X^{d \cdot 2^{j-1}} - \zeta^{s_i \cdot 2^{j-1}})(X^{d \cdot 2^{j-1}} - \zeta^{s_{i+2^{-j}D} \cdot 2^{j-1}})$$

for $i \in [0, 2^{-j}D) \cup [D, D + 2^{-j}D)$. Denote $i = e_1 D + e_2$ for $0 \le e_1 \le 1$ and $0 \le e_2 < 2^{-j}D$, then $s_i = (-1)^{e_1} 5^{e_2}$ and $s_{i+2^{-j}D} = (-1)^{e_1} 5^{e_2 + 2^{-j}D}$. Since ζ is a primitive $4D$-th root of unity and $5^{2^{-j}D} \cdot 2^{j-1} \equiv 2D + 2^{j-1} \bmod 4D$, we have $\zeta^{s_{i+2^{-j}D} \cdot 2^{j-1}} = -\zeta^{s_i \cdot 2^{j-1}}$. Then it follows directly that $F_i^{(j)} = X^{d \cdot 2^j} - \zeta^{s_i \cdot 2^j}$. $\square$

In addition, we denote $F_0^{(\log_2(D)+1)} = \prod_{i \in [2D]} F_i^{(0)} = \Phi_M(X)$.

The Definition of $\mathbb{N}_j$. Suppose $m \in R_{p^r}$, then $\mathbb{N}_j$ can be roughly viewed as the linear transformation that maps $(m \bmod F_i^{(j-1)})_{i \in I_{j-1}}$ to $(m \bmod F_i^{(j)})_{i \in I_j}$, where I_j is the range of i defined in Lemma 1. For the specific definition of $\mathbb{N}_j$, we need to handle the bit-reversal phenomenon to design matrices that can be homomorphic evaluated efficiently. In our case, the bit-reversal primarily arises due to the slots occupied by the two factors that combine into $F_i^{(j)}$ are in an interleaving order. As an example, we illustrate the bit-reversal phenomenon in the computation of $m \bmod F_i^{(2)}$ from $m \bmod F_i^{(1)}$ and $m \bmod F_{i+D/4}^{(1)}$ in Fig. 1. Taking this into consideration, we first define vectors $\boldsymbol{\alpha}_j \in (\mathbb{Z}_{p^r}^d)^L$ for $0 \leq j \leq \log_2(D)+1$ as follows. The vector $\boldsymbol{\alpha}_0$ corresponds to $\alpha = \mathsf{Red}(m) \in \mathcal{E}^L$. For $1 \leq j \leq \log_2(D)$, we define $\boldsymbol{\alpha}_j$ such that

$$\boldsymbol{\alpha}_j[i + k \cdot 2^{-j}D] = (m \bmod F_i^{(j)})[\mathrm{BitRev}_{j,0}(k) \cdot d +: d]$$

for $i \in [0, 2^{-j}D) \cup [D, D + 2^{-j}D)$, $k \in [2^j)$. For $j = \log_2(D)+1$, we define

$$\boldsymbol{\alpha}_{\log_2(D)+1}[k] = m[\mathrm{BitRev}'_{\log_2(D)+1,0}(k) \cdot d +: d]$$

for $k \in [2D]$.

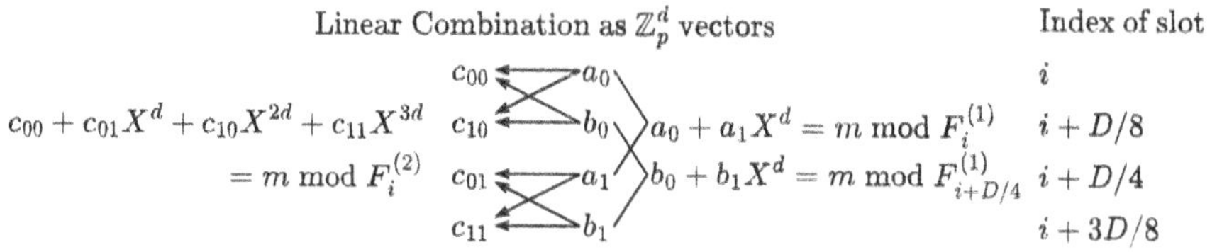

Linear Combination as $\mathbb{Z}_p^d$ vectors Index of slot

Fig. 1. An example of the butterfly structures in $\mathsf{Red}_{\mathrm{BR}}^{-1}$ that leads to bit-reversal. a_i, b_i and c_{ij} are degree $d-1$ polynomials in $\mathbb{Z}_p[X]$.

For $1 \leq j \leq \log_2(D)+1$, we define N_j as the linear transformation that maps $\boldsymbol{\alpha}_{j-1}$ to $\boldsymbol{\alpha}_j$, where the coefficients of m are regarded as independent variables. Denote $\mathsf{Red}_{\mathrm{BR}}^{-1} = \mathsf{N}_{\log_2(D)+1} \circ \ldots \circ \mathsf{N}_1$, then it can be readily checked that

$$\mathrm{BR}'_{\log_2(2dD),\log_2(d)}(\mathsf{Red}_{\mathrm{BR}}^{-1}(\alpha))) = m.$$

Notably, the output of $\mathsf{Red}_{\mathrm{BR}}^{-1}(\alpha)$ is a permutated version of m's coefficients, which is a common phenomenon in fast NTT algorithms. As in [10,23], we will not reorder the slots into their ordinary order by computing the inverse permutation homomorphically. Instead, we directly pass the output of $\mathsf{Red}_{\mathrm{BR}}$ and $\mathsf{Red}_{\mathrm{BR}}^{-1}$ to the next stage of bootstrapping. This will not affect the correctness of bootstrapping, similar to the observations in previous works on CKKS bootstrapping. This is because: (1) the digit removal step is performed in a SIMD manner and is insensitive to the order of the values in the slots; (2) the coefficients in each slot remain as a whole group during the permutation, which makes it possible to repack the output ciphertexts of digit removal.

Let $\mathbf{N}_j \in (\mathbb{Z}_{p^r}^{d \times d})^{L \times L}$ denote the matrix corresponding to N_j. In Lemma 2, we discuss the structure of the $\mathbf{N}_j$s. The proof can be found in Supplementary Materials B in the full version of this paper. An example illustrating the $\mathbf{N}_j$'s for $D = 4$ is provided in Fig. 2 for a better understanding.

$$
\begin{bmatrix} * & & & & * & & & \\ & * & & & & * & & \\ & & * & & & & * & \\ & & & * & & & & * \\ \hline * & & & & * & & & \\ & * & & & & * & & \\ & & * & & & & * & \\ & & & * & & & & * \end{bmatrix}
\begin{bmatrix} *, F_0^{(0)} \\ *, F_1^{(0)} \\ *, F_2^{(0)} \\ *, F_3^{(0)} \\ \hline *, F_4^{(0)} \\ *, F_5^{(0)} \\ *, F_6^{(0)} \\ *, F_7^{(0)} \end{bmatrix}
=
\begin{bmatrix} 0*, F_0^{(1)} \\ 0*, F_1^{(1)} \\ 1*, F_0^{(1)} \\ 1*, F_1^{(1)} \\ \hline 0*, F_4^{(1)} \\ 0*, F_5^{(1)} \\ 1*, F_4^{(1)} \\ 1*, F_5^{(1)} \end{bmatrix},
\qquad
\begin{bmatrix} * & * & & & & & & \\ * & * & & & & & & \\ & & * & * & & & & \\ & & * & * & & & & \\ \hline & & & & * & * & & \\ & & & & * & * & & \\ & & & & & & * & * \\ & & & & & & * & * \end{bmatrix}
\begin{bmatrix} 0*, F_0^{(1)} \\ 0*, F_1^{(1)} \\ 1*, F_0^{(1)} \\ 1*, F_1^{(1)} \\ \hline 0*, F_4^{(1)} \\ 0*, F_5^{(1)} \\ 1*, F_4^{(1)} \\ 1*, F_5^{(1)} \end{bmatrix}
=
\begin{bmatrix} 00*, F_0^{(2)} \\ 10*, F_0^{(2)} \\ 01*, F_0^{(2)} \\ 11*, F_0^{(2)} \\ \hline 00*, F_4^{(2)} \\ 10*, F_4^{(2)} \\ 01*, F_4^{(2)} \\ 11*, F_4^{(2)} \end{bmatrix}
$$

$$
\begin{bmatrix} * & & & & * & & & \\ & * & & & & * & & \\ & & * & & & & * & \\ & & & * & & & & * \\ \hline * & & & & * & & & \\ & * & & & & * & & \\ & & * & & & & * & \\ & & & * & & & & * \end{bmatrix}
\begin{bmatrix} 00*, F_0^{(2)} \\ 10*, F_0^{(2)} \\ 01*, F_0^{(2)} \\ 11*, F_0^{(2)} \\ \hline 00*, F_4^{(2)} \\ 10*, F_4^{(2)} \\ 01*, F_4^{(2)} \\ 11*, F_4^{(2)} \end{bmatrix}
=
\begin{bmatrix} 000*, F_0^{(3)} \\ 010*, F_0^{(3)} \\ 001*, F_0^{(3)} \\ 011*, F_0^{(3)} \\ \hline 100*, F_0^{(3)} \\ 110*, F_0^{(3)} \\ 101*, F_0^{(3)} \\ 111*, F_0^{(3)} \end{bmatrix}
$$

Fig. 2. An illustration of $\mathrm{Red}_{\mathrm{BR}}^{-1}$ for $D = 4$ and $p \equiv 1 \bmod 4$. A '$*$' in matrices stands for a nonzero entry that is a multiple of $\mathbf{I}_d$, while a '$*$' in the vectors means $\log_2(d)$ bits ranging from all zeros to all ones. Each slot stores part of the coefficients of $m \bmod F_i^{(j)}$. The (binary format of) indices of the coefficients are displayed along with the corresponding $F_i^{(j)}$. E.g., '$01*, F_0^{(2)}$' means that this slot stores $(m \bmod F_0^{(2)})[d +: d]$.

Lemma 2. (1) For $j \in [1, \log_2(D)]$, $\mathbf{N}_j$ can be viewed as a $2^j \times 2^j$ diagonal block matrix. Each block has a size of $2^{-j+1}D \times 2^{-j+1}D$, which has three non-zero diagonals indexed by $2^{-j}D \times \{-1, 0, 1\}$.

(2) When viewed as an $L \times L$ block matrix, $\mathbf{N}_{\log_2(D)+1}$ has three non-zero diagonals indexed by $D \times \{-1, 0, 1\}$.

For $j \in [1, \log_2(D) + 1]$, all non-zero entries of $\mathbf{N}_j$ in $\mathbb{Z}_{p^r}^{d \times d}$ are multiples of $\mathbf{I}_d$. All the above properties also hold for $\mathbf{N}_j^{-1}$.

Proof of (1) in Theorem 1. According to Lemma 2, for $j \in [1, \log_2(D)]$, $\mathbf{N}_j$ and $\mathbf{N}_j^{-1}$ can be viewed as

$$
\begin{bmatrix} \mathbf{A}_0 & 0 \\ 0 & \mathbf{A}_1 \end{bmatrix},
$$

where $\mathbf{A}_0$ and $\mathbf{A}_1$ are $D \times D$ matrices, and $\mathbf{A}_t$ is a linear transformation on the t-th hypercolumn of the major dimension for $0 \le t \le 1$. Thus $\mathbf{N}_j$ and $\mathbf{N}_j^{-1}$ are linear transformations on the major dimension.

For $\mathbf{N}_{\log_2(D)+1}$ and its inverse, the t-th hypercolumn of the minor dimension consists of the t-th and $(t + D)$-th slot, where $t \in [D]$. The 2×2 submatrix

$$
\begin{bmatrix} \mathbf{N}_{\log_2(D)+1}[t, t] & \mathbf{N}_{\log_2(D)+1}[t, t + D] \\ \mathbf{N}_{\log_2(D)+1}[t, t + D] & \mathbf{N}_{\log_2(D)+1}[t + D, t + D] \end{bmatrix}
$$

is a linear transformation on the t-th hypercolumn of the minor dimension. Thus both $\mathbf{N}_{\log_2(D)+1}$ and its inverse are linear transformations on the minor dimension.

For $j \in [1, \log_2(D)+1]$, $\mathbf{N}_j$ is a MatMul1D transformation because each entry of $\mathbf{N}_j$ is a multiple of $\mathbf{I}_d$. The indices of nonzero diagonals in $\mathbf{N}_j$ and $\mathbf{N}_j^{-1}$ follow directly from Lemma 2.

3.2   The Case of $p \equiv 3 \bmod 4$

In this case, we have $s_{e_1} = 5^{e_1}$ for $e_1 \in [D]$, and the only dimension in the hypercube is good only if $D = \frac{M}{4}$. According to [31], $\phi_M(X)$ factors into trinomials for $d \geq 2$, i.e.,

$$\Phi_M(X) = \prod_{i \in \mathbb{Z}_{4D}^*/\langle p \rangle} (X^d - (\zeta^i + \zeta^{ip})X^{d/2} + \zeta^{i(p+1)}),$$

where $\zeta \in \mathsf{GF}(p^2)$ is a primitive $4D$-th root of unity, and each factor is an irreducible polynomial in $\mathbb{Z}_p[X]$. Without loss of generality, we can assume that $F_0(X) = X^d - (\zeta + \zeta^p)X^{d/2} + \zeta^{p+1}$, which leads to $F_i(X) = X^d - (\zeta^{s_i} + \zeta^{s_i p})X^{d/2} + \zeta^{s_i(p+1)}$ for $i \in [D]$. Similarly, we have the following lemma.

Lemma 3. *Let* $F_i^{(0)} = F_i$ *for* $i \in [D]$, *and* $F_i^{(j)} = F_i^{(j-1)} F_{i+2^{-j}D}^{(j-1)}$ *for* $1 \leq j \leq \log_2(D)$, $i \in [2^{-j}D]$. *Then it has*

$$F_i^{(j)} = X^{2^j d} - (\zeta^{2^j \cdot s_i} + \zeta^{2^j \cdot s_i p})X^{2^{j-1} d} + \zeta^{2^j \cdot s_i(p+1)},$$

for $0 \leq j \leq \log_2(D)$ *and* $i \in [2^{-j}D]$. *Moreover, the middle term is nonzero except for* $j = \log_2(D)$.

Proof. The proof of the expression of $F_i^{(j)}$ is similar to Lemma 1.

For the middle term, $\zeta^{2^j \cdot s_i} + \zeta^{2^j \cdot s_i p} = 0 \iff \zeta^{2^j \cdot s_i(p-1)} = -1 \iff 2^j \cdot 5^i(p-1) \equiv 2D \bmod 4D$. The remaining is easy to verify. $\square$

The Definition of N_j**.** Suppose $m \in R_{p^r}$, we first define vectors $\boldsymbol{\alpha}_j \in (\mathbb{Z}_{p^r}^d)^L$ for $0 \leq j \leq \log_2(D)$ as follows. The vector $\boldsymbol{\alpha}_0$ corresponds to $\alpha = \mathsf{Red}(m) \in \mathcal{E}^L$. For $1 \leq j \leq \log_2(D)$, we define $\boldsymbol{\alpha}_j$ such that

$$\boldsymbol{\alpha}_j[i + k \cdot 2^{-j}D] = (m \bmod F_i^{(j)})[\mathrm{BitRev}_{j,0}(k) \cdot d +: d]$$

for $i \in [2^{-j}D], k \in [2^j]$.

For $1 \leq j \leq \log_2(D)$, we define N_j as the linear transformation that maps $\boldsymbol{\alpha}_{j-1}$ to $\boldsymbol{\alpha}_j$. Denote $\mathsf{Red}_{\mathrm{BR}}^{-1} = \mathsf{N}_{\log_2(D)} \circ \ldots \circ \mathsf{N}_1$, then it can be checked that

$$\mathrm{BR}_{\log_2(2dD), \log_2(d)}\big(\mathsf{Red}_{\mathrm{BR}}^{-1}(\alpha))\big) = m.$$

In contrast to the case of $p \equiv 1 \bmod 4$, the fact the $F_i^{(j)}$s are trinomials complicates the butterfly structure, turning its outputs from linear combinations of two terms into linear combinations of four terms. For example, given two polynomials $f_0(X) = X^{2k} + sX^k + t$ and $f_1(X) = X^{2k} - sX^k + t$ of degree $2k$, let $l + hX^k \in \mathbb{Z}_p[X]/f_0(X)$ and $l' + h'X^K \in \mathbb{Z}_p[X]/f_1(X)$, where $s, t \in \mathbb{Z}_p$ and $l, h, l', h' \in \mathbb{Z}_p[X]$ with degrees less than k. Denote the polynomial reconstructed from $l + hX^k$ and $l' + h'X^k$ as $a_{00} + a_{01}X^k + a_{10}X^{2k} + a_{11}X^{3k} \in \mathbb{Z}_p[X]/(f_1(X)f_2(X))$, where $a_{00}, \ldots, a_{11}$ are polynomials with degree less than k. Then we have the following *Bruun butterfly* structure, where '$*$' represents a non-zero entry in $\mathbb{Z}_p$.

$$
\begin{bmatrix} a_{00} \\ a_{01} \\ a_{10} \\ a_{11} \end{bmatrix} = \begin{bmatrix} * & * & * & * \\ * & * & * & * \\ & & * & * \\ * & & * & \end{bmatrix} \times \begin{bmatrix} l \\ h \\ l' \\ h' \end{bmatrix}, \quad \begin{bmatrix} l \\ h \\ l' \\ h' \end{bmatrix} = \begin{bmatrix} * & & * & * \\ & * & * & * \\ * & & * & * \\ & * & * & * \end{bmatrix} \times \begin{bmatrix} a_{00} \\ a_{01} \\ a_{10} \\ a_{11} \end{bmatrix}. \tag{3}
$$

In the first layer of $\mathtt{Red}_{\mathrm{BR}}^{-1}$, the i-th Bruun butterfly has two input slots $\boldsymbol{\alpha}_0[i]$ and $\boldsymbol{\alpha}_0[i + D/2]$, where the former stores l and h while the latter stores l' and h'. The output of this butterfly is stored in $\boldsymbol{\alpha}_1[i]$ and $\boldsymbol{\alpha}_1[i + D/2]$.

The natural approach is to store the lower coefficients a_{00} and a_{01} in $\boldsymbol{\alpha}_1[i]$, while the higher ones a_{10} and a_{11} are stored in $\boldsymbol{\alpha}_1[i+D]$, i.e., in a non-bit-reversed order. In this case, for $j \geq 2$, the four inputs to each Bruun butterfly in $\mathtt{N}_j$ lie in four distinct slots, which means each entry in $\boldsymbol{\alpha}_j$ are $\mathbb{Z}_p$-linear combinations of entries in $\boldsymbol{\alpha}_{j-1}$ and each entry of $\mathbf{N}_j$ is a multiple of $\mathbf{I}_d$. We call this way of constructing $\mathtt{N}_j$ as the *Bruun style*. An example of $\mathtt{N}_j$'s for $D = 8$ is given in Fig. 3 for better illustration, while the formal statements about the structure of $\mathtt{N}_j$ are given in Lemma 4 and proved in Supplementary Material B in the full version of this paper.

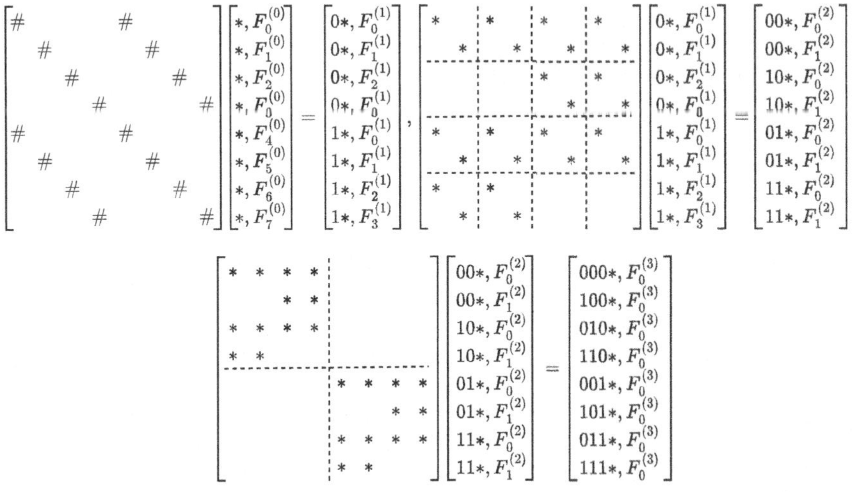

Fig. 3. An illustration of $\mathtt{Red}_{\mathrm{BR}}^{-1}$ in Bruun-style for $D = 8$ and $p \equiv 3 \bmod 4$. A '#' in matrices stands for a nonzero entry with the form of $\begin{bmatrix} a_0\mathbf{I}_{d/2} & a_1\mathbf{I}_{d/2} \\ a_2\mathbf{I}_{d/2} & a_3\mathbf{I}_{d/2} \end{bmatrix}$ for $a_i \in \mathbb{Z}_p$. Other symbols have the same meaning as in Fig. 2.

Lemma 4. (1) *In the Bruun-style decomposition, when viewed as* $D \times D$ *matrices,* $\mathbf{N}_1$ *and its inverse have only three non-zero diagonals indexed by* $D/2 \times \{-1, 0, 1\}$. *Each entry in* $\mathbf{N}_1$ *and* $\mathbf{N}_1^{-1}$ *has the form of* $\begin{bmatrix} a_0 \mathbf{I}_{d/2} & a_1 \mathbf{I}_{d/2} \\ a_2 \mathbf{I}_{d/2} & a_3 \mathbf{I}_{d/2} \end{bmatrix}$ *for* $a_i \in \mathbb{Z}_p$ *that may vary for each entry.*

(2) *For* $j \in [2, \log_2(D)]$, $\mathbf{N}_j$ *can be viewed as a* $2^{j-2} \times 2^{j-2}$ *diagonal block matrix. Each block has a size of* $2^{2-j}D \times 2^{2-j}D$, *which has 7 non-zero diagonals indexed by* $2^{-j}D \times [-3, 3]$. *Each entry in* $\mathbf{N}_j$ *is a multiple of* $\mathbf{I}_d$. *These properties also hold for* $\mathbf{N}_j^{-1}$, *except that the nonzero diagonals of* $\mathbf{N}_j^{-1}$ *are indexed by* $2^{-j}D \times [-3, 2]$.

Reducing the Number of Nonzero Diagonals. As an optimization, we can reduce the number of nonzero diagonals in the Bruun-style decomposition from six or seven to only three by folding some nonzero diagonals inside each entry of $\mathbf{N}_j$.

To achieve this effect, we need to modify the output of the i-th Bruun butterfly in the first layer by storing a_{00} and a_{10} in $\boldsymbol{\alpha}_1[i]$ with a_{01} and a_{11} in $\boldsymbol{\alpha}_1[i+D/2]$, i.e., in a bit-reversed order.

Suppose $m \in R_{p^r}$, we first define vectors $\boldsymbol{\alpha}_j \in (\mathbb{Z}_{p^r}^d)^L$ and $\boldsymbol{\alpha}'_j \in (\mathbb{Z}_{p^r}^{d/2})^{2L}$ for $0 \leq j \leq \log_2(D)$ as follows. The vector $\boldsymbol{\alpha}_0$ corresponds to $\alpha = \mathrm{Red}(m) \in \mathcal{E}^L$. $\boldsymbol{\alpha}'_0$ is defined by $\boldsymbol{\alpha}'_0[2i] = \boldsymbol{\alpha}_0[i][0 +: d/2]$ and $\boldsymbol{\alpha}'_0[2i+1] = \boldsymbol{\alpha}_0[i][d/2 +: d/2]$ for $i \in [D]$. For $1 \leq j \leq \log_2(D)$, we define $\boldsymbol{\alpha}'_j$ such that

$$\boldsymbol{\alpha}'_j[2(i + k \cdot 2^{-j}D) + k_0] = (m \bmod F_i^{(j)})[\mathrm{BitRev}_{j+1,0}(2k + k_0)d/2 +: d/2]$$

for $i \in [2^{-j}D]$, $k \in [2^j]$ and $k_0 \in [2]$. Moreover, $\boldsymbol{\alpha}_j$ is defined by $\boldsymbol{\alpha}_j[i][0 +: d/2] = \boldsymbol{\alpha}'_j[2i]$ and $\boldsymbol{\alpha}_j[i][d/2 +: d/2] = \boldsymbol{\alpha}'_j[2i+1]$ for $i \in [D]$.

For $1 \leq j \leq \log_2(D)$, we define $\mathtt{N}'_j$ as the linear transformation that maps $\boldsymbol{\alpha}_{j-1}$ to $\boldsymbol{\alpha}_j$. Denote $\mathrm{Red}'^{-1}_{\mathrm{BR}} = \mathtt{N}'_{\log_2(D)} \circ \cdots \circ \mathtt{N}'_1$, then

$$\mathrm{Red}'^{-1}_{\mathrm{BR}} = \mathrm{BR}_{\log_2(dD), \log_2(d)-1} \circ \mathrm{Red}^{-1}.$$

We call this kind of $\mathrm{Red}'_{\mathrm{BR}}$ as a *Radix-2-style* one. An example of $\mathtt{N}'_j$'s for $D = 8$ is shown in Fig. 4 while the formal statements about the structure of $\mathtt{N}'_j$ are given in Lemma 5 and its proof is provided in Supplementary Material B in the full version of this paper.

Lemma 5. *In the Radix-2-style* $\mathrm{Red}'^{-1}_{\mathrm{BR}}$, *for* $j \in [1, \log_2(D)]$, $\mathtt{N}'_j$ *can be viewed as a* $2^{j-1} \times 2^{j-1}$ *diagonal block matrix. Each block has a size of* $2^{-j+1}D \times 2^{-j+1}D$, *which has three non-zero diagonals indexed by* $2^{-j}D \times \{-1, 0, 1\}$. *Each entry in* $\mathtt{N}'_j$ *has the form of* $\begin{bmatrix} a_0 \mathbf{I}_{d/2} & a_1 \mathbf{I}_{d/2} \\ a_2 \mathbf{I}_{d/2} & a_3 \mathbf{I}_{d/2} \end{bmatrix}$ *for* $a_i \in \mathbb{Z}_p$ *that may vary for each entry. These properties also hold for* $\mathtt{N}'^{-1}_j$.

Proof of (2) in Theorem 1. Clearly, all $\mathtt{N}_j, \mathtt{N}'_j$ and their inverses are linear transformations on the major dimension because it is the only dimension. The

$$
\begin{bmatrix}
\# & & & & \# & & & \\
 & \# & & & & \# & & \\
 & & \# & & & & \# & \\
 & & & \# & & & & \# \\
\# & & & & \# & & & \\
 & \# & & & & \# & & \\
 & & \# & & & & \# & \\
 & & & \# & & & & \#
\end{bmatrix}
\begin{bmatrix}
X*,F_0^{(0)} \\
X*,F_1^{(0)} \\
X*,F_2^{(0)} \\
X*,F_3^{(0)} \\
X*,F_4^{(0)} \\
X*,F_5^{(0)} \\
X*,F_6^{(0)} \\
X*,F_7^{(0)}
\end{bmatrix}
=
\begin{bmatrix}
X0*,F_0^{(1)} \\
X0*,F_1^{(1)} \\
X0*,F_2^{(1)} \\
X0*,F_3^{(1)} \\
X1*,F_0^{(1)} \\
X1*,F_1^{(1)} \\
X1*,F_2^{(1)} \\
X1*,F_3^{(1)}
\end{bmatrix},
$$

$$
\begin{bmatrix}
\# & \# & & \\
\# & \# & & \\
\# & \# & & \\
\# & \# & & \\
 & & \# & \# \\
 & & \# & \# \\
 & & \# & \# \\
 & & \# & \#
\end{bmatrix}
\begin{bmatrix}
X0*,F_0^{(1)} \\
X0*,F_1^{(1)} \\
X0*,F_2^{(1)} \\
X0*,F_3^{(1)} \\
X1*,F_0^{(1)} \\
X1*,F_1^{(1)} \\
X1*,F_2^{(1)} \\
X1*,F_3^{(1)}
\end{bmatrix}
=
\begin{bmatrix}
X00*,F_0^{(2)} \\
X00*,F_1^{(2)} \\
X10*,F_0^{(2)} \\
X10*,F_1^{(2)} \\
X01*,F_0^{(2)} \\
X01*,F_1^{(2)} \\
X11*,F_0^{(2)} \\
X11*,F_1^{(2)}
\end{bmatrix}
$$

$$
\begin{bmatrix}
\# & \# & & & & \\
\# & \# & & & & \\
 & & \# & \# & & \\
 & & \# & \# & & \\
 & & & & \# & \# \\
 & & & & \# & \#
\end{bmatrix}
\begin{bmatrix}
X00*,F_0^{(2)} \\
X00*,F_1^{(2)} \\
X10*,F_0^{(2)} \\
X10*,F_1^{(2)} \\
X01*,F_0^{(2)} \\
X01*,F_1^{(2)} \\
X11*,F_0^{(2)} \\
X11*,F_1^{(2)}
\end{bmatrix}
=
\begin{bmatrix}
X000*,F_0^{(3)} \\
X100*,F_0^{(3)} \\
X010*,F_0^{(3)} \\
X110*,F_0^{(3)} \\
X001*,F_0^{(3)} \\
X101*,F_0^{(3)} \\
X011*,F_0^{(3)} \\
X111*,F_0^{(3)}
\end{bmatrix}
$$

Fig. 4. An illustration of $\mathrm{Red}'^{-1}_{\mathrm{BR}}$ in Radix-2 style for $D = 8$ and $p \equiv 1 \bmod 4$. A '*' in vectors means $\log_2(d) - 1$ bits ranging from all zeros to all ones while a 'X' means a single bit running from 0 to 1. For example, when $d = 8$, '$X0*$' stands for $(0000, 0001, 0010, 0011, 1000, 1001, 1010, 1011)$. Other symbols have the same meaning as in Fig. 2 and Fig. 3.

indices of the nonzero diagonals stated in Theorem 1 can be directly derived from Lemma 4 and Lemma 5.

According to Lemma 4, the entries of $\mathbf{N}_j$ and $\mathbf{N}_j^{-1}$ are multiples of $\mathbf{I}_d$ if $j \in [2, \log_2(D)]$. Consequently, these linear transformations are in MatMul1D type. The entries of $\mathbf{N}_1$ and $\mathbf{N}_1^{-1}$ have the form

$$
\begin{bmatrix}
a_0 \mathbf{I}_{d/2} & a_1 \mathbf{I}_{d/2} \\
a_2 \mathbf{I}_{d/2} & a_3 \mathbf{I}_{d/2}
\end{bmatrix}
$$

for $a_i \in \mathbb{Z}_p$. These entries generally cannot be represented as a $\mathcal{E}$-linear map. Therefore, these matrices should be implemented as BlockMatMul1D type transformations.

On the other hand, according to Lemma 5, the entries of $\mathbf{N}'_j$ and $\mathbf{N}'^{-1}_j$ have the same form as $\mathbf{N}_1$ in the Bruun-style decomposition. Thus, they should be implemented as BlockMatMul1D as well.

3.3 The Galois Ring Case

In this subsection, we give the proof of Theorem 1 for the case $r > 1$. Again, the derivation is different for the two cases of p.

The Case of $p \equiv 1 \bmod 4$. To begin with, we provide the factorization of $\Phi_M(X)$ over $\mathbb{Z}_{p^r}$ using Hensel's lifting.

Lemma 6. For $p \equiv 1 \bmod 4$, it has $\Phi_M(X) = \prod_{i \in \mathbb{Z}^*_{4D}} (X^d - \zeta^i)$, where $\zeta \in \mathbb{Z}_{p^r}$ is a $4D$-th primitive root of unity.

Proof. Let $\Phi_M(X) = \prod_{i \in \mathbb{Z}_{4D}^*}(X^d - \zeta_0^i)$ be the factorization into irreducible polynomials over $\mathbb{Z}_p$, where $\zeta_0 \in \mathbb{Z}_p$ is a primitive $4D$-th root of unity. By substituting $Y = X^d$, we obtain $\Phi_{M/d}(Y) = \prod_{i \in \mathbb{Z}_{4D}^*}(Y - \zeta_0^i)$. This factorization can be lifted to $\mathbb{Z}_{p^r}$ using Hensel's lemma, giving

$$\Phi_{M/d}(Y) = \prod_{i \in \mathbb{Z}_{4D}^*}(Y - u_i) \text{ for some distinct } u_i \in \mathsf{GR}(p^r).$$

Note that $u_i^{4D} - 1 = \Phi_{M/d}(u_i) = 0$. Furthermore, the u_i's are primitive $4D$-th root of unity due to $u_i \equiv \zeta_0^i \bmod p$ and $\zeta_0^i \in \mathbb{Z}_p$ is a primitive $4D$-th root of unity. Since $\mathbb{Z}_{p^r}^*$ is a cyclic group, we can assume that $u_i = \zeta^i$ for $i \in \mathbb{Z}_{4D}^*$, where $\zeta \in \mathbb{Z}_{p^r}$ is a $4D$-th primitive root of unity. The lemma then follows directly by replacing Y with X^d. □

Note that the hypercube structure for the Galois ring case is identical to that of $r = 1$. Based on the factorization presented in Lemma 6, we can define $F_i^{(j)}$ and prove properties that are analogous to those stated in Lemma 1. Then by defining the linear transformation N_j in the same manner as in Sect. 3.1, we can prove statement (1) of Theorem 1 using the method outlined in Lemma 2.

The Case of $p \equiv 3 \bmod 4$. Again, we first provide the factorization of $\Phi_M(X)$ over $\mathbb{Z}_{p^r}$ using Hensel's lifting.

Lemma 7. *For $p \equiv 3 \bmod 4$, it has $\Phi_M(X) = \prod_{i \in \mathbb{Z}_{4D}^*/\langle p \rangle}(X^d - (\zeta^i + \zeta^{ip})X^{d/2} + \zeta^{i(p+1)})$, where $\zeta \in \mathsf{GR}(p^2; 2)$ is a $4D$-th primitive root of unity and each factor is a polynomial in $\mathbb{Z}_{p^r}[X]$.*

Proof. Let $\Phi_M(X) = \prod_{i \in \mathbb{Z}_{4D}^*}(X^{d/2} - \zeta_0^i)$ be the factorization into irreducible polynomials over $\mathsf{GF}(p^2)$, where $\zeta_0 \in \mathsf{GF}(p^2)$ is a primitive $4D$-th root of unity. By substituting $Y = X^{d/2}$, we get $\Phi_{2M/d}(Y) = \prod_{i \in \mathbb{Z}_{4D}^*}(Y - \zeta_0^i)$ over $\mathsf{GF}(p^2)$. This factorization can be lifted from $\mathsf{GF}(p^2)$ to $\mathsf{GR}(p^r; 2)$ using Hensel's lemma, i.e.,

$$\Phi_{2M/d}(Y) = \prod_{i \in \mathbb{Z}_{4D}^*}(Y - u_i), u_i \in \mathsf{GR}(p^r; 2).$$

Similarly, the u_i's form the complete set of $4D$-th primitive roots of unity in $\mathsf{GR}(p^r; 2)$, and we can assume that $u_i = \zeta^i$ for a primitive $4D$-th root of unity $\zeta \in \mathsf{GF}(p^2)$. It only remains to prove that $(Y^i - \zeta^i)(Y^i - \zeta^{ip}) \in \mathbb{Z}_{p^r}[X]$, which is equivalent to proving both $-(\zeta^i + \zeta^{ip})$ and $\zeta^{i(p+1)}$ are in $\mathbb{Z}_{p^r}$.

Let γ be a primitive element such that $\mathsf{GR}(p^r; 2) = \mathbb{Z}_{p^r}[\gamma]$. According to Sect. 2.2, the unit group $\mathsf{GR}(p^r; 2)^*$ is isomorphic to $C_{p^2-1} \times C_{p^{r-1}} \times C_{p^{r-1}}$, where C_i denotes a cyclic group of order i. Given that $\mathrm{ord}_{\mathsf{GR}(p^r;2)^*}(\gamma) = p^2 - 1$ and $\mathrm{ord}_{\mathsf{GR}(p^r;2)^*}(\zeta) = 4D$ are both coprime to p, it follows that ζ is a power of γ. Furthermore, as $4D$ divides $p^2 - 1$, we can deduce that $\zeta = \gamma^k$ for some integer k that is divisible by $(p^2 - 1)/4D$. Let π be the Frobenius automorphism, we have

$$\pi(\zeta^i + \zeta^{ip}) = \pi(\gamma^{ki} + \gamma^{kip}) = \gamma^{kip} + \gamma^{kip^2} = \gamma^{kip} + \gamma^{ki} = \zeta^i + \zeta^{ip},$$

$$\pi(\zeta^{i(p+1)}) = \pi(\gamma^{ki(p+1)}) = \gamma^{ki(p^2+p)} = \gamma^{ki(p+1)} = \zeta^{i(p+1)}.$$

Thus, $(\zeta^i + \zeta^{ip})$ and $\zeta^{i(p+1)}$ are in $\mathbb{Z}_{p^r}$, and the lemma follows directly.   □

Drawing upon the factorization presented in Lemma 7, we are able to define $F_i^{(j)}$ and establish properties that are same to those stated in Lemma 3. Subsequently, we can construct the linear transformation $\mathtt{N}_j$ in a manner consistent with Sect. 3.2, and validate properties that are same to those in Lemma 4. In addition, it can be verified that the methodology presented in Lemma 5 is still applicable, thereby enabling us to prove statement (2) of Theorem 1.

4   Algorithmic Optimizations of Homomorphic NTT

In this section, we introduce multiple optimizations based on the decomposition in Theorem 1. In Sect. 4.1, we combine consecutive $\mathtt{N}_j$s to realize a tradeoff between level consumption and running time. In Sect. 4.2, we modify the logic of the BSGS-style linear transformation to reduce the number of unhoisted automorphisms for better efficiency. In Sect. 4.3, we discuss the interaction of our decomposed CoeffToSlot/SlotToCoeff with general and thin bootstrapping. Finally, we analyze and compare the asymptotic complexity of the previous and our method in Sect. 4.4.

4.1   Combining Consecutive $\mathtt{N}_j$s

Note that the evaluation of each MatMul1D or BlockMatMul1D consumes a multiply-by-constant depth. Thus evaluating all the $\mathtt{N}_i$s one by one will consume a depth of $\log_2(L)$, which can significantly diminish the remaining depth after bootstrapping when L is large. This issue can be mitigated by combining several consecutive $\mathtt{N}_i$s and evaluating the resulting composite linear transformations as a whole. We note that a similar technique, known as level-collapsing, has been proposed for FFT-based CKKS bootstrapping in [10,23].

The properties of the composite linear transformations can be stated as follows.

Lemma 8. Let $k \in [1, \log_2(D)]$ and $1 \leq j \leq k$.
If $p \equiv 1 \bmod 4$, then it has

$$DiagSet(\mathtt{N}_k \ldots \mathtt{N}_j), DiagSet(\mathtt{N}_j^{-1} \ldots \mathtt{N}_k^{-1}) \subseteq 2^{-k} D \times [-2^{1+k-j} + 1, 2^{1+k-j} - 1]_{2^k}.$$

If $p \equiv 3 \bmod 4$, then it has

$$DiagSet(\mathtt{N}_k \ldots \mathtt{N}_j) \subseteq 2^{-k} D \times [-3(2^{1+k-j} - 1), 3(2^{1+k-j} - 1)]_{2^k},$$

$$DiagSet(\mathtt{N}_j^{-1} \ldots \mathtt{N}_k^{-1}) \subseteq 2^{-k} D \times [-3(2^{1+k-j} - 1), 2(2^{1+k-j} - 1)]_{2^k},$$

$$DiagSet(\mathtt{N}_k' \ldots \mathtt{N}_j'), DiagSet(\mathtt{N}_j'^{-1} \ldots \mathtt{N}_k'^{-1}) \subseteq 2^{-k} D \times [-2^{1+k-j} - 1, 2^{1+k-j} - 1]_{2^k}.$$

Specifically, if $j = 1$, all the RHS become $2^{-k} D \times [2^k]$.

Proof. We prove the conclusions about $\mathrm{DiagSet}(\mathtt{N}_k \ldots \mathtt{N}_j)$ by induction on k. When $k = j$, the conclusions are true due to Theorem 1. Suppose they hold for some k_0 with $j \leq k = k_0 < \log_2(D)$, we prove they still hold for $k + 1$. Since

$$\mathrm{DiagSet}(\mathtt{N}_{k+1} \ldots \mathtt{N}_j) \subseteq \bigcup_{a \in \mathrm{DiagSet}(\mathtt{N}_{k+1})} [a + \mathrm{DiagSet}(\mathtt{N}_k \ldots \mathtt{N}_j)]_D,$$

substituting $\mathrm{DiagSet}(\mathtt{N}_{k+1})$ and $\mathrm{DiagSet}(\mathtt{N}_k \ldots \mathtt{N}_j)$ with the corresponding values in each case will lead to the desired results.

For the inverse transformations, the conclusions can be obtained similarly. □

In the case of $p \equiv 1 \bmod 4$, the composition of multiple $\mathtt{N}_i$ may not be a one-dimensional linear transformation if $\mathtt{N}_{\log_2(D)+1}$ is included. Let ρ_1 be the rotation operation along the minor dimension. According to Theorem 1, $\mathtt{N}_{\log_2(D)+1}$ represents a MatMul1D in the minor dimension, which can be implemented as $\mathtt{N}_{\log_2(D)+1}(m) = \kappa_0(0)m + \kappa_0(1)\rho_1(m)$ for some $\kappa_0(0), \kappa_0(1) \in R_{p^r}$. Thus, for $\mathtt{N} = \mathtt{N}_k \circ \cdots \circ \mathtt{N}_j$ with $1 \leq k \leq \log_2(D)$ as in Lemma 8, which is a one-dimensional linear transformation along the major dimension, the cross-dimensional transformation $\mathtt{N}_{\log_2(D)+1} \circ \mathtt{N}$ can be computed in the form of

$$\mathtt{N}_{\log_2(D)+1} \circ \mathtt{N}(m) = \sum_{i \in \mathrm{DiagSet}(\mathtt{N})} \kappa_1(i)\rho^i(m) + \rho_1 \left(\sum_{i \in \mathrm{DiagSet}(\mathtt{N})} \kappa_2(i)\rho^i(m) \right)$$

for some $\kappa_1(i)$ and $\kappa_2(i) \in R_{p^r}$. This is called a MatMulFull transformation [20].

4.2   Modified BSGS Style Linear Transformations

We note that a large number of slots L implies that the size D of the main dimension is large. Thus the rotation keys for the main dimension should be generated in a baby-step-giant-step (BSGS) way, which can reduce the number of rotation keys from D to about $2\sqrt{D}$. As stated in [20], the BSGS method chooses $g = \lceil \sqrt{D} \rceil$ as the 'giant step'. Denote $h = \lceil D/g \rceil$, it generates the rotation keys for Galois rotations θ^i, where either $i \in [g]$ (i.e., the baby steps) or $i \in g \cdot [h]$ (i.e., the giant steps). Then for a good dimension, it has $\rho = \theta$ and MatMul1D is implemented as

$$T_N(m) = \sum_{k \in [h]} \rho^{gk} \left(\sum_{j \in [g]} \kappa'(j + gk)\rho^j(m) \right), \text{ for } m \in R_{p^r}, \tag{4}$$

where $\kappa'(j + gk) = \rho^{-gk}(\kappa(j + gk))$. The $\rho^j(m)$'s are computed using the hoisting technique, while the ρ^{gk}s cannot be computed with hoisting because they have different inputs. For a bad dimension, MatMul1D is implemented as

$$T_N(m) = \sum_{k \in [h]} \theta^{gk} \left(\sum_{j \in [g]} \kappa'(j + gk)\theta^j(m) + \kappa''(j + gk)\theta^{j-D}(m) \right) \tag{5}$$

for $m \in R_{p^r}$, where $\kappa'(j + gk) = \theta^{-gk}(\mu(j + gk)\kappa(j + gk))$ and $\kappa''(j + gk) = \theta^{-gk}(\mu'(j+gk)\kappa(j+gk))$. Again, $\theta^j(m)$ and $\theta^{j-D}(m)$ are computed with hoisting on m and $\theta^{-D}(m)$ while θ^{gk} are computed without hoisting.

Modified BSGS Method for MatMul1D. For a MatMul1D map $\mathbb{N}$ along the major dimension, define $\text{GiantSet}(\mathbb{N}) = \{\lfloor \frac{[i]_D}{g} \rfloor \mid i \in \text{DiagSet}(\mathbb{N})\}$ and $\text{BabySet}(\mathbb{N}) = \{[i]_D \bmod g \mid i \in \text{DiagSet}(\mathbb{N})\}$. Then, we can replace '$[h]$' with '$\text{GiantSet}(\mathbb{N})$' and '$[g]$' with '$\text{BabySet}(\mathbb{N})$' in Eq. 4 and Eq. 5.

Our key observation is that the matrices that $\text{Red}_{\text{BR}}^{-1}$ splits into usually have either a small GiantSet or a small BabySet. For example, consider the case of $p \equiv 1 \bmod 4$ and $D = 2^{2k}$ for some integer k. Using Theorem 1 and Lemma 8, consider two composite linear transformations $\mathbb{N}^{(1)} = \mathbb{N}_k \ldots \mathbb{N}_1$ and $\mathbb{N}^{(2)} = \mathbb{N}_{2k} \ldots \mathbb{N}_{k+1}$. We have $\text{DiagSet}(\mathbb{N}^{(2)}) = [-2^k + 1, 2^k - 1]$ and $\text{DiagSet}(\mathbb{N}^{(1)}) = 2^k \times [2^k]$. Since $g = h = 2^k$, we have $\text{GiantSet}(\mathbb{N}^{(2)}) = \{-1, 0, 1\}$, $\text{BabySet}(\mathbb{N}^{(2)}) = [2^k]$ and $\text{GiantSet}(\mathbb{N}^{(1)}) = [2^k]$, $\text{BabySet}(\mathbb{N}^{(1)}) = \{0\}$. If $|\text{GiantSet}(\mathbb{N})|$ is small for a linear transformation $\mathbb{N}$, the number of unhoisted automorphisms (i.e., ρ^{gk} and θ^{gk}) in Eq. 4 and Eq. 5 is greatly reduced.

In the other case where $\text{BabySet}(\mathbb{N})$ is small, we exchange the role of j, k to obtain the revised MatMul1D in a good dimension

$$\mathbb{N}(m) = \sum_{j \in \text{BabySet}(\mathbb{N})} \rho^j \left(\sum_{k \in \text{GiantSet}(\mathbb{N})} \kappa'(j + gk)\rho^{gk}(m) \right), \qquad (6)$$

where $\kappa'(j + gk) = \rho^{-j}\kappa(j + gk)$, and the revised MatMul1D in a bad dimension

$$\mathbb{N}(m) = \sum_{j \in \text{BabySet}(\mathbb{N})} \theta^j \left(\sum_{k \in \text{GiantSet}(\mathbb{N})} \kappa'(j + gk)\theta^{gk}(m) + \kappa''(j + gk)\theta^{gk-D}(m) \right),$$

where $\kappa'(j+gk) = \theta^{-j}(\mu(j+gk)\kappa(j+gk))$, $\kappa''(j+gk) = \theta^{-j}(\mu'(j+gk)\kappa(j+gk))$.

Swapping the roles of j and k whenever $|\text{GiantSet}(\mathbb{N})| > |\text{BabySet}(\mathbb{N})|$ ensures that the number of unhoisted automorphisms is minimized while the total number of automorphisms is fixed. This reduces the running time since hoisted automorphisms are cheaper than unhoisted ones.

In our example above, the sparsity of $\text{BabySet}(\mathbb{N}^{(1)})$ relies on the fact that $g = \sqrt{D}$ is a power of 2. However, this is not true if $D = 2^{2k+1}$ for some integer k. Thus, in this case, we choose $g = 2^{k+1}$ and $h = 2^k$ so that the previous optimizations are still valid. Compared to the original choice of g, such choice of g will slightly increase the number of rotation keys from $2^{1.5} \cdot 2^k$ to $3 \cdot 2^k$ by about 6%.

Modified BSGS Method for BlockMatMul1D. The tricks for MatMul1D can be applied to the computation of BlockMatMul1D in either good or bad dimensions.

When HElib computes a BlockMatMul1D transformation, $\rho^i(m)$'s in Eq. 2 are computed for all $i \in [D]$ if the dimension is good. In a bad dimension, $\theta^i(m)$'s are computed for all $i \in [D]$. Let $j = [i]_g$ and $k = \lfloor \frac{i}{g} \rfloor$, these ciphertexts are generated in two steps, (1) $\theta^{gk}(m)$ are generated from m with hoisting for $k \in [h]$, (2) $\theta^i(m) = \theta^j(\theta^{gk}(m))$ are generated from $\theta^{gk}(m)$ with hoisting for $j \in [g]$. Thus, we can still replace $[g]$ with BabySet(N) and $[h]$ with GiantSet(N) for faster computation. The role of giant and baby steps can also be swapped if $|\text{BabySet(N)}| < |\text{GiantSet(N)}|$, which reduces the number of hoisting precomputations from $|\text{GiantSet(N)}| + 1$ to $|\text{BabySet(N)}| + 1$. If they are swapped, $\theta^j(m)$ will be generated from m and $\theta^{j+gk}(m)$ will be computed from $\theta^j(m)$.

4.3   Applying the Decomposition to BGV Bootstrapping

In this subsection, we describe how the decomposition of linear transformations can be deployed into general or thin bootstrapping, including some modifications to them for better efficiency.

Recall that $\text{Decode} = \text{Eval} \circ \text{Red}$ and $\text{Red}^{-1} = \text{BR} \circ \text{Red}_{\text{BR}}^{-1}$, where BR is an order-two permutation of the $L \cdot d$ slot coefficients induced by some bit-reversal map. Then the polynomial $m \in R_{p^r}$ and its slot values α are related as

$$\alpha = \text{Decode}(m) = \text{Eval} \circ \text{Red}(m) = \text{Eval} \circ \text{Red}_{\text{BR}} \circ \text{BR}^{-1}(m).$$

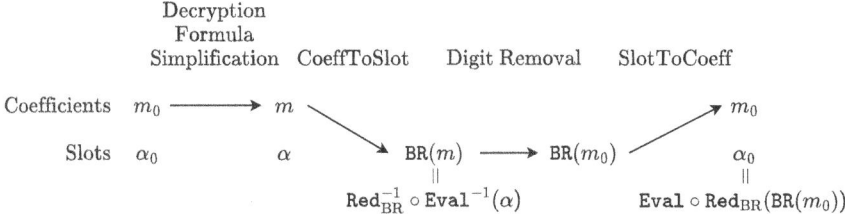

Fig. 5. Workflow of general BGV bootstrapping. The slot values in $\text{BR}(m)$ after CoeffToSlot are identified with $\mathbb{Z}_{p^r}^d$ with respect to the normal basis of $\mathcal{E}$. Other slot values are represented with respect to the power basis of $\mathcal{E}$.

Applying to General Bootstrapping. The workflow of general bootstrapping is illustrated in Fig. 5. Note that the output of CoeffToSlot and the input of SlotToCoeff is a permutated version of m or m_0. This helps to avoid computing BR and its inverse homomorphically, which will be rather expensive.

The CoeffToSlot transformation (corresponding to the $\text{Red}_{\text{BR}}^{-1} \circ \text{Eval}^{-1}$) is followed by a BlockMatMul1D transformation that moves the power basis coefficients of each slot into the normal basis [22]. Denoting this transformation as PtoN, the overall transformation applied is $\text{PtoN} \circ \text{Red}_{\text{BR}}^{-1} \circ \text{Eval}^{-1}$, where PtoN and Eval^{-1} are slot-wise BlockMatMul1D. Denote the split $\text{Red}_{\text{BR}}^{-1}$ as $\text{Red}_{\text{BR}}^{-1} = \text{N}^{(k)} \ldots \text{N}^{(1)}$. As the first optimization, we merge Eval^{-1} with $\text{N}^{(1)}$ to save a multiply-by-constant level, which is a tradeoff between level and time.

Moreover, this is free if $\mathtt{N}^{(1)}$ is already a BlockMatMul1D. This trick is applied to both SlotToCoeff and CoeffToSlot transformations, whether the bootstrapping is a general one or a thin one.

As the second optimization, we merge PtoN with the $\mathtt{N}^{(k)}$ to save a multiply-by-constant level, again increasing its running time if it is not a BlockMatMul1D. However, we can avoid the extra cost by reordering $\mathtt{N}^{(k)}$. If $p \equiv 1 \bmod 4$, all $\mathtt{N}^{(i)}$s are either MatMul1D or MatMulFull. For $p \equiv 3 \bmod 4$, $\mathtt{N}^{(1)}$ is a BlockMat-Mul1D and other $\mathtt{N}^{(i)}$s are either MatMul1D (for Bruun-style decomposition) or BlockMatMul1D (for Radix-2-style decomposition). Each entry of a MatMul1D or MatMulFull used here is a multiple of $\mathbf{I}_d$, which is a linear transformation that multiplies the input $v \in \mathcal{E}$ by some constant in $\mathbb{Z}_{p^r}$. Note that such a multiply-by-integer map remains the same regardless of the basis we use for $\mathcal{E}$ (i.e., the power basis or the normal basis). Thus, PtoN commutes with all $\mathtt{N}^{(i)}$s that are MatMul1D or MatMulFull. It is easy to see that there exists some integer j such that $\mathtt{N}^{(i)}$ is a BlockMatMul1D $\iff i \leq j$. Then we can rewrite the overall linear transformation as

$$\mathtt{N}^{(k)} \circ \ldots \circ \mathtt{N}^{(j+1)} \circ \left(\mathtt{PtoN} \circ \mathtt{N}^{(j)}\right) \circ \mathtt{N}^{(j-1)} \circ \ldots \circ \mathtt{N}^{(2)} \circ \left(\mathtt{N}^{(1)} \circ \mathtt{Eval}^{-1}\right).$$

In this way, we ensure that the number of BlockMatMul1D transformations during SlotToCoeff is minimized to $\max(j, 1)$. Since BlockMatMul1D is usually more time-consuming than MatMul1D, running time is saved by the reordering of transformations.

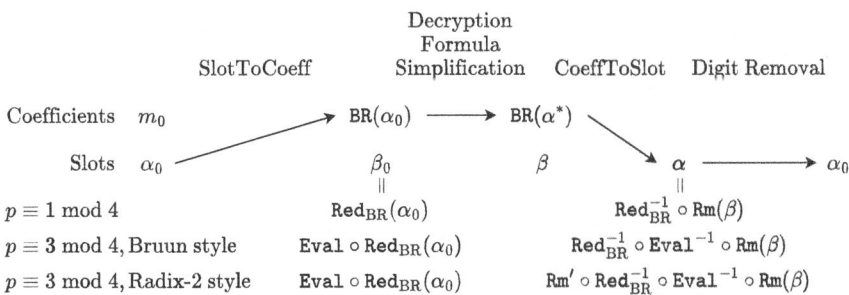

Fig. 6. Workflow of thin BGV bootstrapping. The SlotToCoeff and CoeffToSlot transformations are compositions of different sub-transformations for different parameters. All slot values are represented with respect to the power basis of $\mathcal{E}$.

The workflow of thin bootstrapping is illustrated in Fig. 6. The permutation BR is also not computed homomorphically, similar to that in general bootstrapping.

SlotToCoeff (corresponding to $\mathtt{Eval} \circ \mathtt{Red}_{\mathrm{BR}}$) is performed first on a thin ciphertext, where each slot contains an integer instead of a Galois ring element.

Let the slot values of the input to SlotToCoeff be $\alpha \in \mathcal{E}^L$. If $p \equiv 1 \bmod 4$, each slot in $\mathtt{Red_{BR}}(\alpha_0)$ still stores an integer because the entry in $\mathtt{Red_{BR}}$ is a multiple of $\mathbf{I}_d$. This means the restriction of $\mathtt{Eval}$ on $\mathtt{Red_{BR}}(\alpha_0)$ is an identity map and can be omitted. For $p \equiv 3 \bmod 4$, the value in each slot during the computation of $\mathtt{Red_{BR}}$ lies in the subring $F \subset \mathcal{E}$ satisfying $[F : \mathsf{GR}(p^r)] = 2$ because each entry of $\mathbf{N}_j$ has the form of $\begin{bmatrix} a_0\mathbf{I}_{d/2} & a_1\mathbf{I}_{d/2} \\ a_2\mathbf{I}_{d/2} & a_3\mathbf{I}_{d/2} \end{bmatrix}$ for $a_i \in \mathbb{Z}_p$. This means the linearized polynomials in the $\mathtt{BlockMatMul1D}$ maps of $\mathtt{Red_{BR}}$ and in $\mathtt{Eval}$ can be built on F instead of on $\mathcal{E}$, reducing the highest power of σ in the linearized polynomials from $d - 1$ to 1.

Another feature of thin bootstrapping is that a trace-like map needs to be applied to the ciphertext to clear the extra coefficients introduced by the decryption formula simplification. For a power-of-2 M, Chen and Han found that such a map can be computed efficiently before CoeffToSlot [11]. As their core observation, for $m \in R_{p^r}$ and $0 \le k \le \log_2(M/2)$, there is a map $\mathtt{RM}_k : R_{p^r} \to R_{p^r}$, satisfying $\mathtt{RM}_k(m)[i] = 0$ for $[i]_{2^k} \ne 0$ and $\mathtt{RM}_k(m)[i] = m[i]$ otherwise. The cost of $\mathtt{RM}_k$ is dominated by k homomorphic automorphisms.

In Fig. 6, $\mathtt{Rm}$ and $\mathtt{Rm}'$ clear the extra coefficients in $\mathtt{BR}(\alpha^*)$ introduced by decryption formula simplification into $\mathtt{BR}(\alpha_0)$. Using our FFT-like linear transformations, the permutation $\mathtt{BR}$ satisfies

$$\mathtt{BR} = \begin{cases} \mathtt{BR}'_{\log_2(D)+1,\log_2(d)}, & \text{if } p \equiv 1 \bmod 4 \\ \mathtt{BR}_{\log_2(D),\log_2(d)}, & \text{if } p \equiv 3 \bmod 4, \text{ Bruun-style decomposition} \\ \mathtt{BR}_{\log_2(D),\log_2(d)-1}, & \text{if } p \equiv 3 \bmod 4, \text{ Radix-2-style decomposition} \end{cases}.$$

For $p \equiv 1 \bmod 4$, the indices of the coefficients of $\mathtt{BR}(\alpha_0)$ in Fig. 6 form the set $d \times [2D]$. I.e., $\mathtt{BR}(\alpha^*)[i]$ should be kept by $\mathtt{RM}$ if and only if the lowest $\log_2(d)$ bits of i are all zeros. Thus, we let $\mathtt{RM} = \mathtt{RM}_{\log_2(d)}$ and $\mathtt{RM}'$ be the identity map. Note that we abuse the notation of $\mathtt{RM}_k : R_{p^r} \to R_{p^r}$ here to denote its corresponding map on the slots, which is a $\mathcal{E}^L \to \mathcal{E}^L$ map.

For $p \equiv 3 \bmod 4$ and Bruun-style decomposition, the indices of coefficients of $\mathtt{BR}(\alpha_0)$ form $d \times [D]$ and $\mathtt{RM} = \mathtt{RM}_{\log_2(d)}$ suffices to clear the extra coefficients. For Radix-2-style decomposition, the indices of the coefficients of $\mathtt{BR}(\alpha_0)$ form the set $\{\mathtt{BR}_{\log_2(D),\log_2(d)-1}(i) \mid i \in d \times [D]\} = d/2 \times [D]$. Thus, $\mathtt{BR}(\alpha^*)[i]$ should be kept by $\mathtt{RM}$ if and only if the highest bit and the lowest $\log_2(d) - 1$ bits of i are all zeros. In this case, although we can clear $\mathtt{BR}(\alpha^*)[i]$ with $[i]_{d/2} \ne 0$ using $\mathtt{RM} = \mathtt{RM}_{\log_2(d)-1}$, those undesired coefficients with indices in $d/2 \times [D/2, D-1]$ cannot be cleared. This means that the first $D/2$ slots in $\mathtt{Red}_{\mathtt{BR}}^{-1} \circ \mathtt{Eval}^{-1} \circ \mathtt{RM}(\beta)$ will have the form of $\alpha_i + bX^{d/2}$, with b being the undesired coefficient. Thus, an extra map $\mathtt{Rm}'$ needs to be applied slot-wise to clear b in these slots. We note that $\mathtt{Rm}'$ can also be represented as a linearized polynomial in the subring $F \subset \mathcal{E}$ and can be incorporated into the last $\mathtt{BlockMatMul1D}$ in $\mathtt{Red}_{\mathtt{BR}}^{-1}$ for free.

The optimizations for SlotToCoeff can also be applied to CoeffToSlot. For $p \equiv 1 \bmod 4$, $\mathtt{Eval}^{-1}$ in CoeffToSlot can be omitted because $\mathtt{Rm}(\beta)$ stores an integer in each of its slots. For $p \equiv 3 \bmod 4$, $\mathtt{Rm}(\beta)$ and the intermediate results during the computation of $\mathtt{Red}_{\mathtt{BR}}^{-1}$ store an element in the subring F in each of their slots. Again, this means the linearized polynomials of $\texttt{Eval}^{-1}$ and the $\texttt{BlockMatMul1D}$ maps that $\texttt{Red}_{\mathrm{BR}}^{-1}$ splits into can be built on F instead of on $\mathcal{E}$.

4.4 Asymptotic Complexity Analysis

In this subsection, we discuss the asymptotic complexity of linear transformations in BGV bootstrapping for both our method and the baseline approach. The results are summarized in Table 1. For our method, the depth-time tradeoff of combining $\texttt{Eval}$, $\texttt{N}_j$, and $\texttt{PtoN}$ can be ignored because the maximum number of decompositions is logarithmic in L, rendering the depth consumption negligible in the asymptotic analysis. For the baseline method, we assume that the rotation keys are generated in the BSGS manner, and CoeffToSlot/SlotToCoeff is evaluated without decomposition. The complexity of both methods is estimated by counting the number of unhoisted automorphisms and hoisting precomputation, which are the most computationally expensive operations.

Table 1. Asymptotic complexity of linear transformations in BGV bootstrapping for our method and the baseline method

Complexity	Thin Bootstrapping	General Bootstrapping	
Baseline	$O(\log_2(d) + \sqrt{L})$	$O(d + \sqrt{L})$	
Ours	$O(\log_2(d) + \log_2(L))$	$O(d \cdot \log_2(L))$ for Radix-2-style decomposition	
		$O(d + \log_2(L))$ for other cases	

For the baseline method, the whole CoeffToSlot/SlotToCoeff in thin bootstrapping is a $\texttt{MatMul1D}$ [17,20], requiring a complexity of $O(\sqrt{L})$. For both methods, the complexity of $\texttt{RM}$ and $\texttt{RM}'$ is $O(\log_2(d))$. In general bootstrapping, CoeffToSlot and SlotToCoeff become $\texttt{BlockMatMul1D}$, thus having a complexity of $O(d + \sqrt{L})$ according to [20]. Thus, the total complexity is $O(\log_2(d) + \sqrt{L})$ for thin bootstrapping and $O(d + \sqrt{L})$ for general bootstrapping.

For our method, the complexity of $\texttt{PtoN}$ is $O(d)$ for general bootstrapping, while the complexity of $\texttt{Eval}$ and its inverse is $O(1)$ for thin bootstrapping and $O(d)$ for general bootstrapping. Each $\texttt{N}_j$ in our method has a computational complexity of $O(d)$ with the Radix-2-style decomposition in general bootstrapping, and $O(1)$ with other styles in general bootstrapping (as the only exception, $\texttt{N}_1$ in general bootstrapping with $p \equiv 3 \bmod 4$ costs $O(d)$) and in thin bootstrapping.

5 Implementation

5.1 Experiment Setup

We implemented our approach in BGV bootstrapping based on HElib (commit id 3e337a6) with the optimization in [30]. The code is available at https://github.com/msh086/bgv-bootstrapping-with-homomorphic-NTT. The security level of

BGV parameter sets is estimated using the lattice estimator [2] with commit id `fd4a460`. The experiments are conducted on a machine running Fedora 33 (Workstation Edition) equipped with a 3 GHz Intel Xeon Gold 6248R CPU and 1006 GB of RAM. The compiled program is executed in a single thread, as in previous works on BGV bootstrapping [22,30].

Parameter Selection. We set p to be of the form $2^i \pm 1$ for friendly integer arithmetic, and choose it to correspond to a large number of slots L, ranging from 4096 to 32768. The Hamming weight h of the main secret key is set to 120, aligning with the default value used in HElib. In accordance with previous works [16,22,30], we choose the maximum ciphertext modulus Q to guarantee a security level of at least 80 bits. The Hamming weight of the encapsulated bootstrapping key [6] is chosen to have a security level of at least 128 bits to defend against potential attacks on sparse secrets, which is consistent with the choice in [30]. The selected parameter sets are displayed in Table 2.

Table 2. The parameter sets. h and λ are the Hamming weight and the security level of the main secret key, while h' and λ' are those for the encapsulated bootstrapping key.

ID	p	r	M	L	D	d	$\log_2(Q)$	h	λ	h'	λ'
I	65537		65536	32768	16384	1				26	134.4
II	8191	1	65536	4096	4096	8	1332	120	81.13	24	129.8
III	131071		65536	16384	16384	2				26	133.81

The Decomposition of Red_{bfBR}^{-1}. Recall that we combine consecutive NTT matrices $\mathtt{N}_j$ to reduce the number of levels consumed by homomorphic NTT. We use a list P to represent a partition of $\mathtt{N}_j$'s. The list stores $n_{mats}+1$ integers in an increasing order with $P[0] = 1$ and $\mathtt{N}^{(i)} = \prod_{P[i]\leq j<P[i+1]} \mathtt{N}_j$ for $0 \leq i < n_{mats}$. We use the same P for CoeffToSlot and SlotToCoeff, although we could use different P for more fined-grained performance tuning.

The optimal partition for a fixed n_{mats} can be obtained using the dynamic programming method of Chen et al. [10]. However, their method requires an accurate estimation of the running time, which means one may have to benchmark the running time of a series of basic operations, including hoisting precomputation, hoisted automorphism, non-hoisted automorphism, plaintext-ciphertext multiplication (with plaintext in both double-CRT and non-double-CRT form), and ciphertext summation. Thus, considering the difficulty of obtaining an accurate model of the running time, we choose to determine the partitions experimentally through trial and error, which we believe suffices to demonstrate the effectiveness of our method. The obtained partitions are listed in Table 3.

Table 3. The partitions for general and thin bootstrapping.

	Bootstrapping Type	I	Style	II	III
Partition	Thin	(1, 6, 12, 16)	Bruun	(1, 6, 10, 13)	(1, 7, 12, 15)
			Radix-2	(1, 5, 9, 13)	(1, 6, 10, 15)
	General	(1, 6, 12, 16)	Bruun	(1, 5, 10, 13)	(1, 7, 12, 15)
			Radix-2	(1, 5, 9, 13)	(1, 6, 10, 15)

Table 4. Benchmark results for thin bootstrapping. Capacity refers to the capacity consumed by each stage of bootstrapping. The speedup is computed as the ratio of throughput with respect to the baseline case

Parameter Set		I		II			III		
Method		Baseline	Ours	Baseline	OursBruun	Ours Radix2	Baseline	OursBruun	OursRadix2
Capacity (bits)	Initial	941	941	947	947	947	939	939	939
	SlotToCoeff	39	79	33	70	69	39	85	85
	CoeffToSlot	62	134	56	120	118	64	144	143
	Digit removal	265	264	232	231	232	277	276	277
	Remaining	556	446	610	511	513	540	415	415
Time (sec)	SlotToCoeff	58	4.2	11	3.8	3.1	33	4.8	3.8
	CoeffToSlot	317	12.4	54	14.8	11.6	170	16.1	13.9
	Digit removal	6.0	5.7	5.9	5.9	5.9	6.1	5.5	5.6
	Total	381	22.8	71.5	25.1	21.1	210	26.9	23.7
Throughput (bps)		1.46	19.6	8.53	20.4	24.4	2.57	15.4	17.5
Speedup		1x	13.4x	1x	2.4x	2.9x	1x	6.0x	6.8x
Memory Usage (GB)		398	31	52	9.7	8.8	201	24	24

5.2   Experimental Results

The benchmark results for thin bootstrapping are shown in Table 4 while those for general bootstrapping are in Table 5. For thin bootstrapping, the algorithm proposed in [11] and refined in [17] is chosen as the baseline of comparison. Since the method in [11] only applies to thin bootstrapping, the HElib implementation [22] is taken as the baseline for general bootstrapping. For general bootstrapping, the running time of CoeffToSlot and SlotToCoeff includes the unpacking/repacking procedure before/after digit removal. The capacity needed by the next bootstrapping is subtracted from the remaining capacity, e.g., the capacity required by SlotToCoeff in thin bootstrapping or the decryption formula simplification process. The throughput of the bootstrapping procedure is defined as the remaining capacity divided by the running time, as in [16].

HElib stores the ring constants of a linear transformation (e.g., $\kappa(i)$ in (Eq. 1) in two ways, either as plain R_{p^r} elements or in the double-CRT form. The former format has lower memory cost while the latter leads to faster homomorphic computation at the cost of memory overhead. All constants in baselines and our methods are represented in the double-CRT format. With these constants in double-CRT format, the baselines incur much heavier memory overhead than our method due to the larger number of constants in the baselines.

As shown in the tables, the throughput of thin bootstrapping is improved by 2.4x–13.4x and the throughput of general bootstrapping is improved by 15.2x–55.1x. Although the cases using our method consume more capacity than the baseline cases, they have much shorter running times, outweighing the extra capacity consumption and leading to a higher throughput.

For $p \equiv 3 \bmod 4$, Bruun-style and Radix-2-style decompositions exhibit different running times. For general bootstrapping with a small d or thin bootstrapping (i.e., except for the parameter set II in Table 5), the Radix-2-style decomposition is faster than the Bruun-style decomposition because the NTT/INTT matrices in Radix-2 style have fewer nonzero diagonals. In general bootstrapping with a larger d (i.e., the parameter set II in Table 5), the Bruun-style one is faster than the Radix-2-style one because the computational overhead of BlockMatMul1D over MatMul1D grows with d. Only one of the split NTT/INTT matrices in Brunn style is BlockMatMul1D, while all the NTT/INTT matrices in Radix-2 style are BlockMatMul1D. Thus, the disadvantage of having more BlockMatMul1D outweighs the advantage of having fewer diagonals in each matrix, making the Radix-2-style transformation slower than the Bruun-style one.

Table 5. Benchmark results for general bootstrapping. Capacity refers to the capacity consumed by each stage of bootstrapping. The speedup is computed as the ratio of throughput with respect to the baseline case.

Parameter Set		I		II			III		
Method		Baseline	Ours	Baseline	Ours Bruun	OursRadix2	Baseline	Ours Bruun	Ours Radix2
Capacity (bits)	Initial	918	918	927	927	927	915	915	915
	CoeffToSlot[†]	54	126	86	148	157	91	169	169
	SlotToCoeff[†]	54	126	97	159	154	90	168	168
	Digit extract	281	282	245	246	244	294	293	293
	Remaining	526	382	511	371	370	438	282	282
Time (sec)	CoeffToSlot	321	12.5	1035	20.7	25.3	1636	16.1	14.1
	SlotToCoeff	321	12.5	1035	19.0	21.1	1642	15.8	13.9
	Digit extract	5.9	5.5	46	44	45	11.2	9.8	10.0
	Total	649	31	2116	85	92	3289	42	38
Throughput (bps)		0.81	12.3	0.23	4.4	4.0	0.13	6.7	7.3
Speedup		1x	15.2x	1x	18.7x	17.1x	1x	50.3x	55.1x
Memory Usage (GB)		398	31	744	11.8	13.6	392	24.1	23.6

[†] Currently, SlotToCoeff and CoeffToSlot have similar capacity consumption because they have the same plaintext modulus p^{r+t}. By using the optimization remarked at the end of Sect. 4.3 in [30], the plaintext modulus of SlotToCoeff can be reduced to p^r, leading to a lower capacity cost than CoeffToSlot, as expected in a normal general bootstrapping. The updated benchmark results will be included in the full version of this paper.

Acknowledgments. We thank Mr. Robin Geelen at KU Leuven for identifying the issue with the capacity consumption in Table 5. We also thank the anonymous reviewers for their insightful comments that greatly improved this manuscript. The study is supported by the National Key R&D Program of China (2018YFA0704701, 2020YFA0309705), Shandong Key Research and Development Program (2020ZLYS09), the Major Scientific and Technological Innovation Project of Shandong, China (2019JZZY010133), the Major Program of Guangdong Basic and Applied Research (2019B030302008), Tsinghua University Dushi Program, and the Key Laboratory of Data Protection and Intelligent Management, Ministry of Education, Sichuan University.

References

1. Albrecht, M., Chase, M., Chen, H., Ding, J., Goldwasser, S., Gorbunov, S., Halevi, S., Hoffstein, J., Laine, K., Lauter, K., Lokam, S., Micciancio, D., Moody, D., Morrison, T., Sahai, A., Vaikuntanathan, V.: Homomorphic Encryption Security Standard. Tech. rep., HomomorphicEncryption.org, Toronto, Canada (November 2018)

2. Albrecht, M.R., Player, R., Scott, S.: On the concrete hardness of Learning with Errors. Journal of Mathematical Cryptology **9**(3), 169–203 (2015). https://doi.org/10.1515/jmc-2015-0016

3. Alperin-Sheriff, J., Peikert, C.: Practical Bootstrapping in Quasilinear Time. In: Canetti, R., Garay, J.A. (eds.) Advances in Cryptology – CRYPTO 2013. pp. 1–20. Springer Berlin Heidelberg, Berlin, Heidelberg (2013). https://doi.org/10.1007/978-3-642-40041-4_1

4. Badawi, A.A., Bates, J., Bergamaschi, F., Cousins, D.B., Erabelli, S., Genise, N., Halevi, S., Hunt, H., Kim, A., Lee, Y., Liu, Z., Micciancio, D., Quah, I., Polyakov, Y., R.V., S., Rohloff, K., Saylor, J., Suponitsky, D., Triplett, M., Vaikuntanathan, V., Zucca, V.: OpenFHE: Open-Source Fully Homomorphic Encryption Library. Cryptology ePrint Archive, Paper 2022/915 (2022), https://eprint.iacr.org/2022/915

5. Blatt, M., Gusev, A., Polyakov, Y., Rohloff, K., Vaikuntanathan, V.: Optimized homomorphic encryption solution for secure genome-wide association studies. BMC Medical Genomics **13**(7), 83 (Jul 2020). https://doi.org/10.1186/s12920-020-0719-9

6. Bossuat, J.P., Troncoso-Pastoriza, J., Hubaux, J.P.: Bootstrapping for Approximate Homomorphic Encryption with Negligible Failure-Probability by Using Sparse-Secret Encapsulation. In: Ateniese, G., Venturi, D. (eds.) Applied Cryptography and Network Security. pp. 521–541. Springer International Publishing, Cham (2022). https://doi.org/10.1007/978-3-031-09234-3_26

7. Brakerski, Z., Gentry, C., Vaikuntanathan, V.: (Leveled) Fully Homomorphic Encryption without Bootstrapping. ACM Trans. Comput. Theory **6**(3) (jul 2014). https://doi.org/10.1145/2633600

8. Bruun, G.: z-transform DFT filters and FFT's. IEEE Transactions on Acoustics, Speech, and Signal Processing **26**(1), 56–63 (1978). https://doi.org/10.1109/TASSP.1978.1163036

9. Cantor, D.G., Kaltofen, E.: On fast multiplication of polynomials over arbitrary algebras. Acta Informatica **28**(7), 693–701 (Jul 1991). https://doi.org/10.1007/BF01178683

10. Chen, H., Chillotti, I., Song, Y.: Improved Bootstrapping for Approximate Homomorphic Encryption. In: Ishai, Y., Rijmen, V. (eds.) Advances in Cryptology – EUROCRYPT 2019. pp. 34–54. Springer International Publishing, Cham (2019). https://doi.org/10.1007/978-3-030-17656-3_2

11. Chen, H., Han, K.: Homomorphic Lower Digits Removal and Improved FHE Bootstrapping. In: Nielsen, J.B., Rijmen, V. (eds.) Advances in Cryptology – EUROCRYPT 2018. pp. 315–337. Springer International Publishing, Cham (2018). https://doi.org/10.1007/978-3-319-78381-9_12

12. Cong, K., Moreno, R.C., da Gama, M.B., Dai, W., Iliashenko, I., Laine, K., Rosenberg, M.: Labeled PSI from Homomorphic Encryption with Reduced Computation and Communication. In: Proceedings of the 2021 ACM SIGSAC Conference on Computer and Communications Security. p. 1135–1150. CCS '21, Association for Computing Machinery, New York, NY, USA (2021). https://doi.org/10.1145/3460120.3484760

13. Cooley, J.W., Tukey, J.W.: An Algorithm for the Machine Calculation of Complex Fourier Series. Mathematics of Computation 19(90), 297–301 (1965), http://www.jstor.org/stable/2003354

14. Fan, J., Vercauteren, F.: Somewhat Practical Fully Homomorphic Encryption. Cryptology ePrint Archive, Paper 2012/144 (2012), https://eprint.iacr.org/2012/144

15. Geelen, R.: Revisiting the slot-to-coefficient transformation for BGV and BFV. Cryptology ePrint Archive, Paper 2024/153 (2024). https://cic.iacr.org/i/1/3

16. Geelen, R., Iliashenko, I., Kang, J., Vercauteren, F.: On Polynomial Functions Modulo p^e and Faster Bootstrapping for Homomorphic Encryption. In: Hazay, C., Stam, M. (eds.) Advances in Cryptology – EUROCRYPT 2023. pp. 257–286. Springer Nature Switzerland, Cham (2023). https://doi.org/10.1007/978-3-031-30620-4_9

17. Geelen, R., Vercauteren, F.: Bootstrapping for BGV and BFV Revisited. Journal of Cryptology 36(2), 12 (Mar 2023). https://doi.org/10.1007/s00145-023-09454-6

18. Gentry, C.: Fully Homomorphic Encryption Using Ideal Lattices. In: Proceedings of the Forty-First Annual ACM Symposium on Theory of Computing. p. 169–178. STOC '09, Association for Computing Machinery, New York, NY, USA (2009). https://doi.org/10.1145/1536414.1536440

19. Halevi, S., Shoup, V.: Bootstrapping for HElib. In: Oswald, E., Fischlin, M. (eds.) Advances in Cryptology – EUROCRYPT 2015. pp. 641–670. Springer Berlin Heidelberg, Berlin, Heidelberg (2015). https://doi.org/10.1007/978-3-662-46800-5_25

20. Halevi, S., Shoup, V.: Faster Homomorphic Linear Transformations in HElib. In: Shacham, H., Boldyreva, A. (eds.) Advances in Cryptology – CRYPTO 2018. pp. 93–120. Springer International Publishing, Cham (2018). https://doi.org/10.1007/978-3-319-96884-1_4

21. Halevi, S., Shoup, V.: Design and implementation of HElib: a homomorphic encryption library. Cryptology ePrint Archive, Paper 2020/1481 (2020), https://eprint.iacr.org/2020/1481

22. Geelen, R., Vercauteren, F.: Bootstrapping for BGV and BFV Revisited. Journal of Cryptology 36(2), 12 (Mar 2023). https://doi.org/10.1007/s00145-023-09454-6

23. Han, K., Hhan, M., Cheon, J.H.: Improved Homomorphic Discrete Fourier Transforms and FHE Bootstrapping. IEEE Access 7, 57361–57370 (2019). https://doi.org/10.1109/ACCESS.2019.2913850

24. Hwang, V., Liu, C.T., Yang, B.Y.: Algorithmic Views of Vectorized Polynomial Multipliers – NTRU Prime. In: Pöpper, C., Batina, L. (eds.) Applied Cryptogra-

phy and Network Security. pp. 24–46. Springer Nature Switzerland, Cham (2024). https://doi.org/10.1007/978-3-031-54773-7_2

25. Kim, J., Seo, J., Song, Y.: Simpler and Faster BFV Bootstrapping for Arbitrary Plaintext Modulus from CKKS. Cryptology ePrint Archive, Paper 2024/109 (2024). https://www.sigsac.org/ccs/CCS2024/program/accepted-papers.html

26. Lattigo v5. Online: https://github.com/tuneinsight/lattigo (Nov 2023), ePFL-LDS, Tune Insight SA

27. Lee, D., Min, S., Song, Y.: Functional Bootstrapping for Packed Ciphertexts via Homomorphic LUT Evaluation. Cryptology ePrint Archive, Paper 2024/181 (2024), https://eprint.iacr.org/2024/181

28. Lee, J.W., Kang, H., Lee, Y., Choi, W., Eom, J., Deryabin, M., Lee, E., Lee, J., Yoo, D., Kim, Y.S., No, J.S.: Privacy-Preserving Machine Learning With Fully Homomorphic Encryption for Deep Neural Network. IEEE Access **10**, 30039–30054 (2022). https://doi.org/10.1109/ACCESS.2022.3159694

29. Liu, Z., Wang, Y.: Relaxed Functional Bootstrapping: A New Perspective on BGV/BFV Bootstrapping. In: Chung, K., Sasaki, Y. (eds.) ASIACRYPT 2024. LNCS, vol. 15484, pp. 208–240. Springer, Cham (2024). https://doi.org/10.1007/978-981-96-0875-1_7

30. Ma, S., Huang, T., Wang, A., Wang, X.: Accelerating BGV Bootstrapping for Large p Using Null Polynomials over $\mathbb{Z}_{p^e}$. In: Joye, M., Leander, G. (eds.) Advances in Cryptology – EUROCRYPT 2024. pp. 403–432. Springer Nature Switzerland, Cham (2024). https://doi.org/10.1007/978-3-031-58723-8_14

31. Meyn, H.: Factorization of the Cyclotomic Polynomialx2n+ 1 over Finite Fields. Finite Fields and Their Applications **2**(4), 439–442 (1996). https://doi.org/10.1006/ffta.1996.0026

32. Ng, L.K.L., Chow, S.S.M.: GForce: GPU-Friendly Oblivious and Rapid Neural Network Inference. In: 30th USENIX Security Symposium (USENIX Security 21). pp. 2147–2164. USENIX Association (Aug 2021), https://www.usenix.org/conference/usenixsecurity21/presentation/ng

33. Okada, H., Player, R., Pohmann, S.: Homomorphic Polynomial Evaluation Using Galois Structure and Applications to BFV Bootstrapping. In: Guo, J., Steinfeld, R. (eds.) Advances in Cryptology – ASIACRYPT 2023. pp. 69–100. Springer Nature Singapore, Singapore (2023). https://doi.org/10.1007/978-981-99-8736-8_3

34. Microsoft SEAL (release 4.1). https://github.com/Microsoft/SEAL (Jan 2023), microsoft Research, Redmond, WA

35. Wan, Z.: Lectures on Finite Fields and Galois Rings. G - Reference,Information and Interdisciplinary Subjects Series, World Scientific (2003), https://books.google.com.hk/books?id=uCSVbYMljNIC

Revisiting Key Decomposition Techniques for FHE: Simpler, Faster and More Generic

M. G. Belorgey[1(✉)], S. Carpov[2], N. Gama[3(✉)], S. Guasch[3], and D. Jetchev[2,4,5]

[1] Tune Insight, Lausanne, Switzerland
mariya@tuneinsight.com
[2] Arcium, Baar, Switzerland
[3] SandboxAQ, Palo-Alto, USA
nicolas.gama@sandboxaq.com
[4] IOG, Colorado, Costa Rica
[5] EPFL, Lausanne, Switzerland

Abstract. Ring-LWE based homomorphic encryption computations in large depth use a combination of two techniques: 1) decomposition of big numbers into small limbs/digits, and 2) efficient cyclotomic multiplications modulo $X^N + 1$. It was long believed that the two mechanisms had to be strongly related, like in the full-RNS setting that uses a CRT decomposition of big numbers over an NTT-friendly family of prime numbers, and NTT over the same primes for multiplications. However, in this setting, NTT was the bottleneck of all large-depth FHE computations. A breakthrough result from Kim et al. (Crypto'2023) managed to overcome this limitation by introducing a second gadget decomposition and showing that it indeed shifts the bottleneck and renders the cost of NTT computations negligible compared to the rest of the computation. In this paper, we extend this result (far) beyond the Full-RNS settings and show that we can completely decouple the big number decomposition from the cyclotomic arithmetic aspects. As a result, we get modulus switching/rescaling for free. We verify both in theory and in practice that the performance of key-switching, external and internal products and automorphisms using our representation are faster than the one achieved by Kim et al., and we discuss the high impact of these results for low-level or hardware optimizations as well as the benefits of the new parametrizations for FHE compilers. We even manage to lower the running time of the gate bootstrapping of `TFHE` by eliminating one eighth of the FFTs and one sixth of the linear operations, which lowers the running time below 5.5ms on recent CPUs.

Keyword: homomorphic encryption, gadget decomposition, key switching, bivariate representation, bootstrapping

M. G. Belorgey, S. Carpov, and D. Jetchev—This work has been done by the authors while they were employed at Inpher.

K.-M. Chung and Y. Sasaki (Eds.): ASIACRYPT 2024, LNCS 15484, pp. 176–207, 2025.
https://doi.org/10.1007/978-981-96-0875-1_6

1   Introduction

Homomorphic encryption allows computations on encrypted data without decrypting it. Since the first fully homomorphic encryption (FHE) scheme introduced by Gentry in [18], several improvements, implementations and new designs have been proposed. Most of them are based on the ring version of the Learning-With-Error problem (RingLWE) defined in [30]. Among the most popular schemes today are BFV [17], BGV [5], CKKS [8], FHEW [16] and TFHE [9,10]. Subsequent work [4] has been done on the interoperability of TFHE with the other two schemes (BFV and CKKS).

Most of the basic building blocks of the practical homomorphic encryption schemes (e.g., homomorphic multiplication and relinearization, key switching, automorphisms or bootstrapping) reduce to efficient *homomorphic external products*. The latter are basic operations that are combinations of decompositions of one of the inputs into higher-dimensional tensor with entries of small norms (*gadget decompositions*) and polynomial multiplications in order to control the accumulation of noise in the ciphertexts and ensure correct decryption (see, e.g., [4, Defn.1] and [10, Defn.3.12] for typical examples of external product).

A major line of research has been undertaken on using Residue Number Systems (RNS) in the acceleration of the basic underlying polynomial multiplication operations used for computing external products [19]. The full-RNS approach of [2], originally introduced to accelerate BFV operations (see also [22]) and subsequently applied to other schemes too such as CKKS [7], allows for manipulating large numbers using smaller machine-size moduli and expressing the homomorphic products (internal products) as well as the gadget decompositions of the BFV and CKKS in the NTT domain. Subsequent hardware acceleration efforts have been made to accelerate RNS-variants of NTT for GPU architectures [29,35] and FPGA architectures [15,27,31,34].

One can thus conceptually differentiate two important aspects of optimization of FHE operations: 1) efficient large integer arithmetic (frontend aspect) that is addressed via mathematical techniques such as gadget decompositions; 2) cyclotomic arithmetic (backend aspects) - the need for efficient arithmetic on the backend to support the basic cyclotomic operations - the choice of floating-point arithmetic or integer arithmetic on the backend. Unfortunately, in most practical implementations, the two aspects are often coupled together, thus, limiting the flexibility for optimization techniques. For instance, by nature, the full-RNS approach to gadget decomposition requires modular arithmetic operations on the backend and thus, is bound to NTT leaving little room for really fast FFT-favored operations (such as the optical FFT approach from [24]).

Note that there are essentially two classical approaches to 1): decomposition in base 2^K and CRT decomposition over primes of K bits. Assuming that single elementary operations operate natively over K-bit numbers (e.g., 32-bit or 64-bit integers or floating point numbers with 53-bits of mantissa), the fact that CRT arithmetic is exempt from any carry propagation yields very efficient parallel additions and multiplications of ℓ K-bit numbers in $O(\ell)$ operations, whereas the base-2^K counterpart would struggle between $O(\ell \log \ell)$ and $O(\ell^2)$ multiplications and force these elementary operations in sequential mode. For this reason, a natural choice for homomorphic encryption was to prefer CRT representations for efficient implementations of CKKS and BFV.

A recent breakthrough has been made by Kim et al. towards decoupling 1) and 2) by an approach based on an auxiliary gadget decomposition that replaces expensive modular arithmetic in the computation of the external product by pure arithmetic with small integers via gadget decompositions based on RNS [23].

Note that the RNS-type approach to 1) often has the following drawbacks:

1. *Arithmetic modulo different primes.* The arithmetic has to be carried out modulo different prime numbers of same size, even if they are selected to be as *friendly* as possible, numbers modulo which arithmetic is really efficient are rare (e.g., Mersenne primes, Fermat primes). There is also a small loss from hardware aspects such as the necessity to have one hardware multiplier per prime.

2. *Unfeasibility of bit extraction/coarse noise granularity.* Bit extraction is not possible in CRT domain modulo a product of small primes, the best granularity of HE noise levels is those of the primes: e.g., 16 to 40 bits. As explained in the analysis of the Hecate compiler [25] this impacts negatively the optimal use of homomorphic budget for CRT-based CKKS - one often needs to re-scale the noise to the nearest available level before attempting a homomorphic product after an operation producing less noise (such as a sum, a small linear combination or a trace).

3. *Sub-optimal memory usage with respect to truncations.* Restrictions from high-precision representations to low-precision representations are not simple truncations of limbs (as in the natural base-2^K representation), but require a separate RNS representation.

The above-mentioned carry-less nature and efficiency of parallel CRT multiplications would have been perfect if most homomorphic operations were actual ring operations. However, internal ring multiplications over large numbers never come standalone: first of all, in a BFV or CKKS internal product they always come in packs of N (giving a $O(N\ell)$ complexity to multiply two polynomials modulo $X^N + 1$), and second, they are always followed by an external product that comprises at least ℓ NTTs (so at least $O(\ell N(\ell + \log N))$ if we use the latest double gadget decomposition of [23] and $O(\ell^2 N \log N)$ before). In other words, since $N \gg \ell$: typically, N is between 1024 and 65536 and ℓ is lower than 100, the complexity of an internal BFV or CKKS product remains bounded both asymptotically and practically by the complexity of its underlying external product. This means that as long as we make the external product more efficient, we have some margin to degrade the complexity of the internal multiplication of polynomials up to $O(N\ell^2)$ and still accelerating in almost all cases the running time of CKKS and BFV operations.

It is thus desirable to extend the auxiliary gadget decomposition approach of 1) to the natural 2^K-base large integer representation to overcome the above drawbacks.

Our Contributions

In this work, this is exactly what we achieve - we show how to adapt the *auxiliary gadget decomposition* of [23] to the natural base-2^K representation of numbers and thus, obtain an external product that is simpler and faster.

Our starting point is a common plaintext representation space for all the practical RingLWE-based schemes (BFV, CKKS and TFHE) described in [4]: Let $\mathbb{T} = \mathbb{R}/\mathbb{Z}$ be the real torus (which is the set of real numbers modulo 1) and $\mathcal{R} = \mathbb{Z}[X]/\langle X^N + 1\rangle$ be the ring of polynomials of degree $N - 1$ and coefficients in $\mathbb{Z}$. Then we define the common plaintext representation space to be the $\mathcal{R}$-module $\mathbb{T}_N[X] := \mathbb{R}[X]/\langle X^N + 1\rangle/\mathcal{R}$ (also thought of as *formal* polynomials of degree $N-1$ whose coefficients are in $\mathbb{T}$). We can add torus polynomials together, or multiply them by integer polynomials.

Inspired by the classical Schoenhage–Strassen algorithm for large integer multiplication based on FFT [32], in Sect. 3, we propose a bivariate integral polynomial representation with small coefficients of these formal polynomials where the evaluation on $Y = 2^{-K}$ (K is the limb size) yields a sufficiently accurate approximation of the toric coefficients. Introducing the auxiliary variable implicitly corresponds to having the second gadget decomposition: on one hand, it yields the natural decomposition in base 2^K of toric elements (evaluation at $Y = 2^{-K}$); on the other hand, it provides a plenitude of choice of bivariate polynomials to approximate the given toric polynomial. A careful normalization and reduction yields a representative with small coefficients - the bivariate polynomial representation that is used for efficient external product (see Sect. 3.2), thus making it specifically tuned for TRLWE operations.

Since the space of TRLWE ciphertexts is $\mathbb{T}_N[X]^2$, we express the external product in terms of multiplications of bivariate polynomials with small integer coefficients. It is this reduction that decouples 1) and 2) above - the multiplication can be performed using either FFT or NTT backend arithmetic which we explain in Sect. 6, thus, enabling optimal use of different architectures for hardware optimization.

A major advantage of our representation is that it addresses challenges 1–3. Indeed, our representation supports efficient sums, normalizations, reductions modulo $\mathbb{Z}$, left and right shifts in $O(\ell)$ and products in $O(\ell \log \ell)$ (only bilinear expressions are needed, we do not need higher degree terms in FHE operations!), bit-decompositions and bit-extraction. In addition, the *prefix property* of the natural base-2^K representation yields a memory-efficient way to pass from a higher-precision representation to a lower precision representation. It provides a single-bit noise granularity, thus, enabling efficient compositions as proposed in [4]. The asymptotic complexity matches the best available full-RNS algorithms for both external products of TFHE, and also internal products of CKKS and BFV.

The sequential nature of carry propagation is mitigated by the parallelism induced by the fact that the operations in our external product occur in a SIMD (Single Instruction/Multiple Data) manner over N elements each time. We increase the complexities of the internal multiplications from $O(N\ell)$ to $O(N\ell \log \ell)$, keeping them negligible compared to an external product, and hence, due to the speed-up of the latter ones, also accelerate internal products of CKKS and BFV, so that at the end of the day, by not using any of the CRT of full-RNS techniques, and instead, applying the double-gadget decomposition to old-school base-2^K representations directly, we end up speeding up all the existing homomorphic operations of TFHE, CKKS and BFV.

Our practical experiments and benchmarks support the theoretical evidence: first, Table 1 provides evidence for the number of elementary operations (SIMD products and Discrete Fourier Transforms (DFTs)) in an external product computation in the context of the various FHE building blocks (or more specifically, in the more efficient approach via HalfRGSW introduced in Sect. 3.2). The experiments demonstrate that for FHE parameters $N = 65536$, $\ell \sim 100$ and $K \sim 20$, the cost of SIMD products largely dominates the cost of DFTs, an already strong indication of the parallelization-friendly nature of our approach. Second, we compare our bivariate representation (using both FFT and NTT) to the approach from [23] to demonstrate that, prior to any parallelization or hardware acceleration efforts, we get a better performance (see Table 5). Finally, in Sect. 4 we even manage to lower the running time of the gate bootstrapping of TFHE by eliminating 12.5% of the FFTs and 16.6% of the linear operations.

Future Directions

One of the most important contributions of our work is the flexibility it provides for future hardware acceleration efforts. Everything that we have done in this work is single-core optimizations.

First of all, the normalization and reduction Algorithm 1 (and its extension presented in the full version of the paper [3]) allows for fast AVX and GPU-friendly implementations. The bivariate representation yields several advantages making the parallelization very natural. First, as mentioned, it is directly inspired by the Schoenhage–Strassen algorithm for large integer multiplication based on NTT with complexity $O(n \log n \log \log n)$, where n is the number of bits of the inputs [32]. In fact, the case of large integer multiplication is recovered directly from our bivariate representation by setting $N = 1$ via the evaluation map $\mathcal{R}[Y] \to \mathcal{R}$ given by $f(Y) \mapsto f(2^K)$. In this work, we use the opposite exponent $f(Y) \mapsto f(2^{-K})$, whose output is dense in $\mathbb{R}_N[X]$, since we care more about high precision approximations of products between bounded real-valued polynomials. Note that the Schoenhage–Strassen is an NTT version of the DFT-based fast polynomial multiplication. Even if the original Schoenhage–Strassen algorithm is not completely easy to parallelize, the large degree N on the variable X makes our bivariate polynomial multiplication friendlier for parallel architectures.

Second, a recursive version of DFT or more generally, a Cooley–Tukey transform [12] allows for parallelization on both X and Y variables. The well-known *in-place* and *in-order* variants of the Cooley–Tukey transform opens the door for highly optimized memory usage as well. When the degree on Y is too small, the alternative naïve multiplication, or single iteration of Karatsuba algorithms discussed here can also be performed in-place.

As already mentioned, the trade-off of using FFT and NTT can benefit from the various hardware acceleration initiatives such as GPU acceleration [29], FPGA acceleration [27,34], optical computing [24] (particularly favorable for the FFT approach), ASICs [13] as well as the outcome of the DPRIVE program [14], especially the recent work [6].

Finally, our work opens up the possibility for an efficient implementation of the scheme switching framework Chimera [4] that allows to mix TFHE, CKKS, BFV arithmetic using continuous homomorphic levels. The original proposal was suggesting the use of large numbers fixed-point arithmetic in order to perform efficient additions, multiplication and bit-extraction. Unfortunately, none of the available representations of big numbers in GMP, MPFR are sufficiently efficient in practice, and a CRT representation would not allow efficient bit-extraction either, thus leading to the same setbacks as Full-RNS. For these reasons, the early attempts to implement Chimera were, thus, slow in practice for multiplicative levels ≥ 3. The efficient multi-precision arithmetic we propose in this work, while being compatible with cyclotomic multiplication, bit extraction, and lazy carry propagation make the whole concept practical.

In conclusion, our approach supports the following general principle: instead of one trying to find a numerical representation (e.g., RNS representation) with a gadget decomposition that is not too convoluted, it is more natural to start from the gadget decomposition (e.g., base-2^K representation) and take the output of the gadget decomposition directly as the numerical representation.

2 Preliminaries

Notation

Let $\mathbb{T} = \mathbb{R}/\mathbb{Z}$ be the real torus. For a ring A (e.g., $A = \mathbb{Z}, \mathbb{R}, \mathbb{C}$), let $A_N[X] := A[X]/\langle X^N + 1 \rangle$ be the ring of polynomials modulo $X^N + 1$ with coefficients in A and N a power of 2. In particular, let $\mathcal{R} = \mathbb{Z}_N[X]$, which is also the ring of integers of the cyclotomic field $\mathbb{Q}(\zeta_{2N})$.

Let $\mathbb{T}_N[X] = \mathbb{R}_N[X]/\mathcal{R}$ (a.k.a $\mathbb{R}[X] \bmod X^N + 1 \bmod \mathbb{Z}$) which we view as an $\mathcal{R}$-module (it has no ring structure). Elements of this module can formally be represented using notations borrowed from polynomials, i.e., $a(X) = \sum_{i=0}^{N-1} a_i X^i$ where $a_i \in \mathbb{T}$. Since the coefficient space $\mathbb{T}$ is not a ring, we cannot evaluate these polynomials over any non-integer value, nor multiply two such elements together. However, the notation allows coefficient-wise addition/subtraction of polynomials, projection from and lifts to the continuous ring $\mathbb{R}_N[X]$, and most importantly, we often refer to the module action of $\mathcal{R}$ on $\mathbb{T}_N[X]$ as an *external multiplication* of a by integer polynomial $u(x) = \sum_{i=0}^{N-1} u_i X^i \in \mathcal{R}$ where $u_i \in \mathbb{Z}$ via the natural Cauchy product formula: $(u \cdot a)(X) = \sum_{i=0}^{2N-2} \left(\sum_{j=0}^{i} u_j \cdot a_{i-j} \right) X^i \bmod X^N + 1$.

We denote by $\|.\|_p$ and $\|.\|_\infty$ the standard norms for scalars and vectors over real field or over the integers. By extension, the norms $\|P(X)\|_p$ and $\|P(X)\|_\infty$ of a real or integer polynomial P are the norms of their coefficient vectors. The norm of an element of $\mathbb{T}_N[X]$ is the norm of its centered lift in $\mathbb{R}_N[X]$ with coefficients in $[-1/2, 1/2)$.

Historically, there have been two different lattice-based encryption scheme designs. The first, Learning With Errors (LWE) [30], encrypts modular numbers or even continuous reals modulo 1. The second, Gentry-Sahai-Waters (GSW) [20], focuses on encrypting small integer plaintexts. Polynomial ring extensions were independently added to both schemes: for LWE as early as 2009 [26], and for GSW in 2015 [16]. Later, the formalization of external products established the interconnection between plaintexts of LWE and GSW ciphertexts [9], leading to simplifications in GSW ciphertexts that preserved the external product morphism.

The TRLWE and TRGSW ciphertexts are fundamental to almost all fully homomorphic encryption schemes, including BFV, CGGI (also known under the name TFHE), and CKKS. These ciphertexts can be represented either over integers (without the T in the name) or over real numbers modulo 1 (with the T in the name). TFHE has used both types of ciphertexts since its inception, whereas the original descriptions of BFV and CKKS used only RLWE ciphertexts with ad-hoc key switches for products.

In the Chimera framework [4], the authors explain how to unify and switch between CKKS, BFV, and TFHE using common notations, as well as the minimal set of operations over TRLWE and TRGSW ciphertexts necessary for comprehensive arithmetic. We introduce and use this minimal set of operations as the starting point in our paper.

2.1   TRLWE

TRLWE encrypts elements of a subset of the $\mathcal{R}$-module $\mathbb{T}_N[X]$ called the plaintext space, and which can be finite (TFHE), a discrete subgroup (BFV) or a continuous set of small elements (CKKS). The ciphertexts of μ are of the form $c = (a, b = s \cdot a + \mu + e)$, where $s \in \mathcal{B}$ is the secret key, $a \in_R \mathbb{T}_N[X]$ is uniformly random and the $e \in \mathbb{T}_N[X]$ is chosen randomly from an error distribution with mean zero and suitably chosen standard deviation. Without loss of generality, the keyset $\mathcal{B}$ in this work can refer to binary, ternary keys or small keys. The decryption procedure starts by evaluating the phase function on the ciphertext, that is, by computing $\varphi_s(a, b) := b - s \cdot a$. Since $\varphi_s(a, b) = \mu + e$, the plaintext μ is the mean of the phase (the mean being computed over the random coins in the generation of the noise e during encryption).

- **Parameters**: A security level λ and a minimal noise parameter α.
- **KeyGenTRLWE**(λ, α): A uniformly random binary or ternary key $s \in \mathcal{B} \subset \mathcal{R}$.
- **EncTRLWE**(μ, s, α): Choose a uniform random element $a \in \mathbb{T}_N[X]$ and a small Gaussian error $e \in \mathbb{T}_N[X]$ and return $c = (a, b = s \cdot a + \mu + e)$
- **DecTRLWE**(c, s): Compute the phase $\varphi_s(c)$ and round $\varphi_s(c)$ to the nearest point in the plaintext space (when it is discrete), or returns a close approximation (CKKS).

2.2   Approximate Gadget Decompositions and TRGSW Ciphertexts

A common challenge with various FHE constructions (e.g., GSW) is the control on the accumulation of noise after homomorphic operations. A general technique from lattice-based cryptography to address this problem is a concept known as *flattening gadget* or *gadget decomposition*, that is, a map that transforms a ciphertext into a higher dimensional vector with small $\|.\|_\infty$ while preserving some linear-algebraic properties.

Two classical examples of gadget decompositions are numerical base representations and RNS representations. Since most of the FHE literature uses gadget decompositions on integral values, the decompositions themselves are exact. A notable exception to this principle is TFHE where one uses floating point arithmetic and therefore, an approximate gadget decomposition. Below we recall the basic definition (see also [10, Defn.3.6]):

Definition 2.1 (approximate gadget decomposition for TRLWE samples).
We say that an algorithm $Decomp_{H,\beta,\epsilon}$ *is a valid gadget decomposition on gadget* $H \in (\mathbb{T}_N[X]^2)^{2\ell}$, *quality (or* $\|\|_\infty$*-bound)* β, *and precision* $\epsilon > 0$ *if for any input* $v \in \mathbb{T}_N[X]^2$, *it outputs an element* $u \in \mathcal{R}^{2\ell}$, $\|u\|_\infty \leq \beta$ *such that* $\|u \cdot H - v\|_\infty < \epsilon$.

As already mentioned in [10], there is a canonical approximate gadget decompositions coming from numerical base representations for any base B_g:

$$H^T = \begin{pmatrix} B_g^{-1} \dots B_g^{-\ell} & 0 & \dots & 0 \\ 0 & \dots & 0 & B_g^{-1} \dots B_g^{-\ell} \end{pmatrix}$$

The above notion is important for two main reasons: 1) it allows us to define TRGSW ciphertexts; 2) it allows us to define an external product between TRGSW ciphertexts and TRLWE ciphertexts.

We first recall the TRGSW ciphertexts: the TRGSW encrypts elements of the ring $\mathcal{R}$ with bounded infinity norm. Intuitively, the idea of the original GSW scheme [20] is to encrypt a small plaintext $\mu \in \mathbb{Z}$ into a ciphertext that is a matrix C_μ such that the secret key $\mathbf{s}$ is an approximate eigenvector of C_μ with eigenvalue μ. Such an encryption scheme leads to natural homomorphic addition and multiplication operations that are simply matrix additions and matrix multiplications. The naïve idea does not quite work without gadget decompositions since one cannot control the propagation of the errors in the approximate eigenvalues under homomorphic multiplications. The schemes FHEW and TFHE use a ring-variant of the original scheme, the last one with an approximate gadget decomposition:

Definition 2.2 (TRGSW ciphertexts). *Let* $H \in (\mathbb{T}_N[X]^2)^{2\ell}$ *be a gadget and let* $\mu \in \mathcal{R}$ *be a plaintext with bounded* ℓ_∞*-norm. The space of valid TRGSW ciphertexts for* μ *is* $TRGSW(\mu) := \{Z + \mu H\}$, *where each element of* $Z \in (\mathbb{T}_N[X]^2)^{2\ell}$ *is a valid TRLWE ciphertext of zero.*

2.3   External Products, Relinearization Keys and Internal Products

For the purposes of the current work, we will need a relatively uniform treatment of the various RLWE-based FHE frameworks, most notably, BFV, CKKS and TFHE, as well as their internal products.

It is explained in [4, §2.5] (as well as the particular discussion of BFV and CKKS in Sects. 3 and 4, respectively, of *loc. cit.*) how to uniformize the plaintext spaces for all these schemes and view them as various subgroups of the $\mathcal{R}$-module $\mathbb{T}_N[X]$. Once this is done, the homomorphic internal products of BFV and CKKS are expressed in terms of the following basic primitive, the *external product*, a major operation of interest in the current work:

Definition 2.3 (**TFHE external product**). *Given a flattening gadget H and an approximate gadget decomposition* $Decomp_{H,\beta,\epsilon}$, *the* external product *in* TFHE *is a map*

$$\boxdot : TRGSW \times TRLWE \to TRLWE$$

defined by

$$C \boxdot c := Decomp_{H,\beta,\epsilon}(c) \cdot C,$$

where $C \in TRGSW(\mu_1)$ *and* $c \in TRLWE(\mu_2)$.

One can show [10, Thm. 3.13] that under certain specific noise conditions, the above external product $C \boxdot c$ is a valid ciphertext for $\mu_1 \mu_2$.

Once we have defined this primitive, we use it to express the various internal products, the major idea being the concept of *relinearization* and *relinearization keys* - we refer the reader to [4, pp. 325–326] for a more detailed explanation. The important point is that by using extra key material (relinearization key), one can express the internal product of the BFV scheme in terms of the above external product. More specifically, if we define[1] the relinearization key as RK $= TRGSW(s)$, then for $\star \in \{\text{BFV}, \text{CKKS}\}$ the homomorphic internal product $\boxtimes : \mathbb{T}_N[X]^2 \times \mathbb{T}_N[X]^2 \to \mathbb{T}_N[X]^2$ of two ciphertexts (a_1, b_1) and (a_2, b_2) of plaintexts μ_1 and μ_2, respectively becomes

$$(a_1, b_1) \boxtimes (a_2, b_2) = (C_1, C_0) - \text{RK} \boxdot (C_2, 0), \tag{1}$$

where $C_0 = b_1 \otimes_\star b_2$, $C_1 = a_1 \otimes_\star b_2 + a_2 \otimes_\star b_1$, $C_2 = a_1 \otimes_\star a_2$, the important point being that this ciphertext is a valid encryption of the plaintext $\mu_1 \otimes_\star \mu_2$. Here, $\otimes_\star : \mathbb{T}_N[X] \times \mathbb{T}_N[X] \to \mathbb{T}_N[X]$ indicates a certain product map (depending on the scheme) whose restriction to the plaintext subgroup of $\mathbb{T}_N[X]$ yields the plaintext product.

For instance, if for $\bullet \in \mathbb{T}_N[X]$, $\widetilde{\bullet} \in \mathbb{R}[X]/\langle X^N + 1\rangle$ denotes the unique lift with coefficients in the interval $[-1/2, 1/2]$ then the BFV product $\otimes_{\text{BFV}}$ with plaintext modulo p (Montgomery product) is:

$$\otimes_{\text{BFV}} : \mathbb{T}_N[X] \times \mathbb{T}_N[X] \to \mathbb{T}_N[X], \qquad (u, v) \mapsto p \cdot \widetilde{u} * \widetilde{v}. \tag{2}$$

Similarly, CKKS plaintext products at input level L_{in} are:

$$\otimes_{\text{CKKS}} : \mathbb{T}_N[X] \times \mathbb{T}_N[X] \to \mathbb{T}_N[X],$$

$$(u, v) \mapsto 2^{L_{\text{in}}} \cdot \text{Round}_{2^{-L_{\text{in}}}}(\widetilde{u}) * \text{Round}_{2^{-L_{\text{in}}}}(\widetilde{v}) \tag{3}$$

---

[1] There are many equivalent ways to define the relinearization key. Here, we use an external product and a zero term in the TRLWE ciphertext, which can be propagated in the algorithm and simplified, the original references of Fan–Vercauteren [17] present a key-switching that substitute a key s^2 by s.

In both formulas for (BFV and CKKS product), the symbol $\cdot$ is the external product by an integer, and $*$ represents multiplication in $\mathbb{R}_N[X]$: the input coefficients are first lifted to the real interval $[-1/2, 1/2)$ and in the second case, also rounded to the nearest exact multiple of 2^{-L}. None of these functions is an actual product over the entire space - one needs to restrict the inputs to the subgroups $p^{-1}\mathcal{R}/\mathcal{R}$ and $2^{-L}\mathcal{R}/\mathcal{R}$ of $\mathbb{T}_N[X]$, respectively to obtain products. Yet, the function $\otimes_{\mathsf{BFV}}$ has the property that if u and v are close from i/p and j/p where i and j are integers, their product is close to $(ij \bmod p)/p$, which is handy to encode plaintext arithmetic modulo p. The product $\otimes_{\mathsf{CKKS}}$ has the property that if u and v are at distance $\leq 2^{L+1}$ away from $i/2^L$ and $j/2^L$ where i and j are smaller than 2^ρ, then their product is at distance $2^{L-\rho}$ away from $ij/2^L$, which is good to encode fixed-point number arithmetic on ρ-bits numbers.

2.4 Table of Symbols, Orders of Magnitudes

When reading the paper, different complexities shall intervene in the different theorems. It is important to keep in mind the difference in orders of magnitude, as for instance: having an arithmetic in $O(N^2)$ is prohibitive, and we must absolutely stick to $O(N \log N)$, however $O(\ell^2)$ is perfectly realistic in some scenario.

The parameters N, K and $\tilde{K}$ are set once and for all during parameter and key generation, while L, ℓ, and $\tilde{\ell}$ evolve during a homomorphic evaluation computation, following the noise rate variations: They decrease across homomorphic operations, and are reset to a large value after a bootstrapping.

3 A Bivariate Polynomial Representation

We keep the notation and the setting from Sect. 2. Let K be a limb size. We represent (rational) approximations of elements of $\mathbb{R}[X]/\langle X^N + 1\rangle$ by elements of the (discrete) quotient ring $\mathbb{Z}[X, Y]/\langle X^N + 1\rangle$ (also equal to $\mathcal{R}[Y]$, the polynomials in Y over $\mathcal{R}$) of the bivariate polynomial ring $\mathbb{Z}[X, Y]$. The representations are obtained via the evaluation map (ring homomorphism) on the Y variable

$$\phi_K \colon \mathcal{R}[Y] \to \mathbb{R}_N[X], \qquad P(X, Y) \mapsto P(X, 2^{-K}). \qquad (4)$$

More explicitly, the elements of $\mathcal{R}[Y]$ are represented by bivariate integer polynomials $P(X, Y) = \sum a_{i,j} X^i Y^j$ whose degrees in X are at most $N - 1$. Since the ring homomorphism ϕ_K is clearly not injective, an element of $\mathbb{R}_N[X]$ can have multiple pre-images in $\mathcal{R}[Y]$. We will use this property in a crucial way and will be particularly interested in representatives with small coefficients.

Variable	Range	Meaning
N	$[2^{10}, 2^{16}]$	Power-of-two polynomial modulus: $X^N + 1$
$K, \widetilde{K}$	$[10 - 60]$	Multi-precision representation of Torus elements consist of K-bit limbs (so machine words have at least $2K$ bits to handle products), and gadget decompositions produce $\widetilde{K}$-bit outputs. $\widetilde{K}$ is in general equal to K, but can be chosen smaller in rare circumstances, since $\widetilde{K}$ intervenes in the noise propagation of external products.
L	$[20 - 2000]$	Targeted number of bits of precision of the multiprecision arithmetic (to handle a RLWE ciphertext whose noise rate is $\alpha \approx 2^{-L}$). For a given cryptographic security parameter, each key dimension is associated to a maximal noise level L: for 128-bit security, count $L_{\max} = 20, 880, 1761$ for respectively $N = 2^{10}, 2^{15}, 2^{16}$
$\ell, \widetilde{\ell}, \widetilde{\ell}_A$	[1-100]	Number of limbs per coefficient in a RLWE ciphertext (without tilde) or in a gadget decomposition (with tilde, and/or subscript depending on the context). These ℓ can be thought as $\ell \approx L/K$, it is the main asymptotic parameter in all the complexities, directly related to the number of elementary vector operations. In practice, for the key sizes and precision we consider above, all these ℓ's fall within the range $[1, 100]$

Definition 3.1. A *bivariate polynomial* $P(X, Y) = \sum_{i=0}^{N-1} \sum_{j \geq 0} a_{i,j} X^i Y^j$ *is called* K-*normalized if* $a_{i,j} \in [-2^{K-1}, 2^{K-1})$ *for all* $i = 0, \ldots, N - 1$ *and* $j \geq 1$.

As we are mainly interested in representing elements of $\mathbb{T}_N[X]$, that is, formal polynomials over the torus, we often reduce the coefficients of real polynomials to the real interval $[-1/2, 1/2)$ and hence, we give the following definition:

Definition 3.2. A *bivariate polynomial* $P(X, Y) = \sum_{i=0}^{N-1} \sum_{j \geq 0} a_{i,j} X^i Y^j$ *is* K-normalized *and* reduced *if, in addition to being* K-*normalized, it satisfies* $a_{i,0} = 0$ *for all* $i = 0, \ldots, N - 1$.

We now approximate any element of the $\mathcal{R}$-module $\mathbb{T}_N[X]$ up to an arbitrary precision with K-normalized and reduced bivariate polynomials from $\mathcal{R}[Y]$. The proofs of the lemma and the corollary below are simple consequences of the decomposition of the coefficients in base 2^K.

Lemma 3.1. *For every integer* $L > 0$ *and every polynomial* $Q \in \mathbb{R}_N[X]$, *there exists a* K-*normalized polynomial* $P(X, Y) \in \mathcal{R}[Y]$ *of degree* $\leq \lceil L/K \rceil$ *in* Y *such that* $\|\phi_K(P) - Q\|_\infty \leq 2^{-L}$.

Corollary 3.1. *For every integer* $L > 0$ *and for all elements* $Q \in \mathbb{T}_N[X]$, *there exists a* K-*normalized and reduced polynomial* $P \in \mathcal{R}[Y]$ *of degree* $\leq \lceil L/K \rceil$ *in* Y *such that*

$$\|\phi_K(P) \bmod \mathcal{R} - Q\|_\infty \leq 2^{-L}.$$

Note that the above approximation of the elements $Q \in \mathbb{T}_N[X]$ via bivariate polynomials $P(X,Y) \in \mathcal{R}[Y]$ is reminiscent to a *gadget decomposition* in classical lattice-based cryptography. Intuitively, the presence of the variable Y corresponds to representing a vector in higher-dimensional space with lower $\|.\|_\infty$-norm - a key technique necessary for the design of various FHE schemes (e.g., GSW [21] and TFHE [9]).

The following lemma whose proof is rather formal shows that for any limb size K and any polynomial in $P \in \mathcal{R}[Y]$, there is a unique K-normalized and reduced polynomial Q with the same image under ϕ_K.

Lemma 3.2. *For any limb size K and any polynomial $P(X,Y) \in \mathcal{R}[Y]$, there exists a unique normalized polynomial $Q(X,Y)$ of the same degree in Y such that $\phi_K(P) = \phi_K(Q)$. Additionally, there exists a unique K-normalized and reduced polynomial $Q(X,Y)$ such that $\phi_K(P) = \phi_K(Q) \bmod \mathcal{R}$.*

We are now interested in an efficient algorithm for normalization and reduction of polynomials.

Algorithm 1. Normalization and Reduction

Input: A target precision of L bits (that represents 2^{-L}) and a limb size K

Input: An input polynomial $A(X,Y) = \sum_{k\geq 0} A_k(X)Y^k$ satisfying $\|A\|_\infty < 2^M$

Output: A K-normalized and reduced polynomial $R(X,Y) = \sum_{k=1}^{\ell} R_k(X)Y^k$ of degree $\ell = \lceil L/K \rceil$ in Y such that $\|\phi_K(R) - \phi_K(A)\|_\infty \leq 2^{-L}$.

1: $\mathrm{acc}(X) = 0$
2: **for** $k = \lceil (L+M)/K \rceil$ **downto** 1 **do**
3:     $\mathrm{acc}(X) \leftarrow \mathrm{acc}(X) + A_k(X)$
4:     $R_k(X) \leftarrow \mathtt{centermod}_{2^K}(\mathrm{acc}(X))$
5:     $\mathrm{acc}(X) \leftarrow (\mathrm{acc}(X) - R_k(X))/2^K$
6: **end for**
7: Return $R(X,Y) = \sum_{k=1}^{\ell} R_k(X)Y^k$

Lemma 3.3. *Let K be a limb size and let $L > 0$ be a specified precision. Given a polynomial $A(X,Y) \in \mathcal{R}[Y]$ satisfying $\|A\|_\infty < 2^M$ for some M, Algorithm 1 outputs a K-normalized and reduced polynomial $R(X,Y) \in \mathcal{R}[Y]$ such that $\|(\phi_K(A) - \phi_K(R)) \bmod \mathcal{R}\| \leq 2^{-L}$ in $O((L+M)/K)$ element-wise operations (additions/subtractions or binary shifts) on N-length vectors of integers in $\left(-2^{M+1}, 2^{M+1}\right)$.*

Lemma 3.2 and Algorithm 1 are actually a specialization of Lemma 3.3 and Algorithm 2 to the easier case $K = \tilde{K}$. A proof of the generic case Lemma 3.3 is given in appendix Sect. A.

Using a parameter value M such that $M + 1 < 64$, Algorithm 1 allows for efficient AVX and GPU-friendly implementations.

Since the representations that occur throughout a FHE computation can be parameterized with different limb sizes, we are going to present the general theorems using two limb sizes K and $\widetilde{K}$ that are not necessarily the same. This is why in the full version of the paper [3] we present a slightly more general algorithm that converts a K-representation into a normalized $\widetilde{K}$-representation. Even if slightly more complex than Algorithm 1, it has the same performance.

3.1   Evaluation of External Products

Most homomorphic operations reduce to efficient evaluations of Lipschitz functions. Recall that a function $f\colon \mathbb{T}_N[X] \to \mathbb{T}_N[X]$ is called κ-Lipschitz for some parameter $\kappa > 0$ if $\|f(x) - f(y)\|_\infty \leq \kappa \|x - y\|_\infty$ for all $x, t \in \mathbb{T}_N[X]$. Any continous $\mathcal{R}$-module homomorphism is an external product and is therefore a Lipschitz function (see proof in [3]), that is, $f_u\colon \mathbb{T}_N[X] \to \mathbb{T}_N[X]$, $x \mapsto u \cdot x$. We thus explain how to evaluate efficiently external products. The lemma below formalizes the following simple fact: evaluating f_u up to a certain target precision 2^{-L} amounts to evaluating the reduced and K-normalized representations of the external products $u \cdot 2^{-K}, \ldots, u \cdot 2^{-\widetilde{K}\widetilde{\ell}}$ for sufficiently large $\widetilde{\ell}$.

The following technical lemma enables us to compute a sufficiently good K-normalized and reduced representation of the external product $u \cdot \bullet$ with a prescribed target precision of L bits by providing (in a precomputation) sufficiently good approximations of the external product of u with the negative powers 2^{-Kj}.

Lemma 3.4. Let $u \in \mathcal{R}$ be an integer polynomial and consider a target precision of $L > 0$ bits. Let K and $\widetilde{K}$ be two positive integers (limb sizes). Let $B_1(X,Y), \ldots, B_{\widetilde{\ell}}(X,Y)$ be K-normalized and reduced representations of $u \cdot 2^{-\widetilde{K}}, u \cdot 2^{-2\widetilde{K}}, \ldots, u \cdot 2^{-\widetilde{K}\widetilde{\ell}}$ with precision $(\widetilde{\ell}N)^{-1}2^{-(\widetilde{K}+L-1)}$. For any $\widetilde{K}$-normalized and reduced bivariate polynomial $A(X,Y) = \sum_{i=1}^{\widetilde{\ell}} A_i(X)Y^i \in \mathcal{R}[Y]$,

$$C(X,Y) = \sum_{i=1}^{\widetilde{\ell}} A_i(X)B_i(X,Y) \tag{5}$$

is a (non-reduced) K-representation of $u \cdot \phi_{\widetilde{K}}(A)$ of precision 2^{-L}, i.e.,

$$\left\|\phi_K(C) - u \cdot \phi_{\widetilde{K}}(A))\right\|_\infty \leq 2^{-L} \qquad and \qquad \|C\|_\infty \leq \widetilde{\ell}N2^{K+\widetilde{K}-2}.$$

Proof. The second bound on $\|C\|$ comes from the fact that A and B are resp K and $\widetilde{K}$-normalized, thus each $\|A_i\|_\infty$ and $\|B_i\|_\infty$ are bounded by resp. 2^{K-1} and $2^{\widetilde{K}-1}$. $\phi_K(C) = \sum_{i=1}^{\widetilde{\ell}} A_i\phi_K(B_i) = \sum_{i=1}^{\widetilde{\ell}} A_i(u \cdot 2^{-\widetilde{K}i} + e_i)$ where by definition, each $\|e_i\|_\infty \leq (\widetilde{\ell}N)^{-1}2^{-(K+L-1)}$. Therefore, $\phi_K(C) = u \cdot \phi_{\widetilde{K}}(A) + \sum_{i=1}^{\widetilde{\ell}} A_ie_i$, so the first inequality becomes $\left\|\sum_{i=1}^{\widetilde{\ell}} A_ie_i\right\|$ which is $\leq \sum_{i=1}^{\widetilde{\ell}} N\|A_i\|_\infty\|e_i\|_\infty \leq 2^{-L}$. $\qquad\square$

If we expand further the right-hand side of (5) via $B_i(X,Y) = \sum_{j=1}^{\ell} B_{i,j}(X)Y^j$ for $\ell \leq L+1+\tilde{K}+\log_2 \tilde{\ell}$, we obtain $C(X,Y) = \sum_{j=1}^{\ell} \sum_{i=1}^{\tilde{\ell}} A_i(X)B_{i,j}(X)Y^j$ that can be computed using

- $\ell\tilde{\ell}$ internal polynomial products over $\mathcal{R}$ with inputs of infinity norm bounded by $2^{\tilde{K}-1}$ and 2^{K-1}, respectively and output of norm bounded by $N \cdot 2^{\tilde{K}+K-2}$.
- $\ell\tilde{\ell}$ additions of polynomials whose norm is bounded by $N\tilde{\ell} \cdot 2^{\tilde{K}+K-2}$.

In most FHE operations with GSW ciphertexts such as key switching, relinearization, automorphisms and bootstrapping, $u \in \mathcal{R}$ depends only on the secret key and is thus known in advance of the homomorphic operation. Anything that depends only on u can thus be precomputed in an offline phase (in general during the key generation) and only the cross-terms must be evaluated in an online phase (HE evaluation). With this in mind, should we decide to use DFT over only X, all the multiplications between $A_i(X)$ and $B_{i,j}(X)$ become element-wise products on the DFT space and are performed separately for each power of Y. Therefore, we obtain a nice offline/online phase separation:

Offline Phase (most often during keygen)
- $\ell\tilde{\ell}$ bounded DFT's of $B_{i,j}(X)$ precomputed and given as input
Online Phase
- $\tilde{\ell}$ bounded DFT's of $A_i(X)$
- $\ell\tilde{\ell}$ element-wise multiplications in DFT domain
- $\ell\tilde{\ell}$ element-wise additions in DFT domain
- ℓ bounded iDFT's for the results $C_j(X)$
- $O(\ell)$ element-wise additions, shifts or masks to normalize the result (if needed)

Even if we have ℓ^2 products to evaluate, the online phase requires only a linear number of DFT's/iDFT's instead of a quadratic number. Fundamentally, it is the exact same root cause that lead [23] to its new asymptotic speedup compared to full-RNS. The main advantage here is that we obtain the representation in a natural way from the normalized gadget decomposition on $\mathbb{T}_N[X]$.

3.2   External Products by Secret Polynomials over TRLWE

TRGSW ciphertexts have traditionally been used to multiply TRLWE ciphertexts by a secret integer polynomial $u \in \mathcal{R}$, which is the TRGSW-TRLWE external product from [10]. As noted in [4, p.326], the homomorphic evaluation of the external product $v \rightarrow s \cdot v$ where s is the small TRLWE secret key could be used as an alternative to the traditional relinearization of the quadratic term s^2 originally used in the CKKS and BFV products. This is done via a relinearization key RK = $\text{TRGSW}_s(s)$ using an external product of the form RK $\boxdot$ $(a,0)$ (see [4, Defn.3]). However, once we propagate the zeros in this formula, we realize that the latter requires only half of a TRGSW ciphertext and half of the running time. Also $(a,0)$ has to be treated as a noiseless ciphertext, which seems a bit arbitrary. These points are better formally explained below via a concept that we call HalfRGSW ciphertext[2]. The latter can be used to multiply a secret $u \in \mathcal{R}$ with a public $v \in \mathbb{T}_N[X]$ via the $\boxtimes$ secret-public external product operation:

$$\texttt{HalfRGSW}(u) \boxtimes v \to \texttt{TRLWE}(u \cdot v)$$

rather than via the $\boxdot$ and the full TRGSW ciphertext of s^2.

For a secret $u \in \mathcal{R}$ and ℓ TRLWE ciphertexts of zero $Z := (A|B) \in \mathbb{T}_N[X]^{\ell \times 2}$, the HalfRGSW is defined as

$$\texttt{HalfRGSW}(u) := \left(A, B + u(B_g^{-1}, \ldots, B_g^{-\ell})\right) \in \mathbb{T}_N[X]^{2 \times \ell},$$

Note that for all valid TRLWE encryption $(a, b) \in \mathbb{T}_N[X]^2$ of v the element $\texttt{HalfRGSW}(u) \boxtimes b - \texttt{HalfRGSW}(us) \boxtimes a \in \mathbb{T}_N[X]^2$ is a valid TRLWE ciphertext (under s) of the plaintext $u \cdot v$. That yields a more flexible computation of a ciphertext of $u \cdot v$ instead of computing the traditional external product $\texttt{TRGSW}(u) \boxdot (a, b)$, thus, justifying the principle that *two halves make a whole*. As a bonus, a speed-up can be achieved by using different parameters for the two halves, especially in small levels as in the bootstrapping of TFHE.

Definition 3.3 (bivariate RLWE ciphertexts). *Let K be a limb size. A bivRLWE ciphertext C under a small key $S \in \mathbb{Z}_N[X]$ of the message $m \in \mathbb{T}_N[X]$ is materialized by a tuple $(A, B) \in \mathcal{R}[Y]^2$ of K-normalized and reduced representations whose phase $\varphi_{S,K}(A, B) \underset{def}{=} \phi_K(B) - S \cdot \phi_K(A)$ is equal to $m + e$ where $e \in \mathbb{T}_N[X]$ is a small Gaussian error. We will note $\texttt{bivRLWE}_{S,K,2^{-L}}(m)$ such bivariate RLWE encryption of m with error bound 2^{-L}*

Note that bivRLWE ciphertexts satisfy the following *prefix property*: a higher precision ciphertext with small error yields a lower precision one by simply restricting the representation to the first few limbs (prefix). For instance, when restricting a high precision ciphertext (A, B) of error norm $\leq 2^{-L+1}$ to degrees $\ell_B = \lceil (L+2)/K \rceil$ and $\ell_A = \lceil (L+2+\log_2 \|S\|_1)/K \rceil$ in B and A, respectively, we obtain an encryption of the same plaintext with error $\leq 2^{-L}$. The importance of the *prefix property* is that it is a computation-free version of modulus switching. We assume that all bivRLWE ciphertexts of precision 2^{-L} are instantiated with degrees ℓ_A, ℓ_B in Y. We also consider the bivariate HalfRGSW counterpart:

Definition 3.4 (bivariate HalfRGSW encryptions). *Let $K, \tilde{K}$ be limb sizes, let $u \in \mathcal{R}$ be a small polynomial of norm $\|u\|_1 \leq \kappa$ and let $S \in \mathcal{R}$ be a small key. We define $\texttt{bivHalfRGSW}_{S,K,\tilde{K},2^{-L}}(u)$ (bivariate half RingGSW encryption of u under S with precision L) to be a family of $\texttt{bivRLWE}_{S,K,2^{-L}}$ ciphertexts of $u \cdot 2^{-\tilde{K}}, u \cdot 2^{-2\tilde{K}}, \ldots, u \cdot 2^{-\tilde{\ell}\tilde{K}}$. The family can be restricted to its first $\tilde{\ell} = \lceil (L + 2 + \log_2 \kappa)/\tilde{K} \rceil$ ciphertexts. If the bivHalfRGSW encryption is given in DFT basis, we denote it by $\texttt{bivHalfRGSW}^{\texttt{DFT}}$.*

---

[2] In [11] this ciphertext is called RLev, we could also name it $RK(u)$ since it has the shape of a relinearization key. However the GSW name better depicts the fact that it is a ciphertext not some key material, and most importantly, the $\boxtimes$ morphism is half of the $\boxdot$ operation.

These ciphertexts also satisfy an even stronger prefix property: from any bivHalfRGSW ciphertext C of high precision $\leq 2^{-(L+1)}$, the truncations to degrees ℓ_A, ℓ_B above of its first $\tilde{\ell} = \lceil (L + 2 + \log_2(\kappa))/\tilde{K} \rceil$ bivRLWE ciphertexts form a bivHalfRGSW of the same message with lower precision $\leq 2^{-L}$.

Because of the prefix property, these ciphertexts can be passed to any function that require a lower precision level $L' < L$: in this case, the function will only access the terms of degree $\ell'_A \leq \ell_A$ and $\ell'_B \leq \ell_B$ from the first $\tilde{\ell}' \leq \tilde{\ell}$ elements. This property holds both on paper and also in efficient implementations, where ciphertexts are passed by pointers.

Theorem 3.1 (half external product (secret×public)). *Let $u \in \mathcal{R}$ be a small polynomial of norm $\|u\|_1 \leq \kappa$ for some $\kappa > 0$, let $a \in \mathbb{T}_N[X]$ and let L an output precision parameter. Let $L_\alpha, L_\beta \geq L$ be parameters satisfying $2^{-L_\alpha} + 2^{-L_\beta} \leq 2^{-L}$ and let $L_1 = L_\alpha + \log_2 \kappa$, $\tilde{\ell} = \lceil L_1/K \rceil$ and $L_2 = L_\beta + \tilde{K} + \log_2(N\tilde{\ell})$. If $C_f = (c_1, \ldots, c_{\tilde{\ell}})$ is a $\text{bivHalfRGSW}^{DFT}_{S,K,\tilde{K},2^{-L_2}}$ encryption of u with precision $\leq 2^{-L_2}$ and $A(X,Y) = \sum_{i=1}^{\tilde{\ell}} A_i \cdot Y^i$ is a $\tilde{K}$-normalized and reduced representation of $a \in \mathbb{T}_N[X]$ up to 2^{-L_1} then the ciphertext*

$$C_f \mathbin{\triangle} a = \text{normalizeReduce} \left(\text{iDFT} \left(\sum_{i=1}^{\tilde{\ell}} \text{DFT}(A_i) \cdot c_i \right) \right)$$

is a $\text{bivRLWE}_{S,K,2^{-L}}$ encryption of $u \cdot a$. Homomorphic evaluation of such an external product with $\tilde{\ell} = \lceil L_1/\tilde{K} \rceil$ and $\ell = \lceil (L_2 + \log_2 N + 2)/K \rceil$ requires

- *$\tilde{\ell}$ bounded DFT's of the $A'_i s$ of norm $\leq 2^{\tilde{K}-1}$,*
- *$2\ell\tilde{\ell}$ element-wise addmul's in DFT domain for polynomials of norm $\leq N\tilde{\ell}2^{\tilde{K}+K-2}$,*
- *2ℓ bounded iDFT's for the results $C_j(X)$ with norm bound $N\tilde{\ell}2^{\tilde{K}+K-2}$,*
- *2ℓ element-wise additions/shifts/masks to normalize and truncate the result.*

Proof. Letting $e = a - \sum_{i=1}^{\tilde{\ell}} A_i \cdot 2^{\tilde{K}i}$, we have $\|e\|_\infty \leq 2^{-L_1}$. If $c'_i = \text{iDFT}(c_i)$ for $i = 1, \ldots, \tilde{\ell}$ then $\varphi_{S,K}(c'_i) = u \cdot 2^{-\tilde{K}i} + e_i$ where $\|e_i\|_\infty \leq 2^{-L_2}$. Since $C_f \mathbin{\triangle} a = \text{normalizeRed}(\sum_{i=1}^{\tilde{\ell}} A_i \cdot c'_i)$, it follows that $\varphi_{S,K}(C_f \mathbin{\triangle} a) = \sum_{i=1}^{\tilde{\ell}} A_i \cdot \varphi_{S,K}(c'_i) = u \cdot \left(\sum_{i=1}^{\tilde{\ell}} A_i \cdot 2^{-\tilde{K}i} \right) + \sum_{i=1}^{\tilde{\ell}} A_i \cdot e_i$, and therefore, $\|\varphi_{S,K}(C_f \mathbin{\triangle} a) - u \cdot a\|_\infty \leq \|u \cdot e\|_\infty + \sum_{i=1}^{\tilde{\ell}} \|A_i \cdot e_i\|_\infty \leq 2^{-L_\alpha} + 2^{-L_\beta} \leq 2^{-L}$. The rest of the theorem is a simple count of operations, the degrees of c_i being bounded by ℓ. $\square$

The above theorem applies to the traditional key switching, automorphisms and relinearization operations. To recover the traditional homomorphic product of a secret u by a bivRLWE encrypted ciphertext $(a,b) \in \mathcal{R}[Y]^2$ under a small key $s \in \mathbb{Z}_N[X]$, we can use one bivHalfRGSW ciphertext C_u of u and one bivHalfRGSW ciphertext C_{su} of su, and call the pair $C = (C_u, C_{su})$ a full bivRGSW(u). The full external product is then

$$C \mathbin{\square} (a,b) = C_u \mathbin{\triangle} b - C_{su} \mathbin{\triangle} a. \tag{6}$$

Note that since the norms $\|u\|_1$ and $\|su\|_1$ in the two halves are distinct, Theorem 3.1 suggests the use of distinct parameters for each half. This reflects the natural property that in a RingLWE ciphertext (a, b), it suffices to provide the term b up to a lower precision compared to the term a. In the next section, we show that this speeds up the bootstrapping of TFHE by removing 12.5% of the FFTs and 16.7% of the products and decompositions.

We also merge the final normalizations of the two half-products together to obtain the following

Corollary 3.2 (full external product (secret×secret)). *Let $K, \tilde{K}, \tilde{K}'$ be limb sizes, let $u \in \mathcal{R}$ be a small polynomial, let $v \in \mathbb{T}_N[X]$ be a message, let $s \in \mathcal{R}$ a small key and and $2^{-L} > 0$ be a target output precision. For all $L_\alpha, L_\beta, L_\gamma \geq L$ satisfying $2^{-L_\alpha} + 2^{-L_\beta} + 2^{-L_\gamma} \leq 2^{-L}$, let $L_1 = L_\alpha + \log_2 \|u\|_1$, $\tilde{\ell}_B = \lceil (L_1+2)/\tilde{K} \rceil$, $\tilde{\ell}_A = \lceil (L_1 + 2 + \log_2 \|s\|_1)/\tilde{K}' \rceil$, $L_2 = L_\beta + \tilde{K} + \log_2(N\tilde{\ell}_B)$ and $L'_2 = L_\gamma + \tilde{K}' + \log_2(N\tilde{\ell}_A)$. If $(A, B) \in \mathcal{R}[Y]^2$ is a $\mathtt{bivRLWE}_{s,K}$ of $v \in \mathbb{T}_N[X]$ with noise $\leq 2^{-L_1}$, if $C_u = (c_1, \ldots, c_{\tilde{\ell}})$ is a $\mathtt{bivHalfRGSW}_{s,K,\tilde{K}}$ encryption of u with precision 2^{-L_2} and if $C_{su} = (d_1, \ldots, d_{\tilde{\ell}})$ is a $\mathtt{bivHalfRGSW}_{s,\tilde{K}'}$ encryption of su with precision $2^{-L'_2}$ then*

$$(C_u, C_{su}) \boxdot (a, b) = \mathtt{normalizeRed}\left(\mathtt{iDFT}\left(\sum_{i=1}^{\tilde{\ell}_B} \mathtt{DFT}(B_i) \cdot c_i - \sum_{i=1}^{\tilde{\ell}_A} \mathtt{DFT}(A_i) \cdot d_i \right) \right),$$

is a $\mathtt{bivRLWE}_{S,K,2^{-L}}$ encryption of $u \cdot v$. Here, A and B have been $\tilde{K}'$ and $\tilde{K}$-normalized, respectively. In addition, computing this encryption with $\ell = \lceil (L'_2 + \log_2 N + 2)/K \rceil$ requires at most

- *$\tilde{\ell}_A + \tilde{\ell}_B$ bounded DFT's of the A_i, B_i's of norm $\leq 2^{\tilde{K}-1}$,*
- *$2\ell(\tilde{\ell}_A + \tilde{\ell}_B)$ element-wise $\mathtt{addmul}$'s in DFT domain for polynomials of norm $\leq 2N\tilde{\ell}2^{\tilde{K}+K-2}$,*
- *2ℓ bounded iDFT's for the results $C_j(X)$ with norm bound $2N\tilde{\ell}2^{\tilde{K}+K-2}$,*
- *$\tilde{\ell}_A + \tilde{\ell}_B + 2\ell$ element-wise additions/shifts or masks to normalize and truncate the input ciphertext and the final result.*

Proof. Let $d'_i = \mathtt{iDFT}(d_i)$ and $c'_i = \mathtt{iDFT}(c_i)$, by the same proof as in Theorem 3.1, $\varphi_{S,K}(\sum_{i=1}^{\tilde{\ell}_B} B_i \cdot c'_i) = u \cdot \phi_{\tilde{K}}(B) + e_1$ where $\|e_1\|_\infty \leq 2^{-L_\beta}$ and $\varphi_{S,K}(\sum_{i=1}^{\tilde{\ell}_A} A_i \cdot d'_i) = su \cdot \phi_{\tilde{K}'}(A) + e_2$ where $\|e_2\|_\infty \leq 2^{-L_\gamma}$. Therefore, $\varphi_{S,K}(C \boxdot (A, B))$ is the difference $u \cdot (\phi_{\tilde{K}}(B) - s \cdot \phi_{\tilde{K}'}(A)) + e_1 - e_2 = u \cdot \varphi_{S,K}(A, B) + e_1 - e_2$. Since $\varphi_{S,K}(A, B) = v + e$ where $e \leq 2^{-L_1}$, we have $\|\varphi_{S,K}(C \boxdot (A, B)) - u \cdot v\|_\infty \leq 2^{-L_\alpha} + 2^{-L_\beta} + 2^{-L_\gamma} \leq 2^{-L}$. $\qquad\square$

3.3 Public Linear Combinations

The main difference and advantage of the bivariate representation, over the more classical base-2^K representation is the ability to decouple and delay carry propagation, which leaves the opportunity to do a lot of linear algebra between two normalizations. The bivariate representation is linear over $\mathbb{Z}$ and $\mathbb{Z}_N[X]$, so linear combinations $\sum_{i=1}^{k}(\lambda_i \cdot m_i)$ of ciphertexts can primarily be evaluated termwise. From a normalized representation, if the intent of normalization is to maintain the base arithmetic bounded, e.g. by $O(\ell N 2^{2K})$ like in the external product, it leaves enough room to evaluate more than $\ell N 2^K$ (so more than 100000) simple additions and subtractions before a single normalization is needed. To evaluate linear combinations with larger coefficients, where $\|\lambda_i\|_\infty$ are larger than 2^K, we can use the same strategy as for the external product: decompose the integer coefficients λ_i in base 2^K to represent them under the form $\sum_{j=1}^{p} e_j 2^{Kj}$, and precompute the DFT of the e_j's. ($p = 2$ or 3 terms are sufficient to represent the constant coefficients λ_i that appear in a BFV or CKKS bootstrapping). The linear combination is then easy to apply under this form, and requires only $O(p\ell)$ element-wise products, which is still negligible compared to the cost of an external product.

3.4   Automorphisms in BFV and CKKS

Unlike external products that can operate with very short keys and large noise, BFV and CKKS arithmetic usually operate on much larger parameters, where a single limb is in general the optimal choice. For the rest of the section, we will therefore consider that there is a unique limb size K (i.e. $K = \tilde{K}$).

Automorphisms of $\mathbb{T}_N[X]$ are $\mathcal{R}$-module homomorphisms. These are the *rotation/conjugation* functions $\sigma_k \colon \mathbb{T}_N[X] \to \mathbb{T}_N[X]$ that substitutes the variable X with X^k where k is odd. $\sigma_k(a)$ can be computed efficiently in coefficient space over the bivariate representations $\mathbb{Z}[X,Y]/\langle X^N + 1\rangle$ by treating each power of Y independently and mapping $\sum_{i=1}^{\ell} A_i(X)Y^i$ to $\sum_{i=1}^{\ell} \sigma_k(A_i(X))Y^i$.

Over ciphertexts, we just need to observe that $\sigma(b - sa) = \sigma(b) - \sigma(s) \cdot \sigma(a)$, so given an bivHalfRGSW encryption of $\sigma(s)$, we recover the well known homomorphic evaluation:

Lemma 3.5 (Automorphism in BFV and CKKS). *Let K be a limb size, let $v \in \mathbb{T}_N[X]$ be a message, let σ be an automorphism of $\mathbb{T}_N[X]$ and let L be an output precision parameter. For all $L_\alpha, L_\beta \geq L$ that satisfy $2^{-L_\alpha} + 2^{-L_\beta} \leq 2^{-L}$, if $(a, b) \in \mathcal{R}[Y]^2$ is a bivRLWE$_{s,K}$ encryption of $v \in \mathbb{T}_N[X]$ with noise 2^{-L_α} and $C_{\sigma(s)}$ is a bivHalfRGSW$_{s,K,K}$ of $\sigma(s)$ with noise 2^{-L_β}, then*

$$\boxed{\sigma}((a,b)) = (0, \sigma(b)) - C_{\sigma(s)} \boxtimes \sigma(a)$$

is a bivRLWE$_{s,K}$ encryption of $\sigma(v)$ with noise $\leq 2^{-L}$. Note that we can omit the normalizeReduce operation of the $\boxtimes$ operation in Theorem 3.1 and compute it at the end, after the subtraction. Computing this operation with $\tilde{\ell} = \lceil L_\alpha/K \rceil$ and $\ell = \lceil (L_\beta + \log_2 N + 2)/K \rceil$ requires, as in Theorem 3.1,

- *$\tilde{\ell}$ bounded DFT's of the A_i's, of norm $\leq 2^{K-1}$,*
- *$2\ell\tilde{\ell}$ element-wise addmul's in DFT domain for polynomials of norm $\leq N\tilde{\ell}2^{2K-2}$,*

- 2ℓ *bounded DFT's for the results* $C_{\sigma(s)}(X)$ *with norm bound* $N\widetilde{\ell}2^{2K-2}$,
- 2ℓ *element-wise additions/shifts/masks to normalize and truncate the final result,*
- *(in addition to the computations in Theorem 3.1),* 2ℓ *evaluations of* σ *over the input* A_i *and* B_i, *of norm bound* 2^K.

Proof. We first verify that $\varphi_{s,K}(\boxed{\sigma}((a,b)))$ is close to $\sigma(v)$. We compute the noise level of the output as $\left\|\varphi_{s,K}(\boxed{\sigma}((a,b))) - \sigma(v)\right\|_\infty = \left\|\phi_K(\sigma(b)) - \varphi_{s,K}(C_{\sigma(s)} \triangle \sigma(a)) - \sigma(v)\right\|_\infty = \left\|\sigma(\phi_K(b))) - \sigma(v) - \sigma(s\phi_k(a)) + \sigma(s\phi_k(a)) - \varphi_{s,K}(C \triangle \sigma(a))\right\|_\infty \leq \left\|\sigma(\phi_K(b) - s\phi_K(a) - v)\right\|_\infty + \left\|\sigma(s\phi_K(a)) - \varphi_{s,K}(C_{\sigma(s)} \triangle \sigma(a))\right\|_\infty$. Per the LWE definition, and because σ is an isometry, $\left\|\sigma(\phi_K(b) - s\phi_K(a) - v)\right\|_\infty = \left\|\sigma(e)\right\|_\infty = \left\|e\right\|_\infty \leq 2^{-L_\alpha}$. Per Theorem 3.1, the second term is a (half) external product noise bounded by $\left\|\sigma(s)\sigma(\phi_K(a)) - \varphi_{s,K}(C_{\sigma(s)} \triangle \sigma(a))\right\|_\infty \leq 2^{-L_\beta}$. Summing the two, the output noise is bounded by $2^{-L_\alpha} + 2^{-L_\beta} \leq 2^{-L}$. $\qquad\square$

3.5   Internal Products in BFV and CKKS

In the previous section, we showed how to efficiently compute homomorphic external products and automorphisms using leveled-FFT. We now discuss how to efficiently compute homomorphic internal products between two TRLWE ciphertexts as defined in Sect. 2 and in [4].

Using the notation of Sect. 2, to evaluate a BFV or CKKS product between two RingLWE ciphertexts, we first apply (6) to the relinearization term of (1):

$$\mathtt{TRGSW}(s) \boxdot (P_2, 0) = \mathtt{bivHalfRGSW}(s) \triangle 0 - \mathtt{bivHalfRGSW}(s^2) \triangle P_2$$

After substituting the expression in (1), the internal product becomes

$$(a_1, b_1) \boxtimes (a_2, b_2) = (P_1, P_0) + \mathtt{bivHalfRGSW}(s^2) \triangle P_2, \qquad (7)$$

where $P_0 = b_1 \otimes_\star b_2$, $P_2 = a_1 \otimes_\star a_2$, $P_1 = a_1 \otimes_\star b_2 + b_1 \otimes_\star a_2$ for $\star = \{\mathtt{BFV}, \mathtt{CKKS}\}$ depending on whether one computes the BFV product (2) or the CKKS product (3).

We compute the internal product using that formula by first approximating the inputs by bivariate polynomials via the evaluation ring homomorphism (4). Lifts from the torus to the real fields come for free, and rounding in CKKS is a simple truncation and bit masking operation on the last limb. We then use DFT bivariate polynomial multiplication (in X and Y) to evaluate the products $\otimes_\star$ and hence, compute approximations of P_0, P_1 and P_2. We use DFT over X and Y for the latter which runs in asymptotic complexity $O(\ell \log_2 \ell)$ SIMD operations on vectors of size N. This computation is asymptotically negligible compared to the half TRGSW product $\triangle$ in (7) that requires $2\ell^2$ such SIMD operations. In practice, even for smaller dimensions where one may use polynomial multiplication that is quadratic in ℓ, the run-time of computing $\otimes_\star$ never exceeds 75% of the run-time of computing $\triangle$. We summarize the complexity in the theorem below and provide detailed discussion of the optimizations in the full version of the paper [3].

Theorem 3.2 (CKKS/BFV **product complexity**). *The homomorphic CKKS or BFV product between two* bivRLWE *ciphertexts* (a_1, b_1) *and* $(a_2, b_2) \in \mathcal{R}[Y]^2$ *with a relinearization key* $RK = $ bivHalfRGSW(s^2) *where* s *is the secret key requires:*

- 8ℓ *DFT/IDFTs in* X *(including* 3ℓ *of them for the external product)*
- $2\ell^2 + \min\left(7\ell \log_2 \ell + 9\ell, \frac{3}{2}\ell(\ell-1) + 4\ell\right)$ *SIMD operations (add, mul, addmul or twiddle factors) on vectors of size* N *(including* $2\ell^2$ *for the external product).*
- 3ℓ *SIMD rounding/normalization operations on vectors of size* N *(including* 2ℓ *of them in the external product).*

This lemma shows that as ℓ grows, the asymptotic complexity of an internal product is exactly the same as that of the underlying external product (i.e. $O(\ell^2 N)$) and the overhead induced by the rest of the operations is negligible. In practice, since the SIMD operations dominate, the run-time is at most 1.75 times the running time of the underlying external product for small values of ℓ.

We conclude this section with Table 1, which recalls the number of N-dimensional DFT's and the number of SIMD operations over vectors of $N/2$ complexes, for one half external product (so either one keyswitch or one automorphism), as well as the number of such operations in one CKKS or BFV product. Although the maximal levels for L for 128-bit security are 1761 and 880 for $N = 65536$ and 32768 respectively, we use $L = 1729$ and $L = 865$ as in the implementation provided by the authors of [23] to facilitate the comparison with their work. The table confirms that the larger we can choose the limb size K, the less elementary operations are required. We will show in the following sections that each choice of backend naturally comes with one maximal value of K it can process: for instance, the double floating points FFT is limited to $K = 19$, but other 128-bit constructions can afford larger limb sizes, which we explain in Sect. 6 together with some benchmarks.

Table 1. Number of operations in one half-external product (i.e. one relinearization, one keyswitch, or one automorphism) and in one BFV/CKKS internal product (IP). The rows in bold correspond to the optimal value of K.

$N = 65536$, $L = 1729$						$N = 32768$, $L = 865$				
K	ℓ	# DFTs	# SIMD prods	# IP DFTs	# IP SIMD prods	ℓ	# DFTs	# SIMD prods	# IP DFTs	# IP SIMD prods
16	109	327	23762	763	30278	55	165	6050	385	8927
19	**91**	**273**	**16562**	**637**	**22889**	**46**	**138**	**4232**	**322**	**7016**
22	79	237	12482	553	18683	40	120	3200	280	5600
...										
46	38	114	2888	266	5054	19	57	722	133	1263
49	36	108	2592	252	4536	18	54	648	126	1134
52	**34**	**102**	**2312**	**238**	**4046**	**17**	**51**	**578**	**119**	**1011**

The dominant part of the computation is spent in the SIMD products (or assimilated), the cost of the DFTs remains very small. $K = 19$ is the largest limb-size achieved via float64 FFT whereas $K = 52$ is achieved via 120-bit NTT. Because elementary operations are faster in the first case, it compensates the additional number of operations, and the two backends end up give similar final running time: SIMD products for $N = 65536$ are micro-benchmarked at $27\mu s$ in the float64 scenario, whereas the equivalent counterpart for 120-bit NTT take $93\mu s$. The number of SIMD products per internal product in Table 1 is an upper-bound that considers the best choice between the naive multiplication in $3\ell(\ell - 1)/2$ and the DFT one in $O(\ell \log_2(\ell))$. Because ℓ has to be rounded up to the next power of two, some nodes in the resulting Cooley-Tuckey recursion would compute zeros: these nodes have been eliminated from the count in this table.

4   Accelerating TFHE Gate Bootstrapping

In this section, we show how the concept of halfTRGSW can speed-up the TFHE library [33]. One TFHE gate bootstrapping is computing $n = 630$ successive TRGSW-TRLWE external products. We defer to the noise propagation analysis in [9] and the lattice estimator [1] for the explanations on lattice security but in summary, there are two constraints on the external products:

- *Lattice security constraint.* Any TRLWE or TRGSW ciphertext encrypted with an $N = 1024$ dimensional key (binary or ternary) must have a noise variance parameter of at least $V_{GSW} = 2^{-50}$ (stdev 2^{-25}) to provide 128-bits of security.
- *Correctness of bootstrapping constraint.* Each individual external product output shall make the noise variance grow by at most $\Delta_{max} = 8.4961.10^{-8}$ to ensure that the final ciphertext is decryptable.

Since the ratio between Δ_{max}/V_{GSW} is very small, we have to pick the external product parameters with extreme care. For instance, it is unrealistic to try to take $K = \tilde{K}$, instead, the choice in TFHE is to decrease $\tilde{K}$ as much as needed to contain the noise growth of TRGSW ciphertexts, and maintain K to a fixed value 32, so that TRLWE use a single limb of 32-bits, and correspond to our bivRLWE with $\ell = 1$. Also, the worst-case bounds on noise amplitude increase too fast compared to the reality: as it is shown in LWE, we can use the average-case noise propagation formula, which is essentially a transcription of the worst-case theorems where all noises are assimilated to independent Gaussian samples and the theorem operates on their variance instead of their infinity norm.

With this in mind, in TFHE, the noise propagation of a TRGSW-TRLWE external product (adapted to use the notations of this paper), between a TRGSW ciphertext of error variance V_{GSW} for a decomposition in $\tilde{\ell}$ limbs of $\tilde{K}$ bits, and an input TRLWE ciphertext of noise variance V_{in}, is:

$$V_{out} - V_{in} \leq 2\tilde{\ell}N4^{\tilde{K}-1}V_{GSW} + (1 + \underbrace{N}_{\|S\|_2^2})4^{-\tilde{K}\tilde{\ell}-1}. \tag{8}$$

The choices of $\tilde{K}, \tilde{\ell}$ in TFHE library are 7 and 3, which correspond to a variance growth of $2.2410.10^{-8} < \Delta_{\max}$ per external product. As we know that the running time of TFHE is proportional to the number of FFTs per external products, this number is $2\tilde{\ell} + 2 = 8$.

We can also see that any attempt to reduce the number of FFTs by setting $\tilde{\ell} = 2$ for instance fails, as no more limb size $\tilde{K}$ exists that makes $V_{\text{out}} - V_{\text{in}}$ in Eq. (8) smaller than $\Delta_{\max}$. That's precisely where the concept of HalfRGSW helps: if the input TRLWE is (A, B), and we are allowed to pick different parameters and dimensions $\tilde{K}_A, \tilde{\ell}_A$ and $\tilde{K}_B, \tilde{\ell}_B$, the variance growth bound of Eq. (8) becomes, by analogy with our Corollary 3.2:

$$\left(\tilde{\ell}_A N 4^{\tilde{K}_A - 1} V_{\text{GSW}} + N \cdot 4^{-\tilde{K}_A \tilde{\ell}_A - 1}\right) + \left(\tilde{\ell}_B N 4^{\tilde{K}_B - 1} V_{\text{GSW}} + 1 \cdot 4^{-\tilde{K}_B \tilde{\ell}_B - 1}\right)$$

Not unsurprisingly, the term in $\tilde{K}_A, \tilde{\ell}_A$ is already tight, so the value $(7, 3)$ remains optimal. However the absence of the factor N in the second term (analogue of $\|s\|_1$ in worst-case formulae, which only affects the half external product term in A) gives us much more flexibility on the choices of $\tilde{K}_B, \tilde{\ell}_B$. It turns out that we can finally reduce $\tilde{\ell}_B$ to 2 and use $\tilde{K}_B = 8$. We indeed obtain the following variance growth: $2.986053 \cdot 10^{-8}$ for the half external product in A and $1.1234 \cdot 10^{-8}$ for the one in B, and we verify that the sum $4.10946 \cdot 10^{-8}$ stays $\leq \Delta_{\max}$, and is thus suitable for bootstrapping.

Because of that improvement compared to the TFHE library default parameter set, the number of FFTs in TFHE decreases to $\tilde{\ell}_A + \tilde{\ell}_B + 2 = 7$ instead of 8 per external product (so 12.5% less FFTs), and the other linear operations, decompositions, and matrix multiplications also drop by 16.6%, since the outer loop has only 5 iterations instead of 6.

Table 2. Performance comparison of gate bootstrapping with a n2-standard GCP instance with 64GB of RAM and a 12-th Gen i7-1260p laptop with 64GB of RAM. All the benchmarks are single core.

Library	Instruction set	n2-standard	12-Gen i7-1260p
TFHE-lib, spqlios-fma	AVX2	22.4 ms	10.4 ms
TFHE-rs, TFHE_LIB_PARAMETERS	AVX2	18.2 ms	8.6 ms
	AVX512	14.4 ms	*not supported*
TFHE-rs, DEFAULT_PARAMETERS	AVX2	14.4 ms	7.6 ms
	AVX512	13.7 ms	*not supported*
Our work, halfTRGSW	AVX2	11.2 ms	5.3 ms

We first implemented this concept as a simple patch to the original TFHE library by overriding the tGswExternMulToTLwe function and removing the last iteration of the loop. On a n2-standard Xeon, we already witnessed a decrease of the NAND gate bootstrapping by 3ms which matches the expected theoretical speedup. In order to compare our proof-of-concept to the fastest CPU bootstrapping whose reference implementation is the TFHE-rs library [36], we then extracted and re-implemented the entire blindrotate_woKS loop obtaining another 2x speedup by back-porting the following engineering improvements: from the TFHE-rs optimizations, we used the fast AVX floating-point flooring, conversions to and from integer and bit-decompositions that work on bounded floating-point numbers that are never infinite, NaN, or subnormal. We also dropped completely the round-trip to the int32/int64 and reduced the numbers modulo $\mathbb{Z}$ directly over their floating point bits, so that the entire blind rotate procedure operates solely on the double-floating point precision domain. Finally, we incorporated the latest improvements from fast implementations of Falcon to the complex FFT described in [28, sec.5]: namely instead of evaluating the $\log_2(N/2)$ iterations of the FFT circuit one after the other, we execute them two by two and thus save half of the memory accesses. The last four iterations, that operate contiguously on vectors of 16 complex numbers are run entirely on registers. We did however not backport the DEFAULT_PARAMETERS optimization of TFHE-rs that consists of trading the ring dimension N against an increase of the module dimension, nor any AVX512 optimizations. Our prototype uses therefore only AVX2 instructions. Finally, since we did not have access to a Xeon Platinum, we have run our experiments on two different architectures: one "slow" cloud instance, which is a GCP n2-standard Xeon CPU Cascade Lake at 2.8 GHz with 4 cores, 8vCPU and 64 GB of RAM (left column of Table 2), and one "fast" laptop with a AlderLake Core i7-1260P at 4.7 GHz with 64 GB of RAM (right column of Table 2). The fast laptop does not have AVX512, whose support was discontinued by Intel, but it has a much higher cache and memory access rates than the Cascade Lake counterpart, so timings on this machine are often very close to those published with a bare metal server with a Xeon Platinum: overall, Table 2 gives a neat intuition of the range of performance we can expect depending on the CPU. The combination of the half external product and all the other engineering optimizations described in this paragraph make our new bootstrapping running time as low as 5.3 milliseconds per NAND gate, which is the new single core record, even though it sticks to a traditional ring-lwe parameter-set and does not use any AVX512 instructions.

5   Frontend and Large Number Arithmetic: Bivariate Versus CRT Representations

The main idea in both [23] and the present work is the decoupling of the cyclotomic arithmetic (the backend representation) from the large number arithmetic (the frontend representation) in BFV, CKKS, TFHE and Chimera which, in turn, allows to fully benefit from the small polynomial coefficients produced by the gadget decomposition. Taking one step further, both works suggest a frontend/backend separation where TRLWE ciphertexts are represented non-uniquely by their gadget decomposition: a vector of small polynomials

$\in (\mathbb{Z}_N[X])^\ell$. The content of the vector being the coefficients in Y for the bivariate representation, the centered and reduced coefficients mod q_i for CRT representations, and in general any other gadget-decomposed representation. Similarly, half-TRGSW ciphertexts would correspond to a matrix of $\ell \times 2\ell$ small integer polynomials. The most complex operation that arises in the external product is an efficient vector $\times$ matrix product, where the matrix is preprocessed in an offline phase. The online phase of the product is carried out by the backend API using the appropriate DFTs. Cheaper operations are of course, element-wise additions, scaling, rotations and automorphisms, as well as normalization whose role is to keep the representation small. Depending on the frontend, the bivariate approach benefits from the fact that modulus rescaling just requires a prefix truncation of the normalized representation, but has a $O(\ell.\log_2(\ell)) \otimes_\star$ products. CRT frontends have a more expensive modulus rescaling, but faster $O(\ell)$ internal products. With the operations described in Sect. 3.2, the bivariate and CRT frontends can be instantiated on the same backend API and offer similar performance. CRT frontends should be preferred for use-cases involving large homomorphic matrix products, as the external products and modulus rescaling can in these cases be amortized, and the frontend benefits from the faster $\otimes_\star$ products. On the opposite, the bivariate frontend is preferred when the use cases have fewer internal products and rely on lookup-tables, trace algorithms, circuit bootstrappings or when the homomorphic internal products are sequential. These use cases benefit from the fact that $\otimes_{\mathsf{CKKS}}$ can be instantiated at any noise level L on the bivariate frontend, rather than at integer multiplicative levels (multiples of $\log_2(q_i)$) in the CRT frontend. A more in-depth comparison is provided in [3]. Finally, since the external product is fast on both frontends (the CRT one via [23], and the bivariate one from Sect. 3.2), the half-external product can be used to switch dynamically between both on more complex use cases, which is also interesting from a scheme switching perspective.

6   Backend Arithmetic and Cyclotomic Multiplications: Approximate FFT or NTT

At a low level, we need efficient arithmetic (additions and multiplications) in the cyclotomic ring $\mathcal{R}$ where the coefficients of the polynomials are integers bounded by $B'_{\mathsf{worst}} = 2\ell N 2^{K+\tilde{K}-2}$ in the worst case. We can get a tighter average case bound if we pay closer attention to the expressions present in the previous section. We then notice that it is sufficient for such arithmetic to be able to successfully evaluate, with overwhelming probability, expressions of the form $\sum_{i=1}^{2\ell} a_i(X) \cdot b_i(X)$ where a, b have their coefficients computationally indistinguishable from uniformly distributed in respectively $[-2^{K-1}, -2^{K-1})$ and $[-2^{\tilde{K}-1}, -2^{\tilde{K}-1})$. Indeed, these inputs are base-2^K decompositions of LWE ciphertexts or fresh GSW ciphertexts, and any computational bias against the uniform distribution would form an attack on these schemes. In other words, if we randomize bivRLWE ciphertexts during normalization (e.g. we can always mask them with random ciphertexts of zero), with an overwhelming probability $1 - \varepsilon$

the arithmetic just needs to handle elements of size $B'_{\mathrm{avg}} = C_\varepsilon\sqrt{2\ell N}2^{K+K'-2}$ instead of the worst case $B'_{\mathrm{worst}} = 2\ell N 2^{K+K'-2}$. We will use $C_\varepsilon = 17$ in this section, that corresponds to an error probability $\varepsilon < 2^{-40}$.

We present two equivalently good ways of handling such arithmetic: floating point or fixed-point approximations of the continuous FFT on backends whose mantissa can store B', or NTT over a friendly modulus larger than B'. The underlying arithmetic must be sufficiently atomic to be considered as native operations, therefore we will limit ourselves to 64-bit or 128-bit B'.

In a nutshell, the main result is that each choice of backend is bound to a precision B' and lead to a maximal limb size K: for all practical HE dimensions, the `float64` backend corresponds to $K \leq 19$, the `float128` backend (or fixed-point backends via 104-bit arithmetic in `AVX_IFMA`) would correspond to $K \leq 49$, doing NTT over a 60-bits modulus corresponds to $K \leq 22$, and $K \leq 52$ for a 120-bit modulus. And the key takeaway is that the most important success factor for a backend to be FHE friendly is to support the largest machine-word arithmetic; it is much less important if that arithmetic is modulo a power of two (fixed-point FFT), modulo a user-friendly prime number (NTT), or floating point (FFT).

6.1   Floating Point Backends

The first choice when it comes to FFT on bounded numbers is floating point backends. This algorithm is well studied and has been successfully used in the `TFHE` library since its origins. A naïve application of the formula $B'_{\mathrm{avg}} = C_\varepsilon\sqrt{2\ell N}2^{K+\tilde{K}-2}$ for $K = \tilde{K}$ and provided that we can use the 52 bits of mantissa without loss would bound K around 19. However, a lot of intermediate floating point operations occur between the start of the FFT, the products, the inverse FFT and we have to guarantee that the final error remains bounded by $1/2$ to be recoverable by rounding. We decided to treat the problem experimentally, by sampling uniformly random polynomials $A(X), B(X) \in \mathcal{R}$ with coefficients $\in [-2^{K-1}, 2^{K-1})$, multiplying these two polynomials via $C = iFFT(FFT(A) * FFT(B))$ using 64-bit double-precision floats, and measuring the amplitude and the standard deviation of the error $C - AB$, as a function of N and K. The results are provided in Table 3 and the following paragraphs describe the experiment in more detail. From these measurements, we estimate the probability that a sum of such terms satisfy $\left\|\sum_{i=1}^{2\ell} C_i - A_iB_i\right\|_\infty < 1/2$, which is sufficient to recover the actual result by rounding.

Lemma 6.1. *Let $\ell, N \in \mathbb{N}$ and $\varepsilon > 0$. The maximal value of σ such that with probability $\geq 1 - \varepsilon$, the sum $v = \sum_{i=1}^{2\ell} v_i$ of 2ℓ independent real vectors $v_i \in \mathbb{R}^N$ with independent Gaussian coordinates of mean 0 and stdev σ is bounded by $\|v_\infty\| < 1/2$ is $\sigma \leq 1/\left(\sqrt{16\ell}\,\mathrm{erfinv}\left((1-\varepsilon)^{1/N}\right)\right)$.*

For a target probability error $\varepsilon = 2^{-40}$, $N = 65536$ and $\ell = 100$, the maximum σ is 0.00414. Experimentally we have observed that for those values the largest limb size we can choose is $K = 19$ for 64-bit words. We obtain the same result with $N = 32768$. For completeness, we have run the same experiment with 128-bit words (float128) that have a mantissa of 112 bits. In this case we see that we can choose $K = 48$, however the obtained σ is very close and we could even choose $K = 49$ given that ℓ is going to be much smaller than 100 due to the constraints outlined in Table 1.

Table 3 shows the results of these experiments for different values of K and N for 64-bit (double) and 128-bit (float128) words. The objective is to find the largest value of K for a given error boundary.

Unfortunately, to this date, float128 is not a primitive type on x86 architectures and it's not available in all targets either. Additionally, float128 operations provide a poor performance compared to AVX accelerated doubles. Our experiment shows that due to the increased limb size K, large precision floats have potential, but without any dedicated hardware support, quad floats are not performant enough for our homomorphic backends. As an opening, we could however investigate the newer AVX-IFMA extensions set, whose instructions are already available on most recent commodity CPUs. These instructions allow to easily emulate 104-bit fixed-point arithmetic, and seems to be a perfect hardware-accelerated candidate for FFT computations, on a large limb sizes.

Table 3. Experimental standard deviation of floating point errors after a sum of FFT products for given N and varying K with 64 and 128-bit floats. The columns in bold correspond to the optimal value of K.

N	64-bit representation					128-bit representation					
65536	17	18	**19**	20	21	47	48	**49**	50	51	K
	0.0002	0.0008	**0.0031**	0.0124	0.0498	0.0003	0.0011	**0.00416**	0.0169	0.067	σ
32768	17	18	**19**	20	21	47	48	**49**	50	51	K
	0.0001	0.0005	**0.0021**	0.0085	0.034	0.0002	0.0007	**0.0028**	0.0112	0.0448	σ

6.2   NTT Backends over a Fixed Modulus

As an alternative to FFT over the complex numbers, it is well known that cyclotomic multiplications can also be carried out by NTT, which has been the default choice in the Full-RNS representation and later in [23]. All we need is a choice of one modulus or a product of moduli larger than B' that are NTT-friendly (unlike the frontend-ones in the CRT-representation) and replace all DFTs by NTT. NTT over moduli that are products of 30-bit or 60-bit primes can be accelerated on processors supporting AVX2 extensions of x86 architectures. Note that due to the overhead necessary for modular reductions as well as the missing support for native 64-bit SIMD integer multiplication on AVX2[3], one NTT on a 30-bit modulus requires the same number of clock cycles as one FFT on 64-bit floating points. Similarly, all NVIDIA GPUs provide native support

---

[3] Originally, AVX2 was supporting mainly floating point operations with 32-bit floats and 64-bit doubles - it was much later that integer operations were introduced. Today, not all 64-bit integer operations are supported - e.g., it was only recently that SIMD multiplications of vectors of 64-bit integers were introduced in AVX512 and recently, Intel has disabled AVX512 in AlderLake processors.

for only 32-bit SIMT integer multiplication, thus, requiring emulation for larger (64-bit or more) SIMT integer multiplication.

Therefore, the best trade-off we have under the above constraints is to target 120-bit modulus NTT since the larger supported limb size $K = 52$ reduces the number of elementary operations in an external product: 120-bit NTT with $K = 52$ that has approximately the same running time as the 64-bit floating point FFT counterpart with $K = 19$ (the evidence for the latter can be deduced by combining the data from Table 1 with the micro-benchmarks from Table 4 below).

Table 4. DFT and SIMD arithmetic operations on a Xeon 2.8GHz n2-standard with 64GB of RAM instance. All benchmarks are single core.

backend	float64 FFT		float128 FFT		60-bit NTT		120-bit NTT	
K	19		49		22		52	
N	$64k$	$32k$	$64k$	$32k$	$64k$	$32k$	$64k$	$32k$
DFT/iDFT	$125\mu s$	$57\mu s$	60.3ms	28.4ms	$534\mu s$	$243\mu s$	$1342\mu s$	$541\mu s$
SIMD addmul/twiddle	$27\mu s$	$9\mu s$	2.17ms	1.07ms	$49\mu s$	$28\mu s$	$93\mu s$	$48\mu s$
automorphism	$58\mu s$	$29\mu s$	$68\mu s$	$33\mu s$	$68\mu s$	$33\mu s$	$92\mu s$	$45\mu s$

Comparative micro-benchmarks between floating point and NTT elementary operations are provided in Table 4: one DFT/iDFT operation is either an FFT or an NTT on a consecutive array of N elements. The `float64` and `float128` FFT operations are self-explanatory, whereas in 60-bit or 120-bit NTT, an element x is represented by two or four (lazily-reduced) 64-bit integers equal to x modulo (q_1, q_2) or (q_1, q_2, q_3, q_4), respectively. One SIMD `addmul`/twiddle consists of either one operation $r = r + ab$ over vectors in $\mathbb{C}^{N/2}$ or $(\mathbb{Z}/Q\mathbb{Z})^N$ or one twiddle-factor $(a, b) \to (a + \omega \cdot b, a - \omega \cdot b)$ where ω is a fixed (general) root of unity, whichever is slower. For $N = 32K$ or $64K$, the twiddle factor is in general 10% faster than the `addmul`, despite the fact that it contains one more subtraction, which indicates that these operations are memory-bound. `float64`, and the two NTTs use `AVX2` instructions, whereas `float128` is powered by `libquadmath` and does not benefit from any particular acceleration except for automorphisms that use only copy and sign-bit flipping.

We also provide benchmarks of homomorphic elementary operations in Table 5. We used the same parameter sets: $(N = 65536, L = 1729)$ and $(N = 32768, L = 865)$ as in [23]. The fast CKKS-RNS benchmarks have been run from the source code provided in [23] on the same machine as our own benchmarks. We evaluated the performance on the same machines as in Sect. 4: one n2-standard GCP instance with 64GB of RAM, and one 12-th Gen i7-1260p laptop with 64GB of RAM (Top and Down parts of Table 5). We expect that the performance numbers in these tables will be in constant evolution, as new hardware tend to support larger precision arithmetic. However, unlike what was commonly believed so far, any chip or device that can: either efficiently approximate the complex FFT with reasonable precision, or execute NTT on even just one single NTT-friendly modulus of reasonable size, is suitable for fast homomorphic computations at any depth. The efficiency of such device is directly related to the number of bits of mantissa or modulus it natively supports.

Table 5. Total running time per homomorphic operation over RLWE ciphertexts: CRT representations for full-RNS and [23], bivariate representations in our case. We recall that we use $L = 1729$ and $L = 865$ as in the implementation provided by [23].

Operation	Keyswitch		Automorphism	CKKS product
Size	$N = 64k$	$N = 32k$	$N = 64k$	$N = 64k$
	L=1729	L=865	L=1729	L=1729
Hardware	n2-standard VM Xeon(R) CPU @ 2.8 GHz, 64 GB RAM			
- Full-RNS (best r)	3.111 s	0.359 s	3.279 s	3.311 s
- [23] (best r)	0.965 s	0.161 s	1.134 s	1.155 s
- ours: biv + fft-f64 ($K = 19$)	0.589 s	0.086 s	0.602 s	0.862 s
- ours: biv + ntt120 ($K = 52$)	0.541 s	0.073 s	0.547 s	0.777 s
Hardware	Laptop with Intel Core i7-1260P @ 4.7 GHz, 64 GB RAM			
- Full-RNS (best r)	1.598 s	0.192 s	1.796 s	1.759 s
- [23] (best r)	0.521 s	0.085 s	0.578 s	0.598 s
- ours: biv + fft-f64 ($K = 19$)	0.228 s	0.027 s	0.233 s	0.335 s
- ours: biv + ntt120 ($K = 52$)	0.218 s	0.029 s	0.221 s	0.314 s

Conclusion

In this paper we extend the key decomposition techniques from [23] by using a simpler and more natural base-2^K representation. It allows a better understanding of the parametrization of TFHE, CKKS and BFV schemes, which in turn speeds-up not only the main operations in CKKS and BFV schemes, but also low-depth computations in TFHE.

A   Appendix: Normalization and Reduction Lemma Proof

Proof of Lemma 3.3. Let $n = \lceil (L + M)/K \rceil$ be the number of algorithm iterations. Let $\mathtt{acc}^{(i)}$ be accumulator value after step 3 of iteration i and let $\mathtt{acc}^{(n+1)} = 0$. At iteration i, $n \geq i \geq 1$, we have:

$$\mathtt{acc}^{(i)} = A_i + \epsilon_{i+1} \quad \text{and} \quad R_i = \mathtt{acc}^{(i)} - \epsilon_i 2^K, \tag{9}$$

here $\epsilon_i = \lfloor \mathrm{acc}^{(i)} 2^{-K} \rfloor$ and has integer values. The evaluation of result polynomial at 2^{-K} gives:

$$\phi_K(R) = \sum_{i=1}^{\ell} R_i 2^{-iK} = \sum_{i=1}^{\ell} \left(A_i + \epsilon_{i+1} - \epsilon_i 2^K \right) 2^{-iK}.$$

Expanding the sum and simplifying common expressions we obtain:

$$\phi_K(R) = \sum_{i=1}^{\ell} A_i 2^{-iK} + \epsilon_{\ell+1} 2^{-\ell K} - \epsilon_1$$

Now, we will prove that $\|(\phi_K(A) - \phi_K(R)) \bmod \mathcal{R}\|_\infty$ is smaller than 2^{-L}. We have:

$$\phi_K(A) - \phi_K(R) = A_0 + \sum_{\ell < i} A_i 2^{-iK} - \epsilon_{(\ell+1)} 2^{-\ell K} + \epsilon_1.$$

Observe that terms A_0 and ϵ_1 are integers and are reduced by $\bmod \mathcal{R}$ operation, we obtain:

$$(\phi_K(A) - \phi_K(R)) \bmod \mathcal{R} = \sum_{\ell < i} A_i 2^{-iK} - \epsilon_{\ell+1} 2^{-\ell K}.$$

From (9) it is easy to see that $A_i - \epsilon_i 2^K \equiv R_i - \epsilon_{i+1}$. Using previous relations we have:

$$(\phi_K(A) - \phi_K(R)) \bmod \mathcal{R} = 2^{-(\ell+1)K} (A_{\ell+1} - \epsilon_{\ell+1} 2^K) + \sum_{\ell+1 < i} A_i 2^{-iK}$$

$$= 2^{-(\ell+1)K} R_{\ell+1} + \sum_{\ell+1 < i} A_i 2^{-iK} - \epsilon_{\ell+2} 2^{-(\ell+1)K} = \cdots = \sum_{i=\ell+1}^{n} R_i 2^{-iK} + \sum_{n < i} A_i 2^{-iK}.$$

Looking at the infinity norm we have:

$$\|(\phi_K(A) - \phi_K(R)) \bmod \mathcal{R}\|_\infty = \left\| \sum_{i=\ell+1}^{n} R_i 2^{-iK} + \sum_{n < i} A_i 2^{-iK} \right\|_\infty$$

$$< \left\| \sum_{i=\ell+1}^{n} 2^{-iK+K} + \sum_{n < i} 2^{-iK+M} \right\|_\infty \le 2^{-\ell K+1} \le 2^{-L}.$$

Element-wise operations are on integers in interval $\left(-2^{M+1}, 2^{M+1}\right)$.
The accumulator variable acc (at step 3) has the largest values during algorithm execution. We will prove that its magnitude (i.e. infinity norm) never exceeds 2^{M+1}.

Algorithm step 3 increases accumulator value by at most 2^M and step 5 divides the new value by 2^K. After the first iteration, we have $\|\mathrm{acc}^{(n)}\|_\infty < 2^M$, after second iteration $\|\mathrm{acc}^{(n-1)}\|_\infty < 2^{M-K} + 2^M$ and so on until the last iteration where we have $\|\mathrm{acc}^{(1)}\|_\infty < \sum_{0 \le i < n} 2^{M-iK}$, which is the maximum accumulator magnitude attained during algorithm execution. We can rewrite the last expression as:

$$\left\|\mathrm{acc}^{(1)}\right\|_\infty < \sum_{0\le i<n} 2^{M-iK} = 2^M \cdot \sum_{0\le i<n} 2^{-iK} < 2^M \cdot 2 = 2^{M+1},$$

which proves the accumulator bound.

Complexity Algorithm steps 3-5 are executed $\lceil (L+M)/K \rceil$ times. In each iteration 5 operations are performed: an addition (step 3), 3 shifts (2 in step 4 and 1 in step 5) and a subtraction (step 4). The overall complexity of the algorithm is $5 \cdot \lceil (L+M)/K \rceil$ element-wise operations. □

In this paragraph we introduce Algorithm 2, a general conversion and normalization with two limb size K and $\widetilde{K}$. This algorithm is a slightly more complex than Algorithm 1 with $K = \widetilde{K}$, since it must handle additional binary shifts to synchronize the limb sizes, and thus, the for loop on a single index k is replaced by two while loops and two indexes $k, \widetilde{k}$ that decrease at their respective speed. Besides that, it follows the same principle as the single-limb normalization.

Algorithm 2. Conversion, Normalization and Reduction (from K to $\widetilde{K}$).

Input: A target precision of L bits, an input limb size K and an output limb size $\widetilde{K}$
Input: An input polynomial $A(X,Y) = \sum_{k \in \mathbb{Z}_{\ge 0}} A_k(X)Y^k$ satisfying $\|A\|_\infty \le 2^B$
Output: A $\widetilde{K}$-normalized and reduced polynomial $R(X,Y)$ of degree $\le \lceil L/\widetilde{K} \rceil$ in Y
  such that $\|\phi_{\widetilde{K}}(R) - \phi_K(A)\|_\infty \le 2^{-L}$.
1: $k = \lceil (L+B)/K \rceil$, $\widetilde{k} = \lceil (L+B)/\widetilde{K} \rceil$
2: $\mathrm{acc}(X) = \lfloor A_k(X) \cdot 2^{\widetilde{k}\widetilde{K} - kK} \rceil$
3: **while** $\widetilde{k} > 1$ **do**
4:     **while** $(\widetilde{k}-1)\widetilde{K} < (k-1)K$ **do**
5:         $\mathrm{acc}(X) \leftarrow \mathrm{acc}(X) + A_{k-1}(X) \cdot 2^{(k-1)K - (\widetilde{k}-1)\widetilde{K}}$
6:         $k \leftarrow k - 1$
7:     **end while**
8:     $R_{\widetilde{k}}(X) \leftarrow \mathrm{centermod}_{2^{\widetilde{K}}}(\mathrm{acc}(X))$
9:     $\mathrm{acc}(X) \leftarrow (\mathrm{acc}(X) - R_{\widetilde{k}}(X))/2^{\widetilde{K}}$
10:    $\widetilde{k} \leftarrow \widetilde{k} - 1$
11: **end while**
12: Return $R(X,Y) = \sum_{k=1}^{\lceil L/K \rceil} R_k(X)Y^k$

References

1. M. R. Albrecht, R. Player, and S. Scott. On the concrete hardness of learning with errors. *Journal of Mathematical Cryptology*, 9(3):169–203, 2015.
2. J.-C. Bajard, J. Eynard, M. A. Hasan, and V. Zucca. A full RNS variant of FV like somewhat homomorphic encryption schemes. In *Selected Areas in Cryptography – SAC 2016*, pages 423–442. Springer, 2017.
3. M. G. Belorgey, S. Carpov, N. Gama, S. Guasch, and D. Jetchev. Revisiting key decomposition techniques for FHE: Simpler, faster and more generic. Cryptology ePrint Archive, Paper 2023/771, 2023.
4. C. Boura, N. Gama, M. Georgieva, and D. Jetchev. CHIMERA: combining ring-lwe-based fully homomorphic encryption schemes. *J. Math. Cryptol.*, 14(1):316–338, 2020.
5. Z. Brakerski, C. Gentry, and V. Vaikuntanathan. (leveled) fully homomorphic encryption without bootstrapping. In *Innovations in Theoretical Computer Science 2012*, pages 309–325. ACM, 2012.
6. R. Cammarota. Intel HERACLES: homomorphic encryption revolutionary accelerator with correctness for learning-oriented end-to-end solutions. In *Proceedings of the 2022 on Cloud Computing Security Workshop, CCSW*. ACM, 2022.
7. J. H. Cheon, K. Han, A. Kim, M. Kim, and Y. Song. A full rns variant of approximate homomorphic encryption. *Selected areas in cryptography : ... annual international workshop, SAC ... proceedings. SAC*, 11349:347–368, 2018.
8. J. H. Cheon, A. Kim, M. Kim, and Y. S. Song. Homomorphic encryption for arithmetic of approximate numbers. In *Advances in Cryptology - ASIACRYPT, Part I*, pages 409–437. Springer, 2017.
9. I. Chillotti, N. Gama, M. Georgieva, and M. Izabachène. Faster fully homomorphic encryption: Bootstrapping in less than 0.1 seconds. In *ASIACRYPT 2016, Proceedings, Part I*, volume 10031 of *LNCS*, pages 3–33. Springer, 2016.
10. I. Chillotti, N. Gama, M. Georgieva, and M. Izabachène. TFHE: fast fully homomorphic encryption over the torus. *J. Cryptol.*, 33(1):34–91, 2020.
11. I. Chillotti, D. Ligier, J.-B. Orfila, and S. Tap. Improved programmable bootstrapping with larger precision and efficient arithmetic circuits for tfhe. In M. Tibouchi and H. Wang, editors, *Advances in Cryptology – ASIACRYPT 2021*, pages 670–699, Cham, 2021. Springer International Publishing.
12. J. Cooley and J. Tukey. An algorithm for the machine calculation of complex fourier series. *Mathematics of Computation*, 19(90):297–301, 1965.
13. M. Creeger. The rise of fully homomorphic encryption: Often called the holy grail of cryptography, commercial FHE is near. *ACM Queue*, 20(4):39–60, 2022.
14. DARPA. DARPA:data protection in virtual environments (DPRIVE).
15. K. Derya, A. C. Mert, E. Öztürk, and E. Savas. Coha-ntt: A configurable hardware accelerator for ntt-based polynomial multiplication. *Microprocess. Microsystems*, 89:104451, 2022.
16. L. Ducas and D. Micciancio. FHEW: bootstrapping homomorphic encryption in less than a second. In *EUROCRYPT 2015, Proceedings, Part I*, volume 9056 of *LNCS*, pages 617–640. Springer, 2015.
17. J. Fan and F. Vercauteren. Somewhat practical fully homomorphic encryption. *IACR Cryptol. ePrint Arch.*, page 144, 2012.
18. C. Gentry. Fully homomorphic encryption using ideal lattices. In *Proceedings of the 41st Annual ACM Symposium on Theory of Computing, STOC 2009*, pages 169–178. ACM, 2009.

19. C. Gentry, S. Halevi, and N. P. Smart. Homomorphic evaluation of the aes circuit. In *Advances in Cryptology – CRYPTO 2012*, pages 850–867. Springer, 2012.
20. C. Gentry, A. Sahai, and B. Waters. Homomorphic encryption from learning with errors: Conceptually-simpler, asymptotically-faster, attribute-based. In *Advances in Cryptology - CRYPTO 2013, Part I*, pages 75–92. Springer, 2013.
21. C. Gentry, A. Sahai, and B. Waters. Homomorphic encryption from learning with errors: Conceptually-simpler, asymptotically-faster, attribute-based. In *CRYPTO 2013, Proceedings, Part I*, volume 8042 of *LNCS*, pages 75–92. Springer, 2013.
22. S. Halevi, Y. Polyakov, and V. Shoup. An improved rns variant of the bfv homomorphic encryption scheme. In *Topics in Cryptology – CT-RSA 2019*, pages 83–105. Springer, 2019.
23. M. Kim, D. Lee, J. Seo, and Y. Song. Accelerating he operations from key decomposition technique. In *Advances in Cryptology – CRYPTO 2023: 43rd Annual International Cryptology Conference, Proceedings, Part IV*. Springer-Verlag, 2023.
24. I. Kundu, E. Cottle, F. Michel, J. Wilson, and N. New. The dawn of energy efficient computing: Optically accelerating the fast fourier transform core. In *Photonics in Switching and Computing 2021*. Optica Publishing Group, 2021.
25. Y. Lee, S. Heo, S. Cheon, S. Jeong, C. Kim, E. Kim, D. Lee, and H. Kim. Hecate: Performance-aware scale optimization for homomorphic encryption compiler. In *2022 IEEE/ACM International Symposium on Code Generation and Optimization (CGO)*, pages 193–204, 2022.
26. V. Lyubashevsky, C. Peikert, and O. Regev. *EUROCRYPT*, chapter On Ideal Lattices and Learning with Errors over Rings, pages 1–23. Springer, 2010.
27. A. C. Mert, E. Öztürk, and E. Savas. FPGA implementation of a run-time configurable ntt-based polynomial multiplication hardware. *Microprocess. Microsystems*, 78:103219, 2020.
28. D. T. Nguyen and K. Gaj. Fast falcon signature generation and verification using armv8 neon instructions. In *Progress in Cryptology - AFRICACRYPT 2023*, pages 417–441. Springer, 2023.
29. Ö. Özerk, C. Elgezen, A. C. Mert, E. Öztürk, and E. Savas. Efficient number theorotic transform implementation on GPU for homomorphic encryption. *J. Super comput.*, 78(2):2840–2872, 2022.
30. O. Regev. On lattices, learning with errors, random linear codes, and cryptography. *J. ACM*, 56(6):34:1–34:40, 2009.
31. S. S. Roy, F. Turan, K. Järvinen, F. Vercauteren, and I. Verbauwhede. FPGA-based high-performance parallel architecture for homomorphic computing on encrypted data. In *25th IEEE International Symposium on High Performance Computer Architecture*, pages 387–398. IEEE, 2019.
32. A. Schönhage and V. Strassen. Schnelle Multiplikation grosser Zahlen. *Computing (Arch. Elektron. Rechnen)*, 7:281–292, 1971.
33. TFHE-lib. TFHE: Fast Fully Homomorphic Encryption over the Torus. https://tfhe.github.io/tfhe/.
34. F. Turan, S. S. Roy, and I. Verbauwhede. HEAWS: an accelerator for homomorphic encryption on the amazon AWS FPGA. *IEEE Trans. Computers*, 2020.
35. E. R. Türkoglu, A. S. Özcan, C. Ayduman, A. C. Mert, E. Öztürk, and E. Savas. An accelerated GPU library for homomorphic encryption operations of BFV scheme. In *IEEE International Symposium on Circuits and Systems*, 2022.
36. Zama. TFHE-rs: A Pure Rust Implementation of the TFHE Scheme for Boolean and Integer Arithmetics Over Encrypted Data, 2024. https://github.com/zama-ai/tfhe-rs.

Relaxed Functional Bootstrapping: A New Perspective on BGV/BFV Bootstrapping

Zeyu Liu$^{(\boxtimes)}$ and Yunhao Wang

Yale University, New Haven, CT, USA
zeyu.liu@yale.edu

Abstract. BGV and BFV are among the most widely used fully homomorphic encryption (FHE) schemes, supporting evaluations over a finite field. To evaluate a circuit with arbitrary depth, bootstrapping is needed. However, despite the recent progress, bootstrapping of BGV/BFV still remains relatively impractical, compared to other FHE schemes.

In this work, we inspect the BGV/BFV bootstrapping procedure from a different angle. We provide a generalized bootstrapping definition that relaxes the correctness requirement of regular bootstrapping, allowing constructions that support only certain kinds of circuits with arbitrary depth. In addition, our definition captures a form of functional bootstrapping. In other words, the output encrypts a function evaluation of the input instead of the input itself.

Under this new definition, we provide a bootstrapping procedure supporting different types of functions. Our construction is 1–2 orders of magnitude faster than the state-of-the-art BGV/BFV bootstrapping algorithms, depending on the evaluated function.

Of independent interest, we show that our technique can be used to improve the batched FHEW/TFHE bootstrapping construction introduced by Liu and Wang (Asiacrypt 2023). Our optimization provides a speed-up of 6x in latency and 3x in throughput for binary gate bootstrapping and a plaintext-space-dependent speed-up for functional bootstrapping with plaintext space smaller than $\mathbb{Z}_{512}$.

1 Introduction

Fully Homomorphic Encryption (FHE) allows one to securely compute over encrypted data without the knowledge of the secret key or interaction with the owner of the data, thus resulting in a very strong primitive. FHE was first realized by Gentry in the groundbreaking work [27]. Since then, there have been lots of works trying to improve the efficiency of FHE [6–9,17,18,21,22,28].

These works follow a similar paradigm as Gentry's original work: a ciphertext contains some initial noise and each operation (e.g., multiplications and additions) introduces some additional noise; the initial parameter provides some noise budget, and if the noise budget is used up when carrying out operations

© International Association for Cryptologic Research 2025
K.-M. Chung and Y. Sasaki (Eds.): ASIACRYPT 2024, LNCS 15484, pp. 208–240, 2025.
https://doi.org/10.1007/978-981-96-0875-1_7

(i.e., the noise has grown to be close to some threshold), computations cannot be continued. This is thus called the Leveled Homomorphic Encryption (LHE). To make LHE indeed FHE, one needs an additional operation: bootstrapping.

Essentially, bootstrapping takes a ciphertext with a relatively large error (i.e., only a small amount of noise budget left) and outputs a new ciphertext encrypting the same plaintext with a relatively small error (i.e., a large amount of noise budget left). With bootstrapping, one can evaluate circuits of arbitrary depths. Bootstrapping itself is very costly and a lot of work has been done to improve the efficiency of bootstrapping (e.g., [13,16,18,21,50]).

Among all the FHE schemes, one critical line of work is BGV/BFV [6,7,22], which has a very important property called "Same Instruction Multiple Data" (SIMD), i.e., one BFV ciphertext encrypts a vector of $D \gg 1$ $\mathbb{Z}_t$ elements (in D slots). Then, any operation over a ciphertext is done over all these D $\mathbb{Z}_t$ elements (element-wise). The state-of-the-art framework for BGV/BFV bootstrapping was first introduced in [32] and later improved in [14,25,26,56]. While the most recent work [56] has asymptotically achieved a very efficient construction (requiring only a logarithmic number of ciphertext multiplications), the practicality is still relatively limited. Concretely, to bootstrap for a single element (amortized over D slots) in $\mathbb{Z}_{257}$, the state-of-the-art BFV bootstrapping construction takes ~ 0.17 s [56]. The main issue is that to design a suitable bootstrapping scheme for arbitrary circuits, these works make use of some algebraic structure to improve the efficiency and thus do not take full advantage of the SIMD capability of BGV/BFV. Thus, the amortized cost of every slot is still relatively large.

However, in some cases, supporting arbitrary circuits might be an overkill. In some circuits, there might exist some sub-circuit C such that the output is only a subset of the entire plaintext space $\mathbb{Z}_t$, or only a subset of $\mathbb{Z}_t$ is taken as input. In other words, we have $C : \mathcal{X} \to \mathcal{Y}$ where $\mathcal{Y} \subset \mathbb{Z}_t$, or $C' : \mathcal{X}' \to \mathcal{Y}'$ where $\mathcal{X}' \subset \mathbb{Z}_t$. This means that if the bootstrapping comes after C or before C', only the plaintext values in $\mathcal{Y}$ or $\mathcal{X}'$ need to be bootstrapped, respectively. Conditional branching serves as a great example here: if $x \in [u, v]$,[1] outputs y; if $x \in [u', v']$, outputs y'. This branching can then be modeled as a circuit $f : \mathcal{X}_f \to \mathcal{Y}_f$, where $\mathcal{X}_f := [u, v] \cup [u', v']$ and $\mathcal{Y}_f := \{y, y'\}$. Both $\mathcal{X}_f$ and $\mathcal{Y}_f$ are only a (small) subset of $\mathbb{Z}_t$.

In fact, such circuits are common in many applications, like oblivious permutation [23], PSI with computation [35], secure machine learning [20,36,41,42,52], and so on. See Sect. 7 for more examples and detailed discussions. Therefore, the first natural question we ask in this paper is:

Can we achieve better efficiency by relaxing the requirement of supporting arbitrary circuits? In other words, if we only allow bootstrapping input to be a subset of the entire plaintext space, can we do bootstrapping more efficiently?

Another inefficiency of regular bootstrapping comes from the fact that, as a standalone component, the bootstrapping procedure itself does not directly contribute to evaluating the target circuit. Every effort spent on bootstrapping is an extra cost. Therefore, the second question we pose is:

---

[1] $[u, v]$ denotes $\{u, u + 1, \ldots, v\}$.

Can we achieve better efficiency by embedding bootstrapping into the circuit? In other words, can we do bootstrapping while evaluating a circuit like C or C' without introducing much overhead?

In this paper, we make solid progress in both directions. Due to space reasons, please see our full version [51] for deferred details and clarifications.

1.1 Our Contribution

Definition of Generalized Functional Bootstrapping. We propose a new generalized definition of BFV bootstrapping. The definition captures the most fundamental requirement of bootstrapping (i.e., the output ciphertext has a larger noise budget than the input ciphertext), but also allows some relaxation on the functionality: the output ciphertext does not need to provide correctness for *all* plaintexts, but only a predetermined subset of the plaintext space. In other words, for the input ciphertexts encrypting *invalid plaintexts* (i.e., not in that subset), the construction may output a ciphertext encrypting an arbitrary plaintext, since an expected output is not defined. This relaxation allows us to develop more efficient bootstrapping constructions for valid inputs.

Moreover, the definition captures a form of *functional bootstrapping*, which means that the output encrypts $f(x)$ instead of x, where x is the valid input plaintext and f is some predetermined function. This allows the bootstrapping itself to be embedded into the circuit for better efficiency.

As an auxiliary property, we define *closeness*, which captures how the output behaves when the inputs are invalid. Instead of arbitrary output for invalid input, the algorithm returns the expected output of some valid input points *close* to the invalid input in the plaintext space. This property provides extra flexibility and might be useful in some applications.

Constructions of Generalized Functional Bootstrapping. In addition, we show a general framework for this (relaxed) BFV bootstrapping. While our framework cannot be used to achieve regular bootstrapping, we show that it can be used to efficiently achieve relaxed bootstrapping while evaluating three different types of functions:

- Point functions: the function takes m points and maps them to m points. This type of function is like an arbitrary lookup table, but only the specified m points are valid inputs, where $m \ll t$ for t being the plaintext modulus. The runtime is essentially linear in $c \cdot m$ (where c is some tuneable parameter) instead of t as in regular BFV bootstrapping constructions.
- Range functions: the function takes k ranges and maps them to k points, each range containing m consecutive points[2]. This type of function is more limited, but can be evaluated more efficiently: even if there are $m \cdot k$ valid input points, the runtime cost is only $(m + c) \cdot k$ instead of $c \cdot m \cdot k$.
- Unbalanced range functions: the function takes 2 ranges and maps them into 2 different points, where the first range contains m_1 points and the second

---

[2] Each range may contain a different amount of points, but for simplicity here, we assume they all have m points.

range contains $m_2 \gg m_1$ points. This is a special case of the range functions. However, with $m_2 \gg m_1$, we construct a bootstrapping scheme running in $m_1 + c + \log(t)$ time, which is much more efficient than the $m_1 + m_2 + 2c$ (the efficiency of applying the algorithm for the general range functions). We also extend this result to functions with $k > 2$ ranges, where the k-th range is larger than all the other ranges combined. In this case, our construction can evaluate it more efficiently than evaluating it as normal range functions.

We implement our construction as a C++ library, and show that it is indeed concretely more efficient than regular BFV bootstrapping: the amortized cost is about 1–2 orders of magnitude faster than regular BFV bootstrapping, depending on the function that is evaluated by our functional bootstrapping procedure.

To showcase the practicality of our construction, in Sect. 7 we specifically demonstrate that our relaxed functional bootstrapping constructions could bring a 20x speedup to oblivious permutation [23] compared to using the bootstrapping from prior works, and also discuss some other applications that could take advantage of our constructions.

Batched LWE Ciphertexts Bootstrapping. As an independent contribution, we show that our techniques can be applied to improve the batched functional bootstrapping construction for LWE ciphertexts introduced by [50]. Our benchmark shows that for binary-gate batched bootstrapping, our construction is about 3x faster than [50]. Moreover, with optimizations allowing the runtime to scale with the plaintext space, our construction greatly brings down the overall bootstrapping runtime for smaller plaintext space. Compared to the uniform runtime for any plaintext space smaller than $\mathbb{Z}_{512}$ in the prior work, our work is more efficient when considering the functional/programmable bootstrapping for plaintext space with 3–8-bit.

1.2   Related Work

BFV Bootstrapping. All the prior works about BFV bootstrapping are regular bootstrapping whose goal is simply to reduce the error (or equivalently increase the noise budget) of the input ciphertexts [6,14,22,26,32]. This allows one to evaluate circuits with arbitrary depth.

In Table 1, we compare our result with the prior works on regular BFV bootstrapping [14,25,26,32,56]. Our protocol supports several different types of functions: f_{pts} maps a random set $\mathcal{X}$ to another random set $\mathcal{Y}$, with $|\mathcal{Y}| \leq |\mathcal{X}| \leq \lfloor t/r \rfloor$ (for $\mathbb{Z}_t$ being the plaintext space, and $r = O(\sqrt{h})$ where h is the hamming weight of the BFV secret key); f_{ranges} represents a range-to-point mapping for multiple ranges, while f_{ub} maps one range to some point and the other much larger range[3] to another point (i.e., an unbalanced range mapping). Note that f_{ranges} and f_{ub} both map ranges to points and both require the ranges to be separated by r (for example, if the inputs are composed of k ranges, we need

---

[3] Can be almost as large as all the other points in $\mathbb{Z}_t$.

$[u_i - r/2, v_i + r/2] \cap [u_j - r/2, v_j + r/2] = \emptyset$ for all $i \neq j \in [k]$). f_1 and f_2 are two additional types of functions that serve as stepping stones toward our final construction, where f_1 is the identity function on a subset of $\mathbb{Z}_t$ with static intervals r, and f_2 is its generalized version with potentially small static intervals.

The closenessproperty is a new property we define additional to standard correctness (which does not put any constraint on invalid inputs): for any invalid input, the output still needs to be the outputs of one of the closest ℓ valid input points to that invalid input. This property can be useful in some applications but is not a hard requirement as constructions may take advantage of not having it for better efficiency. See Sect. 7 for further discussion regarding applications (with and without closenessrequirement).

In Sect. 5.2, we provide an alternative construction to evaluate the type f_{ranges} (i.e., type (2) function of our result). This alternative construction is more efficient when the k-th range is larger than the other $k - 1$ ranges combined and provides k-closeness (Definition 2). Let the total size of the first $k - 1$ ranges be S. The depth is $\log(S + r(k - 1)) + \log(t)$; number of scalar multiplications is S; and the number of non-scalar multiplications is $S + \log(t)$. To avoid extra complexity, we do not include it in the table.

From Table 1, we can see that the total cost of our construction is dependent on the functions and thus more fine-grained. For example, for f_{pts}, if $|X| = O(1)$, our construction cost can also be $O(1)$ (as $r = O(\sqrt{h})$ and h is viewed as a constant in prior works [26, Section 7.2]). Note that since function f_1, f_2 can be treated as special cases of f_{pts}, they achieve the same efficiency asymptotically as f_{pts}. On the other hand, although f_{ub} is also a special case of f_{ranges}, f_{ub} is both asymptotically and concretely more efficient when $|v_1 - u_1| \ll |v_2 - u_2|$ (due to symmetry, it also works for functions with $|v_1 - u_1| \gg |v_2 - u_2|$).

Lastly, our construction supports a lot more slots: N compared to N/d. In practice, $d \gg 1$. For example, for the parameters tested in [14], $N/d \approx \sqrt{N}$ (we refer readers to the caption of Table 1 for more detailed parameter definitions). Thus, prior works inherently support a lot fewer slots due to their techniques and can hardly be extended. Thus, our amortized efficiency is much better than prior works.

Method-wise, our construction uses a different idea to reduce costs. [14, 26, 32] focuses on temporarily enlarging the plaintext space to accommodate the partial decryption value. In more detail, when computing $b - \langle \vec{a}, \mathsf{sk} \rangle$ for ciphertext $(\vec{a}, b)$,[4] instead of computing it over $\mathbb{Z}_{t^\circ}$, they compute it over $\mathbb{Z}_{t^{\circ'}}$ for some $e' > 1$ satisfying $b - \langle \vec{a}, \mathsf{sk} \rangle \ll t^{e'}$ when evaluated in the integer domain; thus, they obtain $k \cdot t + m + \epsilon < t^{e'}$ for some integer k. To recover m, one of their main steps is then to remove $k \cdot t$. In contrast, our construction directly computes the partial decryption over $\mathbb{Z}_t$, and thus do not need this step.

A recent work [56] explores the algebraic structure of the plaintext space, they can reduce the number of non-scalar multiplications from $O(\sqrt{p})$ to $O(\log(p))$ (other works in the table has $O(\sqrt{p})$ non-scalar multiplications instead). Despite

---

[4] Notice that for readability, we use LWE ciphertext as an illustration here, while in the construction, we use RLWE ciphertext instead.

Table 1. Asymptotic behavior of our construction compared to prior works on regular BFV bootstrapping (ignoring some constants). $[a, b, c] := \{a, a + c, a + 2c, \ldots, b\}$ (i.e., the set of all the integers $x \in [a, b]$ such that $x - a$ divides c), where c divides $b - a$, p is some small prime satisfying $\gcd(p, m) = 1$, $e \geq 1$, the plaintext space is given as p^e, and d the multiplicative order of p in $\mathbb{Z}_{2N}^*$. t is some prime satisfying $t \equiv 1 \bmod 2N$, and $r = O(\sqrt{h})$ is the modulus switching error range. Concretely speaking, for most practical parameters benchmarked in our work and prior works, $t \approx p^e$ (or $t \gg p^e$ for some parameters [25,56]). h is the hamming weight of the secret key, and $r = O(\sqrt{h})$. At a high level, ℓ-closenessmeans that the output of all the out-of-the-range invalid inputs are mapped to the evaluation result of one of their closest ℓ valid inputs. Depth here means the multiplicative depth of the bootstrapping circuit. Due to space reasons, most of the pseudocode are deferred to our full version [51], so please refer to our full version [51] for the same table with better readability and pointers.

	Supported functions	Depth	# of scalar multiplications	# of non-scalar multiplications	Plaintext space	# slots	Closeness (Definition 2)
Regular BFV Bootstrapping [14,25,26,32,56]	Identity function over the entire plaintext space	$\log(h) + \log\log(p^e)$	$\log_p(h) \cdot (\log_p(h) + e) \cdot p$ $\frac{(\log_p(h) \cdot (\log_p(h) + e) \cdot p)}{d}$	$\frac{(\log_p(h) \cdot (\sqrt{e} + \log_p(h)) \cdot \log p)}{(\log_p(h) \cdot (\sqrt{e} + \log_p(h)) \cdot \log p)/d}$	$R(p^e, d)$ $\mathbb{Z}_{p^e}$	N/d	N/A
Our result	(1) $f_{\mathsf{pts}} : X \to Y$ $X, Y \subset \mathbb{Z}_t$	$\log(|X| \cdot r)$	$|X| \cdot r$	$\sqrt{|X| \cdot r}$	$\mathbb{Z}_t$	N	$\ell = |\mathcal{Y}|$, if $|X| = \frac{t-1}{r}$; no, i.e.
	(2) $f_{\mathsf{ranges}}(m) = y_i$ if $m \in [u_i, v_i]$ $u_i, v_i, y_i \in \mathbb{Z}_t, i \in [k], k \geq 2$	$\log(\sum_{i \in [k]} (|v_i - u_i| + r))$	$\sum_{i \in [k]} (|v_i - u_i| + r)$	$\sqrt{\sum_{i \in [k]} (|v_i - u_i| + r)}$			$\ell = 2$ with overhead (Remark 4)
	(3) $f_{\mathsf{ub}}(m) = y_i$ if $m \in [u_i, v_i]$ $u_i, v_i, y_i \in \mathbb{Z}_t, i \in [2]$	$\log(|v_1 - u_1| + r) + \log(t)$	1	$|v_1 - u_1| + r + \log(t)$			$\ell = 2$
Our result (Stepping stone)	(4) f_1 : identity function over $[0, t-1, r]$	$\log(t)$	t	$\sqrt{t}$			$\ell = 2$
	(5) $f_2 : [u, v, r'] \to Y$ $u, v, r' \in \mathbb{Z}_t, Y \subset \mathbb{Z}_t$	$\log(r(v - u)/r')$	$r(v - u)/r'$	$\sqrt{r(v - u)/r'}$			$\ell = 2$, if $r' = r$; $\ell = |\mathcal{Y}|$, o.w.

their interesting techniques and great asymptotic improvement, it still only supports N/d slots, and concretely, the construction is only about 1.6x faster than the prior constructions [14]. We provide a concrete comparison in Sect. 6.

Recent Concurrent Works. There are two very recent concurrent and independent works [38,53] on regular BGV/BFV bootstrapping. They have different pros and cons compared to our work. Another very recent work [40] also studies BGV/BFV functional bootstrapping. They have similar functionality as ours, but since they follow ideas from prior regular BGV/BFV bootstrapping works (in Table 1), their construction has worse efficiency than ours. Due to space constraints, we discuss these works in our full version [51] in more detail, from both an analytical and concrete point of view.

CKKS Bootstrapping. CKKS bootstrapping is another line of work [5,13, 33,34,39,43,44]. Similar to regular BFV bootstrapping, CKKS bootstrapping also only supports (approximate) identity function. Unlike BFV, CKKS instead computes with (approximate) real numbers. Therefore, their decryption process takes a different strategy from our construction or the BFV bootstrapping: they use sine to approximate a mod function, and then use a polynomial function to approximate the sine function. This path also makes it inherently hard to support any form of functional bootstrapping.

(Batched) FHEW/TFHE Bootstrapping. FHEW/TFHE bootstrapping [18,21,45] focuses on bootstrapping for a single LWE ciphertext. Recently, some works bootstrap multiple LWE ciphertexts at the same time, denoted as batched bootstrapping [29,48–50,54,55]. This line of work also supports arbitrary function evaluation during bootstrapping. Looking ahead, some of our techniques can be applied to improve the batched bootstrapping method proposed in [50], as discussed in Sect. 8.

Functionality-wise, our major advantage over batched FHEW/TFHE bootstrapping is that our bootstrapping is embedded inside BFV circuits. One can easily perform multiplications and additions before or after our bootstrapping, which is inherently hard in the FHEW/TFHE case.

2   Preliminary

Let N be a power of two. Let $[u, v, r]$ denote the range from u to v with step value r (i.e., $[u, v, r] := \{u, u + r, u + 2r, \ldots, v\}$ and r divides $u - v$). Let $\mathcal{R} = \mathbb{Z}[X]/(X^N + 1)$ denote the $2N$-th cyclotomic ring where N is a power-of-two, and $\mathcal{R}_Q = \mathcal{R}/Q\mathcal{R}$ for some $Q \in \mathbb{Z}$. Let $[n]$ denote the set $\{1, \ldots, n\}$. Let $\vec{a}$ denote a vector and $\vec{a}[i]$ denote the i-th element of $\vec{a}$. Similarly, if A is a matrix, let $A[i][j]$ denote the element on the i-th row and j-th column of matrix A. Let $\|\vec{x}\|_\ell$ denote the ℓ-norm for vector $\vec{x}$ (calculated as $(\sum_{i \in |\vec{x}|} \vec{x}[i]^\ell)^{1/\ell}$). If $x \in \mathcal{R}$, let $\|x\|_\ell$ denote the ℓ-norm of the coefficient vector of x, and let $x[i]$ denote the i-th coefficient of x. Unless otherwise specified, the key is taken implicitly and correctly for functions (e.g., $\mathsf{Dec}(\mathsf{ct})$ where ct is some LWE ciphertext and Dec is the decryption procedure of LWE scheme). All the divisions (i.e., a/b or $\frac{a}{b}$) and roundings (i.e., $\lceil \cdot \rfloor, \lceil \cdot \rceil, \lfloor \cdot \rfloor$) are performed in real numbers. All the other operations (including a^{-1}) are performed in finite field $\mathbb{Z}_t$ for some prime t (where t is specified if not obvious), unless otherwise noted.

2.1   B/FV Leveled Homomorphic Encryption

The BFV leveled homomorphic encryption scheme is first introduced in [6] using standard LWE assumption, and later adapted to ring LWE assumption by [22].

Given a polynomial $\in \mathcal{R}_t = \mathbb{Z}_t[X]/(X^N + 1)$, the BFV scheme encrypts it into a ciphertext consisting of two polynomials, where each polynomial is from a larger cyclotomic ring $\mathcal{R}_Q = \mathbb{Z}_Q[X]/(X^N + 1)$ for some $Q > t$. We refer t as the plaintext modulus, Q as the ciphertext modulus, and N as the ring dimension. t satisfies that $t \equiv 1 \bmod 2N$, where N is a power of two.[5]

Plaintext Encoding. In practice, instead of having a polynomial in $\mathcal{R}_t = \mathbb{Z}_t[X]/(X^N + 1)$ to encrypt, applications usually have a vector of messages $\vec{m} =$

---

[5] Note that this is the relationship between t, N does not need to be satisfied in general (e.g., see [30,31] for the general encoding). However, throughout our paper, we suppose it holds to maximize the concrete efficiency and thus introduce it this way for simplicity.

$(m_1, \ldots, m_N) \in \mathbb{Z}_t^N$. Thus, to encrypt such input messages, BFV first encodes it by constructing another polynomial $y(X) = \sum_{i \in [N]} y_i X^{i-1}$ where $m_i = y(\zeta_j)$, $\zeta_j := \zeta^{3^j} \bmod t$, and ζ is the $2N$-th primitive root of unity of t. Such encoding can be done using an Inverse Number Theoretic Transformation (INTT), which is a linear transformation represented as matrix multiplication.

Encryption and Decryption. The BFV ciphertext encrypting $\vec{m}$ under $\mathsf{sk} \leftarrow \mathcal{D}$ has the following format: $\mathsf{ct} = (a, b) \in \mathcal{R}_Q^2$, which satisfies $b - a \cdot \mathsf{sk} = \lfloor Q/t \rfloor \cdot y + e$ where $\lfloor Q/t \rfloor \cdot y \in \mathcal{R}_Q$ and y is the polynomial encoded in the way above, and e is a small error term sampled from a Gaussian distribution over $\mathcal{R}_Q$ with some constant standard deviation.

Symmetric key encryption can be done by simply sampling a random a and constructing b accordingly using sk. Public key encryption can also be achieved easily but it is not relevant to our paper so we refer the readers to prior works (e.g., [6,22,37]) for details.

Decryption is thus calculating $y' \leftarrow \lceil (t/Q) \cdot (b - a \cdot \mathsf{sk}) \rfloor \in \mathcal{R}_t$ (note that $(b - a \cdot \mathsf{sk})$ is done over $\mathcal{R}_Q$), and then decodes it by applying a procedure to revert the encoding process (which is also a linear transformation). For simplicity, we assume BFV.Dec also embeds the decoding procedure and thus outputs plaintext $y' \in \mathbb{Z}_t^N$ in the decoded form directly (instead of a polynomial $y \in \mathcal{R}_t$). Similarly, we assume BFV.Enc contains the encoding process, thus taking a plaintext $y' \in \mathbb{Z}_t^N$. In addition, define $\mathsf{PartialDec}(\mathsf{sk}, \mathsf{ct} = (a, b) \in \mathcal{R}_Q^2) := b - a \cdot \mathsf{sk} \in \mathcal{R}_Q$ (i.e., decryption without performing the rounding to $\mathcal{R}_t$).

BFV Operations. BFV essentially supports addition, multiplication, rotation, and polynomial function evaluation, satisfying the following property:

- (Addition) $\mathsf{BFV.Dec}(\mathsf{ct}_1 + \mathsf{ct}_2) = \mathsf{BFV.Dec}(\mathsf{ct}_1) + \mathsf{BFV.Dec}(\mathsf{ct}_2)$
- (Multiplication) $\mathsf{BFV.Dec}(\mathsf{ct}_1 \times \mathsf{ct}_2) = \mathsf{BFV.Dec}(\mathsf{ct}_1) \times \mathsf{BFV.Dec}(\mathsf{ct}_2)$
- (Rotation) $\mathsf{BFV.Dec}(\mathsf{rot}(\mathsf{ct}, j))[i] = \mathsf{BFV.Dec}(\mathsf{ct})[i + j \pmod{N}], \forall i, j \in [N]$
- (Polynomial evaluation) $\mathsf{BFV.Dec}(\mathsf{BFV.Eval}(\mathsf{ct}, f)) = f(\mathsf{BFV.Dec}(\mathsf{ct}))$, where $f : \mathbb{Z}_t \rightarrow \mathbb{Z}_t$ is a polynomial function. Note that this is implied by addition and multiplication.
- (Vector-matrix multiplication) $\mathsf{BFV.Dec}(\mathsf{ct} \times A) = \mathsf{BFV.Dec}(\mathsf{ct}) \times A$, where $A \in \mathbb{Z}_t^{N \times D}$ for any $D > 0$.

Given a BFV ciphertext ct and its corresponding secret key sk, we also assume that its noise budget can be derived via interface $\mathcal{B}(\mathsf{sk}, \mathsf{ct})$. A noise budget is essentially the gap between the plaintext encrypted under ct and the noise inside ct, which is used to allow operations (e.g., multiplications) over the ciphertexts. For simplicity, $\mathcal{B}$ with subscripts is also used to refer to hardcoded noise budget bounds (e.g., $\mathcal{B}_{\mathsf{in}}$ represents the noise budget requirement of the input).

All operations are operated over the entire plaintext vector $m \in \mathbb{Z}_t^N$ (element-wise). Thus, all messages need to be evaluated using the same polynomial f by default. This is also known as the Single Instruction Multiple Data (SIMD) property of BFV. Note that vector-matrix multiplication can be realized using scalar multiplication (implied by addition) and rotation. All of these BFV operations are used as blackboxes in our main constructions and we refer the readers to [6,22,30,32,37] to see how these operations are accomplished in detail. In this paper, we sometimes directly refer to the interfaces (e.g., Dec) for short without the BFV prefix (e.g., BFV.Dec).

3   Definition of Generalized BFV Bootstrapping

We first define a more general BFV bootstrapping procedure.[6] As discussed in Sect. 1, the main goal of this generalized definition is to capture (1) the relaxation that not the entire plaintext space needs to be valid, and for the invalid plaintexts, the corresponding correctness does not need to be guaranteed by the construction; (2) the bootstrapping itself contains an evaluation of a given function, thus making the bootstrapping procedure itself more useful and can be embedded directly into the circuit without inducing stand-alone bootstrapping overhead. These two properties are captured as follows: given a function $f : \mathcal{X} \to \mathcal{Y}$ and input ciphertext encrypting $x \in \mathcal{X}$, after the bootstrapping procedure, the output ciphertext encrypts $y = f(x) \in \mathcal{Y}$. If $x \notin \mathcal{X}$, the output is not defined, and thus can be arbitrarily decided by the construction.

The definition also captures the most basic requirement of bootstrapping: the output ciphertext has more noise budget (or equivalently less noise) compared to the input ciphertext, such that bootstrapping can be used to support circuits with arbitrary depth.

Formally, the general BFV bootstrapping procedure is defined as follows, consisting of two PPT algorithms:

- $\mathsf{pp} = (N, t, \mathcal{B}_{\mathsf{in}}, \mathcal{B}_{\mathsf{out}}, \mathcal{F}, \mathsf{pp}_{\mathsf{aux}}), \mathsf{sk}, \mathsf{btk} \leftarrow \mathsf{Setup}(1^\lambda)$: Setup takes a security parameter λ, and outputs a secret key sk, a bootstrapping key btk, and a public parameter pp including ring dimension N, plaintext space t, input noise budget $\mathcal{B}_{\mathsf{in}}$, output noise budget $\mathcal{B}_{\mathsf{out}}$, a function family $\mathcal{F}$, and auxiliary public parameters $\mathsf{pp}_{\mathsf{aux}}$.
- $\mathsf{ct}' \leftarrow \mathsf{Boot}(\mathsf{pp}, \mathsf{btk}, f, \mathsf{ct})$: takes the public parameter pp, a bootstrapping key btk, a function $f \in \mathcal{F}$, a ciphertext ct and outputs a ciphertext ct'.

Definition 1 (Correctness). *The bootstrapping procedure is correct, if it satisfies the following: let* $(\mathsf{pp} = (N, t, \mathcal{B}_{\mathsf{in}}, \mathcal{B}_{\mathsf{out}}, \mathcal{F}, \mathsf{pp}_{\mathsf{aux}}), \mathsf{sk}, \mathsf{btk}) \leftarrow \mathsf{Setup}(1^\lambda)$, *for any function* $f : \mathcal{X} \to \mathcal{Y} \in \mathcal{F}$ *(where* $\mathcal{X}, \mathcal{Y} \subseteq \mathbb{Z}_t$ *and* $|\mathcal{X}| \geq |\mathcal{Y}| \geq 2$*),[7] any honest input ciphertext* ct *with* $\mathcal{B}(\mathsf{sk}, \mathsf{ct}) \geq \mathcal{B}_{\mathsf{in}}$, *let* $\mathsf{ct}' \leftarrow \mathsf{Boot}(\mathsf{pp}, \mathsf{btk}, f, \mathsf{ct})$, $\vec{m} \leftarrow \mathsf{Dec}(\mathsf{sk}, \mathsf{ct}) \in \mathbb{Z}_t^N$, $\vec{m}' \leftarrow \mathsf{Dec}(\mathsf{sk}, \mathsf{ct}') \in \mathbb{Z}_t^N$, *it holds that:*

$$\Pr\left[\begin{array}{l} \forall i \in [N], \ if \ \vec{m}[i] \in \mathcal{X}, f(\vec{m}[i]) = \vec{m}'[i] \\ \wedge \ \mathcal{B}(\mathsf{sk}, \mathsf{ct}') \geq \mathcal{B}_{\mathsf{out}} > \mathcal{B}_{\mathsf{in}} \end{array} \right] \geq 1 - \mathsf{negl}(\lambda)$$

---

[6] We focus on BFV in this work, but all our results can be directly transformed to BGV with minimum modification (e.g., with techniques in [3, Sec A]).

[7] For $|\mathcal{Y}| = |[y]| = 1$, a trivial yet valid bootstrapping is to directly output a BFV ciphertext with all slots encrypting y.

In some cases, applications may require that even if $x \notin \mathcal{X}$, the result does not "deviate" too much (such that the error can be predicted and algorithmically handled). To capture this demand, we define an additional property we call "ℓ-closeness". Essentially, it means that even if $x \notin \mathcal{X}$, the output ciphertext encrypts $y \in \mathcal{S}$, where $\mathcal{S} \subseteq \mathcal{Y}$ contains the evaluation results of the ℓ points of $\mathcal{X}$ that are the "closest" to x (for a point $x' \in \mathcal{X}$, the smaller $|x - x'|$ is, the closer x' and x are).

Note that this property is auxiliary to the regular correctness, and may not be needed in some applications (see Sect. 7 for discussion). Looking ahead, some of our constructions achieve the closenessproperty while some do not. The ones that do not achieve it take advantage of such further relaxation to achieve even better efficiency. With these in mind, we define ℓ-closenessformally as follows.

Definition 2 (ℓ-closeness). *The bootstrapping procedure is ℓ-close, if it satisfies the following: for the same quantifiers as correctness; for all $x \in \mathbb{Z}_t \setminus \mathcal{X}$, let $y_{x,1}, \ldots, y_{x,|\mathcal{Y}|}$ denote all the points in $\mathcal{Y}$ satisfying $|f_x^{-1}(y_{x,1}) - x| \leq |f_x^{-1}(y_{x,2}) - x| \leq \cdots \leq |f_x^{-1}(y_{x,|\mathcal{Y}|}) - x|,$[8,9] and $\mathcal{S}_x := \{y_{x,1}, \ldots, y_{x,\ell}\}$; it holds that for all $i \in [N]$, if $\vec{m}[i] \notin \mathcal{X}$: $\Pr\left[f(\vec{m}[i]) \in \mathcal{S}_{\vec{m}[i]}\right] > 1 - \mathsf{negl}(\lambda)$[10]*

Remark 1. The regular BFV bootstrapping, which only supports $\mathcal{F} = \{I\}$ with $I : \mathbb{Z}_t \to \mathbb{Z}_t$ being the identity function, is a special case of our definition.

Remark 2. Naturally, we want at least $\mathcal{B}_{\mathsf{out}} > \mathcal{B}_{\mathsf{in}} + \mathcal{B}_\times$, where $\mathcal{B}_\times$ is the noise budget needed for one multiplication. Thus, after every bootstrapping, the output ciphertext can perform at least one multiplication (which implies one addition for BFV) before the next bootstrapping. However, for generality, we simply require $\mathcal{B}_{\mathsf{out}} > \mathcal{B}_{\mathsf{in}}$, the minimum requirement for a non-trivial bootstrapping scheme (*without* evaluating a non-identity function), and leave the value of $\mathcal{B}_{\mathsf{out}} - \mathcal{B}_{\mathsf{in}}$ to be tuned based on applications during setup.

4   Our General Framework for Bootstrapping

In this section, we propose a (relaxed) BFV bootstrapping framework. In Sect. 4.1, we start with a simple function (the identity function over a subset of the plaintext space) to show how the general framework works. Then in Sect. 4.2, we use a generalized type of function to show how the framework can be used for more versatile functions. These two types of functions work as stepping stones to fully introduce our framework. We later show in Sect. 5 how the framework works for more general types of function families.

---

[8] Let $f_x^{-1}(y)$ denote a point z where $f(z) = y$ and $z - x = \min_{z' \in \mathcal{X}, f(z')=y}(z' - x)$. In other words, $f_x^{-1}(y)$ outputs a point that is (1) a valid input in $\mathcal{X}$; and (2) is the close to x among all possible points z' satisfying $f(z') = y$.

[9] If $|f_x^{-1}(y_{x,i}) - x| = |f_x^{-1}(y_{x,j}) - x|$ for $i \neq j$, then any order is accepted.

[10] The randomness is taken over the input ciphertext and the generated keys.

4.1 Bootstrap for Identity Function f_1 over $[0, t-1, r]$

As a stepping stone, let us first consider the identity function. Different from prior works that focus on identity mapping on all values in $\mathbb{Z}_t$, we define f_1 with input consisting of a set of points $\mathcal{X} \subset \mathbb{Z}_t$. This allows us to construct a more efficient bootstrapping scheme.

Let $\mathcal{X} := [0, t-1, r]$, for some $1 \leq r < t$ (r to-be-fixed later). Denote $\vec{m} \in \mathbb{Z}_t^N \leftarrow \mathsf{Dec}(\mathsf{sk}, \mathsf{ct}_{in})$, where ct_{in} is the input ciphertext, sk is the corresponding secret key, t is the plaintext space, and N is the ring dimension. Our goal is to compute $\mathsf{ct}_{out} \leftarrow \mathsf{Boot}(\cdot, \cdot, \mathsf{ct}_{in}, f_1)$ such that for all $i \in [N]$, if $\vec{m}[i] \in \mathcal{X}$, $\vec{m}'[i] = \vec{m}[i]$, where $\vec{m}' \leftarrow \mathsf{Dec}(\mathsf{sk}, \mathsf{ct}_{out})$.

Decoding the Input Ciphertext. Recall that as introduced in Sect. 2, to encrypt a message $\vec{m} \in \mathbb{Z}_t^N$, BFV constructs a ciphertext ct that encrypts a polynomial $y(X)$ encoding $\vec{m}$. Formally speaking, let $\mathsf{ct} = (a, b) \in \mathcal{R}_Q^2$, it holds that $b - a \cdot \mathsf{sk} \approx \lfloor Q/t \rfloor \cdot y$, where $y(X) = \sum_{i \in [N]} y[i] X^{i-1} \in \mathcal{R}_t$, satisfying $\vec{m}[i] = y(\zeta_i)$ (where $\zeta_i := \zeta^{3^i}$) for all $i \in [N]$ (ζ is the $2N$-th primitive root of unity of t). Thus, the very first step for bootstrapping (i.e., homomorphic decryption) is to perform a decoding, homomorphically changing the encrypted $y(X)$ into $m(X) := \sum_{i \in [N]} \vec{m}[i] X^{i-1}$ by computing $\mathsf{ct}_1 \leftarrow \mathsf{ct} \cdot U^\mathsf{T}$ homomorphically with:

$$
U := \begin{pmatrix}
1 & \zeta_0 & \zeta_0^2 & \cdots & \zeta_0^{N-1} \\
\vdots & \vdots & \vdots & \ddots & \vdots \\
1 & \zeta_{\frac{N}{2}-1} & \zeta_{\frac{N}{2}-1}^2 & \cdots & \zeta_{\frac{N}{2}-1}^{N-1} \\
1 & \bar{\zeta}_0 & \bar{\zeta}_0^2 & \cdots & \bar{\zeta}_0^{N-1} \\
\vdots & \vdots & \vdots & \ddots & \vdots \\
1 & \bar{\zeta}_{\frac{N}{2}-1} & \bar{\zeta}_{\frac{N}{2}-1}^2 & \cdots & \bar{\zeta}_{\frac{N}{2}-1}^{N-1}
\end{pmatrix} \in \mathbb{Z}_t^{N \times N} \quad \text{as the } \mathsf{SlotToCoeff} \text{ step in [50]}.
$$

Switching Modulus. Now we have a ciphertext $\mathsf{ct}_1 = (a_1, b_1) \in \mathcal{R}_Q^2$, encrypting $m(X) \in \mathcal{R}_t$ defined above. Recall that the plaintext space of the underlying BFV scheme is $\mathbb{Z}_t$. Therefore, to homomorphically decrypt ct_1, we need to first match the modulus by performing a modulus switching: $\mathsf{ct}_2 \leftarrow \lceil t \cdot (a_1, b_1)/Q \rfloor \in \mathcal{R}_t^2$. Notice that with $\mathsf{ct}_1 = (a_1, b_1)$ satisfying $b_1 - a_1 \cdot \mathsf{sk} = \alpha \cdot m + e$ (where $\alpha = \lfloor Q/t \rfloor$), for some small noise term $e \in \mathcal{R}_Q$. After modulus switching, we have $\mathsf{ct}_2 = (a_2, b_2)$ satisfying $b_2 - a_2 \cdot \mathsf{sk} = m + e'$, where $e'(X) := \sum_{i \in [N]} e'[i] X^{i-1} \in \mathcal{R}_t$ is some noise term dominated by the error introduced through modulus switching, which might "contaminate" the correct message m.

Fortunately, we do not need to correctly decrypt all possible values in $\mathbb{Z}_t$, but instead, only consider the correct decryption of $m[i] \in [0, t-1, r]$; for invalid values in $\mathbb{Z}_t \setminus [0, t-1, r]$, we do not need to guarantee the correctness per Definition 1. Therefore, we fix r to be the smallest positive integer such that $\Pr[\|e'[i]\| < r/2] \geq 1 - \mathsf{negl}(\lambda)$ for all $i \in [N]$.[11]

This means that for $m[i] \in [0, t-1, r]$, $m[i] + e'[i] \in (m[i] - r/2, m[i] + r/2)$, Rounding $m[i] + e'[i]$ to the nearest value in $[0, t-1, r]$ then gives us exactly $m[i]$,

---

[11] For simplicity, we assume r divides $t-1$. This is w.l.o.g because we can make the range $[0, t-t', r]$ where $t-t'$ is the largest multiple of r with $t > 0$. This change does not affect the main point or technique of this paper.

which provides the correct decryption. Formally speaking, with $\mathsf{ct}_2 = (a_2, b_2)$, let $m'(X) := \sum m'[i]X^{i-1} \leftarrow b_2 - a_2 \cdot \mathsf{sk}$, it holds that $r\left\lceil\frac{m'[i]}{r}\right\rceil = \vec{m}[i] \in \mathbb{Z}_t$, for all $i \in [N]$, except with negligible probability. With these, we proceed to introduce how the homomorphic decryption is done.

Analysis of t and r. One may wonder whether this t is always possible to achieve given that we need $t > r$. Luckily, this is easy: since the modulus switching error, as mentioned in [21, Lemma 5], is $O(\sqrt{h})$ where h is the hamming weight of the secret key.[12] Thus, we simply need to set $t = \omega(\sqrt{h})$. To utilize the full SIMD power of the BFV scheme, one needs to set $t > N$ such that $t \equiv 1 \bmod 2N$ (as discussed in Sect. 2), and thus $t = \Omega(N) = \omega\sqrt{h}$ (for ternary or binary secret keys). Note that prior works [14,25,26,32,56] similarly require the keys to be ternary or binary (or more commonly a sparse key with some fixed hamming weight), as they need to bound the wrap-around over $\mathbb{Z}_t$ as well to perform the digit extraction method. Furthermore, most existing implementations of BFV [1,4,57] use a ternary secret key. Thus, we believe our parameter setting is easily achievable.

Homomorphic Decryption. The final step is to homomorphically decrypt ct_2. Note that now $\mathsf{ct}_2 \in \mathcal{R}_t^2$, and the plaintext modulus is t. Therefore, we can simply homomorphically compute $b_2 - a_2 \cdot \mathsf{sk}$ over $\mathbb{Z}_t$ by utilizing the free mod operation. Compared to prior works [14,26,32], which need to perform plaintext space switching, our construction is much simpler. In more detail, our homomorphic decryption is carried out in two steps:

- First, given $\mathsf{ct}_2 = (a_2, b_2) \in \mathcal{R}_t^2$, we evaluate a partial decryption process $\mathsf{PartialDec}(\mathsf{sk}, \mathsf{ct}_2)$, which computes $b_2 - \mathsf{ct}_{\mathsf{sk}} \times A_2$, where $\mathsf{ct}_{\mathsf{sk}}$ is the encrypted sk under BFV, $A_2 := \begin{pmatrix} a_2[1] & a_2[2] & a_2[3] & \cdots & a_2[N] \\ -a_2[N] & a_2[1] & a_2[2] & \cdots & a_2[N-1] \\ -a_2[N-1] & -a_2[N] & a_2[1] & \cdots & a_2[N-2] \\ \vdots & \vdots & \vdots & \ddots & \vdots \\ -a_2[2] & -a_2[3] & -a_2[4] & \cdots & a_2[1] \end{pmatrix} \in \mathbb{Z}_t^{N \times N}$ (i.e., the matrix representation of ring element $a \in \mathcal{R}_t$), and $\mathsf{ct}_{\mathsf{sk}} \times A_2$ is homomorphically computed as a vector-matrix multiplication. The resulting ciphertext is denoted as ct_3.

- With ciphertext ct_3 encrypting $(m'[1], \ldots, m'[N]) \in \mathbb{Z}_t^N$ (recall that $m' = m + e'$ for some small error e'), we then simply need to compute $r\left\lceil\frac{m_i'}{r}\right\rceil$ over $\mathbb{Z}_t$ for all $i \in [N]$. This can be done by interpolating a function $f_{\mathsf{post}}(x) : \mathbb{Z}_t \to \mathbb{Z}_t$, s.t., for all $x \in \mathbb{Z}_t$, $f_{\mathsf{post}}(x) = r\lceil\frac{x}{r}\rfloor$ via Lagrange interpolation. The resulting ciphertext, denoted as $\mathsf{ct}_{\mathsf{out}}$, encrypts the same message as $\mathsf{ct}_{\mathsf{in}}$ as desired.

Bootstrapping Key and Noise Setup. Lastly, we discuss what the bootstrapping key contains. Since we need to homomorphically decrypt the ciphertext ct_2,

---

[12] Note that this is the modulus switching error of the LWE ciphertexts, which we can achieve by simply transforming one RLWE ciphertext to N LWE ciphertexts using the SampleExtract procedure as discussed incite [18]. One may also simply bound the modulus switching error of RLWE as discussed in [37], which is $O(\sqrt{N})$ for binary/ternary secrets.

Algorithm 1. BFV Bootstrapping for $f_1 : [0, t-1, r] \rightarrow [0, t-1, r]$

1: **procedure** Setup(1^λ)
2:     Select $(N, Q, \mathcal{D}, \sigma, \mathcal{B}_{in}, \mathcal{B}_{out}, t)$ satisfying the following while minimizing the overall computation cost of Boot below:
3:         (1) RLWE$_{N,Q,\mathcal{D},\chi_\sigma}$ holds.
4:         (2) Select the minimum $\mathcal{B}_{in}$ such that a BFV ciphertext with ring dimension N, plaintext space t, and noise budget $\mathcal{B}_{in}$, is enough to evaluate SlotToCoeff.
5:         (3) Select the minimum Q such that a fresh BFV ciphertext with ring dimension N, plaintext space t, and ciphertext space Q, after evaluating PartialDec followed by f_{post}, still has $\mathcal{B}_{out} = \mathcal{B}_{in} + 1$ noise budget remaining. ▷ $\mathcal{B}_{out}$ can be replaced by any number dependent on applications.
6:     Let r be the error bound such that $\Pr[\|\mathsf{err}(\mathsf{sk}, \mathsf{ct}_3)\| < r/2] \geq 1 - \mathsf{negl}(\lambda)$, where ct_3 is in line 16 below.
7:     Let $\mathsf{pp}_{bfv} := (N, Q, \mathcal{D}, \sigma, t)$.
8:     $\mathsf{sk}, \mathsf{btk} \leftarrow \mathsf{KeyGen}(1^\lambda, \mathsf{pp}_{bfv})$
9:     $\mathcal{F}_1 := \{f_1(x) := x \text{ iff } x \in [0, t-1, r]\}$
10:    **return** $\mathsf{pp} = (N, t, \mathcal{B}_{in}, \mathcal{B}_{out}, \mathcal{F}_1, \mathsf{pp}_{aux} = r), \mathsf{sk}, \mathsf{btk})$.
11: **procedure** Boot($\mathsf{pp} = (N, t, \mathcal{B}_{in}, \mathcal{B}_{out}, \mathcal{F}, \mathsf{pp}_{aux} = r), \mathsf{btk}, \mathsf{ct}_{in}, f_1$)
12:    If $f_1 \notin \mathcal{F}_1$, abort.
13:    $f_{post}(x) := r \lfloor \frac{x}{r} \rfloor$
14:    $\mathsf{ct}_1 \leftarrow \mathsf{ct}_{in} \times U^\mathsf{T}$ (evaluated homomorphically)
15:                                    ▷ Recall that U is defined in Section 4.1 and this step is SlotToCoeff
16:    $\mathsf{ct}_2 \leftarrow \mathsf{ModSwitch}(\mathsf{ct}_1, t)$
17:    Parse $\mathsf{ct}_2 = (a_2 = \sum_{i \in [N]} a_{2,i} X^{i-1}, b_2 = \sum_{i \in [N]} b_{2,i} X^{i-1}) \in \mathcal{R}_t^2$
18:    Let A_2 be the matrix representation of a_2, and $\vec{b}_2 \leftarrow (b_{2,i})_{i \in [N]} \in \mathbb{Z}_t^N$
19:    $\mathsf{ct}_3 \leftarrow \vec{b}_2 - \mathsf{ct}_{sk} \times A_2$ (evaluated homomorphically)   ▷ i.e., PartialDec($\mathsf{ct}_2, \mathsf{sk}$)
20:    $\mathsf{ct}_{out} \leftarrow \mathsf{BFV}.\mathsf{Eval}(\mathsf{evk}, \mathsf{ct}_3, f_{post})$
21:    **return** ct_{out}.

---

we need to include ct_{sk} which is the encrypted sk under BFV. Moreover, BFV public keys pk and BFV evaluation keys evk, the keys needed to evaluate the circuits in the construction (e.g., the relinearization key and the rotation keys[13]), are all included in the bootstrapping key.

We also need to specify the input noise budget and output noise budget. $\mathcal{B}_{in}$ is set to be enough for evaluating the SlotToCoeff step, and Q to be large enough to evaluate f_{post} such that afterwards there are still at least $\mathcal{B}_{out} > \mathcal{B}_{in}$ noise budget left.

To finalize the algorithm of BFV bootstrapping for our identity function f_1, we need to do some preparation work in the Setup phase, including choosing all public parameters such as the ring dimension N and the plaintext space t. The bootstrapping keys are generated as discussed above. Finally, we define $f_{post}(x) := r \lceil \frac{x}{r} \rceil$. The procedure is formalized in Algorithm 1.

---

[13] For simplicity, we assume all possible rotation keys are generated. Later, we discuss how to only generate the necessary ones.

Theorem 1. *Algorithm 1 is a correct BFV functional bootstrapping (Definition 1) procedure with function family $\mathcal{F} := \{f(x) = x, \forall x \in [0, t-1, r]\}$ where t, r are from* pp *generated by* Setup, *assuming the correctness of BFV. Furthermore, it is 2-close(Definition 2).*

Proof. Given that the underlying BFV is correct (i.e., all the homomorphic evaluations are completed as expected given enough noise budget), let $\vec{m} \leftarrow$ Dec(sk, ct$_{\text{in}}$) $\in \mathbb{Z}_t^N$, ct$_1 = (a_1, b_1) \in \mathcal{R}_Q^2$, $m_1 \leftarrow \lceil (t/Q)(b_1 - a_1 \cdot \text{sk}) \rfloor$ (i.e., BFV decryption without the decoding process), it holds that $m_1 = \sum_{i \in [N]} \vec{m}[i] X^{i-1} \in \mathcal{R}_t$, by condition (2) (that there is enough noise budget for SlotToCoeff). Let ct$_2 = (a_2, b_2) \in \mathcal{R}_t^2$, $m_2 := \sum_{i \in [N]} m_2[i] X^{i-1} \leftarrow b_2 - a_2 \cdot \text{sk} \in \mathcal{R}_t$, Then, it holds that $\Pr[m_2[i] \in (\vec{m}[i] - r/2, \vec{m}[i] + r/2)] \geq 1 - \text{negl}(\lambda)$ for all $i \in [N]$, by condition (3) (that the error range r is large enough). Thus, let $\vec{m}_3 \leftarrow$ Dec(sk, ct$_3$) $\in \mathbb{Z}_t^N$, for all $i \in [N]$, $\vec{m}_3[i] = m_2[i]$. Lastly, let $\vec{m}_4 \leftarrow$ Dec(sk, ct$_{\text{out}}$) $\in \mathbb{Z}_t^N$, we have $\vec{m}_4[i] = r \cdot \left\lceil \frac{\vec{m}_3[i]}{r} \right\rfloor = r \cdot \left\lceil \frac{m_2[i]}{r} \right\rfloor$ for all $i \in [N]$ by f_{post} and condition (3) (that there is enough noise budget to evaluate PartialDec and f_{post}). Since we have $m_2[i] \in (\vec{m}[i] - r/2, \vec{m}[i] + r/2)$, then if $\vec{m}[i] \in [0, t-1, r]$, we have $\vec{m}_4[i] = \vec{m}[i]$ for all $i \in [N]$.

The 2-closenessproperty is straightforward. The intuition is that the invalid input points are "rounded" to the two nearest valid input points. In more detail, let $x = \vec{m}[i]$, and let $z_{x,i} \leftarrow f_x^{-1}(y_{x,i})$ for $i \in [1, 2]$ and $y_{x,i}$ in Definition 2; let $d_1 \leftarrow x - z_{x,1}$, $d_2 \leftarrow x - z_{x,2}$, (where $z_{x,j}$ are per closeness definition). Note that we have $d_2 = r - d_1$ and $d_2 \geq r/2 \geq d_1$. For 2-closenessto not hold, err(sk, ct$_3$) $> r/2 + d_1$, which happens with negl(λ) by condition (3).

Biased rounding for invalid inputs. In addition to 2-closeness, there is another property of our construction with respect to invalid inputs. At a high level, an invalid input rounds to the nearest valid input with high probability p and rounds to the second nearest valid input with $1 - p$, where $p \gg 1 - p$ as long as the invalid input is obviously closer to one input than the other (i.e., $d_1 \ll d_2$ using the notations in the proof).

4.2   Bootstrapping for $f_2 : [u, v, r'] \to \mathcal{Y}$

We now extend the above identity function into a more general function family: $\mathcal{F}_2 = \{f_2 : [u, v, r'] \to \mathcal{Y}\}$, where $u, v, r' \in \mathbb{Z}_t$, and $\mathcal{Y}$ being any subset of $\mathbb{Z}_t$ with $|\mathcal{Y}| \leq |[u, v, r']| = \frac{t-1}{r}$.[14] It is easy to see that f_1 is the special form with $u = 0, v = t - 1, r' = r$ and $\mathcal{Y} = [u, v, r']$.

Preprocess the Input Ciphertext with f_{pre}. The very first challenge is that if we have $r' < r$ (call that r is set to be the error bound of modulus switching), after multiplying the ciphertext with t/Q during the modulus switching step, the encrypted messages will be contaminated by the error incurred and thus the decryption process fails.

---

[14] Note that if $|[u, v, r']| < \frac{t-1}{r}$, we can either pad dummy elements to follow the same bootstrapping procedure or apply a more efficient way, introduced in Sect. 5.1.

To resolve this issue, we first "preprocess" the input ciphertexts by stretching the small intervals r' to be r the error bound: in this case the encrypted messages would survive the modulus switching procedure. In more detail, we construct a bijective mapping $f_{\mathsf{pre}}(x) : [u, v, r'] \to [0, t-1, r]$, defined as $f_{\mathsf{pre}}(x) := (x - u) \cdot r \cdot (r')^{-1}$. Before we perform the original SlotToCoeff process as the first step discussed above, we first homomorphically evaluate f_{pre} over the input ciphertext $\mathsf{ct_{in}}$ (which means by the SIMD property we evaluate $f_{\mathsf{pre}}(\vec{m}[i])$ for all $i \in [N]$ and $\vec{m}$ being the message vector encrypted under $\mathsf{ct_{in}}$).

A New f_{post} Function. As before, after preprocessing, we perform SlotToCoeff and modulus switching. The resulting ciphertext encrypts $\vec{m}' \in \mathbb{Z}_t^N$ such that $r \cdot \lceil \vec{m}'[i]/r \rceil = f_{\mathsf{pre}}(\vec{m}[i])$ for all $i \in [N]$. Here comes the second challenge: instead of simple identity mapping, which requires nothing else other than output $\vec{m}'$ in our previous construction[15], $\mathcal{Y}$ as the output set of f_2 can be any arbitrary subset of $\mathbb{Z}_t$ with size $\leq |\frac{t-1}{r'}|$.

Thus, we need a new function $f_{\mathsf{post}}(x) : \mathbb{Z}_t \to \mathbb{Z}_t$ to map $\vec{m}'$ onto the corresponding values in $\mathcal{Y}$, i.e., $f_{\mathsf{post}}(x) = f_2(f_{\mathsf{pre}}^{-1}(r \cdot \lceil x/r \rceil))$. Note that since f_{pre} is bijective, f_{pre}^{-1} always exists. The correctness is as follows:

$$f_{\mathsf{post}}(\vec{m}'[i]) = f_2(f_{\mathsf{pre}}^{-1}(r \cdot \lceil \vec{m}'[i]/r \rceil)) = f_2(f_{\mathsf{pre}}^{-1}(f_{\mathsf{pre}}(\vec{m}[i]))) = f_2(\vec{m}[i])$$

Regarding the Setup phase, we set $\mathcal{B}_{\mathsf{in}}$ to be large enough to evaluate *any* degree one function (to accommodate the noise growth in the worst case), since

---

Algorithm 2. BFV Bootstrapping for $f_2 : [u, v, r'] \to \mathcal{Y}$

1: **procedure** Setup(1^λ)
2:    Same as the Setup in Algorithm 1, except for that lines 4, 5, and 9 are changed to the following:
3:    line 4: (2) Select the minimum $\mathcal{B}_{\mathsf{in}}$ such that a BFV ciphertext with ring dimension N, plaintext space t, and noise budget $\mathcal{B}_{\mathsf{in}}$, is enough to evaluate SlotToCoeff followed by any degree-1 polynomial function.
4:    line 5: (3) Select the minimum Q such that a fresh BFV ciphertext with ring dimension N, plaintext space t, and ciphertext space Q, after evaluating PartialDec followed by an arbitrary degree-t polynomial function, still has $\mathcal{B}_{\mathsf{out}} = \mathcal{B}_{\mathsf{in}} + 1$ noise budget remaining.
5:    line 9: $\mathcal{F}_2 := \{f_2(x) : [u, v, r'] \to \mathcal{Y} \mid (u, v, r' \in \mathbb{Z}_t) \wedge (\mathcal{Y} \subset \mathbb{Z}_t) \wedge (|\mathcal{Y}| \leq |[u, v, r']| = \frac{t-1}{r})\}$
6: **procedure** Boot$(\mathsf{pp} = (N, t, \mathcal{B}_{\mathsf{in}}, \mathcal{B}_{\mathsf{out}}, \mathcal{F}_2, \mathsf{pp_{aux}} = r), \mathsf{btk}, \mathsf{ct_{in}}, f_2)$ ▷ For the sake of space, we call the GeneralFramework function defined in Algorithm 3.
7:    If $f_2 \notin \mathcal{F}_2$, abort.
8:    Let the input domain of f_2 be $[u, v, r]$.
9:    $f_{\mathsf{pre}}(x) := (x - u) \cdot r \cdot (r')^{-1}$
10:    $f_{\mathsf{post}}(x) = f_2(f_{\mathsf{pre}}^{-1}(r \cdot \lceil x/r \rceil))$
11:    $\mathsf{ct_{out}} \leftarrow \mathsf{GeneralFramework}(\mathsf{pp}, \mathsf{btk}, \mathsf{ct_{in}}, f_{\mathsf{pre}}, f_{\mathsf{post}})$
12:    **return** $\mathsf{ct_{out}}$.

---

[15] Note that even if we do have an identity mapping (i.e., $\mathcal{Y} = [u, v, r']$), the f_{post} in the previous section is not enough as we need to revert the influence of f_{pre}.

f_{pre} is at most a degree-1 polynomial. Similarly, for f_{post} to be at most degree-$(t-1)$, we set Q large enough to accommodate an arbitrary degree-$(t-1)$ function. We formalize our construction in Algorithm 2. As since the proof is very similar to that of Theorem 1, we defer it to our full version [51] for space.

Theorem 2. *Algorithm 2 is a correct BFV functional bootstrapping (Definition 1) procedure for function family $\mathcal{F}_2 := \{f_2 := [u,v,r'] \to \mathcal{Y} \mid (u,v,r' \in \mathbb{Z}_t) \land (\mathcal{Y} \subset \mathbb{Z}_t) \land (|\mathcal{Y}| \le |[u,v,r']| = \frac{t-1}{r})\}$, assuming the correctness of BFV. Furthermore, if it $|\mathcal{Y}|$-closeness(Definition 2).*

2-Closeness. When extending f_1 to f_2, the 2-closenessproperty cannot be satisfied easily. The reason is that now f_{pre} maps a point $\notin \mathcal{X}$ into an arbitrary point. This point is then "rounded" to one of the two closest points in $[0, t-1, r]$ as for f_1, when evaluating f_{post}. The only exception is that when $r' = r$, f_{pre} simply shifts the inputs. In this case, $|\mathcal{Y}|$-closeness is improved to 2-closeness.

4.3   General Framework

We now introduce the general framework abstracted from the constructions we described above for the two function families. Looking ahead, the rest of the work highly relies on this framework, and only small local changes are made for different function families.

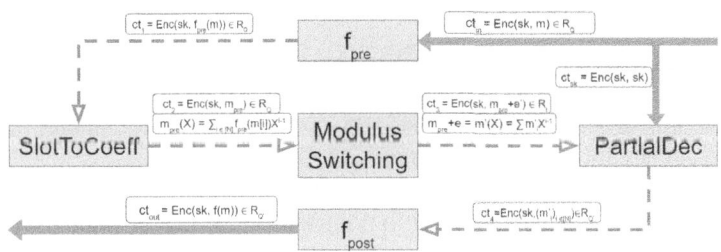

Fig. 1. The high-level illustration of our generalized framework

The general framework is straightforward, a visualization is provided in Fig. 1. It is formalized in Algorithm 3, where KeyGen is used to generate bootstrapping keys given f_{pre} and f_{post}; and GeneralFramework is used to formalize our general Boot procedure. Note that setting up the noise budgets is not included, since it is more function-family-dependent and we leave it to the setup algorithm for each function family. To avoid repetition, all of our procedures directly call the ones in Algorithm 3 as sub-procedures (except for Algorithm 1 served as the starting point).

Algorithm 3. General Framework

1: **procedure** KeyGen(1^λ, pp_{bfv})
2:     Prase $pp_{bfv} = (N, Q, \mathcal{D}, \sigma, t)$.
3:     Generate BFV secret key $sk = \sum_{i \in [N]} s_i X^{i-1} \leftarrow \mathcal{D}$, and let $\vec{s} := (s_i)_{i \in [N]} \in \mathbb{Z}_t^N$.
4:     Generate fresh encryption of BFV secret key $sk \leftarrow \mathcal{D}$.
5:     Generate $ct_{sk} \leftarrow \mathsf{Enc}(sk, \vec{s})$ with pp_{bfv} [16]
6:     Generate BFV public key pk and evaluation key evk, using sk.
7:     Let $btk := (pk, evk, ct_{sk})$.
8:     **return** sk, btk.

9: **procedure** GeneralFramework(pp, $btk = (pk, evk, ct_{sk})$, $ct_{in}, f_{pre}, f_{post}$)
10:     $ct_1 \leftarrow \mathsf{BFV.Eval}(evk, ct_{in}, f_{pre})$
11:     $ct_2 \leftarrow ct_1 \times U^\mathsf{T}$ (evaluated homomorphically)
12:         $\triangleright$ Recall that U is defined in Section 4.1 and this step is SlotToCoeff
13:     $ct_3 \leftarrow \mathsf{ModSwitch}(ct_2, t)$
14:     Parse $ct_3 = (a_3 = \sum_{i \in [N]} a_3[i] X^{i-1}, b_2 = \sum_{i \in [N]} b_3[i] X^{i-1}) \in \mathcal{R}_t^2$
15:     Let A_2 be the matrix representation of a_3, and $\vec{b}_3 \leftarrow (b_3[i])_{i \in [N]} \in \mathbb{Z}_t^N$
16:     $ct_4 \leftarrow \vec{b}_3 - ct_{sk} \times A_3$ (evaluated homomorphically) $\triangleright$ i.e., PartialDec(ct_2, sk)
17:     $ct_{out} \leftarrow \mathsf{BFV.Eval}(evk, ct_4, f_{post})$
18:     **return** ct_{out}.

Optimization. For the best concrete performance, we also use some techniques to optimize some specific steps of our framework. Due to space reasons, we move the optimization discussion to our full version [51].[17]

5   A More Fine-Grained Construction

In this section, we make our construction's efficiency more fine-grained: i.e., dependent on the function families it needs to support.

Recall that for all the constructions introduced in Sect. 4, the circuits for evaluating f_{post}, which is of degree $O(t)$, have $O(t)$ multiplications. Notice that t needs to be at least $2N + 1$ to allow N slots for the best-amortized efficiency. In some applications, t needs to be even larger to allow a larger finite field computation. The efficiency is therefore greatly hampered. A natural question is can we make the number of multiplications and the degree of f_{post} $o(t)$?

Unfortunately, if we are mapping $O(t)$ of $\mathbb{Z}_t$ elements into $\mathbb{Z}_t$ elements (which is indeed the case for all the functions introduced above), we need a polynomial function of degree $\Omega(t)$. This makes it intuitively impossible to improve the efficiency asymptotically. Thus, in this section, we discuss some other function families with a more limited input domain (e.g., simply mapping $z \in \mathbb{Z}_t$ to $y \in \mathbb{Z}_t$ and $z' \neq z \in \mathbb{Z}_t$ to $y' \neq y \in \mathbb{Z}_t$), and show how to support them by evaluating a polynomial with a much smaller degree and thus provide better efficiency.

---

[17] Note that both our asymptotic behavior and the one in prior works shown in Table 1 assumes using the Paterson-Stockmeyer algorithm discussed in Algorithm 3.

5.1 Point Functions

Two-Point Functions. We start with the simplest case: a function mapping two points to two points. We formalized this two-point mapping function as follows: $f_{2\text{points}}(x) = \begin{cases} y & \text{if } x = z \\ y' & \text{if } x = z' \end{cases}$ where $z \neq z', y \neq y' \in \mathbb{Z}_t$.[18]

We apply our generalized framework introduced in Sect. 4 by passing the correct $f_{\text{pre}}, f_{\text{post}}$ accordingly. Similar to the general issue discussed in Sect. 4.2, since $z \neq z'$ can be arbitrary, f_{pre} needs to be used to scale the intervals $|z - z'|$ by mapping z to v and z' to v' such that $|v - v'| \geq r$, where r again is the error bound. For simplicity, we choose $v = 0, v' = r$. Thus, $f_{\text{pre}}(x) := r(x-z)(z'-z)^{-1}$. If $x = z$, $f_{\text{pre}}(x) = 0$; if $x = z'$, $f_{\text{pre}}(x) = r$.

Then, for f_{post}, we simply need to (homomorphically) map the ciphertext resulting from the partial decryption to y or y'. Formally: $f_{\text{post}}(x) = \begin{cases} y & \text{if } x \in (-r/2, r/2) \\ y' & \text{if } x \in (r/2, 3r/2) \end{cases}$ Note that this function only has $< 2r \ll t$ roots[19], which means that the degree of the function and the number of multiplications to evaluate this polynomial are both $O(r)$ instead of $O(t)$.

Now we discuss how to extend this idea to support more than 2 points.

Revisiting Function Family $\mathcal{F}_2$. Let us first take a closer look at the function discussed in Sect. 4.2: $f_2 : [u, v, r'] \to \mathcal{Y} \in \mathcal{F}_2$, $u, v, r' \in \mathbb{Z}_t$, and $\mathcal{Y} \subset \mathbb{Z}_t$, and let $S := |[u, v, r']|$, we have $|\mathcal{Y}| \leq S \leq \frac{t-1}{r}$. The reason why the degree of f_{post} for f_2 needs to be $O(t)$ is that $S = \frac{t-1}{r}$, and by mapping all the inputs within error bound r to their corresponding outputs, we are eventually mapping all points $\in \mathbb{Z}_t$. In other words, if we make S strictly less than $\frac{t-1}{r}$, the pre-processing and post-processing can be evaluated by polynomials with degree $< t$.

To be more specific, denote f_2' to be this variant of f_2 with $S < \frac{t-1}{r}$. To perform functional bootstrapping for f_2', the preprocessing function remains unchanged: $f_{\text{pre}}(x) := (x - u) \cdot r \cdot (r')^{-1}$, and set $f_{\text{post}}(x) = f_2'(f_{\text{pre}}^{-1}(r \cdot \lceil x/r \rceil))$, for $x \in [-r/2, (S - 1) \cdot r + r/2]$.

The difference between the bootstrapping procedure for f_2 and f_2' is that now f_{pre} has S roots and f_{post} has $S \cdot r$ roots, which largely reduces the degree and number of multiplications needed when S is small.

Multi-Point Mapping Function Family. The above high-level idea can be extended to a more general multi-point mapping function family $\mathcal{F}_{\text{pts}} = \{f_{\text{pts}} : \mathcal{X} \to \mathcal{Y}, \mathcal{X}, \mathcal{Y} \subseteq \mathbb{Z}_t, |\mathcal{Y}| \leq |\mathcal{X}|\}$. Denote $S = |\mathcal{X}|$, and let $\mathcal{X} = \{x_1, \ldots, x_S\}$. Similarly, to map the input to $[0, (S - 1) \cdot r, r]$. we define $f_{\text{pre}}(m) := i \cdot r$ if $m = x_i$. Then, the post-processing function remains mostly the same: $f_{\text{post}}(x) := f_{\text{pts}}(f_{\text{pre}}^{-1}(r \cdot \lceil x/r \rceil))$, for $x \in [-r/2, (S - 1) \cdot r + r/2]$.

By interpolating $f_{\text{pre}}, f_{\text{post}}$ of polynomials with degree $S, S \cdot r$ respectively, we have the construction for a general multi-point mapping function. For space

---

[18] Note that if $y = y'$, the construction is trivial. Simply return $\mathsf{Enc}(\mathsf{sk}, y)$ suffices, as the correctness definition does not explicitly define the behavior for $f(x)$ if $x \notin \{z, z'\}$.

[19] Recall that $r = O(\sqrt{h})$ where h is the hamming weight of the secret key.

reasons, we defer the pseudocode to and the proof of the following theorem is similar to our full version [51].

Theorem 3. *Algorithm 4 in our full version [51] is a correct BFV functional bootstrapping (Definition 1) procedure for function family $\mathcal{F}_{\mathsf{pts}} := \{f_{\mathsf{pts}} : \mathcal{X} \rightarrow \mathcal{Y} \mid \mathcal{X}, \mathcal{Y} \subset \mathbb{Z}_t, |\mathcal{Y}| \leq |\mathcal{X}| = S < \frac{t-1}{r}\}$, with t is from pp generated by Setup, assuming the correctness of BFV.*

Remark 3. Notice that when $S \ll t$, i.e., the input set $\mathcal{X}$ is very sparse over $\mathbb{Z}_t$, a low degree (with degree $\ll S$) function may already be enough to map $\mathcal{X}$ to $\mathcal{X}'$ such that for all $i \neq j \in \mathcal{X}'$, $|i - j| > r$. After obtaining $\mathcal{X}'$, we simply set $f_{\mathsf{post}}(m) := f_{\mathsf{pts}}(x)$ for $m \in [f_{\mathsf{pre}}(x) - r/2, f_{\mathsf{pre}}(x) + r/2], x \in \mathcal{X}$ (thereby $f_{\mathsf{pre}}(x) \in \mathcal{X}'$). I.e., f_{post} checks every possible $x \in \mathcal{X}$, and if m is within $r/2$ points for any of the $f_{\mathsf{pre}}(x)$, return $f_{\mathsf{pts}}(x)$.

Furthermore, if $\forall i \neq j \in \mathcal{X}$, we have $|i-j| > r$, then there is no pre-processing needed to scale the intervals in between. See Sect. 6 for a concrete example. For simplicity, in the formal construction, we consider the worst-case scenario and treat the degree of f_{pre} to be S.

ℓ-closeness. For f_{pts}, ℓ-closeness does not hold for any ℓ unless $S = \frac{t-1}{r}$ which goes back to f_2. This is because the f_{post} domain now only covers a subset of $\mathbb{Z}_t$ while the invalid input may become any point in $\mathbb{Z}_t$ before computing f_{post}.

5.2   Range Functions

Now instead of only allowing points, we focus on function mapping ranges (i.e., $[a,b]$ for $a < b \in \mathbb{Z}_t$) to points. Naively, we can treat a range $[a,b]$ simply as $b-a$ points, $a, b \in \mathbb{Z}_t$, and we reuse the scheme of the point-to-point functions above for range-to-point functions. However, this naive approach not only limits the efficiency but suffers from having at most $\frac{t-1}{r}$ points across all ranges.

Fortunately, it turns out that if the ranges are well-separated, we could again construct a bootstrapping scheme with much better performance. Formally, define $\mathcal{F}_{\mathsf{ranges}} := \{f_{\mathsf{ranges}} : (\mathcal{X}_i)_{i \in [k]} \rightarrow \mathcal{Y}\}, \mathcal{X}_i \subset \mathbb{Z}_t, \mathcal{Y} = \{y_1, \ldots, y_k\} \subset \mathbb{Z}_t, k > 1,$

and: $f_{\mathsf{ranges}}(m) = \begin{cases} y_1 \text{ if } m \in \mathcal{X}_1 \\ y_2 \text{ if } m \in \mathcal{X}_2 \\ \cdots \\ y_k \text{ if } m \in \mathcal{X}_k \end{cases}$, where $\mathcal{X}_i = [u_i, v_i], \forall i \in [k]$; furthermore, for

all $i \neq j \in [k]$, $[u_i - r/2, v_i + r/2] \cap [u_j - r/2, v_j + r/2] = \emptyset$, where r is the error bound. Figure 2 depicts a high-level view of an example f_{ranges} input $\mathcal{X}$.

Notice that for such a type of function, no pre-processing is needed and we safely set f_{pre} to be the identity function, and then set $f_{\mathsf{post}}(m) := y_i$ if $m \in (u_i - r/2, v_i + r/2), \forall i \in [k]$. Let $\mathcal{X} := \bigcup \mathcal{X}_{i \in [k]}$. Since f_{post} has $|\mathcal{X}| + k \cdot r$ roots[20],

---

[20] Technically speaking, since it is $(a_i - r/2, b_i + r/2)$, it only has $|\mathcal{X}| + k(r - 1)$ roots. However, it is distracting to either make the range check non-symmetric (i.e., change to $(a_i - r/2, b_i + r/2]$) or calculate the number of roots more exactly (i.e., $k(r - 1)$ instead of kr). Therefore, for here and also the rest of the paper, we estimate the number of roots roughly for better readability.

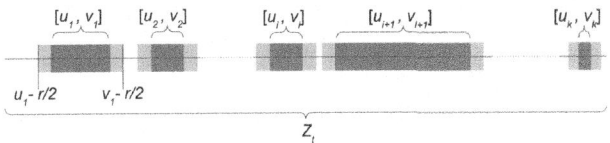

Fig. 2. Depiction of the $\mathcal{X}$ of an example f_{ranges} over $\mathbb{Z}_t$.

it has degree $|\mathcal{X}| + k \cdot r - 1$. We formalize our construction in Algorithm 4 and defer the proof of the following theorem to our full version [51] as it is similar to the proof of Theorem 1.

Algorithm 4. BFV Bootstrapping for f_{ranges}

1: Let S, k be two publicly known variables, where S denotes the size of the input domain, and k denotes the total number of ranges.

2: **procedure** Setup(1^λ)

3:   Same as the Setup in Algorithm 1, except for that lines 4 and 9 are changed to the following respectively:

4:   line 5: (3) Select the minimum Q such that a fresh BFV ciphertext with ring dimension N, plaintext space t, and ciphertext space Q, after evaluating homomorphic decryption followed by an arbitrary degree-$(S + r \cdot k - 1)$ polynomial function, still has $\mathcal{B}_{\text{out}} = \mathcal{B}_{\text{in}} + 1$ noise budget remaining.

5:   line 9: $\mathcal{F}_{\text{ranges}} := \{ f_{\text{ranges}} \mid (f_{\text{ranges}} \text{ with the following format}) \wedge (k > 1) \wedge (\mathcal{X}_i = [u_i, v_i] \subset \mathbb{Z}_t, [u_i - r/2, v_i + r/2] \cap [u_j - r/2, v_j + r/2] = \emptyset, \forall i \neq j \in [k]) \}$

6: $f_{\text{ranges}}(m) = \begin{cases} y_1 & \text{if } m \in \mathcal{X}_1 \\ y_2 & \text{if } m \in \mathcal{X}_2 \\ \cdots \\ y_k & \text{if } m \in \mathcal{X}_k \end{cases}$

7: **procedure** Boot($\text{pp} = (N, t, \mathcal{B}_{\text{in}}, \mathcal{B}_{\text{out}}, \mathcal{F}_{\text{ranges}}, \text{pp}_{\text{aux}} = r), \text{btk}, \text{ct}_{\text{in}}, f_{\text{ranges}}$)

8:   If $f_{\text{ranges}} \notin \mathcal{F}_{\text{ranges}}$, abort.

9:   $f_{\text{pre}}(m) := m$

10: $f_{\text{post}}(m) := y_i$ if $m \in (u_i - r/2, v_i + r/2), \forall i \in [k]$ (interpolated as a polynomial with degree at most $S + k \cdot r - 1$)

11: $\text{ct}_{\text{out}} \leftarrow \text{GeneralFramework}(\text{pp}, \text{btk}, \text{ct}_{\text{in}}, f_{\text{pre}}, f_{\text{post}})$

12: **return** ct_{out}.

Theorem 4. *Algorithm 4 is a correct BFV functional bootstrapping (Definition 1) procedure for function family defined on line 6, assuming the correctness of BFV.*

Remark 4 (ℓ-closeness for f_{ranges}). While our construction does not naturally support 2-closenessfor f_{ranges}, it can be achieved with some overhead. We modify f_{post} to be: $f_{\text{post}}(m) = \begin{cases} y_i & \text{if } (u_i - r/2, v_i + r/2), \forall i \in [k] \\ f_{\text{post}}(m') & \text{Otherwise} \end{cases}$, where $m' \in \mathcal{X}$ satisfying $m' - m \in \mathbb{Z}_t = \min_j (j - m), \forall j \in \mathcal{X}$. In this case, 2-closenessis straightforward (similar to the proof of Theorem 1). The overhead with this new f_{post} is then essentially $\frac{t}{|\mathcal{X}|+kr}$, which may be relatively insignificant (depending on the input function). The worst-case overhead is essentially bounded by $\frac{t}{2r}$ (and recall that evaluating f_{post} is only one component of the entire process).

Alternatively, in Sect. 5.2 provides an alternative way to evaluate f_{ranges} (with different efficiency tradeoffs) and provides k-closenessfor free.

5.3   Two Unbalanced Ranges

If we have $\mathcal{X} = \mathcal{X}_1 \cup \mathcal{X}_2$ with two ranges only, denote $S_1 = |\mathcal{X}_1|, S_2 = |\mathcal{X}_2|$, the method above would need a degree-$(S_1 + S_2 + 2r - 1)$ function with $S_1 + S_2 + 2r$ multiplications. However, if we assume that the sizes of these two ranges are extremely unbalanced, w.l.o.g., $S_2 \gg S_1$, we are able to further reduce the computation work down to $S_1 + r + \log(t) + 1$ multiplications, which can be much more efficient. Formally, we define: $\mathcal{F}_{\text{ub}} := \{f_{\text{ub}} : \mathcal{X}_1, \mathcal{X}_2 \to y_1, y_2\}, \mathcal{X}_{i \in [2]} \subset \mathbb{Z}_t, y_{i \in [2]} \in \mathbb{Z}_t$, such that: $f_{\text{ub}}(m) = \begin{cases} y_1 \text{ if } m \in \mathcal{X}_1 \\ y_2 \text{ if } m \in \mathcal{X}_2 \end{cases}$ where $\mathcal{X}_i = [u_i, v_i], |\mathcal{X}| = S_i$ for $i \in [2]$ and $S_1 \ll S_2$.

Regarding the more detailed construction, we again set f_{pre} to be the identity function, but use a new post-processing function $f_{\text{post}}(m) := (\prod_{i \in (u_1 - r/2, v_1 + r/2)} (m - i))^{t-1} \cdot (y_2 - y_1) + y_1$. The correctness analysis is as follows: recall that after homomorphic decryption, input $m[i] \in \mathcal{X}_1 = [u_1, v_1]$ is mapped to $(u_1 - r/2, v_1 + r/2)$. Thus, $c \leftarrow \prod_{i \in [u_1 - r/2, v_1 + r/2]} (m - i) = 0$, if $m[i] \in [u_1, v_1]$ and $c \in \mathbb{Z}_t, c \neq 0$ for $m[i] \notin \mathcal{X}_1$. By Fermat's Little Theorem, raising a non-zero field element up to $t - 1$ would result in 1, i.e., $c^{t-1} = 1$ for all $c \in \mathbb{Z}_t, c \neq 0$. Therefore, $c^{t-1} = 0$ if $m[i] \in [u_1, v_1]$ and 1 otherwise. Lastly, we evaluate $c^{t-1} \cdot (y_2 - y_1) + y_1$ so that the result would be y_1 if $m[i] \in \mathcal{X}_1$ and y_2 otherwise.

It is not hard to see that f_{post}, though with degree $(S_1 + r - 1) \cdot t + 1$, only needs $S_1 + r + \log(t) + 1$ multiplications for evaluation. The pseudocode and proof are deferred to our full version [51] (proof is similar to that of Theorem 1).

Theorem 5. *Algorithm 5 in our full version [51] is a correct BFV functional bootstrapping (Definition 1) procedure for the function family defined on line above, assuming the correctness of BFV. Furthermore, it is 2-close (Definition 2).*

Remark 5. For this construction, essentially, instead of treating the input domain as $\mathcal{X}_1, \mathcal{X}_2$, we are treating it as $\mathcal{X}_1 = [u_1, v_1], \mathcal{X}_2' := \mathbb{Z}_t \setminus [u_1 - r, v_1 + r]$. In other words, the actual function we evaluate is as follows: $f_{\text{ub}}'(m) = \begin{cases} y_1 \text{ if } m \in \mathcal{X}_1 \\ y_2 \text{ if } m \in \mathcal{X}_2' \end{cases}$. Since there are only two possible results, 2-closenessis satisfied for free.

5.4   Generalized Unbalanced Ranges

Moreover, we can extend this two-unbalanced-ranges setting to multiple ranges, when one of them still has a dominant size. Formally, for k ranges $\mathcal{X}_1, \ldots \mathcal{X}_k$ that are well separated, let $\mathcal{X}_i = [u_i, v_i]$, $S_i = |\mathcal{X}_i|$, w.l.o.g., we assume $S_k > \sum_{i=1}^{k-1} S_i$. By applying a similar way to evaluate this type of function, we only need $2\left(\sum_{i=1}^{k-1} S_i + r(k-1)\right) + \log(t)$ multiplications, instead of $\sum_{i=1}^{k} S_i$. For S_k much larger than $\sum_{i=1}^{k-1} S_i$, this evaluation might be more efficient. Notice that this generalized unbalanced case evaluates the exact same function as f_{ranges} defined in Sect. 5.2, but we utilize its "unbalanced" property and thus evaluate it with an alternative method.

The construction is as follows. Let $\mathcal{X}'_i := (u_i - r/2, v_i + r/2)$ for all $i \in [k]$. Again f_{pre} is the identity function. To set f_{post}, we first define:

$$h(m) := \begin{cases} y_1 - y_k & \text{if } m \in \mathcal{X}'_1 \\ y_2 - y_k & \text{if } m \in \mathcal{X}'_2 \\ \cdots \\ y_{k-1} - y_k & \text{if } m \in \mathcal{X}'_{k-1} \end{cases} \quad \text{and } h(m) \text{ has degree } \sum_{i=1}^{k-1}(S_i + r). \text{ Then, we}$$

define $g(m) := \prod_{j \in \mathcal{X}'_i, i \in [k-1]}(x - j)$ $g(m)$ also has degree $\sum_{i=1}^{k-1}(S_i + r)$. Lastly, we define $f_{\text{post}}(m) := h(m) \cdot (1 - g(m)^{t-1}) + y_k$. [21]

For $m \in \mathcal{X}'_i$ for all $i \in [k-1]$, $h(m) = y_i - y_k$, and $g(m) = 0$. Therefore, $h(m) \cdot (1 - g(m)^{t-1}) + y_k = (y_i - y_k) \cdot (1 - 0^{t-1}) + y_k = y_i$ as expected. On the other hand, if $m \in \mathcal{X}'_k$, $g(m) \neq 0$. Therefore, $h(m) \cdot (1 - g(m)^{t-1}) + y_k = h(m) \cdot (1 - 1) + y_k = y_k$.

With regard to the efficiency, both h, g requires $2\sum_{i=1}^{k-1}(S_i + r)$ multiplications, and therefore, in total, f_{post} requires $2\sum_{i=1}^{k-1}(S_i + r) + \log(t) + 1$ multiplications. On the other hand, the degree of the function is $(\sum_{i=1}^{k-1}(S_i + r))(t - 1)$.

We defer the pseudocode of our construction and proof to our full version [51].

Theorem 6. *Algorithm 6 in our full version [51] is a correct BFV functional bootstrapping (Definition 1) procedure for function family defined above, assuming the correctness of BFV. Furthermore, it is k-close (Definition 2).*

6   Evaluation

We implemented our algorithms proposed above in a C++ library, based on the SEAL [57] library. We benchmark these schemes on several parameter settings on a Google Compute Cloud e2-standard-4 with 16 GB RAM.

---

[21] Notice that f_{ub} is a special case of this construction, as for f_{ub} in Sect. 5.2, $h(m) = y_1 - y_2$ is simply a constant function and thus does not require any evaluation. Therefore, the cost is $S_1 + r + \log(t)$ for f_{ub} instead of $2S_1 + 2r + \log(t)$.

6.1   Performance of Our Construction

Parameter Selection. We choose BFV parameters as follows: $N = 32768, t = 65537, \sigma = 3.2$. We use ternary secret keys with a hamming weight of 512.[22] The ciphertext modulus Q is chosen according to each function as specified in Table 2. These parameters guarantee > 128-bit security by LWE estimator [2] for all the function families we have tested (except for f_{ub}, which provides 106-bit of security, but for better comparison, we remain N, t, σ unchanged but reduce the security). To guarantee that the modulus switching error is bounded by r except with 2^{-40} probability,[23,24] we choose $r = 128$ (thus $r/2 = 64$).

We benchmark all the functions we described, including f_1 (i.e., the identity function over $[0, 65536 = t - 1, 128 = r]$) in Algorithm 1; f_2 (i.e., mapping each point in $[a, b, r']$ to an arbitrary point $y \in \mathbb{Z}_t$) in Algorithm 2; point functions f_{pts} (i.e., several points to several points); range functions f_{ranges} (i.e., several ranges to several points); and unbalanced range functions f_{ub} (i.e., two unbalanced ranges to two points).

As r is fixed, the input of f_2 can be at most $\frac{t-1}{r} = 512$ points. Therefore, we choose $f_2 : [0, 1022, 2] \to \mathcal{Y}$ where $\mathcal{Y}$ is a random subset of $\mathbb{Z}_{65537}$ with 512 points. For $f_{pts} : \mathcal{X} \to \mathcal{Y}$ where $\mathcal{X} \subset \mathbb{Z}_{65537}$, we choose two different functions: the first function maps $\{0, 32768\}$ to two different random points, i.e., $\mathcal{X}$ and $\mathcal{Y}$ only contain two points, and thus achieve the best possible performance; the second one demonstrates a more general functionality by mapping eight random points to eight random points. For f_{ranges}, we choose two well-separated ranges each containing 127 points. For f_{ub}, we choose two very unbalanced ranges, one of which is of size $r - 1$ and the other being $t - 2r + 1$.

Performance Analysis. As shown in Table 2, our amortized runtime is about 1–2 orders of magnitude faster than regular BFV bootstrapping: both for the

---

[22] Our construction replies on sparse keys in the same way as prior works. We can extend our key to be uniform, but r needs to be increased accordingly, since $r = O(\sqrt{h})$ for h being the hamming weight.

[23] We choose security parameter $\delta = 40$ which is the same as in [50], since the error probability is statistical, and 40 is a relatively popular and reasonable statistical security parameter. Prior works in BGV/BFV bootstrapping instead choose error probability via evaluation: based on our private communication with the authors of the prior works, it was chosen such that no overflow happens during benchmarking tests. To our knowledge, other BFV bootstrapping works do not explicitly discuss how they choose the concrete numbers, and thus we follow the parameter in [50]. Asymptotically, $r = O(\sqrt{\delta})$ when fixing other parameters.

[24] According to [15], 2^{-40} gives ~ 50-bit of security for IND-CPA-D (introduced in [46]). To achieve 128-bit security of IND-CPA-D, roughly a failure probability of 2^{-120} is needed. To accommodate this, our error range grows from 128 to ~ 216 and thus the effective plaintext space (for f_1, f_2) is reduced from 512 points to ~ 302 points (and correspondingly other function families). Thus, our amortized per bit runtime would be just slightly increased. Furthermore, note that adjusting the IND-CPA-D security level would also affect the runtime in all prior works as well, which will thus maintain our advantage, if not further increase.

Table 2. Batched bootstrapping for binary gates using our technique compared to the unoptimized construction in [50]. Notice that based on the BFV parameter we choose, all our constructions guarantee > 128-bit security except for f_{ub} which is of 106-bit security; all our constructions are evaluated on input with 35-bit noise budget, except for f_{pts_3} which needs input with 125-bit noise budget. See Sect. 6 "Parameter selection" for details. The runtimes of prior works are taken directly from their papers. We use a basic GCP instance which does not grant us extra advantage over the runtime. As a comparison, for [25], our instance time is ~1.2x slower than the numbers reported.

Function Family	Input Domain	# of slots	Ciphertext Modulus	Output Noise Budget	Total Runtime (sec)	Runtime per slot (ms)	Runtime per bit (ms)
Identity function f_1 over $[0, t-1, r]$, Algorithm1	$[0, 65536, 128]$	32768	830	181	370.6	11.3	1.26
$f_2 : [u, v, r'] \to \mathcal{Y}$ $u, v, r' \in \mathbb{Z}_t$, $\mathcal{Y} \subset \mathbb{Z}_t$, Algorithm2	$[0, 1022, 2]$				370.2	11.2	1.24
$f_{pts_1} : \mathcal{X} \to \mathcal{Y}$, $\mathcal{X}, \mathcal{Y} \subset \mathbb{Z}_t$, $|\mathcal{X}| = |\mathcal{Y}| = 2$	$\{0, 32768\}$		590	198	48.5	1.5	1.50
$f_{pts_2} : \mathcal{X} \to \mathcal{Y}$, $\mathcal{X}, \mathcal{Y} \subset \mathbb{Z}_t, |\mathcal{X}| = |\mathcal{Y}| = 8$, without pre-scale on $\mathcal{X}$	$\{57004, 46969, 21931, 39030, 59092, 9965, 30013, 58301\}$		650	194	64.5	2.0	0.67
$f_{pts_3} : \mathcal{X} \to \mathcal{Y}$, $\mathcal{X}, \mathcal{Y} \subset \mathbb{Z}_t, |\mathcal{X}| = |\mathcal{Y}| = 8$, with pre-scale on $\mathcal{X}$				181	68.5	2.1	0.70
$f_{ranges}(m) = y_i$ if $m \in [u_i, v_i]$, $u_i, v_i, y_i \in \mathbb{Z}_t, i \in [k], k \geq 2$,	Two ranges: $[-63, 63]$ & $[32704, 32831]$		630	205	58.4	1.8	0.23
$f_{ub}(m) = y_i$ if $m \in [u_i, v_i]$, $u_i, v_i, y_i \in \mathbb{Z}_t, i \in [2]$,	Two ranges: $[-63, 63]$ & $\mathbb{Z}_{65537} \setminus [-127, 127]$		1070	180	89.3	2.7	0.18
Regular BFV bootstrapping [56] 128-bit security	$\mathbb{Z}_{257}$	128	881	507	22.0	173.0	21.62
Regular BFV bootstrapping [25] 66-bit security	$\mathbb{Z}_{127^2}$	2268	1134	330	95.0	42.0	3.00
Regular BFV bootstrapping [14] 126-bit security	$\mathbb{Z}_{257^2}$	128	806	245	42.0	328.0	20.50

runtime per slot and the runtime per effective bit (i.e., the runtime per slot divided by the effective input plaintext space in bits). Our functionality is slightly different from prior works: we only support correctness over a subset of the plaintext space, but we also allow a look-up table evaluation.

[56] has the plaintext space to be much smaller than the other regular bootstrapping constructions because enlarging the plaintext space requires some nontrivial modification to their construction. Therefore, they also have a relatively limited input domain (containing only 257 points). Among all of the regular BFV bootstrapping works, [25] provides the best performance but with a relatively low security guarantee (only 66 bits). To guarantee > 100 bit security, their performance will be further reduced. As mentioned in [56], the techniques in [25,56] might be combined to achieve a better regular BFV bootstrapping construction, but it is still unlikely to be comparable with our constructions (again, they provide a stronger functionality by considering all values in the plaintext space as valid inputs). The main reason we outperform the regular bootstrapping framework by around 1 to 2 orders of magnitude, is that we make full use of 32768 slots per ciphertext.

f_1 and f_2 have roughly the same runtime and the same input noise budget requirement, as the evaluation of f_{pre} is combined with the SlotToCoeff step

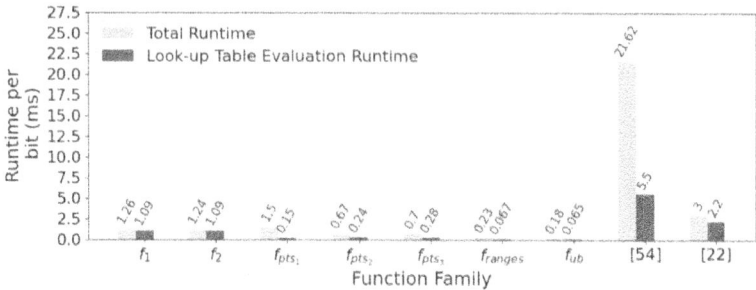

Fig. 3. Bar chart illustration of total runtime and look-up table evaluation time per bit. Note that [25] provides only 66-bit of security while our construction and [56] both provide about 128-bit security.

(recall that for f_2, f_{pre} is simply a degree-1 function)[25] They both evaluate over 512 different points, thus requiring f_{post} to have degree $t - 2$ (as $512 \cdot r = t - 1 = 65536$). Therefore, they are both the slowest among all the different types of functions. Also, as discussed, these two types of functions can be viewed as special cases of f_{pts}.

For f_{pts}, we test a function for two points, for which is the most efficient non-trivial function our protocol works. Such a function takes only about 1.5ms per slot. To show more generality, we also test functions with 8 points. All the points are randomly chosen. For the points we randomly chose, no f_{pre} is needed as they are all separated by at least $r = 128$. In this case, the runtime is only slightly slower than f_{pts} with two points. However, to show the worst case, a function of degree 7 is needed as the preprocessing function. We also benchmark it to show the difference. In this case, f_{pre} is a degree 7 function and therefore requires the input noise budget to be 90 bits more. The runtime is roughly the same. Note that, however, for such a small number of points (e.g., 8 points), it is more likely that f_{pre} does not need any preprocessing (or at least only a lower degree function, thus introducing little overhead, if any).

For f_{ranges}, each range contains 127 points. Therefore, there are a total of 254 points. However, the runtime is even faster than f_{pts} with only 8 points. This is because it only requires a degree-$254 + 2r = 510$ postprocessing function; in contrast f_{pts} with 8 points already requires the postprocessing function to have degree $8 \cdot r = 1024$. For the unbalanced ranges, we use $[-63, 63]$ and $\mathbb{Z}_t \setminus [-127, 127]$, containing 65409 points. However, it is also easy to see that the runtime is only slightly slower than the range function with two small ranges. The only drawback is that $\log(Q)$ is required to be very large since f_{post} is a function of degree $\sim 2r \cdot t$.

---

[25] Since f_2 is only degree 1, the scalar multiplication can be saved by changing the SlotToCoeff matrix U to be multiplied with this scalar first. See detailed description in our full version [51] paragraph "Combining SlotToCoeff and f_{pre}".

Runtime Breakdown. As shown in Fig. 3, for some functions like f_1, f_2, the look-up table evaluation takes the majority of time, as their f_{post} has a much higher degree than the other ones. However, for all of the functions, our runtime is still greatly better than both of the prior works (and their breakdown is taken from the papers).

Comparison with Other FHE Bootstrapping. Since it is hard to directly compare to other FHE bootstrapping schemes concretely (as distinct schemes differ a lot in terms of settings), we give a brief high-level discussion. For CKKS, functional bootstrapping is particularly challenging as during bootstrapping, a polynomial approximation of the sine function is used. To capture functional bootstrapping, a polynomial approximation of that function together with sine needs to be done, which is very inefficient. Therefore, to the best of our knowledge, CKKS cannot easily support (even relaxed) functional bootstrapping. On the other hand, for FHEW/TFHE, while they natively support functional bootstrapping, they do not naturally support additions and multiplications before or after bootstrapping. Therefore, our method provides more flexibility (while the performance can be comparable when $|\mathcal{X}| = p$ where p is the plaintext space of FHEW/TFHE, based on our estimation with the numbers in [50] and Sect. 8).

7   Applications

In this section, we discuss some applications that can take advantage of our constructions. We first discuss one application in very recent work in detail and compare the result using our scheme with the results using prior works. We then introduce some potential applications at a high level.

7.1   Oblivious Permutation via BFV

A recent work [23] proposes a way to homomorphically permute a database with N entries. Essentially, it allows the server to obliviously permute a database using BFV such that the decrypted result is indistinguishable from a randomly permuted database. The permutation randomness comes from the client, but it takes only $o(N)$ communication: the server first uses a BFV-encrypted seed provided by the client and a BFV-friendly PRG to generate $O(N \log(N))$ random bits homomorphically; then, it homomorphically evaluates the Thorp shuffle (or equivalently, a butterfly shuffle) using these random bits. The Thorp shuffle consists of $h = O(\lambda)$ consecutive rounds, where each round divides the database into $N/2$ pairs of entries and then swaps each pair using a random bit. For example, if $N = 2$, the swap operation homomorphically computes $\mathsf{DB}'[1] \leftarrow \mathsf{DB}[1] \cdot r + \mathsf{DB}[2] \cdot (r - 1)$ and $\mathsf{DB}'[2] = \mathsf{DB}[2] \cdot r + \mathsf{DB}[1] \cdot (r - 1)$. If $r = 1$, $\mathsf{DB}' = \mathsf{DB}$, and $\mathsf{DB}' = \mathsf{DB}[2]\|\mathsf{DB}[1]$ otherwise. After performing h such rounds (over all pairs) for some security parameter λ, the database looks like a uniformly permuted database (when querying only $q = o(N)$ entries).

One main nice property of the Thorp shuffle is that the whole shuffle process only involves this homomorphic swap, which only depends on the database entries $DB[i]$ and the random binary bits. Thus, to perform a homomorphic Thorp shuffle over a database, we first encode $DB[i]$ into some valid input set $\mathcal{X}$. For example, if $DB[i]$ has 3 bits (as used in the evaluation section of [23]), we can encode each entry into an element in $\mathcal{X}$ with $|\mathcal{X}| = 8$. In this case, when bootstrapping is needed (between two rounds of swapping), we only need to bootstrap an identity function over $\mathcal{X}$ instead of the entire plaintext space. This application is thus well suited to our relaxed bootstrapping (even without the closenessproperty).

With this high-level idea, we estimate the concrete improvement by applying our construction to such as oblivious permutation process. As shown in [23], for a database of length $N = 2^{23}$ (each entry has 3 bits), the Thorp shuffle requires 416 levels. Using our scheme, with the function being an identity function over $\mathcal{X}$ of size 8 (e.g., $\mathcal{X} = \{0, 2r, \ldots, 14r\}$, where r is the error bound), and setting the ciphertext modulus to be 860 bits (providing ≈ 128 bits of security), each bootstrapping of our construction allows about 13 levels of multiplications (about 400 bits of noise budget left). We can encode the entire database to $3N/32768/3 = 256$ BFV ciphertexts. Each ciphertext requires $416/13 = 32$ bootstrapping. Thus, in total, it takes $256 \times 32 \times 91 = 745472\,\text{s}^{26}$, which is about 207 h.

On the other hand, in the prior works [56], encoding the entire database requires $3N/128/8 = 24576$ ciphertexts. Each bootstrapping gives ≈ 19 levels of multiplications (about 507 bits of noise budget left). Thus, in total, it takes $24576 \times 416/19 \times 22 \approx 11894784\,\text{s}$ (each of their bootstrapping takes 22 s), which is about 3304 h. Similarly, it takes about 4587 h when using [14], and about 670 h when using [25]. Notice that [25] only offers 66-bit security, while the other two prior works and ours provide $\approx$128 bit security.

With our work, under a similar security guarantee, the bootstrapping time can be reduced by >20x. Furthermore, since our construction supports more slots, there are less ciphertexts needed to pack the entire database. Therefore, the homomorphic Thorp shuffle can be evaluated more efficiently by having fewer regular (non-bootstrapping) ciphertext operations[27]. See [23] for a more detailed discussion and estimation.

7.2   Other Potential Applications

We then discuss some other potential applications that benefit from our construction. We start with applications that do not require closeness. Such applications have a hard requirement: the input must be within $\mathcal{X}$.

PIR/PSI with Computation. Private information retrieval (PIR) [19] allows one to retrieve a data entry from the database without revealing which data entry

---

[26] In Table 2, we use ciphertext modulus of 650 bits instead of 860 bits. Using 860, which is essentially the maximum for 128-bit security, our bootstrapping takes about 91 s using GCP e2-standard-4.

[27] Note that a more recent version of this paper uses a larger database size. However, the analysis and our advantages remain *exactly* the same.

is retrieved. PIR with computation [47] further allows computing some function over the retrieved data entry (or multiple data entries for batch-PIR). Since the data entry can be encoded (e.g., as a multiple of r, the error range introduced in Sect. 4.1), we can use relaxed functional bootstrapping (e.g., Algorithm 1) to compute this function (or at least a sub-module of this function). Such a method can also be used for Private Set Intersection with computation [35], whose construction indeed requires a lot of bootstrapping operations, which can be replaced with our relaxed functional bootstrapping. Note that since PSI requires two-sided privacy, more careful handling is required when designing the function to not leak any database information (e.g., use noise flooding), or use other techniques like Oblivious PRF [11].

Access Control. Within an organization, access control is needed to perform some action (e.g., data retrieval [10]). To realize such access control, BFV can be used in the following way. During a private data retrieval (i.e., retrieval of some documents without revealing which document it is), the user provides their identity, which corresponds to some permission level l. Then, the document also has some requirements q. The server, after obtaining q (without learning what q is) under BFV, can compute some access control function $f(q, l)$. If the result is 1, the returning ciphertext contains the document. Otherwise, the returning ciphertext contains only 0. l, q, f can all be easily encoded in a way that our relaxed functional bootstrapping supports. For example, let $|l - q| > r$ by encoding l, q accordingly, and let f checks whether $l > q$. This check can then be realized using our range function in Algorithm 4.

We then discuss some applications that may require the additional flexibility provided by closenessdefined in Definition 2.

Secure Machine Learning. Machine learning (ML) using FHE has been a long-standing popular topic [20,36,41,42,52]. One major bottleneck of using FHE for ML is bootstrapping. By the nature of the fuzziness in ML, some small deviations from the model are tolerable. In this case, a relaxed functional bootstrapping satisfying 2-closenesscan be used to evaluate some parts of the ML model (e.g., evaluating the activation function): any invalid inputs are simply rounded to the two nearest valid inputs. Furthermore, since the ML training process is repetitive (every batch or epoch shares the same activation function for example), our relaxed functional bootstrapping is then a perfect fit to guarantee the error budget is increased after each activation function evaluation.

Fuzzy PSI. Another natural application is fuzzy PSI [24]. Fuzzy PSI returns the elements that are similar instead of identical as in PSI. Therefore, if the fuzziness definition (e.g., the correctness definition in [12,58]) allows the borderline elements to be decided either way, we can use our relaxed functional bootstrapping in the following way. We first set a range $[u, v]$ to be the range for the similarity. In other words, if two elements a, b satisfying $|a - b| \in [u, v]$, the functionality should return 1; otherwise, the functionality should return 0. The issue is that the elements within $[u - r, v + r]$ may return either 0 or 1. However, due to the fuzziness definition, these are borderline cases and may be decided either way. Furthermore, with some of our constructions (Algorithm 1), the closer the difference is to $[u, v]$ the larger the probability our algorithm returns 1, which may be further preferred (discussed in Sect. 4.1).

There are many other potential examples, like homomorphic comparisons, private branching, fixed-point arithmetic using BFV/BGV, and so on. We leave a more detailed application-based follow-up to future works.

8   Extension to Batched FHEW/TFHE Bootstrapping

Of independent interest, our techniques can be applied to improve the batched FHEW/TFHE bootstrapping algorithm in [50]. Essentially, batched FHEW/TFHE bootstrapping is to take $2N$ LWE ciphertexts each encrypting either 0 or 1 and output the NAND result of each pair of them. Another application is that given N LWE ciphertexts each encrypting a message $x \in \mathbb{Z}_p$ for some $p \geq 2$, output an encryption of $f(x)$'s for some function f over $\mathbb{Z}_p$ that serves like a look-up table. This is called the batched functional bootstrapping.

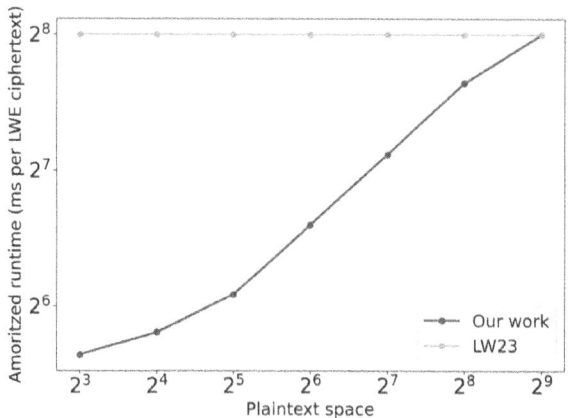

Fig. 4. Comparison between our work on batched functional bootstrapping and [50].

Our Optimization. In [50], for both a binary gate bootstrapping and a functional bootstrapping, the bootstrapping gate contains a degree-$(t-1)$ function. We observe that instead, for a binary gate bootstrapping, we only need a degree-$(3r-1)$ function, and for a k-bit functional bootstrapping, only a degree-$(k \cdot r - 1)$ function is needed. We defer recalling the construction of [50] and how the optimization is done in detail in our full version [51].

Benchmark and Comparison. For the NAND gate, since the degree now is much lower, instead of using $N = 32768$ for the underlying BFV as in [50], we use $N = 16384$ together with $\log(Q) \approx 420$, which further reduces the runtime. We use other parameters exactly the same as in [50, Section 10], except that we are using ternary keys for the LWE secret keys. The total runtime is 24.5 s and the amortized runtime is 1.5 ms per slot. Compared to the total runtime of 155 s and the amortized runtime of 4.7 ms in [50][Table 2], our total runtime (i.e., the latency) is about 6x faster than [50], and the amortized runtime (i.e., the throughput) is about 3x faster.

Furthermore, we show that for p being 3–8 bits for functional bootstrapping, we achieve a speed up as shown in Fig. 4.

References

1. Lattigo v2.1.1. Online (December 2020). ePFL-LDS. http://github.com/ldsec/lattigo
2. Albrecht, M.R., Player, R., Scott, S.: On the concrete hardness of learning with errors. J. Math. Crypt. **9**(3), 169–203 (2015)
3. Alperin-Sheriff, J., Peikert, C.: Practical bootstrapping in quasilinear time. In: Canetti, R., Garay, J.A. (eds.) Advances in Cryptology – CRYPTO 2013. pp. 1–20. Springer Berlin Heidelberg, Berlin, Heidelberg (2013)
4. Badawi, A.A., et al.: OpenFHE: open-source fully homomorphic encryption library. Cryptology ePrint Archive, Paper 2022/915 (2022). https://eprint.iacr.org/2022/915, commit: 122f470e0dbf94688051ab852131ccc5d26be934
5. Bossuat, J.P., Mouchet, C., Troncoso-Pastoriza, J., Hubaux, J.P.: Efficient bootstrapping for approximate homomorphic encryption with non-sparse keys. In: Canteaut, A., Standaert, F.X. (eds.) Advances in Cryptology – EUROCRYPT 2021. pp. 587–617. Springer International Publishing, Cham (2021)
6. Brakerski, Z.: Fully homomorphic encryption without modulus switching from classical gapsvp. In: Proceedings of the 32nd Annual Cryptology Conference on Advances in Cryptology — CRYPTO 2012 - Volume 7417, p. 868–886. Springer-Verlag (2012)
7. Brakerski, Z., Gentry, C., Vaikuntanathan, V.: (leveled) fully homomorphic encryption without bootstrapping. ACM Trans. Comput. Theor. (TOCT) **6**(3), 1–36 (2014)
8. Brakerski, Z., Vaikuntanathan, V.: Efficient fully homomorphic encryption from (standard) LWE. In: Ostrovsky, R. (ed.) 52nd FOCS, October 22–25, 2011, pp. 97–106. IEEE Computer Society Press (2011)
9. Brakerski, Z., Vaikuntanathan, V.: Fully homomorphic encryption from ring-LWE and security for key dependent messages. In: Rogaway, P. (ed.) CRYPTO 2011. LNCS, vol. 6841, pp. 505–524. Springer, Heidelberg, Germany (Aug 14–18, 2011)
10. Camenisch, J., Dubovitskaya, M., Neven, G.: Oblivious transfer with access control. In: Al-Shaer, E., Jha, S., Keromytis, A.D. (eds.) ACM CCS 2009, November 9–13, 2009, pp. 131–140. ACM Press (2009)
11. Casacuberta, S., Hesse, J., Lehmann, A.: SoK: oblivious pseudorandom functions. IEEE EuroS&P 2022 (2022). https://eprint.iacr.org/2022/302
12. Chakraborti, A., Reiter, M.K., Fanti, G.C.: This paper is included in the proceedings of the 32nd USENIX security symposium. In: USENIX 2023 (2023). https://api.semanticscholar.org/CorpusID:245537395
13. Chen, H., Chillotti, I., Song, Y.: Improved bootstrapping for approximate homomorphic encryption. In: Ishai, Y., Rijmen, V. (eds.) Advances in Cryptology – EUROCRYPT 2019. pp. 34–54. Springer International Publishing, Cham (2019)

14. Chen, H., Han, K.: Homomorphic lower digits removal and improved FHE bootstrapping. In: Nielsen, J.B., Rijmen, V. (eds.) EUROCRYPT 2018, Part I. LNCS, vol. 10820, pp. 315–337. Springer, Heidelberg, Germany (Apr 29 – May 3, 2018)

15. Cheon, J.H., Choe, H., Passelègue, A., Stehlé, D., Suvanto, E.: Attacks against the INDCPA-D security of exact FHE schemes. In: CCS (2024)

16. Cheon, J.H., Han, K., Kim, A., Kim, M., Song, Y.: Bootstrapping for approximate homomorphic encryption. In: Annual International Conference on the Theory and Applications of Cryptographic Techniques. pp. 360–384. Springer (2018)

17. Cheon, J.H., Kim, A., Kim, M., Song, Y.: Homomorphic encryption for arithmetic of approximate numbers. In: International Conference on the Theory and Application of Cryptology and Information Security. pp. 409–437. Springer (2017)

18. Chillotti, I., Gama, N., Georgieva, M., Izabachène, M.: Faster fully homomorphic encryption: Bootstrapping in less than 0.1 seconds. In: Cheon, J.H., Takagi, T. (eds.) Advances in Cryptology – ASIACRYPT 2016. pp. 3–33. Springer, Heidelberg (2016). https://doi.org/10.1007/978-3-662-53887-6_1

19. Chor, B., Goldreich, O., Kushilevitz, E., Sudan, M.: Private information retrieval. In: 36th FOCS, pp. 41–50. IEEE Computer Society Press (1995)

20. Dalvi, A., Jain, A., Moradiya, S., Nirmal, R., Sanghavi, J., Siddavatam, I.: Securing neural networks using homomorphic encryption. In: 2021 International Conference on Intelligent Technologies (CONIT), pp. 1–7 (2021). https://doi.org/10.1109/CONIT51480.2021.9498376

21. Ducas, L., Micciancio, D.: FHEW: Bootstrapping Homomorphic Encryption in Less Than a Second. In: Oswald, E., Fischlin, M. (eds.) Advances in Cryptology – EUROCRYPT 2015. pp. 617–640. Springer, Berlin, Heidelberg (2015)

22. Fan, J., Vercauteren, F.: Somewhat practical fully homomorphic encryption. Cryptology ePrint Archive, Report 2012/144 (2012). https://ia.cr/2012/144

23. Fisch, B., Lazzaretti, A., Liu, Z., Papamanthou, C.: ThorPIR: single server PIR via homomorphic thorp shuffles. In: CCS 2024 (2024)

24. Freedman, M.J., Nissim, K., Pinkas, B.: Efficient private matching and set intersection. In: Cachin, C., Camenisch, J. (eds.) EUROCRYPT 2004. LNCS, vol. 3027, pp. 1–19. Springer, Heidelberg, Germany (May 2–6, 2004)

25. Geelen, R., Iliashenko, I., Kang, J., Vercauteren, F.: On polynomial functions modulo p^e and faster bootstrapping for homomorphic encryption. In: Eurocrypt 2023 (2023). https://eprint.iacr.org/2022/1364

26. Geelen, R., Vercauteren, F.: Bootstrapping for BGV and BFV revisited. J. Cryptol. **36**(2) (2023)

27. Gentry, C.: Fully homomorphic encryption using ideal lattices. In: Proceedings of the Forty-First Annual ACM Symposium on Theory of Computing, pp. 169–178 (2009)

28. Gentry, C., Sahai, A., Waters, B.: Homomorphic encryption from learning with errors: conceptually-simpler, asymptotically-faster, attribute-based. In: Canetti, R., Garay, J.A. (eds.) CRYPTO 2013, Part I. LNCS, vol. 8042, pp. 75–92, Aug. 18–22, 2013. Springer, Heidelberg (2013)

29. Guimarães, A., Pereira, H.V.L., van Leeuwen, B.: Amortized bootstrapping revisited: simpler, asymptotically-faster, implemented. In: Asiacrypt 2023 (2023). https://eprint.iacr.org/2023/014

30. Halevi, S., Shoup, V.: HElib (2014). https://github.com/homenc/HElib

31. Halevi, S., Shoup, V.: Design and implementation of HElib: a homomorphic encryption library. Cryptology ePrint Archive, Report 2020/1481 (2020). https://eprint.iacr.org/2020/1481

32. Halevi, S., Shoup, V.: Bootstrapping for HElib. J. Crypt. **34**(1), 7 (2021)
33. Han, K., Hhan, M., Cheon, J.H.: Improved homomorphic discrete Fourier transforms and FHE bootstrapping. IEEE Access **7**, 57361–57370 (2019). https://doi.org/10.1109/ACCESS.2019.2913850
34. Han, K., Ki, D.: Better bootstrapping for approximate homomorphic encryption. In: Cryptographers' Track at the RSA Conference. pp. 364–390. Springer (2020)
35. HU, J., Chen, J., Dai, W., Wang, H.: Fully homomorphic encryption-based protocols for enhanced private set intersection functionalities. Cryptology ePrint Archive, Paper 2023/1407 (2023). https://eprint.iacr.org/2023/1407
36. Juvekar, C., Vaikuntanathan, V., Chandrakasan, A.: GAZELLE: a low latency framework for secure neural network inference. In: Enck, W., Felt, A.P. (eds.) USENIX Security 2018, pp. 1651–1669. USENIX Association (2018)
37. Kim, A., Polyakov, Y., Zucca, V.: Revisiting homomorphic encryption schemes for finite fields. In: ASIACRYPT 2021. p. 608–639. Springer (2021)
38. Kim, J., Seo, J., Song, Y.: Simpler and faster BFV bootstrapping for arbitrary plaintext modulus from CKKS. Cryptology ePrint Archive, Paper 2024/109 (2024). https://eprint.iacr.org/2024/109
39. Kim, S., Park, M., Kim, J., Kim, T., Min, C.: Evalround algorithm in CKKS bootstrapping. In: Asiacrypt 2022 (2022). https://eprint.iacr.org/2022/1256
40. Lee, D., Min, S., Song, Y.: Functional bootstrapping for FV-style cryptosystems. Cryptology ePrint Archive, Paper 2024/181 (2024). https://eprint.iacr.org/2024/181
41. Lee, J.W., et al.: Privacy-preserving machine learning with fully homomorphic encryption for deep neural network. IEEE Access **10**, 30039–30054 (2022). https://doi.org/10.1109/ACCESS.2022.3159694
42. Lee, J.W., Lee, E., Kim, Y.S., No, J.S.: Rotation key reduction for client-server systems of deep neural network on fully homomorphic encryption. In: Guo, J., Steinfeld, R. (eds.) Advances in Cryptology, ASIACRYPT 2023, pp. 36–68. Springer, Singapore (2023). https://doi.org/10.1007/978-981-99-8736-8_2
43. Lee, J.W., Lee, E., Lee, Y., Kim, Y.S., No, J.S.: High-precision bootstrapping of RNS-CKKS homomorphic encryption using optimal minimax polynomial approximation and inverse sine function. In: EUROCRYPT 2021, pp. 618–647 (2021)
44. Lee, Y., Lee, J.W., Kim, Y.S., No, J.S.: Near-optimal polynomial for modulus reduction using l2-norm for approximate homomorphic encryption. IEEE Access **8**, 144321–144330 (2020). https://doi.org/10.1109/ACCESS.2020.3014369
45. Lee, Y., et al.: Efficient FHEW bootstrapping with small evaluation keys, and applications to threshold homomorphic encryption. In: Hazay, C., Stam, M. (eds.) Advances in Cryptology, EUROCRYPT 2023, pp. 227–256. Springer, Cham (2023). https://doi.org/10.1007/978-3-031-30620-4_8
46. Li, B., Micciancio, D.: On the security of homomorphic encryption on approximate numbers. In: EUROCRYPT 2021 (2021)
47. Lin, C., Liu, Z., Malkin, T.: XSPIR: efficient symmetrically private information retrieval from ring-LWE. In: Atluri, V., Di Pietro, R., Jensen, C.D., Meng, W. (eds.) ESORICS 2022, Part I. LNCS, vol. 13554, pp. 217–236. Springer, Heidelberg (2022). https://doi.org/10.1007/978-3-031-17140-6_11
48. Liu, F.H., Wang, H.: Batch bootstrapping i: A new framework for simd bootstrapping in polynomial modulus. In: Hazay, C., Stam, M. (eds.) Advances in Cryptology – EUROCRYPT 2023. pp. 321–352. Springer Nature Switzerland, Cham (2023)

49. Liu, F.H., Wang, H.: Batch bootstrapping i: bootstrapping in polynomial modulus only requires o (1) FHE multiplications in amortization. In: Hazay, C., Stam, M. (eds.) Advances in Cryptology – EUROCRYPT 2023, pp. 321–352. Springer, Cham (2023)

50. Liu, Z., Wang, Y.: Amortized functional bootstrapping in less than 7ms, with $\tilde{O}(1)$ polynomial multiplications. In: Asiacrypt 2023 (2023). https://eprint.iacr.org/2023/910

51. Liu, Z., Wang, Y.: Relaxed functional bootstrapping: a new perspective on BGV/BFV bootstrapping. Cryptology ePrint Archive, Paper 2024/172 (2024)

52. jie Lu, W., Huang, Z., Hong, C., Ma, Y., Qu, H.: PEGASUS: bridging polynomial and non-polynomial evaluations in homomorphic encryption. In: 2021 IEEE Symposium on Security and Privacy, pp. 1057–1073. IEEE Computer Society Press (2021)

53. Ma, S., Huang, T., Wang, A., Wang, X.: Accelerating BGV bootstrapping for large p using null polynomials over $\mathbb{Z}_{p^e}$. Cryptology ePrint Archive, Paper 2024/115 (2024). https://eprint.iacr.org/2024/115

54. Miccianco, D., Sorrell, J.: Ring packing and amortized FHEW bootstrapping. In: 45th International Colloquium on Automata, Languages, and Programming, ICALP 2018. Leibniz International Proceedings in Informatics (LIPIcs), vol. 107. Schloss Dagstuhl–Leibniz-Zentrum fuer Informatik (2018)

55. Micheli, G.D., Kim, D., Micciancio, D., Suhl, A.: Faster amortized FHEW bootstrapping using ring automorphisms. Cryptology ePrint Archive, Paper 2023/112 (2023). https://eprint.iacr.org/2023/112

56. Okada, H., Player, R., Pohmann, S.: Homomorphic polynomial evaluation using Galois structure and applications to BFV bootstrapping. In: Asiacrypt 2023 (2023). https://eprint.iacr.org/2023/1304

57. Microsoft SEAL (2020). https://github.com/Microsoft/SEAL

58. Uzun, E., Chung, S.P., Kolesnikov, V., Boldyreva, A., Lee, W.: Fuzzy labeled private set intersection with applications to private real-time biometric search. In: Bailey, M., Greenstadt, R. (eds.) USENIX Security 2021, pp. 911–928. USENIX Association (2021)

NTRU-Based Bootstrapping
for MK-FHEs Without Using
Overstretched Parameters

Binwu Xiang[1,2,3], Jiang Zhang[2(✉)], Kaixing Wang[2,4], Yi Deng[1,3],
and Dengguo Feng[2]

[1] Key Laboratory of Cyberspace Security Defense, Institute of Information
Engineering, CAS, Beijing, China
{xiangbinwu,deng}@iie.ac.cn
[2] State Key Laboratory of Cryptology, P.O. Box 5159, Beijing 100878, China
zhangj@sklc.org, wangkaixing22@mails.ucas.ac.cn, fengdg@263.net
[3] School of Cyber Security, University of Chinese Academy of Sciences,
Beijing, China
[4] School of Computer Science and Technology, University of Chinese Academy
of Sciences, Beijing, China

Abstract. Recent attacks on NTRU lattices given by Ducas and van
Woerden (ASIACRYPT 2021) showed that for moduli q larger than the
so-called fatigue point $n^{2.484+o(1)}$, the security of NTRU is noticeably
less than that of (ring)-LWE. Unlike NTRU-based PKE with q typically
lying in the secure regime of NTRU lattices (i.e., $q < n^{2.484+o(1)}$), the
security of existing NTRU-based multi-key FHEs (MK-FHEs) requiring
$q = O(n^k)$ for k keys could be significantly affected by those attacks.

In this paper, we first propose a (matrix) NTRU-based MK-FHE for
super-constant number k of keys without using overstretched NTRU
parameters. Our scheme is essentially a combination of two components
following the two-layer framework of TFHE/FHEW:

- a simple first-layer matrix NTRU-based encryption that naturally
  supports multi-key NAND operations with moduli $q = O(k \cdot n^{1.5})$
  only linear in the number k of keys;
- and a crucial second-layer NTRU-based encryption that supports
  an efficient hybrid product between a single-key ciphertext and a
  multi-key ciphertext for gate bootstrapping.

Then, by replacing the first-layer with a more efficient LWE-based multi-
key encryption, we obtain an improved MK-FHE scheme with better
performance. We also employ a light key-switching technique to reduce
the key-switching key size from the previous $O(n^2)$ bits to $O(n)$ bits.

A proof-of-concept implementation shows that our two MK-FHE
schemes outperform the state-of-the-art TFHE-like MK-FHE schemes
in both computation efficiency and bootstrapping key size. Concretely,
for $k = 8$ at the same 100-bit security level, our improved MK-FHE
scheme can bootstrap a ciphertext in 0.54 s on a laptop and only has

This work was done while I was a visiting student in the group of Dr. Jiang Zhang
during 2021–2024 at State Key Laboratory of Cryptology, Beijing, China.

K.-M. Chung and Y. Sasaki (Eds.): ASIACRYPT 2024, LNCS 15484, pp. 241–270, 2025.
https://doi.org/10.1007/978-981-96-0875-1_8

a bootstrapping key of size 13.89MB, which are respectively 2.2 times faster and 7.4 times smaller than the MK-FHE scheme (which relies on a second-layer encryption from the ring-LWE assumption) due to Chen, Chillotti and Song (ASIACRYPT 2019).

1 Introduction

Multi-key Fully Homomorphic Encryption (MK-FHE) has emerged as a critical cryptographic primitive, facilitating secure computations on encrypted data contributed by multiple users in cloud environments. At STOC 2012, López-Alt, Tromer and Vaikuntanathan constructed the first MK-FHE scheme [27] which supported a-priori bounded number of keys. Clear and McGoldrick presented a GSW-type MK-FHE based on the Learning With Errors (LWE) problem [14]. Subsequently, Mukherjee and Wichs streamlined this approach and obtained a two-round Multi-Party Computation (MPC) protocol in the common random string model by proposing another LWE-based MK-FHE [30]. Both [30] and [14] are static in the sense that the keys involved in the homomorphic computation have to be determined at the beginning and do not support homomorphic computation on ciphertexts under new keys.

Peikert and Shiehian [31] introduced the concept of dynamic MK-FHE, where the resulting ciphertexts from previous homomorphic evaluations can be employed in subsequent homomorphic computations involving additional keys. A related concept, known as fully dynamic MK-FHE, was proposed by Brakerski and Perlman [8], which even does not need to know the total number of all possible keys during the setup. Chen, Chillotti and Song [9] proposed a dynamic TFHE-like MK-FHE scheme with efficient bootstrapping, but it requires a large number of bootstrapping keys (approximately 90MB for each party in the two-party case), limiting the applicability in resource-constrained environments such as the Internet of Things (IoT), blockchain, and GPU acceleration [29,32,34]. Recently, Kwak et al. [25] presented another variant of the TFHE-like MK-FHE scheme with asymptotically better computational efficiency but with much worse noise growth and larger bootstrapping keys (more than 214MB for each party in the two-party case).

Even if the first MK-FHE was based on NTRU lattices [27], the research on NTRU-based MK-FHE schemes was indeed suffered from the sublattice attacks in [2,10,16,20,23]. [1] In particular, the scheme in [27], adhering to the frameworks outlined in BGV [7] or BFV [18], had an error of magnitude about $\tilde{O}(n^{\tau k})$ and a moduli $q > \tilde{O}(n^{\tau k})$ for correctness, where τ is a small constant. However, Ducas and van Woerden [16] showed that the NTRU problem (including its matrix version [19]) with large moduli $q > n^{2.484+o(1)}$ and ternary secret could be significantly easier than its ring-LWE counterpart using similar parameters. Recently, Hough, Sandsbråten and Silde [21] showed that this conclusion still

---

[1] One way to avoid the sublattice attacks is to increase key size, but this can cause noise to escalate rapidly, potentially preventing even a single homomorphic multiplication. Therefore, ternary secret keys are typically preferred for efficiency.

Table 1. Experimental comparison between our MK-FHEs and two related ones [9, 25].

Scheme	Security	First layer		Second layer	Runtime(s)				Boot. Key(MB)			
		Assum.	Key Dist.	Assum.	$k=2$	$k=4$	$k=8$	$k=16$	$k=2$	$k=4$	$k=8$	$k=16$
CCS [9]	100	LWE	binary	RLWE	0.07	0.33	1.19	\	89.82	96.38	102.94	\
KMS [25]	100	LWE	binary	RLWE	0.14	0.44	1.17	2.86	214.61	285.22	250.06	285.31
Ours (Alg. 1)	100	MNTRU	ternary	NTRU	0.07	0.28	0.82	2.74	38.31	38.31	38.31	38.31
Ours (Alg. 2)	100	LWE	binary	NTRU	0.05	0.21	0.54	2.61	13.89	13.89	13.89	13.89
Ours (Alg. 1)	128	MNTRU	ternary	NTRU	0.14	0.40	1.55	6.84	72.5	72.5	92.69	112.87
Ours (Alg. 2)	128	LWE	binary	NTRU	0.06	0.23	0.76	4.21	17.45	17.45	17.45	25.83

holds for Gaussian secret of NTRU with such overstretched parameter, which puts a crucial limitation on the number k of keys in existing NTRU-based MK-FHEs [13, 27]. Although the problem of obtaining MK-FHE with larger k can be somehow eased by using very sparse secrets [36], the construction of NTRU-based MK-FHE schemes with super-constant $k = \omega(1)$ in the standard and secure parameter regime of NTRU lattices (e.g., uniform ternary keys with $q < n^{2.484+o(1)}$), to the best of our knowledge, is still open.

1.1 Our Results

In this work, we first propose a (matrix) NTRU-based MK-FHE for super-constant number k of keys without using overstretched NTRU parameters. Our construction basically consists of two components following the two-layer framework of the TFHE/FHEW scheme in [11, 15] and the MK-FHE scheme in [9]: a simple first-layer encryption for homomorphic NAND operations and a more complex second-layer encryption for gate bootstrapping. Specifically, our first-layer is an encryption scheme based on the matrix version of the NTRU problem (a.k.a., MNTRU [19]) which naturally supports multi-key NAND operation with moduli $q = O(k \cdot n^{1.5})$ only linear in the number k of keys, and can thus support a sub-linear number k of keys for $q < n^{2.484+o(1)}$. Our second-layer is a new and crucial NTRU-based encryption (more precisely, a Hint-NTRU based encryption, see technical overview below) which supports an efficient hybrid product between a single-key ciphertext and a multi-key ciphertext for gate bootstrapping. Then, by using our second-layer encryption as a building block, we also present an improved MK-FHE scheme with better performance by replacing the first layer with an LWE-based multi-key encryption. We further reduce the key-switching key size from previous $O(n^2)$ to $O(n)$ bits by using a light key-switching technique. As the TFHE-like MK-FHE in [9], our proposed two MK-FHEs inherently support dynamic homomorphic computation on ciphertexts under new keys.

We implement our two schemes in experiment using the OpenFHE library [4]. In Table 1, we provide an experimental comparison of our schemes with the two MK-FHEs by Chen, Chillotti and Song (CCS) [9] and by Kwak, Min and Song (KMS) [25]. Since both CCS [9] and KMS [25] only choose parameters achieving 100-bit security, we select two sets of parameters achieving both 100-bit and

128-bit security for a fair comparison, where the concrete security of all set of parameters (as well as the ones in [9,25]) is estimated by using the LWE estimator in [3] and the NTRU estimator in [16] (see Sect. 7.2 for details). From Table 1 one can see that our two MK-FHE schemes are faster and have smaller bootstrapping keys than the MK-FHE schemes in [9,25]. The efficiency improvement over [9,25] is mainly because our NTRU-based second-layer encryption supports a more efficient hybrid product. One can also see that our first MK-FHE scheme with MNTRU-based first-layer ciphertexts (i.e., Algorithm 1) is less efficient than our second one with LWE-based first-layer ciphertexts (i.e., Algorithm 2). The main reason is that Algorithm 1 uses uniform ternary keys which requires a more complex bootstrapping algorithm than that of Algorithm 2 using binary keys (see the technical overview below for more details). For a concrete comparison at the same 100-bit security level, our Algorithm 2 is about 1.4, 1.6 and 2.2 times faster than CCS [9], and 2.8, 2.1 and 2.2 times faster than KMS [25] for $k = 2$, 4 and 8, respectively. Correspondingly, the bootstrapping key size of our Alg. 2 is 6.5, 6.9 and 7.4 smaller than that of CCS [9], and is 15.5, 20.5 and 18 times smaller than that of KMS [25]. For $k = 16$, our Alg. 2 is about 1.1 times faster and 20.5 times smaller than KMS [25] (note that CCS [9] did not provide the parameters for $k = 16$).

1.2   Technical Overview

Before diving into the technical details of our constructions, we begin by recalling the two-layer framework of FHEW/TFHE in [11,15], which was later extended to the multi-key setting in [9]. Basically, the framework consists of two layers of different encryption schemes: the first layer only supports a single homomorphic NAND computation and the second layer is designed to bootstrap the first layer ciphertext to support more NAND operations (namely, the gate bootstrapping). For simplicity, we restricted our attention to the setting where the first layer is an LWE-based encryption, and the second layer is an RLWE-based encryption (namely, the whole scheme is essentially a hybrid scheme under two assumptions). Formally, let n, q be the dimension and moduli of the LWE problem in the first layer, respectively. Let $\mathbf{z} \in \{0,1\}^n$ be the LWE secret of the first layer, and the ciphertext of the first layer has the form of $(b, \mathbf{a}) \in \mathbb{Z}_q^{n+1}$ such that $b + \langle \mathbf{a}, \mathbf{z} \rangle \approx \lfloor q/4 \rfloor \cdot m$ for $m \in \{0,1\}$. Given two first-layer ciphertexts $ct_1 = (b_1, \mathbf{a}_1) \in \mathbb{Z}_q^{n+1}$ and $ct_2 = (b_2, \mathbf{a}_2) \in \mathbb{Z}_q^{n+1}$ encrypting $m_1 \in \{0,1\}$ and $m_2 \in \{0,1\}$, respectively, the homomorphic NAND operation can be simply done by computing $ct' = (b', \mathbf{a}') = (\frac{5q}{8}, \mathbf{0}) - ct_1 - ct_2$ such that $b' + \langle \mathbf{a}', \mathbf{z} \rangle \approx \lfloor q/2 \rfloor \cdot m$ where $m = m_1 \bar{\wedge} m_2$. Moreover, let N, Q be the dimension and moduli of the RLWE problem in the second layer such that N is a power of two and $q = 2N$. Let $R = \mathbb{Z}[X]/(X^N + 1)$ and its quotient ring $R_Q = \mathbb{Z}_Q[X]/(X^N + 1)$. The second-layer RLWE-based encryption is basically a GSW-like encryption under secret key $s \in R$, which given an encryption of the first-layer secret key $\mathbf{z} \in \{0,1\}^n$ under $s \in R$, supports the homomorphic computation of $b' + \langle \mathbf{a}', \mathbf{z} \rangle \approx \lfloor q/2 \rfloor \cdot m$ on the exponent of X (namely, $X^{b' + \langle \mathbf{a}', \mathbf{z} \rangle}$) such that the modulo q operation is free in R_Q (this is because the order of X in R is exactly q due to the choice of $q = 2N$). By multiplying a carefully designed polynomial $r(X) \in R_Q$ to $X^{b'+\langle \mathbf{a}', \mathbf{z} \rangle}$, one can exactly extract an encryption of m on the constant term of the resulting polynomial[2]. The above procedure is also known as blind rotation [5,11,15,26,35].

To extend the above framework to the multi-key setting, it suffices to design a first-layer encryption that supports multi-key NAND operation and a second-layer GSW-like encryption that supports multi-key blind rotation. Note that given a ciphertext $ct_1 = (b_1, \mathbf{a}_1) \in \mathbb{Z}_q^{n+1}$ under a single-key secret key $\mathbf{z}_1$, by appending $(k-1)n$ zeros one can easily obtain a ciphertext $\overline{ct}_1 = (b, \mathbf{a}_1, \cdots, \mathbf{a}_k) = (b_1, \mathbf{a}_1, \mathbf{0}, \cdots, \mathbf{0}) \in \mathbb{Z}_q^{kn+1}$ that encrypts the same message under the set of keys $\{\mathbf{z}_i\}_{1 \le i \le k}$ because of $b + \langle \mathbf{a}_1, \mathbf{z}_1 \rangle = b + \sum_{i=1}^{k} \langle \mathbf{a}_i, \mathbf{z}_i \rangle$. This means that the multi-key NAND operation can be trivially done as in the single-key setting.

The multi-key blind rotation is more complex and non-trivial because we essentially need a way to generate the blind rotation evaluation key that encrypts a set of first-layer secrets $\{\mathbf{z}_i\}_{1 \le i \le k}$ under a set of second-layer secrets $\{s_i\}_{1 \le i \le k}$ on the fly (namely, the set of keys involved in the computation is not known in the setup phase). To handle this, Chen et al. [9] presented an RGSW-like scheme (called uni-encryption) supporting the hybrid product between an MK-RLWE ciphertext and the uni-encryption. Specifically, for a base $B \in \mathbb{Z}$ and $d = \lceil \log_B Q \rceil$, the uni-encryption $\mathsf{UniEnc}(\mu, s) = (\mathbf{d}, \mathbf{f}_0, \mathbf{f}_1) \in R_Q^d \times R_Q^d \times R_Q^d$ that encrypts $\mu \in R_Q$ under the secret $s \in R$ is defined as

$$\mathbf{d} = r \cdot \mathbf{a} + \mu \cdot \mathbf{g} + \mathbf{e}_1 \in R_Q^d, \qquad \mathbf{f}_0 = -s \cdot \mathbf{f}_1 + r \cdot \mathbf{g} + \mathbf{e}_2 \in R_Q^d,$$

where $\mathbf{a} \in R_Q^d$ is a Common Reference String (CRS), $\mathbf{g} = [B^0, \ldots, B^{d-1}] \in \mathbb{Z}^d$ is a gadget vector, $r \in R_Q$ is a random polynomial and $\mathbf{f}_1, \mathbf{e}_1, \mathbf{e}_2 \in R_Q^d$ are d-dimension polynomials in R_Q.

To perform the multi-key blind rotation for an LWE-based first-layer ciphertext $\overline{ct}' = (b', \mathbf{a}_1', \cdots, \mathbf{a}_k')$ under the keys $\{\mathbf{z}_i\}_{1 \le i \le k}$ for some $\mathbf{a}_i' = (a_{i,j}')_{0 \le j < n}$ and $\mathbf{z}_i = (z_{i,j})_{0 \le j < n}$, each party (of index i) independently generates a set of uni-encryption ciphertexts $\{\mathsf{UniEnc}(z_{i,j}, s_i)\}_{0 \le j < n}$ that encrypts $\mathbf{z}_i \in \{0,1\}^n$ under the secret key $s_i \in R_Q$ as the evaluation key. Let

$$\mathsf{CMUX}(z_{i,j}) = \mathbf{1} + (X^{a_{i,j}'} - 1) \cdot \mathsf{UniEnc}(z_{i,j}, s_i)$$

for binary $z_{i,j}$. Since $\mathbf{1}$ can be designed as a noiseless uni-encryption of one and the uni-encryption ciphertext also has homomorphic properties (see Lemma 2), we have $\mathsf{CMUX}(z_{i,j}) = \mathsf{UniEnc}(X^{a_{i,j}' z_{i,j}}, s_i)$. Then, we can initialize the accumulator as a trivial MK-RLWE encryption $\mathsf{ACC}_{in} = (r(X)X^{b'}, \mathbf{0}) \in R_Q^{k+1}$ and recursively compute

$$\mathsf{ACC}_{out} = \mathsf{ACC}_{in} \cdot \prod_{i=1}^{k} \prod_{j=0}^{n-1} \mathsf{CMUX}(z_{i,j}).$$

---

[2] The details on how to set such $r(X)$ can be found in [5,9,12,35]. We omit these details in this paper.

By the fact that the order of X is exactly q for $q = 2N$, one can check that the output ACC_{out} is an MK-RLWE ciphertext that encrypts $r(X) \cdot X^{b' + \sum_{i=1}^{k} \langle \mathbf{a}'_i, \mathbf{z}_i \rangle}$ under the secret $(1, s_1, \cdots, s_k) \in R^{k+1}$. And by carefully designing the rotation polynomial $r(X)$, the message in the constant term can be exactly $\lfloor Q/4 \rceil \cdot m$. Finally, by using the sample extraction as in [22], we can extract an MK-LWE encryption $\overline{ct}'' = (b'', \mathbf{a}''_1, \ldots, \mathbf{a}''_k) \in \mathbb{Z}_Q^{kN+1}$ that encrypts $\lfloor Q/4 \rceil \cdot m$ under the secret $(\mathbf{s}_i)_{i \in [k]} \in \mathbb{Z}^{kN}$ where $\mathbf{s}_i$ is the coefficient vector of s_i. Then by performing the multi-key LWE modulus-switching from Q to q and key-switching from $(\mathbf{s}_i)_{i \in [k]} \in \mathbb{Z}^{kN}$ to $(\mathbf{z}_i)_{i \in [k]} \in \mathbb{Z}^{kn}$, we finish the bootstrapping and get a refreshed MK-LWE ciphertext.

As sketched above, in order to obtain a (matrix) NTRU-based MK-FHE, it suffices to design a first-layer MNTRU-based encryption that supports multi-key NAND operation and a second-layer NTRU-based GSW-like encryption that supports efficient hybrid product for multi-key blind rotation.

First-Layer Matrix NTRU-Based Multi-Key Encryption. We begin by first recalling the single-key MNTRU ciphertext in [5]. Formally, let n, q be two positive integers. The single-key MNTRU ciphertext that encrypts a message bit $m \in \{0, 1\}$ in [5] is defined as $\mathbf{c} := (\mathbf{e} + \lfloor \frac{q}{4} \rceil \cdot \mathbf{m}) \cdot \mathbf{F}^{-1} \in \mathbb{Z}_q^n$ where the secret key $\mathbf{F} \in \mathbb{Z}^{n \times n}$ is an invertible matrix, $\mathbf{e} \in \mathbb{Z}_q^n$ is a random vector from $\mathbb{Z}_q^n$, and $\mathbf{m} = (m, 0, \ldots, 0) \in \mathbb{Z}^n$. Note that this can be actually viewed as a standard MNTRU ciphertext that encrypts a message vector $\lfloor \frac{q}{4} \rceil \cdot \mathbf{m} \cdot \mathbf{F}^{-1} = (*, 0, \ldots, 0) \in \mathbb{Z}^n$ with a single non-zero term, whose security can be based on either a KDM-form MNTRU assumption (which essentially assumes that the standard MNTRU encryption is KDM-secure as in [5,35], we refer to Sect. 2.4 for a formal definition), or the matrix inhomogeneous NTRU (MiNTRU) assumption with a more complex distribution for error $\mathbf{e}$ in [19]. We prefer to the former assumption because a circular-secure/KDM-secure assumption is common for constructing FHEs with bootstrapping (e.g., [5,35]), and designing FHEs without circular-secure/KDM-secure assumptions is actually a long-term open problem. We now extend the above single-key ciphertext to the multi-key setting, and naturally define the multi-key MNTRU ciphertext as a vector of the form $\overline{ct} = (\mathbf{c}_1, \cdots, \mathbf{c}_k) \in \mathbb{Z}_q^{kn}$ such that

$$\langle \mathbf{c}_1, \mathrm{col}_0(\mathbf{F}_1) \rangle + \cdots + \langle \mathbf{c}_k, \mathrm{col}_0(\mathbf{F}_k) \rangle = \left\lfloor \frac{q}{4} \right\rceil \cdot m + e$$

where k denotes the number of involved keys, e is a small noise and $\mathrm{col}_0(\mathbf{F}_i) = (f_{i,j})_{0 \leq j < n}$ is the first column of the secret matrix $\mathbf{F}_i$.

Since a constant cannot be treated as a noiseless ciphertext in our MNTRU-based multi-key encryption (which is unlike the LWE-based one in [9]), we have to create an additional evaluation key $evk_i = (\mathbf{e}_i + \lfloor \frac{5q}{8} \rceil \cdot (1, \mathbf{0})) \cdot \mathbf{F}_i^{-1} \in \mathbb{Z}_q^n$ encrypting the constant $\frac{5q}{8}$ for performing the NAND gate evaluation. Now, given two multi-key MNTRU ciphertexts $\overline{ct}_1 = (\mathbf{c}_1, \cdots, \mathbf{c}_{k_1}) \in \mathbb{Z}_q^{k_1 n}$ and $\overline{ct} = (\mathbf{c}_1, \cdots, \mathbf{c}_{k_2}) \in \mathbb{Z}_q^{k_2 n}$, let k be the maximum number of different keys involved in $\overline{ct}_1$ and $\overline{ct}_2$. By reorganizing the components and padding empty slots with zeros, we can extend the ciphertexts $\overline{ct}_1$ and $\overline{ct}_2$ to $\overline{ct}'_1, \overline{ct}'_2 \in \mathbb{Z}^{kn}$ under the secret $(\mathbf{F}_j)_{j \in [k]}$. Then, the NAND gate operation can be done by computing

$$\overline{ct}' = (\ \underbrace{\mathbf{0}, \cdots, \mathbf{0}}_{(i-1)n \text{ zeros}}, evk_i, \underbrace{\mathbf{0}, \cdots, \mathbf{0}}_{(k-i)n \text{ zeros}}\ ) - \overline{ct}'_1 - \overline{ct}'_2 \in \mathbb{Z}_q^{kn}.$$

Second-Layer NTRU-Based Uni-Encryption. Now, we give our NTRU-based uni-encryption scheme that supports efficient hybrid product for multi-key blind rotation. Let B, d be two integers and $d = \lceil \log_B Q \rceil$. Specifically, each party i takes a uniformly random CRS $\mathbf{a} \in R_Q^d$ and sets the public key $\mathbf{b}_i = -\mathbf{a} \cdot s_i + \mathbf{e}_i \in R_Q^d$ where s_i is the secret of the second layer for party i, $\mathbf{e}_i$ is a d-dimensional polynomial vectors. Party i can encrypt a plaintext $\mu_i \in R_Q$ into a uni-encryption ciphertext $\mathsf{UniEnc}(\mu_i, s_i) = (\mathbf{d}_i, \mathbf{f}_i) \in R_Q^d \times R_Q^d$ under secret key s_i such that

$$\mathbf{d}_i = r_i \cdot \mathbf{a} + \mu_i \cdot \mathbf{g} + \mathbf{e}_{i,1} \in R_Q^d, \qquad \mathbf{f}_i = \mathbf{e}_{i,2} \cdot s_i^{-1} + r_i \cdot \mathbf{g} \cdot s_i^{-1} \in R_Q^d,$$

where r_i is a polynomial with small coefficients, $\mathbf{e}_{i,1}, \mathbf{e}_{i,2}$ are d-dimensional polynomial vectors and $\mathbf{g} = [B^0, \ldots, B^{d-1}] \in \mathbb{Z}^d$ is a gadget vector. Note that our NTRU-based uni-encryption ciphertext only contains two polynomials in R_Q (while the MK-FHE scheme [9] and its variant [25] have to store three polynomials), which allows us to save both computation and storage for a hybrid product. Because the same s_i is used in both $\mathbf{b}_i = -\mathbf{a} \cdot s_i + \mathbf{e}_i$ and $\mathbf{f}_i = \mathbf{e}_{i,2} \cdot s_i^{-1} + r_i \cdot \mathbf{g} \cdot s_i^{-1}$, the above construction essentially relies on the hardness of a KDM-secure assumption and a variant of the NTRU problem called Hint-NTRU [17]. As discussed in [17], with a suitable choice of secret and error distributions, the Hint-NTRU problem is at least as hard as the inhomogeneous NTRU problem [19].

The single-key KDM-form NTRU ciphertext that encrypts a message $\mu \in R_Q$ in [35] is defined as $c := (g + \mu)/s$ where the secret key $s \in R$ is an invertible polynomial, $g \in R_Q$ is a random polynomial from R_Q. We can extend the above single-key ciphertext to the multi-key setting, and naturally define the multi-key NTRU (MK-NTRU) ciphertext under the secret $(s_i)_{i \in [k]}$ as a vector of the form $(c_i)_{i \in [k]} \in R_Q^k$ such that $\sum_{i=1}^k c_i s_i = g' + \mu$ where k denotes the number of involved keys, g' is a small noise. To homomorphically multiply the MK-NTRU ciphertext by a uni-encryption that encrypts μ_i of party i, we compute the following inner products: $u_j = \langle \mathbf{g}^{-1}(c_j), \mathbf{d}_i \rangle$ for $1 \leqslant j \leqslant k$, and compute $v = \sum_{j=1}^k \langle \mathbf{g}^{-1}(c_j), \mathbf{b}_j \rangle$. Then we output $\overline{\mathbf{c}}' = (c'_1, \ldots, c'_k) \in R_Q^k$ where $c'_i = u_i + \langle \mathbf{g}^{-1}(v), \mathbf{f}_i \rangle$ and $c'_j = u_j$ for $j \neq i$. One can check that $\overline{\mathbf{c}}'$ is an MK-NTRU ciphertext that encrypts $\mu \cdot \mu_i$ (we defer the proof and security analysis to Sect. 4). It is important to note that our MK-NTRU ciphertext consists of k polynomials in R_Q, which is one less than that of the MK-RLWE ciphertext in [9,25]. This means our hybrid product only needs $d(2k + 1)$ multiplications in R_Q, which is $2d$ less than that of the MK-FHE schemes in [9,25].

Bootstrapping First-Layer Matrix NTRU-Based Multi-Key Ciphertexts. Now, we show how to bootstrap first-layer matrix NTRU-based multi-key ciphertexts. Formally, Given a multi-key MNTRU ciphertext $\overline{ct}' = (\mathbf{c}'_1, \cdots, \mathbf{c}'_k) \in \mathbb{Z}_q^{kn}$ satisfying $\sum_{i=1}^{k} \langle \mathbf{c}'_i, \mathrm{col}_0(\mathbf{F}_i) \rangle \approx \lfloor \frac{q}{2} \rceil m$ for some $\mathbf{c}'_i = (c'_{i,j})_{0 \leq j < n}$ where $\mathrm{col}_0(\mathbf{F}_i) = (f_{i,j})_{0 \leq j < n} \in \{-1, 0, 1\}^n$ is the first column of the secret matrix $\mathbf{F}_i$, the gate bootstrapping consists of three steps: blind rotation, modulus switching and key-switching. Recall the previous multi-key blind rotation is to homomorphically decrypt an MK-LWE ciphertext with a binary secret key distribution on the exponent [9,25]. One issue we encounter is that in our MNTRU scheme, the secret key follows a ternary distribution. Therefore, we need to extend this method to accommodate ternary secret key distributions. To solve this issue, we employ the ternary CMUX gate $1 + \left(X^{c'_{i,j}} - 1 \right) \cdot f^{+}_{i,j} + \left(X^{-c'_{i,j}} - 1 \right) \cdot f^{-}_{i,j} = X^{c'_{i,j} f_{i,j}}$ first used in [5] where

$$\begin{cases} f^{+}_{i,j} = 1, & \text{if } f_{i,j} = 1 \\ f^{+}_{i,j} = 0, & \text{otherwise} \end{cases}, \quad \begin{cases} f^{-}_{i,j} = 1, & \text{if } f_{i,j} = -1 \\ f^{-}_{i,j} = 0, & \text{otherwise} \end{cases} \quad \text{for } 0 \leq j < n.$$

Another issue is that in previous methods [9] the accumulator can be initialized as a trivial MK-RLWE encryption. However, this feature is not satisfied for our MK-NTRU ciphertext. Noticed that if we set the initial accumulator as $\mathsf{ACC}_{in} = (r(X), \mathbf{0}) \in R_Q^k$ for some rotation polynomial $r(X) \in R_Q$, we have the fact $\langle \mathsf{ACC}_{in}, \mathbf{s} \rangle = r(X)s_1$ where $\mathbf{s} = (s_1, \cdots, s_k) \in R^k$ is the secret keys of k keys used in hybrid product. Fortunately, we can effectively address this challenge by carefully designing the evaluation key. Specifically, party i creates a set of ciphertexts as follows:

- For $i = 1$, given secret key $\mathrm{col}_0(\mathbf{F}_1) = (f_{1,0}, \ldots, f_{1,n-1}) \in \{-1, 0, 1\}^n$, create a set of ciphertexts that encrypts $\mathrm{col}_0(\mathbf{F}_1)$ under s_1 as follows:

$$\begin{cases} \mathbf{evk}^{+}_{1,0} = \mathsf{UniEnc}(f^{+}_{1,0}/s_1, s_1) \\ \mathbf{evk}^{-}_{1,0} = \mathsf{UniEnc}(f^{-}_{1,0}/s_1, s_1) \end{cases}, \quad \begin{cases} \mathbf{evk}^{+}_{1,j} = \mathsf{UniEnc}(f^{+}_{1,j}, s_1) \\ \mathbf{evk}^{-}_{1,j} = \mathsf{UniEnc}(f^{-}_{1,j}, s_1) \end{cases} \quad \text{for } 1 \leq j < n,$$

- For $i \neq 1$, given secret key $\mathrm{col}_0(\mathbf{F}_i) = (f_{i,0}, \ldots, f_{i,n-1}) \in \{-1, 0, 1\}^n$, create a set of ciphertext that encrypts $\mathrm{col}_0(\mathbf{F}_i)$ under s_i as follows:

$$\mathbf{evk}^{+}_{i,j} = \mathsf{UniEnc}(f^{+}_{i,j}, s_i), \mathbf{evk}^{-}_{i,j} = \mathsf{UniEnc}(f^{-}_{i,j}, s_i) \text{ for } 0 \leq j < n.$$

Recall that in the previous scheme [9,25], the uni-encryption ciphertexts can be publicly generated even when the plaintext is known. This feature is crucial for the CMUX gate evaluation. But our KDM-form evaluation keys $\mathbf{evk}^{+}_{1,0}$ and $\mathbf{evk}^{-}_{1,0}$ given above don't satisfy this requirement. We address this issue with minimal additional cost by additionally constructing an auxiliary ciphertext $\mathbf{evk}^{*}_{1,0} = \mathsf{UniEnc}(1/s_1, s_1)$. In this case, the CMUX gate in the first iteration can be computed as

$$\mathsf{CMUX}(f_{1,0}) = \mathbf{evk}^{*}_{1,0} + \left(X^{c'_{1,0}} - 1 \right) \cdot \mathbf{evk}^{+}_{1,0} + \left(X^{-c'_{1,0}} - 1 \right) \cdot \mathbf{evk}^{-}_{1,0},$$

which is a uni-encryption of $X^{c'_{1,0}f_{1,0}}/s_1$. In other iterations, we slightly revised the CMUX gate as

$$\mathsf{CMUX}(f_{i,j}) = 1 + \left(X^{c'_{i,j}} - 1 \right) \cdot \left(\mathbf{evk}_{i,j}^+ - X^{-c'_{i,j}} \cdot \mathbf{evk}_{i,j}^- \right),$$

where $\mathbf{1}$ is a noiseless uni-encryption of one.

We now describe our bootstrapping algorithm. Firstly, we initialize the accumulator as $\mathsf{ACC}_{in} = (r(X), \mathbf{0}) \in R_Q^k$ and compute the hybrid product of ACC_{in} and $\mathsf{CMUX}(f_{1,0})$ to obtain $\mathsf{ACC}_{1,0}$. Since $\mathsf{CMUX}(f_{1,0}) = \mathsf{UniEnc}(X^{c'_{1,0}f_{1,0}}/s_1, s_1)$, one can easily check that $\mathsf{ACC}_{1,0}$ is an MK-NTRU ciphertext that encrypts $r(X) \cdot X^{c'_{1,0}f_{1,0}}$. Next we compute $\mathbf{evk}'_{1,1} = \mathbf{evk}_{1,1}^+ - \mathbf{evk}_{1,1}^- \cdot X^{-c'_{1,1}}$ to obtain a uni-encryption for $f_{1,1}^+ - f_{1,1}^- \cdot X^{-c'_{1,1}}$. Then we compute the hybrid product between $(X^{c'_{1,1}} - 1)\mathsf{ACC}_{1,0}$ and $\mathbf{evk}'_{1,1}$, and $\mathsf{ACC}_{1,0}$ to obtain $\mathsf{ACC}_{1,1}$. We can check that $\mathsf{ACC}_{1,1}$ is an MK-NTRU ciphertext that encrypts

$$r(X) \cdot X^{c'_{1,0}f_{1,0}} \left(1 + (X^{c'_{1,1}} - 1) \cdot (f_{1,1}^+ - f_{1,1}^- \cdot X^{-c'_{1,1}}) \right) = r(X) \cdot X^{c'_{1,0}f_{1,0} + c'_{1,1}f_{1,1}}.$$

We can iteratively absorb $X^{c'_{i,j}f_{i,j}}$ for $i \in [k]$ and $0 \le j < n$ to obtain an MK-NTRU ciphertext $\mathsf{ACC}_{k,n-1}$ that encrypts $r(X) \cdot X^{\sum_{i=1}^{k} \sum_{j=0}^{n-1} c'_{i,j}f_{i,j}}$. Furthermore, by carefully designing $r(X)$ we can ensure that the constant term of $r(X) \cdot X^{\sum_{i=1}^{k} \sum_{j=0}^{n-1} c'_{i,j}f_{i,j}}$ equals $\left\lfloor \frac{Q}{4} \right\rfloor \cdot m$.

Another issue is that after multi-key blind rotation, we obtain an MK-NTRU ciphertext under the modulus Q instead of a multi-key MNTRU-based first-layer ciphertext. Therefore, we use the modulus switching technique to switch the modulus from Q back to q and we design a key-switching method to switch the MK-NTRU ciphertext back to MNTRU first-layer ciphertext, resulting in a refreshed multi-key MNTRU ciphertext of encryption $\left\lfloor \frac{q}{4} \right\rfloor \cdot m$, which is convenient for the next NAND gate computation.

Bootstrapping First-Layer Multi-key LWE Ciphertexts. Recall that the multi-key LWE ciphertext (after NAND gate) that encrypts a message bit $m \in \{0,1\}$ in [9] under the secret $(1, \mathbf{z}_1, \cdots, \mathbf{z}_k) \in \mathbb{Z}^{kn+1}$ is defined as a vector of the form $\overline{ct}' = (b', \mathbf{a}'_1, \ldots, \mathbf{a}'_k) \in \mathbb{Z}_q^{kn+1}$ such that $b' + \sum_{i=1}^{k} \langle \mathbf{a}'_i, \mathbf{z}_i \rangle \approx \lfloor q/2 \rfloor \cdot m$ for some $\mathbf{a}'_i = (a'_{i,j})_{0 \le j < n} \in \mathbb{Z}_q^n$. Our second-layer encryption scheme can also be modified to bootstrap such a standard first-layer multi-key LWE ciphertext $\overline{ct}'$. Similarly, it requires us to carefully design the evaluation key. Details can be found in Sect. 6 and we skip it here.

After blind rotation, we get an MK-NTRU ciphertext $\mathbf{c} = (c_1, \cdots, c_k) \in R_Q^k$ under the secret key $(s_1, \cdots, s_k) \in R^k$ instead of an MK-LWE ciphertext. Then we can extract a multi-key LWE ciphertext $\overline{ct}'' = (0, \mathbf{a}''_1, \cdots, \mathbf{a}''_k) \in \mathbb{Z}_Q^{kN+1}$ under the secret key $(1, \mathbf{s}_1, \cdots, \mathbf{s}_k) \in \mathbb{Z}^{kN+1}$ where $\mathbf{s}_i$ is the coefficient vector of s_i. Subsequently, by performing a modulus switching, we can switch the modulus from Q back to q.

Finally, we only need to perform one key-switching to switch the secret key from $(1, \mathbf{s}_1, \cdots, \mathbf{s}_k) \in \mathbb{Z}^{kN+1}$ back to the secret key $(1, \mathbf{z}_1, \cdots, \mathbf{z}_k) \in \mathbb{Z}^{kn+1}$. However, in previous key-switching methods [9,25] the key-switching keys are substantially larger than the evaluation keys. For example, the evaluation key measures 19.7 MB, whereas the key-switching keys occupy a much larger 70.1 MB of storage space in [9]. This size discrepancy presents a significant challenge and warrants attention. To solve this issue, we propose a light key-switching method. Let B_{ks} be an integer, $d_{ks} = \lceil \log_{B_{ks}} q \rceil$. To switch an MK-LWE ciphertext under the secret $(1, \mathbf{s}_1, \cdots, \mathbf{s}_k) \in \mathbb{Z}^{kN+1}$ to the secret $(1, \mathbf{z}_1, \cdots, \mathbf{z}_k) \in \mathbb{Z}^{kn+1}$, the previous method is to create a set of LWE ciphertexts that encrypts $vB_{ks}^l s_{i,j}$ under $\mathbf{z}_i$ for party i where $i \in [k], j \in [0, \cdots, N-1], l \in [0, \cdots, d_{ks}-1], v \in [1, \cdots, B_{ks}-1]$. Instead, we pack these LWE ciphertexts of party i into a small number of RLWE ciphertexts, and the server can extract them as LWE ciphertexts almost for free using sample extraction. This approach reduces the key-switching key size from $\tilde{O}(kn^2)$ bits to $\tilde{O}(kn)$ bits, which can be of independent interest to other schemes (e.g., the single-key FHEs [11,12,15,26,35]) as well.

1.3 Organization

After giving some background in Sect. 2, we present a multi-key matrix NTRU-based encryption scheme in Sect. 3. In Sect. 4, we present our new hybrid product. We show how to use our new hybrid product to bootstrap the multi-key matrix NTRU-based and LWE-based ciphertexts in Sect. 5 and Sect. 6, respectively. Finally, we report our implementation in Sect. 7.

2   Preliminaries

2.1   Notation

The set of real numbers (integers) is denoted by $\mathbb{R}$ ($\mathbb{Z}$, resp.). Vectors and matrices are denoted as lowercase bold letters (e.g. $\mathbf{a}$, $\mathbf{b}$) and uppercase bold letters (e.g. $\mathbf{A}$, $\mathbf{B}$), respectively. The $i + 1$-th column of a matrix $\mathbf{A}$ is denoted by $\mathrm{col}_i(\mathbf{A})$ and $\mathbf{A}_{i,j}$ denotes the element in the i-th row and j-th column.

The inner product of two vectors $\mathbf{a}$ and $\mathbf{b}$ is denoted by the symbol $\langle \mathbf{a}, \mathbf{b} \rangle$. The index set $[k]$ represents the set of integers $\{1, 2, ..., k\}$. For positive integers q, Q and power of two N, by R and R_q (resp., R_Q) we denote the $2N$-th cyclotomic ring $R = \mathbb{Z}[X]/(X^N + 1)$ and its quotient ring $R_q = R/qR$ (resp., $R_Q = R/QR$).

For polynomial $a = \sum_{i=0}^{N-1} a_i X^i \in R$, we use $\mathsf{Cof}(a)$ to denote the coefficient vector of a, and we denote the N-dimensional anti-circulant matrix of a by

$$\mathcal{A}(a) := \begin{pmatrix} a_0 & a_1 & \cdots & a_{N-1} \\ -a_{N-1} & a_0 & \cdots & a_{N-2} \\ \vdots & \ddots & \ddots & \vdots \\ -a_1 & -a_2 & \cdots & a_0 \end{pmatrix} = \begin{pmatrix} (\mathsf{Cof}(a)) \\ (\mathsf{Cof}(a \cdot X)) \\ \vdots \\ (\mathsf{Cof}(a \cdot X^{N-1})) \end{pmatrix}.$$

We use $\leftarrow$ to denote sampling an element uniformly at random from some distribution. By $\|\cdot\|$ and $\|\cdot\|_\infty$, we denote the ℓ_2 and ℓ_∞ norms. By $\lceil\cdot\rceil$, $\lfloor\cdot\rfloor$ and $\lfloor\cdot\rceil$ we denote the ceiling, floor and round function, respectively.

2.2 Gadget Decomposition

For integers q, B, let $d = \lceil \log_q B \rceil$ and $\mathbf{g}_{q,B} = [B^0, \ldots, B^{d-1}] \in \mathbb{Z}^d$ be a gadget vector. We write $\mathbf{g}$ when q and B are clear from the context. For an integer $k \geq 1$, the gadget matrix is defined as

$$\mathbf{G}_k = \mathbf{I}_k \otimes \mathbf{g}^t = \begin{bmatrix} \mathbf{g}^t & 0 & \ldots & 0 \\ 0 & \mathbf{g}^t & \ldots & 0 \\ \vdots & \vdots & \ddots & \vdots \\ 0 & 0 & \ldots & \mathbf{g}^t \end{bmatrix} \in \mathbb{Z}^{dk \times k}.$$

For any $a \in \mathbb{Z}$, the gadget decomposition of a is defined as its signed decomposition in base B as $\mathbf{g}^{-1}(a) = (a_0, \cdots, a_{d-1})$ with each $a_i \in (-B/2, B/2]$ such that $a = \langle \mathbf{g}^{-1}(a), \mathbf{g} \rangle$. The definition can be naturally extended to any polynomial in R_q. For any $a = \sum_{i=0}^{N-1} a_i X^i$, we define $\mathbf{g}^{-1}(a) = \sum_{i=0}^{N-1} \mathbf{g}^{-1}(a_i) X^i$.

In practice, we can ignore the first element of $\mathbf{g}^{-1}(a)$ and $\mathbf{g}$ to obtain $\mathbf{g}^{-1}(a) = (a_1, \cdots, a_{d-1})$ which satisfies $a \approx \langle \mathbf{g}^{-1}(a), \mathbf{g} \rangle$, thereby achieving optimization in both computation and storage.

2.3 Multi-key Fully Homomorphic Encryption

Let $\mathcal{M}$ be the message space with arithmetic structure. Let k be the bound of the involved keys. A multi-key FHE scheme is a tuple of PPT algorithms (Setup, KeyGen, Enc, Dec, Eval) having the following properties:

- Setup (1^λ): Given the security parameter λ, outputs a public parameter pp.
- KeyGen(pp): Outputs a public key pk and secret key sk.
- Enc(m, pk): Given the public key pk and a message $m \in \mathcal{M}$, output a ciphertext ct. For convenience, we assume that ct contains an index to pk.
- Dec $(\overline{ct}_j, \{sk_i\}_{i \in T_j})$: Let $T_j \subseteq [k]$ be a set. Given a ciphertext $\overline{ct}_j$ corresponding to a set of keys $T_j \subseteq [k]$ and a tuple of secret keys $\{sk_i\}_{i \in T_j}$, outputs the message $m \in \mathcal{M}$.
- Eval $(\mathcal{C}, (\overline{ct}_1, \cdots, \overline{ct}_l), \{pk_i\}_{i \in T})$: Let $T = T_1 \cup \cdots \cup T_\ell$. Given a circuit $\mathcal{C}$, a set of public keys $\{pk_i\}_{i \in T}$ and a tuple of multi-key ciphertexts $\overline{ct}_1, \cdots, \overline{ct}_l$ where each ciphertext $\overline{ct}_j$ is evaluated using $pk_{T_j} = \{pk_d, \forall d \in T_j\}$ for $j \in [l]$, outputs a ciphertext $\overline{ct}$.

Compactness. We say that a multi-key FHE scheme is compact if there exists a polynomial $poly(\cdot, \cdot)$ such that the length of a ciphertext associated with k keys is bounded by a polynomial $poly(\lambda, k)$.

Correctness. Let $\overline{ct}_j$ be a ciphertext (associated with the set T_j) such that $\mathsf{Dec}\left(\overline{ct}_j, \{sk_i\}_{i \in T_j}\right) = m_j$ for $1 \leq j \leq l$. Let $\mathcal{C} : \mathcal{M}^\ell \to \mathcal{M}$ be a circuit and $\overline{ct} \leftarrow \mathsf{Eval}\left(\mathcal{C}, (\overline{ct}_1, \cdots, \overline{ct}_l), \{pk_i\}_{i \in T}\right)$ for $T = T_1 \cup \cdots \cup T_\ell$. We say that a multi-key FHE scheme is correct if

$$\Pr\left[\mathsf{Dec}\left(\overline{ct}, \{sk_i\}_{i \in T}\right) \neq \mathcal{C}\left(m_1, \ldots, m_l\right)\right] = \mathrm{negl}(\lambda).$$

2.4   Hard Problems

Let q, n, Q be three integers, and N a power of two. Let $R_Q = \mathbb{Z}_Q[X]/\left(X^N + 1\right)$. Let χ_e (resp., χ_e') be a noise distribution over $\mathbb{Z}$ (resp., R_Q). Let χ_s (resp., χ_s') be a secret distribution over $\mathbb{Z}$ (resp., R).

The LWE Problem [33]. The decisional $\mathrm{LWE}_{n,q,\chi_s,\chi_e}$ problem is to distinguish the following two distributions:

- $\{(\mathbf{A}, \mathbf{b} = \mathbf{A} \cdot \mathbf{s} + \mathbf{e}) | \mathbf{A} \leftarrow \mathbb{Z}_q^{k_1 \times n}, \mathbf{s} \leftarrow \chi_s^n, \mathbf{e} \leftarrow \chi_e^{k_1}\}$,
- $\{(\mathbf{U}, \mathbf{v}) | \mathbf{U} \leftarrow \mathbb{Z}_q^{k_1 \times n}, \mathbf{v} \leftarrow \mathbb{Z}_q^{k_1}\}$.

The decisional $\mathrm{LWE}_{n,q,\chi_s,\chi_e}$ assumption says that it is hard for any PPT algorithms to solve decisional $\mathrm{LWE}_{n,q,\chi_s,\chi_e}$ with non-negligible advantage over a random guess.

The RLWE Problem [28]. The decisional $\mathrm{RLWE}_{N,Q,\chi_s',\chi_e'}$ problem is to distinguish the following two distributions:

$$\{(\mathbf{a}, \mathbf{b} = \mathbf{a} \cdot s + \mathbf{e}) | \mathbf{a} \leftarrow R_Q^{k_2}, s \leftarrow \chi_s', \mathbf{e} \leftarrow \chi_e'^{k_2} \quad \text{and} \quad \{(\mathbf{u}, \mathbf{v}) | \mathbf{u}, \mathbf{v} \leftarrow R_Q^{k_2}\}\}.$$

The decisional $\mathrm{RLWE}_{N,Q,\chi_s',\chi_e'}$ assumption says that it is hard for any PPT algorithms to solve decisional $\mathrm{RLWE}_{N,Q,\chi_s',\chi_e'}$ with non-negligible advantage over a random guess.

The NTRU Problem [5,35] (in the vector form). For an integer d, the decisional $\mathrm{NTRU}_{N,Q,\chi_s',\chi_e'}$ problem is to distinguish the following two distributions:

- $\{(g_0/f, \cdots, g_{d-1}/f) | f \leftarrow \chi_s', g_0, \cdots, g_{d-1} \leftarrow \chi_e'\}$,
- $\{(u_1, \cdots, u_d) | u_1, \cdots, u_d \leftarrow R_Q\}$.

The decisional NTRU assumption (in the vector form) says that it is hard for any PPT algorithms to solve decisional $\mathrm{NTRU}_{N,Q,\chi_s',\chi_e'}$ with non-negligible advantage over a random guess.

The matrix NTRU Problem [16,19]. The decisional matrix $\mathrm{NTRU}_{n,q,\chi_s,\chi_e}$ problem is to distinguish the following two distributions:

$$\{\mathbf{G} \cdot \mathbf{F}^{-1} | \mathbf{F} \leftarrow \chi_s^{n \times n}, \mathbf{G} \leftarrow \chi_e^{m \times n}\} \quad \text{and} \quad \{\mathbf{U} | \mathbf{U} \leftarrow \mathbb{Z}_q^{m \times n}\}.$$

The decisional matrix $\mathrm{NTRU}_{n,q,\chi_s,\chi_e}$ assumption says that it is hard for any PPT algorithms to solve decisional matrix $\mathrm{NTRU}_{n,q,\chi_s,\chi_e}$ with non-negligible advantage over a random guess.

The Hint-NTRU Problem [17] (in the vector form). The decisional Hint-$\mathrm{NTRU}_{N,Q,\chi_s',\chi_e'}$ problem is to distinguish the following two distributions:

- $\{(\mathbf{h} = \mathbf{e}_1/s, \mathbf{a}, \mathbf{b} = \mathbf{a} \cdot s + \mathbf{e}_2) | s \leftarrow \chi'_s, \mathbf{e}_1, \mathbf{e}_2 \leftarrow \chi'^d_e, \mathbf{a} \leftarrow R^d_Q\}$,
- $\{(\mathbf{u}, \mathbf{v}, \mathbf{w}) | \mathbf{u}, \mathbf{v}, \mathbf{w} \leftarrow R^d_Q\}$.

The decisional Hint-NTRU$_{N,Q,\chi'_s,\chi'_e}$ assumption says that it is hard for any PPT algorithms to solve decisional Hint-NTRU$_{N,Q,\chi'_s,\chi'_e}$ with non-negligible advantage over a random guess.

In Eurocrypt 2024, Esgin, Espitau, Niot et al. [17] first introduced the Hint-NTRU problem, asserting that an adversary against Hint-NTRU can break the indistinguishability of the inhomogeneous NTRU instance [19] for appropriate choices of parameters.

As the FHE schemes in [5,19,35], our MK-FHEs essentially rely on the KDM-security of the (matrix) NTRU problems and Hint-NTRU problems. We formally define the problems below.

The KDM-form NTRU Problem [35] (in the vector form). For an arbitrarily chosen (and public known) $m \in R_Q$ and integers B, d, the decisional KDM-form NTRU$_{N,Q,\chi'_s,\chi'_e}$ problem is to distinguish the following two distributions:

- $\{((g_0 + B^0 \cdot m)/f, \cdots, (g_{d-1} + B^{d-1} \cdot m)/f) | f \leftarrow \chi'_s, g_0, \cdots, g_{d-1} \leftarrow \chi'_e\}$,
- $\{(u_1, \cdots, u_d) | u_1, \cdots, u_d \leftarrow R_Q\}$.

The decisional KDM-form NTRU$_{N,Q,\chi'_s,\chi'_e}$ assumption says that it is hard for any PPT algorithms to solve decisional KDM-form NTRU$_{N,Q,\chi'_s,\chi'_e}$ with non-negligible advantage over a random guess.

The KDM-Form Matrix NTRU Problem. For an arbitrarily chosen (and public known) $\mathbf{M} \in \mathbb{Z}^{m \times n}_q$, the decisional KDM-form matrix NTRU$_{n,q,\chi_s,\chi_e}$ problem is to distinguish the following two distributions:

$$\{(\mathbf{G} + \mathbf{M}) \cdot \mathbf{F}^{-1} | \mathbf{F} \leftarrow \chi^{n \times n}_s, \mathbf{G} \leftarrow \chi^{m \times n}_e\} \quad \text{and} \quad \{\mathbf{U} | \mathbf{U} \leftarrow \mathbb{Z}^{m \times n}_q\}.$$

The decisional KDM-form matrix NTRU$_{n,q,\chi_s,\chi_e}$ assumption says that it is hard for any PPT algorithms to solve decisional KDM-form matrix NTRU$_{n,q,\chi_s,\chi_e}$ with non-negligible advantage over a random guess.

Note that the standard (matrix) NTRU problem is essentially a special case of the KDM-form (matrix) NTRU problem with $m = 0$ or $\mathbf{M} = 0$. Intuitively, the hardness of the KDM-form (matrix) NTRU problem is equivalent to the KDM-security of the standard (matrix) NTRU encryption which encrypts m/f or $\mathbf{G} \cdot \mathbf{F}^{-1}$ [5,35]. We also note that the matrix inhomogeneous NTRU (MiNTRU) problem considered in [19] is basically a special case of our KDM-form matrix NTRU problem with $\mathbf{M}$ being fixed to a gadget matrix. As shown in [19], for an appropriate choice of error distributions, the above KDM-form matrix NTRU problem is polynomially equivalent to the MiNTRU problem, which in turn is not easier than a trapdoor version of the standard LWE problem [19].

The KDM-Form Hint-NTRU Problem (in the vector form). For an arbitrarily chosen (and public known) $m \in R_Q$, integers B, d and gadget vector $\mathbf{g} = (B^0, \cdots, B^{d-1})$, the decisional KDM-form Hint-NTRU$_{N,Q,\chi'_s,\chi'_e}$ problem is to distinguish the following two distributions:

- $\{((\mathbf{e}_1 + \mathbf{g} \cdot m)/s, \mathbf{a}, \mathbf{b} = \mathbf{a} \cdot s + \mathbf{e}_2)|s \leftarrow \chi'_s, \mathbf{e}_1, \mathbf{e}_2 \leftarrow \chi'^d_e, \mathbf{a} \leftarrow R^d_Q\}$,
- $\{(\mathbf{u}, \mathbf{v}, \mathbf{w})|\mathbf{u}, \mathbf{v}, \mathbf{w} \leftarrow R^d_Q\}$.

The decisional KDM-form Hint-NTRU$_{N,Q,\chi'_s,\chi'_e}$ assumption says that it is hard for any PPT algorithms to solve decisional KDM-form Hint-NTRU$_{N,Q,\chi'_s,\chi'_e}$ with non-negligible advantage over a random guess.

Note that the standard Hint-NTRU problem is essentially a special case of the KDM-form Hint-NTRU problem with $m = 0$. Essentially, the hardness of the KDM-form Hint-NTRU problem is equivalent to the KDM-security of the standard Hint-NTRU encryption which encrypts m/s.

3   First-Layer Matrix NTRU-Based Multi-Key Encryption

In this section, we propose a first-layer multi-key encryption HE that supports multi-key NAND operation in a natural way based on the matrix NTRU assumption. Formally, our construction HE = (Setup, KG, Enc, MK-Dec, MK-NAND) consists of five algorithms below:

- HE.Setup(1^λ): Given the security parameter λ, set the matrix dimension n, ciphertext modulus q, secret distribution χ_s and error distribution χ_e over $\mathbb{Z}$. Return the public parameter $pp = (n, q, \chi_s, \chi_e)$.
- HE.KG(pp): Sample $\mathbf{F} \leftarrow \chi_s^{n \times n}$ until $\mathbf{F}^{-1}$ exists in $\mathbb{Z}_q^{n \times n}$. Define $sk := \mathbf{F}$. Create a public evaluation key as $evk := (\mathbf{e} + \lfloor 5 \cdot q/8 \rfloor \cdot (1, \mathbf{0})) \cdot \mathbf{F}^{-1} \in \mathbb{Z}_q^n$, where $\mathbf{e} \leftarrow \chi_e^n$. Output (evk, sk).
- HE.Enc($m, \mathbf{F}$): Given $m \in \{0, 1\}$, sample $\mathbf{e}' \leftarrow \chi_e^n$. Let $\Delta := \lfloor q/4 \rfloor$ and output

$$\mathbf{c} = (\mathbf{e}' + \Delta \cdot (m, \mathbf{0})) \cdot \mathbf{F}^{-1} \in \mathbb{Z}_q^n.$$

- HE.MK-Dec($\overline{ct}, \{\mathbf{F}_i\}_{i \in [k]}$) : Given a ciphertext $\overline{ct} = (\mathbf{c}_1, \cdots, \mathbf{c}_k) \in \mathbb{Z}_q^{kn}$ after NAND gate evaluation under the secret key $(\mathbf{F}_1, \cdots, \mathbf{F}_k) \in (\mathbb{Z}_q^{n \times n})^k$, which satisfies $\sum_{i=1}^k \langle \mathbf{c}_i, \mathrm{col}_0(\mathbf{F}_i) \rangle \approx \lfloor \frac{q}{2} \rfloor m$. Compute

$$\left\lfloor \frac{2 \cdot \sum_{i=1}^k \mathbf{c}_i \cdot \mathrm{col}_0(\mathbf{F}_i)}{q} \right\rceil \in \mathbb{Z}_2.$$

- HE.MK-NAND($\overline{ct}_1, \overline{ct}_2, evk_i$) : Given $\overline{ct}_1 = (\mathbf{c}_{1,j_1}, \cdots, \mathbf{c}_{1,j_{k_1}}) \in \mathbb{Z}_q^{k_1 n}$ satisfying $\sum_{i=j_1}^{j_{k_1}} \langle \mathbf{c}_{1,i}, \mathrm{col}_0(\mathbf{F}_i) \rangle \approx \lfloor \frac{q}{4} \rfloor m_1, \overline{ct}_2 = (\mathbf{c}_{2,j_1}, \cdots, \mathbf{c}_{2,j_{k_2}}) \in \mathbb{Z}_q^{k_2 n}$ satisfying $\sum_{i=j_1}^{j_{k_2}} \langle \mathbf{c}_{2,i}, \mathrm{col}_0(\mathbf{F}_i) \rangle \approx \lfloor \frac{q}{4} \rfloor m_2$ and the evaluation key evk_i of party $i \in [k]$ as inputs, let k be the maximum number of different keys involved in $\overline{ct}_1$ and $\overline{ct}_2$. Extend $\overline{ct}_i = (\mathbf{c}_{i,j_1}, \cdots, \mathbf{c}_{i,j_{k_i}}) \in \mathbb{Z}_q^{k_i n}$ to the ciphertext $\overline{ct}'_i = \left(\mathbf{c}'_{i,1}, \ldots, \mathbf{c}'_{i,k} \right) \in \mathbb{Z}_q^{kn}$ where

$$\mathbf{c}'_{i,j} = \begin{cases} \mathbf{c}_{i,\ell} & \text{if } j = j_\ell \text{ for some } \ell \in [k_i] \\ \mathbf{0} & \text{otherwise} \end{cases}$$

for $i \in \{1,2\}$ and $j \in [k]$. Compute the homomorphic NAND gate homomorphically as follows:

$$\overline{ct} = (\ \underbrace{\mathbf{0}, \cdots, \mathbf{0}}_{(i-1)n \text{ zeros}}, evk_i, \underbrace{\mathbf{0}, \cdots, \mathbf{0}}_{(k-i)n \text{ zeros}}\ ) - \overline{ct}'_1 - \overline{ct}'_2 \in \mathbb{Z}_q^{kn}.$$

By Lemma 1, we show the correctness of the NAND gate evaluation.

Lemma 1. *For $i \in \{1,2\}$, let $\overline{ct}_i = (\mathbf{c}_{i,j_1}, \ldots, \mathbf{c}_{i,j_{k_i}}) \in \mathbb{Z}_q^{k_i n}$ be the ciphertext that encrypts m_i under the secret key $(\mathbf{F}_{j_1}, \ldots, \mathbf{F}_{j_{k_i}}) \in (\mathbb{Z}_q^{n \times n})^{k_i}$ with noise $\mathbf{e}_i$, satisfying $\langle \mathbf{c}_{i,j_1}, \mathrm{col}_0(\mathbf{F}_{j_1}) \rangle + \cdots + \langle \mathbf{c}_{i,j_{k_i}}, \mathrm{col}_0(\mathbf{F}_{j_{k_i}}) \rangle = \lfloor \frac{q}{4} \rfloor \cdot m_i + e_{i,0}$, where $e_{i,0}$ is the first element of $\mathbf{e}_i$. Let evk_i be the evaluation key of party i with a noise $\mathbf{e}$. Let e_0 be the first element of $\mathbf{e}$. Let $\overline{ct} = \mathsf{HE.MK\text{-}NAND}(\overline{ct}_1, \overline{ct}_2, evk_i)$. If $|e_0 - e_{1,0} - e_{2,0}| < \frac{q-12}{8}$ then $\mathsf{HE.MK\text{-}Dec}(\overline{ct}, \{\mathbf{F}_i\}_{i\in[k]})$ outputs $\mathsf{NAND}(m_1, m_2) = 1 - m_1 m_2$.*

Proof. Let $\overline{\mathbf{F}} = (\mathrm{col}_0(\mathbf{F}_j))_{j\in[k]}$. For $1 \leq i \leq 2$, let $\overline{ct}'_i = (\mathbf{c}'_{i,1}, \cdots, \mathbf{c}'_{i,k})$ be the extended ciphertext of $\overline{ct}_i$. By definition, we have $\langle \overline{ct}'_i, \overline{\mathbf{F}} \rangle = e_{i,0} + \lfloor \frac{q}{4} \rfloor m_i$. Let e_0 be the first element of $\mathbf{e}$, then

$$\langle \overline{ct}', \overline{\mathbf{F}} \rangle = \left\langle (\mathbf{0}, \cdots, \mathbf{0}, \mathbf{e} + \lfloor 5 \cdot q/8 \rfloor \cdot (1, \mathbf{0}) \cdot \mathbf{F}_i^{-1}, \mathbf{0}, \cdots, \mathbf{0}) - \overline{ct}'_1 - \overline{ct}'_2, \overline{\mathbf{F}} \right\rangle$$

$$= \frac{5q}{8} + e_0 + \epsilon - \left(e_{1,0} + \frac{q}{4} m_1 + m_1 \epsilon_1 \right) - \left(e_{2,0} + \frac{q}{4} m_2 + m_2 \epsilon_2 \right)$$

$$= e_0 - e_{1,0} - e_{2,0} \pm \frac{q}{8} + \epsilon - m_1 \epsilon_1 - m_2 \epsilon_2 + \frac{q}{2} (1 - m_1 m_2),$$

where $\epsilon, \epsilon_1, \epsilon_2$ are round-off errors and $|\epsilon| \leq \frac{1}{2}, |\epsilon_1| \leq \frac{1}{2}, |\epsilon_2| \leq \frac{1}{2}$, respectively. Let $e = \epsilon - m_1 \epsilon_1 - m_2 \epsilon_2$, we have $|e| \leq \frac{3}{2}$. The output of $\mathsf{HE.MK\text{-}Dec}(\overline{ct}, \{\mathbf{F}_i\}_{i\in[k]})$ is

$$\left\lfloor \frac{2}{q} \cdot (e + e_0 - e_{1,0} - e_{2,0} \pm \frac{q}{8} + \frac{q}{2} (1 - m_1 m_2)) \right\rceil.$$

Thus, the output is equal to $1 - m_1 m_2$ as long as $|\frac{2}{q} \cdot (e + e_0 - e_{1,0} - e_{2,0} \pm \frac{q}{8})| < \frac{1}{2}$, which implies $|e_0 - e_{1,0} - e_{2,0}| < \left(\frac{1}{2} - \frac{1}{4} - \frac{3}{q} \right) \cdot \frac{q}{2} = \frac{q-12}{8}$. $\qquad \square$

Theorem 1 (Security of HE). *Let $pp = (n, q, \chi_s, \chi_e)$ be some parameters such that the KDM-form matrix NTRU problem is hard. Then, for any $m \in \mathbb{Z}_q$, if $(evk, \mathbf{F}) \leftarrow \mathsf{HE.KG}(pp)$, $\mathbf{c} \leftarrow \mathsf{HE.Enc}(m, \mathbf{F})$, it holds that the joint distribution $(evk, \mathbf{c})$ is computationally indistinguishable from uniform over $\mathbb{Z}_q^n \times \mathbb{Z}_q^n$.*

Note that our multi-key construction is essentially a natural extension of the single-key MNTRU encryption based on the KDM-form MNTRU problems in [5]. The proof is similar and directly, we omit the details.

4 Second-Layer NTRU-Based Uni-Encryption

In this section, we present a second-layer NTRU-based uni-encryption that supports an efficient hybrid product.

Our uni-encryption $\Pi = (\mathsf{Setup}, \mathsf{KG}, \mathsf{UniEnc}, \mathsf{HbProd})$ consists of four algorithms:

- $\mathsf{Setup}(1^\lambda)$: Given the security parameter λ, set the polynomial degree N, ciphertext modulus Q, gadget vector dimension d, secret distribution χ'_s and error distribution χ'_e over R. Generate a random vector $\mathbf{a} \leftarrow R_Q^d$. Return the public parameter $pp' = (N, Q, d, \mathbf{a}, \chi'_s, \chi'_e)$.
- $\mathsf{KG}(pp')$: Sample a polynomial $s \leftarrow \chi'_s$ uniformly at random until s^{-1} exists in R_Q and a noise $\mathbf{e} \leftarrow \chi'^d_e$. Compute the public key $\mathbf{b} = -\mathbf{a} \cdot s + \mathbf{e}$ and output $(s, \mathbf{b})$.
- $\mathsf{UniEnc}(\mu, s)$: For a message $\mu \in R_Q$ and a secret key s, sample $r \leftarrow \chi'_s$ uniformly at random, and noise $\mathbf{e}_1, \mathbf{e}_2 \leftarrow \chi'^d_e$. Compute the ciphertext $\mathbf{d} = r \cdot \mathbf{a} + \mu \cdot \mathbf{g} + \mathbf{e}_1 \in R_Q^d$ and $\mathbf{f} = \mathbf{e}_2 \cdot s^{-1} + r \cdot \mathbf{g} \cdot s^{-1} \in R_Q^d$ and output $(\mathbf{d}, \mathbf{f}) \in R_Q^d \times R_Q^d$.
- $\mathsf{HbProd}(\overline{\mathbf{c}}, \{\mathbf{b}_j\}_{j \in [k]}, (\mathbf{d}_i, \mathbf{f}_i))$: Given an NTRU-based multi-key ciphertext $\overline{\mathbf{c}} = (c_1, \cdots, c_k) \in R_Q^k$, the public keys $\{\mathbf{b}_j\}_{j \in [k]}$ of k keys involved in $\overline{\mathbf{c}}$, and a uni-encryption $(\mathbf{d}_i, \mathbf{f}_i)$ of party i as inputs, return an MK-NTRU ciphertext $\overline{\mathbf{c}}' \in R_Q^k$ as follows:
  (a) Compute the following inner products:
  $$u_j = \left\langle \mathbf{g}^{-1}(c_j), \mathbf{d}_i \right\rangle \text{ for } 1 \leqslant j \leqslant k,$$
  $$v = \sum_{j=1}^{k} \left\langle \mathbf{g}^{-1}(c_j), \mathbf{b}_j \right\rangle.$$

  (b) Output $\overline{\mathbf{c}}' = (c'_1, \ldots, c'_k) \in R^k$ where
  $$c'_j = \begin{cases} u_i + \left\langle \mathbf{g}^{-1}(v), \mathbf{f}_i \right\rangle & \text{if } j = i, \\ u_j & \text{otherwise.} \end{cases}$$

By Lemma 2, we show that our uni-encryption supports homomorphic additions. In Lemma 3, we establish the correctness and estimate noise bound. For the detailed formal proofs, see the full version.

Lemma 2. *Let* $\mathsf{UniEnc}(\mu_1, s) = (\mathbf{d}_1, \mathbf{f}_1), \mathsf{UniEnc}(\mu_2, s) = (\mathbf{d}_2, \mathbf{f}_2) \in R_Q^d \times R_Q^d$ *be two uni-encryption ciphertexts. We define the homomorphic addition between* $\mathsf{UniEnc}(\mu_1, s)$ *and* $\mathsf{UniEnc}(\mu_1, s)$ *as*

$$\mathsf{UniEnc}(\mu_1, s) + \mathsf{UniEnc}(\mu_2, s) = (\mathbf{d}_1 + \mathbf{d}_2, \mathbf{f}_1 + \mathbf{f}_2),$$

which is also a uni-encryption ciphertext that encrypts $\mu_1 + \mu_2$ *under the secret* s. *And for a monomial* u *with ternary coefficient,* $u \cdot \mathsf{UniEnc}(\mu_i, s) = (u \cdot \mathbf{d}_i, u \cdot \mathbf{f}_i)$ *is also a uni-encryption ciphertext that encrypts* $u \cdot \mu_i$ *under the secret* s.

Moreover, if the variance of the noise distribution used in generating uni-encryption is $Var(e)$, *then the noise variance of the ciphertext* $(\mathbf{d}_1 + \mathbf{d}_2, \mathbf{f}_1 + \mathbf{f}_2)$ *and* $u \cdot \mu_i$ *is bounded by* $2Var(e)$ *and* $Var(e)$, *respectively.*

Lemma 3 (Hybrid Product). *Let* $\overline{c} = (c_1, \cdots, c_k) \in R_Q^k$ *be an MK-NTRU ciphertext under the secret key* $\mathbf{s} = (s_1, \cdots, s_k) \in R^k$, *and let* $\{\mathbf{b}_j\}_{j \in [k]}$ *be the public keys of* k *keys associated with* $\overline{c}$. *Let* $(\mathbf{d}_i, \mathbf{f}_i) \leftarrow \mathsf{UniEnc}(\mu_i, s_i)$ *be the uni-encryption of* $\mu_i \in R_Q$ *for party* i, *and let* $\overline{c}' \leftarrow \mathsf{HbProd}(\overline{c}, \{\mathbf{b}_j\}_{j \in [k]}, (\mathbf{d}_i, \mathbf{f}_i))$ *be the output of the hybrid product, we have that* $\langle \overline{c}', \mathbf{s} \rangle \approx \mu_i \langle \overline{c}, \mathbf{s} \rangle$.

Moreover, if the noise variance in generating $(\mathbf{d}_i, \mathbf{f}_i)$ *and* $\{\mathbf{b}_j\}_{j \in [k]}$ *is* $Var(e)$ *and the variance of the secret is* $Var(s)$, *then the variance of the increased noise in the resulting ciphertext is upper bounded by* $(2kN Var(s) + 1) \frac{B^2}{12} dN Var(e)$.

In the following, we will use $\sigma_{HP1}^2 = (Var(s)kN + 1) \frac{dNB^2}{12} Var(e)$, and $\sigma_{HP2}^2 = Var(s)kN \frac{dNB^2}{12} Var(e)$ to denote the variance of the increased noise (with respect to the input ciphertext) for the hybrid product.

By Theorem 2, we show that our NTRU-based Uni-Encryption is provably IND-CPA secure in the standard model.

Theorem 2 (Security of the second-layer NTRU-based Uni-Encryption). *Let* $pp' = (N, Q, d, \mathbf{a}, \chi'_s, \chi'_e) \leftarrow \mathsf{Setup}(1^\lambda)$ *be the parameters such that standard* $\mathsf{RLWE}_{N,Q,\chi'_s,\chi'_e}$ *and the KDM-form* $\mathsf{Hint\text{-}NTRU}_{N,Q,\chi'_s,\chi'_e}$ *assumptions hold, we have that our second-layer NTRU-based Uni-Encryption is provably IND-CPA secure in the standard model.*

The proof of Theorem 2 follows directly from the RLWE and the KDM-form Hint-NTRU assumptions via a standard hybrid argument. We defer this proof to the full version.

5 Bootstrapping First-Layer Matrix NTRU-Based Multi-key Ciphertexts

In this section, we describe how to apply our second-layer NTRU-based hybrid product to bootstrap a first-layer matrix NTRU-based multi-key ciphertext. In Sect. 5.1, we described the multi-key NTRU modulus switching technique. In Sect. 5.2, a key-switching technique is introduced to transform an MK-NTRU ciphertext back into a multi-key matrix NTRU ciphertext. In Sect. 5.3, we present the bootstrapping algorithm and analyze its correctness. The complete proofs of all Lemmas and Theorems are deferred to the full version of the paper.

5.1 Modulus Switching for MK-NTRU Ciphertext

To transform an MK-NTRU ciphertext from modulus Q to q, we can multiply it by q/Q and round the result to the nearest integer.

Lemma 4. *Given an MK-NTRU ciphertext $\overline{c} = (c_1, \cdots, c_k) \in R_Q^k$ that encrypts $m \in \{0, 1\}$ with secret key $\mathbf{s} = (s_1, \cdots, s_k) \in R^k$, where $\sum_{i=1}^{k} c_i s_i = \lfloor \frac{Q}{4} \rceil m + e$, the MK-NTRU modulus switching procedure $\mathsf{NModSwitch}(\overline{c}, q)$ is defined as*

$$\mathsf{NModSwitch}(\overline{c}, q) = (c_1', \cdots, c_k') = \left(\sum_{i=0}^{N-1} \left\lfloor \frac{q}{Q} c_{1,i} \right\rceil X^i, \cdots, \sum_{i=0}^{N-1} \left\lfloor \frac{q}{Q} c_{k,i} \right\rceil X^i \right),$$

where $c_{j,i}$ denotes the i-th coefficient for c_j ($j \in [k]$). Then, $(c_1', \cdots, c_k')$ is an MK-NTRU ciphertext that encrypts the same message under the secret key $\mathbf{s} \in R^k$. Moreover, if the noise variance of $\overline{c}$ is $Var(e)$, then the noise variance of the ciphertext after modulus switching is bounded by $(\frac{q}{Q})^2 Var(e) + 1 + \frac{\sum_{i=1}^{k} \|s_i\|}{12}$.

For this modulus switching, we denote $\sigma_{NMS}^2 = 1 + \frac{\sum_{i=1}^{k} \|s_i\|}{12}$ as the variance of the increased noise (relative to the input ciphertext).

5.2 Key-Switching from MK-NTRU Ciphertext to the Base Scheme

In this subsection, we define a pair of two algorithms $(\mathsf{MN.KSKG}, \mathsf{MN.KS})$ for key switching the MK-NTRU ciphertext to the MNTRU-based first layer multi-key ciphertext as follows:

- $\mathsf{MN.KSKG}(s_i, \mathbf{F}_i)$: Given matrice $\mathbf{F}_i \in \mathbb{Z}_q^{n \times n}$, polynomial $s_i \in R$ as inputs, the algorithm first samples matrice $\mathbf{E}_i \leftarrow \mathbb{Z}_q^{Nd_{ks} \times n}$ from some noise distribution over $\mathbb{Z}_q$ and outputs

$$\mathbf{KSK}_i = (\mathbf{E}_i + \mathbf{G}_N \cdot \mathcal{A}(s_i) \cdot \mathbf{M}) \cdot \mathbf{F}_i^{-1} \in \mathbb{Z}_q^{(N \cdot d_{ks}) \times n},$$

  where $\mathcal{A}(s_i)$ denotes the anti-circulant matrix of s_i and $\mathbf{M} \in \mathbb{Z}_q^{N \times n}$ is a matrix with entries being all zeros except for $\mathbf{M}_{0,0} = 1$.
- $\mathsf{MN.KS}(\overline{c}, \{\mathbf{KSK}_i\}_{i \in [k]})$: Input an NTRU-based multi-key ciphertext $\overline{c} = (c_1, \cdots, c_k) \in R_q^k$ that encrypts a polynomial with constant coefficient $m \in \{0, 1\}$ and the key-switching keys $\{\mathbf{KSK}_i\}_{i \in [k]}$ of keys associated with $\overline{ct}$, it first computes

$$\hat{\mathbf{c}}_i = \left(\mathbf{g}^{-1}(c_{i,0}), \cdots, \mathbf{g}^{-1}(c_{i,N-1}) \right)$$

  where $(c_{i,0}, \cdots, c_{i,N-1})$ is the coefficient vector of c_i. Then it computes

$$\mathbf{c}_i = \hat{\mathbf{c}}_i \cdot \mathbf{KSK}_i$$

  for $i \in [k]$ and outputs $\overline{ct} = (\mathbf{c}_1, \cdots, \mathbf{c}_k)$.

Lemma 5 (Key-switching for MK-NTRU ciphertext). *Let $\mathbf{F}_1, \cdots, \mathbf{F}_k \in \mathbb{Z}_q^{n \times n}$ and $s_1, \cdots, s_k \in R$ be k matrices and polynomials, respectively. Let $\overline{c} = (c_1, \cdots, c_k) \in R_q^k$ be an MK-NTRU ciphertext that encrypts a polynomial with constant coefficient $m \in \{0, 1\}$ under the secret key $(s_1, \cdots, s_k) \in$*

R^k. Then, for any $\mathbf{KSK}_i = \mathsf{MN.KSKG}(s_i, \mathbf{F}_i)$, we have that the output of $\mathsf{MN.KS}(\overline{\mathbf{c}}, \{\mathbf{KSK}_i\}_{i\in[k]})$ is a matrix NTRU based ciphertext that encrypts $m \in \{0,1\}$ under the secret key $\{\mathbf{F}_1, \cdots, \mathbf{F}_k\} \in \mathbb{Z}_q^{(n\times n)k}$.

Moreover, if the variance of the noise in $\overline{\mathbf{c}}$ is $Var(e)$, and the variance of the noise distribution used in generating $\mathbf{KSK}_i$ is $Var(e_{ks})$, then the variance of the noise in the resulting ciphertext $\overline{ct}$ is upper bounded by

$$k\frac{B_{ks}^2}{12}Nd_{ks}Var(e_{ks}) + Var(e).$$

We use the symbol $\sigma_{NKS}^2 = k\frac{B_{ks}^2}{12}Nd_{ks}Var(e_{ks})$ to denote the variance of the increased noise (with respect to the input ciphertext) for key-switching.

5.3   Bootstrapping

In this subsection, we define a pair of algorithms $(\mathsf{MN.BSKG}, \mathsf{MN.BSEval})$ for bootstrapping an MNTRU-based first-layer multi-key ciphertext as follows:

- $\mathsf{MN.BSKG}(\mathbf{F}_i)$: Given a matrix $\mathbf{F}_i \in \mathbb{Z}_q^{n\times n}$ as input, run $(s_i, \mathbf{b}_i) \leftarrow KG(pp')$ and set the public key as $\mathbf{PK}_i = \mathbf{b}_i$. Let $(f_{i,j})_{0\le j<n} = \mathrm{col}_0(\mathbf{F}_i)$ be the first column of the secret matrix $\mathbf{F}_i$. For $(f_{i,j})_{0\le j<n}$, let

$$\begin{cases} f_{i,j}^+ = 1, \text{ if } f_{i,j} = 1 \\ f_{i,j}^+ = 0, \text{ otherwise} \end{cases}, \quad \begin{cases} f_{i,j}^- = 1, \quad \text{if } f_{i,j} = -1 \\ f_{i,j}^- = 0, \quad \text{otherwise} \end{cases} \text{ for } 0 \le j < n.$$

  - For $i = 1$, given secret key $\mathrm{col}_0(\mathbf{F}_1) = (f_{1,0}, \ldots, f_{1,n-1}) \in \{-1, 0, 1\}^n$, create a set of ciphertexts that encrypts $\mathrm{col}_0(\mathbf{F}_1)$ under s_1 as follows:

$$\begin{cases} \mathbf{evk}_{1,0}^+ = \mathsf{UniEnc}(f_{1,0}^+/s_1, s_1) \\ \mathbf{evk}_{1,0}^- = \mathsf{UniEnc}(f_{1,0}^-/s_1, s_1) \end{cases}, \begin{cases} \mathbf{evk}_{1,j}^| = \mathsf{UniEnc}(f_{1,j}^|, s_1) \\ \mathbf{evk}_{1,j}^- = \mathsf{UniEnc}(f_{1,j}^-, s_1) \end{cases} \text{ for } j \ne 0,$$

  and creates an auxiliary ciphertext $\mathbf{evk}_{1,0}^* = \mathsf{UniEnc}(1/s_1, s_1)$. The evaluation key is defined as $\mathbf{EVK}_1 = (\mathbf{evk}_{1,0}^*, \{\mathbf{evk}_{1,j}^+, \mathbf{evk}_{1,j}^-\}_{0\le j<n})$.
  - For $i \ne 1$, given secret key $\mathrm{col}_0(\mathbf{F}_i) = (f_{i,0}, \ldots, f_{i,n-1}) \in \{-1, 0, 1\}^n$, create a set of ciphertext that encrypts $\mathrm{col}_0(\mathbf{F}_i)$ under s_i as follows:

$$\mathbf{evk}_{i,j}^+ = \mathsf{UniEnc}(f_{i,j}^+, s_i), \mathbf{evk}_{i,j}^- = \mathsf{UniEnc}(f_{i,j}^-, s_i) \text{ for } 0 \le j < n.$$

  The evaluation key is defined as $\mathbf{EVK}_i = (\{\mathbf{evk}_{i,j}^+, \mathbf{evk}_{i,j}^-\}_{0\le j<n})$. Then it computes the key-switching key $\mathbf{KSK}_i = \mathsf{MN.KSKG}(s_i, \mathbf{F}_i)$, and outputs $(\mathbf{EVK}_i, \mathbf{KSK}_i)$.
- $\mathsf{MN.BSEval}(\overline{ct}, \{\mathbf{PK}_i, \mathbf{EVK}_i, \mathbf{KSK}_i\}_{i\in[k]}, r)$: Given a multi-key MNTRU ciphertext $\overline{ct} = (\mathbf{c}_1, \cdots, \mathbf{c}_k) \in \mathbb{Z}_q^{kn}$ that encrypts $m \in \{0, 1\}$ under the secret key $\mathbf{F}_1, \cdots, \mathbf{F}_k \in \mathbb{Z}_q^{n\times n}$, the key-triple $\{\mathbf{PK}_i, \mathbf{EVK}_i, \mathbf{KSK}_i\}_{i\in[k]}$, and a rotation polynomial $r \in R_Q$ as inputs, computes and returns $\overline{ct}'$ as described in Algorithm 1.

Algorithm 1. MN.BSEval($\overline{ct}, \{\mathbf{PK}_i, \mathbf{EVK}_i, \mathbf{KSK}_i\}_{i \in [k]}, r$)

Input:

  A multi-key MNTRU ciphertext $\overline{ct} = (\mathbf{c}_1, \cdots, \mathbf{c}_k) \in \mathbb{Z}_q^{kn}$;

  The key-triple $\{\mathbf{PK}_i, \mathbf{EVK}_i, \mathbf{KSK}_i\}_{i \in [k]}$;

  A rotation polynomial $r(X) \in R_Q$.

Output:

  A multi-key MNTRU ciphertext $\overline{ct}' \in \mathbb{Z}_q^{kn}$.

1: $\hat{ct} = (\hat{\mathbf{c}}_1, \cdots, \hat{\mathbf{c}}_k) \leftarrow \left\lfloor \frac{2N \cdot \overline{ct}}{q} \right\rceil \in \mathbb{Z}_{2N}^{kn}$

2: $\mathsf{ACC} \leftarrow (r(X), \mathbf{0}) \in R_Q^k$

3: **for** $i = 1; i < k + 1; i = i + 1$ **do**

4:   **for** $j = 0; j < n; j = j + 1$ **do**

5:     **if** $i = 1, j = 0$ **then**

6:       $\mathbf{evk}_{1,0} \leftarrow \mathbf{evk}_{1,0}^* + (X^{\hat{c}_{1,0}} - 1)\mathbf{evk}_{1,0}^+ + (X^{-\hat{c}_{1,0}} - 1)\mathbf{evk}_{1,0}^-$

7:       $\mathsf{ACC} \leftarrow \mathsf{HbProd}(\mathsf{ACC}, \{\mathbf{PK}_l\}_{l \in [k]}, \mathbf{evk}_{1,0})$

8:     **else**

9:       $\mathbf{evk}_{i,j} \leftarrow \mathbf{evk}_{i,j}^+ - \mathbf{evk}_{i,j}^- \cdot X^{-\hat{c}_{i,j}}$

10:       $\mathsf{ACC} \leftarrow \mathsf{ACC} + \mathsf{HbProd}((X^{\hat{c}_{i,j}} - 1)\mathsf{ACC}, \{\mathbf{PK}_l\}_{l \in [k]}, \mathbf{evk}_{i,j})$

11:     **end if**

12:   **end for**

13: **end for**

14: $\mathsf{ACC} \leftarrow \mathsf{NModSwitch}(\mathsf{ACC}, q)$

15: $\overline{ct}' \leftarrow \mathsf{MN.KS}(\mathsf{ACC}, \{\mathbf{KSK}_i\}_{i \in [k]})$

16: **return** $\overline{ct}'$

Theorem 3 (Bootstrapping MNTRU-based Ciphertexts). *Let q, Q be two positive integers. Given a multi-key MNTRU ciphertext $\overline{ct} = (\mathbf{c}_1, \cdots, \mathbf{c}_k) \in \mathbb{Z}_q^{kn}$ that encrypts $m \in \{0, 1\}$ under the secret key $\mathbf{F}_1, \cdots, \mathbf{F}_k \in \mathbb{Z}_q^{n \times n}$, Algorithm 1 outputs a refreshed multi-key MNTRU ciphertext that encrypts the same message $m \in \{0, 1\}$. And the noise of the refreshed ciphertext is bounded by a Gaussian with standard deviation*

$$\beta = \sqrt{\frac{q^2}{Q^2}((2kn + 3)\sigma_{HP1}^2 + kn\sigma_{HP2}^2) + \sigma_{NMS}^2 + \sigma_{NKS}^2}$$

where σ_{HP1}^2, σ_{HP2}^2 are the variance of the increased noise for the hybrid product described in Sect. 4, σ_{NMS}^2 and σ_{NKS}^2 are the variance of the increased noise for modulus switching and key switching for NTRU described in Sect. 5.1 and 5.2, respectively.

Theorem 4. *If the standard deviation of refreshed noise for the output in Algorithm 1 satisfies Theorem 3 except with negligible probability and the modulus satisfies $q = \tilde{O}(kn^{1.5})$, then the output of Algorithm 1 can be correctly decrypted except with negligible probability.*

6 Bootstrapping First-Layer Multi-key LWE Ciphertexts

In this section, we describe how to modify our second-layer scheme to bootstrap a standard first-layer multi-key LWE ciphertext. In Sect. 6.1, we describe the modulus switching for multi-key LWE ciphertext. In Sect. 6.2, we propose a light-key switching technique. In Sect. 6.3, we present the bootstrapping algorithm and analyze its correctness. The full proofs of all Lemmas and Theorems are presented in the full version of the paper.

6.1 Modulus Switching for Multi-key LWE Ciphertext

The modulus switching from Q to q can be easily achieved by multiplying the targeted ciphertext with q/Q, and rounding the results to the nearest integer.

Lemma 6 (Modulus Switching for Multi-Key LWE ciphertext). *Given as input a multi-key LWE ciphertext* $\overline{ct} = (b, \mathbf{a}_1, \cdots, \mathbf{a}_k) \in \mathbb{Z}_Q^{kN+1}$ *under secret key* $\mathbf{s} = (1, \mathbf{s}_1, \cdots, \mathbf{s}_k) \in \mathbb{Z}^{kN+1}$, *the LWE modulus switching procedure is defined as*

$$b' = \left\lfloor \frac{q}{Q} b \right\rceil \quad and \quad \mathbf{a}'_i = \left\lfloor \frac{q}{Q} \mathbf{a}_i \right\rceil \quad for \; i \in [k].$$

Then, $(b', \mathbf{a}'_1, \cdots, \mathbf{a}'_k)$ *is a multi-key LWE ciphertext that encrypts the same message under the same secret key* $\mathbf{s} \in \mathbb{Z}^{kN+1}$. *Moreover, if the noise variance of* $\overline{ct}$ *is* α^2, *then the noise variance of the ciphertext after modulus switching is bounded by* $(\frac{q}{Q})^2 \alpha^2 + \frac{1 + \sum_{i=1}^k \|\mathbf{s}_i\|}{12}$.

For modulus switching, we denote $\sigma^2_{LMS} = \frac{1 + \sum_{i=1}^k \|\mathbf{s}_i\|}{12}$ as the variance of the increased noise (relative to the input ciphertext).

6.2 Light Key Switching for Multi-key LWE Ciphertext

Let $(b, \mathbf{a}_1, \cdots, \mathbf{a}_k) \in \mathbb{Z}_q^{kN+1}$ be an MK-LWE ciphertext under $(1, \mathbf{s}_1, \cdots, \mathbf{s}_k) \in \mathbb{Z}^{kN+1}$. To switch the secret from $(1, \mathbf{s}_1, \cdots, \mathbf{s}_k) \in \mathbb{Z}^{kN+1}$ to $(1, \mathbf{z}_1, \cdots, \mathbf{z}_k) \in \mathbb{Z}^{kn+1}$ for some $\mathbf{s}_i = (s_{i,j})_{0 \leq j \leq N-1}$ and $\mathbf{z}_i = (z_{i,j})_{0 \leq j < n}$. In prior methods [9,25], each party i independently generates the key switching key as a set of LWE ciphertexts that encrypts each value $v \cdot B_{ks}^l \cdot s_{i,j}$ under the secret $\mathbf{z}_i = (z_{i,j})_{0 \leq j < n}$ where $j \in \mathbb{Z}_N, l \in \mathbb{Z}_{d_{ks}}, v \in [B_{ks} - 1]$ (See Appendix A). Instead, we sequentially decode those values

$$\{B_{ks}^0 s_{i,0}, 2B_{ks}^0 s_{i,0}, \cdots, (B_{ks} - 1)B_{ks}^{d_{ks}-1} s_{i,N-1}\}$$

into the coefficients of t polynomials $m_1(X), \cdots, m_t(X)$ in $R_q = \mathbb{Z}_q[X]/(X^N + 1)$ where $t = (B_{ks} - 1)d_{ks}$.

In this setting, for any value $v \cdot B_{ks}^l \cdot s_{i,j}$, one can check that it be decoded in x-th coefficient $m_y(X)$ polynomial where $\left\lceil y = \frac{(B_{ks}-1)(jd_{ks}+l)+v}{N} \right\rceil$ and $x = (B_{ks} - 1)(jd_{ks} + l) + v - 1 \mod N$. To perform key-switching, we only need to employ the sample extraction algorithm in [22] (Sec. IV, step 1), which we refer to as SamExt for clarity, to extract the corresponding LWE ciphertext from the RLWE ciphertext at the desired position. Notably, we only need to extract the first n coefficients.

Formally, we define two algorithms (ML.PKSKG, ML.KS) as follows.

- ML.PKSKG($\mathbf{z}_i, \mathbf{s}_i$): Given two vectors $\mathbf{z}_i = (z_{i,0}, \cdots, z_{i,n-1}) \in \mathbb{Z}^n$, $\mathbf{s} = (s_{i,0}, \cdots, s_{i,N-1}) \in \mathbb{Z}^N$ and two integers q, B_{ks} as input, the algorithm computes $d_{ks} = \lceil \log_{B_{ks}} q \rceil$ and sets $z_i = \sum_{j=0}^{n-1} z_{i,j} X^j + 0 X^n \cdots + 0 X^{N-1} \in R_q$. Then it decodes the values $v \cdot B_{ks}^l s_{i,j}$ into t polynomials $m_1(X), \cdots, m_t(X)$ where $j \in \mathbb{Z}_N$, $l \in \mathbb{Z}_{d_{ks}}$, $v \in [B_{ks} - 1]$ as described above. Then it samples polynomial $a'_{i,j} \in R_q$ uniformly at random and $e_{i,j} \in R_q$ from some noise distribution and computes $\mathbf{PKSK}_{i,j} = (b'_{i,j}, a'_{i,j})$ where $b'_{i,j} = a'_{i,j} \cdot z_i + e_{i,j} + m_j(X) \in R_q$ for $j \in [t]$. Finally, it outputs $\mathbf{PKSK}_i = \{\mathbf{PKSK}_{i,j}\}_{j \in [t]}$ as the key-switching key of party i.

- ML.KS($\overline{ct}, \{\mathbf{PKSK}_i\}_{i \in [k]}$): Given as input a multi-key LWE ciphertext

$$\overline{ct} = \left(b = \sum_{i=1}^{k} \langle \mathbf{a}_i, \mathbf{s}_i \rangle + e + \lfloor \tfrac{q}{4} \rceil \cdot m, \mathbf{a}_1, \cdots, \mathbf{a}_k \right) \in \mathbb{Z}_q^{kN+1}$$

for $\mathbf{a}_i = (a_{i,j})_{j \in \mathbb{Z}_N} \in \mathbb{Z}_q^N$ and the key-switching keys $\{\mathbf{PKSK}_i\}_{i \in [k]}$ of keys associated with $\overline{ct}$, the algorithm first computes $\mathbf{g}^{-1}(a_{i,j}) = (v_{i,j,l})_{l \in \mathbb{Z}_{d_{ks}}}$ for each $i \in [k]$ and $j \in \mathbb{Z}_N$ and then computes as follows:

  - Key reconstruction. Extrac LWE ciphertexts

$$\{(b'_{i,j,l,v_{i,j,l}}, \mathbf{a}'_{i,j,l,v_{i,j,l}})\}_{i \in [k], j \in \mathbb{Z}_n, l \in \mathbb{Z}_{d_{ks}}}$$

where $b'_{i,j,l,v_{i,j,l}} = \left\langle \mathbf{a}'_{i,j,l,v_{i,j,l}}, \mathbf{z}_i \right\rangle + e_{i,j,l,v_{i,j,l}} + v_{i,j,l} \cdot s_{i,j} \cdot B_{ks}^l$ from $\{\mathbf{PKSK}_i\}_{i \in [k]}$.

  - Key switching. Compute

$$b'_i = \sum_{j=0}^{N-1} \sum_{l=0, v_{i,j,l} \neq 0}^{d_{ks}-1} b'_{i,j,l,v_{i,j,l}} \quad \text{and} \quad \mathbf{a}'_i = \sum_{j=0}^{N-1} \sum_{l=0, v_{i,j,l} \neq 0}^{d_{ks}-1} \mathbf{a}'_{i,j,l,v_{i,j,l}},$$

and let $b' = b + \sum_{i=1}^{k} b'_i$. Finally, the algorithm outputs a multi-key LWE ciphertext $\overline{ct}' = (b', \mathbf{a}'_1, \ldots, \mathbf{a}'_k) \in \mathbb{Z}^{kn+1}$.

Lemma 7 (Key-switching for MK-LWE ciphertext). *Let $\mathbf{s}_1, \cdots, \mathbf{s}_k \in \mathbb{Z}^N$ and $\mathbf{z}_1, \cdots, \mathbf{z}_k \in \mathbb{Z}^n$ be some vectors. Let $\overline{ct} = (b, \mathbf{a}_1, \cdots, \mathbf{a}_k) \in \mathbb{Z}^{kN+1}$ be a multi-key LWE ciphertext that encrypts $m \in \{0, 1\}$ under the secret key $(1, \mathbf{s}_1, \cdots, \mathbf{s}_k) \in \mathbb{Z}^{kN+1}$. Let $\mathbf{PKSK}_i = \mathsf{ML.PKSKG}(\mathbf{z}_i, \mathbf{s}_i)$ be the key-switching key of party i. We have that $\overline{c}' = \mathsf{ML.KS}(\overline{ct}, \{\mathbf{PKSK}_i\}_{i \in [k]}) \in \mathbb{Z}_q^{kn+1}$ is a valid multi-key LWE ciphertext that encrypts the same message $m \in \{0, 1\}$ under the secret key $(1, \mathbf{z}_1, \cdots, \mathbf{z}_k) \in \mathbb{Z}^{kn+1}$.*

Moreover, if the variance of the noise in $\overline{ct}$ is $Var(e)$ and the variance of the noise distribution used in generating $\mathbf{PKSK}_i$ is $Var(e_{ks})$, we have that the variance of the noise after key-switching is upper bounded by $Var(e) + kd_{ks}NVar(e_{ks})$.

For key switching, we denote $\sigma_{LKS}^2 = kd_{ks}NVar(e_{ks})$ as the variance of the increased noise.

The correctness of our light key switching for multi-key LWE ciphertexts is guaranteed by Lemma 7. We now proceed to provide the necessary security analysis.

Security. Our ML.PKSKG's security can be theoretically based on the standard RLWE and NTRU assumptions as long as the secret in **PKSK** has sufficient large entropy for appropriate choices of parameters.

Specifically, the RLWE ciphertexts generated by our ML.PKSKG basically use a secret key z_i chosen from a distribution always having zeros in the last $N - n$ coefficients over R_q, which is different from standard RLWE ciphertexts. However, as long as z_i has sufficient large entropy for appropriate choices of parameters, the corresponding RLWE instances well fit the setting of Entropic RLWE problem, which in turn is provably hard under the standard RLWE and NTRU (a.k.a DSPR) assumptions [6].

Regarding concrete security, one often translates an RLWE instance in dimension N into N samples of LWE instances in the same dimension N, as the best-known lattice attacks do not seem to offer additional advantages in solving RLWE compared to standard LWE, and one can naturally treat a single RLWE instance as N samples of LWE instances corresponding to a public anti-circular matrix defined by the ring multiplication.

In our case, as the last $N - n$ coefficients of the secret key are zeros, it is equivalent to treat the last $N - n$ columns of the public (anti-circular) matrix as zeros when we translate the RLWE instance into LWE instances. In particular, our RLWE instance in ML.PKSKG can be translated into N samples of LWE instances in dimension n (instead of N for a standard RLWE instance). We have actually taken this into account when choosing our concrete parameters using the LWE estimator [3] in Sect. 7.

6.3   Bootstrapping

In this subsection, we define a pair of algorithms (ML.BSKG, ML.BSEval) for bootstrapping an MK-LWE ciphertext as follows:

- ML.BSKG($\mathbf{z}_i$): Given a secret key $\mathbf{z}_i = (z_{i,j})_{0 \leq j < n} \in \{0,1\}^n$ as input, the algorithm first runs $(s_i, \mathbf{b}_i) \leftarrow \mathsf{KG}(pp')$ and sets the public key as $\mathbf{PK}_i = \mathbf{b}_i$.
  - For $i = 1$, given secret key $\mathbf{z}_1 = (z_{1,j})_{0 \leq j < n} \in \{0,1\}^n$, create a set of ciphertexts that encrypts $\mathbf{z}_1$ under s_1 as follows:

$$\mathbf{evk}_{1,0} = \mathsf{UniEnc}(z_{1,0}/s_1, s_1), \quad \mathbf{evk}_{1,j} = \mathsf{UniEnc}(z_{1,j}, s_1) \text{ for } j \neq 0$$

and creates an auxiliary ciphertext $\mathbf{evk}_{1,0}^* = \mathsf{UniEnc}(1/s_1, s_1)$. The evaluation key is defined as $\mathbf{EVK}_1 = (\mathbf{evk}_{1,0}^*, \{\mathbf{evk}_{1,j}\}_{0 \leq j < n})$.

- For $i \neq 1$, given secret key $\mathbf{z}_i = (z_{i,j})_{0 \leq j < n} \in \{0,1\}^n$, create a set of ciphertexts as follows

$$\mathbf{evk}_{i,j} = \mathsf{UniEnc}(z_{i,j}, s_i) \text{ for } 1 \leq j < n.$$

The evaluation key is defined as $\mathbf{EVK}_i = (\{\mathbf{evk}_{i,j}\}_{0 \leq j < n})$.
Then it computes the key-switching key $\mathbf{PKSK}_i = \mathsf{ML.PKSKG}(\mathbf{z}_i, \mathbf{s}_i)$, and outputs $(\mathbf{EVK}_i, \mathbf{PKSK}_i)$.

- $\mathsf{ML.BSEval}(\overline{ct}, \{\mathbf{PK}_i, \mathbf{EVK}_i, \mathbf{PKSK}_i\}_{i \in [k]}, r)$: Given a multi-key LWE ciphertext $\overline{ct} = (b, \mathbf{a}_1, \cdots, \mathbf{a}_k) \in \mathbb{Z}_q^{kn+1}$ under the secret $(1, \mathbf{z}_1, \cdots, \mathbf{z}_k) \in \mathbb{Z}^{kn+1}$, the key-triple $\{\mathbf{PK}_i, \mathbf{EVK}_i, \mathbf{PKSK}_i\}_{i \in [k]}$, and a rotation polynomial as inputs, computes and returns $\overline{ct}'$ as described in Algorithm 2.

Algorithm 2. $\mathsf{ML.BSEval}(\overline{ct}, \{\mathbf{PK}_i, \mathbf{EVK}_i, \mathbf{PKSK}_i\}_{i \in [k]}, r)$

Input:
    A multi-key LWE ciphertext $\overline{ct} = (b, \mathbf{a}_1, \cdots, \mathbf{a}_k) \in \mathbb{Z}_q^{kn+1}$;
    The key-triple $\{\mathbf{PK}_i, \mathbf{EVK}_i, \mathbf{PKSK}_i\}_{i \in [k]}$;
    A rotation polynomial $r(X) \in R_Q$.
Output:
    A multi-key LWE ciphertext $\overline{ct}' \in \mathbb{Z}_q^{kn+1}$.
1: $\hat{ct} = (\hat{b}, \hat{\mathbf{a}}_1, \cdots, \hat{\mathbf{a}}_k) \leftarrow \left\lfloor \frac{2N \cdot \overline{ct}}{q} \right\rceil \in \mathbb{Z}_{2N}^{kn+1}$
2: $\mathsf{ACC} \leftarrow (r(X)X^{\hat{b}}, \mathbf{0}) \in R_Q^k$
3: **for** $i = 1; i < k + 1; i = i + 1$ **do**
4:     **for** $j = 0; j < n; j = j + 1$ **do**
5:         **if** $i = 1, j = 0$ **then**
6:             $\mathbf{evk}_{1,0} \leftarrow \mathbf{evk}_{1,0}^* + (X^{\hat{a}_{1,0}} - 1)\mathbf{evk}_{1,0}$
7:             $\mathsf{ACC} \leftarrow \mathsf{HbProd}(\mathsf{ACC}, \{\mathbf{PK}_l\}_{l \in [k]}, \mathbf{evk}_{1,0})$
8:         **else**
9:             $\mathsf{ACC} \leftarrow \mathsf{ACC} + \mathsf{HbProd}((X^{\hat{a}_{i,j}} - 1)\mathsf{ACC}, \{\mathbf{PK}_l\}_{l \in [k]}, \mathbf{evk}_{i,j})$
10:        **end if**
11:     **end for**
12: **end for**
13: $\overline{ct}_1 \leftarrow \mathsf{SamExt}(\mathsf{ACC})$
14: $\overline{ct}_2 \leftarrow \mathsf{LModSwitch}(\overline{ct}_1, q)$
15: $\overline{ct}' \leftarrow \mathsf{MN.KS}(\overline{ct}_2, \{\mathbf{PKSK}_i\}_{i \in [k]})$
16: **return** $\overline{ct}'$

Theorem 5 (Bootstrapping LWE-based Ciphertexts). *Let q, Q be two positive integers. Given a multi-key LWE ciphertext $\overline{ct} = (b, \mathbf{a}_1, \cdots, \mathbf{a}_k) \in \mathbb{Z}_q^{kn+1}$ that encrypts $m \in \{0,1\}$ under the secret key $(1, \mathbf{z}_1, \cdots, \mathbf{z}_k) \in \mathbb{Z}^{kn+1}$, Algorithm 2 outputs a refreshed multi-key LWE ciphertext that encrypts the same message $m \in \{0,1\}$. The noise of the refreshed ciphertext is bounded by a Gaussian with standard deviation*

$$\beta = \sqrt{\frac{q^2}{Q^2}((kn+1)\sigma_{HP1}^2 + kn\sigma_{HP2}^2) + \sigma_{LMS}^2 + \sigma_{LKS}^2},$$

where σ_{HP1}^2, σ_{HP2}^2 are the variance of the increased noise for hybrid product described in Sect. 4, σ_{LMS}^2 and σ_{LKS}^2 are the variance of the increased noise for modulus switching and key switching for LWE ciphertexts described in Sect. 6.1 and Sect. 6.2, respectively.

Theorem 6. *If the standard deviation of the noise for the output in Algorithm 2 satisfies Theorem 5 except with negligible probability and the modulus satisfies $q = \tilde{O}(kn^{1.5})$, then the output of Algorithm 2 can be correctly decrypted except with negligible probability.*

7 Analysis and Implementation

In this section, we first analyze the computational complexity and key size of our algorithms proposed in Sect. 5 and Sect. 6, and then give a comparison to the prior works. Finally, we present the implementation results.

7.1 Analysis and Comparison

In Table 2, we give a theoretical comparison of the bootstrapping algorithms among our MK-FHEs, CCS [9] and its variant KMS [25], where n is lattice dimension, k is the number of keys, d is the gadget decomposition dimension, #mul denotes the number of multiplications in R_Q for performing the bootstrapping, and #R_Q (resp.,#*bits*) denotes the number of R_Q elements (resp., bits) for storing the evaluation key (resp., key-switching key) at each party. One can see that our Algorithm 2 outperforms CCS [9] and KMS [25] in both the evaluation key size and the computational efficiency. Algorithm 1 and Algorithm 2 have the same computational complexity, but the evaluation key size of Algorithm 1 is almost twice that of Algorithm 2. This is primarily because the secret key of the first layer in Algorithm 1 is ternary, which requires us to employ a more complex CMUX gate. Moreover, the noise magnitude in the KMS scheme is larger, which means that larger parameters need to be chosen in implementation, resulting in higher costs.

7.2 Recommended Parameters

We observe that the state-of-the-art works CCS [9] and KMS [25] only achieve a security level of 100 bits, as noticed in [1]. For a fair comparison, we first select parameters that support 2, 4, 8, and 16 participants with a minimum security level of 100 bits. We also give a set of parameters that support up to 2, 4, 8, and 16 participants with the standard 128-bit security. The recommended parameter sets are presented in Table 3.

Table 2. Comparison of different bootstrapping methods among ours vs. [9,25]

Method	#mul	$\#R_Q$	$\#bits$	noise
CCS [9]	$4k(k+1)nd$	$3dn$	$nNB_{ks}d_{ks}\log_2 Q_{ks}$	$\tilde{O}(kn^{1.5})$
KMS [25]	$4nkd^2 + 2k(2k+3)d$	$(4n+3)d$	$nNB_{ks}d_{ks}\log_2 Q_{ks}$	$\tilde{O}(kn^2)$
Ours (Alg. 1)	$(2k+1)knd$	$(4n+2)d$	$nNd_{ks}\log_2 Q_{ks}$	$\tilde{O}(kn^{1.5})$
Ours (Alg. 2)	$(2k+1)knd$	$(2n+2)d$	$2N(B_{ks}-1)d_{ks}\log_2 Q_{ks}$	$\tilde{O}(kn^{1.5})$

For LWE instances, we use a uniform binary key distribution and set the noise standard deviation to 1.9. We use the LWE estimator [3] to determine the concrete security[3]. For MNTRU instances, we use a uniform ternary key distribution and set the noise standard deviation to 0.5 (resp., 0.75) for 128-bit (resp., 100-bit). For the second-layer NTRU ciphertexts, we fix the noise standard deviation to 0.4 (resp., 0.25) for 128-bit (resp., 100-bit) security with a uniform ternary secret key. To determine the concrete security, two recent types of attacks are considered. One is the Dense Sublattice Discovery (DSD) attack, which focuses on recovering a basis vector from the dense sublattice within the NTRU lattice. The other one is the Secret Key Recovery (SKR) attack, aiming to directly recover a vector of the short lattice basis by the lattice attacks. Ducas and van Woerden identified the fatigue point at $Q = N^{2.484+o(1)}$, where the modulus Q is such that for values above Q, the DSD attack becomes more efficient than SKR [16]. They have also provided an NTRU estimator[4]. One can use it to determine the BKZ block size β' required for the DSD attack or SKR attack to break the (M)NTRU problem. To convert β' to the concrete security, we use the cost model $T(d,\beta) := 2^{0.292\cdot\beta'+16.4+\log_2(8\cdot d)}$ (in the NTRU setting $d = 2N$) as in [5,24].

Table 3. Parameters Sets for Our MK-FHE.

k	First layer					Second layer				Estimate
	Assumption	(n,q,B_{ks},d_{ks})	$\log_n q$	Key Dist.	Noise Dist	(N,Q,B,d)	$\log_N Q$	Key Dist.	Noise Dist.	Security
2						$(2048, 2^{27}, 2^9, 3)$				
4	LWE	$(500, 32749, 32, 3)$	$1.67 < 2.484$	binary	$\sigma = 1.9$	$(2048, 2^{27}, 2^9, 3)$	$2.45 < 2.484$	ternary	$\sigma = 0.25$	100
8						$(2048, 2^{27}, 2^9, 3)$				
16						$(2048, 2^{27}, 2^9, 3)$				
2						$(2048, 2^{27}, 2^9, 3)$				
4	LWE	$(635, 32749, 32, 3)$	$1.61 < 2.484$	binary	$\sigma = 1.9$	$(2048, 2^{27}, 2^9, 3)$	$2.45 < 2.484$	ternary	$\sigma = 0.4$	128
8						$(2048, 2^{27}, 2^9, 3)$				
16						$(2048, 2^{27}, 2^7, 4)$				
2						$(2048, 2^{27}, 2^9, 3)$				
4	MNTRU	$(560, 45181, 32, 4)$	$1.69 < 2.484$	ternary	$\sigma = 0.75$	$(2048, 2^{27}, 2^9, 3)$	$2.45 < 2.484$	ternary	$\sigma = 0.25$	100
8						$(2048, 2^{27}, 2^9, 3)$				
16						$(2048, 2^{27}, 2^9, 3)$				
2						$(2048, 2^{27}, 2^7, 4)$				
4	MNTRU	$(765, 45181, 32, 4)$	$1.61 < 2.484$	ternary	$\sigma = 0.5$	$(2048, 2^{27}, 2^7, 4)$	$2.45 < 2.484$	ternary	$\sigma = 0.4$	128
8						$(2048, 2^{27}, 2^6, 5)$				
16						$(2048, 2^{27}, 2^5, 6)$				

---

[3] https://github.com/malb/lattice-estimator.
[4] https://github.com/WvanWoerden/NTRUFatigue.

7.3   Experimental Results

All experiments run on the same laptop with a 12th Gen Intel(R) Core(TM) i9-12900H @2.50 GHz and 32 GB RAM, running Ubuntu 20.04.6 LTS. We use the OpenFHE library (v1.1.1) [4] to implement the proposed algorithms. Our codes are publicly available at https://github.com/SKLC-FHE/MKFHE. In Table 4, we present the implementation results with the state-of-the-art works CCS [9] and KMS [25], as detailed below. CCS* is implemented in C++ with the TFHE library[5], while KMS and CCS** are implemented in Julia[6].

Table 4. Timings and key sizes for bootstrapping

Scheme	λ	Hybrid Product	Runtime(s)				EVK(MB)				KSK (MB)
			2	4	8	16	2	4	8	16	
CCS* [9]	100	RLWE	0.07	0.33	1.09	\	19.69	26.25	32.81	\	70.13
CCS** [9]	100	RLWE	0.12	0.42	1.61	11.36	39.85	53.12	66.38	159.21	54.38
KMS [25]	100	RLWE	0.14	0.44	1.17	2.86	105.86	176.47	141.31	176.56	108.75
Alg. 1	100	**NTRU**	0.07	0.28	0.82	2.74	29.56	29.56	29.56	29.56	8.75
Alg. 2	100	**NTRU**	**0.05**	**0.21**	**0.54**	**2.61**	**13.21**	**13.21**	**13.21**	**13.21**	**0.68**
Alg. 1	128	**NTRU**	0.14	0.40	1.55	6.84	60.55	60.55	80.74	100.92	11.95
Alg. 2	128	**NTRU**	0.06	0.23	0.76	4.21	16.77	16.77	16.77	25.15	0.68

From Table 4 one can see that, for parameters at 100-bit security, the bootstrapping time of our Alg. 1 is the same as CCS [9], and 2 times faster than KMS [25]. Correspondingly, the bootstrapping key size of our Alg. 1 is 2.3 times smaller than that of CCS [9], and 5.6 times smaller than that of KMS [25]. For $k = 4$ and 8, our Alg. 1 is about 1.2 and 1.5 times faster than CCS [9], and 1.6 and 1.4 times faster than KMS [25]. Correspondingly, the bootstrapping key size of our Alg. 1 is 2.5 and 2.7 smaller than that of CCS [9], and is 7.4 and 6.5 times smaller than that of KMS [25]. For $k = 16$, our Alg. 1 is approximately the same as KMS [25] and 7.4 times smaller than KMS [25]. For $k = 16$, we did not report CCS's implementation in C++ because the parameters they provided only support up to $k = 8$. Moreover, our Alg. 2 is about 1.4, 1.6 and 2.2 times faster than CCS [9], and 2.8, 2.1 and 2.2 times faster than KMS [25] for $k = 2$, 4 and 8, respectively. Correspondingly, the bootstrapping key size of our Alg. 2 is 6.5, 6.9 and 7.4 smaller than that of CCS [9], and is 15.5, 20.5 and 18 times smaller than that of KMS [25]. For $k = 16$, our Alg. 2 is about 1.1 times faster and 20.5 times smaller than KMS [25]. Moreover, due to the influence of the first-layer ternary key, Algorithm 1 exhibits slightly inferior performance compared to Algorithm 2.

---

[5] https://github.com/ilachill/MK-FHE.
[6] https://github.com/SNUCP/MKTFHE.

Acknowledgements. We thank the anonymous reviewers of ASIACRYPT 2024 and Huanhuan Chen for their helpful comments and suggestions on earlier versions of our paper. This paper is supported by the National Key Research and Development Program of China (Grant No. 2022YFB2702000), the National Natural Science Foundation of China (Grant Nos. 62022018, 61932019), and the Strategic Priority Research Program of Chinese Academy of Sciences (Grant No. XDB0690200).

A   Key-Switching for Multi-Key LWE Ciphertext in [9, 25]

- LWE.KSKG($\mathbf{z}_i, \mathbf{s}_i$): Given two vectors $\mathbf{z}_i = (z_{i,0}, \cdots, z_{i,n-1}) \in \mathbb{Z}^n$, $\mathbf{s} = (s_{i,0}, \cdots, s_{i,N-1}) \in \mathbb{Z}^N$ and two integer q, B_{ks} as input, the algorithm first computes $d_{ks} = \lceil \log_{B_{ks}} q \rceil$ and sets $\mathbf{g} = (B_{ks}^0, \cdots, B_{ks}^{d_{ks}-1})$. Then it samples vector $\mathbf{a}_{i,j,l,v} \leftarrow \mathbb{Z}^n$ uniformly at random and $e_{i,j,l,v} \in \mathbb{Z}_q$ from some noise distribution and computes $\mathsf{ksk}_{i,j,l,v} = (b_{i,j,l,v}, \mathbf{a}_{i,j,l,v})$ where $b_{i,j,l,v} = -\mathbf{a}_{i,j,l,v} \cdot \mathbf{z}_i + e_{i,j,l,v} + v \cdot s_{i,j} \cdot B_{ks}^l$ for all $j \in \mathbb{Z}_N$, $l \in \mathbb{Z}_{d_{ks}}$, $v \in [B_{ks} - 1]$. Finally, it outputs $\mathbf{KSK}_i = \{\mathsf{ksk}_{i,j,l,v}\}$ as the key-switching key of party i.
- LWE.KS($\overline{ct}, \{\mathbf{KSK}_i\}_{i \in [k]}$): Given as input a multi-key LWE ciphertext $\overline{ct} = (b, \mathbf{a}_1, \cdots, \mathbf{a}_k) \in \mathbb{Z}^{kN+1}$ and the key-switching keys $\{\mathbf{KSK}_i\}_{i \in [k]}$ of keys associated with $\overline{ct}$, the algorithm computes $\mathbf{g}^{-1}(a_{i,j}) = (v_{i,j,l})_{l \in \mathbb{Z}_{d_{ks}}}$ for each $i \in [k]$ and $j \in \mathbb{Z}_N$ and then compute

$$b_i' = \sum_{j=0}^{N-1} \sum_{l=0, v_{i,j,l} \neq 0}^{d_{ks}-1} b_{i,j,l,v_{i,j,l}} \quad \text{and} \quad \mathbf{a}_i' = \sum_{j=0}^{N-1} \sum_{l=0, v_{i,j,l} \neq 0}^{d_{ks}-1} \mathbf{a}_{i,j,l,v_{i,j,l}},$$

and let $b' = b + \sum_{i=1}^{k} b_i'$. Finally, the algorithm outputs a multi-key LWE ciphertext $\overline{\mathbf{c}}' = (b', \mathbf{a}_1', \ldots, \mathbf{a}_k') \in \mathbb{Z}^{kn+1}$.

References

1. Akin, Y., Klemsa, J., Önen, M.: A practical TFHE-based multi-key homomorphic encryption with linear complexity and low noise growth. In: ESORICS 2023. LNCS, vol. 14344, pp. 3–23. Springer (2023), https://doi.org/10.1007/978-3-031-50594-2_1
2. Albrecht, M., Bai, S., Ducas, L.: A subfield lattice attack on overstretched NTRU assumptions. In: CRYPTO 2016. LNCS, vol. 9814, pp. 153–178. Springer (2016), https://doi.org/10.1007/978-3-662-53018-4_6
3. Albrecht, M.R., Player, R., Scott, S.: On the concrete hardness of learning with errors. J. Math. Cryptol. 9(3), 169–203 (2015), http://www.degruyter.com/view/j/jmc.2015.9.issue-3/jmc-2015-0016/jmc-2015-0016.xml
4. Badawi, A.A., Bates, J., Bergamaschi, F., Cousins, D.B., Erabelli, S., Genise, N., Halevi, S., Hunt, H., Kim, A., Lee, Y., Liu, Z., Micciancio, D., Quah, I., Polyakov, Y., Saraswathy, R.V., Rohloff, K., Saylor, J., Suponitsky, D., Triplett, M., Vaikuntanathan, V., Zucca, V.: OpenFHE: Open-source fully homomorphic encryption library. In: Proceedings of the 10th Workshop on Encrypted Computing & Applied Homomorphic Cryptography. pp. 53–63. ACM (2022), https://doi.org/10.1145/3560827.3563379

5. Bonte, C., Iliashenko, I., Park, J., Pereira, H.V., Smart, N.P.: Final: Faster FHE instantiated with NTRU and LWE. In: ASIACRYPT 2022. LNCS, vol. 13792, pp. 188–215. Springer (2022), https://doi.org/10.1007/978-3-031-22966-4_7

6. Brakerski, Z., Döttling, N.: Lossiness and entropic hardness for ring-LWE. In: TCC 2020. LNCS, vol. 12550, pp. 1–27. Springer (2020), https://doi.org/10.1007/978-3-030-64375-1_1

7. Brakerski, Z., Gentry, C., Vaikuntanathan, V.: (leveled) fully homomorphic encryption without bootstrapping. In: ACM Trans. Comput. Theory. vol. 6, pp. 13:1–13:36 (2014). https://doi.org/10.1145/2633600

8. Brakerski, Z., Perlman, R.: Lattice-based fully dynamic multi-key FHE with short ciphertexts. In: CRYPTO 2016. LNCS, vol. 9814, pp. 190–213. Springer (2016). https://doi.org/10.1007/978-3-662-53018-4_8

9. Chen, H., Chillotti, I., Song, Y.: Multi-key homomorphic encryption from TFHE. In: ASIACRYPT 2019. LNCS, vol. 11922, pp. 446–472. Springer (2019). https://doi.org/10.1007/978-3-030-34621-8_16

10. Cheon, J.H., Jeong, J., Lee, C.: An algorithm for NTRU problems and cryptanalysis of the GGH multilinear map without a low-level encoding of zero. LMS J. Comput. Math. 19(A), 255–266 (2016). https://doi.org/10.1112/S1461157016000371

11. Chillotti, I., Gama, N., Georgieva, M., Izabachène, M.: Faster fully homomorphic encryption: Bootstrapping in less than 0.1 seconds. In: ASIACRYPT 2016. LNCS, vol. 10031, pp. 3–33 (2016). https://doi.org/10.1007/978-3-662-53887-6_1

12. Chillotti, I., Gama, N., Georgieva, M., Izabachène, M.: TFHE: fast fully homomorphic encryption over the torus. J. Cryptol. 33(1), 34–91 (2020). https://doi.org/10.1007/S00145-019-09319-X

13. Chongchitmate, W., Ostrovsky, R.: Circuit-private multi-key FHE. In: PKC 2017. LNCS, vol. 10175, pp. 241–270. Springer (2017). https://doi.org/10.1007/978-3-662-54388-7_9

14. Clear, M., McGoldrick, C.: Multi-identity and multi-key leveled FHE from learning with errors. In: CRYPTO 2015. LNCS, vol. 9216, pp. 630–656. Springer (2015). https://doi.org/10.1007/978-3-662-48000-7_31

15. Ducas, L., Micciancio, D.: FHEW: bootstrapping homomorphic encryption in less than a second. In: EUROCRYPT 2015. LNCS, vol. 9056, pp. 617–640. Springer (2015). https://doi.org/10.1007/978-3-662-46800-5_24

16. Ducas, L., van Woerden, W.: NTRU fatigue: How stretched is overstretched? In: ASIACRYPT 2021. LNCS, vol. 13093, pp. 3–32. Springer (2021). https://doi.org/10.1007/978-3-030-92068-5_1

17. Esgin, M.F., Espitau, T., Niot, G., Prest, T., Sakzad, A., Steinfeld, R.: Plover: Masking-friendly hash-and-sign lattice signatures. In: EUROCRYPT 2024. LNCS, vol. 14656, pp. 316–345. Springer (2024), https://doi.org/10.1007/978-3-031-58754-2_12

18. Fan, J., Vercauteren, F.: Somewhat practical fully homomorphic encryption. IACR Cryptol. ePrint Arch. p. 144 (2012), http://eprint.iacr.org/2012/144

19. Genise, N., Gentry, C., Halevi, S., Li, B., Micciancio, D.: Homomorphic encryption for finite automata. In: ASIACRYPT 2019. LNCS, vol. 11922, pp. 473–502. Springer (2019), https://doi.org/10.1007/978-3-030-34621-8_17

20. Gentry, C., Szydlo, M.: Cryptanalysis of the revised NTRU signature scheme. In: EUROCRYPT 2002. LNCS, vol. 2332, pp. 299–320. Springer (2002). https://doi.org/10.1007/3-540-46035-7_20

21. Hough, P., Sandsbråten, C., Silde, T.: Concrete NTRU security and advances in practical lattice-based electronic voting. Cryptology ePrint Archive p. 933 (2023), https://eprint.iacr.org/2023/933

22. Kim, A., Deryabin, M., Eom, J., Choi, R., Lee, Y., Ghang, W., Yoo, D.: General bootstrapping approach for rlwe-based homomorphic encryption. IEEE Trans. Computers **73**(1), 86–96 (2024). https://doi.org/10.1109/TC.2023.3318405

23. Kirchner, P., Fouque, P.A.: Revisiting lattice attacks on overstretched NTRU parameters. In: EUROCRYPT 2017. LNCS, vol. 10210, pp. 3–26 (2017). https://doi.org/10.1007/978-3-319-56620-7_1

24. Kluczniak, K.: NTRU-v-um: Secure fully homomorphic encryption from NTRU with small modulus. In: CCS 2022. pp. 1783–1797. ACM (2022), https://doi.org/10.1145/3548606.3560700

25. Kwak, H., Min, S., Song, Y.: Towards practical multi-key TFHE: parallelizable, key-compatible, quasi-linear complexity. In: PKC 2024. LNCS, vol. 14604, pp. 354–385. Springer (2024), https://doi.org/10.1007/978-3-031-57728-4_12

26. Lee, Y., Micciancio, D., Kim, A., Choi, R., Deryabin, M., Eom, J., Yoo, D.: Efficient FHEW bootstrapping with small evaluation keys, and applications to threshold homomorphic encryption. In: Hazay, C., Stam, M. (eds.) EUROCRYPT 2023. LNCS, vol. 14006, pp. 227–256. Springer (2023). https://doi.org/10.1007/978-3-031-30620-4_8

27. López-Alt, A., Tromer, E., Vaikuntanathan, V.: On-the-fly multiparty computation on the cloud via multikey fully homomorphic encryption. In: STOC 2012. pp. 1219–1234. ACM (2012), https://doi.org/10.1145/2213977.2214086

28. Lyubashevsky, V., Peikert, C., Regev, O.: On ideal lattices and learning with errors over rings. In: EUROCRYPT 2010. LNCS, vol. 6110, pp. 1–23. Springer (2010). https://doi.org/10.1007/978-3-642-13190-5_1

29. Morshed, T., Aziz, M.M.A., Mohammed, N.: CPU and GPU accelerated fully homomorphic encryption. In: HOST 2020. pp. 142–153. IEEE (2020). https://doi.org/10.1109/HOST45689.2020.9300288

30. Mukherjee, P., Wichs, D.: Two round multiparty computation via multi-key FHE. In: EUROCRYPT 2016. LNCS, vol. 9666, pp. 735–763. Springer (2016). https://doi.org/10.1007/978-3-662-49896-5_26

31. Peikert, C., Shiehian, S.: Multi-key FHE from LWE, revisited. In: TCC 2016-B. LNCS, vol. 9986, pp. 217–238 (2016). https://doi.org/10.1007/978-3-662-53644-5_9

32. Peralta, G., Cid-Fuentes, R.G., Bilbao, J., Crespo, P.M.: Homomorphic encryption and network coding in IoT architectures: Advantages and future challenges. Electronics **8**(8), 827 (2019), https://doi.org/10.3390/electronics8080827

33. Regev, O.: On lattices, learning with errors, random linear codes, and cryptography. J. ACM **56**(6), 34:1–34:40 (2009). https://doi.org/10.1145/1568318.1568324

34. Shrestha, R., Kim, S.: Chapter ten - integration of IoT with blockchain and homomorphic encryption: Challenging issues and opportunities. vol. 115, pp. 293–331 (2019). https://doi.org/10.1016/BS.ADCOM.2019.06.002

35. Xiang, B., Zhang, J., Deng, Y., Dai, Y., Feng, D.: Fast blind rotation for bootstrapping FHEs. In: CRYPTO 2023. LNCS, vol. 14084, pp. 3–36. Springer (2023), https://doi.org/10.1007/978-3-031-38551-3_1

36. Xu, K., Tan, B.H.M., Wang, L., Aung, K.M.M., Wang, H.: Multi-key fully homomorphic encryption from NTRU and (R)LWE with faster bootstrapping. Theor. Comput. Sci. **968**, 114026 (2023). https://doi.org/10.1016/J.TCS.2023.114026

Homomorphic Sign Evaluation with a RNS Representation of Integers

Philippe Chartier[1,2]($\boxtimes$), Michel Koskas[1], Mohammed Lemou[1,3], and Florian Méhats[1,4]

[1] Ravel Technologies, 75 rue de Richelieu, 75002 Paris, France
{michel.koskas,florian.mehats}@raveltech.io,
mohammed.lemou@univ-rennes.fr
[2] INRIA, Rennes, France
philippe.chartier@inria.fr
[3] CNRS, Rennes, France
[4] University of Rennes 1, Rennes, France

Abstract. In the context of *fully-homomorphic-encryption*, we consider the representation of large integers by their decomposition over a product of rings (through the *Chinese Remainder Theorem*) and introduce a new algorithm for the determination of the sign solely through the knowledge of ring-components. Our implementation with 128 bits of security delivers a correct result with a probability higher than $1 - 10^{-12}$ in less than 140 ms for 32-bit integers on a laptop.

Keywords: fully homomorphic encryption · residue number system · sign · functional bootstrapping

1   Introduction

On top of the two elementary arithmetic operations (addition and multiplication) included by design in all fully-homomorphic-encryption (FHE) systems, many real-world applications require comparisons[1]. As a consequence, algorithms aimed at computing the sign[2] of a message have been developed for the most prominent classes of FHE crypto-systems, that is to say FHEW/TFHE schemes for boolean circuits [23], Brakerski-Gentry-Vaikuntanathan (BGV), Brakerski/Fan-Vercauten (BFV) schemes for messages in finite fields [16,26] and Cheon-Kim-Kim-Song (CKKS) scheme for real and complex messages [9,18,19]. We refer to [23] for an evaluation of the comparative merits of these various algorithms and for a description of what appears, up to our knowledge, as the

---

P. Chartier—On leave from INRIA, M. Lemou—On leave from CNRS, F. Méhats—On leave from University of Rennes 1.

[1] This is in particular the case for training neural networks [3,17] –or more generally statistical learning [10]– or requesting databases.

[2] The comparison of two messages a and b boils down to the determination of the sign of $a - b$.

© International Association for Cryptologic Research 2025
K.-M. Chung and Y. Sasaki (Eds.): ASIACRYPT 2024, LNCS 15484, pp. 271–296, 2025.
https://doi.org/10.1007/978-981-96-0875-1_9

most recent technique for the large-precision evaluation of the sign. However, none of the literature cited above is concerned with the sign evaluation of large-integers from its residues (encryptions thereof). It is precisely the objective of this work (see also [7]) to introduce a method for determining the sign for a FHE crypto-system based on a *residue number system* (RNS).

Using the Chinese Remainder Theorem (CRT) in order to build a FHE library is indeed a well-known theoretical alternative to the binary representation of large numbers (say 32-bits or 64-bits) and their treatment by circuits (see for instance papers on the TFHE [11] and FHEW [14] protocols). The advantage of the representation of numbers of $\mathbb{Z}/p\mathbb{Z}$ by their moduli in a product of rings of $\mathbb{Z}/p_1\mathbb{Z} \times \cdots \times \mathbb{Z}/p_\kappa\mathbb{Z}$ lies in the fact that each ring can be handled separately as far as additions and multiplications are concerned. In the companion paper and corresponding patent [6,8] by the same authors, a modification of the bootstrap procedure is introduced which aims at allowing (without extra computational cost) larger values of the pairwise coprime integers p_i's and thus values of $p = \prod_{i=1}^\kappa p_i$ up to 2^{64}. However, as aforementioned, one key aspect of the manipulation of large sets of data is the necessity to order and sort them: at the core of all FHE-library, should lie the possibility to determine the sign of a single number. Until now, this has prevented the use of the CRT in the context of FHE as the homomorphic determination of the sign has long been considered as a difficult question[3].

In this paper, we present a solution of this problem in the context of FHEW/TFHE encryption protocols. More precisely, we show how to compute with the help of homomorphic operations and several functional bootstrappings, an encrypted value of the sign of any element $\mu \in \mathbb{Z}/p\mathbb{Z}$ from the FHEW-encryptions c_i of its residues $\mu_i \in \mathbb{Z}/p_i\mathbb{Z}$ for $i = 1, \ldots, k$. To this aim, we first compute a series of scalings by $\bar{p}^r, r = 0, \ldots, r_{max}$, of the reconstructed ciphertext of the message μ

$$c^{[r]} = \sum_{i=1}^{k} (\bar{p}^r v_i \bmod p_i) c_i$$

where the v_i's are obtained in a standard way from the Bezout coefficients. A crucial observation is that the noise embedded in c does not grow with r (owing to the mod p_i's) and consequently becomes smaller as compared to the message $\bar{p}^r \mu$ encrypted in $c^{[r]}$. We then show that among the consecutive magnifications of μ (again, in encrypted version), one allows to determine safely its sign. The idea is the following: given a noisy value $\mu + e$ with $\mu \in \mathbb{R}/p\mathbb{Z}$, its sign is ambiguous as soon as μ is close to 0 (or by action of the modulo, close to $\pm\frac{p}{2}$). In this case however, computing $\bar{p}\mu + e'$ with $|e'| \approx |e|$ alleviates the ambiguity as long as $\bar{p}\mu$ does not approach too closely from $\frac{p}{2}$ or is larger than $\frac{p}{2}$. If the sign can not be determined with sufficient confidence, i.e. if $\bar{p}\mu$ is still small, then one can repeat the operation. The result is then carried out through a cascade of linear combinations whose aim is to preserve the relevant information. This last trick

---

[3] Note that the use of a RNS is not *per se* a particular good choice if no other homomorphic computation than the sign is required.

is to a large extent similar to the one used in [4,5]. We prove rigorously the correctness of the algorithm with very high probability for appropriate parameters and we explain how to choose them.

We finally conclude with some implementation results which demonstrate the efficiency of our algorithm: for instance, we are able to homomorphically compare two 32-bit integers in just 140 ms that with a probability of an incorrect decryption smaller than 10^{-12} and a security level of 128 bits. In the light of the pioneering paper [21] and its recent developments [1,2,22,28], let us stress that the model of security envisaged in this paper achieves only indistinguishability under chosen plaintext attacks (IND-CPA) and does not allow the adversary to observe decryption results as in the IND-CPA^D model[4] introduced in [21]. Now, recalling that, to the best of our knowledge, no sign algorithm with a *RNS encoding of cleartexts* is available in the literature, a direct comparison is not possible. In that respect, one of the leading FHE libraries[5] based on TFHE, reports comparison times (93 ms) 33% smaller for 32-bit integers. However, it is important to notice that within our implementation, addition and multiplication are distributed over the rings and thus a lot faster (our multiplication of two 32-bit integers takes 28 ms as compared to the 251 ms announced by TFHE-rs)[6]. In applications to neural networks for instance, a weighted sum of the output x_i, $i = 1, \ldots, n$ of n neurons is passed through an activation function (say a *RELU* function) to produce the output: if the data are encrypted integers, this requires n homomorphic multiplications, $n - 1$ additions, a homomorphic Heaviside function (a tiny modification of the sign) and a last multiplication. Based on the figures given above, a crude estimate of the computational time for one layer gives

$$(n + 1) \times 28 + (n - 1) \times 0.0014 + 140 \text{ and } (n + 1) \times 251 + (n - 1) \times 118 + 93$$

milliseconds for respectively our implementation and THFE-rs, leading to a factor 10 acceleration already for $n = 16$. Alleviating the obstacle of the sign, even though its computation can not be distributed over the rings, thus allows to exploit in practice the full potential of RNS. The principal contribution of this paper can thus be summed up as follows.

Main Result: *Let p be a product of pairwise coprime integers p_i, $i = 1, \ldots, \kappa$. There exists an efficient algorithm, which, given FHEW-encryptions c_i of the residues $\mu_i \in \mathbb{Z}/p_i\mathbb{Z}$ for $i = 1, \ldots, \kappa$ of $\mu \in \mathbb{Z}/p\mathbb{Z}$, delivers a FHEW-encryption*

---

[4] As the algorithm proposed here relies on several bootstraps, the determination of its IND-CPA^D-security level requires further investigations and discussions. Nevertheless, let us already note that smaller probabilities of incorrect decryptions may be simply obtained by considering larger cyclotomic rings, thus rendering the current IND-CPA^D-attacks more difficult.

[5] Namely THFE-rs by Zama, see https://docs.zama.ai/tfhe-rs/getting-started/benchmarks..

[6] The computation of an addition is even faster as it doesn't require any bootstrap: it takes just 14 microseconds for 32-bits integers in the RNS representation, as compared to the 118 ms claimed for TFHE-rs.

c of its sign, namely $\text{sign}(\mu) \in \mathbb{Z}/3\mathbb{Z}$, *with very high probability of correct decryption and in less than* 100 *ms for* 32-*bits integers.*

2   Background and Setting of the Problem

2.1   Notations and Preliminaries on the Chinese Remainder Theorem

For all integer $p \geq 2$, the main representative of $\mu \in \mathbb{R}/p\mathbb{Z}$, denoted by $[\mu]_p$, will be taken in the interval $[-p/2, p/2[$, and the norm of μ is $|\mu| = |[\mu]_p|$. Throughout the paper, for all interval $I \subset \mathbb{R}$ of length smaller than p, for any $\mu \in \mathbb{R}/p\mathbb{Z}$, we shall say that $\mu \in I$ if there exists $k \in \mathbb{Z}$ such that $[\mu]_p - kp \in I$.

Consider an integer p of the form

$$p = \prod_{i=1}^{k} p_i$$

where the integers $p_i \geq 3$ are assumed to be odd and pairwise coprime, i.e.

$$\forall\, 1 \leq i < j \leq k, \quad p_i \wedge p_j = 1.$$

Any element μ in the set $\mathbb{Z}_p$ may be represented unambiguously (owing to the Chinese Remainder Theorem) by its coordinates

$$(\mu_1, \ldots, \mu_k) \in \mathbb{Z}_{p_1} \times \cdots \times \mathbb{Z}_{p_k}$$

with

$$\mu_i = \mu \bmod p_i, \quad i = 1, \ldots, k.$$

The Chinese Remainder Theorem states that the map

$$\Phi : \mathbb{Z}_p \to \mathbb{Z}_{p_1} \times \cdots \times \mathbb{Z}_{p_k}$$
$$\mu \mapsto (\mu_1, \ldots, \mu_k) = (\mu \bmod p_1, \ldots, \mu \bmod p_k)$$

is an isomorphism with inverse

$$\Phi^{-1} : \mathbb{Z}_{p_1} \times \cdots \times \mathbb{Z}_{p_k} \to \mathbb{Z}_p$$
$$(\mu_1, \ldots, \mu_k) \mapsto \mu = \sum_{i=1}^{k} \widehat{p}_i^{-1} \widehat{p}_i \, \mu_i \bmod p$$

where $\widehat{p}_i = p/p_i$ and where $\widehat{p}_i^{-1}$ denotes the inverse of $\widehat{p}_i$ in $\mathbb{Z}_{p_i}$, determined as a Bezout coefficient by Euclide's algorithm.

2.2   LWE Encryption and Functional Bootstrapping

In this section we recall the definition of LWE ciphertexts [27], and the properties of the functional bootstrapping procedure needed by our algorithm. The LWE cryptosystem is parametrized by a plaintext modulus p_i, a ciphertext modulus q and the secret dimension n. As in the BFV, FHEW and TFHE schemes, we shall encrypt any message in $\mathbb{Z}_{p_i}$ in the most significant digits of integers of $\mathbb{Z}_q$. The LWE encryption of a message $\mu_i \in \mathbb{Z}_{p_i}$ under (secret) key $s \in \mathbb{Z}^n$ is a vector $c = \mathrm{LWE}_s^{n,q,p_i}(\mu_i) = (a,b) \in \mathbb{Z}_q^{n+1}$ such that[7]

$$b = \langle a, s \rangle + \lfloor q\mu_i/p_i \rceil + e \bmod q$$

where $e \in \mathbb{Z}_q$ is the so-called noise, which is picked from a centered Gaussian distribution during secret-key encryption. For all ciphertext $c = (a,b) = \mathrm{LWE}_s^{n,q,p_i}(\mu_i)$, the so-called phase is the quantity

$$\varphi_s(c) := b - \langle a, s \rangle \in \mathbb{Z}_q$$

and we shall denote the error term associated to c by

$$\mathrm{Err}(c) = \varphi_s(c) - q\mu_i/p_i.$$

Introducing the *rounding error*

$$\delta_i := \lfloor q\mu_i/p_i \rceil - q\mu_i/p_i,$$

we have $\mathrm{Err}(c) = e + \delta_i \in \mathbb{Q}$ with $|\delta_i| \leq \frac{1}{2}$. The message μ_i is recovered by first computing the approximate decryption function

$$\varphi_s(c) = \lfloor q\mu_i/p_i \rceil + e = q\mu_i/p_i + \mathrm{Err}(c) \bmod q$$

and then rounding its main representative to the closest multiple of q/p_i. Decryption is correct if $|\mathrm{Err}(c)| < \frac{q}{2p_i}$. Now, if $p = \prod_{i=1}^k p_i$ is as in the previous section, the encryption of any (possibly large) integer $\mu \in \mathbb{Z}_p$ will be the set of encryptions $\mathrm{LWE}_s^{n,q,p_i}(\mu_i)$ of its components μ_i for $1 \leq i \leq k$.

Homomorphic arithmetic operations intrinsically increase the level of noise up to a point where the message can not decrypted. The *bootstrapping* procedure introduced by Gentry [15] and its generalisations to the evaluation of functions have been designed to re-encrypt a message with a lower noise without having to decrypt it beforehand. Ducas and Micciancio [14], and later on in a faster version, Chillotti et al. [11,12], have introduced a very efficient bootstrapping based on the polynomial rings (see also [20,24] for further improvements), whose details we shall not give here[8]. In the rest of this section, we nevertheless present its main properties for later use in the paper.

The FHEW/TFHE functional bootstrapping algorithm uses the polynomial ring

$$\mathcal{R}_{N,p'} = \mathbb{Z}_{p'}[X]/(X^N + 1)$$

where N is a power-of-two, so that $X^N + 1$ is the $2N$-th cyclotomic polynomial. The underlying idea of this method consists in the homomorphic implementation of a function

$$f_v : \mu \in \mathbb{Z}_{2N} \mapsto f_v(\mu) = \mathrm{coeff}_0\left(X^\mu v(X) \bmod (X^N + 1)\right) \in \mathbb{Z}_{p'} \qquad (2.1)$$

---

[7] When $p_i = q$, the message $\mu_i \in \mathbb{Z}_q$ is not rescaled and the corresponding $\mathrm{LWE}_s^{n,q,q}(\mu_i)$ ciphertext will be denoted shortly as $\mathrm{LWE}_s^{n,q}(\mu_i)$.

[8] For a thorough description of the technique in the RNS context, we refer the reader to [6].

where coeff$_0$ selects the constant term of a polynomial and where $v \in \mathcal{R}_{N,p'}$ is the so-called *test-polynomial*, whose choice determines the characteristics of the functional bootstrapping. Note that this function f_v defined on $\mathbb{Z}_{2N}$ satisfies the negacyclic constraint

$$f_v(\mu + N) = -f_v(\mu). \tag{2.2}$$

Proposition 1. *Let c be a* $\mathrm{LWE}_s^{n,q}$ *ciphertext. For a given test-polynomial $v \in \mathcal{R}_{N,p'}$, there exists a homomorphic evaluation of the function f_v (a so-called "blind rotation") that provides a ciphertext*

$$c' = \mathrm{LWE}_s^{n,q',p'} \left(f_v(2N\varphi_s(c)/q + \delta(c)) \right),$$

where the term $\delta(c)$ comes from specific rounding approximations on the ciphertext c after a rescaling. Moreover, the variance of the refreshed error associated to the ciphertext c' is constrained by security requirements only and does not depend on the error of the original ciphertext c.

Owing to this result, the key feature of the functional bootstrapping is that, if p_i is odd and small enough, then for any target function $F : \mathbb{Z}_{p_i} \mapsto \mathbb{Z}_{p'}$, it is possible to choose the test polynomial $v(X)$ such that

$$\forall \mu \in \mathbb{Z}_{p_i}, \quad f_v\left(\lfloor 2N\mu/p_i \rceil + \varepsilon\right) = F(\mu)$$

as soon as ε is small enough. This enables to obtain a $\mathrm{LWE}_s^{n,q',p'}(F(\mu))$ ciphertext from a $\mathrm{LWE}_s^{n,q,p_i}(\mu)$ ciphertext, with a refreshed error. In the special case where $p' = p_i$, $q' = q$ and F is the identity function, this operation is a bootstrapping in the usual sense.

2.3   Setting of the Problem

We define the sign of an element $\mu \in \mathbb{Z}_p$ for odd p as the sign of its main representative

$$\mathrm{sign}(\mu) = \begin{cases} -1 & \text{if } [\mu]_p \in \left\{-\dfrac{p-1}{2}, \ldots, -1\right\}, \\ 0 & \text{if } [\mu]_p = 0, \\ +1 & \text{if } [\mu]_p \in \left\{1, \ldots, \dfrac{p-1}{2}\right\}. \end{cases}$$

Our aim in this paper is the following.

Objective: *Find the encrypted value of the sign of an element of $\mathbb{Z}_p$ from the encrypted values of its components. More precisely, given the k values*

$$c_i = \mathrm{LWE}_s^{n,q,p_i}(\mu_i) \in \mathbb{Z}_q^{n+1}, \quad i = 1, \ldots, k,$$

we aim at obtaining

$$\mathrm{LWE}_s^{n,q,3} \left(\mathrm{sign} \circ \Phi^{-1}(\mu_1, \ldots, \mu_k) \right),$$

where the sign $\in \{-1, 0, 1\}$ *has been identified with an element of* $\mathbb{Z}_3$.

Remark 1. By linearity of LWE-encryption, the ciphertext $c = \sum_{i=1}^{k} [\widehat{p}_i^{-1}]_{p_i} c_i$ is an encrypted value of $\mu = \Phi^{-1}(\mu_1, \ldots, \mu_k)$, i.e. $c = \text{LWE}_s^{n,q,P}(\mu)$ with an error $\text{Err}(c)$. A probability estimate (see Appendix) of $\text{Err}(c)$ shows that the decryption of c gives a wrong value with high probability (more than 0.5) for $(p_1, p_2, p_3, p_4, p_5, p_6, p_7, p_8) = (7, 11, 13, 17, 19, 23, 25, 27)$ with nominal assumptions on the errors $\text{Err}(c_i)$, $i = 1, \ldots, k$ in the rings. This renders the determination of μ intractable as such and one should look for an algorithm to evaluate its sign without knowing it exactly.

3   The Sign Algorithm for Plaintexts

To introduce our method, let us examine a toy problem where we want to determine the sign of an integer $\mu \in \mathbb{Z}_p$, but instead of knowing its components μ_i, we only have at hand some noisy values $\widetilde{\mu}_i \in \mathbb{R}$ satisfying $\widetilde{\mu}_i = \mu_i + e_i$. We assume having an estimate on the error terms, more precisely $|e_i| \leq \varepsilon/k$, for some $0 < \varepsilon \leq 1/(2\bar{p} + 2)$, and where $\bar{p} \geq 3$ is an odd rescaling parameter whose role will be made precise further on. Trying to reconstruct μ from the noisy values yields the approximate value

$$\widetilde{\mu}^{[0]} := \Phi^{-1}(\widetilde{\mu}_1, \ldots, \widetilde{\mu}_k) = \sum_{i=1}^{k} [\widehat{p}_i^{-1}]_{p_i} \widehat{p}_i \, \widetilde{\mu}_i = \mu + e^{[0]} \bmod p,$$

with

$$e^{[0]} = \sum_{i=1}^{k} [\widehat{p}_i^{-1}]_{p_i} \widehat{p}_i \, e_i.$$

We have the estimate

$$|\widetilde{\mu}^{[0]} - \mu| = |e^{[0]}| \leq \frac{p}{2} \sum_{i=1}^{k} |e_i| \leq \frac{\varepsilon}{2} p.$$

If $\frac{\varepsilon}{2} p \geq 1$, the signs of $\widetilde{\mu}^{[0]}$ and μ may be different and it is clear that knowing $\widetilde{\mu}^{[0]}$ may not be sufficient to determine the sign of μ.

The following function will be useful (the scaling by $2N$, unnatural here, prepares its use with ciphertexts in next section).

Definition 1. *Let* $0 \leq \varepsilon \leq 1$ *and* $N \geq 1$ *an integer. We introduce the function* g_ε *on* $\mathbb{R}/(2N\mathbb{Z})$ *by*

$$g_\varepsilon(\mu) = \begin{cases} +1 & \text{if } \mu \in]\varepsilon N, N - \varepsilon N[, \\ -1 & \text{if } \mu \in]-N + \varepsilon N, -\varepsilon N[, \\ 0 & \text{otherwise.} \end{cases}$$

Note that g_ε is odd and satisfies the negacyclic constraint (2.2).

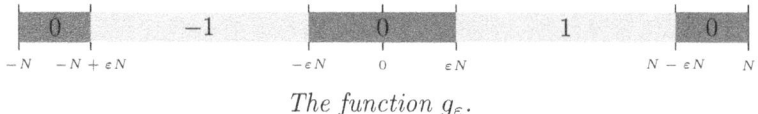

The function g_ε.

Proposition 2. *For $p \in \mathbb{N}^*$, $3 \leq \bar{p} < p$ and odd integer and $0 < \varepsilon < \frac{1}{2(\bar{p}+1)}$, let us consider a noisy value of $\mu \in \mathbb{R}/p\mathbb{Z}$ of the form*

$$\tilde{\mu}^{[0]} = \mu + e^{[0]} \mod p \text{ with } |e^{[0]}| \leq \varepsilon \frac{p}{2} < 1. \tag{3.1}$$

The following statements hold

(i) if $g_\varepsilon(2N\tilde{\mu}^{[0]}/p) = 1$, then $\text{sign}(\mu) = 1$;
(ii) if $g_\varepsilon(2N\tilde{\mu}^{[0]}/p) = -1$, then $\text{sign}(\mu) = -1$;
(iii) if $g_\varepsilon(2N\tilde{\mu}^{[0]}/p) = 0$, then $\bar{p}\mu$ and μ have the same sign.

Proof. We first assume that $g_\varepsilon(2N\tilde{\mu}^{[0]}/p) = 1$. This means that

$$\tilde{\mu}^{[0]} \in]\frac{\varepsilon}{2}p, \frac{p}{2} - \frac{\varepsilon}{2}p[$$

so that, from (3.1), we have

$$\mu \in]0, \frac{p}{2}[,$$

i.e. $\text{sign}(\mu) = 1$. Similarly, if $g_\varepsilon(2N\tilde{\mu}^{[0]}/p) = -1$, then we have $\text{sign}(\mu) = -1$.

We now assume that $g_\varepsilon(2N\tilde{\mu}^{[0]}/p) = 0$. Necessarily $\bar{p}\mu$ and μ have the same sign: as a matter of fact, either $\mu = 0$, or $\mu > 0$ or $\mu < 0$. If $\mu = 0$, then $\bar{p}\mu = 0$. If $\mu > 0$, then

$$\mu^{[0]} \in] -\varepsilon\frac{p}{2}, \varepsilon\frac{p}{2}] \cup [\frac{p}{2} - \varepsilon\frac{p}{2}, \frac{p}{2}[\cup [-\frac{p}{2}, -\frac{p}{2} + \varepsilon\frac{p}{2}[$$

and it stems from (3.1) and $0 < \mu < \frac{p}{2}$ (note that $\frac{p}{2} + \varepsilon\frac{p}{2} < 0$ owing to $0 < \varepsilon < 1$), that

$$\mu \in]0, \varepsilon p] \cup [\frac{p}{2} - \varepsilon p, \frac{p}{2}[$$

If μ lies in the first interval, we have

$$0 < \bar{p}\mu \leq \varepsilon\bar{p}p \leq \frac{\bar{p}}{2(\bar{p}+1)}p \leq \frac{p}{2} - \varepsilon p, \tag{3.2}$$

while if μ lies in the second interval ($\mu \in [\frac{p}{2} - \varepsilon p, \frac{p}{2}[$), we have

$$\frac{p}{2} - \mu \in]0, \varepsilon p]$$

and similarly we get

$$0 < \bar{p}(\frac{p}{2} - \mu) \leq \frac{p}{2} - \varepsilon p,$$

which is equivalent to

$$\varepsilon p \leq \bar{p}\mu - \frac{\bar{p}-1}{2}p < \frac{p}{2}.$$

We recall that $\bar{p}$ is odd, so $\frac{\bar{p}-1}{2}$ is an integer, which yields $\bar{p}\mu \in [\varepsilon p, \frac{p}{2}[$. Consequently, in both cases, we have $\text{sign}(\bar{p}\mu) = +1 = \text{sign}(\mu)$. If $\mu < 0$, by considering $-\mu > 0$ we get that $\text{sign}(\bar{p}\mu) = -1 = \text{sign}(\mu)$. The claim is proved.

We now consider the following approximation of $\bar{p}\mu$:

$$\widetilde{\mu}^{[1]} := \sum_{i=1}^{k} [\widehat{\bar{p}p_i}^{-1}]_{p_i} \widehat{p}_i \, \widetilde{\mu}_i = \bar{p}\mu + e^{[1]} \bmod p, \quad \text{with} \quad e^{[1]} = \sum_{i=1}^{k} [\widehat{\bar{p}p_i}^{-1}]_{p_i} \widehat{p}_i \, e_i.$$

Since we have the same estimate

$$|\widetilde{\mu}^{[1]} - \bar{p}\mu| = |e^{[1]}| \leq \frac{p}{2} \sum_{i=1}^{k} |e_i| \leq \frac{\varepsilon}{2} p, \tag{3.3}$$

the same reasoning as above leads to the fact that if $g_\varepsilon(2N\widetilde{\mu}^{[1]}/p) = +1$ (resp. $= -1$) then $\text{sign}(\bar{p}\mu) = \text{sign}(\mu) = +1$ (resp. $= -1$). In other words, in the case $g_\varepsilon(2N\widetilde{\mu}^{[0]}/p) = 0$, the quantity $g_\varepsilon(2N\widetilde{\mu}^{[1]}/p)$ is an estimator of the sign of μ with no false positive.

One can iterate on this method, considering all the rescalings

$$\widetilde{\mu}^{[r]} := \sum_{i=1}^{k} [\widehat{\bar{p}^r p_i}^{-1}]_{p_i} \widehat{p}_i \, \widetilde{\mu}_i = \bar{p}^r \mu + e^{[r]} \bmod p \text{ with } e^{[r]} = \sum_{i=1}^{k} [\widehat{\bar{p}^r p_i}^{-1}]_{p_i} \widehat{p}_i \, e_i, \tag{3.4}$$

for $r \in \mathbb{N}$. By an induction argument, one can easily generalize the above proof and show that, if $g_\varepsilon(2N\widetilde{\mu}^{[0]}/p) = \ldots = g_\varepsilon(2N\widetilde{\mu}^{[r-1]}/p) = 0$, then all the terms $\bar{p}^r\mu, \bar{p}^{r-1}\mu, \ldots, \bar{p}\mu$ and μ have the same sign and, moreover, if $g_\varepsilon(2N\widetilde{\mu}^{[r]}/p) = +1$ (resp. $= -1$) then $\text{sign}(\mu) = +1$ (resp. $= -1$).

In fact, the number of required rescalings can be bounded *a priori*. To see this point, we state a technical Lemma.

Lemma 1. *Let $3 \leq \bar{p} < p$ be odd integers, let $0 < \varepsilon \leq \frac{1}{2(\bar{p}+1)}$ and let $\mu \in \mathbb{R}/p\mathbb{Z}$. Consider the sequence $(\bar{p}^r \mu)_{r \geq 0}$. The following statements hold true.*

(i) If $\mu \in]0, \varepsilon p]$, then there exists $r^* \in \mathbb{N}^*$ such that for all $0 \leq r < r^*$, one has $\bar{p}^r \mu \in]0, \varepsilon p]$ and $\bar{p}^{r^*} \mu \in]\varepsilon p, \frac{p}{2} - \varepsilon p]$.
(ii) If $\mu \in [\frac{p}{2} - \varepsilon p, \frac{p}{2}[$, then there exists $r^* \in \mathbb{N}^*$ such that for all $0 \leq r < r^*$, one has $\bar{p}^r \mu \in [\frac{p}{2} - \varepsilon p, \frac{p}{2}[$ and $\bar{p}^{r^*} \mu \in [\varepsilon p, \frac{p}{2} - \varepsilon p[$.
(iii) If $\mu \in [-\varepsilon p, 0[$, then there exists $r^* \in \mathbb{N}^*$ such that for all $0 \leq r < r^*$, one has $\bar{p}^r \mu \in [-\varepsilon p, 0[$ and $\bar{p}^{r^*} \mu \in [-\frac{p}{2} + \varepsilon p, -\varepsilon p[$.
(iv) If $\mu \in]-\frac{p}{2}, -\frac{p}{2} + \varepsilon p[$, then there exists $r^* \in \mathbb{N}^*$ such that for all $0 \leq r < r^*$, one has $\bar{p}^r \mu \in]-\frac{p}{2}, -\frac{p}{2} + \varepsilon p[$ and $\bar{p}^{r^*} \mu \in]-\frac{p}{2} + \varepsilon p, -\varepsilon p]$.

Proof. Items *(iii)* and *(iv)* can be directly deduced from *(i)* and *(ii)* by $\mu \to \frac{p}{2}+\mu$. Note indeed that, $\bar{p}$ being odd, we have $\bar{p}^r \frac{p}{2} = \frac{p}{2} \bmod p$ for all $r \geq 0$.

Let us prove *(i)*. We thus assume that $\mu \in]0, \varepsilon p]$. Let $r^* \geq 1$ be the largest integer such that $\bar{p}^r \mu \in]0, \varepsilon p]$ for all $0 \leq r \leq r^* - 1$ (such an integer exists given that $\bar{p}^0 \mu \in]0, \varepsilon p]$ and that the *real* sequence $\bar{p}^r \mu \to +\infty$ when $r \to +\infty$). By construction, we have $\bar{p}^{r^*-1} \mu \leq \varepsilon p < \bar{p}^{r^*} \mu \leq \frac{p}{2} - \varepsilon p$, which yields

$$r^* = 1 + \left\lfloor \log_{\bar{p}} \left(\frac{\varepsilon p}{\mu} \right) \right\rfloor.$$

Moreover, replacing μ by $\bar{p}^{r^*-1}\mu \in]0, \varepsilon p]$ in (3.2), we obtain $\bar{p}^{r^*} \mu \leq \frac{p}{2} - \varepsilon p$. We have proved *(i)* (Fig. 1).

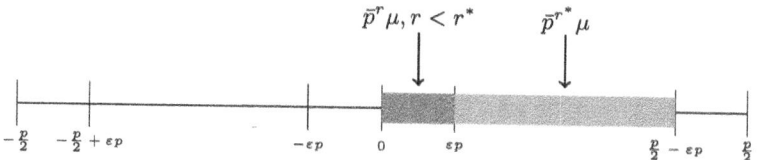

Fig. 1. *Case (i) of Lemma 1.*

In order to prove *(ii)*, we now assume that $\mu \in [\frac{p}{2} - \varepsilon p, \frac{p}{2}[$. Then $\frac{p}{2} - \mu \in]0, \varepsilon p]$ so Item *(i)* can be applied to $\frac{p}{2} - \mu$. Setting $r^* = 1 + \left\lfloor \log_{\bar{p}} \left(\frac{\varepsilon p}{p/2 - \mu} \right) \right\rfloor$, one has

$$\forall 0 \leq r \leq r^* - 1, \quad \bar{p}^r \left(\frac{p}{2} - \mu \right) \in]0, \varepsilon p] \quad \text{and} \quad \bar{p}^{r^*} \left(\frac{p}{2} - \mu \right) \in \left] \varepsilon p, \frac{p}{2} - \varepsilon p \right].$$

By substracting $p/2$, this yields

$$\forall 0 \leq r \leq r^* - 1, \quad \bar{p}^r \mu - \frac{\bar{p}^r - 1}{2} p \in \left[\frac{p}{2} - \varepsilon p, \frac{p}{2} \right[\text{ and } \bar{p}^{r^*} \mu - \frac{\bar{p}^{r^*} - 1}{2} p \in \left[\varepsilon p, \frac{p}{2} - \varepsilon p \right[.$$

Since $\frac{\bar{p}^r - 1}{2}$ is an integer for all $r > 0$, the proof of *(ii)* is complete (Figs. 2, 3 and 4).

Remark 2. By considering the smallest and largest positive values in $\mathbb{Z}_p$, that is to say $\mu = 1$ and $\mu = \frac{p-1}{2}$, with $\varepsilon \leq \frac{1}{2(\bar{p}+1)}$, we can bound from above r^* by

$$r^* \leq r_{max} = 1 + \left\lfloor \log_{\bar{p}} \left(\frac{p}{\bar{p} + 1} \right) \right\rfloor.$$

In order to prepare the adaptation of this algorithm to ciphertexts, we summarize in the following proposition the result that we have proved.

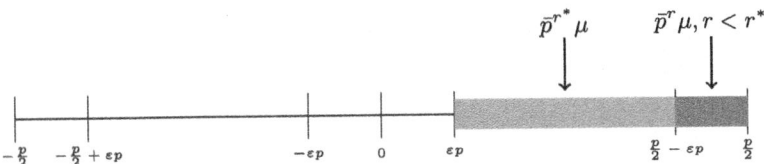

Fig. 2. *Case (ii) of Lemma 1.*

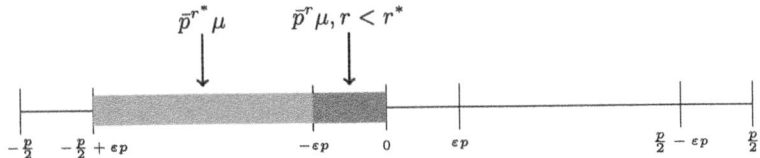

Fig. 3. *Case (iii) of Lemma 1.*

Proposition 3. *Let $3 \leq \bar{p} < p$ be odd integers and let $0 < \varepsilon \leq \frac{1}{2(\bar{p}+1)}$. Let $\mu \in \mathbb{Z}_p$ and consider a sequence of real numbers $\mu^{[r]} \in \mathbb{R}/(2N\mathbb{Z})$, defined for $r = 0, 1, \ldots, r_{max} = 1 + \left\lfloor \log_{\bar{p}} \left(\frac{p}{\bar{p}+1} \right) \right\rfloor$, and satisfying*

$$|\mu^{[r]} - 2N\bar{p}^r\mu/p|| \leq \varepsilon N. \tag{3.5}$$

Then, there exists $r^* \geq 0$ such that

1. *if $\mu > 0$ then $g_\varepsilon(\mu^{[r^*]}) = 1$ and for all $0 \leq r < r^*$, $g_\varepsilon(\mu^{[r]}) = 0$;*
2. *if $\mu < 0$ then $g_\varepsilon(\mu^{[r^*]}) = -1$ and for all $0 \leq r < r^*$, $g_\varepsilon(\mu^{[r]}) = 0$;*
3. *if $\mu = 0$ then $g_\varepsilon(\mu^{[r]}) = 0$ for all $r \geq 0$,*

where the function g_ε was introduced in Definition 1.

As a direct application of this proposition, one can directly determine the sign of μ by a lexicographic comparison of $(g_\varepsilon(2N\widetilde{\mu}^{[0]}/p), g_\varepsilon(2N\widetilde{\mu}^{[1]}/p), \ldots, g_\varepsilon(2N\widetilde{\mu}^{[r_{max}]})/p)$ with $(0, 0, \ldots, 0)$. Equivalently, we can state the

Corollary 1. *Let $3 \leq \bar{p} < p$ be odd integers, let $0 < \varepsilon \leq \frac{1}{2(\bar{p}+1)}$ and let $\mu \in \mathbb{Z}_p$. Denote $\mu_i = \mu \bmod p_i$ and let g_ε be the function given in Definition 1. If for*

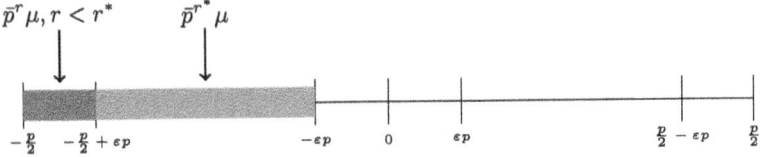

Fig. 4. *Case (iv) of Lemma 1.*

$0 \le r \le r_{max} = 1 + \left\lfloor \log_{\bar{p}} \left(\frac{p}{\bar{p}+1} \right) \right\rfloor$, *we define $\tilde{\mu}^{[r]}$ by (3.4), where the noisy values $\tilde{\mu}_i \in \mathbb{R}/p_i\mathbb{Z}$ satisfy $|\tilde{\mu}_i - \mu_i| \le \varepsilon/k$, then we have*

$$\text{sign}(\mu) = \text{sign} \left(\sum_{r=0}^{r_{max}} 2^{r_{max}-r} g_\varepsilon(2N\tilde{\mu}^{[r]}/p) \right). \tag{3.6}$$

As a matter of fact, either all values $g_\varepsilon\left(2N\tilde{\mu}^{[r]}/p)\right)$ remain null, and the sum accordingly, or the first non-vanishing value (either 1 or −1) dominates the sum (owing to the scaling factors $2^{r_{max}-r}$). We hereafter illustrate Corollary 1 with $\bar{p} = 13$ and $r_{max} = 8$ in the case where $\mu \in]0, \varepsilon p]$ (Table 1).

Table 1. Values of the inner sum (row S) of (3.6) with $M = 2^{r_{max}-r^*}$ and $\mu > 0$.

r	$\tilde{\mu}^{[r]}$	Interval	$g_\varepsilon\left(2N\tilde{\mu}^{[r]}/p\right)$	S
0	$\approx \mu$	$]0, \varepsilon p]$	0	0
⋮	⋮	⋮	⋮	⋮
r^*-1	$\approx \bar{p}^{r^*-1}\mu$	$]0, \varepsilon p]$	0	0
r^*	$\approx \bar{p}^{r^*}\mu$	$]\varepsilon p, \frac{p}{2} - \varepsilon p]$	1	M
r^*+1	$\approx \bar{p}^{r^*+1}\mu$	$[-\frac{p}{2}, \frac{p}{2}[$	$\in \{-1,0,1\}$	$\ge M - \frac{M}{2} = \frac{M}{2}$
⋮	⋮	⋮	⋮	⋮
r_{max}	$\approx \bar{p}^{r_{max}}\mu$	$[-\frac{p}{2}, \frac{p}{2}[$	$\in \{-1,0,1\}$	$\ge M - \frac{M}{2} - \ldots - 1 = 1$

4   The Homomorphic Sign Algorithm

With the notations introduced in Sect. 2, we consider a plaintext $\mu \in \mathbb{Z}_p$ encoded by its CRT components μ_i, $1 \le i \le k$, which are encrypted as $c_i = \text{LWE}_s^{n,q,p_i}(\mu_i)$, with errors $\text{Err}(c_i)$. Our aim is to obtain an encrypted value of $\text{sign}(\mu)$. Three steps are necessary to adapt the above algorithm from plaintexts to ciphertexts.

4.1   Rescaling Ciphertexts

The first step consists in rescaling the ciphertexts c_i by factors $\bar{p}^r$. The following result is an adaptation of Proposition 3.

Proposition 4. *Let $3 \le \bar{p} < p$ be odd integers and let $0 < \varepsilon \le \frac{1}{2(\bar{p}+1)}$. Consider the sequence*

$$c^{[r]} = \sum_{i=1}^k [\bar{p}^r \widehat{p_i}^{-1}]_{p_i} c_i, \qquad r = 0, \ldots, r_{max} = 1 + \left\lfloor \log_{\bar{p}} \left(\frac{p}{\bar{p}+1} \right) \right\rfloor \tag{4.1}$$

of encrypted values $\text{LWE}_s^{n,q,p}(\bar{p}^r\mu)$ and denote, for all $\text{LWE}_s^{n,q}$ ciphertext c,

$$\widetilde{\varphi}_s(c) := 2N\varphi_s(c)/q + \delta(c) \in \mathbb{Z}_{2N}, \tag{4.2}$$

where $\delta(c)$ was defined in Proposition 1. Suppose that, for all r, we have the estimate

$$\left|2N\,Err(c^{[r]})/q + \delta(c^{[r]})\right| \le \varepsilon N. \tag{4.3}$$

Then, there exists $r^* \in \{0, \dots, r_{max}\}$ such that

1. if $\mu > 0$ then $g_\varepsilon(\widetilde{\varphi}_s(c^{[r^*]})) = 1$ and for all $0 \le r < r^*$, $g_\varepsilon(\widetilde{\varphi}_s(c^{[r]})) = 0$;
2. if $\mu < 0$ then $g_\varepsilon(\widetilde{\varphi}_s(c^{[r^*]})) = -1$ and for all $0 \le r < r^*$, $g_\varepsilon(\widetilde{\varphi}_s(c^{[r]})) = 0$;
3. if $\mu = 0$ then $g_\varepsilon(\widetilde{\varphi}_s(c^{[r]})) = 0$ for all $r \ge 0$,

where the function g_ε was defined in Definition 1.

Proof. This result is a direct application of Proposition 3. Indeed, setting $\mu^{[r]} = \widetilde{\varphi}_s(c^{[r]})$, we have

$$\mu^{[r]} = \widetilde{\varphi}_s(c^{[r]}) = 2N\varphi_s(c^{[r]})/q + \delta(c^{[r]})$$

$$= \frac{2N}{q}\left(q\bar{p}^r\mu/p + Err(c^{[r]})\right) + \delta(c^{[r]})$$

$$= 2N\bar{p}^r\mu/p + \frac{2N}{q}Err(c^{[r]}) + \delta(c^{[r]}).$$

Therefore, (4.3) yields, for all r,

$$\left|\mu^{[r]} - 2N\bar{p}^r\mu/p\right| = \left|\frac{2N}{q}Err(c^{[r]}) + \delta(c^{[r]})\right| \le \varepsilon N,$$

which enables to apply this Proposition 3.

Remark 3. Piecewise constant functions may also be obtained through an elaboration of the same technique as for the sign. To this aim, it is sufficient to notice (i), that the Heaviside function $H(\mu)$ can be emulated through the same procedure by attributing the value 0 instead of -1 to all torus-elements in $[-\frac{p}{2} + \frac{\varepsilon}{2}p, -\frac{\varepsilon}{2}p]$ in the definition of g_ε and (ii), that all piecewise constant functions f on the discrete torus $[-\frac{p}{4}, \frac{p}{4}]$ are linear combinations of translated Heaviside functions $f(x) = \sum_i \alpha_i H(x - \beta_i)$ where the α_i's are integers and the β_i's are elements of $[-\frac{p}{4}, \frac{p}{4}]$.

4.2   Emulating g_ε Through Bootstrapping

Having computed the rescaled ciphertexts $c^{[r]}$ for $0 \le r \le r_{max}$ by formula (4.1), the second step of the sign algorithm consists in a functional bootstrapping of each $c^{[r]}$ in order to compute an encrypted version of $g_\varepsilon(\widetilde{\varphi}_s(c^{[r]}))$. To this aim, we have to define a suitable test-polynomial $v(x)$.

More precisely, we aim in this subsection at constructing a test-polynomial $v^\kappa(X) \in \mathcal{R}_{N,2N}$ such that the associated function defined by (2.1) satisfies

$$\forall \mu \in \mathbb{Z}_{2N}, \qquad f_{v^\kappa}(\mu) = 2^\kappa g_\varepsilon(\mu), \qquad (4.4)$$

where $0 \leq \kappa \leq \log N$ is a scaling factor so as to emulate the function g_ε, rescaled, in an encrypted form through a bootstrapping procedure (according to Proposition 1).

By construction, function g_ε is a piecewise constant function, with discontinuities only at points

$$\mu = \pm\varepsilon N + \alpha N, \quad \alpha \in \mathbb{Z}$$

while function $\nu \in \mathbb{R}/\mathbb{Z} \mapsto f_{v^\kappa}(\lfloor 2N\nu \rceil)$ may have jumps only at points

$$\frac{1}{2} + \beta, \quad \beta \in \mathbb{Z}.$$

In order not to introduce possible biases from roundings, we thus require that

$$\pm\varepsilon N + \alpha N = \frac{1}{2} + \beta, \quad \alpha \in \mathbb{Z}, \beta \in \mathbb{Z} \quad \text{i.e.} \quad \varepsilon = \frac{1}{2N} + \frac{\alpha}{N}, \quad \alpha \in \mathbb{Z}. \quad (4.5)$$

Under the constraint that $0 < \varepsilon \leq \frac{1}{2(\bar{p}+1)}$ we thus get (assuming $N \geq 3(\bar{p}+1)$ which is always satisfied in practice)

$$0 \leq \alpha \leq \left\lfloor \frac{N}{2(\bar{p}+1)} - \frac{1}{2} \right\rfloor \qquad (4.6)$$

and we take the largest possible value for ε in order to alleviate the constraint (4.3). Now, a key feature of functional bootstrapping based on blind rotation is that for any function F defined from $\mathbb{Z}_{2N}$ to $\mathbb{Z}$ and such that

$$\forall j \in \mathbb{Z}_{2N}, \quad F(j+N) = -F(j),$$

there exists a unique polynomial $v \in \mathbb{Z}[X]/(X^N + 1)$ such that the function f_v defined by (2.1) satisfies

$$\forall j \in \mathbb{Z}_{2N}, \qquad f_v(j) = F(j).$$

Its coefficients v_j are given by $v_j = F(-j)$, $j = 0, \dots, N-1$.

For a given α in (4.5), it is thus enough to define F on $\{0, \dots, N-1\}$ as follows:

$$\begin{aligned} \forall 0 \leq j \leq \alpha, & \qquad F(j) = 0, \\ \forall \alpha + 1 \leq j \leq N - \alpha - 1, & \qquad F(j) = 2^\kappa, \\ \forall N - \alpha \leq j \leq N - 1, & \qquad F(j) = 0, \end{aligned}$$

so that

$$v_j^\kappa := F(-j), \qquad j = 0, \dots, N-1,$$

that is to say

$$v_0^\kappa = \ldots = v_\alpha^\kappa = 0,$$
$$v_{\alpha+1}^\kappa = \ldots = v_{N-\alpha-1}^\kappa = -2^\kappa,$$
$$v_{N-\alpha}^\kappa = \ldots = v_{N-1}^\kappa = 0. \tag{4.7}$$

For these specific choices of ε and v^κ, the equality (4.4) is satisfied.

4.3   Implementing the Homomorphic Lexicographic Comparison

Arguing as for Corollary 1, it is clear from Proposition 4 that the sign of $\mu \in \mathbb{Z}_p$ can be obtained from the expression

$$\sum_{r=0}^{r_{max}} 2^{r_{max}-r} g_\varepsilon(\tilde{\varphi}_s(c^{[r]})). \tag{4.8}$$

Assuming for a while that $2^{r_{max}} \leq N$ and using that the addition is homomorphic, an encryption of (4.8) is

$$\sum_{r=0}^{r_{max}} \mathrm{LWE}_s^{n,q,2N}\left(2^{r_{max}-r} g_\varepsilon(\tilde{\varphi}_s(c^{[r]}))\right) = \sum_{r=0}^{r_{max}} \mathrm{LWE}_s^{n,q,2N}\left(f_{v^{r_{max}-r}}(\tilde{\varphi}_s(c^{[r]}))\right). \tag{4.9}$$

According to Subsect. 2.2, we can bootstrap directly $c^{[r]}$ onto the encryption of $f_{v^{r_{max}-r}}(\tilde{\varphi}_s(c^{[r]}))$, by using the test-polynomial $v^{r_{max}-r}(X)$, and sum up homomorphically to obtained the desired ciphertext (4.9).

However, the noise in (4.9) is determined by the output noise of the boostrapping procedure. This may render the decryption of (4.9) incorrect, as soon as the noise is non zero (indeed, the smallest non zero value in (4.8) may be ± 1). In order to overcome this difficulty, we first replace the sum (4.8) into sub-sums of m terms as follows, where we have supposed, for the sake of simplicity, that $r_{max} + 1 = m^\ell$, where by definition $\ell = \log_m(r_{max} + 1)$. We suppose also that $2^{m+1} \leq N$. Let $\tilde{\varepsilon}$ be defined by

$$\tilde{\varepsilon} = \frac{1}{2N} + \frac{\tilde{\alpha}}{N} \quad \text{with} \quad \tilde{\alpha} = \frac{N}{2^{m+1}} - 1, \tag{4.10}$$

and consider

$$g_{\tilde{\varepsilon}}\left(\sum_{r_0=0}^{m-1} 2^{\log N - r_0 - 1} g_{\tilde{\varepsilon}}\left(\sum_{r_1=0}^{m-1} 2^{\log N - r_1 - 1} g_{\tilde{\varepsilon}}\left(\ldots \sum_{r_{\ell-1}=0}^{m-1} 2^{\log N - r_{\ell-1} - 1} g_\varepsilon(\tilde{\varphi}_s(c^{[j_\mathbf{r}]}))\right)\right)\right) \tag{4.11}$$

with

$$j_\mathbf{r} = \sum_{i=0}^{\ell-1} r_i m^{\ell-1-i}, \qquad \mathbf{r} = (r_0, \ldots, r_{\ell-1}).$$

Now, the smallest non zero values in this new sum is larger than $2^{\log N - m} > 1$, which authorizes some noise in the encrypted form of (4.11). Note that the innermost loop involves g_ε, while all other loops resort to $g_{\tilde\varepsilon}$. There is indeed no reason to use the same value of ε given that the space of messages on which we evaluate $g_{\tilde\varepsilon}$ is different. Arguing in a similar way as for ε, we require that $\tilde\varepsilon = \frac{1}{2N} + \frac{\tilde\alpha}{N}$ with $\alpha \in \mathbb{Z}$ and $\tilde\varepsilon < \frac{1}{2^{m+1}}$ leading to (4.10).

It is easy to check that, by Proposition 4 and as formula (4.8), this new expression (4.11) also gives the sign of μ. Using once again the homomorphy of the addition and the bootstrapped version of g_ε, we obtain an encryption of the sign of μ from the sequence of ciphertexts $c^{[k]}$ through the expression

$$\widehat{F}\left(\sum_{r_0=0}^{m-1}\widetilde{F}_{r_0}\left(\sum_{r_1=0}^{m-1}\widetilde{F}_{r_1}\left(\cdots\sum_{r_{\ell-1}=0}^{m-1}F_{r_{\ell-1}}\left(c^{[j_r]}\right)\right)\right)\right)$$

where we have denoted, for any LWE ciphertext c,

$$F_j(c) := \mathrm{LWE}_s^{n,q,2N}\left(f_{v^{\log N-j-1}}(\tilde\varphi_s(c))\right), \quad \widetilde{F}_j(c) := \mathrm{LWE}_s^{n,q,2N}\left(f_{\tilde v^{\log N-j-1}}(\tilde\varphi_s(c))\right)$$

and

$$\widehat{F}(c) := \mathrm{LWE}_s^{n,q,3}\left(f_{\hat v}(\tilde\varphi_s(c))\right)$$

with $\tilde v^\kappa$ and $\hat v$ obtained from the following adaptations of Formula (4.7):

$$\tilde v_0^\kappa = \ldots = \tilde v_{\tilde\alpha}^\kappa = 0, \quad \tilde v_{\tilde\alpha+1}^\kappa = \ldots = \tilde v_{N-\tilde\alpha-1}^\kappa = -2^\kappa, \quad \tilde v_{N-\tilde\alpha}^\kappa = \ldots = \tilde v_{N-1}^\kappa = 0, \tag{4.12}$$

$$\hat v_0 = \ldots = \hat v_{\tilde\alpha} = 0, \quad \hat v_{\tilde\alpha+1} = \ldots = \hat v_{N-\tilde\alpha-1} = -1, \quad \hat v_{N-\tilde\alpha} = \ldots = \hat v_{N-1} = 0. \tag{4.13}$$

The corresponding algorithm is illustrated in Fig. 5, in a special case.

Remark 4. Note that the factors 2^j used here could be replaced by other choices. This one is optimal in the context of the sign but is not compatible with some other piecewise constant functions.

The following proposition states the conditions under which our algorithm works.

Proposition 5. *Let $3 \le \bar p < p$ be odd integers and let ε be given by (4.5), where the integer α satisfies (4.6). Let $\mu \in \mathbb{Z}_p$ and consider encryptions of its CRT components $c_i = \mathrm{LWE}_s^{n,q,p_i}(\mu_i)$. Consider the sequence $c^{[r]}$, for $r = 0, \ldots, r_{max} = 1 + \left\lfloor \log_{\bar p}\left(\frac{p}{\bar p+1}\right)\right\rfloor$ defined by (4.1). Assume that (4.3) is satisfied for all r and that each LWE ciphertext S_i defined in Algorithm 1 as an argument of a function $\widetilde{F}_j$ or of $\widehat{F}$ satisfies the estimate*

$$|2N\,\mathrm{Err}(S_i)/q + \delta(S_i)| \le N/2^{m+1} - 1. \tag{4.14}$$

Then Algorithm 1 provides an $\mathrm{LWE}_s^{n,q,3}(\mathrm{sign}(\mu))$ ciphertext with an error bounded independently of the c_i's.

Algorithm 1. Homomorphic determination of the sign

For $r = 0, \ldots, m^\ell - 1$ **do**

$\quad c^{[r]} = \sum_{i=1}^{k} [\bar{p}^r \widehat{p}_i^{-1}]_{p_i} c_i \quad$ with $c_i \in \mathbb{Z}_{2N}^{n+1}$

End

$S_0 = 0$

For $r_0 = 0, \ldots, m - 1$ **do**

$\quad S_1 = 0$

$\quad$ **For** $r_1 = 0, \ldots, m - 1$ **do**

$\qquad \cdots$

$\qquad S_{\ell-2} = 0$

$\qquad$ **For** $r_{\ell-2} = 0, \ldots, m - 1$ **do**

$\qquad\quad S_{\ell-1} = 0$

$\qquad\quad$ **For** $r_{\ell-1} = 0, \ldots, m - 1$ **do**

$\qquad\qquad r = r_{\ell-1} + m r_{\ell-2} + \ldots + m^{\ell-2} r_1 + m^{\ell-1} r_0$

$\qquad\qquad S_{\ell-1} = S_{\ell-1} + F_{r_{\ell-1}}(c^{[r]})$

$\qquad\quad$ **End**

$\qquad\quad S_{\ell-2} = S_{\ell-2} + \widetilde{F}_{r_{\ell-2}}(S_{\ell-1})$

$\qquad \cdots$

$\qquad S_1 = S_1 + \widetilde{F}_{r_1}(S_2)$

$\quad$ **End**

$\quad S_0 = S_0 + \widetilde{F}_{r_0}(S_1)$

End

Return $\widehat{F}(S_0)$

Proof. Thanks to Propositions 1 and 4, and by (4.4), we already know that the innermost loop, the only one that involves g_ε, is correct. Moreover, each S_i to be bootstrapped in the next steps with the function $g_{\widetilde{\varepsilon}}$ is an $\text{LWE}_s^{n,q,2N}(\Sigma_i)$ ciphertext, where Σ_i is under the form

$$\Sigma_i = \sum_{j=0}^{m-1} 2^{\log N - j - 1} \xi_j \qquad \text{with} \quad \xi_j \in \{-1, 0, 1\}.$$

These values belong to the set

$$\frac{N}{2^m} \mathbb{Z}_{2^{m+1}-1} = \{0, \pm N/2^m, \pm 2N/2^m, \pm 3N/2^m, \ldots, \pm (2^m - 1)N/2^m\}.$$

Hence, owing to the formulae (4.12) or (4.13) of the test-polynomials $v(X)$ used in this bootstrap, only three cases have to be examined:

- if $\Sigma_i = 0$, then $\widetilde{F}_j(S_j)$ is a correct bootstrap if $|\widetilde{\varphi}_s(S_i)| \leq \widetilde{\alpha}$;
- if $\Sigma_i > 0$, then $\widetilde{F}_j(S_j)$ is a correct bootstrap if $\widetilde{\alpha} + 1 \leq \widetilde{\varphi}_s(S_i) \leq N - \widetilde{\alpha} - 1$;
- if $\Sigma_i < 0$, then $\widetilde{F}_j(S_j)$ is a correct bootstrap if $-N + \widetilde{\alpha} + 1 \leq \widetilde{\varphi}_s(S_i) \leq -\widetilde{\alpha} - 1$.

Since $\widetilde{\alpha} = N/2^{m+1}$, it can be observed that each of these three conditions is satisfied when (4.14) is fulfilled.

$$
\begin{array}{cccc}
c^{[0]} \quad c^{[1]} & c^{[2]} \quad c^{[3]} & c^{[4]} \quad c^{[5]} & c^{[6]} \quad c^{[7]} \\
\downarrow \quad \downarrow & \downarrow \quad \downarrow & \downarrow \quad \downarrow & \downarrow \quad \downarrow \\
F_0(c^{[0]}) + F_1(c^{[1]}) & F_0(c^{[2]}) + F_1(c^{[3]}) & F_0(c^{[4]}) + F_1(c^{[5]}) & F_0(c^{[6]}) + F_1(c^{[7]}) \\
= & = & = & = \\
S_2^{(0)} & S_2^{(1)} & S_2^{(2)} & S_2^{(3)} \\
\downarrow & \downarrow & \downarrow & \downarrow \\
\widetilde{F}_0(S_2^{(0)}) \quad + \quad \widetilde{F}_1(S_2^{(1)}) & & \widetilde{F}_0(S_2^{(2)}) \quad + \quad \widetilde{F}_1(S_2^{(3)}) \\
= & & = \\
S_1^{(0)} & & S_1^{(1)} \\
\downarrow & & \downarrow \\
\widetilde{F}_0(S_1^{(0)}) \quad + \quad \widetilde{F}_1(S_1^{(1)}) \\
= \\
S_0 \\
\downarrow \\
\widehat{F}(S_0)
\end{array}
$$

Fig. 5. Computation of the sign function for $m = 2$ and $\ell = 3$: each arrow represents a bootstrap.

4.4 Correctness of the Associated Sign Function for a Specific Implementation of Bootstrap

In this subsection, we show that our method is of practical interest by estimating its probability of success in a typical implementation. We shall consider the TFHE bootstrapping introduced in [11,12], extended to messages in the discrete tori $\mathbb{T}_{p_i} = \frac{1}{p_i}\mathbb{Z}_{p_i}$. In order to make our Proposition 1 more precise, let us make a few assumptions. We refer to [12] (see e.g. Algorithm 1 in this paper) for the definition of the parameters B_g and ℓ_g involved in the gadget decomposition (and, also, we only consider the case where the associated $k_g = 1$). We assume that the keys are binary for simplicity and that the ciphertext to be boostrapped is in $\text{LWE}_{\tilde{s}}^{N,q}$ for some parameters N and q. If $\mathbb{B}$ denotes the set $\{0,1\}$, the vectorial secret keys for LWE ciphertexts belong to $\mathbb{B}^N$ and the polynomial secret keys for RLWE ciphertexts belong to $\mathbb{B}[X]/(X^N + 1)$, where we recall that N is a power-of-two.

Before performing a blind rotation on an $\text{LWE}_{\tilde{s}}^{N,q}$ encryption, a keyswitching is usually applied to bring this ciphertext to an $\text{LWE}_s^{n,q}$ one for some smaller n and key $s \in \mathbb{B}^n$. The deviation term $\delta(c)$ in Proposition 1 comes from rounding the mask $(a_i)_{i=1,\dots,n}$ of the $\text{LWE}_s^{n,q}$ ciphertext $c = (a, b)$ at the beginning of the blind rotate process. More precisely, an instanciation of blind rotation leads to[9]

$$
2N\varphi_s(c)/q + \delta(c) = \left\lfloor 2Nb/q - \frac{1}{2}\sum_{i=1}^{n}\delta_i \right\rceil - \sum_{i=1}^{n}\lceil 2Na_i/q \rceil \, s_i,
$$

---

[9] The trick of substracting the term $\frac{1}{2}\sum_{i=1}^{n}\delta_i$ to $2Nb/q$ before rounding improves the total rounding error.

where we have denoted $\delta_i = 2Na_i/q - \lfloor 2Na_i/q \rfloor$. Since $b = \sum_i a_i s_i + \varphi_s(c)$, we compute

$$\delta(c) = \left\lfloor \sum_{i=1}^{n}(s_i - 1/2)\delta_i + 2N\varphi_s(c)/q \right\rceil - 2N\varphi_s(c)/q,$$

and denoting $\gamma = -\sum_{i=1}^{n}(s_i - 1/2)\delta_i - 2N\varphi_s(c)/q$, this yields

$$\delta(c) = \sum_{i=1}^{n}(s_i - 1/2)\delta_i + \gamma - \lceil \gamma \rceil.$$

Since we have assumed that $s_i \in \{0,1\}$ for all i, we finally get the estimate

$$|\delta(c)| \leq \frac{1}{2}\left(1 + \sum_{i=1}^{n}|2Na_i/q - \lfloor 2Na_i/q \rfloor|\right). \tag{4.15}$$

Moreover, following, [] the variance of the refreshed error of the output $c' = \text{LWE}_s^{N,q,p'}$ (we take $q' = q$) can be computed as[10]

$$\sigma_{out}^2 := \text{Var}(\text{Err}(c')) = n\left(1 + \frac{N}{2}\right)q^2\frac{B_g^{-2\ell_g}}{12} + 2nN\ell_g\frac{B_g^2 + 2}{12}\sigma_{BK}^2,$$

where σ_{BK} is the standard deviation for the noise sampled to generate the RGSW bootstrap keys. Finally, we shall make the standard assumption [13,25] that the Central Limit Theorem applies and that the output error $\text{Err}(c')$ can be well approximated by a gaussian random variable.

A very conservative estimate of the correctness of the sign function can be obtained by computing the probability that all the bootstraps involved in Algorithm 1 are correct. Assuming that all the $e_i = \text{Err}(c_i)$ associated to the c_i's involved in formula (4.1) are independent sub-gaussian random variables with parameters $\sigma(e_i)$, and that the terms in the sum in the right-hand side of (4.15) are uniformly distributed independent random variables and as such sub-gaussian with parameter $1/(2\sqrt{3})$, we may obtain the following upper bound of the probability of getting an incorrect sign by computing the probability that at least one condition on the errors in Proposition 5 is not satisfied. In other terms, we have

$$\mathbb{P}_{fail} \leq \mathbb{P}_{fr} + \mathbb{P}_{or} \tag{4.16}$$

where $\mathbb{P}_{fr}$ is the probability that one of the bootstrap of the innermost loop of Algorithm 1 fails and $\mathbb{P}_{or}$ is the probability that one of the bootstrap of the outer loops of Algorithm 1 fails.

---

[10] We assume here that B_g is even.

Lemma 2. *Assuming that all the $e_i = Err(c_i), i = 1, \ldots, k$ are independent sub-gaussian random variables with parameters $\sigma(e_i)$, and that each rounding error term in (4.15) is sub-gaussian with parameter $1/(2\sqrt{3})$, we have*

$$\mathbb{P}_{fr} \leq 2 \sum_{r=0}^{r_{max}} \exp\left(-(\varepsilon - 1/(2N))^2/(8\sigma_r^2)\right) \qquad (4.17)$$

where

$$\sigma_r^2 = \sum_{i=1}^{k} [\bar{p}^r \widehat{p_i}^{-1}]_{p_i}^2 \left(\sigma(e_i)/q\right)^2 + n/(192N^2) + \sigma_{out,ks}^2, \qquad r = 0, \ldots, r_{max}, \qquad (4.18)$$

and where $\sigma_{out,ks}$ is the standard deviation of the keyswitch amplification error, i.e. the additional error generated after transforming an encryption $\mathrm{LWE}_{\tilde{s}}^{N,q}$ into an encryption $\mathrm{LWE}_{s}^{n,q}$. We recall that

$$\sigma_{out,ks}^2 = \frac{N}{2} \frac{B_{ks}^{-2\ell_{ks}}}{12} + N\ell_{ks}\frac{B_{ks}^2 + 2}{12}\sigma_{ks}^2,$$

where σ_{ks} is the switching key and where B_{ks} and ℓ_{ks} are the usual parameters in a keyswitching operation.

Moreover, assuming that the sums obtained in the outer loops of Algorithm 1 and used as input of further bootstraps are LWE ciphertexts whose errors are independent sub-gaussian variables with common parameter $\sqrt{m}\sigma_{out}$, we have

$$\mathbb{P}_{or} \leq \frac{2r_{max}}{m-1} \exp\left(-(1/2^m - 1/N)^2/(32\widetilde{\sigma}_r^2)\right) \qquad (4.19)$$

where

$$\widetilde{\sigma}_r^2 = m\sigma_{out}^2/q^2 + n/(192N^2) + \sigma_{out,ks}^2.$$

Proof. The first statement (4.17) follows from the upper-bound

$$\mathbb{P}_{fr} \leq \sum_{r=0}^{r_{max}} \mathbb{P}\left(|Err(c^{[r]})/q + \delta(c^{[r]})/(2N)| \geq \varepsilon/2\right)$$

and from Markov's inequality. For the second statement, we have to estimate from above the probability $\mathbb{P}_{incbo}$ that one bootstrap $\widetilde{F}_{r_i}(S_i), r_i \in \{0, \ldots, m-1\}$, of a sum S_i involved in the outer loops of Algorithm 1 is incorrect. Recall that each S_i is of the form $S_i = e + \sum_{j=0}^{m-1} 2^{\log N - j - 1}\xi_j$, where the ξ_j's take their values in $\{\pm 1, 0\}$ and e is a sub-gaussian variable with parameter $\sqrt{m}\sigma_{out}$. According to Proposition 5, we have

$$\mathbb{P}_{incbo} \leq \mathbb{P}\left(|e/q + \delta(S_i)/(2N)| \geq 1/2^{m+2}\right)$$

and using again Markov's inequality yields (4.19). Note that the number of such bootstraps is

$$m^{\ell-1} + m^{\ell-2} + \ldots + m^1 + m^0 = \frac{r_{max}}{m-1}.$$

An Example

For instance, consider the situation where

$$p = 7 \times 11 \times 13 \times 17 \times 19 \times 23 \times 25 \times 27 = 5019589575 > 2^{32}$$

and $\bar{p} = 13$. We take $m = 3$, $\ell = 2$ and compute $r_{max} = 8$. Maximizing (4.6), we obtain $\alpha = 36$.

We compute successively the Bezout coefficients associated with $(p_i, p/p_i)$ for $i = 1, \ldots, 8$ and the growth factors in (4.18). We have the following table:

p_j	7	11	13	17	19	23	25	27	$(\sum_j [\bar{p}^r \widehat{p}_j^{-1}]_{p_j})^2$
$[\widehat{p}_j^{-1}]_{p_j}$	2	3	-2	1	4	6	-3	5	104
$[13\widehat{p}_j^{-1}]_{p_j}$	-2	-5	0	-4	-5	9	11	11	393
$[13^2\widehat{p}_j^{-1}]_{p_j}$	2	1	0	-1	-8	2	-7	8	187
$[13^3\widehat{p}_j^{-1}]_{p_j}$	-2	2	0	4	-9	3	9	-4	211
$[13^4\widehat{p}_j^{-1}]_{p_j}$	2	4	0	1	-3	-7	-8	2	147
$[13^5\widehat{p}_j^{-1}]_{p_j}$	-2	-3	0	-4	-1	1	-4	-1	48
$[13^6\widehat{p}_j^{-1}]_{p_j}$	2	5	0	-1	6	-10	-2	-13	339
$[13^7\widehat{p}_j^{-1}]_{p_j}$	-2	-1	0	4	2	8	-1	-7	139
$[13^8\widehat{p}_j^{-1}]_{p_j}$	2	-2	0	1	7	-11	12	-10	423

As cryptographic parameters, let us take the following values, corresponding to a security[11] of $\lambda = 80$ bits. For simplicity in this example, we assume that $n = N$ so that the contribution of the keyswitching can be removed.

N	q	σ_{BK}	B_g	ℓ_g
1024	2^{64}	1.3×10^7	2^{13}	2

We assume moreover that the ciphertexts c_i have been obtained by a bootstrap with the same parameters, i.e. for $i = 1, \ldots, k$, we take $\sigma(e_i) = \sigma_{out}$. This set of parameters yields

$$\sigma_{out}^2/q^2 = 2.14 \times 10^{-11}, \quad \widetilde{\sigma}_r = 5.09 \times 10^{-6}, \quad \mathbb{P}_{fr} \leq 1.19 \times 10^{-12} \quad \mathbb{P}_{or} \leq 7.25 \times 10^{-41}$$

so, finally,

$$\mathbb{P}_{fail} \leq 1.2 \times 10^{-12}.$$

This proves the efficiency of our method. Note that the number of bootstraps involved in one homomorphic evaluation of the sign is $r_{max} + 1 + \frac{r_{max}}{m-1} = 13$ here, which is less than an homomorphic multiplication (which can be done with $2k = 16$ bootstraps).

5 Performance Results

In the next tableaux, we give the computational times of the sign determination for integers of various sizes (from 8 bits to 64 bits). In order to emphasize the global interest of the RNS representation which is very beneficial for a

---

[11] According to the lattice estimator https://github.com/malb/lattice-estimator.

multi-threaded execution, we also include the computational times of elementary operations $+, \times$ obtained in our implementation[12]. The set of parameters used is obviously identical for all operations $\times, =, \text{Sign}, +$ in each line of Figs. 6 and 7. All the cleartext numbers under consideration are integers with various numbers of bits, from 16 to 64, and all computations are made on an average laptop. Note that for the sake of better readability the algorithm is used here with the same values $m = 3$ and $\ell = 2$ for all benchmarks. Better performances are obtained by optimizing the parameters in each situation (for a given security parameter, given size of integers and given error probability) and this work is ongoing. For instance, as stated in the abstract, our algorithm delivers a correct result with a probability error below 10^{-12} and a security of 128 bits in less than 100 ms for 32-bit integers.

Type	Security	$\mathbb{P}_{\text{fail}}$	$\times$	$=$	Sign	$+$
$U8$	80 bits	$1.e-5$	$7.96\,ms$	$14.74\,ms$	$40.02\,ms$	$5.92\,\mu s$
$U8$	80 bits	$1.e-9$	$8.59\,ms$	$15.69\,ms$	$43.19\,ms$	$5.89\,\mu s$
$U8$	80 bits	$1.e-12$	$8.93\,ms$	$16.11\,ms$	$44.63\,ms$	$5.91\,\mu s$
$U8$	100 bits	$1.e-5$	$18.18\,ms$	$33.78\,ms$	$92.10\,ms$	$5.93\,\mu s$
$U8$	100 bits	$1.e-9$	$19.85\,ms$	$36.56\,ms$	$98.23\,ms$	$5.92\,\mu s$
$U8$	100 bits	$1.e-12$	$16.40\,ms$	$26.34\,ms$	$91.16\,ms$	$8.97\,\mu s$
$U8$	128 bits	$1.e-5$	$26.56\,ms$	$48.85\,ms$	$132.7\,ms$	$14.02\,\mu s$
$U8$	128 bits	$1.e-9$	$28.62\,ms$	$50.70\,ms$	$137.35\,ms$	$14.05\,\mu s$
$U8$	128 bits	$1.e-12$	$27.98\,ms$	$51.29\,ms$	$138.33\,ms$	$13.98\,\mu s$
$U16$	80 bits	$1.e-5$	$17.91\,ms$	$15.50\,ms$	$42.38\,ms$	$11.91\,\mu s$
$U16$	80 bits	$1.e-9$	$18.37\,ms$	$16.45\,ms$	$46.01\,ms$	$11.79\,\mu s$
$U16$	80 bits	$1.e-12$	$20.25\,ms$	$17.82\,ms$	$50.11\,ms$	$11.95\,\mu s$
$U16$	100 bits	$1.e-5$	$38.78\,ms$	$34.62\,ms$	$94.76\,ms$	$11.96\,\mu s$
$U16$	100 bits	$1.e-9$	$52.55\,ms$	$46.54\,ms$	$126.62\,ms$	$11.93\,\mu s$
$U16$	100 bits	$1.e-12$	$47.52\,ms$	$40.75\,ms$	$108.58\,ms$	$14.89\,\mu s$
$U16$	128 bits	$1.e-5$	$35.52\,ms$	$54.46\,ms$	$151.95\,ms$	$20.93\,\mu s$
$U16$	128 bits	$1.e-9$	$60.09\,ms$	$52.47\,ms$	$145.40\,ms$	$28.18\,\mu s$
$U16$	128 bits	$1.e-12$	$61.62\,ms$	$53.56\,ms$	$145.91\,ms$	$28.16\,\mu s$

Fig. 6. Computation times on milliseconds (except for the addition in microseconds)

Appendix

The sign of $\mu \in \mathbb{Z}_p$ can not be determined from the signs of its components $(\mu_1, \dots, \mu_k)$. This can be easily seen on the following example with $k = 2$, $p_1 = 3$ and $p_2 = 5$: both $2 \in \mathbb{Z}_{15}$ and $7 \in \mathbb{Z}_{15}$ have positive signs, while their

---

[12] Our code includes here a keyswitch from $(N + 1)$-dimensional LWEs to $(n + 1)$-dimensional LWEs where n depends on the security parameter (in practice, $460 \leq n \leq 600$).

Type	Security	$\mathbb{P}_{\text{fail}}$	$\times$	$=$	Sign	$+$
$U32$	80 bits	$1.e-5$	$7.96\,ms$	$14.74\,ms$	$40.02\,ms$	$5.92\,\mu s$
$U32$	80 bits	$1.e-9$	$8.59\,ms$	$15.69\,ms$	$43.19\,ms$	$5.89\,\mu s$
$U32$	80 bits	$1.e-12$	$8.93\,ms$	$16.11\,ms$	$44.63\,ms$	$5.91\,\mu s$
$U32$	100 bits	$1.e-5$	$18.18\,ms$	$33.78\,ms$	$92.10\,ms$	$5.93\,\mu s$
$U32$	100 bits	$1.e-9$	$19.85\,ms$	$36.56\,ms$	$98.23\,ms$	$5.92\,\mu s$
$U32$	100 bits	$1.e-12$	$16.40\,ms$	$26.34\,ms$	$71.16\,ms$	$8.97\,\mu s$
$U32$	128 bits	$1.e-5$	$26.56\,ms$	$48.85\,ms$	$132.7\,ms$	$14.02\,\mu s$
$U32$	128 bits	$1.e-9$	$28.62\,ms$	$50.70\,ms$	$137.35\,ms$	$14.05\,\mu s$
$U32$	128 bits	$1.e-12$	$27.98\,ms$	$51.29\,ms$	$138.33\,ms$	$13.98\,\mu s$
$U64$	80 bits	$1.e-5$	$17.91\,ms$	$15.50\,ms$	$42.38\,ms$	$11.91\,\mu s$
$U64$	80 bits	$1.e-9$	$18.37\,ms$	$16.45\,ms$	$46.01\,ms$	$11.79\,\mu s$
$U64$	80 bits	$1.e-12$	$20.25\,ms$	$17.82\,ms$	$50.11\,ms$	$11.95\,\mu s$
$U64$	100 bits	$1.e-5$	$38.78\,ms$	$34.62\,ms$	$94.76\,ms$	$11.96\,\mu s$
$U64$	100 bits	$1.e-9$	$52.55\,ms$	$46.54\,ms$	$126.62\,ms$	$11.93\,\mu s$
$U64$	100 bits	$1.e-12$	$47.52\,ms$	$40.75\,ms$	$108.58\,ms$	$14.89\,\mu s$
$U64$	128 bits	$1.e-5$	$35.52\,ms$	$54.46\,ms$	$151.95\,ms$	$20.93\,\mu s$
$U64$	128 bits	$1.e-9$	$60.09\,ms$	$52.47\,ms$	$145.40\,ms$	$28.18\,\mu s$
$U64$	128 bits	$1.e-12$	$61.62\,ms$	$53.56\,ms$	$145.91\,ms$	$28.16\,\mu s$

Fig. 7. Computation times in milliseconds (except for the addition in microseconds)

components are respectively $(-1, 2) \in \mathbb{Z}_3 \times \mathbb{Z}_5$ and $(1, 2) \in \mathbb{Z}_3 \times \mathbb{Z}_5$ with signs $(-1, 1)$ and $(1, 1)$ respectively. This shows that the value of μ has to some extent to be computed through Φ^{-1} in order to evaluate its sign: denoting $c_i = (a_i, b_i)$ and $c = (a, b)$, we have

$$
\begin{aligned}
b - \langle a, s \rangle &= \sum_{i=1}^{k} [\widehat{p}_i^{-1}]_{p_i} b_i - \sum_{i=1}^{k} \langle [\widehat{p}_i^{-1}]_{p_i} a_i, s \rangle = \sum_{i=1}^{k} [\widehat{p}_i^{-1}]_{p_i} (b_i - \langle a_i, s \rangle) \\
&= \sum_{i=1}^{k} [\widehat{p}_i^{-1}]_{p_i} ((q/p_i)\mu_i + \mathrm{Err}(c_i)) \bmod q \\
&= (q/p) \sum_{i=1}^{k} \widehat{p}_i^{-1} \widehat{p}_i \, \mu_i + \sum_{i=1}^{k} [\widehat{p}_i^{-1}]_{p_i} \mathrm{Err}(c_i) \bmod q \\
&= (q/p)\mu + \mathrm{Err}(c) \bmod q,
\end{aligned}
$$

with

$$
\mathrm{Err}(c) = \sum_{i=1}^{k} [\widehat{p}_i^{-1}]_{p_i} \mathrm{Err}(c_i).
$$

In practice, the errors $\mathrm{Err}(c_i)$, for $i = 1, \ldots, k$, are the sum of a fixed rational (the rounding error) and of a sub-gaussian random variable e_i with parameter $\sigma(e_i)$, that is to say such that

$$
\mathbb{E}(e^{\lambda e_i}) \leq e^{\frac{1}{2}\sigma^2(e_i)\lambda^2}.
$$

Neglecting rounding errors and using standard estimates, it is straightforward to show that the decryption of c in $\mathbb{Z}_p$ coincides with μ with probability

$$\mathrm{erf}\left(\frac{q}{2\sqrt{2}\sigma(e)p}\right)$$

with parameter $\sigma(e) = \sqrt{[\widehat{p_1}^{-1}]_{p_1}^2\sigma^2(e_1) + \ldots + ([\widehat{p_k}^{-1}]_{p_k}^2\sigma^2(e_k)}$. Now, assuming, for instance, that the parameters $\sigma(e_i) = \frac{q}{2\sqrt{2}p_i\theta}$ have all been adjusted so as to ensure a correct decryption in $\mathbb{Z}_{p_i}$ with a given probability $\mathrm{erf}(\theta)$, the probability that the decryption of μ fails can be bounded from below by

$$1 - \mathrm{erf}\left(\frac{q}{2\sqrt{2}\sigma p}\right) \geq \sqrt{\frac{e}{2\pi}}\,\exp\left(-\frac{2\theta^2 p_{max}^2}{kp^2}\right),$$

where $p_{max} = \max_{i=1,\ldots,k} p_i$. This bound shows that the decryption of c is incorrect with a probability higher than 0.5 for $(p_1, p_2, p_3, p_4, p_5, p_6, p_7, p_8) = (7, 11, 13, 17, 19, 23, 25, 27)$ and $1 - \mathrm{erf}(\theta) = 10^{-10}$ in the rings. This renders the determination of μ intractable as such and one should look for an algorithm to evaluate its sign without knowing it exactly.

References

1. A. Alexandru, A. Al Badawi, D. Micciancio and Y. Polyakov, *Application-Aware Approximate Homomorphic Encryption: Configuring FHE for Practical Use*, Cryptology ePrint Archive, Paper 2024/203, 2024, https://eprint.iacr.org/2024/203
2. J.-P. Bossuat, A. Costache, C. Mouchet, L. Nürnberger and J.R. Troncoso-Pastoriza, *Practical q-IND-CPA-D-Secure Approximate Homomorphic Encryption*, Cryptology ePrint Archive, Paper 2024/853, 2024, https://eprint.iacr.org/2024/853
3. F. Bourse, M. Minelli, M. Minihold, and Pascal Paillier, *Fast homomorphic evaluation of deep discretized neural networks*, Advances in Cryptology - CRYPTO, 483–512, Springer, 2018
4. F. Bourse, O. Sanders, and J. Traoré, *Improved secure integer comparison via homomorphic encryption*, Cryptographers' Track at the RSA Conference, 391–416, Springer, 2020
5. Carlton, R., Essex, A., Kapulkin, K.: Threshold properties of prime power subgroups with application to secure integer comparisons, Cryptographers' Track at the RSA Conference, 137–156. Springer, Heidelberg (2018)
6. P. Chartier, M. Koskas, M. Lemou, and F. Méhats, *Fully Homomorphic Encryption on large integers*, Cryptology ePrint Archive, 2024
7. P. Chartier, M. Koskas, M. Lemou, and F. Méhats, *Method for homomorphically determining the sign of a message by dilation, associated methods and devices*, Patent no WO2023242429 - 12/21/2023. Number and date of prority : FR2205957 - 17/06/2022
8. P. Chartier, M. Koskas, M. Lemou, and F. Méhats, Homomorphic encryption method and associated devices ans system. Patent no WO2022129979 - 06/23/2022. Number and date of priority : PCT/IB2020001147 - 12/18/2020

9. J. H. Cheon, D. Kim, and D. Kim, *Efficient homomorphic comparison methods with optimal complexity*, Proceedings of International Conference on the Theory and Application of Cryptology and Information Security, 221–256, 2020
10. H. Chen, R. Gilad-Bachrach, K. Han, Z. Huang, A. Jalali, K. Laine, and K. Lauter, *Logistic regression over encrypted data from fully homomorphic encryption*, Cryptology ePrint Archive, Report 2018/462, 2018
11. Chillotti, I., Gama, N., Georgieva, M., Izabachène, M.: Faster Fully Homomorphic Encryption: Bootstrapping in Less Than 0.1 Seconds. In: Cheon, J.H., Takagi, T. (eds.) ASIACRYPT 2016. LNCS, vol. 10031, pp. 3–33. Springer, Heidelberg (2016). https://doi.org/10.1007/978-3-662-53887-6_1
12. Chillotti, I., Gama, N., Georgieva, M., Izabachène, M.: TFHE: Fast fully homomorphic encryption over the torus. Journal of Cryptology **33**(1), 34–91 (2020)
13. A. Costache, B. R. Curtis, E. Hales, S. Murphy, T. Ogilvie and R. Player, *On the precision loss in approximate homomorphic encryption*, Cryptology ePrint Archive, Report 2022/162, 2022
14. Ducas, L., Micciancio, D.: FHEW: Bootstrapping Homomorphic Encryption in Less Than a Second. In: Oswald, E., Fischlin, M. (eds.) EUROCRYPT 2015. LNCS, vol. 9056, pp. 617–640. Springer, Heidelberg (2015). https://doi.org/10.1007/978-3-662-46800-5_24
15. C. Gentry, *Fully homomorphic encryption using ideal lattices*, 41st Annual ACM Symposium on Theory of Computing, 169–178. ACM Press, 2009
16. I. Iliashenko, and V. Zucca, *Faster homomorphic comparison operations for BGV and BFV*, Proceedings on Privacy Enhancing Technologies, 2021
17. M. Izabachène, R. Sirdey, and M. Zuber, *Practical fully homomorphic encryption for fully masked neural networks*, Cryptology and Network Security - 18th International Conference, CANS, 24–36. Springer, 2019
18. E. Lee, J.-W. Lee, J.-S. No, and Y.-S. Kim, *Minimax approximation of sign function by composite polynomial for homomorphic comparison*, IEEE Transactions on Dependable and Secure Computing, 2021
19. Lee, E., Lee, J.-W., Kim, Y.-S., No, J.-S.: Optimization of homomorphic comparison algorithm on RNS-CKKS scheme. IEEE Access **10**, 26163–26176 (2022)
20. Y. Lee, D. Micciancio, A. Kim, R. Choi, M. Deryabin, J. Eom, and D. Yoo, *Efficient FHEW Bootstrapping with Small Evaluation Keys, and Applications to Threshold Homomorphic Encryption*, Advances in Cryptology – EUROCRYPT 2023
21. B. Li, D. Micciancio, *On the Security of Homomorphic Encryption on Approximate Numbers*, In: Canteaut, A., Standaert, FX, (eds) Advances in Cryptology, EUROCRYPT 2021, Lecture Notes in Computer Science, vol 12696, Springer
22. B. Li, D. Micciancio, M. Schultz and J. Sorrell, *Securing Approximate Homomorphic Encryption Using Differential Privacy*, In: Dodis, Y., Shrimpton, T. (eds) Advances in Cryptology, CRYPTO 2022, Lecture Notes in Computer Science, vol 13507, Springer
23. Z. Liu, D. Micciancio, and Y. Polyakov, *Large-precision homomorphic sign evaluation using FHEW/TFHE bootstrapping*, IACR Cryptol. ePrint Arch., 2021/1337, 2021
24. D. Micciancio, and Y. Polyakov, *Bootstrapping in FHEW-like Cryptosystems*, Association for Computing Machinery, New York, NY, USA, 17–28, 2021
25. S. Murphy, R. Player, *A Central Limit Framework for Ring-LWE Decryption*, Cryptology ePrint Archive, Report 2019/452, 2019
26. H. Narumanchi, D. Goyal, N. Emmadi, and P. Gauravaram, *Performance analysis of sorting of fhe data: Integer-wise comparison vs bit-wise comparison*, 2017 IEEE

31st International Conference on Advanced Information Networking and Applications (AINA), 902–908, 2017

27. Regev, O.: On lattices, learning with errors, random linear codes, and cryptography. Journal of the ACM (JACM) **56**(6), 1–40 (2009)

28. R. Schwerdt, L. Benz, W. Beskorovajnov, S. Eilebrecht, J. Müller-Quade and A. Ottenhues, *Sender-binding Key Encapsulation*, Cryptology ePrint Archive, Paper 2023/127, 2023, https://eprint.iacr.org/2023/127

Low Communication Threshold Fully Homomorphic Encryption

Alain Passelègue$^{(\boxtimes)}$ and Damien Stehlé

CryptoLab Inc., Lyon, France
{alain.passelegue,damien.stehle}@cryptolab.co.kr

Abstract. This work investigates constructions of threshold fully homomorphic encryption with low communication, i.e., with small output ciphertexts and small partial decryption shares. In this context, we discuss in detail the technicalities for achieving full-fledged threshold FHE, and put forward limitations regarding prior works, including an attack against the recent construction of Boudgoust and Scholl [ASIACRYPT 2023]. In light of our observations, we generalize the definition of threshold fully homomorphic encryption by adding an algorithm which allows to introduce additional randomness in ciphertexts before they are decrypted by parties. In this setting, we are able to propose a construction which offers small ciphertexts and small decryption shares.

1 Introduction

Fully homomorphic encryption (FHE) [Gen09] allows to perform arbitrary computations on encrypted data. It has found numerous applications in cryptography. One of the vanilla applications is the delegation of heavy computation to a server: by encrypting data to the server, the server can perform the computation homomorphically on encrypted data to get an encryption of the result without learning any information about the raw input data nor the result. Yet, the data owner, who owns the FHE decryption key, can decrypt the evaluated ciphertext to get the plain result of the computation. Threshold fully homomorphic encryption [AJL+12, BGG+18] extends FHE in the multi-client setting: the decryption key is split between N parties so that to decrypt a ciphertext, each party must partially decrypt the ciphertext using its share of the key.[1] The plaintext is recovered by combining these partial decryptions. Threshold FHE has tremendous applications, including multi-party computation, universal thresholdizer, and delegation of computation over private data owned by multiple parties. In the latter scenario, each party can encrypt its data and upload it on a server. Anyone can ask the server to perform (homomorphic) computation over the joint data; yet, to learn the result of a computation, all parties must jointly decrypt the result, which allows parties to manage access to their data by possibly refusing decryption depending on the evaluated function.

---

[1] We focus on the N-out-of-N case of threshold FHE, in which all N parties must participate during decryption.

© International Association for Cryptologic Research 2025
K.-M. Chung and Y. Sasaki (Eds.): ASIACRYPT 2024, LNCS 15484, pp. 297–329, 2025.
https://doi.org/10.1007/978-981-96-0875-1_10

The most basic idea to turn an FHE scheme into a threshold scheme is as follows: FHE schemes have ciphertexts of the form $(\mathbf{a}, b)$ where $\mathbf{a} \in \mathbb{Z}_q^n$, and where $b = -\mathbf{a}^\mathsf{T}\mathbf{s} + \mu + e$ with $\mathbf{s} \in \mathbb{Z}_q^n$ being the secret key, μ the underlying plaintext, and e a small error term.[2] Decrypting such a ciphertext using $\mathbf{s}$ is done by computing $\mathbf{a}^\mathsf{T}\mathbf{s}$ and adding it to b to recover $\mu + e$ which is close to μ.[3] Transforming such a scheme into a threshold variant can be done by splitting the secret key $\mathbf{s}$ as $\mathbf{s} = \mathbf{s}_1 + \cdots + \mathbf{s}_N \bmod q$ and giving one share $\mathbf{s}_i$ of the key to each user P_i [BD10]. Decryption is then replaced by two algorithms (PartDec, FinDec). The first one is run by each party using its share of the key to compute a partial decryption share of the ciphertext, while the second one combines all partial decryption shares to recover the actual plaintext. At a high level, PartDec consists in computing $\mathsf{p}_i := \mathbf{a}^\mathsf{T}\mathbf{s}_i$, and $\mathbf{a}^\mathsf{T}\mathbf{s}$ is reconstructed in FinDec by adding all p_i's; $\mu + e$ is then recovered by computing $\mathbf{a}^\mathsf{T}\mathbf{s} + b$ as in the non-threshold case.

Obviously, this approach is not secure: each of P_i's partial decryption $\mathbf{a}^\mathsf{T}\mathbf{s}_i$ of a ciphertext $(\mathbf{a}, b)$ provides a linear equation in $\mathbf{s}_i$, therefore $\mathbf{s}_i$ can be recovered by Gaussian elimination given sufficiently many partial decryptions. An alternative way to see the problem is to observe that parties recover $\mu + e$ when decrypting, and then, if μ is known, they recover e. Given μ, e, and a ciphertext $(\mathbf{a}, \mathbf{a}^\mathsf{T}\mathbf{s} + \mu + e)$, one can then recover a linear equation $(\mathbf{a}, \mathbf{a}^\mathsf{T}\mathbf{s})$ in $\mathbf{s}$ and recover the secret key via Gaussian elimination. While this is not an issue in the non-threshold setting since decryption requires $\mathbf{s}$ anyway, the global secret key $\mathbf{s}$ should remain hidden to parties in the threshold setting. Hence, it is crucial that partial decryptions hide the value of the error term of the ciphertext e.

The solution proposed in [AJL+12, BGG+18] is to add a noise term $\mathfrak{d}_i$ to p_i, i.e., defining $\mathsf{p}_i := \mathbf{a}^\mathsf{T}\mathbf{s}_i + \mathfrak{d}_i$ where $\mathfrak{d}_i$ is an independent error term. Denoting $\mathfrak{d} := \sum_{i \in [N]} \mathfrak{d}_i$, the combination of partial shares during FinDec then allows to recover $\mu + e + \mathfrak{d}$ instead $\mu + e$. Regarding correctness of decryption, this is still fine as long as $e + \mathfrak{d}$ is small compared to μ and, hopefully, adding this error term now guarantees security by hiding e and therefore $\mathbf{s}$. The main question is then: *what is the minimal magnitude for $\mathfrak{d}_i$'s in order to guarantee security of the construction?* Ideally, one wants $\mathfrak{d}_i$ to be as small as possible, since the larger it gets, the larger one must set other parameters of the scheme to ensure correctness (and also to ensure security, which decreases as the ratio q/e increases).

Prior Works. Early works have shown that adding an exponential noise term allows to guarantee the security of the scheme. Indeed, consider $\mathfrak{d}_i$ of magnitude $\Omega(2^\lambda B)$ where λ denotes the security parameter and B is a bound on the magnitude of the error term e of the ciphertext $(\mathbf{a}, \mathbf{a}^\mathsf{T}\mathbf{s} + \mu + e)$ to be decrypted.

---

[2] The most efficient FHE instantiations actually rely on Ring-LWE, i.e., replace $\mathbf{a}, \mathbf{s}$, μ and e by ring elements a, s, μ and e. We use LWE notations in the introduction.

[3] The plaintext μ can be a scaled version of a message. An additional rounding operation removes the error term for exact schemes (e.g., BGV [BGV12], B/FV [Bra12, FV12], DM/CGGI [DM15, CGGI16], or discrete versions of CKKS [DMPS24, BCKS24, BKSS24]), while approximate schemes (CKKS [CKKS17]) keep the approximate result $\mu + e$, seeing e as part of the approximation error of the computation over $\mathbb{R}$ or $\mathbb{C}$.

Then, the distribution of $\mu + e + \mathfrak{d}$ is statistically close to that of $\mu + \mathfrak{d}$, which is independent of e. Security follows: even if parties $P_1, \ldots, P_{N-1}$ get corrupted by an attacker, the last partial decryption share p_N of P_N allows the attacker to recover $\mu + e + \mathfrak{d}$, which is statistically close to $\mu + \mathfrak{d}$. The latter can be sampled publicly given the result μ of the decryption. Hence, the attacker learns statistically nothing about e and therefore s, or equivalently s_N, remains hidden.

While this provides security, exponential noise flooding induces a significant overhead in terms of efficiency, since the scheme must be correct even for exponentially large decryption error terms. Notably, the partial decryption shares p_i's include an exponential error term and must hence be very large, leading to high communication cost between parties. Consequently, several recent works have tried to reduce the magnitude of $\mathfrak{d}$ in order to improve the efficiency of the construction. The main work in this area is a recent paper by Boudgoust and Scholl [BS23a], which aims to build threshold FHE using a security analysis based on the Rényi divergence. The Rényi divergence has proven to be a powerful tool to reduce the magnitude of noise terms required in security analyses in the context of lattice-based signatures [BLL+18]. Yet, for primitives whose security is based on indistinguishability-based games such as FHE, the Rényi divergence has not been very successful. This contrasts with signatures, whose unforgeability security notion is a search-based game.

Two other recent works [CSS+22, DWF22] have also attempted to provide constructions relying on analysis based on the Rényi divergence in order to reduce the magnitude of the noise term added during partial decryption. It turns out that none of these works provides a valid solution to the above problem. In [DWF22], the authors only claim an extremely weak security statement, where security holds only for a single partial decryption. In [CSS+22], the authors propose a security analysis based on so-called public sampleability and claim security for threshold FHE based on DM/CGGI with polynomially many decryption queries. The security claim is again rather weak, since the adversary is selective (the adversary must declare its encryption and evaluation queries before seeing challenge ciphertexts). Furthermore, their argument for public sampleability (see the proof of Theorem 2 in [CSS+22]) relies on a distribution for the randomness r which can depend on the error underlying an evaluated ciphertext. For public sampleability, this distribution should be independent of the challenge bit, but the error underlying an evaluated ciphertext could depend on the plaintexts involved in the computation (hence on the challenge bit) even though the result of the computation is independent of the challenge bit.

In [DDK+23], the authors provide an intermediate step to efficient threshold FHE, based on DM/CGGI, by proposing the following approach: practical parameters are used to encrypt and evaluate computation, but before partial decryption is performed, a ciphertext is passed through a "switch-n-squash" process. The latter bootstraps a ciphertext to sufficiently large parameters while keeping the noise small, so that it is possible to flood the noise during threshold decryption of the resulting (large) ciphertext. This allows to have half of the communication reduced (communication towards the server) but decryption shares remain large due to (exponential) noise flooding.

Finally, note that theoretical solutions to threshold FHE exist using generic MPC techniques (e.g., [BJKL21, Shi22] implies an N-out-of-N threshold FHE with $\mathsf{poly}(\lambda)$-size decryption shares), but none of these results achieves practical efficiency. However, focusing only on threshold PKE instead of FHE, a recent work by Micciancio and Suhl [MS23] provides an elegant solution (in the N-out-of-N threshold setting) from LWE via a careful analysis of the noise distributions. Our main construction follows a similar analysis as theirs, but for fully homomorphic encryption.

1.1 Our Contributions

First, we remark that only adding a small error term during partial decryption cannot succeed for some classical schemes (e.g., B/FV or CKKS). This is due to the error distribution during homomorphic computation and has already been observed in the context of IND-CPA-D security for CKKS [LMSS22]. Hence, to circumvent this issue, a natural direction is to further rely on techniques to sanitize the noise during homomorphic computation, such as relying on circuit-private FHE, as proposed in [BS23a]. Unfortunately, we show that the transform from [BS23a] fails to provide threshold security, by proposing a circuit-private FHE scheme which is insecure when plugged into their transform. In addition, relying on sanitization techniques (which induce randomized evaluation) rises a challenging question about the model: security of sanitization is guaranteed based on the (private) internal randomness of evaluation. Relying on randomized evaluation in the threshold setting then questions which party does the randomized evaluation, and what can we hope from this approach if the party doing the evaluation (and therefore knowing its internal randomness) is corrupted?

Based on these observations, we extend the definition of threshold FHE by adding an additional algorithm which allows an uncorrupted party (we assume it is a server) to process on evaluated ciphertexts before parties run partial decryption. This randomized operation, termed ServerDec, uses randomness unknown to parties. Our definition matches the standard threshold FHE definition when ServerDec is deterministic (or, equivalently, void).

We then propose a construction guaranteeing security in this setting. Our main construction is round optimal, and relies on two flooding steps: ServerDec adds an exponential noise to ciphertexts after evaluation, but also compresses them. Hence, ciphertexts fed to partial decryptions are small, and we prove that adding a very small noise in PartDec is sufficient for security. In the context of delegation of computation on a trusted server, this means that the communication from the server to the parties as well as between parties is small, even if exponential noise flooding is used on the server side.

We complete our work by providing a few more contributions in the full version of this paper. First, we propose a protocol designed for threshold delegation of computation over private data. It is not a threshold FHE scheme properly speaking: our protocol requires an additional round before partial decryption. A specific party (distinct from the server, but possibly one of the partial decryptors) needs to process the evaluated ciphertext before the other parties can run partial decryption. On the positive side, our protocol is only based on circuit-private (non-threshold) FHE and threshold public-key encryption. Hence it can avoid any (exponential) noise flooding by relying on circuit-private transforms (e.g., [DS16,BPMW16,Klu22,BI22]). Second, we describe connections between various security notions for FHE, notably an indistinguishability-based notion of threshold security, IND-CPA-D security, and a weak form of circuit-privacy.

1.2 Technical Overview

We start our technical overview by describing vulnerabilities in prior attempts to achieve threshold FHE with small partial decryption shares.

Our first observation is a direct generalization of known results in the context of the CKKS approximate FHE scheme. Recall that a CKKS ciphertext $(\mathbf{a}, b)$ with $b = \mathbf{a}^\mathsf{T}\mathbf{s} + \mu + e$ is decrypted by returning $\mu + e = b + \mathbf{a}^\mathsf{T}\mathbf{s}$. In [LM21], the authors show that decryption results can be exploited to mount so-called IND-CPA-D attacks, which simply exploit the fact that the decryption equation is a linear equation in $\mathbf{s}$. It is shown in [LMSS22] that adding a Gaussian noise $\mathfrak{d}$ to the decryption result $\mu + e$ allows to prevent such attacks, but the magnitude of the noise needs to be exponential in the security parameter. This was generalized to the threshold variant of CKKS in [KS23]. The attack exploits the fact that when multiplying two CKKS ciphertexts encrypting μ_0, μ_1 with error terms e_0, e_1, the error term of the resulting ciphertext is of the form $\mu_0 e_1 + \mu_1 e_0 + e'$ where $\|e'\| \ll \|\mu_0 e_1 + \mu_1 e_0\|$. Hence, the error distribution is highly-dependent on the underlying plaintexts. Two computations leading to the same result could therefore have vastly different error terms because they have different intermediate values, and hiding the bias during decryption requires to add an exponentially large noise term. We observe that in the context of threshold FHE, this attack does not exploit any specificity of CKKS. Since B/FV has identical noise propagation during homomorphic multiplications as CKKS, similar lower bounds on $\mathfrak{d}$ are also required to guarantee the security of threshold B/FV. Hence, it seems that, in general, only adding a small error term during partial decryption cannot be a solution to obtain threshold security. This motivates the use of sanitization, to make the noise of the result independent of the intermediate values.

An Attack Against the Boudgoust-Scholl Transform. In [BS23a], the authors show that a circuit-private FHE scheme can be turned into a threshold FHE scheme satisfying a one-way security notion by secret-sharing the secret key between parties and adding an error term of magnitude growing with Q_D to partial decryption, where Q_D is an upper bound on the number of decryptions made. Note that Q_D can be much lower than exponential in the security parameter. This is made possible by a security analysis based on the Rényi divergence, thanks to the fact that one-way security is a search-based security game. Then, the authors claim that the one-way threshold FHE schemes can be turned into an IND-CPA threshold FHE schemes via a transform based on hard-core bit predicates. We refer the reader to Sect. 3 for details about the transform.

Unfortunately, we show that this transform fails to provide IND-CPA security of the resulting threshold FHE scheme. We construct a circuit-private FHE scheme which results in an insecure threshold FHE scheme once plugged into the transform. Let us now provide a simplified overview of the attack. Consider a (circuit-private, threshold) FHE scheme whose ciphertexts have the form $(\mathbf{a}, \mathbf{a}^\mathsf{T}\mathbf{s} + \mu + e)$. The adversary's goal is to distinguish an encryption of μ_0 from an encryption of μ_1 given access to a (partial) decryption oracle. Let $(\mathbf{a}^*, b^*)$ denote the challenge ciphertext, where $b^* = \mathbf{a}^{*\mathsf{T}}\mathbf{s} + \mu^{(\beta)} + e^*$, where $\beta \in \{0, 1\}$ is the challenge bit. Further assume that it is possible, via the circuit-private evaluation, to transform a ciphertext encrypting a plaintext μ into another ciphertext encrypting the same plaintext, but whose error term e' is now of the form $\mu^\mathsf{T}\mathbf{s}$. We emphasize that this does not contradict circuit-privacy.[4] Our attack exploits the fact that the adversary can ask decryption of ciphertexts whose underlying plaintext depends on $\mathbf{a}^*$. Specifically, our attacker submits an encryption query whose plaintext encodes the most significant bits $[\mathbf{a}^*]$ of $\mathbf{a}^*$, applies the above circuit-private mechanism, and then asks for decryption of the result. Ignoring the small noise term added during partial decryption, the adversary then recovers an error term of the form $[\mathbf{a}^*]^\mathsf{T}\mathbf{s}$ with $[\mathbf{a}^*]$ being the most significant bits of $\mathbf{a}^*$, and putting the bits in the appropriate slots, it can then subtract the most significant bits of $\mathbf{a}^{*\mathsf{T}}\mathbf{s}$ from b^* to guess the value of β, leading to a distinguishing attack and contradicting the security of the transform. The attack being adaptive (it involves a query that depends on the challenge ciphertext), it might be possible to prove the security of the transform in a selective case, requiring the adversary to declare all its encryption and evaluation queries before seeing the challenge ciphertext. However, this model is much weaker than ours and than the model considered in [BS23a]. (At the time of writing, the current eprint version [BS23b] of [BS23a] considers selective security, the update having being made based on our notification of a proof flaw to the authors.)

A Generalized Definition of Threshold FHE. Given our first observation, it seems that sanitizing evaluated ciphertexts such that the error term is independent of the underlying plaintexts is a good start. This can be done by randomizing evaluation (e.g., using circuit-private evaluation), but it poses a definitional issue: in threshold FHE, any party can be corrupted, hence if a party performs the evaluation and gets corrupted, the randomness used during the evaluation is revealed to the adversary. In this case, there is no randomness in the evaluation and one cannot rely on it to argue about security, falling back to the prior issues.[5]

---

[4] Another issue that could be noticed is that e' has no reason to be small or might not even be properly defined. We assume this is not the case, only for simplifying the overview. Our actual attack avoids this issue.

[5] Note that relying on randomized evaluation also induces issues for some applications of threshold FHE to threshold cryptography. We provide an example with threshold signatures. The construction from [BGG+18] of threshold signature from threshold FHE requires parties to homomorphically evaluate a deterministic signing algorithm,

To circumvent this issue, we modify the definition of threshold FHE by adding an algorithm termed ServerDec. We define a threshold FHE scheme as a tuple (KeyGen, Enc, Eval, ServerDec, PartDec, FinDec) where KeyGen, Enc, Eval, PartDec, and FinDec are the usual threshold FHE algorithms. ServerDec is an additional, public-key, randomized algorithm, which can be performed on fresh or evaluated ciphertexts, and before partial decryption. It returns a ciphertext which fits the input format of PartDec. We suppose that ServerDec is executed by an uncorrupted party (e.g., the server) and uses randomness that remains unknown to all parties (and therefore to the adversary). We recover the prior syntax of threshold FHE when ServerDec is void (or equivalently, when it is deterministic). Note that, assuming homomomorphic evaluation is performed on an uncorrupted server as for delegation of computation, ServerDec can be performed directly following the Eval algorithm by the server. It may seem that it could then be integrated directly in Eval algorithm, but adding an explicit algorithm increases flexibility: for instance, ServerDec might convert ciphertext into a format which prevents further homomorphic evaluation. Also, adding an explicit ServerDec algorithm allows Eval to possibly remain deterministic. Finally, it allows to identify precisely the sources of security. Considering an adversary which corrupts all first $N - 1$ users, the security is guaranteed thanks to the remaining uncorrupted randomness, i.e., (1) the internal randomness of ServerDec, and (2) the randomness held by P_N (its share s_N of the key and its internal randomness of PartDec).

Speaking of security, we define a simulation-based security notion which closely follows prior notions from [BGG+18]. It is actually slightly stronger: adaptive queries and multi-hop evaluations are permitted. In short, our security notion requires that an adversary corrupting at most $N - 1$ parties should not learn any valuable information beyond the value of the underlying plaintext. This is modeled by the existence of an efficient simulator which takes as input information available to the adversary (the corrupted shares of the secret key as well as the plaintext underlying the ciphertext to be decrypted), and returns a simulated ciphertext as well as simulated partial decryption shares for all parties. We further require that the distribution of the simulation is indistinguishable from that of the real ciphertext produced by ServerDec and of the honestly generated partial decryption shares.

Double-Flood-and-Round Threshold FHE. Our main result is a construction of threshold FHE with low communication. We call our technique *Double-Flood-and-Round*. consider a generic FHE scheme whose ciphertexts have the above form $(\mathbf{a}, \mathbf{a}^\mathsf{T}\mathbf{s} + \mu + e)$ over $\mathbb{Z}_Q$ for some (exponentially) large modulus $Q = p \cdot q_{\mathsf{dec}}$ with $p = \Omega(2^\lambda)$ and $q_{\mathsf{dec}} = \mathsf{poly}(\lambda)$. The key generation, encryption, and evaluation algorithms are directly inherited from the under-

---

where the signing key is encrypted, and to reveal partial decryptions of the resulting ciphertext as partial signatures. For correctness, it is crucial that all parties evaluate the same signature (which is why it is chosen deterministic), but also the same ciphertext: randomized evaluation is not an option. However, an analysis based on Rényi divergence shows that a noise growing with Q_D suffices in this setting [ASY22].

lying FHE scheme, except that the secret key $\mathbf{s}$ is additively secret shared as $\mathbf{s} = \mathbf{s}_1 + \cdots + \mathbf{s}_N \bmod q_{\mathsf{dec}}$. Our technique is to first rely on exponential noise flooding to sanitize evaluated ciphertexts before partial decryption. This is done by the ServerDec algorithm. It takes a ciphertext $(\mathbf{a}, b) \in \mathbb{Z}_Q^n \times \mathbb{Z}_Q$ and returns a ciphertext $(\mathbf{a}', b') \in \mathbb{Z}_{q_{\mathsf{dec}}}^n \times \mathbb{Z}_{q_{\mathsf{dec}}}$ with:

$$\mathbf{a}' = \left\lfloor \frac{1}{p} \cdot \mathbf{a} \right\rceil_{\sigma_0} \quad , \quad b' = \left\lfloor \frac{1}{p} \cdot (b + \mathfrak{E}) \right\rceil_{\sigma_1} \quad .$$

where $\lfloor \cdot \rceil_\sigma$ denotes a randomized Gaussian rounding, which on input $x \in \mathbb{R}$ returns an element from $\mathcal{D}_{\mathbb{Z}, x, \sigma}$, and where $\mathfrak{E}$ is an exponentially large Gaussian noise term. Via standard noise flooding, the error term $\mathfrak{E}$ statistically hides the error term from b. Moreover, thanks to the rescaling to $q_{\mathsf{dec}} = \mathsf{poly}(\lambda)$, the ciphertext $(\mathbf{a}', b')$ sent to parties to be partially decrypted is only $(n+1) \log(q_{\mathsf{dec}})$-bit long. PartDec and FinDec then follow the same design as before.

We are able to prove that adding a very small amount of noise (whose magnitude is even independent of the number of decryptions Q_D) during partial decryption suffices to guarantee security. Specifically, a ciphertext $(\mathbf{a}', b')$ returned by ServerDec is of the form $(\mathbf{a}', \mathbf{a}'^{\mathsf{T}} \mathbf{s} + \mu + e')$, where e' has the form $\left\lfloor \frac{1}{p} \cdot (\mathbf{r}_0^{\mathsf{T}} \mathbf{s} + \mathfrak{E}) \right\rceil_{\sigma_1}$ with $\mathbf{r}_0$ denoting the (Gaussian) rounding error of $\mathbf{a}$, i.e., $\mathbf{r}_0 = \mathbf{a} - p \cdot \mathbf{a}'$. Therefore, following a similar approach as the proof of [BLP+13, Lemma 3.5], one can show that e' is statistically close from a Gaussian distribution whose standard deviation is $\sqrt{(\sigma_0 \|\mathbf{s}\|)^2 + (\sigma_{\mathsf{flood}}/p)^2 + \sigma_1^2}$. Assuming $\|\mathbf{s}\|$ is publicly known, this distribution is publicly sampleable. Thanks to this clean distribution of e', the rest of the security analysis is analogous to the recent proof of security of lattice-based threshold public-key encryption from [MS23].

A partial decryption of $(\mathbf{a}', b')$ computed by party P_N owning $\mathbf{s}_N$ is of the form $\mathbf{a}'^{\mathsf{T}} \mathbf{s}_i + \mathfrak{d}_i$. Sampling $\mathfrak{d}_N$ from $\mathcal{D}_{\mathbb{Z}, \eta}$, we then obtain that the view of an adversary corrupting all parties $P_1, \ldots, P_{N-1}$ (and therefore $\mathbf{s}_1, \ldots, \mathbf{s}_{N-1}$) is a triple $(\mathbf{a}', \mathbf{a}'^{\mathsf{T}} \mathbf{s} + \mu + e', \mathbf{a}'^{\mathsf{T}} \mathbf{s}_N + \mathfrak{d}_N)$, and adding $\mathbf{a}'^{\mathsf{T}} \sum_{i \in [N-1]} \mathbf{s}_N$ to the third term, it is then a triple of the form:

$$(\mathbf{a}', \mathbf{a}'^{\mathsf{T}} \mathbf{s} + \mu + e', \mathbf{a}'^{\mathsf{T}} \mathbf{s} + \mathfrak{d}_N) \ ,$$

with $e' \sim \mathcal{D}_{\mathbb{Z}, \sqrt{(\sigma_0 \|\mathbf{s}\|)^2 + (\sigma_{\mathsf{flood}}/p)^2 + \sigma_1^2}}$ and $\mathfrak{d}_N \sim \mathcal{D}_{\mathbb{Z}, \eta}$. Assuming LWE, we prove the above distribution is computationally indistinguishable from a triple:

$$(\mathbf{a}', b', b' + \mathfrak{h}) \ ,$$

where $\mathfrak{h} \leftarrow \mathcal{D}_{\sigma_{\mathfrak{h}}}$ with $\sigma_{\mathfrak{h}} := \sqrt{(\sigma_0 \|\mathbf{s}\|)^2 + (\sigma_{\mathsf{flood}}/p)^2 + \sigma_1^2 + \eta^2}$. The latter distribution is publicly sampleable if $\|\mathbf{s}\|$ is known, which does not hurt the analysis.

We further note that the partial decryption shares can be rounded, in order to lower communication (we do not use this for security). This explains why the construction is called double-round-and-flood. As a final remark, note that our input FHE ciphertexts are not compact by default, as they are defined over a large modulus Q. This problem is solved by relying on transciphering, e.g., using [BCK+23]. Hence, all communications are small, and only the steps run by the server are dealing with large ciphertexts.

Additional Contributions. We provide a few more contributions in the full version of this paper. First, in addition to our double-flood-and-round threshold FHE construction, we propose an alternative protocol for delegation of computation in a threshold setting which combines threshold public key encryption with circuit-private FHE. The idea is the following: users generate a threshold PKE public key and shares of the secret key. A special party, termed the *transcryptor*, which could be a trusted third party or one of the users, generates a pair of keys for a (circuit-private) FHE scheme and keeps the secret key for itself while revealing the public key to the server and all users. We assume that the transcryptorand the server are not colluding and that communications between every party is done via secure channels (e.g., using authenticated symmetric encryption). The server receives data from each user, encrypted under the FHE public key, via secure channels. Then, to perform a computation C over data $\mu_1, \ldots, \mu_N$, the server homomorphically evaluates $\mathsf{ThEnc_{tpk}} \circ \mathsf{C}$ on the data, where ThEnc denotes the encryption algorithm of the threshold PKE scheme and tpk its public key. The result is an FHE encryption of a threshold PKE encryption of $\mathsf{C}(\mu_1, \ldots, \mu_N)$. Then, this ciphertext is sent to the transcryptor, which decrypts it using the FHE secret key, and broadcasts $\mathsf{ThEnc_{tpk}}(\mathsf{C}(\mu_1, \ldots, \mu_N))$ to all users. This step adds a communication round compared to approaches based on threshold FHE in which the outputs of $\mathsf{ServerDec}$ computed by the server can be directly decrypted by all parties: it is not possible to avoid this additional round since the party (here, the server) performing evaluation must be independent of the FHE secret key holder. The protocol completes decryption of the result by having all parties jointly decrypting the threshold PKE ciphertext using their shares of the decryption key.

Assuming circuit-privacy of the underlying FHE scheme and simulation security of the underlying threshold PKE scheme, this protocol achieves simulation security. This is proven by simulating the view of an adversary by simulating $\mathsf{ThEnc_{tpk}}(\mathsf{C}(\mu_1, \ldots, \mu_N))$ using the threshold PKE simulator, and by replacing the ciphertext computed by the server with a fresh FHE encryption of this simulated threshold PKE ciphertext. Using circuit-private FHE directly allows to avoid the use of exponential noise flooding when circuit-privacy is achieved by mechanisms such as those from [DS16, BPMW16, Klu22, BI22].

We also complete the paper with discussions about various advanced security notions for FHE, including threshold security, IND-CPA-D security, and circuit-privacy, and provide connections between these notions.

Additional Related Work. In [ASY22], the authors construct threshold signatures based on threshold FHE techniques, again by relying on an analysis based on the Rényi divergence to reduce the magnitude of the added noise. We emphasize that the authors do not build a threshold FHE scheme, but only use FHE as a building block ina threshold flavour as part of their threshold signature construction. The reduction does not rely on the security of thresh-old FHE: the authors directly prove unforgeability (a search-based game) of the threshold signature by arguing that a small noise is sufficient.

2 Preliminaries

Notation. For any integer $N \geq 1$, we let $[N]$ denote the set $\{1, \ldots, N\}$. Vectors and matrices are written in bold letters. Vectors are column vectors. For a vector $\mathbf{x}$, we let $\mathbf{x}^\mathsf{T}$ denote its transpose. Given a finite set S, we let $U(S)$ denote the uniform distribution over S. The notation log refers to the natural logarithm. We use the notations $\mathsf{negl}(\lambda) = \lambda^{-\omega(1)}$ and $\mathsf{poly}(\lambda) = \lambda^{O(1)}$, where λ refers to the security parameter. For X, Y two distributions over a countable set Ω, the statistical distance between X and Y is defined as $\Delta(X, Y) := \frac{1}{2} \sum_{\omega \in \Omega} |\Pr[X = \omega] - \Pr[Y = \omega]|$.

For an integer $x \in \mathbb{Z}$, a modulus $q > 0$, and an integer $N > 0$, we let Share denote the standard additive secret sharing algorithm which takes as input (x, N, q), samples $(x_1, \ldots, x_{N-1}) \leftarrow U(\mathbb{Z}_q^{N-1})$, and returns $(x_1, \ldots, x_N)$ with $x_N = x - \sum_{i \in [N-1]} x_i \bmod q$.

2.1 Gaussian Distributions

Definitions. For an integer $n > 0$ and $\sigma > 0$, we define the n-dimensional Gaussian function $\rho_\sigma : \mathbb{R}^n \to (0, 1]$ as:

$$\rho_\sigma(\mathbf{x}) := \frac{1}{\sigma^n} \exp\left(\frac{-\pi \|\mathbf{x}\|^2}{\sigma^2}\right) \ .$$

We say that a random variable X over $\mathbb{R}^n$ follows the Gaussian distribution of standard deviation σ and center $\mathbf{c} \in \mathbb{R}^n$, denoted $\mathcal{D}_{\mathbf{c}, \sigma}$, if its density function is $\rho_X : \mathbf{x} \mapsto \rho_\sigma(\mathbf{x} - \mathbf{c})$. Similarly, a random variable X over $\mathbb{Z}^n$ follows the discrete Gaussian distribution of standard deviation parameter σ and center parameter $\mathbf{c}$ if the probability mass function of X is given by:

$$\Pr[X = \mathbf{x}] = \frac{\rho_\sigma(\mathbf{x} - \mathbf{c})}{\rho_\sigma(\mathbb{Z}^n)} \ .$$

We let $\mathcal{D}_{\mathbb{Z}^n, \sigma, \mathbf{c}}$ denote the n-dimensional discrete Gaussian distribution of standard deviation parameter σ and center parameter $\mathbf{c}$, and drop the index $\mathbf{c}$ if $\mathbf{c} = \mathbf{0}$. We also remark that $\mathcal{D}_{\mathbb{Z}^n, \sigma} = \mathcal{D}_{\mathbb{Z}, \sigma}^n$. The definition generalizes to shifted supports $\mathbb{Z}^n - \mathbf{c}$. These distributions are efficiently sampleable for all σ (see, e.g., [BLP+13, Section 5.1]).

Gaussian Rounding. In our main construction, we rely on randomized Gaussian roundings: for a standard deviation parameter $\sigma > 0$, we let $\lfloor \cdot \rceil_\sigma$ denote the Gaussian rounding operation which, on input a value $x \in \mathbb{R}$ returns a sample from $\mathcal{D}_{\mathbb{Z}, x, \sigma}$, or equivalently, samples z from $\mathcal{D}_{\mathbb{Z} - x, \sigma}$ and returns $x + z$. We extend it to vectors in a component-wise manner.

Elementary results. We prove the following smudging lemma in the full version of the paper.

Lemma 2.1. *Let $\sigma > 0$ and $c_0, c_1 \in \mathbb{Z}$. Then:*

$$\Delta\left(\mathcal{D}_{\mathbb{Z},c_0,\sigma}, \mathcal{D}_{\mathbb{Z},c_1,\sigma}\right) \leq O\left(\frac{|c_0 - c_1|}{\sigma}\right) .$$

In particular, for $\lambda > 0$, $c \in \mathbb{Z}$ and $\sigma > \Omega(c2^\lambda)$, we have $\Delta(\mathcal{D}_{\mathbb{Z},\sigma}, \mathcal{D}_{\mathbb{Z},c,\sigma}) < 2^{-\lambda}$.

We finally recall the following results about lattice Gaussians. They are expressed in terms of the smoothing parameter $\eta_\varepsilon(\mathbb{Z}^n)$, defined, for arbitrary $\varepsilon > 0$ and integer $n \geq 1$, as the smallest $s > 0$ such that $\rho_{1/s}(\mathbb{Z}^n \setminus \{\mathbf{0}\}) \leq \varepsilon$. By [GPV08, Lemma 3.1], we know that $\eta_\varepsilon(\mathbb{Z}^n) \leq \sqrt{\log(2n(1 + 1/\varepsilon))/\pi}$.

Lemma 2.2. *[Reg05, Corollary 3.10] Let $n \geq 1$, $\mathbf{a}, \mathbf{s} \in \mathbb{R}^n$ and $\sigma, \psi > 0$. Assume that $(1/\sigma^2 + (\|\mathbf{s}\|/\psi)^2)^{-1/2} \geq \eta_\varepsilon(\mathbb{Z}^n)$ for some $\varepsilon < 1/2$. Then, the distribution of $\mathbf{x}^\mathsf{T}\mathbf{s} + e$ where $\mathbf{x} \leftarrow \mathcal{D}_{\mathbb{Z}^n + \mathbf{a}, \sigma}$ and $e \leftarrow \mathcal{D}_\psi$ is at statistical distance at most 4ε from $\mathcal{D}_{\sqrt{(\sigma\|\mathbf{s}\|)^2 + \psi^2}}$.*

Lemma 2.3. *[Pei10, Theorem 3.1] Let $n \geq 1$ and $\sigma, \psi > 0$ with $\sigma \geq \eta_\varepsilon(\mathbb{Z}^n)$ for some $\varepsilon < 1/2$. If sampling $\mathbf{x} \leftarrow \mathcal{D}_\psi$ and $\mathbf{y} \leftarrow \mathcal{D}_{\mathbb{Z}^n - x, \sigma}$, the distribution of $\mathbf{x} + \mathbf{y}$ is at statistical distance at most 8ε from the discrete Gaussian distribution $\mathcal{D}_{\mathbb{Z}^n, \sqrt{\sigma^2 + \psi^2}}$.*

2.2   Hardness Assumptions

We first remind the standard LWE assumption.

Definition 2.4. *Let $n, m, q, \psi > 0$, and $\chi_\mathbf{s}$ denote a distribution over $\mathbb{Z}^n$. These parameters are function of the security parameter λ. The $\mathsf{LWE}_{n,m,q,\psi,\chi_\mathbf{s}}$ assumption states that the distributions*

$$(\mathbf{A}, \mathbf{As} + \mathbf{e}) \quad and \quad (\mathbf{A}, \mathbf{u})$$

are computationally indistinguishable, where $\mathbf{A} \leftarrow U(\mathbb{Z}_q^{m \times n})$, $\mathbf{s} \leftarrow \chi_\mathbf{s}^n$, $\mathbf{e} \leftarrow \mathcal{D}_{\mathbb{Z}^m, \psi}$ and $\mathbf{u} \leftarrow U(\mathbb{Z}_q^m)$.

Our main construction relies on the following yaLWE assumption (yet another LWE assumption), which is implied by the standard LWE assumption, as we explain below. It combines the Reused-**A** LWE and Known-Norm LWE assumptions considered in [MS23].

Definition 2.5. *Let $n, m, q, \sigma, \eta > 0$ and $\chi_\mathbf{s}$ denote a distribution over $\mathbb{Z}^n$. These parameters are function of the security parameter λ. The $\mathsf{yaLWE}_{n,m,q,\sigma,\eta,\chi_\mathbf{s}}$ assumption states that the distributions*

$$(\mathbf{A}, \mathbf{As} + \mathfrak{e}, \mathbf{As} + \mathfrak{d}, \|\mathbf{s}\|) \quad and \quad (\mathbf{A}, \mathbf{u}, \mathbf{u} + \mathfrak{h}, \|\mathbf{s}\|)$$

are computationally indistinguishable, where $\mathbf{A} \leftarrow U(\mathbb{Z}_q^{m \times n})$, $\mathbf{s} \leftarrow \chi_\mathbf{s}^n$, $\mathfrak{e} \leftarrow \mathcal{D}_{\mathbb{Z}^m, \sigma}$, $\mathfrak{d} \leftarrow \mathcal{D}_{\mathbb{Z}^m, \eta}$, $\mathbf{u} \leftarrow U(\mathbb{Z}_q^m)$ and $\mathfrak{h} \leftarrow \mathcal{D}_{\mathbb{Z}^m, \sqrt{\sigma^2 + \eta^2}}$.

Lemma 2.6. *Let $n, m, q, \sigma_s, \sigma_e$ and $\eta > 0$, with $\sigma_e \geq \sqrt{2}\sigma_s \geq \Omega(\sqrt{\lambda + \log n})$ and $\sigma_s \leq \mathsf{poly}(\lambda)$. Assume that $\chi_s = \mathcal{D}_{\mathbb{Z}^n, \sigma_s}$. If the $\mathsf{LWE}_{n,m,q,\psi,\chi_s}$ assumption holds for $\psi = (\sqrt{\sigma_e^{-2} + \eta^{-2}})^{-1/2}$, then the $\mathsf{yaLWE}_{n,m,q,\sigma_e,\eta,\chi_s}$ assumption holds.*

This essentially follows from [MS23, Corollary 3 and Lemma 9]. In the latter, the authors prove that $\mathsf{LWE}_{n,m,q,\psi,\chi_s}$ implies the Reused-**A** $\mathsf{LWE}_{n,m,q,\sigma_s,\eta,\chi_s}$ assumption. The latter assumption precisely corresponds to our $\mathsf{yaLWE}_{n,m,q,\sigma_s,\eta,\chi_s}$ except for $\|\mathbf{s}\|$ which is kept secret. (Reused-**A** LWE considers $\chi_s = U(\mathbb{Z}_q^n)$, but the analysis from [MS23] generalizes to arbitrary secret key distributions χ_s.) Then, Lemma 2.6 follows by the same observation as for Known-Norm LWE in the same work: any solver for the search variant of $\mathsf{yaLWE}_{n,m,q,\sigma_s,\eta,\chi_s}$ yields a solver for the search variant of Reused-**A** $\mathsf{LWE}_{n,m,q,\sigma_s,\eta,\chi_s}$, by first guessing $\|\mathbf{s}\|$ (this guess being correct with probability $1/\mathsf{poly}(\lambda)$ as long as $\|\mathbf{s}\| = \mathsf{poly}(\lambda)$); then one can rely on [MM11] to relate the search and decision variants. Note that [MS23, Lemma 9] requires the same distribution for the coordinates of $\mathbf{s}$ and $\mathbf{e}$. In our application (and in the statement of Lemma 2.6), we use larger a larger standard deviation parameter for the coefficients of $\mathbf{e}$ than for those of $\mathbf{s}$. Reducing the same-noise variant to the latter one is achieved by adding Gaussian noise to the second and third coordinates of the yaLWE sample. The sum of two discrete Gaussians is indeed very close to a discrete Gaussian (see [BF11, Lemma 4.12]).

3   Limitations from Prior Works

We start by discussing prior attempts to build threshold FHE with small partial decryption shares. Threshold FHE (and variants of it) has received a lot of attention in the last few years and some works (notably [BS23a, CSS+22]) claim to obtain efficient constructions based on an analysis relying on the Rényi divergence. We already pointed issues with [CSS+22] in the introduction and now focus on explaining technical issues with [BS23a]. We first discuss about the need for randomness before partial decryption happens to achieve threshold FHE with small partial decryption shares, then detail our analysis of [BS23a].

3.1   On the Need for Randomness Before Partial Decryption

For the approximate FHE scheme CKKS, lower bounds were proven in [LMSS22] regarding the amount of (Gaussian) noise to be added after decryption, in order to achieve IND-CPA-D security (see full version of the paper for a precise definition) when the evaluation algorithm Eval of the scheme is deterministic. The authors proved that decryption needs to add a noise of magnitude $\Omega(2^{\lambda/4})$, and a similar lower bound was recently proven in the threshold setting (still for CKKS only) in [KS23, Theorem 12]. (The result is written in the case of multi-key FHE but extends to threshold FHE.) Our first observation is that these results do not rely on any specificity of CKKS, except on the fact that the noise after multiplication of two ciphertexts, encrypting μ_1, μ_2 and with noise terms e_1, e_2, is of the form $\mu_1 e_2 + \mu_2 e_1 + e'$ with $\|e'\| \ll \|\mu_1 e_2 + \mu_2 e_1\|$. This noise propagation is also that of the (exact) B/FV FHE scheme. The lower bound can then be extended to any threshold FHE scheme with such a format, and in particular to B/FV. This is not surprising, given that IND-CPA-D can be seen as a particular case of threshold FHE security (see full version of the paper for details). In short, this is due to the fact that CKKS decryption corresponds to (noiseless) PartDec as defined earlier.

To obtain the lower bound, we consider four challenge queries of the form

$$(\mu_1^{(0)}, \mu_1^{(1)}) = (0, B), \quad (\mu_2^{(0)}, \mu_1^{(1)}) = (0, B) \ ,$$
$$(\mu_3^{(0)}, \mu_3^{(1)}) = (0, B), \quad (\mu_4^{(0)}, \mu_4^{(1)}) = (0, -B) \ .$$

We then evaluate $\mu_1 \mu_2 + \mu_3 \mu_4$, which leads to an encryption of 0 (computed as $0^2 + 0^2$ or as $B^2 - B^2$ respectively, depending on the challenge bit β). The fact that intermediate plaintexts are 0 is one case and of magnitude B in the other case implies that the underlying error of the result is simply e' for $\beta = 0$, while it is of the form $Be + e'$ with e' small relative to Be for $\beta = 1$. This difference in magnitude can be further amplified by making not just 4 queries but $4t$ queries of the same form and evaluating $\sum_{i \in [t]} (\mu_{1,i} \mu_{2,i} + \mu_{3,i} \mu_{4,i})$. As explained in the introduction, partial decryptions allow to recover the error, up to the error added by each partial decryption. Hence, unless partial decryption adds an exponential error, there is an efficient distinguisher based on the evaluation error, and the scheme is not secure. We refer the reader to [LMSS22] for more details. The main technicality lies in the fact that, outputting a guess based on which of the two shifted Gaussians in more likely to have generated the challenge sample essentially provides an efficient distinguisher whose advantage is the statistical distance between the Gaussians, and an exponential flooding is required to make this statistical distance negligible.

As a consequence, it seems that relying on sanitization techniques to remove dependencies between the error term and the plaintexts involved in the computation is needed to obtain efficient threshold constructions without exponential noise flooding during partial decryption. This is what is done in [BS23a], by relying on circuit-private FHE. However, adding randomness before partial decryption rises another question: which party adds this randomness? If this is a party, then it has to be honest, uncorrupted, and even in this case, it is not clear that any security can be guaranteed with respect to this party, since it knows the randomness which serves as source of security. This is what motivates our generalization of threshold FHE, defined in the next section (Sect. 4): we add a ServerDec operation which processes the evaluated ciphertext to add randomness; we assume it is run by a trusted third-party (e.g., a server), so that none of the (possibly corrupted) parties knows the internal randomness of this step. Before we move on to our definition, let us analyze [BS23a] in more details.

3.2   A Construction Based on Circuit-Private FHE

In [BS23a], the authors proposed a transformation which allows to convert a One-Way-CPA (OW-CPA), circuit-private, threshold FHE into an IND-CPA threshold FHE. The precise definition of OW-CPA threshold FHE is not relevant for our work and we refer the reader to [BS23a] for more details. IND-CPA threshold FHE is similar to our Definition A.1, though it suffers from minor caveats. Indeed, in their security notions, the adversary does not have access to two distinct oracles OEval and ODec but only to a single oracle OEvalDec which combines evaluation of a circuit C with partial decryption of the resulting ciphertext. While this could be fine, the issue with their definition is that this oracle only reveals the partial decryption shares to the adversary and does not reveal the evaluated ciphertext which was decrypted. Note that, since the ciphertext is obtained by a circuit-private evaluation, it is not possible for the adversary to compute the decrypted ciphertext by itself. In practice, parties (and therefore the adversary) must know the ciphertext to be able to decrypt it, so OEvalDec should reveal both the ciphertext and the partial decryption shares when Eval is randomized. Yet, the fact that the ciphertext distribution is correlated to that of partial decryptions makes it much harder to analyze security. (Also, again, this rises the question of who does the evaluation since randomness plays a central role in security.)

Beside this definitional issue, our main contribution in this section is an attack against the transform. We start by briefly recalling the transform. Let ThFHE $=$ (KeyGen, Enc, Eval, PartDec, FinDec) be a OW-CPA, circuit-private, threshold FHE scheme. The authors suggest to construct an IND-CPA threshold FHE from this OW-CPA threshold FHE scheme by tweaking encryption and evaluation as follows.

- To encrypt a message $\mu \in \{0,1\}^\delta$: sample $(s_1, \ldots, s_\delta) \leftarrow U(\mathcal{M}^\delta)$ and $x \leftarrow U(\mathcal{M})$ where $\mathcal{M}$ denote the message space of the OW-CPA scheme – we assume that x has large min-entropy (i.e., that $\mathcal{M}$ is large); compute $\mathsf{ct} \leftarrow \mathsf{Enc_{pk}}(x)$ and $r_i := \langle x, s_i \rangle \oplus \mu_i$ for $i \in [\delta]$; return $(\mathsf{ct}, (s_i)_{i \in \delta}, (r_i)_{i \in \delta})$.
- To evaluate a circuit C, one first unmasks the r_i's homomorphically using the encryption of x (and known s_i's) to compute an FHE encryption of μ, and then performs Eval of C on the resulting ciphertext.

Let us first remark that unmasking can be done directly on ciphertexts, and therefore one can assume that a message μ is simply encrypted using the OW-CPA scheme (up to some changes in the noise distribution). Therefore, the above transform would imply that a OW-CPA (circuit-private) threshold FHE scheme is actually IND-CPA-secure without any change. In the full version of the paper, we show that this is actually correct for *non-threshold* FHE schemes, assuming the scheme satisfies a mild form of circuit-privacy. The proof relies on a rewinding argument. However, if the attacker can make decryption queries (e.g., for threshold or IND-CPA-D security), the rewinding argument blows up the number of decryption queries and its seems very challenging to extend our result without this blow-up.[6]

3.3   An Attack Against the [BS23a] Transform

To attack the transform, we construct a threshold circuit-private FHE scheme which is does not satisfy their claimed security notion once plugged into their transform.

Syntax of Our Scheme. We consider a (threshold) FHE scheme with the following syntax. This corresponds in particular to some instantiations of B/FV or CKKS. The scheme uses a chain of moduli $q_\ell > q_{\ell-1} > \cdots > q_0$, providing $\ell+1$ levels of computation. Define $\mathcal{R} = \mathbb{Z}[X]/(X^N + 1))$ for N a power of 2, and $\mathcal{R}_q = \mathcal{R}/q\mathcal{R}$ for $q \geq 2$. A ciphertext at level i is of the form $\mathsf{ct} = (a, -as + \mu + e)$ with $a, s, e \in \mathcal{R}_{q_i}$, where $\mu \in \mathcal{R}$ is a polynomial encoding a plaintext.

Let $\mathsf{ct}_0, \mathsf{ct}_1$ denote two level-$(i + 1)$ ciphertexts with $\mathsf{ct}_\beta^{(i+1)} = (a_\beta, -a_\beta s + \mu_\beta + e_\beta)$ for $\beta \in \{0, 1\}$. We assume that multiplying two level-$(i+1)$ ciphertexts leads to a level-i ciphertext $ct^{(i)}$ whose error term is of the form $\frac{q_i}{q_{i+1}} \cdot (\mu_0 e_1 + \mu_1 e_0 + e')$ where e' satisfies $\|e'\| \ll \|\mu_0 e_1 + \mu_1 e_0\|$. In the case of B/FV and CKKS, decreasing e' is obtained by increasing the q_i's.

We consider a circuit-private threshold FHE scheme with the above format and consider three consecutive moduli $q_2 > q_1 > q_0$ of the modulus chain. We assume that:

- fresh/evaluated ciphertexts are at level 0 (i.e., encryption, challenge, and evaluation queries all return level-0 ciphertexts);
- the public parameters contain a level-2 encryption of 1, denoted $\mathsf{ct}_{\mathsf{pp}}^{(2)}$;
- the (circuit-private) evaluation of a circuit C has the following form: it starts by performing a *circuit-private* evaluation of C resulting in a level-2 ciphertext $\mathsf{ct}_{\mathsf{priv}}^{(2)}$; then, the following post-processing is performed:
    1. both level-2 ciphertexts $\mathsf{ct}_{\mathsf{priv}}^{(2)}$ and $\mathsf{ct}_{\mathsf{pp}}^{(2)}$ are rescaled to level 1 by applying the map $c \mapsto \lfloor \frac{q_1}{q_2} \cdot c \rceil$; this results in two level-1 ciphertexts denoted $\mathsf{ct}_{\mathsf{priv}}^{(1)}$ and $\mathsf{ct}_{\mathsf{pp}}^{(1)}$, respectively;
    2. the ciphertexts $\mathsf{ct}_{\mathsf{priv}}^{(1)}$ and $\mathsf{ct}_{\mathsf{pp}}^{(1)}$ are multiplied, resulting in a level-0 ciphertext $\mathsf{ct}_{\mathsf{res}}^{(0)}$, which is returned as the output of the evaluation.
- partial decryption of a ciphertext (a, b) with a partial key s_j returns $as_j + \mathfrak{d}$ with $\mathfrak{d}$ being a noise of amplitude $\approx Q_D$, where Q_D denote an upper bound on the number of decryption queries made by the adversary (as suggested by the analysis based on the Rényi divergence from [BS23a]).

---

[6] Recall that, the OW-CPA threshold FHE construction proposed in [BS23a] requires to add a noise term of magnitude $O(Q_D)$ during partial decryption, with Q_D an upper bound on the number of decryption. Hence, if the reduction blows up the number of decryption queries to argue threshold IND-CPA security, then the amount of flooding noise shall be increased accordingly.

We now add two comments on the evaluation procedure. As $\mathsf{ct}_{\mathsf{pp}}^{(1)}$ is an encryption of 1, the ciphertext $\mathsf{ct}_{\mathsf{res}}^{(0)}$ properly decrypts to the result of the computation. Further note that the evaluation process is circuit-private since the post-processing is circuit-independent and applies to a circuit-private evaluated ciphertext $\mathsf{ct}_{\mathsf{priv}}^{(2)}$.

Finally, we assume that $q_0 \leq \mathsf{poly}(\lambda \cdot N \cdot Q_D)$, which suffices to enable correct decryption.

The Attack. Our threshold IND-CPA attack starts as follows:

1. The attacker makes a challenge query (μ_0, μ_1) using scalar plaintexts. Let $\mathsf{ct}^* = (a^*, -a^*s + \mu_\beta + e^*)$ denote the resulting level-0 challenge ciphertext.
2. The attacker requests an encryption of the most significant bits of a^* (i.e., of a polynomial whose coefficients are the MSB of that of a^*; let us denote its encoding as $[a^*]$), resulting in a level-i ciphertext $\mathsf{ct}_1^{(0)}$.
3. The attacker requests an evaluation of the identity circuit on $\mathsf{ct}_1^{(0)}$, resulting in a level-0 ciphertext $\mathsf{ct}_2^{(0)}$.
4. The attacker finally requests all partial decryptions of $\mathsf{ct}_2^{(0)}$.

Note that the decryption query is valid as the underlying plaintext, which corresponds to the MSB of the a^*-part of ct^*, is independent of μ_β and therefore the decryption query does not reveal information about β.

Before completing the attack, let us analyze the various noise terms. By definition, $\mathsf{ct}_1^{(0)}$ is a level-0 ciphertext. When the identity circuit is evaluated, the circuit-private evaluation of the circuit is first run, ending up with a level-2 ciphertext $\mathsf{ct}_2^{(2)}$ of the form $(a_2^{(2)}, -a_2^{(2)}s + [a^*] + e_2^{(2)})$, which is then rescaled to a level-1 ciphertext $\mathsf{ct}_2^{(1)}$. Finally, it is multiplied to the rescaling $\mathsf{ct}_{\mathsf{pp}}^{(1)}$ of $\mathsf{ct}_{\mathsf{pp}}^{(2)}$. We have, for $k \in \{2, 1\}$:

$$\mathsf{ct}_{\mathsf{pp}}^{(k)} = (a_{\mathsf{pp}}^{(k)}, b_{\mathsf{pp}}^{(k)}) \quad \text{with} \quad a_{\mathsf{pp}}^{(k)}s + b_{\mathsf{pp}}^{(k)} = [1] + e_{\mathsf{pp}}^{(k)} \ ,$$

where $[1]$ denotes the polynomial encoding of plaintext 1, and

$$\mathsf{ct}_2^{(k)} = (a_2^{(k)}, b_2^{(k)}) \quad \text{with} \quad a_2^{(k)}s + b_2^{(k)} = [a^*] + e_2^{(k)} \ .$$

Recall that $a_2^{(1)} := \lfloor \frac{q_1}{q_2} \cdot a_2^{(2)} \rceil$. Let r_2 denote the rounding error $r_2 := \frac{q_1}{q_2}a_2^{(2)} - a_2^{(1)}$. Then, the error term $e_2^{(1)}$ is $\lfloor r_2 s + \frac{q_1}{q_2}e_2^{(2)} \rceil$. By increasing q_2/q_1, we can make the error term $e_2^{(1)}$ dominated by $r_2 s$.

Similarly, letting r_{pp} denote the rounding error $r_{\mathsf{pp}} := \frac{q_1}{q_2}a_{\mathsf{pp}}^{(2)} - a_{\mathsf{pp}}^{(1)}$, we see that the error term $e_{\mathsf{pp}}^{(1)}$ is dominated by $r_{\mathsf{pp}}s$. Note that r_{pp} is publicly computable since $a_{\mathsf{pp}}^{(2)}$ is part of the public parameters and the rescaling operation is deterministic.

Finally, by definition of the scheme, multiplying $\mathsf{ct}_{\mathsf{pp}}^{(1)}$ with $\mathsf{ct}_2^{(1)}$ leads to an encryption $\mathsf{ct}_2 = (a_2, b_2)$ of $[a^*]$ with $b_2 = -a_2 s + [a^*] + e_2$ where the error term e_2 is of the form $[a^*]r_{\mathsf{pp}}s + r_2 s + e'$, where e' is small compared to the other terms. This error is then approximately $[a^*]r_{\mathsf{pp}}s$.

To complete the attack, we observe that the decryption of ct_2 allows the attacker to learn $a_2 s_j + \mathfrak{d}_j$ for $j \in [N]$, with N being the number of parties. Write $\mathfrak{d} := \sum_{j \in [N]} \mathfrak{d}_j$. Then, summing all partial decryptions with b_2, the adversary can recover $[a^*] + e_{\mathsf{dec}}$ where $e_{\mathsf{dec}} = \frac{q_i}{q_{i+1}} \cdot ([a^*] r_{\mathsf{pp}} s + [1] r_2 s + e') + \mathfrak{d}$, where $\|e'\| \ll \|[a^*] r_{\mathsf{pp}} s + [1] r_2 s\|$. Since the attacker knows $[a^*]$, it can recover e_{dec}.

The attacker knows r_{pp}, hence it can compute $r_{\mathsf{pp}} ct^* = (a^* r_{\mathsf{pp}}, a^* s r_{\mathsf{pp}} + \mu_\beta r_{\mathsf{pp}} + e^* r_{\mathsf{pp}})$ and subtract a scaling of e_{dec} to the right-hand term. This has the effect of making the term $a^* s r_{\mathsf{pp}}$ small, as $[a^*]$ corresponds to the MSB of a^*. We then obtain a polynomial $\mu_\beta r_{\mathsf{pp}} + e_{\mathsf{small}}$, where $\|e_{\mathsf{small}}\| \ll q_0$. As the error term e_{small} is small compared to q_0, which is itself $\leq \mathsf{poly}(\lambda \cdot N \cdot Q)$, the error e_{small} is not sufficiently large to hide $\mu_\beta r_{\mathsf{pp}}$. By setting $\mu_0 = 0$ and $\mu_1 = [1]$, the attacker can guess β with non-negligible advantage based on the largeness of $\mu_\beta r_{\mathsf{pp}} + e_{\mathsf{small}}$.

Error in the Analysis of the [BS23a] Transform. We can trace our attack back to an error in the analysis of [BS23a, Theorem 3]: the issue lies in how [BS23a, Lemma 2] is applied in the proof. We borrow the notations from [BS23a, Lemma 2]. The set Z may depend on X, the first input of the extractor, but it cannot depend on its second input (the uniform distribution over $\{0, 1\}^{n\delta}$). This implies that Z should not depend on the Goldreich-Levin bits s_j's in the proof of [BS23a, Theorem 3]. However, in that proof, it could depend on them: the s_j's are revealed in clear as part of the ciphertexts so the adversary could submit an encryption (or an evaluation) query whose plaintext (or circuit) depends on prior s_j's.

4 A Generalized Definition of Threshold FHE

In this section, we provide a generalization of the definition of threshold fully homomorphic encryption which allows to introduce (uncorrupted) randomness to a ciphertext before it is fed to partial decryption. We focus on N-out-of-N threshold FHE for readability and since our main construction (Sect. 5) handles only this setting. However, our definition extends to arbitrary monotone access structures. As already discussed, we consider that a trusted third-party (e.g., a server performing the computation) performs a public-key randomized pre-processing operation on ciphertexts before they can be partially decrypted. Specifically, the server applies an algorithm termed ServerDec, transforming a ciphertext into a form that is adequate for partial decryption by users. Using this terminology, evaluation could be deterministic and ServerDec randomized. We remark that, if ServerDec is void (or is deterministic), we recover the prior definition of threshold FHE.

We consider a simulation-based security notion inspired by [BGG+18]. Specifically, assume that the attacker corrupts parties $P_1, \dots, P_{N-1}$ (and therefore knows $sk_1, \dots, sk_{N-1}$). Let ct denote a ciphertext to be decrypted. It is first processed through ServerDec. The result of this operation is a ciphertext ct_{dec} which can be partially decrypted by all parties. Our security notion requires that ct_{dec} and the partial decryptions of ct_{dec} do not reveal more information than the plaintext μ underlying $\mathsf{ct}_{\mathsf{dec}}$ and what is already known by the adversary. This is enforced by the existence of a simulation which outputs a simulated $\mathsf{ct}_{\mathsf{dec}}$ and partial decryptions whose distribution is indistinguishable from that of the real ones. The sources of security are then clearly identified: (1) the internal randomness of $\mathsf{ServerDec}$ and (2) the randomness of the uncorrupted party P_N (i.e., the partial secret key sk_N and the internal randomness $\mathfrak{d}_N$ used when running $\mathsf{PartDec}$).

We now formalize our generalized definition of threshold functional encryption with the additional $\mathsf{ServerDec}$ algorithm.

Definition 4.1 (Threshold FHE). *A threshold fully homomorphic encryption scheme is a tuple of PPT algorithms* $\mathsf{ThFHE} = (\mathsf{KeyGen}, \mathsf{Enc}, \mathsf{Eval},$ $\mathsf{ServerDec}, \mathsf{PartDec}, \mathsf{FinDec})$ *with the following properties. Let* $\mathcal{M}$ *denote the plaintext space,* $\mathcal{C}$ *the ciphertext space,* $\mathcal{C}_{\mathsf{dec}}$ *the processed ciphertext space, and* $\mathcal{M}_{\mathsf{share}}$ *the space of partial decryption shares.*

- $\mathsf{KeyGen}(1^\lambda, 1^N)$ *takes as input a security parameter, a number of parties N, and returns public parameters* pp *containing descriptions of* $\mathcal{M}, \mathcal{C}, \mathcal{C}_{\mathsf{dec}}$, *a public key* pk, *an evaluation key* ek, *and N secret key shares* $\mathsf{sk}_1, \ldots, \mathsf{sk}_N$;
- $\mathsf{Enc}(\mathsf{pp}, \mathsf{pk}, \mu)$ *takes as input public parameters* pp, *a public key* pk, *and a plaintext* $\mu \in \mathcal{M}$ *and returns a ciphertext* $\mathsf{ct} \in \mathcal{C}$;
- $\mathsf{Eval}(\mathsf{pp}, \mathsf{ek}, \mathsf{C}, \mathsf{ct}_1, \ldots, \mathsf{ct}_\ell)$ *takes as input public parameters* pp, *an evaluation key* ek, *a circuit* $\mathsf{C} : \mathcal{M}^\ell \to \mathcal{M}$ *of arbitrary arity $\ell \geq 0$, and ℓ ciphertexts* $\mathsf{ct}_1, \ldots, \mathsf{ct}_\ell$, *and returns a ciphertext* $\mathsf{ct} \in \mathcal{C}$;
- $\mathsf{ServerDec}(\mathsf{pp}, \mathsf{pk}, \mathsf{ct})$ *takes as input public parameters* pp, *a public key* pk, *and a ciphertext* $\mathsf{ct} \in \mathcal{C}$ *and returns a ciphertext* $\mathsf{ct}_{\mathsf{dec}} \in \mathcal{C}_{\mathsf{dec}}$;
- $\mathsf{PartDec}(\mathsf{pp}, \mathsf{sk}_i, \mathsf{ct}_{\mathsf{dec}})$ *takes as input public parameters* pp, *a partial decryption key* sk_i, *and a ciphertext* $\mathsf{ct}_{\mathsf{dec}} \in \mathcal{C}_{\mathsf{dec}}$, *and returns a partial decryption* $\mathsf{p}_i \in \mathcal{M}_{\mathsf{share}}$.
- $\mathsf{FinDec}(\mathsf{pp}, \{\mathsf{p}_i\}_{i \in [N]})$ *takes as input public parameters* pp *and a set of partial decryptions* $\{\mathsf{p}_i\}_{i \in [N]}$ *in* $\mathcal{M}_{\mathsf{share}}$, *and returns a plaintext* $\mu' \in \mathcal{M} \cup \{\bot\}$.

To ease notation, the public parameters pp *are implicit for the rest of the paper. We require the following properties.*

Correctness. *For any* $\lambda, N > 0$, $\ell \geq 0$, $\mathsf{C} : \mathcal{M}^\ell \to \mathcal{M}$, *and* $(\mu_1, \ldots, \mu_\ell) \in \mathcal{M}^\ell$, *we have:*

$$\Pr\left[\mathsf{FinDec}(\{\mathsf{p}_i\}_{i \in [N]}) = y \,\middle|\, \begin{array}{l} (\mathsf{pk}, \mathsf{ek}, (\mathsf{sk}_i)_{i \in [N]}) \leftarrow \mathsf{KeyGen}(1^\lambda, 1^N) \\ \mathsf{ct}_j \leftarrow \mathsf{Enc}(\mathsf{pk}, \mu_j), \forall j \in [\ell] \\ \mathsf{ct} \leftarrow \mathsf{Eval}(\mathsf{ek}, \mathsf{C}, \mathsf{ct}_1, \ldots, \mathsf{ct}_\ell) \\ \mathsf{ct}_{\mathsf{dec}} \leftarrow \mathsf{ServerDec}(\mathsf{pk}, \mathsf{ct}) \\ \mathsf{p}_i \leftarrow \mathsf{PartDec}(\mathsf{sk}_i, \mathsf{ct}_{\mathsf{dec}}), \forall i \in [N] \end{array}\right] \geq 1 - \mathsf{negl}(\lambda),$$

where $y = \mathsf{C}(\mu_1, \ldots, \mu_\ell)$ *and the probability is over the internal coins of the algorithms.*

Compactness. *There exists a polynomial p such that, for any* $\lambda, N > 0$, *and execution of* $\mathsf{KeyGen}(1^\lambda, 1^N)$, *we have:*

$$\log |\mathcal{C}|, \log |\mathcal{C}_{\mathsf{dec}}|, \log |\mathcal{M}_{\mathsf{share}}| \leq p(\lambda, N) \ .$$

Definition 4.2 (Threshold Simulation Security). *A threshold FHE scheme* ThFHE = (KeyGen, Enc, Eval, ServerDec, PartDec, FinDec) *is simulation-secure if it satisfies the following two properties:*

- *the sub-scheme* (KeyGen, Enc) *is* IND-CPA-*secure;*
- *there exists a PPT simulator* Sim *such that the experiments depicted in Fig. 1 are computationally indistinguishable; specifically, we require that for any PPT adversary* $\mathcal{A} = (\mathcal{A}_0, \mathcal{A}_1)$,

$$\mathsf{Adv}_{\mathcal{A}}^{\mathsf{SimThFHE}} := \left| \Pr[\mathcal{A}(\mathsf{Exp}_{\mathsf{real}}^{\mathsf{ThFHE}}(1^\lambda, 1^N)) = 1] - \Pr[\mathcal{A}(\mathsf{Exp}_{\mathsf{ideal}}^{\mathsf{ThFHE}}(1^\lambda, 1^N)) = 1] \right|$$

is negligible.

Our definition fixes a minor issue in [BGG+18, Definition 5.5]. In the latter definition, a state st is returned by Sim_1 when simulating KeyGen and fed as input to Sim_2. With this syntax, Sim_1 could run the actual KeyGen algorithm and st could contain all shares $(\mathsf{sk}_1, \ldots, \mathsf{sk}_N)$ of the secret key sk. In this case, Sim_2 can simply run the real evaluation/decryption algorithms, and simulation is perfect, but vacuous. Therefore, this definition could be trivially satisfied. In our definition, the public and partial keys revealed to the adversary are sampled identically in both experiments, using the KeyGen algorithm. It is very similar to the original definition from [JRS17] which did not suffer from the above minor issue, but our definition is slightly more general as it is multi-hop, adaptive (and we only require computational indistinguishability). It does not seem obvious to us that multi-hop, adaptive security is implied by single-hop, selective security since decryption results of multi-hop evaluation queries can be correlated.

Threshold Public-Key Encryption. We also define a Threshold PKE scheme ThPKE = (KeyGen, Enc, PartDec, FinDec) based on our definition of Threshold FHE by requiring Eval and ServerDec to be vacuous algorithms. A definition of simulation-based security is also obtained from simplifying the above definition by removing the OEval oracle and the ServerDec step in the oracle ODec (Step 4 in Fig. 1).

5 Double-Flood-and-Round Construction

In this section, we propose an N-out-of-N threshold FHE scheme with small partial decryption shares. The design of our scheme is fairly generic and can be adapted to most FHE schemes for exact computations. We start by specifying some high-level structure for the underlying scheme.

$\mathsf{Exp}^{\mathsf{ThFHE}}_{\mathsf{real}}(1^\lambda, 1^N)$:
1: $(\mathsf{pk}, \mathsf{ek}, (\mathsf{sk}_i)_{i \in [N]}) \leftarrow \mathsf{KeyGen}(1^\lambda, 1^N)$
2: $\mathsf{ctr} \leftarrow 0, \mathsf{L} \leftarrow \emptyset$
3: $(\mathcal{S}, \mathsf{st}) \leftarrow \mathcal{A}_0(\mathsf{pk})$ with $|\mathcal{S}| = N - 1$
4: $\mathsf{out} \leftarrow \mathcal{A}_1^{\mathsf{OEnc}, \mathsf{OEval}, \mathsf{ODec}}(\mathsf{pk}, (\mathsf{sk}_i)_{i \in \mathcal{S}}, \mathsf{st})$
5: Return $(\mathsf{out} = \mathsf{real})$

$\mathsf{Exp}^{\mathsf{ThFHE}}_{\mathsf{ideal}}(1^\lambda, 1^N)$:
1: $(\mathsf{pk}, \mathsf{ek}, (\mathsf{sk}_i)_{i \in [N]}) \leftarrow \mathsf{KeyGen}(1^\lambda, 1^N)$
2: $\mathsf{ctr} \leftarrow 0, \mathsf{L} \leftarrow \emptyset$
3: $(\mathcal{S}, \mathsf{st}) \leftarrow \mathcal{A}_0(\mathsf{pk})$ with $|\mathcal{S}| = N - 1$
4: $\mathsf{out} \leftarrow \mathcal{A}_1^{\mathsf{OEnc}, \mathsf{OEval}, \mathsf{OSim}}(\mathsf{pk}, (\mathsf{sk}_i)_{i \in \mathcal{S}}, \mathsf{st})$
5: Return $(\mathsf{out} = \mathsf{ideal})$

$\mathsf{OEnc}(\mu)$:
1: $\mathsf{ct} \leftarrow \mathsf{Enc}(\mathsf{pk}, \mu)$
2: $\mathsf{ctr} \leftarrow \mathsf{ctr} + 1$
3: $\mathsf{L}[\mathsf{ctr}] \leftarrow (\mu, \mathsf{ct})$
4: Return ct

$\mathsf{ODec}(j)$:
1: If $j > \mathsf{ctr}$:
2:     Return $\bot$
3: $(\mu, \mathsf{ct}) \leftarrow \mathsf{L}[j]$
4: $\mathsf{ct}_{\mathsf{dec}} \leftarrow \mathsf{ServerDec}(\mathsf{pk}, \mathsf{ct})$
5: $\mathsf{p}_k \leftarrow \mathsf{PartDec}(\mathsf{sk}_k, \mathsf{ct}_{\mathsf{dec}})$, for $k \in [N]$
6: Return $(\mathsf{ct}_{\mathsf{dec}}, (\mathsf{p}_k)_{k \in [N]})$

$\mathsf{OEval}(\mathsf{C}, (i_1, \dots, i_\ell)))$:
1: For $j \in [\ell]$:
2:     $(\mu_j, \mathsf{ct}_j) \leftarrow \mathsf{L}[i_j]$
3: $\mathsf{ct} \leftarrow \mathsf{Eval}(\mathsf{ek}, \mathsf{C}, \mathsf{ct}_1, \dots, \mathsf{ct}_\ell)$
4: $\mathsf{ctr} \leftarrow \mathsf{ctr} + 1$
5: $\mu \leftarrow \mathsf{C}(\mu_1, \dots, \mu_\ell)$
6: $\mathsf{L}[\mathsf{ctr}] \leftarrow (\mu, \mathsf{ct})$
7: Return ct

$\mathsf{OSim}(j)$:
1: If $j > \mathsf{ctr}$:
2:     Return $\bot$
3: $(\mu, \mathsf{ct}) \leftarrow \mathsf{L}[j]$
4: $(\mathsf{ct}_{\mathsf{dec}}, (\mathsf{p}_k)_{k \in [N]}) \leftarrow \mathsf{Sim}(\mathsf{pk}, \mu, (\mathsf{sk}_i)_{i \in \mathcal{S}})$
5: Return $(\mathsf{ct}_{\mathsf{dec}}, (\mathsf{p}_k)_{k \in [N]})$

Fig. 1. Simulation security games for Threshold FHE.

5.1 Structure of the Underlying FHE Scheme

Let λ denote a security parameter. Let $\mathsf{FHE} = (\mathsf{FHE.KeyGen}, \mathsf{FHE.Enc}, \mathsf{FHE.Eval}, \mathsf{FHE.Dec})$ denote an FHE scheme with the following structure.

1. The public parameters include two dimensions $m \geq n \geq 1$, a modulus $Q \geq 2$, a secret key distribution χ_s over $\mathbb{Z}^n$ whose samples have norms $\leq \mathsf{poly}(\lambda)$, and three distributions χ_e, χ_v and χ_f over $\mathbb{Z}$. All these are functions of λ, and the distributions are assumed to be efficiently sampleable.
2. The key pair is of the form:[7]

$$\mathsf{pk} = [\mathbf{A}|\mathbf{b}] \quad \text{with} \quad \mathbf{b} := -\mathbf{A}\mathbf{s} + \mathbf{e} \ , \quad \mathsf{sk} = \mathbf{s} \ ,$$

with $\mathbf{A} \leftarrow U(\mathbb{Z}_Q^{m \times n})$, $\mathbf{s} \leftarrow \chi_s$ and $\mathbf{e} \leftarrow \chi_e^m$. We have $\mathsf{pk} \cdot (\mathsf{sk}, 1)^\mathsf{T} = \mathbf{e} \bmod Q$.

---

[7] We ignore the evaluation key ek in our description and our proof. This is common even for non-threshold schemes: security of FHE relies on the additional assumption that security still holds given ek (which typically involves a circular security assumption).

3. Encrypting a plaintext $\mu \in \mathcal{M}$ starts by encoding μ into some plaintext $\mu' = \mathsf{Encode}_q(\mu) \in \mathbb{Z}_Q$ (e.g., by setting $\mu' = \Delta \cdot \mu$ for some scaling factor Δ). Then encryption first computes $\mathsf{ct}_0, \mathsf{ct}_1$ with:

$$\mathsf{ct}_0 := \mathbf{v}^\mathsf{T}\mathbf{A} + \mathbf{f}^\mathsf{T} \ , \quad \mathsf{ct}_1 := \mathbf{v}^\mathsf{T}\mathbf{b} + f' + \mu' \ ,$$

with $\mathbf{v} \leftarrow \chi_v^m$, $\mathbf{f} \leftarrow \chi_f^n$ and $f' \leftarrow \chi_f$. Note that this setting handles the case where both $\mathbf{f}$ and f' are zero (for instance in FHE schemes where the leftover hash lemma is relied upon for IND-CPA). The ciphertext is $\mathsf{ct} = (\mathsf{ct}_0, \mathsf{ct}_1)$.

4. The decryption algorithm Dec is split into two steps $(\mathsf{Dec}_1, \mathsf{Dec}_2)$, as follows. Let ct be its input ciphertext (which can be either a fresh ciphertext or the result of an homomorphic computation).
   (a) $\mathsf{Dec}_1(\mathsf{sk}, \mathsf{ct})$ returns $z := \mathsf{ct}_0 \cdot \mathsf{sk} + \mathsf{ct}_1 \bmod Q$.
   (b) $\mathsf{Dec}_2(z)$ returns $\mu := \mathsf{Decode}_Q(z)$. Importantly, it does not use sk; it might be void, notably in the case of an LWE version of CKKS, whereas it typically involves a rounding or a modular reduction in exact schemes.

   We assume that $z = \mu' + e_{\mathsf{eval}}$ where $\mu' = \mathsf{Encode}_Q(\mu)$ is an encoding of the plaintext μ corresponding to ct and e_{eval} is an error term with bounded magnitude $|e_{\mathsf{eval}}| \leq B_{\mathsf{eval}}$ for some $B_{\mathsf{eval}} > 0$. We refer to e_{eval} as the evaluation error.

Our framework captures most known (LWE-based) FHE schemes. It does not directly capture GSW, in which messages are encoded as $\mu \cdot \mathbf{G}$ for $\mathbf{G}$ the gadget matrix and encrypted as $\mathsf{ct} = \mathbf{R} \cdot \mathsf{pk} + \mathbf{F} + \mu \cdot \mathbf{G}$. We could generalize our description to also encompass GSW but it would hurt the readability regarding the decryption procedure, hence we chose this less general but simpler description.

5.2   Construction

As already mentioned, a simple solution to obtain a threshold FHE (even for general access structure or when the computation is performed by parties) is to have the parties add an exponential noise term after decryption such that no information about their partial decryption key is revealed to other. Yet, a significant drawback of the noise flooding approach is the size of the output ciphertexts, as the modulus needs to be large enough to tolerate the addition of this large noise term at decryption. To mitigate this, we propose a different approach, in which exponential noise flooding is performed on the server side. Computation by the server is performed with a large modulus Q which tolerates exponential noise-flooding, and the ciphertext is then rounded to a smaller modulus $q_{\mathsf{dec}} \ll Q$, before being sent to the users. This modulus remains sufficiently large for the users to be able to add some limited noise term to guarantee security without impacting decryption correctness. After performing its partial decryption, a user can round the decryption share to an even smaller modulus: indeed, there is no more noise that needs to be added, and it is only required that the combination of the current noises does not impact correctness. Overall, the successive roundings allow to minimize bandwidth consumption.[8]

---

[8] Another drawback of exponential flooding, which our construction does not address, is the need for an LWE parametrization with exponential noise rate.

The scheme is described in Figs. 2 and 3. To ease description, our scheme does not include the second rounding (performed after partial decryption). We briefly discuss this optimization at the end of this section. The construction relies on a perfectly correct FHE scheme that fulfills the constraints of Sect. 5.1. For the sake of simplicity, we consider an FHE scheme that encodes a plaintext μ over $\mathbb{Z}_Q$ as $\mathsf{Encode}_Q(\mu)$ such that for $Q = pq_{\mathsf{dec}}$, it holds that: $1/p \cdot \mathsf{Encode}_Q(\mu) = \mathsf{Encode}_{q_{\mathsf{dec}}}(\mu)$. For example, this holds if plaintexts are encoded in the most significant bits of the ciphertexts, i.e., $\mathsf{Encode}_Q(\mu) = Q/t \cdot \mu$, with t denoting the plaintext modulus (e.g., as done in B/FV).

We only describe the procedures $\mathsf{KeyGen}, \mathsf{ServerDec}, \mathsf{PartDec}, \mathsf{FinDec}$ in Figs. 2 and 3, as the encryption and evaluation procedures Enc and Eval are identical to those of the underlying FHE scheme (and operate over $\mathbb{Z}_Q$ with Q being the larger modulus). The scheme involves two noise flooding parameters σ_{flood} and η. The first flooding parameter σ_{flood} is used for exponential flooding, while the second parameter η is used for small flooding during partial decryption. It also involves two moduli $Q = pq_{\mathsf{dec}}$ and q_{dec} with $q_{\mathsf{dec}} \ll Q$ (we use $p \approx 2^\lambda$). $\mathsf{ServerDec}$ uses randomized Gaussian roundings. We reveal the norm of the secret key $\|\mathsf{sk}\|$ in the public parameters. This is only to ease simulation in our security analysis. In practice, the scheme is at least as secure if $\|\mathsf{sk}\|$ is not given, since removing it only restricts the information available to an attacker.

▶ $\mathsf{KeyGen}(1^\lambda, 1^N)$:
1: Construct $Q = p \cdot q_{\mathsf{dec}}$ with $q_{\mathsf{dec}} \ll Q$ and the secret key dimension n
2: Sample $(\mathsf{sk}, \mathsf{pk}) \leftarrow \mathsf{FHE}.\mathsf{KeyGen}(1^\lambda)$ with modulus Q
3: Define public parameters pp containing Q, p, q_{dec} as well as $\|\mathsf{sk}\|$
4: Sample $(\mathsf{sk}_1, \ldots, \mathsf{sk}_N) \leftarrow \mathsf{Share}(\mathsf{sk}, N, q_{\mathsf{dec}})$
5: Return $(\mathsf{sk}_1, \ldots, \mathsf{sk}_N, \mathsf{pk}, \mathsf{pp})$

Fig. 2. Key generation of double-flood-and-round threshold FHE.

The communication involved between parties after the computation is limited, as only the small modulus q_{dec} is involved. However, communication before the computation, to provide inputs to the server, remains large as we encrypt over $\mathbb{Z}_Q$. This may be solved using transciphering (see, e.g., [BCK+23] and references therein).

The construction can be adapted to further reduce the bandwidth. The users could apply a second rounding step after their partial decryption, e.g., by returning $\lfloor q_{\mathsf{out}}/q_{\mathsf{dec}} \cdot \mathsf{p}_i \rceil \bmod q_{\mathsf{out}}$ for $q_{\mathsf{out}} < q_{\mathsf{dec}}$, in order to further reduce the size of communication with other parties. Security follows from that of the base

▶ ServerDec(pk, ct):
1: $ct_{fresh} \leftarrow Enc_{pk}(0)$
2: $ct_{in} \leftarrow ct + ct_{fresh}$
3: $\mathfrak{E} \leftarrow \mathcal{D}_{\sigma_{flood}}$
4: Parse ct_{in} as $(ct_{in,0}, ct_{in,1}) \bmod Q$
5: $ct_{in,1} \leftarrow ct_{in,1} + \mathfrak{E}$
6: $ct_{dec,0} := \left\lfloor \frac{1}{p} \cdot ct_{in,0} \right\rceil_{\sigma_0} \bmod q_{dec}$
7: $ct_{dec,1} := \left\lfloor \frac{1}{p} \cdot ct_{in,1} \right\rceil_{\sigma_1} \bmod q_{dec}$
8: $ct_{dec} := (ct_{dec,0}, ct_{dec,1})$
9: Return ct_{dec}

▶ PartDec(sk_i, ct_{dec}):
1: Parse ct_{dec} as $(ct_{dec,0}, ct_{dec,1})$
2: Sample $\mathfrak{d}_i \leftarrow \mathcal{D}_{\mathbb{Z},\eta}$
3: $p_i \leftarrow ct_{dec,0} \cdot sk_i + \mathfrak{d}_i \bmod q_{dec}$
4: Return p_i

▶ FinDec(ct_{dec}, $\{p_i\}_{i \in [N]}$):
1: Parse ct_{dec} as $(ct_{dec,0}, ct_{dec,1})$
2: $z \leftarrow \sum_{i \in [N]} p_i + ct_{dec,1} \bmod q_{dec}$
3: $\mu \leftarrow \mathsf{Decode}_{q_{dec}}(z)$
4: Return μ

Fig. 3. Decryption procedures of double-flood-and-round threshold FHE.

construction since the modified scheme provides strictly less information to the adversary. Functionality is preserved as long as parameters are carefully selected to ensure correctness.

5.3 Analysis of the Double-Flood-and-Round Construction

Let B_{eval} be an upper bound on $|ct \cdot sk - Encode_Q(\mu)|$ for any ciphertext ct that can be produced by a combination of encryptions and evaluations, and where μ is the underlying plaintext of ct. We assume that fresh ciphertexts also have decryption noises that are bounded by B_{eval} in absolute value (this follows from the definition of B_{eval} if FHE.Eval does not do anything for the empty circuit).

Theorem 5.1. *Let* ThFHE *denote the above double-flood-and-round construction. It is a correct and secure threshold fully homomorphic encryption scheme, assuming that:*

- *the decoding procedure of the underlying FHE scheme satisfies*

$$\mathsf{Decode}_{q_{dec}}\left(\mathsf{Encode}_{q_{dec}}(\mu) + e\right) = \mu \; ,$$

  for any plaintext μ and e with $|e| \leq \sqrt{\lambda} \cdot \sigma_{dec}$ and where σ_{dec} is defined as $\sqrt{(\sigma_0 \|s\|)^2 + (\sigma_{flood}/p)^2 + \sigma_1^2 + N\eta^2}$;
- *the underlying FHE scheme is* IND-CPA*-secure;*
- $\sigma_0, \sigma_1 = \Omega(\sqrt{\lambda + \log n})$ *and* $\sigma_{flood} = \Omega(p\|sk\|\sqrt{\lambda + \log n})$;
- $\sigma_{flood} = \Omega(2^\lambda B_{eval})$;
- $yaLWE_{n,Q_D,q_{dec},\sigma_e,\eta,\chi_s}$ *holds for* $\sigma_e = \sqrt{(\sigma_0\|s\|)^2 + (\sigma_{flood}/p)^2 + \sigma_1^2}$;

- $\mathsf{LWE}_{n,Q,\chi_f,\chi_s}$ holds.

In the above, the variable Q_D refers to the number of decryption queries made by the adversary. We assume that $Q_D \leq \mathsf{poly}(\lambda)$.

Proof. We prove correctness and threshold simulation security independently. IND-CPA security follows from that of the underlying FHE scheme.

Correctness. Let $\mathsf{ct}_{\mathsf{dec}} = (\mathsf{ct}_{\mathsf{dec},0}, \mathsf{ct}_{\mathsf{dec},1})$ denote a ciphertext obtained from the server after it applied $\mathsf{ServerDec}$. We define the rounding error $\mathbf{r}_0$ of $\mathsf{ct}_{\mathsf{dec},0}$ as:

$$\mathbf{r}_0^\mathsf{T} := \mathsf{ct}_{\mathsf{in},0} - p \cdot \mathsf{ct}_{\mathsf{dec},0} \ .$$

By definition, since $\mathsf{ct}_{\mathsf{dec},0} \sim \mathcal{D}_{\mathbb{Z}^n, \frac{1}{p} \cdot \mathsf{ct}_{\mathsf{in},0}, \sigma_0}$, we have $\mathbf{r}_0 \sim \mathcal{D}_{p\{\frac{1}{p} \cdot \mathsf{ct}_{\mathsf{in},0}\} + p\mathbb{Z}^n, p\sigma_0}$, where $\{\cdot\}$ denotes the fractional part defined as $\{x\} := x - \lfloor x \rfloor$ for any $x \in \mathbb{R}$. Assume that $\mathsf{ct}_{\mathsf{in},1} = \mathsf{ct}_{\mathsf{in},0} \cdot \mathsf{sk} + \mu' + e_{\mathsf{eval}} + e_{\mathsf{fresh}}$, where e_{eval} is the decryption noise of the input ct of $\mathsf{ServerDec}$ and e_{fresh} is the decryption noise of $\mathsf{ct}_{\mathsf{fresh}}$ (recall that $\mathsf{ct}_{\mathsf{in}} = \mathsf{ct} + \mathsf{ct}_{\mathsf{fresh}}$). We then have, modulo q_{dec}:

$$
\begin{aligned}
\mathsf{ct}_{\mathsf{dec},1} &= \left\lfloor \frac{1}{p} \cdot (-(p \cdot \mathsf{ct}_{\mathsf{dec},0} + \mathbf{r}_0^\mathsf{T}) \cdot \mathsf{sk} + \mu' + e_{\mathsf{eval}} + e_{\mathsf{fresh}} + \mathfrak{E}) \right\rceil_{\sigma_1} \\
&= -\mathsf{ct}_{\mathsf{dec},0} \cdot \mathsf{sk} + \left\lfloor \frac{1}{p} \cdot (-\mathbf{r}_0^\mathsf{T} \cdot \mathsf{sk} + \mu' + e_{\mathsf{eval}} + e_{\mathsf{fresh}} + \mathfrak{E}) \right\rceil_{\sigma_1} \\
&= \mathsf{Encode}_{q_{\mathsf{dec}}}(\mu) - \mathsf{ct}_{\mathsf{dec},0} \cdot \mathsf{sk} + \left\lfloor \frac{1}{p} \cdot (-\mathbf{r}_0^\mathsf{T} \cdot \mathsf{sk} + e_{\mathsf{eval}} + e_{\mathsf{fresh}} + \mathfrak{E}) \right\rceil_{\sigma_1} \ . \quad (1)
\end{aligned}
$$

Let $\mathsf{p}_i = \mathsf{PartDec}(\mathsf{sk}_i, \mathsf{ct}_{\mathsf{dec}})$, and recall that $\mathsf{p}_i = \mathsf{ct}_{\mathsf{dec},0} \cdot \mathsf{sk}_i + \mathfrak{d}_i$, with $\mathfrak{d}_i \leftarrow \mathcal{D}_{\mathbb{Z},\eta}$ for $i \in [N]$. Then, we have, modulo q_{dec}:

$$
\begin{aligned}
\mathsf{FinDec}((\mathsf{p}_i)_{i \in [N]}) &= \left(\sum_{i \in [N]} \mathsf{p}_i \right) + \mathsf{ct}_{\mathsf{dec},1} \\
&= \mathsf{ct}_{\mathsf{dec},0} \cdot \mathsf{sk} + \mathsf{ct}_{\mathsf{dec},1} + \sum_{i \in [N]} \mathfrak{d}_i \\
&= \mathsf{Encode}_{q_{\mathsf{dec}}}(\mu) + \mathfrak{e} + \sum_{i \in [N]} \mathfrak{d}_i \ , \quad (2)
\end{aligned}
$$

where $\mathfrak{e} := \left\lfloor \frac{1}{p} \cdot (-\mathbf{r}_0^\mathsf{T} \cdot \mathsf{sk} + e_{\mathsf{eval}} + e_{\mathsf{fresh}} + \mathfrak{E}) \right\rceil_{\sigma_1}$. We finally obtain:

$$\mathsf{FinDec}((\mathsf{p}_i)_{i \in [N]}) = \mathsf{Encode}_{q_{\mathsf{dec}}}(\mu) + e_{\mathsf{dec}} \bmod q_{\mathsf{dec}} \ ,$$

with $e_{\mathsf{dec}} = \mathfrak{e} + \sum_{i \in [N]} \mathfrak{d}_i$. Correctness follows as long as $|e_{\mathsf{dec}}|$ is sufficiently small to enable correct decoding to μ. In our security analysis below, we show in the proof of Lemma 5.3 that e_{dec} follows a distribution which is statistically close to $\mathcal{D}_{\mathbb{Z},\sigma_{\mathsf{dec}}}$, where $\sigma_{\mathsf{dec}} = \sqrt{(\sigma_0 \|\mathbf{s}\|)^2 + (\sigma_{\mathsf{flood}}/p)^2 + \sigma_1^2 + N\eta^2}$. By standard

Gaussian tail bounds, the samples have magnitudes $\leq \sqrt{\lambda}\sigma_{dec}$ with overwhelming probability.

Threshold Simulation. As for all known examples of LWE-based FHE scheme, we ignore the evaluation key in our security analysis. Our actual security claim is then obtained by additionally assuming that security still holds provided the extra information contained in the evaluation key. This is the standard circular security assumption underlying FHE schemes.

Our proof proceeds by a sequence of hybrids. The KeyGen, Enc and Eval algorithms are modified in none of them and encryption and evaluation queries are answered by running the corresponding algorithms. Hence, we only focus on handle decryption queries.

Let $\mathcal{A}$ denote an adversary. Without loss of generality, assume that $\mathcal{A}$ corrupts parties $1, \ldots, N-1$ so that it knows $sk_1, \ldots, sk_{N-1}$. Our objective is to prove that the real experiment distribution $\mathsf{Exp}_{real}^{ThFHE}$ is computationally indistinguishable from the simulated one $\mathsf{Exp}_{ideal}^{ThFHE}$, which can be run directly given the information of $\mathcal{A}$ (i.e., given the corrupted partial keys and the plaintexts underlying the ciphertexts that are queried to the decryption oracle, but without sk nor sk_N). The simulator Sim is given in Fig. 4.

▶ $\mathsf{Sim}(pk, \mu, (sk_1, \ldots, sk_{N-1}))$:
1: $ct_{dec,0} \leftarrow U(\mathbb{Z}_{q_{dec}}^n)$
2: $ct_{dec,1} \leftarrow U(\mathbb{Z}_{q_{dec}})$
3: $\mathfrak{d}_i \leftarrow \mathcal{D}_{\mathbb{Z},\eta}$ for $i \in [N-1]$
4: $p_i \leftarrow ct_{dec,0} \cdot sk_i + \mathfrak{d}_i$ for $i \in [N-1]$
5: $\mathfrak{h} \leftarrow \mathcal{D}_{\sigma_{\mathfrak{h}}}$ where $\sigma_{\mathfrak{h}} := \sqrt{(\sigma_0\|s\|)^2 + (\sigma_{flood}/p)^2 + \sigma_1^2 + \eta^2}$
6: $p_N \leftarrow \mathsf{Encode}_{q_{dec}}(\mu) + \mathfrak{h} - ct_{dec,1} - \sum_{i \in [N-1]} ct_{dec,0} \cdot sk_i$
7: Return $(ct_{dec,0}, ct_{dec,1}, p_1, \ldots, p_N)$.

Fig. 4. Simulator for the double-flooding-and-round threshold FHE.

Let ct denote a ciphertext held by the server and for which the adversary is requesting decryption. Let μ denote the underlying plaintext. Note that ct could be a fresh encryption of μ or the result of a homomorphic computation whose underlying plaintext is μ. We aim to prove that $ct_{dec} \leftarrow \mathsf{ServerDec}(pk, ct)$, the ciphertext revealed by the server to all parties, and $p_N \leftarrow \mathsf{PartDec}(sk_N, ct_{dec})$, the partial decryption of the uncorrupted party N, are computationally indistinguishable from those provided by the simulator Sim. We proceed by a hybrid argument, first considering the real distribution in $\mathsf{Exp}_{real}^{ThFHE}$.

Hyb$_0$. This is the adversary's view in $\mathsf{Exp}_{real}^{ThFHE}$. Given the constraints we imposed on the underlying FHE scheme, the ciphertext $ct = (ct_0, ct_1)$ to be decrypted satisfies:

$$ct_0 \cdot sk + ct_1 = \mu' + e_{eval} \bmod Q \ ,$$

with $\mu' = \mathsf{Encode}_Q(\mu)$ and $|e_{\mathsf{eval}}| \leq B_{\mathsf{eval}}$.

Hyb$_1$. In this first hybrid, we change how $\mathsf{ct}_{\mathsf{in}}$ is defined by the challenger. We remind that, as for ct, the ciphertext $\mathsf{ct}_{\mathsf{in}}$ is held by the server and is never revealed to the adversary. The latter only sees $\mathsf{ct}_{\mathsf{dec}}$, which is produced from $\mathsf{ct}_{\mathsf{in}}$.

In this hybrid, when the adversary makes a decryption query for a ciphertext ct encrypting a plaintext μ', the server now samples $(\mathsf{ct}_{\mathsf{in},0}, \mathsf{ct}_{\mathsf{in},1})$ and $\mathsf{ct}_{\mathsf{dec}}$ as follows:

- it samples $\mathsf{ct}_{\mathsf{in},0} \leftarrow \mathbf{a}^{\mathsf{T}}$ with $\mathbf{a} \leftarrow U(\mathbb{Z}_Q^n)$;
- it sets $\mathsf{ct}_{\mathsf{in},1} \leftarrow -\mathbf{a}^{\mathsf{T}} \cdot \mathsf{sk} + \mu' + \mathfrak{E}$, where $\mathfrak{E} \leftarrow \mathcal{D}_{\sigma_{\mathsf{flood}}}$;
- the rest of the decryption proceeds as before.

We claim that games **Hyb$_0$** and **Hyb$_1$** are computationally indistinguishable. The detailed analysis is provided in Lemma 5.2.

We recall the correctness equation (Eq. (2)):

$$\left(\sum_{i \in [N]} \mathsf{p}_i \right) + \mathsf{ct}_{\mathsf{dec},1} = \mathsf{Encode}_{q_{\mathsf{dec}}}(\mu) + \mathfrak{e} + \sum_{i \in [N]} \mathfrak{d}_i \bmod q_{\mathsf{dec}} \ , \tag{3}$$

where $\mathfrak{e}$ is now $\mathfrak{e} := \left\lfloor \frac{1}{p} \cdot (-\mathbf{r}_0^{\mathsf{T}} \cdot \mathsf{sk} + \mathfrak{E}) \right\rceil_{\sigma_1}$, with $\mathbf{r}_0 \sim \mathcal{D}_{p\{\frac{1}{p} \cdot \mathsf{ct}_{\mathsf{in},0}\} + p\mathbb{Z}^n, p\sigma_0}$.

Hyb$_2$. In this hybrid, we change how the partial decryption p_N of the uncorrupted party is computed as well as how $\mathsf{ct}_{\mathsf{dec},1}$ is sampled. Simplifying Eq. (3) above, we obtain that, in **Hyb$_1$**, the partial decryption p_N satisfies:

$$\mathsf{p}_N := \mathsf{Encode}_{q_{\mathsf{dec}}}(\mu) + \mathfrak{e} + \mathfrak{d}_N - \mathsf{ct}_{\mathsf{dec},1} - \sum_{i \in [N-1]} \mathsf{ct}_{\mathsf{dec},0} \cdot \mathsf{sk}_i \ . \tag{4}$$

Motivated by this equation, in **Hyb$_2$**, we now sample $\mathsf{ct}_{\mathsf{dec},1}$ as $\mathsf{ct}_{\mathsf{dec},1} \leftarrow U(\mathbb{Z}_{q_{\mathsf{dec}}})$ and set p_N as:

$$\mathsf{p}_N := \mathsf{Encode}_{q_{\mathsf{dec}}}(\mu) + \mathfrak{h} - \mathsf{ct}_{\mathsf{dec},1} - \sum_{i \in [N-1]} \mathsf{ct}_{\mathsf{dec},0} \cdot \mathsf{sk}_i \ ,$$

with $\mathfrak{h} \leftarrow \mathcal{D}_{\sigma_{\mathfrak{h}}}$ and $\sigma_{\mathfrak{h}} := \sqrt{(\sigma_0 \|\mathbf{s}\|)^2 + (\sigma_{\mathsf{flood}}/p)^2 + \sigma_1^2 + \eta^2}$.

We claim that games **Hyb$_1$** and **Hyb$_2$** are computationally indistinguishable. The detailed analysis is provided in Lemma 5.3. Note that the distribution in this game no longer depends on sk_N and is therefore sampleable by the adversary given its known information, since $\sigma_0, \sigma_1, p, \sigma_{\mathsf{flood}}, \|\mathbf{s}\|, \eta$ are public parameters. The view is identical to the one provided by the Sim algorithm from Fig. 4.

This completes the proof of Theorem 5.1. $\qquad\square$

Lemma 5.2. *Assuming that $\sigma_{\mathsf{flood}} = \Omega(2^\lambda B_{\mathsf{eval}})$ and that $\mathsf{LWE}_{n,Q,\chi_f,\chi_s}$ holds, games* **Hyb$_0$** *and* **Hyb$_1$** *are computationally indistinguishable.*

Proof. For simplicity, we focus on simulating a single decryption query: the general case where multiple decryption queries are made is obtained by a standard hybrid argument.

Let $\mathsf{ct} = (\mathsf{ct}_0, \mathsf{ct}_1)$ denote a ciphertext corresponding to a decryption query made by the adversary. First, we recall that a fresh encryption $\mathsf{ct}_{\mathsf{fresh}}$ of 0 is added to the ciphertext ct at Step 2 of $\mathsf{ServerDec}(\mathsf{ct})$ to produce $\mathsf{ct}_{\mathsf{in}}$. It is of the form $\mathsf{ct}_{\mathsf{fresh}} = (\mathsf{ct}_{\mathsf{fresh},0}, \mathsf{ct}_{\mathsf{fresh},1})$ with $\mathsf{ct}_{\mathsf{fresh},0} = \mathbf{v}^{\mathsf{T}}\mathbf{A} + \mathbf{f}^{\mathsf{T}}$ and $\mathsf{ct}_{\mathsf{fresh},1} = -\mathsf{ct}_{\mathsf{fresh},0} \cdot \mathbf{s} + e_{\mathsf{fresh}}$. Here $\mathbf{v} \leftarrow \chi_v^m$, $\mathbf{f} \leftarrow \chi_f^n$ and the noise term e_{fresh} satisfies $|e_{\mathsf{fresh}}| \leq B_{\mathsf{eval}}$. Further, given our assumptions regarding the underlying FHE scheme, the ciphertext $\mathsf{ct} = (\mathsf{ct}_0, \mathsf{ct}_1)$ to be decrypted satisfies:

$$\mathsf{ct}_0 \cdot \mathbf{s} + \mathsf{ct}_1 = \mu' + e_{\mathsf{eval}} \bmod Q \ ,$$

with $\mu' = \mathsf{Encode}_Q(\mu)$ and $|e_{\mathsf{eval}}| \leq B_{\mathsf{eval}}$. Overall, the ciphertext $\mathsf{ct}_{\mathsf{in}}$ is of the form $(\mathsf{ct}_{\mathsf{in},0}, \mathsf{ct}_{\mathsf{in},1})$ with:

$$\mathsf{ct}_{\mathsf{in},0} = \mathbf{v}^{\mathsf{T}}\mathbf{A} + \mathbf{f}^{\mathsf{T}} + \mathsf{ct}_0$$

and

$$\mathsf{ct}_{\mathsf{in},1} = -\mathsf{ct}_{\mathsf{in},0} \cdot \mathbf{s} + e_{\mathsf{fresh}} + e_{\mathsf{eval}} + \mathfrak{E} + \mu' \ .$$

Note that $|e_{\mathsf{fresh}} + e_{\mathsf{eval}}| \leq 2B_{\mathsf{eval}}$. By Lemma 2.1, taking $\sigma_{\mathsf{flood}} = \Omega(2^{\lambda}B_{\mathsf{eval}})$, the above distribution of $\mathsf{ct}_{\mathsf{in}}$ is statistically indistinguishable from sampling $\mathsf{ct}_{\mathsf{in}}$ as:

$$\mathsf{ct}_{\mathsf{in},0} = \mathbf{v}^{\mathsf{T}}\mathbf{A} + \mathbf{f}^{\mathsf{T}} + \mathsf{ct}_0 \quad , \quad \mathsf{ct}_{\mathsf{in},1} \leftarrow -\mathsf{ct}_{\mathsf{in},0} \cdot \mathbf{s} + \mathfrak{E} + \mu' \ .$$

Finally, note that $\mathsf{ct}_{\mathsf{in},1}$ no longer contains information about $\mathbf{v}, \mathbf{f}$ apart from that carried by $\mathsf{ct}_{\mathsf{in},0}$. In the above, we can hence replace $\mathbf{v}^{\mathsf{T}}\mathbf{A} + \mathbf{f}^{\mathsf{T}}$ by a uniformly random value over $\mathbb{Z}_Q^n$, under the LWE assumption. As a result, the distribution of $\mathsf{ct}_{\mathsf{in}}$ is computationally indistinguishable from a pair of the form $(\mathbf{a}^{\mathsf{T}}, -\mathbf{a}^{\mathsf{T}}\mathbf{s} + \mathfrak{E} \mid \mu')$ where $\mathbf{a} \leftarrow U(\mathbb{Z}_Q^n)$, which is precisely the distribution of $\mathsf{ct}_{\mathsf{in}}$ in $\mathbf{Hyb}_1$. $\square$

Lemma 5.3. *Assuming that* $\mathsf{yaLWE}_{n,Q_D,q_{\mathsf{dec}},\sigma_e,\eta,\chi_s}$ *holds, games* $\mathbf{Hyb}_1$ *and* $\mathbf{Hyb}_2$ *are computationally indistinguishable.*

Proof. We aim to prove that the view of the adversary in games $\mathbf{Hyb}_1$ and $\mathbf{Hyb}_2$ are computationally indistinguishable. In both games, the ciphertext $\mathsf{ct}_{\mathsf{in}}$ is defined as $(\mathsf{ct}_{\mathsf{in},0}, \mathsf{ct}_{\mathsf{in},1}) \leftarrow (\mathbf{a}^{\mathsf{T}}, \mathbf{a}^{\mathsf{T}}\mathsf{sk} + \mu' + \mathfrak{E})$. Then the vector $\mathsf{ct}_{\mathsf{dec},0}$ is computed as

$$\mathsf{ct}_{\mathsf{dec},0} \leftarrow \left\lfloor \frac{1}{p} \cdot \mathbf{a}^{\mathsf{T}} \right\rceil_{\sigma_0} \bmod q_{\mathsf{dec}} \ ,$$

which is revealed to the adversary. Note that, since $\mathbf{a} \sim U(\mathbb{Z}_Q^n)$ and p divides Q, since only $\mathsf{ct}_{\mathsf{dec}}$ is revealed to the adversary, one can directly sample $\mathsf{ct}_{\mathsf{dec},0}$ uniformly over $\mathbb{Z}_{q_{\mathsf{dec}}}^n$. Using the same notation as before (in the proof of correctness), we define the rounding error of $\mathsf{ct}_{\mathsf{dec},0}$ as $\mathbf{r}_0^{\mathsf{T}} := \mathsf{ct}_{\mathsf{in},0} - p \cdot \mathsf{ct}_{\mathsf{dec},0}$, and recall that, by definition, we have $\mathbf{r}_0 \sim \mathcal{D}_{p\{\frac{1}{p} \cdot \mathsf{ct}_{\mathsf{in},0}\} + p\mathbb{Z}^n, p\sigma_0}$.

The adversary's view in $\mathbf{Hyb}_1$ is then $(\mathsf{ct}_{\mathsf{dec},0}, \mathsf{ct}_{\mathsf{dec},1}, (\mathsf{p}_i)_{i \in [N]})$ where $\mathsf{ct}_{\mathsf{dec},0}$ is defined as above, and $(\mathsf{p}_i)_{i \in [N-1]}$ can be computed directly by the adversary since it knows $\mathsf{sk}_1, \ldots, \mathsf{sk}_{N-1}$ and $\mathsf{ct}_{\mathsf{dec},0}$. It remains to deal with $\mathsf{ct}_{\mathsf{dec},1}$ and p_N. By adapting Equation (1) to $\mathbf{Hyb}_1$, we have, modulo q_{dec}:

$$\mathsf{ct}_{\mathsf{dec},1} = \mathsf{Encode}_{q_{\mathsf{dec}}}(\mu) - \mathsf{ct}_{\mathsf{dec},0} \cdot \mathsf{sk} + \left\lfloor \frac{1}{p} \cdot (-\mathbf{r}_0^\mathsf{T} \cdot \mathsf{sk} + \mathfrak{E}) \right\rceil_{\sigma_1} .$$

Further, from Eq. (4), we have, modulo q_{dec}:

$$\mathsf{p}_N = \mathsf{Encode}_{q_{\mathsf{dec}}}(\mu) + \left\lfloor \frac{1}{p} \cdot (-\mathbf{r}_0^\mathsf{T} \cdot \mathsf{sk} + \mathfrak{E}) \right\rceil_{\sigma_1} + \eth_N - \mathsf{ct}_{\mathsf{dec},1} - \sum_{i = \in [N-1]} \mathsf{ct}_{\mathsf{dec},0} \cdot \mathsf{sk}_i .$$

Since μ, $\mathsf{ct}_{\mathsf{dec},0}$ and $(\mathsf{sk}_i)_{i \in [N-1]}$ are known to the adversary, and replacing $\mathsf{ct}_{\mathsf{dec},1}$ in the second equation the right hand side of the first equation, we observe that it suffices to focus on the quantities (defined modulo q_{dec}):

$$\mathsf{ct}'_{\mathsf{dec},1} := -\mathsf{ct}_{\mathsf{dec},0} \cdot \mathsf{sk} + \left\lfloor \frac{1}{p} \cdot (-\mathbf{r}_0^\mathsf{T} \cdot \mathsf{sk} + \mathfrak{E}) \right\rceil_{\sigma_1} \quad \text{and} \quad \mathsf{p}'_N := -\mathsf{ct}_{\mathsf{dec},0} \cdot \mathsf{sk} - \eth_N .$$

The partial decryption noise $\eth_N$ having a distribution that is symmetric aroung 0, up to inverting the sign, letting $\mathbf{a} := -\mathsf{ct}_{\mathsf{dec},0}$ and $\mathbf{s} := \mathsf{sk}$, we then have:

$$\mathsf{ct}'_{\mathsf{dec},1} = \mathbf{a} \cdot \mathbf{s} + \mathfrak{e} \bmod q_{\mathsf{dec}} \quad \text{and} \quad \mathsf{p}'_N = \mathbf{a} \cdot \mathbf{s} + \eth_N \bmod q_{\mathsf{dec}} ,$$

where $\mathfrak{e} := \left\lfloor \frac{1}{p} \cdot (-\mathbf{r}_0^\mathsf{T} \cdot \mathsf{sk} + \mathfrak{E}) \right\rceil_{\sigma_1}$.

Recall that $(1/p) \cdot \mathbf{r}_0^\mathsf{T}$ follows the distribution $\mathcal{D}_{\{\frac{1}{p} \cdot \mathsf{ct}_{\mathsf{in},0}\} + \mathbb{Z}^n, \sigma_0}$ and $\mathfrak{E}/p$ follows the distribution $\mathcal{D}_{\frac{1}{p}\sigma_{\mathsf{flood}}}$. Therefore, applying Lemma 2.2, assuming $(1/\sigma_0^2 + (p\|\mathsf{sk}\|/\sigma_{\mathsf{flood}})^2)^{-1/2} \geq \eta_\varepsilon(\mathbb{Z}^n)$ for some $\varepsilon < 1/2$, the distribution of $-(1/p) \cdot \mathbf{r}_0^\mathsf{T} \cdot \mathsf{sk} + \mathfrak{E}/p$ is at statistical distance at most 4ε from $\mathcal{D}_{\sqrt{(\sigma_0\|\mathsf{s}\|)^2 + (\sigma_{\mathsf{flood}}/p)^2}}$. The smoothing condition is fulfilled, thanks to the assumptions on σ_0 and σ_{flood}. By definition of Gaussian rounding and thanks to the latter observation, we can then apply Lemma 2.3. Assuming $\sigma_1 \geq \eta_\varepsilon(\mathbb{Z})$ for some $\varepsilon < 1/2$, we then obtain that the distribution of $\mathfrak{e}$ is within statistical distance 8ε of the discrete Gaussian $\mathcal{D}_{\mathbb{Z}, \sqrt{(\sigma_0\|\mathsf{s}\|)^2 + (\sigma_{\mathsf{flood}}/p)^2 + \sigma_1^2}}$. The smoothing condition is fulfilled, thanks to the assumption on σ_1.

Define $\sigma_{\mathfrak{e}} := \sqrt{(\sigma_0\|\mathsf{s}\|)^2 + (\sigma_{\mathsf{flood}}/p)^2 + \sigma_1^2}$. Now that we have proven that $\mathfrak{e}$ is statistically close from $\mathcal{D}_{\mathbb{Z}, \sigma_{\mathfrak{e}}}$, the rest of the proof is similar to the simulation proof for threshold PKE from [MS23], since $\mathsf{ct}_{\mathsf{dec}}$ is essentially a fresh PKE ciphertext now. Recall that $\eth_N \sim \mathcal{D}_{\mathbb{Z}, \eta}$. The pair $(\mathsf{ct}'_{\mathsf{dec},1}, \mathsf{p}'_N)$ precisely corresponds to a sample for the yaLWE problem, for secret $\mathbf{s}$. Thanks to the privacy of Share, the adversary has no information about $\mathbf{s}$ (except the knowledge of $\|\mathbf{s}\|$ which is publicly available), even given $\mathsf{sk}_1, \ldots, \mathsf{sk}_{N-1}$, since the latter are identically distributed as $\mathsf{sk}'_1, \ldots, \mathsf{sk}'_{N-1}$ where $(\mathsf{sk}'_1, \ldots, \mathsf{sk}'_N) \leftarrow$ Share$(\mathbf{0}, N, q_{\mathsf{dec}})$, which are independent of $\mathbf{s}$. Assuming that yaLWE$_{n, q_{\mathsf{dec}}, \sigma_{\mathfrak{e}}, \eta, \chi_{\mathbf{s}}}$ holds, we obtain that $(\mathsf{ct}'_{\mathsf{dec},1}, \mathsf{p}'_N)$ from $\mathbf{Hyb}_1$ is computationally indistinguishable from a pair $(\mathsf{ct}'_{\mathsf{dec},1}, \mathsf{p}'_N)$ sampled as:

$$\mathsf{ct}_{\mathsf{dec},1} \leftarrow U(\mathbb{Z}_{q_{\mathsf{dec}}}) \quad \text{and} \quad \mathsf{p}_N \leftarrow \mathsf{ct}_{\mathsf{dec},1} + \mathfrak{h} ,$$

with $\mathfrak{h} \leftarrow \mathcal{D}_{\sigma_{\mathfrak{h}}}$ where $\sigma_{\mathfrak{h}} := \sqrt{(\sigma_0 \|\mathbf{s}\|)^2 + (\sigma_{\mathsf{flood}}/p)^2 + \sigma_1^2 + \eta^2}$.

Since $\sigma_0, \sigma_1, p, \sigma_{\mathsf{flood}}, \|\mathbf{s}\|$ and η are public parameters, the latter distribution is publicly sampleable and precisely corresponds to the distribution generated by our simulator, i.e., to the distribution in $\mathbf{Hyb}_2$ (up to the terms known to the adversary that we ignored above for simplicity).

We complete the proof of Lemma 5.3 by applying a hybrid argument on all ciphertexts for which a decryption query is made. $\square$

5.4 Open Problems

The construction can be extended to a t-out-of-N threshold FHE, by relying on Shamir secret sharing or linear integer secret sharing [DT06]. However, we do not know how to adapt the security analysis, in particular how to simulate all $N - t + 1$ partial decryptions that are not available to the adversary. We now describe a way to partially circumvent this difficulty, by relying on N-out-of-N threshold FHE. For each subset $\mathcal{S} \subseteq [N]$ of size t, compute a t-additive secret sharing of sk. This leads to $\binom{N}{t}$ independent additive secret sharings of sk. Then, the partial key of each party P_i is the union of shares of the key for each valid set $\mathcal{S}$ such that $i \in \mathcal{S}$. This induces a significant blow-up, but for small choices of t and N, the overhead is limited.

Similarly, while the scheme can be extended to the ring setting, extending the analysis to rely on ring-LWE [SSTX09, LPR10] seems challenging. Most of the proof extends to the ring setting, but there is one specific difficulty that arises: revealing $\|\mathbf{s}\|$ is sufficient to obtain a simulator in the LWE case, it does not seem to be no longer the case in the ring setting. Letting $s \in \mathcal{R} = \mathbb{Z}[X]/(X^N + 1)$ denote the secret key (with N a power of 2), directly extending the analysis would require to reveal the covariance $s\bar{s}$ where $\bar{s}$ denotes the polynomial $s(X^{-1})$. It may however be possible to extend the security analysis to the ring setting by relying on the extension of ring-LWE proposed in [MS23, Section 5.3] (in the context of threshold PKE).

Acknowledgments. We thank Katharina Boudgoust and Peter Scholl for fruitful discussions, as well as Intak Hwang, Seonghong Min and Yongsoo Song for helpful feedback on a prior version of this work.

A   Indistinguishability-Based Security for Threshold FHE

Below, we provide an indistinguishability-based security notion for threshold FHE, termed Th-IND-CPA-security. Indistinguishability definitions for ThFHE have been proposed in prior works (e.g., in [JRS17, BS23a, KS23]). Our definition is similar in flavour though it is slightly more general. In particular, it is multi-hop and adaptive.

Definition A.1 (Threshold-IND-CPA Security). *We say that a threshold FHEscheme* ThFHE = (KeyGen, Enc, Eval, ServerDec, PartDec, FinDec) *is* Q_D-

Th-IND-CPA *secure, if for all PPT adversaries* $\mathcal{A} = (\mathcal{A}_0, \mathcal{A}_1)$ *making at most* Q_D *decryption queries, we have:*

$$\left| \Pr[\mathcal{A}(\mathsf{Exp}_1^{\mathsf{Th\text{-}IND\text{-}CPA}}(1^\lambda, 1^N)) = 1] - \Pr[\mathcal{A}(\mathsf{Exp}_0^{\mathsf{Th\text{-}IND\text{-}CPA}}(1^\lambda, 1^N)) = 1] \right| \leq \mathsf{negl}(\lambda),$$

where the experiment is described in Fig. 5.

$\mathsf{Exp}_b^{\mathsf{Th\text{-}IND\text{-}CPA}}(1^\lambda, 1^N, 1^t)$:
1: $(\mathsf{pk}, \mathsf{ek}, \mathsf{sk}_1, \ldots, \mathsf{sk}_N) \leftarrow \mathsf{KeyGen}(1^\lambda, 1^N)$
2: $\mathsf{ctr} \leftarrow 0, \mathsf{L} \leftarrow \emptyset$
3: $(\mathcal{S}, \mathsf{st}) \leftarrow \mathcal{A}_0(\mathsf{pk})$ with $\mathcal{S} \subset [N]$ and $|\mathcal{S}| < N$;
4: $b \leftarrow \mathcal{U}(\{0, 1\})$
5: $b' \leftarrow \mathcal{A}_1^{\mathsf{OEnc}, \mathsf{OChall}_b, \mathsf{OEval}, \mathsf{ODec}}(\mathsf{pk}, (\mathsf{sk}_i)_{i \in \mathcal{S}}, \mathsf{st})$
6: Return $(b' = b)$

$\mathsf{OEnc}(\mu)$:
1: $\mathsf{ct} \leftarrow \mathsf{Enc}(\mathsf{pk}, \mu)$
2: $\mathsf{ctr} \leftarrow \mathsf{ctr} + 1$
3: $\mathsf{L}[\mathsf{ctr}] \leftarrow (\mu, \mu, \mathsf{ct})$
4: Return ct

$\mathsf{OChall}_b(\mu_0, \mu_1)$:
1: If $|\mu_0| \neq |\mu_1|$:
2:     Return $\bot$
3: $\mathsf{ct} \leftarrow \mathsf{Enc}(\mathsf{pk}, \mu_b)$
4: $\mathsf{ctr} \leftarrow \mathsf{ctr} + 1$
5: $\mathsf{L}[\mathsf{ctr}] \leftarrow (\mu_0, \mu_1, \mathsf{ct})$
6: Return ct

$\mathsf{OEval}(C, (i_1, \ldots, i_\ell))$:
1: For $j \in [\ell]$:
2:     $(\mu_0, \mu_1, \mathsf{ct}_j) \leftarrow \mathsf{L}[i_j]$
3: $\mathsf{ct} \leftarrow \mathsf{Eval}(\mathsf{ek}, C, \mathsf{ct}_1, \ldots, \mathsf{ct}_\ell)$
4: $\mathsf{ctr} \leftarrow \mathsf{ctr} + 1$
5: $\mu_0 \leftarrow C(\mu_{0,1}, \ldots, \mu_{0,\ell})$
6: $\mu_1 \leftarrow C(\mu_{1,1}, \ldots, \mu_{1,\ell})$
7: $\mathsf{L}[\mathsf{ctr}] \leftarrow (\mu_0, \mu_1, \mathsf{ct})$
8: Return ct

$\mathsf{ODec}(j)$:
1: If $j > \mathsf{ctr}$:
2:     Return $\bot$
3: $(\mu_0, \mu_1, \mathsf{ct}) \leftarrow \mathsf{L}[j]$
4: If $\mu_0 \neq \mu_1$:
5:     Return $\bot$
6: $\mathsf{ct}_{\mathsf{dec}} \leftarrow \mathsf{ServerDec}(\mathsf{pk}, \mathsf{ct})$
7: $\mathsf{p}_k \leftarrow \mathsf{PartDec}(\mathsf{sk}_k, \mathsf{ct}_{\mathsf{dec}})$, for $k \in [N]$
8: Return $(\mathsf{ct}_{\mathsf{dec}}, (\mathsf{p}_k)_{k \in [N]})$

Fig. 5. Q_D-Th-IND-CPA security game for Threshold FHE.

Lemma A.2. *Let* ThFHE *be a simulation-secure threshold FHE scheme. Then,* ThFHE *is* Th-IND-CPA *secure.*

Proof. For any Th-IND-CPA adversary, one can run it by replacing replies to its decryption queries by simulated answers using the simulator for ThFHE. Then, any adversary having non-negligible advantage contradicts simulation security of ThFHE. □

References

[AJL+12] Gilad Asharov, Abhishek Jain, Adriana López-Alt, Eran Tromer, Vinod Vaikuntanathan, and Daniel Wichs. Multiparty computation with low communication, computation and interaction via threshold FHE. In *EUROCRYPT*, 2012.

[ASY22] Shweta Agrawal, Damien Stehlé, and Anshu Yadav. Round-optimal lattice-based threshold signatures, revisited. In *ICALP*, 2022.

[BCK+23] Youngjin Bae, Jung Hee Cheon, Jaehyung Kim, Jai Hyun Park, and Damien Stehlé. HERMES: efficient ring packing using MLWE ciphertexts and application to transciphering. In *CRYPTO*, 2023.

[BCKS24] Youngjin Bae, Jung Hee Cheon, Jaehyung Kim, and Damien Stehlé. Bootstrapping bits with CKKS. In *EUROCRYPT*, 2024.

[BD10] Rikke Bendlin and Ivan Damgård. Threshold decryption and zero-knowledge proofs for lattice-based cryptosystems. In *TCC*, 2010.

[BF11] Dan Boneh and David Mandell Freeman. Linearly homomorphic signatures over binary fields and new tools for lattice-based signatures. In *PKC*, 2011.

[BGG+18] Dan Boneh, Rosario Gennaro, Steven Goldfeder, Aayush Jain, Sam Kim, Peter M. R. Rasmussen, and Amit Sahai. Threshold cryptosystems from threshold fully homomorphic encryption. In *CRYPTO*, 2018.

[BGV12] Zvika Brakerski, Craig Gentry, and Vinod Vaikuntanathan. (leveled) fully homomorphic encryption without bootstrapping. In *ITCS*, 2012.

[BI22] Florian Bourse and Malika Izabachène. Plug-and-play sanitization for TFHE. *IACR eprint 2022/1438*, 2022.

[BJKL21] Fabrice Benhamouda, Aayush Jain, Ilan Komargodski, and Huijia Lin.Multiparty reusable non-interactive secure computation from LWE. In *EUROCRYPT*, 2021.

[BKSS24] Youngjin Bae, Jaehyung Kim, Eias Suvanto, and Damien Stehlé. Bootstrapping small integers with CKKS. In *ASIACRYPT*, 2024.

[BLL+18] Shi Bai, Adeline Langlois, Tancrède Lepoint, Amin Sakzad, Damien Stehlé, and Ron Steinfeld. Improved security proofs in lattice-based cryptography: Using the Rényi divergence rather than the statistical distance. *Journal of Cryptology*, 2018.

[BLP+13] Zvika Brakerski, Adeline Langlois, Chris Peikert, Oded Regev, and Damien Stehlé. Classical hardness of learning with errors. In *STOC*, 2013.

[BPMW16] Florian Bourse, Rafaël Del Pino, Michele Minelli, and Hoeteck Wee. FHE circuit privacy almost for free. In *CRYPTO*, 2016.

[Bra12] Zvika Brakerski. Fully homomorphic encryption without modulus switching from classical GapSVP. In *CRYPTO*, 2012.

[BS23a] Katharina Boudgoust and Peter Scholl. Simple threshold (fully homomorphic) encryption from LWE with polynomial modulus. In *ASIACRYPT*, 2023.

[BS23b] Katharina Boudgoust and Peter Scholl. Simple threshold (fully homomorphic) encryption from LWE with polynomial modulus. *IACR eprint 2023/016*, 2023. Version dated 16 July 2024.

[CGGI16] Ilaria Chillotti, Nicolas Gama, Mariya Georgieva, and Malika Izabachène. Faster fully homomorphic encryption: Bootstrapping in less than 0.1 seconds. In *ASIACRYPT*, 2016.

[CKKS17] Jung Hee Cheon, Andrey Kim, Miran Kim, and Yong Soo Song. Homomorphic encryption for arithmetic of approximate numbers. In *ASIACRYPT*, 2017.

[CSS+22]   Siddhartha Chowdhury, Sayani Sinha, Animesh Singh, Shubham Mishra, Chandan Chaudhary, Sikhar Patranabis, Pratyay Mukherjee, Ayantika Chatterjee, and Debdeep Mukhopadhyay. Efficient threshold FHE with application to real-time systems. *IACR eprint 2022/1625*, 2022. Version dated 18 July 2024.

[DDK+23]   Morten Dahl, Daniel Demmler, Sarah El Kazdadi, Arthur Meyre, Jean-Baptiste Orfila, Dragos Rotaru, Nigel P. Smart, Samuel Tap, and Michael Walter. Noah's ark: Efficient threshold-fhe using noise flooding. In *WAHC*, 2023.

[DM15]   Léo Ducas and Daniele Micciancio. FHEW: bootstrapping homomorphic encryption in less than a second. In *EUROCRYPT*, 2015.

[DMPS24]   Nir Drucker, Guy Moshkowich, Tomer Pelleg, and Hayim Shaul. BLEACH: cleaning errors in discrete computations over CKKS. *Journal of Cryptology*, 2024.

[DS16]   Léo Ducas and Damien Stehlé. Sanitization of FHE ciphertexts. In *EUROCRYPT*, 2016.

[DT06]   Ivan Damgård and Rune Thorbek. Linear integer secret sharing and distributed exponentiation. In *PKC*, 2006.

[DWF22]   Xiaokang Dai, Wenyuan Wu, and Yong Feng. Key lifting : a more efficient weak MKFHE scheme in the plain model against rational adversary. *IACR eprint 2022/055*, 2022.

[FV12]   Junfeng Fan and Frederik Vercauteren. Somewhat practical fully homomorphic encryption. *IACR eprint 2012/144*, 2012.

[Gen09]   Craig Gentry. *A fully homomorphic encryption scheme*. PhD thesis, 2009.

[GPV08]   Craig Gentry, Chris Peikert, and Vinod Vaikuntanathan. An efficient and parallel gaussian sampler for lattices. In *STOC*, 2008.

[JRS17]   Aayush Jain, Peter M. R. Rasmussen, and Amit Sahai. Threshold fully homomorphic encryption. In *eprint 2017/257*, 2017.

[Klu22]   Kamil Kluczniak. Circuit privacy for fhew/tfhe-style fully homomorphic encryption in practice. *IACR eprint 2022/1459*, 2022.

[KS23]   Kamil Kluczniak and Giacomo Santato. On circuit private, multikey and threshold approximate homomorphic encryption. In *IACR eprint 2023/301*, 2023.

[LM21]   Baiyu Li and Daniele Micciancio. On the security of homomorphic encryption on approximate numbers. In *EUROCRYPT*, 2021.

[LMSS22]   Baiyu Li, Daniele Micciancio, Mark Schultz, and Jessica Sorrell. Securing approximate homomorphic encryption using differential privacy. In *CRYPTO*, 2022.

[LPR10]   Vadim Lyubashevsky, Chris Peikert, and Oded Regev. On ideal lattices and learning with errors over rings. In *EUROCRYPT*, 2010.

[MM11]   Daniele Micciancio and Petros Mol. Pseudorandom knapsacks and the sample complexity of LWE search-to-decision reductions. In *CRYPTO*, 2011.

[MS23]   Daniele Micciancio and Adam Suhl. Simulation-secure threshold PKE from LWE with polynomial modulus. In *IACR eprint 2023/1728*, 2023.

[Pei10]   Chris Peikert. An efficient and parallel Gaussian sampler for lattices. In *CRYPTO*, 2010.

[Reg05]   Oded Regev. On lattices, learning with errors, random linear codes, and cryptography. In *STOC*, 2005.

[Shi22]   Sina Shiehian. mrNISC from LWE with polynomial modulus. In *SCN*, 2022.

[SSTX09]   Damien Stehlé, Ron Steinfeld, Keisuke Tanaka, and Keita Xagawa. Efficient public key encryption based on ideal lattices. In *ASIACRYPT*, 2009.

Bootstrapping Small Integers With CKKS

Youngjin Bae[1]([envelope]) [iD], Jaehyung Kim[1] [iD], Damien Stehlé[2] [iD],
and Elias Suvanto[1,3] [iD]

[1] CryptoLab Inc., Seoul, Republic of Korea
{youngjin.bae,elias.suvanto}@cryptolab.co.kr, jaehk@stanford.edu
[2] CryptoLab Inc., Lyon, France
damien.stehle@cryptolab.co.kr
[3] University of Luxembourg, Esch-sur-Alzette, Luxembourg

Abstract. The native plaintexts of the Cheon-Kim-Kim-Song (CKKS) fully homomorphic encryption scheme are vectors of approximations to complex numbers. Drucker *et al.* [J. Cryptol.'24] have showed how to use CKKS to efficiently perform computations on bits and small bit-length integers, by relying on their canonical embeddings into the complex plane. For small bit-length integers, Chung *et al.* [IACR eprint'24] recently suggested to rather rely on an embedding into complex roots of unity, to gain numerical stability and efficiency. Both works use CKKS in a black-box manner.

Inspired by the design by Bae *et al.* [Eurocrypt'24] of a dedicated bootstrapping algorithm for ciphertexts encoding bits, we propose a CKKS bootstrapping algorithm, SI-BTS (small-integer bootstrapping), for ciphertexts encoding small bit-length integers. For this purpose, we build upon the DM/CGGI-to-CKKS conversion algorithm from Boura *et al.* [J. Math. Cryptol.'20], to bootstrap canonically embedded integers to integers embedded as roots of unity. SI-BTS allows functional bootstrapping: it can evaluate an arbitrary function of its input while bootstrapping. It may also be used to batch-(functional-)bootstrap multiple DM/CGGI ciphertexts. For example, its amortized cost for evaluating an 8-bit look-up table on 2^{12} DM/CGGI ciphertexts is 3.75ms (single-thread CPU, 128-bit security).

We adapt SI-BTS to simultaneously bootstrap multiple CKKS ciphertexts for bits. The resulting BB-BTS algorithm (batch-bits bootstrapping) allows to decrease the amortized cost of a binary gate evaluation. Compared to Bae *et al.*, it gives a 2.4x speed-up.

Keywords: Fully Homomorphic Encryption · Bootstrapping · Binary Circuits · Functional Bootstrapping

1 Introduction

The diverse Fully Homomorphic Encryption (FHE) schemes handle different primary data types. In BGV/BFV [BGV12,Bra12,FV12], a plaintext is a vector of elements in a finite field. DM/CGGI [DM15,CGGI16a] considers bits,

K.-M. Chung and Y. Sasaki (Eds.): ASIACRYPT 2024, LNCS 15484, pp. 330–360, 2025.
https://doi.org/10.1007/978-981-96-0875-1_11

and can be extended to process small bit-length integers [CJP21,KS22]. Finally, CKKS [CKKS17] enables computations on vectors of (approximations to) complex numbers. Even though computations on a second data type can be expressed as computations on a first data type, this incurs a "data type translation" cost. For example, simulating a multiplication between reals with a boolean circuit may incur a large extra cost. For this reason, it can be tempting to choose an FHE scheme whose primary data type matches the considered application, to maximize efficiency. In this work, we go against this intuition, and consider the efficiency of CKKS for computations on small integers, including bits.

Recently, Drucker et al. [DMPS24] used CKKS to perform computations on vectors of bits, obtaining impressive performance in terms of throughput: thanks to the SIMD nature of CKKS, when the computations to be performed are sufficiently large, the amortized cost of homomorphically evaluating a binary gate becomes very small. The main idea of [DMPS24] is to view the bit $b \in \{0,1\}$ as a real/complex number and map a vector of such bits to a CKKS plaintext. The latter encoding adds a small noise to the bits. By interpreting binary gates as bivariate polynomials, one can then evaluate binary circuits with CKKS. To handle the noise increase, the authors of [DMPS24] propose to use a noise-cleaning polynomial, which implements the identity function on $\{0,1\}$ with a vanishing derivative on those points. The vanishing derivatives allow to square the noise, i.e., to double the accuracy. We stress that with CKKS, it is possible to reduce the encryption noise without bootstrapping, since the noise is part of the message. In [ADE+23], following a suggestion from [DMPS24], the authors proposed to use such noise cleaning only after every few gates rather than after every gate, leading to improved throughput. This was used to homomorphically evaluate AES multiple times in parallel. The throughput was further lowered in [BCKS24], which introduced variants of the CKKS bootstrapping algorithm [CHK+18] specifically designed for binary data. Borrowing the figures from [BCKS24, Table 2], evaluating a binary gate with CKKS has an amortized cost of 17.6µs in single-thread CPU (where amortization is over slots and the multiple sequential gates that can be applied between two consecutive bootstraps). For sufficiently large computations, this compares favorably to [DM15,CGGI16a], which typically consumes around 10ms per binary gate [CGGI16b]. Interestingly, the bootstrapping algorithms from [BCKS24] are compatible with DM/CGGI ciphertexts. By relying on fast ring packing [BCK+23], one then obtains a CKKS-based DM/CGGI bootstrapping algorithm for multiple ciphertexts which outperforms other DM/CGGI bootstrapping when the number of ciphertexts to be bootstrapped is around 200.

Drucker et al. [DMPS24] also considered viewing small bit-length integers as real/complex numbers and using CKKS to perform SIMD homomorphic computations on integers. The cost increases fast with the bit-length, notably because of the considered noise-cleaning strategy. The integer is homomorphically decomposed in base 2 by repeatedly computing the most significant bit. The latter is quite costly as this discontinuous function is implemented using a precise polynomial approximation of a step function. The bits are then cleaned individually before being recombined in a cleaned integer. In [CKKL24], Chung *et al.* considered a different path for enabling small bit-length integer computations with CKKS. Instead of embedding an integer $m \in [0, t)$ for some small t into $\mathbb{C}$ using the identity function, they exploit t-th roots of unity and send m to $\exp(2i\pi m/t)$. By restricting the CKKS plaintext space to small balls around these t points, discrete computations can be performed via numerically stable polynomial interpolations. Indeed, Lagrange's interpolation on equispaced points of the real line suffers from huge oscillations, which is known as Runge's phenomenon. On the contrary, roots of unity make the interpolating polynomial nicely converge to the target function (assuming it is sufficiently smooth). Similarly to binary circuits [DMPS24], the noise grows with homomorphic operations and the data points progressively become less separated. This is also handled with a noise-cleaning polynomial evaluation.

The works above on small integers use CKKS bootstrapping in a black-box manner. This raises the following questions: As in the case of bits, can CKKS bootstrapping be adapted for small bit-length integers? Can we obtain a CKKS-based batch-bootstrapping algorithm for multiple DM/CGGI ciphertexts for small integers? Similarly to DM/CGGI functional/programmable bootstrapping [CJP21, KS22], can we bootstrap and evaluate a function simultaneously?

Contributions. We introduce two new CKKS bootstrapping algorithms for plaintexts respectively encoding small bit-length integers and bits.

The first algorithm, SI-BTS (for small integer bootstrapping), bootstraps ciphertexts whose plaintexts are integers of small bit-sizes (e.g., 8 bits). It can be combined with an arbitrary table look-up, at no extra cost, providing a CKKS analogue to functional bootstrapping [CJP21, KS22] in the context of the DM/CGGI fully homomorphic encryption scheme. Like in [CIM19], several functions of the same plaintexts can be evaluated for a cost that is significantly less than that of applying the functional bootstrap multiple times. Finally, as the inputs and outputs of SI-BTS are compatible with DM/CGGI ciphertexts, SI-BTS can be used to perform functional bootstraps on multiple DM/CGGI ciphertexts at once, rather than running the DM/CGGI functional bootstrapping algorithm in parallel on the multiple ciphertexts.

The second algorithm, BB-BTS (for batch-bits bootstrapping), bootstraps in one go multiple CKKS ciphertexts for bits. For a single ciphertext, it essentially corresponds to the BinBoot algorithm from [BCKS24]. As its cost grows slowly with the number of batched ciphertexts (up to some integer bit-length), when several ciphertexts are considered, it leads to a large throughput improvement compared to [BCKS24].

Implementation. We implemented SI-BTS and BB-BTS in the C++ HEaaN library [Cry22]. For Int-BTS, we designed parameter sets optimizing latency, primarily focusing on obtaining an efficient algorithm for batch functional bootstrapping of DM/CGGI ciphertexts. As showed by its multiple uses (see, e.g., [CJP21, CHMS22, TCBS23]) the importance of functional bootstrapping cannot be overstated. For BB-BTS, we designed parameter sets optimizing throughput.

Table 1 illustrates the performance of CKKS-based functional bootstrapping for integers of various bit-sizes. We compare the performance to the functional bootstrapping algorithm of DM/CGGI [KS22] and to the BFV/BGV-based functional bootstrapping algorithms of [LW23]. The DM/CGGI figures are retrieved from the tfhe-rs benchmarks page, and correspond to a similar computing environment (single-thread CPU).[1]

Table 1. Comparison for look-up table evaluations for various input bit-sizes. The figures for [KS22] only provide 100-bit security, while all others aim at 128-bit security.

	Number of input LWE ciphertexts	Number of input/output bits	Total time	Amortized time
[Zam24]	1	2	6.4 ms	6.4 ms
		4	12.9 ms	12.9 ms
		6	104 ms	104 ms
		8	489 ms	489 ms
[KS22]	1	8	21 s	21 s
[LW23]	2^{15}	9	220 s	6.7 ms
This work	2^{12}	2	3.20 s	0.78 ms
		4	6.41 s	1.57 ms
		6	11.0 s	2.67 ms
		8	15.4 s	3.75 ms
		10	50.3 s	12.3 ms

Table 2 focuses on throughput for binary gate evaluations. The run-time figures for [LMSS23] and [LW24] are borrowed from the corresponding papers. The figures for [BCKS24] and [DMPS24] are borrowed from [BCKS24], and we included only the 'improved version' figures for [DMPS24]. All the experiments were on similar computing environments (single-thread CPU). Our batch bits bootstrapping (BB-BTS) that bootstraps 5 ciphertexts in parallel gives 2.38x faster amortized gate evaluation time than the state-of-the-art [BCKS24]. In this figure, we considered $k = 5$ batched ciphertexts in parallel because it shows the best performance, as illustrated in Table 7. As we increase the batch number k, the amortized bootstrapping time decreases at first but it starts to increase at some point. This is because the cost of BB-BTS depends on k and the benefit of simultaneously computing several bootstrappings is offset by the increased cost. For a more detailed analysis on the effect of k, we refer to Sect. 6.2.

---

[1] Choosing the number of input LWE ciphertexts to be as large as 2^{12} is somewhat necessary to reduce the amortized bootstrapping time. If one uses a smaller number of input LWE ciphertexts instead, one may consider CKKS bootstrapping for fewer slots (i.e., thin bootstrapping). However, as the overall bootstrapping time scales sublinearly with the number of slots, using fewer slots is less efficient in terms of amortized bootstrapping time.

Table 2. Throughput comparison for BB-BTS. Here number of plaintext slots refers to the number of bits being bootstrapped per single (batched) bootstrapping. All figures correspond to parameters aiming at 128-bit security.

	Number of plaintext slots	Amortized bootstrapping time per gate
[LMSS23]	1	6.49 ms
[LW24]		1.5 ms
[DMPS24]	2^{16}	27.7μ s
[BCKS24]		17.6μ s
This work	$5 \cdot 2^{16}$	7.39μ s

1.1 Technical Overview

Modulus Consumption in Bootstrapping. To explain our contributions, we first highlight what makes conventional bootstrapping costly and how this is handled with the bootstrapping algorithm from [BCKS24] for bits. CKKS performs plaintext operations on $\mathbb{C}^{N/2}$ by manipulating ciphertexts belonging in R_q^2 where $R_q = \mathbb{Z}[X]/(X^N + 1)$ for some power-of-two integer N. The modulus q may vary but, for any given N, it is bounded from above as else the underlying hard problem, a variant of Ring-LWE [SSTX09, LPR10], does not provide sufficient security. The primary homomorphic operations are component-wise addition, multiplication and complex conjugation, as well as cyclic rotations of the vector coefficients. While many additions, conjugations and rotations can be performed without significant difficulties, repeated multiplications are more difficult to support. They involve a rescaling operation that decreases the modulus q of the ciphertext by a number of bits that grows linearly with the precision of the plaintexts considered in the computations. Therefore, the current modulus directly limits the number of sequential multiplications that can be subsequently performed, if one is restricted to the primary operations mentioned above. The CKKS bootstrapping procedure [CHK+18] takes as input a low-modulus ciphertext and outputs a high-modulus ciphertext that decrypts to the same message, up to some noise. Homomorphic computations can then be run endlessly. Despite many improvements [CCS19, HK20, LLL+21, BTPH22, KPK+22, LLK+22] (among others), CKKS bootstrapping still suffers from two main drawbacks: first, its run-time is high; second, it itself requires significant multiplicative depth and hence consumes a large amount of modulus. Modulus consumption in bootstrapping is a main factor in the efficiency of CKKS: a lower modulus consumption in bootstrapping provides more room for useful computations, helping for throughput; it may also allow to choose a smaller N, which helps for latency.

When it comes to modulus consumption, the two main components of bootstrapping are a linear evaluation phase called CtS (for coefficients to slots), and a non-linear evaluation phase called EvalMod (for evaluation of modular reduction). The other linear phase called StC consumes less modulus, and the remaining bootstrapping component, ModRaise, creates modulus. The input of CtS is a ciphertext whose underlying plaintext is $\mathbf{V} \cdot (\mathbf{x} + \mathbf{I})$, where $\mathbf{V}$ is a matrix that is closely related to the discrete Fourier transform, $\mathbf{x}$ is a vector containing the message and satisfying $\|\mathbf{x}\|_\infty < 1/2$, and $\mathbf{I}$ is a vector whose coordinates are bounded integers. The main task of bootstrapping is to remove $\mathbf{I}$. CtS is a homomorphic multiplication by $\mathbf{V}^{-1}$: its output is a ciphertext that decrypts to $\approx \mathbf{x} + \mathbf{I}$. EvalMod evaluates, on all coordinates in parallel, a polynomial that approximates the function $x + I \mapsto x$ on a relevant domain. The modulus consumption is driven by two aspects. First, all computations are performed in some precision that is larger than the bit-size of the manipulated data, i.e., $x + I$ with an accuracy that provides enough meaningful bits of the message encoded in x. Second, this per-level modulus consumption is multiplied by the multiplicative depth of CtS and EvalMod.

The first aspect above explains why the BinBoot bootstrapping algorithm from [BCKS24] consumes little modulus and could even be implemented with ring degree as low as $N = 2^{14}$. BinBoot was designed for bootstrapping plaintexts corresponding to bits, encoded into reals as proposed in [DMPS24]. A bit $b \in \{0,1\}$ is represented by a real $b + \varepsilon$ for some ε satisfying $|\varepsilon| \ll 1$. An essential aspect of BinBoot is that the bit b is encoded into x as $x \approx b/2$. This is in sharp contrast to using an x that satisfies $|x| \ll 1$ as is the case in most other CKKS bootstrapping algorithms. As a result, a small precision suffices for bootstrapping computations: one only needs to handle I and a few more bits to capture a good estimate of b. Further, the multiplicative depth of EvalMod is itself limited as the manipulated data has low bit-size.

As a minor contribution, we note that the cleaning strategy from [BCKS24] can be modified to lower bootstrapping modulus consumption. Error cleaning increases the precision of the bit b, i.e., reduces the magnitude of ε in $b + \varepsilon$. In [BCKS24], cleaning is performed before bootstrapping, and the plaintext is represented on sufficiently many bits to capture this accuracy. Instead, one can perform bootstrapping with a lower precision and clean the error after bootstrapping. Consistently, the accuracy of the plaintext can be decreased. This saves only a few bits of modulus per multiplication level, but this saving is multiplied by the multiplicative depth of bootstrapping.

Bootstrapping Integers with Low Modulus Consumption. To minimize modulus consumption in bootstrapping, we would like that the pre-CtS plaintext $\mathbf{V} \cdot (\mathbf{x} + \mathbf{I})$ is such that $\mathbf{x}$ contains m in its most significant bits, as in [BCKS24]. We have two embeddings of integers $m \in [0, t)$ into complex numbers at hand: either encode m as $m \in \mathbb{C}$ (up to some noise) or as $\exp(2i\pi m/t) \in \mathbb{C}$ (up to some noise). CtS works with both encodings. Oppositely, the subsequent bootstrapping step should remove I using a polynomial evaluation, which can be more or less difficult depending on the choice of encoding and scaling. Let us examine the four possibilities at hand:

- map $m/t + I$ to m/t (for all $m \in \mathbb{Z} \cap [0, t)$ and all integer I in some range);
- map $m/t + I$ to $\exp(2i\pi m/t)$;
- map $\exp(2i\pi m/t) + I$ to m/t (for all $m \in \mathbb{Z} \cap [0, t)$ and all Gaussian integer $I = I_1 + iI_2$ with I_1 and I_2 in some range);
- map $\exp(2i\pi m/t) + I$ to $\exp(2i\pi m/t)$.

In principle, any of these can be handled by using a polynomial approximation around the distinguished points (interpolation may not suffice, as the distinguished points are noisy). For a growing value of t, the first interpolation task converges to finding a polynomial approximation of the $y \mapsto y \bmod 1$ function. For the remaining three, let us only consider the real part, to simplify: the second function is $y \mapsto \cos y$, the third is $y \mapsto \arccos(y \bmod 1)$ and the fourth is $y \mapsto \arccos(\cos y)$. Out of these, only the second one is differentiable, making it more suitable for polynomial interpolation. We hence choose the second mapping. Conveniently, the usual EvalMod phase of CKKS bootstrapping is typically implemented by a polynomial approximation to a trigonometric function, so that it can be readily replaced by an "EvalExp" that sends $m/t + I$ to

$$\exp\left(2i\pi\left(\frac{m}{t} + I\right)\right) = \exp\left(2i\pi\frac{m}{t}\right) .$$

Indeed, the complex exponential can be computed with a cosine evaluation for the real part and a sine evaluation for the complex part. Further, these can be evaluated efficiently by relying on the double-angle formula. Overall, the resulting bootstrapping, which we refer to as IntRootBoot, sends a ciphertext that contains the integer m embedded as $m/t \in \mathbb{C}$ to a root of unity $\exp(2i\pi m/t) \in \mathbb{C}$.

Interestingly, using EvalExp to bootstrap integers stored in the most significant bits has already been considered in [BGGJ20], in the context of converting DM/CGGI ciphertexts to CKKS ciphertexts. Also, by taking $t = 2$ and considering only the real part, one recovers the BinBoot algorithm from [BCKS24].

An Improved Tool-Box for Roots of Unity. To obtain good efficiency, we first extend the toolbox for homomorphically manipulating t-th roots of unity. First, we revisit the analysis of the IntRootBoot algorithm from [BGGJ20]. We focus on modulus consumption. By using the sparse-secret encapsulation technique from [BTPH22], one can ensure that $|I| \leq 15$ with probability extremely close to 1, so that $5 + \log t$ bits of precision suffice to represent $I + m/t$. A few extra bits are needed to separate the data points, and a little over $(\log N)/2$ bits should be added to handle the inherent inaccuracy of CKKS homomorphic computations. For moderate values of t and $N = 2^{16}$, this adds up to as low as ≈ 30 bits of precision for the elementary CKKS operations, whereas other CKKS bootstrapping algorithms often consider up to 45 or 50 bits of precision. Recall that this modulus gain is multiplied by the multiplicative depth of bootstrapping, which is typically over 10.

We also propose improvements for interpolation from complex roots of unity, which was studied in [CKKL24]. Note that such an interpolation seems necessary for FHE based on IntRootBoot. Indeed, the input complex-plane embedding is $m \mapsto m$ whereas the output embedding is $m \mapsto \exp(2i\pi m/t)$. One then needs to convert roots of unity back to integers at some stage, to be able to use IntRootBoot again. As a first remark, we observe that any monomial x^i for $0 \leq i < t$ can be replaced by $\overline{x}^{t-i}$, as we are only interested in t-th roots of unity. As homomorphic conjugation does not consume modulus, this provides a total degree reduction by a factor 2 and hence allows to save one multiplicative depth. Second, we consider the noise-cleaning functionality. A cleaning function of degree $t + 1$ was proposed in [CKKL24]. Instead, we investigate combined interpolation and cleaning. This may be achieved using Hermite interpolation (which extends Lagrange interpolation by imposing that the derivatives of the polynomial vanish at all interpolation points). For t-th roots of unity, we expect Hermite interpolation to provide polynomials of degree $2t$. This would already be interesting compared to [CKKL24], as evaluation and cleaning could be achieved in depth $1 + \log t$ instead of $1 + 2 \log t$. We decrease depth consumption further than this by designing bivariate polynomials in x and $\overline{x}$ of degree $t - 1$ that properly interpolate and clean (note that replacing x^i by $\overline{x}^{t-i}$ for large values of i in the Hermite interpolation indeed decreases the degree but does not preserve the cleaning functionality). This also saves one multiplication depth, down to $\log t$.

New Bootstrapping Algorithms. The design rationale of our first bootstrapping algorithm, SI-BTS, starts from the observation that BinBoot is wasteful. For a single bit of interest, a multiplication consumes more than 20 bits of modulus. For this consumption, we may as well consider small integers rather than bits: the required CKKS precision is about the same, but much more data is handled. SI-BTS hence considers an input ciphertext whose underlying plaintext is a vector $\mathbf{m} \in \mathbb{Z}^{N/2}$ with each coefficient in $[0, t)$ for some integer t. It then calls IntRootBoot, to obtain a high-modulus ciphertext that decrypts to $\exp(2i\pi\mathbf{m}/t)$. If t remains small, the multiplicative depth of the approximate complex exponential evaluation does not grow, as we rely on good polynomial approximations to the sine and cosine functions on a whole interval containing $2 \cdot 15 = 30$ periods, even for $t = 2$. Once we have $\exp(2i\pi\mathbf{m}/t)$, we could keep this format and perform computations on roots of unity as described in [CKKL24]. However, at some stage, we should switch back to integers to apply SI-BTS again. This is achieved by a polynomial interpolation on the roots of unity. Further, we propose to combine the first interpolation after the exponential evaluation with cleaning: this consumes only one extra multiplicative depth compared to a simple interpolation but allows to lower the precision inside bootstrapping (as the output ciphertext is subsequently cleaned). As the approach allows any interpolation from complex roots of unity to integers, we can simultaneously evaluate an arbitrary function from $[0, t)$ to $[0, t)$ at no extra cost. Finally, we note that the input format of SI-BTS closely matches that of DM/CGGI ciphertexts and use it to provide a CKKS-based batch functional bootstrapping algorithm for DM/CGGI.

Our second algorithm, BB-BTS, takes as input many ciphertexts for bits and bootstraps them in a batch. More concretely, assume we have k input CKKS ciphertexts, each of which encrypts a vector $\mathbf{b}_j \in \{0, 1\}^{N/2}$. We could execute Binboot k times in parallel. Alternatively, we pack the data into a single ciphertext by homomorphically performing a linear combination $\sum_{0 \le j < k} 2^j \mathbf{b}_j$, resulting into a vector whose coefficients are integers in $[0, 2^k)$. We then use IntRootBoot to obtain a high-modulus ciphertext that decrypts to the vector of roots of unity $\exp(2i\pi(\sum_j 2^{j-k} b_j))$ (for each slot). To recover individual high-modulus ciphertexts that encrypt the $\mathbf{b}_j$'s, we perform k polynomial interpolations $\exp(2i\pi(\sum_j 2^{j-k} b_j)) \mapsto b_j$. Due to the recursive structure of roots of unity of power-of-two orders, these interpolations are far from arbitrary, allowing for an efficient implementation even for moderate k. Finally, we clean the error terms of the individual bits in parallel. This is far thriftier than cleaning the roots of unity and then converting to integers.

2   Background on CKKS

For a power-of-two $N \ge 1$ and $q \ge 2$, we define the rings $\mathcal{R} = \mathbb{Z}[X]/(X^N + 1)$ and $\mathcal{R}_q = \mathcal{R}/q\mathcal{R}$. We let i denote the complex imaginary unit. We let $\bar{x}$ denote the complex conjugate of $x \in \mathbb{C}$. Vectors are denoted in bold lower-case. The notation log refers to base-2 logarithm.

2.1   Encodings

We define the Discrete Fourier Transform (DFT) $\mathsf{DFT} : \mathcal{R} \to \mathbb{C}^{N/2}$ as

$$\mathsf{DFT}(p(X)) = (p(\zeta_j))_{0 \le j < N/2} \ ,$$

where $\zeta_j = \zeta^{5^j}$ for a complex $2N$-th root of unity $\zeta \in \mathbb{C}$. Its inverse iDFT : $\mathbb{C}^{N/2} \to \mathcal{R}$ is the inverse Discrete Fourier Transform (iDFT). In the CKKS scheme, messages are elements of $\mathbb{C}^{N/2}$, up to some accuracy quantified by a scaling factor $\Delta > 0$. To encode a message $\mathbf{z} \in \mathbb{C}^{N/2}$ into a plaintext $\mathsf{pt} \in \mathcal{R}$ with a scaling factor Δ, one uses the encoding map $\mathsf{Ecd} : \mathbb{C}^{N/2} \to \mathcal{R}$ defined as

$$\mathsf{Ecd}(\mathbf{z}) = \lfloor \Delta \cdot \mathsf{iDFT}(\mathbf{z}) \rceil \ .$$

The decoding map is defined as $\mathsf{Dcd}(m) = \mathsf{DFT}(m)/\Delta$.

As put forward in [DMPS24], one may focus on a subset of $\mathbb{C}$ to handle discrete data. For example, a bit $b \in \{0, 1\}$ can be viewed as a complex number $b \in \mathbb{C}$. *Bits encoding* maps a vector $\mathbf{b} \in \{0, 1\}^{N/2}$ to $\mathsf{Ecd}(\mathbf{b}) \in \mathbb{C}^{N/2}$. For integers in $[0, t)$ for some arbitrary $t > 0$, one may extend the latter encoding of bits by using the inclusion $\mathbb{Z} \cap [0, t) \subset \mathbb{C}$: an integer vector $\mathbf{v} \in \mathbb{Z}^{N/2}$ is encoded to a plaintext $\mathsf{Ecd}(\mathbf{v}) \in \mathbb{C}^{N/2}$. We will refer to the latter as *integers encoding*. Another way to embed small integers in the complex plane is to use complex roots of unity. As showed in [CKKL24], such an encoding is advantageous in the context of evaluating look-up tables in CKKS, from the perspective of numerical stability. Let $\phi_t : \mathbb{Z}_t \to \mathbb{C}$ denote the map $m \mapsto e^{2\pi i \cdot m/t}$. The *roots-of-unity encoding* of a vector $\mathbf{v} \in \mathbb{Z}_t^{N/2}$ is $\mathsf{Enc} \circ \phi_t^{N/2}$, where $\phi_t^{N/2}$ is the evaluation of ϕ_t on all coefficients of $\mathbf{v}$ in parallel.

CKKS computations induce error growth. If we start with good approximations to encodings as above (for bits, integers or roots-of-unity), computations may lead to less precise approximations. In order to keep the plaintexts close to the expected encodings, it was suggested in [DMPS24] to use cleaning functions to reduce the error. For instance, for bits encoding, one may consider the polynomial $h_1(x) = 3x^2 - 2x^3$ initially introduced in [CKK20]: it has minimal degree such that $h_1(0) = 0$, $h_1(1) = 1$ and $h_1'(0) = h_1'(1) = 0$. In particular, it satisfies the following cleaning property.

Lemma 1. *For all $b \in \{0, 1\}$ and $\varepsilon \in [-1, 1]$, we have:*

$$|h_1(b + \varepsilon) - b| \leq 3|\varepsilon|^2 + 2|\varepsilon|^3 \ .$$

Note that $3|\varepsilon|^2 + 2|\varepsilon|^3$ is much smaller than $|\varepsilon|$, if $|\varepsilon|$ is sufficiently small.

In [DMPS24], the authors suggested to clean small integers by extracting bits (with a homomorphic evaluation of binary decomposition), cleaning bits using h_1 and then recombining the cleaned bits. For roots of unity, the authors of [CKKL24] considered the polynomial $((t + 1)x - x^{t+1})/t$.

2.2 Ciphertexts and Elementary Operations

A CKKS ciphertext for a message $\mathbf{z} \in \mathbb{C}^{N/2}$ for a secret key $s \in \mathcal{R}$ is a pair $(a, b) \in \mathcal{R}_q$ such that $a \cdot s + b \approx \mathsf{Ecd}(\mathbf{z})$. In that case, we say that the ciphertext encrypts $\mathbf{z}$ in its slots. Sometimes, we have $a \cdot s + b \approx \Delta \cdot z'$ for some scaling factor Δ and where z' starts with the real parts of the coefficients of $\mathbf{z}$ and continues with the imaginary parts. In this case, we say that $\mathbf{z}$ is encrypted in the coefficients.

The homomorphic addition algorithm add takes as input two ciphertexts modulo q and outputs a ciphertext that decrypts to the sum of the plaintexts underlying the input ciphertexts (for encryption with respect to both slots and coefficients). The homomorphic conjugation algorithm conj takes as input a ciphertext modulo q and outputs a ciphertext that decrypts to the coefficient-wise complex conjugate of the plaintext underlying the input ciphertext (for slots-encryption). We will not explicitly need homomorphic rotation in this work. Note that these algorithms preserve the ciphertext modulus q.

The homomorphic multiplication algorithm mult takes as input two ciphertexts for a common modulus q and a common scaling factor Δ. It outputs a ciphertext whose underlying plaintext is close to the coefficient-wise product of the plaintexts underlying the input ciphertexts (for slots-encryption). The modulus of the output ciphertext is $q' \approx q/\Delta$.

Note that for a given ring degree N, the ciphertext modulus q cannot exceed some value if one wants to maintain sufficient security. As multiplications decrease the ciphertext modulus, the number of multiplications that one can perform sequentially while only relying on the operations mentioned so far is bounded. For this reason, the CKKS literature always considers a chain of moduli $q_0 < q_1 < \ldots$ corresponding to multiplication levels. The integer q_0 is called the base modulus.

2.3   Bootstrapping

Bootstrapping allows one to regain modulus: it takes as input a ciphertext with a small modulus and outputs a ciphertext with higher modulus, whose underlying plaintext is close to the plaintext underlying the input ciphertext. Bootstrapping consists of the following four components.

- **Slots-to-Coefficients** (StC). Given a ciphertext that encrypts a complex vector $\mathbf{z} \in \mathbb{R}^{N/2}$ in its slots, we convert it to a ciphertext that encrypts $\mathbf{z}$ in its coefficients. This can be realized via homomorphic evaluation of DFT.
- **Modulus Raising** (ModRaise). Given a ciphertext ct at the base modulus q_0 encrypting a plaintext $m \in \mathcal{R}$, we regard it as a ciphertext encrypting $m + q_0 I \in \mathcal{R}$ without modulus. This increases the ciphertext modulus, while adding a small multiple of the base modulus.
- **Coefficients-to-Slots** (CtS). To prepare the removal of the $q_0 I$ term introduced in the coefficients by ModRaise, we convert the ciphertext to the slot-encoded format. This is realized with homomorphic evaluation of iDFT.
- **Homomorphic Modular Reduction** (EvalMod). We remove the $q_0 I$ term by homomorphically evaluating the "modulo-q_0" function (in a SIMD manner). Since modular reduction is discontinuous, one may set parameters in a way that ensures that there is a gap between m and q_0, so that it suffices to approximate the "modulo-q_0" function only on small intervals around integer multiples of q_0. This is achieved by a polynomial approximation to the $x \mapsto (q_0/2\pi) \cdot \sin(2\pi x/q_0)$ function.

In this work, we consider StC-*first bootstrapping*, which executes EvalMod ∘ CtS ∘ ModRaise ∘ StC. This requires to start the process at a modulus larger than q_0 so that StC is completed at the base modulus q_0.

Real bootstrapping is restricted to ciphertexts whose underlying plaintexts are in $\mathbb{R}^{N/2}$ (in slots). *Complex bootstrapping* works for plaintexts in $\mathbb{C}^{N/2}$. The main difference lies in the EvalMod function, whose correctness holds if its input ciphertext decrypts to a real vector. If the vector is complex, one extracts the real and imaginary parts using homomorphic conjugation just before EvalMod, runs EvalMod twice in parallel, and finally recombines the outputs into a single ciphertext that encodes the desired complex vector.

In [BCKS24], the EvalMod function was adapted to handle binary data ciphertexts (i.e., with $\mathbf{z} \in \{0,1\}^{N/2}$). At the bottom modulus, i.e., just before ModRaise, the ciphertexts encode $\mathbf{z}$ in their most significant bits, and a properly scaled version of the sine function is used to bootstrap (other variants are considered in [BCKS24], such as evaluating a binary gate and bootstrap at once).

3   Improving the Roots-of-Unity Toolbox

In this section, we consider the efficiency of some homomorphic computations involving roots-of-unity encodings.

We first revisit the conversion algorithm from [BGGJ20], from DM/CGGI ciphertexts to a CKKS ciphertext. We observe that the main step of this algorithm bootstraps a ciphertext for integers into a ciphertext for roots of unity. We provide a depth-consumption analysis, based on the observation that the data of interest is encrypted in the most significant bits. We then consider the task of evaluating look-up-tables using roots-of-unity encodings, and decrease the required depth compared to [CKKL24]. Finally, we introduce an extension of interpolation that also decreases the error of a roots-of-unity encoding, for a multiplicative depth that is twice lower than the depth required to interpolate and clean, based on the tools from [CKKL24].

3.1   Revising Chimera's Conversion from DM/CGGI to CKKS

Below, we study an algorithm introduced in [BGGJ20, Section 4.1], in the context of converting multiple DM/CGGI ciphertexts to a CKKS ciphertext. This conversion algorithm handles three difficulties. The first one is of a packing nature: a DM/CGGI ciphertext contains a single small integer as plaintext, whereas a CKKS ciphertext can store up to N (when using coefficients-encoding, or slots-encoding with real and imaginary parts). In this subsection, we do not consider this aspect. The second difficulty is that a DM/CGGI ciphertext has a small modulus, typically with magnitude similar to the base modulus q_0 of CKKS. The third difficulty is of a scaling nature: in DM/CGGI, the plaintext lies in the most significant bits of the ciphertext (sometimes with some margin to allow for one homomorphic addition), whereas in a CKKS ciphertext, the most significant bits are typically not used. Such a plaintext scaling prevents the use of conventional CKKS bootstrapping, as it makes it very difficult to approximate the discontinuous "modulo-q_0" function (see Sect. 2.3). More concretely, a coefficients-encoded CKKS ciphertext $(a, b) \in \mathcal{R}_q^2$ with DM/CGGI plaintext scaling would be such that $a \cdot s + b \approx (q/t) \cdot z$, where s is the secret key and $z \in \mathcal{R}_t$ is the plaintext. Oppositely, a typical CKKS ciphertext would satisfy $a \cdot s + b \approx (\Delta/t) \cdot z$ with $\Delta \ll q$.

Putting aside the packing of multiple DM/CGGI ciphertexts, the algorithm from [BGGJ20, Section 4.1] can be revisited as a transformation from a low-level coefficients-encoding CKKS ciphertext for a plaintext in the most significant bits into a high-level roots-of-unity-encoding CKKS ciphertext. We revisit it as a CKKS bootstrapping algorithm from slots-encoded integers to slots-encoded roots of unity for the same data.

We assume that the input ciphertext decrypts to a vector (in slots) that corresponds to a vector $\mathbf{m} = \mathbf{z} + \boldsymbol{\varepsilon}$ in $\mathbb{C}^{N/2}$ where $\mathbf{z}$ is an integer vector with coefficients in $[0, t)$ and the error term $\boldsymbol{\varepsilon}$ satisfies $\|\boldsymbol{\varepsilon}\|_\infty \ll 1$. We choose the scaling factor Δ_0 at the base modulus q_0 as $\Delta_0 = q_0/t$, so that for ciphertexts modulo q_0, the message is coefficients-encoded in the most significant bits. IntRootBoot, described in Algorithm 1, proceeds as follows.

- It runs StC to put the message in the coefficients. The message is then placed in the most significant bits, by choice of Δ_0.

- It runs ModRaise to increase the ciphertext modulus. The message can then be described as $(q_0/t)\cdot m + q_0\cdot I \in \mathcal{R}$ for some $I \in \mathcal{R}$. Note that it can be rewritten as $(q_0/t)(m + tI)$: the aim of the subsequent steps is to homomorphically reduce $m + tI$ modulo t to remove the tI term.
- It runs CtS to put the message in the slots. It uses homomorphic conjugation to compute the real part.
- It runs EvalExp, which is the homomorphic evaluation of the function $x \mapsto e^{2\pi i x/t}$. Note that after ModRaise, the message is interpreted as $m + tI$, and the exponential function can be implemented using homomorphic conjugation and the trigonometric functions $x \mapsto \sin(2\pi x/t)$ and $\mapsto \cos(2\pi x/t)$ (using the identity $e^{ix} = \cos(x) + i\sin(x)$).

The above extends to a complex bootstrapping algorithm, i.e., for an input plaintext $\mathbf{m} = \mathbf{z} + \varepsilon$ in $\mathbb{C}^{N/2}$ where both the real and imaginary parts of $\mathbf{z}$ are integer vectors with coefficients in $[0, t)$. This is achieved by appropriately adapting Steps 2 and 3 of Algorithm 1, as discussed in Sect. 2.3.

Algorithm 1: IntRootBoot

Setting: $\Delta_0 = q_0/t$.
Input : $\mathsf{ct} = \mathsf{Enc}_{\mathsf{sk}}(\mathbf{z} + \varepsilon) \in \mathcal{R}_q^2$ with $\mathbf{z} \in \{0, 1, \ldots, t-1\}^{N/2}$ and $\|\varepsilon\|_\infty \ll 1$.
Output: $\mathsf{ct}_{\mathsf{out}} \in \mathcal{R}_Q^2$.
1 $\mathsf{ct}' \leftarrow \mathsf{CtS} \circ \mathsf{ModRaise} \circ \mathsf{StC}(\mathsf{ct})$;
2 $\mathsf{ct}'' \leftarrow (\mathsf{conj}(\mathsf{ct}') + \mathsf{ct}')/2$;
3 $\mathsf{ct}_{\mathsf{out}} \leftarrow \mathsf{EvalExp}(\mathsf{ct}'')$;
4 **return** $\mathsf{ct}_{\mathsf{out}}$.

Let $\mathsf{ct} = \mathsf{Enc}_{\mathsf{sk}}(\mathbf{z} + \varepsilon) \in \mathcal{R}_q^2$ be an input ciphertext encoding an integer vector $\mathbf{z} \in \{0, 1, \ldots, t-1\}^{N/2}$ with an error ε satisfying $\|\varepsilon\|_\infty \ll 1$. Assume that homomorphic operations StC, ModRaise, StC and conj and EvalExp give sufficiently high precision. Then the output $\mathsf{ct}_{\mathsf{out}}$ of Algorithm 1 encrypts the vector $(e^{2\pi i(z_j + \varepsilon_j)/t})_{0 \le j < N/2}$, up to a tiny error. The latter is close to $e^{2\pi i z_j/t}$. Indeed, the difference can be bounded from above as follows, for all j:

$$
\begin{aligned}
|e^{2\pi i(z_j + \varepsilon_j)/t} - e^{2\pi i z_j/t}| &= |e^{2\pi i z_j/t}| \cdot |e^{2\pi i \varepsilon_j/t} - 1| \\
&= |e^{2\pi i \varepsilon_j/t} - 1| \\
&\le |\sin(2\pi\varepsilon_j)| + |\cos(2\pi\varepsilon_j) - 1| \\
&= |\sin(2\pi\varepsilon_j)| + |2\sin^2(\pi\varepsilon_j)| \\
&\le 2\pi\|\varepsilon\|_\infty + 2\pi^2\|\varepsilon\|_\infty^2 .
\end{aligned}
$$

Apart from EvalExp, all operations are as in CKKS bootstrapping. EvalExp can be performed using the formula $e^{ix} = \cos(x) + i\sin(x)$. Homomorphic evaluations of sin and cos have been extensively explored throughout the CKKS literature (see, e.g., [CHK+18,LLL+21]), as it is a key ingredient of CKKS bootstrapping algorithms. An approach is to perform EvalExp by homomorphically evaluating the sine function twice (once for $\sin(2\pi x)$ and once for $\cos(2\pi x) = \sin(\pi/4 - 2\pi x)$). The cost is then roughly twice that of EvalMod. As EvalMod and CtS have similar costs (the other bootstrapping steps being less costly), the total cost of IntRootBoot is a little larger than the cost of the conventional CKKS bootstrapping.

We now argue that IntRootBoot consumes relatively little modulus. Since conventional CKKS bootstrapping and IntRootBoot both evaluate StC, CtS and EvalMod/EvalExp, the multiplicative depth consumption is the same. However, as there is no gap between message and modulus at the base level (corresponding to modulus q_0), we may use relatively smaller scaling factors during CtS and EvalMod, leading to a reduction of modulus consumption. For concreteness, let us assume that we are interested in integers in $[0, t)$, with an accuracy of $\gamma_{acc} = \log \|\varepsilon\|_\infty$ bits, and an FHE computing noise of γ_{noise}. The FHE noise is typically slightly above $(\log N + \log h)/2$, where h is the Hamming weight of the secret key (to fix the ideas, one may consider that $\gamma_{noise} = 12$). For each level in CtS and EvalExp, the scaling factor must have $\approx \log(2I_{\max}) + \log t + \gamma_{acc} + \gamma_{noise}$ bits, to represent the I term with coefficients in $[-I_{\max}, I_{\max}]$, the integer vector $\mathbf{z}$ under scope, the accuracy bits and the FHE computing noise. By using the sparse secret encapsulation technique from [BTPH22], the integer I belongs to $[-15, 15]$ with probability extremely close to 1, leading to $\log(2I_{\max}) = 5$. In the StC levels, there is no need for these first 5 bits, as the I term vanishes due to the use of appropriate roots of unity. This gives the following rough approximation to modulus consumption:

$$\mathsf{ModCons}_{\mathsf{IntRootBoot}} \approx (\ell_{\mathsf{CtS}} + \ell_{\mathsf{EvalExp}}) \cdot (5 + \log t + \gamma_{acc} + \gamma_{noise})$$
$$+ \ell_{\mathsf{StC}} \cdot (\log t + \gamma_{acc} + \gamma_{noise}) \ ,$$

where ℓ_{CtS}, ℓ_{EvalExp} and ℓ_{StC} respectively refer to the multiplicative depths of CtS, EvalExp and StC.

By using conventional bootstrapping, one would need to consider a gap to encode the integer to be bootstrapped, to make it small compared to the bottom modulus, to enable a polynomial approximation to the "modulo-q_0" function. In practice, one often chooses a gap of $\gamma_{gap} \approx 10$ bits. This gap is added to the modulus consumption of all levels of CtS and EvalExp. This implies that IntRootBoot consumes $\approx (\ell_{\mathsf{CtS}} + \ell_{\mathsf{EvalExp}}) \cdot \gamma_{gap}$ fewer bits of modulus than conventional CKKS bootstrapping. For bootstrapping techniques that are currently used, this most often amounts to more than 100 bits.

3.2   Interpolation for Roots of Unity

We now consider the task of homomorphically evaluating a look-up table, from the $e^{2\pi ij/t}$'s for some integer $t \geq 2$ and $j \in \{0, 1, \ldots, t-1\}$ to arbitrary complex values $(y_j)_{0 \leq j < t}$. Concretely, we aim at finding a function f such that $f(e^{2\pi ij/t}) = y_j$ for all $0 \leq j < t$, which can be homomorphically evaluated with good efficiency and low modulus consumption. It was observed in [CKKL24] that complex t-th roots of unity provide good numerical stability when it comes to polynomial interpolation. We argue below that complex conjugation can help performing look-up table evaluations on such points.

Suppose that $f : x \mapsto f_0 + f_1 x + \ldots + f_{t-1} x^{t-1}$ is the Lagrange interpolation from the $e^{2\pi i j/t}$'s to the y_j's. In full generality, evaluating f requires depth $\log t$. Now, note that we may as well evaluate

$$g : x \mapsto \left(f_0 + f_1 x + \ldots + f_{\lfloor t/2 \rfloor} x^{\lfloor t/2 \rfloor} \right)$$
$$+ \left(f_{t-1} \overline{x} + f_{t-2} \overline{x}^2 + \ldots f_{\lfloor t/2 \rfloor + 1} \overline{x}^{t-(\lfloor t/2 \rfloor + 1)} \right) .$$

Indeed, on the $e^{2\pi i j/t}$'s, the values x^i and $\overline{x}^{t-i}$ coincide. Note that g requires a homomorphic conjugation. As homomorphic conjugation does not consume depth and g has degree twice less than f, it can be evaluated with one less multiplicative depth.

3.3   Combined Interpolation and Cleaning for Roots of Unity

We now describe another interpolation strategy, which simultaneously interpolates and increases the accuracy of the discrete data points. A first approach would be to use Hermite interpolation, i.e., extending Lagrange interpolation with the condition that the derivative of the polynomial cancels on the interpolation points. The cancelling derivatives imply a decrease of the noise, similarly to the h_1 function from Sect. 2.1. As there are twice more conditions, this polynomial has degree $< 2t$. Note that the complex conjugation approach of the previous subsection does not apply. It would result in a bivariate polynomial in x and $\overline{x}$ which is not differentiable. It preserves the evaluations of the initial polynomial, but there is no a priori reason for the noise-cleaning functionality to be preserved. For example, the polynomial $f(x) = 3x/2 + x^3/2$ cleans for inputs in $\{-1, 1\}$. However, the function $g(x) = 3x/2 + \overline{x}/2$ is equal to f on $\{-1, 1\}$ but without any cleaning functionality since $g(1 + e) = 1 + 3e/2 - \overline{e}/2$ has non-vanishing linear terms in e and $\overline{e}$.

We now explain how to exploit complex conjugation to obtain a combined interpolation and noise-cleaning functionality. Let f be the Lagrange interpolation polynomial, from the roots of unity to the desired y_j's. We consider the following function, which may be viewed as a bivariate polynomial in x and $\overline{x}$:

$$h : x \mapsto f_0 + \sum_{k=1}^{\lfloor t/2 \rfloor} \frac{f_k}{t} \left(k\overline{x}^{t-k} + (t-k)(k+1)x^k - k(t-k)x^{k+1}\overline{x} \right)$$
$$+ \sum_{k=\lfloor t/2 \rfloor + 1}^{t-1} \frac{f_k}{t} \left((t-k)x^k + k(t-k+1)\overline{x}^{t-k} - k(t-k)\overline{x}^{t-k+1}x \right)$$

Observe that each f_i is multiplied by a trinomial in x and $\overline{x}$ such that each monomial $x^a \overline{x}^b$ satisfies $a - b = k \bmod t$. The trinomials are chosen so that the evaluation of any of these in the t-th roots of unity is equal to 1, so that the evaluation of h is exactly the same as that of f. Further, the trinomials are such that when evaluated in $x + \varepsilon$ and $\overline{x} + \overline{\varepsilon}$, the partial derivatives with respect to ε and $\overline{\varepsilon}$ cancel in the t-th roots of unity. This property provides the cleaning functionality. We stress that there is flexibility in the choice of the monomials appearing in the trinomials, and that we opted to have a pattern, as well as some symmetry between the first half and the second half. The total degree of h is $\max(t-1, 4)$, and h can be evaluated with multiplicative depth $\log t$ (when $t \geq 4$), i.e., one less than the polynomial obtained with Hermite interpolation.

Lemma 2. *There exists a constant $C > 0$ such that the following holds. Let $t \geq 2$ and $y_0, \ldots, y_{t-1} \in \mathbb{C}$. Let f be the univariate polynomial of degree $< t$ such that $f(e^{2\pi i j/t}) = y_j$ for all $0 \leq j < t$, and h be as above. Then, for all $0 \leq j < t$ and $\varepsilon \in \mathbb{C}$ with $|\varepsilon| \leq 1/(t-1)$, we have:*

$$\left| h(e^{2\pi i j/t} + \varepsilon) - y_j \right| \leq C \cdot t^3 \cdot \max_j |f_j| \cdot |\varepsilon|^2 \ .$$

Proof. Let $\zeta = e^{2\pi i j/t}$ for some arbitrary $0 \leq j < t$. Replacing x by $\zeta + \varepsilon$ in the definition of h, we see that it can be expressed as a bivariate polynomial in ε and $\overline{\varepsilon}$. By using the relation $\overline{\zeta} = \zeta^{-1}$ and using the definition of f, we obtain that the constant term of that bivariate polynomial is

$$h(\zeta) = f_0 + f_1 \cdot \zeta + \ldots + f_{t-1}\zeta^{t-1} = y_j \ ,$$

where the second equality is by definition of f.

It may then be checked that the terms linear in ε and $\overline{\varepsilon}$ sum to 0. Therefore, in order to bound $|h(\zeta+\varepsilon) - y_j|$, it suffices to consider the terms of total degree 2 or more in ε and $\overline{\varepsilon}$. For this purpose, we will use the following inequality, which holds for all integer $n > 2$, all $x \in \mathbb{C}$ with $|x| \leq 1$ and all $u \in \mathbb{C}$ with $|u| \leq 1/n$:

$$\left| (x + u)^n - x^n - nx^{n-1}u \right| \leq n^2 |u|^2 \ .$$

By using the facts that $|\zeta| = 1$ and $|\varepsilon| \leq 1/(t-1)$, the triangle inequality and the above inequality, we have:

$$|h(\zeta + \varepsilon) - y_j| \leq C \cdot t^3 \cdot \max_j |f_j| \cdot |\varepsilon|^2 \ ,$$

for some (absolute) constant C.   □

An interesting particular case is the interpolation for the identity function. This provides a cleaning functionality. Taking $f(x) = x$ in the above definition of h, we obtain the function:

$$x \mapsto \frac{1}{t} \left(\overline{x}^{t-1} + 2(t-1)x - (t-1)x^2\overline{x} \right) \ .$$

It has degree $\max(3, t-1)$. It may be compared to the cleaning polynomial $x \mapsto ((t+1)x - x^{t+1})/t$ considered in [CKKL24], of degree $t+1$. For t's chosen as powers of two, this provides a saving of one multiplicative depth.

3.4   Polynomial Multi-evaluation

We now consider the task of evaluating the bivariate polynomials of Sects. 3.2 and 3.3, by viewing it as a variant of homomorphically evaluating several polynomials on the same input.

Consider first the case of a single polynomial $P = P_0 + P_1 x + \ldots + P_{d-1} x^{d-1}$. A naive version of the Paterson-Stockmayer algorithm [PS73] proceeds as follows:

1. (Initialization) Compute $1, x, \ldots, x^{\sqrt{d}-1}$ and $x^{\sqrt{d}}, x^{2\sqrt{d}}, x^{2^2\sqrt{d}}, \ldots$;
2. (Baby steps) Compute

$$\pi_0 = P_0 + P_1 x + \ldots + P_{\sqrt{d}-1} x^{\sqrt{d}-1} \ ,$$

$$\vdots$$

$$\pi_{\sqrt{d}-1} = P_{d-\sqrt{d}} + P_{d-\sqrt{d}+1} x + \ldots + P_{d-1} x^{\sqrt{d}-1} \ ;$$

3. (Giant steps) Compute $\pi_0 + \ldots + x^{d-\sqrt{d}} \pi_{\sqrt{d}-1}$ with a binary recursion.

Homomorphically, this amounts to $\approx 2\sqrt{d}$ ciphertext-ciphertext multiplications, half of them in the initialization and the other half in the giants steps. As ciphertext-ciphertext multiplications are significantly more costly than plaintext-ciphertext multiplications, this dominates the cost. Note further that the multiplicative depth is $\log d$.

Now, consider a scenario in which we would like to homomorphically evaluate k polynomials $P^{(0)}, \ldots, P^{(k-1)}$ on the same ciphertext. By applying the above algorithm k times, one obtains a cost dominated by $\approx 2k\sqrt{d}$ ciphertext-ciphertext multiplications. Now, observe that the initialization can be shared across the polynomial evaluations, the number of ciphertext-ciphertext multiplications can be decreased to $\approx (k+1)\sqrt{d}$. This can be decreased further by modifying the balance between the baby steps and giant steps, as follows.

1. (Initialization) Compute $1, x, \ldots, x^{\sqrt{kd}-1}$ and $x^{\sqrt{kd}}, x^{2\sqrt{kd}}, x^{2^2\sqrt{kd}}, \ldots$;
2. (Baby steps) For all $0 \le i \le \sqrt{d/k}$ and $0 \le j \le k$, compute

$$\pi_i^{(j)} = P_{i\sqrt{kd}}^{(j)} + P_{1+i\sqrt{kd}}^{(j)} x + \ldots + P_{\sqrt{d}-1+i\sqrt{kd}}^{(j)} x^{\sqrt{kd}-1} \ ;$$

3. (Giant steps) For all $0 \le j \le k$, compute $\pi_0^{(j)} + x^{\sqrt{kd}} \pi_1^{(j)} + \ldots + x^{d-\sqrt{kd}} \pi_{\sqrt{kd}-1}^{(j)}$ using $x^{\sqrt{kd}}, x^{2\sqrt{kd}}, x^{3\sqrt{kd}}, \ldots$ and a binary recursion.

The number of ciphertext-ciphertext multiplications then decreases to $\approx 2\sqrt{kd}$. At the same time, the multiplicative depth is preserved.

In Sect. 3.2, the function to be evaluated is the sum of a polynomial in x and a polynomial in $\bar{x}$. This may be handled similarly as above for $k = 2$, by computing the baby step for x and applying homomorphic conjugation on its output. Note that homomorphic conjugation adds a small cost that is independent of the degree d.

The function h in Sect. 3.3 can be handled similarly, with four polynomial evaluations. Indeed, it can be expressed as:

$$h(x) = f_0 + (P_f(x) + P_{f^r}(\bar{x})) - \bar{x}x\,(Q_f(x) + Q_{f^r}(\bar{x}))\ ,$$

where the polynomial f^r is the reversal of f, i.e., with $f_k^r = f_{t-k}$ for $k \in \{1, \dots, t-1\}$, and:

$$P_f(x) = \sum_{k=1}^{t-1} \alpha_{f,k} x^k \quad \text{with} \quad \alpha_{f,k} = \begin{cases} \frac{f_k}{t}(t-k)(k+1) & \text{if } k \le t/2 \\ \frac{f_k}{t}(t-k) & \text{otherwise} \end{cases} ,$$

$$Q_f(x) = \sum_{k=1}^{\lfloor t/2 \rfloor} -\frac{f_k}{t} k(t-k) x^k\ .$$

4   Bootstrapping Small Integers

We now present our bootstrapping algorithm for small integers, as well as its extension to multi-function functional bootstrapping and its application to batch-bootstrapping multiple DM/CGGI ciphertexts for small integers.

4.1   SI-BTS

Assume that the plaintext underlying the input ciphertext is a vector $\mathbf{m}$ of small integers, between 0 and $t-1$ for some $t \ge 2$, and one wants to obtain a ciphertext whose plaintext is also a vector $\mathbf{y}$ of small integers, so that $y_j = f(m_j)$ for all $0 \le j < N/2$. Here f is an arbitrary function from integers in $[0, t)$ to integers in $[0, t)$. (We could consider different sets for inputs and outputs, but keep them identical for the sake of simplicity.)

For this purpose, SI-BTS (given in Algorithm 2) first uses IntRootBoot, and then interpolate from the t-th root of unity $\exp(2i\pi m/t)$ to the integer $f(m)$ by using the combined interpolation and cleaning from Sect. 3.3. If cleaning is not necessary (for example, if it occurred soon earlier in the computations or is to be performed soon after), then one may optionally rely on the interpolation algorithm from Sect. 3.2. We however recall that it is interesting to clean together with a polynomial interpolation on the roots of unity, as it consumes only one additional multiplicative level compared to only interpolating (compared to $\approx \log t$ levels for a separate cleaning).

Converting from roots-of-unity embedding to integer embedding is important to be able to run SI-BTS again. However, in some cases, it may be interesting to postpone this conversion rather than performing it in bootstrapping, and keep the roots-of-unity embedding for a while. For example, for evaluating table look-ups, roots-of-unity embedding has been showed quite advantageous (see [CKKL24]). In this case, one can replace the interpolation of Step 2 by the one that sends $\exp(2i\pi x/t) \mapsto \exp(2i\pi f(x)/t)$ for all $0 \le x < t$.

Correctness follows by inspection. We now adapt the modulus consumption of the end of Sect. 3.1 to the SI-BTS algorithm. In Sect. 3.1, we already estimated

---

Algorithm 2: Small Integer (Functional) Bootstrapping (SI-BTS)

Input : A CKKS ciphertext decrypting to $\approx \mathbf{m} \in \mathbb{C}^{N/2}$ in the slots, where $m_j \in \mathbb{Z} \cap [0,t)$ for all $0 \leq j < N/2$; a function $f : \mathbb{Z}_t \to \mathbb{Z}_t$.

Output: A CKKS ciphertext whose modulus is no smaller, and decrypting to $\approx (f(m_j))_j \in \mathbb{C}^{N/2}$ in the slots.

Keys : IntRootBoot bootstrapping, conjugation and relinearization keys.

1 Run IntRootBoot on ct;

2 Homomorphically evaluate, with cleaning, the function that maps $\exp(2i\pi x/t)$ to $f(x)$ for all $0 \leq x < t$; for this purpose, use Section 3.3; let ct be the output ciphertext;

3 **return** ct.

---

the modulus consumption of Step 1. As seen in Sect. 3.3, we may interpolate and clean at Step 2, with $\log t$ multiplicative levels. At that stage, we do not need to represent the integer I any more, so that a level corresponds to the same amount of modulus as in StC.

$$\text{ModCons}_{\text{SI-BTS}} \approx (\ell_{\text{CtS}} + \ell_{\text{EvalExp}}) \cdot (5 + \log t + \gamma_{acc} + \gamma_{noise}) \qquad (1)$$
$$+ (\ell_{\text{StC}} + \log t) \cdot (\log t + \gamma_{acc} + \gamma_{noise}) \ ,$$

where ℓ_{CtS}, ℓ_{EvalExp} and ℓ_{StC} respectively refer to the multiplicative depths of CtS, EvalExp and StC. The quantity γ_{noise} corresponds to the bit-size of the noise induced by homomorphic operations and γ_{acc} corresponds to the accuracy of the representations of the $(\log t)$-bit integers. We insist that this estimate is rough, and we refer the reader to Sect. 6 for concrete experimental data. We note that γ_{acc} is not constant throughout the computation: it first decreases because of homomorphic computations, and it is then replenished at Step 2. We do not consider this variation in (1). Similarly, the quantity γ_{noise} varies depending on the type of homomorphic operations performed. It can be seen in (1) that when t is small, the modulus consumption grows very slowly, as the terms linear in $\log t$ are 'somewhat hidden' by $\gamma_{acc} + \gamma_{noise}$, and, to a lesser extent, by $\ell_{\text{CtS}} + \ell_{\text{StC}} + \ell_{\text{EvalExp}}$. However, as t increases, the growth rate eventually becomes quadratic in $\log t$.

In terms of cost, the situation is similar. For small t, the cost will be dominated by Step 1, but when t increases, the cost of Step 2 will eventually become dominant.

4.2   Multi-output SI-BTS

The SI-BTS algorithm can be extended to evaluate several functions f_i for a given input m. This may be viewed as a CKKS (and hence SIMD) analogue to the DM/CGGI multi-output bootstrap algorithm from [CIM19].

Algorithm 2 is then modified as follows. Step 1 is run only once, while Step 2 can benefit from the multi-evaluation algorithm of Sect. 4.2. Overall, if K is the number of functions being evaluated in parallel, the cost of Step 1 is independent of K, while the cost of Step 2 essentially grows with $\sqrt{K}$ (the ciphertext-ciphertext multiplications being the most expensive component of polynomial evaluation). For a small K and a small t, the cost of Step 2 is limited compared to the cost of Step 1, so that several functional bootstraps can be performed for essentially the same cost as a single one. When t and K are larger, Step 2 dominates and the cost increase is more visible.

4.3   Batch Functional Bootstrapping of DM/CGGI Ciphertexts

SI-BTS is particularly useful when one wishes to perform multiple DM/CGGI functional bootstraps in parallel. This gives an extension of the batch DM/CGGI bootstrapping from [BCKS24], which was restricted to evaluating a binary gate.

Recall that a CGGI/DM ciphertext can be viewed as an LWE version of our coefficient-integer-encoded ciphertext, where the plaintext integer lies in the most significant bits of the ciphertext. More concretely, a ciphertext $\mathsf{ct} \in \mathbb{Z}_q^n$ for some integers n and q decrypts to an integer $m \in [0, t)$ under a key $\mathsf{sk} \in \{-1, 0, 1\}^n$ if:

$$\langle \mathsf{ct}, \mathsf{sk} \rangle = \frac{q}{t} m + e \bmod q \ ,$$

where $|e| \ll q/t$. For efficiency purposes, the modulus q is typically very small (e.g., it can have 12 bits).

Now, assume we are given $\leq N$ such ciphertexts $(\mathsf{ct}_j)_{0 \leq j < N}$, decrypting to integers $(m_j)_{0 \leq j < N}$ under a common key sk. These ciphertexts can be packed into a single coefficients-encoded CKKS ciphertext, by relying on a ring-packing procedure (see [CGGI17,BCK+23], among others). This provides a ciphertext $(a, b) \in R_{q_0}^2$ for the base CKKS modulus q_0 and for a key $s \in R$ such that

$$a \cdot s + b \approx \frac{q'}{t} \left(m_0 + m_1 \cdot X + \ldots + m_{N-1} X^{N-1} \right) \ .$$

Note that the base CKKS modulus q_0 is typically larger than q. The change of modulus from q to q_0 is implemented by scaling and rounding. Ring packing requires a dedicated evaluation key (some form of CKKS encryption of sk under s).

One then uses IntRootBoot (without StC) to bootstrap this CKKS ciphertext and evaluate an arbitrary function by interpolation. Complex bootstrapping may be used if there are $> N/2$ input ciphertexts ct_j. Finally, we run StC to put the message back in the coefficients, and by properly rearranging the coefficients of the obtained RLWE ciphertext, we obtain the desired LWE-format DM/CGGI ciphertexts.

5   Batch Bits Bootstrapping

In the previous section, we have seen how to bootstrap ciphertexts whose underlying plaintexts encode small integers, for a cost (mostly driven by bootstrapping modulus consumption) that is not significantly higher than that of bootstrapping bits. It is hence tempting to use such an approach to batch-bootstrap bits, by packing them into integers, to increase the throughput for binary circuits.

5.1 BB-BTS

Let us assume we aim at simultaneously bootstrapping $k \geq 1$ CKKS ciphertexts whose underlying plaintexts correspond to bits, encrypted into slots. The goal is to bootstrap these ciphertexts together, for a cost that is significantly lower than bootstrapping them individually using the algorithm from [BCKS24].

Our approach is as follows. We first pack the data into a single ciphertext. More concretely, we create a single ciphertext such that for any $j \leq N/2$, the j-th slot contains a k-bit integer obtained by concatenating the bits in the j-th slots of the input ciphertexts. Then we apply IntRootBoot with 2^k-th roots of unity, to obtain a roots-of-unity slots-encoded ciphertext. The next step is to extract the individual bits from the roots-of-unity ciphertexts by running k interpolations (one for each bit). Finally, we decrease the noise of the resulting slots-encoded ciphertexts for bits, by using the h_1 cleaning function (see Sect. 2). This procedure is summarized in Algorithm 3.

Algorithm 3: Batch Bits Bootstrapping (BB-BTS)

Input : $k \geq 1$ slots-encoded ciphertexts $\mathsf{ct}_0, \ldots, \mathsf{ct}_{k-1}$ for vectors in $\{0,1\}^{N/2}$.
Output: $k \geq 1$ slots-encoded ciphertexts $\mathsf{ct}'_0, \ldots, \mathsf{ct}'_{k-1}$ for the same vectors of bits, at a higher modulus.
Keys : IntRootBoot bootstrapping, conjugation and relinearization keys.
1 Homomorphically evaluate $m_0, \ldots, m_j \mapsto \sum_j 2^j m_j$ on the input ciphertexts; let ct be the output ciphertext;
2 $\mathsf{ct} \leftarrow \mathsf{IntRootBoot}(\mathsf{ct})$;
3 For all $0 \leq j < k$, set ct'_j as the ciphertext obtained by homomorphically interpolating from $\exp(2\pi i(\sum_{0 \leq \ell < k} b_\ell 2^\ell)/2^k)$ to b_j;
4 For all $0 \leq j < k$, set ct'_j as the ciphertext obtained by homomorphically evaluating h_1 on ct'_j;
5 **return** $\mathsf{ct}'_0, \ldots, \mathsf{ct}'_{k-1}$.

Correctness follows from inspection. We now analyze modulus consumption, by adapting the end of Sect. 3.1. Step 2 has been studied in Sect. 3.1. As seen in Sect. 3.2, we may interpolate at Step 3 with $k - 1$ multiplicative levels. At that stage, we do not need to represent the integer I any more, but we still need to represent k-bit data points. Finally, evaluating the h_1 polynomial requires two multiplicative levels, and the data of interest has a single bit at that stage. Overall, the modulus consumption is as follows:

$$
\begin{aligned}
\mathsf{ModCons}_{\mathsf{BB\text{-}BTS}} \approx\ & (\ell_{\mathsf{CtS}} + \ell_{\mathsf{EvalExp}}) \cdot (5 + k + \gamma_{acc} + \gamma_{noise}) \\
& + (k - 1) \cdot (k + \gamma_{acc} + \gamma_{noise}) \\
& + (\ell_{\mathsf{StC}} + 2) \cdot (1 + \gamma_{acc} + \gamma_{noise})\ ,
\end{aligned} \tag{2}
$$

where the variables $\ell_{\text{CtS}}, \ell_{\text{EvalExp}}, \ell_{\text{StC}}, \gamma_{acc}$ and γ_{noise} are as before. It may seem that cleaning the ciphertexts may not be necessary, depending on how noisy they currently are. Indeed, if their noise is limited, then one may first evaluate some binary gates and postpone cleaning. However, cleaning at the end of bootstrapping allows us to lower the bootstrapping modulus consumption, and we argue that it should hence be viewed as a component of bootstrapping. Concretely, the quantity γ_{acc} is smaller for Steps 2 and 3 than it is at Step 4. When k is small, its impact is limited, because of the terms $\gamma_{acc} + \gamma_{noise}$, for the precision, and $\ell_{\text{CtS}} + \ell_{\text{EvalExp}} + \ell_{\text{StC}} + 2$, for the multiplicative depth. However, when k increases, the modulus consumption eventually grows quadratically in k.

For the cost, the situation is similar. For small k, one expects Step 2 to dominate the cost. When k increases, the cost of Step 2 remains almost constant, but those of Steps 3 and 4 grow. The highest throughput is achieved when the cost and modulus consumption of these steps is correctly balanced with the cost and modulus consumption of Step 2.

We note that using complex bootstrapping allows to improve throughput further, as CtS and StC can then handle twice more data for the same cost. However, EvalExp and Steps 2 and 3 of BB-BTS are then run twice in parallel.

5.2 Extracting Bits

It could be tempting to view Step 3 as a multi-evaluation and use the algorithm described in Sect. 4.2. One could even avoid Step 4 by cleaning the noise in Step 3, by using the approach given in Sect. 3.3, and save one multiplicative depth. However, it seems preferable to exploit the fact that the interpolation polynomials for extracting bits are not generic at all. For example, the least significant bit b_0 can be obtained from $\exp(2i\pi(\sum_{0 \le \ell < k} b_\ell 2^\ell)/2^k)$ by raising it to the 2^{k-1}-th power to obtain $(-1)^{b_0} = -2b_0 + 1$ and then correct the result to b_0. As showed in the following lemma, the interpolation polynomials for the subsequent bits are also very sparse.

Lemma 3. *Let $k \ge 1$ and $0 \le j < k$. Define $P_{k,\ell} \in \mathbb{C}[x]$ as the minimal degree polynomial that maps $\exp(2i\pi(\sum_{0 \le \ell < k} b_\ell 2^\ell)/2^k)$ to b_j, for all $b_0, \ldots, b_{k-1} \in \{0,1\}$. Then $P_{k,\ell}$ has at most $1 + 2^\ell$ non-zero coefficients, for monomials of degrees 0 and odd multiples of 2^{k-j-1} that are $< 2^k$.*

Proof. We prove the result by induction on k. It may be checked that it holds for $k = 1$, and we now assume that $k \ge 2$. We now consider two cases, depending on the value of j. Assume first that $j < k-1$. Note that for any bits $b_0, \ldots, b_{k-1}$, raising the 2^k-th root of unity $\exp(2i\pi(\sum_{0 \le \ell < k} b_\ell 2^\ell)/2^k)$ to the power 2^{k-j-1} gives the 2^{j+1}-th root of unity $\exp(2i\pi(\sum_{0 \le \ell \le j} b_\ell 2^\ell)/2^{j+1})$. By unicity of interpolating polynomials of small degree, we then obtain that

$$P_{k,j}(x) = P_{j+1,j}(x^{2^{k-j-1}}) \ .$$

The induction hypothesis gives the result. We now consider the remaining case, i.e., $j = k - 1$. Using the observation that

$$\exp\left(\frac{2i\pi}{2^k}\left(2^{k-1} + \sum_{0 \le \ell < k-1} b_\ell 2^\ell\right)\right) = -\exp\left(\frac{2i\pi}{2^k}\left(0 + \sum_{0 \le \ell < k-1} b_\ell 2^\ell\right)\right),$$

we observe that for any θ in the set of interpolating points, we have that $-\theta$ belongs to the set of interpolating points and one is mapped to $0 = -1/2 + 1/2$ whereas the other one is mapped to $1 = 1/2 + 1/2$. This implies that the shifted interpolation polynomial $P_{k,k-1} - 1/2$ is odd. In particular, its non-zero coefficients can only be for odd powers of x.   □

As an illustration, we give the list of $P_{4,\ell}$'s below.

$$P_{4,0} = \frac{1}{2} - \frac{1}{2}x^8,$$

$$P_{4,1} = \frac{1}{2} + \alpha_4 x^4 + \alpha_{12} x^{12},$$

$$P_{4,2} = \frac{1}{2} + \alpha_2 x^2 + \alpha_6 x^6 + \alpha_{10} x^{10} + \alpha_{14} x^{14},$$

$$P_{4,3} = \frac{1}{2} + \alpha_1 x + \alpha_3 x^3 + \alpha_5 x^5 + \alpha_7 x^7 + \alpha_9 x^9 + \alpha_{11} x^{11} + \alpha_{13} x^{13} + \alpha_{15} x^{15},$$

where:

$$\begin{bmatrix} \alpha_4 \\ \alpha_{12} \end{bmatrix} = \begin{bmatrix} -0.25 + 0.25i \\ -0.25 - 0.25i \end{bmatrix}, \quad \begin{bmatrix} \alpha_2 \\ \alpha_6 \\ \alpha_{10} \\ \alpha_{14} \end{bmatrix} \approx \begin{bmatrix} -0.125 + 0.3018i \\ -0.125 + 0.0518i \\ -0.125 - 0.0518i \\ -0.125 - 0.3018i \end{bmatrix}, \quad \begin{bmatrix} \alpha_1 \\ \alpha_3 \\ \alpha_5 \\ \alpha_7 \\ \alpha_9 \\ \alpha_{11} \\ \alpha_{13} \\ \alpha_{15} \end{bmatrix} \approx \begin{bmatrix} -0.0625 + 0.3142i \\ -0.0625 + 0.0935i \\ -0.0625 + 0.0418i \\ -0.0625 + 0.0124i \\ -0.0625 - 0.0124i \\ -0.0625 - 0.0418i \\ -0.0625 - 0.0935i \\ -0.0625 - 0.3142i \end{bmatrix}.$$

We now describe a multi-evaluation algorithm specifically designed for evaluating the $P_{k,\ell}$'s for $0 \le \ell < k$. The shape of the polynomials to be evaluated makes it suitable for an adapted version of the Paterson-Stockmeyer algorithm [PS73]. It is possible to use the algorithm described in Sect. 4.2 to evaluate these multiple polynomials, but such an approach wastes the potential speed-ups stemming from the **sparsity** of the coefficients, as well as the fact that $\alpha_i X^i = \overline{\alpha_{16-i} X^{16-i}}$ for every i. We instead write the polynomial $P_{k,\ell}$ as

$$P_{k,\ell}(X) = \frac{1}{2} + X^{2^{k-\ell-1}} Q_{k,\ell}(X^{2^{k-\ell}}) + \overline{X^{2^{k-\ell-1}} Q_{k,\ell}(X^{2^{k-\ell}})},$$

with $\deg(Q_{k,\ell}) \le 2^{\ell-1}$. We then sequentially use the Paterson-Stockmeyer algorithm evaluating a polynomial of degree d in $2\sqrt{d}$ non-scalar multiplications, for each $Q_{k,\ell}$. The total number of non-scalar multiplications for evaluating all polynomials follows a geometric sum of ratio $1/\sqrt{2}$, since $\lfloor \deg(Q_{k,\ell})/2 \rfloor =$

$\deg(Q_{k,\ell-1})$. The resulting number of ciphertext-ciphertext multiplications is $\simeq 3.4 \cdot 2\sqrt{2^{k-2}}$.

To further optimize the algorithm for extracting bits, one can recycle the setup basis to evaluate all polynomials $Q_{k,\ell}$'s. Assume that $Q_{k,\ell}$ has degree 2^{2u-1}. The baby-step phase of the Paterson-Stockmeyer algorithm computes $1, x, x^2, \ldots, x^{u-1}, x^u, x^{2u}, x^{4u}, \ldots$. Since $Q_{k,\ell-1}(X^2) = Q_{k,\ell}(X) \bmod (X^{2^k} - 1)$ for $1 \leq \ell < k$ with $\deg(Q_{k,\ell-1}) = \lfloor \deg(Q_{k,\ell})/2 \rfloor$, half of the baby-step basis (the odd-indexed elements) becomes useless. The other half is still sufficient to run the Paterson-Stockmeyer algorithm. The baby-step phase is thus recycled across the polynomial evaluations. However, the baby-step basis may be unbalanced compared to the giant-step basis after too many recyclings. This strategy alone is suboptimal to minimize the number of nonscalar multiplications. To handle this issue, we extend the baby-steps basis, which results in twice less recursive calls for polynomial evaluation. The halved baby-step basis $1, x^2, \ldots, x^{u-2}$ becomes extended to $1, x^2, \ldots, x^{u-2}, x^u, \ldots, x^{2u-2}$ and the giant-step basis starts now at x^{2u} as described in Algorithm 4.

Algorithm 4: BitExtract

Setting: Compute $u \leftarrow 2^{\lfloor \log 2(\sqrt{t}) \rfloor}$, $bs = \{1, x^2, x^4, x^6, \ldots, x^{u-2}\}$ and
$gs = \{x^u, x^{2u}, x^{4u}, x^{8u}, \ldots, x^{2^{v-1}u}\}$.

Input   : $x \leftarrow \mathsf{Enc}_{\mathsf{sk}}(\mathbf{z} + \boldsymbol{\varepsilon}) \in \mathcal{R}_q^2$ with $\mathbf{z} \in \{e^{2i\pi 0/t}, e^{2i\pi 1/t} \ldots, e^{2i\pi(t-1)/t}\}^{N/2}$ and $\|\boldsymbol{\varepsilon}\|_\infty \ll 1/t$.

Output: $\mathsf{ct}_{\mathsf{out}} \in \mathcal{R}_Q^2$.

1 $\mathsf{tmp}_{k-1} \leftarrow \frac{1}{4} + x \cdot \mathsf{PS}(Q_{k,k-1}, bs, u/2, gs, v)$;

2 $\mathsf{ct}_{k-1} \leftarrow \mathsf{tmp}_{k-1} + \overline{\mathsf{tmp}_{k-1}}$;

3 $bs' \leftarrow \{bs_{2i}\}_i$;

4 $\mathsf{tmp}_{k-2} \leftarrow \frac{1}{4} + x^2 \cdot \mathsf{PS}(Q_{k,k-2}, bs', u/4, gs, v)$;

5 $\mathsf{ct}_{k-2} \leftarrow \mathsf{tmp}_{k-2} + \overline{\mathsf{tmp}_{k-2}}$;

6 $bs'' \leftarrow \{bs'_{2i}\}_i$;

7 $bs''' = bs'' \cup \{x^u, x^{u+4}, \ldots, x^{2u-4}\}$;

8 $gs' = \{gs_{i+1}\}_i$;

9 $\mathsf{tmp}_{k-3} \leftarrow \frac{1}{4} + x^4 \cdot \mathsf{PS}(Q_{k,k-3}, bs''', u/4, gs', v-1)$;

10 $\mathsf{ct}_{k-3} \leftarrow \mathsf{tmp}_{k-3} + \overline{\mathsf{tmp}_{k-3}}$;

11 Repeat Steps 3-10 for the next bits starting from $(u/4, v-1)$;

12 **return** $\mathsf{ct}_{\mathsf{out}}$.

BitExtract is setting the polynomials basis for the Paterson-Stockmeyer polynomial evaluation of $Q_{k,k-1}$. Since it is a polynomial in x^2, only even exponent monomials are computed. Step 1 calls the polynomial evaluation method, abbreviated as PS, taking as arguments the setup basis for baby-steps and giant-steps and their sizes u and v. Step 2 computes the value of $P_{k,k-1}$ with respect to the formula above. The next polynomial $Q_{k,k-2}$ is smaller. Step 3 is thus halving the bs polynomial basis as explained above. Similarly, Steps 4 and 5 compute $P_{k,k-2}$ from $Q_{k,k-2}$. Step 6 is again halving bs as the algorithm moves to the evaluation of $Q_{k,k-3}$. To balance it with the giant-steps, Step 7 extends the baby-steps basis, which saves a recursive level in giant-steps at Step 8. Steps 9 and 10 evaluate $Q_{k,k-3}$. The next bits are recovered by continually decreasing bs and gs to evaluate $P_{k,\ell}$ with the formula until $\ell = 0$.

6   Experiments

We now describe proof-of-concept implementations, based upon the C++ HEaaN library [Cry22], and report experiment results based on them. These were run on a single-threaded CPU (i.e., Intel Xeon Gold 6242 at 2.8GHz with 502GiB of RAM) running Linux. In the experiments, the variable N denotes the ring degree of the bootstrapping parameter, N_{LWE} denotes the dimension of LWE samples where $N_{\mathsf{LWE}} < N$, h and $\tilde{h}$ denote the Hamming weights of the dense and sparse secret keys respectively (we rely on the sparse secret encapsulation technique from [BTPH22]), $\log_2(QP)$ denotes the maximum switching key modulus, $dnum$ denotes the gadget rank of the gadget decomposition, and $depth$ denotes the remaining multiplicative depths after IntRootBoot. All parameter sets considered in this section reach 128-bit security, according to [APS15]. Note that the security of our new bootstrapping can be analyzed exactly in the same as for conventional CKKS, as we built our scheme upon CKKS without modifying any aspect related to security.

6.1   Bypassing DM/CGGI

As described in Sect. 4.3, we combined the ring packing from [BCK+23] (i.e., HERMES), the IntRootBoot algorithm borrowed from [BGGJ20], and our adaptation of the roots-of-unity look-up table of [CKKL24], to bypass DM/CGGI bootstrapping. We have implemented j-bits to j-bits look-up table for $j \in \{2, 4, 6, 8, 10\}$. As the precision for the look-up table interpolation depends on j, we designed optimized parameters for each value of j, as shown in Table 3. Since DM/CGGI is generally effective on processing one or a small number of inputs, we mainly targeted the better latency on small number of inputs. When designing the bootstrapping parameters, we minimized degrees/depths for look-up table evaluations. We also used thin bootstrapping with complex slots, i.e., used fewer slots than available in the ring, to obtain a further latency gain as well as an accuracy improvement.

In Table 4, we batch-evaluated look-up tables for 2^{12} LWE samples of dimension 2^{12}, in all experiments. The method can be generalized to look-up table evaluations on 2^{ℓ} LWE ciphertexts of dimension 2^k. Note that k cannot be too small as a function of the integer bit-length j, as one needs to increase the modulus and dimension to encrypt more bits in a DM/CGGI ciphertext.

Table 3. Parameters we used for the look-up table implementations. *depth* refers the multiplicative depth after IntRootBoot. The $\log_2(q)$ columns correspond to the primes used for ciphertext modulus, with Base, StC, Mult, Extract, EvalExp and CtS referring to bit-sizes and numbers of primes of the corresponding steps. The column $\log_2(p)$ refers to the bit-sizes and numbers of temporary primes for switching keys. Each parameter set is designed to provide the exact depth required to evaluate an arbitrary look-up table on the required number of bits.

	N	$(h, \tilde{h})$	$\log_2(QP)$	$dnum$	$depth$
Param-LUT-2-to-2	2^{14}		440	16	4
Param-LUT-4-to-4	2^{15}		786	4	6
Param-LUT-6-to-6	2^{15}	$(256, 32)$	799	11	8
Param-LUT-8-to-8	2^{15}		869	12	10
Param-LUT-10-to-10	2^{16}		1378	5	12

	$\log_2(q)$					$\log_2(p)$
	Base	StC	Mult and Extract	EvalExp	CtS	
Param-LUT-2-to-2	26	27	26×4	26×8	24×2	27
Param-LUT-4-to-4	33	25×2	33×6	33×8	29×2	61×3
Param-LUT-6-to-6	35	33×2	35×8	35×8	33×2	36×2
Param-LUT-8-to-8	35	33×2	35×10	35×8	33×2	36×2
Param-LUT-10-to-10	42	42×3	42×12	42×8	42×3	61×4

More concretely, our method for batch-evaluating look-up tables on $N_{\mathsf{LWE}} = 2^k$ LWEs of dimension N_{LWE} consists of the following steps:

1. (Ring pack) Map the input LWE ciphertexts into a single N_{LWE}-dimensional RLWE ciphertext. Embed the N_{LWE}-dimensional RLWE ciphertext into an N-dimensional RLWE ciphertext. We consider the N-dimensional RLWE ciphertext as a sparsely packed RLWE ciphertext with $N_{\mathsf{LWE}}/2$ complex slots.
2. (IntRootBoot) Apply IntRootBoot for $N_{\mathsf{LWE}}/2$ out of N slots (i.e., using thin bootstrapping) on the result of the previous step, to get an RLWE ciphertext.
3. (Interpolation) Perform a polynomial interpolation with cleaning functionality.
4. (StC and LWE extraction) Apply thinly-packed StC on the result of the previous step. Decompose the N-dimensional RLWE ciphertext into N_{LWE}-dimensional ciphertexts and extract LWE ciphertexts.

To ensure compatibility with DM/CGGI parameters that have LWE dimensions N_{LWE} that are not 2^k, one can perform pre-processing on the input and post-processing on the output. For the pre-processing, we can simply embed the given LWE ciphertexts into 2^k-dimensional LWE ciphertexts by padding with zeros. For the post-processing, we can switch from dimension 2^k to dimension N_{LWE} LWE as done in CGGI bootstrapping [CGGI16a].

Table 4. Performance evaluation for look-up-tables with various numbers of input/output bits. The second row corresponds to the precision of the integers. The amortized time is computed as total time divided by the number of input LWE ciphertexts. Each reported timings is obtained by averaging over 10 experiments, whereas the precision is maximized over all 10 experiments and all slots.

Number of bits of the input/output	2	4	6	8	10
$-\log \|e\|_\infty$	5.4	12.5	12.8	8.7	18.8
HERMES execution time (sec)	0.671	0.717	0.72	0.757	0.76
IntRootBoot execution time (sec)	2.36	4.84	8.09	9.3	18
Interpolation time (sec)	0.09	0.66	1.95	5.1	31.1
StC and LWE extraction time (sec)	0.077	0.19	0.196	0.194	0.39
Total time for look-up table evaluation (sec)	3.2	6.4	11	15.4	50.3
Amortized look-up-table evaluation time (ms)	0.78	1.57	2.67	3.75	12.26

Table 5. Performance evaluation for multi-output look-up tables for various numbers of look-up tables. The second row corresponds to the precision of the integers. We used parameter Param-LUT-8-to-8 to evaluate several 8-bits to 8-bits look-up tables at once on the same input. Each reported timings is obtained by averaging over 10 experiments, whereas the precision is maximized over all 10 experiments and all slots.

Number of look-up tables evaluated	1	2	3	4
$-\log \|e\|_\infty$	8.7			
HERMES execution time (sec)	0.757			
IntRootBoot execution time (sec)	9.3			
Hermite Interpolation time (sec)	5.1	7.1	9.5	10.6
StC and LWE extraction time (sec)	0.194	0.42	0.67	0.77
Total time for look-up table evaluation (sec)	15.4	17.6	20.2	21.4
Amortized look-up-table evaluation time (ms)	3.75	2.14	1.65	1.3

In Table 5, we report experiments for multi-function evaluation (see Sect. 4.2) in the context of batch-bootstrapping DM/CGGI ciphertexts. We used Identity, Square, Cube, Backwards : $\{0, \cdots, 2^8 - 1\} \rightarrow \{0, \cdots, 2^8 - 1\}$ for the functions, which are defined as $\mathsf{Identity}(x) = x$, $\mathsf{Square}(x) = x^2 \pmod{2^8}$, $\mathsf{Cube}(x) = x^3 \pmod{2^8}$, and $\mathsf{Backwards}(x) = 2^8 - 1 - x$.

6.2   Batch Bits Bootstrapping

We instantiated the batch bits bootstrapping (BB-BTS) described in Sect. 5. For bit extraction, we followed the strategy described in Sect. 3.3. Below, we report

Table 6. Parameter we used for batch bits bootstrapping. Here $\log_2(q)$ denotes the primes used for ciphertext modulus, with Base, StC, Mult, Extract, EvalExp and CtS referring to bit-sizes and numbers of primes of the corresponding steps. $\log_2(p)$ refers to the bit-size and number of temporary primes for switching keys.

	N	$(h, \tilde{h})$	$\log_2(QP)$	$dnum$	$depth$
Param-BB-BTS	2^{16}	$(256, 32)$	1585	3	24

$\log_2(q)$					$\log_2(p)$
Base	StC	Mult and Extract	EvalExp	CtS	
35	60×1	30×24	35×7	35×3	60×7

efficiency measurements and provide a comparison to the bits bootstrapping algorithm from [BCKS24]. For a fair comparison, we chose the same ring degree $N = 2^{16}$ and measured the execution time in a similar computing environment. BB-BTS however requires a different CKKS parametrization, which we describe in Table 6. The number of levels reserved for cleaning is estimated as in [BCKS24] (once after 4 sequential gate evaluations).

BB-BTS allows to bootstrap many encrypted bits for the cost of a single (heavier) bootstrapping. In order to quantify the throughput gain, we consider the execution time of BB-BTS and the amount of computation that can be done between two consecutive bootstraps. The amortized gate evaluation time is defined as

$$\frac{T_{\text{BB-BTS}}}{n \times \ell \times k},$$

where $T_{\text{BB-BTS}}$ denotes the BB-BTS time, n denotes the number of slots for bootstrapping, ℓ denotes the number of remaining levels after BB-BTS excluding the levels reserved for cleaning, and k denotes the number of bits. This definition is a generalization of the amortized gate evaluation time used in [BCKS24, Section 5.2]. The detailed results are provided in Table 7. Note that our bit extraction method BitExtract consumes one more multiplicative level for each additional bit. If ℓ_1 denotes the number of useful levels when $k = 1$, then $\ell \approx \ell_1 - k$, and one sees that the term $1/(\ell \times k)$ decreases when k increases, until k reaches approximately $\ell_1/2$. If k further increases, then the amortized cost increases as well, as the number of useful levels becomes too low. This phenomenon limits the speedup factor. For Param-BB-BTS, the speedup factor of BB-BTS on k bits compared to BB-BTS on 1 bit (which is slightly slower than the method in [BCKS24]) is thus bounded from above as $\approx 4.5 = (24 - 6)/4$. This neglects the fact that run-time also grows with k.

Table 7. Performance evaluation of BB-BTS for the parametrization in Table 6 (i.e., Param-BB-BTS). Here $\|e_{\mathsf{BB\text{-}BTS}}\|_\infty$ denotes the maximum error of BB-BTS across all the slots and ciphertexts.

Number of ciphertexts (2 bits per slot)	1	2	3	4	5	6	7	8
Number of bits per slot	2	4	6	8	10	12	14	16
Number of levels after bit extraction	23	22	21	19	18	17	16	15
$-\log_2(\|e_{\mathsf{BB\text{-}BTS}}\|_\infty)$	12	11	10	9	8	7	6	5
Number of levels reserved for cleaning	6	6	5	5	5	5	5	4
IntRootBoot execution time (sec)	24.0	23.3	23.8	23.8	23.7	23.5	23.6	24.5
Bit extraction time (sec)	0.106	0.862	2.50	4.94	7.80	12.5	20.7	34.3
Amortized gate evaluation time (μs)	21.6	11.5	8.36	7.83	**7.39**	7.62	8.78	10.2

Regarding the amortized gate evaluation time, the experimental optimum is obtained when bootstrapping 10 bits (i.e., 5 ciphertexts) together. In that case, we obtain an amortized gate evaluation time of $7.39\mu s$. Recall that [BCKS24] reached $17.6\mu s$ per binary gate, i.e., our BB-BTS reaches an amortized gate cost that is **2.38**x smaller.

References

[ADE+23] E. Aharoni, N. Drucker, G. Ezov, E. Kushnir, H. Shaul, and O. Soceanu.E2E near-standard and practical authenticated transciphering. IACR eprint 2023/1040, 2023.

[APS15] M. R. Albrecht, R. Player, and S. Scott. On the concrete hardness of learning with errors. *J. Math. Cryptol.*, 2015. Software available at https://github.com/malb/lattice-estimator (commit fd4a460).

[BCK+23] Y. Bae, J. H. Cheon, J. Kim, J. H. Park, and D. Stehlé. HERMES: Efficient ring packing using MLWE ciphertexts and application to transciphering. In *CRYPTO*, 2023.

[BCKS24] Y. Bae, J. H. Cheon, J. Kim, and D. Stehlé. Bootstrapping bits with CKKS. In *EUROCRYPT*, 2024.

[BGGJ20] C. Boura, N. Gama, M. Georgieva, and D. Jetchev. CHIMERA: combining ring-LWE-based fully homomorphic encryption schemes. *J. Math. Cryptol.*, 2020.

[BGV12] Z. Brakerski, C. Gentry, and V. Vaikuntanathan. (Leveled) fully homomorphic encryption without bootstrapping. In *ITCS*, 2012.

[Bra12] Z. Brakerski. Fully homomorphic encryption without modulus switching from classical GapSVP. In *CRYPTO*, 2012.

[BTPH22] J.-P. Bossuat, J. Troncoso-Pastoriza, and J.-P. Hubaux. Bootstrapping for approximate homomorphic encryption with negligible failure-probability by using sparse-secret encapsulation. newblock In *ACNS*, 2022.

[CCS19] H. Chen, I. Chillotti, and Y. Song. Improved bootstrapping for approximate homomorphic encryption. In *EUROCRYPT*, 2019.

[CGGI16a] I. Chillotti, N. Gama, M. Georgieva, and M. Izabachène. Faster fully homomorphic encryption: Bootstrapping in less than 0.1 seconds. In *ASIACRYPT*, 2016.

[CGGI16b] I. Chillotti, N. Gama, M. Georgieva, and M. Izabachène. TFHE: Fast fully homomorphic encryption library (version 1.1), 2016. Software available at https://tfhe.github.io/tfhe/.

[CGGI17] I. Chillotti, N. Gama, M. Georgieva, and M. Izabachène. Faster packed homomorphic operations and efficient circuit bootstrapping for TFHE. In *ASIACRYPT*, 2017.

[CHK+18] J. H. Cheon, K. Han, A. Kim, M. Kim, and Y. Song. Bootstrapping for approximate homomorphic encryption. In *EUROCRYPT*, 2018.

[CHMS22] O. Cosseron, C. Hoffmann, P. Méaux, and F.-X. Standaert. Towards case-optimized hybrid homomorphic encryption - featuring the Elisabeth stream cipher. In *ASIACRYPT*, 2022.

[CIM19] S. Carpov, M. Izabachène, and V. Mollimard. New techniques for multi-value input homomorphic evaluation and applications. In *CT-RSA*, 2019.

[CJP21] I. Chillotti, M. Joye, and P. Paillier. Programmable bootstrapping enables efficient homomorphic inference of deep neural networks. In *CSCML*, 2021.

[CKK20] J. H. Cheon, D. Kim, and D. Kim. Efficient homomorphic comparison methods with optimal complexity. In *ASIACRYPT*, 2020.

[CKKL24] H. Chung, H. Kim, Y.-S. Kim, and Y. Lee. Amortized large look-up table evaluation with multivariate polynomials for homomorphic encryption. IACR eprint 2024/274, 2024.

[CKKS17] J. H. Cheon, A. Kim, M. Kim, and Y. Song. Homomorphic encryption for arithmetic of approximate numbers. In *ASIACRYPT*, 2017.

[Cry22] CryptoLab. HEaaN library, 2022. Available at https://heaan.it/.

[DM15] L. Ducas and D. Micciancio. FHEW: Bootstrapping homomorphic encryption in less than a second. In *EUROCRYPT*, 2015.

[DMPS24] N. Drucker, G. Moshkowich, T. Pelleg, and H. Shaul. BLEACH: Cleaning errors in discrete computations over CKKS. *J. Cryptol.*, 2024.

[FV12] J. Fan and F. Vercauteren. Somewhat practical fully homomorphic encryption. IACR eprint 2012/144, 2012.

[HK20] K. Han and D. Ki. Better bootstrapping for approximate homomorphic encryption. In *CT-RSA*, 2020.

[KPK+22] S. Kim, M. Park, J. Kim, T. Kim, and C. Min. EvalRound algorithm in CKKS bootstrapping. In *ASIACRYPT*, 2022.

[KS22] K. Kluczniak and L. Schild. FDFB: Full domain functional bootstrapping towards practical fully homomorphic encryption. *TCHES*, 2022.

[LLK+22] Y. Lee, J.-W. Lee, Y.-S. Kim, Y. Kim, J.-S. No, and H. Kang. High-precision bootstrapping for approximate homomorphic encryption by error variance minimization. In *EUROCRYPT*, 2022.

[LLL+21] J.-W. Lee, E. Lee, Y. Lee, Y.-S. Kim, and J.-S. No. High-precision bootstrapping of RNS-CKKS homomorphic encryption using optimal minimax polynomial approximation and inverse sine function. In *EUROCRYPT*, 2021.

[LMSS23] C. Lee, S. Min, J. Seo, and Y. Song. Faster TFHE bootstrapping with block binary keys. In *AsiaCCS*, 2023.

[LPR10] V. Lyubashevsky, C. Peikert, and O. Regev. On ideal lattices and learning with errors over rings. In *EUROCRYPT*, 2010.

[LW23] Z. Liu and Y. Wang. Amortized functional bootstrapping in less than 7 ms, with $\widetilde{O}(1)$ polynomial multiplications. In *ASIACRYPT*, 2023.

[LW24] Z. Liu and Y. Wang. Relaxed functional bootstrapping: A new perspective on BGV/BFV bootstrapping. IACR eprint 2024/172, 2024.

[PS73] M. S. Paterson and L. J. Stockmeyer. On the number of nonscalar multiplications necessary to evaluate polynomials. *SIAM J Comput*, 1973.

[SSTX09] D. Stehlé, R. Steinfeld, K. Tanaka, and K. Xagawa. Efficient public key encryption based on ideal lattices. In *ASIACRYPT*, 2009.

[TCBS23] D. Trama, P.-E. Clet, A. Boudguiga, and R. Sirdey. A homomorphic AES evaluation in less than 30 seconds by means of TFHE. In *WAHC*, 2023.

[Zam24] Zama. TFHE-rs: A pure rust implementation of the TFHE scheme for boolean and integer arithmetics over encrypted data. (version 0.6.1), 2024. Software available at https://github.com/zama-ai/tfhe-rs.

Digital Signatures

Practical Blind Signatures in Pairing-Free Groups

Michael Klooß[1]($\boxtimes$), Michael Reichle[1], and Benedikt Wagner[2]

[1] Department of Computer Science, ETH Zurich, Zurich, Switzerland
{michael.klooss,michael.reichle}@inf.ethz.ch
[2] Ethereum Foundation, Berlin, Germany
benedikt.wagner@ethereum.org

Abstract. Blind signatures have garnered significant attention in recent years, with several efficient constructions in the random oracle model relying on well-understood assumptions. However, this progress does not apply to pairing-free cyclic groups: fully secure constructions over cyclic groups rely on pairings, remain inefficient, or depend on the algebraic group model or strong interactive assumptions. To address this gap, Chairattana-Apirom, Tessaro, and Zhu (CTZ, Crypto 2024) proposed a new scheme based on the CDH assumption. Unfortunately, their construction results in large signatures and high communication complexity. In this work, we propose a new blind signature construction in the random oracle model that significantly improves upon the CTZ scheme. Compared to CTZ, our scheme reduces communication complexity by a factor of more than 10 and decreases the signature size by a factor of more than 45, achieving a compact signature size of only 224 Bytes. The security of our scheme is based on the DDH assumption over pairing-free cyclic groups, and we show how to generalize it to the partially blind setting.

1 Introduction

A blind signature scheme [17] is a special digital signature scheme with a two-party signing process. Namely, a Signer, who possesses the secret key, interacts with a User holding the message intended for signing. Once the signing interaction terminates, the User should hold a signature for the message that can be verified with respect to the Signer's public key. It is crucial that the scheme upholds the following security and privacy properties [35,51]: *One-More Unforgeability* asserts that the User can not generate valid signatures on its own, i.e., without engaging in the signing protocol with the Signer; *Blindness* ensures that during the signing process, the User's message remains undisclosed to the Signer. More precisely, the Signer can not link the message-signature pair to the interaction. These two properties render blind signatures a versatile privacy-preserving tool.

M. Klooß—Work done at Aalto University. The author's affiliation changed before publication.

K.-M. Chung and Y. Sasaki (Eds.): ASIACRYPT 2024, LNCS 15484, pp. 363–395, 2025.
https://doi.org/10.1007/978-981-96-0875-1_12

They have found use in various domains, including but not limited to anonymous credentials [12,13] and electronic cash [17,46].

Recent Progress. For a long time, constructions of blind signatures faced considerable challenges, characterized by prohibitive inefficiency [29], reliance on strong assumptions [5,8,17,24,31], complexity leveraging [28,29] or limited security guarantees [3,33,36,51]. Even in the random oracle model [6], a fully secure and efficient blind signature scheme based on well-studied assumptions remained an elusive goal. Recently, progress in two distinct directions has been made, both contributing significantly to the resolution of this longstanding issue: The first line of work [15,32,41] uses cut-and-choose techniques to turn weakly secure but efficient constructions into fully secure ones while avoiding the use of strong assumptions. The second line of work [20,38,40] draws inspiration from a generic construction due to Fischlin [22]. By carefully exploiting the algebraic structure of specific instantiations and with major modifications of Fischlin's proof technique, these works provide practical blind signatures based on established assumptions. Notably, among the aforementioned constructions, the practical ones heavily rely on algebraic properties of lattices [20], pairings [15,32,40], or the RSA setting [15,38].

The Pairing-Free Setting. A long-standing goal in the realm of digital signature variants and in cryptography in general is to understand if and how pairings can be avoided [11,14,18,30,47,54,55]. This endeavor holds both scientific intrigue and practical merit: operations in pairing-friendly groups are more expensive, and pairing-free groups enjoy a broader library support.

Unfortunately, as we have seen above, the lines of work [15,32,41] and [20,40] so far did not yield practical blind signatures over pairing-free cyclic groups. And while there are promising works trying to close this gap, they all fall short in meeting the desired objectives entirely. Specifically, while some works [19,37,54] yield very efficient pairing-free blind signature based on established assumptions, their analysis relies on the algebraic group model [25]. Conversely, the very recent work by Chairattana-Apirom, Tessaro, and Zhu [16] avoids the use of the algebraic group model. They give efficient constructions based on interactive variants of CDH, along with a non-interactive CDH-based construction utilizing techniques from [32]. Unfortunately, this latter construction has signatures containing $\Theta(\lambda)$ many group elements, where λ is the security parameter. In contrast to that, signatures in the most efficient pairing-based construction [40] contain only a small constant number of group elements.

Our Goal. The goal of this work is to close this gap by providing a new blind signature scheme over pairing-free cyclic groups, that (1) is based on well-studied cryptographic hardness assumptions, (2) avoids idealizations other than the random oracle model, and (3) is practically efficient, without the λ overhead in signature size.

1.1 Our Contribution

We achieve our goal by constructing a practical blind signature scheme in pairing-free groups, which we compare with the state-of-the-art in Tables 1 and 2. To summarize, our scheme comes with the following key characteristics:

- *Unforgeability.* One-more unforgeability holds based on the DDH assumption in the random oracle model. Notably, our proof avoids the need for rewinding, resulting in a tighter security bound in contrast to CTZ-3 [16], which is the only other scheme achieving full one-more unforgeability in pairing-free groups without the algebraic group model.
- *Blindness.* Our scheme is statistically blind, and we show that it naturally generalizes to the setting of partially blind signatures [2]. This is the first scheme supporting partial blindness in this regime[1].
- *Efficiency.* Our scheme is both concretely and asymptotically efficient. Especially, comparing to CTZ-3 [16], we reduce the communication complexity by a factor of more than 10, and the signature size from 10.5 Kilobytes to 224 Bytes, see Table 2).

Technically, our starting point is the pairing-based construction by Katsumata, Reichle, and Sakai [40]. We turn this construction into a pairing-free variant by replacing the pairing with a (blindly issued) non-interactive proof. It is worth noting that a straightforward substitution would yield only a weaker notion of one-more unforgeability, similar to CTZ-1 and CTZ-2 [16]. However, through a strategically devised security proof, we can circumvent this issue, achieving full one-more unforgeability. A second twist allows us to avoid rewinding, another improvement over CTZ-3 [16]. Further, we revist the security of Fischlin's straightline extractable proof to achieve statistical blindness for our scheme. Notably, this is in contrast to [40], which is only computationally blind.

1.2 Related Work

Here, we discuss related work on blind signatures. We focus primarily on recent efficient and secure constructions in the random oracle model [6]. We give a comparison of blind signature schemes in pairing-free cyclic groups in Table 1.

Foundations of Blind Signatures. Blind signatures have been introduced by Chaum in 1982 [17] in the context of electronic cash. Pioneering works are by Juels, Luby, and Ostrovsky [35], by Fischlin [22], and by Pointcheval and Stern [51]. Namely, Juels, Luby, and Ostrovsky have demonstrated that blind signatures can generically (and inefficiently) be constructed from one-way trapdoor permutations via secure two-party computation. Fischlin also gave a generic construction of round-optimal (i.e., two moves) blind signatures. On the other hand, Pointcheval and Stern have shown the security of efficient three-move blind signatures in the random oracle model, as long as only polylogarithmically many signatures are issued concurrently. Since then, several impossibility results have

---

[1] It is not obvious how to modify CTZ [16] to achieve partial blindness.

Table 1. Comparison of concurrently secure blind signature schemes in the discrete logarithm setting without pairings. All constructions rely on the random oracle model, and schemes above the line additionally require the algebraic group model. We compare the assumptions and security and the communication complexity and signature size in terms of number of group elements and number of field elements. The schemes CTZ-1 and CTZ-2 [16] only satisfy a weaker variant of one-more unforgeability.

Scheme	Assumption	Full OMUF	Moves	Communication	Signature
Cl-Schnorr [26]	OMDL, mROS	✓	3	$2\mathbb{G} + 3\mathbb{Z}_p$	$1\mathbb{G} + 1\mathbb{Z}_p$
Abe [1,37]	DLOG	✓	3	$\lambda + 3\mathbb{G} + 6\mathbb{Z}_p$	$2\mathbb{G} + 6\mathbb{Z}_p$
TZ [54]	DLOG	✓	3	$2\mathbb{G} + 4\mathbb{Z}_p$	$4\mathbb{Z}_p$
Snowblind [19]	DLOG	✓	3	$2\mathbb{G} + 4\mathbb{Z}_p$	$1\mathbb{G} + 2\mathbb{Z}_p$
CTZ-1 [16]	CT-OMCDH	✗	4	$5\mathbb{G} + 5\mathbb{Z}_p$	$1\mathbb{G} + 4\mathbb{Z}_p$
CTZ-2 [16]	CT-OMCDH	✗	5	$5\mathbb{G} + 5\mathbb{Z}_p$	$1\mathbb{G} + 4\mathbb{Z}_p$
CTZ-3 [16]	CDH	✓	4	$\Theta(\lambda)(\lambda + \mathbb{G} + \mathbb{Z}_p)$	$\Theta(\lambda)(\lambda + \mathbb{G} + \mathbb{Z}_p)$
Ours	DDH	✓	4	$\Theta(\lambda)(\lambda + \mathbb{G} + \mathbb{Z}_p)$	$2\mathbb{G} + 5\mathbb{Z}_p$

Table 2. Comparison of the concrete efficiency of concurrently secure blind signature schemes in the discrete logarithm setting without pairings. We exclude constructions in the algebraic group model and constructions that do not achieve full one-more unforgeability for this comparison. We assume $\lambda = 128$ and that group and field elements are represented using 256 bit. See the full version [42] for the parameter script.

Scheme	Assumption	Full OMUF	Moves	Communication	Signature
CTZ-3 [16]	CDH	✓	4	27.12 Kilobytes	10.50 Kilobytes
Ours	DDH	✓	4	2.46 Kilobytes	224 Bytes

been proven [4,23,49]. For example, Fischlin and Schröder have ruled out certain statistically blind three-move constructions from non-interactive assumptions in the standard model [23].

Strong Assumptions or Idealized Models. In addition to generic constructions mentioned earlier, several more direct constructions exist, relying on complexity leveraging [28,29] or non-standard q-type or interactive assumptions [24,29,31,45]. Also, there are blind variants of BLS signatures and RSA-full-domain hash signatures [5,8], which are very efficient and round-optimal. However, these constructions rely on interactive one-more variants of the underlying assumptions, e.g., one-more CDH. If one is willing to rely on the algebraic group model [25], there are several efficient constructions of blind signatures in pairing-free groups [19,37,54]. A recent scheme due to Fuchsbauer and Wolf [27] outputs regular Schnorr signatures [52]. In terms of assumptions, their result can be interpreted in two ways: one can assume the security of Schnorr signatures [52] with respect to a fixed hash function, which is an interactive assumption; alternatively, one can rely on the discrete logarithm assumption by treating the hash function as a random oracle. In this latter case, however, their protocol proves relations defined by the random oracle in generic SNARK, which has unclear security implications and is highly non-standard.

Cut-and-Choose Constructions. The starting point of this line of work lies in efficient constructions of blind signatures with weak security guarantees [3,33,34,36,51] based on witness indistinguishable linear identification schemes [44]. Specifically, these schemes are insecure if more than polylogarithmically many signatures are issued concurrently. This is not only an artifact of the security proof but can be exploited in a practical attack [7,53,56]. By extending a classical construction of Pointcheval [50], Katz, Loss, and Rosenberg have introduced boosting [41], a technique to turn the aforementioned polylogarithmically-secure blind signatures into fully secure ones: during the Nth signing interaction, the Signer and User engage in a 1-of-N cut-and-choose, which results in communication and computation scaling linearly in N. Subsequently, Chairattana-Apirom et al. [15] have improved communication to scale logarithmically in N. They have also developed two concretely efficient constructions leveraging the cut-and-choose idea. Building on one of these constructions (called PI-Cut-Choo), Hanzlik, Loss, and Wagner [32] have proposed a construction called Rai-Choo. This scheme is stateless and round-optimal, and both computation and communication are independent of N. It relies on the CDH assumption in the pairing-setting. On the downside, signatures in Rai-Choo contain $\Theta(\lambda)$ many group elements. The latest achievements in this line of work are the pairing-free constructions by Chairattana-Apirom, Tessaro, and Zhu [16]. While two of their constructions are very efficient, they rely on interactive assumptions and only achieve a weaker version of unforgeability. The third construction, which achieves full unforgeability and relies only on CDH has signatures containing $\Theta(\lambda)$ many group elements due to techniques inherited from Rai-Choo. Hence, this line of work did not yet result in a fully secure and efficient scheme with constant[2] signature size over pairing-free groups.

Fischlin and its Descendants. In addition to the line of work using cut-and-choose outlined above, a second line of constructions managed to construct schemes that are practical and rely on conservative assumptions. This line of work draws inspiration from Fischlin's generic construction [22] but introduces several modifications to the proof technique to enable efficient implementations. Specifically, del Pino and Katsumata [20] efficiently instantiate this framework from lattice assumptions, while Katsumata, Reichle, and Sakai [40] give two constructions utilizing pairings. Kastner, Nguyen, and Reichle [38] present a construction relying on pairing-free groups and the strong RSA assumption.

However, this line of research has not yet yielded an efficient scheme with constant signature size over pairing-free groups alone. Our contribution can be viewed as adapting the second construction proposed by Katsumata, Reichle, and Sakai to the pairing-free setting. Doing this naively would result in a weaker form of unforgeability as for the first two constructions in [16]. With a clever twist, we can prove full unforgeability.

---

[2] Constant signature size here means a constant (in λ) number of group elements.

1.3   Technical Overview

Here, we give an informal overview of our techniques. Our starting point will be the pairing-based blind signature scheme by Katsumata, Reichle, and Sakai [40]. As this scheme is already very efficient, our main technical goal is to eliminate the use of pairings.

Our Starting Point: Pairing-Based Blind Signatures. Let us briefly recall the construction by Katsumata et al. [40]. To this end, let $\mathbb{G}$ be a pairing-friendly group generated by $G \in \mathbb{G}$. The basis of the scheme is a signature scheme obtained from the Boneh-Boyen identity-based encryption [9], for which signatures $\sigma = (S_1, S_2)$ have the structure

$$S_1 = uV + s(\overline{m}U + H), \quad S_2 = sG. \tag{1}$$

Here, $s \in \mathbb{Z}_p$ is sampled uniformly during the signing process, $u \in \mathbb{Z}_p$ is the secret key, $U = uG$, V, and H are public group elements, and $\overline{m}$ is a hash of the message to be signed. Verification leverages the pairing. In the construction by Katsumata, Reichle, and Sakai, such signatures are issued blindly as follows:

1. The User sends a Pedersen commitment C to $\overline{m}$. It also includes a proof π_{Ped}, proving knowledge of the commitment randomness and $\overline{m}$;
2. The Signer homomorphically computes a blinded version σ_C of the signature σ from the commitment C and sends it to the User;
3. The User can remove the commitment randomness to obtain an actual signature σ'. For blindness, it is also essential that the User rerandomizes the signature into a fresh valid signature σ before outputting it.

In [40] and in this work, π_{Ped} has to be straightline-extractable. Due to their instantiation of π_{Ped}, [40] relies on DDH for blindness. We follow a different approach and instantiate π_{Ped} by revisiting the security of randomized Fischlin's transform [21,43]. Consequently, our instantiation is statistically blind. We refer to the technical part of this paper for details.

Towards a Pairing-Free Scheme. We now want to eliminate the use of the pairing from the scheme. For that, we first observe that we can port the underlying signature scheme into the pairing-free setting. Essentially, we include a proof π in the signature that proves that Eq. (1) holds. That is, the signature is now $\sigma = (S_1, S_2, \pi)$. We observe that such a proof can be constructed very efficiently from a Σ-protocol.

While this works in the non-blind setting, computing such a signature σ interactively and blindly turns out to be challenging: the User needs to obtain π, but it does not know a suitable witness to do so. Especially, the witness includes the secret key $u \in \mathbb{Z}_p$. On the other hand, we cannot just let the Signer generate the proof π, because the statement is the rerandomized signature σ, which we want to keep hidden from the Signer.

To overcome this first challenge, our starting point is an approach similar to [16]. Namely, as π is constructed from an appropriate Σ-protocol, we can issue π

interactively and blindly. Roughly, we adapt the techniques of [16] to our setting, and obtain a pairing-free variant of the construction by Katsumata et al. [40] with blind issuance.

Full Unforgeability Fails. Equipped with (a sketch of) our scheme, let us now move our attention to the security proof, concretely, the proof of one-more unforgeability. The natural idea would be to translate the security proof from the pairing-based construction [40] to our setting. Unfortunately, when doing that naively, we can not achieve full one-more unforgeability. To understand this, the reader may first recall that in the one-more unforgeability game, the adversary can interact with the Signer in multiple signing sessions. It wins the game, if it outputs valid signatures for more messages than it *completed* signing interactions[3]. Additionally, the reader may recall the structure of our current blind signing protocol:

1. The Signer and the User interact similarly to the pairing-based scheme sketched above. This means that the Signer sends σ_C to the User which allows the User to compute a signature (S_1, S_2) of the underlying pairing-based scheme [40];
2. The Signer and the User interactively (and blindly) compute the proof π;

Now, assume that we have an adversary interacting 20 times with the Signer, but only completing 7 interactions. Say the remaining 13 interactions end after the first of the two stages above. Now, if an adversary outputs 8 valid message-signature pairs, it is deemed successful in the one-more unforgeability game. However, the reduction from [40] does not apply, as the adversary essentially finished $13 > 8$ interactions of the pairing-based protocol and learned σ_C. Conceptually, the reduction would leak σ_C to the adversary too early, and σ_C contains a solution to a hard problem (specifically, CDH). A similar issue with a different underlying scheme also appeared in [16]. The authors manage to circumvent the issue by outputting a commitment to the signature at first, in the second, and then opening the commitment only in the very last message of the protocol. While this is elegant, it also causes some overhead in terms of efficiency. As we will see next, for our scheme it is possible to prove unforgeability *without* further modifying the signing protocol.

Achieving Full Unforgeability. Our high-level approach for showing full one-more unforgeability is to eliminate information about σ_C from singing interactions that are not finished. To this end, we observe that σ_C is pseudorandom as long as the adversary never learns π, so intuitively, it should not give the adversary any information it can use for its forgeries. To be more concrete, let us assume for the sake of this overview that the reduction knows ahead of time which signing interactions are not finished[4]. Then, the reduction will simply

---

[3] We could show a weaker form of one-more unforgeability similar to CTZ-1 and CTZ-2 [16], in which the adversary has to output valid signatures for more messages than it *started* signing interactions.

[4] Naively, this requires guessing aborted sessions which leads to an exponential security loss. Our approach actually relies on a slightly more sophisticated argument.

send a random σ_C to the adversary. To get an intuition for why that works, observe from Eq. (1) that (S_1, S_2) is indistinguishable from random by the DDH assumption applied to (sG, H, sH). Coming back to our example from above, the adversary would now only learn $7 < 8$ such σ_C's, and the proof of the pairing-based scheme applies.

Avoiding Rewinding. So far, we have omitted an important detail: the reduction of the pairing-based scheme [40] does (of course) not know the secret key, which is part of the witness for the proof π. It is thus not clear how the reduction can issue π to the User interactively[5]. A similar problem appears in [16], so let us briefly review their solution. Roughly [16] employs an *OR proof* for π. That is, π ensures that the signature is valid *or* the Signer knows the discrete logarithm of some group element $X \in \mathbb{G}$ output by the random oracle. The reduction then makes sure to know this discrete logarithm, which allows simulating π. Finally, the reduction either obtains a valid signature, which allows to finish the proof as before, or the discrete logarithm of X. For the latter, the reduction is required to *rewind* the adversary, leading to a highly non-tight security bound.

To avoid rewinding, we make the following twist: we replace X with a Diffie-Hellman (DH) tuple **D**. In particular, π now ensures that either σ is well-formed or **D** is a DH tuple. Interestingly, this comes at *no* additional cost in signature size. Intuitively, as we are no longer proving knowledge of a witness, but rather membership in a language, rewinding should not be needed.

Turning this into a formal proof requires a careful sequence of hybrid games, as outlined next. Initially, the game simulates the Signer as in the real protocol, which means that the proof π is computed via the *signature branch*, i.e., using the witness which testifies the validity of the signature. Also, **D** is not a DH tuple. Then, soundness (not knowledge soundness!) of the proofs π contained in the forgery guarantees that all signatures in the forgery are valid (because **D** is *not* a DH tuple). Call this event E, our strategy is to preserve E while simulating π using the DH branch. If so, we can argue as above that CDH is solved if the adversary is successful. To carry this out, we need to switch **D** to a valid DH tuple. We want to use DDH to argue that the probability of E does not change significantly when we make this change. To do this formally, we need to present a reduction that interpolates between the two games and *efficiently* evaluates whether E occurs. Doing this naively is equivalent to solving DDH in the first place! The crucial insight here is that this can be done efficiently using the signing key u and the discrete logarithm h of H. Once we are in a game where **D** is a valid DH tuple, we can use the corresponding DH witness to simulate π. Then, if E occurs in this last game, we can reduce to CDH as discussed above[6].

Generalizing to Partial Blindness. Partial blindness allows the Signer and User to agree on a common message τ that is signed together with the (hid-

---

[5] Non-interactively and without blindness, this can be done in a standard way, using honest-verifier zero-knowledge and by programming the random oracle.

[6] The final reduction does not need to check if E occurs, and hence it neither needs the secret key u nor the discrete logarithm h of H.

den) message m. This property is useful for many privacy-preserving applications. To obtain partial blindness, we employ the design principle from Abe and Okamoto [3]. That is, the vector $\mathbf{D}$ is output by a random oracle H_{ddh} on input τ. Otherwise, the entire protocol remains unchanged. By carefully applying the techniques sketched above, we can prove partial blindness.

1.4 Organization of this Paper

In Sect. 2, we provide the relevant cryptographic definitions. In Sect. 3, we sketch the pairing-free signature scheme that underlies our construction. To improve readability, we first provide an unblinded version of our protocol in Sect. 4 and prove one-more unforgeability. In Sect. 5, we provide the full protocol and its blindness proof. The Signer in this protocol is the same as in Sect. 4, which means that one-more unforgeability follows as in Sect. 4.

2 Preliminaries

Let $\lambda \in \mathbb{N}$ be the security parameter. We use standard notations for probability, algorithms and distributions[7]. We write $A(\mathsf{in}_A) \longleftrightarrow B(\mathsf{in}_B)$ for interactive protocols between parties A and B with input in_A and in_B, respectively. Within algorithmic descriptions, we denote by **req** C that the algorithm outputs $\perp$ if the condition C is false. When describing games, we denote by **abort if** C that the game outputs 0 if the condition C is false. Throughout, we denote by $\mathbb{G}$ a group of prime order p with generator $G \in \mathbb{G}$. We generally use additive notation for $\mathbb{G}$. Throughout, group elements G are capital, whereas elements x in $\mathbb{N}$ or $\mathbb{Z}_p$ are lowercase. Vectors of elements $\mathbf{G}$ or $\mathbf{x}$ are bold, and generally indexed $\mathbf{G} = (G_1, \cdots, G_n)$ or $\mathbf{x} = (x_1, \cdots, x_n)$, respectively.

Assumptions. Throughout the paper, we let $\mathbb{G}$ be a group of prime order p with generator $G \in \mathbb{G}$. As common, this should be understood as implicitly being a family of groups, i.e., $\mathbb{G} = \mathbb{G}_\lambda$ is implicitly parameterized by the security parameter λ. We briefly recall the DL, CDH and (Q-)DDH assumptions and refer to the full version [42] for formal definitions. While DDH implies Q-DDH, CDH and DL tightly, these assumptions will be convenient to prove security later. Below, let $a, b, c \xleftarrow{\$} \mathbb{Z}_p$. The DL assumption states that given G and aG it is hard to compute a. The CDH assumption states that it is hard given (G, aG, bB) to compute $(ab)G$. The DDH assumption states that it is hard to distinguish a real Diffie-Hellman tuple $(G, aG, bB, (ab)G)$ from a random tuple (G, aG, bB, cG). The Q-DDH assumption states that it is hard to distinguish Q random Diffie-Hellman tuples from random Q tuples.

---

[7] We use $x := v$ for assignment of value v to x (and $x \leftarrow v$ if x is updated with value v), $x \leftarrow A(\mathsf{in})$ for (probabilistic) algorithms A on input in, and $x \xleftarrow{\$} \mathcal{D}$ for sampling from distribution $\mathcal{D}$. (If $\mathcal{D}$ is a set, this denotes sampling from $\mathcal{D}$ uniformly and independently at random).

(Partially) Blind Signatures. We define the primitive of interest, namely, blind signatures [17]. For convenience, we directly define partially blind signatures [2] and note that plain blind signatures are the special case in which τ is fixed, i.e., $|\mathcal{T}| = 1$.

Definition 1 (Partially Blind Signature Scheme). *A partially blind signature scheme with message space $\mathcal{M}$ and common message space $\mathcal{T}$ is a tuple of PPT algorithms* BS $=$ (KeyGen, S, U, Verify) *with the following syntax:*

- KeyGen(1^λ): *outputs a pair of keys* (vk, sk). *We assume that* sk *includes* vk *implicitly.*
- S(sk, τ) $\longleftrightarrow$ U(vk, m, τ): S *takes as input a secret key* sk *and common message* $\tau \in \mathcal{T}$. U *takes as input a key* vk, *a message* $m \in \mathcal{M}$ *and common message* $\tau \in \mathcal{T}$. *After the execution,* U *returns a signature* σ *and we write* $\sigma \leftarrow \langle$S(sk, τ), U(vk, m, τ)$\rangle$.
- Verify(vk, m, τ, σ) *is deterministic and takes as input public key* vk, *message* $m \in \mathcal{M}$, *a common message* τ, *and a signature* σ, *and outputs* $b \in \{0, 1\}$.

Definition 2 (Correctness). *A partially blind signature* BS *is correct with correctness error* γ_{err} *if for all* (vk, sk) $\in$ KeyGen(1^λ) *and all* $m \in \mathcal{M}, \tau \in \mathcal{T}$, *it holds that*

$$\Pr[\sigma \leftarrow \langle\text{S(sk}, \tau), \text{U(vk}, m, \tau)\rangle : \text{Verify(vk}, m, \tau, \sigma) = 1] \geq 1 - \gamma_{\text{err}}(\lambda).$$

Intuitively, a (partially) blind signature scheme should not allow any user to obtain signatures without interacting with the Signer. This is modeled by the notion of one-more unforgeability, which states that after completing $k - 1$ signing sessions on some common message τ^*, an adversary can not output valid signatures on k messages with common message τ^*.

Definition 3 (One-More Unforgeability). *Let* BS $=$ (KeyGen, S, U, Verify) *be a blind signature scheme. Consider an algorithm $\mathcal{A}$ and the following game:*

1. *Run* (vk, sk) $\leftarrow$ KeyGen(1^λ) *and let $\mathcal{O}$ be an interactive oracle simulating* S(sk, $\cdot$).
2. *Run* $\tau, ((m_1, \sigma_1), \ldots, (m_k, \sigma_k)) \leftarrow \mathcal{A}^{\mathcal{O}}$(vk), *where $\mathcal{A}$ can query $\mathcal{O}$ in an arbitrarily interleaved way.*
3. *Output 1 if and only if all $m_i, i \in [k]$ are pairwise distinct, $\mathcal{A}$ completed at most $k - 1$ interactions with $\mathcal{O}$ on input τ, and for each $i \in [k]$ it holds that* Verify(vk, m_i, τ, σ_i) = 1.

We denote by AdvOMUF$_{\mathcal{A}}^{\text{BS}}(\lambda)$ *the probability that the above game outputs 1. We say that* BS *is one-more unforgeable (OMUF), if for every PPT algorithm $\mathcal{A}$, it holds that* AdvOMUF$_{\mathcal{A}}^{\text{BS}}(\lambda) = \text{negl}(\lambda)$.

To protect the privacy of users, blind signatures should satisfy blindness. Intuitively, blindness states that a malicious signer can not link the signing interaction to the message-signature pair (except for the common message τ). We emphasize that we consider the malicious signer blindness, i.e., the malicious signer can freely choose the public key and arbitrarily deviate from the protocol.

Definition 4 (Partial Blindness). *Let* BS $=$ (KeyGen, S, U, Verify) *be a blind signature scheme. For an algorithm* $\mathcal{A}$ *and bit* $b \in \{0, 1\}$*, consider the following game:*

1. *Run* $(\text{vk}, m_0, m_1, \tau, st) \leftarrow \mathcal{A}(1^\lambda)$.
2. *Let* $\mathcal{O}_0$ *be an interactive oracle simulating* U(vk, m_b, τ) *and* $\mathcal{O}_1$ *be an interactive oracle simulating* U$(\text{vk}, m_{1-b}, \tau)$.
3. *Run* $st' \leftarrow \mathcal{A}^{\mathcal{O}_0, \mathcal{O}_1}(st)$*, where* $\mathcal{A}$ *has arbitrary interleaved one-time access to* $\mathcal{O}_0$ *and* $\mathcal{O}_1$*. Let* σ_b, σ_{1-b} *be the local outputs of* $\mathcal{O}_0, \mathcal{O}_1$*, respectively.*
4. *If* $\sigma_0 = \bot$ *or* $\sigma_1 = \bot$*, run* $b' \leftarrow \mathcal{A}(st', \bot, \bot)$*. Else, run* $b' \leftarrow \mathcal{A}(st', \sigma_0, \sigma_1)$*.*
5. *Output* b'*.*

We denote by AdvPBlind$_{\mathcal{A}}^{\text{BS}}(\lambda)$ *difference between the probability that the above game with* $b = 0$ *outputs 1 and the probability that the game with* $b = 1$ *outputs 1. We say that* BS *satisfies partial blindness if* AdvPBlind$_{\mathcal{A}}^{\text{BS}}(\lambda) = \text{negl}(\lambda)$*.*

Relations and Σ-Protocols. Next, we define Σ-protocols for NP-relations. We start by defining NP-relations.

Definition 5 (NP-Relation and Language). *Let* R $\subseteq \{0, 1\}^* \times \{0, 1\}^*$ *be a binary relation. We say that* R *is an NP-relation, if there are polynomials p and q such that* R *can efficiently be decided and for every* $(x, w) \in R$*, we have* $|x| \leq p(\lambda)$ *and* $|w| \leq q(|x|)$*. We denote by* $\mathscr{L}_R = \{x \in \{0, 1\}^* \mid \exists w \text{ s.t. } (x, w) \in R\}$ *the language induced by* R*.*

Let R be an NP-relation with statements x and witnesses w. A Σ-protocol for an NP-relation R for language $\mathscr{L}_R$ with challenge space $\mathcal{CH}$ is a tuple of PPT algorithms $\Sigma = $ (Init, Resp, Verify) such that

- Init(x, w): given a statement $x \subset \mathscr{L}_R$ and a witness w, outputs a first flow message (*i.e.*, commitment) A and a state st, where we assume st includes (x, w),
- Resp(st, c): given a state st and a challenge $c \in \mathcal{CH}$, outputs a third flow message (*i.e.*, response) z,
- Verify(x, A, c, z): given a statement $x \in \mathscr{L}_R$, a commitment A, a challenge $c \in \mathcal{CH}$, and a response z, outputs a bit $b \in \{0, 1\}$.

We call the tuple (A, c, z) the *transcript* and say that they are *valid for* x if Verify(x, A, c, z) outputs 1. When the context is clear, we simply say it is valid and omit x. Next, we define the standard notions of correctness, special honest-verifier zero-knowledge, and (2-)special soundness.

Definition 6 (Correctness). *Let* R *be an NP-relation and* $\Sigma = $ (Init, Resp, Verify) *be an Σ-protocol for* R*. We say Σ is correct, if for all* $(x, w) \in R$*,* $(A, st) \leftarrow$ Init(x, w)*,* $c \in \mathcal{CH}$*, and* $z \leftarrow$ Resp(st, c)*, it holds that* Verify$(x, A, c, z) = 1$*.*

Definition 7 (Special HVZK). *Let* R *be an NP-relation and* $\Sigma = $ (Init, Resp, Verify) *be a Σ-protocol for* R*. We say that Σ is special honest-verifier zero-knowledge (HVZK), if there exists a PPT zero-knowledge simulator* Sim *such* *that for any (potentially unbounded) adversary $\mathcal{A}$, it holds that for any $(\mathbb{x}, \mathbb{w}) \in \mathsf{R}$ and $c \in \mathcal{CH}$ that $\mathsf{D}_{\mathsf{real}} = \mathsf{D}_{\mathsf{sim}}$ for*

$$\mathsf{D}_{\mathsf{real}} := \{(A, c, z) \mid A \leftarrow \mathsf{Init}(\mathbb{x}, \mathbb{w}), z \leftarrow \mathsf{Resp}(\mathsf{st}, c)\},$$
$$\mathsf{D}_{\mathsf{sim}} := \{(A, c, z) \mid (A, z) \leftarrow \mathsf{Sim}(\mathbb{x}, c)\}.$$

In this work, we write HVZK for short.

Definition 8 (Special Soundness). *Let R be an NP-relation and $\Sigma = (\mathsf{Init}, \mathsf{Resp}, \mathsf{Verify})$ be a Σ-protocol for R. We say that Σ is (2-)special sound, if there exists a deterministic PT extractor Ext such that given two valid transcripts $\{(A, c_b, z_b)\}_{b \in [2]}$ for statement $\mathbb{x}$ with $c_0 \neq c_1$, along with x, outputs a witness $\mathbb{w}$ such that $(\mathbb{x}, \mathbb{w}) \in \mathsf{R}$.*

Non-interactive Proof Systems. Here, we define straightline-extractable non-interactive zero-knowledge proofs. We limit ourselves to security in the random oracle model. Efficient constructions are known in this case, e.g., using the Fischlin transformation [21], but also [39,43,48].

Definition 9 (Non-Interactive Proof System). *A non-interactive proof system NIPS for NP-relation R using a random oracle H is a pair NIPS = (Prove, Ver) of PPT algorithms with access to a random oracle, where*

- $\mathsf{Prove}^{\mathsf{H}}(\mathbb{x}, \mathbb{w})$: *generates a proof π given $(\mathbb{x}, \mathbb{w}) \in \mathsf{R}$.*
- $\mathsf{Ver}^{\mathsf{H}}(\mathbb{x}, \pi)$: *verifies a proof π for statement $\mathbb{x}$ and outputs 0 or 1.*

Note that out definitions of zero-knowledge simulator and knowledge extractor are independent of an adversary, in particular, they are straightline by definition.

Definition 10 (Correctness). *Let NIPS = (Prove, Ver) be a non-interactive proof system for a relation R. It has correctness error γ_{err} if for all $(\mathbb{x}, \mathbb{w}) \in \mathsf{R}$, it holds that*

$$\Pr\left[\pi \leftarrow \mathsf{Prove}^{\mathsf{H}}(\mathbb{x}, \mathbb{w}) \; : \; \mathsf{Ver}^{\mathsf{H}}(\mathbb{x}, \pi) = 1\right] \geq 1 - \gamma_{\mathsf{err}}(\lambda),$$

where the probability is over the choice of H and the randomness of Prove, Ver. We call NIPS correct if $\gamma_{\mathsf{err}}(\lambda) = \mathrm{negl}(\lambda)$. We say it is perfectly correct if $\gamma_{\mathsf{err}} = 0$.

Definition 11 (Witness Indistinguishability). *Let NIPS = $(\mathsf{Prove}^{\mathsf{H}}, \mathsf{Ver}^{\mathsf{H}})$ be a non-interactive proof system for a relation R in the random oracle model. Let $\mathcal{A}$ be an algorithm which makes at most $Q = Q(\lambda)$ queries to H and let*

$$\mathsf{AdvWI}_{\mathcal{A}}^{\mathsf{NIPS}}(Q, \lambda) = \Pr\left[b \leftarrow \mathcal{A}^{\mathsf{H}, \mathcal{O}_0}(1^{\lambda}): b = 1\right] - \Pr\left[b \leftarrow \mathcal{A}^{\mathsf{H}, \mathcal{O}_1}(1^{\lambda}): b = 1\right],$$

where $\mathcal{O}_i(\mathbb{x}, \mathbb{w}_0, \mathbb{w}_1)$ returns $\mathsf{Prove}^{\mathsf{H}}(\mathbb{x}, \mathbb{w}_i)$ for $i \in \{0, 1\}$. We call NIPS statistically (resp. computationally) witness indistinguishable (WI), if for any unbounded (resp. PPT) adversary $\mathcal{A}$, the advantage $\mathsf{AdvWI}_{\mathcal{A}}^{\mathsf{NIPS}}(\lambda)$ is negligible.

For knowledge soundness, the extractor must compute a witness from an accepting proof and all adversarial random oracle queries. In particular, extraction is straightline. We say that knowledge soundness is relaxed if the witness is for a relaxed relation $\tilde{R} \supsetneq R$. We refer to $\tilde{R}$ as the knowledge relation.

Definition 12 (Relaxed Knowledge Soundness). *Let* $\mathsf{NIPS} = (\mathsf{Prove}, \mathsf{Ver})$ *be a non-interactive proof system for a relation* R *and let* $\tilde{R} \supseteq R$ *be an NP-relation. Let* Ext *be a PPT algorithm. Let* $\mathcal{A}$ *be an oracle algorithm and let*

$$\mathsf{Real}_{\mathcal{A}}(\lambda) := \Pr\left[b \leftarrow \mathcal{A}^{\mathsf{H}, \mathcal{O}_{\mathsf{Ver}}}(1^{\lambda}): b = 1\right],$$
$$\mathsf{Ideal}_{\mathcal{A}}(\lambda) := \Pr\left[b \leftarrow \mathcal{A}^{\mathsf{H}, \mathcal{O}_{\mathsf{Ext}}}(1^{\lambda}): b = 1\right].$$

Here, $\mathcal{A}$ *has (black-box) access to the random oracle* H *and to an oracle* $\mathcal{O}_{\mathsf{Prove}}$ *or* $\mathcal{O}_{\mathsf{Ext}}$*, which are as follows:*

- $\mathcal{O}_{\mathsf{Ver}}(\mathrm{x}, \pi)$*: Return* $\mathsf{Ver}(\mathrm{x}, \pi)$*.*
- $\mathcal{O}_{\mathsf{Ext}}(\mathrm{x}, \pi)$*: If* $\mathsf{Ver}(\mathrm{x}, \pi) = 1$ *and* $(\mathrm{x}, \mathrm{w}) \notin \tilde{R}$ *for* $\mathrm{w} \leftarrow \mathsf{Ext}(\mathcal{Q}, \mathrm{x}, \pi)$*, return* 0*. Else, return* 1*. Here,* $\mathcal{Q}$ *denotes the set of* $\mathcal{A}$*'s* H *queries.*

The advantage of $\mathcal{A}$ *against knowledge soundness is* $\mathsf{AdvKS}_{\mathcal{A}}^{\mathsf{NIPS}, \tilde{R}}(\lambda) := |\mathsf{Real}_{\mathcal{A}}(\lambda) - \mathsf{Ideal}_{\mathcal{A}}(\lambda)|$*. We say that* Ext *is a knowledge extractor for* NIPS *and knowledge relation* $\tilde{R}$*, if for every PPT algorithm* $\mathcal{A}$*, the advantage* $\mathsf{AdvKS}_{\mathcal{A}}^{\mathsf{NIPS}, \tilde{R}}(\lambda)$ *is negligible in* λ*. We say that* NIPS *is knowledge sound, if there is a knowledge extractor for* NIPS*.*

Remark 1. Any non-interactive proof system meeting above requirements is sufficient for our blind signature construction, and we present it using the proof system in a black-box way. For concreteness, we will use a variant of the Fischlin transformation [21,43], which is detailed in the full version [42].

3   Signatures Based on the Boneh-Boyen IBE

It is well-known that signatures can generically be constructed from identity-based encryption (IBE) [10]. Our starting point towards constructing blind signatures is the Boneh-Boyen identity-based encryption scheme [9]. Note that without any modification this scheme would rely on pairings, and so would the derived signature scheme. Here, we provide a pairing-free variant of this signature scheme. As this scheme is the basis for our partially blind signature, we also provide a common message $\tau \in \{0,1\}^*$ as parameter.

Overview. Let $\mathsf{H_M} \colon \{0,1\}^* \to \mathbb{Z}_p$ be a random oracle. For any $m \in \{0,1\}^*$, denote by $\overline{m} := \mathsf{H_M}(m)$. A signature on a message $m \in \{0,1\}^*$ consists of two group elements S_1 and S_2 such that

$$S_1 = uV + s(\overline{m}U + H), \quad S_2 = sG, \tag{2}$$

where $V, H, U = uG \in \mathbb{G}$ are part of the public key and $s \in \mathbb{Z}_p$. To verify such a signature without a pairing, signatures in our variant also contain a proof π, which informally shows that one of the following holds:

(i) (S_1, S_2) satisfy Eq. (2) for $U = uG$, or

(ii) $\mathbf{D} = \mathsf{H}_{\mathsf{ddh}}(\tau)$ is a DDH-tuple, where $\mathsf{H}_{\mathsf{ddh}} \colon \{0,1\}^* \to \mathbb{G}^2$ is a random oracle for common message $\tau \in \{0,1\}^*$.

Point (ii) is technically not required for the signature scheme itself but will be useful for the security proof of our (partially) blind signature construction (cf. Sect. 4), where it allows simulating the signer.

Notation. To improve readability, we introduce two functions below, where the reader should think of the element X as representing $X = \overline{m} \cdot U + H$. We define a function that captures the statement (i). For $V \in \mathbb{G}$, we define $\phi_{G,V}^{\mathsf{BB}} \colon \mathbb{G} \times \mathbb{Z}_p^2 \to \mathbb{G}^3$ as follows:

$$\phi_{G,V}^{\mathsf{BB}}(X, (s, u)) = \begin{pmatrix} u \cdot V + s \cdot X \\ s \cdot G \\ u \cdot G \end{pmatrix}. \tag{3}$$

If (X, G) are clear from the context, we write $\phi_0 = \phi_{G,V}^{\mathsf{BB}}$ for short. Note that $\phi_0(X, \cdot)$ is linear for fixed input X. We also define R_{bb} with induced language $\mathscr{L}_{\mathsf{bb}}$ as follows:

$$\mathsf{R}_{\mathsf{bb}} := \{(\mathbbm{x}_0, \mathbbm{w}_0) \mid \mathbf{S} = \phi_0(X, (s, u))\},$$
$$\text{where } \mathbbm{x}_0 = (G, V, X, \mathbf{S}) \in \mathbb{G}^6, \; \mathbbm{w}_0 = (s, u) \in \mathbb{Z}_p^3.$$

We also define a linear function that captures statement (ii). That is, for $D_1 \in \mathbb{G}$, we define $\phi_{D_1}^{\mathsf{DDH}} \colon \mathbb{Z}_p \to \mathbb{G}$ as follows:

$$\phi_{G,D_1}^{\mathsf{DDH}}(d_2) = \begin{pmatrix} d_2 \cdot G \\ d_2 \cdot D_1 \end{pmatrix}. \tag{4}$$

If D_1 is clear from the context, we write $\phi_1 = \phi_{G,D_1}^{\mathsf{DDH}}$ for short. Similarly, we define $\mathsf{R}_{\mathsf{ddh}}$ with induced language $\mathscr{L}_{\mathsf{ddh}}$ as follows:

$$\mathsf{R}_{\mathsf{ddh}} := \{(\mathbbm{x}_1, \mathbbm{w}_1) \mid (D_2, D_3) = \phi_1(d_2)\},$$
$$\text{where } \mathbbm{x}_1 = (G, D_1, D_2, D_3) \in \mathbb{G}^4, \; \mathbbm{w}_1 = d_2 \in \mathbb{Z}_p.$$

3.1   Construction

Let $\Sigma_0 = (\mathsf{Init}_0, \mathsf{Resp}_0, \mathsf{Verify}_0)$ and $\Sigma_1 = (\mathsf{Init}_1, \mathsf{Resp}_1, \mathsf{Verify}_1)$ be Σ-protocols with challenge space $\mathbb{Z}_p$ for the relations R_{bb} and $\mathsf{R}_{\mathsf{ddh}}$ defined above, respectively. Denote by Sim_1 the HVZK simulator of Verify_1. Let $\mathsf{H}_\Sigma, \mathsf{H}_\mathsf{M}, \mathsf{H}_{\mathsf{ddh}}$ be random oracles mapping into $\mathbb{Z}_p, \mathbb{Z}_p$ and $\mathbb{G}^2$, respectively. We define the signature BBSig in the following.

BBSig: Pairing-free signature based on Boneh-Boyen IBE [9]

- KeyGen(1^λ):
    1. Sample $u \xleftarrow{\$} \mathbb{Z}_p$ and set $U := uG$. Sample $H, V, D_1 \xleftarrow{\$} \mathbb{G}$.
    2. Output $\mathsf{vk} := (G, U, H, V, D_1)$ and $\mathsf{sk} := u$.
- Sign(sk, m, τ):
    1. Set $(D_2^\tau, D_3^\tau) := \mathsf{H}_{\mathsf{ddh}}(\tau)$ and $\mathbf{D}^\tau := (D_1, D_2^\tau, D_3^\tau)$.
    2. Set $\overline{m} := \mathsf{H}_\mathsf{M}(m)$ and $X := \overline{m}U + H$.
    3. Sample $s \leftarrow \mathbb{Z}_p$ and set $\mathbf{S} := \phi_0(X, (s, u))$.
    4. Compute a proof π as follows:
        (a) Let $(\mathtt{x}_0, \mathtt{x}_1)$ be as above [a] and set $\mathtt{w}_0 := (s, u)$.
        (b) Sample $c_1 \xleftarrow{\$} \mathbb{Z}_p$ and set $(\mathbf{A}_1, z_1) \leftarrow \mathsf{Sim}_1(\mathtt{x}_1, c_1)$.
        (c) Run $(\mathbf{A}_0, \mathsf{st}_0) \leftarrow \mathsf{Init}_0(\mathtt{x}_0, \mathtt{w}_0)$.
        (d) Set $c := \mathsf{H}_\Sigma((\mathtt{x}_b, \mathbf{A}_b)_{b \in \{0,1\}}, m)$ and $c_0 := c - c_1$.
        (e) Run $\mathbf{z}_0 \leftarrow \mathsf{Resp}_0(\mathsf{st}_0, c_0)$.
        (f) Set $\pi := (\mathbf{A}_0, \mathbf{A}_1, c, c_0, \mathbf{z}_0, z_1)$.
    5. Output $\sigma_\mathsf{bb} := (S_1, S_2, \pi)$.
- Verify($\mathsf{vk}, m, \tau, \sigma_\mathsf{bb}$):
    1. Parse σ_bb as $\sigma_\mathsf{bb} = (S_1, S_2, \pi)$ and π as $\pi = (\mathbf{A}_0, \mathbf{A}_1, c, c_0, \mathbf{z}_0, z_1)$.
    2. Set $(D_2^\tau, D_3^\tau) := \mathsf{H}_\mathsf{ddh}(\tau)$ and $\mathbf{D}^\tau := (D_1, D_2^\tau, D_3^\tau)$.
    3. Let $(\mathtt{x}_0, \mathtt{x}_1)$ be as above [a].
    4. Set $\mathbf{S} := (S_1, S_2, U)$, $\overline{m} := \mathsf{H}_\mathsf{M}(m)$ and $X := \overline{m}U + H$.
    5. Set $c' := \mathsf{H}((\mathtt{x}_b, \mathbf{A}_b)_{b \in \{0,1\}}, m)$ and $c_1 := c' - c_0$.
    6. Output 0 if $\mathsf{Verify}_0(\mathtt{x}_0, \mathbf{A}_0, c_0, \mathbf{z}_0) = 0$.
    7. Output 0 if $\mathsf{Verify}_1(\mathtt{x}_1, \mathbf{A}_1, c_1, z_1) = 0$.
    8. Otherwise, output 1.

---

[a] That is, $\mathtt{x}_0 := (G, V, X, \mathbf{S})$ and $\mathtt{x}_1 := (G, \mathbf{D}^\tau)$.

Note that above, π functions essentially as proof for the disjunctive relation $R_\mathsf{bb} \cup R_\mathsf{ddh}$. Also, the first flow $\mathbf{A}_0, \mathbf{A}_1$ can be omitted from the proof π since these values can be recomputed given $(c, c_0, \mathbf{z}_0, z_1)$.

3.2 Security Analysis

We provide a useful lemma which we employ in our proof of one-more unforgeability (cf. Theorem 1). Roughly, it shows that it is hard to output a tuple (S_1, S_2) such that $(G, V, X_{\overline{m}^*}, S_1, S_2, U) \in \mathscr{L}_\mathsf{bb}$, where $\overline{m}^* \in \mathbb{Z}_p$ is chosen selectively and $X_{m^*} := \overline{m}^* U + H$. This even holds if the adversary is given oracle access to an oracle that outputs (S_1, S_2) such that $(G, V, X_{\overline{m}}, S_1, S_2, U) \in \mathscr{L}_\mathsf{bb}$ for $\overline{m} \neq \overline{m}^*$. Note that this corresponds almost to selective unforgeability of BBSig except that the common message τ and the proof π is ignored. This can be shown via the puncturing strategy from [9] and we provide a formal proof in the full version [42].

Lemma 1 (Selective Security of BBSig). *For any algorithm $\mathcal{A}$, let $\epsilon_\mathcal{A}^\mathsf{BB}$ be the probability that the following game outputs 1:*

1. *Run* $(\overline{m}^*, \mathsf{st}_{\mathcal{A}}) \leftarrow \mathcal{A}(1^\lambda)$.
2. *Sample* $u \xleftarrow{\$} \mathbb{Z}_p$ *and set* $U := uG$.
3. *Sample* $(H, V) \xleftarrow{\$} \mathbb{G}$ *and set* $X_{m^*} := \overline{m}^* U + H$.
4. *Run* $(S_1^*, S_2^*) \leftarrow \mathcal{A}^{\mathcal{O}}(G, U, H, V, \mathsf{st}_{\mathcal{A}})$, *where* $\mathcal{O}$ *is given as:*
   - $\mathcal{O}(\overline{m})$: *Output* $\perp$ *if* $\overline{m} = \overline{m}^*$. *Otherwise, sample* $s \xleftarrow{\$} \mathbb{Z}_p$, *set* $X_{\overline{m}} = \overline{m} \cdot U + H$, *and compute* $\mathbf{S} := \phi_0(X_{\overline{m}}, (s, u))$. *Then return* (S_1, S_2).
5. *Set* $\mathbf{x}_0^* := (G, V, X_{\overline{m}^*}, S_1^*, S_2^*, U)$ *and output* 1 *if and only if* $\mathbf{x}_0^* \in \mathscr{L}_{\mathsf{bb}}$.

Then, for any PPT algorithm $\mathcal{A}$, *there exists some PPT algorithm* $\mathcal{B}$ *with running time similar to* $\mathcal{A}$ *such that*

$$\epsilon_{\mathcal{A}}^{\mathsf{BB}} \leq \mathsf{AdvCDH}_{\mathcal{B}}^{\mathbb{G}}(\lambda).$$

4 Non-blind Interactive Signing Protocol

With BBSig signatures as introduced in Sect. 3 at hand, we now move closer to our blind signature construction. The goal of this section is to define an interactive protocol for obtaining BBSig signatures from the Signer. More precisely, what we construct here is a blind signature scheme that satisfies one-more unforgeability, but is *not* blind at this point. We stress that consequently, the protocol presented in this section is not our final blind signature scheme. We will take care of blindness and present our final signing protocol in Sect. 5.

4.1 Construction

Let $\mathsf{NIPS}_{\mathsf{Ped}} = (\mathsf{NIPS}_{\mathsf{Ped}}.\mathsf{Prove}^{\mathsf{H}_{\mathsf{Ped}}}, \mathsf{NIPS}_{\mathsf{Ped}}.\mathsf{Ver}^{\mathsf{H}_{\mathsf{Ped}}})$ be a NIPS proof system with random oracle $\mathsf{H}_{\mathsf{Ped}} : \{0,1\}^* \to \mathcal{Y}_{\mathsf{Ped}}$ with image space $\mathcal{Y}_{\mathsf{Ped}}$ for the relation

$$\mathsf{R}_{\mathsf{Ped}} := \{(\mathbf{x}, \mathbf{w}) \mid C = \overline{m} U + t G\}, \text{ where } \mathbf{x} = (C, U, G), \; \mathbf{w} = (\overline{m}, t). \quad (5)$$

In addition, our construction makes use of random oracles $\mathsf{H}_{\mathsf{M}} : \{0,1\}^* \to \mathbb{Z}_p$, and $\mathsf{H}_{\Sigma} : \{0,1\}^* \to \mathbb{Z}_p$, and $\mathsf{H}_{\mathsf{ddh}} : \{0,1\}^* \to \mathbb{G}^2$. We now present our construction.

PreBS: Unblinded interactive signing protocol for BBSig signatures

- $\mathsf{KeyGen}(1^\lambda)$: Output $(\mathsf{vk}, \mathsf{sk}) \leftarrow \mathsf{BBSig}.\mathsf{KeyGen}(1^\lambda)$.
- $\mathsf{S}(\mathsf{sk}, \tau) \longleftrightarrow \mathsf{U}(\mathsf{vk}, m, \tau)$: The signing protocol proceeds in 4 moves and is given in Fig. 1.
- $\mathsf{Verify}(\mathsf{vk}, m, \tau, \sigma_{\mathsf{bb}})$: Output $b \leftarrow \mathsf{BBSig}.\mathsf{Verify}(\mathsf{vk}, m, \tau, \sigma_{\mathsf{bb}})$.

Remark 2 (Optimizations). The signer can omit sending $T_3 = U$, as this value is specified in vk. Also, as discussed in Sect. 3, the values $(\mathbf{A}_0, A_1)$ can be omitted from the proof π within the output signature σ_{bb}.

$S(sk, \tau)$	$U(vk, m, \tau)$
	1: $\quad t \xleftarrow{\$} \mathbb{Z}_p, \overline{m} := H_M(m),$
	2: $\quad C := \overline{m}U + tG$
	3: $\quad \mathbb{x}_{Ped} := (C, U, G), \mathbb{w}_{Ped} := (\overline{m}, t)$
	4: $\quad \pi_{Ped} \leftarrow NIPS_{Ped}.Prove^{H_{Ped}}(\mathbb{x}_{Ped}, \mathbb{w}_{Ped})$

$$\xleftarrow{\qquad C, \pi_{Ped} \qquad}$$

5: $\quad \mathbb{x}_{Ped} := (C, U, G)$

6: $\quad \textbf{req } NIPS_{Ped}.Ver^{H_{Ped}}(\mathbb{x}_{Ped}, \pi_{Ped}) = 1$

7: $\quad s \xleftarrow{\$} \mathbb{Z}_p, \mathbb{w}_0 := (s, sk)$

8: $\quad X_C := C + H, \mathbf{T} := \phi_0(X_C, \mathbb{w}_0)$

9: $\quad \mathbb{x}_0^C := (G, V, X_C, \mathbf{T}), \mathbb{x}_1 := (G, \mathbf{D}^\tau)$

10: $\quad c_1 \xleftarrow{\$} \mathbb{Z}_p, (\mathbf{A}_1, z_1) \leftarrow Sim_1(\mathbb{x}_1, c_1)$

11: $\quad (\mathbf{A}_0^C, st_0) \leftarrow Init_0(\mathbb{x}_0^C, \mathbb{w}_0)$

$$\xrightarrow{\qquad (\mathbf{T}, \mathbf{A}_0^C, \mathbf{A}_1) \qquad}$$

	12: $\quad \mathbf{S} := \mathbf{T} - (t \cdot T_2, 0, 0)^T$
	13: $\quad \mathbf{A}_0 := \mathbf{A}_0^C - (t \cdot A_{0,2}^C, 0, 0)$
	14: $\quad X := \overline{m}U + H$
	15: $\quad \mathbb{x}_0 := (G, V, X, \mathbf{S}), \mathbb{x}_1 := (G, \mathbf{D}^\tau)$
	16: $\quad c := H_\Sigma((\mathbb{x}_b, \mathbf{A}_b)_{b \in \{0,1\}}, m)$

$$\xleftarrow{\qquad c \qquad}$$

17: $\quad c_0 := c - c_1$

18: $\quad \mathbb{z}_0 \leftarrow Resp_0(st_0, c_0)$

$$\xrightarrow{\qquad \mathbb{z}_0, z_1, c_0 \qquad}$$

	19: $\quad \pi := (\mathbf{A}_0, \mathbf{A}_1, c, c_0, \mathbb{z}_0, z_1)$
	20: $\quad \sigma_{bb} := (S_1, S_2, \pi)$

Fig. 1. An (unblinded) signing session for PreBS for message $m \in \{0, 1\}^*$ and common message $\tau \in \{0, 1\}^*$. The signer aborts (*i.e.*, outputs $\perp$) if for condition C, **req** C is evaluated for false C. Recall that H_Σ maps into $\mathbb{Z}_p$ and that $\mathbf{D}^\tau := (D_1, D_2^\tau, D_3^\tau)$ for $(D_2^\tau, D_3^\tau) := H_{ddh}(\tau)$. Also, recall that $vk = (G, U, H, V, D_1) \in \mathbb{G}^5$ and $sk = u \in \mathbb{Z}_p$.

4.2 Security Analysis

Correctness follows from inspection and we will give a correctness proof for our final scheme later. As already mentioned, PreBS is not blind. Here, we show one-more unforgeability. As we instantiate $NIPS_{Ped}$ (in the full version [42]) with a relaxed knowledge sound NIPS, the extractor Ext_{Ped} only extracts a witness for the relaxed knowledge relation

$$\tilde{R}_{\mathsf{Ped}} := \{(\mathbb{x}, \mathbb{w}) \mid \mathbb{w}G = U \vee (\mathbb{x}, \mathbb{w}) \in \mathsf{R}_{\mathsf{Ped}}\}, \quad \text{where } \mathbb{x} = (C, U, G). \quad (6)$$

In particular, we show that if $\mathsf{NIPS}_{\mathsf{Ped}}$ is (straightline) knowledge sound with knowledge relation $\tilde{R}_{\mathsf{Ped}}$, then PreBS is one-more unforgeable under the DDH assumption.

Theorem 1 (One-More Unforgeability). *Denote by p the order of group* $\mathbb{G}$. *For any PPT adversary* $\mathcal{A}$ *that causes at most Q random oracle queries, there are reductions* $\mathcal{A}_{\mathsf{KS}}, \mathcal{A}_{\mathsf{DL}}, \mathcal{A}_{\mathsf{DDH}}$, *and* $\mathcal{A}_{\mathsf{CDH}}$ *with running time similar to* $\mathcal{A}$ *such that*

$$\mathsf{AdvOMUF}_{\mathcal{A}}^{\mathsf{PreBS}}(\lambda) \leq \frac{4 \cdot Q^2 + 3 \cdot Q + 4}{p-1} + \mathsf{AdvKS}_{\mathcal{A}_{\mathsf{KS}}}^{\mathsf{NIPS}_{\mathsf{Ped}}, \tilde{R}_{\mathsf{Ped}}}(\lambda) + \mathsf{AdvDL}_{\mathcal{A}_{\mathsf{DL}}}^{\mathbb{G}}(\lambda)$$

$$+ Q^2 \left(10 \cdot \mathsf{AdvDDH}_{\mathcal{A}_{\mathsf{DDH}}}^{\mathbb{G}}(\lambda) + \mathsf{AdvCDH}_{\mathcal{A}_{\mathsf{CDH}}}^{\mathbb{G}}(\lambda) \right).$$

Before we give the proof, let us remark that the quadratic loss is due to partial blindness. For standard blindness, there is only a factor Q before the sum instead of Q^2 and $4 \cdot Q^2$ is replaced with $4 \cdot Q$.

Proof. Let $\mathcal{A}$ be a PPT adversary against one-more unforgeability of PreBS. Denote by $Q_\Sigma, Q_M, Q_{\mathsf{ddh}}, Q_{\mathsf{Ped}}$ the number of oracle queries to $\mathsf{H}_\Sigma, \mathsf{H}_M, \mathsf{H}_{\mathsf{ddh}}, \mathsf{H}_{\mathsf{Ped}}$, respectively, including the queries made by the game (*e.g.*, during signing queries or during signature verification). Denote by Q_S the number of $\mathcal{A}$'s signing queries. Denote by $\mathsf{Ext}_{\mathsf{Ped}}$ the extractor of $\mathsf{NIPS}_{\mathsf{Ped}}$.

We proceed with a sequence of games. For each game Game i, we denote the probability that the game outputs 1 by ε_i.

Game 0 (Honest). This game is the real one-more unforgeability experiment for scheme PreBS and adversary $\mathcal{A}$ with random oracles $\mathsf{H}_{\mathsf{ddh}}, \mathsf{H}_M, \mathsf{H}_{\mathsf{Ped}}$ and H_Σ. The game first samples $\mathsf{vk} = (G, U, H, V, D_1)$ and sk via $\mathsf{PreBS}.\mathsf{KeyGen}$. The adversary $\mathcal{A}$ obtains verification key vk as input and access to the random oracles, as well as both signing oracles $\mathcal{O}_{\mathsf{S}_1}, \mathcal{O}_{\mathsf{S}_2}$, and outputs a common message τ^* and forgeries $(m_j^*, \sigma_j^*)_{j \in [k]}$. The game outputs 1 iff $\mathcal{O}_{\mathsf{S}_2}$ was queried at most $k-1$ times with common message τ^*, all messages $(m_j^*)_{j \in [k]}$ are pairwise-distinct, and all signatures verify (*i.e.*, $\mathsf{Verify}(\mathsf{vk}, m_j^*, \tau^*, \sigma_j^*) = 1$). Note that each signing session is identified by a session identifier sid which is provided as input in $\mathcal{O}_{\mathsf{S}_1}$ and $\mathcal{O}_{\mathsf{S}_2}$. Recall that the signing oracles behave as follows:

- $\mathcal{O}_{\mathsf{S}_1}(\mathsf{sid}, C, \pi_{\mathsf{Ped}})$:   Check   the   proof π_{Ped} and abort if $\mathsf{NIPS}_{\mathsf{Ped}}.\mathsf{Ver}^{\mathsf{H}_{\mathsf{Ped}}}(\mathbb{x}_{\mathsf{Ped}}, \pi_{\mathsf{Ped}}) = 0$ for $\mathbb{x}_{\mathsf{Ped}} := (C, U, G)$. Sample $s \xleftarrow{\$} \mathbb{Z}_p$ and set $\mathsf{w}_0 := (s, \mathsf{sk})$. Next, set $\mathbf{T} := \phi_0(X_C, \mathsf{w}_0)$ for $X_C := C + H$ and $\mathbf{D}^\tau := (D_1, \mathsf{H}_{\mathsf{ddh}}(\tau))$. Prepare both statements $\mathbb{x}_0^C := (G, V, X_C, \mathbf{S})$ and $\mathbb{x}_1 := (G, \mathbf{D}^\tau)$. For the Σ_1 proof, sample $c_1 \xleftarrow{\$} \mathbb{Z}_p$ and simulate $(\mathbf{A}_1, z_1) \leftarrow \mathsf{Sim}_1(\mathbb{x}_1, c_1)$. For the Σ_0 proof, sample first flow $(A_0^C, \mathsf{st}_0) \leftarrow \mathsf{Init}_0(\mathbb{x}_0^C, \mathsf{w}_0)$. Store $(\mathbf{z}_1, c_1, \mathsf{st}_0)$ as state for session sid and output $(\mathbf{T}, \mathbf{A}_0^C, \mathbf{A}_1)$.

- $\mathcal{O}_{S_2}(\mathsf{sid}, c)$: Retrieve $(\mathbf{z}_1, c_1, \mathsf{st}_0)$ from the state for sid (and abort if this is not possible). Compute challenge $c_0 := c - c_1$ and response $\mathbf{z}_0 \leftarrow \mathsf{Resp}_0(\mathsf{st}_0, c_0)$ for the Σ_0 proof. Output $(\mathbf{z}_0, z_1, c_0)$

We provide a detailed description in the full version [42]. By definition, we have

$$\mathsf{AdvOMUF}_{\mathcal{A}}^{\mathsf{PreBS}}(\lambda) = \varepsilon_0.$$

Game 1 (Abort if $\mathsf{H_M}$ collision). The game aborts if there are collisions for $\mathsf{H_M}$. More precisely, it aborts if there are queries $x \neq x'$ such that $\mathsf{H_M}(x) = \mathsf{H_M}(x')$. A standard birthday-bound argument yields that

$$|\varepsilon_0 - \varepsilon_1| \leq \frac{Q_M^2}{p}.$$

Game 2 (Extract $(\overline{m}, t)$ from C). We change the first signer oracle $\mathcal{O}_{S_1}$. Namely, whenever the adversary sends a commitment C with a proof π_{Ped} in its first message of a signing interaction, the game uses the extractor of $\mathsf{NIPS}_{\mathsf{Ped}}$ to extract a preimage $(\overline{m}, t) \in \mathbb{Z}_p^2$ for C, and aborts its entire execution if π_{Ped} verifies but extraction fails. In more detail, we modify the first part of the signer oracle (oracle $\mathcal{O}_{S_1}$) as follows. Initially, it proceeds as in Game 1 until the check $\mathsf{NIPS}_{\mathsf{Ped}}.\mathsf{Ver}^{\mathsf{H_{Ped}}}(\mathbb{x}_{\mathsf{Ped}}, \pi_{\mathsf{Ped}}) = 1$. If the check fails, it outputs $\bot$ as before. Else, the game sets $\mathbb{w}_{\mathsf{Ped}} \leftarrow \mathsf{Ext}_{\mathsf{Ped}}(\mathcal{Q}_{\mathsf{H_{Ped}}}, \mathbb{x}_{\mathsf{Ped}}, \pi_{\mathsf{Ped}})$ and parses $(\overline{m}, t) := \mathbb{w}_{\mathsf{Ped}}$. (Recall that $\mathcal{Q}_{\mathsf{H_{Ped}}}$ denotes the queries to $\mathsf{H_{Ped}}$ made by $\mathcal{A}$ and the game.) The game aborts its entire execution if parsing $\mathbb{w}_{\mathsf{Ped}}$ fails or $C \neq \overline{m}U + tG$.

Let us analyze the advantage of $\mathcal{A}$ in Game 2. Roughly, we need to ensure that extraction succeeds and that the extracted witness $\mathbb{w}_{\mathsf{Ped}}$ is an opening for C, i.e., $(\mathbb{x}_{\mathsf{Ped}}, \mathbb{w}_{\mathsf{Ped}}) \in \mathsf{R}_{\mathsf{Ped}}$. But because the soundness relation is *relaxed*, it is possible that $(\mathbb{x}_{\mathsf{Ped}}, \mathbb{w}_{\mathsf{Ped}}) \notin \mathsf{R}_{\mathsf{Ped}}$. Instead, the extracted witness for relation $\tilde{\mathsf{R}}_{\mathsf{Ped}}$ might be the discrete logarithm u of U (cf. Eq. (6)). Since the adversary $\mathcal{A}$ provides the proof π_{Ped} and u is kept (computationally) hidden from $\mathcal{A}$, this should occur with negligible probability. But because u is also required to simulate the signing oracles, we cannot immediately reduce to the DLOG assumption, and a few intermediate games are required. Roughly, starting with Game 1, we first move to a game where the signing oracles can be simulated without the secret key $\mathsf{sk} = u$. Then, we add an abort condition if $(\mathbb{x}_{\mathsf{Ped}}, \mathbb{w}_{\mathsf{Ped}}) \notin \mathsf{R}_{\mathsf{Ped}}$, where we can now upper bound the abort probability under the DL assumption. Finally, we revert back the changes (keeping the abort condition), and obtain Game 2. This is formalized in Lemma 2 below. We provide a proof in the full version [42].

Lemma 2. *There are reductions $\mathcal{A}_{\mathsf{KS}}, \mathcal{A}_{\mathsf{DDH}}^i$ for $i \in [2]$ and $\mathcal{A}_{\mathsf{DL}}$ with running time close to that of $\mathcal{A}$ such that*

$$|\varepsilon_1 - \varepsilon_2| \leq \mathsf{AdvKS}_{\mathcal{A}_{\mathsf{KS}}}^{\mathsf{NIPS}_{\mathsf{Ped}}, \tilde{\mathsf{R}}_{\mathsf{Ped}}}(\lambda) + \mathsf{AdvDL}_{\mathcal{A}_{\mathsf{DL}}}^{\mathbb{G}}(\lambda) + \frac{4}{p-1} + \sum_{i \in [2]} \mathsf{AdvDDH}_{\mathcal{A}_{\mathsf{DDH}}^i}^{\mathbb{G}}(\lambda).$$

Game 3 (Guess τ^*). Informally, we now guess the first query to $\mathsf{H}_{\mathsf{ddh}}$ such that τ^* is provided as input. More formally, the game samples $q_\tau^* \xleftarrow{\$} [Q_{\mathsf{ddh}}]$ at its start. When the adversary outputs its forgeries with common message τ^* in the end, the challenger additionally checks whether τ^* was queried for the first time to $\mathsf{H}_{\mathsf{ddh}}$ on the q_τ^*-th query to $\mathsf{H}_{\mathsf{ddh}}$. If not, the game aborts its execution.

Recall that the challenger's $\mathsf{H}_{\mathsf{ddh}}$ queries count towards Q_{ddh}. Furthermore, note that the challenger sets $(D_2^{\tau^*}, D_3^{\tau^*}) := \mathsf{H}_{\mathsf{ddh}}(\tau^*)$ when it verifies $\mathcal{A}$'s forgeries, so such a query exists. Next, observe that the guess q_τ^* is hidden from $\mathcal{A}$, and so the probability that the challenger guesses this query is at least $1/Q_{\mathsf{ddh}}$, even conditioned on Game 2 outputting 1. We get that

$$\varepsilon_2 \leq Q_{\mathsf{ddh}} \cdot \varepsilon_3.$$

Observe that the game evaluates $\mathsf{H}_{\mathsf{ddh}}$ on τ in the first signer oracle $\mathcal{O}_{\mathsf{S}_1}$ to compute $(D_2^\tau, D_3^\tau) := \mathsf{H}_{\mathsf{ddh}}(\tau)$. Thus, if $\mathcal{A}$ succeeds, the game knows the forgery's common message τ^* when the first query to $\mathcal{O}_{\mathsf{S}_1}$ with τ^* is made. This will be useful later.

Game 4 (Guess unsigned $\overline{m}^*$ in forgery). We guess the first query q_m^* to H_{M} such that the following two conditions hold:

1. The input $m_{q_m^*}$ to the q_m^*-th H_{M} query is part of $\mathcal{A}$'s forgeries.
2. No session with common message τ^* is *completed* if $\overline{m} = \mathsf{H}_{\mathsf{M}}(m_{q_m^*})$ is extracted from the commitment C (see Game 2).

Again, the game aborts its execution if the guess was incorrect. If $\mathcal{A}$ is successful, then $\mathcal{A}$'s forgeries $(m_j^*, \sigma_j^*)_{j \in [k]}$ with common message τ^* contain k distinct messages. Because we have ruled out collisions for H_{M} (see Game 1), the hashed messages $(\overline{m}_j^*)_{j \in [k]}$ are also pairwise distinct, where $\overline{m}_j^* = \mathsf{H}_{\mathsf{M}}(m_j^*)$. Furthermore, there are at most $k-1$ completed sessions with common message τ^* and each corresponding call to the first oracle $\mathcal{O}_{\mathsf{S}_1}$, exactly one message $\overline{m} \in \mathbb{Z}_p$ is extracted from C via $\mathsf{Ext}_{\mathsf{Ped}}$. In conclusion, one of the k distinct $\overline{m}_j^*$ was never extracted from C within a completed session. Thus, there is an index $j \in [k]$ such that $m_{q_m^*} := m_j^*$ fulfils the above conditions (also counting the challenger's queries).

The probability that the challenger guesses q_m^* correctly is $1/Q_{\mathsf{M}}$ and the guess q_m^* is hidden from the adversary. Thus, we have

$$\varepsilon_3 \leq Q_{\mathsf{M}} \cdot \varepsilon_4.$$

In the following, we denote by $\overline{m}^* := \mathsf{H}_{\mathsf{M}}(m_{q_m^*})$. Note that if $\mathcal{A}$ is successful, we can assume that $\overline{m}^*$ is known by the game from the start on[8]. Also, we stress that the game aborts only if both signer oracles $\mathcal{O}_{\mathsf{S}_1}$ and $\mathcal{O}_{\mathsf{S}_2}$ are executed with extracted $\overline{m}^*$ and common message τ^*, i.e., such a signing interaction is completed. In particular, it is possible that $\overline{m}^*$ is extracted in $\mathcal{O}_{\mathsf{S}_1}$ if the session will not be completed.

---

[8] The game samples $\overline{m}^*$ at random at the beginning of the game and outputs $\overline{m}^*$ in the q_m^*-th query to H_{M}.

Game 5 (Sample DDH tuples if $\tau \neq \tau^*$). From now on, the game samples real DDH tuples in H_{ddh} except in the q_τ^*-th query. That is, the game now holds an initially empty table $T_{ddh}[\cdot] := \bot$. Whenever random oracle H_{ddh} is queried on an input τ and the hash value is not yet defined, the game samples $d_2 \xleftarrow{\$} \mathbb{Z}_p$ and sets $(D_2^\tau, D_3^\tau) := (d_2 G, d_2 D_1)$ instead of $(D_2, D_3) \xleftarrow{\$} \mathbb{G}^2$. Additionally, witness d_2 is stored in the table, i.e., $T_{ddh}[\tau] := d_2$. Importantly, the output on the q_τ^*-th H_{ddh} query (*I.e.*, $(D_2^{\tau^*}, D_3^{\tau^*})$) and all subsequent queries on the same input remain unchanged. Note that by design, we have $\mathbf{D}^\tau \in \mathscr{L}_{ddh}$ for $\tau \neq \tau^*$. Clearly, there is a reduction $\mathcal{B}_1$ on Q-DDH with $Q = Q_{ddh}$ with running time similar to $\mathcal{A}$ such that

$$|\varepsilon_4 - \varepsilon_5| \leq \mathsf{AdvQDDH}_{\mathcal{B}_1}^{\mathbb{G}}(Q_{ddh}, \lambda).$$

Game 6 (Use DDH witness for Σ_1 if $\tau \neq \tau^*$). Now, the game computes the Σ_1 transcript $(\mathbf{A}_1, c, z_1)$ for $\tau \neq \tau^*$ via the witness $T_{ddh}[\tau]$. More precisely, in $\mathcal{O}_{S_1}$ with $\tau \neq \tau^*$, the game samples $c_1 \xleftarrow{\$} \mathbb{Z}_p$ and $(\mathbf{A}_1, \mathsf{st}_1) \leftarrow \mathsf{Init}_1(\mathbb{x}_1, \mathbb{w}_1)$, where $\mathbb{w}_1 := T_{ddh}[\tau]$ and $\mathbb{x}_1 := (G, \mathbf{D}^\tau)$. In $\mathcal{O}_{S_2}$ with $\tau \neq \tau^*$, the game computes $z_1 \leftarrow \mathsf{Resp}_1(\mathsf{st}_1, c_1)$.

Recall that in Game 5, the game samples $c_1 \xleftarrow{\$} \mathbb{Z}_p$ and $(\mathbf{A}_1, z_1) \leftarrow \mathsf{Sim}_1(\mathbb{x}_1, c_1)$. It follows by perfect HVZK of Σ_1, that the Σ_1 transcripts $(\mathbf{A}_1, c_1, z_1)$ in Game 5 and Game 6 are identically distributed. Thus, we have

$$\varepsilon_5 = \varepsilon_6.$$

Game 7 (Simulate Σ_0 if $\tau \neq \tau^*$). The game now simulates the Σ_0 transcript $(\mathbf{A}_0, c_0, \mathbf{z}_0)$ via HVZK in $\mathcal{O}_{S_1}$ and $\mathcal{O}_{S_2}$ for all $\tau \neq \tau^*$. In more detail, if $\tau \neq \tau^*$ in $\mathcal{O}_{S_1}$, the game computes $\mathbf{A}_0^C$ via

$$c_0 \xleftarrow{\$} \mathbb{Z}_p, \ (\mathbf{A}_0^U, \mathbf{z}_0) \leftarrow \mathsf{Sim}_0(\mathbb{x}_0, c_0).$$

In $\mathcal{O}_{S_2}$ for $\tau \neq \tau^*$, the game sets $c_1 := c - c_0$ and outputs $\mathbf{z}_0$ from $\mathcal{O}_{S_1}$. The other response z_1 is computed via $\mathbb{w}_1$ as introduced in Game 6.

Recall that in Game 6, the game sets $c_1 \xleftarrow{\$} \mathbb{Z}_p$ and $c_0 := c - c_1$. Thus, the challenges (c_0, c_1) follow the same distribution in Game 6 and Game 7. Also, observe that in Game 6, the Σ_0 transcript is generated honestly. Thus, by perfect HVZK of Σ_0, we have that

$$\varepsilon_6 = \varepsilon_7.$$

Let us take a closer look at the signer oracle in Game 7 for two specific cases, namely if (1) $\tau \neq \tau^*$, or (2) $\tau = \tau^*$ and the game has extracted $m = \overline{m}^*$ from C. Recall that in the signer oracle $\mathcal{O}_{S_1}$, the game defines the vector $\mathbf{T} := \phi_0(X_C, \mathbb{w}_0)$ for $X_C = C + H$ and $\mathbb{w}_0 = (s, \mathsf{sk})$ where $s \in \mathbb{Z}_p$ is random. Precisely, this means that $\mathbf{T} = (\mathsf{sk}V + s(C + H), sG, U)$. Now, observe that if (1) occurs, then due to the change in Game 7, the challenger uses the witness $\mathbb{w}_0 = (s, \mathsf{sk})$ only to sample $\mathbf{T}$. Similarly, if (2) occurs, then the challenger uses the witness $\mathbb{w}_0 = (s, \mathsf{sk})$ to sample $\mathbf{T}$ and in $\mathcal{O}_{S_2}$ to compute $\mathbf{z}_0$. Due to the abort condition in Game 4, $\mathcal{O}_{S_2}$

is never invoked in case (2). In conclusion, if (1) or (2) occurs, the challenger only uses w_0 to sample $\mathbf{T}$ in the signing oracles.

Game 8 (Send random T in some sessions). We change the signer oracle $\mathcal{O}_{S_1}$ again, for the cases (1) and (2) mentioned above. Namely, recall that until now, the signer oracle defined the vector $\mathbf{T} := \phi_0(X_C, w_0)$. In this game, $\mathbf{T}$ is sampled differently. Namely, if (1) or (2) occurs, then the game samples $T_1, T_2 \xleftarrow{\$} \mathbb{G}$ at random and sets $T_3 := U$. Intuitively, since (H, sG, sH) form Diffie-Hellman tuples and are included in the definition of $\mathbf{T}$ in Game 7, replacing sH by a random element should be indistinguishable and make the first component of $\mathbf{T}$ random.

More formally, we construct a reduction $\mathcal{B}_2$ that breaks Q-DDH if $\mathcal{A}$ can distinguish between Game 7 and Game 8. The reduction $\mathcal{B}_2$ obtains tuples $(G, H_1, (H_{2,i}, H_{3,i})_{i \in [Q_S]})$ from the Q-DDH game and samples $\mathsf{vk} = (G, U, H, V, D_1)$ as in Game 7, except that $H := H_1$. Then, $\mathcal{B}_2$ proceeds to simulate Game 7 to adversary $\mathcal{A}$ with the aforementioned vk except that in the i-th invocation of $\mathcal{O}_{S_1}$, it also checks whether either case (1) or case (2) occurs. If so, $\mathcal{A}$ sets

$$\mathbf{T} := (uV + (m \cdot \mathsf{sk})H_{2,i} + tH_{2,i} + H_{3,i}, H_{2,i}, U),$$

else it sets $\mathbf{T} = \phi_0(X_C, w_0)$ for $w_0 = (s, \mathsf{sk})$ and random $s \xleftarrow{\$} \mathbb{Z}_p$ as before. As discussed above, $\mathcal{B}_2$ can proceed as before. That is, $\mathcal{B}_2$ computes $\mathbf{A}_0^C$ and $\mathbf{A}_1$ as in Game 7 and outputs $(\mathbf{T}, \mathbf{A}_0^C, \mathbf{A}_1)$. Also, $\mathcal{B}_2$ simulates $\mathcal{O}_{S_2}$ as in Game 7. When $\mathcal{A}$ outputs its forgeries, $\mathcal{B}_2$ outputs $b' := 1$ if $\mathcal{A}$ succeeds, and $b' := 0$ otherwise.

Note that the verification key vk that is output by $\mathcal{B}_2$ is identically distributed to vk in Game 7 and Game 8. Further, if we have $H = hG, H_{2,i} = s_i G$ and $H_{3,i} = (h \cdot s_i)G$ for all $i \in [Q_S]$, then if event (1) or (2) occurs in the i-th $\mathcal{O}_{S_1}$ query, it holds that

$$\begin{aligned} T_1 &= uV + (m \cdot \mathsf{sk})H_{2,i} + tH_{2,i} + H_{3,i} \\ &= uV + (s_i \cdot m)U + (s_i \cdot t)G + (h \cdot s_i)G \\ &= uV + s_i(mU + tG) + s_i H \\ &= uV + s_i(C + H), \end{aligned}$$

and $T_2 = s_i G, T_3 = U$. This is exactly the distribution of $\mathbf{T}$ in Game 7. Otherwise, we have $H = hG, H_{2,i} = s_i G$ and $H_{3,i} \xleftarrow{\$} \mathbb{G}$ for all $i \in [Q_S]$. If event (1) or (2) occurs in the i-th $\mathcal{O}_{S_1}$ query, then $\mathbf{T}$ follows the distribution of $\mathbf{T}$ in Game 8, as $H_{3,i}$ functions as a one-time pad. In case neither event (1) nor (2) occurs, $\mathbf{T}$ follows the distribution in Game 7 and Game 8 in $\mathcal{O}_{S_1}$ by design. The running time of $\mathcal{B}_2$ is roughly that of $\mathcal{A}$. In conclusion, we have

$$|\varepsilon_7 - \varepsilon_8| \leq \mathsf{AdvQDDH}_{\mathcal{B}_2}^{\mathbb{G}}(Q_S, \lambda).$$

Game 9 (Abort if forgeries not in $\mathscr{L}_{\mathsf{bb}}$). Now, we make the game abort if one of the adversary's forgeries $\sigma_j^* = (S_{1,j}^*, S_{2,j}^*, \pi_j)$ for message m_j^* satisfies

$(G, V, X_j^*, S_{1,j}^*, S_{2,j}^*, U) \notin \mathscr{L}_{bb}$ with $X_j^* = \overline{m}_j^* U + H$. Here, $\overline{m}_j^* := \mathsf{H_M}(m_j^*)$ denotes the hashed message as before. In more detail, this is done efficiently as follows: The game initially samples $h \xleftarrow{\$} \mathbb{Z}_p$ and sets $H = hG$ to set up the verification key vk. Further, when $\mathcal{A}$ outputs its forgeries $(m_j^*, \sigma_j^*)_{j \in [k]}$ with common message τ^*, the game parses $\sigma_j^* = (S_{1,j}^*, S_{2,j}^*, \pi_j)$. Then, the game checks that for all $j \in [k]$, it holds that

$$S_{1,j}^* = uV + (\overline{m}_j^* \cdot u) S_{2,j}^* + h S_{2,j}^*. \tag{7}$$

This check is efficient using knowledge of h and u. The game aborts if the check fails. Otherwise it proceeds as before.

Denote $\mathbb{x}_1^* := (G, \mathbf{D}^{\tau^*})$ and $\mathbb{x}_{0,j}^* := (G, V, X_j^*, S_{1,j}^*, S_{2,j}^*, U)$. Roughly, we have $\mathbb{x}_1 \notin \mathscr{L}_{ddh}$ except with probability $1/p$. Then, soundness of π_j ensures except with negligible probability that $\mathbb{x}_{0,j} \in \mathscr{L}_{bb}$ which is equivalent to Eq. (7).

More formally, let us analyze the probability that for some $j \in [k]$, Eq. (7) does not hold. First, we proof two useful claims. The first claim follows from soundness of the Fiat-Shamir transformation and the second claim links Eq. (7) with $\mathscr{L}_{bb}$.

Proposition 1. *For every* $\mathsf{H_\Sigma}$ *query* $((\mathbb{x}_b, \mathbf{A}_b)_{b \in \{0,1\}}, m)$ *with* $\mathbb{x}_0 \notin \mathscr{L}_{bb}$ *and* $\mathbb{x}_1 \notin \mathscr{L}_{ddh}$, *there exists* $(c_0, c_1, \mathbf{z}_0, z_1)$ *such that*

$$tr_0 := (\mathbf{A}_0, c_0, \mathbf{z}_0) \text{ is valid for } \mathbb{x}_0 \tag{8}$$

$$tr_1 := (\mathbf{A}_1, c_1, z_1) \text{ is valid for } \mathbb{x}_1 \tag{9}$$

$$c^* := \mathsf{H_\Sigma}((\mathbb{x}_b, \mathbf{A}_b)_{b \in \{0,1\}}, m_j^*) = c_0 + c_1 \tag{10}$$

with probability at most $1/p$.

Proof (Proposition 1). Observe that due to special soundness of Σ_1 and because $\mathbb{x}_1 \notin \mathscr{L}_{ddh}$, there is at most one challenge $c_1 \in \mathbb{Z}_p$ such that there exists a response z_1 with valid transcript $tr_1 = (\mathbf{A}_1, c_1, z_1)$ for $\mathbb{x}_1$. Similarly, since $\mathbb{x}_0 \notin \mathscr{L}_{bb}$, the same argument applies: There exists exactly one challenge c_0 such that there exists a response z_1 with valid transcript $tr_0 = (\mathbf{A}_0, c_0, \mathbf{z}_0)$. Thus, the pair (c_0, c_1) is determined by $(\mathbb{x}_b, \mathbf{A}_b)_{b \in \{0,1\}}$ due to Eqs. (8 and 9). Further, because $(\mathbb{x}_b, \mathbf{A}_b)_{b \in \{0,1\}}$ is part of the input of the $\mathsf{H_\Sigma}$ query that determines c^*, the value c^* is distributed uniformly and independently from (c_0, c_1). Then, the probability that Eq. (10) holds is at most $1/p$. □

Proposition 2. *Equation 7 holds if and only if* $(G, V, X_j^*, S_{1,j}^*, S_{2,j}^*, U) \in \mathscr{L}_{bb}$.

Proof (Proposition 2). Denote $U = uG$. The claim follows due to

$$\text{Equation (7)} \iff S_{1,j}^* = u \cdot V + (\overline{m}_j^* \cdot u) S_{2,j}^* + h S_{2,j}^*$$
$$\iff S_{1,j}^* = u \cdot V + (\overline{m}_j^* \cdot u \cdot s_{j,2}^*) G + (h \cdot s_{j,2}^*) G \wedge S_{2,j}^* = s_{j,2}^* G$$
$$\iff S_{1,j}^* = u \cdot V + s_{j,2}^* (\overline{m}_j^* U + H) \wedge S_{2,j}^* = s_{j,2}^* G$$
$$\iff S_{1,j}^* = u \cdot V + s_{j,2}^* \cdot X_j^* \wedge S_{2,j}^* = s_{j,2}^* G$$
$$\iff (G, V, X_j^*, S_{1,j}^*, S_{2,j}^*, U) \in \mathscr{L}_{bb}$$

□

Let us assume that $\mathcal{A}$ outputs forgeries with common message τ^* such that Game 8 outputs 1. This occurs with probability ε_8 by definition. Further, let us assume that $(G, \mathbf{D}^{\tau^*}) \notin \mathscr{L}_{\mathsf{ddh}}$ (which holds except with probability $1/p$). Denote by $\mathbb{x}_{0,j}^* = (G, V, X_j^*, S_{1,j}^*, S_{2,j}^*, U)$ the statements within $\mathcal{A}$'s forgeries as above. Observe that Eqs. (8) to (10) are satisfied because all k forgeries are valid. Thus, Propostion 1 yields via a union bound over all H_Σ queries that except with probability Q_Σ/p, it holds for all $j \in [k]$ that $\mathbb{x}_{0,j}^* \in \mathscr{L}_{\mathsf{bb}}$. Due to Propostion 2 this implies that Eq. (7) holds for $j \in [k]$. In total, the above considerations yield that

$$|\varepsilon_8 - \varepsilon_9| \le \frac{Q_\Sigma + 1}{p}.$$

We emphasize that it will be essential for the following changes that the winning condition of this game can still be evaluated efficiently.

Game 10 (Sample DDH tuple if $\tau = \tau^*$). In this game, we change how the q_τ^*-th query to $\mathsf{H}_{\mathsf{ddh}}$ (*I.e.*, the query with $\tau = \tau^*$) is answered. Namely, on this query, the challenger samples $d_2 \xleftarrow{\$} \mathbb{Z}_p$ and sets $(D_2^{\tau^*}, D_3^{\tau^*}) := (d_2 G, d_2 D_1)$ instead of $(D_2^{\tau^*}, D_3^{\tau^*}) \xleftarrow{\$} \mathbb{G}^2$. The witness d_2 is stored in the table $\mathsf{T}_{\mathsf{ddh}}[\tau^*]$. Other outputs of $\mathsf{H}_{\mathsf{ddh}}$ remain unchanged. We can easily construct a reduction $\mathcal{A}_{\mathsf{DDH}}^3$ against DDH with running time similar to $\mathcal{A}$ and with

$$|\varepsilon_9 - \varepsilon_{10}| \le \mathsf{AdvDDH}_{\mathcal{A}_{\mathsf{DDH}}^3}^{\mathbb{G}}(\lambda).$$

Note that now, we have $\mathbf{D}^\tau \in \mathscr{L}_{\mathsf{ddh}}$ for all common messages τ.

Game 11 (Use DDH witness for Σ_1 if $\tau = \tau^*$). We change the signer oracle again, for the case that $\tau = \tau^*$. Namely, the Σ_1 transcript $(\mathbf{A}_1, c, z_1)$ is now computed via the witness $\mathbb{w}_1^* := \mathsf{T}_{\mathsf{ddh}}[\tau^*]$ and is no longer simulated via HVZK. That is, in $\mathcal{O}_{\mathsf{S}_1}$ with τ^*, the game samples $c_1 \xleftarrow{\$} \mathbb{Z}_p$ and $(\mathbf{A}_1, \mathsf{st}_1) \leftarrow \mathsf{Init}_1(\mathbb{x}_1, \mathbb{w}_1)$, where $\mathbb{w}_1 := \mathsf{T}_{\mathsf{ddh}}[\tau]$ and $\mathbb{x}_1 := (G, \mathbf{D}^{\tau^*})$. In $\mathcal{O}_{\mathsf{S}_2}$ with τ^*, the game then computes $z_1 \leftarrow \mathsf{Resp}_1(\mathsf{st}_1, c_1)$.

It follows (as in Game 6) from HVZK of Σ_1 that the Σ_1 transcripts $(\mathbf{A}_1, c, z_1)$ for $\tau = \tau^*$ in Game 10 and Game 11 are distributed identically. In conclusion, we have

$$\varepsilon_{10} = \varepsilon_{11}.$$

Game 12 (Simulate Σ_0 if $\tau = \tau^*$). We change the signer oracle a final time, for the case that $\tau = \tau^*$. Concretely, in $\mathcal{O}_{\mathsf{S}_1}$ with τ^*, the game computes $c_0 \xleftarrow{\$} \mathbb{Z}_p$ and $(\mathbf{A}_0^C, \mathbb{z}_0) \leftarrow \mathsf{Sim}_0(\mathbb{x}_0^C, c_0)$ for $\mathbb{x}_0^c := X_C := C + H$. In $\mathcal{O}_{\mathsf{S}_2}$ with τ^*, the game sets $c_1 := c - c_0$ and outputs $\mathbb{z}_0$ from $\mathcal{O}_{\mathsf{S}_1}$. The other branch (i.e., z_1) is computed via $\mathbb{w}_1$ as in Game 11.

It follows (as in Game 7) that in Game 11 and Game 12, the challenges c_0 and c_1 follow the same distribution and that the Σ_0 transcripts $(\mathbf{A}_0, c_0, \mathbb{z}_0)$ are identically distributed (by HVZK of Σ_0). Thus, we have that

$$\varepsilon_{11} = \varepsilon_{12}.$$

A complete description of Game 12 is given in Fig. 2. The game sets up the verification key vk as in KeyGen, except that it knows the discrete logarithm h of H. It also guesses a hash value $\overline{m}^* = H_M(m_j^*)$ such that m_j^* is a forgery's message but no signing session with common message τ^* is finished such that $\overline{m}^*$ is extracted from π_{Ped}, where τ^* is the forgeries' common message. Roughly, the game then simulates the signing oracles as follows. In $\mathcal{O}_{S_1}$, the game outputs $\mathbf{T} = (T_1, T_2, U)$ computed honestly only if $\tau = \tau^*$ and $\overline{m} \neq \overline{m}^*$ (otherwise random $T_1, T_2 \overset{\$}{\leftarrow} \mathbb{G}$ are chosen). The Σ_1 transcripts $(\mathbf{A}_1, c_1, z_1)$ in $\mathcal{O}_{S_1}$ and $\mathcal{O}_{S_2}$ are computed via a DDH witness for $\mathbf{D}^\tau$ via $(\Sigma_1.\text{Init}, \Sigma_1.\text{Resp})$, and the Σ_0 transcripts $(\mathbf{A}_0, c_0, \mathbf{z}_0)$ are simulated via HVZK of Σ_0. In the end, the challenger aborts if the forgeries are not in $\mathcal{L}_{\text{bb}}$ (as in Eq. (7) via h). We stress that h is only required to check Eq. (7) in Game 12 and this is only done after $\mathcal{A}$ output its forgeries.

Reduction to CDH. Finally, there exists a reduction $\mathcal{A}_{\text{CDH}}$ such that $\varepsilon_{12} \leq \text{AdvCDH}^{\mathbb{G}}_{\mathcal{A}_{\text{CDH}}}(\lambda)$. This follows via Lemma 1. In more detail, let us construct a reduction $\mathcal{B}_3$ that outputs $\mathbf{x}_0^* \in \mathcal{L}_{\text{bb}}$ for the game described in Lemma 1, hereafter denoted by Game BB. Note that $\mathcal{B}_3$ has access to an oracle $\mathcal{O}(\lambda)$ that on input $\overline{m}$ outputs values (S_1, S_2). First, $\mathcal{B}_3$ samples $\overline{m}^* \overset{\$}{\leftarrow} \mathbb{Z}_p$ and obtains (G, U, H, V) after providing $\overline{m}^*$ to Game BB. Next, $\mathcal{B}_3$ samples $D_1 \overset{\$}{\leftarrow} \mathbb{G}$ and sets vk $= (G, U, H, V, D_1)$. Also, $\mathcal{B}_3$ initializes the counters ctr_{ddh} and ctr_M to 0, samples q_m^* and q_τ^* at random, and initializes $\tau_{q_\tau^*} := \perp$. It then invokes $\mathcal{A}$ on input vk and simulates the oracles in Game 12 to $\mathcal{A}$ as follows.

- $H_M, H_{\text{ddh}}, H_\Sigma, H_{\text{Ped}}, \text{Next}, \mathcal{O}_{S_2}$: Simulated as in Game 12. We remark that for H_M, the value $\overline{m}^*$ is output on the q_m^*-th query. Also, note that Game 12 aborts if $\overline{m}^*$ is extracted from C in $\mathcal{O}_{S_1}$.
- $\mathcal{O}_{S_1}$: Check that π_{Ped} verifies and output $\perp$ if not. Else, extract $(\overline{m}, t)$ such that $C = \overline{m}U + tG$ from π_{Ped}. If $\tau \neq \tau_{q_\tau^*}$, then set $\mathbf{T} \overset{\$}{\leftarrow} \mathbb{G}^2 \times \{U\}$ as in Game 12, else set $(S_1, S_2) \leftarrow \mathcal{O}(\overline{m})$ and $\mathbf{T} := (S_1 + t \cdot S_2, S_2, U)$. Then, proceed as in Game 12.

When $\mathcal{A}$ outputs its forgeries (m_j^*, σ_j^*) on common message τ^*, $\mathcal{B}_3$ checks whether there is a message m_j^* such that $H_M(m_j^*) = \overline{m}^*$. Finally, $\mathcal{B}_3$ parses $(S_1^*, S_2^*, \pi^*) = \sigma_j^*$ and outputs (S_1^*, S_2^*) to Game BB.

Clearly, the simulated vk is distributed as in Game 12. Also, it is easy to check that $\mathcal{B}_3$'s simulation of Game 12 is efficient and the running time of $\mathcal{B}_3$ is roughly that of $\mathcal{A}$. It remains to show that $\mathbf{T}$ is identically distributed if $\tau = \tau_{q_\tau^*}$. Denote by u the (unknown) discrete logarithm of U. Recall that by definition (cf. Lemma 1), $\mathcal{O}(\overline{m})$ outputs values (S_1, S_2) with $S_1 = uV + sX_{\overline{m}}$ and $S_2 = sG$, where $s \overset{\$}{\leftarrow} \mathbb{Z}_p$ and $X_{\overline{m}} = \overline{m}U + H$. Note that the simulated (T_2, T_3) follow the distribution of Game 12, and due to

$$T_1 = S_1 + tS_2 = uV + sX_{\overline{m}} + (t \cdot s)G$$
$$= uV + s(\overline{m}U + H + tG) = uV + s(C + H),$$

the simulated T_1 is also distributed as in Game 12. In conclusion, the view of $\mathcal{A}$ is as in Game 12 and with probability at least ε_{12}, there is a message m_j^* with $\mathsf{H_M}(m_j^*) = \overline{m}^*$ and Eq. (7) holds (where $h = \mathsf{DLOG}_G(H)$). As shown in Game 9, this implies that $(G, V, X_{\overline{m}^*}, S_1^*, S_2^*, U) \in \mathscr{L}_{\mathsf{bb}}$ for $X_{\overline{m}^*} := \overline{m}^* U + H$. Due to Lemma 1, there is an adversary $\mathcal{A}_{\mathsf{CDH}}$ with running time similar to $\mathcal{A}$ such that $\varepsilon_{12} \leq \mathsf{AdvCDH}_{\mathcal{A}_{\mathsf{CDH}}}^G(\lambda)$. By collecting all the bounds and using the tight equivalence of Q-DDH and DDH, we obtain the statement.   □

5   Blind Interactive Signing Protocol

In this section, we explain how the unblinded protocol from Sect. 4 can be turned into a partially blind signature BS.

5.1   Construction

We construct a partially blind signature BS by blinding the signing protocol of PreBS (cf. Sect. 4). The requirements are identical to PreBS. That is, let $\mathsf{NIPS_{Ped}}$ be a NIPS proof system with random oracle $\mathsf{H_{Ped}}$ for Pedersen openings (see Eq. (5) for the exact relation). Also, let $\mathsf{H_M} : \{0,1\}^* \to \mathbb{Z}_p$, and $\mathsf{H_\Sigma} : \{0,1\}^* \to \mathbb{Z}_p$, and $\mathsf{H_{ddh}} : \{0,1\}^* \to \mathbb{G}^2$ be random oracles.

Our blinding essentially follows the same approach as prior works. The blinding of the statement X as X_C is already present in the unblinded signature, as the proof π_{Ped} is constructed relative to it and required for the OMUF reduction; the statement $\mathbf{D}^\tau$ corresponding to common message τ remains unblinded throughout. Except for the blinding, the only additional change is that the user now *verifies the signer's response*. Otherwise, it may output invalid "signatures", making interactions linkable.

BS: **Partially blind signature**
– $\mathsf{KeyGen}(1^\lambda)$: Output $(\mathsf{vk}, \mathsf{sk}) \leftarrow \mathsf{BBSig.KeyGen}(1^\lambda)$.
– $\mathsf{S}(\mathsf{sk}, \tau) \longleftrightarrow \mathsf{U}(\mathsf{vk}, m, \tau)$: The *blinded* signing protocol proceeds in 4 moves and is given in Fig. 3.
– $\mathsf{Verify}(\mathsf{vk}, m, \tau, \sigma_{\mathsf{bb}})$: Output $b \leftarrow \mathsf{BBSig.Verify}(\mathsf{vk}, m, \tau, \sigma_{\mathsf{bb}})$.

Remark 3 (Notation). In Fig. 3, we follow the convention that variables with a star, such as $\mathbf{A}_0^*$ or c^* are sent to the signer or received by the user. Variables with a prime, such as $\mathbf{A}_0'$ and c_0' are random masks to ensure blindness. Other variables are usually outputs, such as $\mathbf{A}$. Sometimes, this convention is broken for consistency with the unblinded protocol, e.g., for C.

5.2   Security Analysis

We show that BS is correct and partially blind in the random oracle model. One-more unforgeability follows via Theorem 1 under the same conditions.

Game 12 (One-more Unforgeability)	$\mathcal{O}_{S_1}(\mathrm{sid}, C, \pi_{\mathsf{Ped}})$

Game 12 (One-more Unforgeability)

1: $\forall H \in \{\mathsf{H}_{\mathsf{ddh}}, \mathsf{H}_{\Sigma}, \mathsf{H}_{\mathsf{M}}, \mathsf{H}_{\mathsf{Ped}}\}, \mathcal{Q}_H[\cdot] := \bot$
2: $\mathcal{SID} := \emptyset, \mathcal{Q}_T[\cdot] := 0$
3: $\mathsf{common}[\cdot] := \bot, \mathsf{state}[\cdot] := \bot, \mathsf{round}[\cdot] := \bot$
4: $\mathsf{ctr}_{\mathsf{M}} := 0, q_m^* \xleftarrow{\$} [Q_{\mathsf{M}}], \overline{m}^* \xleftarrow{\$} \mathbb{Z}_p$ // Game 4
5: $\mathsf{ctr}_{\mathsf{ddh}} := 0, q_\tau^* \xleftarrow{\$} [Q_{\mathsf{ddh}}], \tau_{q_\tau^*} := \bot$ // Game 3
6: $h \xleftarrow{\$} \mathbb{Z}_p, H := hG$
7: $u \xleftarrow{\$} \mathbb{Z}_p, V \xleftarrow{\$} \mathbb{G}, U := uG$
8: $\mathsf{vk} := (G, U, H, V, D_1), \mathsf{sk} := u$
9: $\mathsf{oracles} := (\mathcal{O}_{S_1}, \mathcal{O}_{S_2}, \mathsf{H}_{\mathsf{ddh}}, \mathsf{H}_{\Sigma}, \mathsf{H}_{\mathsf{M}}, \mathsf{H}_{\mathsf{Ped}})$
10: $(\tau^*, (m_j^*, \sigma_j^*)_{j \in [k]}) \leftarrow \mathcal{A}^{\mathsf{oracles}}(\mathsf{vk})$
11: **abort if** $\mathsf{queried}[\tau^*] \geq k$
12: **abort if** $\exists j \in [k], \mathsf{Verify}(\mathsf{vk}, m_j^*, \tau^*, \sigma_j^*) = 0$
13: **abort if** $\exists (i, j) \in [k]^2, i \neq j, m_i^* = m_j^*$
14: **abort if** $\forall j \in [k], \mathsf{H}_{\mathsf{M}}(m_j^*) \neq \overline{m}^*$ // Game 4
15: **abort if** $\tau^* \neq \tau_{q_\tau^*}$ // Game 3
16: $\mathsf{parse}\ (S_{1,j}^*, S_{2,j}^*, \pi_j)_{j \in [k]} \leftarrow (\sigma_j^*)_{j \in [k]}$ // Game 9
   abort if $\exists j \in [k], S_{1,j}^* \neq S_j$ // Game 9
17:    $S_j := uV + (\mathsf{H}_{\mathsf{M}}(m_j^*) \cdot u) S_{2,j}^* + h S_{2,j}^*$
18: **return** 1

$\mathsf{H}_{\mathsf{ddh}}(\tau)$

1: $\mathsf{ctr}_{\mathsf{ddh}} \leftarrow \mathsf{ctr}_{\mathsf{ddh}} + 1$ // Game 3
2: **if** $\mathsf{ctr}_{\mathsf{ddh}} = q_\tau^*$ **then** $\tau_{q_\tau^*} := \tau$ // Game 3
3: **if** $\mathcal{Q}_{\mathsf{H}_{\mathsf{ddh}}}[\tau] = \bot$ **then**
4:    $d_2 \leftarrow \mathbb{Z}_p, \mathsf{T}_{\mathsf{ddh}}[\tau] \leftarrow d_2$ // Game 5, Game 10
5:    $(D_2^\tau, D_3^\tau) := (d_2 G, d_2 D_1)$ // Game 5, Game 10
6:    $\mathcal{Q}_{\mathsf{H}_{\mathsf{ddh}}}[\tau] \leftarrow (D_2^\tau, D_3^\tau)$
7: **return** $\mathcal{Q}_{\mathsf{H}_{\mathsf{ddh}}}[\tau]$

$\mathsf{H}_{\mathsf{M}}(m)$

1: $\mathsf{ctr}_{\mathsf{M}} \leftarrow \mathsf{ctr}_{\mathsf{M}} + 1$ // Game 4
2: **if** $\mathcal{Q}_{\mathsf{H}_{\mathsf{M}}}[m] = \bot$ **then**
3:    **if** $\mathsf{ctr}_{\mathsf{M}} = q_m^*$ **then** $\overline{m} := \overline{m}^*$ // Game 4
4:    **else** $\overline{m} \xleftarrow{\$} \mathbb{Z}_p$
5:    **abort if** $\exists m, \mathcal{Q}_{\mathsf{H}_{\mathsf{M}}}[m] = \overline{m}$ // Game 1
6:    $\mathcal{Q}_{\mathsf{H}_{\mathsf{M}}}[m] \leftarrow \overline{m}$
7: **return** $\mathcal{Q}_{\mathsf{H}_{\mathsf{M}}}[m]$

$\mathsf{H}_{\Sigma}(x)$ and $\mathsf{H}_{\mathsf{Ped}}(x)$ and $\mathsf{Next}(\mathrm{sid}, \tau)$

// Identical to H_{Σ} and $\mathsf{H}_{\mathsf{Ped}}$ and Next in Game 0

$\mathcal{O}_{S_1}(\mathrm{sid}, C, \pi_{\mathsf{Ped}})$

1: **req** $\mathsf{round}[\mathrm{sid}] = 1$
2: $\tau := \mathsf{common}[\mathrm{sid}]$
3: $\mathbb{x}_{\mathsf{Ped}} := (C, U, G)$
4: **req** $\mathsf{NIPS}_{\mathsf{Ped}}.\mathsf{Ver}^{\mathsf{H}_{\mathsf{Ped}}}(\mathbb{x}_{\mathsf{Ped}}, \pi_{\mathsf{Ped}}) = 1$
5: $(\overline{m}, t) \leftarrow \mathsf{Ext}_{\mathsf{Ped}}(\mathcal{Q}_{\mathsf{H}_{\mathsf{Ped}}}, \mathbb{x}_{\mathsf{Ped}}, \pi_{\mathsf{Ped}})$ // Game 2
6: **abort if** $C \neq \overline{m} U + t G$ // Game 2
7: $X_C := C + H$
8: $\mathbf{D}^\tau := (D_1, \mathsf{H}_{\mathsf{ddh}}(\tau))$
9: $\mathbb{x}_0^C := (G, V, X_C, \mathbf{S}), \mathbb{x}_1 := (G, \mathbf{D}^\tau)$
10: **if** $\tau \neq \tau_{q_\tau^*} \vee \overline{m}^* = \overline{m}$ **then**
11:    $\mathbf{T} \xleftarrow{\$} \mathbb{G}^2 \times \{U\}$ // Game 8
12: **else**
13:    $s \xleftarrow{\$} \mathbb{Z}_p, \mathsf{w}_0 := (s, \mathsf{sk})$
14:    $\mathbf{T} := \phi_0(X_C, \mathsf{w}_0)$
   // Game 7, Game 12
15: $c_0 \xleftarrow{\$} \mathbb{Z}_p, (\mathbf{A}_0^C, \mathsf{z}_0) \leftarrow \mathsf{Sim}_0(\mathbb{x}_0^C, c_0)$
16: $\mathsf{w}_1 := \mathsf{T}_{\mathsf{ddh}}[\tau]$ // Game 6, Game 11
17: $(\mathbf{A}_1, \mathsf{st}_1) \leftarrow \mathsf{Init}_1(\mathbb{x}_1, \mathsf{w}_1)$ // Game 6, Game 11
18: $\mathsf{state}[\mathrm{sid}] := (\mathsf{z}_0, c_0, \mathsf{st}_1, \overline{m})$
19: $\mathsf{round}[\mathrm{sid}] \leftarrow 1$
20: **return** $(\mathbf{T}, \mathbf{A}_0^C, \mathbf{A}_1)$

$\mathcal{O}_{S_2}(\mathrm{sid}, c)$

1: **req** $\mathsf{round}[\mathrm{sid}] = 1$
2: **req** $c \in \mathbb{Z}_p$
3: $(\mathsf{z}_0, c_0, \mathsf{st}_1, \overline{m}) := \mathsf{state}[\mathrm{sid}]$
4: **abort if** $\overline{m} = \overline{m}^*$ // Game 4
5: $c_1 := c - c_0$ // Game 7, Game 12
6: $z_1 \leftarrow \mathsf{Resp}_1(\mathsf{st}_1, c_1)$ // Game 6, Game 11
7: $\mathsf{queried}[\tau] \leftarrow \mathsf{queried}[\tau] + 1$
8: **return** (z_0, z_1, c_0)

Fig. 2. Description of Game 12, where the differences to Game 0 are highlighted in gray. Note that the changes marked with Game 5, Game 10 (resp. Game 7, Game 12) are introduced for $\tau \neq \tau_{q_\tau^*}$ in Game 5 (resp. Game 7), and later for $\tau = \tau_{q_\tau^*}$ in Game 10 (resp. Game 12). For some condition C, **abort if** C makes the game output 0 if C is true and **req** C makes the oracle output $\bot$ if C is false.

$S(sk, \tau)$	$U(vk, m, \tau)$
	1: $\quad t \stackrel{\$}{\leftarrow} \mathbb{Z}_p$; $\quad \overline{m} := H_M(m)$,
	2: $\quad C := \overline{m}U + tG$
	3: $\quad \mathbb{x}_{\mathsf{Ped}} := (C, U, G)$; $\quad \mathbb{w}_{\mathsf{Ped}} := (\overline{m}, t)$
	4: $\quad \pi_{\mathsf{Ped}} \leftarrow \mathsf{NIPS}_{\mathsf{Ped}}.\mathsf{Prove}^{H_{\mathsf{Ped}}}(\mathbb{x}_{\mathsf{Ped}}, \mathbb{w}_{\mathsf{Ped}})$

$$\xleftarrow{\quad C, \pi_{\mathsf{Ped}} \quad}$$

5: $\mathbb{x}_{\mathsf{Ped}} := (C, U, G)$

6: **req** $\mathsf{NIPS}_{\mathsf{Ped}}.\mathsf{Ver}^{H_{\mathsf{Ped}}}(\mathbb{x}_{\mathsf{Ped}}, \pi_{\mathsf{Ped}}) = 1$

7: $s^* \stackrel{\$}{\leftarrow} \mathbb{Z}_p$; $\quad \mathbb{w}_0 := (s^*, sk)$

8: $X_C := C + H$; $\quad \mathbf{T}^* := \phi_0(X_C, \mathbb{w}_0)$

9: $\mathbb{x}_0^C := (G, V, X_C, \mathbf{T}^*)$; $\quad \mathbb{x}_1 := (G, \mathbf{D}^\tau)$

10: $c_1^* \stackrel{\$}{\leftarrow} \mathbb{Z}_p$; $\quad (\mathbf{A}_1^*, z_1) \leftarrow \mathsf{Sim}_1(\mathbb{x}_1, c_1)$

11: $(\mathbf{A}_0^*, \mathsf{st}_0) \leftarrow \mathsf{Init}_0(\mathbb{x}_0^C, \mathbb{w}_0)$

$$\xrightarrow{\quad (\mathbf{T}^*, \mathbf{A}_0^*, \mathbf{A}_1^*) \quad}$$

	12: $\quad s' \stackrel{\$}{\leftarrow} \mathbb{Z}_p$;
	13: $\quad c_0', c_1' \stackrel{\$}{\leftarrow} \mathbb{Z}_p$;
	14: $\quad \mathbf{z}_0' \stackrel{\$}{\leftarrow} \mathbb{Z}_p^2$; $\quad z_1' \stackrel{\$}{\leftarrow} \mathbb{Z}_p$
	15: $\quad X := \overline{m}U + H = X_C - tG$
	16: $\quad \mathbf{S} := \mathbf{T}^* - (t \cdot T_2, 0, 0)^\mathsf{T} + \phi_0(X, (s', 0))$
	17: $\quad \mathbf{A}_0 := \mathbf{A}_0^* - (t \cdot A_{0,2}^*, 0, 0)^\mathsf{T} + \phi_0(X, \mathbf{z}_0') - c_0'\mathbf{S}$
	18: $\quad \mathbf{A}_1 := \mathbf{A}_1^* + \phi_1(z_1') - c_1'\mathbf{D}^\tau$
	19: $\quad \mathbb{x}_0 := (G, V, X, \mathbf{S})$; $\quad \mathbb{x}_1 := (G, \mathbf{D}^\tau)$
	20: $\quad c := H_\Sigma((\mathbb{x}_b, \mathbf{A}_b)_{b \in \{0,1\}}, m)$

$$\xleftarrow{\quad c^* = c - c_0' - c_1' \quad}$$

21: $c_0^* := c^* - c_1^*$

22: $\mathbf{z}_0^* \leftarrow \mathsf{Resp}_0(\mathsf{st}_0, c_0)$

$$\xrightarrow{\quad \mathbf{z}_0^*, z_1^*, c_0^* \quad} \qquad /\!/\ c_1^* = c^* - c_0^*$$

23: **req** $\mathbf{A}_0^* = \phi_0(X_C, \mathbf{z}_0) - c_0^*\mathbf{T}^*$

24: **req** $\mathbf{A}_1^* = \phi_1(\mathbf{z}_1) - c_1^*\mathbf{D}^\tau$

25: $c_0 = c_0^* + c_0'$; $\quad c_1 = c_1^* + c_1'$ $\quad /\!/\ c = c_0 + c_1$

26: $\mathbf{z}_0 = \mathbf{z}_0^* + \mathbf{z}_0' - c_0 \cdot (s', 0)$

27: $z_1 = z_1^* + z_1'$

28: $\pi := (\mathbf{A}_0, \mathbf{A}_1, c, c_0, \mathbf{z}_0, z_1)$

29: $\sigma_{\mathsf{bb}} := (S_1, S_2, \pi)$

Fig. 3. The blinded version of a signing session of BS. As in the unblinded version (cf. Fig. 1), we have $m, \tau \in \{0,1\}^*$, $vk = (G, U, H, V, D_1) \in \mathbb{G}^5$ and $sk = u \in \mathbb{Z}_p$. The signer aborts (*i.e.*, outputs $\perp$) if for condition C, **req** C is evaluated for false C. Recall that H_Σ maps into $\mathbb{Z}_p$ and that $\mathbf{D}^\tau := (D_1, D_2^\tau, D_3^\tau)$ for $(D_2^\tau, D_3^\tau) := H_{\mathsf{ddh}}(\tau)$. Visually highlighted are the parts which blind the parameters C of the map ϕ_0, the statement $\mathbf{T}$ of the map ϕ_0, the challenge c of the OR-composition, the responses $\mathbf{z}_0$ and z_1. If these parts are removed, except for parameter blinding, then one recovers the unblinded protocol (cf. Fig. 1).

Remark 4 (OMUF of BS*).* Observe that in Fig. 3 only the user-side was modified compared to the protocol in Fig. 1. The signer's code is unchanged. As a consequence, Fig. 3 is one-more unforgeable if the unblinded version is. Indeed, one-more unforgeability considers a malicious user, whose code is adversarial, so only the signer's code is specified and part of the one-more unforgeability game.

Theorem 2 (Correctness). BS *is correct with error* γ_{err}*, where* γ_{err} *is the correctness error of* $\mathsf{NIPS}_{\mathsf{Ped}}$.

Correctness is straightforward.

Theorem 3 (Blindness). *For any (unbounded) adversary $\mathcal{A}$ that causes at most Q queries to the random oracle* $\mathsf{H}_{\mathsf{Ped}}$ *(via its own queries or through the oracles $\mathcal{O}_0$, $\mathcal{O}_1$), then there exists an adversary $\mathcal{A}_{\mathsf{WI}}$ with running time roughly that of $\mathcal{A}$, such that*

$$\mathsf{AdvPBlind}_{\mathcal{A}}^{\mathsf{BS}} \leq 2 \cdot \mathsf{AdvWI}_{\mathcal{A}_{\mathsf{WI}}}^{\mathsf{NIPS}}(Q, \lambda) + \frac{2}{p},$$

where $p = |\mathbb{G}|$ is the group order.

The very high-level idea is that enough randomness is injected to completely randomize the transcript π (which is part of the blind signature), and also the signature (S_1, S_2); here we exploit that R_{bb} yields perfectly randomizable signatures. Moreover, the proof π_{Ped} can be simulated. We give the formal proof of blindness in the full version [42].

Acknowledgment. This work was supported by the Helsinki Institute for Information Technology (HIIT) and was conducted while Michael Klooß was affiliated with Aalto University.

References

1. Abe, M.: A secure three-move blind signature scheme for polynomially many signatures. In: Pfitzmann, B. (ed.) EUROCRYPT 2001. LNCS, vol. 2045, pp. 136–151. Springer, Heidelberg (May 2001). https://doi.org/10.1007/3-540-44987-6_9
2. Abe, M., Fujisaki, E.: How to date blind signatures. In: Kim, K., Matsumoto, T. (eds.) ASIACRYPT'96. LNCS, vol. 1163, pp. 244–251. Springer, Heidelberg (Nov 1996). https://doi.org/10.1007/BFb0034851
3. Abe, M., Okamoto, T.: Provably secure partially blind signatures. In: Bellare, M. (ed.) CRYPTO 2000. LNCS, vol. 1880, pp. 271–286. Springer, Heidelberg (Aug 2000). https://doi.org/10.1007/3-540-44598-6_17
4. Baldimtsi, F., Lysyanskaya, A.: On the security of one-witness blind signature schemes. In: Sako, K., Sarkar, P. (eds.) ASIACRYPT 2013, Part II. LNCS, vol. 8270, pp. 82–99. Springer, Heidelberg (Dec 2013). https://doi.org/10.1007/978-3-642-42045-0_5
5. Bellare, M., Namprempre, C., Pointcheval, D., Semanko, M.: The one-more-RSA-inversion problems and the security of Chaum's blind signature scheme. Journal of Cryptology **16**(3), 185–215 (Jun 2003). https://doi.org/10.1007/s00145-002-0120-1

6. Bellare, M., Rogaway, P.: Random oracles are practical: A paradigm for designing efficient protocols. In: Denning, D.E., Pyle, R., Ganesan, R., Sandhu, R.S., Ashby, V. (eds.) ACM CCS 93. pp. 62–73. ACM Press (Nov 1993). https://doi.org/10.1145/168588.168596

7. Benhamouda, F., Lepoint, T., Loss, J., Orrù, M., Raykova, M.: On the (in)security of ROS. In: Canteaut, A., Standaert, F.X. (eds.) EUROCRYPT 2021, Part I. LNCS, vol. 12696, pp. 33–53. Springer, Heidelberg (Oct 2021). https://doi.org/10.1007/978-3-030-77870-5_2

8. Boldyreva, A.: Threshold signatures, multisignatures and blind signatures based on the gap-Diffie-Hellman-group signature scheme. In: Desmedt, Y. (ed.) PKC 2003. LNCS, vol. 2567, pp. 31–46. Springer, Heidelberg (Jan 2003). https://doi.org/10.1007/3-540-36288-6_3

9. Boneh, D., Boyen, X.: Efficient selective-ID secure identity based encryption without random oracles. In: Cachin, C., Camenisch, J. (eds.) EUROCRYPT 2004. LNCS, vol. 3027, pp. 223–238. Springer, Heidelberg (May 2004). https://doi.org/10.1007/978-3-540-24676-3_14

10. Boneh, D., Franklin, M.K.: Identity-based encryption from the Weil pairing. In: Kilian, J. (ed.) CRYPTO 2001. LNCS, vol. 2139, pp. 213–229. Springer, Heidelberg (Aug 2001). https://doi.org/10.1007/3-540-44647-8_13

11. Boneh, D., Gentry, C., Hamburg, M.: Space-efficient identity based encryption without pairings. In: 48th FOCS. pp. 647–657. IEEE Computer Society Press (Oct 2007). https://doi.org/10.1109/FOCS.2007.64

12. Camenisch, J., Groß, T.: Efficient attributes for anonymous credentials. In: Ning, P., Syverson, P.F., Jha, S. (eds.) ACM CCS 2008. pp. 345–356. ACM Press (Oct 2008). https://doi.org/10.1145/1455770.1455814

13. Camenisch, J., Lysyanskaya, A.: An efficient system for non-transferable anonymous credentials with optional anonymity revocation. In: Pfitzmann, B. (ed.) EUROCRYPT 2001. LNCS, vol. 2045, pp. 93–118. Springer, Heidelberg (May 2001). https://doi.org/10.1007/3-540-44987-6_7

14. Catalano, D., Fiore, D., Gennaro, R., Giunta, E.: On the impossibility of algebraic vector commitments in pairing-free groups. In: Kiltz, E., Vaikuntanathan, V. (eds.) TCC 2022, Part II. LNCS, vol. 13748, pp. 274–299. Springer, Heidelberg (Nov 2022). https://doi.org/10.1007/978-3-031-22365-5_10

15. Chairattana-Apirom, R., Hanzlik, L., Loss, J., Lysyanskaya, A., Wagner, B.: PI-cut-choo and friends: Compact blind signatures via parallel instance cut-and-choose and more. In: Dodis, Y., Shrimpton, T. (eds.) CRYPTO 2022, Part III. LNCS, vol. 13509, pp. 3–31. Springer, Heidelberg (Aug 2022). https://doi.org/10.1007/978-3-031-15982-4_1

16. Chairattana-Apirom, R., Tessaro, S., Zhu, C.: Pairing-free blind signatures from CDH assumptions. In: Reyzin, L., Stebila, D. (eds.) CRYPTO 2024. LNCS, Springer, Heidelberg (Aug 18–22, 2024)

17. Chaum, D.: Blind signatures for untraceable payments. In: Chaum, D., Rivest, R.L., Sherman, A.T. (eds.) CRYPTO'82. pp. 199–203. Plenum Press, New York, USA (1982)

18. Couteau, G., Katsumata, S., Ursu, B.: Non-interactive zero-knowledge in pairing-free groups from weaker assumptions. In: Canteaut, A., Ishai, Y. (eds.) EUROCRYPT 2020, Part III. LNCS, vol. 12107, pp. 442–471. Springer, Heidelberg (May 2020). https://doi.org/10.1007/978-3-030-45727-3_15

19. Crites, E.C., Komlo, C., Maller, M., Tessaro, S., Zhu, C.: Snowblind: A threshold blind signature in pairing-free groups. In: Handschuh, H., Lysyanskaya, A. (eds.) CRYPTO 2023, Part I. LNCS, vol. 14081, pp. 710–742. Springer, Heidelberg (Aug 2023). https://doi.org/10.1007/978-3-031-38557-5_23

20. del Pino, R., Katsumata, S.: A new framework for more efficient round-optimal lattice-based (partially) blind signature via trapdoor sampling. In: Dodis, Y., Shrimpton, T. (eds.) CRYPTO 2022, Part II. LNCS, vol. 13508, pp. 306–336. Springer, Heidelberg (Aug 2022). https://doi.org/10.1007/978-3-031-15979-4_11

21. Fischlin, M.: Communication-efficient non-interactive proofs of knowledge with online extractors. In: Shoup, V. (ed.) CRYPTO 2005. LNCS, vol. 3621, pp. 152–168. Springer, Heidelberg (Aug 2005). https://doi.org/10.1007/11535218_10

22. Fischlin, M.: Round-optimal composable blind signatures in the common reference string model. In: Dwork, C. (ed.) CRYPTO 2006. LNCS, vol. 4117, pp. 60–77. Springer, Heidelberg (Aug 2006). https://doi.org/10.1007/11818175_4

23. Fischlin, M., Schröder, D.: On the impossibility of three-move blind signature schemes. In: Gilbert, H. (ed.) EUROCRYPT 2010. LNCS, vol. 6110, pp. 197–215. Springer, Heidelberg (May / Jun 2010). https://doi.org/10.1007/978-3-642-13190-5_10

24. Fuchsbauer, G., Hanser, C., Slamanig, D.: Practical round-optimal blind signatures in the standard model. In: Gennaro, R., Robshaw, M.J.B. (eds.) CRYPTO 2015, Part II. LNCS, vol. 9216, pp. 233–253. Springer, Heidelberg (Aug 2015). https://doi.org/10.1007/978-3-662-48000-7_12

25. Fuchsbauer, G., Kiltz, E., Loss, J.: The algebraic group model and its applications. In: Shacham, H., Boldyreva, A. (eds.) CRYPTO 2018, Part II. LNCS, vol. 10992, pp. 33–62. Springer, Heidelberg (Aug 2018). https://doi.org/10.1007/978-3-319-96881-0_2

26. Fuchsbauer, G., Plouviez, A., Seurin, Y.: Blind schnorr signatures and signed ElGamal encryption in the algebraic group model. In: Canteaut, A., Ishai, Y. (eds.) EUROCRYPT 2020, Part II. LNCS, vol. 12106, pp. 63–95. Springer, Heidelberg (May 2020). https://doi.org/10.1007/978-3-030-45724-2_3

27. Fuchsbauer, G., Wolf, M.: Concurrently secure blind schnorr signatures. In: Joye, M., Leander, G. (eds.) EUROCRYPT 2024, Part II. LNCS, vol. 14652, pp. 124–160. Springer, Heidelberg, Zurich, Switherland (May 26–30, 2024). https://doi.org/10.1007/978-3-031-58723-8_5

28. Garg, S., Gupta, D.: Efficient round optimal blind signatures. In: Nguyen, P.Q., Oswald, E. (eds.) EUROCRYPT 2014. LNCS, vol. 8441, pp. 477–495. Springer, Heidelberg (May 2014). https://doi.org/10.1007/978-3-642-55220-5_27

29. Garg, S., Rao, V., Sahai, A., Schröder, D., Unruh, D.: Round optimal blind signatures. In: Rogaway, P. (ed.) CRYPTO 2011. LNCS, vol. 6841, pp. 630–648. Springer, Heidelberg (Aug 2011). https://doi.org/10.1007/978-3-642-22792-9_36

30. Gay, R., Hofheinz, D., Kiltz, E., Wee, H.: Tightly CCA-secure encryption without pairings. In: Fischlin, M., Coron, J.S. (eds.) EUROCRYPT 2016, Part I. LNCS, vol. 9665, pp. 1–27. Springer, Heidelberg (May 2016). https://doi.org/10.1007/978-3-662-49890-3_1

31. Ghadafi, E.: Efficient round-optimal blind signatures in the standard model. In: Kiayias, A. (ed.) FC 2017. LNCS, vol. 10322, pp. 455–473. Springer, Heidelberg (Apr 2017)

32. Hanzlik, L., Loss, J., Wagner, B.: Rai-choo! Evolving blind signatures to the next level. In: Hazay, C., Stam, M. (eds.) EUROCRYPT 2023, Part V. LNCS, vol. 14008, pp. 753–783. Springer, Heidelberg (Apr 2023). https://doi.org/10.1007/978-3-031-30589-4_26

33. Hauck, E., Kiltz, E., Loss, J.: A modular treatment of blind signatures from identification schemes. In: Ishai, Y., Rijmen, V. (eds.) EUROCRYPT 2019, Part III. LNCS, vol. 11478, pp. 345–375. Springer, Heidelberg (May 2019). https://doi.org/10.1007/978-3-030-17659-4_12

34. Hauck, E., Kiltz, E., Loss, J., Nguyen, N.K.: Lattice-based blind signatures, revisited. In: Micciancio, D., Ristenpart, T. (eds.) CRYPTO 2020, Part II. LNCS, vol. 12171, pp. 500–529. Springer, Heidelberg (Aug 2020). https://doi.org/10.1007/978-3-030-56880-1_18

35. Juels, A., Luby, M., Ostrovsky, R.: Security of blind digital signatures (extended abstract). In: Kaliski Jr., B.S. (ed.) CRYPTO'97. LNCS, vol. 1294, pp. 150–164. Springer, Heidelberg (Aug 1997). https://doi.org/10.1007/BFb0052233

36. Kastner, J., Loss, J., Xu, J.: The Abe-Okamoto partially blind signature scheme revisited. In: Agrawal, S., Lin, D. (eds.) ASIACRYPT 2022, Part IV. LNCS, vol. 13794, pp. 279–309. Springer, Heidelberg (Dec 2022). https://doi.org/10.1007/978-3-031-22972-5_10

37. Kastner, J., Loss, J., Xu, J.: On pairing-free blind signature schemes in the algebraic group model. In: Hanaoka, G., Shikata, J., Watanabe, Y. (eds.) PKC 2022, Part II. LNCS, vol. 13178, pp. 468–497. Springer, Heidelberg (Mar 2022). https://doi.org/10.1007/978-3-030-97131-1_16

38. Kastner, J., Nguyen, K., Reichle, M.: Pairing-free blind signatures from standard assumptions in the rom. In: Reyzin, L., Stebila, D. (eds.) CRYPTO 2024. LNCS, Springer, Heidelberg (Aug 18–22, 2024)

39. Katsumata, S.: A new simple technique to bootstrap various lattice zero-knowledge proofs to QROM secure NIZKs. In: Malkin, T., Peikert, C. (eds.) CRYPTO 2021, Part II. LNCS, vol. 12826, pp. 580–610. Springer, Heidelberg, Virtual Event (Aug 2021). https://doi.org/10.1007/978-3-030-84245-1_20

40. Katsumata, S., Reichle, M., Sakai, Y.: Practical round-optimal blind signatures in the ROM from standard assumptions. In: Guo, J., Steinfeld, R. (eds.) ASIACRYPT 2023, Part II. LNCS, vol. 14439, pp. 383–417. Springer, Heidelberg (Dec 2023). https://doi.org/10.1007/978-981-99-8724-5_12

41. Katz, J., Loss, J., Rosenberg, M.: Boosting the security of blind signature schemes. In: Tibouchi, M., Wang, H. (eds.) ASIACRYPT 2021, Part IV. LNCS, vol. 13093, pp. 468–492. Springer, Heidelberg (Dec 2021). https://doi.org/10.1007/978-3-030-92068-5_16

42. Kloß, M., Reichle, M., Wagner, B.: Practical blind signatures in pairing-free groups. IACR Cryptol. ePrint Arch. p. 1378 (2024), https://eprint.iacr.org/2024/1378

43. Kondi, Y., shelat, a.: Improved straight-line extraction in the random oracle model with applications to signature aggregation. In: Agrawal, S., Lin, D. (eds.) ASIACRYPT 2022, Part II. LNCS, vol. 13792, pp. 279–309. Springer, Heidelberg (Dec 2022). https://doi.org/10.1007/978-3-031-22966-4_10

44. Okamoto, T.: Provably secure and practical identification schemes and corresponding signature schemes. In: Brickell, E.F. (ed.) CRYPTO'92. LNCS, vol. 740, pp. 31–53. Springer, Heidelberg (Aug 1993). https://doi.org/10.1007/3-540-48071-4_3

45. Okamoto, T.: Efficient blind and partially blind signatures without random oracles. In: Halevi, S., Rabin, T. (eds.) TCC 2006. LNCS, vol. 3876, pp. 80–99. Springer, Heidelberg (Mar 2006). https://doi.org/10.1007/11681878_5

46. Okamoto, T., Ohta, K.: Universal electronic cash. In: Feigenbaum, J. (ed.) CRYPTO'91. LNCS, vol. 576, pp. 324–337. Springer, Heidelberg (Aug 1992). https://doi.org/10.1007/3-540-46766-1_27

47. Pan, J., Wagner, B.: Chopsticks: Fork-free two-round multi-signatures from non-interactive assumptions. In: Hazay, C., Stam, M. (eds.) EUROCRYPT 2023, Part V. LNCS, vol. 14008, pp. 597–627. Springer, Heidelberg (Apr 2023). https://doi.org/10.1007/978-3-031-30589-4_21

48. Pass, R.: On deniability in the common reference string and random oracle model. In: Boneh, D. (ed.) CRYPTO 2003. LNCS, vol. 2729, pp. 316–337. Springer, Heidelberg (Aug 2003). https://doi.org/10.1007/978-3-540-45146-4_19

49. Pass, R.: Limits of provable security from standard assumptions. In: Fortnow, L., Vadhan, S.P. (eds.) 43rd ACM STOC. pp. 109–118. ACM Press (Jun 2011). https://doi.org/10.1145/1993636.1993652

50. Pointcheval, D.: Strengthened security for blind signatures. In: Nyberg, K. (ed.) EUROCRYPT'98. LNCS, vol. 1403, pp. 391–405. Springer, Heidelberg (May / Jun 1998). https://doi.org/10.1007/BFb0054141

51. Pointcheval, D., Stern, J.: Security arguments for digital signatures and blind signatures. Journal of Cryptology **13**(3), 361–396 (Jun 2000). https://doi.org/10.1007/s001450010003

52. Schnorr, C.P.: Efficient signature generation by smart cards. Journal of Cryptology **4**(3), 161–174 (Jan 1991). https://doi.org/10.1007/BF00196725

53. Schnorr, C.P.: Security of blind discrete log signatures against interactive attacks. In: Qing, S., Okamoto, T., Zhou, J. (eds.) ICICS 01. LNCS, vol. 2229, pp. 1–12. Springer, Heidelberg (Nov 2001)

54. Tessaro, S., Zhu, C.: Short pairing-free blind signatures with exponential security. In: Dunkelman, O., Dziembowski, S. (eds.) EUROCRYPT 2022, Part II. LNCS, vol. 13276, pp. 782–811. Springer, Heidelberg (May / Jun 2022). https://doi.org/10.1007/978-3-031-07085-3_27

55. Tessaro, S., Zhu, C.: Threshold and multi-signature schemes from linear hash functions. In: Hazay, C., Stam, M. (eds.) EUROCRYPT 2023, Part V. LNCS, vol. 14008, pp. 628–658. Springer, Heidelberg (Apr 2023). https://doi.org/10.1007/978-3-031-30589-4_22

56. Wagner, D.: A generalized birthday problem. In: Yung, M. (ed.) CRYPTO 2002. LNCS, vol. 2442, pp. 288–303. Springer, Heidelberg (Aug 2002). https://doi.org/10.1007/3-540-45708-9_19

Faster Signatures from MPC-in-the-Head

Dung Bui[1(✉)], Eliana Carozza[1], Geoffroy Couteau[2], Dahmun Goudarzi[3], and Antoine Joux[4]

[1] IRIF, Université Paris Cité, Paris, France
{bui,carozza}@irif.fr
[2] CNRS, IRIF, Université Paris Cité, Paris, France
couteau@irif.fr
[3] Quarkslab, Paris, France
dahmun.goudarzi@gmail.com
[4] CISPA Helmholtz Center for Information Security, Saarbrücken, Germany
joux@cispa.de

Abstract. We revisit the construction of signature schemes using the MPC-in-the-head paradigm. We obtain two main contributions:

- We observe that previous signatures in the MPC-in-the-head paradigm must rely on a salted version of the GGM puncturable pseudorandom function (PPRF) to avoid collision attacks. We design a new efficient PPRF construction that is provably secure in the multi-instance setting. The security analysis of our PPRF, in the ideal cipher model, is quite involved and forms a core technical contribution of our work. While previous constructions had to rely on a hash function, our construction uses only a fixed-key block cipher and is considerably more efficient as a result: we observe a $12\times$ to $55\times$ speed improvement for a recent signature scheme (Joux and Huth, Crypto'24). Our improved PPRF can be used to speed up many MPC-in-the-head signatures.
- We introduce a new signature scheme from the regular syndrome decoding assumption, based on a new protocol for the MPC-in-the-head paradigm, which significantly reduces communication compared to previous works. Our scheme is conceptually simple, though its security analysis requires a delicate and nontrivial combinatorial analysis.

1 Introduction

In this work, we revisit signature schemes constructed from the MPC-in-the-head (MPCitH) paradigm. We make two contributions. Our first contribution appeals to all MPCitH signatures, while our second contribution is in the context of code-based MPCitH signatures:

- We introduce the notion of multi-instance puncturable pseudorandom function (PPRF) together with an extremely efficient instantiation from the AES block cipher, which we formally prove secure in the ideal cipher model. Our

ⓒ International Association for Cryptologic Research 2025
K.-M. Chung and Y. Sasaki (Eds.): ASIACRYPT 2024, LNCS 15484, pp. 396–428, 2025.
https://doi.org/10.1007/978-981-96-0875-1_13

construction can be used as a drop-in replacement to the hash-based PPRF used in most previous MPCitH signatures, and yields significant improvements in both signing time and verification time (e.g., from 12× to 55× in our experiments with the recent scheme of [38]).

– We introduce a new MPCitH signature from the regular syndrome decoding (RSD) problem. We formally prove that its unforgeability tightly reduces to the multi-instance security of the underlying PPRF, showcasing how our new primitive results in better security reduction (hence better efficiency for a target security level). Our new signature scheme relies on a non-trivial combinatorial analysis, and significantly improves over the state-of-the-art scheme of [24] on all aspects (signature size, efficiency, security).

1.1 Faster MPCitH Signatures from a New Multi-instance PPRF

All state-of-the-art MPCitH signature schemes rely at their core on a puncturable pseudorandom function, which allows to generate a large number n of pseudorandom strings such that given an index i, the signer can reveal all pseudorandom values except the i-th one using an "opening" of size $\lambda \cdot \log n$ (where λ is a security parameter). The *de facto* PPRF originally used in prominent works such as Picnic [49] was the GGM PPRF [35], where the PRF evaluation on input i with key K is the i-th leave of a full binary tree with root labeled with K. In GGM, the labels of the two children of a node x are computed as $F(x) = (F_0(x), F_1(x))$ using a length-doubling pseudorandom generator (PRG) $x \mapsto (F_0(x), F_1(x))$. The PRG is typically instantiated as $x \mapsto (x \oplus \pi_0(x), x \oplus \pi_1(x))$ for a pair of random invertible permutations (π_0, π_1): this instantiation yields a provably secure construction in the random permutation model [36] and an extremely fast expansion when instantiating the permutations using the AES block cipher with a fixed key (using commonly available hardware acceleration for AES). However, it was observed in [30] that in the context of signatures, this choice allows for a devastating multi-target attack: after 2^t signature queries, an attacker can find the root of one of the GGM trees using on average 2^{128-t} work, and recover the secret signing key as soon as a collision is found.

In reaction to this attack, Picnic [49] and most recent works on MPCitH signatures, including BBQ [29], Banquet [9], all MPCitH candidates of the recent NIST call for additional post-quantum signatures (SDitH [3], MIRA [6], MiRitH [2], MQOM [32], PERK [1], Ryde [5], and Biscuit [11]) and more, all implement the PRG using a hash function (such as SHAKE), as follows: $F_b(x, i, \mathsf{salt}) \leftarrow H(x\|i\|b\|\mathsf{salt})$, where i is the index of the parent node and salt is some random salt (included in the signature). Unfortunately, because of the hardware support for AES, replacing AES with a hash function is considerably slower (up to 50× slower according to [36]).

A Faster Construction from Ideal Ciphers. The reason for choosing the hash-based construction over the existing AES-based construction comes from the need to add a per-signature salt at every node computation to thwart the multi-target attack; however, AES can only take a fixed 128-bit input. We make the following simple observation: in the AES-based instantiation, instead of relying on a global fixed-key that remains identical across all instances (as was originally done in Picnic [49]), the signer can use a per-signature random AES key that will play the role of the salt (crucially, this key needs not be changed at every node of the tree, avoiding costly re-keying of AES), without having to increase the block size.

A Multi-instance PPRF in the Ideal Cipher Model. The idea in itself is surprisingly simple, and we do not claim it to be particularly novel: the idea of rotating the key has been mentioned in the literature in other contexts, for example, in [45]. Our main contributions here are twofold:

- We introduce the notion of multi-instance PPRFs, capturing the exact security requirement that the PPRF must satisfy to avoid multi-target attacks (in contrast, previous works made a direct proof of the full signature construction by modeling the hash function in the ROM; our approach is much more modular).
- We formally prove that the PPRF instantiated with $\mathsf{F}(x, K_0, K_1) = (x \oplus \mathsf{AES}_{K_0}(x), x \oplus \mathsf{AES}_{K_1}(x))$ is a multi-instance PPRF when AES is modeled as an ideal cipher. Our security analysis is non-trivial and forms a core technical contribution of our work. It relies on the H-coefficient technique of Patarin [26,42].

We further expect our new PPRF to find other applications beyond the scope of MPCitH signatures. We sketch these applications in Appendix of our full-version [23].

On the Security Loss of Our Construction. Our analysis induces a loss of $\log D + 3$ bits of security, where D is the depth of the GGM tree. For example, if $D = 8$, this translates to a loss of 6 bits of security. Before we proceed, we comment on this loss:

- The loss of 3 bits of security comes from bounding the worst-case runtime of the attacker (*i.e.* proving that with probability $2^{-\lambda}$, the attacker must run in time 2^{λ} to break the scheme with high probability). If bound instead the *expected* runtime of the attacker, the loss reduces to 1 bit.
- the $\log_2 D$ loss comes from the D hybrids in the PRG-to-PRF reduction, similar to [35]. This loss is inherent to the construction (*i.e.*, the analysis is perfectly tight on this aspect).

To mitigate the second loss, we suggest the following variant of our construction: instead of relying on a global pair of keys (K_0, K_1) for the full GGM tree, use instead D pairs of keys $(K_0^i, K_1^i)_{i \leq D}$ (stretched from some 2λ-bit signature salt using a PRG), one for each level of the tree. Then, evaluate the GGM tree using the key pair (K_0^i, K_1^i) for nodes that are the i-th level of the tree. This induces a slight increase in the number of AES rekeying ($2D$ instead of 2), but the cost is completely negligible compared to the rest (the reader can think of D as an integer between 8 and 16). We put forth the conjecture that in the ideal cipher model, this yields a multi-instance PPRF with $\lambda - 3$ bits of security (or $\lambda - 1$ if we bound the expected runtime of the attacker instead), where λ is the key length of the block cipher.

Unfortunately, it is not straightforward to adapt our security analysis to this variant: our analysis proceeds via a multi-instance PPRF to multi-instance PRG reduction, followed by a proof of security of the multi-instance PRG in the ideal cipher model. The $\log_2 D$ loss stems from the first reduction, and our variant does not generically remove this loss for an arbitrary multi-instance PRG. We conjecture that it does, however, remove this loss when the PRG is instantiated in the ideal cipher model. Proving this conjecture appears to require analyzing directly the full multi-instance PPRF in the ideal cipher model. We believe that this is not out of reach, but it goes beyond the scope of this work, and we leave it to future work.

Case Analysis: the Signature Scheme of [38]. We expect that replacing the hash-based PPRF with our AES-based construction in existing MPCitH signature schemes will yield to efficiency improvements. The improvement is especially noticeable if the cost of expanding the GGM tree represents a large fraction of the overall runtime. We note that if the most optimized state-of-the-art MPCitH signature, the GGM tree expansion indeed tends to account for most of the running time (for both signing and verification).

To illustrate the concrete efficiency improvements one might expect from using our PPRF, we focus on the recent scheme of [38], an extremely efficient MPCitH signature based on the subfield bilinear collision problem. We run the signature scheme using both the hash-based multi-instance PPRF used in previous works, and our AES-based multi-instance PPRF. In both cases, for fairness of comparison, we include all relevant algorithmic optimizations (this includes an algorithmic optimization introduced in [38] subsequently to our work). We report the results on Table 1 for two sets of parameters:$D = 8$ (fast signing, larger signatures) and $D = 16$ (slower signing, short signatures). We observe a very significant improvement in runtime, from $12\times$ when $D = 8$ up to $55\times$ when $D = 16$. We note that the authors of [38] already integrated our improved PPRF in the latest version of their scheme, to be presented at CRYPTO'24.

1.2   A New MPCitH Signature from Regular Syndrome Decoding

We now turn to our second main contribution, a new construction of MPCitH-based signature from the regular syndrome decoding assumption. This contribution is essentially independent of our multi-instance PPRF[1]; however, it also

---

[1] We initially introduced our improved PPRF and its analysis as an optimization of our new scheme, but since it impacts all state-of-the-art MPCitH signatures, we singled it out as an independent contribution.

Table 1. Case analysis of the impact of using our faster AES-based multi-instance PPRF on the signature scheme of [38] for two sets of parameters: $D = 8$ (fast signing) and $D = 16$ (short signatures) compared to the standard hash-based construction. D denotes the depth of the GGM tree (equivalently, 2^D corresponds to the number of virtual parties in the MPC protocol run "in the head"), and τ to the number of repetitions to achieve 128 bits of security. All schemes run on one core of an AMD EPYC 9374F processor clocked at 3.85GHz.

[38]	D	τ	$|\sigma|$	signing	verification
hash-based PPRF	8	16	6.2 kB	9.24 ms	9.11 ms
	16	8	4.1 kB	1.1 s	1.1 s
AES-based PPRF	8	16	6.2 kB	0.80 ms	0.71 ms
(this work)	16	8	4.1 kB	19.5 ms	19.2 ms

allows us to formally illustrate on a concrete signature scheme how multi-instance PPRFs yield tight and simple proofs of existential unforgeability.

Our starting point is the recent work of [24], that relies on a share conversion technique to build a signature scheme from the regular syndrome decoding problem (RSD). The RSD problem was originally introduced in 2003 in [7] as the assumption underlying the FSB candidate to the NIST hash function competition, and subsequently analyzed in [10, 33, 40], among others (it has also been used and analyzed in many recent works on secure computation, such as [14–18, 27, 37, 44, 46, 48]). It states that given a syndrome $H \cdot x$, where x is a *regular* vector (*i.e.*, a concatenation of unit vectors) and H a random compressive matrix, it is infeasible to recover x. To obtain improved performances compared to [24], we encode the regular syndrome decoding instances using a sparse representation on top of the dense representation used in [24]. Encoding regular syndrome decoding instances in a sparse manner is quite natural and relies on the use of an indicator vector to locate the non-zero positions. However, such a representation is not compatible with the secret sharing techniques that are used to split the key between the virtual parties that are introduced by the MPC-in-the-head paradigm: in order to use sparse representations, we need to develop new conversion techniques involving both types of representations. Along the way, we rely on a mechanism to prevent cheating behavior in the conversion, which requires a highly non-trivial combinatorial analysis. Overall, our signature scheme is more than 30% shorter compared to the scheme of [24] and can use significantly more conservative parameter sets, for similar runtimes.

Results and Comparison. We provide a full implementation of our signature scheme. Our implementation is a proof-of-concept implementation, and did not use any optimizations such as batching, vectorization, or bit slicing. In particular, we note that our implementation does not include the folding optimization that was subsequently introduced in [38], that yields significant efficiency improvements when the AES-based multi-instance PPRF is used (in contrast, it only yields mild improvements when using a hash-based PPRF, in essence because it shaves a cost which is dominant in the AES-based PPRF, but dominated by the cost of hashing in the hash-based PPRF). Nevertheless, our implementation confirms that our scheme exhibits excellent performance. Since [24] does not provide an implementation, we compare our scheme to SDitH, the state-of-the-art MPCitH signature from syndrome decoding [3].

Even when compared to a fully-optimized scheme such as SDitH [3] that makes use of batching techniques and advanced hardware instructions, we observe that our scheme performs particularly well. In addition, we provide tight estimates of the performance improvements that results from integrating the fast folding optimization of [38] to our scheme and to SDitH (while we use the implementation of [38] to obtain runtimes for the faster folding, we note that we do not yet have a full-fledged implementation of our scheme integrating the folding optimization). We leave a fully-optimized implementation of our scheme, integrating the optimization of [38], to future works. We outline below a sample of parameters:

- (fast) signature size 6.5kB, signing time 1.40 ms
- (medium) signature size 5.7 kB, signing time 3.56 ms
- (compact) signature size 4.9 kB, signing time 23.9 ms.

We refer the reader to Table 3 of our full-version [23] for more details on our parameters and implementation. We compared our scheme to SDitH [4], the fastest known code-based signature scheme to date, by running both schemes on the same hardware and for comparable parameter sets. To better isolate the effect of our improved PPRF, we also benchmark SDitH with their PPRF replaced by our improved construction,[2] as well as our scheme using the hash-based PPRF of SDitH. For both, we integrate the folding optimization of [38]. We summarize our benchmarks on Table 2. Even when comparing our unoptimized implementation to the optimized implementation of [3], we observe 3× to 4× runtime improvements for $D = 8$ (with signatures of comparable size).

Another advantage of our signature scheme is its simplicity: while [4] requires fast polynomial operations over large fields, our signature uses only very simple operations on strings such as XORs and cyclic shifts. Eventually, we note that our work and [4] use incomparable variants of syndrome decoding: we use regular syndrome decoding over $\mathbb{F}_2$, while [4] uses syndrome decoding over $\mathbb{F}_{256}$. Both variants have received much less attention than the standard syndrome decoding assumption over $\mathbb{F}_2$ (though we note that RSD over $\mathbb{F}_2$ seems to have received significantly more attention than the variant of [4] over the past two decades).

---

[2] In the conference version of their work, the construction of [4] initially used an *unsalted* GGM tree (instantiated using AES), which we show in Sect. 3 to be insecure (with a concrete attack that breaks the scheme using 2^{40} signatures in time 2^{69}). The authors later fixed this issue in their NIST submission [3], using a proper salted GGM tree instantiated with a hash function.

Table 2. Comparison of the new signature scheme with SDitH for $D = 8$ and $D = 12$, with and without our improved multi-instance puncturable pseudorandom function (denoted AES-PPRF and hash-PPRF respectively) integrating the folding optimization of [38]. All schemes were run on one core of an Intel Core i7 processor 14700KF.

	D	τ	$|\sigma|$	signing time
SDitH (hash-PPRF)	8		178.2 kB	6.82 ms
	12		116.0 kB	46.8 ms
SDitH (AES-PPRF)	8		178.2 kB	6.03 ms
	12		116.0 kB	31.5 ms
Our scheme (hash-PPRF)	8		177.8 kB	4.07 ms
	12		116.1 kB	43.83 ms
Our scheme (AES-PPRF)	8		177.8 kB	0.64 ms
	12		116.1 kB	2.13 ms

Concurrent Work. A concurrent and independent work [28] recently introduced another signature scheme based on the Regular Syndrome Decoding assumption. On a technical level, our approaches differ significantly: [28] combines the VOLE-in-the-Head technique from [8] with a sketching method of [20] to reduce the check of the noise structure to a system of degree-2 equations, which are then proven using the Quicksilver VOLE-based zero-knowledge proof [47]. We use the MPC-in-the-Head methodology with a dedicated share-conversion technique. The signatures of [28] are shorter than ours, e.g., 4 kB versus 4.9 kB for comparable runtimes. Since our techniques are incomparable, we nevertheless expect that they could prove useful in future improved constructions of RSD-based signature, and leave as future work the question of exploring whether our combinatorial techniques could be used to further improve the scheme of [28]. We note that our improved PPRF can be used as a drop-in replacement for the one used in [28] (though it uses VOLE-in-the-Head, the methodology still relies on a similar use of a GGM-style PPRF under the hood) and its use should improve the performances of [28].

1.3 Organization

We introduce some preliminaries in Sect. 2 and provide a technical overview of our main two contributions in Sect. 3 (the improved GGM construction) and Sect. 4 (the new signature scheme) respectively. These sections overview the security analysis of our multi-instance PPRF and the combinatorial analysis of a bound used in the analysis of our signature scheme respectively, which form the core contributions of our work. We describe the construction of our PPRF in Sect. 5 and our signature scheme in Sect. 6. Due to space limitations, we refer reader to our full-version [23] for more details.

2   Preliminaries

Given a set S, we write $s \leftarrow_r S$ to indicate that s is uniformly sampled from S. Given a probabilistic Turing machine $\mathcal{A}$ and an input x, we write $y \leftarrow_r \mathcal{A}(x)$ to indicate that y is sampled by running $\mathcal{A}$ on x with a uniform random tape, or $y \leftarrow \mathcal{A}(x; r)$ when we want to make the random coins explicit. Given an integer $n \in \mathbb{N}$, we denote by $[n]$ the set $\{1, \cdots, n\}$. We use $\lambda = 128$ for the computational security parameter.

Vectors and Matrices. We use bold lowercase for vectors and uppercase for matrices. We write $A \| B$ to denote the horizontal concatenation of matrices A, B, and $A /\!/ B$ to denote their vertical concatenation. We denote by Id_n the $n \times n$ identity matrix. By default, we always view vectors as columns. Given a vector $\mathbf{v}$, we will often write $\mathbf{v} = (\mathbf{v}_1, \cdots, \mathbf{v}_n)$ to indicate that $\mathbf{v}$ is a (vertical) concatenation of n subvectors $\mathbf{v}_i$. We use this slight abuse of notation to avoid the (more precise, but cumbersome) notation $\mathbf{v} = (\mathbf{v}_1^\mathsf{T}, \cdots, \mathbf{v}_n^\mathsf{T})^\mathsf{T}$. Given $\mathbf{u}, \mathbf{v} \in \{0, 1\}^n$, we write $\mathbf{u} \oplus \mathbf{v}$ for the bitwise-XOR of $\mathbf{u}$ and $\mathbf{v}$, and $\mathsf{HW}(\mathbf{u})$ for the Hamming weight of $\mathbf{u}$, i.e., its number of nonzero entries.

Permutations. We let $\mathsf{Perm}(w)$ denote the set of all permutations of $[w]$. In this work, we typically use permutations over $[w]$ to shuffle the entries of a length-w vector, or even to shuffle the *blocks* of a vector which is the concatenation of w blocks. For example, given a vector $\mathbf{v} \in [\mathsf{bs}]^w$ and a permutation $\pi : [w] \mapsto [w]$, we write $\pi(\mathbf{v})$ to denote the vector $(v_{\pi(1)}, v_{\pi(2)}, \cdots, v_{\pi(w)})$. Given a vector $\mathbf{v}$ which is the concatenation of w subvectors $(\mathbf{v}_1, \cdots, \mathbf{v}_w)$, we write $\pi(\mathbf{v})$ to denote the vector $(\mathbf{v}_{\pi(1)}, \cdots, \mathbf{v}_{\pi(w)})$. We will typically apply this to vectors over $\mathbb{F}_2^K$, seen as the concatenation of w vectors over $\mathbb{F}_2^{\mathsf{bs}}$.

Code Parameters. In this work, K always denotes the number of columns in the parity-check matrix H, and k denote the number of its rows. Equivalently, K is the codeword length, and $K - k$ is the dimension of the code. We let w denote the weight of the noise, which will always divide K. We let $\mathsf{bs} \leftarrow K/w$ denote the block size: a w-regular noise vector is sampled as a concatenation of w random unit vectors (the *blocks*) of length bs. We write Reg_w to denote the set of all length-K w-regular vectors.

Compact and Expanded Forms. Given an index $i \in [n]$, we let $\mathbf{e}_i \in \mathbb{F}_2^n$ denote the length-n unit $\mathbb{F}_2$-vector whose i-th entry is 1 given w indices $(i_1, \cdots, i_w) \in [n]^w$, we extend the previous notation to $\mathbf{e_i} = (\mathbf{e}_{i_1}, \cdots, \mathbf{e}_{i_w})$, the concatenation of w unit vectors. We typically manipulate noise vectors represented in *compact form*, i.e., as elements $(i_1, \cdots, i_w)$ of $[\mathsf{bs}]^w$, where each entry

$i_j \in [\mathsf{bs}]$ indicates the position of the 1 in the j-th length-bs unit vector. We let Expand denote the mapping which, given a noise vector $\mathbf{x} = (\mathbf{x}_1, \cdots, \mathbf{x}_w) \in [\mathsf{bs}]^w$, outputs the vector $\mathbf{e_x} = (\mathbf{e_{x_1}}, \cdots, \mathbf{e_{x_w}}) \in \mathbb{F}_2^K$. We call $\mathbf{e_x}$ the *expanded form* of $\mathbf{x}$.

Cyclic Shifts. Given a vector $\mathbf{u} \in \mathbb{F}_2^n$ and $i \in [n]$, we write $\mathbf{u} \downarrow i$ to denote the vector $\mathbf{u}$ cyclically shifted by i steps (in other words, $\mathbf{u} \downarrow i$ is the convolution of $\mathbf{u}$ and $\mathbf{e}_i$). We also use notation $\mathsf{Shift}(\mathbf{u}, i)$ to denote $\mathbf{u} \downarrow i$. We extend the notation to a *block-by-block* cyclic shift of vectors: given a vector $\mathbf{u} \in \mathbb{F}_2^K$, viewed as a sequence of blocks $(\mathbf{u}_1, \cdots, \mathbf{u}_w) \in \mathbb{F}_2^{K/w} \times \cdots \times \mathbb{F}_2^{K/w}$, and a vector of shifts $\mathbf{x} \in [\mathsf{bs}]^w$, we write $\mathbf{u} \downarrow \mathbf{x}$ to denote the vector obtained by shifting the blocks of $\mathbf{u}$ according to $\mathbf{x}$. That is $\mathbf{u} \downarrow \mathbf{x} = (\mathbf{v}_1, \cdots, \mathbf{v}_w)$ where each $\mathbf{v}_i$ is the vector obtained by cyclically shifting (downward) the vector $\mathbf{u}_i$ by $\mathbf{x}_i$ steps. To avoid abusing parenthesis, we view $\downarrow$ as a "top priority" operator: by default, for any other operation op, $\mathbf{u} \downarrow \mathbf{x} \mathsf{opv}$ means $(\mathbf{u} \downarrow \mathbf{x})\mathsf{opv}$ and not $\mathbf{u} \downarrow (\mathbf{xopv})$.

Binary Tree. Given a tree of size 2^D, for each leaf $i \in [2^D]$, we define $\mathsf{CoPath}(i)$ as co-path to i in the tree, *i.e.*, the set of intermediate nodes that can be used to recover all leaves except the i-th one. Denote bit-decompose i as $\sum_{j=1}^{D} 2^{j-1} \cdot i_j$ for $i_j \in \{0,1\}$, the associated value of i-th leaf is defined as $X_i := X_{i_1,\ldots,i_D}$.

2.1 Regular Syndrome Decoding Problem

Given a weight parameter w, the syndrome decoding problem asks to find a solution of Hamming weight w (under the promise that it exists) to a random system of linear equations $H \cdot \mathbf{x}$ over $\mathbb{F}_2$. There exist several well-established variants of the syndrome decoding problem, with different matrix distributions, underlying fields, or noise distributions. In this work, we focus on a relatively well-studied variant known as the *regular syndrome decoding* (RSD) problem, introduced in 2003 in [7] as the assumption underlying the FSB candidate to the NIST hash function competition. In RSD, the solution $\mathbf{x}$ is sampled randomly from the set Reg_w of w-regular vectors (*i.e.*, $\mathbf{x}$ is a concatenation of w unit vectors of length K/w). This variant has been used (and analyzed) quite often in the literature [7,10,14–18,27,33,37,40,44,46,48].

Definition 1 (Regular Syndrome Decoding Problem). *Let K, k, w be three integers, with $K > k > w$. The syndrome decoding problem with parameters (K, k, w) is defined as follows:*

- *(Problem generation) Sample $H \leftarrow_r \mathbb{F}_2^{k \times K}$ and $\mathbf{x} \leftarrow_r \mathsf{Reg}_w$. Set $\mathbf{y} \leftarrow H \cdot \mathbf{x}$. Output $(H, \mathbf{y})$.*
- *(Goal) Given $(H, \mathbf{y})$, find $\mathbf{x} \in \mathsf{Reg}_w$ such that $H \cdot \mathbf{x} = \mathbf{y}$.*

3   Technical Overview:Optimized GGM Trees for Faster MPCitH Signatures

Our starting point is the GGM puncturable pseudorandom function [12,22,35, 39], which is used in all modern MPC-in-the-head signatures. At a high level, all MPC-in-the-head protocols start by letting the prover generate shares of the witness, possibly together with shares of some appropriate preprocessing material, to be distributed among the n virtual parties. Then, in the last round, the prover will reveal $n-1$ out of n shares to the verifier. Since each share appears random, the share of each party P_i can be locally stretched from a short seed seed_i. To maintain correctness, an auxiliary "correction word" aux_n is appended to the seed seed_n of the last party P_n (e.g. to guarantee that the stretched shares XOR to the correct witness).

Puncturable PRFs allow us to significantly optimize this step. A *puncturable pseudorandom function* (PPRF) is a PRF F such that given an input x, and a PRF key k, one can generate a *punctured* key, denoted $k\{x\}$, which allows evaluating F at every point except for x, and does not reveal any information about the value $F.\mathsf{Eval}(k, x)$. Using a PPRF, the prover can define all seeds seed_i as outputs of the PRF, using a master seed seed^* as the PRF key. Then, revealing the key seed^* punctured at a point i suffices to succinctly reveal all seeds $(\mathsf{seed}_j)_{j \neq i}$ while hiding seed_i. Concretely, using the GGM PPRF [35], the prover generates n seeds $\mathsf{seed}_1, \cdots, \mathsf{seed}_n$ as the leaves of a binary tree of depth $\lceil \log_2 n \rceil$, where the two children of each node are computed using length-doubling pseudorandom generators. This way, revealing all seeds except seed_i requires only sending the seeds on the nodes along the co-path from the root to the i-th leave, which reduces the communication from $\lambda \cdot (n-1)$ to $\lambda \cdot \lceil \log_2 n \rceil$.

3.1   On the Use of Salt to Avoid Collisions

As shown in [30], MPC-in-the-head can suffer from collision attacks if the GGM PPRF is used *as is*: after about $2^{\lambda/2}$ signature queries, the adversary is likely to observe two signatures computed with the same master seed seed^*, an event which leaks the secret signing key. To circumvent this issue, previous works have relied in one way or another on a random 2λ-bit salt. However, the use of salt within the GGM PPRF is inconsistent across existing works. As a result, some constructions are either poorly specified or even insecure. Specifically:

- In Banquet [9], and in the more recent work of [4], the seeds $(\mathsf{seed}_1, \cdots, \mathsf{seed}_n)$ are generated from an *unsalted* GGM PPRF, and the salt is only used at the leaves, when stretching the share of each party P_i from its seed as $\mathsf{PRG}(\mathsf{seed}_i, \mathsf{salt})$.
- In [31] and [24], the signature description loosely states that $(\mathsf{seed}_1, \cdots, \mathsf{seed}_n)$ are generated in a tree-based fashion using the master seed seed^* and the salt salt. However, the way the salt is used within the GGM construction is not specified precisely. In particular, the definition of the GGM tree in [31] does not include the salt, and their implementation results only mention that it

has been implemented "using AES in counter mode". The work of [24] does not have an implementation.

We observe that using the salt only at the leaves, as in [4,9], does not shield the signature from collision attacks. The attack is relatively simple:

- The attacker queries m signatures. Each signature will contain some number τ of $\lceil \log_2 n \rceil$-tuples of intermediate PRG evaluations (corresponding to the seeds on co-path to the unopened leave; τ corresponds to the number of repetitions of the underlying identification scheme). Let $(\mathsf{seed}^1, \cdots, \mathsf{seed}^k)$ denote all seeds received this way, where $k = m \cdot \tau \cdot \lceil \log_2 n \rceil$.
- The attacker locally samples random seeds seed and evaluates its two children $(\mathsf{seed}_0, \mathsf{seed}_1) \leftarrow_r \mathsf{PRG}(\mathsf{seed})$, until one of the seed_b collides with some seed^i.
- Since it knows the preimage of seed_b, it recovers the parent seed of seed^i, from which it can compute the seed associated with the unopened leave in one of the signatures.
- Given this seed, and using the salt salt associated to the signature (which is public), the attacker reconstructs all virtual parties' shares, and reconstructs the secret witness (the AES secret key in [9], the syndrome decoding solution in [4]. Using the witness, the attacker can now forge arbitrary signatures.

As should be clear from the above description, we note that adding salt to the leaves has absolutely *no* effect on the security of the signature against this collision attack. Efficiency-wise, after receiving m signatures, the attacker finds a collision in time $2^\lambda / (m \cdot \tau \cdot \lceil \log_2 n \rceil)$. For example, using $\lambda = 128$, $n = 2^{16}$, and $\tau = 9$ (this is a parameter set from [4]), after seeing only $m = 2^{40}$ signatures, the attacker can break the scheme in time $\approx 2^{69}$.

3.2 On the Efficiency of Salted GGM Trees

We believe that the attack pointed above is mostly an issue of the presentation in the respective papers, and that the authors are generally aware of this issue. For example, we observe that the implementation of Banquet[3] correctly fixes the issue, by adding salt within all intermediate computations of the tree. As for [4], while their original implementation suffers from the attack above, the authors recently included their scheme in a NIST submission [3] whose implementation properly deals with this issue. However, the state of affairs remains quite unsatisfying on the *efficiency* front: unsalted GGM trees can be instantiated very efficiently using fixed-key AES [36], which enables the use of Intel's AES-NI instruction set. Unfortunately, the fixed block size of AES makes it hard to add salt. And indeed, existing implementations such as Picnic [25], BBQ [29], Banquet [9], and the recent NIST submissions based on [4], all implement the PRG using a hash function (such as SHAKE), as follows: $\mathsf{seed}_b \leftarrow H(\mathsf{seed}\|i\|j\|b\|\mathsf{salt})$, where i is the index of the parent node, and $j \leq \tau$ is a counter for the repetitions of the identification scheme. Unfortunately, because of the hardware support for

---

[3] https://github.com/dkales/banquet.

AES, replacing AES with a hash function is up to 50× slower. This is especially problematic in recent protocols that use the hypercube technique [4], where the cost of generating the tree dominates the signing time.

3.3   A Fast Salted GGM Tree in the Ideal Cipher Model

We now turn to our contribution: we introduce a new construction of salted GGM tree which matches the efficiency of the fastest *unsalted* GGM trees, but which yields much stronger security guarantees. We provide formal security proof that our new construction is a *multi-instance secure* PPRF, a notion that we introduce. Multi-instance PPRFs can be used as a drop-in replacement for PPRFs in MPCitH signatures. In contrast with standard PPRFs, whose use incurs a security loss proportional to the number of signature queries (as illustrated by our attack), the unforgeability of MPCitH signatures tightly reduces to the multi-instance security of the PPRF.

In essence, our multi-instance PPRF is based on a very simple idea: use the previous top-performing GGM construction from a fixed-key block-cipher, and *use the cipher key as the salt*. While the intuition is very natural, formally proving security is actually quite challenging. Our full proof of security, in the ideal cipher model, is one of the core technical contributions of this work. It relies on the H-coefficient technique of Patarin [26,42] and combines it with a balls-and-bins analysis to measure the number of seed and cipher key collisions, and tightly estimate their impact on security.

Starting Point: a PPRF in the Random Permutation Model. Our starting point is a PPRF construction from [36]. The construction of [36] is a tweak on the original GGM construction, where the PRG is instantiated with the following "Davies-Meyer" function.

$$G : x \rightarrow (\pi_0(x) \oplus x, \pi_1(x) \oplus x).$$

In this construction, (π_0, π_1) are two fixed pseudorandom permutations. Using this PRG, the construction of PPRF proceeds in a tree-based fashion: sample a PPRF key $K \leftarrow_r \{0,1\}^\lambda$. On input $x = (x_1, \cdots, x_n)$, the PPRF F_K returns $G_{x_n}(G_{x_{n-1}}(\cdots G_{x_1}(K)\cdots))$, where G_0, G_1 denote the left and right half of the output of G, respectively. Puncturing x is done by computing all values on the co-path to x in the tree, *i.e.*, the values $G_{\bar{x}_i}(G_{x_{i-1}}(\cdots G_{x_1}(K)\cdots)$ for $i = 2$ to n: knowing the values on the co-path allows reconstructing the entire tree except for $F_K(x)$, whose values are pseudorandom under the security of G. To prove the security of the construction, the authors of [36] rely on the *random permutation model*, where (π_0, π_1) are modeled as two independent random permutations.

In [36], the motivation for introducing the construction is that in practice, π_0, π_1 can be instantiated using the AES block cipher with two fixed keys (K_0, K_1). This allows to evaluate G using two calls to AES, which is extremely fast using the AES-NI hardware instruction set (encrypting with AES using AES-NI takes as little as *1.3 cycle per Byte* according to [41]). Furthermore, the entire construction requires only two executions of the AES key schedule. This GGM construction is to date, by a significant margin, the fastest known PPRF, and it has been featured extensively in recent works on functions secret sharing [13,19–21,34], pseudorandom correlation generators [14–18,27,46,48], and many more. It is also the construction suggested in [4], though as we saw above it is insecure in the context of signatures.

Observing that this fast PPRF construction is typically instantiated using a block cipher suggests the following idea, which is very natural in retrospect: use the above construction, but instantiate (π_0, π_1) using a block cipher (such as AES) and *use the block cipher keys* (K_0, K_1) *as a random salt*. This means that in each instance, the pair (K_0, K_1) will be sampled at random. When using AES, this changes nothing to the efficiency of the construction, since in each instance, one still only has to execute the AES key schedule twice. Yet, now, there is some hope that the use of fresh cipher keys in distinct instances can prevent the collision attack.

Multi-instance PPRF and PRGs. To formalize this idea, we introduce the primitive of multi-instance PPRF. At a high level, we define an N-instance PPRF as a PPRF that additionally takes as input a random salt. In the N-instance security game, N keys $(k_1, \cdots, k_N)$, inputs $(x_1, \cdots, x_N)$, and salts $(\mathsf{salt}_1, \cdots, \mathsf{salt}_N)$ are sampled randomly. The game also samples a bit $b \leftarrow_r \{0, 1\}$. Then, the adversary receives $((x_1, \mathsf{salt}_1), \cdots, (x_N, \mathsf{salt}_N))$ and the N punctured keys $(k_1\{x_1\}, \cdots, k_N\{x_N\})$. If $b = 0$, the adversary additionally receives $(F_k(x_1, \mathsf{salt}_1), \cdots, F_K(x_N, \mathsf{salt}_N))$; else, if $b = 1$, the adversary receives N random outputs $(y_1, \cdots, y_N)$ instead. The adversary outputs a guess b' and wins if $b' = b$. The PPRF is said to be N-instance (t, ε)-secure if the advantage of any t-time adversary in this game is at most ε. Since our constructions use τ parallel calls to a PPRF with the same salt, we generalize the notion to (N, τ)-instance security to capture the setting where N instances of τ repetitions of a PPRF are used, where the salt differ across instances, but not across internal repetitions.

As a first step toward proving the security of our construction, we also introduce the similar (but simpler) notion of (N, τ)-instance (t, ε)-secure PRG, which is a PRG $G : (\mathsf{seed}, \mathsf{salt}) \to (G_0(\mathsf{seed}, \mathsf{salt}), G_1(\mathsf{seed}, \mathsf{salt}))$ that additionally takes some random salt. In the N-instance security game, the adversary attempts to distinguish $(G_0(\mathsf{seed}_i, \mathsf{salt}_i), G_1(\mathsf{seed}_i, \mathsf{salt}_i))_{i \leq N}$ from random given the salts $(\mathsf{salt}_1, \cdots, \mathsf{salt}_N)$ (the game extends to (N, τ)-instance security in a straightforward way, but the description is more tedious). We show that the standard GGM reduction extends to the multi-input setting: an (N, τ)-input (t, ε)-secure PRG implies an (N, τ)-input $(t, D \cdot \varepsilon)$-secure PPRF on input domain $[2^D]$ via a straightforward sequence of hybrids.

A Multi-instance PRG in the Ideal Cipher Model. The crux of the analysis is then to show that our PRG is indeed (N, τ)-instance (t, ε)-secure (for a suitable choice of N, τ, t, ε). Since the PRG now explicitly uses a block cipher, we cannot rely on the random permutation model anymore; instead, we prove security in the *ideal cipher model*, where each key $K \in \{0,1\}^\lambda$ defines a truly random permutation π_K, and all parties are given oracle access to π_K and π_K^{-1} for all K (we measure the running time t of the attacker as its number of queries q to the oracles). Using the H-coefficient technique of Patarin, we formally prove that our construction is an (N, τ)-instance (q, ε)-secure PRG for any N up to $2^{\lambda-1}$, with $\varepsilon \leq \frac{4\tau \cdot \lambda}{\ln \lambda} \cdot \frac{q}{2^\lambda}$, where the term $4\tau\lambda/\ln \lambda$ can be replaced by 8τ when $N \leq 2^{\lambda/2}$ (the above inequality is an approximation, see Theorem 7 for the formal inequality). Our analysis is non-trivial, and the bound stems from a careful analysis of the influence of the number of collisions among seeds on the adversarial advantage. We show that this number can be bounded using standard lemmas on the maximum load of a bin when $2N$ balls are thrown into 2^λ bins.

Concretely, this means that one can use our new multi-instance PPRF construction as a drop-in replacement for previous (much slower) hash-based construction, at the (small) cost of a security loss of $4\tau D\lambda/\ln \lambda$ (or simply $8\tau D$ when we bound the number of signature queries by $2^{\lambda/2}$). For $D = 16$, $\tau = 8$, and $\lambda = 128$, this translates to a loss of 14 bits of security (when the number of queries is up to 2^{127}) or 10 bits of security (for up to 2^{64} queries). Furthermore, we can reduce this loss to 8 bits at the (mild) cost of only guaranteeing that the *expected* runtime of the adversary is above 2^λ.

Additionally, we introduce an optimization that converts (N, τ)-instance (t, ε)-secure PRG to $(\tau \cdot N, 1)$-instance (t, ε)-secure by using a pseudorandom generator to sample the τ salts $(\mathsf{salt}^{i,e})_{e \leq \tau}$ in a given instance from a global salt salt_i for each $i \leq N$. This shaves a factor τ from security loss, which is reduced to 5 bits for $D = 16, \tau = 8, \lambda = 128$. We believe that this is a very reasonable tradeoff in exchange for the benefits of using a much faster AES-based construction. Eventually, we suggest a final optimization that further reduces the security loss to 3 bits (independently of D): using a pseudorandom generator to generate $(\tau \cdot D)$ salts $(\mathsf{salt}^{i,e})_{e \leq \tau, i \leq D}$ from a global salt salt, and evaluating each *level* of each GGM tree with a different salt. Now all salts are sampled randomly, it leads to collisions among $(\mathsf{salt}^{i,e}, \mathsf{seed}^{i,e})_{e \leq \tau, i \leq N}$ happening with a negligible probability. We conjecture that this variant can be proven secure with only 1 bit of loss in the ideal cipher model. Under the hood, we expect the proof of this conjecture to be similar to the proof of our multi-instances PRG based on the H-coefficient technique, however, it requires a considerably more cumbersome direct analysis of the full multi-instance PPRF in the ideal cipher model (without reducing it first to a multi-instance PRG, which is a much simpler object). We leave proving this last conjecture for future work.

4 Technical Overview: New Signature from RSD

We now move to our second main contribution, a new signature scheme from the regular syndrome decoding assumption. We start with a brief high-level overview of the RSD-based signature scheme from [24], since it serves as a starting point for our scheme. Let $H \in \mathbb{F}_2^{k \times K}$ be a matrix and $\mathbf{x} \in \mathbb{F}_2^K$ be a w-regular vector (*i.e.*, a concatenation of w unit vectors). We let $\mathsf{bs} \leftarrow K/w$ denote the *block size* of $\mathbf{x}$. The signature builds upon an efficient n-party protocol which, on input shares of $\mathbf{x}$, checks that (1) $\mathbf{x}$ is a regular vector, and (2) $H \cdot \mathbf{x} = \mathbf{y}$. This n-party protocol is then compiled into a zero-knowledge proof via the MPC-in-the-head paradigm (which we sometimes abbreviate MPCitH), and the proof is further compiled into a signature scheme via Fiat-Shamir. The main idea underlying the protocol of [24] is that each of (1) and (2) above can be checked very efficiently, provided that the parties are given a suitable sharing of $\mathbf{x}$ in each case:

- Given (entry-wise) shares of $\mathbf{x}$ over $\mathbb{Z}_{\mathsf{bs}}$, checking that a block of coordinates $x_1, \cdots, x_{\mathsf{bs}}$ has weight 1 boils down to checking that $\sum_{i=1}^{\mathsf{bs}} x_i = 1 \bmod \mathsf{bs}$, which is a linear equation over $\mathbb{Z}_{\mathsf{bs}}$.
- Given shares of $\mathbf{x}$ over $\mathbb{F}_2$, checking $H \cdot \mathbf{x} = \mathbf{y}$ simply amounts to checking a linear equation over $\mathbb{F}_2$.

Since in the MPC-in-the-head paradigm, checking linear equations is for free, the task of building the protocol reduces to the task of designing a *sharing conversion* protocol, which converts $\mathbb{F}_2$-shares of $\mathbf{x}$ into $\mathbb{Z}_{\mathsf{bs}}$-shares. The next observation of [24] is that converting shares mod-2 of some value x into shares mod-bs can be done very efficiently given precomputed shares mod-2 and mod-bs of the same random bit r, which the prover can generate by themselves. The only missing ingredient is a mechanism to ensure that the prover honestly computes mod-2/mod-bs pairs of the *same* identical random bit. The last, and most involved, observation of [24] is that the verifier can completely dispense with the need to perform this check, by picking a random permutation π of $[K]$ and instructing the prover to shuffle the pairs according to π before running the protocol. Using a careful and non-trivial combinatorial analysis, [24] showed that whenever $\mathbf{x}$ is sufficiently far from being a regular vector (meaning that it has many non-unit blocks), a malicious prover using $\mathbf{x}$ has negligible success probability over the choice of π, even if they use incorrect mod-2/mod-bs pairs. Of course, this does not prevent a malicious prover from using an incorrect but close-to-regular witness. However, by choosing the parameters (K, k, w) in a highly injective setting it can be guaranteed that the *only* close-to-regular solution to $H \cdot \mathbf{x} = \mathbf{y}$ is a regular vector.

4.1 An Alternative Share-Conversion Approach

The approach of [24] yields a competitive signature scheme, but has its shortcomings. Its main efficiency bottleneck stems from the use of shares over $\mathbb{Z}_{\mathsf{bs}}$: because of that, the signature includes several (one for each of the τ repetitions of the basic proof) length-K vectors over $\mathbb{Z}_{\mathsf{bs}}$ (using a CRT trick, this can be reduced to $\mathbb{Z}_{\mathsf{bs}/2}$ whenever $\mathsf{bs}/2$ is odd and ≥ 3). This yields a $O(K \cdot \mathsf{bs})$ communication cost, which is (by a significant margin) the dominant cost of their protocol. To mitigate this cost, the authors set the block size bs to be the smallest possible value $\mathsf{bs} = 6$ (such that $\mathsf{bs}/2 = 3$). In turn, this forces them to rely on RSD with very high weight $w = K/6$, which requires significantly increasing the parameters to compensate for the security loss.

Our first observation is that all of these shortcomings can be eliminated at once by relying on an alternative share conversion approach. Because $\mathbf{x}$ is w-regular, it admits a compressed representation as a list of w integers in $[\mathsf{bs}]$, which indicates the position of the nonzero entry in each of the w unit vectors. Now, observe that if the parties hold shares of w integers $(i_1, \cdots, i_w)$ modulo bs, these can always be interpreted as representing some regular vector $\mathbf{x}$; in other words, given such shares, condition (1) is satisfied by default. The crux of our protocol is a conversion procedure that turns shares of this compressed representation into shares modulo 2 of the "decompressed" regular vector (with which the parties can check the linear equation $H \cdot \mathbf{x} = \mathbf{y}$ for free). Furthermore, this share conversion can again be implemented very efficiently if the parties are given shares of pairs of the same random unit vector in compressed representation and in standard representation. Concretely, given an integer $r \in [\mathsf{bs}]$, let $\mathbf{e}_r$ denote the length-bs unit vector with a 1 at position r. Assume that the n parties, holding shares of some $i \in [\mathsf{bs}]$, are given shares of r modulo bs, and shares of $\mathbf{e}_r$ over $\mathbb{F}_2$. Consider the following simple protocol:

- All parties broadcast their shares of $z = i - r \bmod \mathsf{bs}$ and reconstruct z.
- All parties locally shift cyclically their share of $\mathbf{e}_r$ by z.

After this protocol, all parties end up with shares of the vector $\mathbf{e}_r$ shifted by z, which we denote $\mathbf{e}_r \downarrow z$ (we view vectors as columns, hence the shift by z is downward). Observe that $\mathbf{e}_r \downarrow z = \mathbf{e}_r \downarrow (i - r) = (\mathbf{e}_r \uparrow r) \downarrow i = \mathbf{e}_{\mathsf{bs}} \downarrow i = \mathbf{e}_i$. As in [24], we will let the prover generate w random pairs $(r, \mathbf{e}_r)$ and share them between the virtual parties. To dispense with the need to check that the pairs were honestly generated, we rely on the same strategy and let the verifier sample a random permutation π of $[w]$, and instruct the prover to shuffle the pairs according to π before using them in the protocol. The high-level structure of the MPCitH compiled zero knowledge proof (without optimizations) is below:

- **Parameters and input:** let (K, k, w) be parameters for the syndrome decoding problem, and let $\mathsf{bs} \leftarrow K/w$. The prover holds a w-regular witness $\mathbf{x} \in [\mathsf{bs}]^w$ (in compressed representation) for the relation $H \cdot \mathbf{x} = \mathbf{y}$, where $H \in \mathbb{F}_2^{k \times K}$ and $\mathbf{y} \in \mathbb{F}_2^k$ are public. Let n be the number of virtual parties.
- **Round 1:** the prover samples w pairs $(r_i, \mathbf{e}_{r_i})$ where $r_i \leftarrow_r [\mathsf{bs}]$. We denote $(\mathbf{r}, \mathbf{e}_\mathbf{r})$ the vector of pairs. The prover generates n shares of $\mathbf{e}_\mathbf{r}$ (over $\mathbb{F}_2$) and of $\mathbf{x}, \mathbf{r}$ (modulo bs) distributed between the virtual parties, and commits to the local state of each party.
- **Round 2:** the verifier samples and sends to the prover a random permutation $\pi \leftarrow_r \mathsf{Perm}(w)$. We write $\pi(\mathbf{r})$ (resp. $\pi(\mathbf{e}_\mathbf{r})$) for the vector $(r_{\pi(1)}, \cdots, r_{\pi(w)})$ (resp. $(\mathbf{e}_{r_{\pi(1)}}, \cdots, \mathbf{e}_{r_{\pi(w)}})$).
- **Round 3:** the prover runs in their head the following protocol and commits to the views of all parties:
  - All parties reconstruct $\mathbf{z} = \mathbf{x} - \pi(\mathbf{r})$ and shift their shares of $\pi(\mathbf{e}_\mathbf{r})$, getting shares of $\pi(\mathbf{e}_\mathbf{r}) \downarrow \mathbf{z}$ (the shifting is done blockwise: each $\mathbf{e}_{r_{\pi(i)}}$ is cyclically shifted by z_i). Note that $\pi(\mathbf{e}_\mathbf{r}) \downarrow \mathbf{z} = \mathbf{e}_\mathbf{x}$ (i.e. the "uncompressed" representation of the witness $\mathbf{x}$).

– All parties compute a share of $H \cdot (\pi(\mathbf{e_r}) \downarrow \mathbf{z})$ and broadcast them. All parties check that the shares reconstruct to $\mathbf{y}$.
– **Round 4:** the verifier picks $i \leftarrow_r [n]$ and challenges the prover to open the views of all parties except i.
– **Round 5:** the prover sends the $n - 1$ openings to the verifier, who checks that the views are consistent with the commitments, with each other, and with the output of the protocol being $\mathbf{y}$.

The soundness of the scheme is $\varepsilon = \mathsf{p} + (1/n) \cdot (1 - \mathsf{p})$, where $\mathsf{p} = \mathsf{p}(K, k, w)$ is an upper bound on the probability (over the choice of the random permutation π) that a cheating prover, that commits in the first round to an incorrect witness (*i.e.* a compressed vector $\mathbf{x}^*$ such that $H \cdot \mathbf{e_{x^*}} \neq \mathbf{y}$), manages to generate a valid MPC transcript (*i.e.* finds—possibly incorrect—pairs $(\mathbf{r}, \mathbf{u})$ such that $H \cdot (\pi(\mathbf{u}) \downarrow \mathbf{z}) = \mathbf{y}$, where $\mathbf{z} = \mathbf{x}^* - \pi(\mathbf{r})$). The crux of our analysis lies in computing a tight evaluation of p.

In our final signature, we incorporate multiple optimizations on top of this basic template, including the usual optimization of generating the shares in a tree-based fashion using the GGM puncturable pseudorandom function [12,22, 35,39], but also the more recent hypercube technique from [4], and a number of additional optimizations tailored to our scheme.

In terms of signature size, the dominant cost stems from the size of a share of $\mathbf{x}$ and of w pairs $(r, \mathbf{e}_r)$ (using standard optimizations, all shares except one can be compressed, hence the communication is dominated by the size of a single share, ignoring for now the number of repetitions of the identification scheme). The size of a share of $\mathbf{x}$ together with w pairs $(r, \mathbf{e}_r)$ is $2w \log \mathsf{bs} + K$ bits[4], whereas the size of $\mathbf{x}$ (now shared as a vector over $\mathbb{F}_2^K$) and of the pairs in [24] is $K \cdot (2 + \mathsf{bs}/2)$ bits. This directly incurs a significant reduction in the signature size. Furthermore, with this alternative conversion, using a very small block size is not advantageous anymore, which allows us to explore a much wider range of parameters, resulting in further savings.

4.2 Combinatorial Analysis

Although the high-level strategy—shuffling the random pairs—is the same as in [24], the security analysis is *entirely* different and forms a core technical contribution of our work. Shuffling the prover-generated correlated randomness is a highly non-generic technique, where each new protocol requires a new and dedicated combinatorial analysis.[5] The crux of the proof lies in bounding the success probability of a cheating adversary $\mathcal{A}$ in the following game:

– $\mathcal{A}$ holds a vector $\mathbf{x}^* \in [\mathsf{bs}]^w$ and chooses $\mathbf{r} \in [\mathsf{bs}]^w$ and $\mathbf{u} \in \mathbb{F}_2^K$, such that $\mathbf{u}$ is *not* a regular vector.

---

[4] As in [24], this number is multiplied by a number τ of repetition, but since it is the same in both works, we ignore it in this discussion for simplicity.
[5] To give a sense of how specific the analysis of [24] was, not only does it work only for their type of pairs: it works exclusively for $\mathsf{bs} = 6$, corresponding to pairs of bits shared modulo 2 and modulo 3.

- A uniformly random permutation π is sampled from $\mathsf{Perm}(w)$.
- $\mathcal{A}$ wins iff $H \cdot (\pi(\mathbf{u}) \downarrow (\mathbf{x}^* - \pi(\mathbf{r}) \bmod \mathsf{bs})) = \mathbf{y}$.

Given a bound on $\mathcal{A}$'s winning probability in this game, the rest of the proof follows in a relatively standard way and is similar to previous security proofs of code-based signatures schemes in the MPCitH paradigm, such as [24] (we still provide a full proof in the paper for completeness). Above, note that for any vector $\mathbf{s} \in [\mathsf{bs}]^w$, $\pi(\mathbf{u}) \downarrow \mathbf{s}$ is a regular vector if and only if $\mathbf{u}$ is a regular vector. Note also that whether $\mathbf{x}^*$ is actually a correct witness or not (*i.e.* whether $H \cdot \mathbf{e}_{\mathbf{x}^*}$) does not matter: as long as $\mathbf{u}$ is regular, if $\mathcal{A}$ wins the game above, then an extractor can recover a valid regular solution $\pi(\mathbf{u}) \downarrow (\mathbf{x}^* + \mathbf{r} \bmod \mathsf{bs})$ to the syndrome decoding problem (hence $\mathcal{A}$ "knew" a solution to the problem in the first place). Eventually, note that

$$\pi(\mathbf{u}) \downarrow (\mathbf{x}^* - \pi(\mathbf{r}) \bmod \mathsf{bs}) = \pi(\mathbf{u} \uparrow \mathbf{r}) \downarrow \mathbf{x}^*,$$

hence, the game above simplifies to the following: $\mathcal{A}$ chooses $\mathbf{x}^* \in [\mathsf{bs}]^w$ and $\mathbf{u} \in \mathbb{F}_2^K \setminus \mathsf{Reg}_w$, and wins iff $H \cdot (\pi(\mathbf{u}) \downarrow \mathbf{x}^*) = \mathbf{y}$ holds over the choice of a random permutation π.

Eliminating Spurious Solutions. An immediate issue with the above game is that an adversary *might* win with a very high probability, if the system of equations $H \cdot \mathbf{x} = \mathbf{y}$ admits solutions that are mostly invariant by blockwise permutation. Concretely, assume that there exists a vector $\mathbf{u}^*$ which satisfies $H \cdot \mathbf{u}^* = \mathbf{y}$, and such that $\mathbf{u}^*$ is not a regular vector, yet $\mathbf{v}^*$ is a concatenation of w *identical* vectors from $\mathbb{F}_2^{\mathsf{bs}}$. If this happens, then there is an easy winning strategy: $\mathcal{A}$ sets $\mathbf{u} \leftarrow \mathbf{u}^*$ and $\mathbf{x}^* \leftarrow 0^w$. Since $H \cdot (\pi(\mathbf{u}) \downarrow \mathbf{x}^*) = H \cdot \pi(\mathbf{u}) = H \cdot \mathbf{u}^* = \mathbf{y}$, $\mathcal{A}$ is guaranteed to win. More generally, if $H \cdot \mathbf{x} = \mathbf{y}$ admits a solution $\mathbf{u}$ whose blocks are *mostly* identical, then the equation $H \cdot \pi(\mathbf{u}^*) = \mathbf{y}$ has a relatively large chance to hold simply because $\pi(\mathbf{u}^*)$ has a relatively large chance to be equal to $\mathbf{u}^*$.

Setting up Some Notations. Given a vector $\mathbf{u}$, we let $\mathsf{pn}(\mathbf{u})$ denote $|\{\pi(\mathbf{u}) \mid \pi \in \mathsf{Perm}([w])\}|$. That is, $\mathsf{pn}(\mathbf{u})$ is the number of distinct vectors in $\mathbb{F}_2^K$ which can be obtained by shuffling $\mathbf{u}$ blockwise; we call $\mathsf{pn}(\mathbf{u})$ the *permutation number* of $\mathbf{u}$. Then, given a bound B, we define $\mathsf{PN}_B = \{\mathbf{u} \mid \mathsf{pn}(\mathbf{u}) > B\}$, the set of vectors with a large permutation number. We let X denote the set $\{\mathbf{v} \in \mathbb{F}_2^K : \exists \mathbf{u} \in \mathbb{F}_2^K \setminus \mathsf{PN}_B, \exists \mathbf{x}^* \in [\mathsf{bs}]^w, \mathbf{v} = \mathbf{u} \downarrow \mathbf{x}^*\}$. The set X captures exactly the possible spurious solutions: it contains the vectors $\mathbf{v}$ such that there exists some choice of the shift $\mathbf{x}^*$ such that $\mathbf{v} \uparrow \mathbf{x}^*$ has a small permutation number ($\mathsf{pn}(\mathbf{v} \uparrow \mathbf{x}^*) \leq B$). Denoting $\mathsf{Ker}(H) \oplus \mathbf{y}$ the solutions to $H \cdot \mathbf{x} = \mathbf{y}$, if there is a vector $\mathbf{v} \in X \cap \mathsf{Ker}(H) \oplus \mathbf{y}$, then $\mathcal{A}$ can pick $\mathbf{u}, \mathbf{x}^*$ such that $\mathbf{v} = \mathbf{u} \downarrow \mathbf{x}^*$ with $\mathsf{pn}(\mathbf{u}) \leq B$. This guarantees that with probability at least $1/B$, a random permutation π will satisfy $\pi(\mathbf{u}) = \mathbf{u}$, hence $H \cdot (\pi(\mathbf{u}) \downarrow \mathbf{x}^*) = H \cdot (\mathbf{u} \downarrow \mathbf{x}^*) = H \cdot \mathbf{v} = \mathbf{y}$.

D. Bui et al.

Sampling Highly-Injective Instances. Fix some bound B. To eliminate spurious solutions in X, which an adversary could use to win with probability at least $1/B$, we choose parameters (K, k, w) such that when sampling the regular syndrome decoding instance $(H, \mathbf{y} = H \cdot \mathbf{x})$ (for some $\mathbf{x} \in \mathsf{Reg}_w$), it holds with probability $1 - 1/2^\lambda$, the *only* element of X that also belongs to $\mathsf{Ker}(H) \oplus \mathbf{y}$ is the w-regular solution $\mathbf{x}$. It follows from a standard analysis that this is the case as soon as $\log_2 k \geq \log_2 |X| + \lambda$. To select k, we therefore compute a tight upper bound on $|X|$ (see Lemma 24 of [23]). Counting the number of elements of X is not entirely straightforward due to the fact that we count "up to some blockwise shift", but a closed formula can be established using known bounds for counting k-necklaces (*i.e.* bitstrings counted up to cyclic shifts) by leveraging Pólya's enumeration theorem [43]. Given the formula, we use a short Python program to compute explicitly the bound on $|X|$ and select a suitable parameter k (for a fixed choice of K, w). This also faces some challenges: the formula in Lemma 24 of [23] requires summing binomial coefficients over all *integer partitions* of the weight parameter w (*i.e.*, the number of tuples of distinct positive integers that sum to w). Because w is around 120, its number of integer partitions is too large to simply enumerate. With some careful considerations, we observe that many of these partitions can be eliminated from the counting procedure and leverage this observation to reduce the runtime of the program.

Bounding the Success Probability. We now turn to the crux of the analysis: showing that if $\mathcal{A}$ picks $(\mathbf{u}, \mathbf{x}^*)$ where $\mathsf{pn}(\mathbf{u}) > B$, then their probability of winning the game is at most $O(1/B)$ over the choice of the permutation π. What makes the analysis challenging is that in principle, it could be that some vector $\mathbf{u}$ has a high permutation number, yet *many of its permutations belong to* $\mathsf{Ker}(H) \oplus \mathbf{y}$. The core technical component of the analysis is a proof that with very high probability over the choice of a random syndrome decoding instance $(H, \mathbf{y})$, it will simultaneously hold for *all* vectors $\mathbf{u}$ with $\mathsf{pn}(\mathbf{u}) > B$ that for any choice of shift $\mathbf{x}^*$, $\Pr_\pi[H \cdot (\pi(\mathbf{u}) \downarrow \mathbf{x}^*) = \mathbf{y}] \leq 4/B$. To state the result formally, we define "good" syndrome decoding instances below:

Definition 2 (GOOD_B). *Given a bound B, GOOD_B is defined as the set of syndrome decoding instances $(H, \mathbf{y}) \in \mathbb{F}_2^{k \times K} \times \mathbb{F}_2^k$ such that for every $\mathbf{u} \in \mathsf{PN}_B \setminus \mathsf{Reg}_w$ and for all $\mathbf{x}^* \in [\mathsf{bs}]^w$, $\Pr_{\pi \leftarrow_r \mathsf{Perm}_w}[H \cdot (\pi(\mathbf{u}) \downarrow \mathbf{x}^*) = \mathbf{y}] \leq 4/B$.*

Our main technical result of the analysis is stated below:

Lemma 3 (Most syndrome decoding instances are good).

$$\Pr_{H, \mathbf{y}}[(H, \mathbf{y}) \in \mathsf{GOOD}_B] > 1 - \binom{2B}{5} \cdot \frac{2^{K+1}}{B \cdot 2^{3k}} \cdot \left(10 + \frac{(K/w)^w}{2^k}\right).$$

To parse the above, the reader can consider that $(K/w)^w \ll 2^k$ will hold for our selection of parameters, hence the probability that $(H, \mathbf{y}) \in \mathsf{GOOD}_B$ is of the order of $1 - B^4 \cdot 2^{K - 3 \cdot k}$. For concreteness, the reader can think of K as being around 1550, k as being around 820, w being around 200, and B being around 70, resulting in the above being around $1 - 2^{-630}$.

Key Intuition. We outline the main idea of the proof. Given a vector $\mathbf{u}$ with $\mathsf{pn}(\mathbf{u}) = N$, fix some ordering $\mathbf{u}^{(1)}, \cdots, \mathbf{u}^{(N)}$ of its distinct blockwise permutations, and let $\mathbf{x}^* \in [\mathsf{bs}]^w$ denote some shift. Sample a random matrix $H \leftarrow_r \mathbb{F}_2^{k \times K}$, a random regular vector $\mathbf{x} \leftarrow_r \mathsf{Reg}_w$, and set $\mathbf{y} \leftarrow H \cdot \mathbf{x}$. Let $(\mathbf{v}_1, \cdots, \mathbf{v}_N) \leftarrow ((\mathbf{u}^{(1)} \downarrow \mathbf{x}^*) \oplus \mathbf{x}, \cdots, (\mathbf{u}^{(N)} \downarrow \mathbf{x}^*) \oplus \mathbf{x})$ (note that $H \cdot \mathbf{v}_i = 0$ iff $H \cdot (\mathbf{u}^{(i)} \downarrow \mathbf{x}^*) = \mathbf{y}$). Observe that the $\mathbf{v}_i$ are random variables, but they are set independently of H (since $\mathbf{x}$ is sampled independently from H). Then, for any subset S of t *linearly independent* vectors $\mathbf{v}_i$, it holds that

$$\Pr_{H \leftarrow_r \mathbb{F}_2^{k \times K}} [H \cdot \mathbf{v}_i = 0 \text{ for all } i \in S] = 2^{-k \cdot t}.$$

In other words, whenever the $\mathbf{v}_i$'s are linearly independent, the binary random variables X_i equal to 1 if $H \cdot \mathbf{v}_i = 0$ are independent. Building upon this observation, we show the following: fix an arbitrary subset S of five indices. Then

- S contains a size-3 linearly independent subset with probability 1, and
- S contains a size-4 linearly independent subset, except with probability at most $10 \cdot (K/w)^{-w}$.

Together with the previous bound on the probability that $H \cdot \mathbf{v}_i = 0$ for linearly independent vectors, this yields a probability bound of $10 \cdot (K/w)^{-w}/2^{3 \cdot k} + 1/2^{4 \cdot k}$ that $H \cdot \mathbf{v}_i = 0$ for all $i \in S$. To see why this bound holds, observe that:

- The $\mathbf{v}_i$ are pairwise distinct and nonzero by construction (because $\mathbf{u}$ is assumed to be nonregular, so $\pi(\mathbf{u}) \downarrow \mathbf{x}^*$ is never $\mathbf{0}$, and the $\mathbf{u}^{(i)}$ are distinct by definition).
- If e.g. $(\mathbf{v}_1, \mathbf{v}_2, \mathbf{v}_3)$ are linearly dependent, they therefore need to satisfy $\mathbf{v}_1 \oplus \mathbf{v}_2 \oplus \mathbf{v}_3 = \mathbf{0}$. But then, $\mathbf{v}_1 \oplus \mathbf{v}_2 \oplus \mathbf{v}_4 \neq \mathbf{0}$ (otherwise, we would have $\mathbf{v}_3 = \mathbf{v}_4$, contradicting the fact that the vectors are pairwise distinct). Hence, we are guaranteed to find a size-3 independent subset of vectors in S.
- By the same reasoning, S contains necessarily a 4-tuple of $\mathbf{v}_i$'s that does not XOR to 0, say, $(\mathbf{v}_1, \cdots, \mathbf{v}_4)$ (since if both $(\mathbf{v}_1, \cdots, \mathbf{v}_4)$ and $(\mathbf{v}_1, \cdots, \mathbf{v}_3, \mathbf{v}_5)$ XOR to 0, then $\mathbf{v}_4 = \mathbf{v}_5$). Then, either $(\mathbf{v}_1, \cdots, \mathbf{v}_4)$ is linearly independent (in which case we are done, since we found a 4-independent subset), or it must contain a size-3 subset that XORs to 0.
- For any subset of 3 $\mathbf{v}_i$'s, the probability that they XOR to 0 is at most $(K/w)^{-w}$. This follows from the fact that the $\mathbf{v}_i$'s are equal to $(\mathbf{a} \oplus \mathbf{x}, \mathbf{b} \oplus \mathbf{x}, \mathbf{c} \oplus \mathbf{x})$ for some *fixed* vectors $(\mathbf{a}, \mathbf{b}, \mathbf{c})$, and a uniformly random regular vector $\mathbf{x} \in [\mathsf{bs}]^w$. But then, $\mathbf{v}_1 \oplus \mathbf{v}_2 \oplus \mathbf{v}_3 = 0$ rewrites to $\mathbf{a} \oplus \mathbf{b} \oplus \mathbf{c} = \mathbf{x}$, which happens with probability at most $\mathsf{bs}^{-w} = (K/w)^{-w}$ over the choice of $\mathbf{x}$.

Since there are 10 size-3 subsets of S, the bound follows. To summarize, we fixed a vector $\mathbf{u}$ with $\mathsf{pn}(\mathbf{u}) = N > B$ and a shift $\mathbf{x}^*$, and showed that for every size-5 subset S of $[N]$, the probability that $H \cdot (\mathbf{u}^{(i)} \downarrow \mathbf{x}^*) = \mathbf{y}$ holds simultaneously for all $i \in S$ is at most $10 \cdot (K/w)^{-w}/2^{3 \cdot k} + 1/2^{4 \cdot k}$.

A Careful Union Bound. To finish the proof of Lemma 3, it remains to compute a union bound over all possible vectors $\mathbf{u}$, shifts $\mathbf{x}^*$, and size-5 subsets S. However, a quick calculation shows that a naive union bound does not suffice: first, the number of subsets is $\binom{N}{5}$, but since we only know that $N > B$ is the permutation number of $\mathbf{u}$, we can only bound it by $w!$, which is way too large. Second, the number of vectors $\mathbf{u}$ is 2^K, which is also too large for the union bound to yield a nontrivial result.

We overcome this issue by providing a more careful union bound. First, we divide the distinct blockwise permutations of $\mathbf{u}$, $(\mathbf{u}^{(1)}, \cdots, \mathbf{u}^{(N)})$, into size-$B$ blocks of vectors. We apply the previous bound to all size-5 subsets inside each *block* of vectors, which reduces the factor resulting from the union bound to $(N/B) \cdot \binom{B}{5}$. This suffices to guarantee that in each size-B block, at most 4 vectors $\mathbf{v}_i$ can simultaneously satisfy $H \cdot \mathbf{v}_i = 0$, hence guaranteeing a success probability for $\mathcal{A}$ of at most $4/B$ over the random choice of π. Second, instead of enumerating over all vectors $\mathbf{u}$, we enumerate over all *equivalence classes* of vectors $\mathbf{u}$ which generate the same list $(\mathbf{u}^{(1)}, \cdots, \mathbf{u}^{(N)})$. Each equivalence class contains exactly N vectors, and all equivalence classes are disjoint, and we save a factor N this way from the union bound. Eventually, we finish the union bound by summing over all possible values of $N = \mathsf{pn}(\mathbf{u})$ from $B+1$ to $w!$. This finishes the proof of Lemma 3.

5   Multi-instance PPRFs in the Ideal Cipher Model

In this section, we introduce the notion of *multi-instance* puncturable pseudorandom function. We describe an efficient construction from a block cipher, and formally prove its security in the ideal cipher model.

5.1   Defining Multi-instance Puncturable PRF

Pseudorandom functions [35], are families of keyed functions F_k such that no adversary can distinguish between a black-box access to F_k for a random key k and access to a truly random function. A puncturable pseudorandom function (PPRF) [12,22,39] is a PRF F such that given an input x, and a PRF key k, one can generate a *punctured* key, denoted $k\{x\} = F.\mathsf{Punc}(K, x)$, which allows evaluating F at every point except for x (*i.e.*, there is an algorithm $F.\mathsf{Eval}$ such that $F.\mathsf{Eval}(k\{x\}, x') = F_K(x')$ for all $x' \neq x$), and such that $F_k(x)$ is indistinguishable from random given $k\{x\}$. Then,

Definition 4 ((N, τ)-instance (t, ϵ)-secure PPRF). *A function family $F = \{F_K\}$ with input domain $[2^D]$, salt domain $\{0,1\}^s$, and output domain $\{0,1\}^\lambda$, is an (N, τ)-instance (t, ϵ)-secure PPRF if it is a PPRF which additionally takes as input a salt salt, and for every non-uniform PPT distinguisher $\mathcal{D}$ running in time at most t, it holds that for all sufficiently large λ,*

$$\mathsf{Adv}^{\mathsf{PPRF}}(\mathcal{D}) = |\Pr[\mathsf{Exp}_{\mathcal{D}}^{\mathsf{rw}\text{-}\mathsf{pprf}}(\lambda) = 1] - \Pr[\mathsf{Exp}_{\mathcal{D}}^{\mathsf{iw}\text{-}\mathsf{pprf}}(\lambda) = 1]| \leq \epsilon(\lambda)$$

where the experiments $\mathsf{Exp}_{\mathcal{D}}^{\mathsf{rw}\text{-}\mathsf{pprf}}(\lambda)$ and $\mathsf{Exp}_{\mathcal{D}}^{\mathsf{iw}\text{-}\mathsf{pprf}}(\lambda)$ are defined below.

$\mathsf{Exp}_{\mathcal{D}}^{\mathsf{rw\text{-}pprf}}(\lambda):$	$\mathsf{Exp}_{\mathcal{D}}^{\mathsf{iw\text{-}pprf}}(\lambda):$
- $((K_{j,e})_{j\leq N,e\leq\tau}\leftarrow_r (\{0,1\}^\lambda)^{N\cdot\tau}$	- $((K_{j,e})_{j\leq N,e\leq\tau}\leftarrow_r (\{0,1\}^\lambda)^{N\cdot\tau}$
- $\mathsf{salt}:=(\mathsf{salt}_1,\ldots,\mathsf{salt}_N)\leftarrow_r\{0,1\}^s$	- $\mathsf{salt}:=(\mathsf{salt}_1,\ldots,\mathsf{salt}_N)\leftarrow_r\{0,1\}^s$
- $\mathbf{i}:=((i_{1,e})_{e\leq\tau},\ldots,(i_{N,e})_{e\leq\tau})\leftarrow_r[2^D]^{N\cdot\tau}$	- $\mathbf{i}:=((i_{1,e})_{e\leq\tau},\ldots,(i_{1,e})_{e\leq\tau})\leftarrow_r[2^D]^{N\cdot\tau}$
- $\forall j\leq N,e\leq\tau:K_{j,e}^{i_{j,e}}\leftarrow F.\mathsf{Punc}(K_{j,e},i_{j,e})$	- $\forall j\leq N,e\leq\tau:K_{j,e}^{i_{j,e}}\leftarrow F.\mathsf{Punc}(K_{j,e},i_{j,e})$
- $(y_{j,e})_{j\leq N,e\leq\tau}\leftarrow(F_{K_{j,e}}(i_{j,e},\mathsf{salt}_j))_{j\leq N,e\leq\tau}$	- $(y_{j,e})_{j\leq N,e\leq\tau}\leftarrow_r(\{0,1\}^\lambda)^{N\cdot\tau}$
Output $b\leftarrow\mathcal{D}\big(\mathsf{salt},\mathbf{i},(K_{j,e}^{i_{j,e}},y_{j,e})_{j\leq N,e\leq\tau}\big)$	**Output** $b\leftarrow\mathcal{D}\big(\mathsf{salt},\mathbf{i},(K_{j,e}^{i_{j,e}},y_{j,e})_{j\leq N,e\leq\tau}\big)$

The motivation for adding the parameter τ in Definition 4 stems from our use of PPRFs in signatures: our signature construction uses τ parallel instances of the PPRF using the same salt, while distinct salts are used across distinct signature queries.

Furthermore, we observe our actual construction satisfies a stronger property, in which indistinguishability is preserved even the ideal world experiment does not only sample $(y_1,\cdots,y_N)$ uniformly at random, but also samples "fake" punctured keys $K_j^{x_k}$ uniformly at random over an appropriate domain. This stronger notion is not strictly necessary in our signature construction, but its use simplifies the analysis. Below, we state the definition explicitly for the punctured key domain that corresponds to our (GGM-based) construction, but the notion extends naturally to arbitrary domains.

Definition 5 $((N,\tau)$-instance strongly (t,ϵ)-secure PPRF). *A function family $F=\{F_K\}$ with input domain $[2^D]$, salt domain $\{0,1\}^s$, output domain $\{0,1\}^\lambda$, and punctured key domain $(\{0,1\}^\lambda)^D$ is an (N,τ)-instance (t,ϵ)-secure PPRF if it is a PPRF which additionally takes as input a salt salt, and for every non-uniform PPT distinguisher $\mathcal{D}$ running in time at most t, it holds that for all sufficiently large λ,*

$$\mathsf{Adv}^{\mathsf{PPRF}}(\mathcal{D}) - |\Pr[\mathsf{Exp}_{\mathcal{D}}^{\mathsf{rw\text{-}pprf}}(\lambda)=1]-\Pr[\mathsf{Exp}_{\mathcal{D}}^{\mathsf{iw\text{-}spprf}}(\lambda)=1]|\leq\epsilon(\lambda),$$

where the experiment $\mathsf{Exp}_{\mathcal{D}}^{\mathsf{iw\text{-}spprf}}(\lambda)$ is defined as $\mathsf{Exp}_{\mathcal{D}}^{\mathsf{iw\text{-}pprf}}(\lambda)$, except that the line $\forall j\leq N,e\leq\tau:K_{j,e}^{i_{j,e}}\leftarrow F.\mathsf{Punc}(K_{j,e},i_{j,e})$ is replaced by $\forall j\leq N,e\leq\tau:K_{j,e}^{i_{j,e}}\leftarrow_r(\{0,1\}^\lambda)^D$.

5.2 Constructing Multi-instance Puncturable PRFs

In this section, we introduce the notion of (N,τ)-instance (t,ε)-secure pseudorandom generator, which extends the notion of pseudorandom generators to the multi-instance setting (with salt) analogously to our definition of multi-instance PPRFs. Then, we show that the standard GGM construction extends immediately to the multi-instance setting: (length-doubling) (N,τ)-instance (t,ε)-secure PRGs imply (N,τ)-instance strongly $(t,D\cdot\varepsilon)$-secure PPRFs with input domain $[2^D]$ and punctured key domain $(\{0,1\}^\lambda)^D$. We start by defining (N,τ)-instance (t,ϵ)-secure length-doubling PRGs. Below, to interface more easily with the tree-based GGM construction of PPRFs, we use $(\mathsf{F}_0,\mathsf{F}_1)$ to denote functions that compute the left half and right half of the length-doubling PRG output.

Definition 6 ((N, τ)-instance (t, ϵ)-secure PRG). *A PRG PRG $= (\mathsf{F}_0, \mathsf{F}_1)$ with $\mathsf{F}_b : \{0,1\}^{2\lambda} \to \{0,1\}^\lambda$ is an (N, τ)-instance (t, ϵ)-secure length-doubling PRG if for every non-uniform PPT distinguisher $\mathcal{D}$ running in time at most t, it holds that for all sufficiently large λ,*

$$\mathsf{Adv}^{\mathsf{PRG}}(\mathcal{D}) = |\Pr[\mathsf{Exp}_{\mathcal{D}}^{\mathsf{rw\text{-}prg}}(\lambda) = 1] - \Pr[\mathsf{Exp}_{\mathcal{D}}^{\mathsf{iw\text{-}prg}}(\lambda) = 1]| \le \epsilon(\lambda),$$

where $\mathsf{Exp}_{\mathcal{D}}^{\mathsf{rw\text{-}prg}}(\lambda)$ and $\mathsf{Exp}_{\mathcal{D}}^{\mathsf{iw\text{-}prg}}(\lambda)$ are defined below.

$\mathsf{Exp}_{\mathcal{D}}^{\mathsf{rw\text{-}prg}}(\lambda)$:	$\mathsf{Exp}_{\mathcal{D}}^{\mathsf{iw\text{-}prg}}(\lambda)$:
$-$ $(\mathsf{salt}_1, \mathsf{salt}_2, \ldots, \mathsf{salt}_{2N}) \leftarrow_r \{0,1\}^\lambda$ $-$ $(\mathsf{seed}_{i,e})_{i \le N, e \le \tau} \leftarrow_r (\{0,1\}^\lambda)^{N \cdot \tau}$ $-$ $\forall i \le N, e \le \tau :$ $\quad -$ $y_{2i-1,e} \leftarrow \mathsf{F}_0(\mathsf{seed}_{i,e}, \mathsf{salt}_{2i-1})$ $\quad -$ $y_{2i,e} \leftarrow \mathsf{F}_1(\mathsf{seed}_{i,e}, \mathsf{salt}_{2i})$	$-$ $(\mathsf{salt}_1, \mathsf{salt}_2, \ldots, \mathsf{salt}_{2N}) \leftarrow_r \{0,1\}^\lambda$ $-$ $(y_{i,e})_{i \le 2N, e \le \tau} \leftarrow_r (\{0,1\}^\lambda)^{2N \cdot \tau}$
Output $b \leftarrow \mathcal{D}\big((\mathsf{salt}_i, (y_{i,e})_{e \le \tau})_{i \le 2N}\big)$	**Output** $b \leftarrow \mathcal{D}\big((\mathsf{salt}_i, (y_{i,e})_{e \le \tau})_{i \le 2N}\big)$

We note that the definition extends immediately to PRGs that stretch their seeds by a larger factor. We also remark that in the definition above, we assumed that each of F_0 and F_1 takes a distinct λ-bit salt. The definition can be extended to more general salting procedures, but we defined multi-instance PRG with respect to the way we use salt in our actual construction for notational convenience. Looking ahead, the fact that each F_b takes only λ bits of salt is actually a crucial byproduct of our use of block ciphers, and the main reason why the security analysis becomes highly non-trivial.

Now, given a seed $\mathsf{seed} \leftarrow_r \{0,1\}^\lambda$, salt $\mathsf{salt} := (\mathsf{salt}_0, \mathsf{salt}_1) \leftarrow_r \{0,1\}^{2\lambda}$, and a multi-instance secure PRG $\mathsf{F}_0, \mathsf{F}_1 : \{0,1\}^{2\lambda} \to \{0,1\}^\lambda$, we recursively define a PPRF $\mathsf{PPRF}(\mathsf{seed}, \mathsf{salt}) = \mathsf{PPRF}(\mathsf{seed}, \mathsf{salt}, 2^D)$ over input domain $\{0,1\}^D$ (which we later identify with $[2^D]$) in a tree-based fashion as follows:

- The first layer includes two nodes $X_0 := \mathsf{F}_0(\mathsf{seed}, \mathsf{salt}_0)$, $X_1 := \mathsf{F}_1(\mathsf{seed}, \mathsf{salt}_1)$.
- Each layer of the tree is constructed from the nodes of the previous layer similarly, as follows:

$$\mathsf{PPRF}_{\mathsf{seed}}(\mathsf{salt}, i) = \mathsf{F}_{i_D}\left(\mathsf{PPRF}_{\mathsf{seed}}(\mathsf{salt}, i_1, \ldots, i_{D-1}), \mathsf{salt}\right)$$
$$= \mathsf{F}_{i_D}\left(\mathsf{F}_{i_{D-1}}(\ldots(\mathsf{F}_{i_1}(\mathsf{seed}, \mathsf{salt}), \mathsf{salt}), \mathsf{salt})\right),$$

where $i_1, \cdots, i_D$ denote the bits of i.

As with the standard GGM construction, a punctured key at i is just the co-path to i in the tree, *i.e.*, the set of intermediate nodes that can be used to recover all leaves except the i-th one: $\mathsf{CoPath}_{\mathsf{seed}}(\mathsf{salt}, i) = \mathsf{PPRF}_{\mathsf{seed}}\left(\mathsf{salt}, i_{1,\ldots,\bar{j}}\right)_{j=1,\ldots,D}$. The formal construction is presented in Fig. 1. Due to space limitations, we defer the proof of Theorem 7 to Appendix of our full-version [23]. We note that the proof is a natural extension of the security analysis of the GGM construction [35].

Parameters:

- Two functions $F_0, F_1 : \{0,1\}^{2\lambda} \to \{0,1\}^{\lambda}$. Number of leaves $n = 2^D \in \mathbb{N}$.

Construction:

- Sample $(\mathsf{seed}, \mathsf{salt}) \leftarrow_r \{0,1\}^{3\lambda}$ where $\mathsf{salt} := (\mathsf{salt}_0, \mathsf{salt}_1)$. We use $\mathsf{salt}_0, \mathsf{salt}_1$ for F_0, F_1 respectively. For simplicity, we sometimes write $F_i(\mathsf{seed}, \mathsf{salt}_i)$ as $F_i(\mathsf{seed}, \mathsf{salt})$ for $i \in \{0,1\}$.
- Let $X_0 := F_0(\mathsf{seed}, \mathsf{salt}_0)$, $X_1 := F_1(\mathsf{seed}, \mathsf{salt}_1)$.
- For $i \in [2, D]$, define $X_{b_1,\ldots,b_{i-1},0} = F_0(F_{b_{i-1}}(X_{b_1,\ldots,b_{i-1}}), \mathsf{salt}_0)$, $X_{b_1,\ldots,b_{i-1},1} = F_1(F_{b_{i-1}}(X_{b_1,\ldots,b_{i-1}}), \mathsf{salt}_1)$ where $b_j \in \{0,1\}$ for all $j \in [1, i-1]$.
- We generalize the formula to compute the leaf of the tree as follows: For each $i \in [0, n-1]$, bit-decompose i as $\sum_{j=1}^{D} 2^{j-1} \cdot i_j$ for $i_j \in \{0,1\}$ then:

$$X_i = X_{i_1,\ldots,i_D} = F_{i_D}(F_{i_{D-1}}(X_{i_1,\ldots,i_{D-1}}), \mathsf{salt}_{i_D})$$
$$= F_{i_D}(F_{i_{D-1}}(\ldots(F_{i_1}(\mathsf{seed}_{i_1}, \mathsf{salt}_{i_1}), \mathsf{salt}_{i_{D-1}}), \mathsf{salt}_{i_D})$$

To formalize, the value for each leaf $i \in [0, n-1]$ is denoted as:

$$\mathsf{PPRF}_{\mathsf{seed}}(\mathsf{salt}, i) = F_{i_D}(\mathsf{PPRF}_{\mathsf{seed}}(\mathsf{salt}, i_{1,\ldots,D-1}), \mathsf{salt})$$
$$= F_{i_D}(F_{i_{D-1}}(\ldots(F_{i_1}(\mathsf{seed}, \mathsf{salt}), \mathsf{salt}), \mathsf{salt}))$$

where $i_{1,\ldots,k} = \sum_{j=1}^{k} 2^{k-j} i_j$ for any $k \in [1, D]$.
- We define the co-path $\mathsf{CoPath}(i)$ for each $i = \sum_{j=1}^{D} 2^{j-1} \cdot i_j \in [0, n-1]$ as follows:

$$\mathsf{CoPath}(i) = \mathsf{CoPath}(X_{i_1,\ldots,i_D}) = \{X_{\bar{i}_1}, X_{i_1,\bar{i}_2}, \ldots, X_{i_1,\ldots,\bar{i}_D}\}$$

Formalizing, we have:

$$\mathsf{CoPath}_{\mathsf{seed}}(\mathsf{salt}, i) = \mathsf{PPRF}_{\mathsf{seed}}(\mathsf{salt}, i_{1,\ldots,\bar{j}})_{j=1,\ldots,D}$$

where $i_{1,\ldots,\bar{k}} = \sum_{j=1}^{k-1} 2^{k-j} \cdot i_j + \bar{i}_k$ for any $k \in [1, D]$.

Fig. 1. New construction $\mathsf{PPRF}(\mathsf{seed}, \mathsf{salt}, 2^D)$ of Puncturable PRF

Theorem 7 (PPRF security). *Assume that* $\mathsf{PRG} = (F_0, F_1)$ *with* $F_b : \{0,1\}^{2\lambda} \to \{0,1\}^{\lambda}$ *is an* (N, τ)-*instance* (t, ϵ)-*secure length-doubling PRG. Then the construction* $\mathsf{PPRF}(\mathsf{seed}, \mathsf{salt}, 2^D)$ *described in Fig. 1 is an* (N, τ)-*instance strongly* $(t, D \cdot \epsilon)$-*secure PPRF with input domain* $[2^D]$ *and punctured key domain* $(\{0,1\}^{\lambda})^D$.

5.3 A Multi-instance PRG in the Ideal Cipher Model

In this section, we describe the construction of multi-instance PRG in the ideal cipher model. Our construction itself is not really new, but is a tweak on a construction of [36]. The work of [36] gives a construction of PPRF in the random permutation model, which is obtained by applying the GGM reduction to the following "Davies-Meyer" construction of a length-doubling PRG $G : x \to (\pi_0(x) \oplus x, \pi_1(x) \oplus x)$, where (π_0, π_1) are pseudorandom permutations. The PRG is proven secure in the random permutation model (in the analysis, all parties are given oracle access to π_0, π_1, and their inverses). Our core observation, which is quite simple in hindsight, is that the most efficient instantiation of this construction implements the permutations π_0, π_1 by fixing two keys (K_0, K_1) and defining $\pi_b := E_{K_B}$, where E_{K_B} is a *block cipher* (such as AES). This suggests the following idea: instead of fixing the keys (K_0, K_1), sample them randomly and use them as a salt for the PRG in the multi-instance setting. The candidate multi-instance PRG becomes $G = (\mathsf{F}_0, \mathsf{F}_1) : (x, \mathsf{salt}) \to (E_{\mathsf{salt}_0}(x) \oplus x, E_{\mathsf{salt}_1}(x) \oplus x)$. The formal construction is given in Fig. 2. While the high-level intuition is straightforward, the formal analysis turns out to be considerably more involved. The remainder of this section is devoted to a formal proof that the above construction is an (N, τ)-instance (t, ε)-secure PRG, for parameters $(N, \tau, t, \varepsilon)$ which will be specified later. The proof is in the *ideal cipher model*: in this model, each key $K \in \{0,1\}^\lambda$ defines an independent uniformly random permutation π_K. All parties are given access to an oracle which, on input $(0, K, x)$, outputs $\pi_K(x)$, and on input $(1, K, y)$, outputs $\pi_K^{-1}(y)$.

Definition 8 (Ideal Cipher Oracle). *For every* $K \in \{0,1\}^\lambda$, *let* $\pi_K : \{0,1\}^\lambda \to \{0,1\}^\lambda$ *be a uniformly random permutation over* $\{0,1\}^\lambda$. *The ideal cipher oracle* $\mathcal{O}_\pi$ *is defined as follows:*

- *On input* $(x, K) \in \{0,1\}^\lambda \times \{0,1\}^\lambda$, *outputs* $\pi_K(x)$.
- *On input* (inv, x, K), *outputs* $\pi_K^{-1}(x)$.

Parameters:

- For each $K \in \{0,1\}^\lambda$, $\pi_K : \{0,1\}^\lambda \to \{0,1\}^\lambda$ is a uniformly random permutation.

Construction:

- Sample salt $\leftarrow_r \{0,1\}^{2\lambda}$. parse salt $:= (K_0, K_1)$.
- $\mathsf{F}_b : \{0,1\}^{2\lambda} \to \{0,1\}^\lambda$ is defined as $\mathsf{F}_b(\mathsf{seed}, \mathsf{salt}_b) = \pi_{K_b}(\mathsf{seed}) \oplus \mathsf{seed}$ for $b \in \{0,1\}$ and seed $\in \{0,1\}^\lambda$.

Fig. 2. Multi-instance PRG $\mathsf{F}_0, \mathsf{F}_1$ in the ideal cipher model

Theorem 9. *Let* $\mathsf{F}_0, \mathsf{F}_1$ *be the functions defined in Fig. 2. Let* q *be the number of queries to the oracle* $\mathcal{O}_\pi$. *Then* $(\mathsf{F}_0, \mathsf{F}_1)$ *is an* (N, τ)-instance (q, ϵ)-secure PRG *in the ideal cipher model (where the parties are given oracle access to $\mathcal{O}_\pi$ from Definition 8), where*

$$\varepsilon \leq f_N(\lambda) \cdot q \cdot \left(\frac{1}{2^{\lambda-1}} + \frac{1}{2^\lambda - q} \right) + \frac{4\tau N}{2^{2\lambda}},$$

for some function f_N such that if $N \leq 2^{\lambda-1}$, $f_N(\lambda) \leq \frac{3\tau\lambda\cdot\ln 2}{\ln\lambda+\ln\ln 2}$, and if $N \leq 2^{\lambda/2}$, $f_N(\lambda) \leq 4\tau$.

Due to space limitations, the proof of Theorem 9 is deferred to our full-version [23]. It relies on a careful analysis using Patarin's H-coefficient technique [26,42] and forms one of the core technical contributions of this work.

6   A Signature Scheme from Regular Syndrome Decoding

In this section, we introduce a new signature scheme from the regular syndrome decoding assumption. A signature scheme is given by three algorithms (KeyGen, Sign, Verify). KeyGen returns a key pair (pk, sk) where pk and sk are the public and private key. Sign on an input a message m and the secret key sk, produces a signature σ. Verify, on input a message m, a public key pk and a signature σ, returns 0 or 1. Standard security notions for signature schemes are existential unforgeability against key-only attacks (EUF-KO, Definition 11) and against chosen-message attacks (EUF-CMA, Definition 10).

Definition 10 (EUF-CMA security). *Given a signature scheme* Sig = (Setup, Sign, Verify) *and security parameter λ, we say that* Sig *is* EUF-CMA-*secure if any PPT algorithm $\mathcal{A}$ has negligible advantage in the* EUF-CMA *game, defined as*

$$\mathsf{Adv}_{\mathcal{A}}^{\mathsf{EUF\text{-}CMA}} = \Pr\left[\begin{array}{c} \mathsf{Verify}(\mathsf{pk}, \mu^*, \sigma^*) = 1 \\ \wedge \mu^* \notin Q \end{array} \middle| \begin{array}{c} (\mathsf{sk}, \mathsf{pk}) \leftarrow \mathsf{Setup}(\{0,1\}^\lambda) \\ (\mu^*, \sigma^*) \leftarrow \mathcal{A}^{\mathsf{Sign}(\mathsf{sk}, \cdot)}(\mathsf{pk}) \end{array} \right],$$

where $\mathcal{A}^{\mathsf{Sign}(\mathsf{sk}, \cdot)}$ denotes $\mathcal{A}$'s access to a signing oracle with private key sk *and Q denotes the set of messages μ that were queried to* Sign(sk, ·) *by $\mathcal{A}$.*

Definition 11 (EUF-KO security). *Given a signature scheme* Sig = (Setup, Sign, Verify) *and security parameter λ, we say that* Sig *is* EUF-KO-*secure if any PPT algorithm $\mathcal{A}$ has negligible advantage in the EUF-KO game, defined as*

$$\mathsf{Adv}_{\mathcal{A}}^{\mathsf{EUF\text{-}KO}} = \Pr\left[\mathsf{Verify}(\mathsf{pk}, \mu^*, \sigma^*) = 1 \middle| \begin{array}{c} (\mathsf{sk}, \mathsf{pk}) \leftarrow \mathsf{Setup}(\{0,1\}^\lambda) \\ (\mu^*, \sigma^*) \leftarrow \mathcal{A}(\mathsf{pk}) \end{array} \right].$$

6.1   Description of the Signature Scheme

The key generation algorithm (Fig. 3) randomly samples a syndrome decoding instance $(H, \mathbf{y})$ with solution $\mathbf{x}$. The signing algorithm with secret key sk = $(H, \mathbf{y}, \mathbf{x})$ and message $m \in \{0,1\}^*$ is described on Fig. 1. The verification algorithm with public key pk = $(H, \mathbf{y})$ (matrix H can be computed from PRG with a random seed, the public key size is around 0.09kB), message $m \in \{0,1\}^*$, and signature σ, is described in Fig. 4 of our full-version [23].

Inputs: A security parameter λ.

1. Sample seed $\leftarrow \{0,1\}^{\lambda}$;
2. Set $H \leftarrow \mathsf{PRG}(\mathsf{seed})$ with $H \in \mathbb{F}_2^{k \times K}$;
3. Sample $\mathbf{x} \leftarrow_r [\mathsf{bs}]^w$ and set $\mathbf{y} \leftarrow H \cdot \mathsf{Expand}(\mathbf{x})$ and $\mathsf{sk} \leftarrow (\mathsf{seed}, \mathbf{x})$.

Fig. 3. Key generation algorithm of the signature scheme

An Optimization. For readability, the description of the signing and verification algorithms ignores an optimization that slightly reduces the signature size, but significantly complexifies the description. Concretely, because we know that the vectors u^e should be regular vectors, it suffices to share the $\mathsf{bs} - 1$ first entries $(u_1, \cdots, u_{\mathsf{bs}-1})$ of each block of $\mathbf{u}^e$, since the last one can be reconstructed as $\bigoplus u_i \oplus 1$. This reduces the size of $\mathbf{u}$ from $K = w \cdot \mathsf{bs}$ to $w \cdot (\mathsf{bs} - 1) = K - w$ bits. Consequently, the share u_n^e of u^e need also only be shared over $\mathbb{F}_2^{K-w}$. This reduces by w the size of aux_n^e for each $e \leq \tau$, hence overall by $\tau \cdot w$ the size of the signature. An additional byproduct of this optimization is that it reduces the number of possible "cheating" vectors u^e that a malicious prover could choose, which has some positive repercussions on the size of the RSD parameters (K, k, w) which we can choose (we elaborate in Sect. 7 of our full-version [23] for more details).

Protocol Signing Algorithm

Inputs. A secret key sk and a message $m \in \{0,1\}^*$.
Initialization. Parse sk as $(\mathsf{seed}, \mathbf{x})$.
  – Let $H \leftarrow \mathsf{PRG}(\mathsf{seed})$ and $\mathbf{y} \leftarrow H \cdot \mathsf{Expand}(\mathbf{x})$; // $H \in \mathbb{F}_2^{k \times k}$ is a (pseudo)random matrix in systematic form.
  – Sample $(K_0, K_1) \leftarrow_r \{0,1\}^{\lambda} \times \{0,1\}^{\lambda}$. Set $\mathsf{salt} \leftarrow (K_0, K_1)$.
Phase 1. For each iteration $e \in [\tau]$:
  – Sample $\mathsf{seed}^e \leftarrow_r \{0,1\}^{\lambda}$;
  – For $d = 1$ to D, set $(X_{d,0}^e, R_{d,0}^e, U_{d,0}^e) \leftarrow (0,0,0) \in [\mathsf{bs}]^w \times [\mathsf{bs}]^w \times \{0,1\}^K$;
  – Set $x_n^e \leftarrow \mathbf{x}$, $u_n^e \leftarrow 0$, and $r^e \leftarrow 0$;
  – **For** $i = 1$ **to** $n - 1$:
    1. Compute $\mathsf{seed}_i^e \leftarrow \mathsf{PPRF}_{\mathsf{salt}}(\mathsf{seed}^e, i)$; // Can be computed efficiently by always storing the path to the current node: to move from i to $i+1$, start from the closest ancestor of $i+1$ in the path to leave i.
    2. Set $\mathsf{state}_i^e \leftarrow \mathsf{seed}_i^e$;
    3. $(x_i^e, r_i^e, u_i^e, \cdot_i^e) \leftarrow \mathsf{PRG}(\mathsf{seed}_i^e)$; // $(x_i^e, r_i^e, u_i^e, \cdot_i^e) \in [\mathsf{bs}]^w \times [\mathsf{bs}]^w \times \{0,1\}^K \times \{0,1\}^{\lambda}$.
    4. $x_n^e \leftarrow x_n^e - x_i^e \bmod \mathsf{bs}$, $u_n^e \leftarrow u_n^e \oplus u_i^e$, and $r^e \leftarrow r^e + r_i^e \bmod \mathsf{bs}$;

5. For all $d \leq D$ such that $i[d] = 0$, set: // $i[d]$ is the d-th bit of the integer i.
   - $X_{d,0}^e \leftarrow X_{d,0}^e + x_i^e \bmod \mathsf{bs}$;
   - $R_{d,0}^e \leftarrow R_{d,0}^e + r_i^e \bmod \mathsf{bs}$;
   - $U_{d,0}^e \leftarrow U_{d,0}^e \oplus u_i^e$;
- **On node n:**
   1. Compute $\mathsf{seed}_n^e \leftarrow \mathsf{PPRF}_{\mathsf{salt}}(\mathsf{seed}^e, n)$;
   2. Compute $r_n^e \leftarrow \mathsf{PRG}(\mathsf{seed}_n^e)$;
   3. $r^e \leftarrow r^e + r_n^e \bmod \mathsf{bs}$, $u^e \leftarrow \mathsf{Expand}(r^e)$, and $u_n^e \leftarrow u_n^e \oplus u^e$; // The $(x_i^e)_i$ form n pseudorandom shares of $\mathbf{x} \in [\mathsf{bs}]^w$, the $(r_i^e)_i$ form n pseudorandom shares of $r^e \in [\mathsf{bs}]^w$, and the $(u_i^e)_i$ form n pseudorandom shares of $u^e = \mathsf{Expand}(r^e) \in \{0,1\}^K$.
   4. Define $\mathsf{aux}_n^e \leftarrow (x_n^e, u_n^e)$;
   5. Set $\mathsf{state}_n^e \leftarrow \mathsf{aux}_n^e \| \mathsf{seed}_n^e$ and $,_n^e \leftarrow \mathsf{H}(\mathsf{state}_n^e)$.

Phase 2. 1. $h_1 \leftarrow \mathsf{H}_1(m, \mathsf{salt}, ,_1^1, \cdots, ,_n^1, \cdots, ,_1^\tau, \cdots, ,_n^\tau)$; // Accumulate the commitments inside the hash rather than storing and hashing all at once.

2. $\pi_{\{e \in \tau\}}^e \leftarrow \mathsf{PRG}_1(h_1)$. // $\pi^e \in \mathsf{Perm}([w])$.

Phase 3. For each iteration $e \in [\tau]$:
1. $z^e \leftarrow x - \pi^e(r^e) \bmod \mathsf{bs}$;
2. For $d = 1$ to D, set:
   - $y_{d,0}^e \leftarrow H \cdot \mathsf{Shift}(\pi^e(U_{d,0}^e), z^e)$ and $y_{d,1}^e \leftarrow y_{d,0}^e \oplus \mathbf{y}$;
   - $z_{d,0}^e \leftarrow X_d^e - \pi^e(R_{d,0}^e) \bmod \mathsf{bs}$ and $z_{d,1}^e \leftarrow z^e - z_{d,0}^e \bmod \mathsf{bs}$.

Phase 4. 1. $h_2 \leftarrow \mathsf{H}_2(m, \mathsf{salt}, h_1, (y_{d,b}^e, z_{d,b}^e)_{d \leq D, b \in \{0,1\}, e \leq \tau})$;

2. Set $(b_1^e, \cdots b_D^e)_{e \leq \tau} \leftarrow \mathsf{PRG}_2(h_2)$ and let $i^e \leftarrow \sum_{d=1}^D b_d^e \cdot 2^{d-1}$.

Phase 5. Output $\sigma = \left(\mathsf{salt}, h_1, h_2, (\mathsf{CoPath}_{\mathsf{salt}}(i^e, \mathsf{seed}^e), z^e, ,_{i^e}^e, \mathsf{aux}_n^e)_{c \leq \tau} \right)$.
// aux_n^e is not included if $i^e = n$.

Protocol 1: Signing algorithm of the signature scheme

Protocol Verification Algorithm

Inputs. A public key $\mathsf{pk} = (H, \mathbf{y})$, a message $m \in \{0,1\}^*$ and a signature σ.

1. Split the signature as follows:

$$\sigma = \left(\mathsf{salt}, h_1, h_2, (\mathsf{CoPath}_{\mathsf{salt}}(i^e, \mathsf{seed}^e), z^e, ,_{i^e}^e, \mathsf{aux}_n^e)_{e \leq \tau} \right);$$

2. Recompute $\pi_{\{e \in \tau\}}^e$ where $\pi^e \in \mathsf{Perm}([w])$ via a pseudorandom generator using h_1;
3. Recompute $(b_1^e, \cdots b_D^e)_{e \leq \tau}$ via a pseudorandom generator using h_2 and define $i^e \leftarrow \sum_{d=1}^D b_d^e \cdot 2^{d-1}$;

4. For each iteration $e \in [\tau]$,
   - For $d = 1$ to D:
     - Denote $b = 1 - b_d^e$;
     - Set $(X_{d,b}^e, R_{d,b}^e, U_{d,b}^e) \leftarrow (0, 0, 0) \in [\mathsf{bs}]^w \times [\mathsf{bs}]^w \times \{0,1\}^K$;
     - For each $i \neq i^e$:
       * Recompute seed_i^e from the $\mathsf{CoPath}_{\mathsf{salt}}(i^e, \mathsf{seed}^e)$.
       * If $i \neq n$, recompute $(x_i^e, r_i^e, u_i^e, \ _i^e) \leftarrow \mathsf{PRG}(\mathsf{seed}_i^e)$; else, parse aux_n^e as (x_n^e, u_n^e), and compute $r_n^e \leftarrow \mathsf{PRG}(\mathsf{seed}_n^e)$;
       * If $i[d] = b$, update:
         - $X_{d,b}^e \leftarrow X_{d,b}^e + x_i^e \bmod \mathsf{bs}$;
         - $R_{d,b}^e \leftarrow R_{d,b}^e + r_i^e \bmod \mathsf{bs}$;
         - $U_{d,b}^e \leftarrow U_{d,b}^e \oplus u_i^e$;
     - Recompute $(y_{d,b}^e, z_{d,b}^e)$ by simulating the Phase 3 of the signing algorithm as below:
       - $y_{d,b}^e \leftarrow H \cdot \mathsf{Shift}(\pi^e(U_{d,b}^e), z^e)$;
       - $z_{d,b}^e \leftarrow X_{d,b}^e - \pi^e(R_{d,b}^e) \bmod \mathsf{bs}$;
     - Recompute $(y_{d,1-b}^e, z_{d,1-b}^e)$ as below:
       - $y_{d,1-b}^e \leftarrow y_{d,b}^e \oplus \mathbf{y}$;
       - $z_{d,1-b}^e \leftarrow z^e - z_{d,b}^e \bmod \mathsf{bs}$;
5. Check if $h_1 \leftarrow \mathsf{H}_1(m, \mathsf{salt}, {}_{,1}^1, \cdots, {}_{,n}^1, \cdots, {}_{,1}^\tau, \cdots, {}_{,n}^\tau)$;
6. Check if $h_2 \leftarrow \mathsf{H}_2(m, \mathsf{salt}, h_1, (y_{d,b}^e, z_{d,b}^e)_{d \leq D, b \in \{0,1\}, e \leq \tau})$;
7. Output ACCEPT if both conditions are satisfied.

Protocol 2: Verification algorithm of the signature scheme

Theorem 12. *Assume that* PPRF *is a* (q_s, τ)-*instance* $(t, \epsilon_{\mathsf{PPRF}})$-*secure PPRF, that* PRG *is a* (q_s, τ)-*instance* $(t, \epsilon_{\mathsf{PRG}})$-*secure PRG, and that any adversary running in time* t *has at advantage at most* ϵ_{SD} *against the regular syndrome decoding problem. Model the hash functions* $\mathsf{H}_1, \mathsf{H}_2$ *as random oracles with output of length* 2λ-*bit and the pseudorandom generator* PRG_2 *as a random oracle. Then chosen-message adversary against the signature scheme depicted in Fig. 1, running in time* t, *making* q_s *signing queries, and making* q_1, q_2, q_3 *queries, respectively, to the random oracles* $\mathsf{H}_1, \mathsf{H}_2$ *and* PRG_2, *succeeds in outputting a valid forgery with probability*

$$\Pr[\mathsf{Forge}] \leq \frac{q_s (q_s + q_1 + q_2 + q_3)}{2^{2\lambda}} + \epsilon_{\mathsf{PPRF}} + \epsilon_{\mathsf{PRG}} + \epsilon_{\mathsf{SD}} + \Pr[X + Y = \tau] + \varepsilon_{\mathsf{G}} + \frac{1}{2^\lambda},$$

where $\epsilon = \mathsf{p} + \frac{1}{n} - \frac{\mathsf{p}}{n}$, *with* $\mathsf{p} = 4/B$ *and* $\varepsilon_{\mathsf{G}} = \varepsilon_{\mathsf{G}}(K, k, w, B)$ *is* $\Pr[(H, \mathbf{y}) \notin \mathsf{GOOD}_B]$, *which is defined on Lemma 19 of [23]*, $X = \max_{\alpha \in Q_1}\{X_\alpha\}$ *and* $Y = \max_{\beta \in Q_2}\{Y_\beta\}$ *with* $X_\alpha \sim \mathsf{Binomial}(\tau, \mathsf{p})$ *and* $Y_\beta \sim \mathsf{Binomial}\left(\tau - X, \frac{1}{n}\right)$ *where* Q_1 *and* Q_2 *are sets of all queries to oracles* H_1 *and* H_2.

The proof of Theorem 12 is deferred to Sect. 6.3 of our full-version [23]. Computing the bound p from Theorem 12 requires a dedicated and involved combinatorial analysis which forms a core technical contribution of this work. We cover it extensively in Sect. 6.2 of our full-version [23]. In Sect. 7 of [23], we provide a detailed coverage about how to derive parameters for our scheme, which also requires a careful combinatorial analysis, and report on our implementation.

Acknowledgement. This project has received funding from the European Union's Horizon 2020 research and innovation programme under the Marie Skłodowska-Curie grant agreement No 945332. Dung Bui, Eliana Carozza, and Geoffroy Couteau acknowledge the support of the French Agence Nationale de la Recherche (ANR), under grant ANR-20-CE39-0001 (project SCENE). This work was also supported by the France 2030 ANR Project ANR-22-PECY-003 SecureCompute and by ERC grant OBELiSC (101115790). The work of Dung Bui is supported by Dim Math Innov funding from the Paris Mathematical Sciences Foundation (FSMP) funded by the Paris Ile-de-France Region. The work of Antoine Joux has been supported by the European Union's H2020 Programme under grant agreement number ERC-669891.

References

1. Aaraj, N., Bettaieb, S., Bidoux, L., Budroni, A., Dyseryn, V., Esser, A., Gaborit, P., Kulkarni, M., Mateu, V., Palumbi, M., Perin, L., Tillich, J.: PERK. Tech. rep., National Institute of Standards and Technology (2023), available at https://csrc. nist.gov/Projects/pqc-dig-sig/round-1-additional-signatures

2. Adj, G., Rivera-Zamarripa, L., Verbel, J., Bellini, E., Barbero, S., Esser, A., Sanna, C., Zweydinger, F.: MiRitH — MinRank in the Head. Tech. rep., National Institute of Standards and Technology (2023), available at https://csrc.nist.gov/Projects/ pqc-dig-sig/round-1-additional-signatures

3. Aguilar-Melchor, C., Feneuil, T., Gama, N., Gueron, S., Howe, J., Joseph, D., Joux, A., Persichetti, E., Randrianarisoa, T.H., Rivain, M., Yue, D.: SDitH — Syndrome Decoding in the Head. Tech. rep., National Institute of Standards and Technology (2023), available at https://csrc.nist.gov/Projects/pqc-dig-sig/round-1-additional-signatures

4. Aguilar-Melchor, C., Gama, N., Howe, J., Hülsing, A., Joseph, D., Yue, D.: The return of the SDitH. In: Hazay, C., Stam, M. (eds.) EUROCRYPT 2023, Part V. LNCS, vol. 14008, pp. 564–596. Springer, Heidelberg (Apr 2023)

5. Aragon, N., Bardet, M., Bidoux, L., Chi-Domínguez, J.J., Dyseryn, V., Feneuil, T., Gaborit, P., Joux, A., Rivain, M., Tillich, J., Vinçotte, A.: RYDE. Tech. rep., National Institute of Standards and Technology (2023), available at https://csrc. nist.gov/Projects/pqc-dig-sig/round-1-additional-signatures

6. Aragon, N., Bardet, M., Bidoux, L., Chi-Domínguez, J., Dyseryn, V., Feneuil, T., Gaborit, P., Neveu, R., Rivain, M., Tillich, J.: MIRA. Tech. rep., National Institute of Standards and Technology (2023), available at https://csrc.nist.gov/Projects/ pqc-dig-sig/round-1-additional-signatures

7. Augot, D., Finiasz, M., Sendrier, N.: A fast provably secure cryptographic hash function. Cryptology ePrint Archive, Report 2003/230 (2003), https://eprint.iacr. org/2003/230

8. Baum, C., Braun, L., de Saint Guilhem, C.D., Klooß, M., Orsini, E., Roy, L., Scholl, P.: Publicly verifiable zero-knowledge and post-quantum signatures from vole-in-the-head. In: Handschuh, H., Lysyanskaya, A. (eds.) Advances in Cryptology - CRYPTO 2023 - 43rd Annual International Cryptology Conference, CRYPTO 2023, Santa Barbara, CA, USA, August 20-24, 2023, Proceedings, Part V. Lecture

Notes in Computer Science, vol. 14085, pp. 581–615. Springer (2023), https://doi.org/10.1007/978-3-031-38554-4_19

9. Baum, C., Delpech de Saint Guilhem, C., Kales, D., Orsini, E., Scholl, P., Zaverucha, G.: Banquet: Short and fast signatures from AES. In: Garay, J. (ed.) PKC 2021, Part I. LNCS, vol. 12710, pp. 266–297. Springer, Heidelberg (May 2021)

10. Bernstein, D.J., Lange, T., Peters, C., Schwabe, P.: Really fast syndrome-based hashing. In: Nitaj, A., Pointcheval, D. (eds.) AFRICACRYPT 11. LNCS, vol. 6737, pp. 134–152. Springer, Heidelberg (Jul 2011)

11. Bettale, L., Kahrobaei, D., Perret, L., Verbel, J.: Biscuit. Tech. rep., National Institute of Standards and Technology (2023), available at https://csrc.nist.gov/Projects/pqc-dig-sig/round-1-additional-signatures

12. Boneh, D., Waters, B.: Constrained pseudorandom functions and their applications. In: Sako, K., Sarkar, P. (eds.) ASIACRYPT 2013, Part II. LNCS, vol. 8270, pp. 280–300. Springer, Heidelberg (Dec 2013)

13. Boyle, E., Chandran, N., Gilboa, N., Gupta, D., Ishai, Y., Kumar, N., Rathee, M.: Function secret sharing for mixed-mode and fixed-point secure computation. In: Canteaut, A., Standaert, F.X. (eds.) EUROCRYPT 2021, Part II. LNCS, vol. 12697, pp. 871–900. Springer, Heidelberg (Oct 2021)

14. Boyle, E., Couteau, G., Gilboa, N., Ishai, Y.: Compressing vector OLE. In: Lie, D., Mannan, M., Backes, M., Wang, X. (eds.) ACM CCS 2018. pp. 896–912. ACM Press (Oct 2018)

15. Boyle, E., Couteau, G., Gilboa, N., Ishai, Y., Kohl, L., Resch, N., Scholl, P.: Correlated pseudorandomness from expand-accumulate codes. In: Dodis, Y., Shrimpton, T. (eds.) CRYPTO 2022, Part II. LNCS, vol. 13508, pp. 603–633. Springer, Heidelberg (Aug 2022)

16. Boyle, E., Couteau, G., Gilboa, N., Ishai, Y., Kohl, L., Rindal, P., Scholl, P.: Efficient two-round OT extension and silent non-interactive secure computation. In: Cavallaro, L., Kinder, J., Wang, X., Katz, J. (eds.) ACM CCS 2019. pp. 291–308. ACM Press (Nov 2019)

17. Boyle, E., Couteau, G., Gilboa, N., Ishai, Y., Kohl, L., Scholl, P.: Efficient pseudorandom correlation generators: Silent OT extension and more. In: Boldyreva, A., Micciancio, D. (eds.) CRYPTO 2019, Part III. LNCS, vol. 11694, pp. 489–518. Springer, Heidelberg (Aug 2019)

18. Boyle, E., Couteau, G., Gilboa, N., Ishai, Y., Kohl, L., Scholl, P.: Efficient pseudorandom correlation generators from ring-LPN. In: Micciancio, D., Ristenpart, T. (eds.) CRYPTO 2020, Part II. LNCS, vol. 12171, pp. 387–416. Springer, Heidelberg (Aug 2020)

19. Boyle, E., Gilboa, N., Ishai, Y.: Function secret sharing. In: Oswald, E., Fischlin, M. (eds.) EUROCRYPT 2015, Part II. LNCS, vol. 9057, pp. 337–367. Springer, Heidelberg (Apr 2015)

20. Boyle, E., Gilboa, N., Ishai, Y.: Function secret sharing: Improvements and extensions. In: Weippl, E.R., Katzenbeisser, S., Kruegel, C., Myers, A.C., Halevi, S. (eds.) ACM CCS 2016. pp. 1292–1303. ACM Press (Oct 2016)

21. Boyle, E., Gilboa, N., Ishai, Y.: Secure computation with preprocessing via function secret sharing. In: Hofheinz, D., Rosen, A. (eds.) TCC 2019, Part I. LNCS, vol. 11891, pp. 341–371. Springer, Heidelberg (Dec 2019)

22. Boyle, E., Goldwasser, S., Ivan, I.: Functional signatures and pseudorandom functions. In: Krawczyk, H. (ed.) PKC 2014. LNCS, vol. 8383, pp. 501–519. Springer, Heidelberg (Mar 2014)

23. Bui, D., Carozza, E., Couteau, G., Goudarzi, D., Joux, A.: Faster signatures from MPC-in-the-head. Cryptology ePrint Archive, Paper 2024/252 (2024), https://eprint.iacr.org/2024/252, https://eprint.iacr.org/2024/252

24. Carozza, E., Couteau, G., Joux, A.: Short signatures from regular syndrome decoding in the head. In: Hazay, C., Stam, M. (eds.) EUROCRYPT 2023, Part V. LNCS, vol. 14008, pp. 532–563. Springer, Heidelberg (Apr 2023)

25. Chase, M., Derler, D., Goldfeder, S., Katz, J., Kolesnikov, V., Orlandi, C., Ramacher, S., Rechberger, C., Slamanig, D., Wang, X., et al.: The picnic signature scheme. Submission to NIST Post-Quantum Cryptography project (2020)

26. Chen, S., Steinberger, J.P.: Tight security bounds for key-alternating ciphers. In: Nguyen, P.Q., Oswald, E. (eds.) EUROCRYPT 2014. LNCS, vol. 8441, pp. 327–350. Springer, Heidelberg (May 2014)

27. Couteau, G., Rindal, P., Raghuraman, S.: Silver: Silent VOLE and oblivious transfer from hardness of decoding structured LDPC codes. In: Malkin, T., Peikert, C. (eds.) CRYPTO 2021, Part III. LNCS, vol. 12827, pp. 502–534. Springer, Heidelberg, Virtual Event (Aug 2021)

28. Cui, H., Liu, H., Yan, D., Yang, K., Yu, Y., Zhang, K.: ReSolveD: Shorter signatures from regular syndrome decoding and VOLE-in-the-head. In: PKC 2024, Part I. pp. 229–258. LNCS, Springer, Heidelberg (May 2024)

29. Delpech de Saint Guilhem, C., De Meyer, L., Orsini, E., Smart, N.P.: BBQ: Using AES in picnic signatures. In: Paterson, K.G., Stebila, D. (eds.) SAC 2019. LNCS, vol. 11959, pp. 669–692. Springer, Heidelberg (Aug 2019)

30. Dinur, I., Nadler, N.: Multi-target attacks on the Picnic signature scheme and related protocols. In: Ishai, Y., Rijmen, V. (eds.) EUROCRYPT 2019, Part III. LNCS, vol. 11478, pp. 699–727. Springer, Heidelberg (May 2019)

31. Feneuil, T., Joux, A., Rivain, M.: Syndrome decoding in the head: Shorter signatures from zero-knowledge proofs. In: Dodis, Y., Shrimpton, T. (eds.) CRYPTO 2022, Part II. LNCS, vol. 13508, pp. 541–572. Springer, Heidelberg (Aug 2022)

32. Feneuil, T., Rivain, M.: MQOM — MQ on my Mind. Tech. rep., National Institute of Standards and Technology (2023), available at https://csrc.nist.gov/Projects/pqc-dig-sig/round-1-additional-signatures

33. Finiasz, M., Gaborit, P., Sendrier, N.: Improved fast syndrome based cryptographic hash functions. In: Proceedings of ECRYPT Hash Workshop. vol. 2007, p. 155. Citeseer (2007)

34. Gilboa, N., Ishai, Y.: Distributed point functions and their applications. In: Nguyen, P.Q., Oswald, E. (eds.) EUROCRYPT 2014. LNCS, vol. 8441, pp. 640–658. Springer, Heidelberg (May 2014)

35. Goldreich, O., Goldwasser, S., Micali, S.: How to construct random functions. Journal of the ACM 33(4), 792–807 (Oct 1986)

36. Guo, C., Katz, J., Wang, X., Yu, Y.: Efficient and secure multiparty computation from fixed-key block ciphers. In: 2020 IEEE Symposium on Security and Privacy. pp. 825–841. IEEE Computer Society Press (May 2020)

37. Hazay, C., Orsini, E., Scholl, P., Soria-Vazquez, E.: TinyKeys: A new approach to efficient multi-party computation. In: Shacham, H., Boldyreva, A. (eds.) CRYPTO 2018, Part III. LNCS, vol. 10993, pp. 3–33. Springer, Heidelberg (Aug 2018)

38. Huth, J., Joux, A.: MPC in the head using the subfield bilinear collision problem. In: CRYPTO 2024 (2024), https://eprint.iacr.org/2023/1685

39. Kiayias, A., Papadopoulos, S., Triandopoulos, N., Zacharias, T.: Delegatable pseudorandom functions and applications. In: Sadeghi, A.R., Gligor, V.D., Yung, M. (eds.) ACM CCS 2013. pp. 669–684. ACM Press (Nov 2013)

40. Meziani, M., Dagdelen, Ö., Cayrel, P.L., Yousfi Alaoui, S.M.E.: S-fsb: An improved variant of the fsb hash family. In: International Conference on Information Security and Assurance. pp. 132–145. Springer (2011)

41. Münch, J.P., Schneider, T., Yalame, H.: Vasa: Vector aes instructions for security applications. In: Annual Computer Security Applications Conference. pp. 131–145 (2021)

42. Patarin, J.: The "coefficients h" technique. In: Avanzi, R.M., Keliher, L., Sica, F. (eds.) Selected Areas in Cryptography. pp. 328–345. Springer Berlin Heidelberg, Berlin, Heidelberg (2009)

43. Redfield, J.H.: The theory of group-reduced distributions. American Journal of Mathematics 49(3), 433–455 (1927)

44. Rindal, P., Schoppmann, P.: VOLE-PSI: Fast OPRF and circuit-PSI from vector-OLE. In: Canteaut, A., Standaert, F.X. (eds.) EUROCRYPT 2021, Part II. LNCS, vol. 12697, pp. 901–930. Springer, Heidelberg (Oct 2021)

45. Roy, L.: SoftSpokenOT: Quieter OT extension from small-field silent VOLE in the minicrypt model. In: Dodis, Y., Shrimpton, T. (eds.) CRYPTO 2022, Part I. LNCS, vol. 13507, pp. 657–687. Springer, Heidelberg (Aug 2022)

46. Weng, C., Yang, K., Katz, J., Wang, X.: Wolverine: Fast, scalable, and communication-efficient zero-knowledge proofs for boolean and arithmetic circuits. In: 2021 IEEE Symposium on Security and Privacy. pp. 1074–1091. IEEE Computer Society Press (May 2021)

47. Yang, K., Sarkar, P., Weng, C., Wang, X.: QuickSilver: Efficient and affordable zero-knowledge proofs for circuits and polynomials over any field. In: Vigna, G., Shi, E. (eds.) ACM CCS 2021. pp. 2986–3001. ACM Press (Nov 2021)

48. Yang, K., Weng, C., Lan, X., Zhang, J., Wang, X.: Ferret: Fast extension for correlated OT with small communication. In: Ligatti, J., Ou, X., Katz, J., Vigna, G. (eds.) ACM CCS 2020. pp. 1607–1626. ACM Press (Nov 2020)

49. Zaverucha, G., Chase, M., Derler, D., Goldfeder, S., Orlandi, C., Ramacher, S., Rechberger, C., Slamanig, D., Katz, J., Wang, X., Kolesnikov, V., Kales, D.: Picnic. Tech. rep., National Institute of Standards and Technology (2020), available at https://csrc.nist.gov/projects/post-quantum-cryptography/post-quantum-cryptography-standardization/round-3-submissions

One-More Unforgeability for Multi - and Threshold Signatures

Sela Navot[(✉)] [iD] and Stefano Tessaro [iD]

Paul G. Allen School of Computer Science & Engineering, University of Washington,
Seattle, WA, USA
{senavot,tessaro}@cs.washington.edu

Abstract. This paper initiates the study of one-more unforgeability for multi-signatures and threshold signatures as a stronger security goal, ensuring that ℓ executions of a signing protocol cannot result in more than ℓ signatures. This notion is widely used in the context of blind signatures, but we argue that it is a convenient way to model strong unforgeability for other types of distributed signing protocols. We provide formal security definitions for one-more unforgeability (OMUF) and show that the HBMS multi-signature scheme does not satisfy this definition, whereas MuSig and MuSig2 do. In the full version of this paper, we also show that mBCJ does not satisfy OMUF, as well as expose a subtle issue with its existential unforgeability. For threshold signatures, FROST satisfies OMUF, but ROAST does not.

Keywords: Multi-Signatures · Threshold Signatures · Strong Unforgeability · Provable Security

1 Introduction

There has been growing interest in protocols for distributed generation of signatures, in the form of *threshold signatures* (TS) [21,22] and *multi-signatures* (MS) [28]. While these primitives have been studied for decades, their recent widespread use has been driven by applications in blockchain ecosystems, such as digital wallets [26], and to enforce the need for multiple signatures to authorize a transaction. Threshold signatures are also at the center of standardization efforts by NIST [36] and IETF [17].

Recall that in a t-out-of-n threshold signature, a secret signing key, associated with a public verification key, is secret shared amongst a set of n signers (often as the result of running a distributed key generation protocol). Any subset of at least t signers should be able to sign a message, whereas an adversary corrupting fewer than t signers should not be able to come up with a signature on their own. In multi-signatures, in contrast, parties generate their own keys, independently. Then, any group of signers can come together to generate signature shares and aggregate them into a signature, which can be verified using a verification key obtained by aggregating the verification keys of all involved signers.

© International Association for Cryptologic Research 2025
K.-M. Chung and Y. Sasaki (Eds.): ASIACRYPT 2024, LNCS 15484, pp. 429–462, 2025.
https://doi.org/10.1007/978-981-96-0875-1_14

SECURITY DEFINITIONS. Security definitions for distributed signing are far more challenging than definitions for signatures in isolation. A key point is that issuance of signatures generally involves an *interactive* protocol (this is the case for all pairing-free schemes, such as FROST [5,29] and MuSig/MuSig2 [35,40]), and executions are subject to adversarial corruptions. Often, the adversary can not only corrupt a subset of the signers, but also control communication between signers—this is the case for a common model where inter-signer communication is mediated by a proxy.

This makes it hard to define *when* a signature on a message has been issued, and, in turn, to formalize a notion of unforgeability. A number of works (for example, [6,8,13,19,35]) sidestep this question by considering a message signed as long as a signing session *started* on it. In other cases the definition is tailored to the specific structure of the scheme (for example, in the analysis of MuSig2 [40]) or a very limited class of schemes, as in [5,11], where Bellare et al. put forward a hierarchy of security notions for partially non-interactive threshold signatures.

STRONG UNFORGEABILITY. This paper considers a further challenge in the study of security definitions for TS/MS, namely the definition of strong unforgeability. This standard notion of security for plain signatures ensures that, in addition to achieving regular unforgeability, an adversary cannot come up with a different signature for a message for which it has already seen valid signatures. It is natural to expect that a distributed signing protocol for a strongly unforgeable signature scheme, like Schnorr signatures [42,45], should also ensure strong unforgeability. However, somewhat jumping ahead, we will show that in general this is *not true*: there are strongly unforgeable signature schemes with distributed signing protocol that are not strongly unforgeable.

Beyond theoretical interest, this may be of practical interest in the context of blockchain ecosystems, where multi-signatures are used to generate strongly unforgeable plain signatures [39,50]. Lack of strong unforgeability of plain signatures has attracted attention [31,49,50] and has historically been associated with costly transaction malleability attacks [2,20], warranting the study and prevention of similar weaknesses that may be introduced by the usage of multi-signatures. We point out that such weakness is, to some extent, inherent in probabilistic threshold signature schemes, since not all signers are required to participate in each signing session. When corrupting enough signers, an adversary can obtain multiple signatures for a message even if each honest signer only signs the message once, allowing execution of a malleability attack. Moreover, regardless of the number of corrupt signers, an adversary can obtain more signatures for some message then the maximum number of signature shares that any single signer provided.

Our work on threshold signatures, however, is motivated by NIST's interest in strong unforgeability, which is part of the requirements for submissions to its threshold signatures call [14], and we seek to provide a formalization candidate candidate schemes could use. Furthermore, system designers often assume strong unforgeability in unpredictable ways, especially when the underlying scheme is known to be strongly unforgeable, and it is prudent not to break this guarantee when the signature is issued in a threshold setting.

It turns out that a rigorous definition of strong unforgeability for distributed signing is challenging, as the winning condition requires defining which signatures have been generated by interactive signing protocols subject to adversarial behavior, but it is not always clear how to do this. The security notions of Bellare et al. [5,11], for example, give definitions of strong unforgeability for a limited class of semi non-interactive threshold signatures where the signature is uniquely defined by the input to one of the signing rounds, but this is not a property we expect a protocol to have, and no general definition is known.

THIS PAPER: ONE-MORE UNFORGEABILITY. In order to give a generic definition of strong unforgeability, this paper proposes the notion of *one-more unforgeability* (OMUF) as the better approach to model strong unforgeability. OMUF requires that after a certain number ℓ of executions of the signing protocol for a message m, the adversary can generate no more than ℓ signatures for that message. A similar notion is widely used for blind signatures and was introduced by Poitncheval and Stern [41,43], and we argue that it is natural for distributed signing. In particular, for non-distributed plain digital signatures, OMUF and the classical definition of strong unforgeability are in fact equivalent.

OUR CONTRIBUTIONS. Concretely, we make the following contributions.

- **New Definitions.** We formalize the notion of one-more unforgeability for multi-signature and threshold signature schemes.
- **Attacks.** We show that the HBMS multi-signature scheme [6] does not satisfy one-more unforgeability using a polynomial time attack based on the algorithm of Benhamouda et al. [12] to solve the ROS problem [46]. We also point out that the ROAST threshold signature scheme [44] is not strongly unforgeable using a trivial attack. This is despite the fact that the underlying scheme to HBMS is strongly unforgeable (which we prove in the full version of this paper)[1] and that the standard instantiation of ROAST produces ordinary Schnorr signatures.

  In the full version, we also analyze the multi-signature scheme mBCJ [23], showing that it doesn't satisfy OMUF. This analysis also reveals a subtle issue with the existential unforgeability of mBCJ: while an adversary cannot forge a signature for an unsigned message m, they can use valid signatures for m to forge a signature for the same message but with an arbitrary signing set.
- **Proofs of security.** We prove that the MuSig [35] and MuSig2 [40] multi-signature schemes satisfy our one-more unforgeability definition. We also show that a previous security proof [5,11] implies that FROST [5,18,30] satisfies one-more unforgeability, assuming idealized key generation.

ON UC SECURITY. We stress that in this paper we target game-based definitions of security for distributed signing primitives. An alternative approach is to

---

[1] The full version of this paper will soon be available in the IACR Cryptology ePrint Archive under the same title.

consider schemes with UC Security [15], as done in [33], for example. It is not hard to see that a UC-secure threshold signature which implements signatures for a strongly unforgeable signature scheme has to achieve one-more unforgeability. However, many practical threshold and multi-signatures are not UC secure, and hence our game-based approach is meant to capture strong unforgeability for a broader class of schemes.

2   Preliminaries

GAMES FRAMEWORK. We use the game playing framework of [10] for all security definitions and hardness assumptions, with minor simplifications.

A game consists of an initialization algorithm (INIT), finalization algorithm (FIN), and any number of algorithms that can be queried as oracles. When a randomized algorithm $\mathcal{A}$ (usually called an adversary) plays a game Gm, which we denote by $\mathrm{Gm}(\mathcal{A})$, $\mathcal{A}$ is executed with the output of INIT as its input. $\mathcal{A}$ may query the oracles repeatedly at the cost of a single time unit per query. When $\mathcal{A}$ terminates, FIN is executed with the output of $\mathcal{A}$ and outputs true or false, which is the output of the game. We use $\Pr[\mathrm{Gm}(\mathcal{A})]$ as a shorthand for $\Pr[\mathrm{Gm}(\mathcal{A}) = \text{true}]$ where the probability is taken over the randomness of $\mathcal{A}$ and Gm. A game may have parameters params, such as a group used by the game or the number of permitted queries to some oracle.

All schemes and hardness assumptions in this paper are parameterized by an underlying group $\mathbb{G}$ of publicly known prime order p, and their security parameter is $\log(p)$.

Definition 1. *We define the advantage of an adversary $\mathcal{A}$ against an assumption* ASMP *defined by the game* $\mathrm{Gm}^{\mathrm{asmp}}_{\mathrm{params}}$ *as*

$$\mathbf{Adv}^{\mathrm{asmp}}_{\mathrm{params}}(\mathcal{A}) := \Pr[\mathrm{Gm}^{\mathrm{asmp}}_{\mathrm{params}}(\mathcal{A})].$$

The assumption ASMP *holds if* $\mathbf{Adv}^{\mathrm{asmp}}_{\mathrm{params}}(\mathcal{A})$ *is negligible for all polynomial time adversaries $\mathcal{A}$, where polynomial and negligible are in terms of the security parameter defined by* params.

Definition 2. *Let* S *be a cryptographic scheme with scheme parameters* params *and suppose* DEFN *is a security definition defined by the game* $\mathbf{G}^{\mathrm{defn}}[S]$. *We define the advantage of an adversary $\mathcal{A}$ against* S *as*

$$\mathbf{Adv}^{\mathrm{defn}}_{\mathrm{S}}(\mathcal{A}) := \Pr[\mathbf{G}^{\mathrm{defn}}[S](\mathcal{A})].$$

The scheme S *is* DEFN-*secure if* $\mathbf{Adv}^{\mathrm{defn}}_{\mathrm{S}}(\mathcal{A})$ *is negligible for all polynomial time adversaries $\mathcal{A}$, where polynomial and negligible are in terms of the security parameter defined by* params.

Definitions 1 and 2 convert a game definition to a concrete assumption or security definition. Thus, in the rest of the paper, we only write the game definitions.

All of our security proofs are in the random oracle model (ROM) [9], where hash functions are modeled as random oracles. Our security definitions do not rely on the ROM.

NOTATION. We use multiplicative notation for all groups except for $\mathbb{Z}_p$, which denotes the integers modulus p. Addition and multiplication operations of $\mathbb{Z}_p$ elements are modular. Logarithms use base 2.

In pseudocode, we use $\leftarrow$ for assignment and $\leftarrow\!\!\$$ for randomized assignment. In particular, $x \leftarrow\!\!\$ \, S$ denotes sampling an element uniformly at random from a finite set S and $x \leftarrow\!\!\$ \, \mathcal{A}(x_1, \dots)$ denotes assigning the output of a randomized algorithm $\mathcal{A}$ with uniformly random tape and input $x_1, \dots$ to x. We use $\perp$ to denote an error value, and use subscripts for array indexing. All variables are assumed to be uninitialized until assigned a value. Arrays and lists are one-indexed.

3 Specifications and Usage

3.1 Multi-signatures

A multi-signature scheme allows a group of signers to provide a succinct joint signature for an agreed upon message. More specifically, a valid multi-signature by a group of n signers intends to convince verifiers that each of the n signers have participated in the signing protocol in order to sign this message with this group of signers.

In this paper, we primarily consider multi-signature in the plain public key model [8], the setting where each signer has their own long-standing public key that they generate independently (as opposed to using a distributed key generation protocol). This allows signers to use the same public key with multiple signing groups.

KEY AGGREGATION. A multi-signature scheme supports key aggregation if a signature can be verified using a single short key, called the aggregate key of the group, as opposed to the public keys of all the signers. In particular, MuSig [35] and MuSig2 [40] produce ordinary Schnorr signatures that can be verified with respect to the aggregate key.

BROADCASTING VERSUS AN AGGREGATOR NODE. In our syntax, the signers broadcast the output of each round to all other signers. It is sometimes more efficient to use an aggregator node (may be one of the signers) whose role is to aggregate the output of each signing round and forward it to the signers, as well as output the final multi-signature. Some authors describe schemes this way (for example [27,40]) and every scheme can be described in this manner. Since the aggregator is not trusted and all the information available to the aggregator is also available to the adversary in our security model, using an aggregator node does not affect the unforgeability of schemes.

FORMAL SYNTAX AND CORRECTNESS. A multi-signature scheme MS is a collection of algorithms MS.Kg, $(\text{MS.Sign}_r)_{r=1}^{\text{MS.nr}}$, and MS.Verify, where nr is the number of signing rounds specified by the scheme. A scheme also specifies the last interactive round MS.lir, after which it is possible to construct a multi-signature without knowledge of the signers secret information. If a scheme supports key aggregation, it also has an MS.KeyAgg algorithm accompanied by MS.AggVer for key aggregation and for verification using the aggregated key. The intent of the algorithms is as follows:

Key generation: The randomized algorithm MS.Kg is used for key generation by each signing party individually. It takes no input apart from the scheme parameters and outputs a secret-public key pair.

Signing: The collection of algorithms $(\text{MS.Sign}_r)_{r=1}^{\text{MS.nr}}$ specifies the signing procedures to be run by each signing party, where MS.nr (the number of rounds) is specified by the scheme. Each round takes a subset of the following as input: a message, a vector of public keys along with the signer's index in the vector, the output of previous signing rounds, and some other information saved in the state of at most one signer (including the secret key). The algorithm produces an output and updates the state of the signing party, and the multi-signature is the output of the last round $\text{Sign}_{\text{MS.nr}}$. These algorithms may be randomized.

Key aggregation: If the scheme supports key aggregation, the algorithm MS.KeyAgg takes a list of n public keys $(vk_i)_{i=1}^n$ as input and outputs a single aggregated verification key.

Verification: If MS does not support key aggregation, then it has an algorithm MS.Verify that takes a list of public keys, a signature, and a message as input and returns a boolean value signifying whether the signature is valid. If MS supports key aggregation, it has the algorithm MS.AggVer with the same functionality that takes an aggregated public key as input instead of a list of public keys. In this case, a standard Verify algorithm can be obtained by setting $\text{MS.Verify}((vk_i)_{i=1}^n, m, \sigma) = \text{MS.AggVer}(\text{MS.KeyAgg}((vk_i)_{i=1}^n), m, \sigma)$. Hence, without loss of generality, we will only consider MS.Verify in the correctness and security definitions.

The signers maintain a state st which may change throughout the protocol. In particular, using the convention from [6], each signer i has a long-standing secret key $i.\text{st.sk}$ and public key $i.\text{st.vk}$ as well as information associated with each signing session s that they participate in, denoted by $i.\text{st}_s$. The session state includes $\text{st}_s.n$, $(\text{st}_s.vk_j)_{j=1}^{\text{st}_s.n}$, $\text{st}_s.m$, $\text{st}_s.\text{rnd}$, and $\text{st}_s.\text{me}$ which refers to the number of parties, the public keys of those signers, the message being signed, the last completed signing round, and the index of the party within the signers. It is required that signers refuse requests to run the algorithm Sign_r for a session s if $r \neq \text{st}_s.\text{rnd} + 1$. The state may also include other information such as the output of previous signing rounds or the discrete log of a nonce.

Figure 1 describes an honest execution of a multi-signature scheme and provides a correctness definition.

3.2 Threshold Signatures

A threshold signature scheme allows any subset of sufficient size of a group of signers to provide succinct joint signatures for an agreed upon message. This

---

Algorithm $\mathsf{Exec_{MS}}((vk_i)_{i=1}^n, (sk_i)_{i=1}^n, m)$:

1 For $i = 1, \ldots, n$ do:
2      $i.\mathsf{st}.sk \leftarrow sk_i$, $i.\mathsf{st}.vk \leftarrow vk_i$
3 $\mathsf{out} \leftarrow (0)_{i=1}^n$ // output of current round
4 For $r = 1, \ldots, \mathsf{MS.nr}$ do:
5   For $i = 1, \ldots, n$ do:
6          $(\sigma_i, i.\mathsf{st}) \leftarrow\!\!{}_\$ \mathsf{MS.Sign}_r(i.\mathsf{st}, (vk_j)_{j=1}^n, m, \mathsf{out})$
7      $\mathsf{out} \leftarrow (\sigma_i)_{i=1}^n$
8 Return σ_1

Game $\mathbf{G}_{n,m}^{\mathrm{ms\text{-}cor}}[\mathsf{MS}]$

FIN:

1 For $i = 1, \ldots, n$ do:
2      $(vk_i, sk_i) \leftarrow\!\!{}_\$ \mathsf{MS.Kg}()$
3 $\sigma \leftarrow\!\!{}_\$ \mathsf{Exec_{MS}}((vk_i)_{i=1}^n, (sk_i)_{i=1}^n, m)$
4 Return $\mathsf{MS.Verify}((vk_i)_{i=1}^n, m, \sigma)$

Fig. 1. Top: an honest execution of the signing protocol of a multi-signature scheme MS. Note that signing rounds may only use a subset of the provided input. **Bottom:** a game defining the correctness of a scheme. A scheme satisfies perfect correctness for a natural number n if $\Pr[\mathbf{G}_{n,m}^{\mathrm{ms\text{-}cor}}[\mathsf{MS}]] = 1$ for each supported message m.

allows the group to produce signatures even if some signers are offline, unresponsive, or adversarial. The group has an aggregated group public key for signature verification, and honestly generated signatures by any subset of the signers are valid with respect to that key.

IDEALIZED KEY GENERATION. Typically, threshold signatures require a distributed key generation protocol or a trusted dealer of secret keys. For the sake of simplicity, and in line with the framework of [5,11], we idealize key generation, which allows for simpler security definitions. While this model is not representative of some applications, it is straightforward to extend our definitions to include distributed key generation and other security goals.

AGGREGATOR NODE. As with multi-signature, we require that in each signing round the signers broadcasts the output to all other signers. It is possible to use a single aggregator node to facilitate communication between the signers, which does not affect the unforgeability of a scheme.

FORMAL SYNTAX. A threshold signature scheme TS is a collection of algorithms TS.Kg, $(\mathsf{TS.Sign}_r)_{r=1}^{\mathsf{TS.nr}}$, and TS.Verify, where TS.nr is the number of signing rounds specified by the scheme. The scheme also specifies the last interactive signing round TS.lir, after which it is possible to construct a threshold-signature without knowledge of the signers secret information. The intent of the algorithms is as follows:

Key generation: We use idealized key generation, where the randomized algorithm TS.Kg takes the number of signers n and the threshold t as input and outputs the keys for each signer $(sk_i, vk_i)_{i=1}^{n}$ and an aggregate verification key $\tilde{vk}$.

Signing: The collection of algorithms $(\text{TS.Sign}_r)_{r=1}^{\text{TS.nr}}$ specifies the signing procedure to be run by each participating signing party, and TS.nr (the number of rounds) is specified by the scheme. Each round takes a subset of the following as input: a message, a vector of public keys who participate in the session, the output of previous signing rounds, and other information saved in the state of at most one signer (including the secret key). The algorithm produces an output, as well as updates the state of the signing party. The threshold signature is the output of the last round $\text{Sign}_{\text{TS.nr}}$. These algorithms may be randomized.

Verification: The verification algorithm takes an aggregated public key $\tilde{vk}$, a message, and a threshold signature as an input and returns a boolean value signifying whether the signature is valid.

As in the case of multi-signatures, signers have a state st which is updated through the protocol. For each signer i the state $i.\text{st}$ includes the fields $\text{st}.n$ and $\text{st}.t$ denoting the number of signers in the group and the required threshold for signatures, $\text{st}.vk$ and $\text{st}.sk$ denoting the signers own public and secret keys, $(\text{st}.vk_j)_{j=1}^{n}$ denoting the public keys of all signers in the group as well as the group verification key $\text{st}.\tilde{vk}$, and $\text{st}.me$ denoting the index of signer i in the signing group. Additionally, signers hold information for each session s that they participate in, which includes $\text{st}_s.m$ (the message being signed) and $\text{st}_s.\text{rnd}$ (the most recent signing round they completed). It is assumed and required that signers refuse requests to run the algorithm Sign_r for a session s if $r \neq \text{st}_s.\text{rnd}+1$.

Figure 2 describes an honest execution of a threshold signature scheme and provides a correctness definition.

4   Existential and Strong Unforgeability

Figure 3 defines existential and strong unforgeability for plain (single signer) digital signature schemes.

In both security games, the adversary is given an input public key vk and attempts to forge a signature σ for a message m of their choice that is valid for the said key. The adversary also has access to a signing oracle that they can query for signatures on adaptively chosen messages. To win, the adversary needs to output a *non-trivial* forgery. For existential unforgeability, a forgery (m, σ) is non-trivial if m was not a signing oracle query. For strong unforgeability (m, σ) is non-trivial if σ was not a signing oracle response on query m. Thus, a strongly unforgeable scheme guarantees that every signature that an adversary possesses was obtained from the signing oracle, or equivalently that the adversary cannot obtain more signatures for a message than the number of such signature produced by the signing oracle.

Algorithm $\mathsf{Exec_{TS}}(\tilde{vk}, (vk_i)_{i=1}^n, S, (sk_i)_{i \in S}, t, m)$:

1 Initialize the state of each signer $i \in S$ with $i, sk_i, (vk_j)_{j=1}^n, \tilde{vk}, t$ and initialize $i.\mathsf{st}_1$ with S, m
2 $\mathsf{out} \leftarrow (0)_{i \in S}$ // output of current round
3 For $r = 1, \dots, \mathsf{TS.nr}$ do:
4   For $i \in S$ do:
5        $(\sigma_i, i.\mathsf{st}) \leftarrow\!\!{\scriptstyle\$}\ \mathsf{TS.Sign}_r(i.\mathsf{st}, (vk_i)_{i=1}^n, S, m, \mathsf{out})$
6     $\mathsf{out} \leftarrow (\sigma_i)_{s \in S}$
7 Return σ_i for some $i \in S$

Game $\mathbf{G}_{n,t,m}^{\mathsf{ts-cor}}[\mathsf{TS}]$

FIN:

1 $((sk_i, vk_i)_{i=1}^n, \tilde{vk}) \leftarrow\!\!{\scriptstyle\$}\ \mathsf{TS.Kg}(n, t)$
2 $S \leftarrow\!\!{\scriptstyle\$}\ \{R \in \mathcal{P}(\{1, \dots, n\}) : |R| \geq t\}$ // $\mathcal{P}$ denotes the power set
3 $\sigma \leftarrow\!\!{\scriptstyle\$}\ \mathsf{Exec_{TS}}(\tilde{vk}, (vk_i)_{i=1}^n, S, (sk_i)_{i \in S}, t, m)$
4 Return $\mathsf{TS.Verify}(\tilde{vk}, m, \sigma)$

Fig. 2. Top: an honest execution of the signing protocol of a threshold signature scheme TS. Note that signing rounds may only use a subset of the provided input. **Bottom:** a game defining the correctness of a scheme. A scheme satisfies perfect correctness for a group size n and a threshold t if $\Pr[\mathbf{G}_{n,t,m}^{\mathsf{ts-cor}}[\mathsf{TS}]] = 1$ for each message m that is supported by TS.

In this section, we extend the definition of strong unforgeability to multi- and threshold signature using one-more unforgeability.

4.1   Extending Strong Unforgeability to Multi-signatures

Existential unforgeability of multi-signature in the plain public key model is an extension of the existential unforgeability definition for plain signatures. In the standard definition, the adversary is given a public key vk of an "honest signer" as input, and is able to query a signing oracle in which the honest signer completes the signing algorithms for messages and signing groups chosen by the adversary. If the scheme contains multiple signing rounds, then the adversary may also adaptively choose the input to each signing round as well as interweave the rounds of different signing sessions. The adversary wins if they output a non-trivial valid signature for a message m and a group of public keys $(vk_i)_{i=1}^n$ that contains vk, where non-trivial means that the signing oracle did not complete a signing session to sign m with this group of signers.

Extending strong unforgeability to multi-signature schemes is more challenging. The natural security goal is the guarantee that every valid signature was legitimately obtained, but it is unclear how to formalize this goal into a precise definition. First, an interaction with the signing oracle does not output a multi-signature but a signature share, whereas the winning condition for the

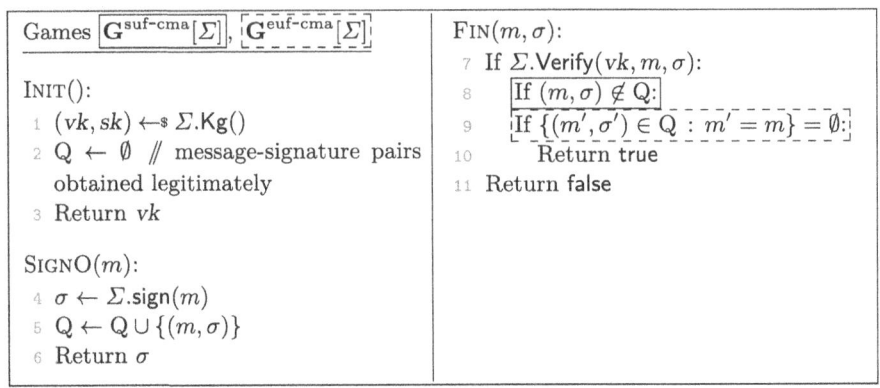

Fig. 3. Games used to define the existential and strong unforgeability of a single signer digital signature scheme Σ. The definition for strong unforgeability, $\mathbf{G}^{\text{suf-cma}}$, contains all but the dashed box. The definition for existential unforgeability, $\mathbf{G}^{\text{euf-cma}}$, contains all but the solid box.

adversary includes producing a valid multi-signature. Furthermore, the single signature share may not uniquely define the aggregate signature, which also depends on input from signers that are controlled by the adversary. Therefore, simply tracking the outputs of the signing oracle does not allow us to distinguish between trivial and non-trivial forgeries.

Thus, we turn to a different approach to defining strong unforgeability. For plain signatures, strong unforgeability is equivalent to the guarantee that an adversary cannot obtain more valid signatures for each message than the number of shares obtained legitimately via the signing oracle. This notion does apply to multi-signatures, and can be formalized using *one-more unforgeability*. In our strong unforgeability definition, we count how many signature shares the adversary obtains from the signing oracles for each message and signing group, and require that the adversary cannot compute more valid signatures. Thus, a secure scheme guarantees that the adversary cannot obtain more signatures than those that can be computed trivially from the shares it obtained from the signing oracles.

We put this notion into a game definition in Fig. 4, which compares it with the definition of existential unforgeability. Note that the only difference between the existential and strong unforgeability games is the winning condition, and whenever an adversary wins the existential unforgeability game it also wins the strong unforgeability game. Hence, strong unforgeability implies existential unforgeability, as expected.

AT WHICH ROUND IS A MESSAGE SIGNED. Some authors (for example [6,8,13, 35]) consider a forgery for a message and a group of signers trivial if the adversary initiated a signing session with those parameters. However, for multi-round schemes, an adversary should not be able to obtain a signature unless all interactive signing rounds have been completed.

Games $\boxed{\mathbf{G}^{\text{suf-ms}}[\text{MS}]}$, $\boxed{\mathbf{G}^{\text{euf-ms}}[\text{MS}]}$

INIT():
1 $(vk, sk) \leftarrow_\$ \text{MS.Kg}()$ // generates keys and initializes state
2 $Q \leftarrow$ Empty Dictionary
3 Return vk

SIGNO$_j(s$, SOME SUBSET OF $\{m, k, (vk_i)_{i=1}^n, \text{out}\})$:
4 // An oracle for each $j \in \{1, \ldots, \text{MS.nr}\}$
5 $\sigma \leftarrow_\$ \text{MS.Sign}_j(\text{input of SIGNO}_j)$
6 If $\sigma = \bot$: return $\bot$
7 If $j = \text{MS.lir}$: // on last interactive signing round
8   If $Q[((\text{st}_s.vk_i)_{i=1}^n, \text{st}_s.m)]$ uninitialized:
9          $Q[((\text{st}_s.vk_i)_{i=1}^n, \text{st}_s.m)] \leftarrow 1$
10   Else:
11         $Q[((\text{st}_s.vk_i)_{i=1}^n, \text{st}_s.m)] \leftarrow Q[((\text{st}_s.vk_i)_{i=1}^n, \text{st}_s.m)] + 1$
12 Return σ

FIN($k, (vk_i)_{i=1}^n, m, (\sigma_j)_{j=1}^\ell)$:
13 If $vk_k \neq vk$: return false
14 If $\sigma_i = \sigma_j$ for some $i \neq j$: return false
15 For $j = 1, \ldots, \ell$ do:
16   If not $\text{MS.Verify}((vk_i)_{i=1}^n, m, \sigma_j)$:
17   Return false
18     $\boxed{\text{If } Q[(vk_i)_{i=1}^n, m] \text{ initialized and } Q[(vk_i)_{i=1}^n, m] \geq \ell:}$
19     $\overline{\text{If } Q[(vk_i)_{i=1}^n, m]} \text{ initialized:}$
20   Return false
21 Return true

Fig. 4. Games used to define the existential and strong unforgeability of a multi-signature scheme MS. The definition for strong unforgeability, $\mathbf{G}^{\text{suf-ms}}$, contains all but the dashed box. The definition for existential unforgeability, $\mathbf{G}^{\text{euf-ms}}$, contains all but the solid box.

Thus, in our syntax a scheme specifies its last interactive signing round, MS.lir. It is expected that after querying the signing oracle for the last interactive round the adversary can produce a multi-signature, but not before, for both existential and strong unforgeability. Therefore, our security game registers that a legitimate multi-signature has been provided only on calls to the signing oracle for the last interactive round.

WHICH SIGNING ROUNDS ARE MESSAGE AND GROUP DEPENDENT. In some multi-signature schemes, some signing rounds can be completed before the message to sign or the identities of the signers in the group are determined (for example, [40, 47]). Our definitions support such schemes by allowing each scheme to define the input for each signing round in our syntax and security definitions.

TOY STRONGLY UNFORGEABLE SCHEME. We present a toy multi-signature scheme in the full version of this paper to help demonstrates the difference and separation between existential and strong unforgeability.

COMPARISON TO OMUF OF BLIND SIGNATURES. While we refer to our security notion as one-more unforgeability, it is more similar to the so called *strong one-more unforgeability* of blind signatures. Whereas existential one-more unforgeability of blind signatures typically refers to the notion that an adversary cannot come up with $\ell + 1$ signatures for distinct messages after completing ℓ signing sessions, strong OMUF does not require the messages to be distinct.

Our approach to defining OMUF and strong OMUF of blind signatures are similar. On one hand, if the number of message-signature pairs exceeds the number of signing sessions, there must be one message that has been signed fewer times than the number of signatures the adversary produced for that message, breaking our definition of OMUF. Conversely, if for some message the adversary can produce more signatures than the number of sessions that signed it, we can extend this to an attack producing more message-signature pairs than the number of signing executions.

4.2 Strong Unforgeability of Threshold Signatures

As with multi-signature, we define strong unforgeability for threshold signatures using one-more unforgeability.

One of the challenges with threshold signatures is the abundance of different security definitions, even for existential unforgeability. In this paper, we only formally define strong unforgeability that corresponds to the simple TS-UF-0 unforgeability definition of [5,11]. We also discuss stronger definitions of existential unforgeability, and how to extend them to strong unforgeability.

EXISTENTIAL AND STRONG UNFORGEABILITY. A t-out-of-n threshold signature scheme with n signers and a signing threshold t can only provide security as long as less than t of the signers are corrupted, since otherwise the corrupt signers can produce signatures by following the protocol. Thus, we enforce that less than t of the signers are corrupt in all security games. The adversary can query the honest signers for signature shares via a signing oracle, and may also adaptively choose the input to each signing round and interweave the rounds of different signing sessions. The adversary wins if they obtain a non-trivial valid signature for the group public key.

Existential unforgeability (TS-UF-0) considers signatures for a message m trivial if the adversary has obtained some signature share for m via the signing oracle, or more specifically if all signing rounds of the signing protocol for m were completed by a signing oracle, up to the last interactive round (which is defined by the scheme). As with multi-signatures, extending this notion to strong unforgeability calls for one-more unforgeability. The strong unforgeability game counts how many signatures shares the adversary obtains from the signing oracle for each message, and the adversary wins if they can produce more signature than that for some message. This corresponds to the adversary obtaining more threshold signatures than the number they can trivially obtain using the signing oracle signature shares, had the adversary corrupted $t - 1$ signers.

Figure 5 provides our game definition, compared with the definition of existential unforgeability. Note that as with multi-signature, whenever an adversary wins the existential unforgeability game they also win the strong unforgeability game, and therefore strong unforgeability implies existential unforgeability.

OTHER CONSIDERATIONS. As with multi-signatures, our definition supports schemes where the message to sign is selected after the first signing round by allowing the scheme to define which input is taken by each signing round. Our definition also considers a message signed by the signing oracle if it completes the last interactive signing round, as opposed to the first round as is done in some prior work ([19], for example).

STRONGER SECURITY GOALS. It is natural to seek stronger security goals for threshold signatures for the case where the adversary corrupts less than $t - 1$ signers. In particular, a forged signature may not be considered trivial whenever the adversary obtained a signature share from a single honest signer for this message; instead, a forgery should only be considered trivial if the adversary obtained a partial signature from $t - |CS|$ signers (where $|CS|$ is the number of signers corrupted by the adversary). For existential unforgeability, this is precisely the distinction between TS-UF-0 and the stronger TS-UF-1 in [5,11].

Using one-more unforgeability, we can extend US-UF-1 to strong unforgeability. To do this, we require that $t - |CS|$ signature shares from distinct signers must be used to construct each threshold signature, and that no partial signature can be used to construct two threshold signatures. In other words, a scheme that satisfies this security goal would guarantee that the maximum number of signatures the adversary can obtain for a message m is no more than the maximum number of threshold signatures the adversary could have constructed if each threshold signature used $t - |CS|$ signature shares obtained via the signing oracle from distinct signers and no signature share is used twice.

Some constructions (for example [1,3,19,32]) seek to provide security against adversaries who adaptively choose which signers to corrupt. In the corresponding security definition, the adversary does not have to input the set of corrupted servers in advance, but can at any point choose to corrupt a signer and obtain their private keys and state. These definitions can easily be generalized to strong unforgeability using one-more unforgeability.

Lastly, it is straightforward to generalize definitions that include a concrete distributed key generation protocol ([16], for example) to strong unforgeability using one more unforgeability by changing the winning condition, as we have done.

PREVIOUS STRONG UNFORGEABILITY DEFINITIONS. In [5,11], Bellare et al. study the strong unforgeability of threshold signature schemes that are semi non-interactive, meaning they have a single signing round that requires signers to know the message and signing subset, and for which a signature is uniquely defined by the input to the last interactive signing round (called the leader request). While the class appears limited, it contains the scheme FROST and is thus of practical interest.

They present multiple strong unforgeability definitions, the weakest of which (TS-SUF-2) considers a forgery trivial only if there exist a leader request for which $t - |CS|$ honest signers replied with a signature share (where $|CS|$ denotes the number of corrupted signers). This definition is stronger than our definition, and any scheme that satisfies TS-SUF-2 satisfies our strong unforgeability definition, as we show in Sect. 6.1 (where we also present their definition in detail). Conversely, in the full version of this paper we present a toy scheme that satisfies our strong unforgeability definition but not TS-SUF-2.

Concretely, the fact that TS-SUF-2 implies our strong unforgeability definition means that the results in [5,11] prove that FROST 1 [30] and FROST 2 [18] are strongly unforgeable by our definition (assuming idealized key generation).

5   Multi-signature Schemes

5.1   Analysis of HBMS

In [6] Bellare and Dai present HBMS ("Hash-Based Multi-Signature"), a two round multi-signature scheme, and prove its existential unforgeability using the discrete log assumption in the random oracle model. We will show that HBMS does not satisfy our definition of strong unforgeability by providing a concrete polynomial time attack by an adversary who corrupts at least one signer and can participate in concurrent signing sessions. The attack uses the algorithm of Benhamouda et al. [12] to solve the ROS problem [46], which broke the unforgeability of many multi-signature schemes including an older variant of MuSig [34].

In the attack the adversary completes the first signing round of ℓ concurrent signing sessions for some $\ell \geq \lceil \log_2(p) \rceil$, where each session has the same group of signers and the same message and p is the order of the underlying group. Then, the adversary completes the signing sessions to obtain one multi-signature from each, and uses the output of those sessions to construct an additional signature for the same message. Thus, the adversary obtains $\ell+1$ multi-signatures, of which ℓ are obtained legitimately and one is a forgery, breaking strong unforgeability.

The attack is practical against a group who produces signatures together repeatedly, and it can be carried out by a single malicious signer regardless of the number of signers in the group. We emphasize, however, that it does not compromise the existential unforgeability of HBMS nor violate existing security proofs.

We point out that HBMS is strongly unforgeable against adversaries that don't exploit the fact that HBMS is an interactive multi-signature scheme. In other words, if we assume an atomic execution of the signing protocol and no corrupt signers, then HBMS is strongly unforgeable. This distinction highlights the risk of integrating a multi-signature scheme in place of a strongly unforgeable single signer digital signature scheme, even if the multi-signatures are indistinguishable from the standard signatures. In the full version of this paper we

---

Games $\boxed{\mathbf{G}_{n,t}^{\text{suf-ts}}[\text{TS}]}$, $\overline{\left[\mathbf{G}_{n,t}^{\text{euf-ts}}[\text{TS}]\right]}$

INIT(CS):

1 Require $CS \subseteq \{1, \ldots, n\}$ and $|CS| < t$: // corrupt set
2 $HS \leftarrow \{1, \ldots, n\} \setminus CS$ // honest parties
3 $Q \leftarrow$ Empty Dictionary // tracks legit signatures
4 $((vk_i, sk_i)_{i=1}^n, \tilde{vk}) \leftarrow\!\!\text{\$}\ \text{TS.Kg}(n, t)$ // generates keys and initializes state
5 Return $\tilde{vk}, (vk_i)_{i=1}^n, (sk_j)_{j \in CS}$

SIGNO$_j(k, s, \text{SOME SUBSET OF } \{m, S, \text{out}\})$:

6 // An oracle for each $j \in \{1, \ldots, \text{TS.nr}\}$
7 If $k \notin HS$: return $\bot$
8 $\sigma \leftarrow\!\!\text{\$}\ k.\text{TS.Sign}_j(\text{input to SIGNO}_j)$
9 If $\sigma = \bot$: return $\bot$
10 If $j = \text{TS.lir}$: // on last interactive signing round
11   If $Q[\text{st}_s.m]$ uninitialized: $Q[\text{st}_s.m] \leftarrow 1$
12   Else: $Q[\text{st}_s.m] \leftarrow Q[\text{st}_s.m] + 1$
13 Return σ

FIN($m, (\sigma_j)_{j=1}^\ell$):

14 If $\sigma_i = \sigma_j$ for some $i \neq j$: return false
15 For $j = 1, \ldots, \ell$ do:
16   If not $\text{TS.Verify}(\tilde{vk}, m, \sigma_j)$:
17   Return false
18 $\boxed{\text{If } Q[m] \text{ initialized and } Q[m] \geq \ell:}$
19 $\overline{\left[\text{If } Q[m] \text{ initialized:}\right]}$
20   Return false
21 Return true

Fig. 5. Game used to define the existential and strong unforgeability of a threshold-signature scheme TS with a threshold t out of n. The definition for strong unforgeability, $\mathbf{G}^{\text{suf-ts}}$, contains all but the dashed box. The definition for existential unforgeability, $\mathbf{G}^{\text{euf-ts}}$, contains all but the solid box.

formally define this weaker security notion (which we call non-interactive strong unforgeability), and prove that it is satisfied by HBMS.

THE HBMS SCHEME. We describe the scheme informally. A formal description of the scheme is given in Figure 9 of [6].

HBMS involves three hash functions: H_0 with codomain $\mathbb{G}$ and H_1, H_2 with codomain $\mathbb{Z}_p$, where $\mathbb{G}$ is a multiplicative group of order p with a generator g provided by the scheme parameters. For key generation, each signer i of the n signers samples a secret key x_i uniformly at random from $\mathbb{Z}_p$ and a public key $X_i \leftarrow g^{x_i}$. The aggregate key is $\tilde{X} \leftarrow \prod_{i=1}^n X_i^{H_2(i, X_1, \ldots, X_n)}$.

To sign a message m with a group of signers $(X_i)_{i=1}^n$, the scheme involves two interactive signing rounds. In the first round, given the message and signing group as input, each signer i calculates $h \leftarrow H_0(X_1, \ldots, X_n, m) \in \mathbb{G}$, samples r_i

and s_i uniformly at random from $\mathbb{Z}_p$, and computes a commitment $M_i \leftarrow h^{s_i} g^{r_i}$ which is sent to every other signer. In the second round, each signer receives a list of commitments $(M_1, \ldots, M_n)$ from all the signers and computes $T \leftarrow \prod_{i=1}^n M_i$. Each signer then computes the challenge $c \leftarrow H_1(T, \tilde{X}, m)$ and the reply $z_i \leftarrow r_i + x_i \cdot c \cdot H_2(i, X_1, \ldots, X_n)$, and sends (s_i, z_i) to every other signer. Finally, every signer can now compute the final signature (T, s, z) where $s \leftarrow \sum_{i=1}^n s_i$, $z \leftarrow \sum_{i=1}^n z_i$, and $T \leftarrow \prod_{i=1}^n M_i$.

To verify a signature (T, s, z) with respect to public keys $(X_1, \ldots, X_n)$ and a message m, the verifier computes $h \leftarrow H_0(X_1, \ldots, X_n, m)$ and $\tilde{X} \leftarrow \prod_{i=1}^n X_i^{H_2(i, X_1, \ldots, X_n)}$, and returns true if and only if the equation

$$g^z h^s = T \cdot \tilde{X}^{H_1(T, \tilde{X}, m)}$$

holds. Note that during verification the entire vector of public keys is needed for computing h, and hence HBMS does not support key aggregation. Perfect correctness is easy to verify, and [6] proves the existential unforgeability of HBMS.

THE ATTACK. We will present an attack in the two signers setting where one signer is corrupt, which is sufficient to break our definition of strong unforgeability. It is easy to generalize it to a setting with more signers, as long as at least one signer is corrupt.

Let S_1 be a corrupt signer controlled by the adversary and S_2 an honest signer (with whom the adversary can communicate via a signing oracle). Let m be a message of the adversary's choice and pick $\ell \geq \lceil \log_2(p) \rceil$. Each signer $S_i \in \{S_1, S_2\}$ proceeds with the key generation honestly by picking $x_i \leftarrow_\$ \mathbb{Z}_p$ and $X_i \leftarrow g^{x_i}$ and computing $\tilde{X} \leftarrow X_1^{H_2(1, X_1, X_2)} X_2^{H_2(2, X_1, X_2)}$.

Now, for each $j \in \{1, \ldots, \ell\}$, the adversary opens a signing session with signing group (X_1, X_2) and message m, and receive a nonce $N_j = h^{s_j} g^{r_j}$ from the honest signer S_2, where $h \leftarrow H_0(X_1, X_2, m)$. For each $j \in \{1, \ldots, \ell\}$ and $b \in \{0, 1\}$, the adversary samples $\bar{r}_j^b$ and $\bar{s}_j^b$ uniformly at random from $\mathbb{Z}_p$ and computes $\overline{N}_j^b \leftarrow h^{\bar{s}_j^b} g^{\bar{r}_j^b}$ and $\overline{T}_j^b \leftarrow N_j \cdot \overline{N}_j^b$ as well as $\bar{c}_j^b \leftarrow H_1(\overline{T}_j^b, \tilde{X}, m)$. The adversary must also ensure that all of the $\overline{T}_j^{b_j}$ are distinct and that $\bar{c}_j^0 \neq \bar{c}_j^1$ for each j by regenerating the nonces if needed.

Now, define the group homomorphisms $\rho_+ : (\mathbb{Z}_p)^\ell \to \mathbb{Z}_p$ and $\rho_\times : \mathbb{G}^\ell \to \mathbb{G}$ given by

$$\rho_+(g_1, \ldots, g_\ell) = \sum_{j=1}^\ell \frac{2^{j-1} g_j}{\bar{c}_j^1 - \bar{c}_j^0}$$

and

$$\rho_\times(g_1, \ldots, g_\ell) = \prod_{j=1}^\ell g_j^{\frac{2^{j-1}}{\bar{c}_j^1 - \bar{c}_j^0}}.$$

Let $T_{\ell+1} \leftarrow \rho_\times(N_1, \ldots, N_\ell)$ and calculate $c_{\ell+1} \leftarrow H_1(T_{\ell+1}, \tilde{X}, m)$. Let $d \leftarrow c_{\ell+1} - \rho_+(\bar{c}_1^0, \ldots, \bar{c}_\ell^0)$ and write it in binary as $d = \sum_{j=1}^\ell 2^{j-1} b_j$ for some $b_1, \ldots, b_\ell \in \{0, 1\}$, which is possible since $\ell \geq \lceil \log_2(p) \rceil$.

Next, continue to the second round of each signing session j by sending $\overline{N}_j^{b_j}$ to the honest signer and obtaining the returned signature shares s_j and z_j. The adversary can now obtain ℓ legitimate signatures for the message m by computing

$$\sigma_j \leftarrow (\overline{T}_j^{b_j}, s_j + \overline{s}_j^{b_j}, z_j + \overline{r}_j^{b_j} + x_1 \cdot \overline{c}_j^{b_j} \cdot H_2(1, X_1, X_2))$$

for each $j \in \{1, \ldots, \ell\}$, as well as a forgery

$$\sigma_{\ell+1} \leftarrow (T_{\ell+1}, \rho_+(s_1, \ldots, s_\ell), \rho_+(z_1, \ldots, z_\ell) + c_{\ell+1} \cdot x_1 \cdot H_2(1, X_1, X_2)).$$

We will prove below that all $\ell + 1$ signatures $(\sigma_1, \ldots, \sigma_\ell, \sigma_{\ell+1})$ are valid for the message m and signing group (X_1, X_2), and that they are all distinct with high probability. This implies that the adversary obtained $\ell + 1$ valid signatures after only completing ℓ signing oracle signing sessions, breaking the strong unforgeability of HBMS.

VALIDITY OF $\sigma_1, \ldots, \sigma_\ell$. Since all of the $\overline{T}_j^{b_j}$ are distinct, all of the σ_j are distinct for $j \in \{1, \ldots, \ell\}$. Also note that each of those signatures was obtained legitimately with both signers following the protocol, and hence by the perfect correctness of HBMS they are valid.

VALIDITY OF $\sigma_{\ell+1}$. The signature $\sigma_{\ell+1} = (T_{\ell+1}, \rho_+(s_1, \ldots, s_\ell), \rho_+(z_1, \ldots, z_\ell) + c_{\ell+1} \cdot x_1 \cdot H_2(1, X_1, X_2))$ is the forged signature, and is the only one that is not trivial to obtain.

For the distinctiveness of $\sigma_{\ell+1}$, note that the collection $\{\overline{T}_1^{b_1}, \ldots, \overline{T}_\ell^{b_\ell}\}$ is selected uniformly at random from all subsets of $\mathbb{G}$ of cardinality ℓ, independently of $(N_1, \ldots, N_\ell)$. Hence, the probability that is contains $T_{\ell+1} = \rho_\times(N_1, \ldots, N_\ell)$ is $\frac{\ell}{|\mathbb{G}|} \approx \frac{\log_2(p)}{p}$, which is very small. Hence, with large probability, $T_{\ell+1} \neq \overline{T}_j^{b_j}$ and therefore $\sigma_{\ell+1} \neq \sigma_j$ for all $j \in \{1, \ldots, \ell\}$.

We will now verify that $\sigma_{\ell+1}$ is valid. To check its validity, we must verify that

$$g^{\rho_+(z_1, \ldots, z_\ell) + c_{\ell+1} \cdot x_1 \cdot H_2(1, X_1, X_2)} \cdot h^{\rho_+(s_1, \ldots, s_\ell)} = T_{\ell+1} \cdot \tilde{X}^{c_{\ell+1}}$$

where $h \leftarrow H_0(X_1, X_2, m)$. Starting from the right-hand side, we have that

$$T_{\ell+1} \cdot \tilde{X}^{c_{\ell+1}} = \rho_\times(N_1, \ldots, N_\ell) \cdot (X_1^{H_2(1, X_1, X_2)} X_2^{H_2(2, X_1, X_2)})^{c_{\ell+1}} =$$
$$= g^{\rho_+(r_1, \ldots, r_\ell)} \cdot h^{\rho_+(s_1, \ldots, s_\ell)} \cdot g^{(x_1 \cdot H_2(1, X_1, X_2) + x_2 \cdot H_2(2, X_1, X_2))c_{\ell+1}}.$$

Applying Lemma 1, which states that $c_{\ell+1} = \rho_+(\overline{c}_1^{b_1}, \ldots, \overline{c}_\ell^{b_\ell})$, we can simplify the equation to

$$= h^{\rho_+(s_1, \ldots, s_\ell)} g^{x_1 \cdot H_2(1, X_1, X_2)c_{\ell+1} + \rho_+(r_1, \ldots, r_\ell) + x_2 \cdot H_2(2, X_1, X_2) \cdot \rho_+(\overline{c}_1^{b_1}, \ldots, \overline{c}_\ell^{b_\ell})}$$

and therefore, since ρ_+ is homomorphic and $z_j = r_j + x_2 \cdot H_2(2, X_1, X_2) \cdot \overline{c}_j^{b_j}$ for each j,

$$= h^{\rho_+(s_1, \ldots, s_\ell)} g^{x_1 \cdot H_2(1, X_1, X_2)c_{\ell+1} + \rho_+(z_1, \ldots, z_\ell)}$$

which is what we wanted to prove. Hence, $\sigma_{\ell+1}$ is a valid signature.

Lemma 1. *By the construction above,* $c_{\ell+1} = \rho_+(\overline{c}_1^{b_1}, \ldots, \overline{c}_\ell^{b_\ell})$.

This lemma is at the heart of the attack, and the construction allowing this lemma to hold is precisely the algorithm of [12] to solve the ROS problem.

Proof (Lemma 1). By definition $\sum_{j=1}^{\ell} 2^{j-1} b_j = c_{\ell-1} - \rho_+(\overline{c}_1^0, \ldots, \overline{c}_\ell^0)$. Hence, to prove the lemma, it is sufficient to show that

$$\rho_+(\overline{c}_1^{b_1}, \ldots, \overline{c}_\ell^{b_\ell}) - \rho_+(\overline{c}_1^0, \ldots, \overline{c}_\ell^0) = \sum_{j=1}^{\ell} 2^{j-1} b_j.$$

Starting from the left-hand side, we have that

$$\rho_+(\overline{c}_1^{b_1}, \ldots, \overline{c}_\ell^{b_\ell}) - \rho_+(\overline{c}_1^0, \ldots, \overline{c}_\ell^0) = \sum_{j=1}^{\ell} \frac{2^{j-1}(\overline{c}_j^{b_j} - \overline{c}_j^0)}{\overline{c}_j^1 - \overline{c}_j^0}.$$

For each j, we have that $\frac{2^{j-1}(\overline{c}_j^{b_j} - \overline{c}_j^0)}{\overline{c}_j^1 - \overline{c}_j^0}$ is equal to 0 whenever b_j is 0 and is equal to 2^{j-1} whenever b_j is 1. Consequently, $\frac{2^{j-1}(\overline{c}_j^{b_j} - \overline{c}_j^0)}{\overline{c}_j^1 - \overline{c}_j^0} = 2^{j-1} b_j$. Thus,

$$\rho_+(\overline{c}_1^{b_1}, \ldots, \overline{c}_\ell^{b_\ell}) - \rho_+(\overline{c}_1^0, \ldots, \overline{c}_\ell^0) = \sum_{j=1}^{\ell} 2^{j-1} b_j$$

which is what we wanted to prove.

5.2 Analysis of MuSig

In this section we prove the strong unforgeability of the multi-signature scheme MuSig which consists of three interactive signing rounds and supports key aggregation, presented in [35].

We emphasize that only the 3-round version of MuSig is strongly unforgeable, whereas the prior two-round version [34] is insecure [12,23].

THE SCHEME. We now describe the scheme informally. A formal description of the scheme using our syntax for multi-signatures can be found in Fig. 6.

The scheme involves a group $\mathbb{G}$ of prime order p with a generator g and the hash functions H_{com}, H_{sign}, and H_{agg} with codomain $\mathbb{Z}_p$ that are used for commitments, signing, and key aggregation respectively. In key generation, each signing party generates a private key $sk \leftarrow_\$ \mathbb{Z}_p$ and a public key $vk \leftarrow g^{sk}$. The aggregate public key for a group of n signers with public keys $vk_1, \ldots, vk_n$ is computed by

$$\tilde{vk} \leftarrow \prod_{i=1}^{n} vk_i^{H_{\mathsf{agg}}(i, vk_1, \ldots, vk_n)}.$$

In the first signing rounds, each signer k chooses $r_k \leftarrow_\$ \mathbb{Z}_p$, computes $R_k \leftarrow g^{r_k}$, and sends a commitment $t_k \leftarrow H_{\mathsf{com}}(R_k)$ to all the other signers. In the second round, each signer k receives the commitments $t_1, \ldots, t_n$ from all other signers, and sends R_k to all other signers. In the third round, the signer receives nonces $R_1, \ldots, R_n$ from all the signers and verifies the commitments by checking that $t_i = H_{\mathsf{com}}(R_i)$ for each i. Then, they compute $R \leftarrow \prod_{i=1}^{n} R_i$, the aggregate public key $\tilde{\mathsf{vk}}$ as described above, and a challenge $c \leftarrow H_{\mathsf{sign}}(\tilde{\mathsf{vk}}, R, m)$. Then, they output a signature share $z_k \leftarrow r_k + sk_k \cdot c \cdot H_{\mathsf{agg}}(k, \mathsf{vk}_1, \ldots, \mathsf{vk}_n)$. Now, any of the signer can output the multi-signature (R, z) where $z \leftarrow \sum_{i=1}^{n} z_i$.

A signature (R, z) is valid with respect to an aggregated verification key $\tilde{\mathsf{vk}}$ and a message m if and only if

$$g^z = R \cdot \tilde{\mathsf{vk}}^{H_{\mathsf{sign}}(\tilde{\mathsf{vk}}, R, m)}.$$

MuSig satisfies perfect correctness, and the verification of a MuSig multi-signature with respect to an aggregated key $\tilde{\mathsf{vk}}$ is identical to the verification of a standard Schnorr signature.

WHICH SIGNING ROUNDS ARE MESSAGE DEPENDENT. The signers in MuSig do not use the message in the first two signing rounds. Thus, it is natural to ask whether it is possible to pre-execute the first two signing rounds before the message to sign arrives. If so, the scheme would involve a single interactive signing round when the message arrives, resulting in an almost non-interactive signature scheme (this property is claimed by MuSig2 [40], for example). The original MuSig paper [35] does not provide an explicit answer to this question.

The answer, however, is no. Such a shortcut leads to the scheme no longer being existentially unforgeable [37,38]. For security, the signers must associate each signing execution with a message and a signing group when executing the second signing round (the "reveal" round of the nonce shares). Our security proof only applies in this setting.

PRIOR SECURITY PROOFS FOR MUSIG. The existential unforgeability of MuSig is proved in [6,13,35]. These proofs, however, use a security definition that considers a forgery trivial whenever the adversary opened a signing oracle signing session with the corresponding message and group of signers, regardless of whether the signing session was completed. Consequently, these proofs do not rule out adversaries who complete the first two signing rounds for some message and then forge a signature without completing the third signing round. This is problematic since the third signing round is where signers verify the commitments sent in previous rounds, and it is the only round where the signers use their private keys.

We fill this gap by providing a security proof of strong unforgeability, and consequently existential unforgeability, using a definition that considers a forgery trivial only if the honest signer has completed all interactive rounds of a signing session with the corresponding message and public keys. This stronger definition comes at the cost of a looser reduction than the reduction in [6] by a factor of

---

Scheme $\mathsf{MuSig}_{\mathbb{G},g,H_{\mathsf{agg}},H_{\mathsf{com}},H_{\mathsf{sign}}}$:

$\mathsf{MuSig.nr} = 4$

$\mathsf{MuSig.lir} = 3$

$\mathsf{KeyGen}()$:

1 $x \leftarrow_{\$} \mathbb{Z}_p$; $X \leftarrow g^x$
2 $\mathsf{st.sk} \leftarrow x$; $\mathsf{st.vk} \leftarrow X$
3 Return $(sk = x, vk = X)$

$\mathsf{KeyAgg}(vk_1, \ldots, vk_n)$:

4 Return $\prod_{i=1}^n vk_i^{H_{\mathsf{agg}}(i,vk_1,\ldots,vk_n)}$

$\mathsf{AggVer}(m, \sigma, \tilde{vk})$:

5 $(R, z) \leftarrow \sigma$
6 Return $[g^z = R \cdot \tilde{vk}^{H_{\mathsf{sign}}(\tilde{vk},R,m)}]$

$\mathsf{Sign}_1()$:

7 $\mathsf{st.}j \leftarrow \mathsf{st.}j + 1$; $j \leftarrow \mathsf{st}_j$
8 $\mathsf{st}_j.r \leftarrow_{\$} \mathbb{Z}_p$; $\mathsf{st}_j.R \leftarrow g^{\mathsf{st}_j.r}$
9 $\mathsf{st}_j.t \leftarrow H_{\mathsf{com}}(\mathsf{st}_j.R)$
10 $\mathsf{st}_j.\mathsf{rnd} \leftarrow 1$
11 Return $\mathsf{st}_j.t$

$\mathsf{Sign}_2(j, (t_i, vk_i)_{i=1}^n, m)$:

12 If $\mathsf{st}_j.\mathsf{rnd} \neq 1$, $vk_k \neq \mathsf{st.vk}$, or $\mathsf{st}_j.t \neq t_k$:
13   Return $\bot$
14 $\mathsf{st}_j.m \leftarrow m$; $\mathsf{st}_j.n \leftarrow n$; $\mathsf{st}_j.k \leftarrow k$
15 For i from 1 to n:
16   $\mathsf{st}_j.t_i \leftarrow t_i$; $\mathsf{st}_j.vk_i \leftarrow vk_i$
17 $\mathsf{st.rnd} \leftarrow 2$
18 Return $\mathsf{st}_j.R$

$\mathsf{Sign}_3(j, R_1, \ldots, R_n)$:

19 If $\mathsf{st}_j.\mathsf{rnd} \neq 2$ or $R_{\mathsf{st}_j.k} \neq \mathsf{st}_j.R$:
20   Return $\bot$
21 If $\exists i$ such that $\mathsf{st}_j.t_i \neq H_{\mathsf{com}}(R_i)$:
22   Return $\bot$
23 $\tilde{vk} \leftarrow \mathsf{KeyAgg}(\mathsf{st}_j.vk_1, \ldots, \mathsf{st}_j.vk_n)$
24 $R \leftarrow \prod_{i=1}^n R_i$
25 $c \leftarrow H_{\mathsf{sign}}(R, \tilde{vk}, \mathsf{st}_j.m)$
26 $a \leftarrow H_{\mathsf{agg}}(\mathsf{st}_j.k, \mathsf{st}_j.vk_1, \ldots, \mathsf{st}_j.vk_n)$
27 $z \leftarrow \mathsf{st}_j.r + x \cdot c \cdot a$
28 $\mathsf{st}_j.\mathsf{rnd} \leftarrow 3$
29 Return (R, z)

$\mathsf{Sign}_4(R, z_1, \ldots, z_n)$:

30 Return $(R, \sum_{i=1}^n z_i)$

Fig. 6. A description of the MuSig scheme over a group $\mathbb{G}$ of order p and generator g. The fourth round is often omitted since it can be performed by any observer of the protocol.

approximately q_s, where q_s denotes the maximum number of signing sessions opened by the adversary.

OUR RESULT, CHAIN REDUCTIONS, AND THE XIDL. In [6], Bellare and Dai construct a chain of reductions from the discrete log problem to their definition of the existential unforgeability of MuSig. One of the links in the chain is the Random Target Identification Logarithm (XIDL) game in Fig. 7, and they show that it is hard whenever the discrete log assumption (Fig. 7) holds, as written in Lemma 2.[2]

In Lemma 3, we prove that MuSig is strongly unforgeable in the random oracle model if winning the XIDL is hard. The combination of these lemmas proves the strong unforgeability of MuSig in the ROM under the discrete log assumption.

Lemma 2 (DL → XIDL in the ROM; a combination of Theorems 3.2 and 3.4 of [6]). *Let $\mathbb{G}$ be a group of order p with generator g. Let q_1, q_2 be positive*

---

[2] They also achieve tighter security bounds using the algebraic group model [24], but this is orthogonal to this paper.

Game $\mathrm{Gm}_{\mathbb{G},g}^{\mathrm{dl}}$	Game $\mathrm{Gm}_{\mathbb{G},g,q_1,q_2}^{\mathrm{xidl}}$
INIT():	INIT():
1 $x \leftarrow\!\!\$\ \mathbb{Z}_p; X \leftarrow g^x$	1 $x \leftarrow\!\!\$\ \mathbb{Z}_p; X \leftarrow g^x$
2 Return X	2 $j \leftarrow 0; i \leftarrow 0$
	3 Return X
FIN(x'):	
3 Return $[x = x']$	NEWTARGET(S): // at most q_1 queries.
	4 $j = j + 1; S_j \leftarrow S$
	5 $e_j \leftarrow\!\!\$\ \mathbb{Z}_p; T_j \leftarrow S_j \cdot X^{e_j}$
	6 Return e_j
	CHALLENGE(j_{sel}, R): // at most q_2 queries
	7 $i \leftarrow i + 1; R_i \leftarrow R$
	8 $Y_i \leftarrow T_{j_{\mathrm{sel}}}; c_i \leftarrow\!\!\$\ \mathbb{Z}_p$
	9 Return c_i
	FIN(I, z):
	10 Return $[g^z = R_I \cdot Y_I^{c_I}]$

Fig. 7. The Discrete Log (DL) and the Random Target Identification Logarithm (XIDL) games in a group $\mathbb{G}$ with a generator g of prime order p.

integers. Let $\mathcal{A}_{\mathsf{xidl}}$ be an adversary against $\mathrm{Gm}_{\mathbb{G},g,q_1,q_2}^{\mathrm{xidl}}$. Then, an adversary $\mathcal{A}_{\mathsf{dl}}$ can be constructed so that

$$\mathbf{Adv}_{\mathbb{G},g,q_1,q_2}^{\mathrm{xidl}}(\mathcal{A}_{\mathsf{xidl}}) \leq \sqrt{q_2\left(\sqrt{q_1 \cdot \mathbf{Adv}_{\mathbb{G},g}^{\mathrm{dl}}(\mathcal{A}_{\mathsf{dl}})} + \frac{q_1}{p}\right)} + \frac{q_2}{p}$$

and the running time of $\mathcal{A}_{\mathsf{dl}}$ is approximately four times the running time of $\mathcal{A}_{\mathsf{xidl}}$.

We omit the proofs of Lemma 2 since it is non-trivial and can be found in the referenced paper.

Lemma 3 (XIDL → SUF of MuSig in the ROM). *Let $\mathbb{G}$ be a group of prime order p. Let g be a generator of $\mathbb{G}$. Let $\mathsf{MS} = \mathsf{MuSig}[\mathbb{G}, g]$ be the associated multi-signature scheme, with its hash functions modeled as random oracles. Let $\mathcal{A}_{\mathsf{ms}}$ be an adversary for the game $\mathbf{G}^{\mathrm{suf\text{-}ms}}[\mathsf{MS}]$ and assume the execution of $\mathcal{A}_{\mathsf{ms}}$ has at most q_0, q_1, q_2, q_s distinct queries to H_{com}, H_{agg}, H_{sign}, and SIGNO_1, the number of signing parties in queries to signing oracle queries and FIN is at most n, and the number of signatures it outputs is at most ℓ. Let $q = q_0(q_0 + n \cdot q_s) + (q_s + q_1 + 1)^2 + q_2(q_s + q_1 + 1) + q_s(q_2 + q_s) + n \cdot q_s(q_0 + n \cdot q_s)$. Then, there exists an adversary $\mathcal{A}_{\mathsf{xidl}}$ for the game $\mathrm{Gm}_{\mathbb{G},g,q_1+q_s+1,q_2+\ell}^{\mathrm{xidl}}$ such that*

$$\mathbf{Adv}_{\mathsf{MS}}^{\mathrm{suf\text{-}ms}}(\mathcal{A}_{\mathsf{ms}}) \leq (1 + q_s)\mathbf{Adv}_{\mathbb{G},g,q_s+q_1+1,q_2+\ell}^{\mathrm{xidl}}(\mathcal{A}_{\mathsf{xidl}}) + \frac{q}{p}$$

and the running time of $\mathcal{A}_{\mathsf{xidl}}$ is similar to that of $\mathcal{A}_{\mathsf{ms}}$.

We now describe the proof idea for Lemma 3, and include a formal proof in the full version of this paper.

Proof Idea for Lemma 3. We describe informally how to win the XIDL game with high probability given an adversary that breaks the strong unforgeability of MuSig in the ROM.

SESSION PARAMETERS AND SIGNATURE TYPES. Each execution of the third signing round of the signing oracle uses a specific aggregate public key $\tilde{vk}$, aggregate nonce R, and message m. We refer this tuple $(R, \tilde{vk}, m)$ as the session parameter of this signing session.

Now consider an adversary $\mathcal{A}_{ms}$ in the random oracle model. If they wish to complete a signing session with the signing oracle, then for each corrupt signer they must provide a commitment t_i as input to the second signing round and then an R_i for the third signing round satisfying $H_{com}(R_i) = t_i$. To have a non-negligible probability of completing the signing session, they must have called the random oracle H_{com} with input R_i before providing the input to the second signing round. Thus, whenever the adversary calls SIGNO_2 with input $(m, X_1, \ldots, X_n, t_1, \ldots, t_n)$, the reduction can recover all of the R_i and compute the session parameters.

Now suppose $\mathcal{A}_{ms}$ breaks the strong unforgeability of MuSig. At the end of the game it outputs ℓ valid signatures $(R_j, z_j)_{j=1}^{\ell}$, where the R_j's are all distinct, for some message m and a group of keys $X_1, \ldots, X_n$ with aggregated key $\tilde{vk}$. Each of these signatures must fall into one of the following cases:

Case 1: $(R_j, \tilde{vk}, m)$ was the session parameters for some signing oracle signing session that executed the third signing round.

Case 2: $(R_j, \tilde{vk}, m)$ was the session parameters for some signing oracle signing session that executed the second signing round, but not the third.

Case 3: $(R_j, \tilde{vk}, m)$ was not the session parameters for any signing oracle signing session.

Since $\mathcal{A}_{ms}$ wins the strong unforgeability game, at most $\ell - 1$ signing oracle sessions with message m and keys $X_1, \ldots, X_n$ completed the third signing round. Hence, at most $\ell - 1$ signatures fall into Case 1 and at least one signature falls into Case 2 or 3. We refer to such signatures as "forgeries."

USING A FORGERY TO WIN XIDL. Let X denote the output of the XIDL INIT procedure, which the reduction sets to be the public key of the honest signer.

Now, suppose (R, z) is a valid multi-signature for a message m and a group of public keys $vk_1, \ldots, vk_n$ with $vk_k = X$. If the key aggregation exponent $H_{agg}(k, vk_1, \ldots, vk_n)$ is an XIDL target[3] and $c = H(R, \tilde{vk}, m)$ is a challenge obtained from the XIDL's CHALLENGE oracle with input R, then (R, z) wins

---

[3] The above procedure works for the case where there exist a unique k such that $vk_k = X$. If more than one such k exists, then we can program the random oracle so that $\sum_{\{k : X_k = X\}} H(k, vk_i, \ldots, vk_n)$ is an XIDL target and the hash function values appear uniformly random. See the formal proof for more details.

the XIDL game. Thus, we program the random oracle so that responses to $H_{\mathsf{agg}}(k, vk_1, \ldots, vk_n)$ queries are indeed XIDL targets and c is an XIDL challenge corresponding to that target. It remains to show how to simulate the signing oracle so that we can program the random oracle in such a way.

HOW TO SIMULATE THE SIGNING ORACLE. In order to construct a reduction, we must simulate the signing oracle without knowing the secret key of the honest signer. We use the standard technique of simulating the Schnorr signing oracle without knowledge of the public key.

1st round: The reduction simply outputs a random commitment $t_k \leftarrow_{\$} \mathbb{Z}_p$.

2nd round: The reduction picks a uniformly random signature share and challenge $z_k, c \leftarrow_{\$} \mathbb{Z}_p$, chooses a nonce-share $R_k \leftarrow g^{z_k} X^{-c \cdot H_{\mathsf{agg}}(k, vk_1, \ldots, vk_n)}$, and sets $H_{\mathsf{com}}(R_k) \leftarrow t_k$ so the commitment from the first round holds. As explained before, the reduction can now recover the session parameters $(R, \tilde{X}, m)$ even though R is not yet known to the adversary. Therefore, it programs the random oracle $H_{\mathsf{sign}}(R, \tilde{vk}, m) \leftarrow c$, and outputs the nonce share R_k.

3rd round: The reduction outputs the partial signature z_k that it generated when simulating the second signing round. It is a valid signature share by construction.

GUESSING WHICH SESSION PARAMETERS ARE FOR FORGERY. When simulating the signing oracle for a session with parameters $(R, \tilde{vk}, m)$, we program the random oracle challenge $H_{\mathsf{sign}}(R, \tilde{vk}, m) \leftarrow c$ for a c that we selected before determining R. Therefore, the reduction cannot use that challenge to win the XIDL game. This is why it needs a forgery.

Suppose the forgery is (R, z) and that is valid for a message m and an aggregated key $\tilde{X}$. If the forgery falls into Case 3 (the cases are defined at the beginning of the proof idea) we can use it to win the XIDL game, since its session parameters $(R, \tilde{X}, m)$ were not used by the signing oracle and thus the corresponding challenge is an XIDL challenge. However, if the forgery falls into Case 2, then the reduction programmed $H_{\mathsf{sign}}(R, \tilde{vk}, m) \leftarrow c$ when simulating SIGNO_2 and thus we cannot use it directly to win the XIDL game.[4]

To win the XIDL game using this type of forgery, the reduction generates an integer ρ uniformly at random from $\{1, \ldots, q_s, q_s + 1\}$ where q_s refers to the maximum number of signing sessions that can be opened by the adversary. Then, it simulates all signing sessions of index different from ρ as described above. For the ρ_{th} session, however, it runs the first two signing rounds of the signing session honestly by picking the nonce share R_k first, then generating the commitment and programming the signing oracle $t_k \leftarrow H_{\mathsf{com}}(R_k) \leftarrow_{\$} \mathbb{Z}_p$. Once the session parameters $(R, \tilde{vk}, m)$ are known at the initiation of the second round we can program the random oracle $H_{\mathsf{sign}}(R, \tilde{vk}, m) \leftarrow c$ where c is an XIDL challenge.

---

[4] Previous MuSig security proofs do not consider signatures of Case 2 as forgeries, since they consider a forgery trivial whenever the adversary initiated a signing session with the signing oracle for the corresponding message.

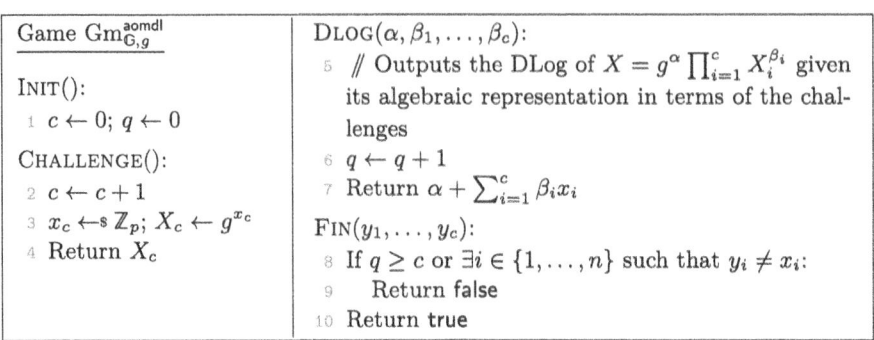

Fig. 8. The Algebraic One More Discrete Log (AOMDL) game in a group $\mathbb{G}$ with a generator g of prime order p.

Note that the reduction cannot simulate the third signing round of the ρ_{th} signing session and will have to abort if the adversary asks for it. It will, however, be able to win the XIDL game if the adversary outputs a forgery that falls into Case 2 with the session parameters of the ρ_{th} signing session.

Thus, if the adversary outputs a forgery that falls into Case 2, and we chose ρ so it corresponds to the session with the same parameters as the forgery, then we win the XIDL game. Hence, if the adversary produces a forgery that falls into Case 2 then we win the XIDL game with probability of at least $\frac{1}{q_s+1}$. If the adversary outputs a forgery that falls into Case 3, then we win if we were able to simulate all signing oracle queries, which is guaranteed if we chose $\rho = q_s + 1$ and thus we win with a probability of at least $\frac{1}{q_s+1}$. Since every successful adversary against the strong unforgeability of MuSig must provide a forgery that falls into Case 2 or 3, this means that if an adversary breaks the strong unforgeability of MuSig then the reduction wins the XIDL game with probability of approximately $\frac{1}{q_s+1}$.

We include a formal proof in the full version of this paper.

5.3   Analysis of MuSig2

We prove the strong unforgeability of the multi-signature scheme MuSig2 [40], a two round multi-signature scheme, under the Algebraic One More Discrete Log assumption of [40] (a weaker falsifiable variant of the One More Discrete Log assumption [7], defined in Fig. 8).

MuSig2 requires only two interactive signing rounds, of which one can be preprocessed before the message to sign and the set of signers have been determined. It also supports key aggregation and produces ordinary Schnorr signatures with respect to the aggregated signing key.

Our strong unforgeability proof of MuSig2 is nearly identical to its original existential unforgeability proof [40], and we strive to use similar structure and notation when presenting the proof as well as reuse as much of it as possible. The similarity of our proof to the existential unforgeability proof serves as evidence that our definition of strong unforgeability is straightforward to use.

THE SCHEME. We will describe the scheme informally. A formal description using our syntax for multi-signatures can be found in the full version of this paper.

The scheme uses a group $\mathbb{G}$ of prime order p with a generator g and three hash functions H_{agg}, H_{nonce}, and H_{sign} with codomain $\mathbb{Z}_p$. Key generation and aggregation is the same as in MuSig,[5] where each signer generates the keys $sk \leftarrow_{\$} \mathbb{Z}_p$ and $vk \leftarrow g^{sk}$ and the aggregate verification key for a group of n signers is $\tilde{vk} \leftarrow \prod_{i=1}^{n} vk_i^{H_{\mathsf{agg}}(i, X_1, \ldots, X_n)}$.

In the first signing round each signer k generates four[6] random values $r_{k,1}, \ldots, r_{k,4} \leftarrow_{\$} \mathbb{Z}_p$ and sends $R_{k,\ell} \leftarrow g^{r_{k,\ell}}$ for each $\ell \in \{1, \ldots, 4\}$ to all other signers. In the second round, on input $((vk_i, R_{i,1}, \ldots, R_{i,4})_{i=1}^{n}, m)$, each signer k computes $R_\ell \leftarrow \prod_{i=1}^{n} R_{i,\ell}$ for $\ell \in \{1, \ldots, 4\}$, the aggregate verification key $\tilde{vk}$, and $b \leftarrow H_{\mathsf{nonce}}(\tilde{vk}, R_1, \ldots, R_4, m)$. Then each signer computes the aggregate nonce $R \leftarrow \prod_{\ell=1}^{4} R_\ell^{(b^{\ell-1})}$, the challenge $c \leftarrow H_{\mathsf{sign}}(\tilde{vk}, R, m)$, and their partial signature $z_k \leftarrow \sum_{\ell=1}^{4} r_{k,\ell} \cdot b^{\ell-1} + c \cdot sk_k \cdot H_{\mathsf{agg}}(k, X_1, \ldots, X_n)$ which they send to all other signers. The final multi-signature is given by $(R, \sum_{i=1}^{n} z_i)$, which can be computed by any of the signers.

A multi-signature (R, z) can be verified with respect to a message m and an aggregate verification key $\tilde{vk}$ by checking that $g^z = R \cdot \tilde{vk}^{H_{\mathsf{sign}}(\tilde{vk}, R, m)}$, which is identical to the verification of a standard Schnorr signature. MuSig2 satisfies perfect correctness.

AGGREGATOR NODE. In the setting with an aggregator node, the communication cost of MuSig2 can be reduced by having the aggregator compute the R_j's instead of the signers. More specifically, after the first signing round the aggregator receives $(R_{i,1}, \ldots, R_{i,4})_{i=1}^{n}$ and computes $R_\ell \leftarrow \prod_{i=1}^{n} R_{i,\ell}$ for $\ell \subset \{1, \ldots, 4\}$. The R_ℓ's can now be used as the input to the second signing round of each signer, as opposed to all of the $R_{i,\ell}$'s.

This shortcut does not affect the existential and strong unforgeability of MuSig2, since an adversary can compute the R_ℓ's given the $R_{i,\ell}$'s, and because given a uniformly random R_ℓ an adversary can simulate a selection of $R_{1,\ell}, \ldots, R_{n,\ell}$ that appear uniformly random and have product R_ℓ. Therefore, without loss of generality, we do not consider this shortcut in our proof.

STRONG UNFORGEABILITY. The strong unforgeability of MuSig2 is given in the following lemma, which we prove in the full version of this paper.

---

[5] We slightly deviate from the original MuSig2 scheme by writing $\tilde{vk} \leftarrow \prod_{i=1}^{n} vk_i^{H_{\mathsf{agg}}(i, X_1, \ldots, X_n)}$, as opposed to $\tilde{vk} \leftarrow \prod_{i=1}^{n} vk_i^{H_{\mathsf{agg}}(X_i, X_1, \ldots, X_n)}$. This follows the convention of [6], which views the public keys of the signing group as a list as opposed to a multi-set in the security definitions.

[6] There is a simpler variant of MuSig2 that uses only two nonces [40] that we do not consider in this paper. Its security proof relies on the algebraic group model.

Lemma 4 (AOMDL → SUF of MuSig2 in the ROM). *Let* $\mathbb{G}$ *be a group with prime order* p *and generator* g. *Let* $\mathsf{MS} = \mathrm{MuSig2}[\mathbb{G}, g]$, *where its hash functions are modeled as random oracles. Let* $\mathcal{A}_{\mathrm{ms}}$ *be an adversary against* $\mathbf{G}^{\mathrm{suf\text{-}ms}}[\mathsf{MS}]$ *making at most* q_s *queries to the signing oracle* SIGNO_1 *and* q_h *queries to each random oracle. Let* $q = 4q_h + 3q_s + 2$. *Then, there exists an algorithm* $\mathcal{D}$ *such that*

$$\mathbf{Adv}^{\mathrm{suf\text{-}ms}}_{\mathsf{MS}}(\mathcal{A}_{\mathrm{ms}}) \leq \left(2q^3 \left(\mathbf{Adv}^{\mathrm{aomdl}}_{\mathbb{G}, g}(\mathcal{D}) + \frac{32q^2 + 12}{p} \right) \right)^{1/4}$$

and $\mathcal{D}$ *runs in approximately 4 times the runtime of* $\mathcal{A}_{\mathrm{ms}}$.

5.4   Analysis of mBCJ

We only introduce the conclusions of our analysis of mBCJ, without justification. Readers are referred to the full version of this paper for our attacks.

In [4], Bagherzandi et al. present BCJ, a two-round multi-signature scheme. Approximately a decade later, Drijvers et al. found an error in the security proof of BCJ and a sub-exponential attack against its existential unforgeability when concurrent signing sessions are permitted [23], using Wagner's algorithm for the generalized birthday problem [48]. The algorithm of Benhamouda et al. to solve the ROS problem [12] improves this attack to polynomial time. In the same paper [23], Drijvers et al. present mBCJ, a modification of the scheme which prevents the attack.

The modified scheme mBCJ is nearly identical to BCJ, except that some scheme parameters (the "commitment parameters") are computed as the hash of the message being signed, as opposed to public parameters that are the same for every signing session. Thus, a forged mBCJ signature on an unsigned message has to be valid for the corresponding commitment parameters, which are different from the parameters used by the signing oracle for signing different messages. The information gained from the signing oracle is now useless for forging a signature for an unsigned message, and the BCJ attack no longer works. Signing oracle queries for the same message, however, use the same commitment parameters and can assist the adversary in forging an additional signature for the same message. In the full version of this paper, we use this observation to modify the attack against BCJ to break the one-more unforgeability of mBCJ.

A more surprising result is a subtlety regarding the existential unforgeability of mBCJ. As mBCJ is originally presented [23], the commitment parameters are a function of the message being signed, but not of the aggregate verification key. This means that a small modification of our one-more unforgeability attack allows the adversary to forge a signature that is valid for an arbitrary signing set. The impact of the attack is as follows: if the adversary starts ℓ concurrent signing sessions for a message m with the honest signer, they can forge a multi-signature for the same message but with a group of signers of the adversary's choice (which may be different from the group used for signign oracle queries). We point out that this does not contradict the security proof of [23], since in their security definition such a forgery is not considered a win for the adversary. It does, however, render the scheme not existentially unforgeable according to many definitions in literature (notably that of Bellare and Neven [8]). We refer readers to the full version of this paper for the attack details.

6   Threshold Signatures Schemes

6.1   Comparison to Previous SUF-TS Definition, and FROST

In [5,11], Bellare et al. provide a hierarchy or unforgeability definitions for a limited class of threshold signature schemes. As part of this hierarchy, they define strong unforgeability for schemes that satisfy the following properties:

Semi non-interactive: The scheme has at most one pre-processing signing round, which takes no input and outputs a pre-processing token pp. Additionally, the scheme has a single signing round that takes the message, the set of participating signers, as well as the pre-processing tokens of all participants as input. The input to the message dependent signing round is called a leader request, denoted lr, with fields $lr.m$, $lr.S$, and $(lr.\mathsf{pp}_i)_{i \in S}$.

Strong-verification: The scheme has an additional strong verification algorithm SVerify, which verifies a signature with respect to a public key and a leader request. It is required that for each leader request lr and aggregated public key $\tilde{vk}$ there exist at most one signature σ such that $\mathsf{SVerify}(\tilde{vk}, lr, \sigma) = \mathsf{true}$. Correctness requires that $\mathsf{SVerify}(\tilde{vk}, lr, \sigma) = \mathsf{true}$ whenever all (of the t or more) signers in S honestly computed σ with lr as the input to the message dependent signing round.

While this class of schemes appears limited, it contains FROST, and is therefore of practical interest.

The hierarchy of strong unforgeability definitions in [5,11] begins at TS-SUF-2, the weakest of their definitions, that both the FROST 1 [30] and FROST 2 [5,18] variants satisfy under the one-more discrete log assumption [7] in the random oracle model (Theorem 5.3 and 5.1 of [11]). This definition considers an adversary who corrupts c out of n signers, where $c < t$. A secure scheme guarantees that if an adversary obtains a valid signature σ on a message m, then there exist a leader request lr with the same message that was signed by at least $t - c$ honest signers and $\mathsf{SVerify}(\tilde{vk}, lr, \sigma) = \mathsf{true}$. Figure 9 shows this definition using our syntax, and compares it to our strong unforgeability definition when restricted to the same class of schemes.

RELATIONSHIP BETWEEN TS-SUF-2 AND OUR DEFINITION. We claim that a TS-SUF-2 secure scheme is also one-more unforgeable according to our definition by showing that any adversary that wins $\mathbf{G}^{\mathsf{suf\text{-}ts}}$ can be modified to win $\mathbf{G}^{\mathsf{ts\text{-}suf\text{-}2\text{-}crypto22}}$ with the same probability and no significant increase in runtime. Note that this implies the one-more unforgeability of FROST 1 and FROST 2 under the OMDL assumption in the ROM.

Suppose there exists an adversary $\mathcal{A}$ that wins $\mathbf{G}_{n,t}^{\text{suf-ts}}[\text{TS}]$ with probability p. To construct an adversary $\mathcal{A}'$ that plays $\mathbf{G}_{n,t}^{\text{ts-suf-2-crypto22}}[\text{TS}]$ we can simply execute $\mathcal{A}$ (since the two games have access to the same oracles, with the same behavior) and maintain a set L of the leader requests that $\mathcal{A}$ inputs to SIGNO_2 (and receives a non-$\perp$ response). If A wins $\mathbf{G}_{n,t}^{\text{suf-ts}}[\text{TS}]$, it must come up with valid distinct signatures $(\sigma_j)_{j=1}^{\ell}$ for some message m such that $\ell \geq |\{lr \in L: lr.m = m\}|$. Hence, there exist some σ_j for which $\text{SVerify}(\tilde{vk}, lr, \sigma_j) = \text{false}$ for all $lr \in \{lr' \in L: lr'.m = m\}$, and thus $\mathcal{A}'$ can use σ_j to win $\mathbf{G}_{n,t}^{\text{ts-suf-2-crypto22}}[\text{TS}]$. Note that $\mathcal{A}'$ has roughly the same runtime as $\mathcal{A}$, and it wins $\mathbf{G}_{n,t}^{\text{ts-suf-2-crypto22}}[\text{TS}]$ with probability p.

We note that TS-SUF-2 is strictly stronger than our one-more unforgeability definition. In the full version of this paper we present a toy scheme that is one-more unforgeable but does not satisfy TS-SUF-2.

6.2   Analysis of ROAST

In FROST-like threshold signature schemes [16,19,25,30,47] signing a message involves selecting a signing subset (of sufficient size), after which it is required that each signing set member participates in a signing session honestly, else signature generation fails. This leads to a lack of robustness, losing one of the main advantages of threshold signatures over multi-signatures.

ROAST [44] is a simple wrapper algorithm that adds robustness to such a scheme Σ by executions the Σ signing protocol multiple times with different signing sets until one is successful. The only requirements on the underlying scheme are the following:

Identifiable aborts: Signers that do not participate honestly in a Σ signing sessions can be detected with overwhelming probability.

Semi non-interactive: Σ has one signing round that requires knowing the signing set, potentially in addition to a "pre-processing" signing round that can be executed before the signing set is selected.

The canonical schemes that satisfy these properties are FROST 1 [25] and FROST 3 [44]. ROAST also uses an aggregator who facilitates communication between the signers and is trusted for robustness, but not for unforgeability.

We argue that the robustness of ROAST comes at the cost of strong unforgeability. ROAST does not satisfy any notion of strong or one-more unforgeability, even if Σ is strongly unforgeable. This is in spite of the fact that ROAST does not fit our syntax and security definition for threshold signatures. It remains an important open problem to define strong unforgeability for a class of schemes that contains ROAST and construct a strongly unforgeable alternative.

THE SCHEME. We describe the scheme informally, and a formal description can be found in Figure 4 of [44].

Suppose Σ is a non-robust and semi non-interactive threshold signature scheme that supports identifiable aborts. Let S denote a signing group of size n

---

Game $\boxed{\mathbf{G}_{n,t}^{\text{ts-suf-2-crypto22}}[\mathsf{TS}]}$ $\overline{\mathbf{G}_{n,t}^{\text{suf-ts}}[\mathsf{TS}]}$

INIT(CS):

1 Require $CS \subseteq \{1,\ldots,n\}$ and $|CS| < t$: // corrupt parties

2 $HS \leftarrow \{1,\ldots,n\} \setminus CS$ // honest parties

3 $\boxed{Q \leftarrow \text{Empty Dictionary} \text{ // tracks who signed each } lr}$

4 $\overline{Q \leftarrow \text{Empty Dictionary} \text{ // num of signers for each } m}$

5 $((vk_i, sk_i)_{i=1}^n, \tilde{vk}) \leftarrow\!\!{}_\$ \mathsf{TS.Kg}(n,t)$ // generate keys and initialize state

6 Return $\tilde{vk}, (vk_i)_{i=1}^n, (sk_j)_{j \in CS}$

SIGNO$_1(k)$:

7 If $k \notin HS$: return $\bot$

8 $\mathsf{pp} \leftarrow\!\!{}_\$ k.\mathsf{TS.Sign}_1()$

9 Return pp

SIGNO$_2(k, s, m, S, (\mathsf{pp}_i)_{i \in S})$:

10 If $k \notin HS$: return $\bot$

11 $lr = (m, S, (\mathsf{pp}_i)_{i \in S})$; $\sigma \leftarrow\!\!{}_\$ k.\mathsf{TS.Sign}_2(s, lr)$

12 If $\sigma = \bot$: return $\bot$

13 $\boxed{\text{If } Q[lr] \text{ initialized: } Q[lr] \leftarrow Q[lr] \cup \{k\}; \text{ Else: } Q[lr] \leftarrow \{k\}}$

14 $\overline{\text{If } Q[m] \text{ initialized: } Q[m] \leftarrow Q[m] + 1; \text{ Else: } Q[m] \leftarrow 1}$

15 Return σ

$\boxed{\text{FIN}(m, \sigma)}$:

16 // $\mathbf{G}^{\text{ts-suf-2-crypto22}}$ game only

17 If not $\mathsf{TS.Verify}(\tilde{vk}, m, \sigma)$: return false

18 For each $lr \in Q$:

19   If lr has message m and $|Q[lr]| \geq t - |CS|$ and $\mathsf{SVerify}(\tilde{vk}, lr, \sigma)$:

20   Return false

21 Return true

$\overline{\text{FIN}(m, (\sigma_j)_{j=1}^\ell)}$:

22 // $\mathbf{G}^{\text{suf-ms}}$ game only

23 If $\sigma_i = \sigma_j$ for some $i \neq j$: return false

24 For $j = 1,\ldots,\ell$ do:

25   If not $\mathsf{TS.Verify}(\tilde{vk}, m, \sigma_j)$: return false

26 If $Q[m]$ initialized and $Q[m] \geq \ell$: return false

27 Return true

Fig. 9. Game $\mathbf{G}^{\text{ts-suf-2-crypto22}}$ used to define TS-SUF-2 for a threshold signature scheme TS in [5,11] (adjusted to our syntax), compared to our strong unforgeability definition $\mathbf{G}^{\text{suf-ts}}$ restricted to schemes where TS-SUF-2 is defined.

with a signing threshold t. The key generation and verification in ROAST are the same as those of Σ.

To sign a message m, the aggregator maintains a set R of available signers, initially adding signers to R whenever they complete the pre-processing round.

Whenever $|R| \geq t$, the aggregator picks a subset $T \subseteq R$ with $|T| = t$, initiates a Σ signing session with the message m for the signers of T, and removes them from R. Whenever a signer completes a signing session and another pre-processing round honestly, it is added back to R. The protocol terminates when one of the signing session produces a valid Σ signature.

This protocol is guaranteed to produce a valid signature whenever t of the signers are honest and responsive. Furthermore, since Σ supports identifiable aborts each signer can sabotage at most one Σ signing session, and thus ROAST terminates within a number of sessions that is at most the number of corrupt signers.

INCOMPATIBILITY WITH OUR UNFORGEABILITY DEFINITIONS. ROAST is inherently incompatible with our unforgeability definitions. To begin, the number of interactive signing rounds is not determined until the protocol terminates, and our syntax does not support such schemes. This issue can be circumnavigated with some syntactical overhead by allowing schemes to adaptively choose the number of signing rounds. More importantly, however, the signers cannot tell whether a signing round is the last interactive signing round. Thus, even in an honest execution, they cannot determine at which signing round the aggregator should be able to construct a threshold signature. In the context of our security definition, the unforgeability game cannot tell at which signing oracle query to increase the count of signatures obtained legitimately.

BREAKING STRONG UNFORGEABILITY. While it remains an open problem to formally define strong unforgeability for ROAST-like schemes, we show that ROAST does not satisfy any notion of strong unforgeability.

Consider, for instance, a group of 100 signers with a signing threshold of 67 and a corrupt aggregator that wishes to obtain many signatures for some message m. Even if all signers are honest, the aggregator can ask each signer to participate in multiple Σ signing sessions with various signing sets and obtain as many as $\binom{100}{67} \approx 3 \times 10^{26}$ signatures for m. This is despite the fact that each signer participated in a single ROAST session.

Acknowledgments. We thank the anonymous Asiacrypt 2024 reviewers for their insightful feedback, and for suggesting that mBCJ is not strongly unforgeable. This research was supported in part by NSF grants CNS-2026774, CNS-2154174, a JP Morgan Faculty Award, a CISCO Faculty Award, and a gift from Microsoft.

References

1. Almansa, J.F., Damgård, I., Nielsen, J.B.: Simplified threshold RSA with adaptive and proactive security. In: Vaudenay, S. (ed.) Advances in Cryptology – EUROCRYPT 2006. Lecture Notes in Computer Science, vol. 4004, pp. 593–611. Springer, Heidelberg, Germany, St. Petersburg, Russia (May 28 – Jun 1, 2006). https://doi.org/10.1007/11761679_35
2. Andrychowicz, M., Dziembowski, S., Malinowski, D., Mazurek, Ł: On the malleability of bitcoin transactions. In: Brenner, M., Christin, N., Johnson, B., Rohloff, K.

(eds.) Financial Cryptography and Data Security, pp. 1–18. Springer, Berlin Heidelberg, Berlin, Heidelberg (2015)

3. Bacho, R., Loss, J., Tessaro, S., Wagner, B., Zhu, C.: Twinkle: Threshold signatures from ddh with full adaptive security. In: Joye, M., Leander, G. (eds.) Advances in Cryptology - EUROCRYPT 2024, pp. 429–459. Springer Nature Switzerland, Cham (2024)

4. Bagherzandi, A., Cheon, J.H., Jarecki, S.: Multisignatures secure under the discrete logarithm assumption and a generalized forking lemma. In: Ning, P., Syverson, P.F., Jha, S. (eds.) ACM CCS 2008: 15th Conference on Computer and Communications Security. pp. 449–458. ACM Press, Alexandria, Virginia, USA (Oct 27–31, 2008). https://doi.org/10.1145/1455770.1455827

5. Bellare, M., Crites, E.C., Komlo, C., Maller, M., Tessaro, S., Zhu, C.: Better than advertised security for non-interactive threshold signatures. In: Dodis, Y., Shrimpton, T. (eds.) Advances in Cryptology – CRYPTO 2022, Part IV. Lecture Notes in Computer Science, vol. 13510, pp. 517–550. Springer, Heidelberg, Germany, Santa Barbara, CA, USA (Aug 15–18, 2022). https://doi.org/10.1007/978-3-031-15985-5_18

6. Bellare, M., Dai, W.: Chain reductions for multi-signatures and the HBMS scheme. In: Tibouchi, M., Wang, H. (eds.) Advances in Cryptology – ASIACRYPT 2021, Part IV. Lecture Notes in Computer Science, vol. 13093, pp. 650–678. Springer, Heidelberg, Germany, Singapore (Dec 6–10, 2021). https://doi.org/10.1007/978-3-030-92068-5_22

7. Bellare, M., Namprempre, C., Pointcheval, D., Semanko, M.: The one-more-RSA-inversion problems and the security of Chaum's blind signature scheme. Journal of Cryptology **16**(3), 185–215 (Jun 2003). https://doi.org/10.1007/s00145-002-0120-1

8. Bellare, M., Neven, G.: Multi-signatures in the plain public-key model and a general forking lemma. In: Juels, A., Wright, R.N., De Capitani di Vimercati, S. (eds.) ACM CCS 2006: 13th Conference on Computer and Communications Security. pp. 390–399. ACM Press, Alexandria, Virginia, USA (Oct 30 – Nov 3, 2006). https://doi.org/10.1145/1180405.1180453

9. Bellare, M., Rogaway, P.: Random oracles are practical: A paradigm for designing efficient protocols. In: Denning, D.E., Pyle, R., Ganesan, R., Sandhu, R.S., Ashby, V. (eds.) ACM CCS 93: 1st Conference on Computer and Communications Security. pp. 62–73. ACM Press, Fairfax, Virginia, USA (Nov 3–5, 1993). https://doi.org/10.1145/168588.168596

10. Bellare, M., Rogaway, P.: The security of triple encryption and a framework for code-based game-playing proofs. In: Vaudenay, S. (ed.) Advances in Cryptology – EUROCRYPT 2006. Lecture Notes in Computer Science, vol. 4004, pp. 409–426. Springer, Heidelberg, Germany, St. Petersburg, Russia (May 28 – Jun 1, 2006). https://doi.org/10.1007/11761679_25

11. Bellare, M., Tessaro, S., Zhu, C.: Stronger security for non-interactive threshold signatures: BLS and FROST. Cryptology ePrint Archive, Report 2022/833 (2022), https://eprint.iacr.org/2022/833

12. Benhamouda, F., Lepoint, T., Loss, J., Orrù, M., Raykova, M.: On the (in)security of ROS. In: Canteaut, A., Standaert, F.X. (eds.) Advances in Cryptology – EUROCRYPT 2021, Part I. Lecture Notes in Computer Science, vol. 12696, pp. 33–53. Springer, Heidelberg, Germany, Zagreb, Croatia (Oct 17–21, 2021). https://doi.org/10.1007/978-3-030-77870-5_2

13. Boneh, D., Drijvers, M., Neven, G.: Compact multi-signatures for smaller blockchains. In: Peyrin, T., Galbraith, S. (eds.) Advances in Cryptology – ASIACRYPT 2018, Part II. Lecture Notes in Computer Science, vol. 11273, pp. 435–464. Springer, Heidelberg, Germany, Brisbane, Queensland, Australia (Dec 2–6, 2018). https://doi.org/10.1007/978-3-030-03329-3_15

14. Brandão, L.T.A.N., Davidson, M.: Notes on threshold EdDSA/Schnorr signatures. Tech. Rep. NIST IR 8214B ipd, National Institute of Standards and Technology, Gaithersburg, MD (2022), https://doi.org/10.6028/NIST.IR.8214B.ipd

15. Canetti, R.: Universally composable security: A new paradigm for cryptographic protocols. In: 42nd Annual Symposium on Foundations of Computer Science. pp. 136–145. IEEE Computer Society Press, Las Vegas, NV, USA (Oct 14–17, 2001). https://doi.org/10.1109/SFCS.2001.959888

16. Chu, H., Gerhart, P., Ruffing, T., Schröder, D.: Practical Schnorr threshold signatures without the algebraic group model. In: Crypto 2023 (Aug 19–24, 2023). https://doi.org/10.1007/978-3-031-38557-5_24

17. Connolly, D., Komlo, C., Goldberg, I., Wood, C.A.: Two-Round Threshold Schnorr Signatures with FROST. Internet-Draft draft-irtf-cfrg-frost-10, Internet Engineering Task Force (Sep 2022), https://datatracker.ietf.org/doc/draft-irtf-cfrg-frost/10/, work in Progress

18. Crites, E., Komlo, C., Maller, M.: How to prove Schnorr assuming Schnorr: Security of multi- and threshold signatures. Cryptology ePrint Archive, Paper 2021/1375 (2021), https://eprint.iacr.org/2021/1375

19. Crites, E., Komlo, C., Maller, M.: Fully adaptive Schnorr threshold signatures. In: Advances in Cryptology – CRYPTO 2023 (Aug 2023)

20. Decker, C., Wattenhofer, R.: Bitcoin transaction malleability and mtgox. In: Kutyłowski, M., Vaidya, J. (eds.) Computer Security - ESORICS 2014. pp. 313–326. Springer International Publishing, Cham (2014)

21. Desmedt, Y.: Society and group oriented cryptography: A new concept. In: Pomerance, C. (ed.) Advances in Cryptology – CRYPTO'87. Lecture Notes in Computer Science, vol. 293, pp. 120–127. Springer, Heidelberg, Germany, Santa Barbara, CA, USA (Aug 16–20, 1988). https://doi.org/10.1007/3-540-48184-2_8

22. Desmedt, Y., Frankel, Y.: Threshold cryptosystems. In: Brassard, G. (ed.) Advances in Cryptology – CRYPTO'89. Lecture Notes in Computer Science, vol. 435, pp. 307–315. Springer, Heidelberg, Germany, Santa Barbara, CA, USA (Aug 20–24, 1990). https://doi.org/10.1007/0-387-34805-0_28

23. Drijvers, M., Edalatnejad, K., Ford, B., Kiltz, E., Loss, J., Neven, G., Stepanovs, I.: On the security of two-round multi-signatures. In: 2019 IEEE Symposium on Security and Privacy. pp. 1084–1101. IEEE Computer Society Press, San Francisco, CA, USA (May 19–23, 2019). https://doi.org/10.1109/SP.2019.00050

24. Fuchsbauer, G., Kiltz, E., Loss, J.: The algebraic group model and its applications. In: Shacham, H., Boldyreva, A. (eds.) Advances in Cryptology – CRYPTO 2018, Part II. Lecture Notes in Computer Science, vol. 10992, pp. 33–62. Springer, Heidelberg, Germany, Santa Barbara, CA, USA (Aug 19–23, 2018). https://doi.org/10.1007/978-3-319-96881-0_2

25. Gennaro, R., Goldfeder, S.: Fast multiparty threshold ECDSA with fast trustless setup. In: Lie, D., Mannan, M., Backes, M., Wang, X. (eds.) ACM CCS 2018: 25th Conference on Computer and Communications Security. pp. 1179–1194. ACM Press, Toronto, ON, Canada (Oct 15–19, 2018). https://doi.org/10.1145/3243734.3243859

26. Gennaro, R., Goldfeder, S., Narayanan, A.: Threshold-optimal DSA/ECDSA signatures and an application to bitcoin wallet security. In: Manulis, M., Sadeghi, A.R., Schneider, S. (eds.) ACNS 16: 14th International Conference on Applied Cryptography and Network Security. Lecture Notes in Computer Science, vol. 9696, pp. 156–174. Springer, Heidelberg, Germany, Guildford, UK (Jun 19–22, 2016). https://doi.org/10.1007/978-3-319-39555-5_9

27. Gennaro, R., Jarecki, S., Krawczyk, H., Rabin, T.: Secure applications of Pedersen's distributed key generation protocol. In: Joye, M. (ed.) Topics in Cryptology – CT-RSA 2003. Lecture Notes in Computer Science, vol. 2612, pp. 373–390. Springer, Heidelberg, Germany, San Francisco, CA, USA (Apr 13–17, 2003). https://doi.org/10.1007/3-540-36563-X_26

28. Itakura, K; Nakamura, K.: A public-key cryptosystem suitable for digital multisignatures. NEC research & development (1983)

29. Komlo, C., Goldberg, I.: Frost: flexible round-optimized Schnorr threshold signatures. In: International Conference on Selected Areas in Cryptography. pp. 34–65. Springer (2020)

30. Komlo, C., Goldberg, I.: FROST: Flexible round-optimized Schnorr threshold signatures. In: Dunkelman, O., Jr., M.J.J., O'Flynn, C. (eds.) SAC 2020: 27th Annual International Workshop on Selected Areas in Cryptography. Lecture Notes in Computer Science, vol. 12804, pp. 34–65. Springer, Heidelberg, Germany, Halifax, NS, Canada (Virtual Event) (Oct 21-23, 2020). https://doi.org/10.1007/978-3-030-81652-0_2

31. Lau, J., Wuille, P.: Dealing with signature encoding malleability. Bitcoin Improvement Proposal 146 (2016), https://github.com/bitcoin/bips/blob/master/bip-0146.mediawiki

32. Libert, B., Joye, M., Yung, M.: Born and raised distributively: Fully distributed non-interactive adaptively-secure threshold signatures with short shares. In: Theoretical Computer Science (2016)

33. Lindell, Y.: Simple three-round multiparty Schnorr signing with full simulatability. IACR Communications in Cryptology $1(1)$ (2024). https://doi.org/10.62056/a36c0l5vt

34. Maxwell, G., Poelstra, A., Seurin, Y., Wuille, P.: Simple Schnorr multi-signatures with applications to bitcoin (deprecated version). Cryptology ePrint Archive, Report 2018/068, version 1 (2018), https://eprint.iacr.org/archive/2018/068/20180118:124757

35. Maxwell, G., Poelstra, A., Seurin, Y., Wuille, P.: Simple Schnorr multi-signatures with applications to bitcoin. In: Design, Code, and Cryptography. pp. 2139–2164 (September 2019)

36. National Institute of Standards and Technology: Multi-Party Threshold Cryptography (2018–Present), https://csrc.nist.gov/Projects/threshold-cryptography

37. Navot, S.: Insecurity of musig and bn multi-signatures with delayed message selection. Cryptology ePrint Archive, Report 2024/437 (2024), https://eprint.iacr.org/2024/437

38. Nick, J.: Insecure shortcuts in musig (2019), https://medium.com/blockstream/insecure-shortcuts-in-musig-2ad0d38a97da

39. Nick, J., Ruffing, T., Jin, E.: Musig2 for bip340-compatible multi-signatures. Bitcoin Improvement Proposal 327 (2022), https://github.com/bitcoin/bips/blob/master/bip-0327.mediawiki

40. Nick, J., Ruffing, T., Seurin, Y.: MuSig2: Simple two-round Schnorr multi-signatures. In: Malkin, T., Peikert, C. (eds.) Advances in Cryptology –

CRYPTO 2021, Part I. Lecture Notes in Computer Science, vol. 12825, pp. 189–221. Springer, Heidelberg, Germany, Virtual Event (Aug 16–20, 2021). https://doi.org/10.1007/978-3-030-84242-0_8

41. Pointcheval, D., Stern, J.: Provably secure blind signature schemes. In: Kim, K., Matsumoto, T. (eds.) ASIACRYPT 1996. LNCS, vol. 1163, pp. 252–265. Springer, Heidelberg (1996). https://doi.org/10.1007/BFb0034852

42. Pointcheval, D., Stern, J.: Security arguments for digital signatures and blind signatures. In: Journal of Cryptology. Journal of Cryptology (May 1998). https://doi.org/10.1007/s001450010003

43. Pointcheval, D., Stern, J.: Security arguments for digital signatures and blind signatures. Journal of Cryptology **13**(3), 361–396 (Jun 2000). https://doi.org/10.1007/s001450010003

44. Ruffing, T., Ronge, V., Jin, E., Schneider-Bensch, J., Schröder, D.: ROAST: Robust asynchronous Schnorr threshold signatures. In: Proceedings of the 2022 ACM SIGSAC Conference on Computer and Communications Security. p. 2551–2564. CCS '22, Association for Computing Machinery, New York, NY, USA (2022). https://doi.org/10.1145/3548606.3560583

45. Schnorr, C.P.: Efficient identification and signatures for smart cards. In: Brassard, G. (ed.) Advances in Cryptology – CRYPTO'89. Lecture Notes in Computer Science, vol. 435, pp. 239–252. Springer, Heidelberg, Germany, Santa Barbara, CA, USA (Aug 20–24, 1990). https://doi.org/10.1007/0-387-34805-0_22

46. Schnorr, C.P.: Security of blind discrete log signatures against interactive attacks. In: Qing, S., Okamoto, T., Zhou, J. (eds.) Information and Communications Security, pp. 1–12. Springer, Berlin Heidelberg, Berlin, Heidelberg (2001)

47. Tessaro, S., Zhu, C.: Threshold and multi-signature schemes from linear hash functions. In: Advances in Cryptology – EUROCRYPT 2023. Lyon, France (Apr 23–27, 2023)

48. Wagner, D.: A generalized birthday problem. In: Yung, M. (ed.) Advances in Cryptology – CRYPTO 2002. Lecture Notes in Computer Science, vol. 2442, pp. 288–303. Springer, Heidelberg, Germany, Santa Barbara, CA, USA (Aug 18–22, 2002). https://doi.org/10.1007/3-540-45708-9_19

49. Wuille, P.: Dealing with malleability. Bitcoin Improvement Proposal 62 (2014), https://github.com/bitcoin/bips/blob/master/bip-0062.mediawiki

50. Wuille, P., Nick, J., Ruffing, T.: Schnorr signatures for secp256k1. Bitcoin Improvement Proposal 340 (2020), https://github.com/bitcoin/bips/blob/master/bip-0340.mediawiki

One Tree to Rule Them All: Optimizing GGM Trees and OWFs for Post-Quantum Signatures

Carsten Baum[1]([✉])[iD], Ward Beullens[2][iD], Shibam Mukherjee[3,4][iD], Emmanuela Orsini[5][iD], Sebastian Ramacher[6][iD], Christian Rechberger[4][iD], Lawrence Roy[7], and Peter Scholl[7][iD]

[1] Technical University of Denmark, Copenhagen, Denmark
cabau@dtu.dk
[2] IBM Research Europe, Zürich, Switzerland
ward@beullens.com
[3] Graz University of Technology, Graz, Austria
shibam.mukherjee@iaik.tugraz.at
[4] Know Center, Graz, Austria
christian.rechberger@tugraz.at
[5] Bocconi University, Bocconi, Italy
emmanuela.orsini@unibocconi.it
[6] AIT Austrian Institute of Technology, Vienna, Austria
sebastian.ramacher@ait.ac.at
[7] Aarhus University, Aarhus, Denmark
peter.scholl@cs.au.dk

Abstract. The use of MPC-in-the-Head (MPCitH) based zero knowledge proofs of knowledge (ZKPoK) to prove knowledge of a preimage of a one way function (OWF) is a popular approach towards constructing efficient post-quantum digital signatures. Starting with the Picnic signature scheme, many optimized MPCitH signatures using a variety of (candidate) OWFs have been proposed. Recently, Baum et al. (CRYPTO 2023) showed a fundamental improvement to MPCitH, called VOLE-in-the-Head (VOLEitH), which can generically reduce the signature size by at least a factor of two without decreasing computational performance or introducing new assumptions. Based on this, they designed the FAEST signature which uses AES as the underlying OWF. However, in comparison to MPCitH, the behavior of VOLEitH when using other OWFs is still unexplored.

In this work, we improve a crucial building block of the VOLEitH and MPCitH approaches, the so-called all-but-one vector commitment, thus decreasing the signature size of VOLEitH and MPCitH signature schemes. Moreover, by introducing a small Proof of Work into the signing procedure, we can improve the parameters of VOLEitH (further decreasing signature size) *without* compromising the computational performance of the scheme. Based on these optimizations, we propose three VOLEitH signature schemes FAESTER, KuMQuat, and MandaRain based on AES, MQ, and Rain, respectively. We carefully explore the

© International Association for Cryptologic Research 2025
K.-M. Chung and Y. Sasaki (Eds.): ASIACRYPT 2024, LNCS 15484, pp. 463–493, 2025.
https://doi.org/10.1007/978-981-96-0875-1_15

parameter space for these schemes and implement each, showcasing their performance with benchmarks. Our experiments show that these three signature schemes outperform MPCitH-based competitors that use comparable OWFs, in terms of both signature size and signing/verification time.

Keywords: Post-Quantum · VOLEitH · Signature Schemes

1   Introduction

The threat of quantum computing has motivated cryptographers to develop digital signatures based on new, supposedly quantum-resistant, hardness assumptions. In order to standardize these new signature schemes, NIST started its first post-quantum (PQ) signature standardization process[1] in 2017, where SPHINCS+ [6,16], Dilithium [30] and FALCON [43] were standardized. With two out of three standardizations relying on hard lattice problems for their security, NIST deemed it necessary to seek additional candidates for standardization whose security is based on a more diverse set of hardness assumptions[2].

Signatures from Zero-Knowledge Proofs. A well-known technique to build a digital signature scheme is to compile a (public-coin, honest-verifier) zero-knowledge (ZK) proof of knowledge, used in an identification protocol, with the Fiat-Shamir transformation (FS). In particular, a zero-knowledge proof of knowledge (ZKPoK) for an NP relation $\mathcal{R}$ is an interactive protocol that allows the prover to prove knowledge of a witness w for a statement x such that $(x, w) \in \mathcal{R}$, without revealing any further information. In the context of signature (and identification) schemes, this is a proof of knowledge of a secret key k such that $y = F_k(x)$, for a given one-way function (OWF) $F_k(\cdot)$.

A powerful and efficient technique to build such ZK proofs for arbitrary NP relations is the MPC-in-the-Head (MPCitH) framework due to Ishai et al. [36]. However, a significant limitation of many MPCitH-based proofs lies in their proof size which scales linearly with the size of the circuit representation of the statement being proven. Nevertheless, MPCitH is particularly effective with small to medium-sized circuits and leads to efficient post-quantum signature schemes. These schemes are either based solely on symmetric primitives, such as AES [13,29,37,45,46] and other MPC-friendly one-way functions (OWFs) like LowMC [4], Rain [29], and AIM [39], or well-studied computational hardness assumptions, including syndrome decoding [3,5,34], the multivariate quadratic problem (MQ) [15,42], the permuted kernel problem [1], and the Legendre PRF [19]. This second approach typically results in a more communication-efficient scheme.

---

[1] https://csrc.nist.gov/Projects/post-quantum-cryptography/post-quantum-cryptography-standardization/Call-for-Proposals.

[2] https://csrc.nist.gov/Projects/pqc-dig-sig/standardization.

VOLE-ZK and FAEST. In 2018, Boyle et al. [22] proposed a new class of prover-efficient (linear complexity) and scalable ZK proofs, which use commit-and-prove protocols instantiated using vector oblivious linear evaluation (VOLE) correlations. Follow-up works [8,12,22,23,27,49–51,53] reduced the constants of the linear proof size, surpassing MPCitH schemes in terms of efficiency, in particular when dealing with very large circuits. Compared to MPCitH schemes, the above VOLE-ZK protocols are limited to the designated-verifier setting only. However, recent work by Baum et al. [7] reconciles the advantages of both worlds, resulting in VOLE-ZK proofs that are publicly verifiable. To achieve this, they introduce a technique called VOLE-in-the-Head (VOLEitH) which bears a surprising resemblance to MPCitH-based protocols. Based on VOLEitH, they proposed the FAEST [9] post-quantum signature scheme.

Similarly to MPCitH signature schemes like Banquet [13], BBQ [45], and Helium [37], FAEST relies on AES [2] as its OWF. However, FAEST outperforms MPCitH-based signatures, by having signatures at least twice as small and with similar or better signing and verification times. This makes the VOLEitH-based FAEST as performant as the most optimized MPCitH-based schemes [37], while relying on a very conservative OWF. At the same time, VOLEitH is a relatively new concept, and it remained unexplored to what extent VOLEitH-based signatures can benefit from selecting different OWFs, such as Rain or random multivariate quadratic maps.

1.1   Our Contributions

In this work, we present improvements to the core building blocks used in VOLE-in-the-head proof systems, as well as alternative one-way function instantiations that optimize prior approaches and lead to more efficient post-quantum signature candidates.

Improved Batch Vector Commitments. VOLE-in-the-head signatures such as those based on MPC-in-the-head, use multiple GGM-based [35] all-but-one vector commitment schemes to generate correlated randomness for the ZK proofs. These vector commitments are then opened at random challenge points as part of the proof, incurring a decommitment size of $\log(N) \cdot \lambda$ bits per vector commitment that must be sent during the opening phase (where N is the length of the vector and λ is the security parameter). These openings are a substantial part of the setup cost of the ZK proof. We provide a new abstraction, called *batch all-but-one vector commitment* (BAVC) schemes, which captures how multiple vector commitments are used in VOLEitH and MPCitH. We observe that, to instantiate the BAVC abstraction more efficiently, one can interleave multiple vector commitments which drastically reduces the opening size. This batching requires the signer to perform rejection sampling when selecting the points to open, reducing the entropy of the challenge space somewhat. While it might seem that this makes the scheme less secure, one can prove that security is actually preserved: since each rejection sampling step requires the prover to perform a hash function call, we can consider rejection sampling as a *proof of work* done during each signing operation. Any attacker must also perform this proof of work to generate a valid signature. We believe that this technique is of independent interest.

FAESTER. This rejection sampling/proof of work idea can be pushed further, using a technique known as "grinding" [18,48]. Proof systems naturally have a tradeoff between signature size, computation, and security, and reducing the security can lead to significant improvements in both signature size and computational efficiency. We do this by further reducing the entropy of the challenge space so that some part of the opening process does not even need to be considered. This makes the VOLEitH proof itself slightly less secure, but the overall signature scheme retains the same security level due to the additional proof of work caused by increased rejection probability. It might seem that this trade-off will naturally lead to longer signing times, but the opposite can actually be the case: reducing the challenge entropy significantly reduces the other signing costs, so the scheme is optimized by finding a balance between the costs of the proof of work and those of the rest of the scheme. We applied BAVC and grinding to the FAEST signature scheme, leading to a new digital signature with a signature size of 4KB (an improvement over all signature schemes using AES OWF) while maintaining or improving upon the signing and verification time of FAEST. We name this new improved signature scheme *FAESTER*.

MandaRain & KuMQuat. AES-based OWFs benefit from decades of public scrutiny. However, AES was not designed for use-cases such as VOLEitH which leaves open the possibility that other OWFs may result in faster signing and verification times, and smaller signature sizes. We survey suitable candidate PRFs, ranging from various recent specialized designs in symmetric cryptography [4,29,31,33,39,44] to various instances of the MQ problem [15]. We select the Rain [29] and MQ [15] PRFs, from which we construct the new MandaRain and KuMQuat signature schemes using our new commitment optimization. These signature schemes have a signature size as small as 2.6KB, lowest among all VOLEitH and MPCitH-based signature schemes. An overview of our results can be seen in Fig. 1.

Allowing Uniform AES Keys in FAEST(ER). In cases where the conservative choice of AES is preferred to alternative OWFs, we show how to tweak the AES proving algorithm so that FAEST and FAESTER can support secret keys that cover the entirety of the AES keyspace. This avoids sampling signing keys via rejection sampling, as done in previous works, so we obtain a simplified key generation algorithm and improve concrete security by 1–2 bits. This improvement comes with no cost in signature size or runtime.

FAEST-d7: Higher-Degree Constraints for AES. We also present a new method of proving AES in VOLE-ZK proof systems, using degree-7 constraints over $\mathbb{F}_2$. Compared with the degree-2 constraints over $\mathbb{F}_{2^8}$ used in the original FAEST

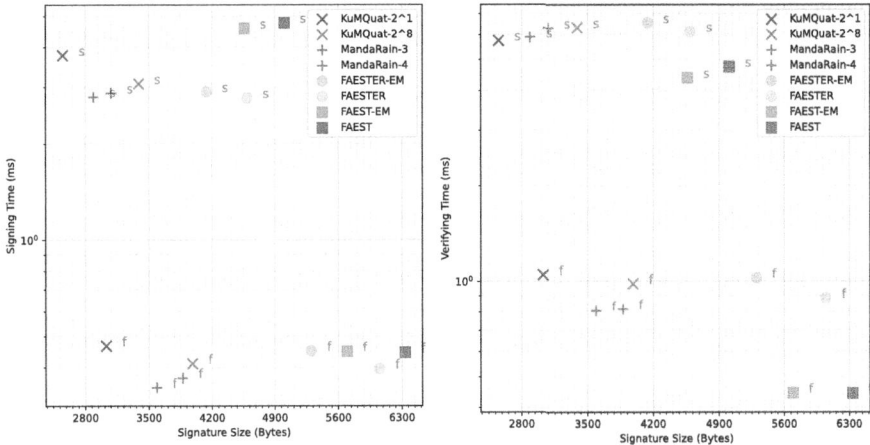

(a) Signing time - Signature Size trade-off, L1 security.

(b) Verification time - Signature Size trade-off, L1 security.

Fig. 1. Signature size and runtime trade-off comparison between the proposed signature schemes with FAEST and FAEST-EM. The slow and fast versions are denoted with s and f respectively. The fast version offers smaller signing and verification time, however, comes with a larger signature size. Similarly, in the slower version, the signature size is smaller but both signing and verification timings are larger.

(and above), we halve the witness size in the ZK proof. Although proving higher-degree constraints does come with some extra costs, we show that signature sizes can be up to 5% smaller in FAEST-d7. We have not yet implemented this variant, but expect signing and verification times to be similar to FAEST. As a contribution of independent interest, we optimize the method for proving high-degree constraints in the QuickSilver proof system [52], greatly improving the efficiency of the prover.

VOLEitH Parameter Exploration. With our implementation[3], we enable a systematic investigation of the parameter set within the VOLEitH paradigm for constructing a signature scheme, providing insights into the effects of different parameters, including those introduced in this work. These insights contribute to further improvements and trade-offs. Table 5 summarizes our signature performance for the L1 security, and in the full version of the paper[4], we include the holistic results for all the security levels. In Fig. 8, we compare our results with the other signature schemes, including the NIST PQ Signature Round 4 candidates.

---

[3] https://github.com/faest-sign/faest-one-tree.

[4] https://eprint.iacr.org/2024/490.

2   Preliminaries

2.1   One-Way Functions

MPCitH and VOLEitH signatures are based on proving knowledge of the preimage to a OWF.[5] In many recent signature schemes like Picnic and FAEST, OWFs are built from a block cipher, according to the following construction.

Construction 1. *A one-way-function* $F(k, x)$ *can be constructed using a block cipher* $E_k(x)$ *by setting* $F(k, x) := (x, E_k(x))$, *where* $E_k(x)$ *denotes the encryption of* x *under the key* k. *The OWF relation is defined as* $((x, y), k) \in R \Leftrightarrow E_k(x) = y$.

The Rain OWF Dobraunig et al. presented a block cipher called Rain [29] with a small number of non-linear constraints, designed to optimize the signature size and time when used as a OWF in MPCitH based signature schemes.[6] The resulting signature scheme, Rainier [29], was the first MPCitH signature scheme with less than 5 KB of signature size.

Below we describe the Rain round function and we refer to Fig. 2 for a graphical overview of Rain with 3 rounds.

The Rain keyed permutation $f_k(x) : \mathbb{F}_2^\lambda \to \mathbb{F}_2^\lambda$ is defined by the concatenation of a small number r of round functions R_i, $i \in [r]$, i.e. $f_k(x) = R_r \circ \cdots \circ R_2 \circ R_1(x)$. Each R_i, $i \in [r]$, is in turn defined as

$$R_i(x) = \begin{cases} \mathbf{M}_i \cdot S(x + k + \mathbf{c}_i) & i \in [1..r) \\ k + S(x + k + \mathbf{c}_r) & i = r. \end{cases}$$

Here, $S : \mathbb{F}_{2^\lambda} \to \mathbb{F}_{2^\lambda}$ is the field inversion function over $\mathbb{F}_{2^\lambda}$ (mapping 0 to 0), $\mathbf{c}_i \in \mathbb{F}_2^\lambda$ is a round constant, $k \in \mathbb{F}_2^\lambda$ the secret key and $\mathbf{M}_i \in \mathbb{F}_2^{\lambda \times \lambda}$ an invertible matrix.

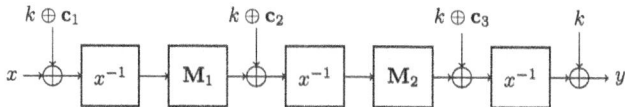

Fig. 2. The Rain encryption function with $r = 3$ rounds. $\mathbf{M}_i$ denotes the multiplication with an unstructured invertible matrix over $\mathbb{F}_2$ in the i-th round.

---

[5] See full version for definitions.

[6] Rain is not a typical block cipher like AES, but rather specifically designed for MPCitH use cases, where it requires that an adversary has access to only one plaintext-ciphertext (*pt-ct*) pair per secret key. When constructing signature schemes, this condition is easily satisfied as pk contains the only *pt-ct* pair known to an adversary.

In the VOLEitH setting, similar to MPCitH schemes, the linear layer has a much smaller impact on the performance in comparison to the non-linear layer. Thus to improve diffusion, the authors of Rain decided to use different round constants $\mathbf{c}_i$ and linear matrices $\mathbf{M}_i$ for each round. Rain comes in two settings, namely Rain-3 with 3 rounds and Rain-4 with (more conservative) 4 rounds. Despite detailed cryptanalysis carried out by the authors, the best known attacks [41,54] extend only to two rounds.

Multivariate Quadratic (MQ) OWF. One can also build a OWF from the well-known Multivariate Quadratic problem.

Definition 1. *(Multivariate Quadratic Problem). Let $\mathbb{F}_q$ be a finite field and $\mathsf{MQ}_{n,m,q}$ be the set of multivariate maps over $\mathbb{F}_q$ with n variables and m components of the form $\{\mathbf{x}^T \cdot \mathbf{A}_i \cdot \mathbf{x} + \mathbf{b}_i^T \cdot \mathbf{x}\}_{i \in [m]}$, where $\mathbf{A}_i \in \mathbb{F}_q^{n \times n}$, are randomly sampled upper triangular matrices and $\mathbf{b}_i \in \mathbb{F}_q^n$ are uniformly sampled vectors. Given $F \in \mathsf{MQ}_{n,m,q}$ and $\mathbf{y} = (y_1, \ldots, y_m) \in \mathbb{F}_q^m$, the MQ problem asks to find $\mathbf{x}$ such that $F(\mathbf{x}) = \mathbf{y}$, i.e. $\left(y_i := \mathbf{x}^T \cdot \mathbf{A}_i \cdot \mathbf{x} + \mathbf{b}_i^T \cdot \mathbf{x}\right)_{i \in [m]}$.*

The MQ problem has been extensively used in cryptography and used to build both trapdoor [17,40] and one-way signature schemes [15,47]. We construct the one-way function $E_{\mathbf{x}}(\mathsf{seed}) = \mathbf{y}$ from the MQ problem, where seed is the input to a pseudorandom generator G such that $\mathbf{A}_1, \ldots, \mathbf{A}_m, \mathbf{b}_1, \ldots, \mathbf{b}_m \leftarrow G(\mathsf{seed})$. Therefore, when constructing a one-way signature scheme from the MQ problem, $(\mathbf{x}, \mathsf{seed})$ becomes the sk and $(\mathbf{y}, \mathsf{seed})$ becomes the pk (similar to MQOM [15]).

2.2   VOLEitH Signatures

We now give an overview of the VOLEitH framework as the ZK-proof system underlying FAEST. A more detailed introduction of the VOLE-in-the-Head approach is available in the full version.

A *vector oblivious linear evaluation* (VOLE) correlation of length m is a two-party correlation between a prover $\mathcal{P}$ and a verifier $\mathcal{V}$ defined by a random global key $\Delta \in \mathbb{F}_{2^k}$, a set of random bits $u_i \in \mathbb{F}_2$, a random VOLE tag $v_i \in \mathbb{F}_{2^k}$ and VOLE keys $q_i \in \mathbb{F}_{2^k}$ such that $q_i = u_i \cdot \Delta - v_i, i = 0, \ldots, m-1$. $\mathcal{P}$ obtains u_i, v_i while $\mathcal{V}$ obtains Δ, q_i. The correlations commit $\mathcal{P}$ to the u_i's as linearly homomorphic commitments, allowing efficient proof systems (see [11] for an overview). One of the main drawbacks of such VOLE-based ZK schemes is that of being inherently designated verifier since the verifier $\mathcal{V}$ needs to know its part of the VOLE correlation to verify the proof, which has to remain secret from the prover for the proof to be sound.

Using VOLEitH, Baum et al. realized a *delayed* VOLE functionality that allows the prover to generate values u_i, v_i of VOLE correlations independently of Δ, q_i and to generate them later instead. This delayed VOLE functionality can in turn be realized from vector commitments (VCs). The main steps of the interactive ZK proof can be computed as before, and only after these, in the last stage of the protocol, the verifier will choose and send to the prover the random value Δ of the correlation. At this point, $\mathcal{P}$ will open the homomorphic

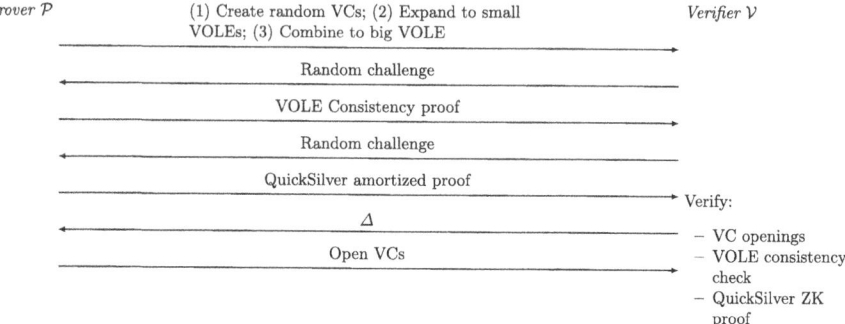

Fig. 3. Main steps of the VOLEitH-based Zero-Knowledge proof in FAEST

commitments and send to $\mathcal{V}$ information which allows it to reconstruct the q_is in the VOLE correlations, check the openings and thus the proof. This guarantees public verifiability, as the final VOLE correlation is defined by the random value Δ chosen as the last step of the proof by the verifier, after all other proof messages have been fixed. Concretely, to obtain the desired soundness, it is necessary to run τ instances of VOLEitH such that $\tau \cdot k = \lambda$. The main steps of the resulting ZK proof using the VOLEitH technique are depicted in Fig. 3.

3   Improving Batch Vector Commitments

In this section, we present our result on batch vector commitments (VCs) in the random oracle (RO) model. We start by providing a formal definition of a batch all-but-one vector commitment scheme (BAVC) with abort in the opening phase. This can be used in FAEST, and more generally in VOLEitH-based protocols, as well as in most of the known MPC-in-the-head schemes. By making the properties of the used GGM-based instantiation explicit, we manage to achieve an optimized construction that results in shorter signatures.

Informally, a batch all-but-one vector commitment scheme (BAVC) is a two-phase protocol between two PPT machines, a *sender* and a *receiver*. In the first phase, called the *commitment phase*, the sender commits to multiple vectors of messages while keeping them secret; in the second phase, the *decommitment phase*, all but one of the entries of each vector are opened. The vectors may have different lengths. We require the binding and hiding properties of regular commitments, and additionally also that the messages at the *unopened indices* remain hidden, even after opening all other indices of each committed vector. In addition, we do not allow the sender to choose the messages, which instead are just random elements from the message space $\mathcal{M}$. This definition captures how vector commitments are used in MPC-in-the-head or VOLE-in-the-head constructions.

Let τ be the number of vectors, and let the α-th vector have length N_α for $\alpha \in [\tau]$. We will denote by i_τ the index of vector τ that remains unopened and by I the vector $(i_1, \ldots, i_\tau)$ comprising all the indices that remain unopened.

Definition 2 (BAVC). *Let H be a random oracle. A* (non-interactive) batch all-but-one vector commitment scheme BAVC *(with message space $\mathcal{M}$) in the RO model is defined by the following PPT algorithms, where all of them have access to a RO, and obtain the security parameter 1^λ as well as $\tau, N_1, \ldots, N_\tau$ as input:*

Commit() $\rightarrow$ (com, decom, $(m_1^{(\alpha)}, \ldots, m_{N_\alpha}^{(\alpha)})_{\alpha \in [\tau]}$): *output a commitment* com *with opening information* decom *for messages* $(m_1^{(\alpha)}, \ldots, m_N^{(\alpha)})_{\alpha \in [\tau]} \in \mathcal{M}^{N_1 + \cdots + N_\tau}$.

Open(decom, I) $\rightarrow$ decom$_I \vee \perp$: *On input an opening* decom *and the index vector $I \subset [N_1] \times \cdots \times [N_\tau]$, output $\perp$ or an opening* decom$_I$ *for I.*

Verify(com, decom$_I$, I) $\rightarrow ((m_j^{(\alpha)})_{j \in [N_\alpha] \setminus \{i_\alpha\}})_{\alpha \in [\tau]} \vee \perp$: *Given a commitment* com, *an opening* decom$_I$, *for an index vector I, as well as the index vector I, either output all messages* $(m_j^{(\alpha)})_{j \in [N_\alpha] \setminus \{i^\alpha\}}$ *(accept the opening) or $\perp$ (reject the opening).*

We now define correctness for the commitment scheme. We allow the sender to potentially abort for certain choices of I during Open. Looking ahead, this does not pose any problem if the abort probability is low, as aborts only happen during signature generation.

Definition 3 (Correctness with aborts). BAVC *is* correct with aborts *if for all $I \subset [N_1] \times \cdots \times [N_\tau]$, the following outputs True*

$$(\text{com}, \text{decom}, M) \leftarrow \text{Commit}()$$
$$\forall \, \text{decom}_I \leftarrow \text{Open}(\text{decom}, I)$$
$$output \; \text{decom}_I = \perp \vee \text{Verify}(\text{com}, \text{decom}_I, I) = M$$

with all but a negligible probability, where $M = (m_1^{(\alpha)}, \ldots, m_N^{(\alpha)})_{\alpha \in [\tau]}$.

Informally, we say that a commitment scheme is extractable-binding if there exists an extractor Ext such that for any commitment opening, the extracted message is equal to the opened message. More formally, we have the following definition.

Definition 4 (Extractable-Binding). *Let BAVC be defined as above in the RO-model with RO H. Let Ext be a PPT algorithm such that*

- Ext$(Q, \text{com}) \rightarrow ((m_j^{(\alpha)})_{j \in [N_\alpha]})_{\alpha \in [\tau]}$, *i.e., given a set Q of query-response pairs of random oracle queries, and a commitment com, Ext outputs the committed messages. (Ext may output $m_j^{(\alpha)} = \perp$, e.g. if committed value at this index is invalid.)*

For any $\tau, N_\alpha = poly(\lambda)$, define the straightline extractable-binding game for BAVC *and stateful adversary $\mathcal{A}^H$ with oracle access to the random oracle H as follows:*

1. com $\leftarrow \mathcal{A}^H(1^\lambda)$
2. $((\overline{m}_1^{(\alpha)}, \ldots, \overline{m}_N^{(\alpha)})_{\alpha \in [\tau]}) \leftarrow$ Ext(Q, com), *where Q is the set $\{(x_i, H(x_i))\}$ of query-response pairs of queries $\mathcal{A}$ made to H.*
3. $(((m_j^{(\alpha)})_{j \in [N_\alpha] \setminus \{i_\alpha\}})_{\alpha \in [\tau]}, \text{decom}_I, I) \leftarrow \mathcal{A}^H(\text{com})$.
4. *Output 1 (success) if:*
   Verify$(\text{com}, \text{decom}_I, I) = ((m_j^{(\alpha)})_{j \in [N_\alpha] \setminus \{i_\alpha\}})_{\alpha \in [\tau]}$,
   but $m_j^{(\alpha)} \neq \overline{m}_j^{(\alpha)}$ for some $\alpha \in [\tau], j \in [N_\alpha] \setminus \{i_\alpha\}$.
   Else output 0 (failure).

We say BAVC *is* straightline extractable *w.r.t.* Ext *if any PPT adversary $\mathcal{A}$ has a negligible probability of winning the extractable binding game. We denote the advantage, i.e. probability to win, by* AdvEB$_\mathcal{A}^{\text{BAVC}}$.

We define the n-hiding real-or-random game where $0 < n \leq \tau$. Here, the attacker has to guess if claimed committed values for the first n commitments at the hidden index are correct or not. We allow for a parameter n to permit hybrids in security proofs.

Definition 5 (Hiding (real-or-random)). *Let* BAVC *be a vector commitment scheme in the RO-model with random oracle H. The* selective hiding *experiment for* BAVC *with $\tau, N_\alpha = poly(\lambda)$, parameter n and stateful $\mathcal{A}$ is defined as follows.*

1. $\overline{b} \leftarrow \{0, 1\}$
2. $(\text{com}, \text{decom}, (\overline{m}_1^{(\alpha)}, \ldots, \overline{m}_N^{(\alpha)})_{\alpha \in [\tau]}) \leftarrow$ Commit()
3. $I \leftarrow \mathcal{A}^H(1^\lambda, \text{com})$, *where $I \in [N_1] \times \cdots \times [N_\tau]$.*
4. decom$_I \leftarrow$ Open(decom, I)
5. $m_j^{(\alpha)} \leftarrow \overline{m}_j^{(\alpha)}$ *for $j \in [N_\alpha] \setminus \{i_\alpha\}, \alpha \in [\tau]$.*
6. *Set* $m_{i_\alpha}^{(\alpha)} \leftarrow \begin{cases} random\ from\ \mathcal{M} & if\ \overline{b} = 0 \wedge \alpha \leq n \\ \overline{m}_{i_\alpha}^{(\alpha)} & otherwise \end{cases}$
7. $b \leftarrow \mathcal{A}((m_j^{(\alpha)})_{j \in [N_\alpha]}, \text{decom}_i)$.
8. *Output 1 (success) if: $b = \overline{b}$, else 0 (failure).*

The advantage AdvSelHide$_{\mathcal{A}, i}^{\text{BAVC}}$ *of an adversary $\mathcal{A}$ is defined by $|$Pr$[\mathcal{A}$ wins and $n = i] - \frac{1}{2}|$ in the hiding experiment. We say* BAVC *is selectively hiding if every PPT adversary $\mathcal{A}$ has a negligible advantage of winning* AdvSelHide$_{\mathcal{A}, i}^{\text{BAVC}}$ *for all $i \in [\tau]$.*

Note that the GGM-based VC scheme of [7] can be defined using our definitions as well. We show this in the full version of the paper.

3.1 Optimized Batch All-but-One Vector Commitments

The GGM-based [35] VC construction has been extensively used both in MPCitH based signature schemes like Picnic [24], BBQ [45], Banquet [13], Helium [37] and also VOLEitH-based FAEST to construct the commitment scheme. It expands a random seed into a tree of Pseudorandom values by recursively applying a length-doubling Pseudo Random Generator (PRG) to each seed. To obtain a VC, the prover commits to the tree leaves to represent one vector commitment towards the verifier. Then, at a later stage, it can reveal parts of the leaves by opening intermediate seeds (i.e. inner nodes of the tree), allowing the verifier to check the opening against the VC. MPCitH-based signatures usually generate a forest of τ such trees in parallel, whose roots are generated from a single seed. This approach (which we recap in the full version) allows expressing τ VCs as one BAVC.

One Big Tree Instead of τ Small Ones. We now describe an optimization of this construction, where instead of generating a forest of τ trees with $N_1, \ldots, N_\tau$ leaves each, we generate a single GGM tree with $L = \sum_{i=1}^{\tau} N_i$ leaves. Opening all but τ leaves of the big tree is more efficient than opening all but one leaf in each of the τ smaller trees, because with high probability some of the active paths in the tree will merge relatively close to the leaves, which reduces the number of internal nodes that need to be revealed. Importantly, we map entries of the individual vector commitments to the leaves of the tree in an interleaved fashion. The first τ leaves of the tree correspond to the first entry of the τ vector commitments, the next leaves correspond to the second entries, and so on. The other way around would force the τ unopened leaves to be spaced far apart, which is detrimental to the number of nodes that need to be revealed. The number of internal nodes that need to be revealed depends on I, which would cause some variability in the size of the signature. To prevent this, we fix a threshold $\mathsf{T_{open}}$ for the number of internal nodes in an opening, and we let the Open algorithm abort if the number of nodes exceeds $\mathsf{T_{open}}$. The value of $\mathsf{T_{open}}$ controls a trade-off between the opening size of BAVC and the success probability of BAVC.Open.

Towards formalizing our optimized BAVC scheme $\mathsf{BAVC_{opt}}$, let $\mathsf{PRG}: \{0,1\}^\lambda \to \{0,1\}^{2\lambda}$ be a PRG, $\mathsf{H}: \{0,1\}^* \to \{0,1\}^{2\lambda}$ be a collision-resistant hash function (CRHF) and $\mathsf{G}: \{0,1\}^\lambda \to \{0,1\}^\lambda \times \{0,1\}^{2\lambda}$ be a PRG and CRHF. We define the scheme $\mathsf{BAVC_{opt}}$, which is parameterized by the number of vectors τ, the lengths of the vectors $N_1, \ldots, N_\tau$, and the opening size threshold $\mathsf{T_{open}}$. Let $\pi : [L-1, 2L-2] \to \{(\alpha, i)\}_{1 \le i \le N_\alpha}$ be a bijective mapping from roots of the GGM tree to positions in the vector commitment.

<u>Commit</u>():

1. Set $k \leftarrow \{0,1\}^\lambda$ and let $k_0 \leftarrow k$.
2. For $i \in [0, L-2]$, compute $(k_{2i+1}, k_{2i+2}) \leftarrow \mathsf{PRG}(k_i)$ to create a tree with L leaves $k_{L-1}, \ldots, k_{2L-2}$.
3. Deinterleave the leaves:
   $\{\mathsf{sd}_1^{(\alpha)}, \ldots, \mathsf{sd}_{N_\alpha}^{(\alpha)}\}_{\alpha \in [\tau]} \xleftarrow{\pi} \{k_{L-1}, \cdots, k_{2L-2}\}$.

4. Compute $(m_i^{(\alpha)}, \mathsf{com}_i^{(\alpha)}) \leftarrow \mathsf{G}(\mathsf{sd}_i^{(\alpha)})$, for $\alpha \in [\tau]$ and $i \in [N_\alpha]$.
5. Compute $h^{(\alpha)} \leftarrow \mathsf{H}(\mathsf{com}_1^{(\alpha)}, \ldots, \mathsf{com}_{N_\alpha}^{(\alpha)})$ for $\alpha \in [\tau]$ and $h \leftarrow \mathsf{H}(h^{(1)}, \ldots, h^{(\tau)})$.
6. Output the commitment $\mathsf{com} = h$, the opening $\mathsf{decom} = k$ and the messages $(m_1^{(\alpha)}, \ldots, m_{N_\alpha}^{(\alpha)})_{\alpha \in [\tau]}$.

$\underline{\mathsf{Open}}(\mathsf{decom} = k, I = (i^{(1)}, \ldots, i^{(\tau)}))$:

1. Recompute k_j for and $j \in [0, \ldots, 2L - 2]$ from k as in Commit.
2. Let $S = \{k_{L-1}, \ldots, k_{2L-2}\}$.
3. For each $\alpha \in [\tau]$, remove $k_{\pi^{-1}(\alpha, i^{(\alpha)})}$ from S.
4. For i from $i = L - 2$ to 0:
    If $k_{2i+1} \in S$ and $k_{2i+2} \in S$ then replace both with k_i.
5. If $|S| \leq \mathsf{T}_{\mathsf{open}}$ output the opening information $\mathsf{decom}_I = ((\mathsf{com}_{i^{(\alpha)}}^{(\alpha)})_{\alpha \in [\tau]}, S)$, otherwise output $\bot$.

$\underline{\mathsf{Verify}}(\mathsf{com} = h, \mathsf{decom}_I = (\{\mathsf{com}_{i^{(\alpha)}}\}_{\alpha \in [\tau]}^{(\alpha)}, S), I = (i^{(1)}, \ldots, i^{(\tau)}))$:

1. Recompute $\mathsf{sd}_i^{(\alpha)}$ from decom_I, for each $\alpha \in [\tau]$ and $i \neq i^{(\alpha)}$ using the available keys in S, and compute $(m_i^{(\alpha)}, \mathsf{com}_i^{(\alpha)}) \leftarrow \mathsf{G}(\mathsf{sd}_i^{(\alpha)})$.
2. Compute $h^{(\alpha)} = \mathsf{H}(\mathsf{com}_1^{(\alpha)}, \ldots, \mathsf{com}_{N_\alpha}^{(\alpha)})$ for each $\alpha \in [\tau]$.
3. If $h \neq \mathsf{H}(h^{(1)}, \ldots, h^{(\tau)})$ output $\bot$.
4. Output $((m_i^{(\alpha)})_{i \in [N_\alpha] \setminus \{i^{(\alpha)}\}})_{\alpha \in [\tau]}$.

Lemma 1 (Extractable Binding). *Decompose* $\mathsf{G} \colon \{0,1\}^\lambda \rightarrow \{0,1\}^{2\lambda}$ *into* $\mathsf{G}(x) := (\mathsf{G}_1(x), \mathsf{G}_2(x))$ *and suppose* G_2, H *are straight-line extractable. Then* $\mathsf{BAVC}_{\mathsf{GGM}}$ *is straight-line extractable-binding according to Definition 4: Given any adversary* $\mathcal{A}$ *breaking the extractable-binding of* $\mathsf{BAVC}_{\mathsf{opt}}$ *with advantage* AdvEB *we can construct a PPT adversary breaking extractability on* G_2, H *with advantage*

$$\mathsf{AdvEB} \leq L \cdot \mathsf{Adv}_{\mathsf{G}_2} + (\tau + 1) \cdot \mathsf{Adv}_{\mathsf{H}}.$$

Proof. The proof is similar to [7, Lemma 1]. We extract Ext after obtaining $\mathsf{com} = h$ using the straight-line extractability of G_2, H. For this, we first find $h^{(1)}, \ldots, h^{(\tau)}$ which hash to h, and then $\mathsf{com}_i^{(\alpha)}$ for each $i \in [N_\alpha], \alpha \in [\tau]$, in both cases using extractability of H. Then, we extract $\mathsf{sd}_i^{(\alpha)}$ from $\mathsf{com}_i^{(\alpha)}$ using the extractability of G_2, and compute $m_i^{(\alpha)}$ using G_1.

Assume $\mathcal{A}$ breaks extractable binding, i.e. provides values during Open which differ from the extracted $h^{(\alpha)}, \mathsf{com}_i^{(\alpha)}, \mathsf{sd}_i^{(\alpha)}$. Then, our constructed adversary will simply guess in advance at which index $\mathcal{A}$ will break extractability of G_2, H and play the extractability game at that index. This guess leads to the loss outlined in the statement.

Lemma 2 (Selectively Hiding). *Given any adversary* $\mathcal{A}$ *breaking the selective hiding of* $\mathsf{BAVC}_{\mathsf{GGM}}$ *for parameter* n *with advantage* $\mathsf{AdvSelHide}_n$ *we can construct a PPT adversary breaking the pseudorandomness of* G, PRG *with advantage*

$$\mathsf{AdvSelHide}_n \leq \lceil \log_2(L) \rceil \cdot \mathsf{Adv}_{\mathsf{PRG}} + \mathsf{Adv}_{\mathsf{G}}.$$

Proof. The proof is similar to [7, Lemma 2]. By using that the GGM construction is a puncturable PRF according to [20] and since we know the unopened index I for each commitment vector, and in particular for vector n, in advance, one can iteratively replace the unopened PRG seeds k_i on the path from the root to $\mathsf{sd}_{i(n)}^{(n)}$ *which are not seeds on paths to* $\mathsf{sd}_{i(1)}^{(1)}, \ldots, \mathsf{sd}_{i(n-1)}^{(n-1)}$ as well as the output of $\mathsf{G}(\mathsf{sd}_{i(n)}^{(n)})$ with uniformly random values. For this to be possible, we fully randomize the seeds on the paths to $\mathsf{sd}_{i(1)}^{(1)}, \ldots, \mathsf{sd}_{i(n-1)}^{(n-1)}$ first, to allow for any hybrids distinguishing at indices n to $n+1$ to be meaningful. The bound then follows from the maximal number of hybrids possible.

4   Using BAVCs in FAEST

When generating a FAEST signature, the signing algorithm initially samples τ independent VC instances, in order to set up the underlying VOLE-in-the-head-based ZK proof. Then, in the last round of the ZK proof (i.e. as output of the RO call to H_2^3 which generates the last λ-bit challenge chal_3), the individual indices that are opened in each VC, i.e. the set $I \in [N_1] \times \cdots \times [N_\tau]$, are chosen using the injective decoding function DecodeChallenge. Therefore, modifying the FAEST scheme to work with one BAVC instance instead of τ independent VC instances is straightforward: sample the τ vector commitments using one instance of BAVC, and open them all simultaneously based on chal_3. However, more modifications are necessary since BAVC does not necessarily enjoy perfect completeness, whereas the standard GGM-based VC used in FAEST does. Hence, it will happen that the signer cannot open a BAVC commitment based on a challenge chal_3, and hence some signing attempts will abort.

Instead, we make the following changes to the FAEST signing algorithm: To handle aborts in the Open algorithm, we add a counter value ctr to the input of H_2^3. If the challenge chal_3 decodes to a sequence of indices I for which Open fails, then the signing algorithm repeatedly increases ctr and hashes again until it reaches a challenge for which Open succeeds. The counter ctr is included in the signature to allow for efficient verification.

Security of the Modification. The FAEST scheme has been proven secure both in [7] and [9]. While the proof in [7] is more modular, arguing security by modifying the proof of [9] is more straightforward.

The proof of [9] says that for every query to the H_2^3 there are at most 2 out of 2^λ challenge responses that can lead to a forgery, because challenges correspond one-to-one with field elements $\Delta \in \mathbb{F}_{2^\lambda}$, and to cheat, the adversary needs Δ to be a root of a non-zero quadratic polynomial in the Quicksilver check. The proof then considers a union bound over all Q queries to H_2^3 to obtain the term $Q/2^{\lambda-1}$ in the bound on the forgery probability of the adversary. The same proof strategy still works for the signing algorithm with counter, because for every query to H_2^3 there are still at most two challenges that map to the roots of the Quicksilver polynomial.

Using Fewer and Shorter Vector Commitments. In the original FAEST scheme we need to have $\prod_{\alpha=1}^{\tau} N_\alpha \geq 2^\lambda$, because the λ-bit challenges need to map injectively to index sequences $I \in [N_1] \times \cdots \times [N_\tau]$. In the setting with aborts, we only need the *non-aborting* challenges to map injectively to index sequences I. Therefore, as an additional optimization, we can choose to reduce the number and/or the length of some of the vectors (reducing the signature size or the signing and verification time respectively), at the cost of increasing the probability of a restart (which slows down signing). Concretely, we set parameters such that $\sum_{\alpha=1}^{\tau} \log N_\alpha = \lambda - w$, and let $I \leftarrow \mathsf{DecodeChallenge}(\mathsf{chal}_3)$ injectively decode the first $\lambda - w$ bits of chal_3. If some of the remaining w bits of chal_3 are nonzero, or if $\mathsf{Open}(I)$ aborts, then the signing algorithm tries again with the next counter. The verifier rejects the signature if the last w bits of chal_3 are not all zero. Since there are still at most two challenges that map to the roots of the Quicksilver polynomial, this optimization does not affect the security proof. The relevant part of the original FAEST and the optimized FAEST signing algorithm are given in Algorithm 1 and Algorithm 2 (Fig. 4). Another way to look at this optimization is that we increase efficiency by giving up w bits of security and that we regain security by making the prover solve a proof of 2^w work for each forgery attempt.

4.1   Benchmarking the Optimized FAEST and FAEST-EM

We call our optimized FAEST and FAEST-EM signature versions, which benefit from the improved BAVC constructions, FAESTER and FAESTER-EM respectively. They have more parameters which allow to fine-tune their efficiency, and we describe their effects below.

When considering the non-optimized BAVC, the previous VOLEitH signatures FAEST and the recently proposed ReSolved [25] are limited to the signature size and signing/verification runtime trade-off only with respect to τ, the number of "small" VOLEs. Even though flexible, such a trade-off provides an exponential correlation between the signature size and signing time as shown in Fig. 5.

With the optimized BAVC, our proposed signature schemes, including FAESTER, enjoy both improved performance and an improved signature size-runtime trade-off. Our experiments show an improvement in the signature size of around 10% for FAESTER when compared to FAEST, in the L1 setting, while maintaining a similar runtime, as shown in the trade-off plot in Fig. 5. As a direct consequence of this improvement, FAESTER is the first signature scheme using standard AES with a signature size of 4.5KB. Similarly, FAESTER-EM enjoys a signature size of less than 4KB, with similar signing times. We refer to the full version for FAESTER performance for the L3 and L5 security levels.

Figure 8 shows the benefits of our new optimized BAVC for different signature schemes. Table 4 presents our recommended parameter choices for different signature schemes. In the FAEST NIST submission [9], the slow and the fast versions represented by (s) and (f) respectively were only determined by τ as shown in the first 4 rows. However, for the optimized FAESTER and FAESTER-EM,

Algorithm 1 FAEST Signing	**Algorithm 2** FAESTER Signing
$\ldots$	$\ldots$
$\text{chal}_3 \leftarrow H_2^3(\text{chal}_2\|\tilde{a}\|\tilde{b};\ \lambda)$	$\text{ctr} \leftarrow 0$
$I \leftarrow \mathsf{DecodeChallenge}(\text{chal}_3)$	**retry:**
$\text{decom}_I \leftarrow \mathsf{BAVC.Open}(I)$	$\text{chal}_3 \leftarrow H_2^3(\text{chal}_2\|\tilde{a}\|\tilde{b}\|\text{ctr};\ \lambda)$
$\sigma \leftarrow \sigma\|\text{decom}_I$	$I \leftarrow \mathsf{DecodeChallenge}(\text{chal}_3[0:\lambda -$
return σ	$w-1])$
	$\text{decom}_I \leftarrow \mathsf{BAVC.Open}(I)$
	if $\text{decom}_I = \bot$ or $\text{chal}_3[\lambda - w : \lambda] \neq$
	0^w **then**
	$\quad \text{ctr} \leftarrow \text{ctr} + 1$
	$\quad$ **go to retry**
	end if
	$\sigma \leftarrow \sigma\|\text{decom}_I\|\text{ctr}$
	return σ

Fig. 4. Signing with FAEST vs signing with FAESTER.

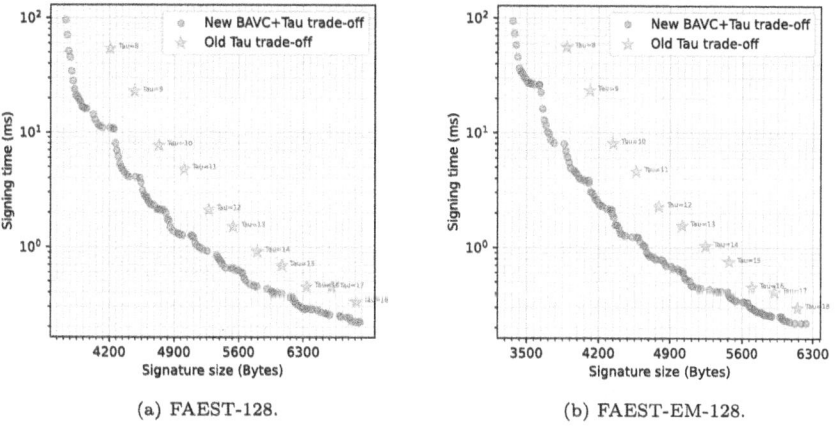

(a) FAEST-128.   (b) FAEST-EM-128.

Fig. 5. FAEST(-EM) τ-signature size and signing time trade-off.

along with the proposed new signature schemes, we also consider the optimal w and $\mathsf{T_{open}}$ parameter as described above. We refer to Table 5 for the FAESTER optimized implementation benchmarks.

5   New VOLEitH Signature Schemes

We present three new signature schemes constructed following the footsteps of FAESTER using the optimized BAVC, however, instantiated with different OWFs. The first two variants take advantage of the Rain and MQ OWFs, discussed in Sect. 2.1 and 2.1 respectively, to achieve the lowest signature sizes (less than 3 KB) among all MPCitH and VOLEitH signature schemes. The third variant uses AES but with a different approach to proving the S-box, which reduces signature sizes by up to around 5%. We also show how to tweak the original AES proof in FAEST, to allow use of the full AES keyspace, instead of restricting to a subset of all keys.

5.1 MandaRain: VOLEitH + Rain

The MandaRain signature scheme uses two instantiations of the Rain OWF, namely Rain-3 and Rain-4 which use 3 and 4 rounds respectively. Rain has the same block size as its security parameter λ, thus unlike FAEST and FAESTER, Rain can circumvent the need for multiple evaluations of the OWF. The parameters of Rain that we use for MandaRain can be found in Table 1.

Table 1. Rain Parameters

Instance	Security level	State	Rounds
Rain-3-128	L1	$\mathbb{F}_2^{128}$	3
Rain-3-192	L3	$\mathbb{F}_2^{192}$	3
Rain-3-256	L5	$\mathbb{F}_2^{256}$	3
Rain-4-128	L1	$\mathbb{F}_2^{128}$	4
Rain-4-192	L3	$\mathbb{F}_2^{192}$	4
Rain-4-256	L5	$\mathbb{F}_2^{256}$	4

Table 2. MQ Parameters

Instance	Security level	Field	$m = n$
MQ-2^1-L1	L1	$\mathbb{F}_{2^1}$	152
MQ-2^8-L1	L1	$\mathbb{F}_{2^8}$	48
MQ-2^1-L3	L3	$\mathbb{F}_{2^1}$	224
MQ-2^8-L3	L3	$\mathbb{F}_{2^8}$	72
MQ-2^1-L5	L5	$\mathbb{F}_{2^1}$	320
MQ-2^8-L5	L5	$\mathbb{F}_{2^8}$	96

We prove Rain using the VOLEitH NIZK proof as described in Sect. 2.2, with the optimized BAVC (Sect. 3.1). The prover uses as a witness the secret key k together with the internal state after each round, except for the last round which can be derived from the public key. This gives a total witness length of $l = r\lambda$ bits for r rounds, and proving consistency requires r multiplication checks in $\mathbb{F}_{2^\lambda}$. See Table 3 for a summary of the non-linear complexity of the Rain-3 and Rain-4 OWFs. Compared to the other OWFs, Rain has the smallest number of non-linear constraints that must be checked in ZK resulting in not only a very small signature size but also a competitive signing and verification time. Refer to Table 4 for details on the MandaRain parameters. Similarly to FAEST, Fig. 6 presents the parameter set exploration to find the most suitable parameter sets for signature size/runtime trade-offs with and without the BAVC optimization. We see that the signature size can be as small as around 2.8KB for the same or better signing runtime. Refer to Table 5 for the MandaRain optimized implementation benchmarks at the L1 security level. For L3 and L5 benchmarks, refer to the full version.

Table 3. Non-linear complexity of VOLEitH signature schemes using different OWFs.

Description	FAEST			FAEST-EM		
λ	AES-128	AES-192	AES-256	AES-EM-128	AES-EM-192	AES-EM-256
No. of S-Boxes in key expansion	40	32	52	0	0	0
No. of S-Boxes in encryption	160	192	224	160	288	448
Total no. of $\mathbb{F}_{2^8}$ constraints	200	416	500	160	288	448
	FAESTER			FAESTER-EM		
λ	AES-128	AES-192	AES-256	AES-EM-128	AES-EM-192	AES-EM-256
No. of S-Boxes in key expansion	40	32	52	0	0	0
No. of S-Boxes in encryption	160	192	224	160	288	448
Total no. of $\mathbb{F}_{2^8}$ constraints	200	416	500	160	288	488
	MandaRain-3			MandaRain-4		
λ	Rain-3-128	Rain-3-192	Rain-3-256	Rain-4-128	Rain-4-192	Rain-4-256
No. of S-Boxes in encryption	3	3	3	4	4	4
Total no. of $\mathbb{F}_{2^\lambda}$ constraints	3	3	3	4	4	4
	KuMQuat-2^1			KuMQuat-2^8		
λ	MQ-$\mathbb{F}_{2^1}$-L1	MQ-$\mathbb{F}_{2^1}$-L3	MQ-$\mathbb{F}_{2^1}$-L5	MQ-$\mathbb{F}_{2^8}$-L1	MQ-$\mathbb{F}_{2^8}$-L3	MQ-$\mathbb{F}_{2^8}$-L5
Total no. of $\mathbb{F}_{2^n}$ constraints	152	224	320	48	72	96

5.2 KuMQuat: VOLEitH + MQ

Using a OWF relying on the MQ problem (Sect. 2.1), we obtain the smallest witness size, and hence the smallest signature size among all VOLEitH and MPCitH signature schemes.

Proving an MQ evaluation in VOLEitH is conceptually straightforward: the witness is the solution $\mathbf{x} \in \mathbb{F}_q^n$ to the system of equations, and there are m quadratic constraints to verify. One challenge is that a naive approach using QuickSilver would require $O(mn^2)$ multiplications in $\mathbb{F}_{2^\lambda}$. In Sect. 2.1, we describe some optimizations that reduce this to just $O(mn^2 q/\lambda)$ multiplications.

Although the runtime of KuMQuat is not as fast as MandaRain, it still has signing and verification speeds comparable to those of FAEST, for signatures of around half the size. Table 2 shows the MQ parameter choices for our experiments chosen according to the security estimation from [14,32]. We set $m = n$ (as in MQOM) and choose a field $\mathbb{F}_{2^k}$ for a power k.

The field size of the MQ problem and security level determines the choice of n (see Sect. 2.1), which in turn influences the key and signature sizes and the runtime as shown in Table 5. We refer to Table 4 for the recommended parameter choice for the L1 security level. For L3 and L5, parameter choices, we refer to the full version. Note that the signature size of KuMQuat depends only mildly on the MQ parameters m, n. One could therefore choose to increase n, m to massively increase the margin of safety against MQ-solving attacks without growing the signature size much.

The key difference between MQOM and KuMQuat is unlike the fully-randomized linear combination of constraints in MQOM, we take several fixed linear combinations of constraints in KuMQuat (which can be precomputed because they are fixed), then later take a random linear combination of these combined constraints as part of QuickSilver. Another way of looking at this (for

Table 4. VOLEitH signature schemes and their parameters. We denote the signature schemes as SCHEME-$\lambda_{s/f}$. l is the number of VOLE correlations required for the NIZK proof. w and T_{open} are the values for the optimized BAVC as described in Sect. 4. τ is the number of VOLE repetitions determining the choice between s (slow) and f (fast) versions. k_0 and k_1 are bit lengths of small VOLEs. B is the padding parameter affecting the security of the VOLE check. Secret key (sk), public key (pk) and signature sizes are in bytes.

Signature Scheme	OWF $E_{sk}(x)$	l	w	T_{open}	τ	τ_0	τ_1	k_0	k_1	sk size	pk size	sig. size
FAEST-128$_s$*	AES128$_{sk}(x)$	1600	–	–	11	7	4	12	11	16	32	5006
FAEST-128$_f$*	AES128$_{sk}(x)$	1600	–	–	16	0	16	8	8	16	32	6336
FAEST-EM-128$_s$	AES128$_x(sk) \oplus sk$	1280	–	–	11	7	4	12	11	16	32	4566
FAEST-EM-128$_f$	AES128$_x(sk) \oplus sk$	1280	–	–	16	0	16	8	8	16	32	5696
FAEST-d7-128$_s$	AES128$_{sk}(x)$	800	–	–	11	7	4	12	11	16	32	4790
FAEST-d7-128$_f$	AES128$_{sk}(x)$	800	–	–	16	0	16	8	8	16	32	6020
FAESTER-128$_s$*	AES128$_{sk}(x)$	1600	7	102	11	0	11	11	11	16	32	4594
FAESTER-128$_f$*	AES128$_{sk}(x)$	1600	8	110	16	8	8	8	7	16	32	6052
FAESTER-EM-128$_s$	AES128$_x(sk) \oplus sk$	1280	7	103	11	0	11	11	11	16	32	4170
FAESTER-EM-128$_f$	AES128$_x(sk) \oplus sk$	1280	8	112	16	8	8	8	7	16	32	5444
FAESTER-d7-128$_s$	AES128$_{sk}(x)$	800	5	102	11	0	11	11	11	16	32	4374
FAESTER-d7-128$_f$	AES128$_{sk}(x)$	800	6	110	16	8	8	8	7	16	32	5732
MandaRain-3-128$_s$	Rain-3-128$_{sk}(x)$	384	7	100	11	7	4	12	11	16	32	2890
MandaRain-3-128$_f$	Rain-3-128$_{sk}(x)$	384	8	108	16	0	16	8	8	16	32	3588
MandaRain-4-128$_s$	Rain-4-128$_{sk}(x)$	512	7	101	11	7	4	12	11	16	32	3082
MandaRain-4-128$_f$	Rain-4-128$_{sk}(x)$	512	8	110	16	0	16	8	8	16	32	3876
KuMQuat-2^1-L1$_s$	MQ-2^1-L1$_{sk}(x)$	152	7	99	11	7	4	12	11	19	35	2555
KuMQuat-2^1-L1$_f$	MQ-2^1-L1$_{sk}(x)$	152	4	102	16	0	16	8	8	19	35	3028
KuMQuat-2^8-L1$_s$	MQ-2^8-L1$_{sk}(x)$	384	7	100	11	7	4	12	11	48	64	2890
KuMQuat-2^8-L1$_f$	MQ-2^8-L1$_{sk}(x)$	384	4	108	16	0	16	8	8	48	64	3588

*The full key version of FAEST and FAESTER share the same parameters as the reduced key version of them for all security levels (L1, L3 and L5).

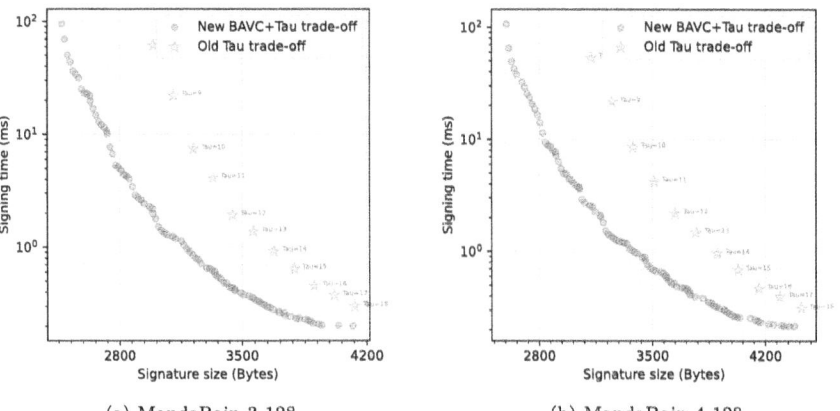

(a) MandaRain-3-128.   (b) MandaRain-4-128.

Fig. 6. MandaRain τ-signature size and signing runtime trade-off.

$q = 2$) is that we take the m-bit output of the MQ function and reinterpret it as a sequence of (m/λ) elements of $\mathbb{F}_{2^\lambda}$, before taking a random linear combination like in MQOM. Having fewer constraints to randomly combine reduces the computational cost (assuming a faster-than-schoolbook implementation of extension field arithmetic) (Fig. 7).

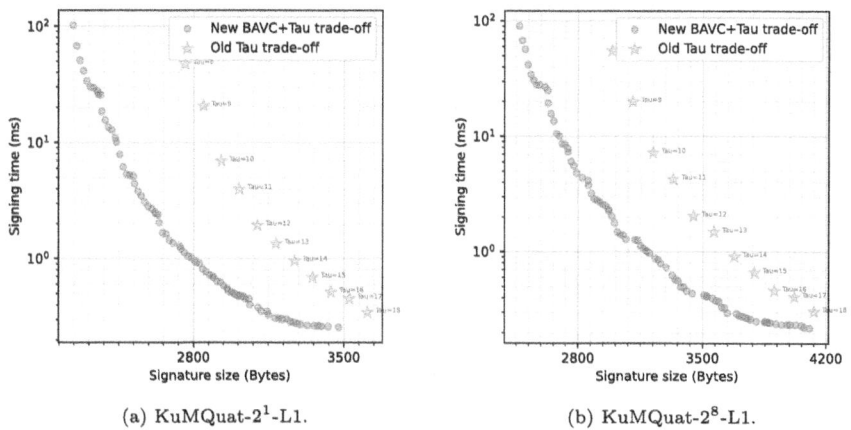

(a) KuMQuat-2^1-L1.

(b) KuMQuat-2^8-L1.

Fig. 7. KuMQuat τ-signature size and runtime trade-off.

Optimizations. One implementation difficulty with KuMQuat is the computational cost of the OWF. The MQ function itself has $mn(n + 3)/2$ terms[7] (see Definition 1), each with coefficients in $\mathbb{F}_q$, and evaluating the constraints with QuickSilver requires calculating the same number of terms over $\mathbb{F}_{2^\lambda}$. While this seems to require $\tilde{\Theta}(mn^2\lambda)$ work, we used an optimization to reduce this back to just $\tilde{\Theta}(mn^2 \log_2 q)$.

Instead of these m constraints (for $i \in [m]$) over $\mathbb{F}_q$:

$$0 = \sum_{jk} \mathbf{A}_{ijk}\, x_j x_k + \sum_j b_{ij}\, x_j - y_i,$$

we require that $\mathbb{F}_{2^\lambda}$ is a degree $r = \frac{\lambda}{\log_2(q)}$ field extension of $\mathbb{F}_q$, and group the constraints into blocks of r:

$$0 = \sum_{i=ri'}^{ri'+r-1} \alpha^{i-ri'} \left(\sum_{jk} \mathbf{A}_{ijk}\, x_j x_k + \sum_j b_{ij}\, x_j - y_i \right),$$

where α is a generator of $\mathbb{F}_{2^\lambda}$ over $\mathbb{F}_q$. These constraints are equivalent to the original ones, because $\alpha^0, \alpha^1, \ldots, \alpha^{r-1}$ are linearly independent over $\mathbb{F}_q$ since

---

[7] Or $mn(n+1)/2$ in $\mathbb{F}_2$, since then $x^2 = x$ which makes the diagonal of $\mathbf{A}_i$ redundant.

$\mathbb{F}_{2^\lambda}$ is a degree r vector space over $\mathbb{F}_q$. Now, we can precompute this linear combination of constraints

$$\mathbf{A}'_{i'jk} = \sum_{i=0}^{r-1} \alpha^i \mathbf{A}_{(ri'+i)jk}$$

$$b'_{i'j} = \sum_{i=0}^{r-1} \alpha^i b_{(ri'+i)j}$$

$$y'_{i'} = \sum_{i=0}^{r-1} \alpha^i y_{ri'+i}$$

to get $\lceil m/r \rceil$ constraints over $\mathbb{F}_{2^\lambda}$:

$$0 = \sum_{jk} \mathbf{A}'_{i'jk} x_j x_k + \sum_j b'_{i'j} x_j - y'_{i'}.$$

Note that evaluating these constraints for QuickSilver now requires only $\Theta(mn^2/r)$ operations over $\mathbb{F}_{2^\lambda}$. Assuming $\mathbb{F}_{2^\lambda}$ multiplication can be done in $\tilde{\Theta}(\lambda)$ time, this is $\tilde{\Theta}(mn^2 \log_2 q)$ time.

As a final optimization, note that if $r \leq m/r$ then there are exactly r $\mathbf{A}_{ijk}$ elements that get mapped into a single $\mathbf{A}'_{i'jk}$, and that the transformation between them is bijective (and similarly for $\mathbf{b}$ and y). Therefore, sampling all $\mathbf{A}'_{i'}$ uniformly at random from the subset of upper triangular matrices in $\mathbb{F}_{2^\lambda}^{n \times n}$ is equivalent to sampling the original $\mathbf{A}_i$ elements uniformly from the upper triangular matrices in $\mathbb{F}_q^{n \times n}$, for all except very last i'. To save computing this transformation, other than for the last i' we sample the $\mathbf{A}'_{i'}$ and $\mathbf{b}'_{i'}$ directly, instead of going through $\mathbf{A}_{ri'}, \ldots, \mathbf{A}_{ri'+r-1}$. Similarly, for $i' \leq m/r$ we also use $y'_{i'}$ directly in the public key, rather than converting between them and the $\mathbf{y}_i$s.

5.3   Uniform AES Keys in FAEST

When using one-way functions based on AES or Rijndael, as in FAEST(ER) and FAEST(ER)-EM, the main challenge is proving consistency of the non-linear part of the S-box. We denote this by the function

$$S : x \mapsto x^{254} \in \mathbb{F}_{2^8}$$

When proving AES in zero-knowledge, the committed witness is typically used to derive an input/output pair $(x, y) \in \mathbb{F}_{2^8}^2$ for each S-box, and the prover shows that $y = S(x)$ by proving the degree-2 constraint $xy = 1$. However, this only works when x, y are non-zero; this meant that prior works [7,10,26] had to restrict the set of AES keys to those where the input to every S-box is non-zero. This requires adding a rejection sampling step to key generation, and slightly reduces entropy of the signing key, effectively reducing security by 1–2 bits [9, Sec. 10.3.4].

We observe that instead, $y = S(x)$ can be proven for all values of $x, y \in \mathbb{F}_{2^8}$, by the pair of constraints:

$$xy^2 = y \quad \wedge \quad x^2 y = x \tag{1}$$

where the first constraint guarantees that we cannot have $x = 0 \wedge y \neq 0$, and the second ensures against $y = 0 \wedge x \neq 0$.

While these constraints have degree-3 over $\mathbb{F}_{2^8}$, when viewed over $\mathbb{F}_2$, their degree is 2 (since squaring is $\mathbb{F}_2$-linear). In FAEST, the witness is initially committed to over $\mathbb{F}_2$, and only lifted to $\mathbb{F}_{2^8}$ for proving the S-box. So, we can easily modify it to prove (1) by linearly computing commitments to the bits of x^2 and y^2 over $\mathbb{F}_2$, before lifting and proving the pair of degree-2 constraints over $\mathbb{F}_{2^8}$. This doubles the number of constraints that are proven, however, in the end, only a random linear combination of all constraints is checked. This means that we can support uniform AES keys with no impact on proof size.

We implemented this tweaked AES proof by modifying the FAEST implementation (FAEST(ER)-fullkey), and using the same parameters as in FAEST(ER) noticed no change in performance when running the signing and verification benchmarks as shown in Table 5. This is because the main cost of FAEST is the PRG and hashing operations in the BAVC, so merely doubling the number of constraints does not noticeably affect performance. Moreover, due to the absence of rejection sampling when choosing the key, we get a runtime improvement in the key generation algorithm. A similar full-key tweak is also possible for the Rain OWF in MandaRain.

5.4   FAEST-d7: Proving AES via Degree-7 Constraints

We have also investigated an alternative approach to proving knowledge of a preimage for the AES-based OWFs, using higher degree constraints over $\mathbb{F}_2$, rather than quadratic constraints over $\mathbb{F}_{2^8}$. This allows us to use an AES witness of half the size, which in some cases reduces signature size.

FAEST-d7 is based on the variant of the QuickSilver proof system [52] that allows for proving arbitrary degree-d constraints on the committed witness. In particular, we use degree-7 constraints, since the AES S-box and its inverse can both be expressed as degree-7 circuits over $\mathbb{F}_2$.[8] We combine this with a meet-in-the-middle idea: instead of committing to the AES state after every round, the prover only commits to the state of every other round. Given committed states s_i, s_{i+2}, we can now prove consistency by verifying that $R_i(s_i) = R_{i+1}^{-1}(s_{i+2})$, where R_i is the i-th round function. Each pair of neighbouring AES states can thus be verified with a single degree-7 QuickSilver check. The same idea can be applied to the S-boxes in the key schedule.

---

[8] The non-linear part of the S-box maps $x \mapsto x^{254}$ in $\mathbb{F}_{2^8}$. Since 254 has Hamming weight 7, and squaring in $\mathbb{F}_{2^8}$ is $\mathbb{F}_2$-linear, we get degree 7 overall.

Computational Efficiency. In QuickSilver, proving a degree-d circuit $C(x_1, \ldots, x_n)$ requires expressing C as a sum of polynomials $\sum_{i=0}^{d} f_i(x_1, \ldots, x_n)$, where each f_i contains monomials only of degree i. While the f_i's need not be computed explicitly, the prover is required to evaluate each f_i. It's not clear how efficiently this can be done for a complex function like the AES S-box.

We observe that it's not necessary to compute the f_i's at all. Instead, to prove the degree-d circuit C, it suffices for the prover to compute the coefficients of a degree-d *univariate* polynomial, given by $g(y) = C(a_1 + b_1 y, \ldots, a_n + b_n y)$, for values $a_i, b_i \in \mathbb{F}_{2^\lambda}$ known to the prover. Meanwhile, the verifier only needs to evaluate C at a single point. When C is the AES S-box, we estimate the cost for the prover is around 150 multiplications in $\mathbb{F}_{2^\lambda}$. While this is a lot more than the cost of proving 1 multiplication in $\mathbb{F}_{2^8}$, it is still insignificant when compared with all of the PRG and hash calls used in the other components of FAEST. We include further details of this method in the full version of this paper.

Signature Size. The main advantage of this approach is that the total witness size is halved, from e.g. $l = 1600$ to $l = 800$ at the 128-bit security level. However, this does not come for free, since proving degree-d relations with QuickSilver incurs a cost of $d\tau\lambda$ bits in the signature size. Overall, when applied to FAEST variants with an l-bit witness, we reduce the signature size by $\tau l/2 - 5\tau\lambda$ bits. For the Even-Mansour 128-bit variants, we have $l/2 = 5\lambda$, so there is no change in size. However, for the standard AES variants and the higher security Even-Mansour variants, we see a reduction of up to around 5%.

We have not implemented FAEST-d7, but show in Table 4 the signature sizes it obtains, as well as those of the FAESTER-d7 variant incorporating our GGM tree optimizations.

6   Broader Discussion

This section compares the existing VOLEitH and MPCitH signature schemes, including the candidates of NIST's call for Additional Signatures, with our proposed optimized signature schemes.

Benchmark Platform. To benchmark and compare all the implementations fairly, we evaluate only the most optimized implementations of the signature schemes that are openly available. For the NIST candidates, we refer to the submitted optimized implementations. We measure all the run times on a system with an AMD Ryzen 9 7900X 12-Core CPU, 128 GB memory and running Ubuntu 22.04.

Security Assumption. The choice of different OWFs allows for a wide variety of security assumptions one can choose from when constructing a VOLEitH signature scheme. For example, using an AES-based OWF results in a highly conservative security guarantee at the cost of a performance penalty in terms of signature size and runtime. This tradeoff is similar to the previous state-of-the-art MPCitH signature schemes like BBQ, Banquet, Helium which relied on

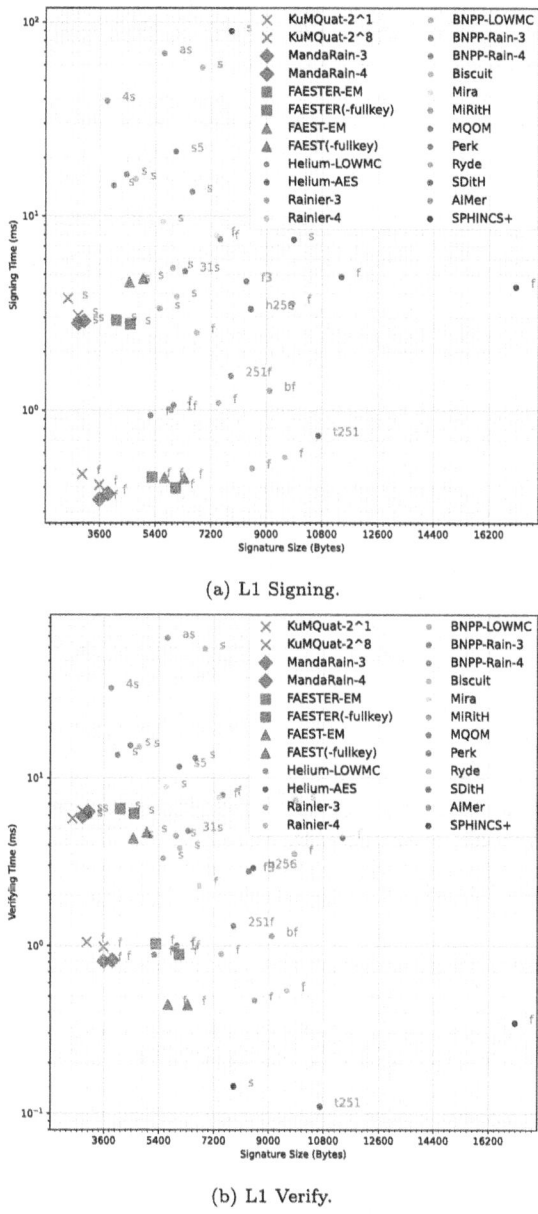

(a) L1 Signing.

(b) L1 Verify.

Fig. 8. Signature size and runtime comparison between state-of-the-art MPCitH and VOLEitH signature schemes. The slow and fast versions are denoted with s and f respectively. Other special versions are denoted by their short names as per their publicly available specification. Due to negligible difference in the performance between the full key and the reduced key version of FAEST and FAESTER, the full key data points are not explicitly included in the figure for better readability and are represented by the reduced key data points.

Table 5. Signing Time (ms), Verification Time (ms), and Signature Size (bytes) of different VOLEitH-based signature schemes (optimized implementations). Slow and fast versions are denoted with s and f respectively.

Scheme	Keygen	Sign	Verify	sk	pk	Signature
FAEST-128$_s$	0.0006	4.381	4.102	16	32	5006
FAEST-128$_f$	0.0005	0.404	0.395	16	32	6336
FAEST-fullkey-128$_s$	0.0003	4.396	4.405	16	32	5006
FAEST-fullkey-128$_f$	0.0003	0.476	0.467	16	32	6336
FAEST-EM-128$_s$	0.0005	4.151	4.415	16	32	4566
FAEST-EM-128$_f$	0.0005	0.446	0.474	16	32	5696
FAESTER-128$_s$	0.0006	3.282	4.467	16	32	4594
FAESTER-128$_f$	0.0005	0.433	0.610	16	32	6052
FAESTER-fullkey-128$_s$	0.0003	2.896	5.734	16	32	4594
FAESTER-fullkey-128$_f$	0.0003	0.371	0.756	16	32	6052
FAESTER-EM-128$_s$	0.0005	3.005	4.386	16	32	4170
FAESTER-EM-128$_f$	0.0005	0.422	0.609	16	32	5444
MandaRain-3-128$_s$	0.0018	2.800	5.895	16	32	2890
MandaRain-3-128$_f$	0.0018	0.346	0.807	16	32	3588
MandaRain-4-128$_s$	0.0026	2.876	6.298	16	32	3052
MandaRain-4-128$_f$	0.0026	0.371	0.817	16	32	3876
KuMQuat-2^1-L1$_s$	0.173	4.305	4.107	19	35	2555
KuMQuat-2^1-L1$_f$	0.172	0.539	0.736	19	35	3028
KuMQuat-2^8-L1$_s$	0.174	3.599	4.053	48	64	2890
KuMQuat-2^8-L1$_f$	0.172	0.400	0.623	48	64	3588

the standard AES OWF and naturally possessed larger signature size and runtime than their competing schemes which relied on optimized but non-standard OWFs like Rainier [29] or Picnic [24]. Switching to AES-EM construction for VOLEitH signature does not give us the most conservative security guarantees like standard AES, however, the general EM construction is already more than two decades old, thus guaranteeing security in a similar ballpark as of AES while still improving both the signature size and runtime considerably. On the other side, optimized OWFs like Rain and AIM [39] are rather new and not that well studied. For example, in 2023, AIM already witnessed two full round attacks [41,54] which were later fixed in AIM2 [38]. Due to the mitigation, as per the authors, the signature scheme AIMER using AIM OWF suffers around 10% runtime penalty. This work does not consider using the AIM OWF for constructing a VOLEitH signature scheme as we conjecture that it will lead to worse runtime due large number of Mersenne exponentiation while still giving a signature size similar to Rain. On the other hand, when considering the KuMQuat signature scheme, we benefit from the MQ problem which relies on a different hardness problem, giving us more choices, when compared to the symmetric primitives like AES, Rain, or AIM. Similarly, in the recently proposed VOLEitH signature scheme ReSolveD [25], their OWF relies on the syndrome decoding problem.

Symmetric Key Primitives. FAEST's zero-knowledge proofs are built out of pseudorandom generators and hash functions, and their instantiation is important for efficiency and security. For consistency with the FAEST and FAEST-EM proposal [9], we use AES-CTR everywhere a PRG is required, and the SHAKE hash function for all random oracle calls, including those at the leaves of the GGM tree.

Parameters. A careful choice of parameters, including the choice of OWF, is crucial for achieving the best performance of the signature scheme. In the previous sections, we extensively demonstrated the impact of w, $\mathsf{T_{open}}$, and τ on the signature size and runtime. Additionally, when considering the MQ OWF, the operational field ($\mathbb{F}_n$) is also a crucial factor determining the performance. For example, KuMQuat-2^1-λ operating in $\mathbb{F}_2$ leads to the smallest signature size, however, has the largest number of non-linear constraints among the other proposed VOLEitH signature schemes leading to a long signing and verification runtime. Alternatively, KuMQuat-2^8-λ leads to a larger signature size, due to more witness bits, however, the number of constraints is roughly 70% smaller, leading to a faster runtime than KuMQuat-2^1-λ.

Key Sizes. The key sizes only depend on the underlying OWF and are not affected by the VOLEitH parameters. With the MQ OWF, for example, the operational field $\mathbb{F}_2^n$ and λ determine the size of sk and pk. The key sizes of MandaRain are determined only by λ.

Signature Size and Runtime. FAEST-EM requires 20–30% less non-linear constraints compared to FAEST, which directly influences both the signature size and the runtime, especially for the slow signature variant with a smaller signature size as shown in Table 5. This holds also true for MandaRain which has the smallest number of non-linear constraints enabling it to enjoy the smallest signature runtime along with the smallest signature size after our proposed KuMQuat signature scheme. Looking at the signature size runtime trade-off, in terms of performance we conclude that MandaRain provides a better signature size runtime trade-off, as it has a slightly larger signature size than KuMQuat, however, to the best of our knowledge, it has the smallest runtime among all VOLEitH and MPCitH based signature schemes. We also looked into the possibility of using NIST standardised ASCON[9] [28] as a OWF for constructing VOLEitH signature scheme. However, due to the design structure of ASCON, our estimates showed us that the signature size will be much worse than that of standard AES even if we can design an ASCON-style permutation for the OWF.[10] One may also question the fitness of other symmetric primitives which are especially designed for

---

[9] https://csrc.nist.gov/news/2023/lightweight-cryptography-nist-selects-ascon.

[10] It might be also interesting to have an analysis on the minimum number of rounds required for security guarantees with ASCON given only one plaintext-ciphertext pair, similar to the security assumptions of Rain or AIM. For AES, this should be conservatively at least 6 rounds as the attack [21,29] costs 2^{120} time and 2^{120} memory for 4.5 AES rounds, which is still worse than Rain-4 non-linear complexity.

use in MPC, Homomorphic Encryption (HE) and ZKP use-cases. Even though several of these primitives focus on reducing the number of multiplications and their multiplicative depth, such primitives are designed while considering adversaries with higher adversary data complexity. The higher the number of rounds required to guarantee security from a key recovery attack increases the number of witness bits that must be communicated to the verifier. For MPCitH or VOLEitH signature schemes, an adversary knows only the public key or one plaintext-ciphertext pair, though. Hence, VOLEitH- or MPCitH-friendly symmetric primitives like Rain and AIM assume that an adversary knows only the public key, requiring them to have as low as only 3 rounds to guarantee security against key recovery attacks.

For fairness, we compare only the optimized implementations of the signature schemes and thus could not include the recent VOLEitH signature ReSolveD [25], as to the best of our knowledge, there exists no optimized implementation for it at the time of writing. However, when comparing the reference implementations of ReSolveD with FAEST and FAEST-EM, we conjecture that the optimized implementation of ReSolveD would be slower than Rain and FAESTER-EM at least, if not also FAESTER. In Fig. 8, we compare our proposed VOLEitH signature schemes with other competitive MPCitH and VOLEitH signature schemes. Here, KuMQuat provides the smallest signature size at a high runtime cost. Whereas, MandaRain provides the best signature size runtime trade-off, where it enjoys the best runtime and gives a signature size only second to KuMQuat. Notably, both MandaRain and KuMQuat are the first VOLEitH signature schemes with signature sizes less than 3 KB. This is also the lowest among all the MPCitH signature schemes. FAESTER, using the optimized BAVC, for the first time achieves a signature size of 4.5 KB while still relying on standard AES. Similarly, FAESTER-EM also enjoys a considerably smaller signature size of just 4.1 KB while relying on AES combined with the EM construction.

Acknowledgements. This work has been supported by: the Defense Advanced Research Projects Agency (DARPA) under Contract No. HR001120C0085, research grant VIL53029 from VILLUM FONDEN, the Independent Research Fund Denmark under project number 0165-00107B (C3PO), the Digital Europe Program under project number 101091642 ("QCI-CAT"), the Horizon Europe Program under grant agreement number 101096435 ("CONFIDENTIAL6G"), the "DDAI" COMET Module managed by Austrian Research Promotion Agency (FFG), and the project "PREPARED" which is funded by Austrian security research programme KIRAS of the Federal Ministry of Finance (BMF).

Any opinions, findings and conclusions or recommendations expressed in this material are those of the author(s) and do not necessarily reflect the views of DARPA. Distribution Statement "A" (Approved for Public Release, Distribution Unlimited).

References

1. Aaraj, N., Bettaieb, S., Bidoux, L., Budroni, A., Dyseryn, V., Esser, A., Gaborit, P., Kulkarni, M., Mateu, V., Palumbi, M., et al.: Perk (2023)
2. Advanced Encryption Standard (AES). National Institute of Standards and Technology, NIST FIPS PUB 197, U.S. Department of Commerce (Nov 2001)
3. Aguilar Melchor, C., Gama, N., Howe, J., Hülsing, A., Joseph, D., Yue, D.: The return of the SDitH. pp. 564–596 (2023). https://doi.org/10.1007/978-3-031-30589-4_20
4. Albrecht, M.R., Rechberger, C., Schneider, T., Tiessen, T., Zohner, M.: Ciphers for MPC and FHE. In: Oswald, E., Fischlin, M. (eds.) Advances in Cryptology - EUROCRYPT 2015 - 34th Annual International Conference on the Theory and Applications of Cryptographic Techniques, Sofia, Bulgaria, April 26-30, 2015, Proceedings, Part I. Lecture Notes in Computer Science, vol. 9056, pp. 430–454. Springer (2015). https://doi.org/10.1007/978-3-662-46800-5_17
5. Aragon, N., Bardet, M., Bidoux, L., Chi-Domínguez, J.J., Dyseryn, V., Feneuil, T., Gaborit, P., Joux, A., Rivain, M., Tillich, J.P., et al.: Ryde specifications (2023)
6. Aumasson, J.P., Bernstein, D.J., Beullens, W., Dobraunig, C., Eichlseder, M., Fluhrer, S., Gazdag, S.L., Hülsing, A., Kampanakis, P., Kölbl, S., Lange, T., Lauridsen, M.M., Mendel, F., Niederhagen, R., Rechberger, C., Rijneveld, J., Schwabe, P., Westerbaan, B.: Sphincs+ – submission to the 3rd round of the nist postquantum project (2022), http://sphincs.org/data/sphincs+-r3.1-specification.pdf
7. Baum, C., Braun, L., Delpech de Saint Guilhem, C., Klooß, M., Orsini, E., Roy, L., Scholl, P.: Publicly verifiable zero-knowledge and post-quantum signatures from VOLE-in-the-head. pp. 581–615 (2023). https://doi.org/10.1007/978-3-031-38554-4_19
8. Baum, C., Braun, L., Munch-Hansen, A., Scholl, P.: MozZ$_{2^k}$arella: Efficient vector-ole and zero-knowledge proofs over $\mathbb{Z}_{2^k}$. In: Dodis, Y., Shrimpton, T. (eds.) Advances in Cryptology - CRYPTO 2022 - 42nd Annual International Cryptology Conference, CRYPTO 2022, Santa Barbara, CA, USA, August 15-18, 2022, Proceedings, Part IV. Lecture Notes in Computer Science, vol. 13510, pp. 329–358. Springer (2022). https://doi.org/10.1007/978-3-031-15985-5_12
9. Baum, C., Braun, L., de Saint Guilhem, C.D., Klooß, M., Majenz, C., Mukherjee, S., Ramacher, S., Rechberger, C., Orsini, E., Roy, L., et al.: FAEST: Algorithm specifications (version 1.1) (2023), https://faest.info/faest-spec-v1.1.pdf
10. Baum, C., Delpech de Saint Guilhem, C., Kales, D., Orsini, E., Scholl, P., Zaverucha, G.: Banquet: Short and fast signatures from AES. pp. 266–297 (2021). https://doi.org/10.1007/978-3-030-75245-3_11
11. Baum, C., Dittmer, S., Scholl, P., Wang, X.: Sok: Vector ole-based zero-knowledge protocols. Cryptology ePrint Archive, Paper 2023/857 (2023), https://eprint.iacr.org/2023/857
12. Baum, C., Malozemoff, A.J., Rosen, M.B., Scholl, P.: Mac'n'cheese: Zero-knowledge proofs for boolean and arithmetic circuits with nested disjunctions. In: Malkin, T., Peikert, C. (eds.) Advances in Cryptology - CRYPTO 2021 - 41st Annual International Cryptology Conference, CRYPTO 2021, Virtual Event, August 16-20, 2021, Proceedings, Part IV. Lecture Notes in Computer Science, vol. 12828, pp. 92–122. Springer (2021). https://doi.org/10.1007/978-3-030-84259-8_4
13. Baum, C., de Saint Guilhem, C.D., Kales, D., Orsini, E., Scholl, P., Zaverucha, G.: Banquet: Short and fast signatures from AES. In: Garay, J.A. (ed.) Public-Key Cryptography - PKC 2021 - 24th IACR International Conference on Practice and

Theory of Public Key Cryptography, Virtual Event, May 10-13, 2021, Proceedings, Part I. Lecture Notes in Computer Science, vol. 12710, pp. 266–297. Springer (2021). https://doi.org/10.1007/978-3-030-75245-3_11

14. Bellini, E., Makarim, R.H., Sanna, C., Verbel, J.A.: An estimator for the hardness of the MQ problem. In: Batina, L., Daemen, J. (eds.) Progress in Cryptology - AFRICACRYPT 2022: 13th International Conference on Cryptology in Africa, AFRICACRYPT 2022, Fes, Morocco, July 18-20, 2022, Proceedings. pp. 323–347. Lecture Notes in Computer Science, Springer Nature Switzerland (2022). https://doi.org/10.1007/978-3-031-17433-9_14

15. Benadjila, R., Feneuil, T., Rivain, M.: MQ on my Mind: Post-Quantum Signatures from the Non-Structured Multivariate Quadratic Problem. Cryptology ePrint Archive (2023)

16. Bernstein, D.J., Hülsing, A., Kölbl, S., Niederhagen, R., Rijneveld, J., Schwabe, P.: The sphincs$^+$ signature framework. In: Cavallaro, L., Kinder, J., Wang, X., Katz, J. (eds.) Proceedings of the 2019 ACM SIGSAC Conference on Computer and Communications Security, CCS 2019, London, UK, November 11-15, 2019. pp. 2129–2146. ACM (2019). https://doi.org/10.1145/3319535.3363229

17. Beullens, W.: MAYO: practical post-quantum signatures from oil-and-vinegar maps. In: AlTawy, R., Hülsing, A. (eds.) Selected Areas in Cryptography - 28th International Conference, SAC 2021, Virtual Event, September 29 - October 1, 2021, Revised Selected Papers. Lecture Notes in Computer Science, vol. 13203, pp. 355–376. Springer (2021). https://doi.org/10.1007/978-3-030-99277-4_17

18. Beullens, W., Kleinjung, T., Vercauteren, F.: Csi-fish: Efficient isogeny based signatures through class group computations. In: Galbraith, S.D., Moriai, S. (eds.) Advances in Cryptology - ASIACRYPT 2019 - 25th International Conference on the Theory and Application of Cryptology and Information Security, Kobe, Japan, December 8-12, 2019, Proceedings, Part I. Lecture Notes in Computer Science, vol. 11921, pp. 227–247. Springer (2019). https://doi.org/10.1007/978-3-030-34578-5_9

19. Beullens, W., Delpech de Saint Guilhem, C.: Legroast: Efficient post-quantum signatures from the legendre prf. In: International Conference on Post-Quantum Cryptography. pp. 130–150. Springer (2020)

20. Boneh, D., Waters, B.: Constrained pseudorandom functions and their applications. pp. 280–300 (2013). https://doi.org/10.1007/978-3-642-42045-0_15

21. Bouillaguet, C., Derbez, P., Fouque, P.: Automatic search of attacks on round-reduced AES and applications. In: Rogaway, P. (ed.) Advances in Cryptology - CRYPTO 2011 - 31st Annual Cryptology Conference, Santa Barbara, CA, USA, August 14-18, 2011. Proceedings. Lecture Notes in Computer Science, vol. 6841, pp. 169–187. Springer (2011). https://doi.org/10.1007/978-3-642-22792-9_10

22. Boyle, E., Couteau, G., Gilboa, N., Ishai, Y.: Compressing vector OLE. In: Lie, D., Mannan, M., Backes, M., Wang, X. (eds.) Proceedings of the 2018 ACM SIGSAC Conference on Computer and Communications Security, CCS 2018, Toronto, ON, Canada, October 15-19, 2018. pp. 896–912. ACM (2018). https://doi.org/10.1145/3243734.3243868

23. Boyle, E., Couteau, G., Gilboa, N., Ishai, Y., Kohl, L., Rindal, P., Scholl, P.: Efficient two-round OT extension and silent non-interactive secure computation. In: Cavallaro, L., Kinder, J., Wang, X., Katz, J. (eds.) Proceedings of the 2019 ACM SIGSAC Conference on Computer and Communications Security, CCS 2019, London, UK, November 11-15, 2019. pp. 291–308. ACM (2019). https://doi.org/10.1145/3319535.3354255

24. Chase, M., Derler, D., Goldfeder, S., Orlandi, C., Ramacher, S., Rechberger, C., Slamanig, D., Zaverucha, G.: Post-quantum zero-knowledge and signatures from symmetric-key primitives. In: Thuraisingham, B., Evans, D., Malkin, T., Xu, D. (eds.) Proceedings of the 2017 ACM SIGSAC Conference on Computer and Communications Security, CCS 2017, Dallas, TX, USA, October 30 - November 03, 2017. pp. 1825–1842. ACM (2017). https://doi.org/10.1145/3133956.3133997
25. Cui, H., Liu, H., Yan, D., Yang, K., Yu, Y., Zhang, K.: Resolved: Shorter signatures from regular syndrome decoding and vole-in-the-head. Cryptology ePrint Archive, Paper 2024/040 (2024), https://eprint.iacr.org/2024/040, https://eprint.iacr.org/2024/040
26. Delpech de Saint Guilhem, C., De Meyer, L., Orsini, E., Smart, N.P.: BBQ: Using AES in picnic signatures. pp. 669–692 (2019). https://doi.org/10.1007/978-3-030-38471-5_27
27. Dittmer, S., Ishai, Y., Ostrovsky, R.: Line-point zero knowledge and its applications. In: Tessaro, S. (ed.) 2nd Conference on Information-Theoretic Cryptography, ITC 2021, July 23-26, 2021, Virtual Conference. LIPIcs, vol. 199, pp. 5:1–5:24. Schloss Dagstuhl - Leibniz-Zentrum für Informatik (2021). https://doi.org/10.4230/LIPICS.ITC.2021.5
28. Dobraunig, C., Eichlseder, M., Mendel, F., Schläffer, M.: Ascon v1.2: Lightweight authenticated encryption and hashing **34**(3), 33 (Jul 2021). https://doi.org/10.1007/s00145-021-09398-9
29. Dobraunig, C., Kales, D., Rechberger, C., Schofnegger, M., Zaverucha, G.: Shorter signatures based on tailor-made minimalist symmetric-key crypto. In: Yin, H., Stavrou, A., Cremers, C., Shi, E. (eds.) Proceedings of the 2022 ACM SIGSAC Conference on Computer and Communications Security, CCS 2022, Los Angeles, CA, USA, November 7-11, 2022. pp. 843–857. ACM (2022). https://doi.org/10.1145/3548606.3559353
30. Ducas, L., Kiltz, E., Lepoint, T., Lyubashevsky, V., Schwabe, P., Seiler, G., Stehlé, D.: Crystals-dilithium: A lattice-based digital signature scheme. IACR Trans. Cryptogr. Hardw. Embed. Syst. **2018**(1), 238–268 (2018). https://doi.org/10.13154/TCHES.V2018.I1.238-268
31. Dunkelman, O., Keller, N., Shamir, A.: Minimalism in cryptography: The even-mansour scheme revisited. In: Pointcheval, D., Johansson, T. (eds.) Advances in Cryptology - EUROCRYPT 2012 - 31st Annual International Conference on the Theory and Applications of Cryptographic Techniques, Cambridge, UK, April 15-19, 2012. Proceedings. Lecture Notes in Computer Science, vol. 7237, pp. 336–354. Springer (2012). https://doi.org/10.1007/978-3-642-29011-4_21
32. Esser, A., Verbel, J.A., Zweydinger, F., Bellini, E.: Cryptographic estimators: a software library for cryptographic hardness estimation. IACR Cryptol. ePrint Arch. p. 589 (2023)
33. Even, S., Mansour, Y.: A construction of a cipher from a single pseudorandom permutation. J. Cryptol. **10**(3), 151–162 (1997). https://doi.org/10.1007/S001459900025
34. Feneuil, T., Joux, A., Rivain, M.: Syndrome decoding in the head: Shorter signatures from zero-knowledge proofs. pp. 541–572 (2022). https://doi.org/10.1007/978-3-031-15979-4_19
35. Goldreich, O., Goldwasser, S., Micali, S.: How to construct random functions (extended abstract). In: 25th Annual Symposium on Foundations of Computer Science, West Palm Beach, Florida, USA, 24-26 October 1984. pp. 464–479. IEEE Computer Society (1984). https://doi.org/10.1109/SFCS.1984.715949

36. Ishai, Y., Kushilevitz, E., Ostrovsky, R., Sahai, A.: Zero-knowledge proofs from secure multiparty computation. SIAM J. Comput. **39**(3), 1121–1152 (2009). https://doi.org/10.1137/080725398
37. Kales, D., Zaverucha, G.: Efficient lifting for shorter zero-knowledge proofs and post-quantum signatures. IACR Cryptol. ePrint Arch. p. 588 (2022), https://eprint.iacr.org/2022/588
38. Kim, S., Ha, J., Son, M., Lee, B.: Mitigation on the AIM cryptanalysis. IACR Cryptol. ePrint Arch. p. 1474 (2023), https://eprint.iacr.org/2023/1474
39. Kim, S., Ha, J., Son, M., Lee, B., Moon, D., Lee, J., Lee, S., Kwon, J., Cho, J., Yoon, H., Lee, J.: AIM: symmetric primitive for shorter signatures with stronger security. IACR Cryptol. ePrint Arch. p. 1387 (2022), https://eprint.iacr.org/2022/1387
40. Kipnis, A., Patarin, J., Goubin, L.: Unbalanced Oil and Vinegar signature schemes. pp. 206–222 (1999). https://doi.org/10.1007/3-540-48910-X_15
41. Liu, F., Mahzoun, M.: Algebraic attacks on RAIN and AIM using equivalent representations. IACR Cryptol. ePrint Arch. p. 1133 (2023), https://eprint.iacr.org/2023/1133
42. Perret, L.: Biscuit: Shorter mpc-based signature from posso
43. Prest, T., Fouque, P.A., Hoffstein, J., Kirchner, P., Lyubashevsky, V., Pornin, T., Ricosset, T., Seiler, G., Whyte, W., Zhang, Z.: Falcon. Post-Quantum Cryptography Project of NIST (2020)
44. Rivest, R.: DESX (1984), Never formally published.
45. de Saint Guilhem, C.D., Meyer, L.D., Orsini, E., Smart, N.P.: BBQ: using AES in picnic signatures. IACR Cryptol. ePrint Arch. p. 781 (2019), https://eprint.iacr.org/2019/781
46. de Saint Guilhem, C.D., Orsini, E., Tanguy, T.: Limbo: Efficient zero-knowledge mpcith-based arguments. In: Kim, Y., Kim, J., Vigna, G., Shi, E. (eds.) CCS '21: 2021 ACM SIGSAC Conference on Computer and Communications Security, Virtual Event, Republic of Korea, November 15 - 19, 2021. pp. 3022–3036. ACM (2021). https://doi.org/10.1145/3460120.3484595
47. Samardjiska, S., Chen, M.S., Hulsing, A., Rijneveld, J., Schwabe, P.: MQDSS. Tech. rep., National Institute of Standards and Technology (2019), available at https://csrc.nist.gov/projects/post-quantum-cryptography/post-quantum-cryptography-standardization/round-2-submissions
48. StarkWare: ethSTARK documentation. Cryptology ePrint Archive, Report 2021/582 (2021), https://eprint.iacr.org/2021/582
49. Weng, C., Yang, K., Katz, J., Wang, X.: Wolverine: Fast, scalable, and communication-efficient zero-knowledge proofs for boolean and arithmetic circuits. In: 42nd IEEE Symposium on Security and Privacy, SP 2021, San Francisco, CA, USA, 24-27 May 2021. pp. 1074–1091. IEEE (2021). https://doi.org/10.1109/SP40001.2021.00056
50. Weng, C., Yang, K., Yang, Z., Xie, X., Wang, X.: Antman: Interactive zero-knowledge proofs with sublinear communication. In: Yin, H., Stavrou, A., Cremers, C., Shi, E. (eds.) Proceedings of the 2022 ACM SIGSAC Conference on Computer and Communications Security, CCS 2022, Los Angeles, CA, USA, November 7-11, 2022. pp. 2901–2914. ACM (2022). https://doi.org/10.1145/3548606.3560667
51. Yang, K., Sarkar, P., Weng, C., Wang, X.: Quicksilver: Efficient and affordable zero-knowledge proofs for circuits and polynomials over any field. In: Kim, Y., Kim, J., Vigna, G., Shi, E. (eds.) CCS '21: 2021 ACM SIGSAC Conference on Computer and Communications Security, Virtual Event, Republic of Korea, November 15 - 19, 2021. pp. 2986–3001. ACM (2021). https://doi.org/10.1145/3460120.3484556

52. Yang, K., Sarkar, P., Weng, C., Wang, X.: QuickSilver: Efficient and affordable zero-knowledge proofs for circuits and polynomials over any field. pp. 2986–3001 (2021). https://doi.org/10.1145/3460120.3484556

53. Yang, K., Weng, C., Lan, X., Zhang, J., Wang, X.: Ferret: Fast extension for correlated OT with small communication. In: Ligatti, J., Ou, X., Katz, J., Vigna, G. (eds.) CCS '20: 2020 ACM SIGSAC Conference on Computer and Communications Security, Virtual Event, USA, November 9-13, 2020. pp. 1607–1626. ACM (2020). https://doi.org/10.1145/3372297.3417276

54. Zhang, K., Wang, Q., Yu, Y., Guo, C., Cui, H.: Algebraic attacks on round-reduced RAIN and full AIM-III. IACR Cryptol. ePrint Arch. p. 1397 (2023), https://eprint.iacr.org/2023/1397

Author Index

© International Association for Cryptologic Research 2025
K.-M. Chung and Y. Sasaki (Eds.): ASIACRYPT 2024, LNCS 15484, pp. 495–496, 2025.
https://doi.org/10.1007/978-981-96-0875-1

GPSR Compliance

The European Union's (EU) General Product Safety Regulation (GPSR) is a set of rules that requires consumer products to be safe and our obligations to ensure this.

If you have any concerns about our products, you can contact us on ProductSafety@springernature.com

In case Publisher is established outside the EU, the EU authorized representative is:

Springer Nature Customer Service Center GmbH
Europaplatz 3
69115 Heidelberg, Germany

The manufacturer's authorised representative in the EU is Springer
Nature Customer Service Centre GmbH, Europaplatz 3, 69115 Heidelberg,
Germany. If you have any concerns regarding our products, please
contact ProductSafety@springernature.com

Printed and bound by CPI Group (UK) Ltd, Croydon, CR0 4YY
05/05/2026
02103581-0005